AUSTRALIA IN THE WAR OF 1939-1945

SERIES ONE
ARMY

VOLUME VII
THE FINAL CAMPAIGNS

AUSTRALIA IN THE WAR OF 1939-1945

SERIES 1 (ARMY)
    I. To Benghazi. *By Gavin Long.*
    II. Greece, Crete and Syria. *By Gavin Long.*
    III. Tobruk and El Alamein. *By Barton Maughan.**
    IV. The Japanese Thrust. *By Lionel Wigmore.*
    V. South-West Pacific Area—First Year. *By Dudley McCarthy.*
    VI. The New Guinea Offensives. *By David Dexter.*
    VII. The Final Campaigns. *By Gavin Long.*

SERIES 2 (NAVY)
    I. Royal Australian Navy, 1939-42. *By G. Hermon Gill.*
    II. Royal Australian Navy, 1942-45. *By G. Hermon Gill.**

SERIES 3 (AIR)
    I. Royal Australian Air Force, 1939-42. *By Douglas Gillison.*
    II. Air War Against Japan, 1943-45. *By George Odgers.*
    III. Air War Against Germany and Italy, 1939-43. *By John Herington.*
    IV. Air Power Over Europe, 1944-45. *By John Herington.*

SERIES 4 (CIVIL)
    I. The Government and the People, 1939-41. *By Paul Hasluck.*
    II. The Government and the People, 1942-45. *By Paul Hasluck.**
    III. War Economy, 1939-42. *By S. J. Butlin.*
    IV. War Economy, 1942-45. *By S. J. Butlin.**
    V. The Role of Science and Industry. *By D. P. Mellor.*

SERIES 5 (MEDICAL)
    I. Clinical Problems of War. *By Allan S. Walker.*
    II. Middle East and Far East. *By Allan S. Walker.*
    III. The Island Campaigns. *By Allan S. Walker.*
    IV. Medical Services of the R.A.N. and R.A.A.F. *By Allan S. Walker and others.*

* Not yet published.

The writers of these volumes have been given full access to official documents, but they and the general editor are alone responsible for the statements and opinions which the volumes contain.

THE
FINAL CAMPAIGNS

by

GAVIN LONG

The Naval & Military Press Ltd

Published by
The Naval & Military Press Ltd
5 Riverside, Brambleside, Bellbrook
Industrial Estate, Uckfield, East Sussex,
TN22 1QQ England
Tel: +44 (0) 1825 749494
Fax: +44 (0) 1825 765701
www.naval-military-press.com
www.military-genealogy.com

In reprinting in facsimile from the original, any imperfections are inevitably reproduced and the quality may fall short of modern type and cartographic standards.

CONTENTS

	Page
Preface	xv
List of Events	xix

Chapter
1. THE FINAL PHASE BEGINS 1
2. PLANS AND PROBLEMS 31
3. THE GENERAL, THE PARLIAMENT AND THE MINISTERS 55
4. LEADERS AND MEN 73
5. THE BOUGAINVILLE CAMPAIGN TAKES SHAPE . 89
6. THE OFFENSIVE OPENS 116
7. TO SLATER'S KNOLL AND SORAKEN . . . 141
8. ACROSS THE HARI: PORTON PLANTATION . . 177
9. THE FLOODS AND THE CEASE FIRE . . . 217
10. OPERATIONS ON NEW BRITAIN . . . 241
11. TAKING OVER AT AITAPE 271
12. ACROSS THE DANMAP 282
13. TO DAGUA: AND ACROSS THE AMUK RIVER . 296
14. MAPRIK AND WEWAK TAKEN 330
15. TAZAKI AND SHIBURANGU 359
16. PLANNING FOR BORNEO—APRIL TO JUNE 1945 . 388
17. TARAKAN: TOWN AND AIRFIELD TAKEN . . 406
18. TARAKAN: THE GARRISON DESTROYED . . 427
19. OBOE SIX OPENS 453
20. SECURING BRITISH BORNEO 472
21. THE SEIZURE OF BALIKPAPAN 502
22. BALIKPAPAN AREA SECURED 532
23. AFTER THE CEASE FIRE 548
24. LOOKING BACK 584

APPENDIXES:
1. Command Problems, S.W.P.A. 1942-1945 . . 590
2. Too Many Generals? 600
3. General Blamey's Appreciation of May 1945 . . 608
4. The Allied Intelligence Bureau 617
5. The Prison Break at Cowra, August 1944 . . 623
6. Order of Battle of the 7th Division at Balikpapan . 625
7. Some Statistics 633
8. Australian Army Unit Histories, War of 1939-45 . 637
9. Abbreviations 639

INDEX 641

ILLUSTRATIONS

	Page
The 25th Battalion advancing towards Little George, Bougainville	92
A patrol of the 42nd Battalion in the Motupena Point area	92
Men of the 42nd Battalion near Mawaraka, Bougainville	92
Aerial view of Japanese gardens in the Monoitu area	92
Headquarters of the 3rd Division at Toko, Bougainville	93
The 2nd Field Regiment disembarking at Toko	93
A patrol of the 24th Battalion searching for Japanese raiders	93
A tank of the 2/4th Armoured Regiment crossing the Puriata River	124
Troops of the New Guinea Infantry Battalion with Japanese prisoners	124
Men of the 24th Battalion advancing along the Buin Road	124
A tractor train on the Buin Road	124
Troops of the 26th Battalion landing on Torokori Island	125
A corduroyed road in northern Bougainville	125
Lieut-General V. A. H. Sturdee, Brigadier H. H. Hammer, Major-General W. Bridgeford and Lieut-General S. G. Savige	125
The Buin Road at the Hongorai River	125
The 2/8th Commando Squadron in the Musaraka area, Bougainville	204
A muddy section of the Buin Road	204
A sodden camp of the 47th Battalion in southern Bougainville	205
The Japanese peace envoy on the bank of the Mivo River	205
Lieut-General Kanda surrenders to Lieut-General Savige	236
Japanese artillery assembled in southern Bougainville after the surrender	236
Sergeant D. E. Sloan giving instructions to a patrol of the 1st New Guinea Infantry Battalion on New Britain	237
A patrol in the Jacquinot Bay area	237
Major-General A. H. Ramsay, Lieut-General J. Northcott, Major-General C. S. Steele and Major-General J. H. Cannan with staff officers of the 5th Division at Jacquinot Bay	268
A wounded man of the 14th/32nd Battalion near Waitavalo, New Britain	268
The 2/11th Battalion advancing from the Danmap River, in the Aitape area of New Guinea	269
The leading company of the 2/11th crossing the Wakip River	269
The 2/11th Battalion in an action against Japanese positions east of Matapau	300
The 2/2nd Battalion near Dagua	301
Wrecked aircraft on Dagua airfield	301
Stretcher bearers of the 2/2nd Battalion on the 1410 Feature	332
Native carriers in the mountains south of Dagua	332
A carrier line taking supplies to the Wonginara Mission area	333
Major-General J. E. S. Stevens and Lieut-Colonel J. A. Bishop	333

	Page
Part of "Farida Force" landing east of Wewak	364
A private of the 2/8th Battalion using a flame-thrower	364
A weapon-pit of the 2/5th Battalion in the Torricellis	365
Carriers climbing Mount Shiburangu	365
Sketch of a Japanese bunker in the Shiburangu area	374
The Blot on the day of its capture by the 2/8th Battalion	380
A Vickers machine-gun crew supporting the 2/6th Battalion during the attack on Ulunkohoitu Ridge	380
Troops of the 2/7th Battalion pass a House Tamboran at Sigora	380
Weary men of the 2/7th resting on a muddy section of the track to Kiarivu	380
A "kai bomber" drops food near Kiarivu	381
The 2/7th Battalion approaching Kiarivu	381
Kiarivu, looking towards Mount Turu	381
Major-General H. C. H. Robertson taking the surrender of Lieut-General Adachi	381
Brigadier D. A. Whitehead, Lieut-General Sir Leslie Morshead and Lieut-Colonel S. J. Douglas	412
An L.S.T. carrying troops of the 26th Brigade for the assault on Tarakan	412
Engineers of the 2/13th Field Company demolishing underwater obstacles at Tarakan	412
Some 2/13th Field Company sappers after breaching underwater obstacles	412
The bombardment of Tarakan	413
Unloading in progress at Tarakan	413
A machine-gun crew of the 2/23rd firing at a Japanese position across the Glenelg Highway, Tarakan	413
Stretcher bearers of the 2/23rd Battalion bringing out a wounded man	413
Red Beach, Tarakan, on the day of the landing	428
Troops of the 2/24th Battalion approach a Japanese pill-box on Tarakan	428
Hill 105, Tarakan	429
Guns bombarding the Joyce feature, Tarakan	429
Snags Track and the Elbow feature, Tarakan	460
A 2/24th Battalion patrol in the Hill 90 area	460
The 24th Brigade's landing on Labuan Island	461
Troops of the 20th Brigade land on Muara Island	461
Lieut-Colonel M. R. Jeanes with General MacArthur and General Morshead on Labuan	476
Men of the 2/43rd Battalion during the attack on Labuan airfield	476
Labuan Island: a jeep ambulance transporting a wounded Chinese girl	476
Questioning refugees on Labuan Island	476
Troops of the 2/17th Battalion patrolling Brunei town	477
Bren gun position of the 2/43rd Battalion north of Labuan airfield	477
Major-General G. F. Wootten and Air Commodore F. R. W. Scherger	477

	Page
Dyaks being questioned at 20th Brigade headquarters, Brunei	477
Burning oil wells at Seria, Borneo	492
Indian troops after release from captivity	493
A patrol of the 2/13th Battalion setting out from Miri, Borneo	493
Landing craft carrying troops of the 7th Division to the assault on Balikpapan	524
Men of the 2/14th Battalion landing from an L.C.I. at Balikpapan on 1st July	524
An L.C.V.P. landing troops at Balikpapan	524
Infantrymen moving inland	524
A Matilda tank advancing through the Balikpapan port area	525
A patrol of the 2/9th Battalion entering Penadjam village	525
The control tower at Manggar airfield	525
General Sir Thomas Blamey with Major-General E. J. Milford and Lieut-General F. H. Berryman	525
Sketch of Waites' Knoll area	529
Sappers of the 2/9th Field Company searching for mines at Balikpapan	540
Stretcher bearers bringing in a wounded man	540
A mortar crew of the 2/2nd Anti-Tank Regiment supporting the advance on Parramatta	540
Directing mortar fire on to Hill 87, Balikpapan	540
Infantry and artillery observers pinned down by fire from Hill 87	541
Men of the 2/12th Battalion in action near Balikpapan	541
A flame-throwing tank with troops of the 2/10th Battalion attacking a Japanese bunker near the Tank Plateau	541
Troops of the 2/10th Battalion, supported by tanks, in action at Balikpapan	541
The surrender ceremony on the U.S.S. *Missouri* at Tokyo Bay, 2nd September 1945	556
Japanese troops dumping ammunition in the sea after the surrender	557
Tokyo, April 1947. The 65th Battalion changing the guard at the Imperial Palace	557

MAPS

	Page
The Allied front in the Far East, December 1944	3
Dutch New Guinea, Borneo and the Philippines	28
Australian and Japanese dispositions in the First Army area, January 1945	60
Bougainville Island	91
New Britain	243
Australian and Japanese formations in Aitape-Wewak area	273
20th Brigade operations	464
Balikpapan operations to 5th July	512

SKETCH MAPS AND DIAGRAMS

The South-West and Central Pacific Areas	16
The Solomon Islands	22
The take-over at Torokina	95
The Numa Numa trail and Sisivie	107
The attack on Little George	108
The attack on Arty Hill	109
Torokina to Numa Numa	111
Pearl Ridge	116
The operations of 31st/51st Battalion towards Soraken	123
Tsimba Ridge	125
Northern Bougainville	127
Operations of the 29th Brigade, January 1945	131
Pagana River area, showing corrections to original map	134
Sipuru-Kieta area	136
The 7th Brigade's advance to the Puriata	144
Slater's Knoll	163
Buin area	171
The 26th Battalion's advance to Soraken	173
The advance from the Puriata to Hiru Hiru	179
15th Brigade, May-June	180
15th Brigade's advance from the Hongorai to the Hari	190
23rd Brigade on the Numa Numa trail	203
Soraken and Porton Plantations	207
Ogorata River to the Porror River	219
Wide Bay area	245
Open Bay area	253

	Page
Operations in central New Britain	254
Bacon Hill area	257
Aitape to Madang	271
To Yambes and the Danmap	276
2/5th Battalion's advance to Bulamita and Amam	282
From the Danmap to the Ninahau	284
19th Brigade's advance to Malin and Abau	285
16th Brigade's advance to the Anumb River	297
17th Brigade's advance from Balif towards Maprik	302
Nilu-Screw River area	305
16th Brigade's advance to the Ninahau River	313
From the Anumb River to But	315
Ninahau River to Kofi	318
16th Brigade's advance to Wonginara Mission and Kofi	320
17th Brigade's advance through Maprik	331
16th Brigade's advance to the Hawain River	339
Wewak area	344
19th Brigade's advance from Boiken to Cape Wom	345
The capture of Wewak	346
Wewak to Madang	355
Hansa Bay to the Sepik River	356
Kalabu to Ilipem	360
17th Brigade's advance to Kiarivu	361
Wewak to Rindogim	371
Japanese last-stand area	384
Borneo and the Philippines—operations of Australian and American forces	390
Diagram—Chain of Command, Tarakan	406
Tarakan Island	408
Japanese dispositions Tarakan, 1st May 1945	409
Advance of the 26th Brigade to 5th May	416
Tarakan, central area, from 6th May onwards	429
Tarakan, south-eastern area, from 6th May	431
North Tarakan	441
Areas of responsibility on Tarakan	447
Borneo	453
Northern Borneo and Sarawak area	455
Landings in Brunei Bay	460
Brunei area	462
Labuan Island	466
"The Pocket", Labuan Island	472

	Page
North Borneo—Beaufort operations	476
The capture of Beaufort—26th-29th June	479
Balikpapan area	503
2/10th Battalion at Parramatta, Balikpapan	517
Stalkudo to Manggar	524
The 2/14th Battalion at Manggar	526
Milford Highway	533
18th Brigade operations, Balikpapan Bay	540
Balikpapan to Sambodja	544
Areas of responsibility of *II Japanese Army* and Allied force commanders	560
Japan	578

PREFACE

IN the earlier volumes of this series the story has generally been told in a chronological fashion, with the object of helping the reader to see the whole problem which faced each military leader day by day and not merely a part of it. The chronicler of Australian military operations in the last year of the war, however, has to describe campaigns in six widely-separated areas. In three of these areas fighting was in progress during all or nearly all of the period. In all of them the operations were not much influenced by what was happening elsewhere. This volume is concerned also with the relations between the Commander-in-Chief and the Ministers in the first half of 1945 and the widespread public and private discussion of his policies and his personality. In the interests of clarity and emphasis it has seemed desirable to tell a large part of the story of the higher planning of the final Australian operations and of General Blamey's relations with the Ministers and the South-West Pacific Command in a narrative unbroken by accounts of the campaigns which the discussions mainly concerned, and to describe the six campaigns each in a self-contained narrative, though inevitably with occasional side glances at other areas.

These narratives are each broken off at the moment when the fighting ceased. Then a single chapter briefly records the part the army played in accepting the surrender of Japanese forces in Australian territory and a large part of Indonesia, and ensuring that the terms of the surrender were carried out, the formation of an Australian contingent for the army of occupation in Japan, and the demobilisation of the wartime army.

The series which this volume concludes is basically a history of military operations in the field. The administrative and technical problems and achievements of the Australian Army in six years of war are touched on only when they directly affected the fighting man or were a subject of discussion between soldiers and statesmen. Largely because of the failure to obtain support for technical and administrative histories of the A.I.F. after the war of 1914-1918 no provision was made for them in this series, except for a medical history.

For a time I worked on an intended appendix to this volume which would record some of the achievements of the wartime army which possessed enduring scientific, educational or economic value: for example, the mapping of practically all the fertile lands of the Australian continent and of most of the outlying territories, the compilation of comprehensive geographical studies of wide areas of the south-west Pacific and east Asia, the work of the Army Education Corps, rehabilitation, the creation in Australia of a large and accomplished team of scholars of the Japanese language, the building of roads and camps, agricultural and forestry development in remote places. To this I intended to add summaries of other large-scale activities of the army which have been referred to only briefly elsewhere in this history: for example, prisoners of war and internees, canteens and clubs, Intelligence, conscientious objectors, the war artists, and so on. It became evident, however, that there would not be room for detailed treatment of such subjects. The student may find much about some of them in unpublished reports and histories of various branches of the army, and a little about most of them in "The Army War Effort", which was produced by the Department of the Army at intervals from 1940 to 1945 and eventually grew into a book of 181 foolscap pages, not counting appendixes. The army's geographical work is described in *The Role of Science and Industry* by D. P. Mellor.

There are other subjects of importance on which only an occasional beam of light is shed in these seven volumes. Indeed, as the series took shape, we all became more and more aware of the size and historical importance of problems and episodes that we could afford only to glance at. The military administration of the colonial territories, the Australian occupation of eastern Indonesia in the later months of 1945 and early 1946, changing attitudes towards conscription, the relationship between regular and citizen soldier, the development of staff work, the growth of the "tail" of the army, and the Army Secretariat's relations with the General Staff are a few of the topics, touched on briefly in these volumes, that await their historians.

In an appendix some command problems referred to at intervals in this volume and the two preceding ones have been recapitulated and re-examined.

Before bidding farewell to the readers of this series I would like to say a little about certain principles that we have followed which have been discussed and sometimes criticised by reviewers and others. As mentioned earlier, the story has been told as a rule with a fairly strict adherence to the time sequence. This was our policy at the outset and, we think, practice confirms its value in military history. A theatre commander is generally obliged to survey his whole area each day and seldom may concentrate for a week or a month on one part of it. If I have been right in describing the various operations of 1945 each as a separate episode, that in itself lends support to the contention that they were strategically of minor importance.

In general we have been hesitant to pass judgment, believing with Bloch that the historian is not a magistrate. Military planning and operations are usually fully discussed by the participants and any differing opinions among senior commanders are usually set out frankly and in detail either at the time or later. When the chronicler has described the events and their outcome and set out the opinions of those who bore the responsibility or part of it, he is perhaps justified in feeling diffident about adding to those opinions an opinion of his own, his own inclinations having been given sufficient latitude in his selection and presentation of evidence and contemporary opinion.

The books in this series have been written in considerably more detail than would be feasible in similar histories produced in larger countries.

In this regard we adopted a tradition established by Dr C. E. W. Bean in his history of the Australian infantry in World War I. At this stage little can usefully be added to Bean's justification of this method in a preface written in 1928. A year later Bean might not have felt impelled to defend his practice, because by that time a procession of books describing the experiences of individual soldiers in that war was being eagerly sought by the public. This volume with its problem of narrating several long and repetitive operations in difficult country has been written in somewhat less detail than the others in the series, but not, I hope, so differently as to create an unwelcome lack of balance.

Throughout the series we have not provided exhaustive references to sources, but have cited them only where they are quoted verbatim or for some other special reason. For this we have been reproved by North American critics. As a rule, however, the sources of most statements are, I think, made evident—whether report, war diary, interview, letter, postmortem comment, or some printed work. Although no bibliographies have been provided, all books and articles on which a writer has relied to an important extent have been named in footnotes.

The degree to which, in the writing of this volume, I have depended upon the correspondence files lent by the trustees of the estate of the late Field Marshal Blamey will be apparent. I owe much to the excellent operational reports of the Commander, Allied Land Forces, drafted during and immediately after the war under the direction of Lieut-Colonel R. W. G. Ogle. These helped to clarify the high-level story and have sometimes influenced the design of my narratives. It is regrettable that these dispatches were not published in 1945 or soon after; perhaps, in the British fashion, as supplements to the *Commonwealth of Australia Gazette*. As it is, they were not even mimeographed, and the whereabouts of only two or three typewritten or fading carbon copies of each of them are known to us.

Among those participants who have helped me with recollections of the events described in this book or with comments on the first draft are:

General Sir John Northcott; Lieut-Generals Sir Frank Berryman, Sir William Bridgeford, Sir Ragnar Garrett, the late Sir Stanley Savige, Sir Vernon Sturdee; Major-Generals J. A. Bishop, P. A. Cullen, T. J. Daly, I. N. Dougherty, K. W. Eather, R. R. Gordon, the late H. H. Hammer and R. King, E. J. Milford, S. H. W. C. Porter, Sir Alan Ramsay, Sir Jack Stevens, J. R. Stevenson, Sir Victor Windeyer, Sir George Wootten; Brigadiers F. O. Chilton, J. Field, J. G. McKinna, the late M. J. Moten, C. H. B. Norman, R. L. Sandover; Colonels R. T. Eldridge, C. H. Grace; Lieut-Colonels B. J. Callinan, B. G. Dawson, H. L. E. Dunkley, O. C. Isaachsen, M. R. Jeanes, H. G. McCammon, J. A. Maitland, G. R. Matthews, W. M. Mayberry, P. K. Parbury, W. E. H. Stanner, G. R. Warfe, J. R. Watch, S. P. Weir; Majors G. W. Bennett, E. J. Cooper, A. C. Robertson, R. P. Serle; Captains L. A. Cameron, G. C. Hart, G. J. Hawke, L. M. Long, R. L. Mathews, E. J. Shattock, T. B. Silk; Lieutenant A. J. T. Ford; Sergeant T. A. G. Hungerford.

I have to thank the Director and staff of the Australian War Memorial for their constant cooperation in providing documents, books and photographs, particularly for the Army series in this history. The valuable contemporary narratives written in 1945 by members of the Military History Section are acknowledged in footnotes. Some of the descriptions and opinions in this volume are based on notes made while I was on Bougainville in January and February 1945, and on the New Guinea mainland, including the coastal sector forward from Aitape, in March and April of that year. I spent some weeks with the 7th Division at Balikpapan and with the 9th Division in British Borneo in August and September.

I am grateful to the two literary assistants who worked on this volume —first Mr James Brill, and later Miss Mary Gilchrist who prepared it for the printer, made the index, and performed many other arduous and necessary tasks. Mr Hugh Groser drew the maps for this as for all other volumes of the history, helped in the later stages by Miss Elaine Oates. In this my last preface I again express my gratitude to my senior research officer, Mr A. J. Sweeting. The history as a whole owes much to his learning, sound judgment and industry and to the devotion which caused him to stick to this task to the end. Finally I wish to record my admiration for the twelve dedicated men who wrote nineteen of the volumes of this history. Probably for each of them the undertaking proved far more exacting than he had expected; for most of them it demanded sacrifice of leisure and opportunity year after year.

G.L.

Canberra,
11th November 1961.

LIST OF EVENTS
FROM SEPTEMBER 1944 TO SEPTEMBER 1945
Events described in this volume are printed in italics

1944	17 Sept	First Allied Airborne Army lands in Holland
	5 Oct	British forces land on mainland of Greece
	6 Oct	*Headquarters 3rd Division opens at Torokina*
	10 Oct	American Third Fleet attacks Okinawa
	11 Oct	American Third Fleet attacks Luzon in the Philippines
	20 Oct	American forces invade Leyte
	23-26 Oct	Naval Battle of Leyte Gulf
	4 Nov	*Troops of 6th Brigade land at Jacquinot Bay*
	8 Nov	*Headquarters 6th Division opens at Aitape*
	13 Nov	*Relief of Americans in Cape Hoskins area of New Britain completed by troops of 5th Division*
	24 Nov	Superfortresses attack Japan from bases in the Marianas
	16 Dec	Germans open counter-offensive in Ardennes
1945	3 Jan	Allies occupy Akyab in Burma
	9 Jan	American forces land on Luzon
	22 Jan	Burma Road re-opened
	4 Feb	Mr Churchill, President Roosevelt and Marshal Stalin meet at Yalta Conference
	19 Feb	American forces land on Iwo Jima
	10 Mar	American forces land on Mindanao
	28 Mar-5 Apr	*Japanese attacks on Slater's Knoll*
	1 Apr	Americans land on Okinawa
	12 Apr	Death of President Roosevelt
	28 Apr	Mussolini shot by partisans in Italy
	30 Apr	Hitler commits suicide in Berlin
	1 May	*Troops of 26th Brigade land on Tarakan Island*
	3 May	Rangoon captured
	7 May	Germany surrenders unconditionally
	8 May	VE-Day
	11 May	*Wewak captured by 6th Division*

10 June		*Troops of 9th Division land at Brunei Bay*
26 June		United Nations Charter signed at San Francisco
1 July		*Troops of 7th Division land at Balikpapan*
5 July		Death of Mr John Curtin
17 July		Potsdam Conference
6 Aug		First atomic bomb dropped on Hiroshima
9 Aug		Atomic bomb dropped on Nagasaki
15 Aug		VJ-Day. All offensive action against Japan comes to an end
2 Sept		Japanese envoys sign the Allied instrument of surrender aboard the U.S.S. *Missouri* in Tokyo Bay.

CHAPTER 1

THE FINAL PHASE BEGINS

IN August and September 1944 the Allied Staffs expected organised German resistance to collapse before the end of the year, but by October it was evident that this hope would not be realised, and that the German Army would survive into the summer of 1945.[1] At the beginning of December General Dwight D. Eisenhower's Allied armies had reached the upper Rhine, the Russians were at Warsaw, Budapest and Belgrade, and in Italy an Allied army was pressing towards the Po. There were some 70 Allied divisions on the Western Front and soon 87 would be deployed for the final offensive; in Italy some 24 Allied divisions faced 27 German and Fascist divisions. About 180 Russian divisions, many greatly depleted, were along the Eastern Front.

In the Far East Japanese armies in Burma were being thrust back from the Chindwin River and were carrying out a successful offensive against Allied airfields in south China; elsewhere their forces had suffered severe defeats. In September 1944 the advance of the Allied forces in the South-West and Central Pacific had reached Morotai, the Palaus and the Marianas. South of this line three Japanese armies lay isolated: one in New Britain, New Ireland and Bougainville; one on the mainland of Australian New Guinea; and one in Dutch New Guinea. The next Allied moves were to be an attack by General Douglas MacArthur's South-West Pacific forces against Mindanao, and by Fleet Admiral Chester W. Nimitz's Pacific Ocean forces against Yap. On 13th September, however, while the British and American leaders were at Quebec considering plans for the defeat of Japan, the American Joint Chiefs of Staff received through Admiral Nimitz a proposal by his subordinate, Admiral William F. Halsey, that Halsey's attack on Yap and MacArthur's on Mindanao be cancelled and instead MacArthur should invade Leyte not on 20th December as planned but as soon as possible. Halsey proposed that his XXIV Corps, then embarking at Hawaii to attack Yap, should be placed at MacArthur's disposal to help on Leyte.

The Joint Chiefs of Staff sought MacArthur's views. He was then in a cruiser watching the invasion of Morotai and wireless silence was being preserved. However, his staff sent a reply to the Joint Chiefs in MacArthur's name stating that he was willing to land on Leyte on 20th October. Thus on 19th October an immense fleet, including six capital ships, 18 escort aircraft carriers, 258 transports and a multitude of smaller craft, was off the coast of Leyte, with the large aircraft carriers in support. The transports carried the Sixth American Army, then comprising two corps.[2]

---

[1] On 5th September General MacArthur predicted to General Berryman (General Blamey's Chief of Staff) that the war against Japan would end in a year.

[2] There had been a proposal that one Australian division be included in each of these corps, but General Blamey would not agree to the scattering of Australian divisions among American formations. His grounds were that his own corps commanders and staffs were more experienced, and that dispersion of Australian divisions would create difficulties of administration and supply.

The American plan was to land X Corps (1st Cavalry and 24th Divisions) near Tacloban on the north-east coast and XXIV Corps (7th and 96th Divisions) at Dulag farther south. Between these two towns were four airfields. The defending force in the Philippines was commanded by General Tomoyuki Yamashita of the *Fourteenth Area Army* whose headquarters were at Manila, where Field Marshal Count Terauchi commanding the whole *Southern Army* had also established his headquarters in April 1944.[3] Yamashita controlled in Luzon an army of four divisions, and in the southern islands the *XXXV Army,* with the *16th Division* on Leyte, *30th* and *100th* on Mindanao, and the newly-constituted *102nd* distributed among the islands to the west. The defenders of Leyte numbered about 27,000.[4]

There was little opposition to the landing because the Japanese had decided to withdraw their main forces from the beaches and concentrate for a counter-attack. They delivered fairly heavy attacks on the beachheads in the first few days, and then opened a counter-offensive on an imposing scale: their main fleet arrived in the western Philippines with the object of sending its main force through San Bernardino Strait and a smaller force through Surigao Strait to destroy the American convoys, while at the same time a diversionary force steamed south from Formosa. On the 24th the opposing carrier-borne aircraft clashed, an American cruiser was mortally hit and a Japanese battleship sunk. That evening the diversionary force was sighted and Admiral Halsey set off in pursuit with his main force. In the night the American Seventh Fleet decisively defeated the Japanese force thrusting through the Surigao Strait, but San Bernardino Strait was left unguarded as a result of Halsey's departure northward, and the main Japanese fleet passed through unnoticed and descended upon Vice-Admiral Thomas C. Kinkaid's Seventh Fleet, whose only carriers were of the small escort type. The Japanese battleships sank one carrier, and their aircraft and a submarine damaged other ships, but American carrier aircraft attacked vigorously. The Japanese admiral, overestimating the force opposing him, turned northward just when, in the opinion of the American admirals, a resounding success was within his grasp. In response to Kinkaid's appeals Halsey broke off and turned south but was too late to intercept the main Japanese battleship force before it steamed back through San Bernardino Strait.

The heavy bombers now took up the pursuit and sank and damaged some vessels. In the various engagements the Japanese had lost 3 battleships, 4 carriers, 10 cruisers, and 11 destroyers. The Americans had lost 3 carriers and 4 smaller warships. It was a great but not an overwhelming victory. Indeed Japanese suicide aircraft now began to cause keen anxiety.

---

[3] As mentioned in earlier volumes a Japanese "Army" was the equivalent of an Allied "Corps", a Japanese "Area Army" the equivalent of an Allied "Army"; the Japanese "Southern Army" resembled an Allied "Army Group".

[4] Immediately after the landing GHQ published a communiqué which could be read only as meaning that there were 225,000 Japanese on Leyte; this, however, was the estimated number in the whole of the Philippines. In December, in a later phase of the operation, the *New York Herald-Tribune* published an editorial in which it spoke of "the imaginative over-emphasis, verging at times on poetic licence, with which General MacArthur's communiqués are wont to report his successes".

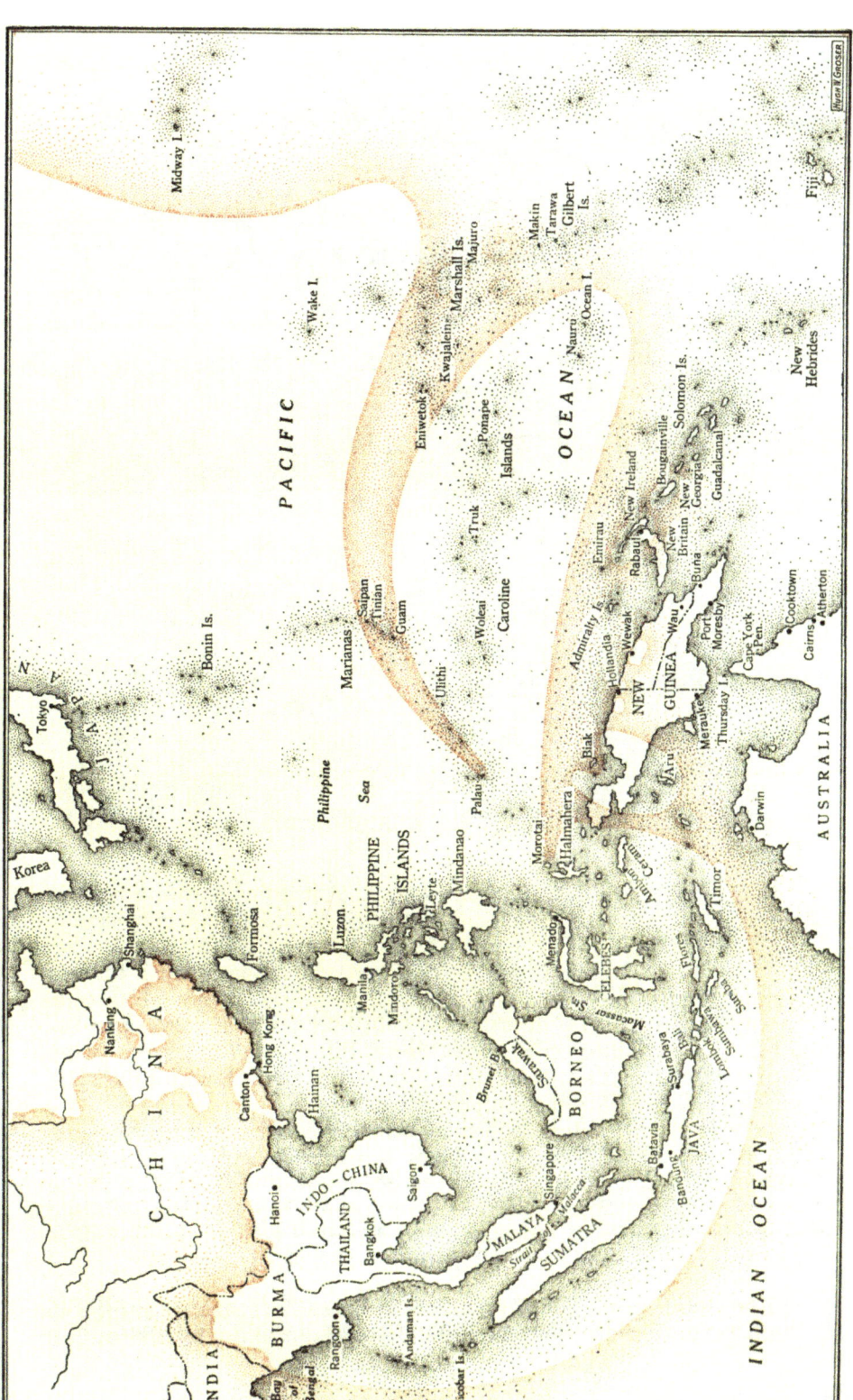

South-West Pacific Area, December 1944

On the 29th and 30th they severely damaged three carriers; and from 29th October to 4th November delivered heavy attacks on the invaders' ships and airfields, and continued to strike although in dwindling force in the following weeks.

Meanwhile the Japanese had brought forward army reinforcements and by 11th November had put ashore on Leyte all or most of the *102nd Division*, the *30th*, the *1st* and the *26th* (the last two from China). MacArthur landed the 32nd American Division on 14th November and the 11th Airborne and 77th by the 23rd, and thus had seven divisions ashore to oppose five Japanese.

The movement of these troops to Leyte had cost the Japanese heavily in transports and naval vessels sunk by air attack, and after bringing in part of their *8th Division* from Manila early in December they ceased trying to reinforce. By the fourth week of December the Japanese army on Leyte was disintegrating. At that stage the Japanese losses were estimated at 56,000 killed; the Americans had lost 3,049 killed or missing.

The American and British Navies now dominated both the Pacific and Indian Oceans and, within the range of their aircraft, the skies above. Of 12 battleships which Japan had possessed when war began or had completed since, only 5 remained; of 20 aircraft carriers (excluding escort carriers) only 5; of 18 heavy cruisers only 6; of 22 light cruisers only 5. The United States Navy on the other hand had greatly increased in the past three years, and possessed, in December 1944, 23 battleships, 24 carriers, 16 heavy and 42 light cruisers. Most of these ships were in the Pacific, where the Australian Navy added a contingent of 4 cruisers and considerable flotillas of smaller ships. A British Pacific Fleet, including the two most modern British battleships and 4 large carriers, was now based on Ceylon.

In the Pacific, up to December 1944, 30 Allied divisions had been in operations—23 American divisions (including 4 of Marines), 6 Australian and one New Zealand. In Burma 13 British Empire divisions—8 Indian, 3 African and 2 British—were deployed, and there were 4 small Chinese divisions with 2 American regiments attached. The armies of General MacArthur and Admiral Nimitz, now poised for the final blows, were together about one-third as large as General Eisenhower's in France would soon be; Admiral Lord Louis Mountbatten's in north Burma about half as strong as Field Marshal Alexander's in Italy.

In November American long-range bombers from bases in the Marianas had thrice attacked Tokyo. As bases closer to Japan were seized and developed, such attacks on Japanese cities would be intensified. Some American leaders hoped that the destruction of cities from the air might persuade the Japanese Government to surrender before American lives had been lost in an assault on the Japanese mainland.

The success of the Allied operations in Europe had brought to the fore the question of re-deploying the British forces once the first main strategical objective—the defeat of Germany—had been achieved. To record the discussions and plans concerning the roles of this and other forces in the Pacific in 1945 it is necessary to go back to 1943. In South-East Asia, then and later, the main military burden was being carried by Indian troops; in the South-West Pacific during 1942 and 1943 by Australian troops and, since the first quarter of 1944, by Americans. If Germany soon collapsed where could room be found in the Asiatic war for forces flying the Union Jack? Preparation of detailed plans for a redeployment of British forces had begun in London in 1943, and the question had been debated and finally decided during 1944.

In September 1943 when the surrender of the Italian Navy made it possible soon to employ the greater part of the Mediterranean Fleet elsewhere, the British Prime Minister, Mr Churchill, was in the United States. He suggested that the Eastern Fleet in the Indian Ocean should be reinforced and, as a first step, that the reinforcements should proceed through the Panama Canal to the Pacific and there spend at least four months gaining experience under American orders.[5]

As a result of discussions at an Allied conference in Cairo in November 1943 the British Chiefs of Staff decided that as soon as possible after the defeat of Germany, then assumed for planning purposes to have taken place by 1st October 1944, the British Fleet should be sent to the Pacific —the main theatre of operations against Japan—and that they should aim at providing also four British divisions based on Australia for service in the Pacific zone. The main British effort on land in 1944 would be made, however, in South-East Asia.

On 30th December the British Chiefs drafted a telegram describing these plans for the information of the Australian and New Zealand Governments and sent it to Mr Churchill, then in Morocco, for approval. This opened "a long and complicated debate which was to end only in September 1944, after involving the Prime Minister and the British Chiefs of Staff in perhaps their most serious disagreement of the war".[6] It is briefly recorded here because from time to time the Australian Government and its military advisers were involved.

Mr Churchill wished the main British effort to be made from the Indian Ocean against Malaya and the Indies. He contended that a Sumatran operation offered greater promise than the plan for sending the British forces to the Pacific. Incidentally he suggested that to base the forces on Australia would involve excessively heavy demands for shipping. Churchill was strongly supported in his insistence on concentration in the Bay of Bengal by the Foreign Office which, on 21st February, presented a memorandum which concluded that

if the [Pacific] strategy . . . is accepted, and if there is to be no major British role in the Far Eastern war, then it is no exaggeration to say that the solidarity of the

---

[5] The following brief account of United Kingdom planning for participation in the Pacific war is chiefly based on J. Ehrman, *Grand Strategy*, Vols V and VI (1956), in the British official *History of the Second World War*.
[6] Ehrman, Vol V, p. 425.

British Commonwealth and its influence in the maintenance of peace in the Far East will be irretrievably damaged.[7]

On the other hand, so far as Australia was concerned, the Prime Minister, Mr Curtin, had made it known to visiting British authorities late in November 1943 that he hoped to see Britain represented in the Pacific, and had caused them to believe that he would welcome the formation of a British Commonwealth Command in the South-West Pacific as a partner to the American command there; or alternatively that the boundaries of South-East Asia Command might be revised to include part of the South-West Pacific Area and Australian forces included in Admiral Mountbatten's command.[8]

On 3rd March Churchill sent the members of the Defence Committee a memorandum[9] (dated 29th February) clearly setting out the problem. In the course of it he wrote:

> The two alternatives open are:
> A. To send a detachment of the British Fleet during the present year to act with the United States in the Pacific and to increase the strength of this detachment as fast as possible, having regard to the progress of the war against Germany. This fleet would be followed at the end of the German war, or perhaps even before it, by four British divisions which would be based on, say, Sydney and would operate with the Australian forces on the left or southern flank of the main American advance against the Philippines, Formosa and ultimately Japan. . . .
> B. To keep the centre of gravity of the British war against Japan in the Bay of Bengal for at least 18 months from now and to conduct amphibious operations on a considerable scale against the Andamans, Nicobars and, above all, Sumatra as resources become available.
>
> The British Chiefs of Staff favour "A", and made an agreement at Cairo after brief discussions with the United States Chiefs of Staff that this should be accepted "as a basis for investigation". Neither I nor the Foreign Secretary was aware of these discussions, though I certainly approved the report by the Combined Chiefs of Staff in which they were mentioned.
>
> Admiral Mountbatten and the South-East Asia Command are in favour of "B", which is perhaps not unnatural since "A" involves the practical elimination of the South-East Asia Command and the immediate closing down of all amphibious plans in the Bay of Bengal.

Churchill added that the Chiefs of Staff considered that British forces based in Australia would be a valuable contribution to the main American operations and would "produce good results upon Australian sentiment towards the Mother Country", and that successful operations in the Pacific would cause Malaya and the Indies to "fall easily into our hands". On the other hand, he pointed out, the Pacific strategy would involve the division of British forces, would place out of offensive action very large forces in the Indian theatre, render idle big bases there and in the Middle East and vastly lengthen the British line of communication. Mr Churchill pointed also to a difficult political question concerning the future of

---

[7] Quoted in Ehrman, Vol V, p. 439.
[8] Ehrman, Vol V, pp. 439-40.
[9] Quoted in Ehrman, Vol V, pp. 441-4.

Britain's Malayan possessions. "If the Japanese should withdraw from them or make peace as the result of the main American thrust, the United States Government would after the victory feel greatly strengthened in its view that all possessions in the East Indian Archipelago should be placed under some international body upon which the United States would exercise a decisive control. They would feel with conviction: 'We won the victory and liberated these places, and we must have the dominating say in their future and derive full profit from their produce, especially oil.' Against this last the British Chiefs of Staff urge that nothing in their plan excludes our attacking the Japanese in Malaya and the Netherlands East Indies in due course from the Pacific."

Churchill added that he would ask President Roosevelt whether American operations in the Pacific really required a detachment of the British Fleet there in 1944 and 1945. He himself deprecated "a hasty decision to abandon the Indian theatre and the prospect of amphibious operations across the Bay of Bengal".

The Chiefs of Staff, in a memorandum presented five days later, expressed disagreement with Churchill's definition of the alternatives. To them it was a choice between a Pacific strategy aimed at obtaining a footing in Japan's inner zone at the earliest possible moment and a Bay of Bengal strategy that could not begin until about six months after Germany's defeat and would be an independent British contribution to the war against Japan. Whatever contribution Britain made, the major credit for the defeat of Japan would go to the Americans. A deadlock seemed to have been reached. General Ismay, Mr Churchill's Chief of Staff, on 4th March warned Churchill of the danger that the Chiefs of Staff would resign, an event that would be "little short of catastrophic" on the eve of the invasion of Europe.

The Australian Government, meanwhile, was wondering what was being done about the decisions reached at the Cairo conference in November, and Mr Curtin sent an inquiry to Mr Churchill on 4th March. Churchill called a conference for 8th March to decide on a reply to this embarrassing question. As a result, on the 11th, Churchill sent a telegram to Curtin in which he said that two broad conceptions were being examined: one that the main weight of the British effort should be directed across the Indian Ocean and brought to bear against the Malay barrier in a west to east thrust using India as the main base; the other that the bulk of the naval forces, together with certain land and air forces, should operate from east to west on the left flank of the United States forces in the South Pacific, with Australia and not India as their main base. He added that before reaching firm conclusions the relative base potentialities of India and Australia should be known, and suggested that Britain should send small parties of administrative experts to Australia.

This proposal ran counter to a principle which the Commander-in-Chief of the Australian Army, General Sir Thomas Blamey, had maintained since 1942, not always with success, that it was not in accordance with long-accepted principles of Imperial defence for one partner in the British

Commonwealth to send independent staffs on military missions to another partner. He considered that such staffs should be integrated into the local staff. The main liaison groups between the South-West Pacific forces (and the Australian Army in particular) and the War Office were then a liaison staff with the Australian Army headed by Major-General R. H. Dewing, and Mr Churchill's personal representative at General MacArthur's headquarters, who was Lieut-General H. Lumsden. The Dewing mission had been appointed in November 1942. Blamey had then objected to it on the ground mentioned above, and on other grounds. In November 1943 he had written to the Chief of the Imperial General Staff, General Brooke, on the subject. The letter said:

> I have been somewhat disturbed of late at the trend of relationships between the Headquarters of the various military forces of the Empire, and particularly between ourselves and W.O. These relationships were laid down originally at the Imperial Conference in 1909, and had been developed steadily until recent years. The pivot of all our relationships was the Imperial General Staff, and although this conception has tended to weaken, the results of its formation still remain, to the immense advantage of the whole of the forces of the Empire.
>
> The main principles that have been enunciated under the aegis of the Imperial General Staff, and determined at various Imperial Conferences, have led to the development of the Empire land forces on identical lines. The result is that throughout the Empire the Army has a common doctrine of war; a common system of organisation, both in relation to the command and staff system, and the organisation of units and formations; common principles and methods of training; and common equipment. The immense advantages of these were demonstrated in the first world war, and again when Empire forces were assembled in Egypt and in Britain in the early days of the present war. Unless the key centre from which these principles radiate, namely, the Imperial General Staff, is maintained, the tendency to drift into differences, already noticeable, will become more and more accentuated. This I believe will be greatly to the detriment of the Imperial Forces jointly and separately.
>
> The tendency in our relations now is to organise Military Missions as opposed to the General Staff conception. While the establishment of Military Missions is probably as good an arrangement as can be made between allied countries, I am perfectly certain that the advantages of combined staffs, of which the Imperial General Staff is the main trunk for the Empire, is a much better solution, and will give greater strength and cohesion to the British Forces, and will ensure the maintenance of the principles already agreed upon at Imperial Conferences.
>
> It is not possible for a Military Mission to get inside the thought of the forces of the country to which it is allocated, because it is itself external to the thinking organisation of the forces of that country. The only way to reach the highest plane in military relationships, for representatives of one portion of the Empire serving in any other part, is to ensure that they shall be part of the organic whole of that portion of the Empire in which they may be employed.
>
> It is probable that Australia was the first to cause a crack in the true relationship. This was due to the fact that it was necessary for us to maintain an agency in England for the procurement of equipment. . . . In its original conception this mission was an off-shoot and was under the control of the Australian representative of the Imperial General Staff at the War Office. Its development, however, has been somewhat away from this.
>
> When Major-General Dewing made a short visit to England, I discussed with him the nature of the British Military Mission here. I have no doubt that he told you that I expressed my opinion as adverse to the change from the Imperial General Staff conception to that of the Military Mission. I also discussed with him—and I understand he raised with you—the question of whether it might be possible to allocate one or two senior officers about the rank of Brigadier from U.K. to

Australia, and reciprocally from Australia to U.K. On mature consideration, however, I do not think that such an arrangement is convenient with the existence of Missions charged with the function of representation, as such officers would find themselves owing allegiance locally to two masters.

The matter has again come to the fore owing to the decision of the Australian Government to establish a High Commissioner in India. Lieut-General Sir Iven Mackay, who has been chosen for the appointment, has asked for a Military Attaché on his staff. I am opposing the suggestion as I feel sure that the present direct communication as between Armies is much more elastic, rapid and confidential than the allocation of a Military Attaché to the High Commissioner could ever be. Moreover it introduces a further centrifugal move at a time when we should be drawing together.

Our tendency at present is to shape our ends in a manner more suited to allied forces rather than to the forces of an entity of which we are integral parts, and I feel that we are going on diverging instead of converging lines.

I should be very glad to hear your views on the matters in question, for I am strongly persuaded that the more closely bound are the Empire forces during the war, the more unified will be the outlook of the Empire Governments in determining matters of common interest in the post-war period.

The letter illustrates two trends in Blamey's thinking, consistently maintained in these years: first, that the United Kingdom and the Dominions should cooperate in military affairs as close and equal partners; second, that the links between the forces of the Empire should not be weakened as an outcome of intimate wartime association with those of the United States.

Brooke deferred a firm expression of opinion on the problem Blamey had raised until it had been discussed by the Dominion Prime Ministers at a meeting to be held early in 1944.

After consulting Blamey, the Chiefs of Staff and MacArthur, Curtin replied to Churchill's telegram of 11th March that substantial information about facilities in Australia had already been provided by them to the Admiralty, War Office and Air Ministry, detailed information had been supplied to the Lethbridge Mission,[1] and other sources of information were readily available through the Australian Service representatives in London and the United Kingdom Army and Air Force Liaison Staff in Australia.[2] The experience of the Australian Staffs in providing base organisations and maintenance for large forces on the mainland and in New Guinea should enable them, in collaboration with the United Kingdom Liaison Staff, to prepare tentative plans. United Kingdom representatives would be welcome but it might be preferable to defer them until plans had progressed further when "best results would probably be obtained by sending representatives of the staffs and advance parties of the Forces concerned". General MacArthur would gladly furnish any opinions that might be desired on the operational aspect of base potentialities of Australia and the operation of forces therefrom. Curtin concluded:

British forces could . . . operate in the South-West Pacific Area only by being assigned to the Commander-in-Chief in accordance with the terms of his directive. A separate system of command could not be established. Furthermore, the base

---

[1] See Volume VI in this series.

[2] The existing liaison machine was already in operation to the extent that Major-General Dewing from 21st March to 3rd April made a reconnaissance of areas in New Guinea in which British divisions might be trained and acclimatised, visiting Donadabu, Wau, Bulolo, Lae and Finschhafen.

facilities on the mainland are under the control of the Commander, Allied Land Forces, who is also Commander-in-Chief of the Australian Military Forces, the Australian Chief of the Naval Staff and the Australian Chief of the Air Staff . . . information should be furnished by these sources and the administrative experts sent to Australia should be attached to the staffs of the respective Australian Services.

Blamey, who foresaw the possibility that the United Kingdom leaders might wish to establish a separate command in the area, was the main author of this final paragraph.[3]

On 30th March the Australian Army Representative in London, Lieut-General Smart,[4] cabled to Blamey's Chief of the General Staff, Lieut-General Northcott, that the general effect of the Australian reply was thought in London to be somewhat discouraging; it was realised that existing machinery could provide the necessary information but it would be of value to have British officers in London who had seen Australia and discussed the problem on the spot. He understood that it was now proposed to send smaller parties to confer with Australian commanders and with General Dewing.

On 13th March President Roosevelt had replied to Mr Churchill's inquiry, mentioned earlier, by saying that there would be no operation in the Pacific in 1944 that would be adversely affected by the absence of a British Fleet detachment, and it did not appear that such a detachment would be needed before the (northern) summer of 1945. He added the opinion that, in view of a recent move of the Japanese main fleet to Singapore,

unless we have unexpected bad luck in the Pacific your naval force will be of more value to our common effort by remaining in the Indian Ocean.

On 20th March Churchill ruled that the Bay of Bengal policy must be maintained and a reconnaissance mission sent to Australia to study potential bases. The Bay of Bengal policy received a rebuff, however, on 21st March when the American Chiefs of Staff stated that once their forces had succeeded in the Formosa-Luzon area the strategic value of operations in Malaya and the Indies would be reduced, and they could not agree to support an operation against Sumatra or any similar operation involving large amphibious commitments in the South-East Asia Command.

The Americans' views were influenced by their wish to establish in China a strategic air force which would bomb Japan and its approaches; to them the Bay of Bengal policy seemed a move in the wrong direction and one which might divert resources from the thrust towards China from northern Burma. They proposed that the Combined Chiefs should order Admiral Mountbatten to concentrate on seizing certain bases in northern Burma before the monsoon. The British Chiefs of Staff disapproved of the Sumatran operation, but had no faith in operations towards China.

---

[3] Blamey Papers: British Cooperation in the Pacific.
[4] Lt-Gen E. K. Smart, DSO, MC, VX133279. (1st AIF; Lt 55 Siege Bty 1915-16; CO 110 How Bty 1918.) QMG AHQ 1939-40; GOC Southern Comd 1940-42; Aust Mil Rep Washington 1942, London 1942-46. Regular soldier; b. Kew, Vic, 23 May 1891. Died 2 May 1961.

Admiral Mountbatten said that he did not think that the operations proposed by the Americans would succeed. Complex discussions followed; the American Chiefs were not persuaded.

Early in April a most unpractical policy came under detailed consideration in London: the joint planners were told to investigate the possibilities of establishing bases in northern and western Australia and "the general strategic concept of an advance on the general line Timor-Celebes-Borneo-Saigon". Within a few days this request in similar but not identical terms reached the planners from both the Prime Minister and the Chiefs of Staff independently.

Thus there were now four proposals in the field: the American leaders wished the main British effort in Asia to be in northern Burma and towards China, in whose military potentialities they had great faith; the British Prime Minister demanded concentration on an eastward drive against the lost colonies of Malaya and the Indies; the British Chiefs of Staff wished a strong British task force to join the Americans in the Pacific; both Churchill (to whom the Chiefs of Staff would not yield) and the Chiefs of Staff (whose plan was not welcomed by the American Chiefs) were now considering a compromise plan—a thrust northward from north Australia.

For planning purposes the target date for this "middle strategy" was fixed at March 1945. The tentative plans provided for an advance to Ambon, by-passing Timor, thence to northern Borneo, perhaps via Menado in Celebes, and on to either Saigon and Malaya or Hong Kong and the China coast at the end of 1945 or early in 1946. The planners pointed out, however, that northern Borneo could be gained more quickly and more economically by passing north of New Guinea and using staging points and sea communications already in Allied hands. Thus there was now a fifth possible policy: an advance to Borneo along the established South-West Pacific route.

The inquiry whether India or Australia had most to offer as the main base was proceeding. The British Chiefs of Staff still wished to send their own missions to examine Australian potentialities. And the Admiralty had already sent Rear-Admiral C. S. Daniel and a staff to the South-West Pacific Area, but Curtin's cablegram of 22nd March caused Churchill to delay Daniel's arrival and it was not until 28th April that he was given permission to make the last lap of his journey to Australia.

At this stage consideration of the proposal to send a larger United Kingdom group to make inquiries in Australia was postponed until the conference of Dominion Prime Ministers was held in London early in May. General Blamey accompanied Mr Curtin to London and, on 5th May he, Admiral Sir Ragnar Colvin and Air Vice-Marshal H. N. Wrigley discussed the problem of the British contingent for the Pacific with the United Kingdom Chiefs of Staff.[5] Blamey and his staff tried to find out what the British intentions were, but without much success at that stage.

---

[5] Colvin was a former First Naval Member; Wrigley commanded RAAF Overseas Headquarters, London.

It was pointed out by the British Chiefs that no British forces could reach the Pacific area before 1945. General MacArthur considered that, after the recapture of the Philippines, the American Navy would control the advance towards Japan while he advanced westward to Borneo. The correct strategy in this phase might be a converging offensive through the Strait of Malacca and across the Bay of Bengal; another possible pincer movement might be developed by other forces under MacArthur operating from north and north-west Australia by way of Timor.

Blamey informed the conference that probably six Australian divisions would be required in forthcoming operations, three to capture Halmahera and three to occupy New Guinea. The British Chiefs of Staff expected that some six British divisions and about 20 air squadrons would be available for the Far East after the collapse of Germany.

At a meeting of the Defence Committee on 10th May a detailed statement of the British forces available for a Pacific strategy and the estimated dates on which they would become operational (assuming that Germany had been defeated by the end of 1944) was presented. It pictured a fleet of 4 battleships, 4 fleet carriers, 10 cruisers and corresponding other vessels being operational late in 1944, and being increased to a fleet of 6 battleships, 5 fleet carriers, 5 light carriers and 25 cruisers late in 1945. Two infantry divisions might arrive from India in January and March 1945 and 3 from European theatres in February, March and April 1945 respectively. The air force would eventually contain 157 squadrons, including 63 R.A.A.F. squadrons (among them being 11 Australian squadrons from Europe and the Middle East), 16 R.N.Z.A.F., and 78 R.A.F. squadrons.

In these discussions three main considerations were uppermost in the minds of the Australian leaders: the desire to have Great Britain strongly represented in the Pacific, a resolve not to upset the command arrangements developed in the past two years, and anxiety lest plans should be made that were beyond the capacity of Australia's manpower.

On 17th May Curtin, in a memorandum to Churchill, raised "the question of the procedure to be followed in order to resolve this question, which is of vital importance to British prestige in the Pacific and to the form and nature of the Australian war effort". Australia did not possess the manpower and material needed to meet all the demands being made on her. He instanced the fact that, at October 1943, United States demands were involving the employment of 75,000 Australians and the figure was expected to reach 100,000 by June 1944; reciprocal Lend-Lease would reach nearly £100,000,000 in 1944. It was presumed that if additional forces were sent to Australia the United Nations would make good the deficiencies which Australia could not supply. The first step, he added, should be a decision by the Combined Chiefs whether the proposed additional forces were to be sent to the Pacific. If they were, Australia would have to begin planning, particularly planning food production. Finally he noted that any variation of the decision whereby the Australian forces had been assigned to the Commander-in-Chief, South-West Pacific

Area could be made only on the recommendation of the Combined Chiefs of Staff and with the approval of the Australian Government. Meanwhile Admiral Daniel on 10th May had cabled to the Admiralty that he could see no reason why the whole proposed naval force could not be supported by Australia by mid-1945.

On 22nd May the British Chiefs of Staff agreed with Blamey that the British reconnaissance parties to go to Australia should be integrated with the Australian Staff and not operate as an independent mission. These parties were to include 17 naval officers, 12 army officers and 4 R.A.F. officers, including those already in Australia.

Mr Curtin had taken with him to London and Washington a proposal that the combat forces of the Australian Army should be reduced to six infantry divisions and two armoured brigades. General MacArthur had already agreed to this proposal, and in Washington, on his return journey, Curtin obtained the approval of the Combined Chiefs of Staff.

On 30th June the representatives of the British Services, led by Daniel, presented to the Australian Chiefs of Staff a revised statement of the requirements of the British forces which it was intended to base in Australia. The estimates were based on the assumption that Germany would be defeated by 1st October 1944. The fleet to be based on Australia was now to include at the outset 2 or 3 battleships, 2 or 3 large carriers, 10 cruisers and corresponding numbers of smaller vessels, and be increased to 4 battleships, a total of 28 carriers of all types, 12 cruisers, 88 L.S.T's and other craft.

It was assumed by the planners, Daniel said, that the British military force to be based in Australia would include five divisions, two tank brigades, some commandos and base troops, the whole force totalling, say, 225,000. It was estimated that 40,000 base troops would arrive from India in February 1945, one division from the Mediterranean in March, two divisions from India and one from England in April, and a division from England in May. The dispatch of the divisions from India was conditional on the situation in Burma permitting it. The divisions were to be ready for operations at various dates between August and October.

The Australian Chiefs of Staff advised the Government that the accommodation of these forces, which would finally total 675,000—equal to about one-tenth of the Australian population—would make heavy demands on materials and labour. (It was as though an additional force of about 5,000,000 were, within a year, to be disembarked in the United Kingdom, or a force of 12,000,000 disembarked in the United States.) A labour force increasing to 26,000 by February would be needed to carry out the necessary building program. To relieve the load to be carried by the railways some 100,000 tons of additional coastal shipping would be needed, and 12,500 men to operate ports and railways. The whole project would depend to a large extent on whether enough coal was available. Probably 15 additional air transport squadrons would be needed. The Chiefs of Staff said that it was essential that a decision about the United Kingdom plans should be made by mid-September so that the necessary work could begin in time. A detailed study of the Australian proposals for accommodating and supplying the proposed forces was prepared; it occupies more than 200 printed pages.

The conclusions reached at the Prime Minister's discussions in London and Washington were set out in an agendum presented to the Australian Advisory War Council and War Cabinet on 5th July and approved by both bodies. In this agendum Curtin quoted from the record of his final discussion with Churchill which ran: "Mr Curtin said it was impossible for him, in the absence of any discussion with his colleagues . . . to commit himself to any changes in the Command arrangements in the South-West Pacific Area. He referred to the history of those Command arrangements. . . . The [Pacific War Council in London] had, to all intents and purposes, ceased to exist, and the Washington body was completely defunct. He therefore had had to deal with General MacArthur as an Allied Commander with Headquarters established in Australia. He feared that there was a danger of the gravest misunderstandings with the United States if Australian Forces were taken away from General MacArthur's direct command and placed under a new Commander."

After the conference in London the British Chiefs of Staff prepared a revised "middle-strategy" plan according to which three Australian divisions supported by a British fleet would attack Ambon. They proposed also that the command arrangements in the South-West Pacific should be altered: that area should become subordinate to the Combined Chiefs instead of the Joint Chiefs, and the British and Dominion forces should operate as "a distinct Command with British Commanders under General MacArthur's supreme direction". They added, however, that this arrangement should be left open to reconsideration at a later date.

At this stage the British Chiefs of Staff learnt that the American time-table was being accelerated to such an extent that the Americans might be in Formosa by the time the Australians, if the "middle strategy" was adopted, were in Ambon. The American Chiefs of Staff now advised the British to concentrate on an offensive from the west against the Netherlands Indies, with Ceylon and not Darwin as the main base; the British Chiefs recommended that an Imperial force should be placed under MacArthur's direction to secure oil installations and air bases in northern Borneo. The difference between Churchill and the Chiefs of Staff was still unresolved after seven months of debate. On 17th July Churchill summoned Mountbatten to London, intending, after discussion with him, to give a final decision.

In June Mountbatten had been directed to concentrate on the north Burma strategy desired by the Americans. He was to develop the air link with China in order to provide more oil and other stores for the forces in China, and was to prepare to develop overland communications with China. During July the Japanese, defeated at Imphal, were in full retreat towards Tiddim and the Chindwin. It seemed that in Burma the tide had turned. After keen discussion it was agreed between the British and

American staffs on 8th September that a plan of Mountbatten's to clear northern Burma to a line Kalewa-Shwebo-Lashio should be adopted and in mid-March 1945 a seaborne and airborne attack on Rangoon should be undertaken.

Meanwhile on 4th July Mr Curtin had sent a telegram to Mr Churchill in which he said that the increasing pace of the American advance might make it unnecessary for large-scale military operations to be undertaken by British Commonwealth forces, but that General MacArthur's weakness at sea could be overcome only by the use of British naval forces.

> It not only would contribute in great measure to the acceleration of the operations, but would be the naval spearhead in a large portion of this campaign (Curtin added). It is the only effective means for placing the Union Jack in the Pacific alongside the Australian and American flags. It would evoke great public enthusiasm in Australia and contribute greatly to the restoration of Empire prestige in the Far East . . . the pace of events here demands immediate action. . . . Britain's war record in relation to her resources is so magnificent that it will bear favourable comparison with any other nation, even if circumstances and the speed of the American program preclude her making an early contribution of land and air forces.

On 12th August Curtin again pressed Churchill for the early dispatch of a British naval force to the Pacific, emphasising that the need was not for a large contribution of sea, land and air forces at some future time but for a naval force as soon as possible. "I am deeply concerned," cabled Curtin, "at the position which would arise in our Far East if any considerable American opinion were to maintain that America fought a war on principle in the Far East and won it relatively unaided while the other Allies, including ourselves, did very little towards recovering our lost property."

On 9th August the British leaders had decided to inform the American Chiefs of Staff that they wished a British fleet to share in the operations against the mainland of Japan or Formosa, but that if this offer was declined in favour of support of MacArthur's operations by the British Fleet they should propose "the formation of a British Empire task force under a British commander, consisting of British, Australian and New Zealand land, sea and air forces, to operate under General MacArthur's Supreme Command". In this event they suggested that control of operations in the South-West Pacific Area should be on the same footing as control of operations in South-East Asia Command except that the American Chiefs of Staff should be the channel of communication for the South-West Pacific Area and the British for South-East Asia Command: that was to say that the South-West Pacific Area should come under the control of the Combined Chiefs and thus Britain would be able to influence it directly.

On 23rd August Churchill replied to Curtin, repeating a cablegram that he had just sent to Washington outlining these conclusions. This cablegram pointed out that the Japanese had increased their strength in Burma from four and a half to ten divisions, and stated that the capture of Myitkyina (which had fallen to Lieut-General Joseph W. Stilwell's American-Chinese force on 3rd August) ruled out "as was always foreseen, any purely defensive policy in north Burma". It was necessary, he said, to protect the air link to China and support the further construction of the Burma Road and the pipe line to Yunnan. Admiral Mountbatten, Churchill added, had put forward alternative plans: either to continue the north Burma operations, or to capture Rangoon by an airborne attack, open that port

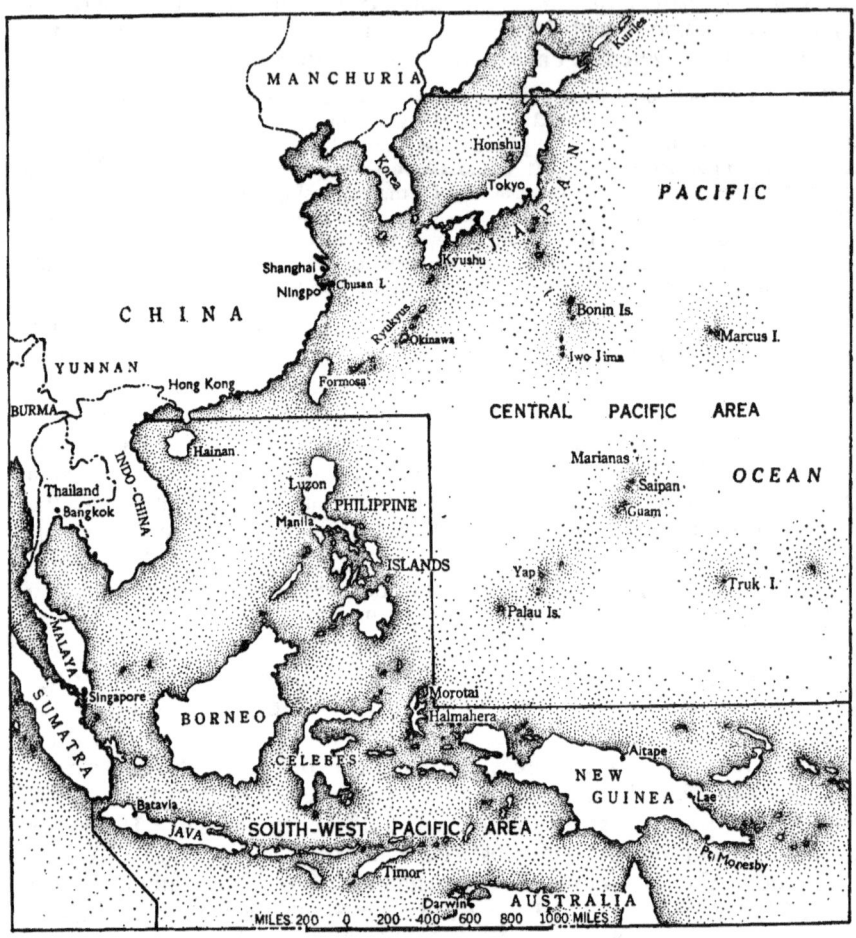

and support the later operations by sea, at the same time cutting the communications of the Japanese armies in north Burma. The British leaders favoured the second course, and were asking the Combined Chiefs of Staff to provide resources for the operations against Rangoon. Meanwhile, the cablegram added, a British fleet was being built up in the Bay of Bengal most of which would not be needed for the operations outlined. By mid-1945 it could take part in the operations leading to the final assault on Japan. But if the American Chiefs of Staff were unwilling to accept this contribution the British Government would discuss as an alternative the "British Empire task force under a British Commander" mentioned above.

Curtin protested strongly against the alternative proposal for British participation, reminding Churchill, on 1st September, that on several occasions he had emphasised that Australia had a deep interest in preserving the existing command arrangements in the South-West Pacific. Government and Opposition leaders were agreed that they should not be varied. He should have been consulted before the new proposal for a British-led British and Dominion force had gone to Washington.

Churchill replied that it had not been suggested that Australian troops should be taken away from General MacArthur. "On the contrary, we have suggested sending to Australia a British naval force which would be combined with the Australian and New Zealand forces already on the spot into a British and Dominion task force under General MacArthur's direct command." Thus the phrase "under a British commander" was now omitted, and did not recur in later discussion of the subject.[6] Churchill added that it was the practice of the Combined Chiefs to draw plans for British and American forces without references to "the various Governments whose forces are included".

Curtin declined to let the matter rest there but (on 16th September) sent Churchill a further cable saying that he felt that he had not misunderstood the task force proposal, and that in principle it did involve a change in the existing direct relationship between the Australian forces and General MacArthur. (Curtin communicated the gist of all these messages to MacArthur.)

Since it was for the sake of prestige that the United Kingdom wished to be represented by forces in the Pacific it was natural that they wished the commander of the proposed task force to be a member of a British Service. Curtin, however, had long since clearly indicated that such a proposal would not be acceptable to Australia; and it seems doubtful whether the British staffs had really thought out the complex command and administrative problems involved, or appreciated the difficulty of defining the spheres of the task force commander on the one hand and Blamey and the Australian Chiefs of Staff on the other. Another aspect was that the proposed commander and his staff would inevitably be new to the area and its problems, whereas the Australians had attained a degree of efficiency in the type of land warfare imposed by conditions in the Pacific and South-East Asia which at that stage was probably unsurpassed.

Meanwhile, on 9th September the American Chiefs had accepted the British proposal for a British task force under a British commander who would be subordinate to MacArthur, but ignored the main proposal concerning participation in the attack on Japan by the British Fleet. Thus one British proposal was unwelcome to the Americans and the other not acceptable to the Australians.

---

[6] In *The Second World War*, Vol V (1952), p. 513, Churchill wrote of "a British and Australian force under an Australian commander", but this suggestion does not seem to have reached the Australian Government.

The command problem, combined with growing uncertainty whether they could spare a military contingent for the proposed task force, made the British leaders the more resolved to obtain acceptance of the offer to send their main fleet to the Central Pacific. And on 12th September the Chief of the Air Staff, Marshal of the R.A.F. Sir Charles Portal, brought forward a new proposal that, after the German collapse, a strong force of British heavy bombers should take part in the long-range bombing of Japan. Consequently, on the eve of a conference at Quebec in August between the British and American leaders, the British were determined to press hard for the employment of the fleet in the Central Pacific and for the employment of their heavy bombers against Japan, and were ready to withdraw the offer of a British Commonwealth task force in the South-West Pacific Area. At the first plenary session at Quebec Mr Churchill offered the main British fleet for service in the Pacific and President Roosevelt promptly accepted it. Churchill then said that the placing of the main British fleet in the Central Pacific would not prevent a detachment from working with General MacArthur if desired, and added that there was "no intention to interfere in any way with General MacArthur's Command".

Later, however, the American Chiefs sent a memorandum to their British colleagues in the course of which they said that they considered that the initial use of the British naval task force should be on the western flank of the advance in the South-West Pacific. This led to long and acrimonious debate in the course of which it became evident that Admirals William D. Leahy and Ernest J. King—two politically aware admirals—did not want the British Fleet to have any share in the main operations in the Pacific and the British Chiefs considered it "for political reasons . . . essential" that it should.[7] Finally the Combined Chiefs agreed that the British Fleet should participate in the main operations against Japan in the Pacific, took note that the British Chiefs withdrew their proposal to form a British Empire task force in the South-West Pacific, and invited the Chief of the Air Staff to put forward proposals about the contribution the R.A.F. could make to the main operations against Japan. Thus, after nine months of debate, the nature of the British contribution in the Pacific was at last agreed upon.

What was the strength and distribution of the Japanese armies now awaiting the final battles? Twenty-six Japanese divisions—one quarter of the total—were in China proper. An additional fourteen were in Manchuria, and thirteen in Japan itself or the Kurile Islands. Thus approximately half the fighting formations were in Japan or deployed against China and possible attack by Russia. Twenty-three divisions, less than a quarter of the total, and some of them now mere fragments, were scattered along the American line of advance or were isolated in areas of American responsibility. Nineteen were in Burma, Malaya and those parts of the Netherlands Indies that lay west of New Guinea. Six lay isolated

---

[7] The minutes of this meeting are reproduced in full in Ehrman, Vol V, pp. 520-3.

in the areas for which Australia would soon take responsibility. These figures do not include numerous independent brigades. All the divisions in Burma, Australian New Guinea and the Central Pacific were veteran formations, as were about two-thirds of those then in the Philippines and Ryukyus, whereas more than half of those in Japan, China and Manchuria had been formed since the war began.

General MacArthur's army and air force had been greatly increased during 1944. At the beginning of that year it had included four army corps: the I, II and III Australian and I American. In March, the XI American Corps had been added, in June the XIV Corps, in July the X Corps and in September the XXIV, temporarily on loan from Admiral Nimitz. At the beginning of the year MacArthur had possessed one American army—Lieut-General Walter Krueger's Sixth; in September a new army—the Eighth, under Lieut-General Robert L. Eichelberger—had been created. In December the Sixth Army (nine divisions) was on Leyte and the Eighth mainly in Dutch New Guinea.[8] Meanwhile in June 1944, as mentioned, the Combined Chiefs of Staff had agreed to an Australian proposal that henceforth Australia would maintain a reduced army of six infantry divisions and two armoured brigades; and the III Australian Corps headquarters had ceased to exist. In October the I Australian Corps was commanded by Lieut-General Sir Leslie Morshead and the II by Lieut-General S. G. Savige.[9]

Of eighteen American divisions that General MacArthur commanded in the third quarter of 1944 six and one-third were employed in the defence of Torokina, Aitape and the New Britain bases. Other divisions were similarly guarding the bases at Morotai, Biak, Hollandia and Sansapor where Japanese forces were still at large, and three divisions were only on loan from Nimitz. If the policy was continued of seizing air bases and manning a defensive perimeter around them with a force generally greater than the enemy force in the area, MacArthur's advance would soon be halted because his army would be fully engaged defending its bases against "by-passed" Japanese. The reconquest of the Philippines would require more divisions than MacArthur could provide unless he was able to use the large part of his force which was tied down in New Guinea and the Solomons. His solution was to hand over the problem of the by-passed garrisons to Australia.

A natural desire that Australians should take a leading part in regaining their own lost territory was reinforced by the decision of February 1943 that conscripted soldiers should not be employed north of the equator. The decisive battles of 1945 would be fought far north of that line. The

---
[8] The divisions on Leyte in late December were the 7th, 24th, 32nd, 38th, 40th, 77th, 96th, 1st Cavalry and 11th Airborne. The 32nd and 40th went to Leyte after being relieved by Australians at Aitape and in New Britain as described below. The XIV Corps (37th and Americal Divisions) was in the Solomons; the 43rd Division and a regiment at Aitape; the 6th at Sansapor; 31st and 33rd at Morotai and Tum; 41st on Biak; 93rd at Hollandia; and 25th at Noumea. The 93rd had formed part of the garrison in the northern Solomons until relieved by Australian troops.
[9] The total strength of the American Army forces in the SWPA in November 1944 was 688,739, including 132,426 in the air force and 5,852 women. The strength of the Australian Army at this time was 423,536, including 25,476 women; of the air force in the SWPA 163,618, including 7,287 women.

three A.I.F. divisions, consisting solely of volunteers, could be sent there or anywhere else in the world, but a proportion of the men in the militia divisions had not volunteered, and their units could not be sent to the Philippines, for example, or northern Borneo, until the conscripts had been subtracted, a process that would entail considerable regrouping and retraining. For example, in October 1944, 13 of the 33 militia infantry battalions had not the 75 per cent of volunteers needed to entitle them to add the letters "A.I.F." in brackets to the name of their battalion, and in the remaining 20 battalions there were small percentages of non-volunteers. Consequently an Australian political problem would be avoided if the partly-militia force—about three divisions—was employed south of the equator.

Throughout 1942 and 1943 (as Blamey had pointed out in a broadcast statement in September) "the great bulk of the land fighting in the South-West Pacific area fell upon the Australian Army". Only after more than two years had the American Army taken over the major share. In the past year, however, a greatly increased American Army, lavishly equipped and strongly supported by sea and air forces, had developed tactics by which it had overcome outlying Japanese garrisons and had gained in confidence and efficiency. It was becoming evident too that, for the sake of enhancing American prestige in the Far East after the war, some American leaders wished the Stars and Stripes alone to float above the major battlefields of 1945.

The association between General MacArthur and the Australian Government (in the persons of Mr Curtin, General Blamey, and the Secretary of the Defence Department, Sir Frederick Shedden) had been harmonious, but nevertheless those who had been close to the American headquarters knew that at least some of its senior members would be happy to snap the link. The cooperation of allies produces many difficulties and irritations, particularly when the larger one is established in the territory of the smaller. And a headquarters staff of which an astute American observer was to write that they considered Washington and perhaps even the President himself to be under the domination of "Communists and British Imperialists",[1] was not likely to find the atmosphere of Australia, a British country with a Labour Government, entirely congenial. In addition the combination of two national armies creates many problems of organisation and equipment, tactics and temperament. It would be satisfactory to MacArthur's headquarters if a separate sphere of action could be found for the Australians; particularly would it be gratifying if one such sphere should be the relief in Australian New Guinea of the American divisions urgently needed in the Philippines.

As early as 22nd November 1943 Mr Curtin had written to General MacArthur pointing out that Australia had a special interest in the employment of her own forces in ejecting the enemy from her New Guinea territories. At that time American forces were engaged or would soon be

---

[1] R. E. Sherwood, *The White House Papers of Harry L. Hopkins*, Vol II (1949), p. 867.

engaged in four areas on Australian territory: Bougainville, New Britain, Saidor, and Aitape-Wewak. General Blamey had long anticipated an American request that Australian troops should take over all areas in Australian New Guinea. On 3rd March 1944, in a letter to Morshead, then commanding in New Guinea, Blamey had said that he envisaged being required soon to garrison the Mandated Islands, and expected to have about eight militia brigades available for this purpose, of which three would probably be in New Guinea, two or three in New Britain and Bougainville, with two at Atherton working reliefs.

On 22nd May 1944 General Northcott had cabled to Blamey, then in London, that Major-General Stephen J. Chamberlin of General Headquarters had said that possibly Australian troops would be required to garrison New Britain, relieving the American division there in November. As he had indicated to Morshead, Blamey planned to garrison the Solomons, New Britain and the mainland of New Guinea, then held by six and a half American divisions, from his three "militia" divisions. Thus he would hold ready for a possible task in the Philippines the veteran 6th, 7th and 9th Divisions.

The plan took more definite shape on 12th July when MacArthur sent Blamey the following memorandum:

1. The advance to the Philippines necessitates a redistribution of forces and combat missions in the Southwest Pacific Area in order to make available forces with which to continue the offensive.

2. It is desired that Australian Forces assume the responsibility for the continued neutralisation of the Japanese in Australian and British territory and Mandates in the Southwest Pacific Area, exclusive of the Admiralties, by the following dates:

    Northern Solomons-Green Island-Emirau Island . 1 Oct 1944
    Australian New Guinea . . . . . . 1 Nov 1944
    New Britain . . . . 1 Nov 1944

3. The forces now assigned combat missions in the above areas should be relieved of all combat responsibility not later than the dates specified in order that intensive preparations for future operations may be initiated.

4. In the advance to the Philippines it is desired to use Australian Ground Forces and it is contemplated employing initially two A.I.F. Divisions as follows:
    One Division—November 1944
    One Division—January 1945

5. It is requested that this headquarters be informed of the Australian Forces available with the dates of their availability to accomplish the above plan and your general comments and suggestions.

In the subsequent discussion MacArthur would not accept a proposal by Blamey that he should hold the perimeters with only seven brigades (little more than one-third of the American forces thus employed) and insisted that he use four divisions—twelve brigades.[2] As a result, at a series of conferences between Blamey's staff and MacArthur's, a directive

---

[2] Blamey proposed putting the 6th and 23rd Brigades (3rd Division) on Bougainville; 13th and 29th (11th Division) on New Britain; and 4th, 7th and 8th (5th Division) on the New Guinea mainland.

was issued by MacArthur on 2nd August that the minimum forces to be employed in the New Guinea areas should be:

Bougainville	4 brigades
Emirau, Green, Treasury and New Georgia Islands	1 brigade
New Britain	3 brigades
New Guinea mainland	4 brigades

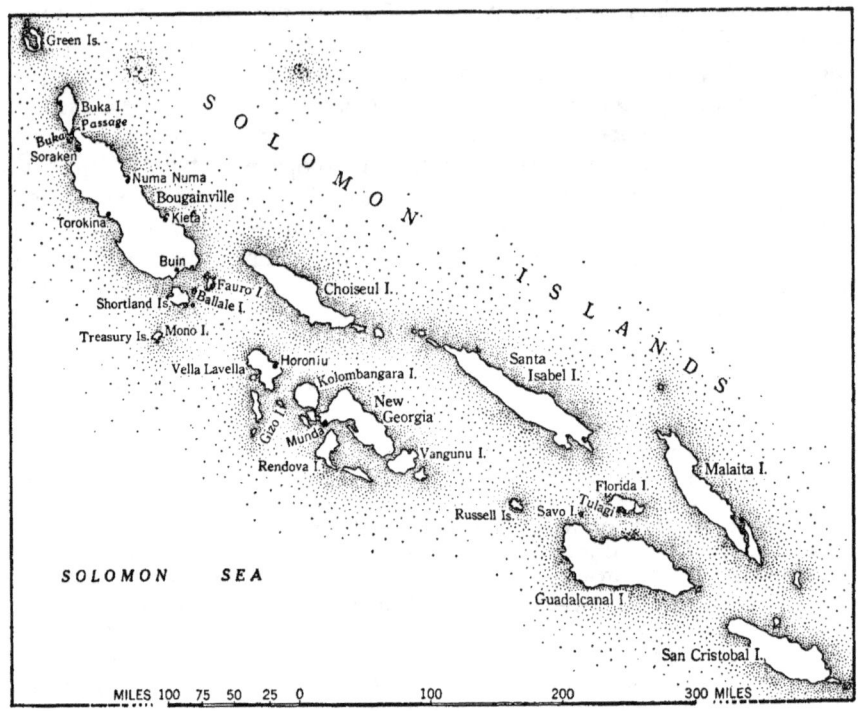

This left a corps of only two divisions for operations farther north with no reserve division. Under a revised arrangement Australian forces were to take over on the outer islands on 1st October, in New Guinea on 15th October, on New Britain on 15th November, and on Bougainville by stages from 15th November to 1st January. MacArthur's insistence that the equivalent of four divisions be employed in the New Guinea areas made it necessary to use one of the A.I.F. divisions there. Only the 6th would be at full strength and ready by 15th October and therefore Blamey chose it to relieve the American Corps at Aitape.[3]

---

[3] The strength and state of availability of the seven Australian divisions on 1st June 1944 were:

	Strength	Available
6th	16,951	At short notice
7th	14,947	In November
9th	13,448	In October
3rd	7,341	Moving to New Guinea
5th	11,693	In New Guinea
11th	8,806	In New Guinea
12th	12,750	Northern Territory garrison

The 1st Armoured Brigade (5,338 strong) and 4th Armoured Brigade (4,719) would be ready for operations in October. The 1st Division, purely a training organisation, was only 4,915 strong.

At this time the estimated strength of the Japanese forces in the three New Guinea areas was:

Bougainville	13,400
New Britain	38,000
Wewak area	24,000

Before the end of the year, however, as a result of information and discussion which will be recorded later, the Bougainville estimate was increased to about 18,000. In fact all these estimates were far too low, as the Intelligence staffs gradually discovered, although the whole truth was not known until after the war had ended. The number in the three areas plus New Ireland totalled not 80,000 but about 170,000 including some 25,000 civilian workers.[4] Eventually 138,200 surrendered, including 12,400 on New Ireland.

The decision that Blamey should employ more troops in New Guinea than Blamey considered necessary was a puzzling one in view of American staff doctrine that when a commander had been allotted a task he himself should decide how to carry it out, and the question arises whether considerations of *amour-propre* were involved: whether G.H.Q. did not wish it to be recorded that six American divisions had been relieved by six Australian brigades (taking into account that one of the seven Australian brigades already had a role in New Guinea and was not part of the relieving force). An even more interesting aspect of the disagreement is that Blamey's proposal seems to indicate that, in July and earlier, he was not contemplating offensive operations on Bougainville and from Aitape, because he could not reasonably have undertaken them with only two brigades in each area. Thus it was the decision of MacArthur, who considered that the Japanese in those areas should not be attacked, to place three instead of two brigades at Aitape and five instead of two in the northern Solomons that made it feasible for the Australians to undertake offensives there, should they so decide.

In preparation for the new phase in which, in General Blamey's words, the army would undertake its "maximum effort during the war", Blamey had held a conference on 11th August at his advanced headquarters at Brisbane, attended by the commanders and senior staff officers of the First Army, New Guinea Force and I Corps and by his own senior staff officers. There he issued instructions that the future roles of the Australian Army would be: first, to occupy the Australian New Guinea areas; and, second, to prepare an A.I.F. Corps for future offensive operations in the South-West Pacific. The headquarters of Lieut-General V. A. H. Sturdee's First Army would move from Atherton to Lae and would command all Australian forces in Australian New Guinea. Blamey directed that from the existing New Guinea Force headquarters, under Lieut-General Savige,

---

[4] The approximate strengths in October 1944 were:

Bougainville	30,000
New Britain	93,000
Aitape-Wewak	31,000

a headquarters of II Corps would be formed (until May 1944 Savige's command had been so named). It would control one division and two brigades. (These were to be the 3rd Division and the 11th and 23rd Brigades.) New Britain would be taken over by one division (the 5th was allotted). The Madang area would continue to be garrisoned by one brigade (the 8th).

The task of II Corps was to defend the air and naval installations on Emirau, Green and Treasury Islands and Munda and, on Bougainville, to "destroy enemy resistance as opportunity offers".[5] The task on New Britain would be to "maintain contact with the Japanese by patrol activity and, without commitment of major forces, endeavour to advance to a line Open Bay-Wide Bay". At Aitape the 6th Division (which might be needed later in the Philippines) was to "defend the airstrip and base area and by patrol activity maintain contact with the enemy in the Wewak area. The commitment of major forces was to be avoided."

In each area there had long been little contact between the American garrisons, manning the defensive perimeters round the bases and airfields, and the Japanese. From the outset the Australian forces were to adopt a more active policy, although in each place, at this stage, a restricted one.

In July Blamey had decided that, in consequence of the movement of General Headquarters to Hollandia and the proposed movement of Advanced G.H.Q. to Leyte, he would form a Forward Echelon of his own headquarters which would move with Advanced G.H.Q. to safeguard Australian interests.[6] Lieut-General F. H. Berryman, now titled "Chief of Staff, Advanced L.H.Q.", commanded this echelon. On 14th November 1944 Blamey approved a re-arrangement of the functions of L.H.Q. in Melbourne and Advanced L.H.Q., as a result of which L.H.Q. took over control of operations in Australia, plus those at Merauke; and Advanced L.H.Q. was defined as "H.Q. for C-in-C Allied Land Forces and C-in-C A.M.F. for dealings with G.H.Q. S.W.P.A. [and] for operations of the A.M.F. outside Australia except for Torres Strait and Merauke areas".[7] The role of the Forward Echelon would be to "move forward with G.H.Q. to assist in the preparation of plans for future employment of the Australian Corps and to initiate movement of troops, equipment and stores to and within the complete area of operations of the Australian Forces abroad". Thus on 7th September, about a fortnight after MacArthur's advanced headquarters was established at Hollandia, the Forward Echelon of Blamey's headquarters had been opened there; and on 15th December Advanced Land Headquarters itself opened at Hollandia.

---

[5] Commander Allied Land Forces, Report on Operations in Australian Mandated Territory, 26 April 1944 to 15 August 1945.

[6] Letter Blamey to the Minister for the Army, Mr F. M. Forde, 26th October 1944.

[7] There had been no changes among the principal staff officers at headquarters in Melbourne since 1943 (although after the death of General Wynter on 7th February 1945 the post of "Lieutenant-General, Administration", would be abolished). Apart from Wynter the principal staff officers were: *Chief of the General Staff* Lt-Gen J. Northcott; *Adjutant-General* Maj-Gen C. E. M. Lloyd; *Quartermaster-General* Maj-Gen J. H. Cannan (since Oct 1940); *Master-General of Ordnance* Maj-Gen L. E. Beavis. Among other senior appointments were: *Military Secretary* Brig A. R. B. Cox; *Major-General of Royal Artillery* Maj-Gen J. S. Whitelaw; *Engineer-in-Chief* Maj-Gen C. S. Steele; *Signals Officer in Chief* Maj-Gen C. H. Simpson; *Director-General of Medical Services* Maj-Gen S. R. Burston.

In the new phase, Blamey would command a total of six subordinate formations: First Army, Second Army, I Corps, Northern Territory Force, Western Command and 11th Division. Lieut-General Sturdee's First Army opened its headquarters at Lae on 2nd October. Under it would be Savige's II Corps with headquarters at Torokina in Bougainville; Major-General A. H. Ramsay's 5th Division on New Britain; Major-General J. E. S. Stevens' 6th Division at Aitape; and the 8th Brigade in the area west of Madang.

The deployment of twelve brigades in New Guinea and the Solomons left in Australia, apart from I Corps training on the Atherton Tableland, only two brigades of infantry. The Second Army—the reserve army—had diminished until its infantry component was one division (the 1st) which, after 8th January 1945 when the 2nd Brigade was disbanded at Wallgrove, would possess only one brigade. In Queensland (under Blamey's direct control) was Major-General A. J. Boase's 11th Division, a reserve divisional headquarters with no infantry brigades under command, as all three brigades normally allotted to it were serving under other commanders in New Guinea. There was now only one brigade (the 12th) in the Northern Territory Force. The garrison of Western Australia (Major-General H. C. H. Robertson's Western Command) had been reduced almost to vanishing point.

On 7th and 21st September 1944 Blamey spoke to the Advisory War Council about the forthcoming operations. Concerning Bougainville he said that Torokina had been an inactive area but the Australian forces would not perhaps be quite so passive. Large-scale operations were not contemplated at present; the enemy strength would be probed and the extent of further operations then determined.

In the last quarter of 1944 the Australian formations relieved the Americans in the various areas, as planned. On 18th October Blamey issued to Sturdee an operation instruction which defined the role of the First Army in the Bougainville, New Britain and Aitape areas as "by offensive action to destroy enemy resistance as opportunity offers without committing major forces".

In order to be able to interpret this to lower formations (Sturdee wrote to Blamey on 31st October), I should be glad if you would give me some advice on the reason for the restriction "without committing major forces".

There seem to be two aspects, one to avoid being so deeply committed that it might be necessary to call for outside assistance if the Japs were unexpectedly stronger than anticipated. The other is that the Jap Garrisons are at present virtually in POW Camps but feed themselves, so why incur a large number of Australian casualties in the process of eliminating them.

If the former is the reason then interpretation is easy, but if it is the latter, then I should like some guidance as to the extent of the casualties that would be justified in destroying these Jap Garrisons.

In the case of Aitape, I realise that 6 Div must be kept on ice for larger operations in 1945. In New Britain I do not have the forces available to do more than keep the Japs confined to the Gazelle Peninsula and by active patrolling eliminate as many as possible.

The real difficulty is with Bougainville, where already there are signs of commanders spoiling, quite laudably, for an all-in fight with the resources at their disposal.

I tried [Brigadier] Barham[8] for some light on the above when I was in Hollandia last week, but he was unable to answer my point.

I realise that there may be some question of prestige that makes the clearing up of Bougainville an urgent necessity, or alternatively of the elimination of the Japs in that area to reduce inter-breeding to a minimum and so avoid the potential trouble of having a half native-Jap population to deal with in the future.

In the course of his reply, written on 7th November, Blamey wrote:

My conception is that action must be of a gradual nature. In the first place our information is imperfect. Before any very definite plans can be made for the destruction of the enemy resistance, it is essential that this information should be greatly enlarged.

This means the early development of patrol action. This again, to my mind, separates itself into two actually overlapping phases. The first is the pushing forward of the native troops into the wild to ascertain the location and strength of the enemy in various places. If this is reasonably successful it should give sufficient information to enable plans to be made to push forward light forces to localities which can be dealt with piecemeal. These light forces would form the nuclei from which patrols would contact and destroy the enemy by normal methods of bush warfare. By such means as these it should be possible, first, to locate the enemy and continually harass him, and, ultimately, prepare plans to destroy him.

Alongside of this, when the enemy is a little more definitely located, every means should be employed, by way of landing parties from small craft, from the air or by other means, to harass and destroy such of his forces as may be located.

The reason for the restriction "without committing major forces" is that it is not desired to formulate plans for a definite advance against main areas of enemy resistance, which will lead to very heavy casualties on our side, until the situation is much clearer. . . .

With regard to Bougainville, our information is far from exact. The . . . latest information produced by our Intelligence . . . shows 25,000 troops, whereas two months ago the estimate was 12,000 to 13,000.

I quite appreciate the desire of commanders for an all-in fight, but the present lack of information and the fact that the enemy strength is unknown on the island make it most desirable that there should be a complete probe and a better knowledge gained before any large commitment is undertaken.

I fully appreciate the undesirability of retaining troops in a perimeter, particularly our Australian troops, over a long period, since this is certain to destroy the aggressive spirit which is essential against the Japanese. I hope, therefore, that there will be a considerable increase in our activity along the lines I have indicated above.

As a result of Blamey's letter Sturdee on 13th November issued a new instruction in which he said that it was considered unwise to undertake major offensive operations to destroy the enemy until more information was available. It added:

In order (a) to obtain the required information, (b) to maintain the offensive spirit in our troops, and (c) to harass the enemy and retain moral superiority over him, offensive operations will consist of patrols and minor raids by land, sea and air, so far as our resources will permit.

Operations will be divided into three phases: A. Patrols and raids . . .; B. Based on the information obtained in Phase A, the preparation of plans for major offensive operations; C. Offensive operations designed to destroy the enemy. Phase C will *not* be undertaken without prior approval from this headquarters.

---

[8] Maj-Gen L. De L. Barham, CBE, NX100292. BGS (Ops & SD) Adv LHQ 1943; Col GS NGF 1943-44; BGS Adv LHQ 1944-45; and other staff and training appointments. Regular soldier; b. Bathurst, NSW, 5 Aug 1900.

It remained to allot a definite role to I Australian Corps. This would depend on American plans.

Before Krueger's army landed on Leyte the American forces in the Pacific had received orders for the next stages of the advance towards Japan. The planning of a proposed assault on Formosa and the China coast had been in progress during most of 1944. On 27th and 28th July 1944 President Roosevelt had met General MacArthur and Admiral Nimitz at Honolulu and discussed future operations. Nimitz wished to by-pass Luzon and MacArthur wished to reoccupy it. Roosevelt decided that Luzon should be reoccupied.[9]

Admiral Nimitz proposed to invade Formosa as soon as General MacArthur's forces were established in the southern and central Philippines. This was to be followed by landings in the Ryukyu and Bonin Islands. A joint staff study of the Formosa operation had been published at Nimitz's headquarters on 23rd August. However, after the Joint Chiefs instructed General MacArthur to invade Leyte two months earlier than had been intended, and Nimitz to by-pass Yap, Nimitz asked his army commanders to express their opinions on a proposal to advance north by way of the Bonins and Ryukyus without landing on Formosa first. It seems probable that Nimitz and his staff preferred to operate as an independent force as they had in the past, and advance on an axis parallel to MacArthur's towards the final objective, delaying the inevitable time when both the predominantly naval force of Nimitz and the predominantly army force of MacArthur must be amalgamated. Lieut-General Robert C. Richardson, commander of the army forces in the Pacific Ocean Area, replied to Nimitz that MacArthur's seizure of Luzon, after Leyte, would enable the Japanese forces operating from Formosa to be neutralised, and the seizure of bases in the Ryukyus to be carried out. The capture of bases in the Bonins would provide alternative bases for bombing attacks on Japan.

Lieut-General Millard F. Harmon, commanding the army air forces in the Pacific Ocean Area, reminded Nimitz that he had earlier suggested the seizure of islands in the Ryukyus as an effective and more economical alternative to an invasion of Formosa. Lieut-General Simon B. Buckner, of the Marines, commander of the Tenth Army to which the capture of Formosa had been allotted, offered a more definite objection. "He informed Admiral Nimitz that the shortages of supporting and service troops in the Pacific Ocean Areas made [Formosa] unfeasible."[1]

On 2nd October Admiral King proposed to the Joint Chiefs that, because of the lack of sufficient troops to execute the assault on Formosa and because the army could not make such troops available until the end of the war in Europe, operations against Luzon, Iwo Jima (in the Bonins)

---

[9] Sherwood, Vol II, p. 801: "The main decision to be made there, as I understand it, was between the Navy plan to devote the ground forces to landings on Formosa, and the MacArthur plan to liberate the Philippines; Roosevelt ultimately decided in favour of the latter, and there were some cynics (especially in the Navy) who remarked in undertones that perhaps the President's choice had been influenced by the thought that the Philippines would provide a more popular victory in an election year." See also W. D. Leahy, *I Was There* (1950), pp. 293-300.

[1] R. E. Appleman, J. M. Burns, R. A. Gugeler and J. Stevens, *The War in the Pacific—Okinawa: The Last Battle* (1948), p. 4, a volume in the official series *United States Army in World War II*. (This summary of United States planning in 1944 is drawn chiefly from this source.)

and the Ryukyus should precede any attack on Formosa. Next day the Joint Chiefs directed MacArthur to invade Luzon on 20th December and Nimitz to seize one or more positions in the Ryukyus by 1st March 1945. On the 5th Nimitz informed his subordinates that his forces would seize Iwo Jima on 20th January and positions in the Ryukyus on 1st March. Thus from bases in Luzon air and naval forces could neutralise the Japanese in Formosa; from Iwo Jima fighter support could be given to B-29's attacking the Japanese mainland; the capture of Okinawa in the Ryukyus would bring American forces within 300 miles of Kyushu, the southernmost of the Japanese islands.

The role of I Australian Corps in these main operations was changed several times in the five months between August 1944 and January 1945. As mentioned, on 12th July MacArthur had said that in the advance to the Philippines he contemplated using one A.I.F. division in November and a second in January. In August, however, G.H.Q. had indicated that the corps would be employed in Luzon about 20th February 1945, when it would land at Aparri on the north coast as a preliminary to the landing of American forces at Lingayen Gulf some 18 days later.

On 5th September 1944 Berryman informed Blamey that MacArthur intended to bring the 6th Division to the Lingayen area on Luzon when it had finished its job at Aitape. He hoped that this would be in March. It would be employed in the final drive on Manila. After the capture of Luzon MacArthur proposed to drive south and use the A.I.F. in British Borneo. If Washington decided to by-pass Luzon in favour of an attack on Formosa by the Central Pacific force, MacArthur proposed to use the A.I.F. in an advance on the Visayas-Luzon axis. On 26th September, in elaboration of this plan, G.H.Q. stated that the task of I Australian Corps would be to establish at Aparri a base whence aircraft could support the operations against Manila; but only if Nimitz's carrier-based aircraft could not ensure the protection of the transports round the north coast of Luzon. If MacArthur had adequate naval support the Aparri operation would be cancelled. Indeed it was becoming evident to those Australians who were close to G.H.Q. that G.H.Q. would prefer not to have Australians playing any notable part in the reconquest of the Philippines. On 7th October Berryman recorded in his diary that MacArthur's Chief of Staff, Lieut-General Richard K. Sutherland, had informed Blamey that

it was not politically expedient for the A.I.F. to be amongst the first troops into the Philippines.

Late in October Blamey's Forward Echelon was informed that the employment of the Australian Corps at Aparri had been cancelled and the future role of the corps would probably be to operate on Mindanao as part of the Eighth American Army, and then to advance into the Netherlands Indies. The 6th, 7th and 9th Australian Divisions would attack Mindanao on 1st March, Jolo Island on 1st April, Kudat on 1st May, and Labuan Island in British Borneo on 1st June. Another phase would be undertaken by XI American Corps: Tarakan on 20th April,

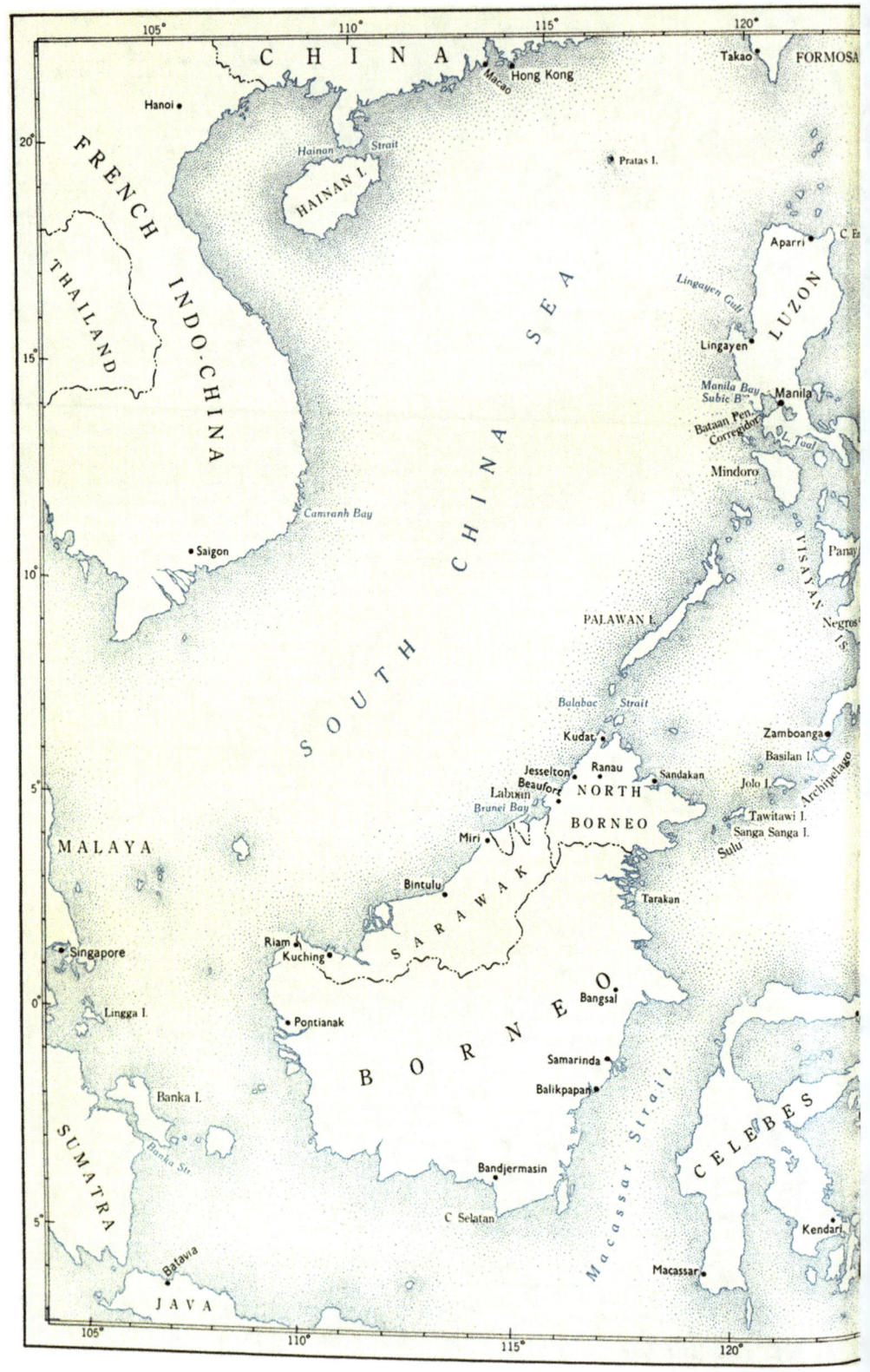

Dutch New Guinea,

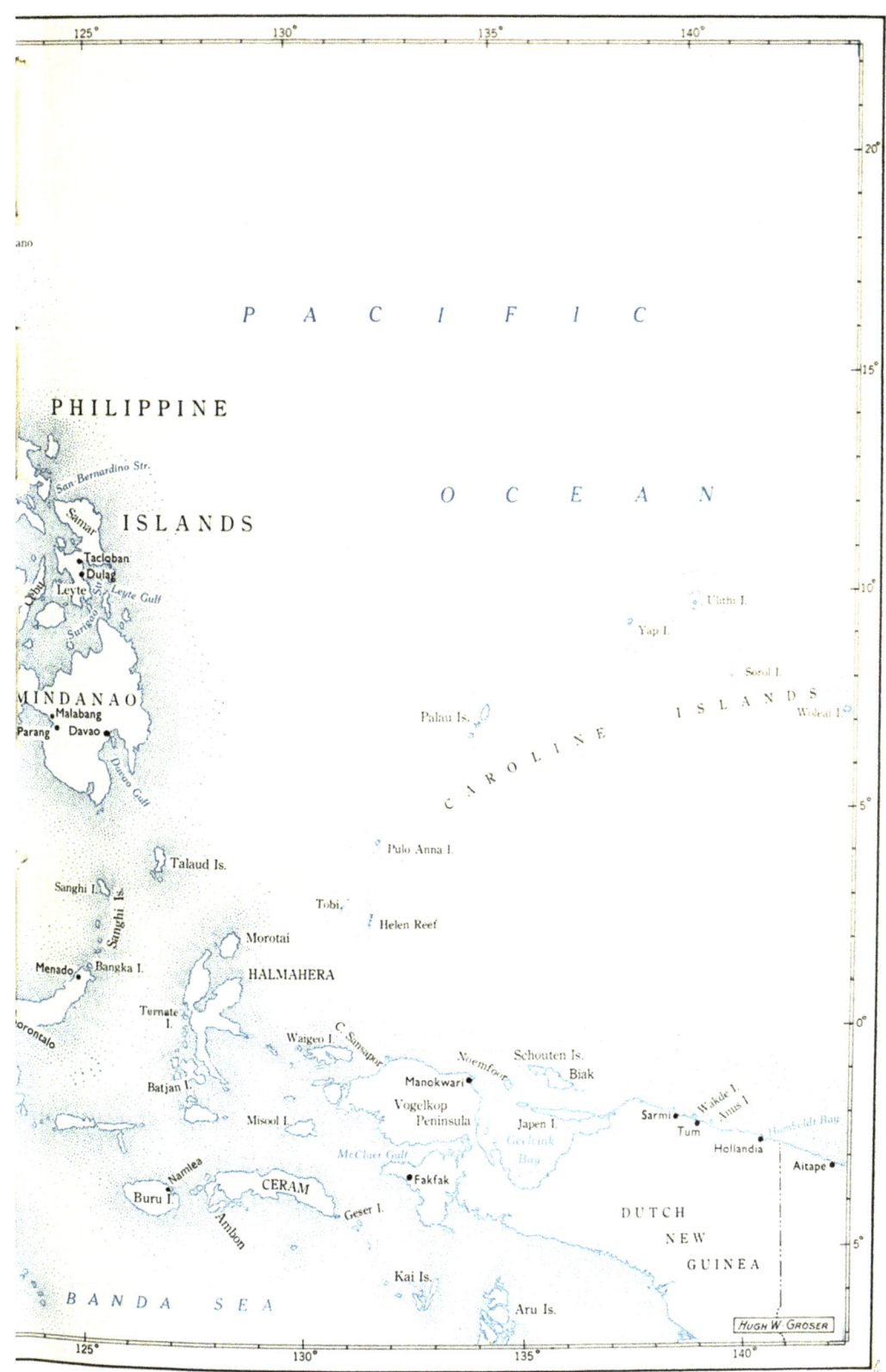

Borneo and the Philippines

Balikpapan on 20th May, Bandjermasin on 10th June, and Surabaya on 10th July. Meanwhile X American Corps was to conduct preliminary operations against Panay, Cebu, Negros, Palawan, Mindoro and the western Visayas. By 20th November, however, these plans were revised, chiefly by the omission of the time-table and the names of the forces that would be employed. On 5th December MacArthur told Blamey that "he would probably want the A.I.F. to clean up Luzon".

On 14th December MacArthur received a telegram from General George C. Marshall in Washington stating that Mountbatten had raised the question of an Australian division being made available to him.[2] MacArthur said that none of his divisions could be removed unless additional troops were sent from the United States. He advised that the matter be "dropped as quietly as possible" since, if it reached the Australian public it would arouse a degree of heated controversy that could only have an adverse effect. MacArthur evidently did not mention the suggestion to the Australian Government. His opinion that the transfer of a division to S.E.A.C. at this stage would have been unpopular was certainly incorrect. As will be seen, the Opposition advocated such a course two months later, Blamey was convinced it would be popular, and there can be no doubt that the troops concerned would have welcomed the opportunity to take part in the drive towards Singapore.

As a preliminary to the invasion of Luzon it had been decided to land on Mindoro, whence the Fifth American Air Force would be within easy reach of Luzon and could protect seaborne communications through the Visayas. The landing on Mindoro was to take place on 5th December, but on 30th November, because the airfields on Leyte were not so far advanced as had been hoped and because of the reduction of Admiral Halsey's carrier force by Japanese suicide bombers, MacArthur postponed Mindoro to 15th December and Luzon to 9th January.

The landing on Mindoro took place on the 15th and by the 19th American engineers and No. 3 Airfield Construction Squadron of the R.A.A.F. had the first airfield ready. On 26th December, Leyte being securely in American hands, though mopping-up would continue for some months, the Sixth American Army handed over the operations in the southern and central Philippines to the Eighth Army, and, on 9th January, the Sixth Army put four divisions ashore in Lingayen Gulf, 150 miles north of Manila. It was in this gulf that the Japanese had made their main landing in December 1941. The huge convoy was attacked by Japanese suicide aircraft and a number of ships were hit, including the battleship *New Mexico* (in which Lieut-General Lumsden, United Kingdom representative at G.H.Q., was killed[3]) and the cruiser *Australia*.

By mid-January five American divisions were firmly established on Luzon and five more were due to land in the next four weeks. This

---
[2] RAAF War History Section, GHQ Papers, No. S.6.
[3] He was succeeded by Lieut-General C. H. Gairdner.
   Lt-Gen Sir Charles Gairdner, KCMG, KCVO, CB, CBE. (1914-18: Lt RA.) GSO1 7 Armd Div 1940-41; GOC 6 Armd Div 1942; CGS North Africa 1943; Prime Minister's Representative in Far East 1945-48. Governor of Western Australia since 1951. Regular soldier; b. 20 Mar 1898.

would leave four divisions—Americal, 24th, 31st and 41st—for the extensive operations in the southern and central Philippines, and the 93rd (Negro) Division in reserve. By March all American divisions under MacArthur's command, except the 93rd, would be employed in operations.

Now that 7, 77 and 96 Divs [of XXIV Corps] are to return to the Pacific Ocean Area (wrote Berryman to Blamey) and now that all U.S. divisions are assigned to tasks, GHQ is giving more attention to the employment of I Aust Corps. . . . G3 [General Chamberlin] is trying to get the Corps into staging areas at Morotai and Hollandia and he thinks that our Corps will be employed in Mindanao and North Borneo. . . .

GHQ Staff Study contemplates the use of 6 Aust Div in North Borneo. If this is so then 6 Aust Div could be replaced by one or two brigades, i.e. 8 Aust Inf Bde and a brigade from New Britain or the Solomons axis. . . .

GHQ estimate that it will take two months to concentrate I Aust Corps in the staging areas and as the ports concerned in Australia and in the staging areas will be able to handle the shipping without delay application is being made to Washington for a definite allotment of shipping for the specific purpose of moving I Aust Corps.

On 20th January G.H.Q. estimated that no ships would be available to move the Australian corps before 1st February; on 24th January that no ships could embark the Australian troops before 7th February; on 29th January it was 15th February; on 1st February it was "not before 22nd February and probably not before 1st March".

Sutherland informed Berryman on 22nd January that the operation against Okinawa, then planned to begin on 16th April, might be postponed, in which event a good deal of amphibious shipping would be available about that time. To make full use of it, MacArthur might speed up his operations, using the 31st American Division, then at Morotai, to capture and establish an air base in the Sulu Archipelago from which to support operations by the A.I.F. in North Borneo, and bringing I Australian Corps forward to Morotai which would be handed over to the A.I.F. as a temporary advanced base. "North Borneo should provide a suitable base for our subsequent operations either against the N.E.I. or Malaya and should also provide a suitable harbour for the Navy."

On 3rd February Berryman informed Blamey that G.H.Q. proposed that the 9th Division should secure the Jesselton-Brunei Bay-Miri area, beginning on 1st April, and later carry out operations against Sandakan and Kuching, probably with paratroops, if Australian prisoners were still there. A brigade of the 7th Division would attack Tarakan on 25th April. The attacks on British Borneo and Tarakan were, in the event, carried out, although not on the dates named, nor, in the case of Tarakan, by a brigade of the 7th Division. After six months of planning G.H.Q. had not yet finally fixed a role for the I Australian Corps and the two divisions it contained.

CHAPTER 2

PLANS AND PROBLEMS

IN the last quarter of 1944 the Australian Army was still shrinking as a result of Government decisions to reduce the intake of men and women into the Services and direct more workers to industry, and of the consequent arrangement that henceforward Australia would maintain only six infantry divisions and two armoured brigades in action or ready for action in the South-West Pacific. To explore manpower policy so far as it affected that army in this phase, it is necessary to turn back to the middle months of 1944.

In a report submitted to the War Cabinet on 3rd May 1944, the Chief of the General Staff, Lieut-General Northcott, estimated that an Australian army with an establishment of 370,500 supported by five months' reinforcements (28,000) and with an estimated 33,000 non-effectives would suffice to carry out the commitments allotted to it. At the end of February, he said, the army had contained 464,000 men and women. It was calculated that even if 20,000 men were released to industries that urgently needed them (as the War Cabinet had ordered in October 1943) the force could be maintained at full strength until December 1944 provided that it received 1,500 men and women a month. However, after the War Cabinet had considered this proposal, it gave the army somewhat fewer than 1,500; out of the 3,000 men and 2,000 women allotted to the three Services each month from 1st May the army was to receive only 420 men and 925 women. Normally 4,000, mostly men, were discharged each month for health and other reasons; consequently the army would to some extent have to live on its own fat in the next six months.

On 2nd August Mr Curtin informed General Blamey that he had directed the Defence Committee to make a further review with the object of reducing the army by an additional 30,000 and the air force by 15,000; of this total 20,000 were to be released by 31st December and the remaining 25,000 by 30th June 1945; these reductions were to be additional to normal wastage. In a letter to Blamey accompanying this minute Curtin recalled that Blamey had informed the Combined Chiefs of Staff that the reduction of the army to six divisions would release some 90,000 men.

Blamey replied on 11th August that the 90,000 related to the total net decrease of army strength for the period from 1st October 1943 to 30th June 1945, including allowance for the reduction of the army by that date to a force of six divisions and two armoured brigades. It had been estimated that in that period discharges and other losses would be 107,000 and effective intake 14,600. These estimates were proving accurate in that actual discharges to 30th June 1944, estimated at 60,000, had been 57,136, and effective intake, estimated at 6,500, had been 6,208. If he had to release 30,000 over and above the estimated 92,400 one of the six infantry divisions Australia had agreed to maintain would have to be disbanded. In addition the army would have to further reduce coast and anti-aircraft defences, and would be unable to maintain many of the services rendered to the navy, air force, American forces and civil population; and there would be "a large deficiency in strength in all field formation units after initial operations".

> During the last two years (he wrote) the combatant organisations have been reduced roughly by half. It is considered that further reductions will greatly reduce the status of Australia and our voice later in important matters of policy.

On 18th September, however, the War Cabinet reduced the army's monthly intake of women from 925 to 500, the intake of men remaining at 420; the total monthly intake for the three Services was henceforth to be 4,020, including 1,020 women.

Blamey wrote a further letter to Curtin on 26th September in the course of which he said that the estimated shortage at June 1945 was about 26,000, in addition to those needed to refill depleted training depots. He estimated that the air force, on the other hand, was 25,000 above establishment (173,000) and could maintain its strength with no further intake of recruits until November 1946. By June 1945 he would have six divisions in action in malarial areas. It would be necessary to disband one militia division as soon as it could be freed from operations in the islands, but that might not be possible until after June 1945. "The effect will be to reduce the A.M.F. below the six divisions and two armoured brigade groups agreed upon at Washington. In fact I have already been compelled, in the endeavour to have the three A.I.F. divisions ready on time, to order the disbandment of the greater part of one of the two armoured brigade groups, retaining little more than the actual armoured regiments of the group."[1] Looking farther ahead Blamey added:

> Even if the C.M.F. division is disbanded when available, there will probably be a period, after the operations at present planned have proceeded for a short time and the A.I.F. Corps has been committed to battle, when it will be so reduced in manpower owing to lack of reinforcements that the scope and duration of its operations will be limited. It will be seen, therefore, that we will probably arrive at the most critical period of the Pacific War with the A.M.F. represented abroad only by much reduced garrisons in the islands immediately to the north and east of Australia.

Finally Blamey suggested that the allotment of manpower to the air force should be related to the number of modern combat aircraft likely to become available to it by the end of 1945 at the latest, that the army's intake "be increased immediately to not less than 1,850 per month as recommended by the Defence Committee", and that the application of that figure be retrospective to 1st July 1944.

The War Cabinet decided on 18th October that Blamey's representations be referred to the Defence Committee for consideration when it made a review, already ordered, of the situation as at 31st December, and directed

---

[1] The 1st Armoured Brigade Group had ceased to exist on 13th October. There were still, however, five armoured regiments. The two brigades—or, indeed, an armoured division—could have been constituted at fairly short notice in the unlikely event of their being needed.

that the committee submit its review in two parts: first on the basis of its direction that each month only 3,000 men and 1,020 women would be allotted to the Services; and second on the basis of the release of an additional 40,000 men from the Services as soon as possible.

Blamey again protested strongly. In a letter written to Curtin on 27th October he repeated his earlier contentions and added:

> I agree the civil population is short of housing and that there is also a shortage of a number of commodities, some of which are important and some of probably less consequence. The same conditions obtain in Britain and elsewhere to a much greater degree. These countries have accepted the conditions of essential privation and stepped up production in order to preserve their striking power, for they appreciate that by this method, and this method alone, can the enemy finally be brought to his knees. . . . The Army deficiency by June 1945 is estimated at 26,000 plus 37,000, total 63,000. During recent weeks references have been made by Ministers to the arduous and difficult times that lie ahead of the armed forces in operations in the very near future. There will be casualties and losses, on what scale nobody knows. One thing, however, is certain. All six divisions and one armoured brigade, with their supporting forces overseas, will be in action. If the Army is to be deficient of 63,000 men as estimated at this vital stage, when the whole of its effective operational strength is employed in operations at one time (which is the maximum effort the Army has been called upon to undertake during the war), then the total force fighting the enemy cannot be adequately supported throughout these operations. The situation is indeed very grave. . . .
>
> If the further reduction of 40,000 is decided upon, I have no alternative but to advise the Government to inform General MacArthur that the Australian Army cannot be maintained at the strength allotted and that it will be necessary to reduce the expeditionary force from one army corps of two divisions and essential service elements to one division. This will bring the Australian expeditionary force to approximately the same dimensions as that of New Zealand.

Curtin replied that he appreciated the desire of the three Services to maintain the greatest possible striking force—that was the wish of the Government—but Australian manpower was "totally inadequate to meet all the demands being made upon it for the Services, for high priority industrial purposes, and to make a contribution to the requirements of the Royal Naval force to be based on Australia". He pointed out that so far no direction that an additional 40,000 be released had been given.

The Defence Committee's review of the situation as it was at 31st December did not come before the War Cabinet until 9th February, when the Ministers decided to confirm their decision of the previous August to reduce the army by a further 30,000 and the air force by 15,000 before 30th June, but to order no more reductions so long as General MacArthur's plans for the employment of the Australian forces were adhered to. Mr Curtin would consult MacArthur with a view to determining when further reductions could be made.

A recommendation by the Defence Committee that the intake of the three Services be raised to 4,200 men a month was not approved; it would remain at 3,000. The monthly intake of women would be reduced from 1,020 to 700. However, the distribution of the men among the three Services was revised in a manner far more satisfactory to the army. The army was allotted 1,500 men a month instead of 420—more than

Northcott had sought in May 1944—the air force 900 instead of 2,280.[2] It was decided that the army's "organisation for active operations" was not to be reduced below the six divisions and two armoured brigades laid down in July. (As we have seen one of these armoured brigades had already been disbanded, though some of its units remained.) When consulted by Curtin, MacArthur replied that his plans contemplated the use of all the Australian forces assigned to his command, whereupon the War Cabinet agreed that no further steps should be taken to reduce the operational strength of the army until the next phase of operations had ended.[3]

In April, however, it was decided that 50,000 men should be released from the army and air force by the end of the year in addition to normal wastage, which would probably amount to about 20,000.[4]

Meanwhile the reduction of the army's establishment in accordance with the agreement made with Washington in mid-1944 had been proceeding. In 1942 it had maintained twelve divisions; by September 1944 eight; in 1945 only six would remain. Of the thirty-two Australian infantry brigades that had existed in 1942, two (A.I.F.) had been lost in Malaya and three (militia) disbanded in Australia in that year, three disbanded in 1943, and three in 1944; another was to be disbanded in January 1945.[5] The reduction between 1st September 1944 and 1st September 1945 is illustrated in the accompanying table, in which it is shown that the reduction in the number of divisional and brigade headquarters was relatively somewhat greater than the reduction in the number of component units.

	Divisions	Armd and Inf Bdes	Inf Bns (excluding Native Bns)	Armd and Cav Regts	Pnr, MG and Parachute Bns	Native Bns
1 Sep 1944	8	23	61	9	10	2
1 Jan 1945	7	22	59	8	9	3
1 May 1945	7	21	59	8	9	4
1 Sep 1945	6	19	56	8	9	6

Did this diminution mean that Australia was not bearing a fair share of the Allied military burden; and did the maintenance of an army of some

---

[2] The expected result of this drop was to be a reduction in the ultimate number of squadrons from 53 to 51.

[3] On 9th January the War Cabinet had approved another means of slightly reducing the army's commitments and saving manpower. It decided that the crews of the fixed batteries of seven defended ports should be removed and the guns left in the charge of maintenance parties. The only forts in Australia where the batteries would be manned would then be at Darwin, Sydney, Fremantle, Brisbane and Torres Strait. This would save 2,900 men and 400 women.

[4] Late in 1944 units learnt that men who wished to begin university courses might be recommended for discharge provided that they had enlisted before they were 21, had three years' service and were qualified; that men who wished to resume medical, dentistry, engineering or science courses might be recommended for discharge if they had completed one year's service, and men who wished to resume other university courses if they had two or three years' service.

[5] The following list shows the brigades, including armoured and motor brigades disbanded from August 1942 when reduction of the establishment of the army began:
1942: 31st, 32nd, 10th, Support Group of 1st Armoured Division.
1943: 2nd Motor, 4th Motor, 6th Armoured, 1st Motor, 30th, 3rd Army Tank, 14th, 28th.
1944: 2nd Armoured, 3rd, 9th, 3rd Motor, 5th, 1st Armoured.
1945: 2nd, 6th (July).

400,000 men to support only the equivalent of seven divisions (including the armoured force) indicate that the commanders were wasting men along the lines of communication? It is not this writer's task to explore the Australian manpower problem of 1944-45 as a whole, but, if the Australian military contribution is examined in isolation, at least this statement can be made in answer to the first question: that in 1945 by maintaining six divisions in the field with their necessary base organisations, 7,000,000 Australians were making a larger contribution of fighting formations, relative to population, than the 130,000,000 Americans or the 45,000,000 people of the United Kingdom even before the defeat of Germany. It seemed certain that by the middle of 1945, when practically all Australian fighting formations would be in the field, the Australian military effort would relatively be far greater than that of any of the Allies.

Early in 1942 the United States leaders had decided to expand the army until, at the end of the year, it included 73 divisions, or about half a division to each million of population; Australia was then maintaining twelve divisions from a population of some 7,000,000. Five of the twelve divisions—6th, 7th, 8th, 9th and 1st Armoured—were of volunteers. These volunteers alone produced a larger fighting army in proportion to population than the United States Army when, finally, the number of its divisions reached 89.

Japan was maintaining one division and a quarter to each million of her population excluding the Koreans and Formosans who, like the subject peoples in occupied territories, were nevertheless a useful addition to her manpower. Germany, however, had succeeded in maintaining more than three German divisions to each million of Germans, partly by economy and good organisation, but largely as a result of the employment of subject peoples in civilian war work.[6]

The second problem—whether the army's "tail" of base and training establishments was too heavy—caused the Ministers considerable concern. Probably most Ministers and civilian Secretaries and most soldiers in forward areas were convinced that it was too large. The War Cabinet's opinion is indicated by a decision of 1st May that final authority to approve the establishments of non-operational units or create new ones should rest with the Minister and not the Commander-in-Chief, and that a War Establishments Investigating Committee be re-established, with a civilian chairman, one member nominated by the Commander-in-Chief, and one by the Secretary of the Department of the Army. Similar provisions were applied to the air force and navy.

Was an army which needed 400,000 men to keep seven divisions in the field in fact wasting its resources? Again the subject is technical and elaborate and a complete answer is beyond the scope of this volume. It seems reasonable, however, again to collect some simple comparisons.

---

[6] Evidence was given at the International Military Tribunal at Nuremberg that by January 1945 4,795,000 foreign civilians were employed on work for the German war effort within the borders of the Germany of 1939, and about 2,000,000 prisoners of war were employed in German-controlled armament factories. However, even in April 1940, Germany, with a population of 80,000,000, had maintained 155 divisions.

In 1940 Mr Churchill, although more learned in military affairs than his colleagues in Australia, had been unable to understand why nearly 3,000,000 men were required to maintain only 34 United Kingdom divisions, plus the oversea garrisons, air defence force and the rest. A division was only 15,500 strong, he argued; its infantry only 6,750. The rifle strength of the 27 British divisions then earmarked for oversea service was therefore only 182,250. What were the remaining two and three-quarter millions doing? In a similar mood to that of the Australian Ministers in 1944, he wrote of "staffs and statics, living well off the nation as heroes in khaki" and declared: "It is necessary . . . that at least a million are combed out of the fluff and flummery behind the fighting troops, and made to serve effective military purposes".[7] At that time there were to be some 86,000 men in the British Army to each division—15,500 in the division and some 70,000 outside it.

Whereas, in 1940, the War Office was thus providing one fighting division for each 86,000 men, and in 1944 the American Army needed approximately 64,000 men per division, the Australian Army leaders in 1945 were providing a division to about 57,000 men.[8] That is not to say that the army contained no drones, or that increases in some base establishments had not been wangled with the object of obtaining promotion for their senior officers, or that a vigilant investigation of establishments was not desirable and Ministerial anxiety to that extent justified; merely that, as armies went, the Australian wartime army seems to have been managed with reasonable economy.[9]

Short though it might be of men the army now suffered no lack of basic weapons. Since 1942 these had been pouring from the factories, and yet since 1942, as we have seen, the establishment of the army, and consequently the number of weapons needed, had been greatly reduced. Thus the army now required 368 25-pounder field guns in the fighting formations and 38 in training units, but it possessed 1,516. It needed 530 2-pounder or 6-pounder tank and anti-tank guns in the fighting units, but possessed 1,941. It was manning 68 3.7-inch anti-aircraft guns and needed five for training; it had 640. Its units needed 9,438 Brens, and it had 21,139;

---

[7] W. S. Churchill, *The Second World War*, Vol II (1949), pp. 620-1.

[8] In December 1944 there were 89 divisions in the American Army of which the aggregate strength (not counting the Air Forces) was about 5,700,000.

[9] A more detailed illustration of the ratio of base troops to fighting troops at this stage can be found in an examination of the force in New Guinea at 20th February 1945. The base and line-of-communication troops under the command of First Army, which controlled all formations in New Guinea, then numbered

Moresby	2,116
Lae	7,859
Madang	903
New Britain	4,061
Bougainville	7,956
Aitape	3,536
Elsewhere	543
Total	26,974

These were organised into some 350 separate units or detachments. Nearly every base area was considerably under strength. For example, the war establishment of the Lae units was 9,158, the actual strength 7,859. In all areas combined there was a deficiency of 309 officers and 4,014 others. Thus some 27,000 base and line-of-communication troops were supporting field forces including one corps headquarters, three divisions and the equivalent of a small fourth division. This was by no means a large "tail" for such a force.

123 carriers and had 3,767—there were few tasks for carriers in island warfare.

In themselves these figures do not convict the army staff of extravagant over-ordering. The order of battle had been reduced by half. In bush warfare fewer heavy weapons were needed than in open warfare and still fewer fighting vehicles and anti-tank guns. The Japanese Navy and Air Force had been broken and consequently the need for anti-aircraft and coast guns had vastly decreased. In short the army possessed the weapons that it would have needed for the large-scale open warfare that it might have been required to undertake in 1942 or early 1943, but it needed only a small proportion of these weapons to arm for jungle warfare the six divisions and the armoured units now committed to battle or ready to embark.

The northward move of MacArthur's headquarters combined with political considerations mentioned earlier created increasing problems for the Australian Commander-in-Chief. General MacArthur from his headquarters now, in February, on Leyte still directed the Australian forces operating in areas from 1,500 to 2,500 miles distant. Blamey, although nominally Commander-in-Chief, Allied Land Forces, had long since ceased to exert any control over American forces and it soon appeared that G.H.Q. wished to limit his control even over the First Australian Army and I Australian Corps. The difficulties inherent in giving command of the South-West Pacific Area not to an Allied headquarters in the sense in which General Eisenhower's was an Allied headquarters, but to an all-American headquarters, were soon to become boldly apparent.

One problem which seemed at first to be of minor importance produced somewhat serious consequences within Australia. G.H.Q. largely retained control of news about Australian operations because the correspondents might write only within the limits of the G.H.Q. daily communiqué in the sense that they might not reveal any important fact (such as the opening of a new operation) not yet mentioned in the communiqué. When MacArthur's headquarters moved forward into the Philippines it was hoped by the Australian staff that he would issue two separate communiqués: one from his advanced headquarters in Leyte about American operations and another from Hollandia about operations in Dutch and Australian New Guinea. On 4th October, however, the Australians learnt that this suggestion would not be adopted.

Through October, November and December no announcement was made in the communiqués that Australian forces were in New Guinea and the Solomons. Probably never in the history of modern war had so large a force, although in action, been hidden from public knowledge for so long. On 4th January its commander, General Sturdee, wrote to Blamey:

> I have been anxiously awaiting some Press announcement that the Australian Army still exists in New Guinea, and it seems that the Australian public must be wondering whether we are still in the war.

By a coincidence, on 5th January, Mr P. C. Spender, a former Minister for the Army, who was visiting New York and was disturbed by the Americans' lack of knowledge of the part Australia was playing, said to a newspaper that MacArthur's communiqués were placing Australia's war effort in a false light. Nothing seemed to be allowed to reach America about the "sizeable and important" operations in which the Australian Army was engaged. This interview was given prominence in the Australian newspapers.

Blamey signalled MacArthur on the 6th suggesting that he should include in his communiqué of two days later a reference to the fact that the Australians had taken over in New Guinea, thus making it possible to release the Australian correspondents' stories which had been banking up for months. On the 8th the acting Minister for Defence, Mr Forde, wrote to MacArthur to inform him that in November the Australian Newspaper Proprietors' Association had expressed the opinion that the methods governing the issue of communiqués militated against adequate reporting of the activities of the Australian Services and suggesting the issue of Australian communiqués; but the acting Prime Minister had replied to the proprietors that any change in the arrangement whereby the G.H.Q. communiqué covered all the forces under its command would require the agreement of all the governments who were parties to the agreement setting up the South-West Pacific Command, and the Australian Government did not think it advisable to seek a variation. The acting Minister suggested to MacArthur that the best answer would be "full treatment of the operations of the Australian forces" in his communiqués, "supplemented by reports from press correspondents".

That day, MacArthur signalled Blamey that his communiqué of the 9th would "carry announcement Australian troops as requested by you". This announcement ran:

> Australian forces have relieved United States Army elements along the Solomons axis, in New Britain and British New Guinea. Continuous actions of attrition at all points of contact have been in progress. So far 372 Japanese have been killed, 20 captured and 10 friendly nationals recovered.

As a result of the appearance of this meagre bulletin the newspapers were able to publish the accumulation of reports and photographs from the northern fronts. The news included an official statement that "earlier announcement" of the presence of Australian troops in Bougainville, New Britain, and the Aitape area "was not possible because it involved the replacement of large bodies of American troops". The published estimates of the strength of the Japanese were: 23,000 in New Guinea, 40,000 in New Britain, and 16,000 on Bougainville. (As mentioned, it was found later that there were actually nearly twice as many in the three areas.)

On the same day Mr Forde announced that "Australian fighting forces" would play a substantial part in the Philippines and Australian naval vessels were in action there, and that he was in touch with General MacArthur about the treatment of Australians in the communiqués.

The newspapers, however, soon ceased to give much prominence to news from Aitape and Bougainville, evidently considering these operations of little interest to Australians compared with the campaigns in Europe and the Philippines. Indeed there had already been indications that the necessity for active operations in the islands might be questioned. As early as 1st November the *Sydney Morning Herald,* for example, in a leading article commenting on a statement by Blamey that "90,000 disciplined and armed Japanese" between Wewak and Bougainville would have to be "rooted out", had predicted "mopping up operations on a very formidable scale"; and seemed a little doubtful as to the necessity for employing large forces in these isolated areas rather than against "active centres of enemy power".

The delayed issue of news about operations in New Guinea brought Blamey into conflict with one of the Ministers. On 17th January the Minister for Information, Mr Calwell,[1] told journalists at Canberra that the responsibility for not informing the public about the Australian operations rested with Army Public Relations and not with his department. Blamey came to the defence of his Directorate of Public Relations and on 18th January issued a statement in which he described the process by which the news was released. He concluded:

It is incredible that these facts and considerations are not known to the Information Minister. I regret the necessity for a public statement on the matter, especially where proper action has been taken to secure the safety of our gallant lads and their American comrades in their passage of perilous waters.

But when a particular section of the army, whose members are serving their country with great fidelity and devotion, is attacked directly from high places, and the basis of such an attack is a direct lie, I would be remiss in my obligations to those under my command if I failed to ensure their public vindication.[2]

---

[1] Hon A. A. Calwell. MHR since 1940; Minister for Information 1943-49, and Immigration 1945-49; Deputy Leader of the Opposition 1951-60, Leader since 1960. Of Flemington, Vic; b. West Melbourne, 28 Aug 1896.

[2] This brief affray was only one incident in a series of clashes, from 1942 onwards, between the Department of Information and the Army's Directorate of Public Relations. The difficulties arose largely from administrative arrangements whereby these two authorities had overlapping or closely-parallel responsibilities. For example, Army Public Relations controlled censorship of news in the field and the Department of Information carried out "publicity censorship" at GHQ and within Australia. This produced friction.

Moreover, from 1942 onwards three separate official organisations were collecting and publishing information about the army. As mentioned in earlier volumes, two official correspondents and several official photographers were appointed to the AIF overseas. They were members of the Department of Information. In 1942 the Minister for the Army, Mr Forde, on his return from a visit to New Guinea wrote to the Minister for Information and to General Blamey expressing the view that an official correspondent should be appointed to furnish reports from New Guinea on the lines of those produced in the earlier war by the official correspondent, C. E. W. Bean. Blamey replied on 18th November that he had no objection to such a plan; but he explained that "during the last world war a very limited number of Press Correspondents were allowed with the AIF and through most of the war I think Dr Bean was practically alone. . . . I think if the reports forwarded by most of the correspondents were allowed free publication, a very good picture of the conditions here would be given. But these are not only subject to censorship here in the field, they are also subject to further censorship in accordance with the directions of GHQ SWPA before they can be published. The effect of this is very frequently to give a much less complete account of the conditions of service in the field than the correspondents themselves submit, and this would equally apply to the work of an official correspondent."

From this distance it seems evident that the need was not for more kinds of writers—and photographers—but fewer. In the forward areas there were some photographers, for example, who were employed by the Department of Information and some who were employed by the Military History Section of the army. Often they worked side by side, taking similar pictures. At various times in New Guinea there were (*a*) newspaper correspondents, (*b*) official or semi-official war correspondents responsible to the Department of Information or to Government broadcasting authorities, (*c*) officers and NCO's of the Public Relations branch who were writing news. In Australia in the period from 1943 to 1945 brochures about the army's achievements were written by the army's Directorate of Public Relations; illustrated, cloth-bound books about the campaigns

In February the prominence given to news from the New Guinea areas dwindled. Maps were very seldom included and thus such reports as appeared were often obscure; and, whereas in January the G.H.Q. communiqué named all the American divisions on Luzon and whence they had come (mostly from New Guinea), the Australian formations and commanders remained anonymous for weeks and, in most instances, months. It was not until 17th March that the Melbourne *Herald,* with the help of Army Public Relations, published a comprehensive article, with maps, and described it as "the first complete picture of where Australian troops are in action today".

For Australia the results of the policies followed by G.H.Q. in the composing of its communiqués had, for three years, been most unhappy. In the years when Australian troops were doing nearly all the land fighting in the area the communiqués had been so phrased that Americans at home were under the impression that it was chiefly their own troops who were engaged; American base troops landed at Finschhafen in 1944, for example, were astonished to find any Australians there. By late-1944 the communiqués, the natural tendency of American correspondents to concentrate on news of their own troops, and the news from Australia that the size of the army was being reduced led to American complaints that Australia was not pulling her weight. This was at a time when the Australian effort was considerably greater, in proportion to population, than the American effort; and the recent reduction of the Australian Army was largely due to the losses suffered in the 18 months to December 1943 when that army had borne practically the whole burden in the South-West Pacific.[3]

---

of each of the Services were published annually by the army's Military History Section in conjunction with the Australian War Memorial; and the Department of Information published booklets and other information about the army and other Services.

Unsound administrative arrangements led to inter-departmental strife, which at length reached such a pitch that, in June 1945, the Minister for Information prepared a War Cabinet agendum recommending, among other things, "that the Directorate of Army Public Relations be abolished as such".

In comparison with the British system the Australian one was confused. The British system produced outstanding results. Under it official writing about the army, for example, was produced by the army's Public Relations branch, which often employed well-known authors. The Ministry of Information "issued" these writings: that is, it was a coordinator, and a link between the Service concerned and the publisher, which was that expert organisation His Majesty's Stationery Office. Each function was clearly defined and each was carried out by people who were highly expert in their fields.

[3] In 1961 the fact that Australian forces formed for a long period the greater part, and always a substantial part, of MacArthur's command seemed unlikely to be recorded in American general histories. For example, in *The Growth of the American Republic* (2 vols; 4th edn 1950), by S. E. Morison and H. S. Commager, there are 78 pages about the progress of the war from 1941 to 1945. In these the only indication that Australian troops took part in the war against Japan is contained in the following passage in Volume II, pp. 717-18: "In the meantime the western prong of this Japanese offensive had been stopped on the north coast of Papua, New Guinea, in the villages of Buna, Gona, and Sanananda. This was done by General MacArthur's command, executed by American and Australian troops under General Eichelberger; and the fighting . . . was the most horrible of the entire war. With the aid of air power the combined army won through, and by the end of January 1943 all Papua up to Huon Gulf was back in Allied hands."

There is no reference to the Australian offensive which opened in 1943, until then perhaps the biggest offensive operation launched against the Japanese. In p. 753 a paragraph begins: "In November 1943 began the first great Pacific offensive. . . ." (The reference is to the landing on Bougainville on 1st November.)

In *A History of the United States Navy* (1948) by D. W. Knox, p. 629, appears the following statement: "Nimitz and MacArthur together used only 26 divisions in combat, of which 6 were Marine and 20 Army divisions, including a comparatively few Australian and New Zealand troops."

As mentioned earlier, at the beginning of February the role of I Australian Corps had not been finally decided, although it seemed probable that it would undertake a series of operations in Borneo. On 3rd February General MacArthur had sent a telegram to General Marshall to say that it was considered of the utmost importance to recover the oilfields of British and Dutch Borneo as soon as possible to provide readily-accessible oil for the advance to Japan. He planned to use the I Australian Corps for these operations but to bring it to the Hollandia-Morotai area would require 87 shiploads of troops and cargo. He asked for authority to retain for some weeks certain Liberty ships then in his area, and asked for 10 trans-Pacific troopships for this period.

At the conference of Allied leaders at Yalta in the Crimea later in February (when Russia agreed to attack Japan two or three months after the defeat of Germany provided a number of concessions were made to her in the post-war settlement) the Joint Chiefs of Staff stated that if invasion of Japan had to be postponed until 1946 because of delays in Europe, operations might be undertaken in 1945 against Hainan, or British Borneo or the Chusan-Ningpo area in China.

Marshall replied to MacArthur's proposal, however, that no ships could then be made available for the Borneo project, that there was an "unmanageable deficit" in shipping in both the Pacific and Atlantic in the first half of 1945 and no remedy unless the war ended in Europe, and that operations in Borneo would have little immediate effect on the war against Japan.

On 15th February Blamey learnt more details of the new plans for the employment of I Corps. G.H.Q. proposed to use the three A.I.F. divisions in an advance to Borneo with Java as a later objective: first taking Tarakan with a brigade if land-based aircraft were available, but, if carrier aircraft were available, taking Balikpapan with a division. It might then be necessary to take Bandjermasin before an assault on Java by a corps of two divisions. In these operations I Corps was to be under the command of the Eighth American Army. This information came from General Berryman, who on 11th February had established the Forward Echelon of L.H.Q. side by side with G.H.Q. on Leyte.

Blamey instructed Berryman strongly to resist the proposal that I Corps be incorporated in an American Army. On the 17th Berryman sent the following signal to Blamey:

I had frank discussion with Chamberlin who today received instructions that Morshead would command the Aust task force and would be under the direct command of GHQ and not under 8th Army. I pointed out that anticipated I Aust Corps HQ was not organised to command the AIF but that Adv LHQ was and that if a task force HQ was formed it would be necessary to integrate Adv LHQ and HQ I Aust Corps. I further pointed out that in the proposed series of operations the task force HQ would have to form a forward tactical HQ in Java and a rear HQ in Morotai or Balikpapan to handle administration and other functions so that in effect we would arrive back to our existing organisation. . . .

Chamberlin said the question was beyond his level and that he could only act on his orders and that he thought General MacArthur would insist on dealing with one commander only and that one of the reasons for changing New Guinea Force to First Aust Army was to enable GHQ to deal direct with First Aust Army.

Thus the plans for the employment of the A.I.F. Corps were still in the melting pot; G.H.Q. intended that it should come forward as a contingent which would be removed from Blamey's command, and intended also to "deal direct" with First Army. Berryman urged Blamey to visit MacArthur.

At this time a letter (dated 15th February) was on its way from Curtin to MacArthur seeking a definite decision about the part Australia was to play. In it Curtin reviewed earlier decisions in some detail and said:

I have been informed by General Blamey that your recent request to Washington for the retention of certain shipping to move the 1st Australian Corps to staging areas in preparation for further operations, has not been accepted. It is understood that this attitude is in accordance with the priority allotted to further operations in the South-West Pacific Area, after the capture of the Philippines, in relation to the war in Europe.

Elements of the 1st Australian Corps have been on the mainland for periods of up to eighteen months and have taken no part in the war since 1943. You may have gathered from press reports that there has been considerable public criticism of the inactivity of the Australian Land Forces which, in a large degree, has arisen from the members of the Forces themselves, a considerable number of whom have been under arms for four and five years. . . .

In view of the great stringency of the manpower position and the heavy pressure that is being brought to bear on the Government to remedy manpower shortages and lift restrictions, I shall be confronted with a difficult situation if so many Australian troops are to be retained in an ineffective role, for it would appear that an all out effort against Japan is unlikely for a considerable period.

It would also seem that when such an effort is mounted, the forces allotted by the respective Allied nations will be much less than the totals now being utilised for the war in the various theatres in Europe and Asia. If these premises are correct, then it would seem that Australia's allocation of forces should be considerably reduced. . . .

The volume of reciprocal aid for the year ending 30th June is estimated at £110,000,000 and, in addition, War Cabinet has approved of programs for works and supplies for the Royal Navy totalling £26,186,100 of which £10,700,000 for foodstuffs is a matter of allocation within the United Kingdom 1945 food program.

. . . it would therefore appear that, after the defeat of Germany, Australia, on the present basis of her effort, will be under greater strain in relation to her resources than the other United Nations. She entered the war in 1939. Except for continued participation in the air war in Europe, her military effort since Japan entered the war has been concentrated in the Pacific. She will therefore experience no direct relief on the defeat of Germany, as will the nations fighting in Europe. . . .

I shall be grateful if you will furnish me with your observations on the various points I have raised in so far as they relate to your responsibilities as Commander-in-Chief of the South-West Pacific Area.

Blamey replied to Berryman's signal of the 17th that he saw no reason why Australian Headquarters should not command and added:

Without having discussed this particular case with Aust Govt I feel assured of complete support on this question. Prefer that matter should not have to be pressed to highest level which I am however prepared to do if necessary. Suggest you discuss the matter quite openly with Chamberlin. Feeling that we are being side-tracked is growing strong throughout country.

Meanwhile Curtin's letter had reached MacArthur and produced swift action. Berryman informed Blamey that G.H.Q. anticipated that from early in March one Liberty ship would berth at Townsville or Cairns daily for 34 days and 8 to 10 troopers would be available over the same period. These should lift the 9th Division and base troops to Morotai by 5th May; and ample shipping should be available to embark the 7th Division and corps troops.

It would seem (wrote Blamey to Shedden on the 19th) that, although Washington refused to allow the retention of ships by General MacArthur, the suggestions contained in the Prime Minister's letter have promptly produced them out of the hat.

One problem seemed to have been solved; another—the American proposal to the effect that the Australian Commander-in-Chief should have no control over forces in the field—remained. Also on 19th February Blamey wrote to Shedden about it.

I think it is desirable that I should put the position, as I see it, for the information of the Prime Minister.

You will recall that, on the establishment of the South-West Pacific Area, General MacArthur was appointed Commander-in-Chief and I was appointed Commander, Allied Land Forces. I understand my appointment was made as part of the general agreement for the acceptance of the set up of the command of the S.W.P. Area. Except during the offensive campaign in the field in New Guinea up to the end of 1943, I have never operated as such.

My requests for American officers to establish a joint staff were met with a face-saving acceptance that was completely ineffective. American troops were brought to this country and later an American army command established. At no stage was I given any information as to the proposals for their arrival or the development of the organisation. In fact, General MacArthur took upon himself the functions of Commander, Allied Land Forces and my own functions were limited to command of the Australian Military Forces.

I have never raised this question definitely before, as I was always of the opinion that the Prime Minister and General MacArthur worked in close consultation and the former was fully informed of and acquiesced in the position. . . . It has been, throughout this war, a definitely accepted principle that our Australian national forces should be under the control of our own Australian commanders. Where, on those odd occasions, this restriction has been lifted, it has been very greatly to the detriment of the Australian Army.

In the position which has now arisen, the Australian Army has been sharply divided into two components:

(a) The First Australian Army, which is dealing with the enemy elements left behind in the New Guinea and adjacent islands area.

(b) The First Australian Corps, which has been made available for offensive operations.

G.H.Q., S.W.P.A. asserts its authority to exercise direct control over the First Australian Army and . . . intends to assume direct control of First Australian Corps for operations now under consideration. . . .

It is obvious to me that the intention of G.H.Q., S.W.P.A. is to treat my headquarters as a purely liaison element. . . .

With regard to the command of New Guinea area, the position is completely unsatisfactory. G.H.Q. claims to exercise direct command, whereas effective command of the land forces is exercised by myself. This is inevitable but, unfortunately, the means to secure fully effective control are not at my disposal. . . .

It is impossible to secure reasonable attention even to maintenance requirements. For example, over 4,000 personnel due for return to their units have been awaiting shipping for weeks at Townsville.

It would be a long story to give all the details of the difficulties of supply and provision resulting from the fact of distant, and I cannot help but feel not sufficiently interested, control of the First Australian Army. . . . It is my view that, unless the authority of the Australian command over Australian national forces is effectively asserted, an undesirable position will arise as far as the Australian troops are concerned, by which they will be distributed under American control and Australian national control of its forces will be greatly weakened.

The insinuation of American control and the elimination of Australian control has been gradual, but I think the time has come when the matter should be faced quite squarely, if the Australian Government and the Australian Higher Command are not to become ciphers in the control of the Australian Military Forces.

On 20th February Berryman informed Blamey that, as forecast earlier, G.H.Q. proposed to use the 6th Division in the Borneo operation and a great part of it was expected to begin combat loading at Aitape about 1st April. G.H.Q. proposed that the headquarters of the 11th Division with the 23rd Brigade and the 8th Brigade less a battalion should relieve the 6th Division. This plan would involve taking 5,000 base troops from First Army. Sturdee telegraphed Blamey on the 21st that it would be impossible to maintain the troops in the operational areas if he lost 5,000 base troops.

On the 22nd Blamey signalled Sturdee and Berryman to defer action on the 6th Division until further orders; the matter was under consideration by the Government. And on the 24th, after seeing Curtin, he signalled Sturdee that all instructions requiring him to prepare for the withdrawal of the 6th Division and base troops were cancelled.

It remained to inform MacArthur that the 6th Division was not available. When it is considered that it was at MacArthur's insistence and against Blamey's wish that the 6th Division had been committed in New Guinea in the first place, the following letter from Curtin to MacArthur on 27th February seems extremely gentle:

I have now been informed by General Blamey that . . . arrangements for the movement of the First Australian Corps are now going ahead, the necessary shipping apparently being available.

It was understood, following our discussions last June when your directive of 12th July was issued for the Australian Forces to assume the responsibility for the continued neutralisation of the Japanese in Australian and British territory and Mandates in the South-West Pacific Area, that two A.I.F. divisions would be used in the advance to the Philippines. The 7th and 9th Divisions were nominated for this purpose, and the 6th Division was included in the Forces disposed in New Guinea. The only operational formation that it is planned should remain in Australia is a brigade at Darwin, so long as this is necessary for the protection of the naval and air bases there. The remaining strength on the mainland, which includes 60,000 B-class men and 20,000 women, is necessary for the maintenance of forces engaged or to be engaged in active operations.

General Blamey now states that it is your desire that the 6th Division should also be allotted as a support for the 7th and 9th Divisions in their prospective operations. He has emphasised the small forces which would be left for the tasks in New Guinea and the other islands, and has pointed out that when the organisation of six divisions was agreed to, it had not been contemplated that the Australian Forces would be actively engaged on operations on several fronts. As the use of a corps of two divisions would alone entail the provision of 30,000 men for base and line of communications units, the proposed use of the 6th Division, together with the position facing the remaining forces in the islands, would make heavy demands on the capacity of Australian manpower to maintain the Australian Army at strength. . . .

I feel that we should adhere to the basis of our previous discussion and limit the Australian component of your spearhead forces to the 7th and 9th Divisions.

General Blamey has also mentioned the question of the higher operational control of the Australian Forces. It is understood from him that the original intention was that the 1st Australian Corps would be commanded by the United States 8th Army and not by the Commander of the Allied Land Forces, but that the latest intention is for it to be under the direct command of General Headquarters.

It was laid down in the 1914-18 war that the Australian Forces serving outside Australia should be organised into and operate as a homogeneous formation appropriate to their strength, and that they should be commanded by an Australian officer. This course was followed in the Middle East in the present war. When the South-West Pacific Area was established, Commanders of the Allied Naval, Land and Air Forces were appointed in your General Order No. 1 of 18th April 1942. The principle which I have mentioned was achieved by the Royal Australian Navy operating under its own Flag Officer who is responsible to the Commander, Allied Naval Forces. In the case of the Royal Australian Air Force, an R.A.A.F. Command was created for operational control of the R.A.A.F. under an Australian Officer who is responsible to the Commander, Allied Air Forces. General Blamey was appointed Commander of the Allied Land Forces which provided for the observance of the principle in respect of the command of the Australian Army. I shall be glad, therefore, if you could inform me of the arrangement that is contemplated in regard to the operational control and command of the First Australian Corps in particular, and of the Australian Land Forces in New Guinea and adjacent islands, and of the manner in which it is proposed to ensure the observance of the basic principle I have mentioned.[4]

That day Berryman had signalled to Blamey:

Chamberlin has insisted that GHQ will only deal with General Morshead task force comd and will not deal with Adv LHQ so consequently there was no reason for Adv LHQ move to Morotai. . . . Efforts by GHQ to bypass Adv LHQ makes planning very difficult and confusing and an early decision is necessary to provide a firm basis for planning. If it is decided that GHQ will only deal with General Morshead during the ops then it will be necessary to integrate part of the staff of Adv LHQ with HQ I Aust Corps.

On 5th March in the course of a reply to Curtin's letter of 15th February, MacArthur wrote:

Original plans for the Philippine campaign contemplated the employment of one Australian division in the initial assault on Leyte and one in the Lingayen landing. General Blamey, however, objected to the plan, stating that he could under no circumstances concur in the use of Australian troops unless they operated as a corps under their own corps commander. It was impossible to utilise the entire corps in the initial landing force and it was therefore necessary to amend the plan, constituting the entire force from American divisions. Plans were then prepared with a view to the employment of the Australian Corps for an operation against Aparri on the northern coast of Luzon, immediately preceding our landing at Lingayen Gulf. The developments of the campaign, however, made it possible to move directly against Lingayen, omitting the Aparri operation with consequent material and vital saving in time. It was then planned to use the corps as the final reserve in the drive across the central plains north of Manila, but the enemy weakness which developed in the tactical situation obviated this necessity.

Current plans contemplate the elimination of the Japanese through a series of comparatively small operations in the central and southern parts of the Philippine

---

[4] Curtin's letter and MacArthur's reply dealt also with the problem of RAAF Command. This is discussed in George Odgers, *Air War Against Japan, 1943-1945* (1957), in the Air series of this history.

archipelago, employing the United States Army troops that are now deployed in forward areas. Concurrently with the later phase of these operations it is proposed to attack Borneo and seize Java by overwater movement. . . . For this operation I have planned to use the Australian Corps . . . operating according to the practice that has consistently been followed in the South-West Pacific Area, under its own task force commander reporting direct to the Commander-in-Chief. It is estimated that the last phase of this operation, the assault upon Java, can be launched by the end of June. . . .

My purpose in projecting this campaign is to restore the Netherlands East Indies authorities to their seat of government as has been done within Australian and United States territory. . . . Immediately upon the re-establishment of the Netherlands East Indies government I propose to report to the Joint Chiefs of Staff that the mission of the South-West Pacific Area has been accomplished and recommend its dissolution. It is contemplated thereafter that there will be a complete reorientation and that the British Empire and the Dutch authorities will collaborate in the complete restoration of their respective territories.

The execution of the plan as above outlined will require not only the full effect of available Australian ground forces, but that of American forces as well. It is proposed to support the Australian ground forces with the R.A.A.F. Command, lending such assistance from the United States Army Air Forces as may be required. It is also hoped that the Seventh Fleet, including the Australian Squadron, will be augmented for this operation by the British Pacific Fleet. . . .

The decision conveyed to me in your letter of 27th February 1945 to limit the Australian component of our assault forces to the 7th and 9th Divisions has been noted. I hope you will not eliminate entirely the possibility of using the 6th Division in the operation outlined above if it becomes a reality.

With reference to the command organisation, we have followed a fixed pattern since the Lae operation. The Commander-in-Chief exercises personal and direct command of assault forces coordinating the action of three principal subordinates:

(a) Naval forces under the Commander,
Allied Naval Forces.
(b) Air Forces under the Commander,
Allied Air Forces.
(c) Ground forces under a Task Force Commander whose organisation is specifically prescribed according to the operation to be undertaken. These forces may vary from a Regimental Combat Team or Brigade Group to an Army and are commanded by an officer of appropriate rank. In the forthcoming operation in which assault forces will include Australian troops, it is contemplated that the Commander would be an Australian officer. While General Morshead has been proposed and is entirely acceptable, I am prepared to accept another officer if designated by the Australian authorities. I consider that the assignment of the Australian Commander should be a matter for determination by the Australians. It is considered to be impossible, however, from an operational viewpoint, for the officer so designated to be concerned with command of Australian troops in New Guinea and Australia. It is essential that the Task Force Commander remain in the field with his troops and that he have no other duties of any kind. Any other course of action would unquestionably jeopardize the success of the operation and impose a risk that could not be accepted.

In this letter Blamey's name was directly mentioned only once and his title never.

Thus MacArthur at length expressed in black and white what Blamey had described as the gradual "insinuation of American control and the elimination of Australian control". It should be remarked, however, that MacArthur's recollection that "since the Lae operation" he, the Commander-in-Chief, had always exercised direct command of ground forces under Task Force commanders of various grades was erroneous. So far as the Australian Army was concerned command of its operations had been exercised, and in appropriate detail, by the Commander-in-Chief of the Australian Army.

At first glance MacArthur's wish to transfer the 6th Division from New Guinea to Borneo may appear as inconsistent as Blamey's opposition to this plan. Six months earlier Blamey had proposed to employ only seven brigades in New Guinea, but MacArthur had insisted on his using twelve. But now, when MacArthur wished to transfer the 6th Division from New Guinea, thus leaving nine brigades there—two more than Blamey had originally wished—Blamey objected, instead of welcoming the belated admission that he had been right in the first place.

In the previous three months, however, the situation had altered. In New Guinea the First Australian Army had become involved in two offensives which were soon to fully tax its strength. At the same time G.H.Q. had been planning operations in Borneo and Java that were likely to be beyond the power of a corps of only two divisions. And, as will be seen, just as G.H.Q. considered it politically inadvisable for Australians to play a leading part in the re-conquest of the Philippines, an American colony, so, evidently, G.H.Q. considered it politically undesirable for American troops to take part in the restoration of Dutch and British control in the Indies.

Blamey travelled to Atherton early in March and went forward to Manila where he met MacArthur on the 14th. The compromise was confirmed that I Australian Corps would operate directly under MacArthur's command, not under the Eighth American Army, and an agreement was reached that "the necessary administrative functions would be performed by Advanced L.H.Q. from Morotai". As a result G.H.Q. dealt directly with I Australian Corps and copies of their correspondence were sent to the Forward Echelon of Blamey's headquarters.

Curtin asked Blamey for his observations on MacArthur's letter of 5th March, and Blamey offered them on 5th April, in a letter which is significant both as indicating to the Government his intentions in New Guinea, and as revealing the increasing and justified coolness of his attitude towards MacArthur.

With reference to [the] paragraph of General MacArthur's letter, commencing "Original plans for the Philippine campaign", the statement made in the first part of the paragraph is true but, I think, not complete. The operation was to have been mounted under an American commander subordinate to General MacArthur and, as the bulk of the troops at that stage were to be Australian, I pointed out that the Australian Corps command and staff were highly trained and were long and well experienced and I saw no reason why it should not be entrusted with this task. The plan as revealed to me required Australians to work in two separate bodies, each under American subordinate commanders.

General MacArthur has always insisted that the difficulties of two different systems of supply made it necessary to ensure that the American and Australian commands should, as far as possible, work independently in the minor field. There was no adequate reason why the Australian corps should not have been employed as a corps under its own commander, since several American corps were employed under American corps commanders during the operations. . . .

I regret that I cannot accept this as a sincere and complete statement of the matter, inasmuch as a whole American corps was brought in ships from the Pacific Ocean Area for these operations and later returned to the Pacific Ocean Area, while the reason given to me why Australian troops could not be moved forward was a lack of shipping.

If it was actually planned to use the Australian corps as a final reserve in the drive across the central plains north of Manila, this was nowhere revealed to me. However, prior to the campaign, General MacArthur stated to me that he would not go into Manila without the Australian corps whom he regarded as essential to deal with the Japanese in that area. I understood that he had informed you in somewhat similar terms.

In spite of the fact that he now claims the enemy weakness obviated the necessity for this, nevertheless very large American forces have been and are being utilised still in this campaign. I would like, however, to bring definitely before your notice that, at Hollandia on my first visit when I proceeded there with the Q.M.G., on the understanding that we were to plan for movement of the Australian Corps from Australia, the American Chief of Staff, General Sutherland, said to me in the presence of General Berryman . . . that it was impossible to use the Australian troops in the Philippines for political reasons. General Berryman immediately made a diary note of this statement.

It will therefore be seen that the paragraph of General MacArthur's letter under notice does not seem to be a full statement of the reasons for the non-use of 1st Australian Corps in the Philippine campaign.

With regard to [the] paragraph of General MacArthur's letter, dealing with current plans. This is in accordance with the instructions I received from General MacArthur. While in Manila recently, I discussed the matter with him and he has requested me to be present for these operations in view of the complicated nature of the command that has developed by reason of its widespread, amphibious and international nature. I have therefore planned to be present for reference and to ensure that the Australian point of view is properly considered.

There is one feature of the forthcoming operations, however, which it is pertinent to consider. There can be no question about the strategical correctness of the seizure of the Philippines, since this aimed straight at the heart of the Japanese ocean area. The whole of the islands comprising the Philippine group have now been seized, giving us direct command of the South China Sea from the northern point of Luzon to the southern point of Palawan.

It would be the logical and strategically correct sequence in the following operations to move down the western coast of Borneo. This would isolate all Japanese forces in Borneo, give a complete control of the South China Sea and facilitate the approach to Malaya.

Current operations do not, however, contemplate such a move. The proposal is to seize two or three points on the east coast of Borneo and to advance from there into Java.

The present proposals envisage the complete destruction of the Japanese in the Philippines and it is proposed in the operations against Borneo and Java to use, in addition to 1st Australian Corps (7th and 9th Divisions) the 6th Australian Division, which is now engaged in operations on the north-east coast of New Guinea. I pointed out what I considered to be an inconsistency in this policy. It did not appear to me to be logical that the plans should contemplate the complete elimination of the Japanese in the Philippines and the withdrawal of Australian Forces from New Guinea before a similar stage had been reached there.

I raised the question with General MacArthur, who said his conception was that the Philippines would be the base for further movement against the Japanese and it was essential that no Japanese should remain in these islands. I pointed out the fact that the withdrawal of Australians from New Guinea before completion of their task in such clearing up would mean they would have to return to complete it.

General MacArthur's staff have since informed me that he will make sufficient landing craft available to allow the 6th Division to seize Wewak.

In view of the intention of the American forces to destroy completely the Japanese in the Philippine Islands, it is my considered opinion that further Australian forces should not be withdrawn from New Guinea until such time as Japanese forces on Australian territory are destroyed also. . . .

I except from this Rabaul. The Japanese forces in this region have been pressed into a comparatively small area. They are well supplied and apparently strong and I consider any attempt to capture this stronghold should be deferred for the present and we should be satisfied to contain it, since we can do so with lesser strength than the enemy force there. . . .

Curtin replied to Blamey on 17th April asking whether he wished to recommend that the Government should make any representation to MacArthur concerning the use of the Australian forces, and whether the operations in the New Guinea area met with MacArthur's approval.

Blamey replied that he did not recommend any action by the Government about the Borneo operations which had now been approved by the Combined Chiefs. The occupation of Tarakan, Brunei and Labuan was strategically sound since it tended to increase the control of the sea area between Malaya and Japan. The operations in New Guinea had been discussed fully with MacArthur. No specific instructions had been given about them. It was a "proper claim" that the 6th Division's operations had MacArthur's approval since they could not be carried out without the allocation by him of the necessary landing craft.

When these discussions opened General Headquarters had already elaborated its outline plan for the employment of I Australian Corps. As first conceived, in February, the OBOE plan as it was named was in six parts. OBOE ONE was to begin on 23rd April when a brigade group of the 6th Division would attack Tarakan Island and enable an airstrip to be established from which aircraft might support the next move (OBOE TWO), which was to be an attack on Balikpapan on 18th May by the 9th Division. Balikpapan would then become an advanced base for OBOE THREE—the occupation on 28th May of Bandjermasin by a brigade group of the 9th Division. (If British carriers were available to support the advance to Java, OBOE THREE was to be omitted.) With air support from Bandjermasin or from British carriers, I Australian Corps, with the 6th and 7th Divisions, two tank battalions and, later, a brigade of the 9th Division, would then undertake the major operation of the series (OBOE FOUR): the seizure of the Surabaya area opening on 27th June and an advance thence west to Batavia and Bandung and east to Lombok Strait. The fifth phase of the plan provided for the consolidation of the remaining areas of the Netherlands Indies, the sixth for the occupation of the remaining areas of Borneo.

After the decision that the 6th Division should not be used in Borneo the plan was amended to provide for the capture of Tarakan by a brigade group of the 9th and of Balikpapan by the remainder of the division. Thus orders were issued on 22nd February for the move of the 9th Division to the staging base at Morotai, and on 1st March planning teams from I Corps, the 9th Division, and the 1st Base Sub-Area were ordered forward to Morotai.

The staff of the Forward Echelon of Land Headquarters produced a staff study for the Tarakan operation by 11th March and General Headquarters a similar study a week later. With these as a basis the Tarakan operation was discussed at a conference at General Headquarters on 17th March and the Balikpapan operation on 20th March. The target date for Tarakan was now set at 29th April and for Balikpapan at 22nd May. By 21st March General Morshead's staff had prepared studies for both operations and Morshead went to Morotai on the 22nd to give preliminary instructions to Major-General G. F. Wootten of the 9th Division.

The proposed operations against Borneo had, despite General Marshall's earlier lack of enthusiasm, won the support of the Joint Chiefs of Staff in March. It seems that the Joint Chiefs were influenced by a desire to find a separate sphere of operations for the British Pacific Fleet, and by Curtin's February letter. The capture of Brunei Bay and the Borneo oilfields would give the British Pacific Fleet a base from which to operate northward or westward; yet the recapture of these British and Dutch possessions by American troops when other objectives were available might be resented in America; therefore Australians should be used, particularly as their Prime Minister was threatening further to reduce the Australian Army if it was not more actively employed.

Thus, on 6th April, General Headquarters informed the Australians that the Joint Chiefs of Staff had cancelled the operation against Bandjermasin and Java. It was proposed instead that a further landing should be made at Brunei Bay by the 7th Division less a brigade group.

The corps staff began planning for these operations, and much paper work had been done when, on 17th April, General Headquarters informed Marshall that the 7th Division would make the attack on Balikpapan, and the 9th less a brigade could undertake the Brunei Bay operation (OBOE SIX). General Headquarters authorised the movement of the 7th Division from Australia to Morotai, as soon as the 9th had finished its movement thither. It was expected that the 7th less one brigade would be at Morotai by 16th June. The target date for Brunei Bay was now set at 23rd May. Later, however, shipping problems and other factors caused further postponement: Tarakan to 1st May, Brunei Bay to 10th June and Balikpapan finally to 1st July.

In April the Joint Chiefs agreed to the program whereby Tarakan, Brunei Bay and Balikpapan would be attacked in that order. On 13th April the British Chiefs of Staff were informed of the plan. They did not at all like an arrangement which seemed likely to defeat their hard-won agreement that the fleet would take part in the main operations against Japan, which, at this stage, it being assumed that Germany would be defeated by the end of May, would open in October or December. In consequence, on 27th April they informed the Joint Chiefs by telegram that they considered the allocation of resources to the operations against Borneo unjustified: Brunei Bay was too far from Japan, could not be ready before the beginning of 1946, and was a long haul from Australia compared with other possible sites at the same distance from Japan. They considered it essential for the effective operation of the British Pacific Fleet to obtain an anchorage and facilities much nearer Japan than Brunei Bay, and suggested Subic Bay in the Philippines.

The Joint Chiefs urged that Brunei Bay had advantages for possible future operations in the Netherlands Indies or the South China Sea, but the British Chiefs replied on 24th May:

> We consider that to develop Brunei Bay . . . would be a waste of the constructional resources at our disposal, especially in view of the fact that the base would not be complete until the end of the year, by which time Singapore may well have been captured.[5]

Nevertheless the 9th Division was landed in Brunei Bay 17 days later.

In February, March and April the American forces had launched their attacks on Iwo Jima and Okinawa. Iwo Jima was defended by some 20,000 Japanese. The Americans put ashore a corps of three divisions of marines —about 82,000 men—and after hard fighting in which about 5,500 Americans were killed, secured the island, which provided a heavy-bomber base only 775 miles from the Japanese mainland.

The expedition against Okinawa was of unparalleled magnitude. The island is 60 miles long and from 2 to 18 miles wide. It was estimated that the defenders numbered about 55,000, including four divisions; in fact there were 77,000, including two divisions, an independent brigade and smaller formations. Against Okinawa the Americans launched the Tenth Army, which included seven divisions and numbered at the outset 183,000 men. Troops were landed on small islands near by on 26th March and on Okinawa proper on 1st April. The invading force had the support of immense naval and air forces and in three months its artillery fired 1,766,000 rounds. The Japanese fought with their usual resolution and in May when the Australians made their first landing in Borneo the long battle was still being fought.

On 6th April the structure of the command in the Pacific had been radically altered. The two prongs of the American advance were now nearing one another, and the main drive would be along a single axis towards the Japanese mainland. In the coming phase the former system whereby each Commander-in-Chief commanded all army, naval and air forces in his area was to be abandoned. General MacArthur now became commander of all American army forces in the Pacific; Admiral Nimitz of all American naval forces. The strategic air force—Twentieth Air Force —would be directly under the Joint Chiefs.

It thus became the more desirable that MacArthur should shed responsibility for the increasingly-remote Japanese-occupied areas to the south and west. Thus on 13th April (the day on which they announced their plans for Borneo) the Joint Chiefs had proposed to the British Chiefs that the whole of the South-West Pacific Area, excluding the Philippines and Hainan, should be included in the South-East Asia Command or as

---

[5] Quoted in J. Ehrman, *Grand Strategy*, Vol VI, p. 226.

a separate command as the British Chiefs thought fit. They proposed that the change should be made on 1st July. The British Joint Planning Staff generally favoured the new proposal, and considered it operationally desirable that the area to be detached should form a single command. At this stage the Australian leaders had not been informed of this plan, though it was likely to interest them closely since the only operations being carried on in the area to be transferred were by Australian troops under Australian command.

On 19th April General MacArthur had seen Generals Morshead and Berryman and discussed the coming operations with them. He spoke with enthusiasm about a wish to have the A.I.F. with him in the final operations against Japan, provided it was not decided that it should join the British in capturing Malaya and the Indies.

"He proposed to use the A.I.F. in CORONET [the final phase of the invasion of Japan] and stressed the advantage to our national prestige," reported Berryman to Blamey. "It was unthinkable that the A.I.F. should be separated from the U.S. Forces after they had been fighting together for three and a half years. If the R.A.N. remains under his command he proposes to hoist his flag in an R.A.N. ship for the OLYMPIC [opening phase of the invasion of Japan] or CORONET operation. . . ."

The suggestions in the Australian Press that the A.I.F. were deliberately kept out of the Philippines operations, MacArthur said to Berryman, were not correct. MacArthur then repeated more or less what he had written on this subject in his letter of 5th March—a letter which Blamey, with good reason, had refused to accept "as a sincere and complete statement of the matter".

It was unfortunate that the history of the relations between G.H.Q. and the Australian Commander-in-Chief should have culminated, with the victory so near, in an exchange of asperities. The causes of this malaise are to be found in the events of the previous three years and in differences of temperament among the principal figures.

G.H.Q. had been formed round MacArthur and the group of staff officers who had emerged with him from the Philippines shocked by the swiftness and severity of their defeat. As has been seen in an earlier volume of this series, this staff throughout 1942 had little confidence in the ability of the forces concentrating in Australia to halt the Japanese advance. Although a skilful, and proper, publicity campaign had given them a high reputation with the American and Australian public, they feared that their standing with Washington was insecure.

The only competent troops this headquarters possessed in the critical months of 1942 had been Australian; and these were commanded generally by leaders of considerably greater experience than those G.H.Q. possessed. The American formations which were sent to the area developed only slowly in skill and confidence and largely failed in their first operations. The war against Japan was two years old before the American divisions were promoted to a major role in the campaign in New Guinea, by which time Australian troops had thoroughly defeated the Japanese army on the New Guinea mainland, and sufficient ships and landing craft were available for oversea movements and more rapid coastwise advances.

In retrospect it seems that from early in 1944 onwards there was a keen, and understandable, desire at G.H.Q. to organise an all-American drive to the Philippines, and perhaps beyond. To allot to Australian divisions the task of relieving the American forces tied up in New Guinea was proper, and a solution acceptable to both the Australian Government and MacArthur. On the other hand the frequent changes of plans for the employment of the A.I.F. Corps in the Philippines, the eventual decision that it should not participate, the neglect to mention Australian operations in the communiqués, and the sometimes devious and often hurtful manner in which the exclusion of General Blamey from the chain of command was carried out were disappointing to the leaders of an army which for two years had borne the heat and burden of the day.[6]

However, the discussions of March and April between the Australian Government and General MacArthur clarified a situation that had become ambiguous and embarrassing. It became clear that MacArthur considered the appointment of Commander Allied Land Forces to have lapsed, and that Blamey's authority should be limited to administrative control of the whole Australian Army and *de facto* operational control of the forces in the New Guinea territories. MacArthur insisted, however, on exercising direct control over the Australian formation—I Australian Corps—which was to serve in Borneo.

These were workmanlike decisions, although they might have been conveyed to the Australian Government and Commander-in-Chief with greater frankness and tact. There were sound political, psychological and technical reasons why MacArthur, after the end of 1943, should not leave his land forces under an Australian commander. At the opening of the northward drive of 1944 the Australian commanders and staffs had more experience and knowledge than the American, but to leave an Australian at the head of a now-large army in which American formations were in a majority, and during a major offensive, would have involved a loss of prestige that the Americans could not have been expected to incur. In addition, because of wide differences of staff methods, tactical doctrines and equipment, it was desirable to employ both Americans and Australians so far as possible under their own commanders and staffs. It was a very much less difficult problem to integrate corps and divisions from five different nations of the British Commonwealth, as in the Middle East, than to integrate Australian and American formations. United Kingdom, Australian, New Zealand and Indian officers and men were trained and equipped similarly, their doctrines and traditions were similar, and, indeed, many of the leaders had previously served side by side in peace and war.

---

[6] For example, Allied Land Forces was no longer listed under the heading "Command Posts" in G.H.Q. orders and instructions. Thus the operation instruction concerning the invasion of Leyte names 15 "command posts" including Allied Air Forces and its Rear Echelon, U.S.A.S.O.S., First Australian Army and so on, but not Allied Land Forces.

In spite of the difficulties imposed by the decision of April 1942 to establish a purely American supreme command in Australia to direct, at that time and for long afterwards, predominantly Australian forces, the system had worked effectively, although some friction was inevitable. In the first place, up to about the end of 1943, it was essential that the tactical command in the field should be Australian. In the next phase it was desirable that the tactical command of the northward advance should be American.

A sequel to this change of policy was the creation of what was virtually a new and independent Allied command in the southern part of the South-West Pacific Area. It came into being from October 1944 onwards without benefit of any decision of the Combined Chiefs of Staff or Joint Chiefs of Staff. MacArthur's insistence that the First Australian Army was directly under his command was not followed up by any effort to influence its operations except in a negative way. In practice it was, after the end of 1944, a rather more independent command than Admiral Halsey's South Pacific Area had been in the period when General MacArthur had "coordinated" its operations with his own. However, although the strategy and tactics in the New Guinea-Solomons area were now directed solely by the Australian command, it depended for shipping almost entirely on remote and uninterested authorities, with results which will be recorded later.

CHAPTER 3

THE GENERAL, THE PARLIAMENT AND THE MINISTERS

BY December 1944 the II Australian Corps in Bougainville and the 6th Division about Aitape had embarked on offensives against the strong Japanese forces in those areas. By the end of February 1945 the II Corps had gained control of most of the western half of Bougainville, and the 6th Division had thrust eastward more than half way to Wewak. In New Britain the 5th Division had advanced, against little opposition, to a line across the neck of the Gazelle Peninsula. The situation of October 1944 had been reversed. Whereas then the American garrisons had been defending bases in these three areas, in February it was the Japanese who were defending their bases.

While the First Australian Army (three divisions and the elements of a fourth) was dealing with the Japanese armies (six divisions) by-passed in Australian New Guinea, the Eighth American Army (four divisions) was performing a similar task in the southern and central Philippines where it faced the remnants of five divisions on Leyte and two divisions and some smaller forces in the other islands; the Sixth American Army (ten divisions), with some help from the Eighth, was fighting in Luzon, where the Japanese had deployed seven infantry divisions and one armoured division, the strongest single Japanese force yet encountered outside China.

In view of the discussion in Australia about the policies adopted by the Australian forces in the New Guinea territories, the operations of the Eighth American Army in Mindanao and the Visayas—the central part of the archipelago—are of special interest. During March and April about one-third of MacArthur's American divisions were employed destroying the Japanese forces in these "by-passed" islands. On 28th February part of the 41st Division occupied Palawan. On 10th March the 41st Division landed at Zamboanga in western Mindanao and on 17th April the X Corps (24th and 31st Divisions) landed on the south coast of that island.[1] On 18th March the 40th Division landed on Panay and on 26th March the Americal Division landed on Cebu. On Leyte "mopping up" was still in progress; the campaign on Leyte would be declared "officially closed" on 30th June, but "mopping up" was then still going on. At that time three American divisions—31st, 41st and Americal—were still in action in the southern and central Philippines, and a division was defending the perimeter on Morotai. Indeed, the American forces employed against

[1] On Mindanao Colonel Wendell Fertig had organised a guerilla force of Filipinos which had harassed the Japanese since 1942 and in March 1945 had seized the Malabang airstrip. This force included several Australians, notably Major Rex Blow, a former lieutenant of the 2/10th Field Regiment, who had escaped from the Japanese at Sandakan in 1943. On 13th April an officer of the American Marines landed in an aircraft at Malabang and on the 16th flew out to Zamboanga with Blow. Both men were taken by small boat to join the invasion convoy which was due to land the X Corps next day. The commander, having heard what they had to say, confirmed a decision, made after receiving the first news of the force at Malabang, to put only one battalion ashore there and land the main force at Parang, 17 miles down the coast.

the Japanese by-passed in the Philippines south of Luzon were never smaller and for much of the time were considerably larger than the Australian forces fighting the stronger Japanese formations in the New Guinea territories. Between 25th December and 8th May the Eighth Army on Leyte alone lost 544 men killed; in the earlier operations in that area the Sixth Army had lost 3,049 killed.

In Luzon at the end of February 1945 the Sixth American Army was fighting round Manila Bay, which was secured early in March.

In the first three weeks of February, as mentioned, the Australian operations ceased to gain much prominence in the newspapers, whose headlines were being given mostly to the fighting in the Philippines and on the Rhine, but, when the Federal Parliament met on 21st February after a recess of two months, the conduct of operations in New Guinea became the subject of criticism which rapidly developed in vehemence. The Opposition based an attack on three main grounds: first, Australian troops were being mis-employed "mopping up" in the islands; secondly, they should be fighting in (*a*) the Philippines or (*b*) South-East Asia; thirdly, they were inadequately equipped. At a later stage violent personal attacks on the Australian Commander-in-Chief were added.

The Leader of the Opposition, Mr Menzies, opened the discussion in a speech during the debate on the Address-in-Reply, in the course of which he said:

Are we to use our major forces primarily for doing what I call "mopping-up operations" in by-passed areas, or should they be used as an integral portion of a British army to deliver those countries in the Far East which have been overrun by Japan? As to that I confess I have very strong views. . . . We have a profound political interest in the restoration of British authority in Burma, Malaya and Singapore, and a profound future interest in the relief and restoration of the Netherlands East Indies. I should like to think . . . that we were able at this time to have a division, or perhaps two divisions, of the Australian Imperial Force fighting with other British troops for the relief of Malaya, and the rescue of those men who were captured at Singapore.[2]

In reply the Attorney-General, Dr Evatt, said that five countries—the United States, the United Kingdom, the Netherlands, Australia and New Zealand—had agreed upon the directive governing the disposition of forces in the S.W.P.A.; the Australian forces were at the disposal of the Supreme Commander, General MacArthur. The Australian Government had loyally conformed to his decisions. There was no role in the theatre that was secondary. He quoted words of praise from MacArthur for Australia's war effort.

Mr Spender questioned the use to which the Australian Army was being put in ridding New Guinea and Bougainville "of Japanese who were supposed to have been left there to wither and famish, but are, in fact, firmly entrenched, well disciplined and adequately equipped and supplied".[3] Mr Forde had said publicly, he added, that all Australian Services would ultimately be in action in the Philippines. He was waiting to hear that

---
[2] *Commonwealth Debates*, Vol 181, p. 58.
[3] *Commonwealth Debates*, Vol 181, p. 68.

the Australian Army was actually engaged there. It was time to discuss whether the manpower was being employed in the most effective way. Australia's position at the peace table would be determined solely by the fighting contribution made by Australia.

Mr Curtin said that he agreed that Australia had a major political and national interest in the British Empire, Malaya, Singapore and the Far East, but she had a major political issue nearer home: to clear out the enemy still in occupation of territories for which the Australian Government was politically responsible.

In the Senate on 28th February the attack reached its second and third phases. Senator McLeay[4] declared that reports were arriving from the front that the equipment of the Australian troops was "far inferior" to that of the Americans. The reports should be investigated. Senator Foll[5] criticised the employment of Australian troops against "besieged Japanese forces" and went on to a direct attack on Blamey.

> The general public has very little faith in him as the Commander-in-Chief, and the Army itself is seething with dissatisfaction . . . the best service he could render to Australia would be to resign.[6]

Foll added that Blamey had "virtually thrown out of this country's service" General Rowell. General Lavarack had been "sacrificed" and sent to Washington, "because of a personal disagreement, apparently". General Bennett was "never given a chance, as others were, to go back and attack his old foe". General Robertson "was sent home and put on the shelf, never to lead his men in action again".[7]

Senator Mattner,[8] quoting passages from soldiers' letters, complained that the army lacked the heavy equipment possessed by the Americans—road-making equipment, amphibious craft and the like; and he declared that the Commander-in-Chief should be "a young and experienced man

---

[4] Hon G. McLeay. Senator 1934-47, 1949-55; Vice-Pres of Executive Council 1938-41; Minister for Commerce 1939-40, for Trade and Customs 1940; PMG and Minister for Repatriation 1940-41, for Supply and Development 1941. B. Port Clinton, SA, 6 Aug 1892. Died 14 Sep 1955.

[5] Hon H. S. Foll. (1st AIF: Gnr 7 Bty AFA 1914-15.) Senator 1917-47; Minister for Interior 1939-40, for Information 1940-41. B. London, 31 May 1890.

[6] *Commonwealth Debates*, Vol 181, pp. 128-9.

[7] Foll had opened this attack a year earlier. In the Senate on 10th February 1944 he had aired a complaint that had already received some publicity in the newspapers and been a subject of gossip. Briefly it was that General Blamey had shelved Generals Rowell, Mackay, Wynter, Lavarack and Morshead. In the House of Representatives on 24th February Mr Archie Cameron had made a similar complaint, but mentioned Generals Mackay, Herring, Lavarack, Rowell and Clowes as those who had been shelved, bringing the total to the imposing figure of seven. In the course of a detailed reply to Cameron the Prime Minister, Mr Curtin, then said:
"The honorable member for Barker had better get it well into his mind that the implied strictures on the Commander-in-Chief that permeated his speech are not shared by the best qualified minds of this country; that there is nothing but admiration for General Sir Thomas Blamey by those who serve under him. There may be there, as there are here, certain disappointed personal ambitions, but there is no professional criticism. There may be in some quarters, as there is in this Parliament, the belief that someone else could do better; but I have been unable to find it among those whom I would regard as most qualified to offer a judgment. . . . I have always regarded it as necessary that I should be able to lay my hands upon somebody who could step into shoes which might become vacant, either because of enemy action or through natural causes. I say . . . with pride and thankfulness, that I have had from the men whom I have entertained in mind, in order to feel sure that we should not be left in the lurch, nothing but the assurance that, if ever the command should come to one of them before the war was over, they would regard its coming as a national calamity." (*Commonwealth Debates*, Vol 177, pp. 576-7.)

[8] E. W. Mattner, MC, DCM, MM. (1st AIF: Lt 6 Army Bde AFA. Maj 13 Fd Regt 1940-42.) Senator 1944-47, and 1949-62. B. Oakbank, SA, 16 Sep 1893.

who has seen service in this war, and is game enough to go to the front and see for himself what is taking place".[9]

On 1st March Blamey, evidently in the hope of halting the personal attacks, wrote a letter to Menzies denying the statements of Senator Foll concerning the shelving of generals and pointing out that "a very great proportion" of his time had been spent "on the Atherton Tablelands and New Guinea".[1]

> The allocation of Australian troops to operations is entirely the responsibility of General MacArthur (he continued) and I have no real say in the matter beyond carrying out the orders I receive. While I have pretty strong feelings on certain of these allocations, I have no right to criticise them.
>
> My chief objection to these criticisms, however, is on account of the evil effect they must have upon the forces. As for myself, you know very well that I do not seek to remain in this office, and would be very happy indeed to be relieved of it. I think it is due to the country's war effort, however, that those responsible for its legislation should not continue to sow seeds of dissent and criticism to the destruction of the morale of the Army.

Menzies replied, on 6th March, advising Blamey to ignore Foll's criticism, and adding that, after Foll's speech, Menzies and several of his members in informal discussion agreed that if today they were appointing a "No. 1" for the Australian Military Forces Blamey would still be their choice. He suggested that the Prime Minister should make a statement indicating the nature of Blamey's responsibilities. "This, I think, would set a great deal of criticism at rest." Menzies added that among his colleagues and friends the real uneasiness related primarily to a feeling that many thousands of young men in the armed forces, including the air force, were under-employed and that the effect of this might be "demoralising and dangerous".

In Parliament the debate had continued. In the House of Representatives on 2nd March the Minister for the Army, Mr Forde, said that some nation had to be responsible for "mopping-up, cleaning out, driving into the sea and annihilating 100,000 fearless fighters of the Japanese Army. They could not be allowed to remain in the islands."[2] It was the opinion of the Government's expert military advisers that Australian troops should be committed to this task. He added that last year some members had complained that some divisions were being overworked; they now contended that Australian troops had been allotted a puny task and should be used elsewhere on difficult and dangerous tasks befitting soldiers of their calibre. He denied that the army was ill-equipped.

In defence of Blamey against his critics Forde said that the actions planned by the Commander-in-Chief and his efficient general staff, "in

---

[9] *Commonwealth Debates*, Vol 181, p. 133.

[1] Blamey's diary shows that, in April, May and part of June 1944, he had attended the Prime Ministers' conferences in London and conferences in Washington. Later in June he had visited Lae and Atherton. In July he had again visited the formations on the Tableland, and in August had been to Merauke and Darwin. In October he had spent about seven days in New Guinea, and in November and December about 14 in New Guinea, including Bougainville and Aitape, and in Leyte. All January and February 1945 had been spent in Melbourne, Canberra, or elsewhere in the south. In the last three weeks of March he was in the Philippines, Morotai and New Guinea, where he visited Bougainville, New Britain and Aitape.

[2] *Commonwealth Debates*, Vol 181, p. 287.

the majority of which the Commander-in-Chief himself participated", combined with American operations, had eliminated the enemy from the areas nearest Australia. It was surely ungrateful now to criticise the leader of the Australian Army. Blamey's task made it necessary for him to keep in touch with his headquarters in Australia as well as with forward units. He considered the criticism "grossly extravagant and most unfair".

Blamey had some defenders among back-benchers as well as among the Ministers. Mr Donald McLeod,[3] for example, said on 15th March that Blamey's direction of the campaigns in the north had been "marked by complete success"; it had been said that he was too old whereas he was "about the same age as General MacArthur" (in fact he was four years younger). "Let the critics, if they have anything against him, come out into the open and state their charges plainly. In the meantime, let us judge the Commander-in-Chief on his record."[4]

From Bougainville on 31st March Blamey made a statement in reply to criticism of the army's equipment. He said that "Australians were never better situated for troops, organisation, administration and supplies"; but there was an immediate shortage of water transport due to the general shipping shortage.

As will be seen later there was little more that could usefully be said about equipment at that time. On 5th April, however, Mr Curtin made an announcement which could be interpreted as meaning that the Government as well as the Opposition lacked confidence in Blamey. He quoted reports from Blamey about transport difficulties then being encountered in and round New Guinea, but added that the acting Minister for the Army, Senator Fraser,[5] would visit the forward areas and report.

In the newspapers at this stage a new field of criticism was being explored: why were the names of the leaders and units then in action not being released for publication?

Blamey's conduct of operations had now been under criticism for some weeks; members of Parliament had charged him with not being "game" to go to the front and with having treated subordinate commanders unjustly, and had urged that he should resign; he had neglected the equipment of his troops; he was too old; the nation had lost confidence in him. On 15th April he retaliated. During a broadcast appeal for subscriptions to a war loan he said:

You may be assured that [the troops'] morale, their fighting capacity, their training and equipment will ensure that their future successes will be no less complete and no less vital than those which they have realised in the past five and a half years of war. But for those troops themselves I have something to say to you. It is this: in no other country have the achievements of a successful army been so belittled as in Australia.

It was different three years ago when the threat of Japanese invasion was very real; when Australian soldiers were fighting desperately to halt the Japanese. It was

---
[3] D. McLeod. (1st AIF: Artillery 1916-19.) MHR 1940-49 and 1951-55. B. Strathmerton, Vic, 29 Oct 1892.
[4] *Commonwealth Debates*, Vol 181, p. 654.
[5] Hon J. M. Fraser. Senator 1937-59; Minister for External Territories 1941-43, for Health and Social Services 1943-46; acting Minister for the Army in 1944-45. Died 27 Aug 1961.

different even when those same soldiers halted the Japanese and turned him back along the long road to Tokyo. Then they were the nation's saviours. The armchair strategists—though fearful—were content to leave the saving of this country to the men who did save it. But now these same amateurs lose no opportunity to publicise their views, without regard to the effect these may have on the self-sacrificing efforts of the troops who are fighting the same battle against the same enemy and in the same type of country as three years ago.

They have advanced little, if any, from the ignorance which characterised their panic of 1942. They seem to have learnt, however, that this country will not tolerate any direct attack on the individual soldier. So they wrap their barbs in other material. They do not suggest that the Japanese is a better soldier than the Australian, but imply that the Australian might be elevated to the Japanese category if he had more arms of a particular type, or vehicles to take him over razorback ridges where no tracked or wheeled vehicle has ever been before or is ever likely to go. . . . They suggest that we should leave this enemy fruit to wither on the vine. . . . It is no mopping-up to those Australians who have to fight it.

It was probably these parts of an address of about 1,000 words that astounded his critics. Mr Spender, for example, was "staggered" that Blamey had used a war loan speech "to engage bitterly in a controversy which had now entered the political field". He added, in the course of a long reply, that Blamey seemed unaware that in democratic countries the general rule is for the Prime Minister or his responsible Minister to answer political criticism and not for any Service chief no matter how exalted his rank.[6]

The newspaper onslaught was no less vehement. In a leading article the *Sydney Morning Herald* found that the general had been "ill-tempered" and "unseemly", and proceeded to attack him in language more vehement than his own, impugning both his honesty and his capacity as a commander.

Next day Curtin, however, told a Press conference that he thought that as Blamey had been severely criticised he might at least be allowed to state his case the same as the critics. "The critics surely can't object to being criticised,"[7] he said.

Mr Menzies referred to the subject in the House of Representatives on 26th April. He said:

I happen to entertain the strongest possible view that it is wrong to use the Australian forces—which, we are told, number hundreds of thousands of men—in operations in those islands which seem to me to have no relation to any first-class strategic objective in this war.[8]

He felt that Australian troops should be engaged in a real drive against the enemy, for example in Malaya or the Netherlands East Indies, instead of doing something which, in his uninformed opinion, could be left until after victory had been achieved. He quoted MacArthur as having said in a communiqué of 16th February: "For all strategic purposes, this completes the campaign in the Solomon Islands." Menzies then said that he

---

[6] *Sydney Morning Herald*, 16th April 1945.
[7] *Sydney Morning Herald*, 17th April 1945.
[8] *Commonwealth Debates*, Vol 181, p. 1126.

New Guinea, main

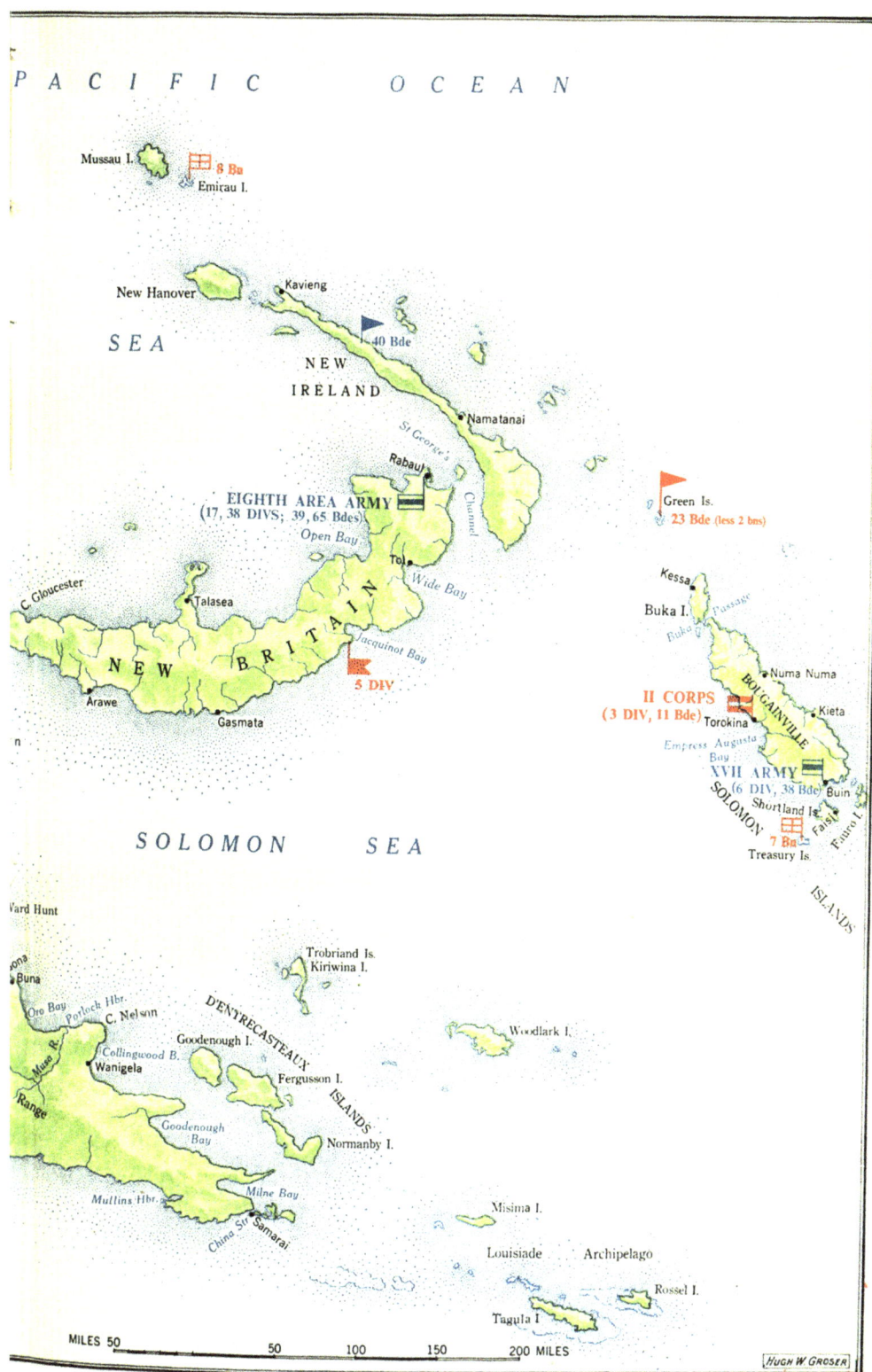

dispositions January 1945

regarded Blamey as a distinguished Australian and a distinguished soldier but his broadcast of 15th April was an "elementary blunder".

No Commander-in-Chief (he said) occupying the place he does, and exercising the authority and responsibility he has, ought to come into the political arena with such an ill-judged and intemperate speech.

Later in his speech Menzies described Blamey's language in this broadcast as "intemperate, unjust and misleading"—adjectives that could justly have been applied also to the language of some of Blamey's critics.

Meanwhile Mr Archie Cameron[9] had offered criticism of Blamey in a Press statement. He charged Blamey with not being in the forward areas enough. Blamey was then in the Northern Territory, whence, on 21st April, his Director-General of Public Relations, Colonel Rasmussen,[1] sent to headquarters in Melbourne a statement for issue to the Press. In it "the official army spokesman" said that "like all personal criticisms that had been directed against the Commander-in-Chief this allegation was notable only for its complete inaccuracy". He had spent more than half of 1944 outside the mainland. Since April 1944 he had travelled 65,000 miles by air, 7,000 miles by sea and 7,500 on land. The statement concluded: "Major Cameron is a comparatively young officer whose name has been on the active list during most of the war but he has not yet put foot outside Australia since its commencement."

Senator Fraser's 12-day visit to the forward areas had ended on 16th April and, on the 24th, Curtin had made a comprehensive statement in the House of Representatives. He defended the offensive policy being adopted by the forces in New Guinea, and said that the Government accepted full responsibility for the operations being carried out by the army. The casualties were remarkably low: 317 Australians killed up to 4th April compared with 5,549 Japanese confirmed killed.

In the Philippines the Americans are clearing the Japanese from the whole of the islands to free the native people, to obtain the use of the resources of the islands, and to free their forces from a prolonged and continuing commitment.[2]

Australia was following the same principle. Curtin then reported the main conclusions reached by Senator Fraser after his visit to the operational areas to investigate the alleged shortages of equipment. There was adequate fighting and engineering equipment on Bougainville and New Britain. In the Aitape-Wewak area, however, floods and unprecedented shipping difficulties due to bad weather had held up the dispatch of certain equipment. Finally Fraser decided that except in New Britain the heavy mechanical equipment could be added to with advantage. Curtin added that General Blamey's comment on this opinion was that the type of operations being carried out did not demand paved roads but, with jeeps, trailers, and six-wheel drive trucks, a cleared earth track sufficed. Concerning shipping, Mr Curtin added, Senator Fraser had said that there

---
[9] Hon A. G. Cameron. (1st AIF: 27 Bn 1916-19. Maj Intell Corps 1942-44.) MHR 1934-56; Minister for Commerce and the Navy 1940; Speaker 1950-56. B. Happy Valley, SA, 22 Mar 1895. Died 9 Aug 1956.
[1] Brig J. H. Rasmussen, V145708. DDPR LHQ 1942-44, DGPR 1944-45. Journalist; of Rutherglen, Vic; b. Rutherglen, 10 Jun 1902. Died 17 Aug 1952.
[2] *Commonwealth Debates*, Vol 181, p. 1028.

were insufficient small craft except in New Britain; and there was a shortage of ships—a world-wide problem.

After his tour Senator Fraser had addressed to the Prime Minister, in addition to the observations contained in the report that was tabled in the House, some general remarks on the operations in New Guinea. In the course of these he said that

> operations should not have been undertaken, except under necessity, until complete fighting, mechanical engineering and small craft equipment, which was necessary for the success of these operations with a minimum casualty rate, had been transported to the operational bases and were available for use.

In Fraser's view practically the whole of the allegations about Australian equipment had been brought about by the fact that American troops always had plenty of heavy mechanical equipment and small craft, and this caused the Australians to compare the inactivity of the American fighting troops when in the areas with the activity of the Australians in "grappling with the enemy with quite good facilities, but in lesser number and spread over a very much greater area". Fraser then wrote critically of a Treasury direction concerning Lend-Lease and American administration of Lend-Lease in the islands; these, he considered, had impeded the smooth transfer of American facilities to the Australian forces.

In Parliament a long and heated debate followed in the course of which many members expressed their views on the aggressive policy being followed in New Guinea and on details of army equipment and organisation, and some continued the stinging attacks on Blamey. The complaints about details of Australian equipment were based on conversations and correspondence with generally anonymous American and Australian soldiers and on newspaper reports, and often were inaccurate or misleading.

However, as Menzies pointed out in the House, the debate had the effect of sifting out the real nature of the problems. So far as equipment was concerned it appeared that it was adequate except that there were shortages of heavy mechanical equipment and light water craft.

Mr Chifley,[3] who was acting Prime Minister because Mr Curtin was ill, spoke in support of Blamey on 27th April, but without marked enthusiasm. General Blamey had a distinguished record. He (Chifley) understood that he was a splendid soldier. "I do not know anything of his other qualities," he added. Blamey's retaliatory broadcast, however, had Chifley's approval.

> Having thrown brickbats at him (he said), honorable gentlemen opposite consider that he should not throw any brickbats in return. It was all right for him to attack the Minister for Information, but when he gave the daily Press and the Opposition a clout, they squealed to high heaven.[4]

On 1st May Australian troops landed at Tarakan. The news that Australians were in action in Borneo was given big headlines in the news-

---

[3] Rt Hon J. B. Chifley. MHR 1928-31 and 1940-51; Treasurer 1941-49, Minister for Post-War Reconstruction 1942-45; Prime Minister 1945-49. B. Bathurst, NSW, 22 Sep 1885. Died 13 Jun 1951.

[4] *Commonwealth Debates,* Vol 181, p. 1189-90.

papers and so was news of a coastwise movement against Wewak a few days later. These events were hailed with enthusiasm. On 5th May the *Sydney Morning Herald,* for example, in a leading article on Tarakan wrote:

> It is to be hoped that the fact that Australian troops are in the front line once more will create in the community at large an adequate appreciation of its debt and responsibilities to them.

For some days Wewak and Tarakan continued to be front-page news. Thenceforward there was little more public criticism of the army's policy and equipment or of the character of Blamey. It remained, however, to unearth the "official army spokesman" of 21st April and to thrash out in the relative privacy of the War Cabinet and the Advisory War Council the rights and wrongs of the New Guinea and Bougainville offensives.

On 3rd May Major-General Rankin[5] in the House of Representatives sought the identity of the "official army spokesman" but was fended off with an uninformative reply. Mr Chifley, however, set off in pursuit of the offender. He wrote to the acting Minister for the Army quoting a decision of the War Cabinet on 18th March 1942 (the date was not mentioned in the letter) that members of the Services were not to make public statements and quoting part but not all of a subsequent Cabinet decision elaborating the first one. Paragraph (ii) of this second decision had originally read:

> All statements in relation to military matters by members of the Services are to be submitted to the Censor, who will consult with representatives of the Services regarding the deletion of information which would be prejudicial to security or public morale.

In Chifley's letter this paragraph was omitted, but the third and final paragraph was included, and numbered (ii). It read:

> The direction relates to statements by all ranks of the Services and covers statements attributed to members of the Forces whose identity is not disclosed.

Chifley concluded that "this resort to anonymous but pseudo-authoritative statements is a contravention of the War Cabinet instruction referred to in sub-paragraph (ii) above, and is to cease forthwith".

On 31st May Blamey named the spokesman. He wrote to the Secretary of the Defence Department:

> The statement in answer to Mr Cameron was prepared by me, and was sent from a forward area to Melbourne for release to the press. Mr Cameron's original allegation was made in the public press and not under the privilege of Parliament. I insist on my right, in common with every other subject of His Majesty, to deal with any attack made upon me, private or public, not made under privilege.

Time passed. On 6th June Fraser sent Blamey's reply to the new Minister for Defence, Mr Beasley.[6] On 18th July Beasley replied to the

---

[5] Maj-Gen G. J. Rankin, DSO, VD. (1st AIF: Comd 4 ALH 1917-18. GOC 2 Cav Div 1937-42.) MHR 1937-49, Senator 1950-57. B. 1 May 1887. Died 28 Dec 1957.
[6] Rt Hon J. A. Beasley. MHR 1928-46; Minister for Supply and Shipping 1941-45, for Defence 1945. B. Werribee, Vic, 9 Nov 1895. Died 2 Sep 1949.

effect that Blamey should have consulted his Minister and that the Government would "defend him from unprovoked attacks". He listed seven speeches made in the House by Ministers since February 1944 replying to criticism of Blamey. Beasley said that he proposed to reply to Rankin's question in the House by quoting Blamey's statement and adding that he had directed Blamey's attention to the War Cabinet instructions, which the army spokesman had contravened. Forde, as Minister for the Army, wrote to Blamey in effect asking him to comment on this reply before it was given. Blamey delayed his reply. Three weeks later the fighting ended. On 21st September the question was again raised in the House and Forde telegraphed Blamey, now in Melbourne. On the 22nd Blamey replied: "Concur proposed reply."

Throughout the five months occupied by this episode, as during the previous two or three years, "army spokesmen" had been making statements to the newspapers at frequent intervals and without being rebuked by the Government. But it seems that the Cabinet decision was never once invoked in the interest of security or even public morale but always, whether by a Minister or a general, to silence or rebuke someone lower down in the chain of command, and not because he had said something harmful, but because he had said anything at all. Thus, on 18th July 1942, Blamey invoked it when rebuking one of his army commanders, Lavarack, who had been quoted in a newspaper article, and on 15th December 1942 he invoked it when rebuking a corps commander, Bennett, in similar circumstances.

On 2nd August 1943 Blamey sought to prevent Chester Wilmot,[7] with whom he had had a dispute in 1942 and whom he had disaccredited as a war correspondent, from broadcasting in Australia interviews with members of the army, but it was pointed out to him that the army had no power over Wilmot, and that the Chief Publicity Censor's interpretation of the War Cabinet's direction was that statements by and interviews with members of the Services *could* be published, after censorship.

On 8th November 1943 Curtin wrote to Forde quoting the War Cabinet's objection to Press statements by General Savige on 4th September and General Herring on 28th October about the Lae-Salamaua operations in New Guinea, and complained incidentally that he had not yet had Blamey's report of these operations. The release of an account of such operations was a matter for the Government. Forde passed the complaint on to Blamey who replied that he had authorised the making of the statements and was under the impression that a certain elasticity was allowed him "although such is not by any means indicated by the War Cabinet Minute".

In every instance quoted above (and they include all that are recorded in the Commander-in-Chief's files) the news item concerned was informative and innocuous.

The regulations of the Services combined with the censorship procedures were sufficient to ensure that officers and men of the Services did not

---

[7] R. W. W. (Chester) Wilmot. War correspondent for ABC 1940-42, for BBC 1944-45. Author and broadcaster; of Melbourne; b. Brighton, Vic, 21 Jun 1911. Killed in aircraft accident 10 Jan 1954. Author of *Tobruk* (1944) and *The Struggle for Europe* (1952).

make improper communications to the Press. If the alleged offender was the head of a Service it was the business of the Minister to deal with him on the merits of the case and with the public interest in mind, and not, as in 1945, by quoting a decision of three years before which had been frequently disregarded.

The Ministers had loyally supported Blamey's policy in New Guinea but nevertheless were uneasy about it. On 7th May Chifley wrote to Blamey and pointed out that General MacArthur had written:

Forces in Bougainville, New Britain and New Guinea have the mission of neutralising the enemy garrisons that have been isolated. These hostile forces are strategically impotent and are suffering a high rate of natural attrition. Australian Forces now engaged are continuing the missions previously assigned American elements. A local Commander in such situations has considerable freedom of action as to methods to be employed. The Australian Commanders have elected to carry out active operations in effecting neutralisation where other Commanders might decide on more passive measures.

Chifley pointed out that Curtin had defended the operations and stated that the Government accepted full responsibility, but a stage had been reached when the Government should have fuller information. He would be glad if Blamey would attend a meeting of the War Cabinet to give an appreciation and answer questions.

The letter reached Blamey at Lae on 12th May. He returned to Australia to attend a meeting of the War Cabinet to be held on the 22nd. Meanwhile, on the 16th, he sent a paper to the acting Minister for the Army in which he said that the end of the war in Europe (Germany had surrendered on 7th May) required that reallocation of the Australian Army be considered. Henceforward the allocation of national forces by the Allies would be on a lower scale. Australia was maintaining one division to each 1,200,000 of population, which was equivalent to about 100 American divisions or 38 British (not including Indian). Not more than half as many divisions could be used against the Japanese. Assuming that 50 American and 20 British divisions were employed, Australia's contribution, on a population basis, should be about three. Three divisions and part of a fourth were already engaged in New Guinea, and two more were either engaged in Borneo or about to move there. It was impossible to foresee when the force in New Guinea could be reduced below two divisions. He suggested that the force to be contributed by Australia to operations outside New Guinea should be one division formed by taking about one-third of the 6th, 7th and 9th. The 7th Division was scheduled for operations against Balikpapan at an early date.

If it is accepted that the Australian military contribution to the Allied effort should be greatly decreased, it is most desirable that the 7th Division should not be committed to this operation on the Borneo mainland, since it will form a commitment where there may be considerable fighting and where we may ultimately be committed to a very large garrison.

Where the Australian contribution should be employed was a purely political and not a strategical question, he added. It was probable that if it was allotted to the South-West Pacific Area it would be included in the force that would reach Japan proper, and that would be most popular with a great many of the troops. The Americans, however, would endeavour to alter its organisation to American pattern. There was also considerable strength of public opinion anxious that the force should participate in operations for the recapture of Singapore. He suggested that even if the main force continued to serve in the South-West Pacific Area a token force should be allotted to South-East Asia Command.[8]

On 22nd May the War Cabinet met to hear Blamey state the reasons for his policy in the islands. The problem before the Australian Ministers and commander was: what policy should the Australian forces have followed in those areas of Australian New Guinea where they had relieved American formations? Should they have sought only to hold the defensive perimeters as the Americans had done, or should they have set out to destroy the enemy, or to attempt some middle course? Hitherto the policy of the Australian commanders had been persistently aggressive. On the Buna-Gona coast in 1942 and 1943 the isolated Japanese force might have been hemmed in until it starved; instead it was attacked and destroyed. On the Huon Peninsula and in the Ramu Valley defensive lines might have been maintained around the captured ports or airfields; instead the enemy was attacked, defeated, and pursued. The practice of holding defensive perimeters round captured airfields had been introduced in the South-West Pacific only in 1944 when American formations took over the main burden.

Blamey presented the War Cabinet with an appreciation dated 18th May.[9] In it he wrote that his object was

> To conduct operations against the enemy with a view to
> (a) destroying the enemy where this can be done with relatively light casualties, so as to free our territory and liberate the native population and thereby progressively reduce our commitments and free personnel from the Army;
> (b) where conditions are not favourable for the destruction of the enemy, to contain him in a restricted area by the use of a much smaller force, thus following the principle of economy.

He pointed out that American operations in New Guinea, New Britain and the Solomons had been designed to secure air bases from which to neutralise the enemy's air power and permit an advance to the Philippines for the purpose of liberating them. Having seized an area for a port and airfields the American Army would form a close perimeter round it and make no effort to seek out the enemy beyond the perimeter; but when it reached the Philippines its policy changed and it sought the complete destruction of the enemy's forces—a change of policy based on political rather than military grounds.[1] The reason given for the American policy in the Australian territories was that the enemy would "wither on the

---

[8] The sequel to this recommendation is recorded in Chapter 16 where the story of the planning of the Borneo operations is resumed.

[9] The appreciation is reproduced in full as Appendix 3.

[1] On 2nd September 1944 MacArthur began a signal sent to all his immediate subordinates except Blamey with the words: "One of the purposes of the Philippine campaign is to liberate the Filipinos."

vine" in a few months, but the policy was now well into its second year and the enemy were still strong and well-organised, cultivating gardens and employing natives to do so, and importing seeds and technical military equipment by aircraft and submarines.

Blamey added that, on reaching Morotai, General MacArthur had said that the enemy forces by-passed in the Australian territories were "strategically impotent", yet six American divisions and one regiment were then disposed in those territories. These American forces were mainly confined within their perimeters; when the enemy had attacked in strength at Torokina and Aitape he was beaten off but not pursued and destroyed and was allowed to re-form. Most of the patrolling outside the perimeters was left to Allied Intelligence Bureau, Angau and Fijian troops.

General Blamey added that when General MacArthur's staff began planning the Philippines campaign they had asked that the American forces be relieved by equivalent Australian forces. However, when General Blamey represented that such large forces were excessive, MacArthur's staff agreed that one Australian division and two brigade groups should relieve the three American divisions in the Solomons, one Australian division (since reduced to two brigades) the one division of Americans in New Britain, and one division the two divisions plus a regiment at Aitape—a saving of the equivalent of three divisions. The fact that the by-passed enemy forces required the deployment of such substantial Australian forces refuted the claim that they were strategically impotent. Just as it was necessary to destroy the enemy in the Philippines so it was necessary that the Australian forces should destroy the enemy in those Australian territories where conditions favoured such action, and so liberate the natives. If Australia waited it could be said that the Americans, having liberated the Philippines, were responsible for the final liberation of the natives in Australian territories, with the result that Australian prestige would suffer both abroad and in the eyes of the natives.

Blamey then discussed the policy adopted in each area where Australians had relieved Americans. In the Solomon Islands three courses were open to him: to continue the American policy, to undertake an all-out offensive with full-scale air and naval support when available, or by aggressive patrolling to gain information of enemy strengths and dispositions (of which the American formation knew little) and, by systematically driving the enemy from his garden areas and bases, to force him into starvation and eventually bring about his total destruction.

He decided that to commit any troops, and particularly Australians, to a passive role of defence was quickly to destroy their morale, create discontent and decrease resistance to sickness. The enemy would have continued his domination of the natives and inflicted a steady flow of casualties on the defenders by sporadic raids. "This course would lower the prestige of the Australian nation throughout the world and particularly would, in the native mind, lower the prestige of the Government to such an extent that it might be difficult to recover on the termination of hostilities."

The second course—a major offensive operation with air and naval support—would have gained control of the enemy's bases, but his forces had become so self-sufficient that it would still be necessary to follow them into the jungle to destroy them; and, in any event, the necessary naval forces were not available. Consequently at Torokina the third course was followed. Active patrolling was undertaken and information obtained. It was decided to probe the enemy's positions and carry out offensive operations with small forces with a view to seeking out and destroying the enemy where found.

> New Britain presented a different problem to New Guinea and the Solomons (he continued). Here we were faced with a force of approximately 56,000 troops. . . . The enemy defences were strong and the enemy themselves well equipped and fed. A major offensive operation with the forces at our disposal was impossible. . . . It was decided to drive the enemy patrols back into the Gazelle Peninsula and then regain control of the major portion of New Britain and contain a large force in the northern end of the island with a considerably smaller one. This is in accordance with the military principle: "A detachment from the main forces is justified if it contains a force superior to itself." In the situation in which I found myself taking over from the Americans, the Japanese, on their side, in certain areas justified this principle.

Blamey added that in the Aitape area in November an American army corps had been "strongly entrenched behind barbed wire with the exception of one regiment on the Driniumor River. A.I.B. patrols were operating to the south but, through lack of support by ground troops, which had been denied to them by the Americans, they were forced to yield large areas to Japanese forces." The enemy had from 24,000 to 27,000 troops, organised in three divisions. He was cultivating gardens, had large stores, and urgent medical and ordnance supplies were brought in by submarines and aircraft. The Australians adopted a plan to advance east on two axes: along the coast to Wewak to destroy the enemy forces and supplies and cut off the forces inland, and into the Torricellis to drive the enemy from his gardens and destroy his organisation and men there.

Blamey appended figures showing, for example, that in the three areas to 18th May 7,958 Japanese dead had been counted, whereas only 573 Australians had been killed or were missing, and 1,433 wounded. He added that, as a result of this aggressive policy, he hoped by the end of the year to be able to reduce the force in the Aitape-Wewak area and the force on Bougainville each to one brigade group.

When Blamey's appreciation was placed before the Advisory War Council on 6th June Sir Earle Page said that insofar as there were political reasons for the change of policy General Blamey had instituted, that was a matter for decision by the Government not General Blamey. The non-Government members had not been informed of the change of policy and were under the impression that the strategy followed was General MacArthur's. A policy of concentrating the forces and reducing each enemy stronghold in turn might have been followed. He was not prepared to take any responsibility for the operations.

Mr Spender said that he could not reconcile the policy of destroying the enemy in two areas and containing them in the third. He was not satisfied that General Blamey's appreciation justified the course he had taken. Mr W. M. Hughes said that the important consideration was: had the operations been successful at relatively small cost? The reports indicated that they were proceeding satisfactorily, losses had been small, and the Australian forces had the task well in hand.

Mr Beasley said that General MacArthur considered that the operations were being carried out with skill and energy. The Government accepted full responsibility for the operations, whose success vindicated the strategy being employed.

At length the Council agreed to Blamey's policy: to destroy the enemy where that could be done with light casualties, but, where conditions were not favourable to the destruction of the enemy, to contain him in a restricted area by the use of a much smaller force.

In his statement to the War Cabinet Blamey said that, when the enemy's organisation in the Solomons, New Britain and New Guinea had been "sufficiently destroyed", he proposed to retain a minimum of Australian troops there and use the Pacific Islands Regiment, with A.I.B. and Angau elements, to develop partisan fighting until the enemy was completely annihilated. Thus he considered that the force on Bougainville might be reduced to two brigades, then progressively to two native battalions. Similarly he looked forward at length to employing only two native battalions on the New Guinea mainland. On New Britain, however, a division of two brigades would be needed, with a brigade in reserve conveniently near in case the enemy attempted to break out of the Gazelle Peninsula.

A letter informing Blamey that both the War Cabinet and the Advisory War Council had recorded their agreement with the "objects" stated at the beginning of his appreciation was not written until 31st July and appears not to have been seen by Blamey until 14th August, the day on which Japan accepted the terms of surrender.

The criticism of the Commander-in-Chief's policies and character had taken five main directions: that the Australian forces should have been employed elsewhere, that the forces in the New Guinea areas should not have adopted the offensive, that those forces were not properly equipped for their task, that General Blamey was not in the forward areas enough and had lost the confidence of the nation and the army, and that he had treated some of his generals unfairly. The charge that Blamey was idling in Melbourne when he should have been in New Guinea was entirely unjust. The foregoing narrative (and the earlier volumes of this series) have shown that the division of his time between the various areas of his command was wisely arranged. The degree in which the forces lacked equipment shall be revealed in the following descriptions of the operations themselves. The deployment of the Australian forces was in

General MacArthur's hands, and the factors which led to their allocation to New Guinea and Borneo have been discussed.

Blamey defended his treatment of some of his generals in a confidential Press conference at Perth on 9th July 1945.[2]

"I think you people have been a little unkind to me," he said. "You have charged me with having got rid of generals. We had twelve divisions to fight the Jap. On arrival of other equipment, other considerations came in and we now have six divisions. Can you tell me what should have been done with the surplus generals? I do know that on every occasion I proposed to terminate a general's appointment, politicians have tried to stop it.

"I want to tell you this about your generals. We have only removed one from his command in the field during this war. That says a great deal for the selection of your commanders. As for my method of dealing with them, we will see what happened to them. General Williams[3] has got a great job and is now head of the Imperial War Graves Commission at a much greater rate of pay than he drew before. General Mackay had his turn in New Guinea. Mr Curtin discussed it with me and decided that the tropics were a bit trying for him and stated that he was agreeable to appoint General Mackay as High Commissioner in India at a considerably increased salary. General Herring has got the most honourable appointment in Victoria, where he is now Lieutenant-Governor. All these men accepted these appointments entirely at their own desire.

"Lavarack has been sidetracked. Nobody thought General Sturdee was sidetracked when he went to Washington. In the opinion of the Government we must have senior commanders to look after our interests in America. Two lieut-generals held the American appointment before General Lavarack. It was then decided that we must have a general with active service in the present war in the appointment, and so General Lavarack took it on. It is the highest paid job that the Australian Army has to offer."

Concerning Rowell, Blamey contended that he "found himself unable to accept the Government's directions" and "had to go". Concerning Bennett, Blamey said that he had told Bennett that he would not have the confidence of his troops in the field.

"The giving and placing of commands is not at my discretion," he said. "They are done under the authority of the Minister for the Army and by direction of the Minister for Defence and I have no authority. Once or twice I have been overruled and it is my business to accept it when I am. Democracy fails if we don't accept the direction of the Government."

In this explanation Blamey did himself less than justice. Most of the criticism of his treatment of his generals had revolved about the names of Lavarack, Bennett and Robertson. In 1942, when the country seemed

---

[2] A note of his statement is among the Blamey Papers.
[3] Maj-Gen T. R. Williams, CMG, DSO, VX139255. (1st AIF: CRE 3 Div 1918.) MGO Mil Bd 1939-40; Chief Mil Adviser to Dept of Munitions 1941-43. Regular soldier; b. Bundaberg, Qld, 10 Apr 1884. Died 23 Oct 1950.

to be threatened with invasion, Lavarack had been appointed army commander in north-eastern Australia, the most likely point of attack; Bennett had been promoted to the corps command in Western Australia, an isolated area and a possible enemy objective; Robertson had the A.I.F. Armoured Division, a *corps d'élite* certain to play a leading role in any operations on the mainland.

At this distance after the event, General Blamey's appreciation of 18th May does not seem to be the last word on the problem of the extent to which offensives should have been undertaken on Bougainville and towards Wewak. It was true that a similar policy was followed by the Eighth American Army in Mindanao and the Visayas and that any criticism by G.H.Q. of the Australian operations was inconsistent with their own practice. But, perhaps, G.H.Q's policy was ill-judged too.

Blamey based his decisions on three main grounds: first, that the isolated Japanese armies were tying down Australian forces which could be used elsewhere and, until made virtually impotent, would continue to do so; secondly, that Australian troops would deteriorate if they remained on the defensive, and were subject to infection with tropical diseases as long as they were in New Guinea; thirdly, that it was politically desirable to regain control of the native peoples of whom Australia was the guardian.

The first contention can be disputed on the ground that extreme difficulty had been found in obtaining any role for Australian troops in the final advance to the Philippines and beyond. In the event American forces were able to carry out unaided all important tasks north of the equator; and most of the Australian units in the "mopping-up" consisted in part of men who could not be sent north of the equator without another amendment of the *Defence Act*. Had the war continued a role might have been found in Java for all available Australian troops, but operations against the Japanese by-passed in Java were open to the same criticism as operations against the Japanese in New Guinea.

Blamey's second contention was denied by the effects of his own policy in New Britain, where the Australian force advanced to the neck of the peninsula and no farther, but continued active patrolling; and in the mountain sector in Bougainville where the main force was halted, but deep patrolling, of a kind seldom excelled in Australian military history, kept the units concerned always tense and confident.

His third contention was based on political considerations of a kind which, as Sir Earle Page pointed out, fall within the sphere of responsibility of the Cabinet rather than the commander of its forces, and it is arguable that he should have sought the direction of the Government on this matter. The Government supported him, but was not consulted in advance.

When MacArthur ordered Blamey to employ twelve brigades in the four New Guinea areas though Blamey considered that seven would suffice (leaving the 6th Division free to move forward with the A.I.F. Corps), Government backing for Blamey's contention might have induced G.H.Q. to change its mind, but Blamey did not enlist the Government's support.

As mentioned earlier, if only seven brigades had been employed the offensives could not reasonably have been undertaken, and it was the insistence of G.H.Q. that larger forces be used that made the offensives possible. General Headquarters, however, was obviously unenthusiastic about the offensives, and yet controlled shipping and aircraft. Therefore it was likely from the beginning that the Australian formations would be short of both ships and planes. In fact, they generally had to fight their way overland although local commanders were convinced that the right answers were fully-supported amphibious operations.

Was it desirable to destroy the *XVII Japanese Army* on Bougainville and the *XVIII Army* round Wewak before they undertook large-scale attacks? The armies were full of courage, but, on the other hand, each had spent much of its strength in a disastrous counter-offensive against the Americans, and was unlikely to attempt other such projects. Indeed, their leaders afterwards said that they welcomed the Australian offensives as giving their armies a useful task to perform for the Emperor.

The cost in Australian soldiers' lives lost in battle in New Guinea in this last year of the war was 1,048 (a grave loss, yet fewer than the number of Australians who would be killed in the following year in automobile accidents: 1,206).

The major decisions affecting the operations were made by Blamey. The narratives which follow will show that the local commanders, although they sometimes strongly emphasised their lack of resources, were never slow in carrying out offensives that had received higher approval. In two long wars the doctrine had been dinned into Australian fighting men from generals to privates that they must press on, must master no-man's land, must attack at every favourable opportunity. It was also characteristic of the national tradition, with its sensitiveness about military honour and its desire that Australian forces should be employed in the decisive battles, that at one time critics at home should charge the Government and the commander with both doing too little and doing too much.

In fact the Australian Army was doing far more than its share in 1945. In New Guinea it was employing larger forces than the Australian Commander-in-Chief had at first desired, and these were spending their strength in unnecessarily aggressive operations. In addition a corps of two divisions was committed to operations in Borneo which were to be a prelude to an invasion of Java. At a time when, because of the German surrender, the effort of every other ally was lessening, the Australian Army was approaching its period of greatest activity. If in 1944 Australia had reduced her fighting formations to three divisions she would have been able, in 1945, to contain the Japanese forces in New Guinea and the Solomons and at the same time would have been maintaining in action in the Pacific an army larger, in proportion to population, than that of any other ally.

CHAPTER 4

LEADERS AND MEN

THE army which had now entered upon its final campaigns, and whose leadership and equipment were the subject of such keen debate at home, was at this time, in many respects, at the peak of its efficiency. More than two years earlier it had established a tactical superiority over the Japanese, and since then it had gained in skill and confidence, and, in particular, in the art of living healthily and cheerfully in tropical bush. Its experience included warfare in many kinds of terrain and climate, and in Africa, Europe, Asia and the South Seas. Its system of training schools was comprehensive and their methods severe. There were 40 schools of various kinds for officers and N.C.O's, and from 1942 to 1945 96,000 courses of one kind or another, varying from four months to a few weeks, had been completed (some individuals doing more than one course). The L.H.Q. Schools ranged from the Officer Cadet Training Unit through which, by August 1945, 7,887 had passed, the Staff School (to produce 1,007), the School of Artillery (14,212) and the Guerilla Warfare School (3,792), to the Cooking and Catering School (3,740), School of Military Law (205), School of Movement and Transport (382) and so on. The training of new recruits, described in an earlier volume, was long and exacting, culminating for young infantrymen in a jungle training course at Canungra in south Queensland so rigorous that life at the front, except for the moments of danger, was often reckoned less trying. The Canungra School was now turning out 4,000 reinforcements a month.

A majority of the senior field commanders were citizen officers. The Commander-in-Chief was a soldier by profession, as were his two chiefs of staff and the commander of the First Army, General Sturdee. The two corps commanders—Generals Morshead and Savige—were citizen soldiers. Each had left Australia in 1940 as a brigadier in the 6th Division. Of the commanders of the six divisions of the striking force four were or had been regulars; all six had served as young officers in 1914-18; the oldest, Wootten, was 51, the youngest, Stevens, 48. Among the twenty-one commanders of infantry or armoured brigades at 1st January 1945 only four had served in the earlier war. The youngest, Sandover,[1] was 34; only two were regulars. Nine had gone overseas in 1940 as battalion commanders. The extent to which the corps that had served in the Middle East, and particularly the division first formed, had inherited the command of the army as a whole was illustrated by the fact that all but one brigade commander had served in the Middle East, and 13 of the 21 had sailed with the 6th Division (then of 12 battalions).

The same trend was evident in the appointment of commanding officers. Of the 59 infantry battalions (on 1st January), 31 were commanded by

---

[1] Brig R. L. Sandover, DSO, ED, WX5. CO 2/11 Bn 1941-43; Comd 6 Bde 1943-45. Accountant and company director; of Perth; b. Richmond, Surrey, England, 28 Mar 1910.

officers who had gone overseas with the 6th Division or its early reinforcements and only five by officers who had served neither in the Middle East nor with the 8th Division.² Only two infantry C.O's—T. J. Daly and J. L. A. Kelly—were regular soldiers.

It was certain that in an army with a relatively small regular officer corps—450 strong in 1945, not including quartermasters and officers of some small specialist corps—and one with so strong a citizen-soldier tradition a majority of the commands would be held by non-regulars. At this stage, however, there was no great shortage of non-regulars qualified to fill staff appointments at least up to the divisional level, and there were good reasons for making an effort to ensure that the post-war regular officer corps contained a due proportion of men who had commanded troops in the field. In the event the Chifley Government's epochal decision soon after the war to establish a small regular army, as distinct from a cadre of regulars within a basically citizen army, led to the appointment to the regular army of a big contingent of regimental officers trained in the A.I.F. with a consequent large increase in the proportion of regular officers with long regimental service in the field.³

The senior general staff and administrative officers on Army and Corps staffs were mostly regulars, but years of active service and strenuous study at the staff schools had brought forward a strong team of non-professional staff officers, so that on 1st January 1945 the G.S.O.1's in each A.I.F. division and nearly all G.S.O.2's of divisions or brigade majors were citizen soldiers.⁴ Unfortunately, this did not mean that a corresponding number of regular officers were freed from staff appointments and were gaining regimental experience. Of the Staff Corps officers commissioned from 1940 to October 1944 and thus mostly aged 20 to 24 just half were already in staff appointments.

Some senior soldiers, both regular and citizen, considered that this was unfortunate from the point of view both of the young officers concerned and of the future of the army generally. In the 9th Division in 1942 and 1943 General Morshead had tried to correct the tendency but without great success. Throughout the army numbers of those young staff officers who had so far had little or no regimental service in the field were striving for transfers to combat units and were willing to drop a step in their wartime rank in order to join the battalion or regiment from which they had been seconded.

Lack of regimental experience reduced not only their general qualifications but their value as staff officers. One citizen soldier who had served

---

² The youngest were four men of 30—P. E. Rhoden, J. D. Carstairs, J. R. Broadbent and W. B. Caldwell—though later in the year C. H. Green was appointed to command a battalion at 25. (In the old A.I.F., with its heavier casualties and rapid expansion, it was not unusual for officers to command battalions at 25 or younger.)

³ At the same time, as a result of the creation of the regular army and of the growing influence of the regular officer corps the proportion of senior ranks held by citizen soldiers was radically reduced. Whereas in 1939 the ratio of regular to citizen generals holding substantive rank on the active list had been 7:7, in 1950 it was 11:0.

⁴ Another citizen soldier, Lieut-Colonel W. T. Robertson, was GSO1 of the 51st Highland Division in Western Europe. He was one of 13 officers who had been lent to the British Army in March 1944 and took part in the operations in Europe. The senior of this group was Lieut-Colonel R. R. McNicoll, a regular, who was a GSO1 at S.H.A.E.F.

on the staff, and later had commanded battalions and brigades in action, wrote after the war:

> As the A.I.F. increased in size from a small expeditionary force to one of many divisions both abroad and in Australia, with expansion and establishment of larger headquarters, ancillary formations, etc., there came an urgent need for skilled staff officers. In the main these officers had to be drawn from existing units. Most of them were civilians in peacetime with no previous staff training. Once again C.O's and higher commanders played fair and made available some of their most promising young officers as students to the Staff College at Haifa and later at Duntroon. In every case the successful graduate was lost to the unit.
>
> From my personal experience I found this type of staff officer, in general, extremely capable, flexible in mind, logical and reasoned in approach, with the added invaluable advantage of having had a good grounding in regimental duties and often experience in command of troops in operations. Unfortunately these essential qualities were not always apparent—partly through lack of opportunity and experience—in the regular staff officer of similar age and rank. Because of this deficiency his approach to his duties was often either timid and uncertain or overbearing and patronising.

In 1944 a committee comprising Major-Generals Vasey and Robertson and Brigadier Combes[5] was appointed by General Blamey to make recommendations on the future organisation and curriculum of the Royal Military College, Duntroon, to meet post-war needs. One recommendation was that graduates entering the permanent army should be appointed regimental officers of permanent units and that they should serve normally for four years before being eligible for secondment to staff or extra-regimental employment; and that, as far as practicable, an officer below the rank of lieut-colonel should not be employed wholly on the staff but should be returned periodically to regimental duty.

The committee recommended also that the name of the Australian Staff Corps be changed to "Australian Command and Staff Corps".

In a large-scale war all armies must be officered largely by non-professional officers, at least in the junior ranks, and some friction is likely to occur between the two groups. In the Australian Army a blunder had been made in 1920 when the regular officer corps had been labelled the "Staff Corps". It was easy to infer from this title that in war the regulars would fill the staff posts and the citizen soldiers would do the fighting. As mentioned earlier in this history the regulars were naturally disgruntled by the slowness of promotion in their own corps and the rapid promotion of citizen officers between the wars, and by the fact that few commands were given to regulars in the 6th, 7th, 8th and 9th Divisions at the outset. (At one stage this injustice was largely rectified when a high proportion of commands in the 1st Armoured Division was given to regulars, but the division was disbanded without having seen action.)

The war provided an opportunity of reducing the isolation of the regular officer corps but, instead, short-sighted administration tended to make it more than ever a "Staff Corps" engaged in instructional and staff work within an army which, from brigade level downwards, was led almost

---

[5] Brig B. Combes, CBE, VP7440. (1st AIF: Lt 14 Bn.) DMO & I AHQ 1939-40; Asst CGS 1940-41; BGS Home Forces 1941-42; Comdt RMC and SS 1942-44, Comdt RMC 1944-45. Regular soldier; b. Goulburn, NSW, 13 Apr 1894. He was the first graduate of the Royal Military College, Duntroon, to become its Commandant.

entirely by citizen officers. However, when the six-year war ended, the Staff Corps contained a large number of officers in their early and middle twenties who had seen much hard service with fighting units in action.

Observation of the relations between regular and citizen officers in both the British and the Australian Armies suggests that those relations might have been greatly improved if the regulars, from the beginning of their training, had been taught two axioms: first that in a total war citizen officers are bound to comprise the great majority and one of the main tasks of the regular is to ensure that this expansion of the officer corps is accomplished smoothly and efficiently; second, that the keen and intelligent citizen officer often brings to his military job valuable civilian experience and after a few years of war may equal the regular in military knowledge and ability.

The dispersal of officers from the corps of three divisions that had served in the Middle East throughout an army that had once been four times as large as that force and even now was more than twice as large (leaving out of account the populous base and training organisations) had entailed the loss to the veteran units of most of their junior leaders of 1941 and 1942, but in each there was still a cadre of specially durable "originals" among the officers and in the ranks. For example, in a battalion of the 6th Division in action east of Aitape, of the 36 officers who had helped to form this battalion in 1939 one was now commanding a division, 3 were commanding brigades, 3 commanding battalions, and 7 were first-grade or second-grade staff officers. Eight had been killed in action, 6 taken prisoner, and the others were widely distributed. There remained with the battalion only two of the original officers, and a sprinkling of original other ranks. Sixteen of its present officers had joined after its return from New Guinea to Australia in 1943. But, although the battalion itself had not been in action since early in 1943, in the previous years it had fought in Africa, Europe and New Guinea, and it now contained also a few veterans transferred from units with different histories, so that in it were men whose experience included service in England in 1940, in Libya in January 1941, in Greece, in Tobruk, on New Britain in 1942, in the early fighting round Kokoda, the subsequent advance through the Owen Stanleys and the long, costly fight at Buna, Gona and Sanananda. Probably only five or six of the subalterns had not been in action before. In this as in other units the tendency was to promote to commissioned rank tried sergeants aged about 25 or more: in four classes graduating from O.C.T.U's in the last half of 1944 40 per cent were aged 28 or over. Thus the new officers coming from the Officer Cadet Training Units were generally considerably older than the regulars of 19 or 20 arriving in smaller numbers from the Royal Military College, Duntroon.

What of the "militia" battalions—many of them now veterans of long campaigns—with their different history? As has been pointed out, a majority of the commanders of these battalions had been drawn from A.I.F. units. Among the majors and captains of a militia battalion there might be one or two young A.I.F. majors or captains, and one or two officers, fairly senior in their ranks, who had been too old to be commissioned in the A.I.F.; the remainder were generally somewhat younger than their opposite numbers in the A.I.F. As a rule they had been commissioned in their battalions in 1940 as youths of 19 or 20, and promoted since. The general view of the officers now leading militia battalions seems to have been that there was little difference between the men of their old units and their new ones, but that the old A.I.F. units contained a higher proportion of forceful leaders both in the ranks and among the officers, and there was probably a greater dash and aggressiveness in the A.I.F. units.

In the militia units the men also tended to be younger than in the A.I.F. This, added to their generally briefer battle experience, caused them, as a group, to be less "browned off" than the veterans in 1945. Many of the men of the 6th Division round Aitape and in the Torricellis had now had about enough of campaigning, but to most of the younger men in II Corps on Bougainville the campaign of 1945 was to be their most telling experience, and they were anxious to prove themselves.

The political and military leaders had long been worried by the existence within their army of two contingents—the volunteer and veteran A.I.F. on the one hand, and the part-volunteer and part-conscript, and less experienced, militia on the other. They had taken measures to erase the differences between the two. One distinction that remained was that the Australian conscript might not be sent north of the equator—a frontier that possessed no military significance. He might die in Dutch New Guinea but not in American Luzon, in Portuguese Timor but not in British Borneo. In any reshaping of the army the military leaders had to take this peculiar political compromise into account.[6]

Measures to bring both A.I.F. and militia to a common standard included sending reinforcements forward to all units from a common pool, except that all non-volunteers went to militia units. In addition lieutenants graduating from the Officer Cadet Training Unit were not as a rule sent back to their own units but were allotted the first appointment that fell vacant. The sweeping manner in which this policy was carried out was deplored by A.I.F. unit commanders.[7] They did not grudge the loss of some of their capable young leaders to the militia, where they could pass on their experience and possibly gain more rapid promotion, but many objected to a policy that made it virtually a rule that a veteran N.C.O. when graduated from the O.C.T.U. would not rejoin his own unit. In the first A.I.F. the opposite policy—generally to return a newly-commissioned officer to his old unit—had been considered a main factor in producing an outstanding fighting force. On the other hand, anything less than a rule to which very few exceptions were permitted[8] would probably not

---

[6] By the end of July 1945 205,000 had transferred from the C.M.F. to the A.I.F.

[7] This and other opinions quoted in this chapter are drawn from numerous interviews recorded in Australia, New Guinea and Borneo mainly in 1944 and 1945.

[8] There were exceptions. For example, Lieutenant T. C. Derrick, VC, DCM, returned from the OCTU to his old battalion, the 2/48th; and Lieutenant R. W. Saunders, an aborigine, returned to the 2/7th, with which he had served in the Middle East and New Guinea. And in 1945 numbers of senior NCO's were commissioned in the field.

have achieved the very desirable result of ensuring that the subalterns joining both A.I.F. and militia units were of even quality. The strength which the young A.I.F. leaders were contributing to the militia will become evident to those who watch the biographical footnotes in the chapters concerning Bougainville and notice how often outstanding company and platoon leaders were men drawn from the veteran divisions. It may be argued, too, that in this sixth year of war it was preferable for men with long service as N.C.O's to begin their life as officers in a new unit, no matter how welcome they would have been in their old one.

On the other hand the fact that A.I.F. units were regarded as being senior and superior to militia ones was not concealed. For example, promising commanding officers who had led militia battalions for a year or more were transferred to A.I.F. battalions as though such a transfer were a promotion.[9] This was a slight that could not fail to be felt by the members of the militia unit concerned. In January 1945 one brigadier on Bougainville wrote a vigorous protest when such a transfer was ordered on the eve of battle, but without effect.

New officers were appointed and recruits sent forward to a unit regardless of whether they came from the State in which it had originally been raised. These practices made life easier for the staff but were widely deplored in the units themselves. Sentiment apart, they imposed practical handicaps. For example, if men of a Queensland battalion were given leave from Atherton and all were Queenslanders they would return from leave more or less at the same time, but if there were West Australians in the unit they would not return until weeks later with consequent disruption of training. Officers who had been transferred to a unit raised in another State said that it was a disadvantage to have relatively little in common with the men of the new unit. (On the other hand some members of regiments that from the time of their formation had contained quotas from several States often considered that it did them good to mix with men from many parts of Australia.) A unit association, supported by wives and mothers in the unit's home State, tended to grow weaker as the proportion of men from that State decreased. This not only tended to lessen the quantity of comforts that the association sent forward but reduced the chances that a wife would be able to join an association where she would meet and exchange news with wives of other men in her husband's unit.

The degree to which units were losing their territorial character is illustrated by the fact that, for example, of 125 men killed or wounded in the 31st/51st (Queensland) Battalion in January and February, 65 were Queenslanders, 24 New South Welshmen, 14 Victorians, and the remainder from the smaller States. (The army numbers of all but eighteen contained "X", indicating that they had volunteered for service in the A.I.F.)

---

[9] For example, P. K. Parbury from the 31st/51st Battalion to the 2/7th; G. R. Warfe from the 58th/59th Battalion to the 2/24th.

A proportion of the men of the militia were now taking a perverse pride in not volunteering.

The term "Chocko" has been changed from a term of opprobrium to a title to be proud of, like the "Rats of Tobruk" or the "Old Contemptibles" (wrote a diarist in 1945). The men call each other "Chocko" as they might say "Mate" or "Digger". They are determined to remain "Chockos" just to show that here was one matter on which the army couldn't order them about. Not even the Commander-in-Chief could make them volunteer and they were going to revel in this freedom.

A reason why some chose not to volunteer was that there was a widespread (and, as it turned out, a very erroneous) belief that the "Chockos" would be sent home as soon as the war ended but that "X numbers" might be retained for garrison duties. It was generally agreed that, as a rule, in mixed units the volunteers were the better soldiers.[1]

In some veteran A.I.F. units the feeling of self-sufficiency that had been born in the Middle East had now developed into an unhappy sense of isolation and neglect. Two or three years overseas, several arduous campaigns, and the multitude of individual problems and frustrations that such a life bred, had combined to convince many that Australia was a "bludgers' paradise", that Australians at home (their own wives and families excepted) were enjoying an easy and profitable time, and cared too little about the war in general and the army in particular, and that the politicians were up to no good.

The fact that even when resting or re-training in Australia most of the fighting soldiers lived on the remote Atherton Tableland, with rare and brief visits south on leave, increased the feeling of isolation. More and more, when he was on leave, the soldier tended not to stay at home and forget the army, but to seek out comrades in arms with whom to talk about old adventures or (grimly congenial topic) the rapid promotion and good pay being won in a manpower-starved country by civilian contemporaries. Some of the soldier's hard feelings towards civilians at this time

---

[1] Australians may be interested in the question whether particular States of the Commonwealth produced disproportionately large quotas of the army's leaders. The following table was compiled from the Staff and Command List for March 1945:

State	Corps, Div, Inf and Armd Bde Comds (excluding regulars)	Comds of Inf, Pnr, MG Bns, Cav and Armd Regts (excluding regulars)	Population 1941 00,000
New South Wales	11	22	28
Victoria	6	25	19
Queensland	1	6	10
South Australia	1	10	6
Western Australia	3	11	4.6
Tasmania	1	2	2.4
Papua	—	1	—
Total	23	77	70

Commanders of artillery and technical units have not been included because a disproportionately large number belonged to New South Wales and Victoria; and regulars because their State of enlistment often was not the place where they had been schooled and spent most of their lives. It will be seen that Western Australia provided more than double its quota of senior infantry leaders, but Queensland only about half. Perhaps these figures may be related to (but not entirely explained by) the fact that before the war Western Australia spent more money in proportion to population on secondary education than any other State, and Queensland (and Tasmania) spent less than other States. The relatively low figures for New South Wales may partly be a result of the fact that the senior officers lost in Malaya came chiefly from that State.

were probably due to his own sense of frustration during the long periods of re-training and waiting. For example, in October 1944, one brigade of the 6th Division had not been in action since Crete in May 1941, and the other brigades had been out of battle for eighteen months or more; the 7th and 9th Divisions were in the middle of their longest periods of inaction since 1941.[2]

For most of the men who had in 1941 eagerly joined the armoured division—it was to be a *corps d'élite,* they believed—the succeeding years had been disappointing. Some armoured units had been disbanded, others were idle in Queensland. Thousands of highly-trained men of the armoured corps had succeeded in "getting a guernsey" by transferring to any units that would take them out of Australia—many went to the army water transport companies. Indeed 1944 and 1945 were years of anti-climax for a big proportion of the men who had enlisted in the first two years of the war. By early 1944 the "second world war" had lasted longer than the first; the Americans had now taken the lead in the South-West Pacific; the Australians were in the background.[3]

Another source of the soldier's resentment towards the civilian world were the sordid conditions of travel, and the often poor quarters and the

---

[2] The following list shows the Middle East campaigns in which each A.I.F. brigade had fought and the approximate number of months served in New Guinea up to August 1944 by all infantry brigades.

Brigade	Middle East	Months in New Guinea
16	Libya, Greece	4
17	Libya, Greece, Syria	12
18	Libya, Siege of Tobruk	6 plus 10
19	Libya, Greece, Crete	nil
20	Siege of Tobruk, El Alamein	8
21	Syria	5 plus 6
24	Siege of Tobruk, El Alamein	7
25	Syria	5 plus 6
26	Siege of Tobruk, El Alamein	7
4		17
6		14
7		17
8		7
11		13
15		16
23		3
29		18

Two brigades—14th and 30th—that had fought in New Guinea no longer existed. Parts of the 16th Brigade served in Crete and Syria, and parts of the 17th in Crete. Some units were in New Guinea longer than the periods here credited to the brigades they belonged to.

[3] The total strength of the army was now 307,000 volunteers of the AIF plus 91,000 compulsorily-enlisted militiamen.

These figures do not include 5,010 men of the AIF and 4,473 of the militia who at the end of 1944 were absent without leave or serving sentences in civil gaols. Throughout the period covered in this volume the number of absentees remained fairly constant. Those from the AIF fluctuated between 4,800 and 5,400; from the militia between 3,900 and 4,500. In July 1945 when all divisions were in action the total was only 400 less than October 1944. It seems that the great majority of these men were habitual absentees and belonged to base units, and that the number absent from fighting formations at any time did not exceed a few hundreds. For example, when, in October 1944, the 15th Brigade was sent to Atherton en route to Bougainville after two months in Victoria, which had followed 18 months service in New Guinea, fewer than 30 men out of 2,200 were absent without leave. From one AIF infantry brigade only three were absent without leave for more than one day in the last quarter of 1944.

The number of AWL's from the divisions fluctuated, probably reaching its maximum at Christmas. "This year the percentage of AWL's from units stationed in Australia should be fairly high," wrote a soldier in December 1944. "In a compartment intended for eight that would have allowed ample seating room from Townsville to Brisbane there were fifteen, seven of whom were AWL. As one absentee said jestingly to a licensed traveller: 'It's bastards like you that make it tough for good fellows like us.' I was surprised to find that the majority of AWL's were not original members or early enlistments who might have had four Christmases away from home, but reinforcements of perhaps one campaign. Only one of the seven AWL's in our carriage wore the Africa Star."

delays on the long journey from New Guinea or Atherton to his home when he went on leave. The camps of fighting formations, when they were resting or re-training in Australia or New Guinea, had become increasingly neat and comfortable, ceremonial had become more elaborate, and standards of dress more exacting. Gardens were planted, roads and paths improved, club rooms built, sports grounds cleared, comfortable furniture cunningly contrived from the most unpromising material. But the soldier's home leave opened with a long and wearisome journey in a crowded train, with meals at railway stations where no eating utensils were provided and the bar was often deliberately closed just before the train arrived. There were delays at uncomfortable leave and transit depots. At the end of the journey hours were sometimes wasted while the man on leave went through formalities that seemed to him unnecessary—and certainly could have been completed in a fraction of the time in the orderly room of his own highly-efficient unit.

In August 1942 the Australian Army, 476,000 strong, had included 14 divisions or their equivalent (1st, 2nd, 3rd, 4th, 5th, 6th, 7th, 9th, 10th, 11th, 1st Armoured, 1st Motor, 2nd Motor and Northern Territory Force). That is, it then required about 34,000 men to maintain a division in the field. In August 1945, when there were six divisions and an armoured brigade, it required some 60,000 men to maintain a division in the field. These figures illustrate the way in which, in this as in other armies, the "tail" of the army tended to grow—a development which, as mentioned earlier, was troubling the Australian Ministers in 1945. In 1942 the men in infantry, cavalry and armour in the Australian Army totalled 137,236, in August 1945 they totalled only 62,097; in 1942 the ordnance corps, on the other hand, totalled 29,079, whereas in 1945 ordnance and its offshoot, the electrical and mechanical engineers, totalled 42,835. In the same period, the artillery had decreased to about half its former strength, but the engineers, signals and the medical corps had remained at about the same strength, though in a smaller army, and a number of ancillary services had been created or enlarged.

For example, in the last six months of 1944 52 officers were promoted to the substantive rank of lieut-colonel: of these only five were infantrymen, two were engineers, and the other arms were not represented. The remaining 45 were in various of the ancillary services.

Similarly in the fourth quarter of 1944 the numbers of lieutenants appointed to various corps were:

Infantry	54	Intelligence . . . 8
Armour	4	Pay 19
Artillery	16	Legal 1
Engineers	27	Provost and Military Prisons 9
Signals	39	Canteens 10
A.S.C.	16	Movement Control . . 1
Ordnance	4	Audit 7
E.M.E.	42	Angau 34
Medical	33	Special List . . . 13
Survey	2	

At this stage the following separate corps existed in addition to those named above, each with its own officers' list:

Amenities Service	Catering Corps
Chaplains' Department	Dental Corps
Education Service	War Graves Service
Hirings	Labour Service
Postal Service	Printing and Stationery Service
Psychology Service	Records Staff
Recruiting Staff	Remounts Service
Salvage Service	Veterinary Corps
Women's Army Service	

In the period covered in this volume members of the Australian Women's Army Service began to serve in New Guinea. As early as 8th September 1943 Blamey had informed the Government that plans had been made to send 200 A.W.A.S. to New Guinea to relieve signalmen at New Guinea Force headquarters and the Moresby base. Nurses and A.A.M.W.S. (Australian Army Medical Women's Service) were already serving in these areas. Blamey had just learnt that, in 1941, when the A.W.A.S. was formed, the War Cabinet directed that none of its members be sent abroad without Cabinet approval. He asked that permission be given. The War Cabinet, however, reaffirmed that A.W.A.S. should not go overseas without its permission and asked whether men were not available. At length the War Cabinet on 15th November 1944 approved of the posting of A.W.A.S. for service in New Guinea provided they volunteered for such service, that they were between the ages of 21 and 35 (40 for officers), and (a curious compromise) that the number of postings did not exceed 500.

In General Blamey's plan an increasingly important role was to be given to native battalions. Indeed, beside the two Australian armies—A.I.F. and militia—a small New Guinea army was now growing up. In October 1944 there were two native battalions—the veteran Papuan Infantry, which had first seen action in 1942, and the 1st New Guinea Battalion, formed in April and May 1944. In October Blamey decided to group these native battalions into a Pacific Islands Regiment, and decided also that a second New Guinea battalion should be raised, and a depot battalion formed. In the event a third New Guinea battalion was constituted in March, and in May the formation of a fourth was ordered. These went most of the way towards replacing the Australian battalions disbanded in the last year of the war.

The New Guinea natives had long since proved that they made splendid troops for bush warfare. They quickly mastered their weapons, being instructed by sight and touch rather than by words; formal drill delighted them—ritual played an important part in their everyday life and military ritual was therefore accepted as being right and proper. They could move in the bush with such stealth and alertness that the risk of being outwitted by Japanese was slight. Their casualties were always relatively low: in about three years of fighting a total of 85 native infantrymen were killed in action and 201 wounded.[4]

The new regiment was attracting enterprising officers and N.C.O's, some with civil experience in New Guinea but most with none. The commanding officers were men who had proved themselves outstanding infantry leaders: T. F. B. MacAdie from the 2/7th Independent Company, for example, Murchison[5] from the 2/3rd Battalion, J. S. Jones from the 2/6th, and C. W. Macfarlane from the 2/7th and 37th/52nd.

At this stage the burden of war was weighing heavily on the New Guinea native—more heavily, man for man, than on the general run of Australian citizens. At the end of 1944 35,387 natives were working as labourers under contract to the forces, the Pacific Islands Regiment would eventually reach a total of 4,700 (of whom perhaps 700 would be Australians), and the Royal Papuan Constabulary had a strength of 2,560 natives.[6] Thousands more were employed as guerillas and locally-recruited carriers. At the peak perhaps 55,000 were serving from a people who, before the war, had been believed to number fewer than 1,000,000; and at this time natives in the thickly-settled areas of eastern New Britain and eastern Bougainville were still under Japanese control and out of reach of the Australian recruiting officer. Angau (the Australian New Guinea Administrative Unit) had placed limits on the percentage of men that might be recruited in an area, and none under 18 might be sent into action. Nevertheless the loss of able-bodied men to these peasant communities, where all food-growing was done with primitive hand tools, caused grave hardships, particularly in areas where houses and gardens had been destroyed as the battle swept over them.

An anthropologist and a district officer, who at this time were assessing war damage suffered by natives, estimated that in the many villages that they had recently visited half the males were absent on military or labour service, and the women, children and older males who remained were gravely underfed as a result of the loss of able-bodied workers. In such communities the absence of even 5 per cent of the men may have ill effects. The birthrate had fallen, with the result that a shortage of workers was likely in future years.

During the war the Australian Army made increasing efforts to educate the troops in non-military subjects and to keep them informed about what was going on in the world.

---

[4] The Royal Papuan Constabulary lost 28 killed in action, the Papuan and New Guinea Battalions 57; 46 indentured labourers were killed in action. Natives serving in the Pacific Islands Regiment and Royal Papuan Constabulary were awarded the following decorations: DCM, 4; GM, 2; MM, 15; BEM, 8; Long Service Medallion, 297; PNG Native Police Valour Badge, 28. Seven were mentioned in dispatches. One was awarded the American Bronze Star.

[5] Brig A. C. Murchison, MC, ED, NX326. 2/3 Bn; CO 2 NG Inf Bn 1945. Bank officer; of Rose Bay, NSW; b. Newcastle, NSW, 27 Oct 1917.

[6] Apart from the Papuan and New Guinea Battalions, 700 island soldiers served in the Torres Strait Light Infantry Battalion. These were rehabilitated in the pearling industry after the war by the Queensland Government. From their earnings they bought their own pearling vessels, and the fleet began to operate at the beginning of 1946. See *Queensland Year Book*, No. 15 (1954), p. 77.

An Australian Army Education scheme, inspired by a similar Canadian project, had been undertaken in the A.I.F. in France and England from May 1918 onwards, and later in the Middle East. The historian of the First A.I.F., Dr C. E. W. Bean, has written that "no part of the A.I.F's war effort more richly repaid the nation";[7] and it was Bean who, on 6th September 1939, wrote to the Minister for the Army pointing out the disabilities the First A.I.F's scheme had suffered through its late start and urging that immediate steps be taken to provide for the physical and mental recreation of the troops. Nothing effective was done at that stage to provide an education scheme, but Bean persisted, other people and organisations became interested, and, in December 1940, the Adjutant-General, Major-General Stantke,[8] in consultation with the Vice-Chancellor of the University of Sydney, Professor R. S. Wallace[9] (who had been an officer in the First A.I.F's education service), Dr Madgwick[1] and Mr Conlon,[2] also of Sydney University, produced a detailed plan. The War Cabinet approved the scheme on 5th March 1941. A few days earlier Madgwick had been appointed to Army Headquarters with the rank of lieut-colonel to administer the scheme, which "began operating seriously in June 1941".[3]

The education service of the First A.I.F. differed in two important respects from the new service. Its officers were inevitably drawn mainly from fighting units whereas the officers of the new service came largely from outside the army; and the first batches of officers of the first service, before beginning work, attended schools at which principles and methods were thrashed out. Perhaps some of the early difficulties which the A.E.S. of 1941-1946 has recorded would have been smaller if it had been possible to develop it to a larger extent from within the army. As it was

> Education officers found that they spent a great deal of their time [in 1941-42] converting those who were openly hostile, instilling enthusiasm into the apathetic, and, by example, demonstrating that the Education Service was not something devised by the Government, or the Army, to keep men quiet or convert them to some political dogma.[4]

The enthusiasm and hard work of the officers and men of the service, however, overcame prejudice and apathy, and this vast experiment in adult education achieved great results. At its peak in October 1945 the service contained 210 officers and 753 other ranks. Up to that time it had been responsible for some 141,000 lectures to aggregate attendances of

---

[7] *Official History of Australia in the War of 1914-1918*, Vol VI (1942), p. 1072. The development of the scheme is described in pp. 1062-1072.

[8] Maj-Gen V. P. H. Stantke, CBE, VP7591. (1st AIF: 29 Bn.) AG 1940-43; Comd Qld L of C Area 1943-45. Regular soldier; b. Fitzroy, Vic, 15 Aug 1886.

[9] Sir Robert Wallace, Kt. Vice-Chancellor, University of Sydney 1928-47. B. Scotland, 1 Aug 1882. Died 5 Sep 1961.

[1] Col R. B. Madgwick, VX89012. Director of Education LHQ 1941-46. Vice-Chancellor, University of New England since 1954. University lecturer; of Sydney; b. North Sydney, 10 May 1905.

[2] Col A. A. Conlon, NX191031. Director of Research LHQ 1943-45. Student; of North Sydney; b. Sydney, 7 Oct 1908. Died 21 Sep 1961.

[3] War History of the Australian Army Education Service 1939-1945. This 116-page typescript report is the source of most of the facts and figures in this brief sketch, but not of some of the opinions it contains.

[4] War History of the A.E.S., p. 6.

8,898,000. It had shown 32,000 film programs (not including the "entertainment" films which were shown by the separate Amenities Service) and provided 31,000 musical recitals. It had enrolled 64,000 students for correspondence courses, and 280 discussion groups and 888 craft groups were at work. By the end of 1945 it had circulated 620,000 books.

The cease-fire in 1945, as in 1918, naturally led to an increase in the opportunities of the service, particularly in the islands. In the First Army area three "Formation Colleges" were soon at work. In II Corps, for example, soldiers wishing to concentrate on education were freed from other duty for 20 hours a week except in certain units, and by September on Bougainville the custom was to devote each morning to education. At the Torokina Rehabilitation Training Centre there was a full-time staff of 36 and, at the peak, 1,700 students, and "the atmosphere of study and industry . . . had to be experienced to be believed".

A big achievement of the service was to reduce the grave degree of illiteracy that existed in Australia. In 1943 the service gave publicity to a conclusion it had reached that 4 per cent of the men of the army were illiterate.[5] The Director-General of Public Relations, Colonel Rasmussen, wrote to Colonel Madgwick on 19th July objecting to the publication of this estimate and pointing out that Tokyo radio had used it for propaganda purposes. He said that "the extremely critical attitude of the public toward the Army . . . can only be encouraged by the publication of material of this kind". Madgwick's contention appears to have been the reasonable one that the discussion of educational standards in the army would encourage outside support for the Education Service; and it seems unlikely that the public would have blamed the army for the illiteracy of its recruits.

The A.E.S. was at times also in conflict with the Directorate of Public Relations concerning a weekly journal named *Salt* which the service published from September 1941 until April 1946. It was digest-size, and the number of its pages increased from 32 at the outset to 64 in June 1944. Its circulation ranged from 55,000 to 180,000. Among its aims were to give uncoloured information about current affairs, to provide a form in which servicemen might express their opinions, and to encourage creative expression by servicemen.

In 1942 *Salt* was subjected to much criticism and its future was discussed by the War Cabinet, which decided, on 31st August, that it was to be continued as a fortnightly, and an air force magazine was to be produced, both under the management of "an editor with journalistic experience, service in the present war, and a knowledge of the psychology of the troops". A senior journalist, Massey Stanley,[6] was appointed, and with Stanley as Managing Editor and Mungo MacCallum[7] as Editor *Salt* went from strength to strength. Stanley won support from the Press by circulating to it summaries and extracts of quotable material in each

---

[5] From 4 to 5 per cent of 68,000 recruits had been found to be illiterate.

[6] Maj M. Stanley, NX58006. 2/4 Fd Amb; Managing Editor *Salt* 1942-44; War correspondent 1945. Journalist; of Canberra; b. Dunedin, NZ, 27 Aug 1902.

[7] Maj M. B. MacCallum, NX139824. Army Education Service (Editor *Salt* 1941-44, Managing Editor 1944-46). Journalist; of Sydney; b. Sydney, 11 Dec 1913.

forthcoming issue of *Salt,* and the War Cabinet agreed to an increase in the size of the journal to 64 pages.

The liberal policies of the group of newspapermen who were producing *Salt* led to conflict with the Director-General of Public Relations. From June 1943 *Salt* was made subject to censorship by the Director-General.

No statement of DGPR's censorial jurisdiction was ever furnished in writing (says the War History of the A.E.S.), with the result that throughout its operation there was considerable difference of opinion between the [Managing] Editor and the DGPR. In July 1942 a reference to Low's creation "Colonel Blimp" was deleted from an article on wartime cartoonists, on the ground that it stimulated "ideas which may be damaging to discipline". In August a Cinesound newsreel of the production of a special election issue was banned, no reason being given. In September the word "bastard" was deleted from a brilliantly written contribution describing a conversation between two soldiers at an advanced dressing station in the heat of battle. In an effort to clarify the DGPR's jurisdiction, the [Managing] Editor restored the word and it appeared in *Salt.* Subsequently paraded to the Adjutant-General, the [Managing] Editor submitted that the DGPR was exceeding his jurisdiction which was that his censorship was confined to security, and conformity with the C-in-C's high policy; and that the residue of authority over *Salt's* contents, including questions of taste and literary standards, remained with the Editor. He stated also that he did not agree with censorship powers being given to an officer hostile to *Salt*—i.e. DGPR; that DGPR had undertaken to write explanations of his deletions, but this had not always been done; and that the Editor had received no verbal or written instructions on the C-in-C's wishes, or the "ethical standards" required. In printing the word "bastard" he had been guided by modern practice—concurrently, the British Minister for Information had condemned objections to it as "spinsterish squeamishness"; the RN sanctioned it in the semi-official documentary film "In Which We Serve", the RAF in the documentary film "Alert" and the AMF in the book "New Guinea Diary".

The Adjutant-General, however, instructed that in future all deletions by DGPR were to be observed.

In the following months, many deletions were made in *Salt* material, partly because no written policy was ever forthcoming for guidance; partly because many items which the Editor thought would obviously be acceptable, were not so; and partly because DGPR and the members of his staff to whom he frequently delegated this duty often appeared to think differently on what was or was not censorable. . . .

In addition to imposing what would generally be called a political censorship, as indicated by the above examples, DGPR censored on grounds of artistic taste, deleting words and phrases from contributed verse of a high standard, and banning contributed drawings on grounds such as "the humour is too grim". An example which subsequently became notorious was the rejection *in toto* of a series of brilliant sketches of soldiers under the shower, showing typical attitudes. None was indecent and all were facing away from the artist.

In addition to *Salt* the Education Service produced from April 1942 onwards what soon was entitled the *Current Affairs Bulletin.* It was published fortnightly, the distribution being one copy to each officer. This journal was intended to form the basis of talks to the troops on current affairs, and a Military Board Instruction of 15th March 1942 laid down that at least 30 minutes a week were to be spent on such work—not as an amenity but as a part of military training. The bulletins were edited by Dr Duncan,[8] Director of Tutorial Classes in the University of Sydney.

---

[8] Professor W. G. K. Duncan. Director of Tutorial Classes, University of Sydney 1934-50; Professor of History and Political Science, University of Adelaide, since 1951. Of Sydney; b. Sydney, 11 Jul 1903.

After the war publication of the *Current Affairs Bulletin* was continued by the Department of Tutorial Classes, University of Sydney, and thus the wartime Education Service lived on not only in a peacetime Army Educational Corps (which in 1961 had 44 officers on its strength, 13 of whom were employed on public relations duties or newspaper production) but in a periodical widely used in the education of civilians both at school and afterwards.

The task of encouraging creative expression was performed also by the Australian War Memorial, which published each year from 1941 onwards a cloth-bound "Christmas book" written and lavishly illustrated by members of the army including the official war artists. From 1942 onwards it published also naval and air force "Christmas books". The army books contained writings by such authors as Gunner Tom Ronan,[9] Trooper Peter Pinney, Captain David McNicoll,[1] Sergeant Lawson Glassop,[2] Lieutenant Shawn O'Leary,[3] Lieutenant Jon Cleary[4] and other writers who were to become well known, or better known, after the war.

While the A.E.S. was helping to inform and educate the soldiers, the Directorate of Public Relations was performing a supplementary task by producing newspapers in the field. In the first volume of this series the prompt and successful establishment in Palestine of *A.I.F. News* was described. In October 1941 a companion newspaper, *Army News,* was established in the Northern Territory, and in November 1942 *Guinea Gold* began publication in New Guinea. When the 9th Division returned from the Middle East the staff of *A.I.F. News* came with it and established a newspaper named *Table Tops* on the Atherton Tableland, where it began publication on 23rd May 1943. Each of these newspapers continued until 1946.

From the outset General Blamey was resolved that the army newspapers should contain no editorial comment. The strength of this resolution was shown, for example, in November 1943, when *Guinea Gold* was a year old. Writing to General Morshead on the 16th of that month Blamey had mentioned a recent article in *Guinea Gold* that was "in the nature of an editorial dealing with pilfering". "It was excellent and, I believe, timely, but it is contrary to my policy to use an Army newspaper for propaganda of any kind. In the first place, troops readily become suspicious of a paper if it contains 'pills'; secondly, this paper is . . . sent to America by a great many American soldiers; thirdly, I do not believe in allowing editors of Army papers to do anything that fashions the outlook of the troops—I

---

[9] Gnr T. M. Ronan, NX52513; 2/3 Anti-Tank Regt. Stockman and drover; b. Perth, 11 Nov 1907. Author of *Strangers on the Ophir* (1946), *Moleskin Midas* (1956) and other works.

[1] Capt D. R. McNicoll, NX52009. 7 Cav Regt, Mil Hist Section, HQ NT Force; War Correspondent 1944-45. Journalist; of Rose Bay, NSW; b. Geelong, Vic, 1 Dec 1914.

[2] S-Sgt L. Glassop, NX24087. 7 Div HQ; First Army Press Unit (*A.I.F. News* and *Table Tops*). Journalist; of Newcastle, NSW; b. Lawson, NSW, 30 Jan 1913. Author of *We Were the Rats* (1944) and other works.

[3] Lt S. H. O'Leary, QX6905. 6 Cav Regt; PRO LHQ. Journalist and broadcaster; of Brisbane; b. Ipswich, Qld, 3 Sep 1916. Author of *Spikenard and Bayonet*.

[4] Lt J. S. Cleary, NX15943. 2/1 Survey Regt; Mil Hist Section. Commercial artist; of Sydney; b. Sydney, 22 Nov 1917. Author of *These Small Glories* (1946), *The Sundowners* (1952), *The Climate of Courage* (1954) and other works.

do not think they are the proper people to do it." He had instructed, he concluded, that no editorial comments were to appear in army newspapers except where the G.O.C. on the spot instructed otherwise.

It would have been wise to have given the Education Service responsibility for providing the army newspapers, confining Public Relations to field censorship, publicity (publications being channelled through the Department of Information) and care of war correspondents; and to have required the editors of army journals and newspapers to be their own censors—all of them seem to have been well qualified to bear this responsibility.

The Amenities Service was complementary to but entirely separate from Army Education. Its tasks included the coordination of the philanthropic organisations working within the army, provision of sports and other entertainment. Amenities officers had been appointed to the A.I.F. when it was overseas, and in the S.W.P.A. General Blamey was prompt in establishing a firmly-founded amenities service. On 3rd July 1942 he wrote to Mr Forde to say that, the actions in the Coral Sea and near Midway Island having removed at least temporarily the menace of immediate invasion, it became necessary for him to make plans to ensure that the considerable forces throughout Australia did not "go stale over a long period of training and preparation". He had therefore established an Amenities Service with Colonel Cohen,[5] formerly Red Cross Commissioner in the Middle East, as director. Blamey considered that the cost of amenities should be met, as in the Middle East, from the profits of the Canteens Service, "a vast cooperative business instituted for the benefit of the troops", the profits of which had always been held to be the property of the troops. He explained to the Minister that it had been customary to return these profits to the troops either by allocation to regimental funds or by paying for entertainment. A "special amenities account" had been established in the Middle East and operated by a committee appointed by the G.O.C. A.I.F. He recommended that, two-thirds of the A.I.F. having returned to Australia, two-thirds of the £35,000 held in this account should be transferred to a Special Amenities Fund to be established in Australia and placed under the control of the Commander-in-Chief.

As a result the War Cabinet agreed to a proposal that 3½ per cent of the turnover of the canteens should be distributed among unit trust funds; 1½ per cent to special amenities, to be spent at the discretion of army or certain other formation commanders; and 1½ per cent to the Special Amenities Fund to which would be added the money from the Middle East Fund and which would be distributed by the Commander-in-Chief.

---

[5] Brig H. E. Cohen, CMG, CBE, DSO, VD. (1st AIF: Comd 6 AFA Bde 1915-18.) Red Cross Commissioner for ME 1940-42; DAG in charge Amenities and Education 1942-44. Solicitor; of Melbourne; b. St Kilda, Vic, 25 Nov 1881. Died 29 Oct 1946.

CHAPTER 5

THE BOUGAINVILLE CAMPAIGN TAKES SHAPE

IN the forthcoming operations in New Guinea the First Army would have more widespread responsibilities than its predecessor, New Guinea Force. From his headquarters at Lae Lieut-General Sturdee controlled four forces deployed in an area that was about 1,000 miles from east to west. Sturdee had not previously held a command in the field in this war. In 1940 he had been appointed to command the 8th Division but after a few weeks had become Chief of the General Staff, an appointment he filled with distinction during the anxious months that followed the entry of the Japanese into the war. In September 1942 he became head of the Australian Military Mission in Washington. His senior staff officer on First Army was Brigadier E. L. Sheehan, who had come to that appointment in 1943 after service on the staff of New Guinea Force and I Corps; his chief administrative officer was Brigadier R. Bierwirth who had held similar appointments on the staff of the 6th Division, Northern Territory Force, and I Corps.[1]

The big base at Lae was well situated to be the headquarters of an army controlling operations throughout the New Guinea territories. It was about 600 miles from Torokina on Bougainville, 450 from Aitape, and 400 from Jacquinot Bay on New Britain and from Emirau Island, its northernmost area of responsibility. From Lae Sturdee and his staff controlled and maintained not only the four main field formations but a total of 134 formations, units, and detachments, including Angau regions and districts, three Area Commands—Madang, Finschhafen and Wau, seven base sub-areas—at Aitape, Torokina, Madang, Lae, Buna, Port Moresby and Milne Bay, fixed defence units at Moresby and Lae, a multitude of engineer and signals units, and many others. The Army headquarters was much concerned with shipping (the shortage of which was a continual anxiety), liaison with the air force (carried out by fourteen air liaison sections) and movement control.

Lae had now grown into a fairly comfortable town of considerable size. Along wide heavily-metalled roads were lines of buildings with concrete or timber floors, walls only half-height to allow the air to circulate, and ceilings of hessian or tar board. Neatly-painted road signs —Wau Avenue, Finschhafen Avenue and so on—guided the traveller. It was long since enemy aircraft had disturbed Lae's tranquillity. Twice a week there was an open-air picture show, and often films not yet seen on the mainland were shown. Here as elsewhere, if a tropical storm broke

---

[1] The senior officers on the staff of the First Army in October 1944 were: *Comd* Lt-Gen V. A. H. Sturdee; *BGS* Brig E. L. Sheehan; *GSO1 (Ops)* Lt-Col J. W. Fletcher; *GSO1 (SD & Trg)* Lt-Col F. W. Speed; *GSO1 (Air)* Lt-Col J. A. Y. Denniston; *GSO1 (Int)* Lt-Col L. K. Shave; *DA&QMG* Brig R. Bierwirth; *DDS&T* Brig P. S. McGrath; *BRA* Brig L. E. S. Barker; *CE* Brig A. G. Torr; *CSO* Col A. D. Molloy; *DDOS* Col J. T. Simpson; *DDME* Col C. A. Jillett; *DMS* Brig J. Steigrad.
There was a total of 183 officers on the staff, though a number of appointments had not been filled.

during the show the audience put on gas capes and went on watching the screen through pouring rain. Five miles away on the banks of the Busu was an officers' club with room for about 200 to dine, served by well-drilled native waiters, and with a fine floor on which officers danced with nurses to music played by a four-man band.

Sturdee's principal opponent was General Hitoshi Imamura of the *Eighth Area Army* whose headquarters were at Rabaul. On New Britain and New Ireland Imamura had the *17th* and *38th Divisions* and also enough independent brigades and regiments to form two more divisions. The *XVII Army* on Bougainville, also under Imamura's command, included the *6th Division*, an independent brigade and other units. On Bougainville and New Britain there were also large bodies of naval troops—far larger than the Australian staffs yet knew.

On the mainland of Australian New Guinea, deployed from west of Wewak to the Sepik, was the *XVIII Army*. Originally it had been part of the *Eighth Area Army* and later of the *Second Area Army,* but now was directly under the command of Field Marshal Count Terauchi of the *Southern Army,* the headquarters which throughout most of the war controlled the Area Armies and Armies employed in the conquest and defence of Japan's new empire south of China.

The largest formation under Sturdee's command was II Corps on Bougainville, led by Lieut-General Savige, who, as mentioned, had been Sturdee's predecessor at the headquarters at Lae until the New Guinea Force staff was renamed II Corps and the First Army assumed control of the whole of Australian New Guinea.

Bougainville is the largest of the Solomon Islands, the chain that forms the north-eastern boundary of the Coral Sea, and, administratively, was part of Australian New Guinea. American troops, having retaken Guadalcanal in 1942, advanced northward along this chain in the next year and on 1st November 1943 their I Marine Corps seized Torokina in Empress Augusta Bay on the western shores of Bougainville. On 15th November the Marines were relieved by the XIV American Corps (Americal and 37th Divisions), which was deployed along an arc about fourteen miles long protecting the airfields at Torokina, with outposts astride the main tracks. The Japanese slowly reorganised and in March 1944 launched a full-scale offensive. It failed, causing them a loss of perhaps 5,000 killed; a total of between 7,000 and 8,000 Japanese were killed and perhaps 16,000 died of sickness during the American occupation.

In late 1944 the Allied base at Torokina was one of several air and naval stations from which intermittent attacks were launched against the isolated Japanese bases in the eastern islands of the New Guinea mandate, principally Buin on Bougainville itself and Rabaul on New Britain. There were also Allied stations at Munda in New Georgia, on the Treasury Islands close to Buin, on the Green Islands north of Bougainville, and on remote Emirau Island north-west of New Ireland. These outer islands had been occupied by New Zealand, American or

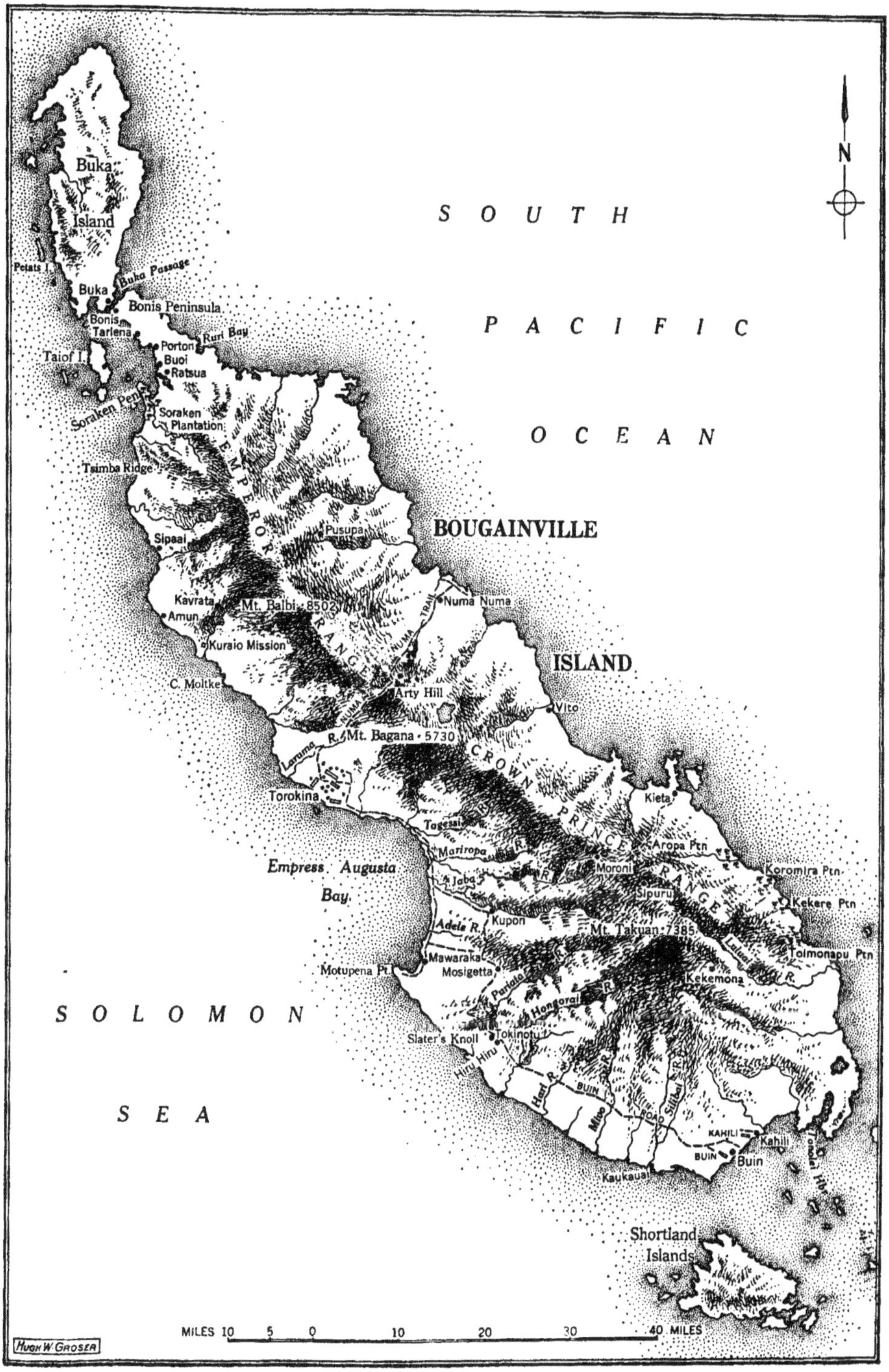
SOUTH
PACIFIC
OCEAN
BOUGAINVILLE
ISLAND
SOLOMON
SEA
N
Buka
Island
Petats I.
Buka
Buka Passage
Bonis Peninsula
Bonis
Tarlena
Porton
Ruri Bay
Taiof I.
Buoi
Ratsua
Soraken Pen.
Soraken
Plantation
Tsimba Ridge
EMPEROR
RANGE
Pusupa
Sipaai
Kavrata
Mt. Balbi 8502
Amun
Kuraio Mission
Numa Numa
NUMA NUMA TRAIL
C. Moltke
Arty Hill
Vito
Mt. Bagana 5730
Laruma R.
CROWN PRINCE RANGE
Torokina
Kieta
Tagessi
Aropa Ptn
Empress Augusta
Bay
Mariropa R.
Moroni
Koromira Ptn
Jaba R.
Sipuru
Kekere Ptn
Adele R.
Kupon
Mt. Takuan 7385
Mawaraka
Luluai R.
Toimonapu Ptn
Motupena Pt.
Mosigetta
Kekemona
Puriata R.
Hongorai R.
Slater's Knoll
Tokinotu
Hiru Hiru
Hari R.
BUIN ROAD
Mivo R.
Silibai R.
KAHILI
Kahili
BUIN
Buin
Kaukauai
Tonolei Hbr.
Shortland
Islands
MILES 10 5 0 10 20 30 40 MILES
HUGH W. GROSER

Fijian troops and were now garrisoned by the 93rd American Division, a Negro formation. The bases at Manus in the Admiralties and in western New Britain completed the encirclement of Rabaul. Japanese sea and air power in the area was now practically non-existent. The last Japanese air attack on Torokina had been made in March by two aircraft, and no Japanese merchant ship had been seen off the island since January. A post-war Japanese report states that the last transport vessel arrived at Buka from Rabaul on 24th November 1943.

Bougainville Island is about 120 miles in length and about 40 miles in width at the widest part. The mountain chain which forms its backbone rises to a height of 8,500 feet at Mount Balbi, an active volcano. The main wide areas of flat country are in the south-west and the east, and it was there that most of the natives lived and most of the plantations had been established—chiefly round Buin and Kieta. On the western side short, fast-flowing streams, fed by a rainfall that averaged 100 inches a year, drained the mountain chain. These streams were from 10 to 80 yards wide, and subject to floods that rose and fell rapidly. The silt which they washed down, plus the sea sand, formed bars across the mouths and these often made it possible to ford otherwise deep rivers. The bars also caused swamps inland from the river mouths. The Torokina plain, however, had the advantage of being formed of a porous mixture of sand and volcanic ash which quickly absorbed the rain. High forest, with dense undergrowth, covered the island to about the 5,000-feet contour where scantier moss forest began. The temperature on the lowlands was generally hot and humid, although the beaches were pleasantly cool at night.

Off the southern end of Bougainville lie three large islands, Shortland, Fauro and Mono, in the Treasury group, and many smaller ones. At the northern end, separated by a narrow passage, lies Buka, and farther north the Green Islands, a circle of land almost completely enclosing a vast lagoon. Except for the Treasury and Green Islands and the area round Torokina on Bougainville, Bougainville and its neighbouring islands were still in the hands of the Japanese.

As mentioned earlier, the XIV American Corps was to be relieved on Bougainville by II Australian Corps whose main components were the 3rd Division (7th, 15th and 29th Brigades) and the 11th and 23rd Brigades. Major-General W. Bridgeford (3rd Division), Brigadier J. Field (7th Brigade) and staff officers flew to Torokina on 4th September for a reconnaissance and for consultations with the commanders and staff of the XIV American Corps and 37th and Americal Divisions. They spent several days touring the area and discussing problems with the Americans and returned to Lae on the 7th. Soon afterwards Field's aircraft crashed in rugged country in New Guinea and he and the crew were missing in the bush for about nine days, but made their way home.

The advanced headquarters of the 4th Base Sub-Area, under Brigadier Vowles,[2] reached Torokina on 11th September and by the first week in

---
[2] Brig E. L. Vowles, MVO, MC, VX101868. (1st AIF: Lt to Maj Arty.) Comd 12 Bde 1943-44, Lae Base Sub-Area 1944, 4 Base Sub-Area 1944-45. Regular soldier; b. Melbourne, 13 Jul 1893.

(Australian War Memorial)
A company of the 25th Battalion moving from Arty Hill to Little George, in the central sector, Bougainville, 30th December 1944.

(Australian War Memorial)
A patrol of the 42nd Battalion in the Motupena Point area, 21st January 1945.

Japanese gardens in the Monoitu area, Bougainville, photographed from an aircraft of No. 5 Squadron, R.A.A.F., April 1945.

(*R.A.A.F.*)

A patrol of the 42nd Battalion moving through swamp in the Mawaraka area, Bougainville, January 1945.

(*Australian War Memorial*)

The headquarters of the 3rd Division and the divisional forward maintenance area, Toko, Bougainville.

(Australian War Memorial)
Men of the 2nd Field Regiment disembarking from an L.C.T. at Toko on 20th March 1945. Natives are helping with the unloading.

(Australian War Memorial)
A patrol of the 24th Battalion moving through bamboo in search of Japanese who raided a battery of the 2nd Field Regiment east of Toko on 28th March 1945.

October the base was ready to receive shipments from Australia. The first American garrisons to be relieved by Australians were those in the outer islands. On 27th September Brigadier A. W. Potts opened the headquarters of the 23rd Brigade on the Green Islands. He placed the 27th Battalion on the Green Islands (where there were still, in December, 6,790 American naval and army men, and 750 New Zealanders—all air force), the 8th on Emirau, and the 7th on Mono with one company at Munda. Thus the brigade freed the 93rd American Division, destined for Morotai.

The 23rd Brigade had been formed in 1940 as part of the 8th Australian Division of the A.I.F. In the early months of the war against Japan one of its battalions had been lost at Rabaul, another on Ambon, and another on Timor; the headquarters and some of its other units remained at Darwin. The brigade had then been re-formed with militia battalions sent north from Victoria and South Australia. After more than two years of garrison duty in the Northern Territory it had gone to north Queensland and thence to a rear area in New Guinea. Now it had been allotted yet another garrison role.

On 23rd October Sturdee, after visiting the four outer islands, informed Blamey that the 23rd Brigade was merely providing airfield guards and the possibility of Japanese attack was remote. He considered that the garrison work could be taken over in January by the 2/2nd Guard Battalion (a security unit mainly of relatively old soldiers) and/or native troops, making the 23rd Brigade available for Bougainville. Blamey, whose proposal that smaller Australian garrisons should take over in the islands had already been rebuffed by G.H.Q., replied that the Guard Battalion was distributed among various headquarters and that the native troops were most valuable for reconnaissance. He would consider the matter further.

In making his proposal Sturdee had probably been influenced by Brigadier Potts, a thrustful commander whose career as a leader of troops in the field had been interrupted when he was transferred from the command of the 21st Brigade after setbacks in the Owen Stanleys in 1942. It was natural that Potts should seek a more active part for his force, among whom were still some who had volunteered for foreign service more than four years before. Thus in November Potts, looking for some action, put forward a proposal that his brigade be regrouped and given one or more of four tasks that he outlined:

(a) General reconnaissance of neighbouring enemy territory.
(b) An operation against Choiseul where some 300 Japanese were believed to be at large.
(c) An operation from the Green Islands against northern Bougainville at Buka Passage (it was estimated that there were some 1,300 Japanese in this area).
(d) An operation against Buka Island, on which were some 1,000 Japanese.

Savige would not agree to any of these expeditions. In his weekly letter to Sturdee on 3rd December he wrote:

Potts with 23rd Bde is very restless, and he has all manner of plans to attack and eliminate the Japanese from Choiseul—the Shortlands—to Buka, etc. I have had to be very definite and firm with him to ensure that he does not embark on any . . . adventures, which would undoubtedly land him and me in trouble. I have issued orders to him that he is not to permit any unit, sub-unit, or individual to move from the islands without my authority.

Nevertheless, sympathetically seeking a more active role for the brigade, Savige proposed that "as early as practicable" the 23rd Brigade should be brought to Torokina, leaving only a battalion in the outer islands; but some months were to pass before MacArthur's headquarters would agree that the garrison of islands where it had formerly deployed a division should so soon be reduced to one battalion, and the 23rd Brigade remained where it was. However, the new posts had spare-time attractions—interesting meetings with Americans and New Zealanders, frequent picture shows, good swimming.

At Torokina Major-General Bridgeford opened the headquarters of the 3rd Australian Division on 6th October. The forces in the area were then still under the command of Major-General Oscar W. Griswold of the XIV American Corps, from whom Lieut-General Savige took over command on 22nd November.[3] The only Australian brigade then on Bougainville was the 7th which, in the previous week, had replaced the 129th and 145th American Regiments on the northern side of the perimeter, which elsewhere was still manned by American troops. The speed of the relief depended on the availability of ships, and many ships were then busy supporting the assault on Leyte. The takeover from the American force was completed in three weeks after the arrival of corps headquarters, as follows:

> 24th November: 2/8th Australian Commando Squadron relieved 164th U.S. Regiment.
> 23rd-25th November: 9th Australian Battalion relieved II/132nd U.S. Battalion.
> 4th-10th December: 29th Australian Brigade relieved 182nd U.S. Regiment and I/132nd U.S. Battalion.
> 11th-12th December: 11th Australian Brigade relieved 148th U.S. Regiment.

Thus the 11th Brigade took over the 37th American Division's sector, the 3rd Division with two brigades the Americal Division's. When the relief was complete the 11th Brigade was in the western coastal sector; the 7th was in the northern sector with an outpost in the hills astride the Numa Numa trail; the 2/8th Commando (after a short term on the left wing) in the east with outposts far afield on the tracks leading over the southern slopes of Mount Bagana; and the 29th Brigade on the south-eastern sector with a detached force on the coast north of the Jaba River. The 11th Brigade was directly under corps command, the 7th, 29th and the commando under the 3rd Division, whose third brigade—the 15th, had not yet arrived from Queensland. Thus the main Australian formation—the 3rd Division—faced the main enemy concentrations, which were in the south of the island.

---

[3] On 9th January XIV Corps, as part of the Sixth Army, landed in Lingayen Gulf on Luzon.

The American air units hitherto in the northern Solomons were replaced by a New Zealand force—No. 1 Group under Group Captain Roberts.[4] In November 1944 this was composed of two fighter squadrons armed

with Corsairs. By January No. 84 Australian Wing[5] (Group Captain Hely[6]) had been added, and in April the New Zealand squadrons were increased to four.[7]

---

[4] Air Cmdre G. N. Roberts, CBE, AFC. Comd NZ Air Task Force 1944-45. Regular air force officer; of Auckland, NZ; b. Inglewood, NZ, 8 Dec 1906.

[5] It included No. 5 (Army Cooperation) Squadron armed with Boomerangs and Wirraways, a detachment of No. 36 Squadron (supply dropping), No. 17 Air Observation Post Flight, equipped with Austers, and No. 10 Local Air Supply Unit.

[6] AVM W. L. Hely, CBE, AFC. Director of Ops RAAF HQ 1941-42; SASO NW Area HQ 1942-43; Director of Plans RAAF HQ 1943-44; Comd 72 Wing 1944, 84 Wing 1944-45. Regular air force officer; b. Wellington, NSW, 24 Aug 1909.

[7] A detailed account of the operations of the RNZAF on Bougainville is given in J. M. S. Ross, *Royal New Zealand Air Force* (1955), a volume of the *Official History of New Zealand in the Second World War 1939-45*.

The Australian commanders were anxious that their troops should be on their best behaviour in Torokina during the weeks when there would be large numbers both of Americans and Australians within the little perimeter. The Australian was paid less than the American and his canteens were less opulently stocked. He was often a shrewd business man, and the American was often an undiscriminating buyer of souvenirs. A routine order of one of the first Australian units to arrive at Torokina directed that "buying or borrowing of our Allies' goods be kept to an absolute minimum", and reminded the men that trading in Government issues was prohibited.

> While the Yanks were ready sellers, they were also ready buyers (wrote a unit historian). . . . For example, whisky brought £10 a bottle, rum and gin about £7, wine £1.10.0 and beer 10/-. As they were not issued to other ranks, the whisky, rum, gin and wine trade was practically monopolised by officers. Some sold it openly or traded it for cigarette lighters, pens, etc. Some got rid of their issue secretly and others gave the job of disposal to their batmen, who sometimes got a cut.[8]

An Australian staff officer annoyed officers of one of the first brigades to arrive by telling them that attention should be paid to compliments because the Americans were "exemplary in that regard"; the officers of Australian infantry considered their men also to be well schooled in military etiquette. The incoming troops found the Americans very friendly and helpful. The elaborate base equipment which the Americans were packing up was in contrast to their own more economical gear, American comforts and amenities particularly being on a scale that seemed to the Australian to be lavish.[9] The amenities now being provided for Australian troops were, however, on a fairly generous scale. For example, in each brigade was an officer and sergeant of the Army Education Service who conducted a library, moved from unit to unit lecturing on current affairs, supervised correspondence courses and produced news sheets. At the base there were fairly large reference libraries. The army's monthly magazine *Salt* and the *Current Affairs Bulletin* were distributed; and, at Lae, *Guinea Gold,* which reached a maximum circulation of 57,000, was printed for circulation throughout the forward areas. A broadcasting station was established at Torokina, as at Lae, Aitape and Jacquinot Bay, and wireless receiving sets were distributed. Both static and mobile cinemas gave shows at the bases and in the brigade areas. The Canteens Service was widely established and its efforts were supplemented by those of the Australian Comforts Fund, the Salvation Army and the Y.M.C.A.

Far more than the Americans the Australians made themselves relatively comfortable in the front line as well as at the base. In the front line the Americans (to Australian eyes) merely existed, often postponing shaving, washing and comfortable messing until they returned to the showers, laundries and mess huts at the base. The Australians in the front line shaved, bathed and washed their clothing every day if possible. The bush

---

[8] S. E. Benson, *The Story of the 42 Aust. Inf. Bn.* (1952), p. 173.

[9] This included some 35,000 cubic feet of refrigeration space, of which about 10,000 was left behind, under the Lend-Lease system. The Australians also bought an ice-cream factory and a soft-drink factory.

carpentry and the engineering devices by which they provided themselves in remote places with reticulated water, efficient kitchens, washing places, and all sorts of furniture had become more ingenious as the years passed.

General Savige was now entering his sixth campaign since 1940—North Africa, Greece, Syria, Wau-Salamaua in 1943, and recently command of New Guinea Force. As mentioned, he took to Torokina the experienced staff that had comprised the headquarters of New Guinea Force until it changed its name and home. His chief staff officer was Brigadier Garrett,[1] who had served on his staff in Greece in 1941; his chief administrative officer, Brigadier Pulver,[2] had been his brigade major in 1939-40. Savige formed strong loyalties, and in his senior commands in the Pacific brought on to his staff officers who had served under him in the 17th Brigade in Africa, Europe and Asia in 1940 and 1941. His artillery commander was Brigadier Cremor,[3] who had led the artillery regiment usually attached to the 17th Brigade in the Middle East fighting.[4]

Major-General Bridgeford of the 3rd Division had not yet commanded a formation in the field, but was a highly-trained soldier with much senior staff experience in Middle East and New Guinea campaigns. In 1918 he had been a major in a machine-gun battalion in France. When the second world war began he had been at the Imperial Defence College in England, where, in 1940, he formed the 25th Australian Brigade from a medley of troops who had been diverted to England in the crisis that followed the defeat in France. Before this brigade left England Bridgeford was ordered to the Middle East as senior administrative officer of I Corps, and he served as such in the campaigns in Greece and Syria; more recently he had held the corresponding post on the headquarters of New Guinea Force.[5]

The four militia brigades now arrived or arriving on Bougainville Island had all seen some active service in New Guinea. The first to enter the line—Brigadier Field's 7th—had fought with distinction at Milne Bay two years before and seen long service in reserve in New Guinea after that; about one-third of the men now in the brigade had been in action at Milne Bay. Lieut-Colonel G. R. Matthews, commanding the 9th Battalion, had

---

[1] Lt-Gen Sir Ragnar Garrett, KBE, CB, NX346. BM 18 Bde 1940; CO 2/31 Bn 1940-41; GSO1 (Ops) I Corps 1943; BGS II Corps 1944-45. CGS 1958-60. Regular soldier; b. Northam, WA, 12 Feb 1900.

[2] Maj-Gen B. W. Pulver, CBE, DSO, VX14. BM 17 Bde 1939-40; DADOS 6 Div 1940-41; AA&QMG 9 Div 1941-42; DA&QMG I Corps and NGF during 1944 and II Corps 1944-45. Regular soldier; b. Maitland, NSW, 12 Sep 1897.

[3] Brig W. E. Cremor, CBE, ED, VX86. (1st AIF: Arty 1918.) CO 2/2 Fd Regt 1940-42; CRA 3 Div 1942-43; CCRA I Corps 1943-44, II Corps 1944-45. Secretary; of Malvern, Vic; b. Hampton, Vic, 12 Dec 1897.

[4] In November 1944 the principal appointments on II Corps included: *Comd* Lt-Gen S. G. Savige; *BGS* Brig A. R. Garrett; *DA&QMG* Brig B. W. Pulver; *GSO1* (*Ops*) Lt-Col E. S. Eyers; *GSO1* (*Int*) Lt-Col E. H. Wilson; *GSO1* (*Liaison*) Lt-Col H. B. Challen; *CE* Brig J. Mann; *CSO* Col R. C. Reeve; *AAG* Lt-Col B. J. O'Loughlin; *DDMS* Col G. B. G. Maitland; *APM* Maj H. McP. Austin; *AQMG* Lt-Col T. H. F. Winchester; *DDST* Col A. J. Stewart; *DDOS* Col S. Johnston; *DDME* Col E. W. Bryceson; *CCRA* Brig W. E. Cremor.

[5] In December 1944 the principal appointments on the 3rd Division included: *Comd* Maj-Gen W. Bridgeford; *GSO1* Col H. G. Edgar; *GSO2* Maj E. G. McNamara; *Senior LO* Maj W. G. T. Merritt; *AA&QMG* Lt-Col K. E. Wheeler; *DAAG* Maj R. C. Tomkins; *DAQMG* Maj D. J. Breheny; *ADMS* Col F. K. Wallace; *Legal* Maj K. P. Rees; *ADOS* Lt-Col W. C. Cayley; *DAPM* Maj R. K. McCaffrey; *CRA* Brig B. E. Klein; *CRE* Lt-Col G. T. Colebatch; *CEME* Lt-Col G. W. Barling; *CO Sigs* Lt-Col L. W. Fargher; *CASC* Lt-Col L. C. Page.

been with the 2/10th in the Middle East; McKinna[6] of the 25th with the 2/3rd Pioneer in North Africa; W. R. Dexter of the 61st had been a platoon commander at Bardia in January 1941, and a company commander in the 17th Brigade in hard fighting outside Salamaua in 1943.

The 29th Brigade had served in the Wau-Salamaua operation and in the final phase in the Ramu Valley. Just before embarking at Brisbane for Torokina it had been reinforced by about 1,000 young soldiers whose average age was 20 years and two months—so many that they formed a majority of the men in the rifle platoons. But so thorough had been their training at Canungra that their commander was later to record that they "reacted with almost miraculous quickness to conditions of battle". Their senior leaders were all men with battle experience in the Middle East. Brigadier R. F. Monaghan, a regular soldier, had commanded battalions in three sectors in 1941 in Syria, and this brigade in the Salamaua operations in 1943. Lieut-Colonel McDonald[7] of the 15th Battalion had led a company of the 2/8th in Libya and Greece; J. H. Byrne of the 42nd had served with the 2/31st Battalion in Syria and New Guinea; Coombes[8] (to take over the 47th Battalion in January) had led a company of the 2/8th at Tobruk, in Greece and in Crete.

The 11th Brigade, commanded by Brigadier J. R. Stevenson, a learned and enterprising soldier, formerly leader of the 2/3rd Battalion in Syria and the Owen Stanleys, was a Queensland group which had been deployed for the defence of Townsville, Cairns and Cape York Peninsula in 1942; thence, early in 1943, part of it had been sent to Merauke in Dutch territory, forming the remote western flank of the force in New Guinea. There it had patrol encounters with the enemy and learnt to live and move in tropical bush. It left one unit—the 20th Motor Regiment—at Merauke; that unit's place was taken in the brigade by the 55th/53rd Battalion. The battalion commanders, Lieut-Colonels Abbot,[9] Kelly and D. J. H. Lovell, had each served in Middle East campaigns, and Kelly and Lovell in New Guinea in earlier operations.

Of the four brigades the last to arrive—the 15th—was the most experienced. Under Brigadier H. H. Hammer, its galvanic leader, it had probably marched over more of New Guinea than any other Allied formation; it had certainly seen more fighting than any other militia brigade. Hammer did not hide his brigade's light under a bushel, and it was largely through this hard-worked formation (and the 7th Brigade at Milne Bay) that the people at home began to become aware of the arduous and important roles that militia formations had played. After some sixteen months of campaigning the 15th had spent two months in Victoria, its home State,

[6] Brig J. G. McKinna, DSO, ED, SX3709. 2/3 Pnr Bn 1940-43; 2/27 Bn 1943; CO 25 Bn 1944-45. Commissioner of Police, South Australia, since 1957. Asst manager; of Kensington Gardens, SA; b. Goodwood, SA, 11 Dec 1906.

[7] Col H. H. McDonald, ED, VX49. 2/8 Bn; CO 15 Bn 1944-45. Furniture manufacturer; of Preston, Vic; b. Maryborough, Vic, 5 Oct 1905.

[8] Lt-Col C. J. A. Coombes, MC, ED, VX55. 2/8 Bn; CO 47 Bn 1945. Policeman; of Northcote, Vic; b. Echuca, Vic, 23 Jan 1908.

[9] Col J. N. Abbot, DSO, ED, NX59. 2/3 Bn; CO 26 Bn 1942-45. Accountant; of Marrickville, NSW; b. Auckland, NZ, 22 Mar 1906. Died 10 Nov 1960.

and on 13th October (with detachments of the 4th Brigade and others) had marched through Melbourne, 2,200 strong, with seven bands, past a saluting base crowded with eminent political and military people, "Tack" Hammer leading the march. Next day it began moving north again. The senior commanding officer, Lieut-Colonel R. R. Marston of the 57th/60th, had served in this brigade since 1927. Lieut-Colonel A. J. Anderson of the 24th had served with the 2/16th in Syria and the 39th at Kokoda; Lieut-Colonel G. R. Warfe of the 58th/59th had been a conspicuously dashing subaltern in Libya and Greece, and commando leader in New Guinea.

Of the twelve infantry battalions on Bougainville Island in December eight were from Queensland—they were all the militia battalions that State possessed. The policy of sending reinforcements to units without regard to which State they came from had somewhat reduced the territorial character of the force, yet, as a rule, more than half of the men of a unit still belonged to its home State. Thus the burden of the coming campaign was to fall particularly heavily on the Queenslanders.[1]

When he was allotted his task in August General Savige had asked for three field artillery regiments, one medium regiment and one mountain battery; he was allotted, however, only two field regiments (the 2nd and 4th) and the 2nd Mountain Battery, and his requests for a machine-gun battalion and a Pioneer battalion were not granted. The 2/8th Commando Squadron, one squadron of the 2/4th Armoured Regiment, and a company of the 1st New Guinea Infantry Battalion were given to him. In response to a request for one landing craft company for operational tasks only and with no responsibility for unloading ships, all of which had to be unloaded by barges since there were no wharves, Savige was given the 42nd.

Soon after his arrival Savige compiled a manual of jungle warfare and had it printed on the spot and circulated—an unorthodox step since such manuals were normally produced at army headquarters and not by field commanders.

I realised (he wrote later) that it was essential to obtain some clear pattern of thinking and action for jungle warfare which would be applicable to all units under command. The multiplicity of tasks and shortage of troops denied the use of schools of instruction. I therefore wrote my textbook *Tactical and Administrative Doctrine for Jungle Warfare*. In accomplishing this task I used Major Travers, who was B.M., 15th Bde, in the Salamaua operations, as a sounding board by getting his reactions chapter by chapter.[2] It was printed and bound in the field and issued to every officer and N.C.O. It worked better than we had a right to expect and, at every opportunity, it was referred to in orders and instructions.

There was, however, some criticism of this manual on the ground that it was based too much on experience when fighting over precipitous

---
[1] When the militia was being maintained at its full establishment about one-third of the units were raised in New South Wales, about one-third in Victoria and the remainder in the four outer States. During the progressive reduction of the force the tendency had been to disband New South Wales and Victorian units and reinforce Queensland and West Australian units, which were deployed farther north or west. As a result, out of the 32 militia battalions that remained, only 8 had originated in New South Wales and 9 in Victoria, but 8 in Queensland, 3 in Western Australia, 2 each in South Australia and Tasmania.

[2] Major B. H. Travers was then GSO2 at Corps headquarters.

mountain trails, whereas much later fighting was on flat coastal country where tanks, mechanical transport and strong concentrations of artillery could be employed.

It has been seen that the first task of II Corps, after freeing the three American divisions employed on Bougainville and the outer islands, was "to gain information which would assist the preparation of a plan for the total reduction of the Japanese troops on Bougainville".[3] At intervals throughout the Japanese occupation of Bougainville parties of the coast-watching organisation, now controlled by the "Allied Intelligence Bureau", had been behind the Japanese lines collecting and sending back such information. In March 1944 the American commanders decided that they were no longer vitally interested in the enemy's activities outside the Torokina perimeter, and the A.I.B. parties were withdrawn. With a view to obtaining more recent Intelligence the Australian commanders in September called upon the A.I.B. to resume its work, and intrepid scouts who, with their trusted natives and their wireless sets, had played so important a part in the partial reconquest of the Solomons in 1942 and 1943, were called forward again. Flight Lieutenant Robinson[4] was sent to Torokina to insert three parties into enemy territory on Bougainville itself, another into New Hanover and another into Choiseul. Thus Lieutenant Bridge,[5] R.A.N.V.R., was chosen to lead a party into northern Bougainville, Flying Officer Sandford[6] a party to operate round Numa Numa, and Lieutenant P. E. Mason, R.A.N.V.R., a party behind Kieta. Sub-Lieutenant Andresen,[7] R.A.N.V.R., was sent to Choiseul and Sub-Lieutenant Bell[8] to New Hanover. By the end of November men had been selected, codes arranged, and parties were ready to set off into the mountains. Bridge, for example, led the veteran Sergeant McPhee,[9] Staff-Sergeant B. F. Nash of the American Army, a native sergeant-major, Yauwiga, and twelve other natives. Sandford's party included Sergeants Wigley[1] and McEvoy,[2] two outstanding scouts. These parties and the native police led by officers of Angau were for a time to prove the main source of information about the enemy.

---

[3] Report on Operational and Administrative Activities of II Australian Corps in the Northern Solomons Area, October 44-August 45.

[4] Sqn Ldr R. A. Robinson, MBE. (1st AIF: 3 MG Bn.) AIB. Plantation inspector; of New Britain; b. Sydney, 19 Jul 1897. Died 4 Oct 1948.

[5] Lt K. W. T. Bridge, DSC, VX77994. "M" and "Z" Special Units; RANVR 1943-45. Patrol officer; of Bougainville; b. Canterbury, Vic, 12 Oct 1907.
The main reasons for the prevalence of naval and air force ranks among these coastwatchers and guerillas were (a) that the coastwatching network had been established by the navy and (b) that, at a later stage, when it was necessary to convert a civilian into an officer in a hurry, it was sometimes found that the air force would do this with less delay than the other Services.

[6] F-Lt N. C. Sandford, DSO. 100 and 11 Sqns; AIB. Plantation manager; of Bougainville; b. Melbourne, 20 Jun 1911.

[7] Sub-Lt A. M. Andresen; RANVR. AIB. Planter and trader; of Solomon Is; b. Balmain, NSW, 14 Nov 1895.

[8] Sub-Lt S. G. V. Bell; RANVR. AIB. Alluvial miner; of Wewak, NG; b. Chillagoe, Qld, 26 Feb 1905.

[9] Lt G. J. McPhee, MC, NX151510; "M" Special Unit. Printing salesman; of Mosman, NSW; b. Mosman, 26 Sep 1921.

[1] Sgt J. H. Wigley, MM, NX71415. RAAF 1940-41; 1 Indep Coy and "M" Special Unit. Timber worker; of Rozelle, NSW; b. Sydney, 21 Oct 1919.

[2] Sgt D. G. McEvoy, BEM, NX20023. 2/1 Pnr Bn and "M" Special Unit. Bricklayer; of Grafton, NSW; b. Grafton, 5 Sep 1917.

The Intelligence staff of XIV American Corps had estimated the strength of the Japanese forces on Bougainville at 12,000, some 5,000 of these being in base units. These, they believed, were all that remained of the *XVII Japanese Army* commanded by Lieut-General Hyakutake, whose headquarters were in the Buin-Faisi area; the *XVII Army* included the *6th Division,* the *38th Independent Brigade,* and other smaller formations.

In October, because Australian forces were going to Bougainville, the Intelligence staff at L.H.Q. began to take a close interest in the strength of the Japanese there, and on 11th October produced an estimate of 25,000 —more than twice the figure stated by G.H.Q. This difference of opinion, one of a series that had occurred between the Australian Intelligence staff and Major-General Charles A. Willoughby, the head of the American Intelligence staff, led to some sharp exchanges. The Australian estimate had been largely based on a report of the *XVII Japanese Army* for March 1944 captured in the Marshall Islands in July, giving the ration strength on Bougainville in late March as 41,200.

On 20th October Willoughby wrote to the Australian Director of Military Intelligence, Brigadier J. D. Rogers, in protest.

Several discrepancies (he wrote) are readily noted in the figures.

(*a*) Under Front Line Strengths it will be noted that total enemy dead in the Torokina operations would amount to 2,651, whereas in excess of 3,000 bodies were actually buried by American troops following the attack.

(*b*) Note also that strength in the L of C Areas increased from the time the attack was begun up to late March (after the battle) when in actual fact a full-scale withdrawal from the area is known to have occurred.

(*c*) The same point is illustrated by taking the numbers reported in the area; a total of 23,102 at the time the 2nd attack was begun as opposed to 21,515 following the operation. The difference here would be 1,587, a ridiculous figure considering the casualties suffered and the withdrawal following the attack.

(*d*) Note that the document specifically says that natives employed as carriers are also listed. There is no reliable basis for estimating or even guessing at the number so employed, i.e. ration reports are not equivalent to strength reports.

(*e*) Lastly, note that in the total strength column, taking the figure from early December (which includes natives) 44,000 and the strength reported in late March 41,200, would admit total casualties of only 2,800 during the entire four month period. In no case do casualties figured from the document coincide; nor do they even approach known enemy dead . . . as has often been the case with Japanese official reports, the particular writer is more concerned in impressing *Imperial Headquarters* with his "valorous deeds" than accuracy. . . .

(*f*) Ration strengths have proved notoriously unreliable in the past and this Section sees no reason to suddenly accept them as accurate now. . . .

Our present strength estimate [is] considered adequate.

Further support for this contention is available in recent PW reports from the area particularly . . . a sergeant who . . . reports a battalion with strength of 119 men, several companies averaging, even after reorganisation, about 100 men each with some as low as 40 and remnants of entire units disbanded to provide men for the companies. Such figures do not support a strength estimate of 25,000. . . .

For the past two years an unwritten practical agreement has been in effect by which any discrepancies in strength estimate between LHQ and GHQ has been settled by inter-camera discussion between the two Order of Battle Sections. In view of this, and in view of the fact that this Section represents the opinion of GHQ, SWPA, the sudden dissemination of this increased strength for Bougainville is suggesting publicly an open discrepancy which is undesirable.

Furthermore, the subject involved is a clear-cut departure, without warning, from a previously most satisfactory process, i.e.

(a) Joint meeting to determine Order of Battle.
(b) Joint agreement on basic totals.
(c) Joint definition of estimates.

This arrangement was faithfully observed in the past; it was found that discrepancies were generally noted in Washington and London and explanations requested; it was simple to adjust locally. Finally, LHQ Intelligence has no source of information beyond that of GHQ Intelligence; they feed out of the same trough.

For professional solidarity, I suggest that this matter be discreetly adjusted in later editions.

Rogers then wrote a memorandum pointing out that the Australian Intelligence Review had on several occasions published estimates at variance with those of Willoughby's staff and quoted five instances in each of which an Australian estimate had varied greatly from G.H.Q's and had been proved more nearly correct. One example was the estimate of the enemy strength at Finschhafen before the Australian attack. The G.H.Q. estimate was 300 to 400, he wrote, the Australian 6,000,[3] which proved an underestimate. "In each of these cases we took the stand after negotiations had failed," wrote Rogers, "in order not to deceive the Commander of our own forces." On 13th November, however, Blamey directed that for publication throughout the Intelligence network the G.H.Q. estimate must be accepted as the official estimate, but where Rogers' staff produced a differing estimate he should inform Blamey.

The problem was further discussed between the staffs at G.H.Q. and L.H.Q. and in mid-December both agreed to accept an estimate of 17,500 "effectives".

The various revisions of this estimate will be recorded later, but probably the reader would prefer at this stage to disperse the fog of war and find out how many Japanese were in fact on Bougainville in October 1944. The true total was somewhere between 37,000 and 40,000, including civilian workers who could be and were incorporated in the military or naval forces; 23,500 Japanese would surrender in August 1945. The exact strength of the Japanese force on Bougainville at other times and its exact casualties will probably never be known—the Japanese burnt many documents, though evidently not so many as they pretended. Two careful studies of the problem were made after the surrender, one being completed by Lieut-Colonel Wilson,[4] the senior Intelligence officer of II Corps, in October 1945, and the other by Captain Campbell[5] of the 23rd Brigade in February 1946, after further interrogation of Japanese officers. Campbell's figures are higher than Wilson's in several places. Campbell found that there were 65,000 Japanese on Bougainville when

---

[3] The Australian estimate was in fact 4,000.

[4] Lt-Col E. H. Wilson, VX27463. GSO1 (Int) Directorate of Mil Int 1943-44, NG Force 1944, II Corps 1944-45. Journalist; of Hawthorn, Vic; b. Mount Gambier, SA, 17 Mar 1906.

[5] Maj D. L. Campbell, VX120319. 15 Bn and HQ 29 and 23 Bdes. Salesman; of East Brighton, Vic; b. Adelaide, 10 Dec 1914.

the Americans landed, the deaths in battle during the American period were 8,200 and the deaths from illness 16,600. Of about 40,000 remaining when the Australians took over, 8,500 were killed in battle or died of wounds and 9,800 died of illness. (Wilson, in the earlier study, had decided that deaths in battle in the American period had been 7,000 and in the Australian period 6,800.[6])

Colonel Hattori in *The Complete History of the Greater East Asia War,* published in 1953, says that 52,000 Japanese remained on Bougainville after the counter-attack against the Americans. Thus if deaths in battle in the American period had been 8,200 the original garrison must have been something over 60,200; if they were 7,000 it must have been something over 59,000. It seems certain that for some months after the big counter-attack Japanese were dying of illness at the rate of about 3,000 a month. Indeed the neglect by the Japanese officers of their own men seems to have been little less callous than their neglect of their prisoners of war.

The Intelligence staff of XIV American Corps had decided that by July or August the enemy had consumed all significant quantities of army rations, and that their morale was low chiefly because of shortage of food and medical supplies but also because of lack of weapons and loss of faith in the high command. The Australian Intelligence staffs largely rejected these conclusions. Documents were captured which showed that in April the Japanese had possessed 750 tons of food, and in the next four months had received about 250 tons from submarines. This food was issued only to troops in contact with the enemy, even though, during July, August and September, about 3,000 Japanese had died, partly of malnutrition, in rear areas. It was decided that a substantial part of this 1,000 tons of food was intact and additional quantities were arriving by submarine and—more important—that by November 1944 a well-planned program of agriculture was providing enough food to sustain all troops on the island.

The Australians had now reached the conclusion that the Japanese had disbanded depleted units to reinforce others and were maintaining a well-disciplined and efficient force. They decided that, at the end of November, the force included the *38th Independent Mixed Brigade,* built round the *81st Regiment,* and the *6th Division* with three depleted infantry regiments —*13th, 23rd* and *45th*. Of these the *38th Brigade* was believed to be chiefly concentrated at Numa Numa, with part of the *81st Regiment* forward on the trail; most of the *13th Regiment* was believed to be round the Jaba River-Gazelle Harbour area, with the *23rd* farther south, and the *45th* round Kieta on the east coast. (All this was later found to be correct.)

The American corps had built some fifty miles of good roads within the perimeter. The Australian commander decided to maintain only about

---

[6] By August 1945 Australian infantry had counted 5,600 bodies of Japanese killed in action, plus 400 found dead later. AIB parties reported 1,076 counted dead.

half of the roads in this base area and concentrate his resources on improving and extending the jeep tracks leading forward. It was found that notable economies could be achieved. For example, along the coast between the little Torokina plain and Kuraio the mountains fall steeply towards the sea, and the first natural approach to the mountain mass east of the coastal ledge was along the Laruma River gorge into the tributary Doiabi gorge and thence up the face of a steep escarpment. The twelve-mile road which the Americans had built along this narrow cleft crossed the rivers twenty-six times over boulder-strewn fords. At the head of the ravine artillery was emplaced ready to fire at unseen targets about three miles away but 2,000 feet above. From the top of the escarpment a track set off across the mountains to Numa Numa. When the Australians arrived the fords were in poor condition; at each a tractor was stationed to haul trucks through the stream and the journey took four hours and a half. By improving the fords the need for tractors was removed and the journey could be made in an hour and a half.

The gun positions in the Doiabi gorge had unusual features. The guns had to be manhandled part-way up the steep slopes on one side of the gully and there placed on platforms. The angle to the crest on the other side of the gully over which the guns had to fire was about 27 degrees. The guns could not have been used effectively without the special incremental charges developed in the war for use in rugged terrain. The incremental charges also had the advantage of giving the shells a steep angle of descent which was important in engaging close targets in hilly country.

In the Japanese-held territory there were native tracks along the coastal plain some of which had been improved sufficiently to carry light vehicles. From Mawaraka southward, for example, the track had been widened to about 12 feet. In the interior a network of footpaths linked the mountain villages, and two main tracks crossed the island over saddles in the mountain chain. One was the Numa Numa trail, mentioned above, connecting Torokina and the east coast, and the other connected the Jaba River with Kieta.

From the outset of the II Corps' operations lack of shipping and particularly of barges (largely a consequence of the lack of ships to bring them forward) was a major handicap. Not only were there not enough barges to make large-scale landings possible but not enough even to carry adequate supplies to forces along the coast and in the outer islands. In the 42nd Landing Craft Company there were in December only 12 craft and even in February only 29,[7] although the establishment was more than 60. The small ships available to II Corps were manned by the 13th Small Ships Company, which, with the 42nd Landing Craft Company, formed

---

[7] These were collected from various sources. Only twelve had arrived for the 42nd Company, twelve had been obtained from the American Navy, five from the British Navy. These five were a gift, approved by the Admiralty, from Rear-Admiral A. G. Talbot whose squadron called at Torokina while escorting ships carrying landing craft forward to the Central Pacific.

the 1st Water Transport Group (Lieut-Colonel Chesterman[8]). The small ships eventually included four 300-ton wooden ships, six 300-ton lighters, and four 66-foot trawlers. The shortage of larger ships to bring in supplies and equipment from Australia was acute. The Australian Government had placed practically all its ships in the Allied pool and the best of them were supporting the operations farther north. At Christmas 1944 II Corps held only three days' reserve rations—apart from those held by the units, which had supplies for up to fourteen days.

Army leaders considered that the American staffs were able to spare enough Australian shipping to ensure the adequate supply of the force on Bougainville, but that the Australian Ministers would not "stand up to the Americans" in this matter. Early in February a diarist on Bougainville wrote:

> Here is being conducted one of the largest single operations the Australian Army has undertaken. One division and a half are engaged, with considerable artillery and some tanks. However, so slender is the supply of shipping that even rations were recently disturbingly low; the outer islands are just managing on supplies provided by an old wooden steamer; the one landing craft company has only one-half of its complement of craft, there is not even a moderate-sized anti-submarine vessel in the area. Yet for more than a year, when there was barely contact with the Japanese force on the island, there were 50,000 troops here, much shipping, large air forces, a lavishly-equipped base.

The leaders in Australia were trying hard, however, to get craft forward to this and other areas. Army Headquarters appealed to the War Office on 11th January 1945 for a ship able to transport from Cairns to Lae, Torokina and New Britain 130 small craft urgently needed there and ready to go. In addition some 27 new craft were being produced each month. The War Office could not help immediately but discovered that the Royal Navy might be able to provide a "heavy lift ship" by the end of March.

General Blamey signalled to General Berryman at G.H.Q. to press firstly for an L.S.D. (Landing Ship, Dock) or alternatively two Liberty ships until movement of these craft had been effected. G.H.Q. replied that all they could do was to load the craft on the decks of the four American ships assigned to take supplies to the Australian forces during February. This method had in recent months resulted in the moving of about 11 craft a month and might move 30 a month in February and March.

Blamey on 10th February asked that the Prime Minister should ask G.H.Q. for the loan of an L.S.D. and he did so on 28th February. Time passed. On 26th March no reply had been received to Mr Curtin's request to G.H.Q. Nine of the 130 craft had been shipped to New Guinea, 23 were moving forward under their own power, and it was decided that 47 more would be sent off under their own power; these ranged from 125-foot wooden cargo vessels to A.L.C.40's (Australian Landing Craft, 66 feet in length and weighing 35 tons). The appeal to G.H.Q. failed to produce

---

[8] Lt-Col C. D. R. Chesterman, OBE, TX2094. RAE I Corps 1940-41, First Army 1942-43, I Corps and NGF 1943; Comd 1 Water Transport Gp 1943-45. Engineer and company director; of Hobart; b. Hobart, 21 Jan 1902.

results. By 30th June 171 craft had been moved forward, largely under their own power.

The Americans had been employing only some 675 native labourers on Bougainville. An additional 500 were allotted to II Corps in October, and in November Savige informed the headquarters of the First Army that by March he would need a total of 1,600 for operational work, and in addition the Base Sub-Area needed 1,300. As operations proceeded and lines of communication lengthened this estimate was found to be too low. By the end of March the 1,500 employed by II Corps were reckoned too few and First Army was informed that 2,000 were needed (apart from the requirements of the base). This figure was reached by recruiting natives locally.

It will be recalled that front-line responsibility was first taken over by Australians on the left of the perimeter. There the Americans had been sending a patrol each week towards Kuraio Mission some 20 miles north along the coast from Torokina. On 6th November Major N. I. Winning's 2/8th Commando Squadron took over this role and made these patrols regularly for the next five weeks, but met the enemy only once—on 9th December, when Lieutenant Astill[9] and five men came upon two unarmed Japanese near Amun, far beyond Kuraio, demanded surrender and, when the Japanese refused, shot them.

The patrols moved part of the way along the coast in barges. They found their maps of the area beyond the perimeter "inaccurate in all respects"—a complaint later to be heard from each sector in turn. Early in December a patrol met at Kuraio three Indian prisoners who had escaped from a Japanese camp in north-east Bougainville. On 12th December the 2/8th Commando handed over this area to the 11th Brigade.[1]

When the road along the Laruma-Doiabi gorge in the central sector reached the escarpment one track branched westward towards a cluster of villages called Sisivie, while the Numa Numa trail proper led east through Piaterapaia which was some four miles beyond the escarpment. On a knoll named George,[2] beyond Piaterapaia, had been established an American outpost; on Little George, about 50 yards beyond, was a Japanese outpost. Each was in view of the other but a kind of informal truce had long existed.

From 23rd to 26th November the 9th Battalion, with the 12th Field Battery and other detachments under command, took over this sector.

---

[9] Lt D. W. Astill, QX24485. 2/8 Indep Coy, 2/8 Cdo Sqn. Clerk; of Brisbane; b. Brisbane, 11 Feb 1921.

[1] The 2/8th Commando Squadron (then named an Independent Company) had been formed in July 1942. From January 1943 to July 1944 it served in the Northern Territory, then moved to New Guinea where it trained until its departure for Torokina in October. Its commander, Winning, had proved himself an enterprising commando leader with the 2/5th Independent Company in the operations round Salamaua in 1942.
Later two novels dealing with experiences on Bougainville were written by members of this company. They are *The Ridge and the River* (1952), by T. A. G. Hungerford and *Road in the Wilderness* (1952), by Peter Pinney.

[2] It had been occupied by "G" (G for George) Company, 132nd American Regiment.

Its supplies were carried by truck up the Laruma River gorge and then manhandled 1,500 feet up the escarpment to the Numa Numa trail.

After almost two years (wrote the 9th Battalion's diarist) the battalion had the honour bestowed on them to face the enemy again. . . . This battalion along with its neighbouring battalions in 7th Brigade were the first Australian troops to retard the advance of the Japanese on Milne Bay in August 1942. . . . The troops are eager and keen to meet the enemy and make full use of their years of training.

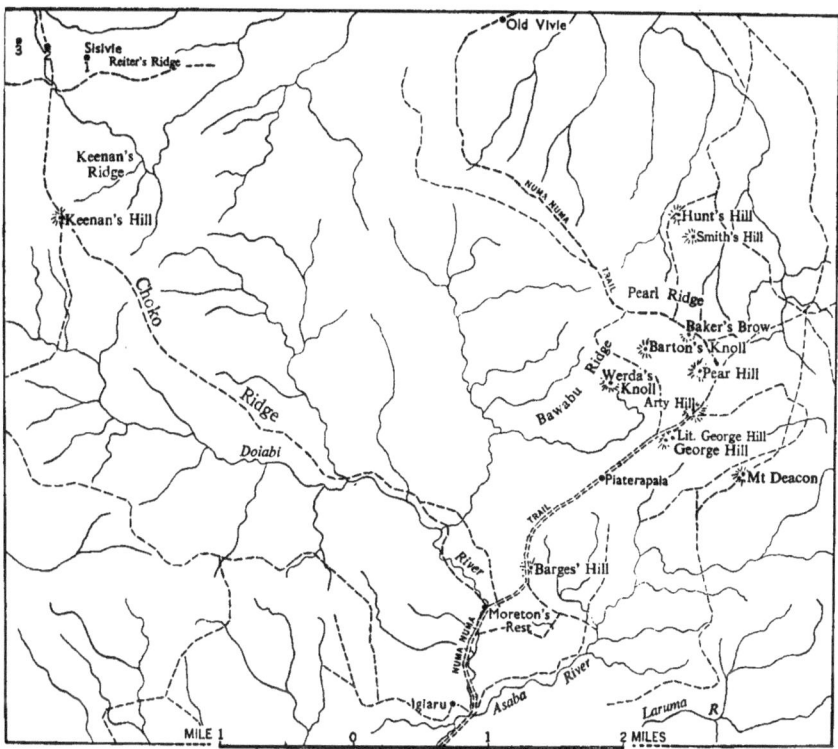

The 9th Battalion's first task was actively to reconnoitre the Sisivie area with a view to attacking it later; and to secure ground from which such an attack could be launched. It had been believed that the main supply route from Numa Numa passed through Sisivie, but captured documents and interrogation of prisoners revealed that Sisivie was merely an outpost and that the Piaterapaia area was the terminus of the enemy's line of communication; consequently the battalion's efforts were concentrated in that direction. At 1.50 p.m. on the 24th one rifle shot was fired from Little George into the battalion's area—the first shot in the Australian operations on Bougainville.

George was a steep-sided knoll only twelve feet wide from crest to crest; on it the forward company occupied an elongated position some

250 yards in length forming a deep salient between Mount Deacon on the east and Bawabu Ridge on the west. Little George was even smaller. Beyond lay a larger feature—Arty Hill, so called because it had been often shelled by artillery and laid bare.

On the 25th a small patrol moved stealthily to the rear of Little George and was fired on, two men being wounded. On the morning of the 29th the battery in the Doiabi Valley fired high-explosive and smoke shells on to Arty Hill, mortars fired smoke bombs on to Little George, and into the smoke a single platoon attacked. At the run the men reached the top of Little George before the Japanese emerged from shelter, opened fire with machine-guns and threw grenades. The attackers did not falter but worked their way forward in pairs, one man firing on a post while the other moved close and threw in grenades. Lieutenant Deacon,[3] the commander, was wounded but carried on. In about half an hour the position was gained. Two Australians had been killed[4] and six wounded, of whom three remained on duty. Twenty Japanese dead lay on the hill, including a lieutenant and a sergeant. The expected enemy counter-attack was made in the evening by about 40 Japanese. It was a frontal thrust and gained no ground. Until dawn the enemy tried in vain to infiltrate.

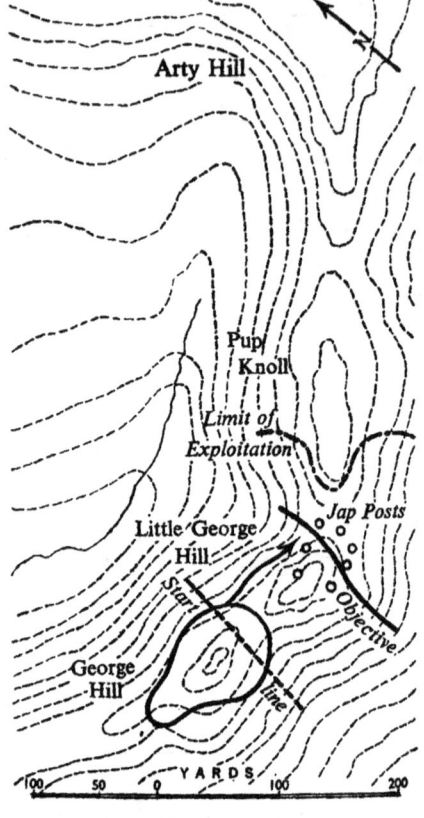

In the next few days patrolling continued. Brigadier Field suggested to Colonel Matthews that he should occupy Sisivie. On 3rd December Lieutenant Mole[5] and his platoon advanced. As they neared the Japanese posts Mole and three men crawled forward. There was a burst of fire which killed the leading man, Private Abbott,[6] and wounded the others. Mole, though mortally wounded, crawled forward to Abbott, found that he was dead, and ordered the whole platoon to withdraw.

---

[3] Capt J. Deacon, MC, VX115580; 9 Bn. Commercial traveller; of Sydney; b. Goulburn, NSW, 23 Oct 1917.

[4] Pte E. Barges, a stretcher bearer (of Yass, NSW) and Pte K. Martin (West Wyalong, NSW). The hill at the Numa Numa roadhead was named Barges' Hill.

[5] Lt C. Mole, NX127054; 9 Bn. Clerk; of Newcastle, NSW; b. Hutton Henry, Durham, England, 6 Dec 1920. Died of wounds 3 Dec 1944.

[6] Pte A. F. Abbott, N196028; 9 Bn. Labourer; of Leadville, NSW; b. Leadville, 7 Jul 1921. Killed in action 3 Dec 1944.

Next day it appeared that the enemy was responding to the Australian thrusts by launching a full-scale encircling attack from heights east and west of the trail—Mount Deacon on the east and Bawabu Ridge on the west. A company of the 61st Battalion was placed to defend the junction of the Doiabi and Asaba Rivers and the heights were shelled; patrols later found that the enemy had abandoned them. Next day the 9th Battalion began moving forward on Bawabu Ridge towards Pearl Ridge[7] which dominated the area to the north and along which it was now evident that the enemy's line of communication ran. On the 13th ten aircraft attacked the enemy's positions for half an hour with naval depth-charges and the artillery shelled them. Under cover of the bombardment a patrol of ten men went forward to Arty Hill to observe, were fired on and lost one man killed and two wounded.

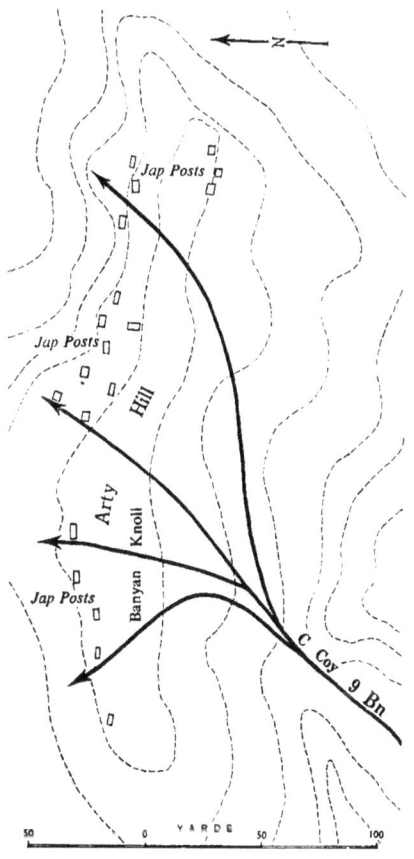

Matthews now planned an attack on Arty Hill by a full company. At 7 a.m. on 18th December Major Blanch's[8] company formed up on the sheltered side of George and Little George, on top of which men of a supporting company were walking about nonchalantly to mislead the enemy into thinking that it was to be another uneventful day. Twelve New Zealand Corsairs attacked the Japanese positions; the battery of the 4th Field Regiment opened fire from its positions in the Laruma River Valley; medium machine-guns fired from Mount Deacon and Bawabu Ridge—that is, from each flank—on to the reverse slope of Arty Hill at ranges up to 1,000 yards. After thirteen minutes of bombardment, the attackers advanced through the smoke along the razor-back ridge which was the only means of approach to the bare hill. Months of intermittent shelling had destroyed the bush and so loosened the soil on the steep slopes that the men had difficulty in scrambling up them. By 8.10 the leading troops were near the crest of Banyan Knoll and were meeting sharp

---

[7] So named by Colonel Matthews after his wife.
[8] Maj J. A. Blanch, VX39161. HQ 8 Div 1940-42; 9 Bn 1944-45. Student; of Melbourne; b. Armadale, Vic, 28 Jul 1920.

small arms fire from Japanese in covered weapon-pits. Grenades were hurled down on them.

They pressed on. Sergeant Allan,[9] commanding the right platoon, led the way to the top of Banyan Knoll, shot a Japanese machine-gunner and himself fell dead. His men carried on up the slopes of Arty Hill. As at Little George, the attackers worked in pairs, one man covering an enemy post with fire while the other attacked from a flank with grenades. After more than an hour of close fighting the position was won and the defenders were digging in and setting up wire in preparation for the probable counter-attack. There was none: a prisoner said that there were not enough men left to attack. Five Australians were killed and 12 wounded of whom 4 remained on duty. Twenty-five Japanese dead were counted, 2 Japanese were taken prisoner, and from 10 to 20 recently-buried bodies were found.[1]

On the 20th the 25th Battalion began to relieve the 9th, which had then been in the line for a month, and was given the task of gaining information in preparation for an attack on the next feature, Pearl Ridge. On the 22nd, after an ineffective air attack, one platoon of the 25th made a probing thrust towards Pearl Ridge from Barton's Knoll, losing one man killed and three wounded. It was estimated that from 80 to 90 Japanese were entrenched on Pearl. Next day a patrol was ambushed beyond Arty Hill and its leader, Lieutenant Smith,[2] was killed.

While these operations were in progress on the Numa Numa trail, the 2/8th Commando, next on the right, had taken over responsibility for the tangled mountain area rising to an altitude of 4,000 feet south and south-east of Mount Bagana, and known as the Hanemo sector. When the commando squadron took over from a company of the 164th American Regiment there had been no contact with the enemy for several weeks, and it was believed that only a handful of Japanese were in the neighbourhood. For five weeks from 24th November, when the relief was completed, a commando troop patrolled but met Japanese only twice, killing two and capturing another. By 27th December, when the 61st Battalion relieved the troop, it was considered that the area was clear and the flank of a force advancing down the coast would be safe.

From the outset, it had been recognised that the southern sector was the principal one, since beyond it lay the main Japanese base, and Savige

---

[9] Sgt D. A. Allan, QX52818; 9 Bn. Sawmiller; of Morayfield, Qld; b. Bangalow, NSW, 18 Apr 1922. Killed in action 18 Dec 1944.

[1] Next day a fighting patrol of two officers and ten men of Captain D. P. Radford's company on the left was ambushed. The leading scout, Private P. B. Barton (of Tumut, NSW) was killed. Corporal M. J. Gillies (Temora, NSW) and Private J. L. Armstrong (Junee, NSW) crept forward to bring in their mate's body but the enemy's fire was too heavy. However, they ensured that he was dead, Armstrong shot one Japanese, and the patrol withdrew through the thick bush. When they reassembled Armstrong was missing, but he reached his company's perimeter next morning. He said that after losing touch he lay in hiding for a time, then, trying to find his way out, walked into an unoccupied enemy position where there were five weapon-pits and a hut. He collected some equipment and papers and, having taken off his boots, crept away. Hearing voices he remained stationary until dark. When he began moving he again met some Japanese but threw a grenade at them and they scattered. Again hearing Japanese, and having no more grenades, he threw his boots at them and ran. Next morning he entered the perimeter still carrying a Japanese bowl and the documents.

[2] Lt K. H. Smith, VX88440; 25 Bn. Farmer; of Boort, Vic; b. Boort, 25 Feb 1921. Killed in action 23 Dec 1944.

had decided to concentrate the 3rd Division in the west and south for that reason, pitting it against the *6th Japanese Division*. On 2nd December General Bridgeford informed his senior officers that the first phase of the operation would be the capture of Mosigetta and Mawaraka, to be used

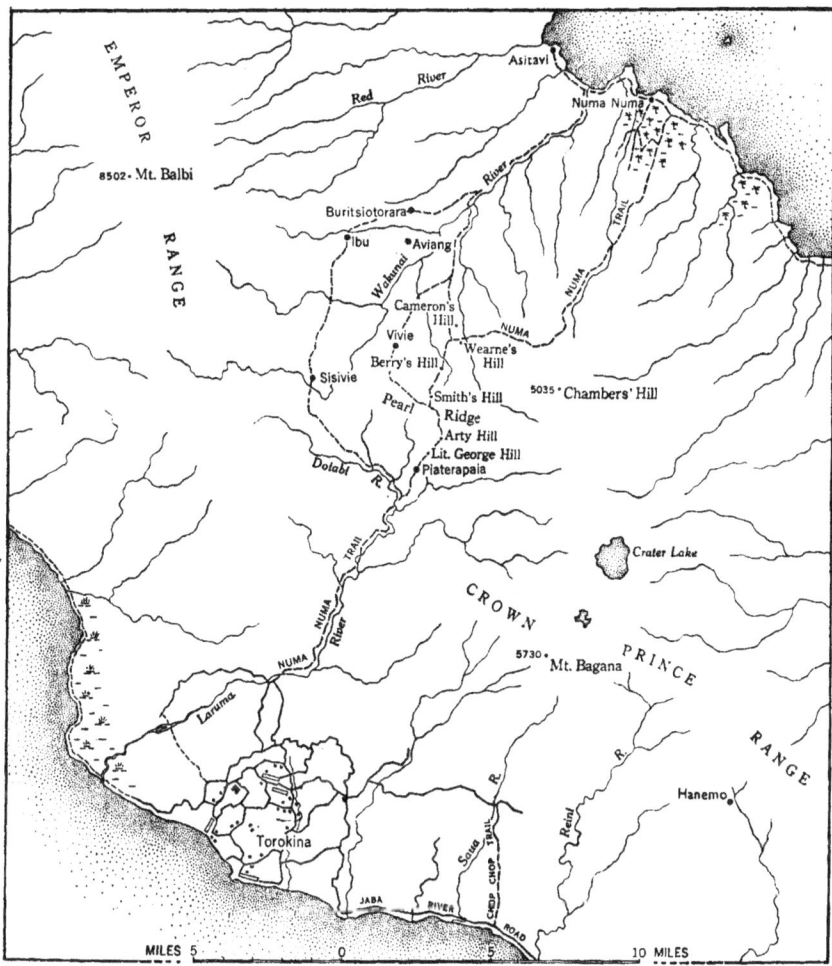

as bases for further advances, but before this operation could be undertaken complete information about the enemy's dispositions was needed. The task of obtaining this information was given to the 29th Brigade Group, in which was included the 2nd Field Regiment and other units. Brigadier Monaghan was instructed not to employ more than one battalion in an attack without the approval of the corps commander. By 10th December the brigade had completed the relief of the 182nd American Regiment.

The southern sector was served by a narrow track near the beach which, between Torokina and the Jaba, crossed a number of streams subject to sudden flooding after heavy rain. When the American regiment was relieved it was maintaining an outpost just north of the mouth of the Jaba, the Japanese an outpost just south of it.

When Monaghan took command he ordered Captain Johnson's[3] company of the 1st New Guinea Battalion stealthily to reconnoitre the bush between the Mariropa and Jaba Rivers. There they met only one Japanese. From the 13th onwards the New Guinea patrols, having crossed the Jaba, explored the country along the south bank, where, on the 16th, they captured a Japanese medical officer (who provided useful information) and surprised and killed four other Japanese. Next day a company of the 15th Battalion crossed the river and established itself. On the 18th (the day of the capture of Arty Hill) a second company of the 15th Battalion landed from barges on the beach well south of the Jaba and later a third company crossed the river. The last two companies were commanded by Major D. Provan and formed a group directly under Monaghan's command.

Next day the 15th Battalion attacked a Japanese post near the river mouth and drove its occupants into an ambush set by the New Guinea Infantry on the road to Kupon. Nine Japanese were killed and the remainder—perhaps ten—fled into the bush. Meanwhile Provan's patrols, advancing without opposition, established a base more than a mile beyond the Tuju River. By the 21st there was evidence that the enemy in response to this rapid move deep into his territory was bringing forward reinforcements, and Monaghan obtained permission to send an additional company (from the 47th Battalion) across the Jaba to join the 15th.

A strong Japanese position flanked by swamps was encountered on the track leading along the south bank of the Jaba on 23rd December and a patrol of New Guinea troops was sent to take it in the rear. From this day onwards the infantry received impressive support from the 2nd Field Regiment. Next day the native soldiers took three prisoners who said that 200 Japanese had left Mosina on the 22nd to launch a counterattack. This attack did not develop. By the 26th patrols had cleared the area south of the Jaba and a platoon of native troops had surprised a strong Japanese patrol and killed eighteen out of perhaps twenty-five. Captured papers and the interrogation of prisoners seemed to indicate that there were one or two battalions of the *13th Japanese Regiment* round Mosina.

Thus by the fourth week of December the tacit truce on Bougainville had been broken. There had been sharp fighting on two of the three main sectors, more than 100 Japanese had been killed, their forward posts in each area had been captured, and they were bringing up reinforcements. On the 23rd the aggressive policy that Bridgeford had adopted (subject to the approval of higher authority) received approval. That day Savige

---

[3] Capt L. R. P. Johnson, NX57084. 2/9 Fd Regt, Angau, 1 NG Inf Bn, 67 Bn BCOF. Police officer, New Guinea Constabulary; of Bellevue Hill, NSW; b. Stanmore, NSW, 21 Apr 1914. Drowned 23 Oct 1946.

issued a crucial instruction: in effect, that he intended to open an offensive. Two of its paragraphs read:

ROLES
8. *3 Aust Div*
Ultimate
To destroy Japanese forces in Southern Bougainville.
Immediate
(a) To conduct operations to clear the enemy from, and to establish control of, the area south from the Jaba River to the Puriata River.
(b) To push forward patrols south of the Puriata River to gain information of and establish contact with Japanese main areas of concentration, in preparation for the next southward move.
(c) To secure and control tracks leading from the east coast on the flank of the line of advance.
(d) To construct necessary tracks in the area of operations to give freedom of movement inland from the coast and parallel to the coast if necessary.
(e) *Employment of Forces*
In carrying out the immediate role, a force exceeding one infantry battalion will not be committed to an attack role without prior approval of 2 Aust Corps.
9. *11 Aust Inf Bde Gp*
(a) To prevent enemy penetration into the Laruma River Valley from the direction of Numa Numa.
(b) To secure the feature known as Pearl Ridge and establish on it firm bases from which to operate patrols towards Numa Numa.
(c) To make no advance beyond Pearl Ridge except by reconnaissance and fighting patrols.
(d) To establish in the Cape Moltke area a firm base for one infantry company and to patrol from there with the object of establishing control in the area Kavrata-Cape Moltke-Amun.
(e) To maintain regular patrols from the perimeter to a minimum depth of 4,000 yards on all lines of approach within the Brigade sector.

"Thus the campaign to destroy the Japanese on Bougainville became resolved into three simultaneous offensives. The ultimate aim in the north was to force the enemy garrison into the narrow Bonis Peninsula and there destroy it. In the central sector the offensive was to clear the enemy from the high ground near Pearl Ridge and then by aggressive patrolling to threaten the important enemy line of communication along the east coast. The main enemy concentration was in the garden area in southern Bougainville and here the decisive battle of the campaign must eventually be fought."[4]

The Allied Intelligence estimates of the whereabouts of the main Japanese formations on Bougainville proved accurate. The main shortcoming was that the strength of the naval troops was underestimated. At the time of the arrival of the Australians there were about 11,000 naval men, including 3,500 civilian workers, on the island; the *87th Garrison Force,* about 4,000 strong, was in the Buka area, and in the south were two strong forces of marines—the *6th Sasebo Special Naval Landing Force* (about 2,000) and the *7th Kure Special Naval Landing Force* (about 1,500). Indeed the naval forces were about as strong in fighting men as the *6th Division.*

During the latter half of 1944 approximately 35 per cent of the Japanese force was on gardening and fishing duty, 15 per cent on transport duty, 30 per cent sick,

---

[4] II Corps report.

and only 20 per cent in the forward areas. The gardens grew sweet potatoes, corn, egg fruit, beans, peanuts and green vegetables. Pawpaws, bananas, coconuts and pineapples were plentiful. There were chickens in every unit's lines.

The policy of concentrating on food production had been made the easier by the fact that it became evident that the Americans did not intend to extend the area that they occupied. General Imamura, at Rabaul, General Hyakutake's senior, favoured a "live and let live" policy. The Japanese believed that they would eventually be reinforced and open a new offensive.

The Japanese first learnt that Australians were arriving on Bougainville from a native who had been at Torokina. The news was confirmed in a broadcast by General MacArthur. Opinions were divided concerning the significance of the change, but, in case it was to lead to an offensive, commanders in the field were ordered to meet all patrols with aggressive action. Hyakutake issued an appreciation in which he stated that the courses open to his enemy if he attacked were (*a*) to land in Gazelle Harbour and at the same time push south across the Jaba, (*b*) to land at Numa Numa and try to cut the north-south line of communication, or (*c*) to land on the south coast between the Hari River and Kaukauai and strike at the main base. The force in the Emperor Range was reinforced from the *38th Brigade*, 3,000 strong, at Numa Numa and the headquarters of the *81st Regiment* moved into the area; the *6th Division* established an advanced headquarters at Mosigetta to control the defence of the Jaba River and Gazelle Harbour. It was considered that the new troops would not be able to attack before the middle of January.

The successful attack on Little George by the 9th Battalion on 29th November, six weeks before it was expected, surprised the enemy commanders and convinced them that the Australians were determined to open an offensive. Reinforcements numbering 450 were hurried into the central area (there were 2,000 troops deployed in or forward of Numa Numa) and Colonel Atsushi Kaneko of the *81st Regiment* took command. A further 1,000 troops were sent from Kieta and the north to Numa Numa. Hyakutake was convinced that the attack on the Numa Numa trail would be accompanied by a landing at its eastern end with the object of severing his force. The quantity of artillery used in the attack on Little George and later Arty Hill convinced the Japanese that a determined thrust was being made. Arty Hill was defended by men of the *5th* and *11th Companies* of the *81st Regiment*.

Meanwhile the *13th Regiment* was attacked on the Jaba River. Lieut-General Kanda of the *6th Division* did not propose to contest the south bank of the river, considering that the crossing was merely a feint and the principal offensive would be made by sea; the main body of the defending force—1,500 men—was retained in the Mosigetta area. By January Kanda estimated that one Australian division, its name yet unknown, was south of the Jaba, with 25 guns.

Although the Australians had thus worked out the dispositions of the principal Japanese military units with some precision, the Japanese had gained little knowledge of their enemy's order of battle and his dispositions. Not even the titles of the major formations were known to them until they were told much later in a broadcast from Australia that troops of the 3rd and 11th Australian Divisions were on Bougainville. The Japanese Intelligence staffs were weak in numbers and training. On Bougainville no Intelligence reports were issued, and, after the surrender, officers were "amazed at the extent of the knowledge the Australians possessed of Japanese units, movements and personalities . . . no system existed in *XVII Army* to produce such results".[5] Their booklet on the Australian

---

[5] This quotation and many of the facts stated in this and later accounts of Japanese operations have been taken from the 23rd Brigade's "History of the Japanese Occupation of Bougainville, March 1942-August 1945", compiled between August 1945 and February 1946 after comprehensive interrogation of the Japanese staff.

Army contained only pre-war information. It seems that throughout the war the Japanese acquired little information about the Order of Battle of the Australian home army beyond what they had probably copied from pre-war publications. Until well into 1942 the Australian Army had continued in a carefree fashion to publish in the telephone directories what amounted to a detailed Order of Battle of the home forces, but the Japanese appear to have missed even that opportunity of bringing their information up to date during 1940 and 1941.

CHAPTER 6

THE OFFENSIVE OPENS

ONE more action was fought by the 7th Brigade in the central sector before it was transferred to the south in consequence of the decision to open a full-scale offensive against the main Japanese force. It will be recalled that the 25th Battalion relieved the 9th at Arty Hill at the end of the third week of December, and that, from the 22nd onwards, the incoming battalion patrolled forward against the new Japanese position on Pearl Ridge, where the enemy force was estimated to number from 80 to 90. An attack was planned for the morning of the 30th, and all four rifle companies were to be used: Lieutenant Shaw's[1] was to advance from Arty Hill and take the north-eastern spur of Pearl, Captain Just's[2] to pass through and take the eastern part of the main ridge, Captain Bruce's[3] to cut the enemy's track to the west and Captain Gabel's[4] to advance from Werda's Knoll to Baker's Brow.

Early in the morning of 30th December aircraft attacked the Japanese positions for about forty minutes, and at 8 a.m. the infantry advanced behind artillery and medium-machine-gun fire. On the right Shaw's company moved along a razor-back only twelve feet in width, with precipitous sides, and broken at a point about 300 yards from the start-line by a bomb crater twelve feet across and ten feet deep. The Japanese were strongly established on the far side of this crater and swept it with fire. Corporal Carter[5] and his section tried to rush across but he was killed, others were wounded, and the attack was halted. The Japanese position was bombarded. Efforts were made to outflank it by sending one platoon to the right and another to the left

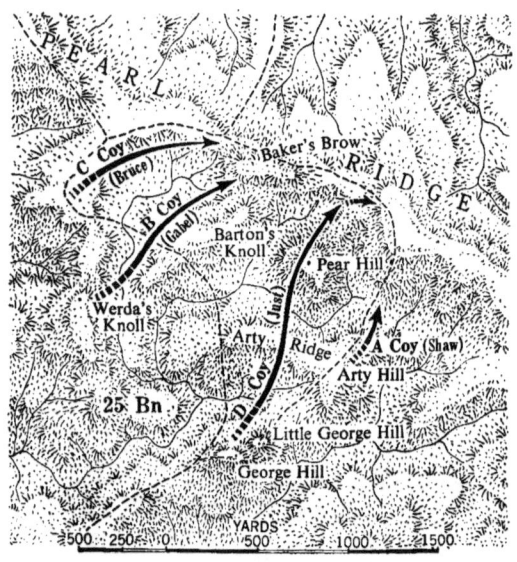

---
[1] Lt B. A. Shaw, NX68272; 25 Bn. Clerk; of Gunning, NSW; b. Gunnedah, NSW, 29 Mar 1919.
[2] Lt-Col M. E. Just, ED, QX36183; 25 Bn. Architectural draftsman; of Toowoomba, Qld; b. Toowoomba, 25 Oct 1920.
[3] Maj W. F. Bruce, VX64391. 25 Bn and staff appointments. Served Korea 1950-51. Regular soldier; b. Sydney, 12 Aug 1917.
[4] Lt-Col C. P. Gabel, ED, NX128782. 3, 7 MG and 25 Bns. Asst grocery manager; of Goulburn, NSW; b. Goulburn, 27 Sep 1918.
[5] Cpl W. E. Carter, NX102959; 25 Bn. Farm hand; of Henty, NSW; b. Culcairn, NSW, 19 Mar 1915. Killed in action 30 Dec 1944.

but these failed because of the heavy fire and the difficulty of moving along the sides of the razor-back ridge, down which the Japanese rolled grenades. After three men had been killed and six wounded the company was ordered, at 4 p.m., to dig in and reorganise.

Bruce's company made slow progress in thick bush, including bamboo, but reached its objective across the Japanese track at 2.45, having killed six Japanese and lost only one man wounded.

After the setback on the right Lieut-Colonel McKinna wisely changed the plan, ordered Just's company to dig in for the present, and approach Pearl Ridge next day by a long and difficult climb along Pear Hill instead of along the narrow spur where the attack had failed.

During the night the leading companies beat off strong counter-attacks. Next day the renewed attack succeeded. Just's company reached the objective by 4.15 p.m. without loss, Gabel's took Baker's Brow at 4.25 p.m., after having killed 13 Japanese, 10 of them having fallen to Lieutenant Chesterton's[6] platoon. It had been a hard fight; 10 Australians had been killed, and 25 wounded; 34 Japanese dead were found and others lay unrecovered on the steep sides of the razor-back; one man was taken prisoner.[7] From the newly-captured heights the Australians could see the sea on both sides of the 30-mile-wide island.

We know now that the attack on Pearl Ridge was launched not against a Japanese company, as was then believed, but against a battalion of fresh troops strongly dug in. Its capture by an Australian battalion whose experience of battle was limited to a brief encounter more than two years before was thus one of the outstanding feats of arms in this campaign and a striking demonstration of the effectiveness of the Australian force's training and tactics. After Arty Hill the survivors of the two companies of the *81st Japanese Regiment* had been withdrawn to Pearl Ridge, where they were reinforced by a fit and keen battalion some 550 strong from the *38th Brigade*, whose commander, Major-General Kesao Kijima, took charge of the whole area. Pearl Ridge was converted into a fortress and from 4 to 6 guns and 20 to 30 mortars were in support. The air strikes preceding the attack caused little damage and few casualties, but were considered nerve-racking. The loss of the ridge after "three days of desperate fighting" was attributed to lack of heavy weapons; Japanese leaders considered that their counter-attacks could not have failed if there had been stronger support by artillery and mortars. The loss of the ridge was regarded as a blow to the prestige of the *38th Brigade*, but the courageous performance of its troops was a source of consolation.

Soon after the capture of Pearl Ridge the 11th Brigade took over the central as well as the northern sector, in accordance with General Savige's instructions. These provided that Brigadier Stevenson should not advance beyond Pearl Ridge, where it was taking about 300 native carriers and

---

[6] Lt J. Chesterton, QX37528; 25 Bn. Farmer; of Proston, Qld; b. Wondai, Qld, 1 Mar 1920.

[7] To 5th January the battalions of the 7th Brigade had suffered the following losses in battle:

	Officers	Other Ranks
9th Battalion	3	42
25th Battalion	3	33
61st Battalion	nil	nil

In the same period one man in the brigade was accidentally killed and six accidentally wounded. Throughout the campaigns of 1945 the ratio of accidental to battle casualties was of this order, as it is always likely to be in bush warfare when men are holding highly-sensitive weapons ready for instant action, and using booby-traps.

five jeeps to supply a battalion group, and that there should be deep patrolling with the object of gaining topographical and tactical information, preventing transfer of reinforcements to the south, and inflicting casualties. Each battalion of the brigade in turn did a tour of duty in the sector.[8]

When the 11th Brigade took over Stevenson decided that effort was being wasted moving supplies forward and had a jeep track built from Barges' Hill to Pearl Ridge. Four jeeps were taken to pieces, carried up the escarpment and assembled on the new track above it. To accelerate the improvement of the road, men of the 16th Field Company under Captain C. C. Wolfe hauled a bulldozer up the 5-in-4 grade of Barges' Hill. The route was reduced to "the least practicable number of straight legs", cleared of undergrowth and roughly levelled with mattocks and shovels. A cable 3,000 feet long was hauled up the hill by 30 infantrymen and 150 natives pulling at 8-foot intervals, and anchored to several trees at Moreton's Rest, 450 feet below the top. On this cable the dozer winched itself up the incline in 60 foot stages. All this took eight days. Beyond Moreton's Rest there were enough strong trees to enable the dozer to climb up along a 300-foot length of cable.

During this phase patrols, generally guided by native police, were sent out for from one day to six days to probe forward through the bush. The 11th Battery relieved the 10th and it replaced its short 25-pounders with long 25-pounders, with their greater range, in order to support these deep patrols more effectively; from posts on Pearl Ridge and Keenan's Ridge observers directed the bombardment of the Japanese positions on the slopes beyond. The firing of the guns, far below at the foot of the Laruma escarpment, could not be heard at Pearl Ridge and the only warning that the Japanese had was the brief whistle of the approaching shells.

Partly as a result of the skilful guidance of the native police the patrols killed many Japanese and suffered relatively small losses. The 26th Battalion, the first to do a tour of duty here, suffered its first death in action on 7th January when a patrol led by Lieutenant Davis[9] met an enemy patrol. Private Smith[1] died of wounds and three corporals were wounded. The hill where the clash occurred was then named Smith's Hill.

Patrolling was carried out persistently and with great skill. While the 55th/53rd Battalion was in the forward position a fighting patrol on 8th February attacked the enemy on Smith's Hill. It was led by Lieutenant Ryan[2] with Lieutenant Ford[3] as artillery observer, and included twelve others.

---

[8] The 26th Battalion from 5th January to 2nd February, the 55th/53rd from 3rd February to 15th March and the 31st/51st from 16th March to 18th April.

[9] Lt A. L. Davis, QX36521; 26 Bn. Clerk; of Longreach, Qld; b. Longreach, 3 Oct 1921.

[1] Pte L. H. Smith, WX26214; 26 Bn. Farmer; of Cunderdin, WA; b. Midland Junction, WA, 24 Apr 1922. Died of wounds 7 Jan 1945.

[2] Lt J. S. Ryan, NX87293; 55/53 Bn. Insurance officer; of Chatswood, NSW; b. Chatswood, 18 Mar 1913. Died of wounds 8 Feb 1945.

[3] Lt A. J. T. Ford, MC, NX109027; 4 Fd Regt. Clerk; of Lane Cove, NSW; b. Waverley, NSW, 1 Apr 1922.

The patrol found signal wires running along the track and began to cut them at intervals. Suddenly the forward scout, Private Elliott,[4] was hit by rifle fire and, as the patrol went to ground, a machine-gun opened up. In the course of the subsequent fight against from fifteen to twenty Japanese, Ryan was seriously wounded while moving forward with Private Paice[5] to recover Elliott. Ryan went on firing; Paice shot two Japanese and continued trying to save Elliott but found that he had been hit again, mortally. Paice then brought Ryan back to the patrol. Ford now rushed forward, retrieved a telephone which had been left when the enemy began shooting, and, from a position close to where contact had been made, directed concentrations from his battery on to the Japanese only 50 yards in front of him; this enabled the patrol to withdraw. Ryan walked back with the patrol but later died of his wounds.

The nature of the deep patrols may be illustrated by drawing on the report of the one which killed the largest number of Japanese. Lieutenant Goodwin[6] and ten infantrymen of the 55th/53rd, with an artillery observer (again Lieutenant Ford) and his team, a native police boy and two native scouts, set out on 2nd March to gain topographical information and information about the enemy, and find suitable supply-dropping points. They were out for five days. On the first morning they saw signs of a Japanese patrol of three some 45 minutes ahead of them and traced their movements. The Australians moved 5,400 yards that day. Next morning near the Numa Numa trail one of the natives reported that Japanese were near by. Goodwin detailed three men to block the track and led three others in from the side to deal with the enemy. They crept stealthily forward and found six Japanese in a lean-to. Goodwin gave each man a target and all six of the enemy were killed. While Goodwin was examining the bodies there was a burst of fire from a ridge overlooking them. The Australians withdrew to dead ground, circled the enemy and marched on into his territory, the Japanese fire continuing for 15 minutes after they had gone. They travelled 7,600 yards that day. The 4th was spent reconnoitring the area they had then reached. Next day they had moved some 5,000 yards on the return journey when scouts reported Japanese round the junction of their native pad and a creek that lay ahead. Goodwin moved the patrol to a ridge overlooking the Japanese and sent three men to cover the track to the west. Goodwin's report says:

> Noise of flowing river covered sounds which might have been made by movement of patrol. The patrol commander then personally positioned each man of the patrol and indicated his target. Thus the eleven members of the patrol made sure of eleven kills on fire being opened after given signal. Approximately seven Japanese rushed from a near-by lean-to. These were immediately engaged by fire from the patrol. The enemy killed by fire totalled 15. In addition fifteen grenades were thrown into area.

---

[4] Pte K. Elliott, N263902; 55/53 Bn. Stove fitter; of Forest Lodge, NSW; b. Stockton, NSW, 17 Oct 1923. Killed in action 8 Feb 1945.

[5] Pte M. F. Paice, DCM, NX73320; 55/53 Bn. Case maker; of Griffith, NSW; b. Temora, NSW, 10 Jan 1919. Died 15 Feb 1956.

[6] Lt L. F. Goodwin, MC, NX27977. 2/4 and 55/53 Bns. Transport driver; of Canberra; b. Yanco, NSW, 15 Dec 1918.

The native police boy claimed 18 killed but patrol commander cannot confirm additional three. From a position overlooking the killing ground LMG and rifle fire was almost immediately opened on patrol. The LMG fire ceased when two grenades were thrown and Owen gun fire was directed at source of enemy fire but results were unobserved. Enemy rifle fire continued and the patrol withdrew. On considering the distance still to be covered back to battalion, the patrol commander decided that the risk of casualties which might be sustained in pressing an attack to search bodies was not justified.

It was then nearly 5 p.m. The patrol moved 700 yards and bivouacked for the night. Next day—the 6th—six hours of marching brought them back to their starting point.

While in this area the 55th/53rd made 36 deep patrols. On one led by Sergeant Greenshields,[7] and lasting four days, 20 Japanese were killed. Lieutenants Goodwin, Campbell[8] and Kayrooz[9] each led out four patrols; Goodwin's killed a total of 26 out of the 107 Japanese killed by all patrols of this battalion.

The next battalion to take over the forward positions was the 31st/51st (Lieut-Colonel Kelly) whose strenuous operations in the northern sector in January and February will be described later. Perhaps the outstanding patrol leader in the 31st/51st was Lieutenant Reiter,[1] who led out three patrols which killed 10 out of the 78 Japanese killed by this battalion's forays. One of these patrols was named by the battalion "the raid on Reiter's Ridge". Reiter and fifteen men were given the task of harassing the Japanese occupying a prominent ridge just east of Sisivie and discovering their strength. They departed from Keenan's Ridge at 5.30 p.m. on 27th March, bivouacked at a former artillery observation post and moved on at 3 a.m. next morning for a dawn attack. At 6 a.m.

the patrol moved in, and throwing grenades and firing L.M.G. occupied a small knoll (its report stated). Two Japanese were killed and one pill-box containing L.M.G. destroyed. Patrol raced down narrow neck to a wide clearing in which several huts were sighted. Phosphorus and H.E. grenades were thrown. In a matter of seconds four more Japanese killed (two in slit trenches, one as he ran and another while abluting). Two were wounded by phosphorus grenades. Three huts were blazing and one (considered to be an ammunition dump) blew up. Enemy opened up with one L.M.G. and fifteen rifles and patrol pulled out with one man wounded.

Instead of hastening them away Reiter assembled his men near by in concealment and watched the enemy. At length Japanese began to move about again, and soon they were washing clothes, chopping wood and performing other tasks. There were from 25 to 30 enemy in the post. The Australians watched throughout the morning and at 12.30 p.m. opened fire with all their weapons. Two Japanese were killed and four more huts set on fire. The enemy fired back, and at 1.15 Reiter withdrew his men and returned to Keenan's Ridge leaving an ambush on the enemy's

---

[7] WO2 F. T. Greenshields, NX113291; 55/53 Bn. Labourer; of Rockdale, NSW; b. Parramatta, NSW, 28 Apr 1920.

[8] Lt L. J. Campbell, NX127563; 55/53 Bn. Master butcher; of Coff's Harbour, NSW; b. Woolgoolga, NSW, 29 May 1918.

[9] Lt L. S. Kayrooz, QX35505; 55/53 Bn. Accountant and salesman; of Ingham, Qld; b. Atherton, Qld, 30 Jul 1918.

[1] Lt F. A. Reiter, MC, MM, VX4024. 2/7 and 31/51 Bns. Dairy farmer; of Korumburra, Vic; b. Meeniyan, Vic, 10 Mar 1918.

track. The ambush party returned later and reported that it had seen no movement.

On the 29th, the day after Reiter's return, a platoon of the 1st New Guinea Infantry Battalion under Lieutenant Martin[2] set out for Buritsiotorara along the Wakunai River. There they found three huts and a large garden with seven Japanese moving about unarmed. Throwing grenades and firing from the hip the native soldiers attacked and killed all seven. Three more who emerged from a hut were chased and killed. Three of the dead men were found to be lieutenants; three machine-guns were captured. Next day at Aviang, 1,200 yards away, seven more Japanese were seen, of whom three including another lieutenant were killed and the others fled.

Other outstanding patrol leaders were: in the 26th Battalion, Lieutenants Chambers,[3] Christie[4] and Wylie[5]; in the 31st/51st, Lieutenants Patterson[6] and Evans.[7] In the brigade's fourteen weeks in this sector 236 Japanese were killed, 15 probably killed, and four prisoners taken, yet the Australians lost only four dead and 19 wounded—evidence of their high standard of training and the quality of the junior leaders.

It soon became evident that the constant harassment of the Japanese, combined with shortage of food, was depressing their spirits. On 4th March a Japanese medical officer who walked into the forward Australian positions and gave himself up said that many of his comrades were in poor condition, possessed surrender pamphlets prepared by the Far Eastern Liaison Office,[8] and would surrender if they could be assured of a safe journey to the Australian lines. Thereupon a F.E.L.O. propaganda unit was brought to Pearl Ridge, and, for several days from 7th March onwards, broadcast to the Japanese that their plight was hopeless and how and where to surrender. Pamphlets were dropped from the air into the Japanese area.

No Japanese surrendered as a result of the propaganda. This may be attributed to the fact that a stricter watch was kept on would-be deserters, and that, soon after the broadcasts began, patrols reported that Smith's Hill garrison included some well-equipped Japanese of big build and in good physical condition, which was thought to indicate that the position had been reinforced or that the former garrison had been relieved.

In fact the strength of the *38th Japanese Brigade* and attached troops in the Numa Numa sector at this stage was about 1,600. The Japanese leaders had reached the conclusion that the Australians had completed preparations for a large-scale

---

[2] Lt J. A. A. Martin, QX14582. 2/9 Fd Regt, 1 NG Inf Bn. Commercial traveller; of Townsville, Qld; b. Sydney, 26 Dec 1905.

[3] Lt A. L. E. Chambers, MC, VX104330; 26 Bn. Bookkeeper; of Oakleigh, Vic; b. Victoria, 15 Apr 1919.

[4] Lt K. MacN. Christie, QX34003. 26 Bn; LO 11 Bde and 5 Div. Costing clerk; of Ingham, Qld; b. Ingham, 6 Mar 1921.

[5] Lt A. Wylie, QX34021; 26 Bn. Rigger; of Innisfail, Qld; b. Kairi, Qld, 12 Sep 1913.

[6] Lt J. G. Patterson, VX5122. 2/6 and 31/51 Bns. Labourer; of Geelong, Vic; b. Portland, Vic, 15 Aug 1921.

[7] Lt W. F. P. Evans, QX34010; 31/51 Bn. Labourer; of Babinda, Qld; b. Paisley, Scotland, 25 Mar 1918.

[8] The Far Eastern Liaison Office controlled "political warfare".

attack from Pearl Ridge, probably by three battalions—one along the Numa Numa trail, one along the Wakunai River trail and the third through Ibu. Finally, they considered, a seaborne force would land and advance on Numa Numa from the north. Thus the Australian force at Pearl Ridge, never more than one battalion, succeeded in its task of keeping the enemy on tenterhooks.

In the northern sector a new phase had opened when, on 31st December, Savige ordered Stevenson "to conduct operations with the object of destroying the enemy garrisons and establishing control along the north-west coast of Bougainville up to the Soraken Harbour". In consequence the 31st/51st Battalion, which already had a company patrolling forward from Kuraio Mission, had been concentrated at Sipaai on 7th January.[9]

Stevenson directed Kelly that, because engineer supplies and native carriers were limited, he should advance by making sweeping inland patrols aimed at driving the enemy down to the coastal belt where they could be annihilated, whereas if they retreated into the mountains it might take months to "winkle" them out. Reports from native scouts suggested that the enemy was reinforcing his positions forward of the Genga River and would fight on that line. While the main body of the 31st/51st advanced astride the coastal track, a long-range patrol was sent inland by way of Totokei toward Lalum, known to be the main village between the Genga River—the probable Japanese defensive line—and Soraken, the Japanese base. On 16th January Captain Titley's[1] company reached Rukussia without incident. This company then moved north along the coastal flank and the first clash with a strong group of Japanese came on 17th January. In sharp fights on the 17th and 18th eight Japanese were killed and three wounded, for a loss of two men wounded. The enemy opened fire with artillery for the first time in this sector, but 14 out of 49 rounds fired failed to explode.

On the 19th the flanking force—a platoon led by Lieutenant A. Roodakoff with Captain Tame[2] of Angau, 12 police boys and 50 porters—advancing towards Lalum through the foothills met from 30 to 40 of the enemy at Kunamatoro. Lance-Sergeant Davies-Griffiths[3] led an attack on the village and in ten minutes the Japanese were overwhelmed. Fourteen Japanese were killed; one Australian was killed and Lieutenant Roodakoff was seriously wounded;[4] after the fight the gallant Davies-Griffiths was missing. At dusk the Australians withdrew carrying the dead and wounded. It was evident that the advancing battalion had encountered the enemy's line of resistance, and that he intended to fight for the Genga.

---

[9] The 31st/51st had taken over this sector early in December from the 2/8th Commando Squadron.

[1] Maj T. H. A. Titley, MC, QX33699; 31/51 Bn. Public accountant; of Charters Towers, Qld; b. Charters Towers, 13 Jan 1909.

[2] Capt S. A. Tame, NX200036. 21 Sqn RAAF 1940-42; Angau 1943-46. Plantation manager; of Buka Passage; b. Cooma, NSW, 6 Jan 1906.

[3] L-Sgt O. L. Davies-Griffiths, QX33557; 31/51 Bn. Clerk; of Atherton, Qld; b. Charters Towers, Qld, 22 Sep 1911. Killed in action 19 Jan 1945.

[4] He was carried in under fire by Constable Suani of the Royal Papuan Constabulary.

On the 19th in an effort to outflank the opposition on the coastal track a patrol was sent inland and then north. It came upon two mountain guns guarded by a sentry, who was taken by surprise and killed, and it captured documents showing the organisation of the *10th Company* of the *81st Regiment* which was evidently opposing the advance.

On the left by 21st January Titley's company was some 800 yards from the Genga River. There the track entered an open garden about 100 yards wide, beyond which on the northern side curved the wooded Tsimba Ridge, the whole forming an amphitheatre. The Japanese dug in on the ridge had an excellent field of fire into the garden area. West from the amphitheatre the high ground stretched some 500 yards to the south bank of the Genga, thus forming an obstacle across and well to the east of the line of advance.

That day efforts were made to outflank this position. The advance was halted by machine-gun and rifle fire, but not before the "Pimple" on Tsimba Ridge had been taken and a machine-gun captured with no loss to the Australians. On the following days patrols pressed forward and it was discovered that there were trenches and pill-boxes along Tsimba Ridge for about 150 yards. On the 23rd two guns of the 2nd Mountain Battery shelled the ridge from 3,100 yards. Next day an attack was launched on the right, but halted by concentrated Japanese fire. On the 25th a wide outflanking movement was begun with the object of attacking the position from the north. One platoon crossed the Genga, some 600 yards inland from Tsimba and was joined next day by the remainder of its company (Captain Shilton[5]). For the next six days

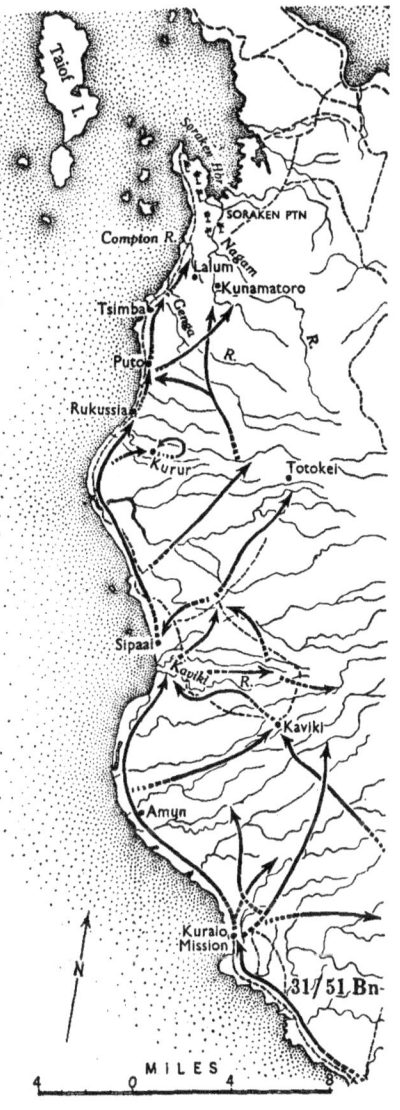

January-February

---

[5] Capt A. L. Shilton, MC, VX3379. 2/5 and 31/51 Bns. Clerk; of Alphington, Vic; b. Heath Hill, Vic, 26 Sep 1918.

the Japanese strongly attacked this bridgehead, but were repulsed with sharp losses. However, the securing of this bridgehead did not loosen the Japanese grip on Tsimba Ridge itself and a set-piece attack, supported by the whole of the 2nd Mountain Battery and a platoon of heavy mortars, was planned for 6th February.

One of the hazards of crossing the Genga (and, later, the Gillman) was the presence of crocodiles. At one crossing Captain Wolfe of the engineers crawled to a tree growing on the bank, placed gelignite round it and felled it across the stream, enabling the men to cross without wading through the water.

Late in January, Brigadier Stevenson suggested that tanks be used in support of the battalion, but General Savige told him that the armour was to be kept to achieve surprise in the southern sector in a later phase.

On 29th January the Japanese launched a particularly fierce attack on the bridgehead across the Genga, broke through one part of the perimeter, and the fighting was so close that men were cut with swords. Shilton organised a counter-attack. From exposed positions Lieutenant Forbes[6] of the mountain battery directed effective fire which helped greatly to break the attack. Next day small parties of the enemy attacked the bridgehead again. An outstanding scout, Private Miles,[7] led out four three-man patrols against these parties and he and his men killed seven and wounded five.

From 8.20 until 9 a.m. on 6th February more than 500 shells and mortar bombs were fired on to Tsimba Ridge. One gun had been brought forward to within 200 yards of the Japanese position. At 9 a.m. two platoons of Captain Harris'[8] company moved to a forming-up place south-east of the amphitheatre and then advanced north-west down a 50-foot incline and up a rise beyond—a distance of about 200 yards. No. 10 Platoon attacked the centre of the ridge from the east and gained its objective by 9.25, killing 5 Japanese and losing 3 killed and 7 wounded. Private Jorgensen[9] courageously rushed a Japanese weapon-pit, killed the two occupants and captured a machine-gun. No. 11 Platoon continued to move north to circle and attack the western part of the ridge from the rear. At 9.30 12 Platoon attacked from the garden area but, having lost four men, were halted. Corporal Miller[1] took command of two sections which had lost contact with the remainder of the platoon and led them forward to the objective under fire which wounded six men. By 11.30 11 Platoon had reached high ground on the western end of the north side of the stronghold but could not advance to the enemy posts on the south side. The surviving Japanese were now surrounded, but the attack had

---

[6] Lt A. J. de B. Forbes, MC, NX138171. 2/11 Fd Regt, 2 Mtn Bty and BCOF. MHR since 1956. Regular soldier; of Adelaide; b. Hobart, 16 Dec 1923.

[7] L-Cpl D. T. G. Miles, MM, QX54772; 31/51 Bn. Farm worker; of Ingham, Qld; b. Ingham, 20 Mar 1920.

[8] Capt M. N. J. Harris, VX5200. 2/6 and 31/51 Bns. Bank officer; of Cobram, Vic; b. Cobram, 12 Mar 1919.

[9] L-Cpl C. C. Jorgensen, MM, Q111747; 31/51 Bn. Carpenter; of Townsville, Qld; b. Gympie, Qld, 25 May 1921.

[1] Cpl G. C. Miller, MM, QX48722; 31/51 Bn. Grocer; of Charters Towers, Qld; b. Charters Towers, 17 Apr 1916.

(*Australian War Memorial*)
Bulldozers towing a tank of the 2/4th Armoured Regiment through the Puriata River on 30th March. Tanks were hurried forward to support the 25th Battalion at Slater's Knoll.

(*Australian War Memorial*)
Troops of the New Guinea Infantry Battalion, attached to the 7th Brigade, with Japanese prisoners taken during a raid in the Barara area, Bougainville, on 23rd March 1945.

(Australian War Memorial)
Troops of the 24th Battalion advancing with a tank along the Buin Road, Bougainville, toward Hiru Hiru on 26th April 1945.

(Australian War Memorial)
A tractor train moving along the Buin Road with supplies for the forward companies of the 24th Battalion, 26th April 1945.

(Australian War Memorial)
A company of the 26th Battalion landed from barges on Torokori Island, off the north-west coast of Bougainville, on 6th May 1945.

(Australian War Memorial)
Corduroyed road serving the 31st/51st Battalion in the Soraken area, northern Bougainville, 7th June 1945.

(Australian War Memorial)
Lieut-General V. A. H. Sturdee (G.O.C. First Army), Brigadier H. H. Hammer (commander of the 15th Brigade), Major-General W. Bridgeford (G.O.C. 3rd Division) and Lieut-General S. G. Savige (G.O.C. II Corps) at the Puriata River, Bougainville, 12th May 1945.

(R.A.A.F.)
The Buin Road at the Hongorai River, 28th July 1945.

cost the Australians 9 men killed and 20 wounded. Such losses were not surprising. There was a continuous communication trench along each crest of the ridge and forward of the trenches were weapon-pits with log roofs commanding a clear field of fire across an area offering practically no cover except at the inner edge of the beach where a line of lofty casuarinas grew.

Next day the enemy counter-attacked and was repulsed, yet he clung doggedly to his remaining pocket on the western tip of the ridge. On the morning of 9th February three aircraft bombed the Japanese positions. Only two of their six bombs exploded, but, after a mortar bombardment, Harris' company advanced and occupied the remainder of the ridge without opposition. It was estimated that 66 Japanese had been killed in the defence of the Tsimba area. Four field and 3 anti-tank guns, 9 machine-guns and 86 rifles were captured. By 10th February the bush south of the Genga River

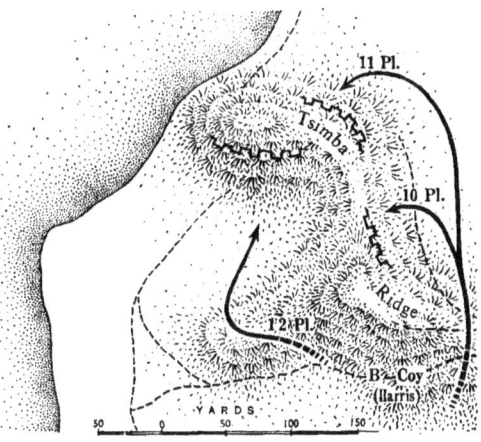

was cleared of the enemy, and patrols had cleared the north bank of the river, after one clash in which 3 Japanese were killed, 3 Australians wounded, and a Japanese 37-mm gun captured. On the 11th the Japanese were forced out of a position astride the track some 150 yards beyond the river. The enemy's artillery was now frequently harassing the advancing battalion.[2] This day shells killed two men, including Lieutenant Bak.[3]

On 4th February Captain Downs'[4] company had departed to clear any enemy from the Kunamatoro area and then swing in to link with the drive up the coast towards Soraken. This company dug in on a ridge overlooking Soraken Plantation and Taiof Island and sent out small patrols. On 7th February a party of Japanese attacked a forward outpost wounding 3 Australians; 4 Japanese were killed and the others withdrew. On 9th February the company advanced and occupied a position 250 yards from the enemy. A party of 20 Japanese were attacked and 2 were killed. Another attack was launched on the 12th, but strongly entrenched automatics plus sniping halted the Australians, who lost 2 killed and 9 wounded. On 19th February 25-pounders, recently arrived at Puto, the barge-

---

[2] The 2nd Mountain Battery was still in support of the 31st/51st. On 14th February Lieutenant Forbes, unable to gain observation in the bush, waded into the sea up to his armpits in full view of the enemy and directed fire from there.

[3] Lt C. J. Bak, QX61455; 31/51 Bn. Shipping clerk; of Cairns, Qld; b. Brisbane, 8 Apr 1920. Killed in action 11 Feb 1945.

[4] Capt H. C. Downs, QX33838; 31/51 Bn. Manager and secretary; of Malanda, Qld; b. Lismore, NSW, 14 Jun 1906. Killed in action 10 Jun 1945.

unloading point through which the force was supplied, and the mountain guns shelled the ridge for 40 minutes. Then the whole company advanced with supporting fire from heavy mortars and machine-guns. One of the men who took part said afterwards:

> The advance was up two spurs: two platoons up the left and one up the right. The Nips were well dug in and the majority were firing American Springfield rifles. We cleared the ridge with grenades and rifles and pushed on to find three pits and a hut in the rear. Two Japs killed by the grenades remained in the pits. The remainder had fled though one was shot careering down the slope. The company pushed on down the ridge which was so narrow that the troops had to move down in single file. Just before dusk one of our men was killed, and during the night the Nips circled about calling out for their mates—the two killed by grenades. The 25-pounders had given the ridge such a pounding that most of the surface soil was loose. . . . During the whole of the attack at Downs' Ridge a big feature was the struggle to get the wounded back. They had to be evacuated over six miles of ridge to Puto. It was a three to four-hour carry and most of it was done at night.

Downs' company pressed on in close touch with the Japanese that day and during the 20th, 21st and 22nd. In the attack and in general skirmishing on the following days the company lost 5 killed and 8 wounded; 12 Japanese dead were counted.

Meanwhile on the coast a series of encircling moves was made cutting the enemy's track behind him. Finally two platoons which had made a wide flanking move reached the coast north of the Gillman River and on the night 20th-21st February the enemy force south of that river withdrew. On the 22nd the 31st/51st (except Downs' company which remained until the 25th) was relieved by the 26th Battalion.[5]

> Papers captured during the operation suggested that the Japanese force on the Genga consisted of about 140 men in December and was reinforced to 390 in January. After the war, however, Japanese officers said that about 900 men, under Lieut-Colonel Shinzo Nakamura, "a master of jungle warfare", were concentrated in the Genga River area to halt any advance up the coast. It was decided not to attempt to deny to the Australians the country south of the Genga area but to stagger them by a sudden show of power on the line of the river. Artillery was brought forward, and a strong position was constructed on Tsimba Ridge, with a flanking force in the Kunamatoro area. The Japanese estimated the Australian force fairly accurately at one battalion with from six to eight guns. The long action was fought with determination on both sides. A Japanese officer stated afterwards that he did not think it possible that the Australians could have received such punishment and still have persisted in their attacks. Nakamura's eventual withdrawal was not considered a defeat but "a necessary tactical move caused by the infiltration of a small enemy group north of the Genga about three-quarters of a mile inland" (presumably Downs' company).

The Corps staff asked Stevenson in the third week of February to capture a Japanese prisoner from one of the islands off the north-west coast with the object of obtaining information. Petats Island, where there were only one or two Japanese, was chosen, and on the night of the 20th-21st February an Angau patrol under Captain Cambridge,[6] accompanied

---
[5] From 17th January to 26th February the 31st/51st Battalion lost 34 killed and 91 wounded. It was estimated that 148 Japanese were killed.

[6] Capt R. C. Cambridge, VX81159. "Z" and "M" Special Units; Angau. Plantation inspector; of Bougainville; b. Windsor, NSW, 11 Aug 1901.

by Major Sampson[7] of the 31st/51st, was landed on the island from a barge and captured a lone sentry. This raid caused the natives on the island to fear reprisals and accordingly the island was again visited on the night of the 24th, four Japanese who had just arrived from Buka were killed, and the 376 native inhabitants removed.

It will be recalled that a party of veteran scouts led by Lieutenant Bridge, R.A.N.V.R., had been ordered to operate behind the enemy's lines in northern Bougainville. Bridge, with Sergeant McPhee and twelve native soldiers led by Sergeant-Major Yauwiga, left Torokina on 24th November,

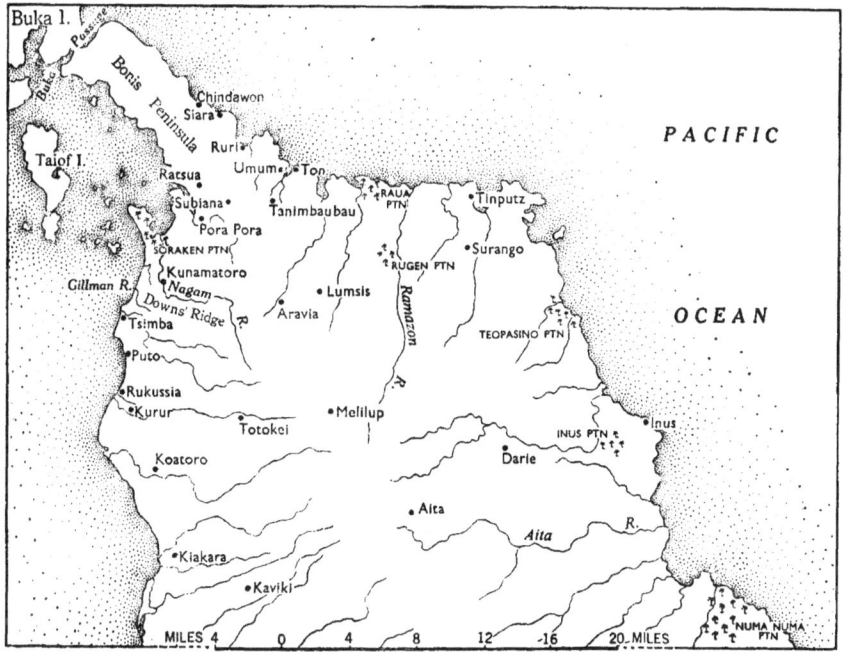

climbed into the mountains, and established a base camp at Aita whence they renewed acquaintance with old friends among the natives. On 12th December they were joined by Flying Officer Sandford's party, which included, as mentioned earlier, Sergeants Wigley and McEvoy of the A.I.F. From the base Sandford sent his men towards Numa Numa, but his operations were interrupted when an aircraft crashed near Aita on 20th December and he had to return to Torokina with the sole survivor. Later in December Bridge's party made two raids on a Japanese camp at Tanimbaubau and rescued 60 Indian prisoners of war, from whom they learnt that the Japanese had shot more than 40 Indian prisoners as a warning after a few (as mentioned earlier) had escaped. As a result

---

[7] Maj R. G. Sampson, MC, QX6063. 2/1 MG Bn 1939-42; 2/3 MG Bn 1942-45; 31/51 Bn 1945. Bank officer; of Launceston, Tas; b. Launceston, 12 May 1914.

of information wirelessed by Bridge's party New Zealand aircraft attacked the camp and killed some 60 Japanese. "Another success at this time," says a report, "was the removal of seven native Kempei (military police agents) who had long worked with the Japanese. Sergeant-Major Yauwiga[8] circulated the rumour that these had been 'double-crossing' the enemy by supplying him with information. On hearing this the Japanese had their agents executed."

A military force usually advances along an "axis", an imaginary line pointing the direction in which the main body is moving, and there are a centre and two flanks, although mountains, the sea or some other obstacle may press the flanks close to the main body. It is difficult, however, to describe the coming operations in the southern sector of Bougainville in these terms. The ultimate objective lay to the south in the Buin area, and to that extent the axis of the advancing force, making its successive landings along the coast, was a north-south line. But enemy forces were concentrated along the east-west rivers and tracks and thus the force, as it moved south, faced east—like a crab. Indeed the hand-painted cover of the musty typewritten "History of Operations—29th Australian Infantry Brigade—29th November 1944-23rd January 1945" shows a large red crab superimposed on a map of the southern end of Empress Augusta Bay; his body rests on the coast, his large left claw grasps the Jaba River, his right reaches for the Puriata, one antenna extends towards Sisiruai on the Tavera, the other towards Makotowa on the Hupai.

This diagram shows the position reached by the brigade in late January. But when, on 23rd December, its role was changed from reconnaissance to attack, the crab lay along the beach north of the Jaba mouth to the mouth of the Tavera, seized on 21st December. Its left claw grasped the Kupon Road at a point about three miles from the Jaba mouth, its right enclosed the Tuju-Tavera area.

The two remaining battalions of the 29th Brigade were now moved south from Torokina, the 47th being made responsible for the country north of the Jaba, the 42nd for the rear area back to the Chop Chop trail. From 22nd December the whole of the 2nd Field Regiment (Lieut-Colonel Parker[9]) was under the command of the 29th Brigade.

On Christmas Day a patrol of the New Guinea Battalion reached the mouth of the Adele River and formed a base there—"Advanced Base A". Next day a further base was established at the mouth of the Hupai, but it was strongly attacked and by the 27th the New Guinea platoon there was withdrawn north of the Tavera. However, the native troops and police were daily proving their value. In December Captain Johnson's company killed 41 Japanese and brought in 8 prisoners. Strong patrols moved stealthily deep into enemy-held country and individual guides were attached to Australian patrols. When natives were employed the chance

---

[8] Yauwiga, an outstanding soldier, was later awarded the D.C.M. for his work during these operations.
[9] Col A. E. H. Parker, DSO, ED, VX104253. CO 2 Fd Regt. Dispatch clerk; of Hampton, Vic; b. Richmond, Vic, 19 Jan 1901.

of being surprised by the enemy was small. Until early in February only two native soldiers of the New Guinea Battalion were killed on Bougainville—one accidentally by an aircraft of the R.N.Z.A.F. whose pilot fired on men seen on a beach, and another when he met a patrol of the 2/8th Commando.[10] None were killed in a clash with the enemy, though they had killed scores of Japanese. Long before a Japanese patrol or ambush knew they were near, the silently-moving natives would be aware of their presence and fade into the bush. It seemed to their European leaders that they possessed another sense denied to Europeans or Japanese. The natives were in good heart. They looked up to Europeans but despised the Japanese, whom they regarded as belonging to an inferior race, a result partly of the Japanese neglect of cleanliness, and partly of their custom of behaving towards the natives as though they were equals. The New Guinea natives could not conceive of people so different being their equals, and, as they did not behave as superiors should, decided that they must be of some lesser breed.

On 28th December Brigadier Monaghan gave orders for a deep advance along the coast; the 15th Battalion was to seize the south bank of the Tavera River with one company, and, if opportunity occurred, to seize the log crossing—Peeler's Post—on the Mendai Track north of the river. Next day a company of the 15th was landed south of the Tavera in spite of heavy seas; Peeler's Post was occupied, and an advance was made by Captain McDonald's[1] company of the 47th Battalion up the Jaba River. Its task was to establish a firm base on the track about half way to the junction with the Pagana and destroy an enemy pocket of resistance which had been holding up the advance along the Jaba. A platoon of the 1st New Guinea Battalion was placed under command with the special task of cutting the signal line from the Japanese post to Japanese headquarters.

A platoon of McDonald's company made several attacks on the enemy post on the 29th but came under heavy fire the origin of which was hard to find because of the dense undergrowth. Meanwhile company headquarters and one platoon had established an ambush east of the Japanese position and the attacking platoon withdrew to a position near by. The company repulsed attacks on the night of the 29th-30th and on the morning of the 30th the Japanese opened fire with a light gun and McDonald and two others were wounded.[2]

The company began to withdraw but encountered an enemy party astride the track. After a sharp fight the Australians dispersed the enemy and reached the battalion perimeter. Meanwhile the company's second-in-command, Captain Wade-Ferrell,[3] had led out a small party to carry

---

[10] This may be regarded as an exception to a claim by the 2/8th Commando that throughout the whole campaign no native was killed while patrolling with it, though it constantly had native groups under command.

[1] Brig S. M. McDonald, MC, VX114129; 47 Bn. Trust officer; of Geelong, Vic; b. Geelong, 12 Jan 1912.

[2] Corporal Owen Russell, MM (of Neutral Bay, NSW), distinguished himself during counter-attacks, continuing to lead his section though twice wounded.

[3] Lt-Col D. H. Wade-Ferrell, MC, NX104287; 47 Bn. Bank officer; of Pymble, NSW; b. Sydney, 13 Feb 1916.

rations and water to the forward troops. They encountered Japanese whom they dispersed after a short engagement. This party then also regained the perimeter.

On the extreme southern wing Lieutenant Rutherford's[4] platoon of the 15th Battalion which, on the 30th, was forming a base south of the Adele from which patrols of New Guinea troops were to probe south and east, was sharply attacked and its communications cut.

A carrier pigeon arrived at battalion headquarters from Rutherford with a message asking for assistance.[5] Lieutenant Moore[6] with a platoon was sent to bring in the isolated men. At 7.20 p.m. Moore was within 30 yards or so of the Japanese who were encircling the isolated Australians and "endeavoured by use of vernacular and slang to persuade 17 Platoon to permit them to enter perimeter", but "every attempt greeted by grenades, Owen and Bren fire". At length the relieving platoon was ordered to return to its company's perimeter, where it arrived some two hours later. The Japanese departed, however, and next morning Rutherford's platoon was withdrawn by barge. Three of its members had been wounded, including Rutherford, but the bodies of 17 Japanese were later found in the neighbourhood.

On 31st December the 42nd Battalion began relieving the 47th to allow it to move down the coast to support the 15th. Meanwhile the 2/8th Commando was arriving in the Jaba area to take over the protection of Monaghan's inland flank.

Each day there were sharp clashes between Australian and Japanese patrols on the tracks south of the Jaba, but the Australians were steadily gaining control of a larger area.[7] On 4th January General Bridgeford instructed Brigadier Monaghan to capture Mawaraka, establish a firm base there and clear the southern hook of Empress Augusta Bay. The 61st Battalion of Field's brigade was to take responsibility for the area between the Tagessi and the Jaba and thus the whole of the 29th would be free to operate south of the Jaba. Monaghan's brigade was re-deployed and by 8th January the 47th was forward with the 15th in support, the 42nd was

---

[4] Lt G. A. Rutherford, VX142225; 15 Bn. Medical student; of Melbourne; b. Melbourne, 9 Jul 1920.

[5] The Corps of Signals Pigeon Service was formed in Australia early in 1942, initially with the object of providing an alternative means of communication between the coast defences of the mainland in an invasion. The service was manned by pigeon fanciers, and pigeon fanciers presented birds to the army until the service possessed 13,500. After the service had established a network covering a great part of the continent, No. 8 Pigeon Section was sent to New Guinea in December 1942. It was found that birds from the south often became ill in New Guinea and local breeding lofts were established. Many other problems produced by the tropical environment were encountered and overcome. For example there were places where birds had to rise 2,000 feet in three miles possibly in rain or mist. The service provided lofts for formations of the Sixth American Army at Saidor, Arawe and Manus, as well as for Australian formations elsewhere in New Guinea.

Pigeons gave particularly valuable service when on several occasions they carried messages from small craft that were in trouble. They were most useful to the 5th Division when it was widely dispersed between Madang and the Sepik. On Bougainville pigeons of No. 1 Section were used by patrols, by small craft, and to carry war correspondents' reports which otherwise would have taken 48 hours to get back to Torokina. In the Torricellis on one occasion six pigeons were dropped by parachute to a patrol that was out of communication and one of them carried a message 45 miles in 50 minutes.

[6] Lt K. W. Moore, QX7360. 2/2 A-Tk Regt and 15 Bn. Clerk; of Brisbane; b. Brisbane, 13 Apr 1917.

[7] In a long fight between a platoon of the 15th and about 20 Japanese on 31st December three Australians were killed, including Private Donald Peeler, son of Staff-Sergeant Walter Peeler, VC, then aged 57 and a prisoner of the Japanese. Peeler's Post was named after Private Peeler.

well south of the Jaba, the 2/8th Commando round the Jaba mouth, the 61st north of it.

Meanwhile, on 5th January, an ambush had been set by a platoon of the 47th at Oxley Ambush[8] on the Jaba-Tuju track and other moves were

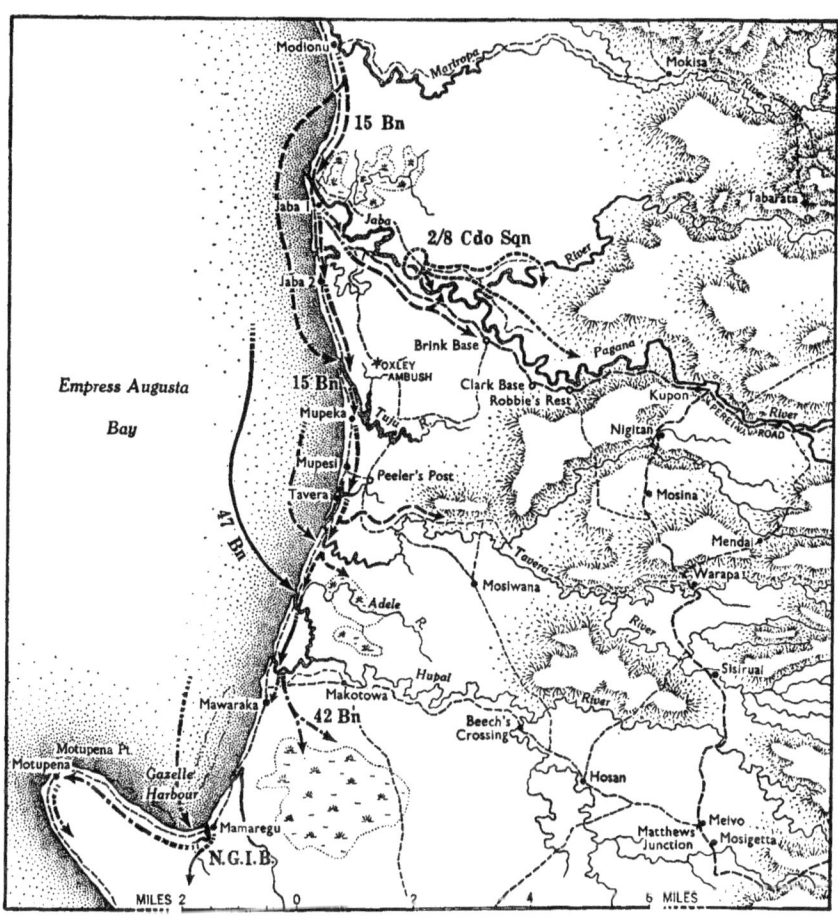

29th Brigade, January 1945

ordered with the object of clearing the Japanese track junctions south of the Jaba. Next day Monaghan recorded "complete success". A company of the 47th occupied "Base A" at the mouth of the Adele (where it counted the bodies of 27 Japanese killed in the earlier fighting), and the mouth of the Tavera was strongly occupied. On 8th and 9th January, as the 15th advanced along the Mendai Track, a road was cut with a bulldozer from the Tavera toward the Adele "in record time" to support the 47th moving south.

[8] Named after Lieutenant P. H. G. Oxley of the 15th.

Lieutenant Light's[9] New Guinea platoon was ordered to cross the Adele on the 9th and Captain Hibberd's[1] company of the 47th was to follow, to discover whether the enemy held the south bank. Light's platoon crossed at 7.35 p.m. on the 9th and were fired on by a machine-gun but, edging forward, found the south bank abandoned. At 8.30 p.m. Hibberd's company landed from a barge on the beach south of the Adele and were being guided forward by Light when an enemy party opened fire.

> The enemy here had a decided advantage situated as he was in a defensive position whilst our troops had only a vague idea of the country (wrote a diarist). The night was pitch black. . . . Troops were obliged to move in single file and . . . hold on to each other's bayonets. Two attempts were made to encircle the enemy—one from the beach and one from the river . . . hampered by lightning flashes which revealed each movement.

At length the company was withdrawn, its role was reconnaissance, and, in any event, there did not seem to be time to dig in before daylight. That evening a Japanese gun opened fire—the first encountered in this area—and its shells caused seven casualties at forward headquarters.

On the 10th Monaghan sent forward to Major Gregory,[2] temporarily commanding the 47th, four anti-tank and two field guns to fire point-blank at the enemy's positions in thick scrub across the Adele. At 6.20 a.m. on the 11th these guns pounded the enemy's posts at ranges of 600 to 800 yards and Japanese guns replied. At 8.20, after Corporal Keed[3] had secured a rope on the south bank in full view of the enemy, a platoon crossed the river by assault boat, supported by mortar and machine-gun fire, and without loss. Next day, however, the forward companies were sharply shelled, and enemy pill-boxes were encountered. They lost 8 killed and 31 wounded but pressed on and seized the Hupai mouth and a log crossing over that river some 800 yards inland.

Monaghan now considered the stage set for the capture of Mawaraka. On 13th January, however, Bridgeford ordered him to halt and secure his position, and to send not more than one battalion of infantry and no artillery south of the Adele. Prisoners' statements, captured papers and patrol reports suggested that the enemy was reinforcing the Kupon-Nigitan-Mendai area on the Australian flank, and the Mawaraka area, and that a strong counter-attack seemed likely. In addition to slowing down the 29th Brigade's advance, Bridgeford sent the 2/8th Commando inland to reconnoitre the Kupon-Mosina-Sisiruai area and discover what the enemy was about. Only one company of the 47th was left south of the Adele.

However, the threat did not develop and patrols pressed on. On the 16th a platoon of the 47th led by Lieutenant Mullaly[4] crossed the

---

[9] Lt M. E. Light, NX106816. 22 Bn and 1 NG Inf Bn. Photographer; of Tamworth, NSW; b. Nambour, Qld, 7 Aug 1916.

[1] Lt-Col H. D. Hibberd, VX104351; 47 Bn. Bank officer; of Bendigo, Vic; b. Malvern, Vic, 11 Mar 1919.

[2] Maj R. C. Gregory, QX6183. 2/2 A-Tk Regt 1940-43; 47 Bn 1943-45. Manufacturer's agent; of Brisbane; b. Brisbane, 22 Dec 1909.

[3] Cpl B. K. Keed, Q101039; 47 Bn. Carpenter; of Inglewood, Qld; b. Coogee, NSW, 29 Sep 1912.

[4] Lt A. E. C. Mullaly, MC, QX35765; 47 Bn. Farmer; of Gympie, Qld; b. Queensland, 19 Jan 1913.

Hupaisapani—the southern mouth of the Hupai—and, supported by mortars, overcame pill-boxes barring the way to Mawaraka. Mullaly himself silenced two pill-boxes with grenades.

On 17th January the 42nd, which had been patrolling on the left flank, began to relieve the 47th; that day a patrol entered Mawaraka without opposition and reported that the enemy's positions were to the east in the direction of Makotowa.

In the following days a long-range patrol of the New Guinea Battalion landed from the sea and probed forward to Motupena Point, where they surprised a Japanese listening post. Meanwhile patrols had moved deep into the Sisiruai area. On the morning of 19th January a patrol led by Lance-Sergeant Cooper[5] of the 15th Battalion with native guides returned to his company having penetrated, he believed, about ten miles into the enemy's area. About 3,000 yards from the base he had come to a deserted village, called by the natives Old Sisiruai 2. Thence they advanced to Sisiruai proper where the Australians saw some 75 Japanese, but were not observed. They went on to a third village, and returned without having been seen. On the 19th Bridgeford ordered Monaghan not to advance beyond Mawaraka, but to await relief by the 7th Brigade.[6]

Meanwhile the 42nd Battalion had been patrolling forward of Mawaraka. On 19th January three patrols set out. One, under Lieutenant P. E. Steinheuer, went through Mawaraka, and along the Mosigetta Road. Lieutenant Collier's[7] platoon moved south through the bush to strike the same road farther east and Lieutenant Lindsay's[8] to strike the road still farther east. They reported the road to be overgrown but capable of carrying trucks. Later all three patrols clashed with Japanese. Lindsay's found a group of pill-boxes surrounded by wire and attacked and took the position, killing seven Japanese. Lindsay remained there and was joined by Collier. The map was so faulty that Lieut-Colonel Byrne was doubtful exactly where they were and a patrol which was sent out to find them was ambushed. Next day (the 20th) the position was found and relieved and patrols moved farther east. Lieutenant Courtney[9] established a post 500 yards farther along the track. On the 23rd the relief of the 29th Brigade by the 7th began and was completed four days later.

In December General Hyakutake ordered the abandonment of Shortland and Fauro Islands so that he could strengthen his reserve at Buin where 70 per cent of the force was now concentrated. He decided that the enemy was determined to conquer Bougainville and realised that the decisive battles must be fought in the south. He ordered, however, that no major battle was yet to be fought even in the southern sector; the object for the present was to delay the enemy and cause him as many casualties as possible.

[5] L-Sgt R. W. F. Cooper, VX117753; 15 Bn. Grocer; of Nhill, Vic; b. Nhill, 16 Jun 1922.
[6] Casualties in the 29th Brigade in these operations were 10 officers and 138 other ranks; 40 men were killed and 108 wounded. It was estimated that 236 Japanese were killed; 8 were captured.
In the first few weeks the 42nd Battalion lost an officer and 7 men drowned when a ferry sank crossing the Tagessi, and one man killed and 7 wounded when a grenade was accidentally exploded.
[7] Lt J. A. Collier, MC, VX8980. 2/5 and 42 Bns. Nurseryman; of St Kilda, Vic; b. Sale, Vic, 30 Aug 1916.
[8] Lt D. C. Lindsay, MC, VX104190; 42 Bn. Orchardist; of Red Hill South, Vic; b. Cowes, Isle of Wight, 18 Dec 1918.
[9] Lt D. A. Courtney, VX104421; 42 Bn. Tea taster; of East Malvern, Vic; b. London, 6 Jan 1921.

"Army staff officers although fully agreeing with the G.O.C's observations were at a loss to account for the allied policy and felt that the actions would make no impression on the course of the war and were absolutely pointless."[1]

When, during January, the Australians continued to advance along the coast the possibility of a sea-borne attack began to seem remote. After the abandonment of Mawaraka the Japanese commanders decided that the time had come to make stronger delaying attacks and risk greater loss of life.

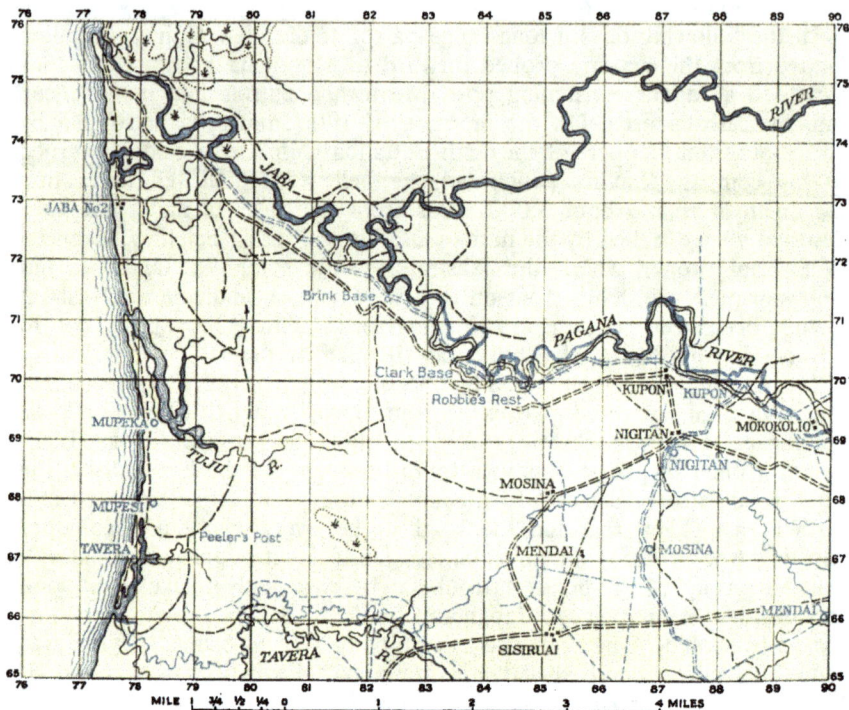

Pagana River area. Corrections and additions to the map originally supplied to the troops are shown in blue.

The possibility of carrying out a sea-borne attack to speed up operations by landing behind the Japanese was fully considered by II Corps. It had to be abandoned as there were insufficient craft to transport troops and ensure their subsequent maintenance. It was considered that any such landing, to be effective, would have had to be made in brigade strength at least.

From 6th January onwards the 2/8th Commando Squadron had relieved companies of the 42nd Battalion to enable them to take part in the southward push. Major Winning considered his new role a somewhat imposing one for such a force.

The area, previously held by a battalion, was large and the responsibility great for a unit of squadron strength without support weapons (he wrote). On 10

---
[1] 23rd Brigade, History of the Japanese Occupation of Bougainville, March 1942-August 1945.

January 4 Battery 2 Aust Field Regiment was placed in support . . . and the doubtful position greatly relieved. Owing to the paucity of information received from 42 Battalion, it was necessary to have patrols traverse and plot the track systems in the immediate vicinity. These two factors prevented long-range patrolling. . . . Most activity was in the B Troop area where patrols made contact on five days along the Perei Road, each time striking the enemy in ambush and finding extreme difficulty, due to the pit-pit (sago) swamps, in manoeuvring off the track. Almost nightly enemy harassed our perimeter, setting off booby-traps and throwing grenades.

From the 6th to the 13th in nine clashes 10 Japanese were killed; one Australian was killed and 5 were wounded.[2]

On 15th January, it will be recalled, the squadron was given a new task: active reconnaissance of the Kupon, Nigitan, Mosina, Mendai, Sisiruai areas, but on the 23rd this was altered to securing Tadolina and Sovele Mission, thus again protecting the flank of the brigade on the coast. The leading section arrived at Sovele on 25th January.

In occasional touch with Winning's squadron on the inland flank were two irregular forces—Angau patrols whose roles were to collect information and do what they could to rescue natives from occupied areas, and Lieutenant Mason's force of tried scouts and natives who had been allotted the mountain area above Kieta.

Winning and Mason, the two commanders in the mountain area, had much in common, and, in particular, each was restless under authority.

Each of these leaders possessed boundless energy, resource and confidence in his own ability and, it appears, his own indestructibility (wrote one who knew them then). Each was contemptuous to a degree of what Winning referred to as "red tape" and other less printable terms. Each invariably saw immediately the shortest route through any difficulty and took it. Winning was constrained by his command to move discreetly, but Mason who knew to the nth degree his own immense value in the campaign, imposed his own conditions and expected them to be met. On those occasions when he was under orders with which he did not agree, he ignored them, arguing that he was the man on the spot and therefore had a better idea of what was needed.

Each man had a thorough understanding of the natives whose friendship was so vital to his role in the campaign. Winning had learned his campaigning in New Guinea with an earlier commando squadron, while Mason had been a planter in the Kieta district of Bougainville. Each had the faculty of inspiring confidence and cooperation in the men he commanded, and each became a legend in his lifetime. It is not surprising that relations of these two men really never progressed beyond the stage of polite toleration, although they worked hand in hand throughout the campaign.

Mason set out with Sergeant Warner,[3] Corporal White[4] and thirty-three natives on 29th November along the Tagessi River. On 4th December he sent his sixteen carriers back to Torokina and continued to Lamparan with local natives carrying. He avoided Orami (whence could be seen Empress Augusta Bay from Torokina to Motupena Point) because the Japanese had a large garden there, and went on over the Crown Prince Range to

---
[2] Corporal Peter Pinney was an outstanding patrol leader in this phase and later.
[3] Sgt K. O. Warner, MM, NX54733; AIB. Farmer and grazier; of Boggabri, NSW; b. Boggabri, 26 Mar 1907.
[4] Sgt B. White, DCM, VX45139. 1 Indep Coy and AIB. Farmer; of Cobden, Vic; b. Mornington, Vic, 24 May 1912.

Sipuru, about 3,500 feet, where, he now knew, the natives, armed largely with captured Japanese rifles, were waging war against the Japanese. At Sipuru the newcomers learnt from the native leader of the Kapikavi people that there were 50 Japanese living on gardens in the neighbourhood, and the Kapikavi natives would have killed them but, hearing of Mason's coming, they considered that they should wait to ask permission. Mason told the native leader to give the enemy an opportunity to surrender and wirelessed to his senior at Torokina, Flight Lieutenant Robinson, Deputy Supervising Intelligence Officer for the Northern Solomons, asking that food be dropped if the enemy surrendered. Robinson replied advising Mason to refrain from guerilla tactics —"the main object at present is to get out informa-

tion and remain unobserved". Mason replied: "There is a war on here."

After this (he wrote later) we carried on in the usual way, but did not report killings, as we could hardly stop here with the enemy being killed all round us, without taking some part.

The Japanese in the Kapikavi country refused to surrender, whereupon the natives killed ten and besieged the survivors. Mason's native scouts brought in five natives who had worked for the Japanese as police. These men had travelled widely and knew much about the enemy's strength and defences, and he enlisted three of them. He was distressed to find that the natives in the area, having obeyed advice contained in propaganda leaflets up to two years before, had left the enemy, then had been hounded from one garden after another and were starving. Mason considered it a grave mistake to tell natives to leave the enemy when there was no plan to rehabilitate them and, a law unto himself in his own territory, always told them to remain with the enemy until the time was ready to revolt. He appealed to Torokina for food for "many native women and children starving owing to having left the Japanese and their gardens", and added: "The men are doing a great job. Have ceased to report their killings. Natives keeping the enemy from the hills and food . . . over a hundred women and children around us starving. All their men are away fighting the Nips." As a result food was dropped.

Mason complained at this stage of delay in obtaining supplies from Torokina. At Torokina Robinson worked under the general direction of the Allied Intelligence Bureau, but under the command of II Corps, and was finding that II Australian Corps was not as easy to work with, from his point of view, as XIV American Corps had been. The American corps had given the A.I.B. group all the equipment it wanted and allowed it great latitude. The II Corps staff at this stage wished to direct its activities in detail. Robinson who was acting under instructions from G.H.Q. sought to be paraded to Savige, who instructed his staff that the A.I.B. were to gain Intelligence in their own way and to be given cooperation. "Although there were some pinpricks later and a certain amount of jealousy," wrote Robinson later, "matters between our organisation and II Australian Corps were cordial, General Savige, Brigadier Garrett and Colonel Wilson were always very helpful and I will go as far as to say appreciative of any efforts we achieved," but the range of stores obtainable was still "very restricted". Robinson recorded also that "warnings of what the north-west season would do to some of [II Corps] beach positions, roads and river bridges was given but unfortunately not accepted".[5]

Meanwhile in Mason's area on 17th December a Japanese patrol twenty-three strong came to Orami (Mason knew that the enemy had found one of his camps near by). Natives harassed the patrol, killing one and wounding six, whom the survivors carried back the way they had come. The previous day natives had ambushed and killed six Japanese.

Before the war Mason, when manager of a plantation at Inus, had known Wong You, a Chinese storekeeper at Kieta. Wong You was now interned at Kieta with other fellow-countrymen. Being within range of Kieta, Mason wrote an unsigned note to Wong You advising him to escape. This was passed by hand from one native to another until it reached Wong You. Three days later (18th December) Mason received a reply, unaddressed and signed "Inus Store", saying that Wong and thirty-five others would escape that night. This Wong did with all but one of his thirty-five. Mason wrote afterwards:

> On 23rd December at 2 p.m. Wong You, carrying his baby son and accompanied by a Cantonese coolie who had escaped from the Japanese with the Bougainville Chinese, arrived at our camp. I had known Wong for over twenty years. He was a capable, friendly, humorous self-made Chinese merchant about 50 years old, of some standing in Kieta. . . . He states that he owed his life to Tashiro, Japanese Intelligence Officer, who had told the officer in charge, who had accused Wong of withholding information concerning myself, that "this man has known Mason twenty years. You he has known only a day. You cannot expect him to betray a lifelong friend to a stranger." Wong, a former shadow of himself with drawn face which was covered with tinea, arrived with a smile on his face and a joke on his lips.

The other Chinese had been left on another track, in accordance with Mason's instructions. There were 11 men, 5 women and 18 children, all

---

[5] A.I.B., Report on Bougainville-New Ireland-Choiseul (B.S.I.P.) Network, 21 Sep 44 to 31 May 1945.

in pitiful condition, having had a ration of 12 pounds of sweet potato a week. Even so they had broken out of the compound and made the long climb to safety. Mason was unsure how the Japanese guard had been disposed of and seems not to have questioned Wong closely, but it appeared that the Chinese had given the guard something to drink that night before the escape.

In the meantime Mason and his agents had induced natives carrying Japanese ammunition and supplies along the tracks from Buin to Numa Numa to desert, and at length had 400 natives and the 35 Chinese assembled at various places in their area, and all had to be fed.

> Information now came that there was a large enemy patrol at Orami (Mason wrote afterwards), another from Kaino coming via Forma, and yet another at Kovidau, who I suspected were searching for the Chinese. They had been planning for some time, according to our information, a mopping-up of the "fifth column" as our natives were called.

Meanwhile a Wirraway that had been sent to drop Christmas rations to Mason crashed. At noon a native brought him a note from Flight Lieutenant Cory[6] and Flying Officer Tucker,[7] the crew, both of whom were injured. So fast did Mason's couriers bring him news that he was reading the note as Torokina began to wireless that the aircraft was overdue. Mason told Cory and Tucker to lie low for the present in the care of the ever-loyal natives of Mau; so they nursed their severe injuries, lived on the cake and Christmas puddings their aircraft had been carrying, and regularly sent cheerful letters to Mason.

Late on Christmas Day natives brought the alarming news that several Japanese patrols had begun to reach the area. The refugee natives fled. Mason, with a small selected party, carried the vital wireless equipment higher into the mountains until they halted on a ridge at 4,000 feet. Next day, believing the Japanese had withdrawn, they returned, but found a patrol of twenty-six Japanese in their old area and marched to Darena. Here, however, difficulties arose with the local natives because of sectarian feeling: the local natives were Roman Catholics and most of those with Mason were Seventh Day Adventists and Methodists, and were refused food. Mason therefore moved down the Luluai River to a hiding-place.

> The food question had now become grave, so we packed off 200 refugees to Torokina and put the Chinese on the road also. . . . I saw all of [the Chinese] as they stumbled by . . . on the road to Tabarata (where an Angau party was to receive them). The island Chinese girls and women are usually shy but these "fell over me" in an endeavour to express their gratitude. They bowed, Japanese fashion, with every word they uttered. . . . They were all in a pitiful condition, barefooted, with an odd assortment of covering. . . . Some natives died on the road, others left their children to die in the bush. One little naked emaciated girl we found was given to natives to care for.

---

[6] F-Lt G. R. I. Cory, DFC. 76, 75, 23, 21 and 5 Sqns. Grazier; of Dalveen, Qld; b. Grafton, NSW, 2 Aug 1910.

[7] F-Lt W. H. Tucker. 33, 38 and 5 Sqns. Schoolteacher; of Bundaberg, Qld; b. Childers, Qld, 3 Jan 1913.

The Chinese refugees reached the area patrolled by the 2/8th Commando on 3rd January, men of the commando and Angau having met them at Tabarata.[8]

A Wirraway dropped "storepedoes" on 31st December and again on 2nd January. As a result Mason's party had enough food for a week or two, provided the 200 natives remaining with him went back to their home areas and took their chances with the Japanese, which they did. On 1st January Cory and Tucker, both still handicapped by their painful injuries, had joined Mason, and on the 3rd Corporal White, with scouts and carriers, set off with them to the Tabarata rendezvous, where they were handed over to the army.

During this time the redoubtable Kapikavi men continued to besiege the Japanese. They now sent news that a column of about 100 Japanese from Buin had marched out to relieve the garrison, but the Kapikavi had ambushed them in a ravine and pelted them with grenades. Only fifteen managed to return to Buin; the others scattered or were killed. An air attack on the Japanese garrison called for by Mason destroyed all the Japanese huts except one, but the Japanese fled to the shelter of a creek while the bombing was in progress.

On the 5th Mason received a signal pointing out that II Corps wanted information from the Buin area and the Siwai District to the west of it which was to be Mason's next area of operations, and adding: "Don't want to stick your neck out unduly." This "riled" Mason; he replied that he would need more men if he was to cover both areas and asked for Sergeant Wigley, Corporal Thompson[9] and Corporal Matthews[1] or the American, Staff-Sergeant Nash, with ten scouts. He was told that they were not available, whereupon he replied that it was

not practical to cover Buin-Siwai from here. Added to our present area would represent three-quarters of Bougainville.

Thus Mason had a triple responsibility: to obtain information for II Corps, to care for the natives over a wide area, and to support a guerilla war that at times was severe and widespread. In January there was much fighting in the headwaters of the Aropa River, where, in one week, twenty-four Japanese were killed. In mid-January some fifty Japanese marched on Forma to raid gardens. "An ambush got four with arrows in the stomach. 'They have got no medicine for that,' the natives said."

---

[8] At this stage native refugees were reaching the coast in considerable numbers. On 14th January Colonel Matthews of the 9th Battalion, which then had a company at Hanemo, wrote in his diary: "At tea time a native police boy came in with an American carbine at the slope, slapped the butt as salute to the Angau officer (Captain F. N. Boisen) and reported that he had completed his mission, which was to bring in the occupants of a native village two days' march away. It is the policy to withdraw complete villages and put the people in a native compound on the Laruma River. Able-bodied men become carriers, the sick are cared for, women and children are safe from Japs. The police boys had been out for 6 days with 2 other boys. About an hour later the village arrived. Old men, old women, all ages to babes in arms, with all the dogs and pigs they owned as well, in single file carrying their possessions on their backs . . . all types of lap laps, army singlets, etc. Dogs barked, pigs squealed, babies cried, natives jabbered and shouted. . . . Bully beef and biscuits issued to all."

[9] Cpl N. D. Thompson, NX34372. 1 Indep Coy and "M" Special Unit. Farm labourer; of Morpeth, NSW; b. West Maitland, NSW, 11 Feb 1915.

[1] Cpl J. Matthews, VX45044. 1 Indep Coy and "M" Special Unit. Dairy farmer; of Heywood, Vic; b. Heywood, 28 Apr 1914.

Mason arranged an air attack on Toborei, headquarters of the Japanese in the Kieta area, and his scouts marked the target with flags and smoke. The camp was wiped out and the natives, waiting in the surrounding bush, killed six Japanese who escaped the bombing. At the end of January, Mason and his group had been in the bush for two months.

The party inserted into Choiseul, where there were some 700 Japanese, consisted initially of Sub-Lieutenant Andresen, Sergeant Selmes,[2] both experienced scouts who knew the Solomons well, and a signaller. For eight days ending on 2nd December a patrol of the 7th Battalion from Mono Island, led by Lieutenant Rhoades[3] (R.A.N.V.R.) of the A.I.B. and Lieutenant Nicholson[4] of the 7th Battalion moved about on Choiseul guided by Andresen's native scouts. Andresen was withdrawn because of illness and later Rhoades took charge. The patrol armed increasing numbers of natives, carried on guerilla warfare and guided air strikes by the New Zealand squadrons. These harassing tactics appear to have been the reason why the Japanese in mid-1945 began to withdraw from Choiseul in barges by night.

---

[2] Sgt J. G. Selmes, NX8040. AASC 6 and 9 Divs; "M" Special Unit. Truck driver; of Gulargambone, NSW; b. Willoughby, NSW, 22 Mar 1915.

[3] Lt-Cdr F. A. Rhoades; RANVR. (1st AIF: Tpr 1 LH Regt 1916-19.) Coastwatcher, AIB. Plantation manager; of Guadalcanal, Solomon Is; b. North Sydney, 26 Jun 1895.

[4] Lt G. L. Nicholson, MM, WX1938. 2/11 and 7 Bns. Secretary; of Perth; b. Noongaar, WA, 30 Jun 1915.

CHAPTER 7

TO SLATER'S KNOLL AND SORAKEN

BY the third week of January the 3rd Division had advanced 13 miles and secured the coast as far south as Mawaraka. General Savige considered that the main enemy force would be unable to offer determined resistance north of the Puriata River, now some 10 miles beyond his leading forces, and that the hard crust of the enemy's defence would be met along that river. For the present, the Japanese were still holding at points on the tracks leading from the coast to the foothills along the three rivers to the north of the Puriata: the Pagana, Tavera, and Hupai. South of the Hupai was Mosigetta, a main track junction and the first of the enemy's big garden areas.

"The time has now arrived," General Savige wrote to General Bridgeford on 21st January, "when swift and vigorous action is necessary to fulfil the task allotted to you in Operation Instruction No. 3, paragraph 8" (the instruction issued on 23rd December). It will be recalled that this had stated that the ultimate role of the 3rd Division was "to destroy Japanese forces in southern Bougainville", and the immediate task was to advance to the Puriata and send patrols beyond it. Savige considered that the Japanese on Bridgeford's front were "weak and off balance".

On the inland flank the 2/8th Commando was now concentrating in the hill country at Sovele Mission whence it could operate from the east against the Japanese strung out between the Pagana and the Hupai while the infantry pressed from the west. On 1st February Savige suggested to Bridgeford that he should use the 2/8th Commando to secure crossings over the Puriata in its area, five miles and more from the coast, and to patrol to the Hongorai if possible; that he should use one battalion to secure a crossing farther west; and another to clear the inland tracks to Mosina and Nigitan. He wished to hold his tanks in reserve until the more open country farther south was reached. The tanks were old, spare parts were short, and he did not wish to wear the tanks out on tasks that infantry and artillery could do. He was considering landing a battalion (the 58th/59th under Lieut-Colonel Mayberry,[1] who had been trained in amphibious operations) at a point on the south coast whence it could cut the main track to Buin, but at length it was decided that there were not enough craft to execute this operation.

The task allotted to the 11th Brigade in the northern sector was to drive the enemy from that end of the island by advancing along the coast and not across the rugged country through which travelled the Numa Numa trail. Savige considered that he might eventually turn the corner and advance south towards Numa Numa.

---

[1] Lt-Col W. M. Mayberry, DSO, VX3272. 2/5 Bn; CO 58/59 Bn 1945. Jackeroo; of Jerilderie, NSW; b. London, 10 Mar 1915.

In the coming phase, as hitherto, only five of Savige's fifteen battalions would be in contact with the enemy. It was not possible to maintain more than those.

Already, on 23rd January, Bridgeford had given the 7th Brigade its roles: to take Mosigetta, clear the enemy from the Kupon-Nigitan-Sisiruai area, and patrol along the Puriata; the 2/8th Commando was to deny to the enemy the track system round Tadolina in the foothills to the east, protecting the flank of the brigade's advance on Mosigetta—a more modest and appropriate role than its former one of "active reconnaissance" into the area now allotted to the infantry. However, when Major Winning soon reported his new area free of the enemy, the squadron's task was again changed, on 2nd February, to reconnaissance of the Puriata crossings inland from a point about four miles from the coast. It was to be maintained by air-dropping until supply by road was possible. Brigadier Field, of the 7th Brigade, planned his operation in three phases. In the first the 61st Battalion would patrol east along the Pagana to Kupon, then south to Nigitan and Mosina; the 25th would patrol along the Tavera to the Mendai-Sisiruai area; the 9th would consolidate a base in the Mawaraka area and patrol. In the second phase the 61st would clear the enemy from the area from Kupon to Sisiruai, the 9th take Mosigetta, and the 25th protect the base at Mawaraka. In the third phase the brigade would be re-grouped for an advance to the Puriata.[2]

Even at this late stage of the war this big Australian force was short not only of heavy equipment such as landing craft and armour but of standard items of infantry equipment. When it began operations the 7th Brigade held only nine wireless sets (No. 108 Mark III of ancient vintage) and no walkie-talkie sets at all. It was entitled to 119 sets of various types including 90 light walkie-talkies.

> Wireless is not only an alternative means of communication (stated the brigade's report). In jungle warfare, patrolling plays an integral part. The use of [light walkie-talkie] sets on short patrols and "108" or "208" sets on long-range patrols is essential to good communication and rapid receipt of information . . . had further wireless sets been made available the amount of line laid (over 600 miles within the brigade) would have been considerably lessened thus obviating the acute shortage which was prevalent owing to transport difficulties.

Each of the tracks along which the battalions would travel was through dense bush, on land sloping up very gradually from the coast. For example, from the sea to Mosigetta the plain rose only some 50 feet above sea level, and for the first few miles about half the area was covered by deep swamp, constantly refilled by rain which, in January and February, fell almost every afternoon. From Beech's Crossing over a tributary of the Hupai the land was higher, and clad with tall trees and light undergrowth. Movement was easier there, and often men could see as much as 50 yards ahead. An old "Government road" led through the bush to

---

[2] The Order of Battle of the 7th Brigade Group on 26th January was: HQ 7 Bde, 9 Bn, 25 Bn, 61 Bn, 20 Pl "E" Coy 2/1 Gd Regt, 2 Fd Regt, 7 Bde Sig Sec, "A" Coy 1 NG Inf Bn, 19 Supply Depot Pl, two Secs 56 Transport Pl, 11 Fd Amb, 241 Light Aid Detachment, Angau detachment.

Mosigetta. Like most such tracks in this area it was from 10 to 15 feet wide and bounded on each side by a deep narrow ditch. In the timbered country the trees met above the track forming a green tunnel, and the secondary growth was so dense as to hide a man standing a yard or two off the track. When the infantry began patrolling forward the tracks were still carpeted with grass, but the jeeps and trucks that followed tore this up and churned the surface into deep mud. At length the worst sections of each track had to be "corduroyed"—paved with logs laid edge to edge —and over these the vehicles would lumber until, as the days passed, they pressed the logs deep into the mire.

The tracks were seldom visible from the air and consequently the targets against which aircraft could be used effectively were relatively few. Field made a practice of inviting each of the pilots of the reconnaissance aircraft to stay with his brigade for a few days and move along the tracks with the infantry so that they could see what the bush hid— roads wide enough to carry heavy trucks entirely concealed by the arching trees. In the Numa Numa sector Brigadier Stevenson organised similar tours for pilots, and also airmen, who enjoyed spending free days with the forward troops.

Along the edges of these tracks the infantry patrols silently advanced. When they met an enemy outpost there would be a burst of fire, then silence again. The advancing patrol would begin a wide outflanking move through the bush on either side of the track. Perhaps when the move had been carried out the enemy would have withdrawn, escaping encirclement. It was a common Japanese device to dig one post at the bole of a large tree and another covering post behind it, each with a narrow escape track cut through the bush and joining the main one behind a bend. When the man or men in the leading post came under heavy fire they could take to the escape track; the machine-gun in the covering post would briefly take up the fight until perhaps its crew also withdrew silently along its narrow pad to join the main track at a point invisible to the attackers. It was easy for the unwary to move along an empty, innocent-seeming track, right up to the forward men, the first warning being a quiet "psst" from the dense bush. "Where are you going?" "Up to Don Company." "We're it."

Part of the 61st Battalion had begun to move south from the Jaba on 15th January. On the 18th and 19th its patrols clashed with the enemy in the area of Brink Base, losing one man killed and two wounded, and killing eight "thin and ragged" Japanese. Thence the 61st advanced systematically, occupying a series of company bases, each ready to meet attack from any direction. On the night of the 23rd-24th, for example, some 40 Japanese probed forward round Clark Base, established that day about a mile forward of Brink Base.[3] Fire was exchanged and grenades thrown, and the Japanese cut the telephone line to battalion

---

[3] These bases were named after Lieutenants F. R. Brinkley and A. G. Clarkson (both of Brisbane).

headquarters, but when the fight was over no Australians had been hit; the Japanese, when they withdrew, left one wounded man behind. By the 30th the 61st had killed 20 Japanese, and their own losses had been 4 wounded in action and 3 in accidents. On 1st February a patrol of 6, including one native soldier, swung south towards Mosina and after moving 2,300 yards clashed with a Japanese force. Lieutenant H. D.

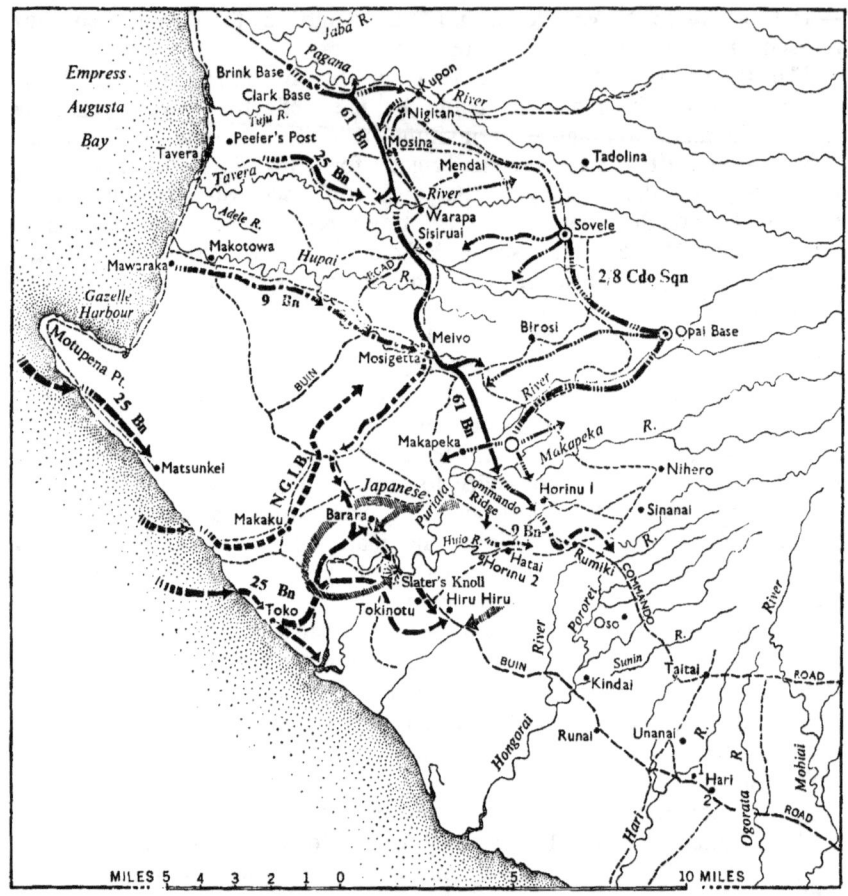

7th Brigade, January-March

Robinson was killed and the patrol withdrew. On the same day, however, other patrols reported Kupon empty of enemy troops and only four Japanese encountered between Kupon and Nigitan. Next day a platoon entered Kupon, the battalion's easternmost objective in this phase. The leading troops of the battalion were now being supplied along a long and muddy track, which the infantry pioneers, and the engineers following behind with their heavy equipment, were striving to improve. A good dropping ground existed near Kupon and on 9th February aircraft dropped some rations, and all were recovered; next day six days' rations for the whole battalion were dropped. On the 9th Mosina was entered.

Natives had reported some thirty Japanese at Warapa south of Mosina. A patrol was sent out, reached Warapa without being seen, and at dawn on the 11th poured fire into the huts there for five minutes, then withdrew. Later 15 bodies—and 13 swords—were found. On the 13th a patrol went to Mendai without meeting any Japanese.

> In all contacts to date (wrote Lieut-Colonel Dexter, commanding the 61st Battalion) the enemy had adopted hit and run tactics. On making contact, our forward troops have returned fire while remainder execute an outflanking move to cut track behind enemy. However, on each occasion the Jap had withdrawn before movement was completed. The counter measure appears to be a wide outflanking move on a previously recced route with the object of setting an ambush behind the enemy before contact is made.

Meanwhile the 2/8th Commando had been closing in from the east. The map was so inaccurate that the move to Sovele Mission placed the squadron 4,000 yards farther forward than was intended. The 61st Battalion were then advancing from Clark Base, some ten miles away. The 2/8th's base at Sovele was the first of a chain of similar bases which the squadron occupied. This one was on a high feature with plenty of open ground on which supplies from the air could be dropped, and had a good water supply near by. The two troops and headquarters formed a ragged perimeter enclosing a far greater area than would normally be considered consistent with safety, since the squadron's most formidable weapon of defence was the Bren. The safety of the position rested mainly on a thorough knowledge of the tracks leading into it, and a system of guards and observation posts manned by natives twenty-four hours a day. Refugees soon began to arrive from the surrounding hills, in long lines. They were laden with their few possessions and captured Japanese weapons, ranging from rifles to heavy machine-guns. Until they could be sent on to the coast, they camped inside the perimeter, and would have presented a considerable liability in the event of an attack, since a great proportion of them were women and children, or old and sick people. They brought information about pockets of Japanese settled in gardens in the area and were eager to help the soldiers exterminate them. At Sovele the squadron came into contact with Musiyama, a native leader who was to prove most valuable in smoothing over differences between the Nargovissi, who lived in the Sovele area, and the Siwais, in whose territory lay Nihero, a village already chosen by Major Winning as a future base.

From Sovele patrols moved out plotting tracks and investigating reports from the natives about enemy parties. After one such reconnaissance two sections led by Captain C. J. P. Dunshea of the 2/8th Commando and an Angau officer, Captain R. Watson, made a surprise attack on 26th January on a group of huts at a large garden. Of probably 25 Japanese who were there, 8 were killed in the fight, 3 next day, and the remainder fled. Useful documents were captured. Three days later another Japanese garden was raided and all 9 occupants killed.

These were promising successes, but Winning believed that his force had been set an unduly heavy task. He was responsible for flank protection of the main force and reconnaissance over a wide area; his base was important to the Angau detachment in its efforts to recover natives from Japanese-occupied areas. But his squadron was tired and depleted. (On the 29th a troop was ordered back to the Jaba mouth; it went there on rafts only to be ordered to return, and after an arduous march reached the base again on the 3rd and 4th February.) The enemy were fit, well-equipped and high-spirited, though it was to their disadvantage that their program compelled them to live in isolated groups cultivating gardens. Winning considered that his best course was to maintain a strong base, strike each scattered group of Japanese and return, maintain light reconnaissance to the west and south-west and security patrols to the south-east, and rely on the natives for information about the mountain areas to the east. Thus, on 2nd February, when (as mentioned above) he was ordered to secure crossings over the Puriata River without delay, Winning asked that an infantry company be based at Sovele, or that the squadron be required not to secure and hold crossings but to harass the enemy in the Makapeka fords area. Savige, however, was convinced that the squadron could secure the crossings. Being short both of men and suitable officers Winning reorganised the squadron into two troops[4] and formed a section of scouts from "old campaigners with good bush sense and ability to handle natives" who were to be given the more difficult reconnaissance tasks. Strong patrols examined the Sisiruai area, the headwaters of the Tavera River and gardens east of Mosigetta. A strong enemy force was found south of Birosi. Tracks along both banks of the upper Puriata were explored.

It will be recalled that the 25th Battalion was to patrol forward along the Tavera and link with the 61st in the Mendai-Sisiruai area. At the outset the company to which this task was allotted met determined opposition by an enemy force established about a mile from the coast on the track along the Tavera River. On 26th January a platoon attack was cancelled after one Australian had been killed and one wounded in an ambush. After each clash the enemy would change his position astride a track that was "little more than a wading passage through swamp knee to neck deep, with movement to either side barred by the swamp. Movement was by single file only."[5] However, patrols pushed gradually forward through this country and by 12th February were established one-third of the way to the Sisiruai villages; on the 14th a patrol from the 61st reached the 25th there.

The country along the Hupai through which the 9th Battalion had to advance was even more swampy than that through which the Tavera

---
[4] Even so he lacked a second-in-command and a signals officer.
[5] 25 Aust Inf Bn Report on Operations in South Bougainville, 16 Jan to 14 Apr 1945.

flowed. Soon after arriving on the Hupai and taking over from the 42nd Battalion, Lieut-Colonel Matthews of the 9th decided that the Japanese he faced were in small scattered groups whose role was to fight delaying actions. On 25th January Field told Matthews, whose main task was to protect the base at Mawaraka, that he might begin moving along the road to Mosigetta but must not go so far that he could not be supplied by jeep. Between Mawaraka and Makotowa lay deep swamps into which patrols of the 9th moved, often waist-deep in water, using pigeons to carry their signals back. On the 26th Matthews wrote:

> Werda's[6] patrol at lunchtime reported that they were in the middle of a swamp, five men exhausted, so I said to withdraw. Tonight they said they were in the middle of the swamp still, perched on trees trying to get some sleep. They will be in tomorrow. Clark's[7] patrol reported by pigeon this morning that they were in a swamp last night and were going to get out this morning. Later message said they were still on their way.

On his return Clark reported that his patrol ran short of food and had to eat the pigeons' blue peas.

That night from 20 to 30 Japanese attacked along the track, while three of their guns shelled the Australian positions farther back, firing some 40 rounds. (It was the first time this battalion had been under artillery fire.) The attack was repulsed, but though there was much firing no Japanese dead were found.

On 27th January patrols reached Makotowa and found Japanese digging in round the garden there. On the morning of the 28th Major Blanch's company of the 9th was sent forward along the Mosigetta Road to take and hold the track at this large garden area. As the leading platoon was circling it, the forward scout, Private Cameron,[8] was killed. While trying to outflank the enemy the leading platoon came under fire from three concealed pill-boxes and two more men were killed and three wounded. Blanch took up a perimeter position astride the road past the garden. A second company (Captain Gaul[9]) was sent forward to cut the track beyond Makotowa; but that evening reported that it had been halted by swamps.[1]

Indeed, during this phase, the infantry were moving along narrow islands in a huge swamp. There was no way of precisely mapping the boundaries of the islands except to patrol them, though aerial photographs helped. These photographs were assembled, sometimes at battalion headquarters, information from patrols was added, and at length each battalion created

---

[6] Lt E. C. Werda, QX55210; 9 Bn. Labourer; of Brisbane; b. Brisbane, 18 Aug 1918.

[7] Lt C. E. Clark, QX41900; 9 Bn. Insurance clerk; of Rockhampton, Qld; b. Rockhampton, 2 Aug 1912.

[8] Pte C. J. Cameron, NX118028; 9 Bn. Farmhand; of Llangothlin, NSW; b. Guyra, NSW, 9 Jun 1921. Killed in action 28 Jan 1945.

[9] Maj A. J. F. Gaul, NX116813; 9 Bn. Regular soldier; b. Warrnambool, Vic, 7 Aug 1915.

[1] On 28th January Captain J. C. Kerridge (of Cheltenham, NSW), the medical officer of the 9th Battalion, and a stretcher bearer were walking along the road 300 yards beyond a company position when they saw two Japanese armed with rifles sitting by the road. The Japanese made signs that they wished to surrender and the Australians disarmed them and took them back. They were thin, poorly clad and lacked boots, and when questioned said that they were artillerymen of the *6th Field Artillery*, who had recently been sent as riflemen to the *2nd Company* of the *13th Regiment*. They had surrendered, they said, because they resented being used as infantry, and because of the lack of food and medical care.

a new map of its own area of perhaps five miles by five. On these the patrols were "briefed". In this instance an aircraft was flown over the swamps south of Makotowa to ascertain the position of the reinforcing company which was found somewhat farther south than was intended. It reached the road east of Makotowa soon after midday on the 30th and during the afternoon parties of fully-equipped Japanese walked from the west into the position it established there; six were killed. It was evident that the enemy was abandoning Makotowa, and next day a jeep was driven along the track to the company east of that place.

In eight days the 9th had advanced 400 yards along the road to Mosigetta. Japanese tactics on these and the following days were to fight from ambush positions flanked by swamps and dense bush, to mine the track, and repeatedly cut the signal lines of the leading Australian groups. They counter-attacked at night using handlines of vine to guide them along the tracks. The Australians' tactics were first to try to overcome opposition with mortar and artillery fire, and if this failed to make a wide and deep outflanking move. During the following weeks the usual aim of such a move would be to penetrate about 1,000 yards behind the Japanese position, establish a perimeter there and patrol back towards the Japanese flanks and rear. Although losses were not heavy, conditions were extremely uncomfortable and there was a constant sense of danger. Officers and men showed signs of strain, and the first self-inflicted wounds recorded on Bougainville occurred at this time. Spirits were improved by the capture on 2nd February of an abandoned 150-mm gun—one of those which had been regularly shelling the area.

During the 3rd several patrols searched the areas to the north and south of the Mosigetta Road and reported some abandoned enemy positions. Some had apparently been sites for 75-mm guns, and small quantities of shell cases and projectiles were scattered around. Among the other equipment were Japanese hurricane lamps with brass candlesticks inside. "These candlesticks were impressed by Padre Ganly,[2] after cleaning, for use on his altar."

General Savige reconnoitred the Puriata sector in an aircraft on the 5th and, later that day, instructed General Bridgeford that a battalion should advance on Mosigetta, and he repeated that the 2/8th Commando should secure crossings over the Puriata about Makapeka. The squadron was ordered so to do, provided the enemy was not defending the crossings when it arrived. By 13th February the squadron had established a new base at Opai, and in the following week found the gardens north of the Puriata to be clear of the enemy. Savige was critical of Winning's failure to secure the fords more promptly. Winning explained that he had to keep pace with the 61st Battalion. Savige informed him, through Colonel Edgar,[3] that the pace of the 61st was no concern of Winning's.

---

[2] Chaplain Rev D. A. Ganly, VX114018; 9 Bn. Church of England clergyman; of Bendigo, Vic; b. Geelong West, Vic, 9 Aug 1913.

[3] Lt-Gen H. G. Edgar, CB, CBE, VX85015. DD of SD (Eqpt) LHQ 1943-44; GSO1 3 Div 1944-45. Regular soldier; b. Wedderburn, Vic, 31 Oct 1903.

On 19th February Savige told Bridgeford that the Chief of the General Staff had said that it was difficult to find replacements and they might have to break up a brigade. Their tactics must be such as to reduce casualties. Indeed it was becoming evident that the II Corps was engaged in a stern struggle against a dogged and formidable enemy force, and might find itself lacking the strength to continue the offensive effectively.

In the southern sector the infantry continued to advance systematically, with a company sweeping round either to the right or the left of the track. Movement was still impeded by swamps and thick undergrowth; nearly every day there was at least one clash with a Japanese rearguard. By 11th February, having crossed a tributary of the Hupai at Beech's Crossing, the leading companies of the 9th were beyond the swamp country and among tall trees standing in thin undergrowth, so that usually men could see 50 yards ahead. The men were happy to be out of the dense swampy bush. Meanwhile the road from the coast was being rapidly improved.

Natives have cleaned out the ditches and cut away all grass on each side (wrote a South Australian diarist). New bridges built, three-ton trucks everywhere and sand spread over the road. Camps of engineers, artillery, sigs, etc., all the way down and the road as busy as Rundle Street on a Friday night.

The battalion was now nearing Mosigetta. Each day abandoned Japanese positions were occupied and one or two straying Japanese were killed. On the 14th eight Corsairs of the R.N.Z.A.F. (the Corsairs had been giving strong support) dropped 1,000-lb bombs ahead of the leading company. On the night of the 14th-15th Japanese guns fired more heavily than usual, expending 110 rounds. The Australians considered that they were using up a dump of ammunition before withdrawing. Next day (the 15th) a patrol from Captain Beech's[4] company reached the junction with the Meivo Track (which was named Matthews' Junction). Later patrols found signs of hasty retreat from the whole neighbourhood. The men dug out freshly-filled holes and found "two anti-tank barrels, many documents, seals, two swords, fountain pens, much money in notes, clothing, medical supplies; a few fires still burning". Next day a platoon under Lieutenant Mulcahy[5] thrust south into the Mosigetta area. This completed the attainment of the 7th Brigade's second phase in this area. On the 17th a company of the 61st Battalion from the north linked with the 9th. They were greeted by a "Welcome" sign erected by the 9th Battalion at the track junction.

A detached company of the 25th Battalion had been given the task of gaining the coast from Motupena Point to the mouth of the Puriata. Consequently, on 25th January, Captain Just's company had been landed by barge on the coast some distance south of Motupena Point and began patrolling along the coast to Matsunkei. Brigadier Field decided to land a platoon of the New Guinea Infantry at a point about a mile farther

[4] Maj A. T. Beech, QX40871; 9 Bn. Apprentice fitter and turner; of Nambour, Qld; b. Brisbane, 6 Nov 1921.
[5] Capt E. R. Mulcahy, QX40835; 9 Bn. Dairy farmer; of Eumundi, Qld; b. Brisbane, 19 Jul 1913.

south whence it would move stealthily towards Mosigetta, and to move Just's company in barges to Toko still farther south, whence it would push inland towards Barara.

On 2nd February a platoon of the 25th was already on the beach at a lagoon well north of Toko, where it killed one Japanese, and then marched south. A second platoon sailed down the coast in a barge. On the way it was signalled into the shore by the New Guinea troops who said that they had found some 30 Japanese at Makaku and placed an ambush between that village and the coast. The platoon landed at 2 p.m. and was joined next day by the platoon moving along the coast. By the 4th the whole company was ashore. In the following days patrols moved inland through dense bush but soon came under fire from a Japanese outpost at a crossing not far from the coast and were held; a patrol probed south to the mouth of the Puriata. By 11th February the company was more than a mile inland. That day Field granted a request by Lieut-Colonel McKinna that he be allowed to land a second company (Captain Corbould[6]) at Toko to assist in an ambitious thrust by this isolated force. Just was to take Barara and Corbould to move through to the ford over which the main southward track passed and ambush the Japanese withdrawing from Mosigetta. Meanwhile the remainder of the 25th was to be ferried to Toko.

The Japanese policy of resisting the southward advance more strongly even if it entailed heavier casualties failed to impose the hoped-for delay of the Australians. Nevertheless the Japanese leaders considered that the *13th Regiment's* "swift damaging hit-and-run tactics" were well executed. However, Mosigetta was at length abandoned and a withdrawal south of the Puriata ordered. The landing at Toko was unexpected and caused an acceleration of this withdrawal.

There now occurred a major crisis in the Japanese command. The young reserve officers were highly critical of the conduct of the campaign and blamed the policies of the older professional officers for the constant reverses. This criticism became so outspoken that, in February, a number of the younger officers were relieved of their commands; perhaps partly as an outcome of this crisis, General Hyakutake suffered a paralysis of his left side. Lieut-General Kanda took command of the *XVII Army* and Lieut-General Tsutomu Akinaga, Chief of Staff of the Army, succeeded him in command of the *6th Division*. "This change of command was regarded favourably by the younger officers, but it soon became apparent that Kanda intended to pursue the same policy as Hyakutake. Kanda was a shrewd, hard, fussy little professional soldier of long experience. He was steeped in tradition and a ruthless commander, but even his bitterest critics admitted his capabilities. Akinaga . . . was a dyed in the wool militarist and a strict disciplinarian. Unused to an active command he was plunged into a situation which was a little out of his depth. One of his staff stated that he spent too much time doing a corporal's job in his forward battalions to be a good divisional commander."[7]

In the country between Mosigetta and the Puriata River only small Japanese rearguards opposed the advance. In a withdrawal such as this, in which it was necessary to coordinate numbers of small groups, the defects of Japanese staff work, and particularly of their communications,

---

[6] Capt R. W. Corbould, VX100095. 39, 7 MG and 25 Bns. Oil company superintendent; of Mildura, Vic; b. Mildura, 25 Aug 1916.

[7] 23rd Brigade, "History of the Japanese Occupation of Bougainville, March 1942-August 1945". (As mentioned, this was written after comprehensive interrogation of the Japanese staff.)

were evident, and many Japanese were killed either as lonely stragglers or in parties that seemed ill-informed about the progress of the withdrawal. The advance on the Puriata was continued by the 25th and 61st Battalions, the 9th being rested. The Australians passed through elaborate Japanese bivouacs with many huts and bomb-proof shelters, and through big gardens.

There were fairly frequent clashes. On 22nd February the 61st Battalion sent out a fighting patrol to drive the enemy from between two company positions. One group of four, including Private Haines,[8] became separated and one man was severely wounded. Haines took command, hoisted the wounded man on his shoulder, and set out, with another man, to carry him through the enemy's lines. Twice he hid the wounded man and drove off enemy parties with his Bren. At nightfall they were within the enemy's perimeter, and hid there waiting for light. At daylight a mortar barrage was brought down on the Japanese and, while it was falling, Haines and his companion got back to the battalion's lines whence Haines led out a patrol which recovered the wounded man. It was found that Haines and his Bren had caused the enemy to abandon their position.

Also on 22nd February, the 25th Battalion advancing from Toko reached Barara, and later that day the track behind the battalion had been made "jeepable" all the way to that point. For five days the leading troops had been living partly on vegetables from Japanese gardens. On 24th February the battalion came to one garden of five acres growing sweet potatoes, peanuts, melons, pumpkins, marrows, paw paws and corn; on 1st March the 61st occupied a garden extending 600 yards by 400. Abandoned pack saddles and horse dung were found. By this time patrols had reached the Puriata along a wide front.

Meanwhile, on 20th February Bridgeford had ordered the 2/8th Commando on the inland flank to seize the fords eastward from a point south of Makapeka, and destroy enemy troops crossing the Puriata from Mosigetta. A section (Lieutenant Perry[9]) had already set ambushes in the area of the Makapeka forks; a second section (Lieutenant Maxwell[1]) took over the area to the west. Between 17th February and 5th March 26 Japanese were killed, mostly in a series of sharp attacks against an enemy force covering one of the main exits from Mosigetta.

This position was discovered in a singular manner. Maxwell's section was in position near the junction of the Makapeka and Puriata Rivers. Nothing was known of any Japanese concentration in the vicinity until one morning a three-man patrol under Corporal Spitz[2] found a well-defined and recently used track leading up the south bank of the Makapeka. The patrol followed it and entered the rear of a Japanese ambush which

---

[8] Pte E. J. Haines, MM, S45748; 61 Bn. Brickyard worker; of West Thebarton, SA; b. Thebarton, 15 April 1923.
[9] Lt R. W. Perry, NX131893; 2/8 Cdo Sqn. Articled clerk; of Bellevue Hill, NSW; b. Randwick, NSW, 2 Dec 1921.
[1] Maj K. J. Maxwell, SX13328; 2/8 Cdo Sqn. Laboratory assistant; of Renmark, SA; b. Adelaide, 13 Jan 1922.
[2] Cpl L. E. Spitz, WX16575; 2/8 Cdo Sqn. Railway ganger; of Nannup, WA; b. Nannup, 5 Jan 1917.

had been established in a commanding position high above the crossing. Spitz, who was in the lead, suddenly saw almost at his feet, the back of a Japanese who, from a very well-concealed slit-trench, was peering through the cover at the river below. Spitz put a burst into the Japanese and, before those in the ambush were really aware of what had happened, the three Australians were well away down the track towards Maxwell's position to report.

In the next few days patrol after patrol crossed the Makapeka River to probe the Japanese positions. Maxwell led out a fighting patrol eight strong to establish the strength of the enemy and try to force them to withdraw by firing on them from an adjoining knoll. When near the Japanese position Maxwell sent Sergeant Brahatis[3] with a Bren gun group to select a fire position while he himself picked a position for a rifle-grenade group. Brahatis' party came under heavy small arms fire. Brahatis attacked immediately with the Bren and silenced one Japanese machine-gun position and engaged another. Maxwell decided that he was not strong enough to overcome the enemy, who were well dug in on the rim of a plateau in approximately platoon strength, and withdrew his men under cover of rifle grenades. Next morning Maxwell reconnoitred the position from the west. Later the entire squadron, aided by an air strike, attacked and took it, securing a ford across the Makapeka (Maxwell's Crossing). The position was named Commando Ridge.

The Australian lines of communication were being steadily improved. By 18th February a strip on which little Auster aircraft could land was open at Mawaraka,[4] which one diarist described as now being "a little city". On the 25th rations were dropped for the first time at Barara. In the forward area the advancing troops were often moving along wide, well-drained tracks, but farther to the rear the rain and the wear and tear caused by heavy vehicles made it difficult to keep the tracks in order. On 25th February the 9th Battalion recorded that it had rained for a week, the mud was knee deep, and trains of six or seven jeeps were being hauled forward by tractors.

Savige now believed that the enemy would use only delaying tactics until the Hari River was reached, but would fight on that river to retain garden areas on which they largely depended for food. He ordered Bridgeford to establish control of the area between the Puriata and the Hari. In a first stage he was to clear to the line of the Hongorai, in a second to clear the country of the enemy to the line Hari River-Monoitu-Kapana. Barge landing points had to be found between the Puriata and Hari and a road built from the coast to link with the road Hiru Hiru-Aku. Bridgeford was to use only one brigade group in the forward area. On 28th February, after Bridgeford received these orders, the 9th Battalion was resting, the 61st was in and forward of Mosigetta from which the

---

[3] WO2 S. Brahatis, DCM, NX101098; 2/8 Cdo Sqn. 3 Bn RAR Korea 1952. Builder's labourer; of Katoomba, NSW; b. Paddington, NSW, 8 Jan 1918.

[4] Named Vernon Strip after Flight Lieutenant W. R. Vernon of No. 5 Squadron RAAF, killed there on 11th January 1945.

enemy had been driven by Captain Hutchinson's[5] company, the 25th was round Barara, the New Guinea company was patrolling to the east between the Puriata and Hongorai, and the 2/8th Commando was harassing the enemy between the two rivers farther to the north.

The 61st continued to probe forward. On 7th March, for example, a patrol of the 61st went to Horinu 2 without meeting any enemy, but next day a platoon patrol opened fire on a party of 15 to 20 and killed six. The guns of the 10th Battery (4th Field Regiment) directed by Captain Koch,[6] the artillery observer with the 61st, drove out the surviving Japanese who were found to have been in occupation of four machine-gun pits and 20 other weapon-pits.

Brigadier Field decided to rest the 61st while the 25th, with the New Guinea company patrolling ahead of it, on 11th March continued to advance to the Hongorai in the western sector and the 2/8th Commando in the eastern. Eventually Field was to establish his headquarters at Toko. It was estimated that 850 men of the *13th Japanese Regiment* were between the Australians and the Hongorai and could be quickly reinforced from beyond the Hari.

Toko had now become a main base. From early in February landing craft had been ferrying supplies thither from both the Adele River and Torokina, and from 7th March small ships carried stores from Torokina to Toko, where landing craft off-loaded them to the beach, an operation greatly hampered by the heavy surf. (At length on 11th April the calmer beach at Motupena Point was used for off-loading the small ships and the cargo was taken on to Toko by road.)

On 4th March the leading company of the 25th Battalion had crossed the Puriata and established a perimeter 200 yards south along the Buin Road. The first man to reach the south bank was Private Galvin[7] and the crossing was named after him.[8] Next day the enemy were easily thrust off a knoll close to the river where it converges with the Buin Road. On the 6th the enemy shelled the area, causing one casualty—the wounding of Private Slater,[9] who carried on at his post until relieved. The knoll was named Slater's. Although some 600 shells were fired into this battalion's area during March he was the only casualty caused by such fire.

The company sent out patrols daily, and on the 9th one of these reported having killed ten Japanese without loss to itself. At the same time it became evident that the enemy intended to dispute the advance vigorously. Often a party of Japanese would advance stealthily at first

---

[5] Maj T. C. Hutchinson, MC, ED, QX40906; 61 Bn. Engineering draftsman; of Brisbane; b. Brisbane, 12 Jan 1910.

[6] Capt A. M. Koch, MC, VX117140; 4 Fd Regt. Costing clerk; of Caulfield, Vic; b. Melbourne, 2 Jan 1918.

[7] Pte P. J. Galvin, Q16917; 25 Bn. Shop assistant; of Sandgate, Qld; b. Murwillumbah, NSW, 17 May 1918.

[8] The following account of the operations of the 25th Battalion in this phase is largely drawn from a narrative compiled in May 1945 by Corporal A. C. Wann of the Military History Section.

[9] Pte C. R. Slater, T101924; 25 Bn. Textile worker; of Beauty Point, Tas; b. Launceston, Tas, 19 Sep 1924.

light, pour machine-gun fire on to Slater's Knoll and then retire to a position some 250 yards along the track. On the 9th a patrol led by Lieutenant King[1] penetrated the Tokinotu area and reported large gardens there.

On the 11th, when, in accordance with the orders outlined above, the battalion was to advance, the leading company found the enemy dug in firmly astride the Buin Road. After several patrol clashes a long duel between mortars opened. Meanwhile two other companies had moved south along the right bank of the river, crossed it and struck out for Tokinotu. They pressed on, reaching a point near the Buin Road after several skirmishes in which two Japanese officers were killed. At length Hiru Hiru was reached, and these companies stood firm and waited for the company to the north to push along the Buin Road and join them. However, this company found that it was fighting a more determined enemy than had been met north of the Puriata. On the 13th Lieutenant Shaw's platoon, which was leading, entered an area in which were recently-dug but unoccupied positions, large enough (as was afterwards found) to harbour two companies. Shaw, who was scouting forward with a corporal, realised just in time that the Japanese intended to reoccupy these positions behind him, and that he was walking into a trap. He and the corporal managed to make their way back. In the ensuing fire fight one Australian was killed and two wounded. The company formed a perimeter. That evening and next day a patrol from Lieutenant Jefferies'[2] company in the south moved along the east side of the Buin Road to Slater's and back along the west side to Jefferies' "firm base" behind the Japanese positions. In heavy rain the leading company pressed on through a bivouac area in which enemy dead were lying unburied.

On the 15th an enemy force thrice vainly counter-attacked this company as the men were digging in. It attacked again on the 16th and 17th. The company was now under fire from three sides. Part of Captain Just's company pressed forward, reached the forward company and all withdrew to Just's perimeter. It was now evident that an aggressive Japanese force of considerable size was active between the leading and the rear companies of the 25th Battalion. Captured documents suggested that reinforcements were moving from Buin towards the Puriata. McKinna decided to make a strong thrust along the Buin Road with Captain McInnes'[3] company on the west of the road, and Just's followed by two platoons of Jefferies' on the east. The aim would be to clear the road as far as the company at Tokinotu.

At 8.30 a.m. on 19th March the attacking companies of the 25th Battalion advanced, supported by fire from artillery, mortars and medium machine-guns, and drove the Japanese from their positions, killing six.

---

[1] Lt B. W. King, NX112256; 25 Bn. Clerk; of Sydney; b. Mosman, NSW, 23 Jun 1923. Killed in action 19 Mar 1945.

[2] Capt R. D. K. Jefferies, DSO, QX36185; 25 Bn. Trainee theatre manager; of Toowoomba, Qld; b. Armidale, NSW, 2 Dec 1920.

[3] Maj R. D. McInnes, MC, QX53202. 25 Bn; 2/Royal Berkshire Regt 1945-46. Trust officer; of Toowoomba, Qld; b. Toowoomba, 12 Apr 1922.

Jefferies' two platoons encountered more Japanese in an extensive system of pill-boxes near the junction of the road with a track leading to Hatai. Jefferies telephoned McKinna for orders. McKinna decided to attack, and himself went forward with a section of machine-guns and a Piat.[4] Jefferies had thirty-five men, and estimated the enemy at fifteen. After a fire fight lasting more than two hours he decided to charge with the bayonet. This entailed borrowing bayonets from Just's company near by, as his platoons, being in patrol formation, were not carrying them. After a final burst of machine-gun fire Jefferies led the men forward. The fire had kept the Japanese underground and the Australians advanced 25 yards before the enemy opened fire. Jefferies was wounded by a grenade, and Lieutenant Chesterton took command. On the right Corporal Gurski's[5] section veered towards a group of pill-boxes from which a damaging fire was coming and, attacking with rifles, bayonets, Brens and grenades, forced the enemy out of some posts and into others farther to the right. After three-quarters of an hour the platoons withdrew to the road leaving 23 enemy dead apart from 6 others seen to fall before reaching their rear positions. Five Australians, including Lieutenants Stewart[6] and King, were killed and 17 wounded, 3 fatally.

The positions to which the enemy had fallen back were located with the help of a scouting Auster aircraft, and McKinna decided to attack again with air and artillery support. Thus, on the morning of the 22nd, eight New Zealand Corsairs bombed the enemy's positions, and accurate fire was brought down by two field batteries, an anti-tank gun, mortars and machine-guns. As soon as the aircraft reported that they had finished with the target, Captain McInnes' company advanced. Corporal Rattey[7] led his section firing a Bren from the hip until he was on top of the first Japanese weapon-pit, when he flung in a grenade and called his men forward. Using the same tactics he killed the Japanese in two more weapon-pits. He then advanced on a Japanese machine-gun post and with his Bren killed one of the team and put the others to flight. Some 2,000 rounds of ammunition were beside the gun. In an hour the Japanese positions were taken, the enemy leaving 18 dead on the field. Five Australians were wounded of whom two remained in action.

On 14th March Field sent Bridgeford a review of "current operations" in which he expressed the opinion that in view of the value of the gardens east of the Hongorai and Hari Rivers the enemy would vigorously contest the crossing of the Hongorai; the enemy appeared to be fighting delaying engagements along the north-south roads eastwards from the Puriata. The 7th Brigade was securing the Tokinotu-Hatai-Rumiki lateral

---

[4] Projector Infantry Tank Attack (now Piat). It was a counterpart of the American Bazooka but with a different firing principle. It succeeded the Boyes anti-tank rifle and fired a 2½-lb H.E. charge with a maximum effective range of 150 yards.

[5] Cpl D. W. Gurski, QX61725; 25 Bn. Foundry packer; of Toowoomba, Qld; b. Laidley, Qld, 21 Jan 1922.

[6] Lt R. K. Stewart, QX33589; 25 Bn. Clerk; of Cairns, Qld; b. Cairns, 17 Nov 1919. Killed in action 19 Mar 1945.

[7] Sgt R. R. Rattey, VC, NX102964; 25 Bn. Farmer; of Barmedman, NSW; b. Barmedman, 28 Mar 1917. (Rattey was awarded the Victoria Cross for this action.)

track. When this had been achieved the line of communications would be shortened, the 61st Battalion could be relieved by the 9th via Toko and Tokinotu and the 2/8th Commando would have a shorter route for supplies. Field added that he considered that the thrust against the Hongorai should be supported by tanks and medium artillery, brought in through Toko. The tanks would "constitute a valuable reserve in support of the two forward battalions to deal with any emergency situation". Medium guns were essential in view of the presence of large-calibre Japanese guns east of the Hongorai.

On 17th March Savige gave Bridgeford permission to move tanks and medium guns to the Toko area and, on the 18th, Bridgeford issued detailed instructions for the coming operation.[8] In these he expressed the opinion that the enemy would "stage his main battle" in the area between the Hongorai and Hari Rivers and would fight a series of delaying actions west of the Hongorai to gain time for re-grouping his forces and completing defence works along the Hongorai guarding the main approaches to the Taitai area. A prisoner had said that if the attack on the Hongorai assumed grave proportions *XVII Army* would send a force, perhaps the *45th Regiment* from Kieta, to move over the foothills and attack the Australian rear. The A.I.B. had reported that there were concentrations in the foothills north-east from Monoitu.

Bridgeford concluded that it would be unwise to advance, except by patrolling, farther east than the Hongorai until the force in the forward area included a striking force of one brigade group, with tanks and heavy artillery, and a reserve of one brigade group to relieve the striking force if need be and maintain the momentum of the attack. Before relieving the striking force the reserve brigade would guard the lines of communication in the forward area. But reinforcement of the forward area depended on ability to maintain more forces. "Road and track construction is, therefore, of urgent priority." The divisional engineers, with all possible speed, were to make a durable truck road from Toko to the Tokinotu area and a corduroy jeep track thence as far forward towards Rumiki and the Hongorai crossing as possible. The 15th Brigade and "B" Squadron of the 2/4th Armoured Regiment would prepare to move to Toko, and the leading battalion would help in this road building. The defence of the Torokina perimeter would be allotted to the 29th Brigade. The wisdom of this re-deployment was confirmed by important Intelligence obtained by the 2/8th Commando which from 9th March onwards had been based at Nihero.

This area (wrote Sergeant Hungerford[9] later) had been a considerable kanaka place on a main Government road to the south. There were two large "house garamuts", or ceremonial sing-sing houses, whose sacsac thatch, although in a ruinous state, proved a boon to the squadron when building shelters. On the west was

---

[8] A fortnight earlier a few Japanese tanks had been located. A New Zealand Corsair pilot reported having seen enemy tanks at Ruri Bay in the north-east of the island. Squadron Leader B. M. H. Palmer, commanding No. 5 Squadron RAAF, led other Corsairs to the target and guided them while they attacked three tanks, all of which they damaged. As a result of this and a later attack two were destroyed but the third was evidently moved away.

[9] Sgt T. A. G. Hungerford, WX14902; 2/8 Cdo Sqn. Of Perth; b. Perth, 5 May 1915.

a high ridge along which the road ran, and in the east a small but swiftly-flowing river, the essential water supply, bucketed through a deep and rocky gorge that was a fine defence.

Between the ridge and the river was a wide basin where the jungle was flattened to make a dropping ground. Headquarters was established on a knoll overlooking the river and the dropping ground, and below headquarters on the ledge immediately above the river a large native camp grew up to accommodate first Angau and the carriers allotted to the squadron, and later on the hordes of refugees who came in for protection.

As usual, the troops were arrayed in a ragged perimeter around the dropping-ground and headquarters, the main reliance for protection being placed on the terrain and the system of "houses-look" on all tracks leading into the position.

The surrounding country was precipitous in the extreme, with razor-back ridges falling sheer into impenetrable gullies and re-entrants, and the whole covered with a dense mat of jungle. One troop was established in a small perimeter about a mile down the road towards Sinanai, where there was a cluster of inhabited places known to be occupied in some numbers by the Japanese. Its job was to report on and if possible prevent any movement of the enemy on Nihero.

Actually, in the early stages before the Japanese had been annoyed into relinquishing Sinanai, it would have been a fairly easy matter for them to force the squadron to evacuate Nihero, but they never realised it. They were held back, it was later discovered, by the report of a warrant officer who conducted a reconnaissance of the position for three days soon after the Australians moved in. He observed the camp from a tall tree on the eastern bank of the river, and was so impressed with the number of kanakas in the area, the widely spread nature of the perimeter, and the size of the dropping ground that had been cleared, that he reported "at least 1,000 white troops were in occupation in Nihero". He later was taken prisoner by some of the "thousand white troops" and proved a mine of information.

Long-range patrols began probing from Nihero as far south as Unanai, Hari and the Buin Road between the Hongorai and Mivo Rivers. On 17th March a patrol under Lieutenant Lawson-Dook[1] attacked five huts in the Sinanai area, killed fourteen Japanese and captured documents. Such attacks had been reduced to a copy-book routine: a patrol looked the position over in the evening and found a good spot from which to launch the attack, the men involved moved in under cover of darkness and at first light poured fire into the huts, usually killing all occupants in their sleep. This patrol of Lawson-Dook's, however, differed in important respects. No suitable spot could be found from which to deliver the broadside, so the patrol waited until the Japanese were at their breakfast and then ran out of the undergrowth—as one of them later described it, "like a football team running on to the field"—lined up under the gaze of the astonished Japanese and "sent them to their ancestors with their rice-bowls still in their hands."

On 11th March Major Winning warned Corps headquarters that several parties each of 12 Japanese were moving towards the Torokina perimeter and one had the task of killing the commander. News of this enterprise excited much interest and some anxiety at Torokina. The 15th Brigade, then garrisoning the perimeter area, took measures to intercept any intruders but none got so far.

---

[1] Lt R. Lawson-Dook, WX12529; 2/8 Cdo Sqn. Compressor driver; of Kalgoorlie, WA; b. Perth, 15 Oct 1915.

A few days later the commando squadron obtained more important information. In ambushes on 18th and 20th March eight Japanese were killed and an order of the *6th Division* dated 16th March was captured indicating that there would be a large-scale Japanese offensive early in April.

The 25th Battalion which was likely to bear the brunt of such an offensive was now deployed with one company in the Tokinotu area, one company across the Hatai Track-Buin Road junction, and the remainder in depth along the Buin Road. McKinna's headquarters and part of Headquarters Company were on Slater's Knoll. Forward of Slater's Knoll the road was now a morass: from 25th to 29th March it was impassable and natives were used to carry supplies forward. Further warning of the impending offensive arrived on the 26th when it was learnt from a captured document that the *23rd Regiment* was concentrating at Oso, and patrols reported large enemy parties moving west. In response to this threat Bridgeford informed Field on the 28th that the squadron of tanks which, fortunately, would begin arriving at Toko next day would be available to him in an emergency.

The Japanese attack was prefaced by a series of raids on the Australian lines of communication and troops in the rear. The eight guns of the 5th Field Battery were in position on the west bank of the Puriata eastward from Toko. At 5.25 a.m. on the 28th a booby-trap exploded in the forest to the rear of the battery. It was not unusual for lightly-set traps to explode without being touched by a man, but Gunner Cheeseman,[2] on guard, fired two bursts in the direction and heard men crashing through the bush. A few minutes later five or six Japanese appeared a few feet from Bombardier Green[3] in a weapon-pit on the left of the battery near the river bank. He fired with his Bren and heard bodies falling into the river. Later two men who had been sent out to disarm the booby-traps, as was usual each morning, were fired on. By midday firing had ceased; the battery suffered no casualties.

Meanwhile on the night of the 27th in the 25th Battalion's area the enemy had been heard moving stealthily on the Buin Road and the east bank of the Puriata near Slater's Knoll. The scouting aircraft reported three large parties of Japanese on the move.

On Slater's Knoll Major Weppner,[4] second-in-command 25th Battalion, supervised the reorganisation of the pit and weapon sightings of battalion headquarters, and after the evening meal called an inspection stand-to. Officers checked on the pits and an hour later the troops stood down. The moon came up and after a while the officers drifted over to hear the evening news from the I.O. Suddenly the wire to "B" echelon went dead.[5]

---

[2] Cpl A. Cheeseman, NX108831; 2 Fd Regt. Photo engraving apprentice; of Randwick, NSW; b. Sydney, 29 May 1923.
[3] Bdr K. E. Green, VX87753; 2 Fd Regt. Carpenter; of Terang, Vic; b. Terang, 27 Oct 1920.
[4] Maj R. Weppner, QX40879; 25 Bn. Advertising contractor, artist and signwriter; of Toowoomba, Qld; b. Colbinabbin, Vic, 30 Aug 1903.
[5] From Corporal Wann's narrative.

The "B" echelon, protected by a company of the 61st Battalion, was only 400 yards to the rear. Immediately runners were sent out to warn the sections round the perimeter. It was then about 8 p.m. At 8.15 about 100 Japanese charged from the rear, screaming and with bayonets fixed. Occasionally one would shout a phrase picked up from attacking Australians—for example, "It's on." The attack was beaten off. The Japanese re-formed and attacked again, first from the direction of the river and then from the south. These thrusts also failed. Next morning 19 enemy dead were found round the perimeter and one wounded man was taken; the Australians had lost 3 killed and 7 wounded. Some of the Japanese survivors, dug in between this perimeter and "B" echelon, fired on a patrol led by Weppner. Another patrol discovered Japanese dug in to the south astride the Buin Road between battalion headquarters and the forward companies.

The 9th Battalion, farther north, guessed that an enemy attack was to be made because of the frequency with which its wires were cut. At 11 p.m. on 28th March a party of Japanese was seen approaching the battalion's rear echelon at Barara astride the Toko-Mosigetta-Buin Road junction, where Major Fry[6] commanded part of Headquarters Company, the transport and quartermaster staffs and others. They possessed only four Bren guns but these were well sited. One Japanese was killed in the initial advance and spasmodic fire continued throughout the night. At 4.45 a.m. in the light of a full moon, and after a prolonged concentration of machine-gun and rifle fire and grenade throwing, about 100 Japanese charged with fixed bayonets. They were driven back and at daybreak withdrew out of range. Soon they could be heard chopping wood, evidently to make stretchers for their wounded. Four Australians were wounded, but the Japanese left 23 dead on the field.

The 29th was comparatively quiet. Chesterton's company of the 25th Battalion was attacked in the morning and afternoon by relatively small enemy parties, and the headquarters of the 25th was again attacked. That morning Japanese attacked also the company of the 61st, killing two Australians and wounding two, but were repulsed. It was estimated that about 70 Japanese were dug in between this company and the headquarters of the 25th. However, a Japanese prisoner taken this day left no doubt that the raids and sporadic attacks were a prelude to a full-scale offensive, so far as the Japanese were able to stage one. He was a sergeant of the *13th Regiment* and said that the whole regiment (probably only 800 or 900 strong) was to be engaged in a battle that was to last five days; each man would carry 15 days' rations, 100 rounds and three grenades.

At 7 a.m. on the 30th (Good Friday) Chesterton's company was strongly attacked; at the time a patrol of 15 was out, leaving only 31 men in the perimeter. The patrol skirted the fight and joined McInnes' company farther north. Thence it was ordered back to Chesterton, but had not arrived when the Japanese, having been once repulsed, attacked again,

---

[6] Lt-Col W. G. Fry, VX117038. 9 Bn; CO 47 Bn 1945. Schoolteacher; of Ballarat, Vic; b. Ballarat, 12 Jun 1909.

and the patrol again returned to the rearward company. During the day the Japanese attacked four times. The last attack, at 1 p.m., was the most severe. After a mortar bombardment the Japanese charged with bayonets fixed, hurling grenades and screaming. Twelve Japanese were killed; one Australian was killed and two were missing. Only 16 remained alive and unwounded in the perimeter, and the survivors withdrew to McInnes' perimeter carrying their wounded. The combined fire-power of the two companies now included one Vickers and fourteen Brens, but three mortars with 250 bombs had been left behind, and in the evening the Japanese brought them into action, dropping bombs throughout the night round Just's company on the east side of the Buin Road, about 500 yards beyond Kero Creek.[7] It was known how many bombs had been left at the abandoned perimeter and the Australians counted the explosions anxiously. Meanwhile a Japanese mortar dropped bombs accurately on McInnes' company, wounding Sergeant Townsley[8] and most of the members of his Vickers gun team.

For considerable periods on the 30th Field's headquarters and McKinna's were out of touch with three of the forward companies. The line to McInnes' combined company was out of action from midday onwards, but that to the company of the 61st was repaired about midday. When Chesterton arrived at McInnes' perimeter he sent back Private Hall[9] with a message that the two companies were together and their position would be held until further orders. Hall followed the signal line 1,100 yards to Just's company arriving at 4.50 p.m.

Bridgeford had now placed Major Arnott's[1] squadron of the 2/4th Armoured Regiment under Field's command and instructed McKinna that he might use a troop of these tanks on the 31st. Meanwhile McInnes' force had been gradually reduced by casualties until it numbered only 83. After midday on the 30th the men had no food and their water-bottles were empty, but more water was obtained by sinking a hole within the perimeter, scooping water out in tins and waiting until the mud settled. The isolated force, now completely surrounded, guessed that Hall had reached the rear companies when, in the evening of the 30th, their own artillery fire fell forward of their perimeter. Many of the attacks on McInnes' force fell on a sector commanded by Sergeant E. N. Jorgensen who exposed himself to Japanese fire while directing his own men and dragging forward ammunition. Although himself wounded he took over a Bren gun whose gunner was disabled and halted a Japanese bayonet charge only a few yards from his position.

---

[7] Battalion headquarters asked Just where the bombs were falling and he told them. Immediately the Japanese altered their deflection. After two more such inquiries and replies had been followed by a switching of Japanese fire, Just realised that they had tapped his line and, in effect, he was ranging the enemy on to his own position.

[8] Sgt C. J. Townsley, QX61658; 25 Bn. Pastoral worker; of Roma, Qld; b. Roma, 23 Nov 1919. (Townsley and another wounded man, Private S. C. White, of Toowoomba, Qld, returned to the gun after treatment.)

[9] Sgt P. J. Hall, MM, QX56727; 25 Bn. Shop assistant; of Toowoomba, Qld; b. Toowoomba, 17 Jan 1924.

[1] Brig K. M. H. Arnott, DSO, ED, NX70790; 2/4 Armd Regt. Grazier; of Murrurundi, NSW; b. Strathfield, NSW, 15 Oct 1906.

The leading tanks of Major Arnott's squadron had run up on to the beach at Toko from landing craft only on the 29th. At 2.30 p.m. Arnott was warned that a troop would be needed in the 25th Battalion's area. To bring the tanks forward to the Buin Road and thence across the Puriata was a severe test for the engineers who were maintaining roads and bridges leading to the battle area.[2] At Coombes' Crossing not far inland from Toko a gully was spanned by a bridge built to carry three-ton trucks. On the 30th the engineers of the 15th Field Company, helped by clerks, cooks and others, completed a bridge to carry the 24-ton Matilda tanks; the four advancing tanks crossed at 2.30 p.m., having been kept waiting only a quarter of an hour. At the Puriata the tanks were waterproofed with canvas and grease in two hours. One bogged in the stream and dropped out of the race. Three crossed with the aid of bulldozers, and reached "B" echelon of the 25th Battalion at 7 p.m. Nothing had been heard of the isolated forward companies since midday, but it was too late to attempt to thrust the tanks forward that night. Field wished to know whether the tanks had reached McKinna. Surprise was essential and the enemy might be listening; it would be inadvisable to use the word "tank" on the telephone. "Arnott's biscuits" were well known in Australia, so McKinna was asked whether "Arnott's biscuits" had arrived and replied that they had.

Next morning the tanks advanced the remaining 400 yards to Slater's and came under McKinna's command. With a composite platoon from the headquarters company they advanced. A bulldozer hauled them through Kero Creek. At 4 p.m. they moved forward from Just's perimeter, now accompanied also by two platoons of his company. With a bulldozer improving the track ahead, the tanks rolled forward until they were about 400 yards from the besieged companies. Thence they advanced to the attack, with the infantry to the right and left.[3] A few minutes earlier the Japanese had opened a fierce attack on McInnes' force—the heaviest of the day. Then the engines of tanks were heard about 100 yards away. McInnes' men, uncertain whether or not they were Japanese tanks, loaded and aimed their Pita. When the Japanese came under fire from the tanks they fled. Sergeant Taylor[4] and Private Hall pressed forward of the tanks towards the perimeter. Eight Japanese were killed by the tanks; 94 more lay dead round the perimeter, killed in the earlier fighting. While McInnes' weary men, escorted by one tank and a platoon of Just's company, marched back along the road, McKinna, with the remaining two tanks and about two platoons of infantry, continued along the road to the abandoned perimeter at the Hatai junction. There the tanks killed 11, and 16 more bodies were found lying where Lieutenant Chesterton's

---

[2] Arnott had reconnoitred the route from Toko to Slater's Knoll on 11th March and had reported that he had seen no country over which tanks could not operate with the help of suitable bridges, waterproofing, bulldozers and powered winches.

[3] The battalions of the 7th Brigade were well prepared for cooperation with tanks, having trained with the 2/6th and 2/8th Armoured Regiments in Papua and with the 2/4th at Madang.

[4] Lt W. J. Taylor, QX54848; 25 Bn. Schoolteacher; of Cleveland, Qld; b. Brisbane, 27 Mar 1917.

men had killed them. The abandoned weapons and ammunition were either salvaged or destroyed lest the Japanese should repeat their achievement of bringing down galling fire on Australian positions with abandoned Australian mortars.

Meanwhile McKinna had ordered that jeeps be sent forward to carry back the wounded. Five set out, drawn by a bulldozer and carrying a total of 26 men. A little north of Just's perimeter they ran into an ambush; three drivers and one man of the escort were killed and most of the remainder left the jeeps and made off the way they had come, covered by fire from Private McGrath[5] who, though severely wounded, continued shooting with his Owen gun until hit again and killed. Craftsman Oliver[6] fired two magazines from his Owen and dived into the scrub where he lay low.

McKinna's group heard the firing and correctly guessed its cause. They moved back along the road with a tank fore and aft. At 6.50 p.m., after having joined the third tank, they attacked the Japanese in the ambush position, killing eleven. Just's company lost three men; Arnott was wounded while going forward to help the wounded men, and Oliver while exposing himself and shouting a warning. It was now too dark to continue moving, so the wounded were made as comfortable as possible in the ditch by the road and the infantry formed a perimeter round tanks and jeeps.

Next morning at 7 a.m. the column crossed Kero Creek and continued north to the Puriata where McInnes' and Just's companies established a perimeter 1,000 yards south of Slater's, Chesterton's going on to battalion headquarters carrying 7 wounded men and escorting 51 walking wounded. In the fighting on 30th and 31st March and 1st April 8 Australians had been killed and 58 wounded; 130 Japanese dead were counted. The enemy was still busy, and that evening (1st April) the line from Slater's to the forward companies was cut again.

For the next three days many small parties of Japanese were seen round Barara and Slater's Knoll and as far north as Mosigetta, evidently reconnoitring and forming up. There were exchanges of fire, but the enemy always made off quickly. Captured papers revealed that the fresh *23rd Japanese Regiment* was in the Barara area preparing to attack. The Australians made ready to fend off the next blow.

On the night of the 4th-5th nearly 200 enemy shells fell round the Australian battery near McKinna Bridge over the Puriata. Just before 5 a.m. on the 5th the lines connecting the 7th Brigade to the 25th Battalion and the 25th Battalion to its forward companies were cut. In a few minutes the posts round Slater's Knoll had been warned that attack was imminent. There were 129 men within the perimeter. Precisely at 5 o'clock Japanese attacked from the north, and almost immediately, as though they had been awaiting this signal, a stronger body attacked from

---

[5] Pte S. W. McGrath, QX63631; 25 Bn. Pig grader; of Toowoomba, Qld; b. Toowoomba, 14 Nov 1914. Killed in action 31 Mar 1945.

[6] Cfn A. R. S. Oliver, MM, NX92169; 2/4 Armd Regt. Barman; of Harden, NSW; b. Moonee Ponds, Vic, 11 Mar 1916.

the south-west. Until 6.20 a.m. wave after wave charged forward and was brought low. Some Japanese fell within four yards of the weapon-pits. The artillery sent over accurate defensive fire, registered the previous day. At dawn the surviving Japanese were heard digging in on dead ground. As the light became clearer, the Australians saw that "enemy dead lay, literally, in heaps in front of the wire", and bodies could be seen scattered over an area some 200 yards square. It was gruesome evidence of the efficient siting of weapons and choice of fields of fire in preparation for expected attack.

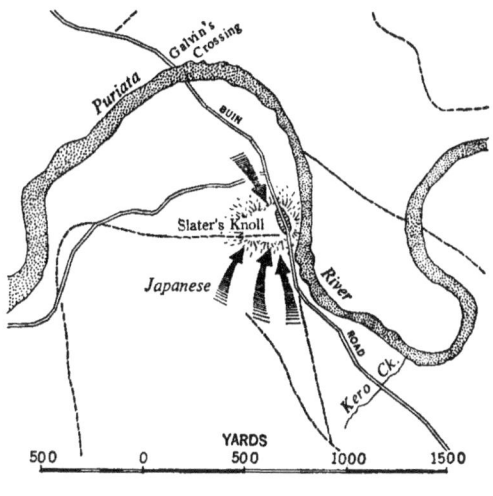

5th April

Twenty minutes after the opening of this attack about 100 Japanese thrust at the two forward companies of the 25th, in a perimeter 1,000 yards along the Buin Road, but were driven off, finally abandoning the effort at 8.30. At 12.50 p.m. two tanks advanced towards Slater's from the "B" echelon position with a company of the 61st Battalion. By 1.45 they were at Slater's where a company of the 25th advanced to mop up the remaining Japanese, covered by the fire of the tanks. One by one small groups of Japanese emerging from cover were shot down. Few escaped.

On 6th April 292 Japanese dead were counted round Slater's Knoll. A bulldozer borrowed from the engineers dug three communal graves in which the enemy dead were buried. Four wounded men were taken. Among the dead were one lieut-colonel (Kawano, commanding the *23rd Regiment*), two majors and many junior officers. Fifteen dead lay round the companies of McInnes and Just, which the main Japanese force by-passed when advancing on battalion headquarters. On the field lay 44 Japanese machine-guns, 219 rifles and 22 swords. Since 28th March a total of 620 Japanese dead had been counted. On the other hand in southern Bougainville from January to April the 25th Battalion, which bore the main force of the attacks from 28th March to 5th April, lost 10 officers and 179 other ranks killed or wounded. At the end of the battle it was 567 strong—270 short. McKinna had led his battalion with great skill and coolness and his men had demonstrated their innate soldierly qualities and the excellence of their training and tactics.

Interrogation of prisoners and examination of captured documents suggested that the Japanese troops assembled for the counter-offensive totalled about 2,400, mostly fresh troops. Since at least 620 Japanese had been killed, and it could be assumed that at least 1,000 had been wounded, it was decided that the main formations engaged—the *13th and 23rd Regiments*—had been made temporarily ineffective. The operations had underlined both the strength and weakness of the Japanese tactics. Their patrolling had been enterprising and thorough. On the other hand their staff work was confused, their artillery fire inaccurate, the practice of invariably cutting signal wires immediately before their attacks robbed them of surprise, and the habit of making repeated charges against strong positions and often from the same direction led to crippling losses.

The operations round Slater's Knoll had demonstrated the effectiveness of employing tanks with the forward companies and on the lines of communication. Field advocated using also machine-gun carriers to patrol the main tracks and bring out wounded.

When it appeared that the Australians were determined to continue advancing south, General Kanda had ordered General Akinaga of the *6th Division* to make a full-scale attack if the Australians crossed the Puriata. His object was to delay the Australians and give time to prepare for the decisive battle, which was to be fought on the line of the Silibai-Porror Rivers with a strong mobile striking force poised in the west.

After the war those who interrogated Japanese officers about this battle found it difficult to reconcile conflicting accounts, evidently not because memories had failed but because the Japanese operation had been "unbelievably confused". The attack was planned by Akinaga, incompetent as a field commander. He had in his division the *13th* and *23rd Regiments*, a field artillery regiment and, in the later stage, a medium artillery regiment. The fighting strength of the battered division was only about 2,700. They believed that there were 400 Australians south of the Puriata.

Officers of both regiments complained afterwards that neither regiment knew what the other was doing. On the first day Colonel Toyoharu Muda's *13th Regiment* believed that it attacked alone. Muda reported that he had taken his objective. But the same day Lieut-Colonel Kawano's *23rd Regiment* attacked a feature and claimed its capture. Akinaga thereupon ordered a further attack to annihilate the remaining enemy forces in the Puriata ford area. Four days later—in moonlight on the morning of the 5th—this attack opened.

The *23rd Regiment* attacked about 1,000 yards to the right of the *13th* and north-east of it. The attack failed, Kawano was killed and the regiment withdrew south to the rear of the *13th*. The *13th Regiment* with 600 men made the main attack from north and east. It made good progress until dawn when the attackers were ordered to dig in until darkness and make full use of grenades and mortars. However, in the afternoon, tanks and artillery fire drove the Japanese from the positions they had gained, and the Japanese commander accepted defeat. All three battalion commanders in the *13th* were killed. After Akinaga had reported his failure Kanda said to his Chief of Staff, Colonel Yoshiyuki Ejima: "It would not have happened if I had been in command. The enemy right flank was wide open. I would have severed his life line and controlled Toko. We could have delayed the enemy for three months."

The Japanese leaders estimated that 1,800 Australians were killed (a perplexing total in view of the fact that they considered that there were only 400 south of the Puriata at the outset). They gave their own casualties as 280 killed, including 30 officers, and 320 wounded (but 620 dead, including 52 officers, were counted).

The Japanese leaders said afterwards that they considered that it was fortunate that the Australians did not exploit their success, since, after the defeat at Slater's, there could have been no organised resistance as far south and east as the Hongorai. They concluded that the length of the supply line was hampering the Australians' rate of progress.

Throughout the operations in the southern and other sectors New Guinea native troops had been strenuously employed. More and more reliance was being placed on them as guides. On 26th March the company of the 1st New Guinea Battalion serving in the southern sector had been withdrawn for a fortnight's rest, though its detached platoon in the central sector remained forward. The company was in need of rest, particularly its European members, whose responsibilities were heavier and, as a rule, more constant than those of their opposite numbers in other units.

In his report for March Captain Hegarty,[7] the medical officer of the 1st New Guinea Battalion, wrote that information from the commanding officer of the battalion and from the company itself made it

> obvious that 90 per cent of the Europeans of this company are exhausted and even now will be ineffective as a fighting force for a minimum of three months. . . . Of the platoon commanders, two . . . have been completely incapacitated for three weeks and the third took ill whilst on leave. Of the N.C.O's, four have been returned to Australia unfit for service outside Australia and every other N.C.O. has spent . . . time in hospital. . . . These Europeans were selected, amongst other things, for good health. . . . There is only one explanation and that is too much work for too long. Four of the five officers have been on service in New Guinea respectively 20, 19, 18 and 16 months.

He pointed out that the officers and N.C.O's had worked for six months on training and camp building and then had been "in action solidly for six months working in succession with three brigades and always with the forward battalion". The natives also had had too little relaxation and about 25 per cent were ineffective at any one time.

During March Savige had been pressing for reinforcements, but without much result. On 4th March he mentioned to Sturdee that the movement to Bougainville of two artillery regiments—the 2/11th and 13th—had been deferred mainly because of lack of shipping. He should, he said, have five field, one medium and one anti-tank regiment, but had only two field regiments, a mountain battery, and a troop of medium guns to cope with a major operation against the *6th Japanese Division* in the south, an "essential operation" on the Numa Numa trail, and an important operation in the north.[8] Sturdee replied that there was no shipping to move new units. As it was, 5,000 men who should be in New Guinea were held up at Townsville.

> As you know (he continued) G.H.Q. controls all shipping and I doubt whether they are the least bit interested in what goes on in Bougainville now that U.S. troops are out of it.

---

[7] Capt V. H. Hegarty, NX200475; RMO 1 NG Inf Bn. Medical practitioner; of Burwood, NSW; b. Burwood, 8 Feb 1918.

[8] The "troop of medium guns" was in fact "U" Heavy Battery. This battery was armed with four 155-mm guns and manned by men of the Port Kembla coast artillery. The battery, commanded by Captain J. I. McKenna (of Ashgrove, Qld), had arrived at Torokina in January and was transported to Toko in landing craft on 3rd and 4th April.

On 11th March Savige informed Sturdee that his infantry units lacked 112 officers, and asked that he be allowed to promote officers from the ranks.[9]

General Blamey had been on Bougainville from 24th to 27th March. About ten days earlier the attacks launched against him in Parliament and Press had reached their climax. The troops had been reading about these and knew that the necessity of the offensive in which they were engaged had been questioned in the House and in the newspapers. On the day of his arrival Blamey was invited to a football match in the area of the 15th Brigade, then in reserve. Savige who accompanied him was anxious lest the spectators—about 7,000 troops—should show signs that they shared the sentiments of the critics at home. But after Blamey had shaken hands with the teams and spun a coin for the captains "the troops broke into cheers which continued until he arrived in his seat" and Blamey seemed "moved and bucked up" by this welcome.

Blamey greatly encouraged Savige on this visit by granting several requests and giving evidence of confidence in him. For example, he approved the commissioning of men from the ranks,[1] promised some L.C.T's and the 2/11th Field Regiment, and agreed that the Base Sub-Area at Torokina should be placed under Savige's command.

In the southern sector patrolling continued. On 7th April a patrol of the 9th Battalion encountered thirty Japanese and killed four. Next day a party of the 61st killed five. The 7th Brigade had now been in action since late January and was weary and depleted. On the 13th Bridgeford ordered the gradual relief of the 7th Brigade by the 15th Brigade, which had not yet been in action on Bougainville. When regrouping was complete the 7th Brigade would move back to Torokina and the 29th would come forward and be responsible for protecting and maintaining the lines of communication. That day the 58th/59th Battalion relieved the 25th in the Slater's Knoll perimeter, and the 24th moved through and occupied a position astride the Buin Road. The 9th remained in the northern area where it pressed on steadily.

On 20th April a platoon of the 9th under Sergeant Lambert[2] with an artillery officer moved out to search the area ahead of a post on the north bank of the Huio River and, if necessary, register the position for artillery fire. It crossed the Huio and established a base; thence a patrol of 11 under Corporal Baker[3] moved forward. After 100 yards it came under fire from a strong party in an ambush position. The men went to ground

---

[9] On 14th March, after Savige had complained that Brigadier Bierwirth of First Army had sent a signal direct to Brigadier Garrett on Savige's staff, Sturdee asked Savige to go to Lae for a rest and a conference. At Lae after a discussion that at times was apparently acrimonious, Sturdee agreed to forbid demi-official correspondence between the two staffs.

[1] On 1st April Savige was given formal permission to commission in the field enough men to fill half the vacancies.

[2] WO2 C. H. Lambert, QX37992; 9 Bn. Farm worker; of Nambour, Qld; b. Brisbane, 22 Aug 1919.

[3] Cpl E. E. Baker, Q100073; 9 Bn. Grocer's assistant; of Kedron, Qld; b. Brisbane, 26 Nov 1920.

until Private Budden[4] deliberately exposed himself, shouting and firing his Bren, and, covered by this fire, the patrol got out. Later Lance-Corporal West,[5] when leading scout, was hit in the shoulder with a dum-dum bullet. The patrol managed to reach the platoon base, whence artillery fire was directed into the enemy's area.

A patrol of thirteen men of the 9th which went out at 8.30 a.m. on 24th April had the task of setting an ambush on a well-worn Japanese track. By 4 p.m. the patrol had not reached its destination and the leader, Sergeant Bolton,[6] decided to establish a perimeter for the night on high ground above a creek. While the men were digging in Bolton saw a Japanese and shot him, and soon the sounds of voices, the smell of cooking, and the discovery of fresh footprints made it evident that the patrol was close to a Japanese bivouac. The patrol began to skirt this area but had gone only 100 yards when a group of Japanese appeared ahead. Bolton, who was leading, fired into the Japanese.

It was a cunning enemy trap (says the unit's report) for no sooner had Sgt Bolton fired his Owen than hell was let loose. The enemy were in position and opened with 3 HMG's, 4 LMG's, numerous rifles and grenade dischargers. Sgt Bolton was seen to clutch his chest and fall mortally wounded. The remainder of the patrol immediately spread out and returned the fire. After some minutes Pte Birch[7] was severely wounded in the knee and fell to the ground where he lay in intense agony. At this stage Pte Norman[8] took command and directed his men to withdraw, but before the command could be carried out Private Roberts,[9] without regard for his own safety, rushed into the position under terrific enemy fire, grasped his wounded mate under the shoulders and dragged him to safety. The patrol then eased out of the position and moved a further 100 yards where Pte Birch had his wounds attended to.

The patrol now had no map and compass because these had been lost with Bolton, but Norman led the men west guided by the sun. They formed a perimeter that night and reached their unit on the 28th.

From 23rd April onwards Colonel Matthews of the 9th had a troop of tanks under his command. By 27th April the 9th had cleared the important lateral track, Tokinotu-Horinu 2-Rumiki, and a company had reached the Hongorai south-east of Rumiki. The battalion was relieved on 2nd May, thus ending the 7th Brigade's extended term in active operations.[1]

During the period of the Slater's Knoll engagement the 2/8th Commando had been active on the inland flank. On 3rd April it carried out a bloody ambush on the Commando Road. A patrol under Lieutenant Killen[2] established the ambush where the road crossed the Taromi River, 3,000 yards east of the Hongorai.

---

[4] Pte H. G. Budden, MM, N168572; 9 Bn. Rabbiter; of Tingha, NSW; b. Tingha, 1 Apr 1923.
[5] L-Cpl A. F. West, NX162355; 9 Bn. Farmer; of Valla, NSW; b. Kempsey, NSW, 27 Apr 1924.
[6] Sgt P. F. Bolton, QX37979; 9 Bn. Traveller; of Tamworth, NSW; b. Tamworth, 13 Feb 1917. Killed in action 24 Apr 1945.
[7] Pte S. G. Birch, N34931; 9 Bn. Labourer; of Wagga Wagga, NSW; b. Grong Grong, NSW, 11 Aug 1917.
[8] Pte A. W. Norman, Q16607; 9 Bn. Labourer; of Brisbane; b. Brisbane, 29 Oct 1917.
[9] Pte R. C. Roberts, MM, NX163354; 9 Bn. Farmer; of Camden, NSW; b. Homebush, NSW, 1 Jan 1924.
[1] In that period the 25th Battalion alone had killed 646 Japanese.
[2] Lt B. G. L. Killen, NX132865; 2/8 Cdo Sqn. Station overseer; of Nyngan, NSW; b. Nyngan, 30 Dec 1923.

Forty to fifty enemy moving up the track disconcertingly halted for a rest in the cleared area which part of the ambush was covering. After a tense 15 minutes in which the enemy smoked and wandered round in scattered, chattering groups, they concentrated ready to move off again. Our patrol opened heavy grenade, automatic and rifle fire which killed 15 of the enemy and probably killed a further ten.[3]

After this ambush no Japanese were seen on the Commando Road for sixteen days.

There had been some anxiety lest the natives beyond the Puriata in this area might be as hostile to the advancing Australians as they were to the neighbouring native tribes north of the river. On 16th March Captain Dunshea took out a patrol to explore the track systems and possible enemy dispositions east of Nihero and discover where the sympathies of the natives lay. The natives proved friendly and ready to swing to the Australian side at the first show of strength. The enemy was disposed in small gardens and not patrolling.

In this area the Japanese seldom retaliated effectively. On 5th April, however, they placed an ambush on the commandos' line of communication where it crossed the Taar River and fired on a patrol bringing in a prisoner. The patrol—two troopers and two police boys—dispersed and the Japanese recovered the prisoner. This was a serious loss because the prisoner had knowledge of the bases from which the A.I.B. and the commando squadron were operating. That afternoon and next day patrols combed the area west of Nihero with orders to destroy the ambushers. They traced them to a House Garamut, where they killed nine Japanese, and later Angau natives captured the only survivor—the commander, a 2nd lieutenant; it was decided that this was a party returning after the attempt to raid the Torokina perimeter.

It will be recalled that at the end of January Lieutenant Mason and his party were in the Sipuru area obtaining information, supporting the natives in their guerilla war against the Japanese, and caring for refugee natives over a wide area. On 9th February Mason learnt that Pilot Officer Stuart,[4] who had been behind the Japanese lines on Bougainville in 1943-44, was leading a party of four, including Sergeant Wigley, south into the Buin-Siwai area. Soon afterwards Mason learnt from his native scouts that a large number of Japanese were assembling at Kovidau and planned to attack him on 16th February. He called for an air attack on Kovidau, but the bombs were dropped on another village five miles away, and soon this Japanese force was camped about two miles from Sipuru, another party was at Orami and a third at Forma.

The enemy continued to mill around us for a couple of days (wrote Mason). The track to our ridge was plain enough owing to heavy traffic backwards and forwards. All tracks seemed to lead to us. Perhaps it appeared too obvious to the enemy. Eventually they moved to Mau. . . . The enemy suffered four casualties by rifle fire and two by arrows before reaching Orami via Mau and Meridau.

---

[3] 2/8 Aust Commando Squadron Report on Operations in Southern Bougainville, Nov 44-Aug 45.

[4] F-O R. Stuart, MC. AIB (RANVR 1943-44; served as civilian with XIV American Corps June-December 1944; RAAF 1944-45). Planter; of Bougainville; b. Mysore, India, 30 Apr 1904.

Roubai who was returning from Torokina with a new rifle found the enemy at Orami and added two Nips to his score. . . . The Japanese left the next morning travelling by moonlight to avoid being ambushed again. . . . It is my opinion that the enemy intended to establish a post at Orami for attacking the 3rd Division's flank at Sovele, only three hours jeepable track from Orami. With hostile natives on their flank and their L of C it was impracticable to hold Orami.

Mason now asked for fuses and explosives to enable him to destroy Japanese ammunition dumps. These arrived, and on 12th March Corporal Narakas and a native leader named Asina blew up a dump near Kieta. At the same time the intrepid Roubai was sent out with ten other natives and two cases of T.N.T. on a double mission: to blow up two other dumps and to bring in Father Muller, a Roman Catholic missionary of German origin, who was in the Arawa Plantation area.

Roubai found one dump guarded by sixteen Japanese; Father Muller was guarded by nine. He reported afterwards that he and his men killed the priest's guard and put him on the road to Mason with a small escort. Roubai and his men then killed the Japanese guarding the dump and blew it up. Mason sent Muller to Torokina.

In February the Japanese sent out a force to relieve their men who were besieged by the Kapikavi natives and succeeded in extricating them and withdrawing to Kekemona, where they dug in. In the fighting 51 Japanese were killed. Indeed the losses inflicted by the native guerillas were now reaching high figures. Mason had sent patrols into the country between Koromira and Toimonapu Plantations where the Japanese were treating the natives well and the natives were working for them. A patrol brought back two envoys and Mason sent these to Torokina to be shown that the Australians were more powerful than the Japanese, and, when the envoys returned, Mason sent them to their own villages to spread the news. Eventually these natives, supported by Mason's scouts, killed by "treachery and surprise" 40 Japanese and took 4 prisoners. These natives then gathered in a remote village for protection against Japanese reprisals. There 14 of them were killed and 45 wounded when an aircraft mistakenly bombed the village.

Until March (wrote Mason) we were in a continual state of alertness. We all slept fully dressed. White and Warner slept with their boots on until the end of March. . . . I always had the pack with the codes and records ready to throw across my shoulders while Warner had his W/T equipment always packed ready, when not in use, for a quick get-away. . . . We had now definitely taken the offensive. I believed that the harder we hit the enemy now, the harder it would be for him to attack us. . . . I had eventually armed thousands of irregulars. Many were armed with bows and arrows and some were given grenades. It was my policy to appoint leaders and sub-leaders to every district. Ammunition, grenades and booby-trap material were only issued to these leaders for distribution and never given to individuals. This was important as everyone wanted to be someone of importance and it gave the leader more power to be able to dispense fighting material to whom he wished. He therefore got unity within his own area and had a responsibility which gave him enthusiasm which he was able to inspire into his men.

At first most Japanese were killed with grenades thrown into their huts, in ambushes, or with booby-traps. At length the Japanese cleared wide areas round their camps and put up palisades; later they dug themselves in. For example, at Moroni, 40 Japanese were dug in, and whenever parties went out to work in the gardens they were protected by a machine-gun team. Nevertheless 23 had been killed by April, and in May 5, including the officer in command, were killed. A party came from Kaino and extricated the survivors. An order had been given that natives should be paid 10 shillings' worth of trade goods for every Japanese killed. Mason declined to do this on the grounds that it would not have increased the killing and goods were difficult to obtain. "We offered to pay handsomely for prisoners but seldom got any. The natives preferred the honour of killing them to payment. Air support would have been more satisfying to the native than remuneration."

In March and April a series of effective air attacks was made on targets indicated by Mason. On 15th April raiders led by Asina destroyed two coast guns and three ammunition dumps on the heights above Kieta harbour. Asina laid the charges in daylight while the Japanese were away for their midday meal. "Our offensive was now in full swing from Buin to Rorovana," Mason wrote. "Confirmed enemy dead were reaching nearly 400 a month. The enemy were now confined to foxholes when not working under cover of machine-guns in the gardens and they only moved about at night, and then avoiding the usual tracks as the shrapnel mines and booby-traps were taking a heavy toll of them." At the end of May Mason was told that Lieutenant Seton[5] (who had been a coast-watcher on Choiseul from October 1942 to March 1944, and on New Britain from August to March 1945) was coming to relieve him. Mason was disappointed that "now that the place was safe and our forces well organised it should be given to somebody else".

Stuart had been attached to the Intelligence staff of the XIV American Corps during its period on Bougainville and had guided a number of long-range patrols. After leave in Australia he arrived back at Torokina early in February, when Mason, Sandford and Bridge were already well established in the mountainous no-man's land. He set off on 17th February with Warrant-Officer Colley,[6] Sergeant Wigley, Corporal Craze,[7] and a party of natives, and on the 20th arrived at Sikiomoni where the natives welcomed them. A camp was made and natives were detailed to watch all tracks. The natives were becoming short of food and Stuart helped them with rations and later distributed 30 rifles.

By the time the 3rd Division was nearing the Hari, Stuart's natives were well organised and were harassing the Japanese by cutting telephone lines, destroying gardens, placing flags on tree tops to guide bombers, and

---

[5] Capt C. W. Seton, DCM, NX91635; AIB. Plantation manager; of Faisi, British Solomon Is; b. Wellingrove Stn, NSW, 14 Jun 1901.

[6] WO2 D. Colley, MM, NX15042. (1st AIF: Anzac Mtd Div Train 1917-19.) I Corps Amn Pk AASC, "M" Special Unit and Angau. Plantation manager; of Mosman, NSW; b. Ingleburn, NSW, 27 Jan 1901.

[7] Cpl W. A. C. Craze, WX13612; "Z" Special Unit. Clerk; of Swanbourne, WA; b. Esperance, WA, 4 Apr 1922.

attacking isolated parties. It was difficult to persuade the natives to take the risk of capturing a prisoner but on 16th March a native brought in a Japanese whom he had persuaded to desert, and who gave useful information.

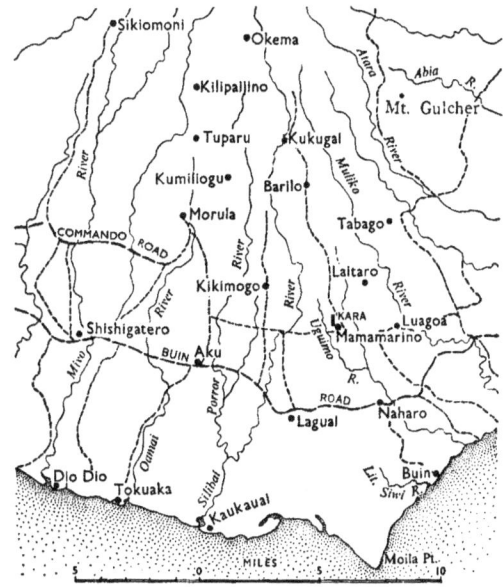

As an outcome of a bombing raid on Japanese headquarters between the headwaters of the Mivo and Silibai Rivers in which the two senior Japanese officers were killed, the natives in that area, hitherto very much afraid of the Japanese, were won over.

On 7th April Stuart's natives attacked a small force of naval men at Okema, and killed the senior officer in the area and three others. This led to the withdrawal of all Japanese from the area north of Kumiliogu and Barilo. About this time Stuart learnt that some missionaries, nuns and about 12 Chinese were held but had a good deal of freedom at Naharo and Laguai. On 12th April natives escorted two priests, Fathers Junkers and Le Breton, and four Chinese into Stuart's camp, and later two nuns, Sisters Ludwig and Ludwina, and two more priests, Fathers Seiller and Griswald arrived.[8]

Meanwhile in the northern sector a difficult operation had been successfully carried out. The main body of the 26th Battalion[9] arrived at Puto to relieve the 31st/51st on 21st February, and its leading companies were

---

[8] See "The Nuns' Patrol" by T. A. G. Hungerford in *Stand-To*, August-September 1950.
[9] The Order of Battle of Callinan's force illustrates the diversity of the specialised groups employed in the field at this time:

	Posted strength	
	Officers	Other ranks
26th Battalion	43	746
HQ 4th Field Regiment	7	60
12th Field Battery	8	181
2nd Mountain Battery	5	97
Platoon 16th Field Company RAE	6	107
Detachment 5th Mobile Meteorological Flight	—	2
Platoon 101st Heavy Mortar Company	3	63
Company 19th Field Ambulance	4	81
Detachment 42nd Watercraft Company	3	42
Detachment 223rd Supply Depot Platoon	1	12
Detachment "B" Corps Wireless Section	—	8
Detachment 11th Brigade Signals	1	16
Detachment Angau	2	6 whites, 249 natives
Detachment 1st Water Transport Signals	—	3
Detachment 102nd Workshops	—	8

Footnote continued next page.

in the forward area that evening. Lieut-Colonel B. J. Callinan (commanding the 26th), an able and experienced leader who had distinguished himself with the 2/2nd Independent Company and later as Force commander on Timor in 1942, gave one company (Captain Gibson[1]) the task of moving round the enemy's coastal flank and cutting his communications, while a second company (Captain McNair[2]) advanced astride the track travelling north about 1,000 yards from the coast, its objective being Lalum, shown on maps as the beginning of a road to Pora Pora. This company found itself flanked by swamps and sent out patrols to find firm ground leading to the foothills on which Lalum was shown to be on the map. On the 24th a patrol reached the east-west track and a company perimeter was established there. Next day, after a fight in which four Japanese were killed, another track junction was seized on the eastern flank and a patrol reached the coast. McNair's company was now astride the enemy's main lines of communication. On the 26th Callinan sent a company (Captain Coleman's[3]) through McNair's to cut the coastal track near the Compton River, outflanking an area which a captured map showed as containing the enemy's main strength.

Meanwhile Gibson's company had cut the tracks leading to the enemy's positions north of the Gillman River—"a maze of tracks covered by logged pill-boxes and recently-dug foxholes joined by communication trenches"—and forced the Japanese out. They abandoned a field gun, two anti-tank guns and a headquarters with office equipment. On the inland flank, where a company of the 31st/51st was still operating, Captain Searles'[4] company of the 26th moved round the enemy's flank on the 23rd but was held by the force strongly sited on Downs' Ridge. On the 25th-26th the enemy, between 30 and 40 strong, was forced out by accurate artillery and mortar fire. The company of the 31st/51st, which had been fighting there for three weeks, was now relieved. Searles' company advanced along the track, met the enemy again on the 27th and withstood two sharp attacks. Throughout this period the enemy regularly shelled the left flank companies and the troops advancing along the coastal track.

	Posted strength	
	Officers	Other ranks
Detachment 102nd Ordnance Field Park	—	5
Detachment II Corps Salvage Unit	—	7
Detachment 72nd Dental Unit	1	4
Detachment 4th Division Provost Company	—	4
Detachment Electrical and Mechanical Engineers	—	5
Detachment ATIS	1	2
Detachment 7th Pigeon Section	—	6
Detachment 1st Pigeon Section	—	2
Detachment 25th Section Field Security Service	—	5
Public Relations Officer and Photographer	1	—
3rd Survey Battery	1	14
Detachment Field Bakery	1	10
Detachment 76th Transport Platoon	1	14
Detachment 2nd Field Survey Company	1	6
Amenities	—	1
HQ 11th Brigade	3	10

[1] Capt J. McL. Gibson, NX124620; 26 Bn. Bank officer; of Harden, NSW; b. Murrumburrah, NSW, 9 Nov 1917.

[2] Capt S. H. H. McNair, NX101320; 26 Bn. Public servant; of Randwick, NSW; b. Randwick, 4 Nov 1916.

[3] Col K. R. G. Coleman, MC, VX133644; 26 Bn. Regular soldier; b. Hobart, 17 Jan 1921.

[4] Maj S. G. Searles, MC, QX36511; 26 Bn. Clerk; of Longreach, Qld; b. Longreach, 4 Oct 1916.

The Australian guns bombarded the enemy's artillery and their fire was effective in stopping some counter-attacks.

The beach-head area having been cleared, McNair's company advanced east to establish a base and send strong patrols farther east to link with Searles' company, still fighting hard. Maps were inaccurate and both companies were encountering well-dug enemy machine-gun posts. By the evening of 3rd March the leading platoons of both companies were close to each other; each indicated its exact position in the dense bush by firing grenades on which the other took compass bearings. After having overcome a post the companies joined on the morning of the 4th and Searles' company went into reserve.

That day Gibson's company moved north along a formed road. A document found on a Japanese sergeant killed that morning gave the dispositions of the enemy forces near the Compton River, and the number of Japanese carrying messages and food killed that day showed that the company was striking the enemy's main line of communication. A series of enemy positions was engaged and captured and on 8th March huts capable of housing about 120 were found; on an enemy map these were marked "old battle headquarters". Farther left Coleman's company had been probing for the enemy's flanks at the mouth of the Compton River.

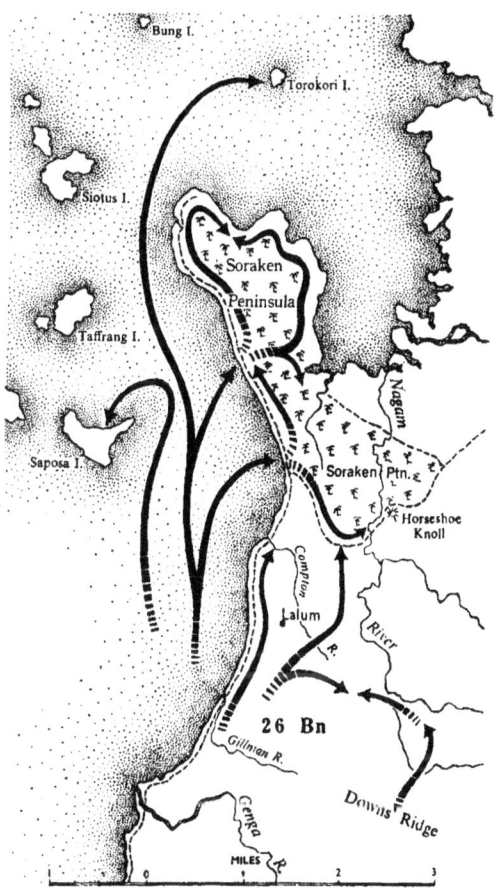

26th Battalion, February-April

Coleman's company continued to advance northward to seize the crossing of the Nagam River. On the 7th and 8th its carrier line was attacked by Japanese. Patrols on the inland flank found the enemy well dug in north of Downs' Ridge. McNair advanced and on 13th March, supported by artillery fire, attacked the position, killed fifteen Japanese and, next day, pursued the survivors.

On the night of the 12th-13th March Searles' company plus an additional platoon landed from the sea in two waves near the southern end of Soraken Plantation, pushed inland to the main track and advanced southward along it. Some Japanese were killed. On the 14th the company was in contact with Gibson's company at the southern end of the plantation. The Japanese made a series of attacks on this force astride their track from the Soraken Peninsula to the Compton and Nagam River areas. Gibson's company advanced through the Soraken Peninsula from its southern boundary to the Nagam River. The enemy were dug in to protect the river crossing, but were forced back to rising ground to the east (later known as Horseshoe Knoll). On the 16th a Japanese signal line was tapped. The Australian lines were cleared of all other traffic and the Japanese line connected to Callinan's tactical headquarters where an interpreter learned that the enemy were greatly worried by the way in which their patrols and runners were disappearing without a trace.[5] Australian patrols continued to harass the Japanese force round Horseshoe Knoll until the 20th when, after continuing losses, it withdrew.

Meanwhile, on 10th March Coleman's company, supported by artillery, had attacked the centre of the enemy's defensive line and overrun the position. An attack on the western part of the line at the mouth of the Compton River was made on the 14th. This position was discovered to be extensive—some 80 by 50 yards—and well dug in. After a long fire fight the company withdrew to its own perimeter having lost four killed, including Lieutenant Compton,[6] and six wounded, among whom was Lieutenant Moore.[7] Four Japanese were certainly killed and probably others. The enemy was ejected on the night of the 16th after accurate artillery bombardment; and on the 19th this company passed through Searles' beach-head.

While two companies were forcing the enemy back from the Nagam River area into the foothills and one was clearing the Compton River area, Callinan delivered another left hook when McNair's company on the night of the 19th-20th was landed some miles to the north. The landing craft were fired on by an anti-tank gun and rifles but the men gained the shore and next morning one platoon was astride the coastal track and another, to the south, had captured the anti-tank gun and a "75", both undamaged and with much ammunition. On the 20th this company linked with the troops moving from the south, who had killed an officer carrying an operation order for the defence of the Soraken Peninsula revealing the whereabouts of the enemy's headquarters and supply base. As a result of the capture of the operation order Coleman's company was moved immediately to the east side of the peninsula to attack the enemy's

---

[5] On another occasion when a Japanese line was tapped the listeners heard their own artillery orders, a result of induction and the swampy nature of the ground. As a result all lines were laid with metallic return, so that two lines were needed. The 11th Brigade laid 541 miles of wire, excluding assault cable.

[6] Lieut J. W. Compton, QX36516; 26 Bn. Branch manager; of Winton, Qld; b. Gayndah, Qld, 12 Mar 1913. Killed in action 14 Mar 1945.

[7] Capt E. H. Moore, MC, NX111499; 26 Bn. Advertising artist; of Milson's Point, NSW; b. Kensington, Vic, 11 Feb 1915.

headquarters. Coleman planned this movement and the subsequent attack with great efficiency and on the 26th organised resistance on the Soraken Peninsula ceased; the battalion had taken its objective after a brilliant series of manoeuvres. The enemy abandoned barges, engines, electrical gear, ammunition and tools. The other companies, patrolling 1,500 yards east of the Nagam River, found abandoned field gun positions containing much ammunition.

Meanwhile two islands off the coast—Taiof and Saposa—had been taken. It was learnt from a native police patrol on the 5th that 25 Japanese had arrived at Taiof and that it was intended to land a field gun there on the night of the 6th. Just before midnight on the 5th-6th Searles' company landed on Saposa, killed four Japanese and captured two anti-tank guns and 20 rifles. Natives now reported that 25 Japanese from Taiof had departed northward on the night of the 3rd; the presence of the rifles suggested that they might return. On the night of the 6th an assault craft loaded with Japanese was engaged by mortars and machine-guns and sunk.

On 10th March an Angau patrol under Captain Cambridge ambushed 11 Japanese left on Taiof Island killing 10 and capturing the warrant-officer in command; later four guns and much equipment were found. An observation post was established giving a view of Soraken harbour, Bonis Peninsula and Buka Passage.

From 22nd February to 4th April, when they were relieved, the 26th Battalion killed and recovered the bodies of 157 Japanese, and were certain that they killed 13 others; 8 additional graves were found; 2 prisoners were taken. They captured 12 guns from 20-mm to 75-mm calibre, 2,650 rounds of artillery ammunition, and 11 machine-guns.

The Japanese forces in the Tarlena area were commanded by Lieut-Colonel Nakamura, mentioned earlier, but the operations in the field were controlled by Captain Matsunami. Under him the force in the Genga-Compton River area was commanded by Captain Kawakami and was built round the *10th Company, 81st Regiment.*

During this period the A.I.B. party behind the enemy's lines in northern Bougainville was sending back detailed information of enemy movements and indicating targets to the supporting aircraft. In February they reported a submarine landing stores at Tinputz. An example of the detailed information obtained is given in the following signal of 21st April:

40 Japs at Ratsua, 46 Umum Gorge, 40 at Ruri, 8 at Chindawon, 50 in kunai behind Ruri, 8 at Tanimbaubau, 100 at Siara, 70 at Ton. 3 field guns at Pora Pora, 2 at Subiana, 1 at Ruri, 1 at Siara, 1 at Chindawon. Large ammunition and stores dump at Umum Gorge.

Flight Lieutenant Sandford's party in the Numa Numa area found that efforts to penetrate to Numa Numa itself were proving "abortive and costly" and was instructed to operate farther north. There they engaged in highly successful guerilla fighting. At Teopasino scouts led by Sergeant Lae and Corporal Sinavina "caught the enemy garrison indulging in physical jerks and 53 were killed by our scouts who suffered only minor casualties". A few days later 17 Japanese were killed near Surango. As a result of these achievements the local people, hitherto apathetic, began to side with Sandford, with the result that he received more information, and, from February onwards, knowledge of enemy movements and dispositions from Inus to Tinputz was fairly complete.

CHAPTER 8

ACROSS THE HARI: PORTON PLANTATION

THE comparative lull which followed the defeat of the Japanese counter-offensive early in April lasted for three weeks. General Savige and General Bridgeford agreed that no attacks should immediately be launched, and that the Japanese should be allowed to exhaust themselves in costly onslaughts. The Japanese, however, were in no position to convenience their enemies by making further heavy attacks. On the other hand the timing of any Australian attacks depended on ability to deliver supplies from the Torokina base. To maintain an effective force in the forward area it was necessary to make roads that would carry either jeeps or 3-ton trucks, and, in some cases, both. Each such road involved laying extensive corduroy and building many bridges across rivers and creeks.

Thus on 19th April, soon after the 15th Brigade had relieved the 7th, Savige, after a visit to the 3rd Division's area, confirmed the plan that Bridgeford should continue to employ only one brigade forward, and that a second brigade (the 29th) should guard and maintain the lines of communication, with one battalion in readiness to counter an enemy movement round the inland flank. He said that one battalion of the leading brigade should advance on the northern axis and one on the southern, while the third was held in close support. Savige had now obtained a third regiment of field artillery—the 2/11th—and he placed it under Bridgeford's command. Because of the difficulty of supply Savige directed that no man who was not "absolutely essential" was to be employed forward of Toko. He gave Bridgeford as his objective the line of the Hari River; the line of the intervening Hongorai River was to be an "intermediate objective".

The total Japanese strength in southern Bougainville was now estimated by the Corps staff at from 10,500 to 11,000, of whom 2,300 were believed to be immediately opposing the 3rd Division, the main concentrations being in the garden areas west of the Hari River. (In fact the Japanese strength in southern Bougainville still exceeded 18,000.)

The incoming 15th Brigade[1] had at the outset been by far the most experienced to arrive on Bougainville. Brigadier Hammer, who had com-

---

[1] The 15th Brigade Group now consisted of:
Headquarters 15th Brigade
24th Battalion
57th/60th Battalion
58th/59th Battalion
15th Brigade Signals Section
Platoon 2/1st Guard Regiment
15th Brigade Flamethrower Platoon
Three troops 2/4th Armoured Regiment
Section 15th Field Company RAE
Company 1st New Guinea Infantry Battalion (less one platoon)
266th Light Aid Detachment
Detachment 3rd Division Provost Company
Detachment 3rd Division Postal Unit
Section 63rd Dental Unit
Detachment Angau
In support were: two troops 2/4th Armoured Regiment, 2nd Field Regiment, "U" Heavy Battery, 15th Field Company (less one section), 11th Field Ambulance.

manded it during arduous operations on the New Guinea mainland in 1943 and 1944, had moulded it into a capable, self-confident force. It had just completed ten weeks of intensive training at Torokina. Hammer himself was a tireless, fiery and colourful leader who would be likely to drive his men hard in the coming operation, encouraging them with vigorously-phrased exhortations. On the day on which the brigade took over the southern sector he distributed an order of the day predicting a long tour of duty with perhaps heavy casualties but expressing confidence in the outcome.

Hammer was resolved to use the artillery, which now included the four 155-mm guns of "U" Heavy Battery, to the utmost, sending out artillery observers with the smallest patrols so that, when they met the enemy, they would be able promptly to bring down the fire of perhaps a regiment of guns. He hoped to herd the enemy into confined areas and there bombard him with guns and mortars. Hammer was enthusiastic about the use of noise to deceive: for example by sending a noisy fighting patrol to one flank and a silent patrol to the other to locate enemy positions and prepare the way for the main attacking force—usually tanks, an infantry battalion and supporting troops. Bulldozers would be used to cut tributary tracks along which tanks could make flanking attacks. Hammer had the advantage of increased air support because there were now four instead of two New Zealand squadrons on the island; the tonnage of bombs dropped increased from 493 in March, to 663 in April, and to 1,041 in May.

The country between the Puriata and the Hari generally resembled that to the west. The coastal plain was some ten miles in width and clad with dense bush above which towered large trees. Big areas of swamp occurred near the coast. East of the Puriata the Buin Road (or "Government Road No. 1") ran 5,000 to 6,000 yards from the coast. The Commando Road (or "Government Road No. 2") was parallel to it, some 5,000 yards farther north. The ground was so sodden that each road had to be corduroyed with logs before it could carry heavy traffic.

The task of advancing along the Buin Road was given to the 24th Battalion (Lieut-Colonel Anderson) with the 58th/59th (Lieut-Colonel Mayberry) protecting its rear and flanks, while the 57th/60th (Lieut-Colonel Webster[2]) advanced down the Commando Road. Hammer intended to develop the lateral track between the two main ones so that he could send tanks across the front into the Rumiki area. Hammer later recorded that when his brigade took over "contact with the Japanese had been completely lost and . . . the enemy situation was most obscure".

The 15th Brigade opened its attack on 17th April when the 24th advanced behind a creeping barrage, with two companies moving forward against enemy positions round Dawe's Creek, and a third making an outflanking move to cut the lateral track to the north. The left forward company reached its objective without encountering any Japanese, but

---

[2] Lt-Col P. G. C. Webster, WX266. 2/11 Bn; 2/48 Bn 1943-45; CO 57/60 Bn 1945. Salesman and agent; of Claremont, WA; b. Bunbury, WA, 6 Mar 1915.

Captain Graham's[3] on the right, with Lieutenant Scott's[4] troop of tanks, became engaged in a vicious fight which lasted until the next afternoon when tanks and leading infantry were 400 yards beyond Dawe's Creek. The tank crews spent the night in two-foot pits with the tanks above them like roofs. Thirty-seven Japanese were killed in this action, and the 24th lost 7 killed and 19 wounded. The 24th pushed on to Sindou Creek where it withstood several sharp counterattacks during the next week, while patrols pushed forward deeply through the bush on either side of the road. One of these, a three-day patrol under Lieutenant N. J. Spendlove, reached the Hongorai about 1,000 yards south of the Buin Road crossing and reported that the river was 30 yards wide with banks eight feet high. On the return journey they observed, unseen, an air bombardment of an enemy position which scattered a party of Japanese and caused "much squealing and cooeeing".

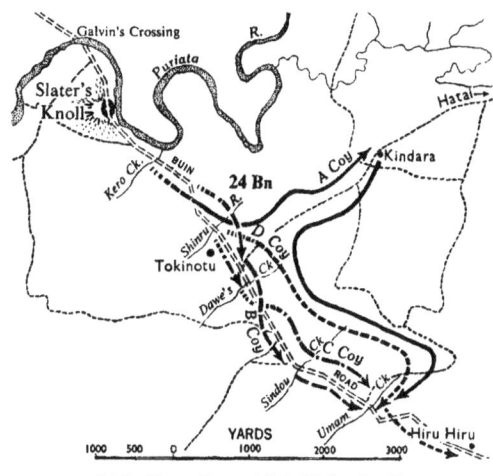

24th Battalion, 17th-25th April

On 23rd April Corporal Nott,[5] an outstanding leader who had taken out many patrols but had never lost a man, led a party 3,000 yards behind the Japanese forward positions to Hiru Hiru, examined the Buin Road there, and later ambushed 12 Japanese of whom five were killed at about 10 yards range.

On 26th April the advance along the Buin Road was resumed. Thirty-six Corsairs of Nos. 14, 22 and 26 Squadrons of the Royal New Zealand Air Force bombed and machine-gunned the enemy's area to within 300 yards of the Australian positions, and so heavily that they cleared the ground of undergrowth for some distance each side of the road. A creeping barrage fired by artillery and mortars preceded the advancing infantry. There was little opposition. By 28th April the 24th was about one-third of the distance from the Puriata to the Hongorai.

It was not until 3rd May that the 57th/60th relieved the 9th in the Rumiki area. The 9th had then been in action for three months and a half and, after the 15th Brigade had begun to take over, was still strenuously patrolling in country where clashes with enemy patrols were fairly frequent. Meanwhile the lateral track to Rumiki had been cleared

---
[3] Col S. C. Graham, OBE, MC, NX76225. 1 Armd Div; attached 7 British Armd Div 1943-44; 24 Bn. Regular soldier; b. Grafton, NSW, 23 Oct 1920.
[4] Lt R. G. Scott, MC, SX11347; 2/4 Armd Regt. Grazier; of Ororoo, SA; b. Ororoo, 2 Jun 1918.
[5] Sgt A. H. Nott, DCM, VX135885; 24 Bn. Trapper; of Rutherglen, Vic; b. Kalgoorlie, WA, 12 Jan 1923.

of the surviving Japanese parties and corduroyed, a task largely done by the infantry of the 58th/59th Battalion.

On their first days in the new area the 57th/60th on the Commando Road had several clashes and lost men—a result, it was decided, of the inexperience of the patrols as a whole. (In the operations in New Guinea in 1943 and 1944 this battalion had had less battle experience than the others in the brigade.) For instance, on 4th May a patrol commanded by Lieutenant

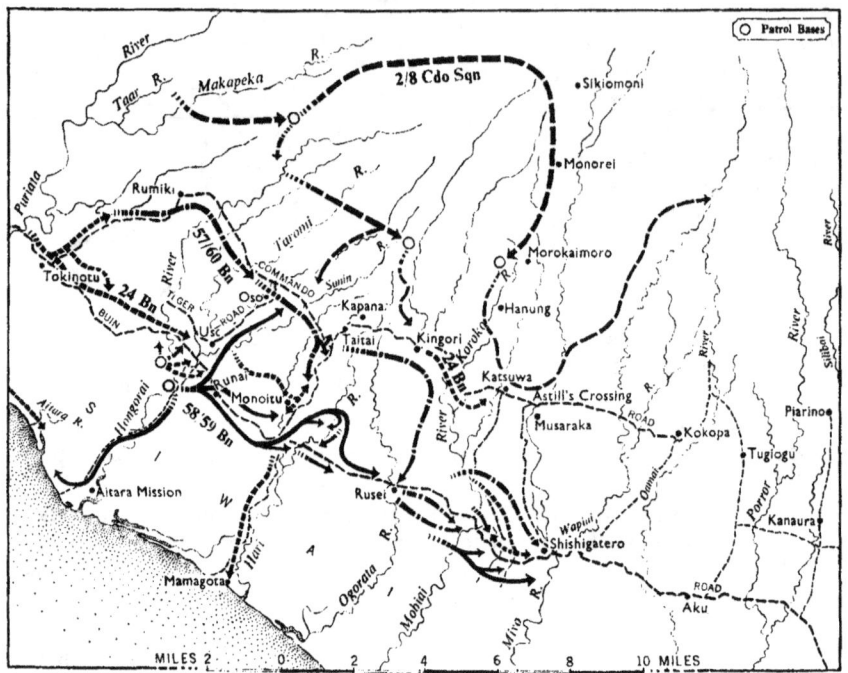

15th Brigade, May-June

Linehan[6] walked into an ambush. Linehan was mortally wounded and as he lay dying ordered his men to press on. In the ensuing fight two others —Lance-Corporal Woolbank[7] and Private Watson[8]—were killed.

Meanwhile on 30th April an artillery forward observation officer, Lieutenant Tarr[9] of the 2nd Field Regiment, who was with a patrol of the 24th Battalion, was missing when the remainder of the patrol returned. His body was found three days later. On 30th April and 2nd May, the 24th, with a troop of tanks reinforcing the leading company, advanced a

---

[6] Lt D. W. Linehan, VX89802; 57/60 Bn. Shop assistant; of Cobram, Vic; b. Cobram, 27 Aug 1917. Killed in action 4 May 1945.

[7] L-Cpl R. B. Woolbank, NX137271; 57/60 Bn. Labourer; of Molong, NSW; b. Molong, 4 Aug 1920. Killed in action 4 May 1945.

[8] Pte C. C. Watson, TX16125; 57/60 Bn. Butcher; of Upper Burnie, Tas; b. Meander, Tas, 11 Jun 1923. Killed in action 4 May 1945.

[9] Lt H. A. Tarr, VX54792; 2 Fd Regt. Bread carter; of Camberwell, Vic; b. North Carlton, Vic, 19 Oct 1914. Killed in action 30 Apr 1945.

total of more than a mile without opposition; they were now nearing the Hongorai. However, on the 4th Lieutenant Lawn's[1] platoon was advancing with two tanks and a bulldozer when the crew of the leading tank came to a log across the road and saw movement in the bush. A burst of machine-gun fire from the tank cut the leaves away and revealed the barrel of a field gun. The first round fired from the tank's 2-pounder disabled the enemy gun and the enemy seemed to flee. Farther ahead, however, a mine exploded at the rear of the second tank. It was discovered that it had been exploded with a wire by a Japanese concealed in the bush.

Henceforward mines and concealed guns were encountered more and more frequently. They were detected chiefly by the practised eyes of the engineer teams of Major Needham's[2] 15th Field Company who became increasingly skilful. Mechanical detectors were defeated by several sorts of mine employed—wooden boxes filled with T.N.T., for example; but their presence was betrayed by protruding fuses, wires, disturbed earth, and confirmed by prodding with a bayonet.

> There were instances where large mines, consisting of many 150-mm and 75-mm shells, were laid underneath corduroy and were so well camouflaged that detection would have been impossible without a significant stick which the enemy had placed by the side of the road. This stick was usually 2 feet to 3 feet high and about 1 inch thick. . . . One mine . . . consisted of a timber hole 8 feet by 5 feet by 3 feet filled with 150-mm, 75-mm shells and 81-mm mortars. This mine was blown *in situ* and created a crater 24 feet in diameter and 10 feet deep.[3]

An impression at this time that the Japanese in this sector were becoming dispirited led to a renewal of "psychological warfare", which, it will be recalled, had already been waged on the central sector, though without visible effect. On several occasions in the first week of May a broadcasting unit of F.E.L.O. spoke to groups of Japanese troops known to be only a few hundred yards away from forward posts of the 24th Battalion. For example, on the morning of the 5th the following address was broadcast in Japanese:

> Soldiers of Japan stop your movement and listen. We are now cooking a good hot meal for our troops, come in and have your first good meal for months. We have for you amongst other things fresh meat, bread and fruit, cigarettes are plentiful and clean clothes and boots are yours for the asking. We do not desire to cause unnecessary killing so we give you this opportunity to come in by walking down the road with your weapons on your backs and your hands in the air with the palms towards your front. You will be well cared for and sent to Australia where thousands of your officers and fellow soldiers are now. Do not die a useless death, come in now and build up to live and serve Japan after the war. Come in now.

Soon after this broadcast Australian troops fired on the Japanese; then a further short broadcast was made telling them that the invitation was still open and fire had been commenced because the first broadcast was not heeded. At 4 p.m. the same day a similar address was broadcast to

---

[1] Lt B. E. Lawn, VX85114; 24 Bn. Regular soldier; of Ballarat, Vic; b. Ballarat, 13 Sep 1914.
[2] Col J. G. Needham, OBE, ED, VX81134. OC 15 Fd Coy. Engineer; of East Malvern, Vic; b. Hobart, 6 Sep 1911.
[3] 15th Field Company, Report on Operations in South Bougainville.

several Japanese in the same locality. About one minute after the broadcast began the Japanese attacked and the talk was discontinued until after the action ceased. Then the following address was given:

> Japanese soldiers do you know the war in Europe is almost over? Yesterday 60 German and Italian divisions surrendered unconditionally. Berlin has fallen. Meanwhile the war fast approaches your homeland. If you continue with your futile resistance here when you are deserted by your High Command, you must surely perish. We offer you a chance to live and work for Japan in the future. Walk down the track with your hands in the air and your weapons across your backs and we will look after you well. Your officers have told you that you will be tortured if you come in. That is not true. It is told you only to ensure that you fight on uselessly. We have waiting for you a good hot meal with fresh meat and plenty of cigarettes or anything else you desire. Be wise come in now, you will be treated well and honourably as are the thousands of your officers and men in our hands. Do not hesitate.

No visible result was achieved by any of these appeals or threats.

References have been made earlier in these volumes to instances where leaflets aimed at depressing the spirits of Australian troops in the Middle East not only failed to do that but had the opposite effect of enhancing their self-esteem and improving their spirits. May not such broadcast addresses as the above have had a similar effect on the Japanese? The Japanese soldier well knew that the Japanese army on Bougainville was isolated and hungry. Each man in the front line knew that his chance of survival was poor. Broadcast addresses such as those quoted above were perhaps likely somewhat to dispel loneliness, and to raise the spirits of the men of those isolated outposts—it must be an important position they were holding and they must be holding it well if the enemy chose to adopt such elaborate and roundabout methods of taking it.

The Australian Army's experience both at the receiving and giving end of "psychological warfare" of this sort suggests that the positive results achieved were not worth the labour that was spent on it. In the years before the outbreak of war the rulers of Germany and Russia had acted on the assumption that intensive preaching could alter the outlook of a community at fairly short notice. Many politicians, administrators and economic planners of the democratic nations developed as great a faith in "propaganda" as Dr Goebbels possessed: if the citizens' outlook was not what was desired, one simply drugged it with "propaganda", and if the required result was not rapidly achieved that was because the drug was not properly mixed and administered.[4] However, Australian experience of battlefield broadcasts and leaflets suggests the possibility that the roots of national character are far too deep for fundamental changes to be brought about in a day, a year, or even several years of exhortation, no matter how cajoling or threatening. It was as futile to attempt to seduce Japanese soldiers from what they regarded as a divinely-appointed duty with the

---

[4] The prevailing attitude is illustrated by the following quotation from *The Australian Economy in War and Reconstruction* (1947), p. 21, by E. Ronald Walker, one-time deputy director-general of the Australian Department of War Organisation of Industry. "Fundamentally the problem of converting a capitalist peacetime economy into a war economy, with an inevitable totalitarian element, is a problem of changing the mental habits of a community. . . . If governments fail in this task, it is due perhaps to ignorance of the art of propaganda rather than any scruples arising from democratic tradition."

offer of a hot meal and a cigarette, or to frighten them with bad news from another front, or even from Japan itself, as it was to try to stop Australians from fighting by showering them with drawings purporting to show Americans embracing their wives. The mental habits of a community and therefore of its soldiers are formed during centuries and are not likely to be basically changed during the relatively brief period of a war.[5]

As the 24th Battalion neared the Hongorai it became evident that the Japanese intended to make the Australians pay a price for each advance, and that they were willing to trade a field gun for a tank at every opportunity. On the 4th and many later occasions leading tanks were fired on at a range of a few yards by guns cleverly concealed beside the track, but in positions from which the Japanese could not hope to extricate them. In other respects also the Japanese tactics were improving and their striking power was strengthened. Each forward Australian battalion was now under frequent artillery fire, evidently directed by Japanese observers who remained close to the Australian advance, and it was this which was now causing most of the casualties. The shells usually burst in the trees and their fragments were scattered over a wide area with lethal effects. To counter the tanks the Japanese were now establishing their positions not astride the track but about 100 yards from it in places where the tanks could not reach them until a side track had been made.

Early in May General Savige received news of a most valuable reinforcement—the headquarters and one additional squadron of the 2/4th Armoured Regiment. This regiment had been formed in November 1942 to take the place in the 1st Armoured Division of the 2/6th when it went into the Buna fighting in New Guinea. It had recently been training at Southport (Queensland), where it was re-armed with Matilda tanks and expanded into a self-contained regimental group with its own technical sections. It was sent to Madang in August 1944, whence, in November, one squadron moved to Aitape to come under the command of the 6th Division, and in December a second squadron (Major Arnott's) was sent to Bougainville. The regiment had not been in battle as a regiment but it had had years of hard training and included a sprinkling of men who had been in action with other cavalry and armoured units. One of these was the commanding officer, Lieut-Colonel Mills,[6] who had been an outstanding cavalry squadron commander in North Africa and Syria.

This reinforcement would enable the relief of the squadron then in action—its tanks were worn and were kept running only by a great amount of maintenance work—and perhaps the employment of tanks in the northern sector.[7] The early relief of Arnott's crews was desirable. The

---

[5] Brigadier Hammer disapproved of the sort of propaganda devised by FELO in his area and suggested a more sentimental approach, with the emphasis on "home and mother, the girl friend, and a quiet life", to the accompaniment of Japanese music. On the Hari three sergeants walked in and surrendered after one such broadcast.

[6] Lt-Col T. Mills, MC, NX174. 6 Cav Regt; CO 2/5 Armd Regt 1943-44, 2/4 Armd Regt 1944-46. Tin miner; of Emmaville, NSW; b. Charters Towers, Qld, 2 Apr 1908.

[7] Early in May an American officer gave the astonishing information that there were 160 medium and light tanks on the Russell Islands, 140 of which had never been used—enough to equip 3 regiments. Brigadier Garrett, who was an experienced tank officer, went to see. The tanks were there but they had received no attention for 15 months and were mere junk, the engines rusted, the electrical gear ruined, and the hulls half full of water.

slow advances along the track entailed arduous periods of up to six hours in closed tanks. Meanwhile, as a result of their experience of using tanks in support of infantry on the narrow tracks travelling through thick forest, Arnott and his officers had worked out a settled tactical doctrine: the leading tank should move fifteen yards ahead of the second, with freedom to fire forward and to each flank from "3 o'clock" to "9 o'clock"; the leading infantry section should be at the rear of the second tank, the second tank supporting the first and being itself protected by the infantry. At night the crews were to run their tanks over shallow pits and sleep below them.

The 24th Battalion made another move forward on 5th May. Lieutenant Yorath's[8] tank troop moved with the leading infantry, firing right and left. At 500 yards the machine-gun in the leading tank (Sergeant Whatley[9]) suffered a stoppage. As the crew were removing it to remedy the defect a concealed field gun opened fire wounding Corporal Clark.[1] A second tank, armed with a howitzer, moved forward, knocked out the field gun and drove off the supporting infantry, who were about 100 strong. Meanwhile, under fire Whatley had lifted Clark out of the tank, carried him to safety, and raced back to his tank. That night the battalion area was sharply bombarded, more than 160 shells falling in it, and in the morning, as Captain Dickie's[2] company was moving forward to relieve Captain J. C. Thomas', about 100 Japanese attacked. A fierce fire fight, in which the tanks also took part, lasted for two hours and a half in dense undergrowth. Some of the Japanese fell only five yards from the forward posts but overran none of them. In one forward pit Private Barnes[3] held his fire until the Japanese were within about 15 yards, then mowed them down, and each time they repeated the attack he did the same. When he had used up his ammunition he carried his gun back, collected more, and returned to his post. Thirteen dead were counted round his pit. At length the Japanese withdrew leaving 58 dead—their heaviest loss in a single action since Slater's—and abandoning two machine-guns. One Australian was killed and 9 wounded. This was the last effort to defend the Hongorai River line. On 7th May the leading company advanced to the river behind a barrage, but met no opposition. The preliminary patrolling and the advance to the Hongorai (7,000 yards in 3 weeks) had cost the 24th heavily—25 killed and 95 wounded; 169 Japanese dead had been counted.

More evidence of the enemy's faulty communications was provided the next night when two Japanese carrying a lantern crossed the Hongorai and walked almost into a company perimeter. When a sentry threw a

---

[8] Lt L. W. Yorath, WX8574; 2/4 Armd Regt. Public servant; of Leederville, WA; b. Fremantle, WA, 31 Mar 1912.

[9] Sgt R. S. Whatley, MM, VX103648; 2/4 Armd Regt. Fibrous plasterer; of Bendigo, Vic; b. Echuca, Vic, 21 Dec 1914.

[1] Cpl F. E. J. Clark, SX23202; 2/4 Armd Regt. Laboratory assistant; of Adelaide; b. Adelaide, 15 Aug 1923.

[2] Capt R. M. Dickie, VX112135; 24 Bn. Laboratory assistant; of Richmond, Vic; b. Scotland, 11 Feb 1916.

[3] Pte L. Barnes, DCM, V180274; 24 Bn. Meat worker; of Footscray, Vic; b. Avenel, Vic, 26 Nov 1921.

grenade they fled, leaving a basket of documents. That day two patrols encountered strong groups of Japanese. In one of them four men were hit and one of these, Private McLennan,[4] was left behind. He crawled away and was not found until four days later, when he was brought in by a patrol of the 58th/59th Battalion.

As the leading battalion and the tanks fought their way forward, the supporting infantrymen and the engineers toiled behind laying corduroy on the road. By the end of the first week of May the 9,300 yards of the Buin Road from Slater's to the Hongorai and 5,000 yards of the lateral Hatai Track had been so treated.

Meanwhile the 57th/60th had also advanced to the Hongorai along the Commando Road from Rumiki. On 6th May a company crossed the river, and that day and the next their ambushes trapped parties of Japanese in the neighbourhood.

On the inland flank the 2/8th Commando Squadron had been patrolling deeply. On 8th April, just before the 15th Brigade replaced the 7th, it had again been brought directly under Bridgeford's command. Major Winning went to Toko to discuss with the staff the future operations of his unit. It was decided that the squadron would reconnoitre and harass the enemy between the Hongorai and the Mobiai Rivers in the general area north of the Buin Road, with the special tasks of locating possible tank obstacles, the enemy's defences and concentrations of strength, and tracks suitable for tank and motor traffic. If considered feasible the headquarters of the *6th Japanese Division* then at Oso was to be raided and ambushes set on the tracks east of the Hongorai. Winning considered that his unit had now been allotted "a role which could be carried out with more purpose and to more effect than at any previous stage in the campaign".[5]

The task, mentioned earlier, of bringing in the missionaries and nuns from Flying Officer Stuart's area somewhat delayed the opening of the new phase, but on 18th April a patrol with the code name "Tiger", under Captain K. H. R. Stephens, established a base on the Pororei River about 3,000 yards north of the Buin Road and thence scouted stealthily to discover the enemy's tracks and dispositions on the Buin Road between the Hongorai and Pororei and on the Commando Road about the Huda River crossing. They found also a secret Japanese track, later named the Tiger Road.

On 21st April, Trooper Kemp[6] and two others of the 2/8th Commando were sent out to obtain information along the Tiger Road and particularly

---

[4] Pte F. D. McLennan, MM, VX93416; 24 Bn. Butcher; of Wodonga, Vic; b. Barmedman, NSW, 22 Aug 1925. McLennan was seriously wounded in the thigh. While he was dragging himself out four Japanese attacked him. He killed three with his Owen gun and the fourth fled; then he dragged himself into the jungle. The patrol could not find him and withdrew. In great pain he began dragging himself towards his own lines using his Owen as a support. On the second night he slept on the edge of an enemy position and next day made notes of the dispositions. He dragged himself on, and that day saw three groups of Japanese. On 11th May, having dragged himself 3,000 yards, he was found by a patrol and carried in bringing information on which effective artillery fire was based. The young McLennan spent the next 4½ years in hospital recovering from his wounds.

[5] 2/8 Aust Commando Squadron Report on Operations in Southern Bougainville, Nov 44-Aug 45.

[6] Tpr G. R. Kemp, MM, NX137928; 2/8 Cdo Sqn. Of Bondi, NSW; b. Sydney, 3 Feb 1923.

to obtain a prisoner. They moved out 2,000 yards and for five hours lay concealed a few feet from the Tiger Road. Finally when a single Japanese approached, Kemp leapt upon him, stunned him with a Bren magazine and brought him to the base.

On the 25th a patrol laid mines on the road and set an ambush. Some hours later eight Japanese arrived and all were killed by mines. Another patrol ambushed and killed four Japanese on the Commando Road and captured a map showing the enemy's proposed defences south of the Hongorai crossing. Other patrols were operating farther east with equal effect. Natives with Lieutenant Clifton's[7] section on 23rd April killed four Japanese near Kapana and captured a lieutenant of the *4th Medium Artillery Regiment*. The section inspected the Hari River crossing and on the 28th attacked an enemy group at Kingori, killing six. Lieutenant Barrett's[8] section sent patrols into the Oso, Taitai and Uso areas, and located near Oso a garrison of 80, which was then shelled by the artillery.

It was discovered that there was no suitable barge-landing point in the Aitara area or at Mamagota, and consequently the rate of advance would be governed largely by the speed with which the Buin Road could be made able to carry 3-ton trucks. Forward of this road supplies had to be carried by jeep trains travelling on corduroyed tracks or dropped from the air. Beyond the corduroy only tracked vehicles could travel, as a rule. Consequently, before the second stage of the advance—from the Hongorai to the Hari—could be completed, it was necessary to pause until enough stores had been brought forward.

It was now estimated that from 1,500 to 1,800 Japanese troops with probably nine guns, including heavy and medium pieces, were west of the Hari. Between the Hari and the Oamai were believed to be from 900 to 1,150 men with eight guns. The enemy could mount a counter-offensive only by withdrawing troops from the base and the gardens. To meet the Australian superiority in artillery, in tanks and in the air, they would need to concentrate behind a tank obstacle, and the next such obstacle was the Hari. A strong reason why they should fight hard on the line of the Hari was that the gardens to the east of it were large enough to feed a fairly big force, but if these gardens were lost, food would have to be carried from distant areas—a very difficult task, particularly in view of the loss of native carriers and the intermittent attacks by native guerillas organised by Stuart's party and Mason's.

Savige issued new instructions: first to advance to the line Hari River-Monoitu-Kapana; and, in a second phase, to advance to the Mivo River. Again only one brigade group would be maintained in the forward zone, its northern battalion being supplied by air-dropping.

Thus the 15th Brigade's battalions on the Hongorai spent the second and third weeks of May patrolling deeply into Japanese territory to gain

---
[7] Lt D. M. Clifton, NX5495. 6 Cav Regt, 2/8 Cdo Sqn. Woolclasser; of Condobolin, NSW; b. Arundle, NSW, 26 May 1918.
[8] Maj A. G. Barrett, VX75804. 2/5 Indep Coy, 2/8 Cdo Sqn. Medical student; of Cobden, Vic; b. Caulfield, Vic, 21 Nov 1922.

information and harass the enemy, and preparing for the next phase—
the advance from the Hongorai to the Hari. The patrolling was intrepid.
For example, on 10th May a small patrol led by Sergeant Langtry[9]
stealthily reached the bridge carrying the Buin Road over the Pororei
River and, near by, spent half an hour concealed in a camouflaged bay
containing a Japanese truck watching groups of up to 30 Japanese moving
up and down the road. On the same day a patrol under Lieutenant Gay[10]
of the 57th/60th, with two native soldiers as guides, set an ambush at a
river crossing about a mile east of the Hongorai. After an hour a Japanese
came to the river to wash. Here was an opportunity to take a prisoner.
One of the natives crept up behind the Japanese, hit him on the head
with a stone, and hauled him screaming into the bush, where he was
bandaged and eventually led back to the battalion's area. In the course
of this preliminary patrolling the 24th Battalion moved a company across
the Hongorai and its patrols found a very strong enemy position estimated
to be manned by 100 on what came to be called Egan's Ridge.

On 13th May Corporal Boswell[11] of the 24th Battalion led out a small
patrol north of the Buin Road towards the Hongorai. It was surprised by
about 50 Japanese armed with machine-guns, light mortars, grenades and
rifles. Boswell and two men with him were pinned down and the others
could not reach them because of the intense fire. Private Barnes killed
one Japanese but an enemy machine-gun opened fire from the rear and a
member of the patrol fell wounded in the fire lane. The men were now
under fire from all the enemy's weapons.

Lance-Corporal O'Connor[1] crawled in a wide circle to the wounded man
and dressed his wounds and then moved under fire to a second wounded
man and looked after him too. The patrol withdrew covered by fire from
O'Connor and Barnes. When Barnes' Bren gun was almost out of ammunition O'Connor sent him to join the rest of the patrol and remained alone
with his Owen gun until he thought that the patrol had all withdrawn.
Then he ran to one of the wounded and was about to carry him out when
three Japanese rushed at him with fixed bayonets. O'Connor killed two
of these and wounded the other. He then dragged his wounded comrade
back and for a time gave covering fire while a man who had been left
behind withdrew.

On the Buin Road the 58th/59th was now taking the lead. Hammer's
plan was that, after a heavy air bombardment, it should make a wide
flanking move on the right some days before the main assault. It would
cut the Buin Road east of the Hongorai while the 24th made a frontal
attack, and the 57th/60th on the left created diversions and attempted to
attract the enemy's attention in that direction. The right was chosen for

---

[9] Maj J. O. Langtry, DCM, VX101703. NGF and 24 Bn. Student; of Balwyn, Vic; b. Melbourne, 2 Dec 1923.
[10] Lt H. W. Gay, MC, VX143577; 57/60 Bn. Glazier; of Preston, Vic; b. Fitzroy, Vic, 26 Jul 1923.
[11] Cpl J. W. H. Boswell, VX104404; 24 Bn. Barman; of East Hawthorn, Vic; b. Brighton, Vic, 16 Apr 1921. Killed in action 13 May 1945.
[1] Cpl O. G. J. O'Connor, DCM, N454252; 24 Bn. Butcher; of Concord, NSW; b. Hornsby, NSW, 2 Nov 1924.

the main flanking move because there seemed to be only light Japanese forces there; it offered the shortest route to the Buin Road, which travelled south-east from the Hongorai to the Hari; and the Aitara Track would enable the final part of the flanking move—the move back to the Buin Road—to be completed without difficulty.

It thus became a task of the 58th/59th to explore the area south of the Buin Road. It sent out five or six-day patrols to set ambushes on the track from the Buin Road to the coast at Mamagota. The intervening bush was so dense and much of the ground so swampy that some patrols reached the track only in time to turn round and return before their rations were exhausted. However, on 10th May one such patrol on its first day out captured a prisoner on the Aitara Track.[2] This Japanese said that 7 men of the *I/23rd Battalion* manned a coastwatching station at Aitara and four more a signal station 1,000 yards east of the point where the track crossed the Hongorai. A telephone line connected both posts and continued to a headquarters in the Runai area. He described how the weapons were sited. On the 12th two fighting patrols set out to attack each station simultaneously, the farther patrol laying a telephone line from the nearer. On the 14th Lieutenant D. J. Brewster leading the Aitara patrol found Aitara Mission deserted and by telephone ordered the other patrol (Sergeant Bush[3] and eight men) to attack the signal post. This post was found to be wired and there were positions for thirty men, but only three were there and all were killed. The prisoner was examined again and revealed that the coastwatching station was not at Aitara Mission but at the mouth of the Aitara River, a mile away. Consequently on the 16th two patrols moved out to attack it and also to destroy a 47-mm gun at the signal station. They found that from 20 to 30 Japanese had now occupied the signal station. Major Pike's[4] company was moved forward to contain this post, which was harassed by mortars and artillery for the next four days while preparations for the main attack continued. Enemy parties made several efforts to reach the beleaguered party and eight Japanese were killed. A patrol to the Aitara area reported it clear of the enemy.

Meanwhile the battalion had sent several other patrols daily across the Hongorai to map the area through which it would advance, avoiding contact with the enemy so as not to reveal a special interest in the area. By the 16th all company commanders had a good knowledge of the country. Finally the engineers chose a crossing and a route thence to the Buin Road was surveyed. Major Sweet[5] of the 58th/59th and Lieutenant

---

[2] Patrols had just been informed that if they took a prisoner they should return to base immediately and would spend the remainder of the time scheduled for the patrol at the unit rest camp.

[3] Sgt J. W. Bush, VX89725; 58/59 Bn. Labourer; of South Corowa, NSW; b. Corowa, 25 Sep 1916.

[4] Maj W. A. Pike, NX97. 2/1 and 58/59 Bns. Clerk; of Mosman, NSW; b. Chatswood, NSW, 14 Apr 1917.

[5] Lt-Col H. G. Sweet, VX7562. 2/5 Bn 1940-43; 58/59 Bn 1943-45. Clerk; of St Kilda, Vic; b. St Kilda, 22 Jun 1918.

Willis[6] of the 15th Field Company picked the area which the battalion would occupy. All this was done without the Japanese being aware of it.

It will be recalled that the 24th had found that a strong enemy force, perhaps 100 strong, occupied Egan's Ridge, dominating the western approaches to the Buin Road. Captain C. J. Egan led out a platoon and two tanks in this direction on the 15th but a tank bellied on a log. As mechanics advanced to help the crew, the Japanese opened fire with a gun and small arms. A 155-mm shell hit the tank killing the gunner, Trooper Hole,[7] and wounding three others and wrecking the tank. An attack which followed was beaten off and the little force withdrew.

Although the main attack across the Hongorai was not to open until 20th May the diversionary advance by the 57th/60th was to begin three days earlier. On the eve of this move Hammer issued an order of the day in a characteristic style. He spoke of his "undying admiration" for and "extreme confidence" in his men and told them that the next few weeks might see the major defeat of the Japanese in south Bougainville. "'Go to battle as you have done in the last month and no enemy can withstand you."

In preparation for the attack and in support of it the four Corsair squadrons of the R.N.Z.A.F.—Nos. 14, 16, 22 and 26—carried out the biggest operation of this kind which the force had undertaken in the Pacific. For eight days from 15th to 22nd May the squadrons attacked along the axis of the Commando and Buin Roads. Each day, except one, from 40 to 63 sorties were made. A total of 185 1,000-lb and 309 lighter bombs were dropped.[8]

On 17th May, supported by 32 Corsairs overhead and the fire of two batteries, the 57th/60th crossed the upper Hongorai and advanced on a wide front astride the Commando Road. The centre company crossed 500 yards north of the ford. The tanks could not negotiate the ford but the infantry attacked down the far bank sending the Japanese off in wild disorder. By 11.35 a.m. the Commando Road beyond the river was secured. Captain J. D. Brookes' company made a wide outflanking move to the Pororei River through difficult country, but reached it at dusk driving off the few Japanese who were at the crossing.

Captain Ross'[9] company, led by native guides, also went wide to cut the road at the Taromi River, 3,000 yards to the south, and Major Wilkie's[1] went north to the Huda River. Next day the infantry pressed on. Brookes' at the Pororei crossing was attacked by 30 Japanese but after a hard

---

[6] Capt J. G. Willis, QX38728. 11 and 15 Fd Coys. Civil engineer; of Brisbane; b. Brisbane, 20 Jul 1920.

[7] Tpr H. E. Hole, SX14145; 2/4 Armd Regt. Dairy farmer; of Kybybolite, SA; b. Harrow, Vic, 5 Sep 1921. Killed in action 15 May 1945.

[8] In support of the 15th Brigade from 22nd April to 30th June the New Zealand squadrons flew 2,262 sorties and dropped 768 tons of bombs. Flying was cancelled because of the weather on only eight days.

[9] Capt W. A. Ross, VX133031; 57/60 Bn. Traveller; of Tocumwal, NSW; b. Swan Hill, Vic, 29 May 1914.

[1] Maj W. H. Wilkie, VX51556; 57/60 Bn. Electrical fitter; of St Kilda, Vic; b. Skipton, Vic, 16 Nov 1912.

fight repulsed them, losing one man (Private Gulley[2]) killed and eight wounded while the Japanese left seven dead. Next day Colonel Webster's headquarters were established on the Torobiru River, a dropping ground had been prepared and supplies dropped; the battalion had seven days' rations, ambushes were established (seven Japanese were killed in ambushes that day) and the battalion was ready to fight again. On the 20th it began patrolling. One party under Lieutenant Paterson,[3] scouting far to the south, found a well-dug Japanese position, set an ambush and killed five, including a sergeant carrying useful documents.

That day, on the Buin Road, the main attack opened. From 8 a.m. until 8.20 on 20th May aircraft bombed the enemy's positions along the road and at 8.30 the 24th Battalion advanced behind a creeping barrage of artillery, mortar and machine-gun fire and with two troops of tanks. Two of the three leading companies soon gained their objectives; the third was held up just short of it by heavy Japanese fire from small arms and artillery, and dug in, having lost 4 killed and 5 wounded.[4] Next day it fought its way to a position dominating the Pororei ford, but Japanese were still holding strongly astride the road farther west; a patrol from a supporting company under Lieutenant Spendlove met a group of some seventy and dug in just west of them. When Captain

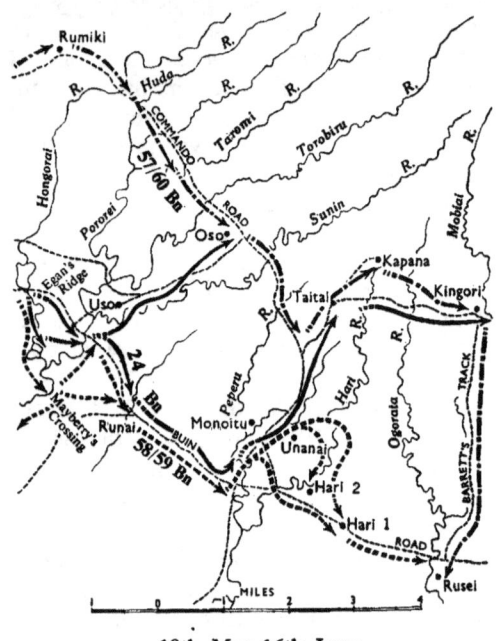

18th May-16th June

Graham's company occupied the high ground on Egan's Ridge it found the whole area to be sown with mines and booby-traps; there were tank mines in the road and booby-traps in the scrub on each side of it. The bomb disposal squad which began working on the mines was blown up, two men being killed. Thereupon all through the morning of the 21st Lieutenant Syrett[5] of the 24th's Pioneer platoon and Sergeant J. A. C.

---

[2] Pte T. Gulley, VX108687; 57/60 Bn. Metal polisher; of East Brunswick, Vic; b. Deniliquin, NSW, 16 Nov 1923. Killed in action 18 May 1945.

[3] Capt H. T. Paterson, VX102740; 57/60 Bn. Clerk; of Darriman, Vic; b. Sale, Vic, 22 Nov 1920.

[4] The killed included Sergeant L. N. McCarthy, only son of Lieutenant L. D. McCarthy who had won the Victoria Cross in 1918.

[5] Lt J. Syrett, GM, NX150794; 24 Bn. Newsagent; of Inverell, NSW; b. Inverell, 9 Sep 1922. On 24th May Syrett was wounded by a booby-trap.

Knight searched for and disarmed mines. At first they used the only available mine detector, but, after it had failed to respond to three improvised mines, Syrett and Knight probed with bayonet and fingers and cleared all mines and traps from the area.

Meanwhile the 58th/59th's wide flanking move on the right had begun along a route bulldozed to the west bank of the Hongorai. On the 18th and 19th there had been some sharp patrol clashes beyond the Hongorai. On 20th May the final pad had been cut to the Aitara Track and tractors had dragged ten trailers loaded with supplies across the river at Mayberry's Crossing. A powerful tractor, newly arrived, dragged the tanks through the deep mud and across the river. Despite the noise the Japanese were evidently oblivious of all these preparations. By 4 p.m. that day the whole battalion except headquarters and the Headquarters Company were in an assembly area east of the Hongorai. Before dawn on the 21st the complete battalion was formed up ready to advance. At 6.30 a.m. Major Pike's company (he had played a leading part in the preliminary patrolling) with Lieutenant Scott's tanks set off eastward. A creek 400 yards forward delayed the tanks so Pike left a platoon with them and advanced with the remainder but was held by some 40 Japanese dug in another 400 yards on. It took a bulldozer an hour to make a crossing over the creek and it was 9.30 a.m. before the tanks reached the forward infantry. They advanced straight up the track sweeping the enemy's position with fire and after half an hour the Japanese broke and fled in disorder, leaving seven dead. Early in the afternoon the battalion was on its objective covering the Buin Road and digging in against the expected counter-attack. Their guns shelled one company position and caused some casualties.

A patrol on the left flank was pinned down by heavy fire from north of the road. Tanks moved forward and fired into the enemy position so effectively that the Japanese fled leaving a 70-mm gun in perfect order, with 100 rounds of ammunition. By nightfall all the objectives had been secured and most localities had been wired in; but the Japanese did not make a counter-attack, probably because an attack so far to their rear had disorganised them.

On 22nd May the powerful tractor mentioned above, dragging a trailer train to the headquarters of the 58th/59th, was ambushed by about 20 Japanese with a 47-mm gun. The tractor was hit and disabled but the escort, reinforced, drove off the attackers and took their gun. On 26th May Captain Hocking's[6] company encountered 20 Japanese astride the Buin Road and drove them off, but booby-traps killed Lieutenant Putnam[7] and wounded 11 others. The Buin Road was now open for traffic, and fighting patrols had mopped-up the whole area and taken a number of prisoners.[8]

---

[6] Capt L. J. Hocking, VX114134; 58/59 Bn. Body-builder; of Geelong, Vic; b. Geelong, 25 Feb 1914.

[7] Lt P. E. Putnam, VX32458; 58/59 Bn. Auctioneer's clerk; of Bendigo, Vic; b. Bendigo, 10 Oct 1918. Killed in action 26 May, 1945.

[8] A detailed account of the 58th/59th's part in this attack appears in *Militia Battalion at War: The History of the 58th/59th Australian Infantry Battalion in the Second World War* (1961), by R. L. Mathews.

In ten days about 500 bombs of up to 1,000 pounds in weight, 7,800 shells and 3,700 mortar bombs had fallen on and about Egan's Ridge. The Japanese endured nine days of this bombardment but after the final blasting, on the 22nd, the infantry advancing to attack found the area abandoned.

> The positions once occupied by the enemy were completely buried under huge piles of debris and the whole area was barren and scarred with shrapnel (says the report of the 15th Brigade). The consistent accuracy of our bombing, shelling and mortaring was evidenced by the complete devastation of the whole area and the destruction of the enemy positions, which were the strongest yet encountered during the operation. A strong odour of dead was noticeable throughout the area but the destruction . . . was so complete that it was impossible to make any search of the original positions for bodies or for abandoned equipment or documents.

The plan had succeeded brilliantly: the enemy forces west of the Hari had been broken. In the attack the 24th Battalion had killed 54 and lost 7 killed and 26 wounded; the 58th/59th had killed 36 and lost one killed and 16 wounded; the 57th/60th had killed 16 and lost 5 killed and 22 wounded.

On the northern flank the 57th/60th now pressed on towards the Oso junction. An attack by three companies was launched on 27th May with the support of aircraft and artillery, and the junction was secured with few casualties. In the new position the 57th/60th were harassed by night raiding parties and artillery fire—the first encountered on the northern road. In one bombardment on 30th May the first shell, bursting in the trees, killed or wounded nine. The same day a Corsair mistakenly strafed one of the companies of the 58th/59th Battalion on the Buin Road and machine-gunned battalion headquarters, killing the Intelligence officer, Lieutenant Wheeler,[9] and wounding the adjutant, Captain R. L. Mathews, and three others.

On 2nd June Corporal Biri, a Papuan soldier of 5 years' service, was sent out with three others to the right flank of an ambush position which was being constructed by 12 Japanese near the Sunin River. When in position near them Biri attacked alone and killed one. The Japanese tried to surround the natives but Biri without trying to take cover set upon them, firing his Owen and hurling challenges and abuse, and kept them from moving. When his Owen jammed he took a rifle and shot two more Japanese whereupon the survivors fled.[1]

On 2nd June the main advance was resumed, the 58th/59th moving forward without opposition through positions which had been "completely devastated by air, artillery and mortars". "Not one enemy was found alive or dead," wrote the battalion diarist, "although a strong smell of death pervaded the whole area." A prisoner taken later in the day said that the air strike had completely demoralised the defenders, and when they heard the tanks approaching they had fled. On the left the 57th/60th reached the Sunin River against slight opposition. On the 3rd and 4th

---

[9] Lt A. B. Wheeler, VX89390; 58/59 Bn. Farmer; of Nhill, Vic; b. Nhill, 13 Oct 1917. Killed in action 30 May 1945.

[1] Corporal Biri was awarded the Military Medal for this action.

the 58th/59th continued the advance, moving slowly because of the need to disarm an unprecedentedly large number of mines and booby-traps—more than 100 in three days—until they reached the Peperu River. Patrols moving stealthily forward to the Hari and across it found evidence of much confusion, many positions dug but unoccupied, and small groups of Japanese at large. It was decided to attack frontally towards the Hari next day.

However, on 6th June many difficulties were encountered. By 12.30 p.m. Captain Bauman's[2] company had advanced only 300 yards when it encountered a strong enemy force that had evidently just come up. This was driven out, but 200 yards farther on, on an escarpment, was another enemy force commanding the whole area. Lieutenant Dent,[3] commanding the supporting troop of tanks, directed Corporal Cooper's[4] tank forward. It bogged and drew heavy fire. Dent took shelter behind it. Corporal Burns'[5] tank advanced and gave support and a bulldozer was brought forward but abandoned after three men had been wounded trying to tie a tow rope to the tank. At length Sergeant Moyle's[6] tank towed Cooper's out and then went forward again to retrieve the bulldozer. Under sharp fire Dent and Lieutenant Dunstan[7] of the engineers attached a tow rope and Moyle's tank dragged the bulldozer to safety. In the day's fighting four Australians, including Bauman, were killed or fatally wounded and sixteen others wounded.

Next day the 58th/59th and tanks, impeded by swampy country, a road scattered with mines, and intermittent shellfire, made some progress against strongly-held Japanese positions. On the 8th Captain E. M. Griff's company of this battalion was sharply attacked, Griff being wounded—the third company commander to become a casualty in a few days.

On 9th June General Blamey visited the 15th Brigade. "Take your time, Hammer," he said to the brigadier. "There's no hurry." It was now clear that the Japanese intended to resist strongly along the approach to the Hari on the Buin Road axis; and the far bank of the Hari was a high escarpment. Hammer therefore decided that the 58th/59th would make a shallow outflanking march to the north and cut the Buin Road some miles east of the Hari while the 57th/60th thrust wide to the south on the far side of the Ogorata and cut the same road near Rusei. At the same time a company of the 24th would operate south of the Buin Road east of the Hari. Success would carry the brigade not only across the Hari but the Ogorata and through a large garden area valuable to the enemy.

---

[2] Capt C. H. Bauman, VX102650; 58/59 Bn. Clerk; of Moonee Ponds, Vic; b. Essendon, Vic, 13 Feb 1919. Died of wounds 11 Jun 1945.

[3] Capt G. C. Dent, NX70810; 2/4 Armd Regt. Insurance clerk; of Mosman, NSW; b. Ashfield, NSW, 11 Sep 1921.

[4] Cpl A. Cooper, WX13523; 2/4 Armd Regt. Labourer; of Southern Cross, WA; b. Southern Cross, 26 Nov 1913.

[5] Cpl T. C. Burns, SX14680; 2/4 Armd Regt. Grazier; of Edenhope, Vic; b. Edenhope, 24 Jan 1909.

[6] Sgt E. F. Moyle, VX61277; 2/4 Armd Regt. Ledgerkeeper; of Burnley, Vic; b. Melbourne, 17 May 1915.

[7] Maj A. R. Dunstan, MC, QX41128. 16 and 15 Fd Coys. Draughtsman; of Gympie, Qld; b. Gympie, 25 Mar 1921.

At a conference on 24th May Bridgeford had expressed the opinion that with his present resources he could not reach Buin before the end of the year. Savige informed him that later he would place the 11th Brigade and the 4th Field Regiment under his command. In the meantime his task was to cross the Hari and push on to the Mivo. Beyond the Hari the 15th Brigade should be relieved by the 29th.

Savige's intention was to advance the 29th Brigade to the Silibai along the present axis. He considered that the enemy would be drawn into the south Silibai area and would denude the northern flank. He then hoped to find a way in on the left flank for the 11th Brigade even if it had to be supplied by air. The 11th Brigade might then attack the Japanese right flank and inflict a decisive defeat. The task of the 2/8th Commando was to reconnoitre a route for the 11th Brigade. With this project in mind Savige on 30th May spent nearly three hours on an air reconnaissance of the Mivo area and the road systems north of Buin. As a result he decided that a movement along the Commando Road, and then on to the lower foothills across the Mivo and Silibai Rivers, and finally an attack southwards would be practicable.

As part of the plan to advance to the Mivo two large patrols from the northern flank were sent out to circle deep into the enemy territory exploring the Commando Road and routes leading south from it to the Buin Road. One commanded by Captain Scott[8] of the 57th/60th numbered some 180 men and included one tank troop, one infantry platoon (Lieutenant Gay), engineers with a bulldozer, and other detachments. It was to advance from Kapana to Kingori destroying the enemy in that area, then south to Rusei—more or less the route of the 57th/60th's advance. One of its objects was to create the impression that the Australians were operating strongly along the northern axis. Another force of the 57th/60th under Lieutenant G. H. Atkinson, about 70 strong, was sent out far along the northern flank to establish a base at Musaraka on the Mivo and obtain information. This was on the fringe of the commando country and both patrols would be dependent on track information obtained by the commando patrols.

The advance of the 57th/60th began on 11th June, that of the 58th/59th on the 12th. The plan of Colonel Mayberry of the 58th/59th was to send two companies and two troops of tanks under Major Pike to gain a position astride the road 2,000 yards east of the Hari, whence a third company, having followed behind, would thrust westward to the Hari taking the enemy in the rear. One company remained near the Hari ford. For four days before the advance began the two artillery regiments and the New Zealand Corsairs had bombarded the area until "it resembled Australian bush after fire". By the early afternoon "Pikeforce" had made its long march and was astride the Buin Road, having encountered little opposition. On the 14th Pike moved east with most of his force towards the Ogorata while one company went west towards the Hari to clear the

---

[8] Maj W. H. Scott, MC, VX81075; 57/60 Bn. Shipping clerk; of Caulfield, Vic; b. Caulfield, 26 Sep 1918.

main road to Pikeforce. In the day the eastern company advanced about 700 yards against stiff opposition; the western company encountered a resolute and well-sited group of Japanese dominating the ford, and between it and the company on the other side of the river.

Daring tactics such as these created situations that could be highly dangerous to supporting troops. At 10.30 a.m. on the 14th a reconnaissance party of five led by Lieut-Colonel Hayes[9] commanding the 2/11th Field Regiment came up to Captain C. C. Cuthbertson's company, which was on the west side of the ford, and (according to the diarist of the 58th/59th Battalion) did not heed a warning but continued along the road. Major Dietrich,[1] however, who was just behind Hayes, heard no warning. At the Hari ford Hayes and his party climbed a 40-foot escarpment beside the road and soon were joined there by Major Pearson[2] and two others. Suddenly Japanese opened fire. Captain Winton[3] who was disarming a booby-trap about 100 yards short of the ford was wounded. The artillery party fired back at the enemy; Dietrich organised covering fire and with two others went forward and brought Winton in. Meanwhile Hayes had been killed by a mine. Three others were wounded.

The ford was not occupied until next day after a heavy bombardment. The road was opened late in the afternoon, but not before some 40 Japanese had suddenly attacked Cuthbertson's company as it was moving east. In the fierce fight which followed two Australians and four Japanese were killed, but this was the last time Japanese appeared on the Buin Road west of the Ogorata, where Pikeforce was now securely dug in.

For its long move through the bush, which began on 11th June, Colonel Webster streamlined his 57th/60th Battalion to three companies, each about 80 strong, a headquarters of 60 and 120 native carriers. The men made slow progress, hacking their way through trackless bush, but achieved almost complete surprise. On the second day the battalion reached a track from Kingori to Rusei—named Barrett's Track after Lieutenant Barrett of the 2/8th Commando. Here some Japanese appeared and a sharp fight followed, but Webster and the main part of the battalion continued on towards the objective. They expected to reach the Buin Road on the 13th but found no sign of it. Next day they pushed on, through swamp and dense bamboo and sago. Seven Japanese were killed in small clashes. It was not until 3.45 p.m. on the 15th that the road was reached.

Meanwhile Scott Force had set out for Kingori on 9th June. The bulldozer and tanks made painfully slow progress, men from the tank crews and such infantry as could be spared having often to corduroy the saturated track with logs before the tanks could move through. On the second day Papuan scouts reported that the enemy was dug in not far ahead.

---

[9] Lt-Col J. M. Hayes, VX147. 2/3 Fd Regt; CO 6 Fd Regt 1943-44, 5 Fd Regt 1944, 2/11 Fd Regt 1945. Bank officer; of Melbourne; b. Melbourne, 22 Jul 1905. Killed in action 14 Jun 1945.

[1] Maj P. W. Dietrich, MC, VX46205; 2/11 Fd Regt. Clothing manufacturer; of Hawthorn, Vic; b. Melbourne, 27 Jun 1908.

[2] Maj J. A. Pearson, VX44225; 2/11 Fd Regt. Architect; of North Balwyn, Vic; b. Colombo, Ceylon, 25 Aug 1908.

[3] Capt J. H. Winton, VX45871; 2/11 Fd Regt. Clerk; of Gardenvale, Vic; b. Armadale, Vic, 14 Nov 1911.

The tanks formed a perimeter. The artillery observer, going forward to direct fire on the Japanese, was wounded. It was the 12th before another artillery observer was forward and fire could be brought down. The tanks advanced and the enemy fled. Thence the force moved slowly to Kapana, through sodden country cut frequently by creeks, and on to Kingori along a good track. At the Mobiai a Papuan patrol was ambushed but extricated itself after inflicting casualties. Scott now turned south towards Rusei along Barrett's Track, which the 57th/60th had already crossed in the course of its advance to Rusei. That afternoon a Japanese field gun concealed by the road opened fire on the leading tank (Corporal Matheson[4]) but the tanks promptly silenced it. On the 16th Scott reached the Buin Road at Rusei and joined the main force. What had this laborious thrust achieved? It demonstrated that tanks could go through the most difficult country with the help of a bulldozer and the labour of infantrymen. Incidentally the tanks maintained the only contact between the 57th/60th Battalion, after its line was cut by the Japanese, and Hammer's headquarters. One tank was in wireless touch with the battalion, the other with squadron headquarters at 15th Brigade.

That morning an armoured patrol from the 58th/59th advanced towards the 57th/60th. On the way a tank was blown up by a mine. The driver, Trooper Dunstan,[5] was killed and the remainder of the crew wounded. The tank lurched into the crater with its engine racing. It could not be stopped because the turret had jammed and the engine raced until it seized. At midday the patrol reached the 57th/60th. Success was now confirmed. On Hammer's orders Webster prepared to send a company eastward towards the Mobiai, and traffic began to pour along the Buin Road to the battalion now, after six days in the bush, linked by a vehicle road with the main force.

"The mass arrival of stores, tanks, jeeps and bulldozers at the one area made a complete traffic jam," wrote the diarist of the 57th/60th. Three troops of tanks and two bulldozers were soon on the spot. It was 3 p.m. before the leading company (Captain Martin[6]) was able to move off with a troop of tanks (Lieutenant Fraser[7]). After advancing only 400 yards from the traffic jam a 150-mm gun 350 yards away hit the forward tank whose magazine exploded killing Trooper Dew,[8] the driver, and wounding Fraser and the others of the crew. The tank was hit twice more and destroyed. It was evident that the Japanese were still in strength west of the Mobiai and determined to make the Australians pay heavily for any ground they gained there. But great success had been achieved. "Thus ended the battalion's last, and undoubtedly its most spectacular,

---

[4] Cpl A. L. Matheson, VX52045; 2/4 Armd Regt. Station hand; of Henty, Vic; b. Casterton, Vic, 14 Feb 1921.

[5] Tpr T. E. Dunstan, SX14036; 2/4 Armd Regt. Student; of Prospect, SA; b. Renmark, SA, 16 Dec 1921. Killed in action 16 Jun 1945.

[6] Capt R. M. Martin, VX81073; 57/60 Bn. Student; of St Kilda, Vic; b. Junee, NSW, 13 Feb 1922.

[7] Lt D. W. H. Fraser, NX113771; 2/4 Armd Regt. Salesman; of Randwick, NSW; b. Hong Kong, 29 Jan 1921.

[8] Tpr L. F. Dew, NX82566; 2/4 Armd Regt. Public servant; of Camperdown, NSW; b. Marrickville, NSW, 6 Oct 1924. Killed in action 16 Jun 1945.

major action in the 1939-45 war," wrote the historian of the 58th/59th. "In 13 days, from 3rd to 15th June, 13,000 yards of territory had been gained from a numerically superior enemy."[9]

It will be recalled that while the main attack from the Hari towards the Mobiai was in progress Atkinson Force (of the 57th/60th) was to move deeply into Japanese territory. It set out on 7th June, moved through Kapana to Katsuwa where it linked with a patrol of the 2/8th Commando, and thence to Astill's Crossing on the Mivo River where it turned south and formed a patrol base in the river bed 1,000 yards south of Musaraka. Next morning a returning line of native carriers encountered some 30 Japanese about 300 yards from Astill's Crossing. The leading escorts engaged the Japanese and the "kai-line" was sent back to the base. Three hours later a second attempt was made to push the kai-line through but again the enemy were across the track. In the light of these events, and of information from the 2/8th Commando that some 60 Japanese were shadowing his force, Lieutenant Atkinson struck camp and moved 3,000 yards north along the east bank of the river. There a new base was formed on the 11th (the main attack had now opened) and thence patrols operated until the 17th, when Atkinson learnt from the 2/8th Commando and Stuart, the guerilla leader, that there were some 180 Japanese round Kingori and perhaps 100 hunting Stuart farther east. Consequently on 18th June Atkinson again moved his base, this time 1,000 yards to the north-west, farther from the Japanese main force and deeper into the commando country.

On the 19th a company of the 24th Battalion under Captain S. C. Graham set out from Taitai through Kingori, where another company of the 24th had established a base on the 14th, to relieve Atkinson. Next morning Lieutenant C. A. Graham[1] of this company was leading a patrol towards Katsuwa ahead of the main column when he encountered about 30 Japanese. A sharp fight followed in which three Australians were wounded, and a number of Japanese were killed or wounded. The main body of the company advanced in extended line to join the patrol then withdrew with it to enable artillery fire to be brought down. Before the guns opened fire Captain Graham was wounded in the foot by a sniper. Lieutenant Whitebrook[2] took command, the enemy were outflanked, and that night the Australians bivouacked on the Koroko River.

On 21st June they moved on through very difficult country, failed to find Katsuwa and instead established a perimeter at a clearing sloping upwards from the river and marked on their map as a likely dropping ground. They set about improving this dropping ground.

Next morning, when most of the force was on patrol and only a handful were left defending its area of the perimeter, some Japanese scouts were seen in the bush. They were fired on and disappeared. About half an

---
[9] R. L. Mathews, p. 207.
[1] Lt C. A. Graham, QX132. 2/9 and 24 Bns. Farm worker; of McKee's Hill, via Casino, NSW; b. Newtown, NSW, 12 Aug 1914.
[2] Capt F. C. Whitebrook, MC, NX139402; 24 Bn. Student; of Glebe Point, NSW; b. Brisbane, 25 Oct 1921.

hour later mortar bombs fell into the perimeter and what seemed like 100 Japanese attacked with fanatical zeal. The fight lasted for two hours. Japanese thrust forward to within a few yards of the posts held by the cooks, under Sergeant Erbs,[3] and one man leapt into a weapon-pit and was clubbed to death. The Australians' ammunition was almost exhausted before the Japanese withdrew, leaving 18 dead. Their fire was wild and no Australian was hit.

Meanwhile Sergeant Langtry, who had led out a patrol before the attack opened, found a strong enemy position astride the Commando Road near Kingori. He attacked but the enemy was too strong. Thereupon he telephoned for artillery support, and moved close to the enemy to direct fire. In the subsequent attack Langtry found the position even larger than he had thought, by-passed it and rejoined his company. When he arrived the company was being fiercely attacked, but he made an encircling move, joined it and helped in the defence.

The company at Kingori had heard the firing in the far distance. At length Private Lancey,[4] a signaller with the company that was being attacked, managed to gain wireless contact with the rear company and it relayed the news to battalion headquarters. Consequently during the afternoon an aircraft made several visits, dropping ammunition and wire to Captain Graham's force. Next day the perimeter was fenced and the artillery ranged on to the wire; the Japanese did not attack again. On 24th June Atkinson Force moved back through Graham Force.

Throughout the period of the 15th Brigade's attacks the 2/8th Commando had been probing forward on the inland flank. On 10th May Captain Dunshea set off to establish a new base near Monorei, near the headwaters of the Mivo. The Tiger patrol (now two sections under Captain Barnes[5]) laid ambushes on the Tiger Road, killing ten and capturing the Regimental Sergeant-Major of the *13th Regiment*. The enemy was now becoming more alert and cautious, and fewer of his foraging parties were to be found moving about. At this stage, after a conference with Brigadier K. E. O'Connell, commanding the artillery of the 3rd Division, it was arranged that an artillery liaison officer (Captain Bott[6]) be attached to the squadron and forward observation officers be attached to patrols to increase their hitting power.

The first such patrol went out from 19th to 26th May into the Taitai and Monoitu areas. It encountered a difficulty already suffered by some earlier commando patrols: the danger of moving behind the Japanese lines now that the supporting artillery and air bombardments were so heavy. The artillery, for their part, were embarrassed by the large areas that should not be shelled because of the possible presence of commando patrols.

---

[3] Sgt A. R. Erbs, VX105842; 24 Bn. Milk factory hand; of Trafalgar, Vic; b. Trafalgar, 30 Aug 1920.

[4] Pte R. Lancey, NX163685; 24 Bn. Clerk; of New Lambton, NSW; b. Newcastle, NSW, 2 Jan 1917.

[5] Maj J. Barnes, NX76555. 2/8 Cdo Sqn; 2/Suffolk Regt 1945-46. Company director; of Strathfield, NSW; b. Cremorne, NSW, 24 Jan 1918.

[6] Capt F. McC. Bott, QX33974; 2/11 Fd Regt. Clerk; of Brisbane; b. Brisbane, 4 Dec 1920.

Eventually it was decided that Major Winning's patrols should not operate within range of the close-support artillery of the brigade.

On 24th May the headquarters of the squadron was opened at Morokaimoro. General Bridgeford had issued an order on 23rd May increasing the strength and re-defining the role of the force on his inland flank. Winning was given command of "Raffles Force", consisting of his own squadron and Captain G. L. Smith's company of the Papuan Infantry Battalion. Its task was to collect information on the flanks and ahead of the main force and harass the enemy's rear.

Winning was disappointed in the results obtained by the Papuan company. The Papuans were successful on fighting patrols of certain types but not in reconnaissance or artillery strikes.

Discipline was not impressive (he wrote), probably due to insufficient Europeans in the establishment. Apart from the company commander, the platoon commanders and sergeants lacked battle experience and experience with natives. The native soldiers feared artillery and would not accompany F.O.O's forward. It was considered more aggressiveness could have been shown on several patrols, and, on investigation, it was found there was friction and mistrust between the Buka natives and the Papuans, who had secretly threatened the Buka guides not to lead them to any targets which could not be overcome easily, or from which escape was likely to be dangerous. This led to considerable use of P.I.B. for escort and security patrolling. . . . The final attitude was that where a definite position for attack could be given, good results could be expected, but it was unwise to give P.I.B. patrols general areas of operations for strikes and ambushes as was done with squadron patrols.

At the new Morokaimoro base huts were built and a strip for Auster aircraft begun. Meanwhile arduous and effective patrolling continued. The report of the squadron gives some examples of the patrol achievements of Captain Dunshea's men, usually in two-men parties with a few natives, between 17th and 31st May: found a group of huts near Ivana River, which was later raided; found and brought down artillery fire on a strong enemy group near Irai; found a field gun which aircraft later destroyed; placed observation posts on the Buin Road which reported movement including the first arrival of naval troops; captured a lieutenant of the *23rd Regiment*; patrolled the coast near the mouth of the Mivo, finding an enemy group and reconnoitring for a possible beach landing.

On 26th May Lieutenant Clifton's section laid an ambush on the Buin Road 400 yards east of the Mobiai ford. A party of 16 entered one end of the ambush while 6 entered the other; 17 were definitely killed and possibly 2 more. Farther east Lieutenant Killen's section, making a series of patrols in the Buin Road area near the Mivo, ambushed a truck near the Mivo crossing and killed 7 of its 10 occupants. Next day it set a nine-man ambush near the Mobiai ford and soon opened fire on a party of Japanese, but almost immediately the Australians were attacked by about 90 Japanese following behind, evidently as part of a pre-arranged drill controlled by whistles. After a fight in which it was estimated that 19 Japanese were killed, the patrol withdrew having had only one man wounded; these Japanese were naval troops—the first encountered in southern Bougainville. Ambushes were set and raids made on enemy camps at frequent intervals. On 2nd June a patrol was sent out to destroy a Japanese post in a garden on the Mobiai, 1,500 yards north of the Buin Road. With two natives Trooper Guerin[7] crawled to within a few feet of the enemy position, then stealthily placed the patrol in positions only a few yards from the enemy. Guerin then led in the attack. One machine-gun began firing from a covered position. Guerin charged and killed the crew with his Owen. Eighteen Japanese were counted, possibly two escaped. No one in the patrol was hit. Later 11 Japanese were killed in an ambush near the Mivo ford; on 16th June Lieutenant Perry's section killed 7 in the same area. However, the main artery in this area—the Buin Road—was so well patrolled by the Japanese that Australian and Papuan patrols had only limited success along it.

During April and May Stuart's Allied Intelligence Bureau party based on Sikiomoni had been sending in detailed information and engaging in guerilla warfare "on the small scale which their position and task permitted"—they were primarily a source of Intelligence. In May they reported the killing of 197 Japanese, mostly with booby-traps. On 17th May Stuart moved his base south-eastward but in June a large enemy force set out to disturb him and he moved eventually into the Mount Gulcher area.

After the war Japanese officers said that in the several severe clashes at the Hari and Ogorata River crossings the uniformity of the Australian tactics—a wide outflanking move to the north accompanied by an artillery barrage—enabled General Akinaga to anticipate the course of action and withdraw before encirclement, using minor tracks parallel to the Buin Road. Since his guns could not be withdrawn across the rivers, the crews were ordered to site their guns for direct fire on advancing tanks. One tank knocked out was considered worth the loss of a gun. The gun crews were allowed to escape as soon as they had hit a tank.

The Japanese were critical of the Australian tactics of repeatedly making a wide outflanking move through the bush combined with a thrust by tanks along the main track. They declared that, because of the weight of the Australian armour, artillery and air support, each river crossing could have been secured more easily by the thrust along the main track combined with a small outflanking movement each side of it. (Hammer's tactics, however, succeeded.)

It will be recalled that in May Seton had relieved Mason as guerilla leader in the Kieta area. According to the report of the II Corps, Seton was by training and predisposition "eminently suited to lead a band of killers". This warrior decided to maintain his headquarters above Kieta which he was determined to capture if he could, and at the same time to send a patrol under Lieutenant Lovett-Cameron[8] and Sergeant Cross[9] along the Luluai Valley and one under Sergeant White and Corporal McGruer[1] north to the Vito area. Lovett-Cameron took up a position covering the Toimonapu, Kekere and Aropa Plantations and, with local partisans, made a series of raids on enemy camps, killing 213 Japanese

---

[7] WO2 J. F. Guerin, SX16061. 2/5 Indep Coy and 2/8 Cdo Sqn. 3 Bn RAR, Korea. Labourer; of Whyalla, SA; b. Millicent, SA, 20 Dec 1917.

[8] Lt H. E. Lovett-Cameron, MC, NX67489; "M" Special Unit. Jackeroo; of Wahroonga, NSW; b. Ceylon, 15 May 1919. Died 13 Jul 1953.

[9] Sgt A. F. Cross, NX18822. 2/1 Pnr Bn and "M" Special Unit. Labourer; of Bingara, NSW; b. Bingara, 29 Sep 1918.

[1] Cpl J. McGruer, NX125050; "M" Special Unit, Accounts clerk; of Vaucluse, NSW; b. Wagga Wagga, NSW, 7 Oct 1921.

in three weeks. They returned to Sipuru on 4th August. White's patrol was less successful, partly because White himself fell ill. However, valuable information was obtained and, in August, an attack on Rorovana killed 32 Japanese.

Mason's guerilla operations, continued by Seton, seem to have been without parallel. Never more than seven Europeans and generally only three took part. When Mason set out he encountered enemy troops only four hours' walk from Torokina, but in a few months his native guerillas had established a reign of terror among well-armed and trained Japanese forces which numbered nearly 2,000 in the Kieta area alone, and in August Seton was preparing to attack and capture Kieta itself. It was estimated that in eight months the partisans killed 2,288 Japanese. For evident reasons nothing was published at the time about the remarkable achievements of these and other guerilla leaders. The work in 1941-1944 of the coastwatching organisation from which most of them were drawn was fully and eloquently described after the war by Commander Eric Feldt in *The Coast Watchers*, but little was published about their guerilla and scouting operations in the final year of the war, and singularly few decorations were bestowed on the leaders for service in that period.

It has been mentioned that from the outset the Australian commanders had disagreed with the direction from General MacArthur's staff that a brigade should be employed in garrisoning Munda and the outer islands—Emirau, Green, Treasury. In December General Savige had submitted to General Sturdee that three companies would suffice, enabling the remainder of the 23rd Brigade to be concentrated at Torokina in reserve. It was not until about three months later—on 20th March—that MacArthur's approval of this plan was received, and so few ships were available that another six weeks passed while the brigade was brought to Bougainville. One company of the 8th Battalion remained on Emirau Island, one on the Green Islands and one was divided between the Treasury Islands and Munda. In June Savige was given permission to withdraw even these companies and the entire brigade was concentrated at Torokina. During its period on the outer islands the brigade, anxious for action, had made a number of small expeditions; there would have been more if General Savige had not restrained the enthusiasm of Brigadier Potts. In November one patrol of the 7th Battalion captured an isolated Japanese on Mono Island in the Treasury group and, as mentioned, another explored Choiseul Island. Patrols of the 27th Battalion discovered that no Japanese remained on several hitherto-occupied islands north of the Green Islands; troops of the 8th Battalion supported an Angau patrol which spent three weeks on New Hanover.

The freeing of the 23rd Brigade enabled Savige to hand over the central sector to it, thus reducing the responsibility of the 11th Brigade to the northern sector. On 19th April Potts took command of the central sector where his 27th Battalion had relieved the 31st/51st. He was ordered not to advance beyond Pearl Ridge, except with patrols. The information brought in by early patrols convinced Potts that the Japanese holding the Berry's Hill-Hunt's Hill area numbered from 40 to 50, and were reinforced from time to time. It was decided to send strong fighting patrols against them.

From 8 a.m. on 10th May twelve Corsairs dropped depth-charges on and machine-gunned Berry's Hill and Little Hunt's Hill for nearly an hour, and from 9 a.m. to 11.25 the field guns and mortars bombarded them. In the afternoon a patrol under Lieutenant Mills[2] advanced through dense bush on to Little Hunt's Hill which had been cleared of foliage by the blast of the depth-charges. After a short exchange of fire in which one Japanese was killed the hill was taken. It appeared to have been occupied by only about ten men. Four Japanese courageously tried to reoccupy the position; two were killed and the others fled. The occupation of this hill brought the forward Australian posts to within 450 yards of Berry's Hill.

Lieut-Colonel Pope[3] planned to take Berry's by sending four strong patrols against it after an air strike. A whole squadron of the New Zealand Air Force dropped bombs on and round Berry's in the morning of the 13th and the patrols moved out. Soon sharp firing was heard from Berry's and later Lieutenant Wolfenden[4] telephoned to Pope that the Japanese occupied it in strength, whereupon "in view of Corps' 'no casualty' policy" Pope ordered a withdrawal. One Australian had been slightly wounded.

However, reports that Japanese with packs on had been seen moving over Berry's led Pope, on 16th May, to decide that it was being abandoned and Wolfenden was again sent forward with a patrol. After calling for artillery fire Wolfenden's patrol advanced on to the hill and found it abandoned. Captain McGee[5] then moved the remainder of his company on to the hill, which had been battered by the air and artillery bombardment. Every post had been hit, the vegetation had been flattened, and several partly-buried corpses and 16 rifles lay around. In the patrolling on earlier days 12 Japanese had been killed on Berry's; a total of about 40 had been killed there by this battalion or the artillery, the Australians losing 3 killed and 2 wounded.

Meanwhile two platoons under Captain Lukyn[6] had been harassing the Japanese garrison of about 15 in the Sisivie area, hoping by continual sniping and harassing to eliminate them. By the 20th it was estimated that 8 had been killed.

---

[2] Lt L. C. Mills, MC, SX25131; 27 Bn. Bank officer; of Adelaide; b. Booleroo Centre, SA, 31 Jul 1919.

[3] Lt-Col A. Pope, DSO, ED, SX2930. 2/27 Bn; CO 27 Bn 1942-45. Assurance inspector; of Leabrook, SA; b. St Albans, Herts, England, 10 Nov 1903.

[4] Lt D. J. Wolfenden, NX113287; 27 Bn. Surveyor's assistant; of Merrylands, NSW; b. Marrickville, NSW, 19 Sep 1918.

[5] Capt T. W. McGee, NX113714; 27 Bn. Bank officer; of Maitland, NSW; b. South Grafton, 10 Sep 1915.

[6] Maj A. F. P. Lukyn, ED, SX2931; 27 Bn. Artist and signwriter; of Adelaide; b. Perth, 19 Oct 1913.

A patrol led by Sergeant Gilligan[7] on 17th May to ascertain whether the enemy still occupied Wearne's Hill and Base Point 3 and harass him, approached Base Point 3 stealthily and found Japanese in position astride the track. Gilligan took one man and a native round a flank and the

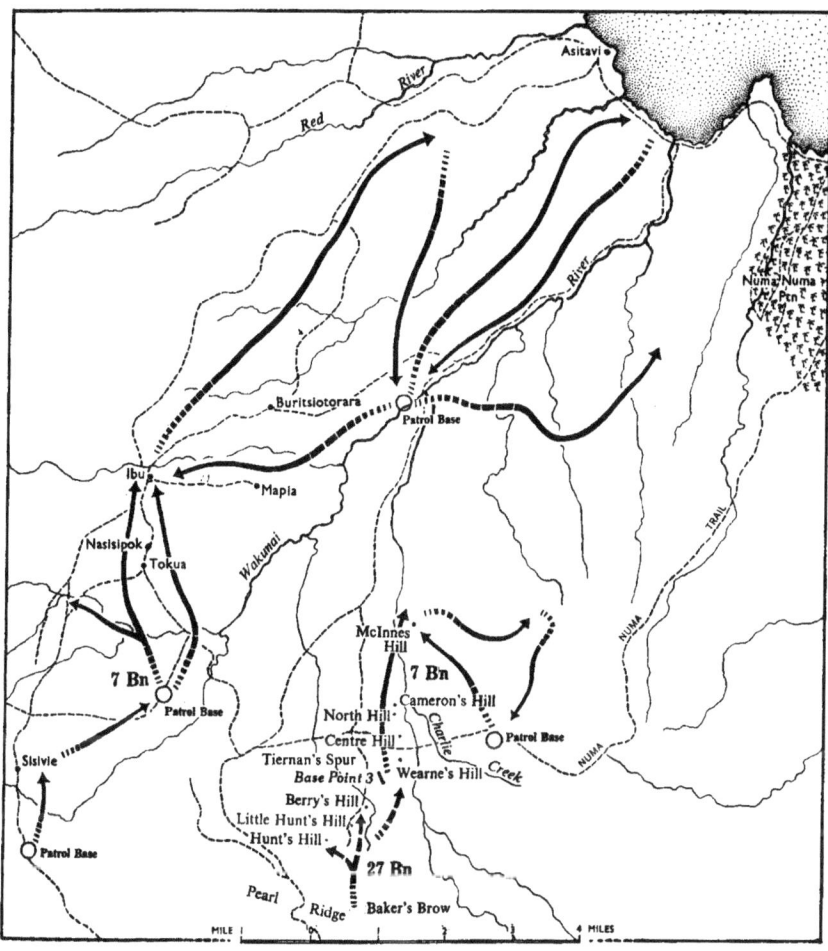

23rd Brigade, April-June

patrol attacked. In a sharp fight lasting 20 minutes eight Japanese were killed and a machine-gun was destroyed before the patrol, under fire from a patrol of six Japanese, withdrew. No Australian was hit.

On 18th May Lieutenant Tiernan[8] led a patrol to spend five days out in the bush and examine Tokua. They found it and observed the enemy

---
[7] Sgt D. M. R. Gilligan, SX26863; 27 Bn. Labourer; of Glenelg, SA; b. Broken Hill, NSW, 11 Apr 1920.
[8] Lt J. A. Tiernan, VX102602; 27 Bn. Clerk; of Wangaratta, Vic; b. Benalla, Vic, 5 May 1916.

for some time; there were 15 to 20 Japanese well dug in. Artillery fire was brought down on the Japanese positions. The patrol report mentions that on the third day a local native armed with one grenade joined the patrol.

From 22nd May onwards a series of patrols were concentrated against Wearne's Hill and Base Point 3. Each moved out and either probed in a new direction or occupied a position from which a further bound could be made.

Early in June Colonel Pope knew that he would soon be relieved by the 7th Battalion. The order that no attack should be made in the central sector had now been lifted, and he decided to take advantage of this change of policy by sending in a company to attack Tiernan's Spur. On the 3rd, after sharp artillery fire, Lieutenant Tiernan's platoon attacked a ridge held by the enemy 200 yards short of the main feature. After a sharp fight it took the position killing 9 Japanese; 5 Australians were wounded. The enemy counter-attacked the company next day without success.

In May and June the 23rd Field Company vastly improved the supply line to the force on the Numa Numa trail by constructing a powered haulage up Barges' Hill. It comprised a 2-foot gauge railway, rising 894 feet in 2,245 feet and with a maximum grade of 1 in 1. It handled 25 one-ton loads a day (600 carrier-loads), and relieved 200 natives for carrying farther forward.

The Papuan Infantry Battalion (Lieut-Colonel S. Elliott-Smith) had arrived at Torokina in May. One company was attached to the 15th Brigade, one (as mentioned) to the 2/8th Commando, one to the 27th Battalion at Pearl Ridge, and one to the battalions in the northern sector. These troops were soon engaged on long-range patrols in all sectors. For example, from 25th May to 5th June a platoon of the Papuan Infantry Battalion under Lieutenant Burns[9] made a notable patrol lasting twelve days, the object being to cut the enemy's track at Mapia and ambush and destroy any Japanese who were encountered. They thoroughly explored the enemy's line of communication, twice ambushing parties travelling along it. On the third day they killed 4 out of a party of 25, on the seventh 7, and on the twelfth day reached home without having lost a man.

In spite of the restrictions imposed on it the 27th came out of the central sector in early June a unit experienced and tested in bush warfare. In six weeks its men had made 48 patrols, and, moving stealthily through the enemy-held area, had launched several small-scale attacks. It had killed 122 Japanese, losing only 4 killed and 9 wounded.

At this stage Savige planned to land a company of the incoming battalion —the 7th—from a corvette on to the coast north of Numa Numa.[10] The plan was abandoned, however, because of the lack of reliable information

---

[9] Capt W. M. Burns, NX50574. 106 Tpt Coy AASC, 2/7 Armd Regt, Papuan Inf Bn. Regular soldier; b. Cootamundra, NSW, 8 Jun 1920.

[10] At one time or another the frigate *Diamantina* and the corvettes *Colac*, *Kiama*, *Lithgow* and *Dubbo* supported II Corps.

(Australian War Memorial)

Troops of the 2/8th Commando Squadron in the Musaraka area, Bougainville, 7th June 1945. Patrols are preparing to move out to attack enemy positions along the Buin Road.

(Australian War Memorial)

A section of the Buin Road, 16th July 1945. The corduroy has been submerged in mud. The jeep and trailer of the 2/11th Field Regiment are carrying water from the Ogorata River.

(*Australian War Memorial*)
A sodden camp of the 47th Battalion in southern Bougainville on 20th July 1945. Weeks of torrential rain have brought operations almost to a standstill.

(*Australian War Memorial*)
First contact between Major Otsu, the Japanese peace envoy, and Australian troops on the bank of the Mivo River, Bougainville, on 18th August 1945. Otsu (left) is accompanied by Superior Private Takeshita, carrying the flags.

about the Japanese strength in the area, and because of the difficulty of supplying even a company there.

For the first four months of the year the Japanese saw nothing to shake their conviction that the Australians would not try to advance overland to Numa Numa. In May, however, they found the Australians (the 27th Battalion) more aggressive and moved back their main strength. In this period they had about 350 men in the forward zone, and about 600 in reserve at Numa Numa. Their orders were to make deep outflanking movements, set ambushes and strike at supply trains. From June onwards, after corvettes had bombarded the north-east coast, a sea-borne landing at Numa Numa was expected daily. This threat added to that of a possible move south along the coast from Ruri Bay, led to the establishment of a composite battalion north of the Wakunai River to meet either contingency, and six field guns were sited for coastal defence.

Meanwhile Flight Lieutenant Sandford had been harassing the Japanese with increasing severity. By the end of May his natives had reported having killed 211 and he was able to patrol from Teopasino to Tinputz without meeting a Japanese. His party then moved south and surprised a body of Japanese troops who had retreated from the north or fled from Inus after air and naval bombardments and were busy building a camp. "The entire complement of 195 was wiped out." In June the camp was reoccupied and Sandford attacked it again, killing all the 50 or so occupants, for a loss of two natives killed. The camp was again reoccupied, this time by more than 300. New Zealand aircraft attacked it on 17th June and about 160 of the Japanese began to flee northward. Sandford's party pursued them and killed 10.

At this stage Captain Robinson[1] was moving into the mountains to relieve Lieutenant Bridge. When he heard a signal from Sandford that about 50 Japanese were moving in his direction, he decided to ambush them and set out to find a suitable position on the Ramazon River where he set three ambushes. On 20th June his men captured two Japanese. On the 22nd he was told from Torokina that 100 more Japanese were on their way towards him. Next day one of his patrols sent word that 50 to 60 Japanese had crossed the Ramazon, 18 had been killed and others hit. Robinson sent word to Aravia and Lumsis villages to muster as many men as they could and join him. On 26th June about 60 Japanese were ambushed near Raua Plantation. The Japanese returned the fire then broke away dragging many wounded. Two police boys were hit but not fatally.

On 29th June one of Robinson's patrols clashed with a party of more than 100 Japanese near Rugen Plantation. After fighting for two hours the Japanese withdrew to a hill in the plantation leaving a captain and 6 others dead. From 8th June to 4th July this party killed 45 Japanese.

Early in July Sandford was relieved by Captain J. H. Mackie.

When [Sandford's] party went into the field few of the natives were friendly, many were bitterly hostile and openly fought with the enemy. Moreover Sandford had had little experience with the A.I.B. previously. Largely by personal influence

---

[1] Maj E. D. Robinson, MC, NX102725. (1st AIF: Sgt 30 Bn.) "M" Special Unit. Hotel proprietor (formerly District Officer in New Guinea); of King's Cross, NSW; b. Doncaster, England, 5 Jan 1897. Died 5 Feb 1961.

Sandford won the natives' support and formed a fighting force of three platoons, each 35 strong, and by splendid organisation and personal leadership welded them into a force which accounted for over 500 Japanese killed.[2]

Early in April (while the Slater's Knoll battle was in progress in the south) the 55th/53rd Battalion had relieved the 26th in the northern sector. By that time the whole of the Soraken Peninsula had been occupied. Across the low coastal strip ahead lay a wide area of swamp; further advance by the main body must eventually be astride a track which was hemmed in by this swamp on the west and the steeply-rising mountains on the east. There were still some Japanese troops in the foothills south of this bottleneck and the incoming battalion was given the task of destroying these and then advancing north to Pora Pora, a village in the defile mentioned above.

In carrying out the instruction to capture Pora Pora Brigadier Stevenson decided that a quick move through the swamps would probably divide the Japanese forces, whereas if he landed at Ratsua and drove inland he would tend to consolidate the enemy round Pora Pora. Consequently he ordered the engineers to develop a jeep road along the old Government Road and to bridge the Nagam River. This was a large undertaking as much of the road had to be corduroyed and the jungle cut back to let the sun in to dry it. Unfortunately the road had not been finished when the advance began.

The 55th/53rd (Lieut-Colonel Henry[3]), now forward in this sector, had not yet been engaged in full-scale action on Bougainville, though it had had six weeks of patrolling in the Numa Numa sector. It was so short of officers at this time that the battalion and the companies lacked seconds-in-command and, even so, five platoons were led by sergeants.

Captured papers showed a secondary track travelling 3,000 to 4,000 yards inland over the foothills to Pora Pora, and Brigadier Stevenson confirmed this by making an air reconnaissance over the area. It was decided to send one company this way while others pressed on along the main coastal route. This company made steady progress along the inland pad, which wound over razor-back ridges covered with thick undergrowth; on 10th April it was about one-third of the way to Pora Pora, and on the 13th only some two miles from it, having made no contact with the enemy. That day Captain Marchant's[5] company, leading astride the coastal track, met the enemy at McKinnon's Ridge. In a sharp fight in which an attempt to outflank the enemy failed, five Australians were killed.[6] Captured documents suggested that a Japanese company 120 strong was guarding the approach to Pora Pora. Two platoons (Lieutenants Lee's[7] and Goodwin's) of Marchant's company now swung east then

---

[2] Report on Operational and Administrative Activities of II Australian Corps in the Northern Solomons Area, October 44-August 45.

[3] Lt-Col T. H. Henry, NX115499. (1st AIF: Pte 26 Bn 1918.) 55/53 Bn (CO 1945). Accountant; of Northbridge, NSW; b. North Sydney, 20 May 1899.

[5] Capt J. L. Marchant, NX127361. 55/53 Bn and staff appointments. Private secretary; of Burwood, NSW; b. London, 31 Jul 1915.

[6] The unit diary records that on this day, having acquired the necessary proportion of volunteers and completed the consequent formalities, the 55th/53rd Battalion became an AIF unit.

[7] Lt H. Lee, QX40924; 55/53 Bn. Labourer; of Brisbane; b. Murwillumbah, NSW, 17 Feb 1915.

north, leaving one platoon (Sergeant McKinnon[8]) at the ridge. On the afternoon of the 16th they encountered a party of Japanese in position and killed nine but others remained. In the following days two lateral tracks were found evidently leading to the Japanese position and on each a strong ambush was set, while artillery fire was brought down. As a result of these tactics the enemy withdrew on 21st April.

During this period Captain Sebbens'[9] company on the inland track had moved forward until it was one mile from Pora Pora. Captain Anderson's[1] company now relieved the platoons on a centre track and all three companies thrust forward to Pora Pora. In the next four days the battalion, supported by artillery fire and under frequent fire from enemy guns, fought its way into the Pora Pora bottleneck. By 30th April the enemy had been forced out, having lost 41 killed, including Captain Arai, commander of the defending force which numbered about 120. The Australian battalion had lost 6 killed (5 in the first clash) and 17 wounded.

Northward of Pora Pora the Bonis Peninsula narrows until at the line Porton Plantation-Tarbut it is only about three miles in width. The advance from Pora Pora made fairly rapid progress and it soon became apparent that the Japanese now intended either to withdraw to a line somewhat farther north in the narrow peninsula or perhaps to abandon the northern end of the island. On 4th May a company of the 55th/53rd, after a clash in which six Japanese were killed, swung west and occupied Ratsua jetty; this enabled supplies to be brought

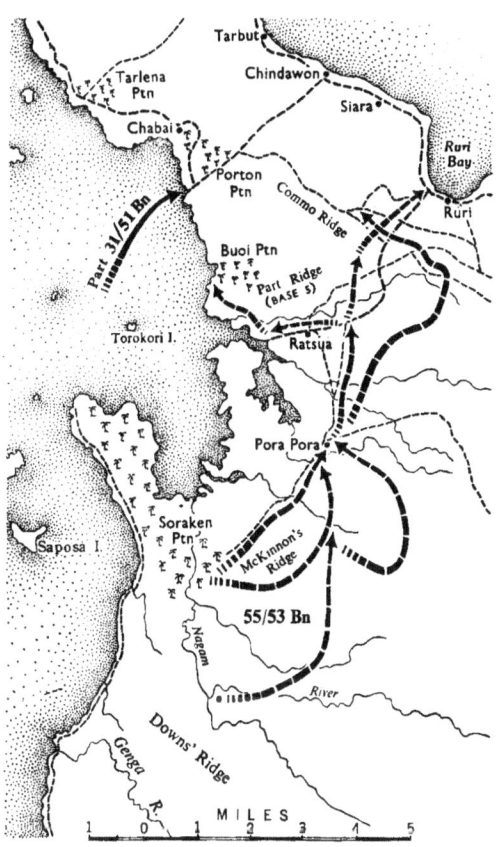

Northern sector, April-June

---

[8] Sgt C. D. McKinnon, NX82457; 55/53 Bn. Cane cutter and dairy farmer; of Ballina, NSW; b. Ballina, 10 Aug 1911.
[9] Capt E. R. Sebbens, NX114054; 55/53 Bn. Cadet valuer; of Bega, NSW; b. Bega, 6 Nov 1918.
[1] Capt D. O. Anderson, NX76325; 55/53 Bn. Credit manager; of Burwood, NSW; b. Burwood, 2 Nov 1917.

in by barge, although the craft were subject to shelling by a long-range gun near Buka Passage. On the 6th Torokori Island was occupied by a company of the 26th Battalion. On the right two columns were moving rapidly towards Ruri Bay on the east coast. Where did the enemy intend to stand?

Corps headquarters asked Stevenson for his views on future operations. He said that he considered that, when the 55th/53rd had cut through to Ruri Bay, the 26th and 31st/51st should be employed to drive north to Buka Passage, the 55th/53rd coming into reserve on the Ratsua-Ruri Bay line. He was told, however, that II Corps would not be able to supply the brigade in Bonis and proposed that he should swing a battalion down the east coast towards Numa Numa, a plan which did not appeal to Stevenson who estimated the enemy's strength in the peninsula at a far higher figure than did the Corps staff. Stevenson wished to maintain the momentum of the advance, but on 7th May he was instructed to halt on the Ratsua-Ruri Bay line—a five-mile frontage of thick jungle—to carry out active patrolling as far north as Tarbut and Tarlena to obtain information, but not to employ more than one battalion forward. On the 9th opposition stiffened. Anderson's company was ambushed approaching Ruri Bay and one man was killed and two wounded; a patrol of the left company under Lieutenant Valentin,[2] moving deeply north through Buoi Plantation towards Porton, ambushed and killed two Japanese just beyond Buoi but, when returning, was itself ambushed not far from Ratsua, Valentin being killed.

Henceforward, beyond the line Ruri Bay-Ratsua inlet the enemy was very aggressive; patrol clashes occurred daily and the Japanese launched fairly strong attacks on the company positions established at intervals across the neck of the peninsula, and began ambushing the Australian supply lines. Nearly every day for some days men were killed in Japanese ambushes. Stevenson allotted the 55th/53rd a company of the 26th to guard the rearward tracks. Not only was Japanese opposition becoming bitter right along the front but the 11th Brigade (which had been in action since January) and the 55th/53rd Battalion in particular were becoming weary. The intermittent shell fire had been galling—the 55th/53rd recorded that more than 700 shells had fallen in their area during their tour of duty. They had lost 17 killed and 26 wounded in their six weeks forward in appallingly swampy country, and had killed 85 Japanese. After a visit to the area Savige agreed that the 55th/53rd should be relieved, and its relief by the 26th was completed by 21st May.

The 26th Battalion was now beginning its second operation in northern Bougainville, after six weeks on the Soraken Peninsula, which it had captured in March. In that area it had no facilities for training and from time to time was under artillery fire; one bombardment had destroyed the ammunition and stores dump.

---

[2] Lt G. Valentin, NX167542; 55/53 Bn. Assurance clerk; of Granville, NSW; b. Ashfield, NSW, 13 Aug 1920. Killed in action 9 May 1945.

Lieut-Colonel Callinan's intention was to drive the infiltrating parties north of the Ratsua-Ruri Bay road. Ahead of him the land was relatively flat but with many small knolls up to 50 feet high on which the Japanese dug their positions. Two companies (Captains Searles and McNair) immediately began thrusting forward in the area south and east of Buoi Plantation, with one platoon holding the coastal flank. Another company (Captain Coleman) was on the right flank at Ruri Bay with the attached company of the Papuan Infantry on its flank. The fourth company made security patrols on the immediate flanks and to the rear where the Japanese were still persistently ambushing supply trains.

Coleman sent out patrols to the north and south and confirmed reports received earlier from Angau that there were no Japanese for 2,000 yards to the south; information from natives was that all the Japanese soldiers had passed through towards Numa Numa, leaving only naval men behind. Coleman therefore concentrated on probing northward.

The companies on the left thrust forward and soon met strong counter-attacks both round Buoi Plantation and on the road leading north. On the east a Papuan patrol commanded by Lieutenant Wall[3] found a strong position north of Ruri, and there and farther north round Siara and Chindawon killed twelve in a series of sharp clashes. It was evident that the enemy occupied strong positions across all tracks leading north into the peninsula, and one battalion on a front of over four miles would have difficulty in making progress—in fact that the 55th/53rd had been meeting sterner opposition than the Corps staff had realised. It was now learnt by the Intelligence officers that the Japanese defending force had been reorganised. The army troops had departed and a naval force of four fresh though small battalions, totalling 1,100 men, had been formed, largely from labour troops with naval officers and N.C.O's. Savige decided that a second battalion (the 31st/51st was now available) should move into the Ratsua-Ruri Bay area to support the 26th.

Thus, on 3rd June, the 31st/51st less two companies took over the western sector. Of the remaining rifle companies, one guarded the beachhead and the observation posts on Taiof and Torokori Islands, and a fourth was held at Soraken. Each battalion had a field battery and a platoon of heavy mortars in support. Against this larger force the Japanese fought strongly, their raiding parties still constantly harassed jeep trains in the rear and little progress was made. The raiding parties were very enterprising: a bomb was exploded one night on the beach outside forward brigade headquarters; next night one was exploded in a landing barge moored at Saposa Island, and another placed in the corps commander's launch but thrown overboard by the coxswain before it exploded. The Japanese inflicted casualties on patrols at fairly frequent intervals.[4] It was evident that the new Japanese naval force was resolute, enterprising and skilful, and every gain would be bought only at the cost of hard fighting;

---

[3] Lt J. D. S. Wall, MC, NX55061; Papuan Inf Bn. Student; of Point Piper, NSW; b. Colombo, Ceylon, 29 Apr 1921.
[4] On 7th June Major W. D. Matthew, who had recently joined the 26th Battalion as a company commander, was fatally wounded while on reconnaissance.

evident too that the 11th Brigade was becoming worn out. After the 26th Battalion had been in the line for three hard weeks its diarist wrote that the campaign had become one of "holding a superior number of enemy by the aggressive action of a tired depleted battalion—companies were no more than half strength and had been in forward areas continuously for four months". The battalion's fighting strength on 3rd June was only 23 officers and 353 other ranks. The constant patrolling, the artillery fire and the raids on jeep trains on tracks well to the rear were wearing down the men's spirits.[5] It was decided to come in behind the Japanese positions on the western flank by landing a reinforced company at Porton Plantation. Such tactics had succeeded early in the year in the south at Toko and in the north on Soraken Peninsula. Might they not succeed again?

At Porton Plantation the coast was fringed by reefs. The coconut plantation itself began almost at the water's edge and extended about 1,000 yards from north to south and from east to west. North and south lay some small plantations. It was believed that about 100 Japanese occupied Porton and scouting aircraft had reported pill-boxes and trenches there. The plan was to land the force by night, secure a foothold, and thence drive east to link with the main force which would push northward, eventually securing the area from Buoi to Porton. The final step would be to secure a line across the narrow neck of the island from Porton to Chindawon. The landing force was 190 strong and was to be embarked in six landing craft.[6]

The plan was that Captain Downs' company would make the initial landing from three L.C.A's (Landing Craft, Assault). Three A.L.C.15's would follow with the remainder of the group; these would guard the beach-head while the rifle company pushed on. The support of the 4th Field Regiment less one battery and of reconnaissance aircraft would be available.

The day after the battalion plan was made, scouting aircraft reported pill-boxes and much activity round Porton. Stevenson asked for an air attack on the pill-boxes but Corps did not consider them a suitable target. In view of the enemy's strength in the area it was decided that the 26th Battalion would take over the whole Ratsua front with one company of the 31st/51st under command, while the remainder of the 31st/51st would concentrate towards Porton; a second platoon of Captain Shilton's company would reinforce the beach-head on the night of the 8th-9th. Stevenson told Downs that, if necessary, another company and battalion headquarters would be sent in.

At 3.57 a.m. on the 8th the first wave of three landing craft, each carrying a platoon of Downs' company, set out for the shore. A local

---

[5] In one such raid, on 11th June, two Japanese wrecked a jeep with a mine, killed Sergeant H. E. Neelssen (of Julia Creek, Qld) and wounded three, including Major A. C. Ralston (of Cremorne, NSW), second-in-command of the 26th Battalion.

[6] The force included "A" Company, 31st/51st Battalion, one platoon of "C" Company, a detachment of mortars, one anti-tank gun, a section of medium machine-guns, detachments of engineers, signals, supply depot, field ambulance and a party from the 4th Field Regiment. The landing craft were 3 LCA's and 3 ALC.15's of the 42nd Australian Landing Craft Company.

native piloted them in. They drifted some 300 yards to the north of the intended landing place—the jetty point—and grounded 50 yards off shore. The men waded forward unopposed, plodded their way over 100 yards of coral and swamp, and by 4.30 had established a company perimeter reaching to 150 yards inland, and just north of three jetties that served the plantation. As soon as the men had scrambled out, the landing craft withdrew to allow the remaining three craft to put more men and the heavy weapons ashore. At 4.35 these craft grounded some 75 yards off shore, but again the men waded to the land. Ten minutes after the second wave of craft had grounded Japanese machine-guns opened fire from the north on the men ashore. One of the craft was able to withdraw but two remained fast; the Japanese fire prevented the unloading of heavy weapons, reserve ammunition or supplies—a great setback for the attackers. The little perimeter, about 100 yards in diameter, which the company had now formed, was soon under somewhat erratic fire from a line of pill-boxes a few hundred yards to the south and another line to the north and east. At 6 a.m. the party ashore established communication with the artillery, and by 6.12 a.m. artillery fire was brought down on the enemy positions to the north-east. It cleared the foliage in places, revealed some of the pill-boxes and silenced several machine-guns. This fire directed by Lieutenant Spark,[7] who was with Downs, was generally extremely accurate.

When it became light, enemy fire opened on the perimeter also from the jetty area. The company, now well dug in, began patrolling forward to destroy the enemy's machine-guns, leaving standing patrols guarding the perimeter, but, after making progress for only 200 to 350 yards, each forward patrol came under heavy fire. They ascertained that the perimeter was within an arc of enemy trenches and pill-boxes with a radius of about 400 yards. During the morning the strength of the enemy increased, and by midday there seemed to be about 100 with at least twelve automatic weapons and they were pressing forward from the north and east. At 8.20 a.m. Downs had signalled: "Unable to attempt get stores from stranded barge stop have no 2-inch or 3-inch mortars stop have no reserve ammunition stop request arrange dropping suitable position available in swamp at 265722. . . ."[8] By 1 p.m. fire was being exchanged at very short range, and returning patrols reported that enemy fire seemed to be coming from their own lines. Three Japanese with a light machine-gun crawled to within ten yards of the foremost pit of the platoon on the left of the perimeter. Private Ward,[9] manning the pit, threw a grenade and then jumped up, ran forward, shot the three Japanese with his rifle and

---

[7] Lt D. F. Spark, MC, NX47054. 2/2 and 4 Fd Regts. Regular soldier; of Artarmon, NSW; b. Hurlstone Park, NSW, 20 Apr 1916. Spark had served in Greece and Crete. He escaped from imprisonment after the fall of Crete and reached Egypt six months later in December 1941. He had been wounded on Bougainville in December and returned to duty in January. He was wounded again at Porton but remained on duty.

[8] The LCA's (which were armoured) had been withdrawn for maintenance on the ground that they could not be relied upon without it.

[9] Sgt K. R. Ward, DCM, WX22431; 31/51 Bn. 3 Bn RAR Korea 1950-54. Process worker; of Victoria Park, WA; b. Victoria Park, 7 Oct 1925.

knocked out the machine-gun. Four more Japanese attacked him and, from cover, he shot these also. Of a patrol of nine led by Lieutenant Smith[1] three men returned reporting that they had become separated. The others were missing. By 6 p.m. mortars were lobbing bombs among the Australians and 15 enemy machine-guns had been counted. It was estimated that 19 Japanese had been killed.

Trucks could be heard in the distance, evidently bringing up reinforcements, and by dusk it was estimated that 300 Japanese were manning the cordon round the Australian company; the observation post on Taiof Island reported that Japanese barges were crossing from Buka Island to Bonis evidently bringing more men forward.

At 9 p.m. a convoy of five Australian landing craft set out for Porton under cover of darkness, with stores, a fresh rifle platoon and a flame-throwing platoon. Four L.C.A's were to land and one A.L.C.15 to stand off while L.C.A's ferried its cargo ashore. Major Sampson of the 31st/51st led the convoy.

The tide was low and the leading craft grounded some distance from the beach under heavy fire from machine-guns and what seemed to be anti-tank guns. After a second attempt to get in closer Captain Leslie,[2] in charge of the landing craft, ordered the L.C.A's to withdraw. After 2.45 a.m. Sampson led a new attempt in one landing craft containing stores and the rifle platoon. When about 200 yards from the beach "a thick belt of fire" was falling in front of the craft and the attempt was abandoned.

Next morning (the 9th) it was decided to withdraw the force late that evening when the armoured landing craft would be in service again. So far losses had been remarkably light—four killed and seven wounded—partly because the perimeter had been formed before the enemy began to shoot and partly because of the inaccuracy of their fire. Throughout the night the Japanese had attacked persistently but were held off. In the morning they launched what was evidently intended as a final blow, thrusting from three sides. Now estimated at over 400 they attacked in waves and were mowed down by the Australian fire. To confuse their enemy they shouted English phrases such as "Watch the right flank", "Throw it in the middle", "It's only me, Jack", and so on. The Australians pulled back towards the beach and at 1 p.m. Downs asked that they be taken off at 8 p.m., not 10 p.m. as arranged, because it would be very difficult to hold the perimeter after dark. At 2.40 p.m. a message from the shore said: "We are now near the beach and getting hell."

The devoted Spark brought down artillery fire within 25 yards of the troops; in the two days 3,700 rounds were fired by the 12th Battery alone. At 4.30 p.m. three landing craft commanded by Leslie went forward to the beach under heavy fire to embark the men and carry them to the

---

[1] Lt N. J. Smith, NX14999. 2/17 and 31/51 Bns. Dairy farmer; of Kiama, NSW; b. Kiama, 28 Apr 1914. Died of wounds 9 Jun 1945.
[2] Capt A. S. Leslie, VX54605; 42 Landing Craft Coy. Insurance clerk; of Kew, Vic; b. Melbourne, 31 Mar 1921.

heavier landing craft which lay close off shore. The wounded were put aboard under intense fire. Then the others dashed back and climbed aboard. The beach was emptied in five minutes. One craft loaded with about 50 men backed out, but two were weighted too heavily and stranded. Not a man had been lost while moving on the beach and scrambling aboard, but a number were hit when they jumped out of the landing craft to lighten it.

A smoke canister landed in some boxes tied on top of the engine of one of the stranded craft. Private Ward, despite intense fire, exposed himself and tried to pick up the canister with his bare hands but it was too hot. With burnt hands he then cut loose the burning boxes with his bayonet and kicked them overboard.

The craft were bullet-proof and this prevented heavier losses. At length, at 10.40 p.m., one of the stranded craft, carrying 14 wounded and 10 unwounded men, drifted off with the tide, but Downs and 60 others, of whom about 12 were wounded, remained besieged in the other stranded craft, now holed by a jagged piece of coral and half full of water. For a time the twin Vickers gun mounted on it was fired at the Japanese on the beach but the enemy's cross fire killed the gunner and damaged the guns. At 1 a.m. Lieutenant Patterson and three men swam to the stranded stores barge farther north to discover whether men might be transferred to it but there they found a hostile native and had to swim away.

Downs' barge was tightly packed with men and because of the wounded lying on the floor movement was almost impossible. Private Crawford,[3] of the Intelligence section, later wrote that

a fierce fire swept the stores barge illuminating the area like day. At the same time a phosphorous grenade was thrown in the stern of our ALCA and Jap automatics opened up from the jetty area. Those in the centre of the barge were swept by fire and in a surge forward to escape the fire several were swept overboard. Captain Downs could not be found after this incident and it is assumed that he was swept out to sea. Several men clambered aboard again, whilst others commenced swimming out to sea and southward. Sharks were seen. . . . Several Japs then swam out and attempted to throw grenades on board. However the troops were alert and picked off the Japs at close range. At 0400 a lone Jap swam around the barge calling out, "I am Johnson, come and help me", and "I am blind and wounded." It was an obvious Jap ruse and easily detected as another Jap was heard on the shore giving out orders and telling the swimmer what to say. . . . At 0430 the swimmer began jabbering violently in Japanese, and was apparently moving back when he was seized by a shark.

At dawn on the 10th—the third day—aircraft appeared overhead and the enemy remained silent. There were now 38 living men on board, with 2 Brens, 5 Owens and 9 rifles. The remaining rations consisted of 8 tins of fruit or vegetables, 3 or 4 of meat and 3 of condensed milk. Corporal Hall[4] issued all the rations. There was no drinking water and the juice from the tinned food was reserved for the wounded. There

---

[3] Cpl W. J. Crawford, W53810; 31/51 Bn. Shipping clerk; of Cottesloe, WA; b. Subiaco, WA, 16 Apr 1925.
[4] WO2 E. D. Hall, QX46767; 31/51 Bn. Bank officer; of Innisfail, Qld; b. South Johnstone, Qld, 31 Aug 1922.

was one large first-aid outfit and some individual field dressings. The survivors in the stranded barge placed Hall in charge. The senior on board was a field ambulance sergeant, but an infantryman was considered a more suitable leader.

> Corporal Hall's defensive plan (wrote Crawford) was as follows: wooden shelves under overlapping sides of ALCA were removed to give protection under the flaps for all troops and placed on top and side of barge to facilitate movement. The wireless set was dismantled and thrown overboard to give further space. Six-inch lengths of copper piping were issued to each man to aid breathing whilst under flaps and when the tide rose. A continuous watch was maintained from the coxswain's enclosure to report on all Jap movements. Weapons were cleaned and oiled with lubricant obtained from engines and distributed evenly to able-bodied troops. Medical kit was placed in charge of a member of 19 Aust Field Ambulance, who distributed morphia and dressings as required.

At 3.30 p.m. on the 10th a concerted effort to rescue these survivors began. An intense and accurate air attack was made on the enemy's positions but did not succeed in hitting a pill-box from which most of the fire directed at the barge was coming. Bombers dropped inflated rubber rafts near the landing craft, but the Japanese fire prevented any men reaching these rafts. Under cover of an artillery smoke screen a landing craft attempted to reach the shore, but enemy fire wounded several of the crew, including the coxswain, and damaged the steering gear so that the craft circled wildly. While this was happening Corporal Hall tried to silence the pill-box with a Bren without success. He then splashed bullets in a line towards it hoping that the aircraft would thus be enabled to find the target, but in vain. The damaged landing craft withdrew.

After dark more Japanese tried to swim out to the craft but were shot at short range.

> By 2300 (wrote Crawford) the intense heat of the day, fatigue and exposure, plus the fact that we had not slept for three days and nights, was beginning to take effect. Men often collapsed due to utter exhaustion, a few were delirious. Men were half deaf from the continual explosion of bombs, shells and machine-gun fire.

At 1 a.m. on the 11th a Japanese succeeded in clambering on to the stern of the barge and firing a machine-gun among the occupants, killing two and wounding others before he himself was shot. Soon afterwards Japanese on shore fired two rounds from an anti-tank gun into the craft, tearing off its stern. Immediately the Australian artillery opened fire and the Japanese fire ceased. This artillery fire raised the spirits of the weary men on the barge, especially when a shell landed among a group of Japanese who were swimming out towards them. In the event of rescue Hall had given orders that the wounded were to go first, then the Owen gunners (who were short of ammunition), then the riflemen and finally the Bren gunners.

The effective artillery fire had been called down by Captain Whitelaw,[5] an artillery observer who was in one of the two A.L.C.15's which were on their way to the stranded craft bearing assault boats. When they were

---

[5] Lt-Col J. Whitelaw, NX76407; 4 Fd Regt. Shipping clerk; of Camberwell, Vic; b. Hawthorn, Vic, 11 Jun 1921.

150 yards from the craft three assault boats, each with 26 life jackets, were launched and led in by Lieutenant Graham.[6] Each had a crew of two sappers of the 16th Field Company. As the boats moved forward all guns of the two batteries fired on the Japanese positions. Two anxious hours passed before Graham's boat returned carrying five rescued men. Both Graham and Corporal Draper,[7] one of his crew, had been wounded. Then the second boat returned carrying seven. They had great difficulty finding the stranded craft because the shore was obscured by the smoke and dust raised by the shelling. At length every living man had been ferried back, the last two boats carrying fourteen and twelve men. Staff-Sergeant Blondell[8] of the engineers made a final search of the stranded craft and was satisfied that no living men remained on board. The rescue craft reached Soraken at 4.30 a.m.

A number of men swam to safety. For example, Gunner Glare[9] swam 5,000 yards from Porton nearly to Torokori Island helping a non-swimmer all the way.

In this enterprise the Australian force lost 23 killed or missing[1] and 106 wounded, of whom 5 killed and 7 wounded belonged to the 42nd Landing Craft Company. It was estimated that 147 Japanese were definitely killed and probably an additional 50. In the infantry 2 officers were killed, 3 wounded and a sixth evacuated suffering exhaustion and exposure; these included both company commanders and all but two of the six platoon commanders. The survivors were Lieutenants Patterson and Reiter, two young veterans from the 6th Division. In the infantry 14 other ranks were killed or missing, 57 wounded; 5 were sent to the field ambulance suffering from exposure, and 9 suffering cuts and bruises.

After the withdrawal from the Genga General Kijima had ordered Lieut-Colonel Nakamura to withdraw his force to Numa Numa, leaving the defence of the Tarlena area and Buka to the naval force. Captain Kato, the senior naval officer in Buka and commander of the *87th Naval Garrison Force* collected a force of 1,400 naval men and 2,000 civilians to defend Bonis Peninsula, but he could arm only one-third of the civilians and of these about 300 were available for front-line duties. Nevertheless this gave him a force of some 2,000 men, mostly well-trained naval veterans. His object was to delay the Australian advance long enough to move equipment from Tarlena to Numa Numa. Numbers of natives and Indian and Indonesian prisoners were employed on this work.

In May Kato issued instructions to his forward commanders that they were to harass the enemy's supply lines, maintain ambushes on all main tracks leading across the island from Ruri Bay to Ratsua, and form and hold a line from Porton Plantation to Tarbut. The force succeeded in carrying out these orders during May and June. Maintenance of the food supply became a big problem because of the withdrawal of men from gardening duties.

---

[6] Capt A. G. Graham, MC, QX36210. 16 Fd Coy and training appointments. Schoolteacher; of Bundamba, Qld; b. Newcastle, England, 4 Apr 1919.
[7] Cpl M. L. W. Draper, MM, QX40914; 16 Fd Coy. Carpenter; of Brisbane; b. Brisbane, 28 Dec 1919.
[8] S-Sgt G. P. Blondell, MM, QX36212; 16 Fd Coy. Bridge builder; of Brisbane; b. Wilston, Qld, 18 Aug 1914.
[9] Gnr E. W. Glare, VX73295; 4 Fd Regt. Mould maker; of Blackburn, Vic; b. Hamilton, Vic, 15 Nov 1915.
[1] The missing included Lieutenant N. J. Smith, two members of whose patrol reached Ratsua through the enemy's lines. They said that Smith had been wounded and had sent them to bring help. Two others, who also escaped, reported having tried to carry Smith in, but the enemy were so close that they had to leave him.

The repulse of the Australian attempt to land near Porton on 8th, 9th and 10th June greatly raised the spirits of the Japanese. "Observers reported that the landing was on a rough strip of beach and the enemy were in difficulties negotiating the reefs. The surrounding high ground commanded an excellent view of the landing point, and presented ideal positions for the siting of automatic weapons." Kato rushed 150 troops to the area from Chabai to reinforce approximately 100 men already in contact. These troops were able to prevent any further enemy landings and the enemy were pushed back to the beach, from where their remaining troops were hurriedly evacuated. Kato estimated that 250 Australians landed and that 60 were killed and 100 wounded; 26 Japanese were killed. If the Japanese report of their own losses is correct, both sides employed and both sides lost approximately the same number of men in this grim action.

The principal object of the landing at Soraken had been to cut the enemy's line of communication and enable the main force to advance. The main force, however, was not able to push ahead because of the stubborn resistance of isolated posts and because the troops were worn out.

CHAPTER 9

THE FLOODS AND THE CEASE FIRE

BY June, after six months of operations, the main Japanese force in south Bougainville had been thrust into an area some 30 miles by 15; in the north the enemy was confined to Buka Island and the narrow Bonis Peninsula; in the east, inland from Numa Numa and Tinputz, they were being increasingly harassed by Australian infantry patrols and the A.I.B. Above Kieta, Captain Mackie of the A.I.B. was planning actually to assault that town with guerilla forces. So far as the main body of the Japanese force was concerned the situation of 1944 had been reversed. Then the American garrison had held a perimeter about fourteen miles in length with some outposts beyond it. The main Japanese force was now hemmed in behind a defended line of about the same length but protecting a somewhat larger area than the Americans' Torokina perimeter had contained.

It was estimated that the strength of the Japanese army on Bougainville was now about 14,500 and that, in the main areas, they were distributed as follows:

Buin	7,850
Shortland, Fauro and near-by islands	1,310
Kieta	1,130
Numa Numa	1,630
Bonis-Buka	1,780
Total	13,700

These totals excluded some other army troops, an estimated 1,500 civilian labourers, and the naval troops—perhaps 3,000—about whom virtually no information could be obtained from captured soldiers. The rough estimate of the total strength was now 19,000 to 20,000.[1]

These figures, based on recent secret information, were considerably higher than the estimates of April, when, as mentioned, the total army strength had been considered to be only about 11,000. Incidentally, there were indications that in the past few months the Buin area had been reinforced from the Shortland and Fauro Islands and Kieta. The strength of the Australian forces on Bougainville was now 32,000, including 7,600 in the Base Sub-Area. At 9th June II Corps was 2,528 below its war establishment, the base 245 below.

Only twenty-eight miles separated the leading Australians from the Japanese base area round Buin, but densely-wooded and wet country made a rapid overland advance impossible. General Savige considered that he

---

[1] The true strength at this time was about 24,000. The estimate of the strength of the army was almost exact, but the naval force, including its civilian workers, was still greatly under-estimated, and hence the error in the total. The actual strengths were:

	Approximately
Naval troops	6,100
XVII Army	13,500
Civilian workers	4,200

did not have enough craft and other equipment to make an effective landing farther along the coast; in any event there were no suitable all-weather landing beaches west of Moila Point, and east of it he would be within range of the Japanese anti-aircraft and coast guns defending their big base. He concluded that the only course was to continue a steady advance along the Buin and Commando Roads.

Savige's problem was to find enough fresh forces to carry out the tasks he planned. It will be recalled that for the coming phase the 3rd Division was to include the 11th, 15th and 29th Brigades; the 7th (formerly part of this division) was in need of rest and leave. Savige hoped to have it and the 15th rested and refreshed for a final assault on the Japanese inner fortress. If the 7th was to be given some leave and the 11th, after a rest, sent to the 3rd Division, the 23rd must take over both central and northern sectors.

From April onwards, in the background of Savige's planning and that of other commanders in Australian New Guinea was the knowledge that their operations were being subjected to increasing criticism in newspapers and Parliament in Australia. The problem faced by the field commanders was expressed in a letter sent by General Sturdee to Savige on 18th July:

> As you are aware as much as I am, we are on rather a hair trigger with operations in Bougainville and in 6 Div area in view of the political hostility of the Opposition and the Press criticism of the policy of operations being followed in these areas. The general policy is out of our hands, but we must conduct our operations in the spirit of the role given us by C. in C., the main essence of which is that we should attain our object with a minimum of Australian casualties. We have in no way been pressed on the time factor and to date have managed to defeat the Japs with very reasonable casualties considering the number of the Japs that have been eliminated.

Meanwhile, on 28th June General Savige had given General Bridgeford, as his next immediate role after securing the line of the Mivo, an advance to the line of the Silibai River, still along the two main tracks—the Buin and Commando Roads. The rate of advance was to be determined by that at which roads and jeep tracks could be built and protection of the line of communication provided by the reserve brigade. At first the 15th Brigade was to be relieved not later than 1st July, but as the battalions of that brigade were already moving up to an attack towards the Mivo, Savige gave permission for the relief to be deferred until their objectives had been reached. Then the 29th Brigade would come forward and secure the Mivo line. This brigade was now commanded by Brigadier N. W. Simpson, a forceful infantry officer who had led the 2/17th Battalion in battle in North Africa and New Guinea.

This account of planning has run somewhat ahead of the narrative of the 3rd Division's operations. As mentioned earlier, the 57th/60th Battalion, having completed its wide outflanking move on 16th June, was on the Buin Road and advancing towards the Mobiai.

On the 17th a company of this battalion tried to outflank the enemy position between it and the Mobiai but was blocked by a Japanese position well north of the road. Next day it made a wider outflanking move and reached the road behind the enemy. There it was attacked but pressed on, and on the 19th the Japanese withdrew, having destroyed the field gun whose presence had prevented the tanks from advancing. In the following days the battalion thrust steadily forward, gaining a few hundred yards at a time, and on the 23rd was close to the Mobiai. There on the 24th a strong and determined enemy force was encountered with a 37-mm gun which scored three hits on the leading tank but failed to damage it. A heavy bombardment failed to dislodge the Japanese that day, but on the 25th they had gone leaving behind their gun, which had been buckled by fire from a tank.

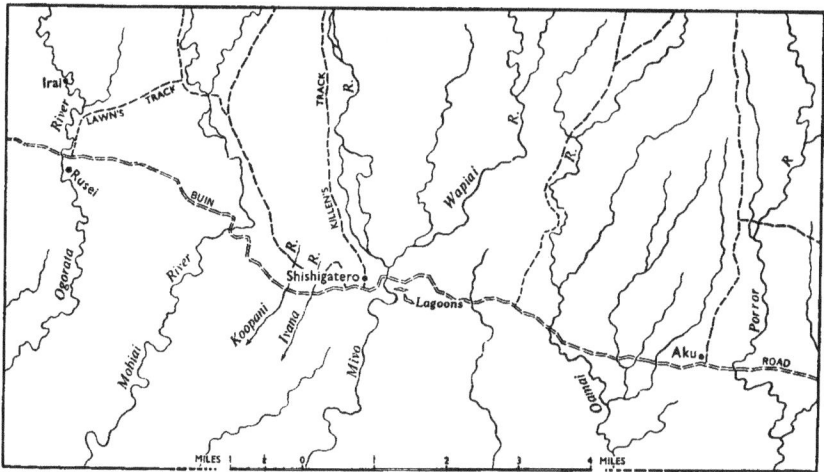

Brigadier Hammer wished to advance to the Mivo before the enemy had recovered and reorganised. His plan was to relieve the 57th/60th Battalion on the Mobiai with the 58th/59th, move the 24th and 57th/60th to Musaraka whence they would advance with tanks round the enemy's northern flank, the 24th to the Buin Road between the Koopani and Ivana Rivers and the 57th/60th to Shishigatero. The 58th/59th would create a diversion across the Mobiai and south of the Buin Road. By the 27th both leading battalions were in the concentration area and a track for tanks had been made on this flank from the Mobiai to a track—Killen's—which ran just west of the Mivo to Shishigatero on the Buin Road.

That day when the 24th Battalion reached the assembly area from which the march to the Buin Road was to begin, the leading company found a party of Japanese in occupation, attacked them, killing nine, and dug in some 200 yards away while the artillery bombarded the enemy. Next day when the 57th/60th reached its area, farther forward, its leading company was attacked by about 100 Japanese as it was digging in. There was a fierce fight lasting half an hour in which 2 Australians were killed and

10 wounded and 11 Japanese dead left on the field. Nevertheless by dusk the battalion was packed and rationed ready to move off early next morning—29th June. All that night it rained, and in the morning there being no sign of the Japanese who had attacked the previous day, two companies, each with a troop of tanks, set off over boggy ground behind an artillery barrage which lifted 200 yards every eight minutes. By 4 p.m. the leading companies were on the Buin Road—their objective. Meanwhile the 24th advanced behind a similar barrage and the devastating bombing and strafing of 44 Corsairs. The bush was so dense that at times the advance of the barrage had to be delayed, but by 3 p.m. one leading company was on the Buin Road at the Ivana River, the other at the Koopani River. At 12.30 p.m. two companies of the 58th/59th with a troop of tanks set out to open the road to the 24th Battalion about 1,000 yards away but met sharp opposition. Lieutenant L. S. Proby led a charge which took one post but by dusk the companies had gained only 300 yards. Thus by the end of the day the 24th had bitten a piece out of the Buin Road about midway between the Mobiai and the Mivo, the 57th/60th was astride the road at the Mivo with Japanese to the east and west; and the 24th was pushing forward to join the 57th/60th.

Throughout this area the road was heavily mined and teams from the 7th Bomb Disposal Platoon (Lieutenant Woodward[2]) were busy.

These boys did a remarkable job (wrote the historian of the 2/4th Armoured Regiment); briefly it consisted of walking down a track through the jungle, in front of the tanks, with infantry creeping through the undergrowth on their flanks, while they prodded an old bayonet into the ground to feel if there were any mines there. The fact that the first sight that the Jap would have of the approach of our troops was that of a tank rolling down the road with a man walking in front brandishing a bayonet and frequently stopping while he deloused and pulled up a mine, didn't appear to worry these fellows.[3]

In the first 10 days of June these bomb disposal men encountered about 20 mines a day ranging from 75-mm to 150-mm shells, usually in clusters of three. Thanks to their skill and devotion this very thorough mining caused no serious delay.

On the 30th the Japanese reacted by steadily shelling the 57th/60th with six guns. This long-range fire caused few losses but the 24th Battalion and engineers of the 15th Field Company who were thrusting along the Buin Road encountered a concealed gun which waited until a bulldozer was only 50 yards away and hit it repeatedly, killing 4 and wounding 6 of the engineers.

The position was a masterpiece of camouflage which accounts for the clearing patrols having not observed it although, as they now know, they had passed within feet of it (wrote a diarist). The gun was completely camouflaged with a cunning wire arrangement in the branches which opened to make a fire lane on being pulled and closed on being released.

---

[2] Capt W. C. Woodward, DSO, VX114949; 7 Bomb Disposal Pl. Joiner; of Hawthorn, Vic; b. Perth, 11 Apr 1918.
[3] *Tank Tracks—The War History of the 2/4th Australian Armoured Regimental Group* (1953), p. 66.

The operations of the 15th Brigade, now nearing their end, had succeeded admirably. The brigade was the most experienced formation on Bougainville. Hammer had the advantage of the support of more heavy weapons than had been used before and he employed them to the full. His wide outflanking moves took time to prepare but probably saved casualties—although the brigade's losses in battle were heavier than those of any other on Bougainville. The outflanking moves were carried out with few casualties; most of the losses were caused in "the many minor battles fought in between the major ones".[4]

During its period in action the 15th Brigade killed and buried 803 Japanese and took 47 prisoners. It is probable that many more were killed by air and artillery bombardments, which were heavy during this phase.

On Bridgeford's orders the 29th Brigade now began to move forward and take over. There were still Japanese on each side of the 57th/60th, and it was soon evident that the incoming troops would have to continue the fight for the line of the Mivo. Each incoming battalion had sharp clashes as it moved up, the 42nd to relieve the 24th, the 47th (now commanded by Lieut-Colonel Fry) to place a company on the Mivo, the 15th to relieve the 57th/60th. On 3rd July as Major McDonald's company of the 47th was coming into its position it was fiercely attacked by from 80 to 100 Japanese. The onslaught continued all day until late in the afternoon when two tanks arrived on the scene with a platoon from the 15th Battalion and dispersed the enemy who were then only 10 yards from the forward weapon-pits. At least 20 Japanese were killed. The tanks brought wire and ammunition to the forward company. There were small attacks on the 4th but on the 5th McDonald's signal line was cut and from 60 to 100 Japanese attacked from several directions. After the infantry and tanks had killed at least 15 Japanese the enemy withdrew. The rain had been incessant and the men were fighting from weapon-pits filled with water. On the 6th line communication with the beleaguered company and tanks was re-established and a fighting patrol took rations forward to it. That day the Japanese began a series of strong attacks on the company of the 15th Battalion nearest the Mivo ford, and shelled it persistently. On 9th July some 70 Japanese attacked with such vigour that some got within the defenders' wire; 34 were killed including 4 officers, and 2 wounded men captured, the Australians losing 2 killed and 4 wounded.

The day on which Simpson's brigade was to cross the Mivo was originally fixed at 3rd July but because of heavy rain it was postponed to the 10th. Meanwhile all battalions sent out patrols, many of which met such fierce opposition that it was soon evident that the enemy intended to offer a determined defence on the Mivo line. Patrols regularly captured useful documents from Japanese ambushed along the tracks leading to

---

[4] The losses in the battalions of the 15th Brigade in this phase were:

	Officers	Other ranks
24th Battalion	11	179
57th/60th Battalion	8	128
58th/59th Battalion	13	196

Of the wounded 74 remained on duty.

their forward positions and a clear picture of the enemy's intentions and dispositions was obtained. A patrol of the 42nd led by Lieutenant Oldfield,[5] ordered to reconnoitre a crossing of the Mivo, found the river in flood, whereupon Oldfield and four others stripped, swam the river and, without weapons, scouted 500 yards beyond it. Because of the weight of the Australian artillery and mortar bombardments the enemy was now digging in less and employing instead a policy of hit-and-run raids and ambushes by parties of from three to ten men.

Before the 10th arrived, the persistent rain caused a second postponement of the next move forward; 24th July was now to be D-day. The rain became heavier. On the 10th even patrols could not cross the flooded Mivo. "Torrential rain flooded the divisional area, reduced the Buin Road to a sea of mud and created a series of islands between the various rivers." On the 17th the rain became still heavier; 8 inches fell in 36 hours. The problem now was not to move troops forward but to feed them where they were. Virtually all the bridges on the line of communication were washed out, all the rivers flooded; the Mivo was running at 12 miles an hour. Soon the forward units could be supplied only by air. It would take weeks to repair the road and bridges. D-day was postponed until late August.

Even deep patrolling now became impossible. The conditions on and beyond the Mivo may be illustrated by an account of a patrol of the 42nd Battalion which set out on 14th July to establish a hidden patrol base about a mile east of the Mivo and about the same distance south of the Buin Road. It was led by Lieutenant R. B. Winter and included his platoon, Lieutenant Smith[6] and a party of the Papuan Infantry, and an artillery observer and his team; it was to be out four days. On the first day, after seeing four parties of Japanese but being unseen by all but one of them, they reached a patrol base already established by Lieutenant Steinheuer on the Mivo about a mile south of the Buin Road. Next day Winter crossed the Mivo and set up his base about a mile to the east. The rain was falling so heavily on the forest that his men could not hear the bursting of ranging shots fired by the artillery. On the fourth day a second patrol under Lieutenant Shaw[7] set out to relieve Winter in due course, but failed to reach him. The rain was becoming heavier and Winter's patrol was running short of food. On such patrols the men spoke in whispers—the excited chattering with which Japanese usually accompanied their movement along the tracks was a main reason for the success of Australians in patrol actions.

Whispering finally got one of the lads down (wrote Winter in his diary);[8] [he] started yelling his head off. What he said about the Nip and all armies in

---

[5] Maj A. S. Oldfield, MC, WX27292; 42 Bn. Printer; of Kalgoorlie, WA; b. Kalgoorlie, 18 Sep 1919.

[6] Lt P. V. Smith, WX17235. 2/7 Armd Regt and Papuan Inf Bn. Public servant; of Gosnells, WA; b. Slough, Bucks, England, 27 Jan 1921.

[7] Lt L. C. Shaw, QX35888; 42 Bn. Motor mechanic; of Rockhampton, Qld; b. Barcaldine, Qld, 6 Aug 1917.

[8] Quoted in S. E. Benson, *The Story of the 42 Aust. Inf. Bn.*, p. 193.

general won't stand repeating. Frightened hell out of me and everyone else. Damn near had to slap his ears off to quieten him. Poor kid only turned 19 the day before we left on this patrol. Seems O.K. now.

The rain discouraged even the carrier pigeons. "Sent a long message to brigade by pigeon," wrote Winter. "The ——— won't fly. Ceiling too low. Up in a tree and not a stone in sight. . . . Bloody sorry I didn't eat them the other night when they were making so much din." On the fifth day out there was still no sign of Shaw and the rations that day were one biscuit per man per meal. Two of the Australians had been wounded, one accidentally, and two had malaria. Sergeant Winter,[9] brother of Lieutenant Winter, arrived back with a small patrol from the Lagoons area to the north where they had killed nine Japanese, and the whole patrol set off westward to the Mivo. On the 19th they recrossed the flooded river. Meanwhile Shaw had crossed the river some distance to the south. The Japanese had now been "stirred up" by the presence of Lieutenant Winter's patrols and there were several clashes, in one of which four Japanese were killed—two by Private Rowbottom,[1] who continued to fire his Bren after his arm had been broken by a grenade—and four Australians wounded. On the 19th and 20th Shaw's patrol was surrounded by swirling waters but after narrow escapes from drowning managed to recross the river with the help of ropes and reached home on the 22nd.

On 16th July the 15th Battalion had sent a patrol across the Mivo. It met a far stronger enemy group which fired with three machine-guns and forced it to withdraw after seven men had been hit. Private Minchin,[2] the forward scout, a youth of just 20, was forced to remain hiding behind a log very close to the enemy. When they advanced he fired with his Owen, killed four, and drove the others to cover. He stayed where he was for nearly two hours, firing on the Japanese whenever they moved while they searched for him with the fire of two machine-guns. The Australian artillery then fired and forced the Japanese out, whereupon Minchin followed them, and slept that night in the jungle just east of their bivouac. Next morning, he moved back through their position, noted the layout, recrossed the Mivo and brought the information back to his company.

On 21st July, Corporal Whitton[3] of the 42nd led out a patrol of four towards the Mivo. After 600 yards, as the leading scout entered a clearing, the patrol was fired on by 10 Japanese. Whitton advanced alone across the clearing firing his Owen. He silenced one machine-gun and then he was hit in the arm and the fore-grip of his gun shot away.

---

[9] Sgt K. N. Winter, MM, QX54865; 42 Bn. Electrician's assistant; of Mount Morgan, Qld; b. Mount Morgan, 13 Aug 1917.
[1] Pte N. K. Rowbottom, MM, TX15099; 42 Bn. Timber carter; of Legerwood, Tas; b. Scottsdale, Tas, 11 Aug 1917.
[2] WO2 R. F. Minchin, DCM, TX9149; 15 Bn. Student; of Hobart; b. Hobart, 3 May 1925.
[3] Cpl S. A. R. Whitton, DCM, NX41284. 17 A-Tk Bty and 42 Bn. Station hand; of Bingara, NSW; b. Bingara, 14 Mar 1912.

He threw grenades into a second enemy machine-gun post killing or wounding six. He then returned to his men and, despite his wound, led a patrol back to clear the enemy out of their position.

Late in July and in early August the rain moderated and patrolling was intensified, long-range patrols penetrating up to and beyond the Oamai River. In a clash on the northern flank on 24th July a patrol of 24 of the 47th Battalion was fiercely attacked by some 60 Japanese. Reinforcements arrived and extricated them but not before 3 Australians had been killed and 11 wounded, including the commander, Lieutenant McLellan,[4] and the artillery observer, Lieutenant Glass.[5]

Glass brought down artillery fire on Japanese positions only 60 yards away and, despite a severe wound in the left arm, continued to fire his sub-machine-gun with his right. McLellan directed the patrol from a stretcher. Soon only 12 men remained unwounded. Finally Corporal Tucker,[6] himself hit in three places, organised the withdrawal of the patrol and its wounded.

On 4th August, Sergeant Steinheuer[7] led a party from the 15th Battalion to patrol the east bank of the Mivo. Crossing the flooded river Lance-Corporal Henderson[8] was swept downstream. Steinheuer and Private Mattingley[9] went to his rescue. Henderson struggled to the east bank and so did Steinheuer and Mattingley. These three, armed only with grenades, patrolled north along the east bank covered by the others from the west bank. Near the Buin Road the Japanese exploded a mine by remote control killing Henderson and wounding Steinheuer. Mattingley gave first aid and brought Steinheuer out across the Mivo.

On 3rd August a deep patrol of the 15th Battalion, led by Lieutenant Young,[1] surprised 15 Japanese in a group of huts well to the east of the Mivo and killed 6, the others fleeing. Next day patrols of the 15th killed 19, and on the 5th a platoon commander and six men from each rifle company crossed the Mivo and patrolled to the Wapiai River reconnoitring the route over which the battalion planned to advance on 17th August.

In this period Japanese patrols were fiercely harassing the Australian lines of communication. At dawn on 5th August when engineers of the 7th Field Company (Major Fitz-Gerald[2]) had partially built a Bailey bridge over the Hongorai, three Japanese appeared at the western end and seemed

---

[4] Lt C. J. McLellan, MC, QX52216; 47 Bn. Public servant; of Bundaberg, Qld; b. Bundaberg, 27 Apr 1916.
[5] Lt R. L. Barnet Glass, MC, VX45395; 2/11 Fd Regt. Cost accountant; of Toorak, Vic; b. Melbourne, 25 Jun 1915.
[6] Cpl G. J. Tucker, MM, QX48064; 47 Bn. Butcher; of Charters Towers, Qld; b. Charters Towers, 7 Oct 1918.
[7] Sgt H. B. Steinheuer, QX62223; 15 Bn. Schoolteacher; of Rockhampton, Qld; b. Rockhampton, 27 May 1910.
[8] L-Cpl R. H. Henderson, WX22639; 15 Bn. Clerk; of Mount Hawthorn, WA; b. Bunbury, WA, 23 Sep 1925. Killed in action 4 Aug 1945.
[9] Pte L. F. Mattingley, MM, QX63502; 15 Bn. Labourer; of Annerley, Qld; b. Brisbane, 17 Jul 1921.
[1] Lt D. H. Young, QX53254; 15 Bn. Ply mill hand; of Carina, Qld; b. Brisbane, 9 Nov 1917.
[2] Maj A. T. Fitz-Gerald, QX22567. OC 7 Fd Coy. Engineer; of Brisbane; b. Melbourne, 16 Dec 1911.

to be determined to blow it up. Sergeant Brown,[3] in charge of the early morning shift, saw them and tried to fire his Owen gun but it jammed. One of the Japanese lit a charge he had placed in position. Brown left his men under cover, obtained more ammunition, went forward and hurled the charge into the river two seconds before it exploded. The Japanese ran away.

On 7th August, a party from this company, going to work in trucks was ambushed by about 35 Japanese just east of Hammer Junction. In an action lasting fifteen minutes seven sappers were killed or mortally wounded and seven less severely wounded.

As a result of this and earlier attacks by Japanese infiltrating ever more boldly the 7th Field Company contrived a truck protected with sandbags and armed it with Bren guns and several Owens and it was used to escort engineer convoys.

The continuance of operations by the infantry depended now, as earlier, on the efforts of the engineers and others who were building and maintaining the roads and bridges. The main road from Torokina to the Mivo, 75 miles long, had been built through virgin coastal scrub on volcanic sandy soil, and through swamp forest, often on clayey soil, cut by many rivers and lagoons. In addition the engineers and infantry had built 21 miles of lateral roads, 25 miles of corduroyed jeep and tank tracks, and more than 50 miles of tracks that were temporarily made capable of carrying tanks or jeeps and then abandoned. In the southern sector the engineers built 30 permanent or semi-permanent bridges totalling 9,500 feet. Frequent flooding made maintenance a heavy task, and the two major floods—the first in April and now this bigger one in July—caused great destruction and much earlier work had to be remade. After the campaign the Chief Engineer of the Corps (Brigadier W. D. McDonald, who had replaced Brigadier Mann[4] in May) recorded that the engineer stores were adequate: 5,000 tons as an initial allotment and 1,700 tons a month thereafter.[5]

On 14th August, a native reported that a large number of Japanese about Hanung wished to surrender and Corporal Geai was sent out with a patrol. Near Hanung three Japanese with hands upraised were met. Geai went forward to take their surrender when he saw a camouflaged machine-gun covering the tracks and several armed Japanese moving stealthily about. He shouted to his men to take cover and opened fire killing the crew of the machine-gun. The patrol was now under intense mortar, rifle and machine-gun fire. Geai was wounded in the arm and hand but rushed forward and killed seven with his Owen. He was now wounded also

---

[3] S-Sgt H. J. Brown, GM, QX40532; 7 Fd Coy. Bridge carpenter; of Brisbane; b. Brisbane, 31 May 1913.

[4] Brig J. Mann, DSO, VX250. (1st AIF: Lt 2 Fd Coy Engrs 1918.) CRE 9 Div 1940-41 and 1941-42; DCE Western Desert Force Apr-Oct 1941; CE First Army 1942-44, NGF 1944, II Corps 1944-45; Comd 1 Aust CE (Wks) 1945. Regular soldier; b. Melbourne, 8 Jul 1897.

[5] On Bougainville the engineers lost 25 killed and 42 wounded not including 8 killed and 13 wounded in the water transport units.

in the leg but carried on and organised a withdrawal. Only one other native was hit.[6]

By the first week in August the rains in southern Bougainville had put a stop to large-scale operations for over a month. News of the dropping of an atomic bomb in Japan convinced the troops that the end of the war was near. On the 9th came news of the dropping of a second atomic bomb and the invasion of Manchuria by the Russians. On the 11th the forward battalions were ordered to withdraw all long-range and fighting patrols forthwith, but to remain on the alert. On the 16th they learnt that fighting was to have ceased the previous day. But when would all the isolated parties of Japanese know what had happened? An Australian patrol searching for the body of a man killed on patrol some days before met a group of Japanese who seemed to have learnt the news: "Neither party knew whether to advance or make off. After observing one another our party returned to company area."[7]

Meanwhile, on the inland flank, commando patrols early in June had found the Commando Road area clear of enemy troops from the Mobiai to the Mivo. Later, however, the enemy began probing vigorously and patrols reached points close to squadron headquarters. Clashes occurred every few days. On 10th July a particularly sharp fight occurred near the Mivo crossing. Lieutenant Smith's[8] section of 18 men found about 40 Japanese foraging in a garden, but they were in small groups and did not present a good target for surprise attack. Smith, therefore, stealthily set an ambush on the track leading to the garden. When the leading enemy party had moved from the garden and was fully enclosed in the ambush the Australians opened fire and killed all these Japanese, but those who remained in the garden opened fire. After an exchange of fire, in which Smith was killed, the Australians withdrew. Next day 20 fresh enemy graves were found.

Major Winning anticipated that, as the brigade was advancing so fast, he would be asked for "information" about the country ahead. Con-

---

[6] Geai, enlisted in May 1941, was awarded the DCM.
[7] The troops at Torokina knew of the surrender on the 15th. That day Gracie Fields, the English singer, had arrived at Torokina. In her autobiography *Sing As We Go* (1960), pp. 151-2, she writes:
"The General who had showed me the jungle clearing where I was to sing that evening came up white-faced with a sort of dazed excitement.
" 'I want you to come with me *now*,' he said. It was midday.
"He took me to the huge clearing. Already it was packed with . . . troops. With all the top brass I stood facing them. The boys must have wondered about the small odd-looking creature I looked, all muffled up in creased khaki.
"The General stepped forward. 'Men, at last I can tell you the only thing you want to know. The Japs have surrendered.' In the second's silence of wonderment and before the cheering could start, he held up his hand. 'I have England's Gracie Fields here. I am going to ask her to sing the Lord's Prayer.'
"He led me to a small wooden box. I got on to it. There was a movement as of a great sea —every man had taken off his cap.
"The matted green of the tall dark jungle surrounded us, but above our clearing the noon sun seared down from the brilliant sky on to . . . bare bowed heads.
"I started to sing. 'Our Father which art in Heaven. . . .' Because of my cold I had to sing in a low key, but there was no sound except my voice. The hushed thousands of men in front of me seemed even to have stopped breathing. Each note and word of the prayer carried across the utter stillness of the rows of bent heads till it was lost in the jungle behind them.
"It was the most privileged and cherished moment of my life.
"I treasure the letters from the many soldiers who have written to me since, telling me it was their most wonderful moment too."
[8] Lt S. H. Smith, SX22393; 2/8 Cdo Sqn. Insurance clerk; of Collinswood, SA; b. St Peters, SA, 17 Dec 1919. Killed in action 10 Jul 1945.

sequently on 7th June a patrol led by Lieutenant Astill moved out along the Commando Road to probe deep into enemy territory. It passed through Kokopa, Tugiogu and Piarino near the Silibai without opposition and on the 9th reconnoitred at Kanaura a force of about 100 Japanese on whom they called down an air attack. Another deep patrol was made by an unusually strong group of 47 led by Captain Martin.[9] They moved south on 5th June travelling to the east of the Mivo. A plan to reconnoitre the coast from Dio Dio to Tokuaka was abandoned because of thick bush and swamp.

As Winning had anticipated, General Bridgeford now instructed Winning to collect information about the Mobiai-Mivo area, Mivo-Oamai and Oamai-Silibai in that order of priority. The first task had already been completed, but on 20th June Lieutenant Lawson-Dook's section set out into the second area and in five days had explored all tracks north of the Buin Road. On 21st June Winning and a few scouts set out to find a new base farther east. This proved a difficult task. Winning hoped to make a base at Kukugai on the upper Silibai River but could not find a site that was defensible and had access to water; in addition the Kukugai area overlooked the Buin plain and the enemy would be able to see the aircraft dropping supplies to the commando squadron and thus take bearings on its camp. Finally Winning established his base farther west at Kilipaijino. By 14th July the base was in use. "The difficulty experienced by me in finding a squadron site and a suitable L of C," he wrote to Lieut-Colonel Hassett[10] of Bridgeford's staff, on 7th July, "is, I think, sufficient answer to the question of moving a brigade group around this flank [the plan being considered by Savige]. It is utterly impracticable. I've ransacked this country to the extent that I'm well towards wearing my second pair of boots out."

A main task at the new base was to gain control of the Buin natives, large numbers of whom were working for the Japanese. It was expected that some 1,200 would be brought in from the Japanese-controlled area. In several respects Winning was now in a situation that differed from his previous ones. He was (in his words) "no longer working on the flank of a [Japanese] force covering its withdrawal" but "on the flank of his main force which . . . has nowhere further to fall back to in Bougainville". In addition he was in an area where large numbers of natives had been working for the Japanese, and one in which an A.I.B. party (Stuart's) had been at work. Winning considered that with the arrival of his stronger force the time had come to replace the A.I.B's "attitude of appeasement" with "a strong disciplinary policy"; in short, that the Angau officer accompanying him should take control of the natives and lay down the law.

---

[9] Capt R. D. Martin, NX70762; 2/8 Cdo Sqn. Salesman; of Coogee, NSW; b. Charlestown, NSW, 9 Jul 1921.

[10] Brig F. G. Hassett, DSO, MVO, OBE, NX322. 2/3 Bn; GSO1 3 Div 1945. CO 3 Bn RAR, Korea, 1951-52. Regular soldier; b. Sydney, 11 Apr 1918. (Hassett was appointed GSO1 of the 3rd Division on 19th February. He arrived at HQ 3rd Division on 1st March and took over from Colonel H. G. Edgar.)

Corps had already proposed late in June that Winning should take over command of Stuart's force, Stuart remaining as Angau adviser, but Stuart objected that he could not do his own job and at the same time look after the 2/8th's needs. The proposal was dropped and Stuart's group continued to send in valuable information until the end of the fighting.

In the meantime Stuart had had his own local problems. On 14th June his scouts reported that an enemy party about 100 strong was moving west towards them from Kikimogo and later that day there was a skirmish between this group and the scouts. Next day the native scouts withdrew, fighting, towards Stuart's base. After losing about 10 men and killing two natives, the Japanese withdrew, but the natives followed up and made a successful night attack. The Japanese pressed on; an air strike failed to reach the right area; and on the night of the 16th-17th and next day Stuart and his men withdrew safely.

Meanwhile the question of control of the new area became submerged in other problems. Winning wrote to Hassett:

> The halting of the 15th Brigade's advance at the Mivo influenced the operations of the 2/8th Commando. The unfavourable flying weather prevented the building up of a reserve of rations large enough to permit strong long-range patrolling; the enemy probed vigorously in the area allotted to the squadron. It was decided not to send patrols south until the brigade was pressing strongly on the Mivo line; and, until the tracks were better secured, to leave the Papuan company at the former base at Morokaimoro.

Anxiety increased when, on 18th July, a courier from the 24th Battalion was ambushed near Kingori and a bag of official and unofficial mail for the squadron was lost. It was suggested by the 3rd Division that the base should be moved, but Winning contended that the Papuan patrols, the native watchers, and the flooded condition of the rivers provided security; and in fact the Japanese appear to have made no use of the valuable information they captured. Winning continued to plan means of gaining control of the natives in the new area. On 25th July he wrote to Hassett:

> I consider it necessary, as do doubtless you, to rake in all kanakas now under Nip control.
> At the moment the situation is:
>   (*a*) the majority of the natives right up to the Muliko is here.
>   (*b*) the minority is in the Mamamarino area, some compounded there.
>
> Many moons ago when the native and the Nip in this area were friendly, the natives below catered to the Nip's sexual lust and supplied him with concubines. Now by virtue of these concubines, the Nip holds a certain proportion of the native populace in thrall. As long as the marys are there the Nip is loth to leave.
> Therefore, by hook and mainly by crook, I'll have to remove the concubines and the natives.
> Have lightly sounded those whom the Nip holds in bondage and I think it can be done by guile. The area will have to be thoroughly sounded and reconnoitred and the information passed rapidly back here.
> Hence the two W/T OP's I mention, each manned by one sig, 1 Int wallah and 1 white scout and two police boys.

A big line of scouts has just completed a sweep through . . . Tugiogu to Astill's Crossing. The only Nips found was a party of 20 at Astill's Crossing. Elsewhere, only odd tracks of a few. There is a red-skin with the Nips from Salamaua area. . . . He'll have to be bumped off as he is too deeply implicated for aught else.

The hold-up on Bde front may be propitious to me in that it gives me time to get the native situation ironed out, before which being done the movement of patrols would be greatly curtailed.

PIB. Intend moving them forward in a few days. I had thought they would strike more around Morokaimoro, and be of some assistance on the flank while I was ironing out the native situation here. Have been disappointed in their performances.

Hope this explains things.

During the early days of August few contacts with the Japanese were made and on the 11th Winning received orders to cancel all long-range and fighting patrols.

On 26th June, General Kanda had issued orders for what he considered would be the final battle. He estimated that the Australians would cross the Mivo River early in August and by the first week in September would be approaching the Silibai. At that stage he would launch an offensive.

His plan provided that Colonel Muda, with the *13th Regiment*, artillery and engineers, totalling 1,200, should move north of and parallel to the Buin Road to a firm base near Taitai. Thence he was to ambush supply trains on the Buin Road between Runai and Rusei, raid vehicle parks and stores, attack small parties of troops, set booby-traps but avoid a major action. A second force of 800 under Major Fukuda of the *23rd Regiment* was to establish a base near the Mivo ford and harass the enemy on the Buin Road between the Mivo and Mobiai. The *4th South Seas Garrison Unit* (about 1,000) was to assemble about Kara Aerodrome, keep the northern road clear, and destroy natives and patrols in the Oamai River and Katsuwa areas. A fourth force of 3,500 men, including the *45th Regiment* from Kieta, the *19th Engineer Regiment, 6th Cavalry* and smaller units, was to concentrate in the Luagoa and Laitaro areas and on the headwaters of the Muliko River, ready to swing south early in September, in combination with the *4th South Seas Garrison Unit*, for a main offensive against the enemy on the Buin Road.

Kanda had reached an agreement with Vice-Admiral Tomoshige Samejima whereby Kanda assumed command of all naval troops except those at Samejima's *Eighth Fleet Headquarters*. A force of 2,500 naval troops was to be formed to man the Silibai River line as far north as the Kanaura area. The remaining naval troops were mostly employed to guard the coast. Thus about 9,000 troops were committed to action; some 8,000 more in the rear area.

When the Australians attacked the Silibai River Kanda's naval troops were to throw them back; promptly the *45th Regiment* and attached troops would attack from the north and force the Australians back to the Mivo. Kanda realised that shortage of food would prevent him from following up this success, and while the Australians were reorganising after their setback all Japanese troops would move back into their inner defences—a line stretching from the mouth of the Little Siwi River north to the Uguimo River and along it to Kara Aerodrome, through Laitaro and Tabago to the Atara River and along it. Within this area, protected by minefields, the Japanese intended to fight the final battle. Within the perimeter would be 4 medium guns, 12 field guns, 70 anti-aircraft guns to be used as field artillery, and 90 medium and 144 light machine-guns—a light armament for perhaps 15,000 men and significant of the rate at which the Australians had been capturing or destroying their weapons. Fukuda had difficulty in carrying out his part in the early stage of this operation, because of the proximity of the Australians to the Mivo ford. On 9th July he attacked them in the Shishigatero area, without success. (This was the attack on a company of the 15th Battalion in which 34 Japanese were killed for a loss of 2 Australians dead.) However, "Fukuda was still able to continue with his harassing tasks to the enemy rear. This force was unable to establish any static defensive localities because of enemy artillery, and Fukuda divided his troops into a number of mobile groups to attack patrols and camp areas."[1] These tactics were considered to have delayed the Australians and prevented them crossing the Mivo in strength during July and early August. (In fact it was the rain not the Japanese that achieved this result.) Thus Kanda was able to continue his re-deployment without undue haste.

On the last day of July Kanda issued a proclamation that the final and decisive battles on Bougainville were imminent; his forces would hurl their entire resources into the task of destroying the enemy; the first attack would open as soon as the enemy reached the Silibai and its object would be to throw them back to the Mivo, after which his force would retire to its inner perimeter, fight there until the last round of ammunition had been fired and then die for the Emperor. Kanda's proclamation added that ships and aircraft were expected from Japan, where, he said, more aircraft were being produced each month than ever before.

He had lost some 18,000 killed or died of illness since the Australians arrived but still commanded 23,500 men.

In June and July in the central sector a fresh battalion had been thrusting forward. Lieut-Colonel H. L. E. Dunkley, commander of the 7th Battalion which had taken over this sector on 7th June, had served with the 2/6th in its Middle East campaigns and with the 2/7th in the Wau-Salamaua operations, and was one of an increasing number of officers who had risen from the ranks to command of a battalion since the war began. His battalion was given a more active role than that permitted to its immediate predecessors. Before Dunkley took over, Savige called him in, emphasised the need to avoid unnecessary casualties, and the unpopularity of the campaign in sections of the Press. He said that he expected the battalion to inflict four times as many losses as it received. In detail the battalion's task would be to capture Wearne's Hill, Base Point 3, Tokua and Sisivie, all of which had been thoroughly reconnoitred by its predecessor, the 27th Battalion, and to establish a company well forward in the Wakunai Valley from which the coastal area could be harassed. From this base the landing of a company north of Numa Numa was to be supported and at length an overland route cutting the island in two via Berry's Hill and the Wakunai River maintained.

However, at this time Flight Lieutenant Sandford, the guerilla leader, who was given the task of finding a suitable landing place on the east coast, was in contact with strong enemy groups, and the plan was deferred for at least four days. On the 14th it was cancelled, and the company on the Wakunai was given the guerilla task of harassing the Japanese round Ibu and Buritsiotorara, avoiding becoming involved with strong bodies of the enemy known to be in the area.

When he took over Dunkley had under his command, in addition to his battalion, Captain Hunt's[2] company of the Papuan Infantry, a platoon of heavy mortars and a detachment of Angau; and he had the support of one battery of the 4th Field Regiment.

---

[1] 23rd Brigade, History of the Japanese Occupation of Bougainville, March 1942-August 1945, p. 30.
[2] Capt L. E. E. Hunt, NX124620; Papuan Inf Bn. Public servant; of Goulburn, NSW; b. Goulburn, 24 Feb 1921.

Before the relief of the 27th Battalion was complete Lieutenant Bonde,[3] an experienced leader with previous service as an N.C.O. in the 2/12th Battalion, had been sent out with a patrol to find a site for the company base on the Wakunai. He set out on 3rd June and on the 6th signalled that he had found an area suitable for a company base and dropping ground—for the troops there could be supplied only from the air—but that there were pro-Japanese natives along the route. Bonde's patrol rejoined its company on the 8th. On the main trail the forward company (Captain Cameron[4]) patrolled aggressively with such promising results that on the 10th Dunkley ordered an attack next day. At 6 a.m. next morning the Japanese themselves attacked the leading platoon but were repulsed. Four hours later, after artillery and mortar fire, the Australians advanced, using a flame-thrower.[5] They gained 300 yards and killed ten Japanese. Sergeant Bennett,[6] gallantly leading the forward platoon, and two others were killed in the day, and two wounded, one (Sergeant Schurr[7]) fatally. Next day patrols found the enemy in position 250 yards farther on and killed two. In the next few days patrols gained more ground.

The next objective was Wearne's Hill, which was patrolled by Sergeant Walsh[8] and a party on 14th June. On the 16th it was hit by 12 Corsairs which dropped depth-charges, blasting away the undergrowth. A platoon attacked taking two positions without loss but meeting heavy opposition at a third where two men were killed and three wounded. In a second attack next day the Japanese again fought back hard and the platoon commander (Lieutenant Baskerville[9]) was wounded. It was possible to maintain only one company forward on the main track and with the existing teams of native carriers this would be so until probably the middle of July when the tramway had been completed to haul supplies up the Barges' Hill escarpment. On the 18th Captain Roberts'[1] company, no longer needed for the east coast landing, relieved Cameron's. Two days later this company attacked the Japanese position on Wearne's, already blasted twice without success, and took it after a sharp fight in which Lieutenant Longmore[2] and three others were killed and two wounded. Longmore appeared to have been hit by a dum-dum bullet, and next day a patrol killed a Japanese who had five rounds of such ammunition.

---

[3] Lt R. R. Bonde, TX450. 2/12 and 7 Bns. Grocer; of Penguin, Tas; b. Myalla, Tas, 27 Apr 1916.

[4] Capt W. O. Cameron, VX114150; 7 Bn. Horticulturist; of Red Cliffs, Vic; b. Mildura, Vic, 12 Aug 1915.

[5] "One flame-thrower was used in this attack with little success (reported the 7th Battalion); light fuel was tried but heat appeared to go upwards and as target was a bunker, under a large standing tree, occupants remained fighting until other means were used. Thick fuel appears most effective for underground defences with head cover."

[6] Sgt A. A. Bennett, VX89415; 7 Bn. Horticulturist; of Merbein, Vic; b. Mildura, Vic, 6 Oct 1916. Killed in action 11 Jun 1945.

[7] Sgt C. H. Schurr, VX89386; 7 Bn. Labourer; of Irymple, Vic; b. Dimboola, Vic, 12 Feb 1918. Died of wounds 12 Jun 1945.

[8] Sgt W. Walsh, VX89400; 7 Bn. Grocer; of Mildura, Vic; b. Ballarat, Vic, 17 Feb 1920.

[9] Lt N. T. Baskerville, WX26483; 7 Bn. Butcher; of Pemberton, WA; b. Pemberton, 28 Sep 1921.

[1] Capt R. Roberts, VX114155; 7 Bn. Storeman; of Wentworth, NSW; b. Wentworth, 12 Oct 1915.

[2] Lt F. R. Longmore, VX117297; 7 Bn. Storeman; of Merbein, Vic; b. Mildura, Vic, 2 Jan 1917. Killed in action 20 Jun 1945.

On the 25th, after the remaining Japanese positions had been much bombarded, the remainder of Wearne's Hill was found to be clear of the enemy. But next day a fighting patrol met sharp opposition on Centre Hill and lost two killed and seven wounded. Here Lance-Corporal Evans,[3] though mortally wounded, continued to direct fire and encourage his comrades. Next day in a platoon attack after an air strike on the same position two were killed and two wounded. In a third platoon attack on the 30th Warrant-Officer Schiele[4] was killed and three wounded. Until 29th June the battalion was supported by the 10th Battery (Major Yott[5]). This battery was now out of range and henceforward support was given by the 2nd Mountain Battery (Major W. R. D. Stevenson).

However, on 6th July, Cameron, whose company had now again taken over the sector, and Keopili,[6] an outstanding native scout, stalked on to Centre Hill and found that the enemy had withdrawn during the night to North Hill, which became the next objective. Artillery and aircraft harassed North Hill and patrols probed forward, and on the 13th a platoon (Lieutenant Elliott[7]) attacked and took it killing seven in a fierce fire fight and later two more. The Japanese forward post was now found to be on Cameron's Hill, 150 yards forward. On the 17th a patrol was ambushed by a Japanese lieutenant and two men, but killed them all without loss to themselves. Next day Lieutenant Neville's[8] platoon took the hill, killing seven in a fight at close quarters and capturing a heavy machine-gun.

Meanwhile on the 13th, 14th and 15th June Captain McInnes'[9] company of the 7th had moved out to a position on the Wakunai two and a half days' march behind the enemy's forward posts. By the 21st they had established observation posts overlooking Inus Point and the big Numa Numa Plantation and their patrols had had several clashes with the enemy. Lance-Sergeant Faux[1] and a party succeeded in laying a line through the mountains to this company's base.

One patrol had a particularly exciting experience. It set out on 27th June to examine and set an ambush on the coastal track—an ambitious venture. Sergeant Clohesy,[2] the leader, set up a base 3,000 yards from the coast, and on the 28th, with ten others including a native scout set out for the coast leaving two signallers, a stretcher bearer and one other man with the wireless set and the native at the base. That evening the signallers sent back a message that the patrol had not returned. Next morning the

---

[3] L-Cpl W. J. Evans, VX63619; 7 Bn. Metal worker; of Bentleigh, Vic; b. Northcote, Vic, 8 Jul 1922. Died of wounds 29 Jun 1945.

[4] WO2 V. G. Schiele, VX89360; 7 Bn. Carpenter; of Red Cliffs, Vic; b. Maitland, NSW, 25 Jan 1919. Killed in action 30 Jun 1945.

[5] Maj B. A. Yott, VX111127. 12 and 4 Fd Regts. Director-manager; of Beaumaris, Vic; b. Malvern, Vic, 9 Jan 1916.

[6] Keopili who, with his brother Supili, had given fine service throughout these operations, was killed in action on patrol on 14th July.

[7] Lt M. H. Elliott, VX89397; 7 Bn. Oil company driver; of Dandenong, Vic; b. Melbourne, 21 Dec 1916.

[8] Lt K. C. Neville, VX114154; 7 Bn. Salesman; of Mildura, Vic; b. Devonport, Tas, 14 Oct 1917.

[9] Capt W. O. McInnes, VX114145; 7 Bn. Horticulturist; of Merbein, Vic; b. Merbein, 23 Jun 1916.

[1] L-Sgt H. L. Faux, VX105374; 7 Bn. Fitter and turner; of Buronga, NSW; b. Mildura, Vic, 21 Mar 1919.

[2] Sgt L. J. B. Clohesy, VX63216; 7 Bn. Grocer; of Rochester, Vic; b. Rochester, 7 Feb 1920.

base was suddenly attacked by fifteen or twenty Japanese. The five occupants fired back from a range of fifteen yards. The native was killed in the fight, and the others at length withdrew, leaving behind packs, the wireless set and a Bren. As the men were making their way back to the company they heard heavy fire from the direction of their base. Clohesy had returned, found eight to ten Japanese in occupation and attacked and driven them off, killing one and probably two others. All the gear was retrieved.

The 7th continued to probe forward on the main track and inflict casualties. On 22nd July a patrol of the Papuan Infantry killed seven at Charlie Creek, the next main obstacle. On 2nd August Sergeant Clohesy's platoon attacked McInnes Hill, the next ridge along the main track, but encountered Japanese who had tunnelled into a low cliff face; these fired at five yards' range, killing two men. Another attack by Lieutenant Bonde's platoon also failed. The trail behind this position was then blocked by a platoon of the 7th and one of Papuans and next day a patrol led by Lieutenant Rush[3] found that the enemy had gone. From McInnes Hill on the 8th a successful attack was made across Charlie Creek.

In June the Japanese round Sisivie had been harassed increasingly and on 12th June Major Blaby,[4] commanding the company there, led out a patrol and found it unoccupied. On 3rd July Tokua was similarly occupied, as a base for probing north towards Ibu. Much patrolling was carried out by this company, one party led by Lieutenant McPhee[5] on 9th July ambushing nine Japanese in gardens at Nasisipok killing five. On the 26th a patrol led to Nasisipok by Lieutenant Murphy[6] found about 30 Japanese in occupation and in the clash Sergeant Midgley[7] was killed and two wounded. On the 30th McPhee took out a patrol of seventeen, including a native guide, to Buritsiotorara. While they were in the bush stealthily observing the Japanese in the village a party of Japanese walked into them; four were killed, including a captain, and the patrol made off.

On the afternoon of 11th August Savige's order to suspend hostilities unless attacked reached Dunkley. On the 13th, however, enemy snipers fired on a forward platoon, killing one man (Private Bahr[8]) and wounding three, including Sergeant Clohesy, mentioned above. Sharp fire was exchanged that day and the next, and on the 15th snipers were still busy and one man was hit. The Australian artillery replied. On the 16th, 17th and 18th leaflets were distributed in the Japanese area by aircraft, by firing them from a mortar, and by Papuan patrols who left them lying on the enemy's tracks, but no Japanese deserted as a result of these devices.

---

[3] Lt G. Rush, VX58109; 7 Bn. Policeman; of Boolarra, Vic; b. Stewkley, Bucks, England, 9 Apr 1913.
[4] Maj K. Blaby, VX114147; 7 Bn. Carpenter; of Merbein, Vic; b. Brighton, Vic, 24 Oct 1916.
[5] Lt N. H. McPhee, VX88143; 7 Bn. Bank officer; of Kew, Vic; b. Canterbury, Vic, 15 May 1917.
[6] Capt J. Murphy, QX42977; 7 Bn. Hotel manager; of Brisbane; b. Murwillumbah, NSW, 19 Sep 1919.
[7] Sgt H. K. Midgley, VX134830; 7 Bn. Horticulturist; of Irymple, Vic; b. Wentworth, NSW, 2 Mar 1918. Killed in action 26 Jul 1945.
[8] Pte E. J. Bahr, V220096; 7 Bn. Farm worker; of Meringur, Vic; b. Jeparit, Vic, 23 Jun 1919. Killed in action 13 Aug 1945.

By the 27th it appeared that the Japanese had retired to Numa Numa. In more than two months in continuous action astride the Numa Numa trail this aggressive battalion killed 181 and probably 17 others, and lost 23 killed and 52 wounded. At the end Dunkley considered his men "never fitter, mentally or physically".

In July Major-General Kijima of the *38th Brigade* decided that the trend of Australian patrolling indicated that the Australians were about to advance down the Wakunai River and Ibu-Asitavi tracks in conjunction with a sea-borne landing at Numa Numa. Kijima recommended withdrawal, but Kanda ordered him to stay and fight, arguing that the troops were not fit to make the long march to the south, that their arrival after August would not help his plan, and that it was desirable to contain the enemy force round Numa Numa as long as possible. Between December 1944 and July 1945 some 1,500 reinforcements were sent to the Numa Numa sector.

When the 23rd Brigade began to take over the northern sector on 20th June the attempted landing at Porton had recently failed and the dogged and enterprising Japanese naval troops were holding firmly across the neck of the Bonis Peninsula. Brigadier Potts was ordered to contain the Japanese in the peninsula and patrol towards Buka Passage. He was to employ only one battalion group for this task on which two battalions of the outgoing brigade had hitherto been used. On the other hand each battalion of the 23rd Brigade was as strong as the 26th and 31st/51st put together. However, as it was estimated that there were 1,200 Japanese on the peninsula and 1,400 on Buka Island, the incoming battalion—the 27th—which had been resting for a little more than a week after its six weeks in the central sector, was to be given a somewhat formidable task, and Potts sought leave to use also his 8th Battalion now being concentrated from the outer islands at Torokina. Savige agreed to this, provided that at all times, two companies were resting. By 28th June the 27th Battalion was in position on the right and the 8th (Major Moran[9]), now in action for the first time, on the left, with the guns of Major Berry's[1] 11th Battery of the 4th Field Regiment in Soraken Plantation.

The track distance through the forward posts was nearly 8,000 yards and the Australian line of communication long and vulnerable. It was impossible to guard all tracks leading south. Japanese parties continued to raid the traffic behind the Australian positions as efficiently as before. Ration trains were ambushed, signal lines cut, mines laid. Indeed the incoming troops found that the situation existing in the central sector was reversed in the north. There constant deep patrols harassed the Japanese behind their lines; here the Japanese, employing a similar policy, were sapping the strength of the Australian force. One day early in July a wood-chopping party was fired on and two men of the field ambulance were killed; the next day a jeep was wrecked by a mine; next day Japanese

---

[9] Maj M. B. Moran, NX114822; 8 Bn. Lecturer; of Tamworth, NSW; b. Bowraville, NSW, 2 Apr 1913.
On 7th July Lieut-Colonel L. J. Loughran took command of the 8th Battalion.

[1] Maj H. J. Berry, VX112236; 4 Fd Regt. Clerk; of North Williamstown, Vic; b. Albert Park, Vic, 15 Dec 1916.

were seen round the headquarters of the 27th; next day Captain Ogden[2] of the 8th was killed by a mine exploded under a jeep train and Lieutenant Webb[3] of the same battalion killed while leading a patrol to lay an ambush. Lieut-Colonel Pope of the 27th placed standing patrols along the main jeep tracks and sought leave to redeploy his battalion. An entry in the diary of the 27th on 1st July indicates the mood of the unit at that time:

> We've been promised tanks but they are yet to be sighted. One Bty 4 Fd Regt only in support, and so far we have no Engrs. The water situation is also difficult. . . . The Bn is occupying 4,000 yds of front, twice the normal frontage for Bn in open warfare. And this country is densely vegetated. The L of C to C Coy is over 3,000 yds long, 2,500 yds of which cannot be covered, and consequently enables the Jap to ambush it just when he likes.

On 21st July the battalion recorded that in four weeks it had made no forward movement yet had lost 7 killed and 17 wounded in patrols and ambushes, 3 killed and 2 wounded by its own mortar fire, 12 wounded by its own booby-traps and 5 in other accidents. Potts wished to attack. Pope was convinced that he could clear the peninsula in a fortnight, but Savige was not willing to undertake further commitments in this area; the concentration was to be in the south. In these circumstances, Potts, unable to maintain an effective number of fighting patrols because so much of his strength was needed to protect his rearward tracks, sought Savige's leave to withdraw from his right flank and concentrate on a 3,000-yard front round Buoi Plantation. This was approved on 22nd July.

Next day—23rd July—the 8th attacked Commo Ridge[4] where the Japanese seemed to be establishing themselves strongly. After a bombardment by aircraft, Captain Reed's[5] company attacked with two tanks belonging to Lieutenant Scott's troop of the 2/4th Armoured Regiment, which had been transferred to this sector early in July.[6] One tank bogged and the other was halted by the swampy ground, and the air strike had been inaccurate; nevertheless the tanks were able to give good supporting fire and the ridge was taken in 20 minutes, six Japanese being killed there and six more by patrols later.

On 29th July a platoon of the Papuan Infantry surprised 25 to 30 Japanese in position covering the Ratsua Road-Umum Track junction. The platoon attacked and killed several Japanese but the survivors manned their defences and forced the Papuans into some old weapon-pits 20 yards away. A native soldier, Oaveta, was hit and called out that he could not

---

[2] Capt R. C. Ogden, VX37393; 8 Bn. Salesman; b. Camberwell, Vic, 26 Oct 1922. Killed in action 7 Jul 1945.

[3] Lt R. G. Webb, WX33831; 8 Bn. Sub-manager; of Geraldton, WA; b. Geraldton, 29 Oct 1919. Killed in action 7 Jul 1945.

[4] Named after a communist who fought well in this area.

[5] Capt S. J. Reed, VX27748; 8 Bn. Schoolteacher; of Melbourne; b. Brunswick, Vic, 4 Oct 1914.

[6] On 2nd August the leader of two tanks accompanying a patrol of the 27th Battalion along the Ruri Bay Road hit a mine made from a 500-lb bomb, which killed three of the crew and wounded eight infantrymen. After this Savige forbade the use of tanks with patrols; they should be employed only with assaulting infantry against a position which had been investigated by infantry patrols.

move. Lance-Sergeant Russell[7] dashed across a fire lane and found Oaveta six feet from an enemy machine-gun pit. He killed the gun's crew with grenades, dragged Oaveta out, dressed his wounds (which were, however, mortal) and withdrew the patrol in good order.

On 1st August a strong patrol of the Papuan Infantry, which was now protecting the open flank on the east, achieved a notable success when it surprised a Japanese ambush party inland from Ruri Bay and in ten minutes killed fourteen with grenades and automatic weapons. Major H. J. Jesser considered this independent role far more satisfactory than his former one of providing parties of native troops to accompany Australian patrols. On 7th August Lieutenant Sheargold[8] took a fighting patrol of Papuans into the midst of the Japanese at Ruri Bay. As it went quietly forward one section moving between the road and the cliffs saw three Japanese. Corporal Maravera killed them all with his Owen gun. Twelve other Japanese who were near by panicked and ran not away from but into the patrol. Seven were killed. Ten more Japanese then appeared from the inland side and were all shot dead, six by one man, Nevato. The patrol withdrew without a single casualty.

The last series of actions in which Australians were engaged on Bougainville were fought by the 8th Battalion. On the afternoon of 24th July two platoons of Major Thompson's[9] company had attacked Base 5 after a bombardment in which a total of 900 shells and mortar bombs were fired. The advancing troops reached the first ridge without difficulty but then ran into heavy fire from well-camouflaged bunkers. Two men were killed and one wounded in the leading section. A section of the neighbouring platoon (Lieutenant Taylor[1]) began an encircling movement but it too came under heavy fire, particularly from a medium machine-gun in a bunker, one man—a Bren gunner—being killed and three wounded. Private Partridge,[2] a young banana grower from northern New South Wales, though wounded in both arm and thigh, then rushed forward under hot fire, retrieved a Bren from beside the dead gunner and exchanged fire with the Japanese bunker. Finding his fire ineffective Partridge put the Bren down and shouted to Corporal Banks,[3] his section leader, that he was going to throw a grenade into the bunker. He went forward with a smoking grenade in one hand and a rifle in the other and threw in the grenade when its fuse was half burnt through. As soon as the grenade burst he dived into the bunker and killed one of the surviving occupants. Other members of the platoon advanced, a second bunker was overcome, and the platoon held its ground long enough to bring in the wounded,

---

[7] L-Sgt A. G. Russell, MM, WX17299; Papuan Inf Bn. Engine cleaner; of Perth; b. Subiaco, WA, 22 May 1922.

[8] Capt R. W. Sheargold, NX105167; Papuan Inf Bn. Bank officer; of Mayfield, NSW; b. Newcastle, NSW, 3 Oct 1922.

[9] Maj C. W. Thompson, NX76249; 8 Bn. Electrical warehouseman; of Hurstville, NSW; b. Warwick, Qld, 26 Jan 1915.

[1] Lt C. W. Taylor, VX114119; 8 Bn. Bank officer; of Stawell, Vic; b. Maryborough, Vic, 19 Mar 1921.

[2] Pte F. J. Partridge, VC, N454409; 8 Bn. Banana grower; of Upper Newee Creek, via Macksville, NSW; b. Grafton, NSW, 29 Nov 1924.

[3] Sgt H. H. Banks, NX193796; 8 Bn. Farm hand; of Yass, NSW; b. Yass, 23 Jul 1923.

(R.N.Z.A.F.)

Lieut-General Kanda, commanding the *XVII Japanese Army* (seated left) surrenders to General Savige (G.O.C. II Australian Corps) at Torokina, Bougainville, on 8th September 1945. Vice-Admiral Baron Samejima sits facing Kanda, who is flanked by two interpreters. Brigadier A. R. Garrett (B.G.S. II Corps) is seated on Savige's right.

(R.N.Z.A.F.)

Japanese artillery assembled in southern Bougainville after the surrender.

(*Australian War Memorial*)
New Britain, 7th February 1945. Sergeant D. E. Sloan of the 1st New Guinea Infantry Battalion giving instructions to a patrol.

(*Australian War Memorial*)
A patrol moving along the beach in the Jacquinot Bay area, New Britain.

this task being organised with great coolness by Private Uebergang.[4] Partridge remained in action until the end.[5] Eight Japanese were killed and probably 3 others; 3 Australians were killed and 5 wounded, including Taylor.

This attack evidently shook the Japanese and on 5th August after careful patrolling, Base 5, now renamed "Part Ridge", was occupied after only light opposition. More than 60 bunkers were in the area, some destroyed by artillery fire. After ensuring that no Japanese remained the company withdrew; on 11th August active patrolling ceased in this and in other sectors.

The long campaign on Bougainville was over except for the formal ceremonies of surrender. On 15th August four aircraft on whose underwings had been painted in Japanese characters "Japan Has Surrendered" flew over the Japanese areas dropping 230,000 leaflets announcing the news. In later chapters the negotiations and ceremonies which followed, here and in other zones, will be described and certain problems common to these and other Australian operations in 1945 discussed.

In the whole campaign on Bougainville 516 Australians were killed or died of wounds and 1,572 were wounded.[6] If the Slater's Knoll period be excepted, the number of Australian deaths ranged from two to 24 a week, the number of counted Japanese dead from 53 to 364 a week. The Japanese staffs burned their papers but, in a detailed investigation after the war, the conclusion was reached that 8,500 Japanese had been killed by the Australians and their native allies on Bougainville and 9,800 died of illness during the Australian period; 23,571 remained out of about 65,000 who had been on the island when the Americans attacked in November 1943, or had arrived soon afterwards.[7]

When the campaign ended the strengths of their infantry regiments, the *19th Engineers,* the marines, and the naval garrison units were: *13th*

---

[4] Pte E. A. Uebergang, MM, VX148237; 8 Bn. Farmer; of Natimuk, Vic; b. Natimuk, 11 Sep 1921.
[5] Partridge was awarded the Victoria Cross for this action.
[6] The battle casualties in infantry, armoured and commando units were:

7 Bde	Offrs	ORs		15 Bde	Offrs	ORs
9 Bn	4	99		24 Bn	11	179
25 Bn	13	202		57/60 Bn	8	128
61 Bn	1	47		58/59 Bn	13	196
11 Bde	Offrs	ORs		23 Bde	Offrs	ORs
26 Bn	7	139		7 Bn	2	70
31/51 Bn	7	218		8 Bn	6	37
55/53 Bn	2	38		27 Bn	3	70
29 Bde	Offrs	ORs			Offrs	ORs
15 Bn	5	102		2/4 Armd Regt	5	38
42 Bn	1	72		2/8 Commando	2	27
47 Bn	7	112		Papuan Inf Bn	3	34
				1 NG Inf Bn	—	17

Admissions to hospital were:
    Malaria 472
    Skin diseases . . . 2,384
    Dysentery, dengue and scrub typhus 672
    Other 8,667
Four officers and 52 others died from causes other than battle wounds.

[7] The Intelligence officer of *XVII Army,* Lieut-Colonel Kiyoshi Miyakawa, in September 1945 gave the number killed in *XVII Army* from November 1944 to August 1945 as 6,870. The above figures were arrived at in February 1946 after further interrogation and calculation.

Regiment, 444; *23rd*, 423; *45th*, 838; *81st*, 690; *19th Engineers*, 704; *6th Sasebo*, 1,683; *7th Kure*, 1,174; *82nd Naval Garrison Force*, 892; *87th Naval Garrison Force*, 2,957, including civilians incorporated in the unit; *88th Naval Garrison Force*, 457. In addition there were technical units, such as the *6th Field Artillery*, 1,403 strong, which were used as infantry.

From an early stage in the operations the troops knew that the value of the campaign, and of their efforts, was being questioned by politicians and newspapers at home. The following extracts from a history of the 42nd Battalion express views fairly widely held:

In the first place the campaign was futile and unnecessary.

At Salamaua men went after the Jap because every inch of ground won meant so much less distance to Tokyo. But what did an inch of ground—or a mile—mean on Bougainville? Nothing!

Whether Bougainville could be taken in a week or a year would make no difference to the war in general. Every man knew this.

The Bougainville campaign was a politicians' war and served no other purpose than to keep men in the fight. They would have been much better employed on the farms, the mines and in building industries in Australia. Why they were not can only be answered by the few who decided that Australians must be kept in the war at all costs.

Every risk taken at Bougainville was one that could not be avoided; every life lost was begrudged. Men fought because there was no alternative. None wanted to lose his life on Bougainville. . . . But despite all this men did fight and fought well. Lieut-Colonel Byrne said of the battalion: "I think that collectively the officers and men of the battalion did a grand job. It was filthy country; they were fighting what appeared to be a useless campaign and they knew it. Men are not fools and even though each man realised he was fighting for something which could benefit his country very little (and in addition his fighting received very little credit or publicity) he carried out orders energetically and in a very fine spirit."[8]

The small amount of publicity given to this and other Australian campaigns of 1945 in the Australian newspapers was undoubtedly a main cause of dissatisfaction. An education officer on Bougainville wrote to the Broadcasting Commission to complain about the dictation-speed news broadcast for the troops. He pointed out that more than half the time was usually given to crimes and accidents in Australia—for example, of the total of 45 minutes 15 had recently been allotted to describing how a man had been bitten by a stingray in St Kilda Baths and how a woman had jumped from an upstairs window, nearly 30 minutes to news of the Russian front, less than a minute each to other fronts, and nothing at all to Bougainville or New Guinea. "The reason for the stingray story as any news editor will affirm, is that 'the public is war-weary and does not want to read about the war', wrote a diarist. 'But the men up here aren't, and they want to know what goes on in the world'." Also they wanted to be assured that the people at home were being told about their achievements.

It was widely agreed that a policy whereby army public relations officers sent personal paragraphs about men fighting on Bougainville to appropriate small-town newspapers had a notable effect on the spirits of the men.

---

[8] Benson, pp. 157-8.

Another unfortunate outcome of the discontent and the political criticism that was linked with it was an order from Land Headquarters dated 21st June which deprived officers below the rank of commanding officer of a unit of the right to censor their own mail, the object evidently being to ensure that their letters did not contain remarks that might be used in public controversy at home. The removal of this time-honoured privilege, particularly at a time when the enemy was on the verge of final defeat and no genuine security considerations were involved was sharply denounced by officers from General Sturdee downwards. Sturdee wrote to the Chief of the General Staff, General Northcott, asking him to discuss the matter with General Blamey with a view to returning to the system which had been in force for over five years "without any dire results so far as I am aware". Savige wrote to Sturdee that the order would "cause deep-seated discontent" and he enclosed extracts culled from officers' letters including: "apparently they do not think that an officer can be trusted", "this comic cuts army", "the crowning achievement of the shiny-seat gents from Victoria Barracks", "those senile simpletons that repose at L.H.Q. for a few hours daily and imagine themselves soldiers".

On the other hand a critical view of critics serving under him was expressed by Brigadier Simpson of the 29th Brigade in his report on the brigade's operations:

Whilst basically there is little difference in the soldier in this Brigade and those of other Brigades in the AMF, I find that there is often an unreasoning resentment of the reputation—hard won in battle over years of service in various theatres of war—of the 6, 7 and 9 Divisions. This stupid attitude of mind is often present in some of the officers whose circumscribed army life had made them very narrow minded, self-satisfied and complacent. The result was a feeling that insufficient notice was being taken by the press and public of the operations in this theatre, an attitude not completely justified. If officers had made the troops realise that the high regard in which this Division is held was the direct result also of a gallant battle record, a high standard of discipline and efficiency, thus creating a reputation that no amount of press publicity can bestow, much of the jealousy would have quickly disappeared. . . . I noticed a tendency among all ranks, including officers, to question vigorously the purpose and soundness of operations in the Solomons. It was necessary to bring to the notice of commanders the danger of permitting unchallenged discussion on such a contentious subject. A certain amount of tactful propaganda was necessary to combat the forceful but often misinformed arguments of certain individuals.

Indeed, the increasing public criticism of the policy of maintaining large-scale offensives against the Japanese on the New Guinea battlefields, and the echoes of that criticism in the letters that the troops were receiving from home, presented the brigade and unit and sub-unit commanders with a difficult problem, particularly as many of them secretly disagreed with the policy. Yet from top to bottom the troops accepted the task as one that had to be done with a whole heart. Brigadier Hammer, for example, wrote afterwards that his brigade's morale

could not have been better if it had been fighting the Alamein battle or capturing Tokyo. Yet every man knew, as well as I knew, that the operations were mopping-up and that they were *not* vital to the winning of the war. So they ignored the Australian papers, their relatives' letters advising caution, and got on with the job in hand, fighting and dying as if it was the battle for final victory.

Discussion whether the offensives were justified is continued later in this volume, but at this stage let it be said that, in the light of later knowledge of the enemy's strength on Bougainville—and even of the knowledge acquired by the second quarter of 1945—the task that the II Corps undertook was too great for its resources. When its offensive opened the Japanese were in greater numerical strength than that part of II Corps which was on Bougainville. In eight months of fighting the Japanese lost about three-sevenths of their number, but in August they were still so strong that the reduction of Buin would undoubtedly have involved longer and costlier operations than those already endured.

CHAPTER 10

OPERATIONS ON NEW BRITAIN

ON the island of New Britain in August 1944 there existed the same kind of tacit truce as on Bougainville and the New Guinea mainland. In each area American garrisons guarded their air bases, the main Japanese forces had been withdrawn to areas remote from the American ones, and, in the intervening no-man's land, Allied patrols, mostly of Australian-led natives, waged a sporadic guerilla war against Japanese outposts and patrols.

In August 1944 one American regimental combat team was stationed in the Talasea-Cape Hoskins area on the north coast, one battalion group at Arawe on the south, and the remainder of the 40th Division, from which these groups were drawn, round Cape Gloucester at the western extremity. The main body of the Japanese army of New Britain—then believed to be about 38,000 strong (actually about 93,000)—was concentrated in the Gazelle Peninsula, but there were coastwatching stations farther west. In the middle area—about one-third of the island—field parties directed by the Allied Intelligence Bureau were moving about, collecting information, helping the natives and winning their support, and harassing the enemy either by direct attack or by calling down air strikes.

New Britain is some 320 miles in length and generally about 50 miles in width, with a mountain spine rising steeply to 8,000 feet. On the south the coastal strip is generally narrow, but suitable landing places are fairly frequent. On the north, east from Cape Hoskins, the coastal strip is wider but very swampy, the shore is mostly reef-bound and landing places are scarce. In addition several of the north-flowing rivers are wide and swift and infested with crocodiles. In the north-west monsoon season, from December to April, the north coast has heavy rain and high winds, while on the south coast it is generally hot and calm. The Gazelle Peninsula, where before the war some 37,000 out of the island's 100,000 people had lived, is approximately 50 miles square and joined to the main part of the island by a neck only 21 miles wide. The largest plantations were within this peninsula, and at its north-eastern corner was Rabaul, for many years the administrative centre of the whole New Guinea territory, and now, in 1944, the main Japanese base in the South-West Pacific and headquarters of the *Eighth Area Army* of General Imamura.

When the relief of the 40th American Division by the 5th Australian was planned it was believed that the Japanese forces on the island included the *17th* and *38th Divisions*, small detachments of the *51st* and *6th Divisions*, the *65th Brigade*, some 22,000 base and line of communication troops, and 2,500 naval men. Japanese air strength at Rabaul was believed to have been reduced to fewer than 30 aircraft and there were no ships in the area except an occasional visiting submarine. When the Australians arrived it was estimated, however, that the Japanese possessed about 150 barges, including large craft able to carry from 10 to 15 tons or 90 men.

It was considered that the Japanese commander had established his main defensive line across the north-eastern corner of the Gazelle Peninsula, along the Warangoi and Keravat Rivers from Put Put on the east to Ataliklikun Bay on the west. (This was so.) Such a line would cover Rabaul and, round it, an area about 28 miles by 16. Forward of this position the enemy appeared to have established delaying forces of varying strength, notably at Waitavalo on Henry Reid Bay. Early in November, at the time when the headquarters of the 5th Division was moving to New Britain, a substantially revised estimate of the enemy's strength and organisation was produced. The total strength was now believed to be not 38,000 but 35,000, the main field formations the *17th* and *38th Divisions,* each with three regiments, and the *39th Brigade*;[1] there were only 12 serviceable aircraft. In January the estimate of the total strength was reduced to 32,000.

Reports about the enemy's food supply were conflicting, but it appeared that they had enough to keep men in fair condition and were growing vegetables on a large scale, and some rice. The principal sources of detailed information about the Japanese on New Britain were the A.I.B. field parties mentioned above, and their agents. In April 1944 a change in the organisation of these field parties was decided upon. Thenceforward they would be concentrated in two groups, one on the north coast and the other on the south.

At this time the Japanese had posts at intervals along the south coast as far west as Awul near Cape Dampier. It was decided that the Australian southern guerilla force would be based at Lakiri, a village in the hills two days' march inland from Waterfall Bay, and in an area into which the enemy had not ventured. It possessed a good site for dropping stores from the air and, as a preliminary, some 25,000 pounds of supplies were dropped there. To give added security to the base the Australian-led native guerillas, commanded at this stage by Captain R. I. Skinner, overcame the enemy's coastwatching posts at Palmalmal and Baien, to the south-west and south-east, respectively, killing 23 and taking three prisoners. None survived at Palmalmal, but two escaped from Baien, and it was learnt later that they reached an enemy post at Milim bearing news of what had happened.

The south coast group was now placed under the command of Captain B. Fairfax-Ross, a former New Guinea planter, who had served as a subaltern in the 18th Brigade in the Middle East. Because of his New Guinea experience he had been transferred to field Intelligence work in August 1942 and had served behind the Japanese lines on the New Guinea mainland in 1943.

Fairfax-Ross' orders were to clear the enemy from the south coast as far east as Henry Reid Bay, 150 miles from the enemy's westernmost

---
[1] In fact there were also: *65th Brigade* and *14th, 34th* and *35th Regiments,* plus several naval combat units. Another independent brigade—the *40th*—was on New Ireland.

New Britain

outpost at Montagu Bay; to contain him within the Gazelle Peninsula; to gather Intelligence; to succour Allied airmen who had been forced down; and help the natives and win or regain their confidence. This was a formidable task for a force comprising five officers (including Flight Lieutenant Hooper[2] as second-in-command, and three platoon commanders, Lieutenants G. B. Black, J. McK. Hamilton and C. K. Johnson), 10 Australian N.C.O's, about 140 native troops, and such native allies as could be maintained on an air delivery of 5,000 pounds of supplies a month. At that stage no air support could be provided south of Cape Cormoran, but aircraft from the Solomons could be called upon to attack points to the north. At the remote base at Lakiri the native troops were trained to shoot and were given "basic field training in the terms of *Infantry Section Leading*".

After the loss of Baien the Japanese reinforced their post at Milim at the south end of Wide Bay until it was 400 strong. Far to the west they retained posts at Massau and Awul and round Cape Beechey. Fairfax-Ross decided to move discreetly into the strongly-held Wide Bay area, advancing through the hills, concentrating first on winning over the natives, and using the air power available from Bougainville as his trump card. At the same time spies would be sent into the Gazelle Peninsula. In the western area also the first task was to gain information.

On 5th June an American patrol from the west led by Lieutenant White[3] of Angau attacked the Awul garrison, which withdrew inland. Black and his platoon thereupon marched from Jacquinot Bay to Lau and Atu. In this area they found that native guerillas about 80 strong had killed 14 Japanese and 14 of their native allies. At Awul they met White and his party. It now seemed that the Japanese from the Atu-Awul area were retreating to the north coast. Guerillas were organised and at Kensina on 18th June, "after pretending to entertain a party of about 50 enemy", the natives attacked and killed 28, losing 5 of their own men. Black's patrol, in pursuit, found the remainder of the enemy about Rang and in an attack on 24th June killed nine, but had to withdraw after losing one native N.C.O. As they moved north and east through hostile territory other Japanese were killed.

In the eastern section in this period Lieutenant Johnson was winning the support of influential natives in the mountains south-west of Wide Bay, where Captain C. D. Bates and Captain English[4] now, like Johnson, due for relief, had also been organising native agents. On 24th June Bates, English, Johnson, who had been on the island since September 1943, and some of their natives were taken off by the destroyer *Vendetta* from

---

[2] F-Lt C. F. Hooper, RAAF; AIB. Newsagent and stationer; of Annandale, NSW; b. Toowoomba, Qld, 23 Oct 1900.

[3] Lt G. J. White, NGX392; Angau. Miner, assayer and planter; b. Hobart, 10 May 1914. Killed in accident 1947.

[4] Capt W. M. English, MBE, VX66764. 2/4 Indep Coy, Angau and "M" Special Unit. Patrol officer; of St Kilda and New Britain; b. Adelaide, 28 Feb 1915.

Cutarp, Johnson being replaced in Fairfax-Ross' force by Lieutenant Sampson.[5]

The Japanese now became very active in the Wide Bay hinterland, punishing natives who had helped the Australians and collecting information, until wholesale reprisals against the Wide Bay people became a possibility. Fairfax-Ross set about persuading the people between Ril on Henry Reid Bay and Milim to move inland secretly to remote areas.

A heavy air attack was made on the main Milim positions on the night of 17th-18th July and as a result the Japanese withdrew some men to a new position away to the west and some men right back to Lemingi in the Gazelle Peninsula.

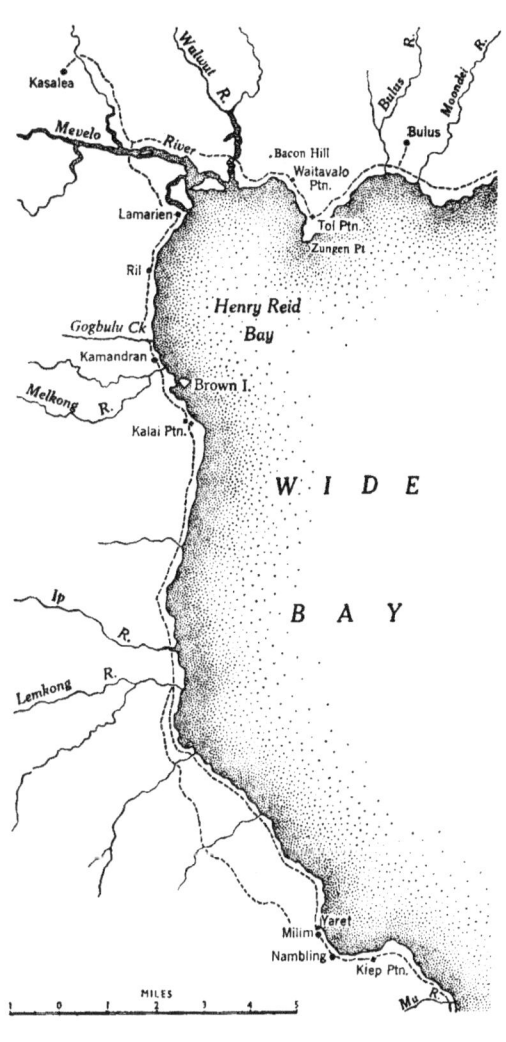

By early September the last of the Japanese stragglers on the south coast west of Wide Bay had been killed; the Japanese had heard many reports of a strong Australian base at Jacquinot Bay—reports circulated by the Australians to dissuade the enemy from advancing westward. This base, although non-existent as yet, was soon to become a reality, and from 5th to 7th September a reconnaissance party, including officers from New Guinea Force and the 5th Division, landed from the corvette *Kiama* and, guided by Black, examined the area.

Fairfax-Ross now planned to reconnoitre Milim with two platoons and, if circumstances were favourable, to attack. In support of this move the South Pacific Area's air force was to bomb Milim on 8th, 9th and 10th

---
[5] Lt J. C. Sampson, QX4869. 2/1 MG Bn and "M" Special Unit. Police officer; of Lake Nash, NT; b. Launceston, Tas, 5 Aug 1911.

August and the sloop *Swan* to bombard it on the 11th. However, because Milim was 16 miles south of the boundary between the Solomons-based air force and the New Guinea-based one, a dispute arose, and whereas Fairfax-Ross had hoped for an attack by perhaps 100 aircraft on three consecutive days from the Solomons, all he got was "an attack by four Beauforts on August 12th which unfortunately missed the target".[6]

The two-platoon force reached Milim unnoticed on 12th August, and found the enemy about 150 strong. At dawn they opened an attack in three groups, one to fire on the houses in the Japanese camp, another to fire from the flank, and the third to intercept any reinforcements from the Yaret position 500 yards to the north. Unfortunately a native fired his rifle during the approach, the enemy manned his defences, and, after a short exchange of fire, the attackers withdrew and placed ambushes across the tracks. The same day the *Swan* bombarded Milim. After three days of inaction on the part of the Japanese four native soldiers crawled into the enemy's position and killed three, whereafter the Japanese fired into the bush at intervals for 36 hours. This fire ceased on the 18th and soon afterwards the position was found to be abandoned; there was much booty including boats and numerous machine-guns. It was discovered that the enemy had withdrawn to Waitavalo.

Fairfax-Ross now moved his forward base to the coast at the Mu River only 6 hours' march from Waitavalo. On 17th and 18th September Fairfax-Ross, Sampson and a platoon, reconnoitring Kamandran, became involved in a fight with a Japanese force about 100 strong. Anticipating that the enemy would retaliate in force the Australians prepared defensive positions and one platoon under Sergeant-Major Josep, an outstanding N.C.O. who had come from the New Guinea Constabulary, was placed on the hillside above Milim to give warning of an enemy advance. On the night of 28th September the Japanese did in fact advance on Milim and on towards the Australian defensive position at the Mu River. Here, however, largely because of Sergeant Ranken's[7] cool handling of his Bren gun, they were repulsed losing 17 killed. Next day about 200 Japanese reinforcements arrived and, in a fire fight with Josep's men whose presence they had not discovered, 16 Japanese and a native ally were killed. The Australians now withdrew inland. Soon the Japanese about 700 strong were in their original positions round Milim, where they remained until heavy air attacks on 6th, 7th and 8th October forced them out again. By 10th October the guerilla force was again concentrated at Lakiri.

At this stage, since the landing of the 5th Division at Jacquinot Bay was soon to take place, Fairfax-Ross was instructed to cease guerilla warfare and concentrate on collecting and passing on information. He placed one platoon covering Jacquinot and Waterfall Bays, another

---

[6] B. Fairfax-Ross, Field Report, A.I.B. Field Activities South Coast New Britain, from April 1944 to March 1945. This report, one of the most systematic and reflective of its kind, contains the makings of a text-book on guerilla warfare with native troops under New Guinea conditions.

[7] Lt J. B. Ranken, MM, VX38868. 1 Indep Coy and "M" Special Unit. Jackeroo; of Broken Hill, NSW; b. Broken Hill, 4 Oct 1919.

watching the coast from Rondahl Harbour to Cape Cormoran and sections covering the inland roads. On 4th November when troops of the 6th Brigade landed at Jacquinot Bay there were no Japanese on the coast south of Henry Reid Bay.

This we could view with a great deal of satisfaction as our labours, and the splendid work of our native troops and free natives associated with us, had now been well rewarded.[8]

Meanwhile a party of three native soldiers, of whom Lance-Corporal Robin was leader, had returned from a four months' patrol into the Gazelle Peninsula as far as the enemy's main defences on the Warangoi River. They had made contact with two devoted agents—Danny Marks William, a Seventh Day Adventist Mission teacher of Put Put, and Ah Ming,[9] a Chinese of Sum Sum Plantation on the east coast—and brought back much information, including estimates of the strength of the garrisons in the outlying part of the eastern side of the peninsula: 200 at Kamandran, 500 at Waitavalo, 500 inland at Lemingi, 320 on the coast from Jammer Bay to Adler Bay, 125 at Sum Sum, 300 at Put Put. On 29th December knowledge of the Japanese dispositions was greatly augmented when Gundo, a former constable of Sattelberg, arrived. He had been in prison where he met Captain J. J. Murphy, captured at Awul in 1943, who told him of the presence of Australian groups on the island. Gundo, who had learnt some Japanese and had been employed as an interpreter, had in consequence a considerable knowledge of the enemy's organisation, depots (excellent air targets), and deployment. He escaped and after many adventures arrived at the A.I.B. base, bringing all this information with him.

On the north coast in September 1944 Lieutenant G. R. Archer had led a guerilla patrol deep into the Gazelle Peninsula. It was out for several weeks and penetrated into Seragi Plantation, near the western tip of the peninsula. On 10th September Archer attacked a Japanese party and put it to flight, killing three and capturing some equipment.

In this month Captain Robinson, a veteran guerilla leader and an experienced New Guinea hand, whose work on Bougainville in mid-1945 has already been mentioned, had on the north coast a force of native troops with three officers and 15 other Australians, mostly senior N.C.O's. Five Europeans and 20 natives were posted in the hills south of Baia. In October the Japanese sent a party forward to Baia and in November became still more active. Shots were exchanged on the beach in Hixon Bay. The enemy (who were also using native troops) moved on and on the night of 13th November tried to cross the Pandi River.

There can be no doubt that the enemy suffered heavy casualties (Robinson reported) as the following morning the canoes or what remained of them were found on the beach completely shot to pieces, quantities of blood were seen in the vicinity—undoubtedly wounded and dead had been removed during the night.

On 19th November, however, the Japanese pressed on in force. More than 100 crossed the Pandi south of its mouth in flat-bottomed boats, and

---

[8] Fairfax-Ross report.
[9] Ah Ming had been providing information since 1942.

about the same time native scouts arrived to report that 50 Japanese were moving along the beach towards the mouth of the river. The Japanese scattered the defenders at the crossing and moved west. One Australian-New Guinea patrol fired on this party as it was resting and hit many.

Robinson now decided to withdraw all his parties to Ea Ea (Nantambu), leaving only 10 native scouts forward. On 20th November Lieutenant Seton reported that 70 Japanese had tried to cross the Pandi at a point some miles inland, but the current prevented them. Seton's patrols engaged these. Fearing that the Japanese might get behind him on an inland track Robinson moved his force to his rear base a few miles south-west of Langeia leaving a forward post at Ulamona. This party withdrew on 21st November when some hundreds of Japanese began to converge on Ulamona from three points. When the Japanese settled in at Ulamona, Robinson withdrew his force, including 400 loyal natives who had evacuated their villages, to the western side of the Balima River near Cape Koas.

Building on the foundations laid by earlier A.I.B. parties in 1942, 1943 and early 1944 the guerilla force had achieved remarkable results in gaining information, winning the support of the natives, and driving the enemy's outposts out of about one-quarter of the island. In the whole operation only two New Guinea soldiers were killed.[1]

The visit of the reconnaissance party to Jacquinot Bay in September was an outcome of a conference between Generals Savige and Ramsay at New Guinea Force headquarters on 24th August, when it was decided to examine both the Jacquinot Bay and Talasea-Hoskins areas and report on their suitability as bases to accommodate a division. Thus from the outset it was intended to establish the incoming force well forward of the existing main bases. The Jacquinot Bay party had decided that the area could house a suitable base: there was shelter for up to six Liberty ships and a site for an airstrip. A second party, examining Talasea and Hoskins, found that both the Talasea and Hoskins sites were less accommodating. On 15th September General Blamey approved the establishment of the new base at Jacquinot Bay and the movement of the 6th Brigade there, less one battalion which was to go to Talasea-Hoskins'.[2] Later in September Savige formally instructed Ramsay that the role of his division was to relieve the American forces on New Britain and protect the western part of that island.

Major-General Ramsay, the commander of the incoming division, was a schoolmaster by profession who had served in the ranks of the artillery

---

[1] Sergeant Kogimara (Loyal Service Medal) of Bogia, and Private Eriwel of Lambom, New Ireland.

[2] A few days later it was decided that the 5th Division was to include:
4th Brigade Group (Brigadier C. R. V. Edgar)
6th Brigade Group (Brigadier R. L. Sandover)
13th Brigade Group (Brigadier E. G. H. McKenzie)
2/2nd Commando Squadron (Major G. G. Laidlaw)
"B" Company, 1 New Guinea Infantry Battalion (Captain H. McM. Lyon)
"D" Company, 1 New Guinea Infantry Battalion (Captain H. R. C. Bernard)
2/14th Field Regiment (Lieut-Colonel R. B. Hone)
The 6th Brigade had formerly been part of the 3rd Division.

in France from 1916 to 1918, had been commissioned in 1919, and was commanding the artillery of the 4th Division when war broke out. He had controlled the artillery of the 9th Division at El Alamein, and commanded the 5th Division in operations on the New Guinea coast earlier in 1944. His leading brigade had not yet been in action as a brigade although one battalion—the 36th—had fought at Gona and Sanananda in the Papuan campaign, and later had taken as reinforcements some men from three battalions which were disbanded after hard fighting in Papua. The brigade commander and the commanding officers, however, were soldiers of wide experience. Sandover, the brigadier since May 1943, had served with the 2/11th Battalion in North Africa and Greece and commanded it on Crete; he was the youngest infantry brigadier in the Australian Army. Caldwell[3] of the 14th/32nd Battalion had proved himself an able company commander in North Africa and Greece; Miell[4] of the 19th had served with the 6th Cavalry in the Middle East; O. C. Isaachsen of the 36th had led a company of the 2/27th in Syria and had now been commanding the 36th for more than two years. The 14th/32nd was a Victorian battalion, the 36th a New South Wales one, and each had largely retained its territorial character. The 19th, originally a New South Wales machine-gun battalion, had absorbed the Darwin Battalion when serving in the Northern Territory and a proportion of its officers were former N.C.O's of the regular army. The 6th Brigade had been in New Guinea since July 1943 training, doing garrison duties and unloading ships; in the opinion of its commander, nine-tenths of the men were anxious lest the war should end before they had heard a shot fired in action.

The landing of one battalion (the experienced 36th was chosen) with its ancillary detachments, 19 in all, at Cape Hoskins, an area already developed by the American forces, seemed to present no difficulties. The first flight of the group landed at Cape Hoskins on 8th October from the transport *Swartenhondt* after a voyage which Colonel Isaachsen considered had demonstrated defective liaison between the army and navy.

> The quarters for troops were found to be in a filthy condition and it was necessary to put a large working party from the battalion on to cleaning it up (he reported). . . . The naval authorities at Finschhafen ordered [the Captain] to sail to Talasea and provided him with charts for that place only. The charts were not even as good as the ones provided in the army terrain studies with the result that the ship nearly ran on to a reef. On arrival at Talasea the Captain was at length persuaded that he should go to Hoskins [using] the chart in the terrain study.

At Hoskins an American battalion gave all the help they could in unloading and fostering the incoming unit. The Australians found that the American battalion was occupying a perimeter with double-apron barbed wire fences, pill-boxes and weapon-pits, but that practically no storage huts were available. For several weeks the 36th Battalion was under the command of the 185th American Regiment and "was receiving orders

---

[3] Lt-Col W. B. Caldwell, DSO, OBE, MC, NX92. 2/2 Bn; CO 14/32 Bn 1942-45. Cadet valuer; of Homebush, NSW; b. Croydon, NSW, 26 Mar 1914.
[4] Lt-Col L. D. Miell, SX1449. 6 Cav Regt 1939-42; CO 19 MG Bn 1942-44, 19 Bn 1944-45. Grazier; of Ororoo, SA; b. Crystal Brook, SA, 4 Oct 1905.

from that regiment, 6 Brigade, and 5 Division, but fortunately these orders did not conflict much".

At Jacquinot Bay, although the A.I.B. patrols continued to report that the area was clear of the enemy, it was decided to provide against the possibility of a sudden attack on the incoming force by providing a naval escort and by landing ready for action; in any event it would be a useful exercise. Thus the two transports carrying the first contingent—the 14th/32nd Battalion group and a company of the 1st New Guinea Infantry Battalion—arrived at Jacquinot Bay on 4th November escorted by the destroyer *Vendetta,* frigate *Barcoo* and sloop *Swan*.[5] The landing was uneventful. Brigadier Sandover considered it fortunate that it was not opposed.

> First Army orders naturally made provision for possible opposition (he wrote), but the landing craft arrived late, the R.A.A.F's "maximum air effort" consisted of one Beaufort which arrived well after H-hour. The troopship was guided to its anchorage by the B.M. in a native canoe. High spot of the trip was the annoyance of base officers who, after watching from armchairs on the wharf the heavily-laden troops disembarking, brought their armchairs out by DUKW and expected the working parties to carry the chairs up with the weapons, ammunition and fighting stores as deck cargo. The chairs were sent back ownerless to the wharf. Incidentally, they were branded A.C.F. [Australian Comforts' Fund]. . . . However, we have nearly reached the war; up to the present the Bde has acquitted itself very creditably. Both of these give cause for gratitude.

After having stood by for two days to cover the landing H.M.A.S's *Swan, Vendetta* and *Barcoo* steamed east and bombarded Japanese positions in Wide Bay. After their departure two naval launches *M.L's 802* and *827* remained in the area available to the 5th Division for intercommunication and patrolling against Japanese barges. In the early stages landing craft were provided by Americans of a company of the 594th Engineer Boat and Shore Regiment; the 41st Australian Landing Craft Company did not arrive until 15th February, and then with only 18 Australian craft, less rugged and powerful than comparable American craft. General Ramsay took over responsibility for New Britain on 27th November. General Sturdee, who had assumed command of all New Guinea operations on 2nd October, had instructed him that, as information about the enemy on New Britain was conflicting and incomplete, it would be unwise to undertake major offensive operations until more information was available. "To undertake such operations would be to court heavy casualties, which the A.M.F. could not afford." Consequently Ramsay should undertake patrols and minor raids "to obtain the required information, to maintain the offensive spirit in our troops, to harass the enemy and retain moral superiority over him". In particular the tasks of the division were to defend the bases; "so far as the maintenance situation would

---

[6] The concentration of the division proceeded slowly because of lack of shipping and the distances involved. For example, the 13th Brigade arrived from Darwin on 26th November, 3rd and 30th December; divisional headquarters and the 2/14th Field Regiment from Lae and Madang on various days from 4th November to 1st January; 4th Brigade between 26th December and 24th February; 2/2nd Commando Squadron not until 16th April.

permit with existing resources, to limit Japanese movement south-west from Gazelle Peninsula"; and to collect information on which future plans could be based.

These fairly modest tasks did not differ greatly from those that had been allotted to the handful of white officers and the few native troops of the A.I.B., who had managed to perform them partly as a result of their skill and enterprise and partly because the Japanese seemed willing to confine themselves to the Gazelle Peninsula, with outposts and occasional patrols in the area immediately to the west.

The A.I.B. on 10th November had given the incoming commander a comprehensive assessment of the temper and tactics of the Japanese on New Britain. It appeared to take the enemy about ten days to make plans and assemble troops in response to a display of force. Recently they had not advanced south of Waitavalo with fewer than 200 troops and equipped with a high proportion of mortars, evidently considering that the best way to deal with guerilla troops was to mortar them. They generally advanced along the tracks and could be ambushed. They showed little tendency to exploit. If a strong Japanese patrol came upon an abandoned A.I.B. camp it would return to the Waitavalo base and there report fictitious successes.

Two days after the arrival of the 36th Battalion at Cape Hoskins on 8th October Colonel Isaachsen sent a patrol along the coast by barge to examine Ulamona, Ubili and Ea Ea and make contact with Captain Robinson's party. It returned next day having seen no Japanese and reported that Ea Ea would provide a suitable flying-boat base and excellent barge harbour in the north-west monsoon season (December to April). Enemy patrols were moving, however, between the Sai and Mavelo Rivers and west of the Mavelo, evidently pressing on towards Robinson. In November Isaachsen with Captain W. A. Money, an officer of the A.I.B. who had been a schooner master on this coast before the war, and a lieutenant of the American 594th E.B.S.R. travelled by barge to Ea Ea examining every harbour on the way. They found that Ea Ea was the only place east of Talasea that provided suitable barge landing points and shelter for large freighters. Thereupon Sandover strongly recommended that if any advance along the coast was to be made it should begin immediately so as to avoid the rough weather of the north-west season due soon to open. Ramsay who, by agreement with the American commander, had now taken over responsibility for the operations on the north coast, informed Sandover that no eastward move was intended yet and he was to confine patrolling to the area west of the Yamule River.

In the first half of November, however, as mentioned earlier, enemy activity south of Open Bay increased and Robinson reported that Japanese patrols had returned to the Pandi River, that strong enemy parties were between Ea Ea and Baia, and a submarine had been seen off Ea Ea. When, on 22nd November, the Japanese reached Ulamona, threatening Robinson's base, the limit of the 36th Battalion's patrolling was immediately extended to the Balima River so that it could give help, and a company was moved to Bialla Plantation on 23rd November and, to Robinson's great relief, began patrolling forward. On 6th December another company was moved to Bialla and the two patrolled along the coast and inland along the Balima. On the night of 1st January one of Robinson's patrols fired on a submarine between Cape Koas and Gulagula. Next day another patrol found that, under this new pressure, the Japanese had withdrawn and the area Ea Ea-Pandi River-Matatoga-Ulamona was clear of the enemy.

Because of this sudden withdrawal and because of the difficulty of beaching barges at Bialla, General Ramsay decided to allow the 36th to advance to Ea Ea, which was the nearest sheltered beach to Bialla, and was covered to the east by the Pandi River and five miles of swamp. Isaachsen was to leave a small detachment at Hoskins to defend the strip and help refuel reconnaissance aircraft;[6] at Ea Ea he was to prevent the enemy filtering west from the peninsula but was to avoid a heavy engagement. Thus on 13th January a company of the 36th landed at Ea Ea and a company of the 1st New Guinea on Lolobau Island, both unopposed. By the end of January the 36th, except for the Hoskins' detachment, but including "D" Company of the 1st New Guinea Battalion (Captain Bernard[7]), was at Ea Ea.

Meanwhile, on the south coast, the remainder of the 6th Brigade was complete at Cutarp by 16th December; there a battery of the 2/14th Field Regiment (Lieut-Colonel R. B. Hone) joined it on 1st January. The brigade's role was to prevent the enemy filtering west from Wide Bay, while the 13th Brigade protected Jacquinot Bay against an enemy approach from north or south.

On the south-west Sandover had under command the 12th Field Company (Major Nelson[8]) less a platoon which was on the north coast. "Work in the initial stages was hampered by poor equipment, but with the assistance of unit pioneer platoons much was accomplished. The poor tracks in the Jacquinot Bay area made heavy demands on engineers, and at one time the only possible method of transporting stores was the inauguration of a tractor train with six jeep-trailers being towed by a tractor."[9]

On 27th and 28th December Lieut-Colonel Caldwell with two companies of the 14th/32nd Battalion and a platoon of Captain H. McM. Lyon's company of the 1st New Guinea Battalion were landed at Sampun. The advance-guard of the force was now approaching the Japanese concentration at the north end of Henry Reid Bay, yet the Japanese, lacking air reconnaissance, not very enterprising in patrolling, and closely watched by the A.I.B. parties, were evidently still unaware of its presence in New

---

[6] The 36th Battalion, using such equipment as they found in the area, repaired this strip, one object being to ensure that its mail arrived earlier than would otherwise have been possible.
[7] Maj H. R. C. Bernard, NX43331; 1 NG Inf Bn. Regular soldier; of Queenscliff, Vic; b. Wollongong, NSW, 22 Aug 1909.
[8] Maj G. J. S. Nelson, VX39028. 2/16 Fd Coy; OC 4 Fd Coy 1943-45, 12 Fd Coy 1945. Civil engineer; of Perth; b. Perth, 2 Jul 1910.
[9] 6 Aust Inf Bde Report on Operations, Sep 44-Apr 45.

Britain.[1] On 7th January Ramsay instructed Sandover to concentrate the whole of the 14th/32nd, with a troop of the 2/14th Field Regiment, at Sampun, and on the 21st to establish a new base at Milim (which had been regularly visited by patrols of the 1st New Guinea Battalion), to secure crossings over the Ip River, and "patrol toward Henry Reid Bay without becoming heavily committed". Sandover was warned on 23rd January that he should soon move the remainder of the brigade to the Kiep-Milim area. This advance was begun on 26th January and completed by 11th February.

Meanwhile, on the north coast, patrols had probed forward from the new base at Ea Ea but met no enemy troops until 27th January when a platoon of native soldiers fired on and put to flight a patrol of Japanese and native troops near Mavelo Plantation. Two days later from 20 to 30 Japanese attacked a section outpost of the 36th Battalion near Baia and it withdrew. A series of small clashes followed culminating in a sharp fight between a large enemy party on the one hand and two New Guinea platoons and one platoon of the 36th on the other. Casualties were inflicted on the Japanese but the New Guinea troops were somewhat unnerved by mortar fire and the detachment withdrew in stages to Baia.

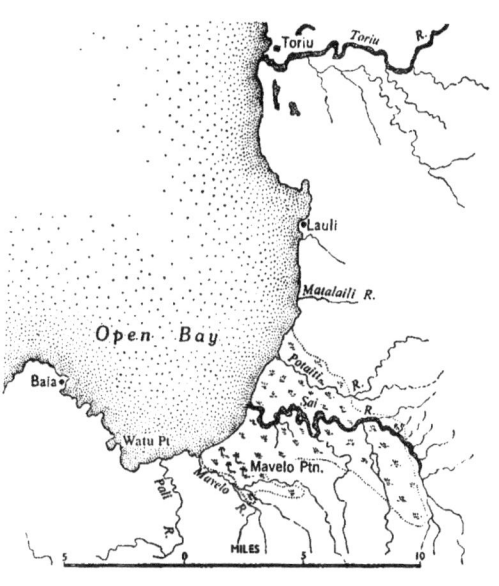

When a company of the 36th moved forward again the Japanese withdrew before they were attacked, but on 9th February two platoons (one Australian and one New Guinea) met an enemy party north of the Mavelo River and withdrew after inflicting casualties. In view of the strength of the enemy patrols it was decided to use patrols one company strong. One such patrol, attempting to cross the Sai River, was attacked by 70 to 80 Japanese, who were repulsed. A second company crossed the Sai farther inland, and circled round to the coast putting to flight a Japanese party there. Isaachsen was then ordered first to withdraw east of the

---

[1] The staff of the 6th Brigade was convinced from study of captured documents that the Japanese had no knowledge that Australians had replaced Americans on the island until Australian stations broadcast the news early in January 1945; and that the heavy mortars which the Japanese brought forward to Tol later that month were sent in response to this broadcast information.

Pali River and then to occupy the line of the Mavelo River. There at dawn on 8th March some 100 Japanese supported by a field gun attacked the leading platoon but were repulsed.

On 3rd March Ramsay had instructed Isaachsen not to establish patrol bases forward of the Mavelo River but to send mobile patrols forward to the Sai River. On 30th March a company landed by barge north of the Sai, met seven Japanese on the Potaiti River and killed or wounded them all. Heavy rain during the first fortnight of April confined patrolling to the area south of the Sai. A.I.B. patrols ahead of the 36th reported that the Japanese were busily building defences in the Matalaili River area; it was evident that his strong patrols from January to March were intended to delay the Australian advance until these were ready. Aircraft attacked

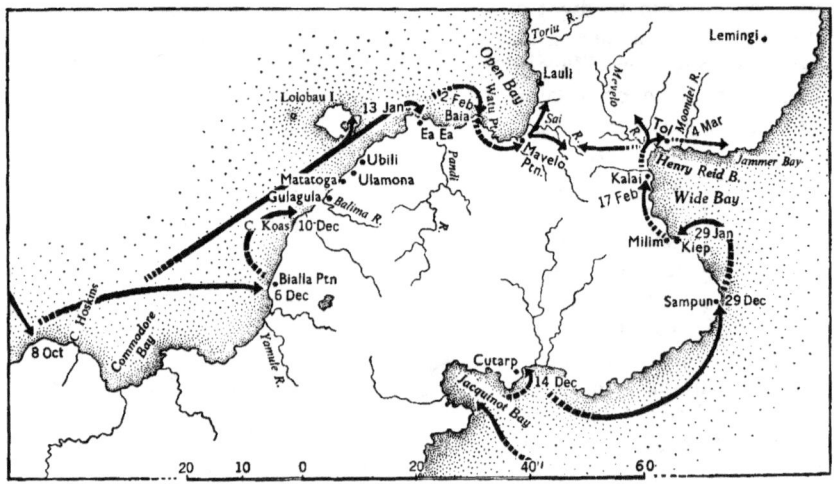

Operations in Central New Britain, October 1944-March 1945

the Japanese positions and on 17th March the sloop *Swan* bombarded them. On 7th April A.I.B. patrols found the defences abandoned and it seemed that the Japanese had withdrawn to the Toriu River. It was decided that their experiences in Wide Bay, described below, had persuaded them that it was unwise to commit their force in small, isolated parties. At the end of April the main body of the 36th was at Watu Point, one company at the mouth of the Mavelo, one company at Ea Ea with a platoon detached at Hoskins. Between the main Australian position at Watu and the main enemy outpost on the Toriu lay a wide area of swamp. Ramsay decided that the battalion group could not safely hold at Lauli and he lacked the means of maintaining any larger force on the north coast.

In December 1944 No. 79 Wing R.A.A.F.—No. 2, No. 18 (N.E.I.) and No. 120 (N.E.I.) Squadrons—was ordered to Jacquinot Bay when the airfield was ready. Its advanced party arrived on 23rd February, but in May, before the wing had been concentrated there, it was ordered north in response to a request by the Netherlands Indies Government that their few squadrons be used over Dutch territory. Later, occasional air attacks and supply-dropping missions were carried out by No. 6 Squadron from Dobodura. In February a detachment of No. 5 Squadron was established at Cape Hoskins for army cooperation.

In comparison with operations elsewhere in the Pacific the air and naval support allotted to the Australian forces throughout New Guinea and the Solomons in 1945 was scanty, but nowhere was it so diminutive as in New Britain. Since the supporting aircraft were based on the mainland of New Guinea requests for air action had to be made 24 hours before it was needed, and the briefing of crews had to be done by signal until early in March when the completion of the Jacquinot Bay airstrip made it possible for them to land there for briefing. From January until March the tactical-reconnaissance aircraft were based at Hoskins where again they had to be briefed by signal, and there were never enough aircraft to do the work required by the forward units. When, in March, these aircraft were based at Jacquinot Bay briefing improved. Also a system of ground to air communications was evolved so that the crews could be briefed in the air. Up to the end of April—that is, during the whole period of offensive operations—no light intercommunication aircraft were available, although they were urgently needed to provide a link with the troops on the north coast, to carry officers forward from divisional headquarters to the 6th Brigade, to enable observation of artillery fire, and to evacuate wounded. The only means of moving from Jacquinot Bay to Hoskins was to make a five-day march across the island or a six-day voyage by barge around it clockwise, and the latter was practically impossible because of the shortage of barges. It took up to three weeks to send a written message from Jacquinot Bay to the north coast.

In Wide Bay the A.I.B. patrols had reported that the enemy's main position was on high ground 800 yards south-west of Kamandran Mission. By 2nd February the 14th/32nd Battalion was firmly established on the Ip River with a troop of artillery two miles southward. By the 6th a company was deployed 3,000 yards north of the river and some 5,000 yards from Kamandran, and soon afterwards patrols had reached Kalai Plantation, which stretched along the coast for two miles southward of Kamandran Mission. Early on 11th February occurred the first clash on this coast between the Japanese and troops of the 5th Division when a small patrol fired on five Japanese. In the meantime a jeep road had been pushed forward to within 3,000 yards of Kalai Plantation.

The steady advance continued. A platoon of Lyon's company of the New Guinea Battalion moved round the left flank and observed enemy parties moving from Kamandran towards Ril; the 14th/32nd was deployed 600 yards south of Kalai with the supporting 28th Battery at the south end of the plantation. On 15th February the New Guinea company set up ambush positions and at 3.15 p.m. about 60 Japanese walked into one of them. The native troops held their fire until the Japanese were very close, then blazed at them killing 20 Japanese and two of their native allies. The ambush party then withdrew, being still outnumbered. That day an A.I.B. patrol reported some 200 Japanese dispersed from the creek bounding the Kamandran area northward for two miles. However, after an attack by Beauforts and some artillery fire the 14th/32nd advanced and found Kamandran abandoned. Sandover established his headquarters and the 19th Battalion on the northern edge of the plantation. Captured papers suggested that there had been an enemy platoon at Kamandran and that there were from 400 to 500 Japanese south of the Mevelo River. The Australians continued to probe forward and by the end of February the 19th Battalion, which had relieved the 14th/32nd at Gogbulu Creek, had secured crossings over the Mevelo River and was patrolling east to the Wulwut (Henry Reid) River, beyond which lay Waitavalo, a ridge overlooking the Waitavalo and Tol Plantations at the eastern end of Henry Reid Bay—the scene, three years before, of the massacre of some 150 Australians endeavouring to escape from Rabaul. Two naval launches patrolled the coast to intercept enemy barges and fired on targets ashore. On one occasion a 3-inch mortar and crew were carried by a launch and bombed targets on Zungen Point, the eastern point of the bay. Almost every night the 2/14th Field Regiment from Kalai Plantation fired across the bay on targets at Waitavalo.

The advancing force was now only about 20 miles from the 36th Battalion on the northern coast of the isthmus, but between them lay a tract of country so rugged that repeated attempts to find a suitable direct track had not yet succeeded.

On 27th February General Sturdee instructed General Ramsay that he was to secure the Waitavalo-Tol area and hold a line not forward of Moondei River-Waitavalo Plantation-Lauli, except that ground necessary for the defence of Tol Plantation could be held. He could send forward of this line such patrols as were necessary to give warning of an enemy attack. This gave the 6th Brigade a somewhat more definite task and led to a long series of fights that was to open on 5th March and last for about six weeks.

In consequence of this order Ramsay, on 3rd March, redefined the role of the 6th Brigade which would now involve crossing the Wulwut River and capturing an elaborate system of Japanese defences along an east-west ridge about 2,500 yards in length and rising steeply from the river and the sea to about 600 feet.

Heavy engineer tasks were involved. Temporary crossings of the Mevelo and Wulwut Rivers had to be made, the jeep track had to be extended behind the advancing infantry, beach-heads improved, and the infantry helped with mine clearings and demolitions. The supporting engineer company was now the 4th Field Company, Major Nelson who had commanded the 12th Field Company remaining to command the incoming one.

The assault was opened on 5th March by the 19th Battalion, commanded since 28th February by Major Maitland.[2] The first effort to cross

---
[2] Lt-Col J. A. Maitland, OBE, ED, WX21. 2/11 Bn 1939-42; 19 Bn 1944-45 (Adm Comd 19 Bn 1945); Instructor (JW and Tactics) Canadian Inf School 1945. Barrister and solicitor; of Perth; b. Clare, SA, 16 Nov 1909.

the river failed because of heavy fire, but at the end of the day one company under Major A. A. Armstrong, with an artillery officer of the 2/14th Regiment, Lieutenant Crompton,[3] was on the east side. In the meantime a company of the 14th/32nd which had relieved the 19th on the Mevelo was fired on by an invisible group of Japanese, evidently trying to cut the tracks behind the attacking force, and lost 2 killed and 3 wounded. On 6th March after artillery fire on Cake Hill Captain Stainlay's[4] company attacked up the steep slope. The leading platoon was pinned down but the others moved left and right and with their support the leading platoon attacked again, and by 10.30 a.m. the Japanese were withdrawing south to Lone Tree Hill leaving 9 killed. One Australian was killed and four wounded. At the end of the day two companies were concentrated on Cake. From Cake onwards the direction of artillery fire was extremely difficult as the observation officers were working in dense rain forest, the fall of shot was rarely visible, and the guns had often to be registered by sound. On the other hand the narrow tracks had all been registered by the many Japanese mortars in the Waitavalo fortress area. The main role of the guns was now to silence these mortars—a difficult task as it soon became evident that they were sheltered in caves where artillery fire became dangerous.

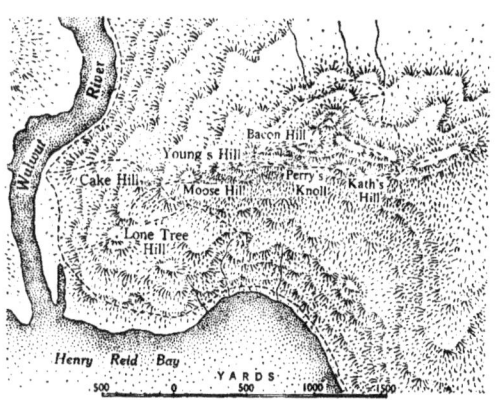

It was difficult for the engineers to maintain communications with the forward infantry. After rain the Wulwut River became a swift torrent; the night after it was bridged a flood came down, the bridge and a ferry boat were swept out to sea, and the forward companies were cut off. The first beach beyond the Wulwut was hard to land craft on and was under mortar fire.

On 7th March after a bombardment (which incidentally removed the lone tree from Lone Tree Hill) Captain Behm's[5] company occupied it without opposition. It now seemed that the Japanese had withdrawn their main force eastward to the higher part of the ridge, because, on the 9th, Major Armstrong's company took Moose Hill with little opposition, and

---

[3] Lt-Col D. H. Crompton, VX101872; 2/14 Fd Regt. Regular soldier; b. Melbourne, 21 Oct 1921.
[4] Maj D. R. Stainlay, MC, NX127371; 19 Bn. Company secretary; of Murwillumbah, NSW; b. Murwillumbah, 26 Oct 1916.
[5] Capt W. J. Behm, QX48769; 19 Bn. Schoolteacher; of Moorooka, Qld; b. Jandowae, Qld, 2 Apr 1916.

early next morning took Young's Hill (named after Lieutenant Young,[6] commanding the leading platoon, who was wounded but remained on duty). About 400 yards to the east stood another knoll the same height as Young's and connected to it by a saddle. About 10.45 the company advanced towards it but after 200 yards came under heavy fire and was halted on the narrow saddle. Soon two platoons were stationary in a narrow perimeter and the third (Lieutenant Perry[7]) was out of touch on the right. The company continued to advance, unobserved, and soon was in the rear of the enemy on Perry's Knoll. Thence it attacked, took the position, and established contact with the rest of the company. Thirteen Japanese dead were counted; the Australians lost two killed and 10 wounded of whom four, including Armstrong, remained on duty. Lieutenant Hunter[8] and a small group made a reconnaissance to the east but were fired on, Hunter and another being wounded. The Japanese suffered still heavier loss when they made a disastrous charge against the company on Perry's at 7.20 p.m. They came under fire from machine-guns on Young's; the men on Perry's held their fire until the enemy was only a few yards away; the attack wilted, and afterwards 25 dead were counted.

Armstrong's company, however, had now been hard hit and next day, when its casualties had mounted to 23, it was withdrawn and Behm's company was concentrated on Perry's and Captain Kath's[9] on Young's. (One company of the 19th was tied down to the task of securing Cake Hill and the northern flank.) In an effort to silence the mortars which were bringing down a galling fire the 2/14th Field Regiment sent 460 rounds over, searching an area 400 yards in depth, and eventually silenced the mortars, although only for the day. On 12th March heavy mortars (the Japanese had improvised mortars to fire 150-mm shells) rained 60 bombs on Perry's and Young's, killing four[1] and wounding nine, including Lieutenant Faul,[2] and temporarily disabling 12 others with bomb blast. It was a day of torrential rain which reduced visibility to a few yards.

On the 13th the artillery again succeeded in silencing the mortars and the five Beauforts made an accurate strike on the main enemy positions. A tunnel was found in the side of a spur (Kath's Hill) running north-east from Perry's. Captain Kath and Lieutenant Worthington[3] were both fatally wounded when Worthington threw a phosphorous grenade into the tunnel and it blew back when the grenade exploded. The Beauforts, mistaking the resultant smoke for a target indicator, strafed the area, but fortunately without hitting anyone.

---

[6] Capt R. A. Young, MC, QX48766; 19 Bn. Insurance agent; of Tweed Heads, NSW; b. Murwillumbah, NSW, 26 Sep 1913.

[7] Lt L. G. Perry, MC, QX50510; 19 Bn. Health inspector; of Toowoomba, Qld; b. Toowoomba, 26 Jun 1912.

[8] Lt R. Hunter, DX897; 19 Bn. Regular soldier; b. Adelaide, 24 Dec 1911.

[9] Capt N. S. Kath, QX48768; 19 Bn. Clerk; of Toowoomba, Qld; b. Toowoomba, 23 Nov 1916. Died of wounds 13 Mar 1945.

[1] Including Lieutenant R. M. Gorrie of the 2/14th Field Regiment and Lieutenant A. J. Anderson, an observer from the 28th Battalion.

[2] Lt H. J. Faul, SX498. 2/10 and 19 Bns. Slaughterman; of Port Lincoln, SA; b. Bordertown, SA, 29 Jan 1911.

[3] Lt S. Worthington, VX54130; 19 Bn. Salesman; of Richmond, Vic; b. Liverpool, England, 3 May 1913. Died of wounds 13 Mar 1945.

By this time the surviving Japanese were all concentrated on Bacon Hill. Sandover decided to relieve the 19th Battalion with the 14th/32nd for the final assault. By 15th March the relief was complete and Captain Sinclair's[4] company of the new battalion was on Kath's and Captain Jack's[5] on Perry's.

Next day two Japanese aircraft appeared and dropped two 100-lb and ten 20-lb bombs round a bridge that had now been built over the Wulwut, killing one and wounding four of the 19th Battalion.[6] About 10 a.m. the forward companies—now Captain Bain's[7] and Jack's—attacked. Jack's company was checked by heavy fire and later in the afternoon Colonel Caldwell ordered that it be extricated. Bain's probed deeply to the northeast and in the afternoon dug in north of Bacon Hill. Bain was wounded and Lieutenant Pugh[8] took command. That day 10 Australians were killed and 13 wounded.

The enemy were now almost surrounded in an area about 500 yards by 500. Caldwell placed Jack in command of both forward companies for an attack on the 17th, to be made from the north, supported by artillery fire directed by Captain Adamson[9] and Lieutenant Longworth[1] of the 2/14th Regiment. Jack's men thrust south and south-east until they were established to the east of Bacon Hill. Then two platoons began clambering westward up the hill about 40 yards apart. Soon they were being heavily grenaded, and the Japanese mortars were dropping bombs round Jack's headquarters just to the rear. A third platoon was sent in on the left to give fire support. Then the men of the forward platoons went in throwing grenades and firing and by 4 p.m. had taken the hill except for two positions. Thirty Japanese broke off and fled. In the day the attacking battalion lost 6 killed and 17 wounded, a number of these being hit carrying wounded men through mortar fire.

On 18th March the mortar fire was intensified from the few remaining enemy positions, and it seemed that the Japanese were firing off their ammunition while they could. The attack was resumed. When Corporal Martin's[2] section was halted on the steep spur by fire from three posts he jumped up shouting, "They can't do that to me", and went on alone, firing

---

[4] Capt E. B. Sinclair, VX117113; 14/32 Bn. Photographic salesman; of East Malvern, Vic; b. East Malvern, 14 Jan 1916. Died of injuries 24 Apr 1945.

[5] Capt R. L. Jack, VX117001; 14/32 Bn. Bank officer; of St Kilda, Vic; b. Bendigo, Vic, 9 Apr 1919.

[6] The Japanese at Rabaul had managed to keep a few aircraft in working order. On 9th March M.L.825 (a "Fairmile"), commanded by Lieutenant H. Venables, RANVR, was a mile and a half off shore, some 10 miles south-west of Cape Orford, when it was attacked by a Zeke, first with bombs and then with machine-gun fire. All guns were soon in action. Three ratings were wounded but the aircraft was hit and crashed into the sea in flames. It sank and no survivors were found.

[7] Capt W. H. Bain, VX117004; 14/32 Bn. Builder; of East Brighton, Vic; b. Moreland, Vic, 6 Jul 1916.

[8] Lt J. N. Pugh, MC, VX117017; 14/32 Bn. Insurance clerk; of Armadale, Vic; b. Moonee Ponds, Vic, 11 Oct 1919.

[9] Capt D. H. Adamson, VX39032; 2/14 Fd Regt. Salesman; of Elsternwick, Vic; b. Lurgan, N Ireland, 27 Jun 1918.

[1] Lt S. P. Longworth, NX66098; 2/14 Fd Regt. Student; of Vaucluse, NSW; b. Sydney, 3 May 1920.

[2] Cpl W. C. Martin, MM, VX73557; 14/32 Bn. Textile operator; of Coburg, Vic; b. Carlton, Vic, 14 Feb 1917.

his Owen and throwing grenades. He forced the enemy out of all three posts, killing five, before he himself was hit. The decisive attack was launched through this foothold. By 3 p.m. all the Japanese had been cleared from Bacon Hill; and a patrol from Kath's, under Lieutenant Lamshed,[3] penetrated to a knoll 800 yards to the east and found no enemy there. No Japanese now remained in the Waitavalo-Tol area. In the five days from the 16th to the 20th 4 officers and 53 others had been killed or wounded. In the next few days fighting patrols probed deeply but few stragglers were found. The 19th relieved the 14th/32nd on 21st March and exploited to the Bulus and Moondei Rivers.

On 28th March General Ramsay ordered that the 13th Brigade should relieve the 6th, and by 12th April this change was complete. Because of the withdrawal of part of the 41st Landing Craft Company and the concentration of the company of the 594th E.B.S.R. preparatory to its departure, the intended relief of the 36th Battalion on the north coast by the 37th/52nd, ordered at this time, was not completed until 19th May, nearly two months after the decision was made.

The division had now achieved its main task; it was firmly established across the neck of the Gazelle Peninsula. Henceforward it was to hold this line and patrol forward of it, but not to thrust farther forward in strength.

On the south coast the division had lost 38 killed and 109 wounded, on the north 4 killed and 13 wounded. The killing of 138 Japanese on the south coast and 68 on the north had been confirmed. Five prisoners had been taken. Strict discipline had kept illness to a remarkably low level: the 6th Brigade, although fighting under difficult conditions, had only 41 malaria casualties.

Four months of patrolling by the infantry and maintenance and routine work by other troops followed the capture of the Waitavalo area. The 13th Brigade (Brigadier McKenzie[4]), now forward on the south coast, was a West Australian formation which had not hitherto been in action. Its battalions were all commanded by officers who had come from A.I.F. battalions: Lieut-Colonel W. S. Melville led the 11th, Lieut-Colonel Horley[5] the 16th, and Lieut-Colonel Brennan[6] the 28th. Its first deep patrol was an eventful one.

On 11th April a platoon of the 16th Battalion under Lieutenant Knight,[7] with Captain Murdoch[8] as an observer, was sent out to reconnoitre a suitable barge-point at Jammer Bay and report recent enemy movement; information suggested that only about twenty Japanese were there. The

---

[3] Lt S. M. Lamshed, SX1065. 2/10 and 14/32 Bns. Press operator; of Seaton Park, SA; b. Moonta, SA, 25 Jun 1919.

[4] Brig E. G. H. McKenzie, MC, ED, WX29558. (1st AIF: Lt 44 Bn.) CO 44 Bn 1939; Comd 13 Bde 1940-45. Sales manager; of Subiaco, WA; b. East Malvern, Vic, 1 Jan 1896. Died 13 Sep 1957.

[5] Lt-Col R. J. Horley, WX11. 2/11 Bn; CO 16 Bn 1942-45. Farmer and grazier; of Northam, WA; b. Coalville, Vic, 8 Jun 1909.

[6] Lt-Col J. G. Brennan, ED, WX3408. 2/28 Bn; CO 28 Bn 1942-45. Auditor and accountant; of West Perth; b. Kalgoorlie, WA, 6 Jul 1906.

[7] Lt J. D. Knight, WX32971; 16 Bn. Clerk; of North Perth; b. East Fremantle, WA, 12 Jun 1919.

[8] Maj R. L. A. Murdoch, WX32981; 16 Bn. Process engraver; of Victoria Park, WA; b. Wagin, WA, 25 Apr 1918.

patrol spent the night of the 12th-13th at a point about one mile from Jammer Bay. Next morning security patrols reported all clear, and the platoon began to form a hidden base from which it intended to send a party forward to the bay. Suddenly, about 7.30 a.m., it was attacked by Japanese who had crept to within 80 yards, and soon advanced, firing, to within 15 yards of the patrol's perimeter. Then the enemy began using mortars from about 100 yards away. The patrol fought the enemy off but not before three Australians had been killed, one mortally wounded, and 13 slightly wounded; one was missing. The wireless set had been out of commission since the 11th. It was decided to withdraw, and in the next half-hour the seriously wounded man was carried out, and the sections thinned out and finally broke contact and withdrew. All the Australians concerned had been in action for the first time, but had behaved calmly, and handled their weapons skilfully, and a dangerous situation was saved.

As a result of patrolling, capture of documents, and information from natives, it was decided that there were now at least 100 Japanese round Jammer Bay and they were digging strong defences: indeed that the occupation of Jammer Bay would probably require an operation on the scale of the one that had been carried out at Tol.

Soon after the capture of Tol Lieut-Colonel B. G. Dawson, commander of the New Guinea Battalion, walked across the island from Ril to Open Bay, thus establishing ground contact between the two parts of the division. (Dawson had made this walk when escaping from Rabaul after the Japanese invasion in 1942.)

In May the 37th/52nd Battalion (Lieut-Colonel Embrey[9]) of the 4th Brigade marched across the island by this route and relieved the 36th which had then been forward on the north coast for about eight arduous months, and the 36th marched across to the south coast. These journeys took five days and a chain of staging camps was set up along the route. Also in May Brigadier McKenzie of the 13th Brigade was invalided to Australia and replaced by Brigadier Winning.[1] McKenzie had commanded this brigade since May 1940—a longer period in command than that of any other Australian infantry brigadier in 1939-45. In June the 2/2nd Commando Squadron arrived at Tol and was concentrated at Lamarien.

In May the airfield at Jacquinot Bay was completed and the New Zealand Air Task Force began moving in. No. 20 Squadron, Royal New Zealand Air Force, began patrolling over the Rabaul area on 29th May. No. 21 Squadron also served at Jacquinot Bay from May until July when it was replaced by No. 19. These were fighter squadrons. One New Zealand bomber squadron was also maintained at Jacquinot Bay from June onwards.

From May onwards most of the deep patrolling was again done by the two companies of the 1st New Guinea Battalion. There were occasional clashes, often with small groups of two or three Japanese sent out to

---

[9] Lt-Col F. J. Embrey, NX127. 2/1 Bn 1939-44; CO 37/52 Bn 1945. Public accountant; of Sydney; b. Sydney, 16 Mar 1913.
[1] Brig R. E. Winning, DSO, OBE, ED, NX44. 2/4 Bn 1939-41; CO 2/8 Bn 1941-43; Comd 3 Bde 1943-44, 12 Bde 1944-45, 13 Bde 1945. Chemist; of Sydney; b. Hurstville, NSW, 9 Apr 1906.

harass the Australians, but the main Japanese outposts were now east of the line beyond which the division was forbidden to advance in force.

The employment of native troops was producing a variety of disciplinary problems. The Australians were collecting a mass of valuable information from natives, but there was evidence that the Japanese too were receiving information by "bush wireless" which circulated at "an alarming rate". Officers were enjoined, in orders distributed in May, to impress on the native soldiers that when they met civilian natives who spoke their tongue "ol tok bilong armi i tambu". There had been a tendency for natives to circulate disparaging remarks about Australian units with which native sub-units had fought; these could harm European status within the Pacific Islands Regiment and were also forbidden. There were other problems of discipline, which at first glance seemed less serious:

> In some cases (said a battalion routine order of 5th May) it has been noticed that when being addressed by European or native N.C.O's soldiers of this battalion have failed to cease smoking and/or remove cigarettes from their mouths. Another irregularity is wearing of cigarettes between the head and ears. These unsoldierly practices will in future be regarded as an offence.

In June the 1st New Guinea Battalion, now temporarily commanded by Major A. R. Tolmer in Lieut-Colonel Dawson's absence at a school, was concentrated on New Britain, "A" Company arriving from Bougainville, "C" from Madang. The two newly-arrived companies began a period of training. The men of the Bougainville company had done invaluable work but had been in operations for seven months with little rest and were tired and debilitated; every man in two platoons that were examined had hookworm. They seemed restless and discontented. The Europeans in the company, as mentioned earlier, were over-tired and their numbers depleted.

On 14th June two New Guinea soldiers were arrested and were about to be charged with having refused to carry out a lawful command when about 50 men of the company marched towards the detention compound armed with rifles and sticks. When ordered by a native N.C.O. to take their rifles to their quarters they did so, but returned to the compound armed with sticks and stones, wrecked it and freed the two prisoners. An inquiry revealed that on Bougainville the native soldiers of the company had agreed that they would free any member who was put in detention; detention was "fashion belong before" and did not now apply to them as fighting soldiers. In the next two days two senior native N.C.O's were threatened by privates, and there was talk of a coming fight between the mainland natives and the New Britain ones. One native told his European sergeant that the time had come for "fighting soldiers" to get European rations.

Tolmer in his report on these incidents concluded that the native soldiers were becoming more educated, and were discontented because of differences between their treatment and the treatment of Europeans; and that natural leaders—sometimes good leaders in action—were arising who were encouraging discontent. Tolmer sought authority to discharge 15 soldiers, all patas (privates). Their periods of service ranged from 13 to 26 months.

On 14th July there was another disturbance in the company from Bougainville which culminated in the release of three prisoners from the unit detention compound. On Brigadier Winning's orders the extreme step was taken of disarming the company and marching it to Jacquinot Bay where a court of inquiry was held. On 19th July there was a disturbance in the company from Madang. Finally the offenders were tried according to civil regulations and six were sentenced to 12 months' and eight to one month's imprisonment.

In a report on this incident Major Tolmer wrote:

> In this type of non-progressive warfare the native soldier is becoming increasingly dissatisfied. The strategy in this area, which has several times been explained to them, is still beyond their comprehension. Our patrols on many occasions contact the enemy, sometimes suffering casualties, and pinpoint his positions with no "follow up" action on the part of the Australian troops. The native soldier's reaction to this is: "Is it worth while?"
>
> The mainland natives . . . dislike being on New Britain, but are most anxious to return to their own country and fight the Japanese who still occupy much of their land.[2]

These tensions, occurring as they did among troops who were giving invaluable service and saving many Australian lives and who were to be allotted a more important role should the war continue into the summer, were very disturbing, particularly to the keen young officers who had formed these battalions. Colonel Dawson of the 1st New Guinea Battalion attributed the troubles to faulty employment of the New Guinea troops by all commanders on Bougainville and New Britain to whom they had been allotted, with the exception of Brigadier Sandover.

When he returned to his command on 8th August, Dawson wrote in his monthly report that the reason for the indiscipline was laxity on the part of the Europeans, and that in its turn was a result of a war establishment which provided so few Europeans that they were overworked. Another reason, he considered, was the splitting up of companies when in operations into small groups under the command of officers who were ignorant of natives and their tactical role.

After the war Dawson, who had been in action first with an A.I.F. infantry battalion, then an Independent Company, and then New Guinea troops, expanded this criticism and propounded doctrines about the employment of New Guinea troops whose soundness seems to have been demonstrated in every area in which they fought, from 1942 to 1945.

> You will readily appreciate (he wrote) from reports of A.I.B. activities, how effective native units can be in deep patrolling, and in driving in enemy outposts. At no stage was 1st N.G.I.B. given the opportunity to operate in this, its true cavalry role. Instead, it was fragmented, and the fragments placed under command of all sorts of Australian infantry officers, very few of whom had the slightest idea of the tactical role in which native troops should be employed. In effect, they were often used so that Australian infantry sub-units, by disposing the natives round their perimeter, could sleep soundly at nights. To get an appreciation of just how absurd this is, one only has to imagine that an infantry platoon commander in the

---

[2] Monthly Report, 1st New Guinea Infantry Battalion, 1 Jul 45 to 31 Jul 45.

desert might ask for a tank, or an A.F.V. of some sort, to be placed under his command and to operate with the platoon to provide local protection. I wonder how many cavalry regiment commanders would have stood for that?

I had no alternative, however, as until the other units of the Pacific Islands Regiment were raised and trained, the 1st N.G.I.B. had to be scattered under several different commands. Not until the war ended did I get the battalion back under my own disciplinary control. It was during this period of fragmentation, and close fraternisation with Australian infantry, away from my personal control, and frequently the control of their experienced company commanders, that a decline took place in the respect in which Europeans were held, and the idea grew that the native soldier should be entitled to expect similar treatment to Australian infantry. . . . Several native platoons had experienced occasions in action when green Australian infantry had not shown up particularly well. . . . These occurrences were the subject of much unfavourable comment by the natives. Quite apart from the abandonment of their correct tactical role, native units should *never under any circumstances* be fragmented and integrated with infantry troops inexperienced in their handling and control. Neither should they be used in a purely infantry role.

[The New Guinea soldier] should remain at all times under the command of those who know him and understand him (he added) and not be farmed out like a library book. Senior commanders should be told not to yield to the temptation to break the unit down under the command of inexperienced infantry junior officers. They should never operate as sub-units in cooperation with other infantry, but should be given their own unit tasks to perform, as a unit, in their correct cavalry role. At no time should senior officers interfere in the internal administration and discipline of native battalions.

Such problems were not confined to New Britain and Bougainville. On 6th August General Sturdee telegraphed from First Army headquarters to the Chief of the General Staff, General Northcott, that serious unrest existed among natives of the Pacific Islands Regiment and the native labourers, particularly at Lae, because of dissatisfaction with their low rates of pay. A spokesman of the regiment had said that the native troops wanted £3 a month instead of the present rate of 10 shillings a month for a private. Angau officers took a very serious view of the unrest. Sturdee himself considered the pay not commensurate with the important work the troops were doing in action.

P.I.R. are natural experts in jungle warfare (he signalled) and few Australians ever reach their individual standards. This all fully realised by native soldiers who feel that their pay of 4d per day and no compensations or pensions most unfair.

Sturdee said that he realised that to pay £3 to New Guinea privates might upset the economy of New Guinea after the war; and recommended £1 a month for a first-year and second-year private, £1 5s for a third-year private; £1 15s for a corporal; £2 10s for a sergeant; and £4 for a warrant-officer. He added that wireless announcements that the Minister for Territories, Mr E. J. Ward, had promised 15 shillings a month as a basic wage for labourers had caused unrest and he, Sturdee, proposed to increase the labourers' wage to 15 shillings. However, he had no power to increase the soldiers' pay.

General Blamey, when he saw this signal, urged that increases in pay be approved immediately. "In view of the serious and important part designed to be played by native troops in releasing white troops early any mass action or mutiny during the next few months would be disastrous."

Events moved quickly and on 9th August Blamey was informed that the Secretaries of the Treasury, the Army, and External Territories had agreed to increased rates and were seeking Ministerial approval. This approval arrived within a week of Sturdee's proposal. Soon, however, the main problem was not pay but demobilisation and rehabilitation.

As a result of this unrest the pay for native privates was increased from 10 to 15 shillings a month after one year's service and to £1 a month after two years' service, the increases being made retrospective for up to six months. Shorts, shirts and European pattern badges of rank were issued to New Guinea soldiers. At the same time discipline was made tighter and compliments more strictly demanded.

Meanwhile, on 15th June 1945, after ten weeks of relatively uneventful patrolling, General Sturdee instructed Major-General Robertson, who had replaced Major-General Ramsay[3] in command of the 5th Division in April, that in order that his units might be more actively employed and thereby their morale and fighting efficiency maintained, they might undertake "minor offensive operations against enemy parties" within the limits of the division's own resources. When General Blamey saw this instruction he objected that it might "easily involve demand for further resources which cannot be met", and instructed that any operations under the new instruction were to be undertaken only with the approval of Sturdee, who must inform Blamey of any such proposals.

In June and July the headquarters staff of the 5th Division, which had served in New Guinea for 32 months, was relieved by that of the 11th Division, of which Major-General K. W. Eather (from the 25th Brigade) took command on 4th August. General Robertson had gone to Wewak a few days earlier to command the 6th Division. Soon, here as elsewhere, it was known that the end of the fighting was near.

On New Britain as in other forward areas the arrival of news that negotiations for a Japanese surrender were in progress was a signal for great revelry: to describe it is to describe what happened in many other places.

> In the Jacquinot Bay area the darkness was broken by coloured flares fired from ships in port; machine-guns rattled; tracers streaked up into the heavens. There was singing and shouting and long blasts from motor horns. . . . In the hospital wards sisters and orderlies sang with the patients. By now several fires were visible as merry-makers ignited some disused buildings in old camp sites. This joyous scene continued until almost morning.[4]

On 15th August when the news arrived that the war was over it was received quietly. Native workers and troops were assembled and told the news—"Japan man 'e cry enough"—and native runners were sent into the hills to spread the news among the villages.

---

[3] General Ramsay, who had commanded the 5th Division since January 1944, changed places with General Robertson who had been commanding the 11th Division.

[4] *Surrender of the Japanese South Eastern Army and Occupation of Rabaul*, by Lieutenant B. A. Harding, Military History Section, 20 Sep 1946.

Next day Gracie Fields and a party of other entertainers arrived at Jacquinot Bay from Bougainville and in the evening performed before 10,000 troops.

> Highlight of the night . . . was a half hour's non-stop entertainment by "Gracie" who at the conclusion of the concert said: "I hope it won't be long before you all pack oop and go H.T.M.—home to Moom." Ten thousand troops had exactly identical hopes and the thunderous cheering showed this in no uncertain manner.[5]

On 4th August the acting commanding officer of the 2/14th Field Regiment, Major Rylah,[6] had asked that the regiment, being the only remaining complete unit of the 8th Division, should be included in the Australian token force which, the Government had announced, was to assist the British in the re-occupation of Singapore. Rylah pointed out that the regiment, formed in December 1940, had served at Darwin from July 1941 to January 1943, and on the New Guinea mainland from late 1943 until December 1944, but up to that time had fired only 25 rounds against the enemy. It had served on New Britain since December 1944. "One of the factors that has sustained the pride and *esprit de corps* of the regiment is the remembrance of the fate of the rest of 8 Div and the desire to do the utmost to avenge and release them has ever been present." The Singapore force, however, was not formed on the scale intended.

It was learnt after the war that the Japanese, in November 1944, suspecting a landing in the Wide Bay area, had sent a force of two infantry companies, a machine-gun company, and a mortar platoon to reinforce the outpost at Tol. In January the main body of this force was round Waitavalo, with a platoon at Kalai Plantation and observation posts along the Wulwut River. The Kalai outpost estimated that a battalion of Australians attacked it and forced it to retreat on 9th February. The Australian force which advanced to the Wulwut River was estimated at two battalions and eight field guns.

On the north coast Lieut-General Yasushi Sakai of the *17th Japanese Division*, in the period from May to September 1944, had small forces aggregating 530 men. The largest was a depleted battalion of the *54th Regiment* at the Toriu and Pondo. There were smaller groups at Massava Bay, Yalom, and Cape Lambert.

After the war a senior officer on General Imamura's staff said that, up to the middle of 1944, they believed that the Allies, having isolated Rabaul, would attack it, probably employing more than ten divisions, including about six Australian divisions. But after mid-1944 when the Allied advance began to head for the Philippines and Japan, they felt that the Allies would advance only gradually overland towards Rabaul and attack it at a time when the advance towards Japan had been halted, or when it had

---

[5] Harding, p. 7.
[6] Maj A. G. Rylah, ED, VX13930; 2/14 Fd Regt. MLA Vic since 1949; Deputy Premier, Chief Secretary and Attorney-General since 1955. Solicitor; of Kew, Vic; b. Kew, 3 Oct 1909.

succeeded, or when the Australian forces had been reorganised and reinforced.[7]

When the Japanese staffs became aware that the Australian force at Open Bay was a small one they decided that the operations in New Britain were a diversion intended to mislead them into believing that important operations were being undertaken, whereas in fact the main body of the Australian Army was going to the Philippines. (American forces had recently landed on Leyte.) Imamura decided that two could play at this game and set about trying to attract Australian reinforcements into this area. Four barges landed 200 men near Ulamona, but, when it was found that the Australian force was even smaller than had been believed, after several clashes the Japanese force was withdrawn by sea to Toriu whence it had come.

There were some Japanese staff officers who found more subtle reasons for the Australian landings: either they were a result of the unwillingness of the Australian Commander-in-Chief to allow his troops to fill a comparatively minor role under American command in the Philippines; or they were part of a political move to enable Australia to claim her mandates after the war.[8] These speculations, of course, contained more than a germ of truth.

From October onwards the Japanese based on the Toriu patrolled between the Sai River and Ea Ea. An outpost watched the landing at Baia of what seemed to be a battalion, and, from Baia, of the advance by sea of a company to Mavelo Plantation.

The Japanese force in the Waitavalo-Tol area numbered 400 to 450 at the outset. Before the final engagement 150 of these had been killed, about half by artillery and mortar fire.

The account of the Japanese side of the action at Waitavalo and Tol, compiled after interrogations in Rabaul after the war, says: "The Australian forces advanced under cover of their bombardment and by clever infiltration captured our water point at our main line of defence. . . . This made it very difficult for our forces to put up a final stand. . . . On 12th March the garrison commander made his decision to fight to the last man. Reinforcements were not sent from Rabaul because our main line . . . was along the Warangoi and Keravat Rivers [and] could not be disturbed. In any case reinforcements would have had to be sent in barges subject to attack from the air. At this time the commander of the *38th Division* sent a message of encouragement to the Tol commander who then attempted a last rally. All men, including those of headquarters units, went out to the [Wulwut] River, and it is assumed that the unit was completely annihilated by 18th March." The force round Tol was out of communication from 15th March onwards.

The staff officer of the *Eighth Area Army* quoted earlier remarked on the Australian policy of establishing offensive bases at points along the

---

[7] S-E Japanese Army Force's War Operation, by Colonel T. Takahasi, 13 Nov 45.
[8] Military History Section, Brief Account of Eastern New Guinea Campaign (compiled by Lieutenant W. N. Prior, after interviewing Japanese staff officers at Rabaul after the war).

roads and advancing step by step, developing the roads as they went so that they would carry motor vehicles. Australian scouts were skilful in concealment, acted promptly and "made puppets of natives skilfully". "The Australian tactics were very steady and the Australian men were very persevering."

After the war the staff of the *Eighth Area Army* at Rabaul said that it had estimated the strength of the whole Australian Army at about seventeen divisions—nearly three times the actual 1945 strength. They were not sure whether the headquarters of the First Army were at Lae or Finschhafen. The only Australian commanders whose names they knew were Generals Blamey and Sturdee. Indeed, here as on Bougainville, the Australians reached the conclusion that Japanese Intelligence work was of a very low order.

> It would appear that the Japanese were anxious to obtain information, as their higher formations carried an extensive Intelligence organisation, but they failed badly because they did not realise that Intelligence of value is obtained by carefully piecing together scraps of information supplied by lower formations and especially by forward troops.[9]

When the fighting ended the main Japanese formations, as before, were concentrated north of the Warangoi-Keravat line. Forward of this line there were, on the east, 1,100 troops in the Put Put-Lemingi-Adler Bay-Jammer Bay area; and, on the west, 520 at posts between Pondo and the Matalaili River.

As mentioned above, by January 1945 the total strength of the Japanese forces on New Britain had been estimated at 32,000 including about 2,500 naval men. By June the estimate was 50,000 plus, perhaps, an additional 10,000 to 15,000 naval men. These figures were still too low, a result (as on Bougainville) largely of failure to obtain adequate information about the naval forces or the large numbers of base troops and civilian workers. In August 1945, the naval troops in the Gazelle Peninsula numbered 16,200 and there were 53,200 soldiers. In addition there were nearly 20,000 civilian workers attached to the army or navy. Close by on New Ireland were 11,100 troops of both Services and 1,200 civilian workers. The grand total of Japanese on New Britain and New Ireland in August 1945 was 101,700.[1] Of these 3,600 were in hospital, not a large total in the circumstances. In this force were 19 generals, 11 admirals, 3,300 other officers of the army and 1,400 of the navy. (In view of the sharp and persistent criticism of the Australian Army by Ministers and others on the ground that it had too many generals, it is interesting to note that, at this time, there were 26 generals in the whole of the Australian Army in Australia and the South-West Pacific Area.)

The strengths of the main Japanese Army formations on New Britain in August were: *17th Division,* 11,429; *38th Division,* 13,108; *39th*

---

[9] 11th Division War Diary, October 1945.

[1] On 20th December 1944 two Koreans who surrendered to the 36th Battalion gave the Japanese strength round Rabaul as about 110,000. The battalion wirelessed this information to divisional headquarters, but was told that division did not consider the information reliable.

(*Australian War Memorial*)

At Jacquinot Bay, New Britain, 9th February 1945. In the foreground, from the left, Major-General A. H. Ramsay (G.O.C. 5th Division), Lieut-General J. Northcott (Chief of the General Staff), Major-General C. S. Steele (Engineer-in-Chief). Behind them, from the left, are: Lieut-Colonel W. T. Briggs (C.R.E. 5th Division), Lieut-Colonel W. B. Maguire (G.S.O.1 5th Division), Lieut-Colonel E. A. Griffin (A.A.&Q.M.G. 5th Division) and Major-General J. H. Cannan (Quartermaster-General).

(*Australian War Memorial*)

At Waitavalo, 16th March 1945, during the attack on Bacon Hill. A wounded man of the 14th/32nd Battalion being helped to the beach.

(Australian War Memorial)
A platoon of the 2/11th Battalion advancing eastward from the Danmap River, Aitape area, 31st December 1944.

(Australian War Memorial)
Men of the leading company of the 2/11th Battalion crossing the Wakip River, 2nd January 1945.

Brigade, 5,073; *65th Brigade*, 2,729; *14th Regiment*, 2,444; *34th Regiment*, 1,879; *35th Regiment*, 1,967. The five independent brigades or regiments contained 19 battalions. Since the naval fighting units amounted to a force of divisional strength, the equivalent of five somewhat depleted divisions was round Rabaul.

Thus the achievements of the 5th Division and the A.I.B. parties on New Britain were remarkable. On the one hand was a Japanese army of over 53,000, most of them in veteran fighting formations, and over 16,000 naval men. On the other was a division of relatively raw troops, although commanded down to unit level by widely-experienced officers. Employing only one brigade in severe fighting, General Ramsay had secured (and General Robertson maintained) a grasp on the central part of New Britain, already virtually cleared of the enemy by the A.I.B. parties, had captured the enemy's forward stronghold round Waitavalo, and had established an ascendancy over the Japanese so complete that they offered no great resistance to fairly deep patrols in the last four months of the war. This was done at a cost of 53 killed, 21 who died of other causes, and 140 wounded.[2]

The air support and the shipping allotted to the Australian force were far from adequate. The responsibility for this rested with General MacArthur and General Blamey. G.H.Q. were not responsible for the fact that the Australians had engaged in more active operations than the Americans, but, even so, they allotted to the Australian forces fewer ships and small craft than their own static garrisons had possessed. From time to time Blamey pressed for more shipping and with some success. It seems, however, that the few transport and light aircraft that were so urgently needed could have been provided with little difficulty by the schools in Australia, the civil airlines, or the big Australian air force farther north, whose crews during part of this time were becoming rebellious because they considered that they were being employed on insignificant tasks.

Why General Imamura at Rabaul showed so little aggressive spirit compared with General Hyakutake of the *XVII Army* on Bougainville or General Hatazo Adachi of the *XVIII Army* at Wewak remains a puzzle. Both the *XVII* and the *XVIII Armies* delivered resolute counter-offensives against the American forces, accepting appalling losses, and, when the Australians began attacking them, they defended every position with all the strength they could find. This was despite the fact that most of the formations composing each army had suffered crushing losses and hardships in earlier campaigns, and by mid-1944 the men were under-nourished and many were sick. The divisions and regiments round Rabaul, on the other

---

[2] The battle casualties in the infantry battalions and artillery regiment were:

	Officers	Other ranks
14th/32nd Battalion	3	61
19th Battalion	7	57
36th Battalion	2	12
37th/52nd Battalion	—	3
11th Battalion	1	3
16th Battalion	—	19
28th Battalion	2	1
2/14th Field Regiment	2	5

hand, had endured less arduous fighting in earlier operations and were fit and well fed. Yet, after the American landings late in 1943, they used only relatively small forces in the main part of New Britain. They allowed guerillas to thrust most of their outpost forces back into the Gazelle Peninsula. The key position at Tol was defended by a force of about battalion strength which the divisional commander exhorted to fight to the last but did not reinforce. In the final stages Imamura had only about 1,600 troops deployed forward of the fortress area, within which he held experienced fighting formations equivalent to five divisions.

CHAPTER 11

TAKING OVER AT AITAPE

THE Wewak campaign was fought in an elongated triangle of country bounded on the north by the sea, on the south by the Sepik River, and in the west more or less by a north-south line through Aitape. Round Aitape the swampy coastal plain extends inland for about eight miles before reaching the foothills of the Torricelli Mountains, but the plain narrows east of Aitape and thereafter the mountains reach down almost to the beach. North from the Torricellis a series of rivers flow rapidly to the sea, all of them subject to sudden flooding. To the south the streams run into the Sepik, a huge river navigable for some 300 miles by vessels drawing about 10 feet of water. Between these south-flowing streams lie a series of steep heavily-timbered ridges and spurs; round Maprik, however, they become slightly less rugged and there are wide areas of kunai grasslands.

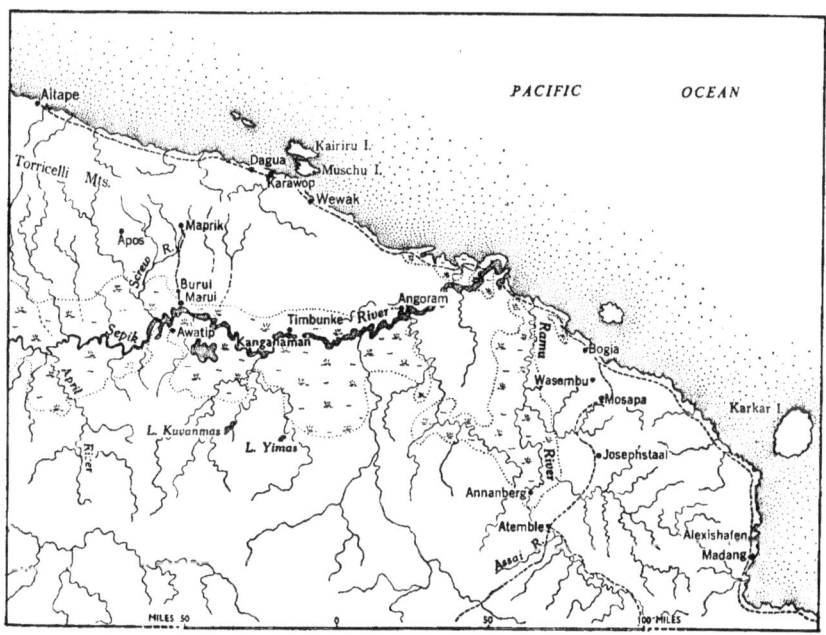

Along the narrow coastal plain between the base of the mountains and the shore the tracks ran along the edge of the beach or a little distance inland, and the surface was often either loose sand or muddy quagmire. In heavy rain the rivers flooded swiftly and violently and swept down great pieces of driftwood which could break through low-level bridges. Only men on foot could move in the mountains rising abruptly on the southern flank. Often the tops of the spurs leading into these ranges were only a few feet wide and offered a multitude of sites for defensive positions exceedingly difficult for infantry to attack or for artillery to range on to.

There were a few miles of motor road in the neighbourhood of Aitape and Wewak and a motor road between Marui and Maprik, which before the war had been an administrative centre and the site of an airfield. In the coastal area the population was sparse but the fertile hill country south of the Torricellis was fairly thickly populated, its many villages being connected by a network of foot tracks.

In this area in October 1944 was deployed the *XVIII Japanese Army*, greatly depleted after its defeat by the Australians in the long campaign in which it was driven westward from Lae and Salamaua in 1943 and early 1944, and by the repulse in July 1944 of its attack on the American garrison protecting the airfield and harbour of Aitape. The Australian Intelligence staffs believed in October that the *XVIII Army* had dwindled to about 30,000. (The true figure was about 35,000.) Lieut-General Adachi's army headquarters were known to be some miles west of Wewak. About 2,000 base troops and infantry were believed to be on Kairiru and Muschu Islands. The *51st Division* (Lieut-General Hidemitsu Nakano) was thought to be deployed in the coastal area from the Sepik to about Karawop; the *20th Division* (Lieut-General Masutaro Nakai) about the But and Dagua airfields and inland to the Maprik area; the *41st Division* (Lieut-General Goro Mano) forward of the Anumb River from the coast to Balif, where its headquarters were established. It was believed that some 3,000 base troops had been dispersed in small groups in the mountains east of the *20th Division's* area with instructions to live off the country.

Broadly speaking the 6th Australian Division considered that it faced three depleted Japanese divisions each reduced to about the strength of a reinforced brigade group. The Australians knew, however, that they themselves were far better equipped, particularly with heavy weapons. They were well fed, and had excellent medical services, and would have fairly strong air support and probably a moderate amount of naval support. The Japanese, on the other hand, were short of food, and many were sick. They had no air or naval forces and there was no hope of any arriving.

The 3rd Base Sub-Area, commanded by Lieut-Colonel J. T. Lang, was to provide a base for the 6th Division, and a reconnaissance party from this unit arrived at Aitape on 15th September. Transports carrying supplies and part of the unit arrived between 12th and 15th October, and when the 6th Division itself began to arrive the base was ready to serve them.[1] Because of the shortage of ships and the means of unloading them— a shortage that would hamper the operations for months—the division could be only trickled into Aitape. Three months and a half elapsed between the arrival of the advanced party and the arrival of the last

---

[1] The 3rd Base Sub-Area at this stage included 36 units and detachments ranging in size from the 17th Works Company, 484 strong, to a Field Security Detachment of three men. Among the units were: the 2/11th General Hospital, 3rd/14th Field Ambulance, 19th Ordnance Depot, 15th Mobile Laundry, Docks Operating Company, 127th Brigade Workshops, 126th General Transport Company.

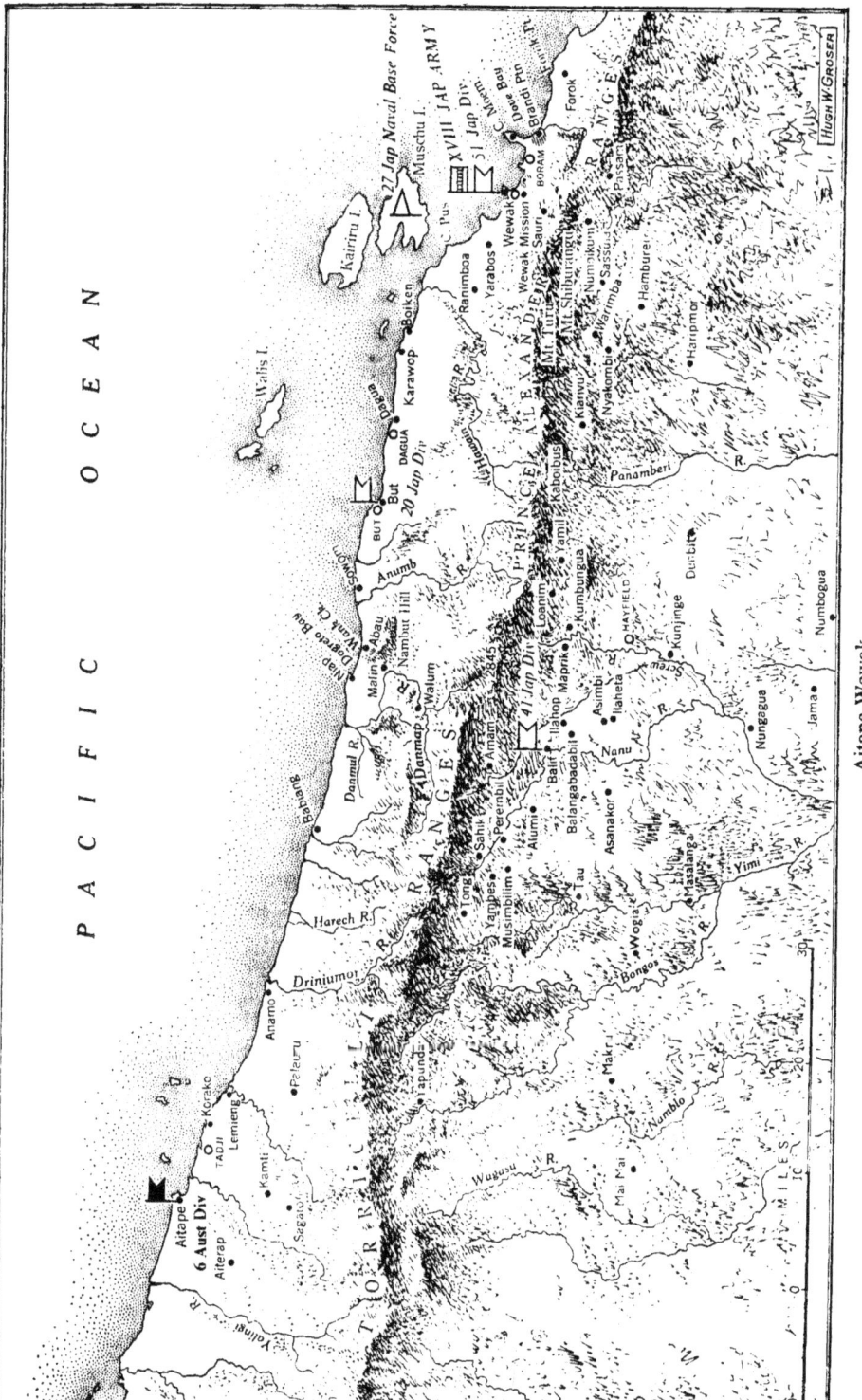

Aitape–Wewak

fighting units. G.H.Q. allocated ships piecemeal to the task. The first was the *Gorgon*, which left Brisbane with base troops on 4th October. Thereafter one ship arrived at Aitape on 19th October, two on 22nd October (with the 2/6th Cavalry (Commando) Regiment and others), one on 23rd October, one on 5th November, one on the 6th, one on the 11th, two on the 12th. By that time the 19th Brigade and a good part of the divisional troops had arrived. The whole 19th Brigade had arrived by 19th November, the 17th Brigade by 7th December and the 16th by 31st December.

The 6th Division—the senior formation of the A.I.F.—had fought in Cyrenaica and Greece in 1940 and 1941 but since then had not been in action as a complete division. In the intervening three years and a half most of its units had seen much fighting both in the Middle East and New Guinea, but some had not been in battle since Crete in May 1941. Five of its battalions had fought in Crete; two, and the divisional cavalry, in Syria. For four months in 1942 the division had ceased to exist; part of it was in Ceylon, part in Australia, and its commander and staff were controlling Northern Territory Force. Its 16th Brigade fought in Papua in 1942 and its 17th Brigade in the Wau-Salamaua operations in 1943. The 19th Brigade spent many months as part of Northern Territory Force and had not yet fought against Japanese. The divisional commander, Major-General Stevens, and two of the infantry brigadiers—R. King of the 16th and Martin[2] of the 19th—had not been in action in New Guinea. Stevens had led a brigade in the Syrian campaign; King a battalion in Cyrenaica, Greece and Syria; Martin a battalion at Giarabub and in Tobruk. The third brigade commander, M. J. Moten, however, had led his brigade during the long and exacting Wau-Salamaua operations of 1943.

In all battalions a substantial number and in some a majority of the officers and a small percentage of the other ranks had served in this division since 1939, and most of Stevens' general and administrative staff were in that category. His G.S.O.1, Lieut-Colonel J. A. Bishop, had served on a brigade staff in North Africa, Greece and Syria, and in 1943 had commanded the 2/27th Battalion in the Ramu Valley. Lieut-Colonel Murphy,[3] his senior administrative officer, was a former regular soldier who had retired in 1923, joined the A.I.F. as a lieutenant in 1940 and, in two years, had become a lieut-colonel. He had served in the Middle East and had come to the 6th Division after twelve months as an instructor at the Senior Staff School.[4]

---

[2] Brig J. E. G. Martin, CBE, DSO, ED, QX6049. CO 2/9 Bn 1939-41; Comd 19 Bde 1941-45. Civil engineer; of Rockhampton, Qld; b. Brisbane, 17 Apr 1904.

[3] Lt-Col W. C. Murphy, OBE, NX354. 2/2 Fd Regt; DAQMG I Corps 1941-42; AA&QMG 6 Div 1942-45. Advertising manager; of Willoughby, NSW; b. Melbourne, 28 Feb 1901.

[4] The senior principal appointments on the staff of the 6th Division in December 1944 were: *GOC* Maj-Gen J. E. S. Stevens; *GSO1* Lt-Col J. A. Bishop; *GSO2* Maj E. Logan; *Snr LO* Maj N. M. Symington; *AA&QMG* Lt-Col W. C. Murphy; *DAAG* Maj D. S. I. Burrows; *DAQMG* Maj C. V. I. Barnden; *Legal Officer* Maj J. R. Nosworthy; *ADMS* Col H. M. Fisher; *ADOS* Lt-Col C. R. Thomson; *CEME* Lt-Col W. H. Mence. The CRA was Brig J. Reddish, the CO Sigs Lt-Col L. N. Tribolet and the COASC Lt-Col J. Talbot.

Air support was to be given by No. 71 Wing, R.A.A.F., commanded by Wing Commander Cooper[5] (but after 27th March by Group Captain Hancock[6]). It included Nos. 7, 8 and 100 Squadrons, equipped with Beauforts and had been operating in support of the American forces at Aitape. Tactical reconnaissance was to be performed by one flight of No. 4 Squadron with Boomerang and Wirraway aircraft.[7] Support was also to be given by aircraft from the American Combat Replacement and Training Centre at Nadzab. Limited numbers of supply aircraft were allotted, as will be recorded later.

The instructions which General Blamey gave to General Sturdee in August have been mentioned earlier, with their indication that in all New Guinea areas the Australian garrisons would be more active than the American garrisons had been. In consequence General Sturdee on 18th October issued to General Stevens an operation instruction in which he defined the division's role thus:

(a) To defend airfield and radar installations in the Aitape-Tadji area;
(b) To prevent movement westward of Japanese forces in the area and seize every opportunity for the destruction of these forces;
(c) To give maximum help to A.I.B. and Angau units in the area in their tasks of gaining Intelligence, establishing patrol bases and protecting the native population.

These A.I.B. and Angau units had been active in the Sepik-Aitape triangle since the time of the landing of American forces at Aitape in April 1944, and the 6th Division came into an area where, from the outset, practically all the deep patrolling had been done by groups of Australians.

In the Aitape area, prior to the arrival of the Division (said the report of the 6th Division), Angau long-range patrols operated without troop support and, for their own protection, inaugurated a type of guerilla warfare. Selected village natives called "sentries" were taught to use grenades and Japanese rifles. The sentries, besides furnishing Intelligence . . . accounted for large numbers of enemy.

This system was continued. As each area was freed the sentries were rewarded and returned to their villages.

The plan for the relief of XI American Corps provided that the corps headquarters and a regiment of the 32nd Division should depart on 10th September, the 31st Division and the remainder of the 32nd on 10th October, and the 43rd Division and 112th Cavalry Regiment on 10th November. Actually the last American troops were not taken off until later than that.

As mentioned, the first Australian fighting unit to arrive at Aitape was the 2/6th Cavalry (Commando) Regiment (Lieut-Colonel Hennessy[8])

---

[5] W Cdr E. W. Cooper, AFC. Comd 73 Sqn 1943, 7 Sqn 1944, 71 Wing 1944-45. Wholesale fruit merchant; of Ashfield, NSW; b. Summer Hill, NSW, 29 Mar 1915.

[6] Air Marshal Sir Valston Hancock, KBE, CB, DFC. Comd 1 Bombing and Air Gunnery School 1940-42; Director of Plans, Allied Air HQ 1942-43; SOA Western Area 1943-44; Comd 100 Sqn and later 71 Wing 1945. AOC Malaya 1957-59; Chief of Air Staff since 1961. Regular air force officer; b. Perth, 31 May 1907.

[7] After 19th March when this flight departed the Beauforts did this work until 18th April when a detachment of No. 5 Squadron arrived.

[8] Lt-Col E. C. Hennessy, DSO, MC, NX8676. 6 Cav Regt; CO 2/6 Cav (Cdo) Regt 1944-45. Of Pine Rocks, via Orange, NSW; b. Lithgow, NSW, 8 Sep 1910.

and, pending the transfer of command to General Stevens, General Sturdee, with the concurrence of the American commander, instructed Hennessy to relieve the American outpost at Babiang and assist the Angau patrols farther forward. The 2/6th Cavalry (Commando) Regiment as a unit had not served in New Guinea before but contained many who had, having absorbed in a reorganisation one of the old Independent companies—the 2/7th, now the 2/7th Commando Squadron.

The 43rd American Division, which now formed the main part of the Aitape garrison, was maintaining standing patrols at Aiterap, Kamti and Palauru as well as Babiang. It had two companies forward of the Driniumor River and the remainder of the division either lightly manning the "main line of resistance" (or perimeter defences) or training. At this stage the A.I.B. had patrols based at Mai Mai and Makru and there was an Angau patrol at the headwaters of the Harech River and another at Yapunda.

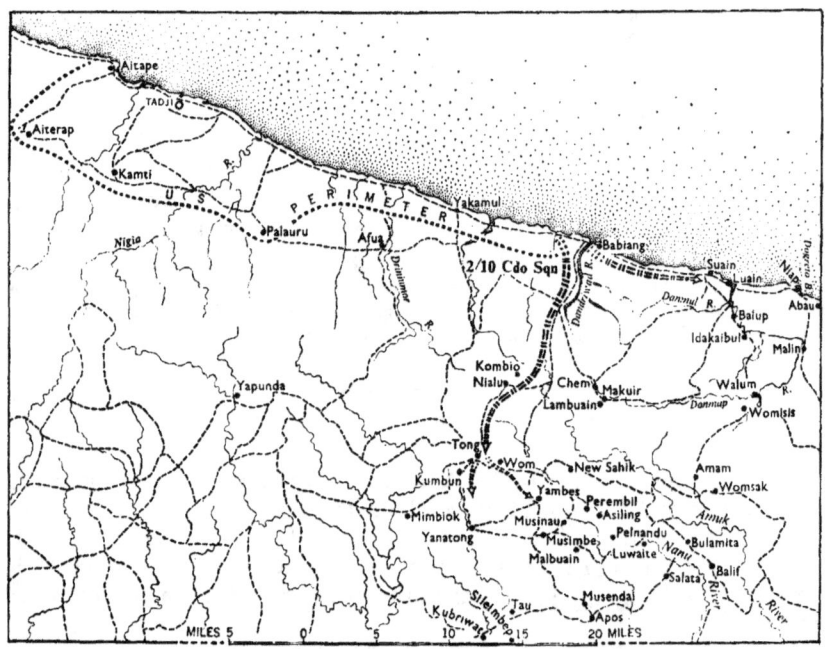

Advance to Yambes and the Danmap, October-December

Little information was available to the division from American sources (wrote Stevens later) as the Americans had had no real contact with the enemy since . . . July and August 1944. It appeared, however, that no organised Japanese force was in the coastal area west of Babiang. Inland and south of the Torricelli Mountains an Angau patrol had twice been driven out of Tong and there was clear evidence that a considerable enemy force was moving westwards. It was considered, therefore, that the enemy had moved a large proportion of his forces inland in order to gain control of the valuable food producing areas there. Several of the main north-south tracks were evidently being used as lines of communication between their coastal and inland forces, the most westerly being the track Abau, Malin, Walum, Amam.[9]

With the object of supplementing his information about the enemy Stevens decided that from the outset there should be vigorous patrolling. Thus, on 27th October, the 2/10th Commando Squadron (Major Wray[1]) relieved a company of the 172nd American Regiment at the outpost at Babiang, at the mouth of the Dandriwad, and, with the help of natives, built a new camp. Thence patrols were carried out each day. On 1st November one of these, at Suain village 10 miles to the east, found 12 dead Japanese who appeared to have died of starvation. On 2nd November a new phase opened when a patrol of six officers and 30 others under Captain Short[2] set out along the Old German Road—the road travelling along or near the shore to Wewak and originally formed during the German possession of this part of New Guinea—with the task of clearing the coastal area as far east as the Danmap River and establishing a base there. It discovered that throughout the area Japanese were moving about in small groups, sometimes unarmed. At Suain Plantation early on the 3rd three were surprised while cooking a meal and killed. A few minutes later two well-equipped Japanese were encountered and one was killed and one escaped. Beyond Suain village two Japanese, only one of them armed, were surrounded and captured. That day and the next other parties were seen; altogether the patrol saw about 40 Japanese, killed 11 for certain and probably 2 more, and had only one of its own men wounded. The fact that the Japanese were surprised at nearly every encounter suggested that they were outpost groups who had been wandering about the area unmolested for so long that they had become careless.

On 3rd November another ambitious patrol set out. It was guided by Captain Cole[3] of Angau and included Captain Woodhouse[4] of the commando squadron, seven other ranks of the squadron, and some native police, and its task was to examine the possibility of establishing a base with a dropping area and landing strip for light aircraft near Yasuar Mission at Tong, deep in the Torricellis. The patrol was in touch with native sentries posted about Kombio, Wom and Yambes and gained a good knowledge of the enemy's dispositions; Yasuar Mission was suitable as a squadron base but the nearest area in which a landing ground could be made was found to be eight hours away.

On 10th November, after the patrol had been at Yasuar Mission for two days, natives reported that Japanese patrols were about, and on the morning of the 12th eight Japanese emerged from the jungle and began advancing on the mission where the Australians, forewarned, were manning their

---

[9] 6th Australian Division Report on Operations Aitape-Wewak Campaign, 26 Oct 44-13 Sep 45.
[1] Maj C. H. W. Wray, NX12264. 6 Cav Regt; OC 2/10 Cdo Sqn. Farmer; of Maclean, NSW; b. Maclean, 14 Nov 1915.
[2] Capt L. T. Short, SX11735. 6 Cav Regt and 2/10 Cdo Sqn. Insurance inspector; of Westbourne Park, SA; b. Adelaide, 17 Oct 1912.
[3] Capt R. R. Cole, MC, NGX46; Angau. Patrol officer; of Ashfield, NSW; b. Dubbo, NSW, 4 Nov 1914.
[4] Capt M. C. Woodhouse, VX8346. 6 Cav Regt and 2/10 Cdo Sqn. Bank officer; of Brighton, Vic; b. Kialla, NSW, 26 Jul 1908.

weapon-pits. All eight were killed. The patrol then withdrew and was back at Babiang on the 14th.

Meanwhile between the 7th and 10th Captain Welsh's[5] troop of the 2/10th Squadron set out with the task of destroying any enemy west of the Danmap area and in the mountain ridges above the German Road. Because the going was so difficult and the available carriers could not cope, the patrol concentrated on the coastal area where it killed four Japanese, including a captain, and captured a prisoner, weapons, and many documents, without loss to itself.

Such patrols continued. On the 10th a Japanese officer and a Chinese coolie surrendered to a small patrol. On the 15th a group of 32 under Short, probing towards Balup, engaged a Japanese party for 45 minutes, and drove it off killing 6 (but losing Trooper Le Brun,[6] killed). On the 19th a patrol of 57 led by Lieutenant Mackinnon,[7] inland from Luain, killed 10 Japanese, and captured three; and observed an air strike on the east side of the Danmap River.

Some of the Japanese killed or captured were in good condition but most were ill-nourished, and their main occupation seemed to be to find food; on the 20th a patrol found "positive evidence of cannibalism" in the foothills south of Suain. Some men were unarmed, and often they were living in twos and threes near sago swamps. The prisoners, who all belonged to the *41st Division,* gave much information. The area as far east as the Anumb was occupied by the *237th Regiment* then comprising two battalions each about 300 strong. The *238th* and *239th Regiments* in the Womisis area were each from 700 to 1,000 strong. Two prisoners said that some men were so hungry that they were eating human flesh, and one that he himself had done so. The *20th Division* between the Anumb and But was about 7,000 strong and the *51st Division,* farther east, with headquarters near Wewak, was probably stronger.

Throughout this period the 2/9th Commando Squadron (Captain Boyd[8]) had been manning the observation posts at Palauru, Kamti and Aiterap, where it had relieved a company of the 172nd American Regiment on 27th October, and maintaining frequent patrols from those posts southward over the Torricellis, but without meeting any Japanese. By 30th November the commando squadrons had killed 73 Japanese, found 12 dead, taken 7 prisoners; and had lost one man killed and one wounded.

Meanwhile on 8th November General Stevens had opened his headquarters at Aitape. Already, under an arrangement with the outgoing American commander, he had issued general instructions to his brigades: the 19th was to relieve the regiment of the 43rd American Division on the Driniumor, the 17th was to relieve the units of the 43rd Division that

---

[5] Capt N. B. Welsh, NX16024. 6 Cav Regt and 2/10 Cdo Sqn. Grazier; of Coogee, NSW; b. Tallangatta, Vic, 14 Dec 1909.
[6] Tpr N. S. Le Brun, VX76818; 2/10 Cdo Sqn. Bricklayer; of Richmond, Vic; b. Sorrento, Vic, 24 Apr 1910. Killed in action 15 Nov 1944.
[7] Capt A. G. Mackinnon, TX2133. 6 Cav Regt and 2/10 Cdo Sqn. Farmer; of Conara, Tas; b. Launceston, Tas, 1 May 1916.
[8] Capt D. G. Boyd, NX12295. 6 Cav Regt, 2/9 Cdo Sqn (acting OC 2/10 Cdo Sqn 1945). Articled clerk; of Peak Hill, NSW; b. Belfast, N Ireland, 3 Aug 1911.

were manning the main line of resistance, and the 16th was to be in reserve. On 13th November General Sturdee's instruction, quoted earlier, had been elaborated by one which required Stevens to conduct minor raids and patrols by land, sea and air "within the resources available", with the object of gaining information on which to base plans for future operations and at the same time maintain an offensive spirit in the troops. The relief of the American force was completed on 26th November, and on that day Stevens assumed full command. Three days earlier he had sought approval to undertake two operations too large to be classed as "minor raids and patrols": to cut the enemy's line of communication through Malin-Walum-Womisis-Amam, and to destroy the enemy east of the Danmap River, D-day to be not before 31st December. These proposals were approved by Sturdee on 13th December, by which date the 19th and 17th Brigades had arrived at Aitape. In the background at this stage was always the consideration that it was possible that the division might be needed at short notice to reinforce I Australian Corps, and consequently it could not yet be committed to a major campaign in the Wewak area.

On 27th November General Stevens had issued "Operation Order 1". In it he expressed the opinion that the enemy would defend the Danmap River area to prevent movement along the coast; and, inland, would use harassing patrols to control the Maprik-Tong area for gardening and foraging. The division's tasks (as mentioned) were to protect the airfield and radar stations; to give maximum assistance to Angau and A.I.B. patrols; and to prevent movement westward of the Japanese forces and seize every opportunity for the destruction of those forces. It was with this third task in view that Stevens had sought approval of an operation to cut the enemy's line of communication from Malin to Amam. He ordered that the 19th Brigade, less most of the 2/11th Battalion, but plus two companies of the 2/3rd Machine Gun Battalion, the 53rd Field Battery and other units and detachments, would relieve the 2/6th Commando Regiment at Babiang by 2nd December and maintain contact on the Danmap River, establish a standing patrol at Afua, prevent enemy movement west of the Driniumor and protect the supply base at Yakamul.[9] The 2/6th Commando Regiment would move the 2/7th Squadron to the Tong area, maintain a base there and gain control of the immediate vicinity, patrol southward and try to establish a forward base at Musu.

The 17th Brigade Group, while improving and maintaining the main line of resistance for local defence of Aitape and the Tadji strip, would, when sufficient troops were available, relieve the 2/9th Squadron, reinforce the Angau patrol at Yapunda, and be prepared to relieve the 2/7th Squadron at Tong, and patrol east to Musu, near Asiling.

In divisional reserve with the 16th Brigade, would be the 2/6th Commando Regiment less two squadrons, and "C" Squadron of the 2/4th Armoured Regiment.

---

[9] The brigade would later have under command the 2/9th and 2/10th Commando Squadrons and the 2/3rd Machine Gun Battalion less two companies; and in support the divisional artillery less a battery.

The 2/7th Commando Squadron (Major A. L. Goode) had relieved the 2/10th at Babiang by 25th November and in accordance with the above orders had moved south. On 1st December Captain Fleming's[1] troop of the 2/7th marched from Nialu (where Cole maintained a base for collecting information from native agents) to Yasuar Mission (at Tong), the remainder of the 2/7th Squadron staying at Yakamul. That afternoon, when half the men were digging in and building huts and the others standing to, Japanese opened fire from the jungle, killing one man and wounding Fleming. In the next five hours a trooper was killed and a police boy wounded. Next morning the enemy had gone. Lieutenant Harrop,[2] now in command, sent a request for reinforcement by the rest of the squadron. On the morning of the 4th Colonel Hennessy, Major Goode and eight others arrived at Tong; and Captain Byrne's[3] troop was on the way. Hennessy decided that Tong was tactically a sound position, the squadron headquarters were established there, and at midday the second troop arrived. Next day he ordered the squadron to clear the Kumbun-Yourang area, farther south, place a troop at Yourang, and patrol south-east. Kumbun was occupied unopposed on the 7th.

In the following days the squadron extended its area of control, establishing outposts at Yasile and Yambes. On 11th December an enemy patrol approached the perimeter held by Byrne's troop at Yambes. The Australians held their fire until the Japanese were 35 to 50 yards away, killed 6 and, during the day, 2 more. There were patrol clashes that day and on the 13th. At 1.30 a.m. on the 15th an enemy force of at least 35 attacked. This time the Australians let the leading Japanese come to within three yards of the perimeter then fired with automatic weapons and threw grenades. After pressing the attack for a while the enemy withdrew, dragging away their wounded and about 10 dead.

On 12th December Stevens had issued an order that the 17th Brigade would, as forecast, relieve the 2/7th Squadron at Tong with not less than a company, and patrol south of the Torricellis west of a north-south line through Musu. From Tong it would patrol south to Mimbiok and Yanatong, south-east to Musimbe and establish a base, and then patrol east and establish a base at Musu. The 2/7th Squadron would move to a base at Makuir and reconnoitre a route via Chem to the Dandriwad River and Babiang, establish a forward base on the Danmap about five miles east of Makuir and carry out other reconnaissance.

Thus by the middle of December the commando regiment had probed forward in the coastal sector to the Danmap, over 40 miles from Aitape, and some 20 miles into the Torricellis without encountering very strong bodies of enemy troops. In addition the parties led by Angau officers were maintaining an Intelligence network farther afield in the Torricellis.

---

[1] Capt R. S. Fleming, VX52857. 2/4 and 2/7th Indep Coys, 2/7 Cdo Sqn. Compositor; of Echuca, Vic; b. Cobram, Vic, 29 Dec 1911.

[2] Capt C. O. Harrop, NX71006; 2/7 Cdo Sqn. Petrol depot superintendent; of Bathurst, NSW; b. Formby, Lancs, England, 30 Nov 1911.

[3] Maj E. F. Byrne, MC, NX58832. 2/7 Indep Coy, 2/7 Cdo Sqn; 9/Royal Sussex Regt 1945. Sharebroker's clerk; of Campsie, NSW; b. Campsie, 23 May 1921.

Not only had the forthcoming actions to be fought either along a coastal plain broken at intervals by rivers liable to flooding, or in inaccessible mountains, but the port was unsuited to the steady maintenance of a large force. By November the north-west monsoon was beginning and it would continue until April. The anchorage at Aitape offered practically no protection from the strong winds, and there was a heavy swell offshore and a surf that sometimes was 6 feet high. There were no jetties and all off-loading or loading had to be done with landing craft. Bulldozers and tractors had to be used to hold the larger landing craft on to the beach and prevent them from broaching. "The smaller landing craft could only dash in to the beach, take on a 2½-ton motor truck which was waiting with its engine switched on, back out to a ship, take on 2½ tons of stores, and then beach again momentarily to allow the motor truck to drive ashore. So a landing craft which was capable of carrying about 14 tons of stores could only be loaded each trip with 2½ tons!"[4]

In addition not only was the port equipped with fewer craft than would have been needed to achieve a swift exchange of garrisons, but priority was, rightly, given to the combat-loading of the American formations which were destined for Leyte.

While XIV American Corps was at Aitape it had control of 150 landing craft and in October was using each day 6 L.C.T's, 41 L.C.M's and 20 DUKW's. The initial planning for working the port at Aitape for the 6th Division provided for 6 L.C.T's, run by an Australian platoon, for handling normal maintenance cargo. But in fact a large force had to be embarked and another one disembarked. The American craft did much of this work, but as the American force departed the number of landing craft diminished. By 27th December 30,000 tons of cargo, 270 vehicles and 2,000 men were awaiting unloading in five transports lying off Aitape, and it was evident that if unloading could not be hastened supplies ashore would be exhausted in the first or second week of January. Sturdee sent a signal to Advanced L.H.Q. to this effect, and Advanced L.H.Q. to G.H.Q., which expressed concern but directed that priority must still be given to the forward movement of the Americans.

By 2nd February only seven days' rations remained at Aitape. As a result of an appeal G.H.Q. directed that priority be given to unloading a transport carrying Australian rations. On 3rd February a company of the 593rd American Boat and Shore Regiment arrived and unloading steadily improved until by April there was no undue delay in getting supplies ashore.

---

[4] "The Wewak Campaign", by Major-General J. E. S. Stevens, *United Service*, November 1947.

CHAPTER 12

ACROSS THE DANMAP

THE first contingent of the 17th Brigade now set out into the Torricellis, where its first task would be to make deep patrols into the Japanese-occupied area. With the object of firmly securing the Tong area whence General Stevens intended to launch an advance early in 1945, Brigadier Moten formed "Piper Force", which included two companies of the 2/5th Battalion and was commanded by Major I. H. McBride. It was to relieve the 2/7th Commando Squadron, ensure that the Tong area was cleared of the enemy, patrol to Mimbiok-Yanatong, and establish bases at Musimbe and Musu near Asiling. Moten instructed McBride to keep his force

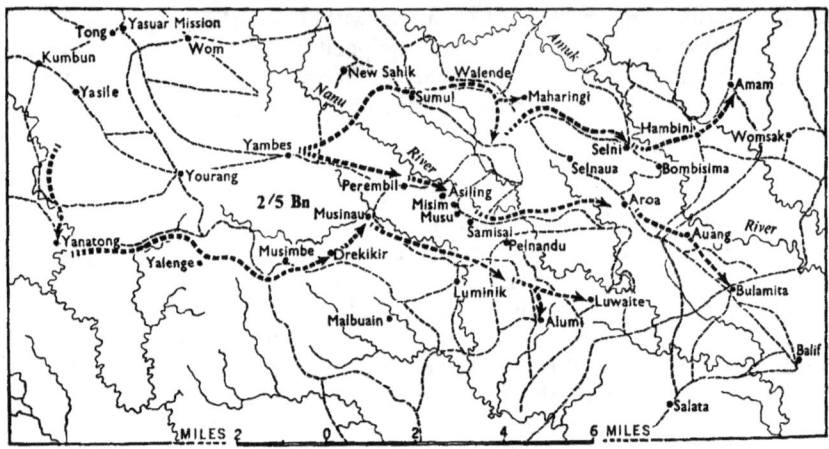

2/5th Battalion, December-January

mobile, make good use of air support, and not become involved in set-piece attacks. On 16th December Piper Force was carried along the coast in vehicles, and next day it set out inland on foot. Despite the sudden flooding of the Harech River it was at Tong by 20th December, and next day had one company at Tong and one based on Yambes.

That day Major Goode of the 2/7th Squadron reported that, except for foraging parties, the area which he had been ordered to patrol had been cleared of the enemy. The squadron had killed 26 Japanese and lost two killed and five wounded; two attached Papuan police had been wounded. The squadron's headquarters were now moved to Lambuain and it began its new task: to clear the Walum area. Walum village was occupied on 30th December after clashes in which several Japanese were killed. Documents captured by the squadron that day indicated that the main enemy line of communication from the coast to Balif was via Walum-Womisis-Womsak.

The enemy groups in the area now entered by Piper Force were apparently engaged mainly in foraging, and at first they moved out, keeping 24 hours ahead of the Australians. No contact was made until the 27th when a patrol of five led by Lieutenant Doneley[1] ambushed 22 Japanese near Perembil and killed 15; Doneley was wounded but carried on and covered the withdrawal of the patrol. The Musimbe area was occupied on the 28th and Musinau on the 29th. Eight more Japanese were killed by patrols up to 1st January. That day the commander of the 2/5th, Lieut-Colonel A. W. Buttrose, arrived, and in the next few days the remainder of the battalion, less one company, reached the area. Piper Force had succeeded in clearing the enemy from the country west of a north-south line through Yambes. Now the 2/5th Battalion was close to the enemy's main defences on a line New Sahik-Perembil-Malbuain-Apos, and faced two Japanese regiments which together were about 1,100 strong.

Meanwhile, in the coastal sector the 19th Brigade had moved forward in accordance with Stevens' orders of 26th November that it should relieve the 2/7th Commando Squadron, clear the enemy from the area west of the Danmap, and concentrate round Babiang and Suain in preparation for operations east of the river. A company of the 2/4th Battalion had therefore relieved the 2/7th Squadron at Suain and Babiang on the 29th and 30th November. In the next 16 days patrols clashed with small groups of Japanese on seven occasions, and killed 28 without loss to themselves. Some of these Japanese were sick and hungry and poorly armed, and some in good condition with their arms and equipment well cared for. About one-quarter of the Japanese who were encountered carried swords. These early patrols made the useful discovery that the presence of groups of Japanese who were living off the land could be detected by the smell of rotting sac sac which became noticeable from a distance of 100 to 200 yards.

On Albu Creek (wrote the diarist of the 2/4th) one party of six Japs was found living in small lean-to shelters in the most appalling conditions of filth and squalor with nothing but a very small quantity of sac sac in the way of food. Yet no more than 400 yards away the same patrol came upon a second party whose quarters were spotlessly clean, equipment laid out in inspection order, mess tins and water bottles polished, and with plenty of food including tinned milk (American), rice, a dark brown paste of Jap make, also tinned, and grain of an unrecognised type.

On 10th December two emaciated Indian prisoners of war were brought in by a patrol. They had been making their way through the bush from Wewak for 45 days. In the following months the arrival of escaped Indian soldiers, brought to New Guinea by the Japanese as labourers, was to become a fairly frequent occurrence.

On 14th December Stevens gave the 19th Brigade a larger task: to capture a line from Abau east of Dogreto Bay to Malin some four miles

---

[1] Lt A. R. Doneley, MC, QX6681; 2/5 Bn. Grazier; of Brisbane; b. Toowoomba, Qld, 18 Apr 1918. Killed in action 6 Jun 1945.

due south, and destroy the enemy between the Danmap and that line.[2] It was estimated that there were some 700 enemy troops mostly of the *237th Regiment* in the area to be captured and perhaps 2,000 to 3,000 in the inland area from Malin to Amam, these, as mentioned, being of the *238th* and *239th Regiments*. Broadly the 19th Brigade's task was to deny the enemy the route from the coast to the Maprik area via Walum.

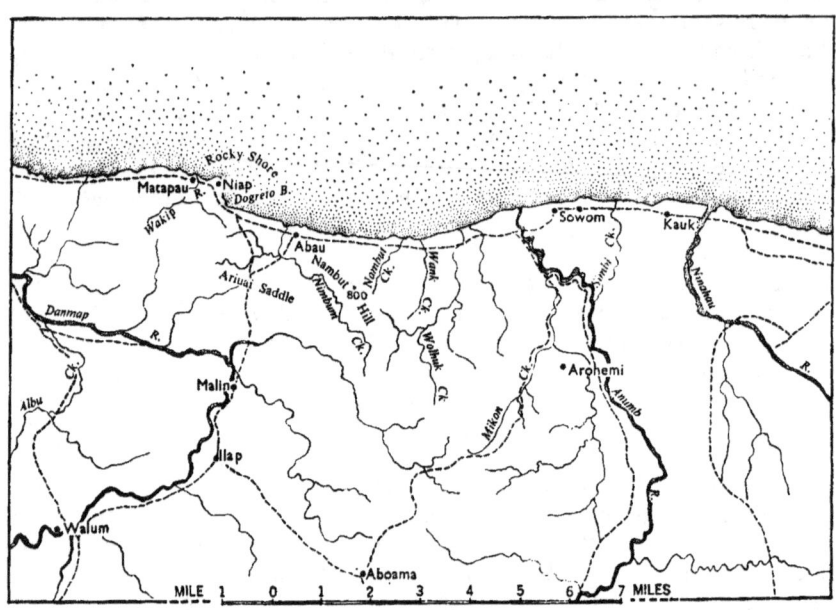

Brigadier Martin ordered the 2/4th to cross the Danmap to seize the ground east of the river, as far as Rocky Point, and to establish a patrol base at Idakaibul to cover the main approaches from Walum and Malin. The 2/11th would then pass through and advance along the coast to Abau, and the 2/8th would take over the Idakaibul base and move east along the upper Danmap to secure the line Ariuai Saddle-Malin. Malin would become a dropping ground for airborne supplies, but, until it was reached, progress would be governed by the number of carriers, then very limited, and the speed at which a road was built east from the Danmap.

By 17th December the main body of the 2/4th Battalion was at Suain, with a company at Idakaibul and one at Babiang. That day at dawn Captain Smith's[3] company crossed the Danmap at the mouth and Smith, with one platoon, reached Lazy Creek. Then a second platoon moved through to Rocky Point, beyond which from 20 to 30 Japanese were

---

[2] The 19th Brigade Group at this stage included its three battalions, a detachment of the 2/4th Armoured Regiment, and the 2/3rd Field Regiment. On 28th December the 2/3rd Machine Gun Battalion less two companies came under command, and on 4th January the 2/6th Commando Regiment.

[3] Capt E. P. A. Smith, MBE, MC, NX5483; 2/4 Bn. Oil company representative; of Cowra, NSW; b. Grafton, NSW, 11 Aug 1914.

seen on the beach and were fired on by the artillery. In the day 18 Japanese were killed and three captured, one Australian being wounded. Next day Major Pegg,[4] commanding the forward companies, led one company to Rocky Point while Smith's moved back to the base through the foothills where it encountered enemy posts, and, in a fight at an ammunition dump just south of Lazy Creek, lost 2 killed and 3 wounded, but killed 7. Captain Cohen's[5] company crossed the Danmap next day and advanced against this enemy group, now estimated to be about 40 strong. It was well led also and ambushed the leading Australian platoon and killed five of them. On the 20th the Danmap was in flood and flowing at 10 to 12 knots. Cohen's company broke contact while the artillery harassed the Japanese, and next day, which was hot and clear, Beaufort bombers bombarded them.

On the 21st the enemy's position was again accurately attacked from the air and the Japanese began to move south, but ran into a standing ambush maintained by Lieutenant Healey's[6] platoon, which killed 28 out of perhaps 40 Japanese and lost one man killed—Private Paff,[7] who had accounted single-handed for a machine-gunner and four riflemen. Next day the 2/11th, which had now come forward, was given the task of keeping in touch with the enemy round Niap, while the 2/4th, with two machine-gun companies under command, defended the area from Lazy Creek to the mouth of the Danmap.

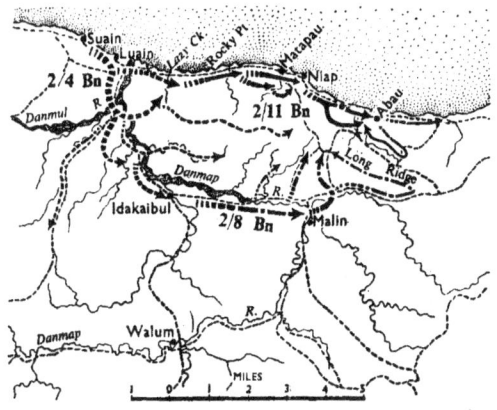

19th Brigade, 17th December-23rd January

Patrolling from Lazy Creek the 2/11th had two sharp clashes with the enemy force west of Niap on 30th and 31st December, three Australians and 11 Japanese being killed. At Matapau village, early on 2nd January, from 30 to 35 Japanese attacked the perimeter of Captain Royce's[8] company. Artillery fire was brought down and the Japanese withdrew leaving six dead. This was the beginning of five days of sharp fighting against Japanese who seemed determined to stop the advance along the Old German Road.

---

[4] Maj F. J. Pegg, NX47; 2/4 Bn. Accountant; of Homebush, NSW; b. Petersham, NSW, 28 May 1912.
[5] Capt P. R. Cohen, QX1258; 2/4 Bn. Bank officer; of Toowoomba, Qld; b. Toowoomba, 6 Jan 1914.
[6] Lt D. G. Healey, MC, NX5992; 2/4 Bn. Bank officer; of Wagga Wagga, NSW; b. Mosman, NSW, 27 Apr 1919. Died 5 Jul 1949.
[7] Pte T. E. Paff, NX69183; 2/4 Bn. Dairy farmer; of Krambach, NSW; b. Nabiac, NSW, 8 Apr 1921. Killed in action 21 Dec 1944.
[8] Maj G. E. Royce, MC, WX248; 2/11 Bn. Accountant; of Claremont, WA; b. Katanning, WA, 15 Oct 1917.

As soon as the enemy's attack had been repulsed Royce's company pushed forward along the road to a spur whence the artillery observer, Captain Lovegrove,[9] might direct fire. A platoon crossed the little Wakip River at 10.20 a.m. but came under fire from Japanese on the steep-sided spur. The infantry withdrew and accurate artillery fire was brought down. At 2.10 p.m. the spur was occupied and from it Lovegrove directed fire on a pocket of Japanese so close that he had "to almost whisper his orders into the phone". In the day 14 Japanese were killed, and two Australians killed and five wounded, of whom four remained on duty. Next day, and on the 4th and 5th, there was sharp fighting round the spur and towards Niap, and on the 6th, after a strike by 11 bombers and a bombardment by the artillery, a platoon attacked across the Wakip but was held by the resolute enemy pocket at Niap. Later in the morning three tanks and a bulldozer were sent forward along the beach whence the bulldozer cut a track to the Old German Road. The tanks advanced along it, they and the infantry moved forward 500 yards, and at 4.42 p.m. Lieutenant Dewar's[1] platoon entered Niap.

Next morning Major Dowling's[2] company joined Dewar (who was mortally wounded later that morning) and thrust towards Dogreto Bay, but met heavy fire and withdrew. On the evening of the 9th Lieutenant Mortimer,[3] commanding the forward platoon, reported that he heard noises which suggested that the enemy was withdrawing, and next morning it was found that he was right. However, the Japanese did not pull back far, and a patrol moving round the slopes above Dogreto Bay was fired on. On the 11th at 10.15 a.m. a platoon and two tanks took up the advance, but the tanks were halted by difficult ground. On 10th January Lieutenant Birrell[4] of Angau led six native constables on a deep patrol up Ulagamagin Creek which reaches the sea in the Matapau area. On the 14th and 15th patrols of the 2/11th probed forward to the slopes above Abau. On the 18th Captain Greenway's[5] company made a flanking movement through the foothills to Nimbum Creek and eventually moved into a position south of Abau whence on the 20th a platoon entered Abau without opposition. By the 23rd patrols had moved as far as "Rocky Foreshore". In its advance from Lazy Creek to beyond Abau the battalion had lost 20 killed and 29 wounded and had killed 118 Japanese.

Meanwhile the 2/8th Battalion (Lieut-Colonel Howden[6]) had been thrusting into the foothills. By 28th December it had been concentrated

---

[9] Capt H. A. Lovegrove, MC, WX3467; 2/3 Fd Regt. Assurance inspector; of Mount Lawley, WA; b. Tambellup, WA, 28 Dec 1912.

[1] Lt R. Dewar, WX7410; 2/11 Bn. Printer; of Cottesloe, WA; b. Subiaco, WA, 14 Mar 1915. Killed in action 7 Jan 1945.

[2] Maj L. E. Dowling, MBE, WX274; 2/11 Bn. Regular soldier; b. Outtrim, Vic, 7 Dec 1910.

[3] Lt W. A. Mortimer, WX983; 2/11 Bn. Truck driver; of Subiaco, WA; b. Elsternwick, Vic, 18 Aug 1916.

[4] Lt J. A. Birrell, MC, NGX355. NGVR and Angau. Bank officer; of Emu Plains, NSW; b. Tenterfield, NSW, 12 Dec 1920.

[5] Capt G. J. Greenway, MC, WX976; 2/11 Bn. Station overseer; of Murchison River, WA; b. Cottesloe, WA, 4 Oct 1903.

[6] Lt-Col W. S. Howden, DSO, ED, VX14047. 2/14 Bn 1940-42; CO 2/8 Bn 1943-45. Bank officer; of Caulfield, Vic; b. Caulfield, 7 Dec 1906.

at Luain, but shortage of native carriers prevented it from maintaining more than a company at Idakaibul, and the planned advance along the Danmap towards Malin had to be delayed. Until 5th January, however, patrols based on Idakaibul and "Fork" (the junction of the eastward-flowing Danmul with the westward-flowing Danmap) patrolled widely. By the 5th enough carriers were available to allow the establishment of patrol bases farther east; the 2/9th Commando Squadron (Major T. G. Nisbet) was placed under Howden's command to patrol the hills south of the Danmap and make contact with the 2/7th Squadron based on Walum. On 8th January the leading company of the 2/8th Battalion entered Malin without opposition. In the first eight days of January the battalion's patrols had killed 23 Japanese without loss to themselves.

In the next three weeks the 2/8th Battalion and the flanking commando squadron patrolled in the rugged country between Nimbum Creek in the north to the upper Danmap in the south, exchanging written signals with brigade headquarters by carrier pigeon. Generally these skilful patrols surprised such groups of Japanese as they came across. On 17th January, however, a commando patrol under Lieutenant Carins[7] met a stronger enemy group and lost one killed and one wounded before it was extricated. Only in one area was effective resistance encountered by the 2/8th Battalion. On Long Ridge on 19th January a patrol under Lieutenant Turnbull,[8] an enterprising and skilful leader, came upon a well-armed party and in a fight lasting an hour and 40 minutes killed 9 and had 4 of their own men wounded. Next day Captain Diffey[9] led out two platoons and an artillery observer, but found that the enemy had hurriedly departed, leaving their dead. On the 24th, however, at the same point a patrol came under heavy fire. One party, then a second and then a third were sent forward to support the patrol and, finally, to extricate it. The Japanese were active and aggressive and began to encircle the covering force. At dusk Diffey took out a platoon to cover a general withdrawal, but before it arrived the whole forward group had withdrawn under cover of darkness. In the long fight the Australians lost 3 killed and 5 wounded and killed 17 Japanese. Captured papers showed that the Japanese belonged to a raiding detachment under orders to advance by way of Long Ridge and retake Malin.

Stevens had now ordered the 16th Brigade to relieve the 19th and it began preparing to move forward. On 21st January there had been an ominous flooding of the Danmap. That day the rising water broke a bridge that the 2/2nd Field Company was building and swept three men out to sea. They were rescued. On the 25th Lieut-Colonel I. Hutchison's 2/3rd Battalion, which was to relieve the 2/8th, moved up to Luain and along the Danmap to Idakaibul. "The mud, the gloomy atmosphere, and

---

[7] Capt T. J. Carins, MC, TX496; 2/9 Cdo Sqn. Student; of Longford, Tas; b. Longford, 28 May 1919.
[8] Lt A. W. J. Turnbull, MC, NX138188; 2/8 Bn. Regular soldier; b. Meekatharra, WA, 19 Jul 1922.
[9] Maj S. C. Diffey, MC, VX6596; 2/8 Bn. Farmer; of Springhurst, Vic; b. Springhurst, 2 Apr 1917.

the prevailing smell of rotting vegetation and sweating bodies strongly recall the Owen Stanley campaign," wrote the battalion diarist. On the 26th the 2/3rd relieved two companies of the 2/8th, but further relief was interrupted next day by disastrous floods. Heavy rain fell almost continuously that day and the rivers rose fast. The machine-gun platoon of the 2/3rd soon found itself on an island in the flooded Danmap near Mima Creek with 30 yards of swirling water on either side. By 9.45 p.m. the river was 12 feet over its banks, the island was covered, the water was roaring so loudly that even shouted conversation was inaudible. It was impossible to take lines across. Trees up to 4 feet in diameter and 60 feet high were being swept past at what seemed like 30 miles an hour. At 10.15 the river had risen another 8 feet.

By watchers on the banks the machine-gunners had last been seen high in trees. The river fell rapidly and by 11 p.m. was down to high-water mark. Meanwhile the almost completed bridge over the Danmap and six other bridges had been swept away and others damaged. A box girder bridge over the Dandriwad at Babiang vanished completely. "A heart breaking scene of devastation," recorded the 2/8th Field Company; the natives told the sappers that there had not been such a flood for 100 years.

The first man of the machine-gun platoon of the 2/3rd to report next morning was Corporal Parkinson,[1] naked, cold, mosquito-bitten, and with a damaged foot, but "still wearing his broad, infectious grin". He had been the last to leave the island. By 10 p.m., he said, the water had covered the island, and large trees were crashing downstream. They then decided to make a break. Several floated off on a big log and others left independently. There was no panic and everyone was in high spirits. Parkinson, a strong swimmer, reached the shore some hundreds of yards downstream where he waited until dawn.

An hour later a second survivor arrived in the battalion area. He could not swim but had been washed ashore on a log. Next came Private Gill,[2] who had been sandwiched between two logs while another passed over his head. He was cut and bruised. Lieutenant Fearnside,[3] the platoon commander (clothed and with compass and pistol), and three others, reached the bank opposite to that on which the battalion was camped. After unsuccessful efforts to get a line across to them, a message was shouted across the river that they were to return to Idakaibul to refit, which they did. Later others arrived back safely, but seven had been drowned. That morning the island was no longer to be seen and great rocks which had not been there the previous day were standing out of the stream.

In the 2/9th Commando Squadron's area heavy rain began on the afternoon of 27th January and by 10.30 p.m. the river had risen 20 feet

---

[1] Sgt F. F. Parkinson, NX7955; 2/3 Bn. Seasonal worker; of Punchbowl, NSW; b. Tempe, NSW, 7 Jul 1921.

[2] Pte L. W. Gill, NX101327; 2/3 Bn. Labourer; of Mayfield West, NSW; b. Newcastle, NSW, 26 Jan 1922.

[3] Lt G. H. Fearnside, NX15033. 2/13 and 2/3 Bns. Clerk; of Epping, NSW; b. Epping, 26 Apr 1917. See "Death on the Danmap" by G. H. Fearnside, *The Bulletin*, 25th April 1956, pp. 21-3. Author of *Sojourn in Tobruk* (1944).

and carried away all trees on the banks, and the water was approaching the forward weapon-pits. The men drew back to higher ground. Next day the river fell somewhat, and on the 29th a patrol managed to cross it to collect rations at Malin. That afternoon five men from Captain Woodhouse's 2/10th Squadron reached the 2/9th in search of rations, and with news that the troop at Walum had been isolated without food for two days, and four men had been drowned. The flood had swept 19 men away but 15 of these had reached the bank of the river.

The 19th Brigade's intrusion into the area east of the Driniumor caused the Japanese heavy loss. The brigade group killed 434 and captured 13; its own losses were 36 killed and 51 wounded. Captured documents later showed that the advance across the Danmap had just forestalled an enemy plan whereby the *II/237th Battalion* was to occupy the line of the Danmap and advance thence to Luain. It was this force which had fought so hard in the foothills from 17th December onwards.

When Lieut-Colonel Buttrose of the 2/5th Battalion took command in the Torricellis it was believed that the headquarters group of the *41st Japanese Division*, 500 to 600 strong, was around Balif; the *238th Regiment*, about 800 strong, around Perembil; and the *239th Regiment*, 500 to 700 strong, in the Womsak and Salata areas. Buttrose ordered that one company should form a base at Musinau and protect the right flank by pressing eastward and patrolling deep to the south; one should secure, in succession, Perembil, Asiling, Misim and Samisai; and a third should advance through Sumul, Walende, Maharingi and Selnaua. The aim was to secure Musu as a base for future operations.

At Perembil the Japanese occupied a strong position on a razor-back ridge and the only approach was up a steep face. Captain L. A. Cameron's company attacked on 3rd January and drove the enemy out, but that night and next day about 40 Japanese made counter-attacks. In the first of them Private Escreet[4] was caught in open ground, but brought his Bren gun into action and engaged the enemy, continuing to fire although thrice wounded. The enemy were finally driven off leaving 19 dead.

Only one aircraft was available for dropping supplies and on the day Perembil was taken Brigadier Moten signalled Colonel Buttrose that, until supplies improved, he should halt his advance but continue aggressive patrolling. The advance was resumed on 8th January with Asiling now an early objective; it was entered without opposition on the 9th. Moten suggested that Samisai rather than Musu be occupied and used as a base for patrols to the south-east. On 11th January Cameron's company gained Samisai where it was relieved by Captain V. M. Walters', newly arrived. Buttrose now ordered Captain Geer's[5] company on the left to secure Maharingi and this was achieved on the 15th.

---

[4] Pte H. G. Escreet, MM, VX13245; 2/5 Bn. Farm worker; of Traralgon, Vic; b. Traralgon, 19 Mar 1914.

[5] Capt A. S. Geer, VX48670; 2/5 Bn. Transport driver; of Orbost, Vic; b. Moonee Ponds, Vic. 11 Dec 1914. Died 11 Jan 1959.

On 12th January, the supply position having improved, Stevens had told Moten that the policy was "to maintain pressure south of the Torricellis and destroy the enemy at every opportunity". Moten thereupon ordered the 2/5th to establish contact with the commando in the Hambini area and to advance south of the Amuk River, to the Nanu River and to Pelnandu. The objective was the capture of Bulamita as a new advanced base. The advance of the 2/5th was resumed in three columns: I. H. McBride's company on the right was aimed at the Luwaite villages, Walters' in the centre at Bulamita, and Geer's on the left at Bombisima.

Each day from 18th January onwards patrols clashed with parties of Japanese and inflicted losses. Near Auang on the 19th 6 were killed and 2 prisoners taken. On 20th January a group of 60 were encountered at Bulamita and 7 killed including 2 officers; this village was occupied on the 22nd, and next day, after an air strike, patrols found Hambini unoccupied. The Beaufort bombers from Tadji, guided by mortar smoke and radio telephone, were making accurate air strikes ahead of the advancing troops almost every day. On the 23rd two Beauforts collided and crashed; the infantry found the wrecks but only one man out of the 10 in the crews had survived. Next day a patrol of 15 led by Sergeant McGreevy[6] encountered an enemy group about 30 strong east of Bulamita and killed 14. Soon afterwards a Japanese foraging party was ambushed at the captured Japanese position. A strong enemy party then approached. The patrol withdrew through the bush and soon heard the Japanese making a banzai charge on the position they had just left.

Buttrose was now calling down air strikes on the Balif villages, where some 300 Japanese were reported. His battalion was now deep in the enemy's territory, and had by-passed groups of stragglers. On 20th January, for example, five Japanese including a medical officer surrendered to a carrying party north-west of Bulamita, whither battalion headquarters moved on 1st February.

By the end of January the battalion had made 77 patrols and had "expedited the enemy's withdrawal" (as the battalion's report put it) from a belt of mountain country about 12 miles from west to east and about 8 from north to south.

In this period a deep patrol was made by Captain Marshall's[7] "Jockforce", comprising himself, Lieutenant Beenie,[8] and 11 others. It left the 2/5th Battalion at Yambes on 12th January and moved south to Yalenge, Sileimbep, and Wogia. In the Wogia area the natives were hostile, resenting the activities of an A.I.B. party that had been there earlier, but Marshall's force was not attacked. Thence they reached an A.I.B. base and, on 28th January, Masalanga where they formed a firm base. On 30th

---

[6] Sgt F. B. McGreevy, MM, QX28549; 2/5 Bn. Miner; of Goodna, Qld; b. Toogoolawah, Qld, 5 Dec 1917.

[7] Capt A. J. Marshall, NX122980. 2/2 Bn and "Z" Special Unit. Zoologist, explorer and author; of Sydney; b. Sydney, 17 Feb 1911.

[8] Lt P. C. Beenie, VX22598. 2/22 and 2/2 Bns. Traveller; of Glenferrie, Vic; b. Glenferrie, 28 Dec 1916.

January they reached a village occupied by Japanese where they killed one and captured documents and gear. On 8th February after further patrols they rejoined the 2/5th Battalion, at Bulamita.

Until early January, because for so long there had been no contact with the enemy, little was known of their strength and dispositions. By that time, however, patrols had captured maps and documents and a more accurate and detailed picture could be constructed. The *41st Division*, holding the Danmap River-Asanakor line, had the *237th Regiment*, about 1,100 strong, on the coast and the *238th* and *239th* south of the Torricellis. The division was about 4,000 strong, but about 1,000 were sick men. The main defensive positions of the *238th* had been at Sumul, Perembil and Malbuain; of the *239th* at Musendai, Apos and Asanakor. As mentioned, the *20th Division* was in reserve to the east, and the *51st* deployed from Wewak to Boiken. At this stage the total strength of the *XVIII Army* was estimated at 21,000—far fewer than the actual numbers.

In the past two years the three divisions of the *XVIII Army* were known to have suffered appalling losses and hardships. The *51st Division* had borne the brunt of the Lae-Salamaua fighting in 1943, and had retreated thence through half the length of Australian New Guinea to Wewak; its *66th Regiment* had been heavily engaged in the battle of the Driniumor River in July and August 1944. A small part of the *20th Division* had fought round Lae and the whole division had fought through the Finschhafen-Ramu Valley operations, suffering grim losses before beginning the costly retreat to Wewak; two of its regiments had lost heavily in the Driniumor battle. One regiment of the *41st Division* had fought at Lae-Salamaua, two in the Finschhafen-Ramu campaign and nearly the whole division in the Driniumor battle. All but one of the nine infantry regiments had made the long retreat from the Huon Peninsula, or even farther south and east, to the Aitape-Wewak area.

The whole army was now running short of food, clothing, weapons, ammunition and medical supplies. Its aircraft had been destroyed and it could expect no naval help. Even if it was not required to fight, its losses from disease would inevitably be very high.

After the defeat of its attack on the Americans round Aitape the *XVIII Army* adopted a policy of withdrawing from contact with the enemy, leaving outpost forces in ambush positions, and dispersing its units over a wide area and particularly in places where they could grow their own food and regain their strength.[9]

---

[9] The account of Japanese operations, intentions and estimates in this and the succeeding three chapters is based on documents captured at the time, and on five post-war sources: *Southeast Area Operations Record, Part III: 18th Army Operations*, Vols IV and V, prepared under the direction of G.H.Q. in Tokyo in 1946 by the "1st Demobilisation Bureau"; a record of the interrogation of Generals Nakai, Nakano, Mano, and Miyake by Brigadiers Moten and Martin at Muschu Island in October 1945; a History of Japanese Operations in New Guinea—Aitape-Wewak Campaign, October 44-September 45, compiled in August 1946 after interviews with General Adachi and Colonel Tanaka of his staff; *Southern Cross, An Account of the Eastern New Guinea Campaign* (Tokyo, 1955), by Lieut-General K. Yoshiwara, General Adachi's one-time Chief of Staff, translated for the War History Section by Miss Doris Heath; and *The Complete History of the Greater East Asia War* (Tokyo, 1953) by Colonel T. Hattori, a translation of which is in the library of the Australian War Memorial.

On their farms the Japanese cultivated sweet potatoes, yams, pawpaws, bananas, maize, tomatoes, pumpkins, cucumbers, peanuts, copra, coconut oil. Machines were devised to crush and refine sago starch. Among the living things they caught and ate to supplement their mainly-starch diet were pigs, dogs, possums, mice, bats, kangaroos, snakes, lizards, frogs, worms, insects of many sorts, maggots, crocodiles, fish, crustaceans and birds.

The supply of ammunition was so short, however, that from 1st February 1945 its use was prohibited for hunting game. Animals and birds had to be trapped.

One consequence of these conditions was that

the method of command became slow and unsatisfactory due to the loss of many excellent staff members, the low physical strength of the soldiers due to the Aitape operation, the bad food after the operation and the conditions which forced them, even the staff members, to work in the fields. Batteries for wireless equipment were not sufficient. . . . A major part of the headquarters communication [was] dependent on laborious trips and on messengers.[1]

Lack of signal equipment helped the commander to conceal from the lower formations discouraging news that might otherwise have come to their ears. Finally only two radio sets were in action, one at army headquarters and one at naval headquarters, and

the groups and units were informed only of those bits of news that the Army considered it necessary for them to know.[2]

Thus, in the brief accounts of Japanese operations in this and the following three chapters the reader should bear in mind that the Japanese troops were often hungry, if not weak from malnutrition, often sick and often lacking much of the equipment then considered essential to a modern army. One result of the shortage of equipment was that large numbers of technical troops could be converted into infantry. The units of the *6th Air Division*, for example, having no aircraft to look after, became fighting units. The infantry regiments were reinforced and reorganised until they had been built to a strength of between 1,000 and 2,500 each.

In the last quarter of 1944 Adachi's orders mainly concerned problems of food production. In his planning he had to keep in mind particularly that little food would be harvested in the gardens from January to April and therefore he must try to hold his gardens at least until this period was over.

During interrogation after the war General Adachi said that, when the Australian offensive opened, he considered that his enemy's plan would be either to attack along the coast with two divisions with Wewak as the objective, or to make an amphibious assault, or to combine both operations. His subordinates said that they expected that, having taken Wewak, their enemy would drive inland, then east along the Prince Alexander Mountains; and attack along the Sepik.

---

[1] 18th Army Operations, Vol IV, pp. 74-5.
[2] 18th Army Operations, Vol V, p. 135.

In October 1944 the *XVIII Army,* as mentioned, was about 35,000 strong. Forward between the Anumb and the Danmap (as the Australians knew) were the *237th Regiment* and other detachments, about 700 men, under Major-General Kikutaro Aozu, formerly commander of the infantry group of the *41st Division,* whose task was to delay and counter any advance along the coast. This force was augmented in December by an improvised group, perhaps of battalion strength. South of the Danmap in November lay the remainder of the *41st Division,* about 4,000 strong, under Lieut-General Mano, with headquarters at Womsak; its role was to counter-attack from the mountains and cut the communications of any force advancing along the coast. In the But-Dagua area, defending the airfields, was the *20th Division* (*79th* and *80th Regiments*) about 8,000 strong; its *78th Regiment* had been sent to Maprik because of lack of food on the coast. Round Wewak was the *51st Division* (*66th, 102nd* and *115th Regiments*), 10,000 strong, and the *Ozihara Force,* 1,000 strong. Muschu and Kairiru Islands were garrisoned by the *27th Naval Base Force* plus some army troops, a total of 5,000 of whom 1,000 were labourers. Some 5,000 base troops are not included in the above totals.

Up to the end of December Adachi did not greatly alter his dispositions or plans, except that "instead of the whole of the *41st Division* being available for counter-attack, part of the division was committed to holding the Australian advance from Tong".[3]

As a result of the pressure by the 19th Brigade, however, Aozu's force was progressively reinforced in the second half of January: by a company of the *80th Regiment,* then a part of the *239th Regiment,* then by a composite unit, and then by the *III/115th Battalion.* It was characteristic of the Japanese to draw reinforcements first from one formation and then another. Aozu now commanded units from each of the three divisions.

On 20th January the headquarters of the *41st Division* was moved to Balif. The main forces under command were then: the *238th Regiment* plus part (about 300) of the *239th* round Salata; the main *239th* and the *54th Garrison Unit* round Bulamita. The 300 men of the *239th* at Salata were ordered to attack the Australians (Buttrose's force) in the rear, and departed on 23rd January with this object, but as a result of marching only at night and losing their way, with consequent shortage of rations, they abandoned the project, and the force arrived back at Salata on 15th February.

The maintenance of the Australian lines of communication was now becoming a major problem. For example, it took the 2/8th Field Company 10 days to put a 236-foot bridge with 42 piles across the Driniumor. About this time the company recorded that "road work progresses slowly owing to unavailability of dozer and shortage of tip trucks". Only one grader was at work on the Rocky Point Road. Still only one transport

---

[3] History of the Japanese Operations in New Guinea—Aitape-Wewak Campaign, October 44- September 45, compiled under the instructions of Brigadier Irving, commanding the 8th Military District, and dated August 1946.

aircraft was available to the 6th Division to supply the force in the Torricellis. Adachi would no doubt have greatly revised his estimate of the Australians' intentions had he known that, largely because of a shortage of shipping and small craft, they were living from hand to mouth.

On 6th January Stevens had informed Sturdee that he would have secured the Abau-Malin-Walum line by the end of January. The division would then have to discontinue the eastward advance because of maintenance difficulties; it would hold the Abau-Walum line and patrol eastward. If, however, "additional maintenance facilities and air support" were provided it would be "possible for the division to adopt a vigorous policy aimed at the destruction of the enemy forces in the Wewak area". He submitted the following three proposals:

(a) *To capture in succession But-Dagua-Wewak*
   Method: Troops to be used:
   6 Aust Div (less one infantry brigade and certain Div troops)
   One infantry battalion to maintain pressure eastwards from Yambes.
   Administration:
   As maintenance by road from Aitape would be impracticable with normal Divisional resources the following facilities would be required:
   (i) *If maintenance be by road*: One heavy general transport company;
   (ii) *If maintenance be by air*: 12 C-47 aircraft;
   (iii) *If maintenance be by sea*: 4 LCTs.
   Suitable small beaches for landing craft exist from inclusive Dogreto Bay eastwards. This operation would free the coastal area, deny the enemy the small amount of supplies he receives by submarine and destroy a substantial part of his force. It would not, however, appreciably affect the enemy forces in the Maprik-Yambes area.

(b) *To destroy enemy forces in the Maprik-Yambes area*
   Method: One infantry brigade group to move south through Walum. One infantry brigade group to maintain pressure in the coastal area. One infantry battalion to maintain pressure eastwards from Yambes.
   Administration:
   Maintenance by air is the only possible means under this plan. Five C-47 aircraft would be required in addition to facilities now available.
   This operation would destroy the enemy forces in their present self-supporting areas or drive them south and east to the swamps of the Sepik River Valley.

(c) *To destroy the enemy forces in the Maprik-Yambes area*
   Method: Drop one Australian paratroop battalion less two companies at Burui to seize airstrip there. Fly into Burui one infantry brigade group by D plus 4.
   Maintain pressure in the coastal area with one infantry brigade group and eastwards from Yambes with one infantry battalion.
   Administration:
   This would require approximately 50 C-47 aircraft based on Tadji from D minus 1 to D plus 4, and 15 C-47s thereafter for maintenance.
   This plan (c) had every prospect of achieving the greatest success. It would prevent the escape of Japanese forces south to the interior, would destroy him or force him out of present self-supporting areas to the coast where his destruction would be easier and where he would find it difficult to survive on local supplies.

For all three of the above plans it was considered the following additional air support would be necessary:
>One Tac R flight
>One squadron attack planes
>Three squadrons medium bombers.[4]

A principle which Stevens considered fundamental to any planning was that an advance along the coast must be accompanied by a thrust through the Torricellis, because there was no point in letting the Japanese merely withdraw from the coast into their garden areas in the mountains or the Sepik Valley. On 10th February, in response to these proposals of 6th January, Sturdee ordered that the 6th Division should continue its advance along the coast towards Wewak "within the limit of its own resources and without becoming involved in a major engagement". "This meant," wrote Stevens later, "that none of the additional facilities . . . were to be made available and that the operations would therefore be conducted under much greater handicaps than those just completed."[5]

---

[4] 6th Australian Division Report on Operations Aitape-Wewak Campaign, 26 Oct 44-13 Sep 45.
[5] 6th Division report.

CHAPTER 13

TO DAGUA: AND ACROSS THE AMUK RIVER

WHILE General Stevens was awaiting a reply to his proposals of 6th January the floods subsided, the repairing of roads and bridges was begun, and Brigadier King's 16th Brigade completed the relief of the 19th in the coastal area. The incoming battalion commanders—P. A. Cullen of the 2/1st, A. G. Cameron of the 2/2nd, and Hutchison of the 2/3rd—had all led battalions in the Papuan operations of 1942 and 1943, and, with few exceptions, the majors and captains had served there as had most of the platoon commanders.[1] The proportion of officers and other ranks who had seen active service in New Guinea was relatively high by reason of the fact that in 1943 the brigade had absorbed large contingents from the battalions of the 30th Brigade, disbanded after their service in Papua.

One task allotted to the new brigade when it was warned to be ready to move forward was to secure the line Malin-Ilap-Aboama if the 19th Brigade had not already done so when it took over. The 19th Brigade had achieved this line, and the principal remaining tasks of the 16th were to harass the enemy by patrolling forward to the Anumb, and to maintain a standing patrol at Walum.[2] The supply problem, made more acute than before by the floods, was partly solved by running landing craft from Aitape to Dogreto Bay, the first beach on the coast where such craft could be employed. On 30th January 80 tons were put ashore, including six trucks, and jeeps and trailers, and thenceforward craft arrived every second or third day.[3]

A document captured in February showed that on 25th January there were 770 Japanese in the groups opposing the Australians on the coast. The *237th Regiment* was still the main element of the force, but, as was usual with the Japanese when on the defensive, several detachments had been added, including those mentioned earlier.

Ahead of the 2/1st Battalion, which took over from the 2/11th in the northern sector on 24th January, lay the narrow coastal plain cut every few

---

[1] In October 1944 the 2/3rd Battalion, for example, had only one captain who had been promoted since 1942, and only five lieutenants whose seniority in the battalion was later than February 1943.

[2] When Brigadier King took over he had the following troops under command in addition to his own brigade:
  2/6th Cavalry (Commando) Regiment
  Squadron 2/4th Armoured Regiment less three troops
  2/3rd Machine Gun Battalion less two companies
  Two sections 2/2nd Transport Platoon
  2/3rd Transport Platoon
  2/21st, 2/22nd and 2/23rd Supply Depot Platoons
  2/7th Field Ambulance
  110th Brigade Workshop
  110th Brigade Ordnance Field Park
  Detachment 6th Division Salvage Unit
  Detachment Australian Army Canteens Service.
In support were the artillery of the division less one regiment and the engineers of the division less two field companies.

[3] In January aircraft chartered from Australian National Airways to conduct a regular service from Australia to Hollandia and beyond began dropping bundles of newspapers to the forward troops. Welcome as this service was, the division as a whole would have preferred to have had some of these aircraft to help supply its force in the Torricellis.

hundred yards by creeks which drained a narrow ridge named Nambut Hill. On the southern side the ridge sloped down to Nimbum Creek. The most easterly position held by the battalion was a platoon post on the westernmost knoll (Haydon Knoll) of Nambut Hill. Cullen sought permission to occupy the whole of Nambut Hill but this was not given.

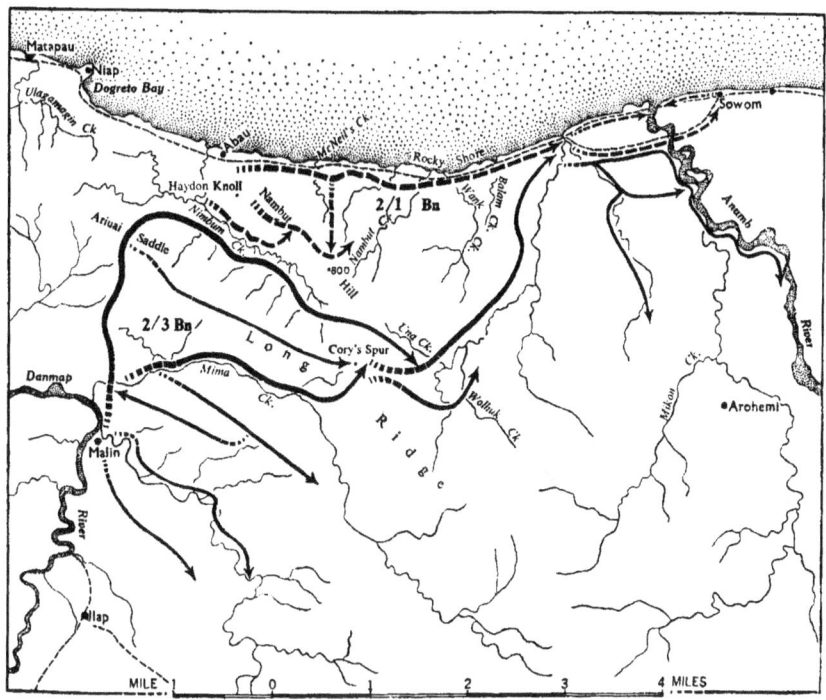

16th Brigade, 24th January-28th February

From 25th to 29th January, however, patrols probed forward along the ridge without seeing any Japanese, until on the 29th one was shot on a knoll by Lieutenant Haydon's[4] platoon which was occupying a patrol base on Haydon Knoll. That night (29th-30th) a Japanese force estimated at about 30, using small arms, grenades and gelignite bombs, made a resolute attack which lasted five hours. The Australians, led with great courage and coolness by Haydon, drove off one assault after another, until the enemy withdrew to a knoll 200 yards to the east, leaving seven dead. Captured papers revealed that these Japanese were part of a battalion sent from Wewak to drive the Australians back across the Danmap. Thus began a fight which lasted three weeks.

---

[4] Lt J. B. Haydon, NX16272. 7 Cav Regt and 2/1 Bn. Station hand; of Quirindi, NSW; b. Lismore, NSW, 15 Nov 1918.

On the 30th a platoon led by Lieutenant Crowden[5] moved through the position on Haydon Knoll to attack the Japanese knoll but came under heavy fire. The Japanese, however, withdrew to a farther knoll. Artillery and mortar fire was brought down on them there but it was soon realised that the position could not be taken except with strong artillery and air support. This was organised and patrols were sent out to investigate possible approaches from the south. As a result of this patrolling Lieut-Colonel Cullen planned, on 4th February, that Captain Kendall's[6] company should attack the hill from the south at a point about 1,000 yards east of the Japanese knoll. Unfortunately the air attack that was to precede the advance had to be cancelled because of the weather, and the attacking company was held by enemy fire when only 100 yards from the summit and eventually withdrawn. Meanwhile Lieutenant McNeil's[7] platoon advancing on the knoll had almost reached the enemy's position but came under heavy fire which killed McNeil and one other; four Japanese were killed. Lieutenant A. D. B. Murray took command, reorganised the platoon, himself carried in McNeil's body under fire and conducted a withdrawal.

Patrolling and bombardment continued. On 7th February after accurate air attacks Lieutenant Gotts'[8] platoon took the knoll where four Japanese were killed and seven other dead were found, but the main enemy force withdrew. The Japanese then held a position—Feature 800—about 400 yards farther east.

On 11th February Captain C. J. Prior's company, probing along the coast took a Japanese position covering McNeil's Creek due north of the summit of Nambut. A platoon climbed south to seek an approach to the summit from that direction, and found no Japanese on the northern slopes.

To the north and east of Mima Creek in the 2/3rd Battalion's area rose Long Ridge, a long steep spur which culminated in a mountain (later named Mount Hutchison) about 3,200 feet above sea level. Here, as mentioned earlier, patrols of the 2/8th Battalion had had several severe clashes with aggressive parties of Japanese. After a patrol had found a track along the top of the spur, Hutchison on 31st January sent out to Long Ridge a force commanded by Lieutenant Cory[9] and including two platoons (Lieutenants Weir[1] and Pope[2]), and an artillery officer (Lieutenant Needham[3]), with eight signallers and 10,000 yards of cable. The

---

[5] Lt C. W. Crowden, TX10303; 2/1 Bn. Buttermaker; of Deloraine, Tas; b. Deloraine, 11 Nov 1918.
[6] Capt C. McI. Kendall, NX34854; 2/1 Bn. Bank officer; of Port Kembla, NSW; b. Wellington, NSW, 27 Sep 1915.
[7] Lt L. McNeil, NX114826; 2/1 Bn. Window dresser; of Newcastle, NSW; b. Newcastle, 30 Mar 1922. Killed in action 4 Feb 1945.
[8] Lt R. J. Gotts, NX15361; 2/1 Bn. Farm manager; of Dunedoo, NSW; b. Wroxham, Norfolk, England, 21 Sep 1911.
[9] Capt G. E. Cory, MC, DCM, NX7864; 2/3 Bn. Motor car salesman; of Uralla, NSW; b. Saumarez, NSW, 23 Dec 1909.
[1] Lt-Col S. P. Weir, MC, NX148640; 2/3 Bn. Regular soldier; b. Canterbury, Vic, 29 Dec 1922.
[2] Lt K. R. Pope, NX59156; 2/3 Bn. Law clerk; of Sydney; b. Sydney, 22 Sep 1917. Died of wounds 6 Feb 1945.
[3] Lt B. Needham, VX621; 2/2 Fd Regt. Clerk; of Brighton, Vic; b. Brighton, 6 May 1919.

task given to Cory's force was to locate and destroy any enemy force on the track along this ridge, verify the existence of the track itself and check the position of streams on each side of the feature. Early on the 31st the men climbed from Mima Creek on to the ridge, there 2,500 feet high, and bivouacked. Next morning they climbed up towards what was later named Cory's Spur. The forward scouts sent back word that there were huts on the top of the slope and that they were occupied by Japanese. Pope's platoon attacked here, killing three while two others escaped. From this point three spurs rose. Cory chose the main one and the force began to advance along a narrow ridge from which rose a series of knolls on each of which unoccupied enemy positions were found. About 4 p.m. the forward scout, Private Perry,[4] surprised a Japanese sentry and killed him silently with his machete, and soon reported a big camp and about 30 Japanese who were unaware of the presence of the Australians.

Cory deployed the force to attack this position, which was on a small plateau. This deployment took about twelve minutes with the Japanese working only a few yards away from the concealed Australians. Then Weir's men charged and had overrun three machine-guns and secured about one-third of the plateau before the Japanese had time to man the weapons that remained. Weir, although wounded, seized one machine-gun and fired it at the enemy. This leading platoon was now pinned down and Cory sent Pope's in. Pope reached Weir, who was in a Japanese foxhole, but before they had time to say much to each other Pope was shot in the head. Sergeant Gooley[5] took charge of Pope's platoon, and his men pressed on throwing grenades and firing Brens and sub-machine-guns but were soon pinned down by the Japanese who had reorganised on the highest part of the plateau. The fire fight continued until it was nearly dark, by which time little ammunition was left. Cory's force then withdrew with its wounded and its spoils but was forced by the darkness to bivouac just a few hundred yards down the very steep side of the mountain. Next morning they returned to the battalion area well satisfied with the battalion's first successful action in this campaign.

There were 33 Japanese dead—confirmed a week later by a count of Japanese graves on the site—including 10 armed with swords and pistols. The captured weapons included 10 pistols, 37 packs full of new equipment, 6 machine-guns of which some had not been fired. Two Australians had been killed or mortally wounded, and 7 wounded. Captured orders showed that the Japanese force was a special raiding force 62 strong and was to link with the forward troops and attack. Another two-platoon patrol of the 2/3rd, under Captain Gibbins,[6] on 9th February found a Japanese

---

[4] L-Cpl J. W. Perry, NX68719; 2/3 Bn. Apprentice tile-layer; of Kogarah, NSW; b. Kogarah, 15 Sep 1924.

[5] Sgt B. V. Gooley, DCM, NX68829; 2/3 Bn. Mill hand; of Casino, NSW; b. Casino, 11 Jun 1919.

[6] Capt G. W. Gibbins, NX12474; 2/3 Bn. Contractor; of Grafton, NSW; b. Sydney, 24 Jun 1916.

position in the vicinity of Cory's Spur and again launched a surprise attack, killing five and taking three machine-guns.[7]

In this period of very vigorous patrol action General Stevens received General Sturdee's decision of 10th February that the division might press on to Wewak, although it would be given no additional resources to help it do so. Promptly Stevens informed his subordinates that he intended to take, in succession, But, Dagua and Wewak, and, in the mountains, to capture Maprik and advance eastward. The 16th Brigade was given the specific preliminary tasks of securing the line of Wank Creek in order to give full protection to the supply base at Dogreto Bay, and then advancing to the Anumb River. Moten was informed that his task would have to be accomplished by a force of one battalion plus a company, two commando squadrons, and service troops, as this was all that the available aircraft could maintain.

After having issued these orders Stevens informed Sturdee that the advance eastward had begun but that "administratively the operation was a complete gamble" because he had no guarantee that the five L.C.T's then at Aitape would remain in his area, and the weather, as it had demonstrated, might dislocate the road, sea and air routes for days on end.

Brigadier King decided as an immediate move that the 2/3rd Battalion on the right would secure the line Wolhuk Creek-Una Creek, and the 2/1st, with a troop of tanks under command, would secure a line Nambut Hill-Nambut Creek. One company of the 2/3rd Machine Gun Battalion, at this stage under the command of the 16th Brigade, was to protect Dogreto Bay and prevent infiltration from the south.

The 2/1st made careful preparations for its attack. The task was given to Captain Givney's[8] company and on the 14th he and a platoon commander looked at the ridge from the air. On the morning of 16th February Givney's men, guided by the Intelligence officer, Lieutenant Begg,[9] moved up the spur from above McNeil's Creek and gained the summit of Feature 800 unnoticed, killing four Japanese on the southern crest and driving others off. Lieutenant Johns'[1] platoon now advanced along the ridge to take the defenders in the rear and met heavy fire about 400 yards to the west which killed two men in the leading section, but next day Johns patrolled to the Australian position on Haydon Knoll, the enemy in between having withdrawn in the night.

Exploiting from Feature 800 on Nambut, a platoon of Givney's company moved north-east down a steep razor-back saddle on 17th February,

---

[7] The report of the 16th Brigade sets out the doctrine concerning attack accepted in this formation at this time: "When the attack is launched and especially if surprise has been effected, the force must at once strike with every weapon and man available and at the same time movement must be maintained. It is fatal for attacking troops to go to ground. . . . Troops who remain on their feet and move quickly from tree to tree run much less risk of becoming casualties even at point blank range. . . . Sufficient reserve should be available to bring through when the assault has lost intensity and the fire fight begins to develop. . . . The only time the soldier becomes so exhausted as to feel incapable of further action is when the officer in command succumbs to fatigue."

[8] Capt E. C. Givney, MC, NX3908; 2/1 Bn. Public servant; of Canterbury, NSW; b. Tenterfield, NSW, 13 Feb 1912.

[9] Lt C. E. Begg, NX106855; 2/1 Bn. Solicitor; of Cremorne, NSW; b. Sydney, 31 Jan 1917.

[1] Lt D. H. Johns, VX108505; 2/1 Bn. Tailor's cutter; of Ormond, Vic; b. Armadale, Vic, 6 Dec 1919.

(*Australian War Memorial*)

Top and bottom: Men of the 2/11th Battalion in an action against Japanese positions east of Matapau, 2nd January 1945.

(*Australian War Memorial*)

(Australian War Memorial)
A company of the 2/2nd Battalion moving westward past Dagua on the way to the 1410 Feature, 25th March 1945.

(Australian War Memorial)
Dagua airfield, New Guinea, on 25th March, four days after it was occupied by the 2/2nd Battalion.

encountered a strong enemy position, and the forward troops came under heavy fire. Warrant Officer Hall[2] and Corporal Graham[3] courageously carried out wounded men under fire and then, with Lance-Corporal Mould,[4] advanced along a narrow ridge and stormed the enemy's position, killing eight. Mould and three others were killed and Hall and three others wounded. Next day 14 Beauforts made an accurate attack on the Japanese here, forcing them to withdraw leaving 14 dead. Thence the Australians exploited down the spur to the coast, and Nambut Hill was entirely in their hands.

Cullen now gave Captain Prior's company the task of continuing the advance along the coast to Nambut Creek. Early on the 19th Lieutenant March's[5] platoon "silently and skilfully" advanced to and captured a knoll overlooking the rocky foreshore at the mouth of the creek, but an enemy machine-gun on the south-east slope fired on a ration party coming behind, killing two and wounding four. Under fire Captain Prior carried out one wounded man and Private Shepherd[6] another.

March's platoon was now cut off and in need of rations and water. A second platoon (Lieutenant Richardson[7]) was sent forward to clear the area, and a company made an outflanking movement to the south while a Wirraway aircraft dropped cylinders containing rations and water to the isolated men. By 5 p.m. Richardson with the help of artillery and mortar fire had driven the Japanese across the creek and was in touch with March. By 22nd February the area up to Balam Creek had been occupied and barges had landed supplies for four days at Wank Creek, where 100 natives arrived next day to help the unloading.[8] Next day a platoon advanced to the Anumb River. That night King ordered Cullen not to continue the advance except with patrols until supplies were assured. The sloop *Swan* arrived on the 28th and bombarded the Sowom and Kauk areas that day, bombarded But on the night of the 26th-27th, and the wireless installations on Kairiru Island on the 28th.

The 2/1st patrols had encountered no further opposition until the 26th when a patrol east of the Anumb was fired on by a field gun from the Sowom area. The gun position was bombarded by artillery and, next day, by aircraft. After the air attack a platoon advanced to west Sowom village, overcame a Japanese group, killing four men, and returned. Another platoon crossed the river farther south at the Old German Road and went 500 yards beyond before being fired on. Artillery fire was brought down and the Japanese withdrew; the patrol moved 1,000 yards along the

---

[2] WO1 R. E. Hall, DCM, QX38356. 49 and 2/1 Bns. Miner; of Cloncurry, Qld; b. Broken Hill, NSW, 12 Jul 1913.
[3] Sgt R. D. Graham, MM, NX73070; 2/1 Bn. Farmer; of Terrigal, NSW; b. Maitland, NSW, 4 Mar 1920.
[4] L-Cpl E. W. Mould, NX107140; 2/1 Bn. Grazier; of Tenterden, NSW; b. Cooma, NSW, 26 Jan 1920. Killed in action 17 Feb 1945.
[5] Lt C. V. March, QX18044. 2/25 and 2/1 Bns. Gardener; of Warwick, Qld; b. Warwick, 19 Nov 1918.
[6] Pte F. W. Shepherd, MM, NX103788; 2/1 Bn. Clerk; b. Naremburn, NSW, 7 Oct 1920.
[7] Lt R. R. Richardson, NX69256; 2/1 Bn. Salesman; of Armidale, NSW; b. Armidale, 15 Aug 1920.
[8] On 27th February the 2/1st Field Ambulance (Lieut-Colonel D. A. Cameron) opened an advanced dressing station, with a surgical team attached, at Wank Creek, thus greatly reducing the distance that seriously wounded men had to be carried for treatment.

German Road. On 28th February the 2/2nd relieved the 2/1st as forward battalion. In this phase the 2/1st had lost 7 killed and 23 wounded, and killed 51 and captured two Japanese.

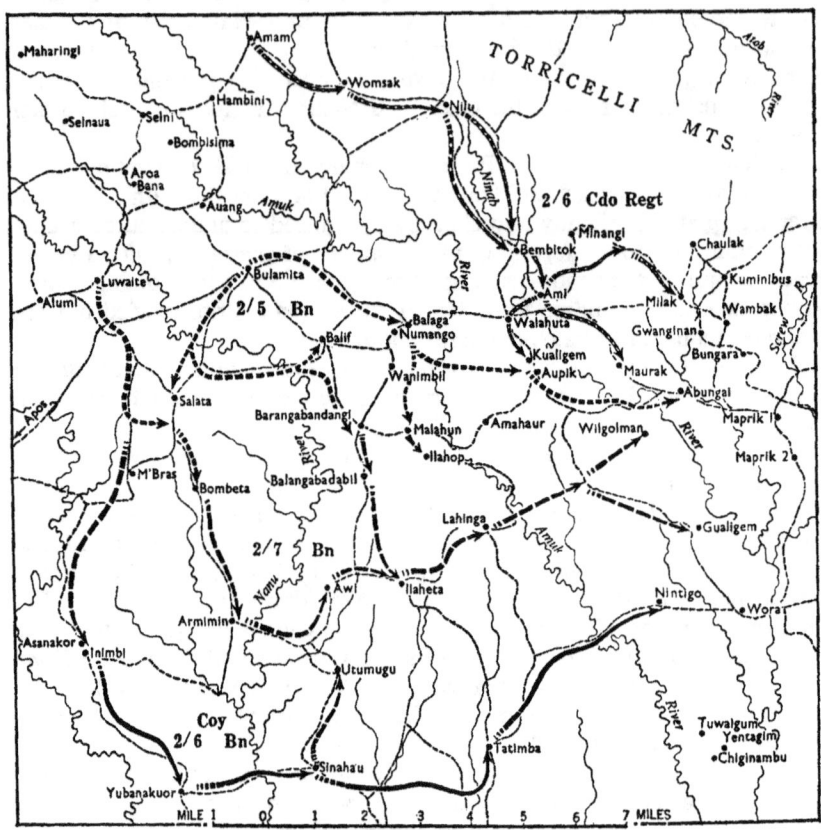

17th Brigade, 1st February-3rd April

In the brigade's inland area patrols from the 2/3rd in the hills had probed north and made contact with both the 2/1st and 2/2nd. On the 28th two platoons under Lieutenant B. H. MacDougal cleared the enemy from a village between Mikon Creek and the Anumb, killing four. Fifteen to 20 Japanese counter-attacked but were driven off. Next day MacDougal called down artillery fire. The first rounds fell among the Australians and killed one and wounded three, but the patrol killed five Japanese.[9]

On 1st February General Adachi ordered General Aozu if necessary to withdraw his force intact on to the *20th Division,* and on the 10th Aozu, hitherto directly under Army command, was placed under the *20th Division.* The 2/1st Battalion delivered a heavier blow to the Japanese round Nambut Hill than the Australians

---

[9] *Action Front* (1961), the history of the 2/2nd Field Regiment, says: "The targets had been plotted from an ordinary survey map and it was 400 yards out."

realised at the time. The *III/115th Battalion* was "defeated" there, the Japanese reported. At Sowom a company of the same battalion was "annihilated", evidently mainly by air and artillery bombardment.

In the Torricellis on 1st February Colonel Buttrose issued orders for an advance by three companies of the 2/5th: one to Salata, one to Balif, and one to the Balaga-Numango area. By 3rd February Salata had been secured after an accurate air attack the previous day; Walters' company entered Bombeta on the 3rd; a patrol found Balif abandoned and Geer's company occupied it on the 6th, when Japanese made an unsuccessful counter-attack losing five men killed. Patrols found that Balaga, however, was held by about 150 Japanese and about 80 were dug in on the Nanu River. Walters' company attacked these with two platoons on 7th February but could not dislodge them.

At the beginning of February the 2/7th Commando Squadron was based on Nilu. The general intention was that the advance on Maprik should be carried out by the 2/6th Cavalry (Commando) Regiment (of which the 2/7th Squadron was a part) and the 2/5th Battalion; Lieut-Colonel Hennessy's advanced headquarters were moved from the coast first to Nilu and then to Ami, and the 2/10th Squadron was brought forward to Ami. On 8th February Moten sent Buttrose and Hennessy a forecast of future operations. He said that the indications were that the enemy's line of withdrawal was to the south and there were few if any Japanese in the Maprik airfield area. The main concentrations seemed to be about Sinahau between the Nanu and Amuk Rivers. The brigade's job was to kill as many Japanese as possible "as part of the process of cleaning up the country". The capture of ground meant nothing at that stage. After the 2/5th Battalion had taken its present objectives attention would be turned to Maprik as a preliminary to a move to the south. The clearing of the Maprik area would be a task for the 2/6th Commando Regiment with some support from the 2/5th Battalion. After Maprik had been taken the 2/5th (or the 2/7th on relief) would turn south and clear the Sinahau area.

Buttrose in reply submitted an outline plan whereby, when Numango and Ilahop had been cleared, he would leave a company at Ilahop to patrol south-east and clear Lahinga, while with two companies he moved south-west from Balif to M'Bras and then south-east to Ilaheta and Sinahau. One company from M'Bras would drive the enemy from Apos, Asanakor, Yubanakuor and Sinahau. This would require the commando to destroy the enemy east of the Amuk, including Walahuta and the Aupik villages.

On 13th February, after a mortar bombardment the previous day, McBride's company took Numango and the battalion was ready to open the next phase. Buttrose, whose headquarters were now at Balif, ordered one company to take Barangabandangi and another Malahun. There was sharp fighting round Barangabandangi, where a fighting patrol came under heavy fire and was ordered to withdraw. The withdrawal was covered by

Corporal Dunlop's[1] section, which Dunlop led to within 15 yards of the Japanese whence the Australians brought accurate fire to bear. Finally Dunlop alone covered the withdrawal of his section. By the 17th, after bombardments from the air and by mortars, Barangabandangi and Malahun had been secured.

At this stage two heavy 4.2-inch mortars manned by a party from the 2/1st Field Regiment arrived forward. This detachment consisted of Lieutenants Tyndale[2] and Wilson[3] with 20 men; in view of the heavy loads they would have to carry Tyndale chose 13 men from the regiment's first Rugby Union team and 6 from the seconds. Six men carried each weapon along muddy tracks into the mountains—two the baseplate, two the barrel, and two the tripod—while two formed an escort. They made their first shoot on Ilahop, where about 90 Japanese were dug in, on 19th February, and their second on the same target on the 21st, firing 43 bombs in all. On the 21st bombers also struck this stronghold.

In this period a strip for light aircraft was completed at Balif, and on 20th February a Piper Cub landed and took off for Aitape with a hospital patient. Thenceforward wounded were flown from Balif and Ami to the 2/11th Hospital at Aitape, thus saving a six-day carry on stretchers over the mountain range.

On 18th February there was a sharp fight at Bombeta where Lieutenant Milton's[4] platoon attacked about 40 Japanese well dug in. After three hours and a half the Japanese withdrew having lost 10 killed of whom Milton himself killed six; only one Australian was wounded. The patrol captured valuable maps and other documents.

At this stage the role of the 2/10th Commando Squadron (Captain Woodhouse) was to protect the left of the 2/5th Battalion, and clear the enemy from the area north-east and east of the Ami villages. This was a populous area with many villages sited along the steep-sided ridges. Water supply was a problem but generally enough was found by digging holes in seepages. After some early easy successes in which the Australians had surprised the enemy the Japanese began to fight stubbornly. The lack of supporting weapons was soon felt and each of the three troops was given a 2-inch mortar, and later a 3-inch mortar section was attached to the squadron. The bomber squadrons from Aitape also gave support.

On 6th February Lieutenant Cater[5] and 23 others had established a patrol base at Bembitok. In the first half of February patrols probed also to the north-east of Ami where five out of 10 Japanese were killed in a sharp clash; and to Walahuta and the Amahaur area where "C" Troop

---

[1] Cpl R. A. Dunlop, DCM, VX4245; 2/5 Bn. Dispatch clerk; of North Fitzroy, Vic; b. Carlton, Vic, 3 Oct 1915.

[2] Capt W. Tyndale, NX3397; 2/1 Fd Regt. Butter factory foreman; of Rockdale, NSW; b. Benalla, Vic, 22 Nov 1914.

[3] Lt A. J. Wilson, NX16062. 2/5 and 2/1 Fd Regts. Salesman; of Keystown, Saskatchewan, Canada; b. Pense, Canada, 18 Dec 1913.

[4] Lt E. J. Milton, MC, VX5292; 2/5 Bn. Caterer; of Bendigo, Vic; b. Watford, England, 16 Nov 1910.

[5] Lt R. B. Cater, NX13276. 6 Cav Regt and 2/10 Cdo Sqn. Grazier; of Wellington, NSW; b Wellington, 23 Jul 1916. Killed in action 20 Feb 1945.

killed ten Japanese. On 20th February Cater's troop attacked Kualigem. Six Japanese were killed but Cater and Lieutenant Liles[6] were killed and five troopers wounded, and the enemy remained in occupation. This position was heavily mortared. Meanwhile a troop of the 2/7th Squadron, based on Walhiga to the north, patrolled deeply up the Atob River and to the headwaters of the Screw River. The remainder of this squadron (Captain F. J. Lomas) arrived at Walhiga by 21st February. One troop moved east, established a patrol base at Kaumala and held it against a counter-attack by 30 or 40 Japanese. By the 26th the squadron had cleared the country to the Nagipem villages, and on 2nd March it established itself at House Copp. Farther south all approaches were found to be strongly guarded.

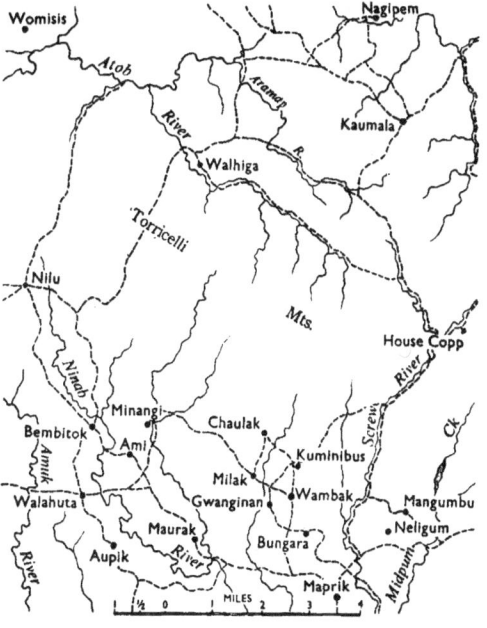

The relief of the 2/5th Battalion by the 2/7th was now in progress and Lieut-Colonel Parbury[7] of the incoming battalion had been in the forward area for about a week. Before the relief was complete, however, Cameron's company of the 2/5th at Malahun had to withstand a sharp counter-attack. At 6.40 a.m. on 23rd February in heavy rain about 60 Japanese attacked from the north, east and south and cut the communications with the rest of the battalion. Ten minutes later some 40 Japanese attacked from the direction of the Amuk River and, 25 minutes after that, 30 attacked from the south-west. All these thrusts were repulsed.

When the attacks were at their height Sergeant Thorn[8] volunteered to lead out a fighting patrol to distract the enemy. With great dash he led this patrol from a flank into the midst of the enemy, inflicting heavy casualties. He then moved round behind the enemy and attacked again. This forced the Japanese to break contact, and enabled the lines of communication to the battalion to be restored.

---

[6] Lt N. J. Liles, QX46939; 2/10 Cdo Sqn. Engine driver; of Innisfail, Qld; b. Esk, Qld, 7 Nov 1919. Killed in action 20 Feb 1945.

[7] Lt-Col P. K. Parbury, DSO, MC, NX69. 2/3 Bn; CO 31/51 Bn 1944, 2/7 Bn 1944-45. Works manager; of Wollongong, NSW; b. Sydney, 16 Sep 1910.

[8] Sgt C. Thorn, DCM, VX14574; 2/5 Bn. Farm worker; of Mildura, Vic; b. Walpeup, Vic, 23 Jul 1914.

In its arduous two months in the Torricellis the 2/5th had certainly succeeded in its task of killing off the enemy: 376 enemy dead had been counted and 12 prisoners taken. The battalion had lost 7 killed and 18 wounded in an advance of about 15 miles on a front that sometimes extended over 11,000 yards. Success was partly due to the generous and mostly accurate air support directed often by radio telephone: 62 strikes had been made in close support of the advancing troops.

During the advance of the 2/5th a large part of the enemy force facing it had withdrawn south into a populous garden area bounded by the Nanu and Amuk Rivers. Stevens wished to push the 17th Brigade east across the Ninab and capture Maprik, the former administrative centre of the Sepik area, but the large force of Japanese that had now accumulated on the southern flank could not be ignored, not only because they would threaten the Australians' communications, but because, if they were passed by, they might drive the natives from villages they had now reoccupied. This would have been a breach of faith, particularly in view of the way in which these local people had

> acted as efficient guides and sentries for our patrols; they built huts, headquarters, medical posts and jungle tracks for our use; they cleared and cleaned the villages previously occupied by an enemy devoid of the most elementary standards of sanitation; they had buried the enemy dead; had voluntarily aided our indentured labour lines . . . and had assisted to evacuate our wounded across the difficult mountain jungle country.[9]

These "sentries" recorded the killing of a Japanese by tying a knot in a piece of twine. In another part of the twine they tied a knot for each enemy observed, and other knots were tied to remind them to report other things they had seen.

The Japanese were now suffering severely as a result of the natives' loyalty to the Australians.

> Once the natives knew where we were (wrote Lieut-General Kane Yoshiwara after the war) they induced aircraft to strafe and bomb us. In addition the natives in the rear rebelled and losses were caused among those of our men who were employed on liaison or food gathering. On top of this at the time rain was falling continuously and the rivers were flooding and the roads were becoming muddy. . . . Now that the enemy were close there were attempts at escape by natives who did not like their task of carrying supplies, and crimes occurred such as the killing of small garrisons. Really, after April 1945, the state of public order on the western front was very disturbed.

If the Australians turned south at this stage they would go farther towards the malarious Sepik country and there would be wide dispersal of their forces. Moten, therefore, on 17th February, had given Hennessy and Parbury instructions to make a wide sweeping movement round the western and south-western flank of the enemy-held area, the move pivoting at first on Balangabadabil and later on Ilahop, the outer flanking company moving through M'Bras, Asanakor, Yubanakuor and then east to the

---

[9] 17th Australian Infantry Brigade Report on Operations in the Aitape-Wewak Area, November 1944-August 1945.

strongly-held Sinahau villages. The flanking company was to move slightly in advance of the rest of the force and press the enemy towards Maprik. This task was given to Major D. O. Hay's company of the 2/6th Battalion, augmented by a section of machine-guns, a detachment of 3-inch mortars, and other detachments.

Some time before this a rumour had been sent out through the natives, from whom the Japanese eventually received it, that a large Australian force was to advance on Maprik through Ami. As was intended, this caused the Japanese to move most of their forces north and north-east and was largely the cause of their pressure on the commando regiment, soon to become even more intense.

When giving instructions to Hay on 21st February Moten said that he considered that there might be 2,000 Japanese living off the country in the southern area, mostly between the Nanu and Amuk Rivers. Hay was to make it his constant aim to drive the enemy east not south, and to destroy them, but without committing his force to a deliberate attack. Maximum use was to be made of air strikes and mortar and medium machine-gun fire to back up patrols.

By the beginning of March the extent to which the Japanese were reinforcing their positions north of Maprik in the 2/10th Squadron's area, and particularly round Kuminibus, Milak and Maurak became more evident. Units of the *20th Japanese Division*, not previously encountered, were identified there. About 100 Japanese established themselves in Bungara and by 7th March the enemy had driven the Australian patrols from Chaulak, Gwanginan and Wambak. About 200 Japanese were found to be occupying Minangi, which was attacked heavily from the air, but without dislodging them. The enemy was now becoming increasingly aggressive, patrolling vigorously, setting ambushes, and reoccupying villages from which they had been manoeuvred in the previous month. They were numerically strong, well organised, and equipped with mortars and grenade dischargers, whose missiles, however, fairly often failed to explode.

Lieutenant Perkins'[1] troop of the 2/10th, 50 strong including mortarmen, now bore the main weight of the enemy's pressure. This troop was round Milak, about two days' march from the nearest support. In the evening of 13th March three native sentries, very alarmed, arrived with the news that "Japan man he come plenty". A quarter of an hour later a Japanese advance-guard of about 12 men appeared. Perkins' troop was then manning the weapon-pits in its perimeter, which was about 50 yards by 70, and in thick bush. The men had four Brens, one 3-inch mortar with 90 bombs, and one 2-inch with 20. The Japanese attacked at 8.30 without avail and maintained harassing fire all night. On the night of the 14th-15th, having now completely surrounded the Australians, they attacked again and were again repulsed. By the 15th the troop was running short of food and ammunition. Four aircraft dropped supplies but these fell 50 yards from the perimeter and half the men had to be sent out to fight for them:

---

[1] Lt K. C. Perkins, MC, NX12843. 8 Cav Regt and 2/10 Cdo Sqn. Mail officer; of Adelong, NSW; b. Adelong, 15 Mar 1915.

they retrieved five cylinders but the enemy got three. That day and on later days aircraft accurately strafed the Japanese to within 50 yards of the perimeter. On the night of the 16th-17th the Japanese attacked persistently and some were killed within three yards of the pits. The Australians were now haggard and weary. Attacks on the night of the 17th-18th were even heavier than the earlier ones, and in the morning 11 Japanese lay dead within a few yards of the perimeter. In the daytime the Australians buried the enemy dead whenever they could, but the stench of the unburied was becoming overpowering. The enemy generally concentrated his force to the north, and often left the Australian line of communication unguarded. Thus on 15th March some native refugees were sent out to Ami. By the 17th patrols had reopened the line of communication and by the 19th the enemy pressure had ceased. During the five-day siege 45 Japanese dead were counted.

During this period Lieutenant Robinson's[2] troop round Maurak was also attacked and ringed with ambushes by an enemy force of about 45. This force too withdrew after suffering fairly heavy losses. Round Aupik Lieutenant J. W. Carr's troop was opposed by about 40 Japanese but here there were only patrol clashes. In March the squadron lost 3 killed and 8 wounded, but counted 91 enemy dead and was certain that more were killed and their bodies taken away. At the end of the month the squadron had been reduced to 198; throughout the long struggle against a far stronger enemy force lack of food and ammunition had often caused anxiety.

> Ammunition remained in short supply during the whole period (wrote the squadron's chronicler). It was impossible to do more than meet the troops' day-to-day requirements. Food was fairly plentiful but essential amenities like tobacco were practically non-existent. . . . The forward troops . . . were reduced to searching Japanese dead for native tobacco. It seems incredible that authority should be so neglectful of its field forces during a time when the troops are going from one victory to another.

"It was apparent," wrote Moten, "that at this stage the enemy had obtained complete initiative in this area. 2/10 Aust Cdo Sqn which had borne the weight of the enemy attacks was completely worn out and the morale of the troops had deteriorated considerably."

On 16th March Captain E. W. A. Price's company of the 2/6th Battalion relieved the 2/7th Squadron at House Copp and next day Lieut-Colonel F. G. Wood took over command of the Ami sector from Lieut-Colonel Hennessy. However, before the 2/10th was relieved it was attacked again round Milak and Maurak. By 23rd March two additional companies of the 2/6th Battalion had relieved the remaining commando troop and Hennessy's weary regiment was moved back to the coast. Price found that in the House Copp area the Japanese had been "stirred up" and were moving about a great deal. On the 18th and 19th two parties of the incoming battalion were ambushed and suffered six casualties.

---

[2] Capt G. A. Robinson, NX2073. 6 Cav Regt and 2/10 Cdo Sqn. Station hand; of Pallamallawa, NSW; b. Northumberland, England, 27 Jan 1907.

Parbury took command in the Balif area on 25th February; that day one of his companies found the north Ilahop villages clear, and next day had moved 1,500 yards south before encountering any Japanese. Ilahop was permanently occupied on 10th March. The battalion's plan was that the Ilahop company on the left would maintain contact with the enemy towards Aupik, and the centre company would advance along a line Bombeta-Ilaheta, while "Hayforce" (under Parbury's command) carried out its wide sweep on the right.

The well-organised enemy attack on Malahun on the 23rd opened a period in which they were more aggressive than hitherto. Sharp clashes occurred daily. On 1st March one platoon drove a small group out of Wanimbil and, on the right, a platoon of Hayforce thrust into Asanakor where it killed three and burnt some huts while the enemy held the rest of the village. Next day Captain A. N. Rooke led a platoon to Asanakor, which was attacked by bombers but not accurately; in the fight Rooke and three others were wounded. On the 3rd Captain V. C. Baird led out two platoons to deal with Asanakor; and on the 5th a patrol entered the village, surprising the Japanese, who withdrew to a higher position to the south-east. The patrol burnt the place down and withdrew.

The vulnerability of the supply line in the Torricellis was again demonstrated at this time. Bad weather made the dropping of supplies impossible for a few days early in March. Soon rations for the natives were almost exhausted, and at a time when 310 indentured carriers had just arrived to replace locally-recruited men. Relief came on the 6th when four Beauforts dropped supplies; next day one Dakota dropped another load.

Hayforce entered Asanakor against only slight opposition on 7th March, and pressed on into Inimbi next day. On the 9th it sent a patrol to Yubanakuor. Next day the 2/7th made a general advance: Captain Pearson's[3] company from Malahun to Ilahop, Captain E. Arnold's to Balangabadabil, Captain Rooke's from Bombeta to Armimin. From the new bases some successful ambushes were carried out: on 18th March Lieutenant Clews[4] and a party ambushed 30 Japanese marching along with full packs towards Aupik and killed eight. On the 19th another ambush killed four on the same track and another near Lahinga killed six. Lieutenant B. W. E. Tyres led a patrol to contact Hay's company now at Sinahau, met 20 Japanese, killed four and drove the others off to the south-east. Hayforce swept on from Sinahau north to Utumugu and east to Tatimba, which was reached on 20th March, the enemy withdrawing generally east and north-east, as Moten hoped they would. On the 28th Hay crossed the Amuk River.

The 2/7th found the enemy holding resolutely in Ilaheta where they resisted for three days despite heavy mortar bombardment and air attack. The enemy occupied a perimeter 25 yards in diameter with an 8-foot drop

---

[3] Col C. M. I. Pearson, MC, VX101992; 2/7 Bn. Regular soldier; b. Kurri Kurri, NSW, 24 Aug 1918.
[4] Lt G. W. Clews, QX23090; 2/7 Bn. Bank officer; of North Rockhampton, Qld; b. Rockhampton, 1 Dec 1916.

on all sides, and held their fire until the attackers were only a few yards away. After one attack had failed a 4.2-inch mortar was sent forward to within 270 yards of the enemy. Lieutenant Wilson (of the 2/1st Field Regiment) directed its fire from a post only 25 yards from the enemy and in the final attack lobbed 13 bombs into the Japanese perimeter. On 20th March a company charged, while bomb splinters flew overhead, and took the position. That day Lieutenant Darryl[5] led out a patrol to raid the headquarters of General Mano's *41st Division* which had just been located. He found that the general had moved the day before, but the patrol killed 14 Japanese in the area.

The 2/7th Battalion noted at this time that the use of natives by the enemy had become more general than before. Wherever contact had been made the Japanese had standing patrols or sentries on all tracks well out from their perimeters; their positions were now more thoroughly prepared and this was taken as indicating that they were resolved to hold them; enemy patrols guided by natives were moving behind the forward company perimeters by night and cutting signal lines.

In the week beginning on 19th March the general plan of the 2/7th Battalion was altered: the companies were concentrated more closely with the general object of driving north-east towards Maprik instead of eastward to the Maprik-Marui road. The area through which the advance was to be made was thickly populated and had many gardens. Most of the muddy tracks followed the ridges and only a few crossed the valleys.

Between 21st and 26th March there was severe fighting on the ground supported by frequent air strikes against the Aupik villages. By the end of the month the concentration of the 2/7th on the west bank of the Ninab was almost complete. By 3rd April all opposition had been cleared along the east side of the river: one company was at Abungai, one at Wilgolman, one at Gualigem and one at Lahinga. The stage was set for the advance to Maprik.

It had been a hard fight and Parbury was anxious that in future he should have more powerful support. On 1st April Lieutenant Tyndale wrote to his commanding officer:

> The C.O. of 2/7 is determined to have a couple of long 25 pdrs here as soon as the Douglas strip is down. He is against mountain guns and said yesterday he would get me two 25s. He won't pay the short 25. If the bringing of long 25's up here involves any argument, we have in our favour the fact that we have men on the spot plus means of communication, so it would be more economical on plane space etc. to just send the guns and ammo along. We must get the job if possible.

When February opened the *41st Japanese Division's* main line of resistance had run through Selni, Luwaite and Salata. During the month "the revolt of the natives" in the Japanese rear areas caused losses and disruption of communications, and led to the reinforcement of those areas; for example, the *5th Shipping Engineer Regiment* was sent to Maprik and the *12th Field Meteorological Unit* and *63rd Air Regiment* were warned to be ready to reinforce Marui. On 25th February Lieut-General

---

[5] Lt L. J. Darryl, MC, NX30055; 2/7 Bn. Transport driver; of North Bondi, NSW; b. Muswellbrook, NSW, 28 May 1918.

Yoshiwara, Adachi's chief of staff, was sent into the mountains with 32 officers from *XVIII Army* headquarters to organise supplies and the protection of the rear of the *41st Division*.

The force deployed east of Maprik was about 1,000 strong, was commanded by Major-General Sadahiko Miyake, the infantry group commander of the *20th Division*, and included mainly the depleted *78th Regiment*, a detachment of marines and a company from the *51st Division*. Its plan had been to make a firm base round Yamil, attack Milak and push on westward. However, while attacking towards Milak, the Australians began to come in from the south towards Maprik, and consequently the advance through Milak was abandoned. On 19th March Miyake was ordered to withdraw on to Jamei.

The Australian advance from Balif brought the front line near groups of Indian prisoners of war organised by the Japanese into labour companies and these were moved back. The Japanese claimed that the Indians were not prisoners but enlisted members of the Japanese Army. According to Lieut-General Yoshiwara, writing after the war, the Indians were moved into an area rich in sago palms "so keen was the G.O.C's moral sense of affection for a friendly nation's troops".

On 11th March 1945 a fresh party of experienced A.I.B. men had arrived at Yambes on their way to take over from Lieutenant K. H. McColl, R.A.N.V.R., who had been operating in the Sepik area. It was led by Captain L. E. Ashton and included two other officers, two signallers, one other rank and some native soldiers. Ashton found Japanese in occupation of Nungagua and "after careful thought"—since his role was to gain information—four Europeans and 14 native soldiers attacked the place on 27th March. Two natives were killed but probably 16 Japanese were killed or wounded and thereafter the local natives cooperated with enthusiasm with the Australians. In April, May and June this party continued probing, gathering Intelligence, and arranging air attacks throughout an area populated by 400 to 500 Japanese troops.

Meanwhile in the coastal sector supply difficulties had produced a lull. At the end of February Brigadier King was convinced that the Japanese had only small outposts west of the Ninahau. Heavy rains, however, had damaged the road forward from Dogreto Bay and it had to be closed to traffic until it had been remade. In this pause King regrouped his forces. In the mountain sector the 2/3rd Machine Gun Battalion, less two companies, but with the 2/9th Commando Squadron under command, relieved the 2/3rd Infantry and was to clear the enemy forward to the Anumb and maintain posts at Walum, Aboama and Malin. On the coast the 2/2nd Battalion was to patrol forward from the Anumb, eventually as far as the Ninahau, and the 2/3rd, concentrated in the coastal area since 3rd March, was to patrol in the foothills to the south.

Up to this time 2/3rd Machine Gun Battalion (less one company) had been holding the line of the Danmap River from the coast southward as a firm base. Lieut-Colonel Gordon[6] with his command group was forward at the headquarters of 2/3rd Infantry Battalion. When Brigadier King told Gordon that he wanted the 2/3rd Machine Gun Battalion to change

---

[6] Maj-Gen R. R. Gordon, CBE, DSO, ED, VX17441. 2/3 MG Bn 1940-45 (CO 1944-45). Railways administrative officer; of Essendon, Vic; b. Essendon, 13 Mar 1907.

its role to that of an infantry battalion when taking over from the 2/3rd
Infantry, Gordon agreed immediately, but the task presented a number of
problems: it left many men without weapons (Numbers 1 and 2 on the
machine-guns, and others, were not equipped with rifles) and the battalion
had no support weapons of any kind. Furthermore, overnight the battalion
undertook a role for which its organisation was not designed and for which
it had not been intensively trained. The adaptability of the battalion in
changing itself at short notice into an infantry battalion was remarkable,
as later operations were to prove.

When he took over the mountain area Gordon began planning an
advance on Arohemi by the 2/9th Commando Squadron (Major Nisbet)
plus a company of the battalion. Arohemi was selected as the objective
because maintenance would have to be by air, and from the
map Arohemi seemed the only suitable dropping ground available
in the advance to the Anumb River. Gordon's plan was that the 2/9th
Squadron with Captain Devonshire's[7] company of the 2/3rd Machine
Gun Battalion under command would capture Arohemi, whither it would
be followed by battalion headquarters and Captain Hewitt's[8] company.

This force set out on 4th March and soon encountered opposition. Five
Japanese were killed on the way and Arohemi was found to be defended
by a force (it was the *III/239th Battalion*) well dug in. An attack that day
failed, Lieutenant Williams[9] and one trooper being killed. It was planned
next day to direct artillery fire on the area from 9 a.m. to 9.30 simultaneously with an attack by aircraft. The artillery officer, Captain Eason,[1]
went forward through dense bush with a small party as escort to within
50 yards of the enemy position to register the artillery. Eason's party
came under fire from a Japanese position. At 8.45 while registration was
in progress word was received that the air strike had been cancelled. It
transpired that the air strike was called off by the R.A.A.F. because of bad
weather, but one flight of Beauforts was already in the air and did not
receive the order. Having learnt of the cancellation of the air strike Nisbet,
the commander on the spot, was proceeding with his attack when the air
strike in fact developed on his own troops, and completely wrecked the
operation. Despite the fact that the strike was put down right on Eason's
post and his signaller and eleven of his escort were either killed or wounded,
Eason stayed put and tried to bring down artillery fire to indicate the
correct target to the aircraft.

Captain Sautelle's[2] troop plus a platoon of the 2/3rd Machine Gun
Battalion (Lieutenant MacFie[3]) advanced on the 6th, in drenching rain,

---

[7] Capt J. W. Devonshire, SX10122; 2/3 MG Bn. Clerk; of Dulwich, SA; b. Adelaide, 31 Aug 1914.

[8] Capt J. S. Hewitt, VX13851. 2/1 and 2/3 MG Bns. Farmer; of Warracknabeal, Vic; b. Warrack-nabeal, 14 Nov 1915.

[9] Lt F. D. Williams, VX42397; 2/9 Cdo Sqn. Sharebroker's clerk; of Melbourne; b. Melbourne, 10 Jul 1918. Killed in action 4 Mar 1945.

[1] Brig R. T. Eason, MC, ED, VX998; 2/2 Fd Regt. Telecommunications technician; of Maidstone, Vic; b. Geelong, Vic, 20 Nov 1913.

[2] Capt J. B. Sautelle, NX12430. 6 Cav Regt and 2/9 Cdo Sqn. Grazier; of Cathcart, NSW; b. Bombala, NSW, 27 Jul 1910.

[3] Lt H. H. MacFie, MC, TX1766; 2/3 MG Bn. Bank officer; of Launceston, Tas; b. Queenstown, Tas, 28 Aug 1919.

and with Eason again directing the artillery, but the enemy, now considered to be about 60 or 70 strong, were firmly established in positions that could be reached only up steep jungle-clad spurs. It was not until the 7th that flanking moves forced the enemy out; he made a stand some distance to the south-east. In the meantime air dropping of supplies proceeded, the supplies sometimes falling in the enemy's area. On 9th March an air strike was called down and the Australians, now reinforced to two companies and the commando squadron, attacked and captured the remaining enemy position. In six days of fighting the force had lost 9 killed and 9 wounded, but had cleared the enemy out of the area west of the Anumb River and killed 39 Japanese. The 2/3rd Machine Gun Battalion was then concentrated at Arohemi, the 2/9th Squadron being sent back to Aitape to rest.

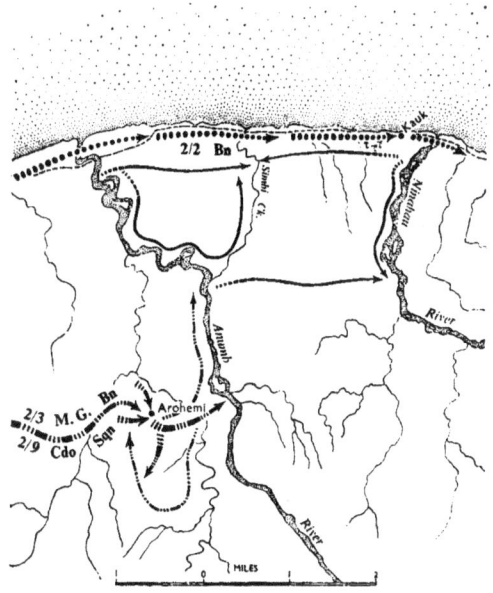

16th Brigade, 2nd-12th March

While the battalion was at Arohemi Warrant Officer Godwin[4] of Angau and a patrol of natives arrived from inland. As Godwin had no orders and was not required elsewhere he volunteered to make long-range reconnaissance patrols. The information gained from these patrols was of very great value in planning the next advance.

Meanwhile the 2/2nd Battalion had the task of probing forward towards Simbi Creek. On the morning of 2nd March Colonel Cameron sent out four patrols to clear the area up to the creek. One of these, under Lieutenant Shanahan,[5] was moving astride the Old German Road when it ran into an ambush from which the enemy did not open fire until within ten yards. The two leading scouts were killed. Shanahan went forward and he too was killed, as was Sergeant McCabe.[6] Sergeant Carnell[7] took command, led four men round the left flank, surprised and killed two

---

[4] Maj J. B. Godwin, MBE, PX102; Angau. Assistant plantation manager; of Roseville, NSW; b. Roseville, 31 Dec 1917.

[5] Lt J. Shanahan, NX7173; 2/2 Bn. Law clerk; of Cessnock, NSW; b. Randwick, NSW, 12 Feb 1912. Killed in action 2 Mar 1945.

[6] Sgt F. J. McCabe, NX125761; 2/2 Bn. Labourer; of Wagga Wagga, NSW; b. Goulburn, NSW, 22 Oct 1918. Killed in action 2 Mar 1945.

[7] Sgt E. J. Carnell, VX105394. 39 and 2/2 Bns. Construction worker; of Geelong West, Vic; b. Hamilton, Vic, 15 Sep 1918.

Japanese and wounded a third, and then charged back along the track killing another. These Japanese had sold their lives dearly.

Meanwhile Lieutenant Thomas'[8] platoon had moved along the coast road to Simbi Creek. As the leading men were crossing the sand bar Japanese fired on them but were driven off leaving five dead. In the course of this fight the platoon sergeant, Hansen,[9] frequently exposed himself to draw the enemy's fire and enable their pits to be located.

In this period the 2/1st Field Company, which had been working on the lines of communication forward of Dogreto Bay, set about bridging the Anumb River, 300 feet wide, 9 feet deep and fast flowing, but rains caused a flood which washed away 150 feet of piled piers. The bridge-building project was abandoned and enough equipment was obtained to instal a ferry capable of taking loaded trucks; hitherto improvised rafts made of drums and timber had been used.

The lack of equipment, bridging and mechanical plant proved a great handicap during this phase. Fortunately the Ninahau River proved fordable after banks had been cut down and the road from Anumb to But proved sufficient to take the brigade traffic with the assistance of tractors. No mechanical plant was available.[1]

Rain continued to disrupt the line of communication from Dogreto Bay, the road to Wank Creek became impassable, and "lack of mechanical equipment so handicapped the engineers that the road had to be temporarily abandoned".[2] It became necessary to depend on craft landing supplies at Wank Creek—when the surf permitted. An observer who travelled on the road to and from Dogreto on 12th and 13th March wrote:

The bridges, of which there are dozens, are named nostalgically after places in the Middle East: Bagush, Sollum, Barrani, Giovanni (no "Berta"), Athens, Larisa. A strong surf dumps on the beach at Dogreto, so strong that the men ram the L.C.M. or L.C.T. ashore, a loaded truck runs off and the craft pulls out as fast as it can, before it broaches. Supply is the only problem, and all here are convinced that as soon as the supplies are forward it will be only a march to But, but with so few L.C.M's the supplies cannot be got forward quickly enough.

The M.D.S. of the 2/1st Field Ambulance is placed just where the road climbs from the beach to go round the Dogreto headland. A sea of mud, with water-carts, 3-tonners, ambulances and jeeps keeping it stirred to a fine paste. A little farther on the mud, splayed out by the moving trucks, is pouring down the side of the hill like thick soup.... That night it rained—about 3 inches, belting down and blowing strongly. Today on the road back our jeep was stuck for about an hour on a shingly stretch of beach at one of the smaller creeks and was eventually winched out by a truck. Then we stuck for a time in the Danmap, but dried out the engine and got clear. In the Driniumor we stuck again with the water not so high as in the Danmap where it had been up to the back seat. Again a truck pulled us out.[3]

---

[8] Lt R. R. Thomas, NX8739; 2/2 Bn. Regular soldier; b. Forbes, NSW, 4 Jul 1917.
[9] Sgt F. J. Hansen, NX23995; 2/2 Bn. Storeman and packer; of Penrith, NSW; b. Goulburn, NSW, 11 Apr 1920.
[1] 16 Aust Inf Bde Report on Operations—Aitape-Wewak Campaign, 23 Jan 45 to 8 May 45. Appendix on Operations of 2/1st Field Company.
[2] 16th Brigade report.
[3] The power and swiftness of the floods were immense. At Aitape one morning troops found that whereas they had been able to see five islands off the coast the night before there were now six. "One was a floating island, a bit weather-beaten but complete with its quota of vegetation," wrote a soldier in a letter home. "It looked like what had once been an island in a river, with the low shrubs that grow on such places, and evidently it had been carried bodily out to sea. It must have been a couple of acres. That sort of thing makes it very difficult for the engineers when they build permanent bridges. One of their best ones, in the big floods, got in the way of an island solid enough to have palm trees growing on it, and island and bridge floated gaily out to sea."

At this stage it seemed evident that the enemy were not strong forward of But. Brigadier King considered he had a choice of two courses. The first was to wait until an adequate road was made up to the forward troops and then advance on But at the pace at which that road could be extended; this would take about two months in all. The second was to make a dash to But in sufficient strength to cover the establishment of a field maintenance centre at the beach there, march the remainder of the

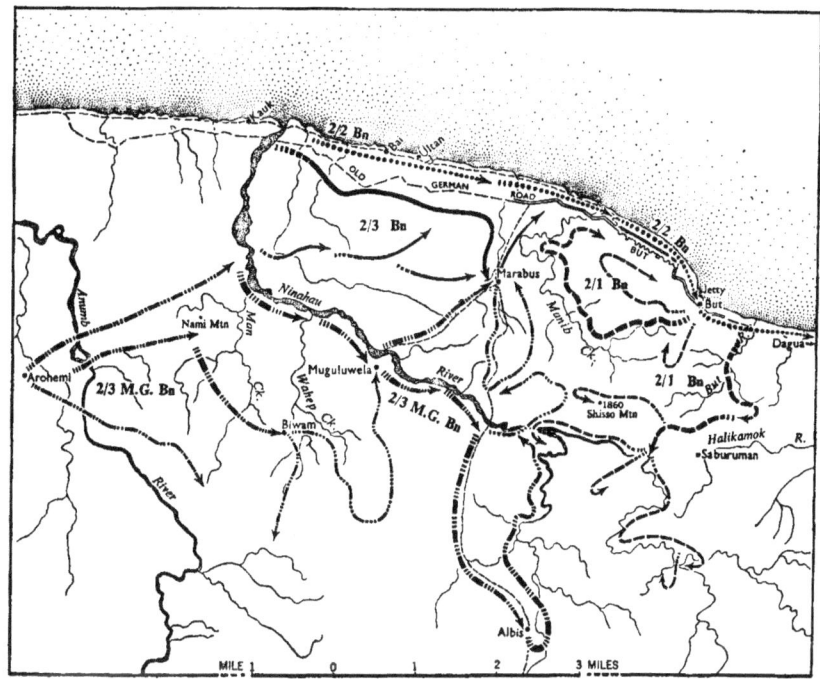

16th Brigade, 13th March-1st April

brigade forward, and ferry the vehicles and heavy equipment to But in landing craft. King decided that Cameron should send a company through to But on 15th March to discover what opposition would be offered between Bai and But, what forces were round But and, in particular, whether guns covered the anchorage. If the patrol could not deal quickly with the opposition, it would return; if the approach to the anchorage was "reasonably clear" the whole battalion would move quickly to But next day.

Already on 12th March a series of patrols had cleared the Japanese from the area west of the first creek beyond the swift, wide Ninahau. Lieutenant Park's[4] platoon, moving along the coast, overcame one Japanese outpost

---

[4] Lt-Col E. N. Park, DSO, ED, NX8942; 2/2 Bn. Jackeroo; of Manilla, NSW; b. Manilla, 5 Dec 1920.

killing four. Lieutenant Evans's[5] platoon was fired on by Japanese from among undergrowth in Kauk Plantation and Sergeant Bathgate[6] was killed and one man wounded. Three Japanese were killed. Lieutenant Ferguson's[7] platoon farther inland killed three Japanese.

On the 14th Cameron gave the task of making the dash to But to Captain J. C. S. Gilmore's company. It would advance to Bai that day and But jetty the next. It moved out at 11 a.m., reached Bai at 1.50, and advanced thence to Ultan where three Japanese were killed. By nightfall the battalion was concentrated about Bai and Ultan. On the 15th Gilmore's company encountered a strong Japanese position east of Ultan and, in the ensuing fight, lost two men killed and two wounded.[8] Next day the artillery fired 400 rounds into the Japanese position but the enemy was not silenced until Lieutenants Park and Bower[9] led their platoons forward in a concerted attack which ended with a bayonet charge. During the action Bower's platoon on the left was held up 15 yards from an enemy position astride the coastal track consisting of four bunkers and several foxholes. Lance-Corporal Stubbs[1] worked his way forward, directed fire on to two bunkers and then rushed them throwing grenades, killing four. He shot three more with his Owen gun and the advance was continued. Ten Japanese in all were killed, and 6 threw away their weapons and fled. Thus, at the outset, the dash to the But airfield met solid resistance.

Captain Derbyshire's[2] company then moved through and thrust along the coast to Manib Creek where it came under the fire of two 75-mm guns (and probably mortars), which dropped 30 to 40 shells along the beach, and a 20-mm gun. Only one man was wounded by this fire, and after dark the battalion moved forward and dug in along the eastern edge of the airfield itself. Next morning Japanese were seen on the airfield and it was evident that they did not know that the Australians had advanced so far in the night; indeed at 9 a.m. the Japanese guns dropped shells 400 yards to the rear of the advancing battalion.

Cameron now ordered Derbyshire to press on to But and establish a beach-head round the jetty. This he did, and by 5 p.m. the whole battalion had formed an arc a mile long embracing the jetty and the eastern end of the airfield. Aircraft dropped supplies, but only 40 per cent were recovered, largely because parachutes drifted out to sea. The confusion into which this swift advance had put the enemy was indicated next morning when field guns sited west of Dagua airfield fired shells into an area

---

[5] Capt J. A. Evans, NX31138. 2/33 and 2/2 Bns. Film dispatch assistant; of Bondi, NSW; b. Annandale, NSW, 1 Oct 1920.

[6] Sgt H. Bathgate, NX47887; 2/2 Bn. Hairdresser; of Kyogle, NSW; b. Maclean, NSW, 17 Jun 1920. Killed in action 12 Mar 1945.

[7] Lt K. Ferguson, QX22661; 2/2 Bn. Storeman; of Wilston, Qld; b. 29 Sep 1918.

[8] That day Lieutenant J. A. Birrell of Angau and five native police returned from a patrol Sowom-Loanim-But, having captured useful papers.

[9] Lt R. R. Bower, NX167518; 2/2 Bn. Schoolteacher; of Gundagai, NSW; b. Singleton, NSW, 11 Mar 1922.

[1] L-Cpl S. B. A. Stubbs, DCM, NX200338. RAAF; 2/2 Bn 1943-45. Farm hand; of Young, NSW; b. Sydney, 5 Feb 1917.

[2] Maj M. Derbyshire, MC, ED, NX12177; 2/2 Bn. Motor trimmer; of Wagga Wagga, NSW; b. Launceston, Tas, 27 Jun 1915.

about a mile and a half west of the jetty. Earlier in the day the guns had opened up on the 2/2nd Battalion as it was moving over the airfield but were promptly silenced by the fire of the only 25-pounder then within range, directed by Major Strong.[3] The Japanese guns were dual-purpose weapons and fired also at the aircraft that was dropping supplies. That day aircraft attacked the enemy's guns and each platoon of Derbyshire's company patrolled deeply. Lieutenant Goldsmith's[4] swept the But airfield killing two Japanese. Lieutenant Jackson's[5] moved into the foothills and found and disabled a 75-mm gun which had been recently used and beside which lay 50 rounds of unexpended ammunition and 30 recently expended. They went on for 500 yards across the But River and back along the coast, killing three stray Japanese.

Lieutenant Cameron's[6] platoon set out at midday also in search of guns in the foothills. Soon they were moving through recently-dug Japanese gardens in one of which, after a skirmish, they found huts that had evidently housed a headquarters, because there were several telephones one of which was ringing as they arrived. Cameron heard a Japanese voice chattering at the other end of the line and broke the instrument. At another group of huts they saw four Japanese walking about unconcernedly. Corporal Donnett[7] led a charge, the men throwing grenades and firing as they advanced. Three Japanese were hit and the fourth leaped away and disappeared. Cameron, following, fell through some sac-sac roofing into a pit and found himself beside the fourth Japanese. He clambered out, and the Japanese was promptly killed. Beyond were more huts. Great quantities of stores were found here, including 63 sacks or drums of rice, 70 cases of stationery, 52 of medical equipment, 200 rifles, many cases of ammunition, much clothing, machines and other equipment that had been in use when the airfield was operating. On the 20th Lieutenant Goldsmith led his platoon along the Old German Road, where five Japanese were killed, to a point west of the Dagua airfield and found and spiked two more field guns.

This was a day of wide patrolling of the newly-invaded area. Lieutenant G. Coyle led four sections inland to the Halikamok River where they met a native who led them to a camp occupied by 10 Japanese who were all killed, but not before a sentry had killed one Australian. Also in the foothills Lieutenant Jarvie's[8] platoon attacked some Japanese dug in on a ridge and drove them off. King ordered Colonel Cameron to secure Dagua airfield next day.

---

[3] Lt-Col J. A. R. K. Strong, MBE, VX102; 2/2 Fd Regt. Architect; of Elsternwick, Vic; b. Three Springs, WA, 3 Jun 1916. Killed in motor-car accident 2 Jul 1960.
[4] Lt-Col D. V. Goldsmith, NX162784; 2/2 Bn. Regular soldier; b. Hobart, 4 Jan 1921.
[5] Lt H. H. Jackson, NX42404. 2/1 Indep Light Tank Sqn and 2/2 Bn. Jackeroo; of Killara, NSW; b. Sydney, 12 Mar 1921.
[6] Lt K. R. Cameron, NX170623; 2/2 Bn. Schoolteacher; of Maroubra, NSW; b. Sydney, 26 Mar 1920.
[7] Sgt A. H. Donnett, DCM, NX42848; 2/2 Bn. Farm worker; of Gulargambone, NSW; b. Gilgandra, NSW, 4 Aug 1921.
[8] Lt J. Jarvie, NX105159; 2/2 Bn. Miner; of Weston, NSW; b. Weston, 28 Jan 1919.

Three Japanese were killed in the advance to Dagua on the 21st. On a ridge overlooking the road were signs that 60 to 70 Japanese had camped there the previous night and hurriedly departed leaving some rifles and equipment.

It was remarkable that the Japanese made no effort to harass the advancing column from positions in the hills overlooking the narrow coastal plain. Apparently the rapid thrust to But had thoroughly disorganised them and they had not yet recovered. On the overgrown Dagua strip, as at But, there were some abandoned aircraft, many rusty engines, and dumps of rusty bombs.

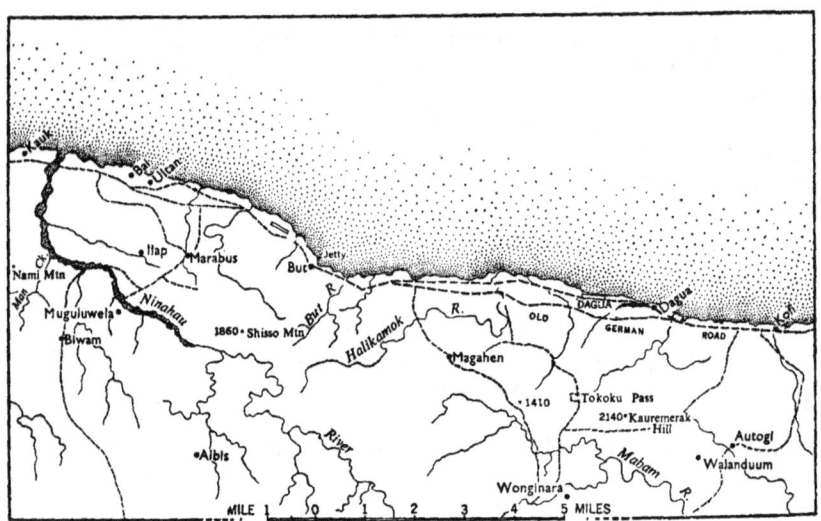

On 17th March King had ordered that the 2/1st Battalion should move forward and arrive at But on the 19th to protect the beach, and that Colonel Cullen should take command of all troops in the beach area. Captured documents and interrogation of prisoners and natives gave a fairly clear picture of the enemy's dispositions at this stage. Aozu's headquarters had evidently been moved back to Muguluwela (actually to "Shisso Mountain") and his plan was apparently to hold a line approximately from Muguluwela to Biwam. His force was about 200 strong including stragglers still between the Anumb and Ninahau Rivers. In the coastal area, the defending force included the *II/80th Battalion, 21st Airfield Battalion* and other detachments, and had apparently withdrawn its main strength into the hills above But. The *80th Regiment* less the *II Battalion* was apparently defending the area from Shisso Mountain—Feature 1860 —east and south-east along Manib Creek and the upper Ninahau River to the But River controlling the tracks Muguluwela-Ninahau River-Halikamok River-Dagua-Yamil.

It now appears that at this stage both remaining regiments of the *20th Division—79th* and *80th*—plus the *237th Regiment* and the *III/115th Battalion*, the *21st Airfield Battalion* and other detachments were forward round But and Dagua. A Japanese report describes the thrust (by Gilmore's company) on the 15th and 16th as having annihilated the forward troops. The *80th Regiment* was ordered to defend But airfield but was forced into the hills.

Despite the recent setbacks the Japanese commander still cherished dreams of glory. In an order of 18th March Adachi wrote: "It is not an impossibility for us, using our original all-out fighting tactics, to annihilate the 50,000 or 60,000 enemy troops with our present fighting power . . . leaving thus an impressive record . . . in the annals of our Army and paying a tribute to the Emperor and to the spirits of our numerous fellow dead."[9]

While the 2/2nd Battalion was advancing to Dagua the 2/3rd Machine Gun Battalion was pressing forward to the upper Ninahau. On 13th and 14th March one patrol reached the Ninahau and destroyed a Japanese headquarters on Man Creek; another patrol was ambushed and lost 3 killed and 4 wounded on the track round Nami Mountain; but the combined patrols manoeuvred the enemy off this ground. The battalion established a dropping ground about two miles inland west of the Ninahau on 18th March, and next day established a base at the junction of Wahep Creek and the Ninahau River. By the 22nd Muguluwela had been occupied and the enemy cleared from the area. After a fierce fight lasting eight hours Captain Hewitt's company captured a strong position 1,000 yards east of Muguluwela, killing nine Japanese. By 30th March the battalion had cleared the area up to a north-south line about two miles beyond Muguluwela, killing 35 Japanese. At the same time Major Clennett's[1] company cleared Biwam and patrolled east and south.

As mentioned, the main enemy strength in the But area was now concentrated in the hills to the south. King gave the 2/2nd Battalion the task of clearing the foothills south of Dagua and destroying the enemy in the Tokoku Pass, while the 2/3rd Battalion outflanked these Japanese by cutting the track leading south from the pass, and then destroyed the enemy in the area Mabam River-Hamsuk-Yalaminuni. The 52nd Battery would be in support. From an intercepted message the total strength of units of the *20th Japanese Division* in the forward area at 26th March was learnt to be 510, of whom probably about 300 were in the front line.

Above Dagua the mountains rose steeply from the plain towards the dominating 1410 Feature—so steeply that in places men had to clamber using hands as well as feet. The track then followed a razor-back ridge only about five feet wide with an almost vertical fall for some distance on either side, the steepness of the descent being obscured by the dense bush thrusting upwards on each flank. This razor-back led to a knoll— a little plateau about 50 yards in diameter. Thence the track fell and then rose again to another small knoll which formed the summit of Feature 1410. The track then descended in a series of steep slopes connected by level bridge-like razor-backs to the Mabam River. On the 22nd patrols

---

[9] 18th Army Operations, Vol IV, p. 182.
[1] Maj B. G. Clennett, TX2097; 2/3 MG Bn. Sawmiller; of Hobart; b. Hobart, 22 Jan 1917.

of the 2/2nd Battalion were sent southward into these hills: Captain Derbyshire's company to Magahen, which was taken against only slight opposition; Captain Lovett's[2] company along the road through the mountains to Wonginara. When they had covered about two miles the leading platoons (Lieutenants Goldsmith and Jackson) moving stealthily, heard chattering and wood-chopping about 100 yards to the left. The Australians

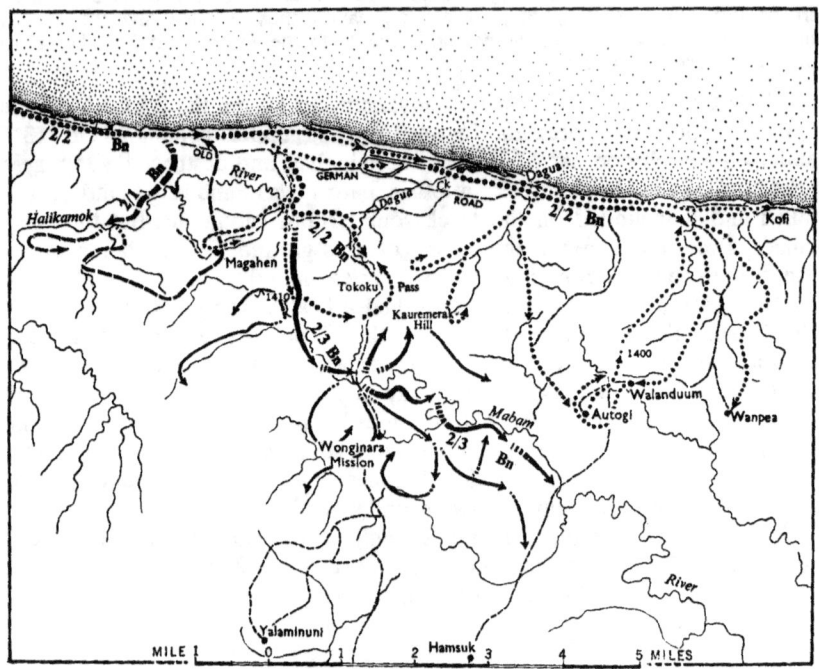

16th Brigade, March-April

worked their way forward until the men of the leading section, under Corporal Chapman,[3] could see six Japanese on the track 100 yards away, and hear others in huts beyond. Chapman moved his men into position and they opened fire. The Japanese scattered, after some had been killed, and a fight began against a force of about 30—the strongest encountered since the first day of the drive to Dagua. The remainder of Goldsmith's platoon moved up and, coolly and skilfully directed by Goldsmith, put in an attack to the huts, killing probably 8 more Japanese; 7 others fled. Under sniping fire the Australians held the ground gained until dusk when, after their three wounded men had been carried out, they withdrew about 800 yards to higher ground covered by Jackson's platoon. The Australians

---

[2] Capt K. H. Lovett, VX100099. 39 and 2/2 Bns. Assistant shire secretary; of Warracknabeal, Vic; b. Echuca, Vic, 23 Dec 1918.

[3] Cpl J. W. Chapman, NX15558; 2/2 Bn. Farm worker; of Boggabri, NSW; b. Portland, NSW, 24 Dec 1919.

had killed 14 at a cost of 3 wounded, one fatally. It was evident that the enemy regarded the track to Wonginara as being of some importance. The artillery observer, Captain Olsson,[4] ranged the guns by moonlight during the night.

From a position in the hills a 75-mm gun fired on Lovett's company and at targets farther north on the morning of the 23rd, but no one was hit and the gun became silent after the Australian artillery opened fire. Lieutenant A. Chowne's platoon patrolled high up on to the 1410 Feature and encountered Japanese in a group of huts. The Australians attacked, killing one; 15 more, with 10 natives, fled into the bush. On the way home Private Core[5] killed two Japanese and wounded a third.

Colonel Cameron's plan was now to send fighting patrols on to the ridges west of Lovett's position with the object of outflanking the Japanese force holding the pass to Wonginara, while Lovett probed southward. At the same time a reconnaissance patrol of five under Chowne, a fearless and skilful leader, was to go right through to Wonginara. On the afternoon of the 24th Park's platoon of Gilmore's company found the enemy digging in on the slopes of 1410 and dispersed them. They left 14 packs behind. Park pressed on and found the enemy well established higher up on the summit of 1410. After 250 shells had been directed into the enemy positions by Captain Powell,[6] the artillery observer, the platoon charged, killed three, and dug in on this dominating feature for the night. Patrols moved out that evening and killed more Japanese making a total of nine in the day's fighting; four Australians were wounded. Park thought a counter-attack likely and formed a perimeter about 30 yards across. It was so cold there at 1,400 feet that at night the men huddled together for warmth.

Another strong group of perhaps 30 Japanese had been encountered that day by Lieutenant Jackson's platoon covering the Wonginara Track itself. In the fight which followed Jackson was gravely wounded. A stretcher bearer, Private Morris,[7] went forward to attend him and was himself hit, but covered Jackson with his own body and dressed his wounds, being hit a second time as he did so. The attackers could not be extricated until dark, after another platoon had been sent forward to help. On the 24th twenty Japanese were killed by the 2/2nd. That night Chowne's patrol arrived back having reached Wonginara without seeing any Japanese and having obtained valuable information including verification of the existence of a line of communication from the Boiken area to the divide between the Ninahau and the Anumb.

The Japanese resistance was steadily increasing in intensity; this was proving the most severe fighting that had taken place so far in the campaign.

---

[4] Maj R. C. Olsson, NX111089; 2/1 Fd Regt. Industrial research officer; of Kogarah, NSW; b. Petersham, NSW, 23 Feb 1919.
[5] Pte M. J. Core, NX119863; 2/2 Bn. Tally clerk; of Coorparoo, Qld; b. Brisbane, 4 May 1922.
[6] Capt R. L. Powell, MC, VX565; 2/2 Fd Regt. Salesman; of Armadale, Vic; b. Thornbury, Vic, 13 Mar 1913.
[7] Pte E. G. Morris, MM, QX30832; 2/2 Bn. Farm worker; of Gayndah River, Qld; b. Gayndah, 1 Sep 1919.

The 2/2nd was now weary and due for a rest, but the final days of this phase were to prove the hardest and costliest. On the night of the 24th-25th Japanese raiding parties cut the lines between Derbyshire's and Lovett's companies. The plan for the day was that Derbyshire should attack through Park's platoon on the 1410 Feature, cut the Wonginara Track to the east, and push north along it to link with Lovett.

Chowne's platoon led the advance from the 1410 Feature. The men were moving along a track on a narrow ridge at about 900 feet when, at 11.20 a.m., the leading scouts were fired on.

The ground consisted of a narrow razor-back about eight feet wide with a high knoll covered with kunai rising abruptly above the general line of the ridge (wrote the battalion diarist).[8] 7 Platoon was under fire moving slowly forward until 1450 when it was found that the Japs, approximately 30, were in well-concealed foxholes among the tree roots and bunkers. The front presented by the edge of the knoll was only wide enough for 3 men to operate at a time. At 1500 hours artillery concentrations were called down, 7 Pl withdrawing 50 yards and at 1720 hrs a mortar H.E. concentration. Jap snipers were located in trees and one enemy was killed and 3 wounded. At 1800 hrs Lt Chowne led 8 Pl up the track in a bayonet charge.

"The artillery concentration had done nothing to shift the Japanese," said an eye-witness soon afterwards. "Chowne took his platoon in yelling like mad and him leading. The men were firing all they had. Chowne had gone 15 yards when he turned his head to urge the men on and a Nip hit him in the head with a bullet. Our men went on, yelling like stone-age men. Private Conway[9] was killed, then Sergeant Austin[1] was wounded. They were 60 yards up the ridge when 7 Platoon [Lieutenant Ferguson] went through them. The Bren gunner from Chowne's platoon, Private McClelland,[2] went on with 7 Platoon and stood on the side of the feature firing his Bren from the shoulder. He went on firing until they took the feature."

Eleven Japanese were killed and the Australians lost three killed or died of wounds (Chowne, Conway and Private Beardow[3]). Lieutenant Ferguson, who was among the wounded, remained on duty. The regimental medical officer, Captain McLennan,[4] moved up to the position and treated the wounded there as it was impossible to evacuate them until daylight.[5]

Next morning (the 26th) Colonel Cameron, with Lieutenant Lee's[6] platoon, moved through Derbyshire's company to reconnoitre the Japanese

---

[8] Lieutenant J. Smiles, the Intelligence Officer of this battalion, kept a war diary of unusual completeness and clarity.
[9] Pte A. W. Conway, NX13471; 2/2 Bn. Labourer; of Ungarie, NSW; b. Ungarie, 22 Apr 1916. Killed in action 25 Mar 1945.
[1] Sgt V. P. Austin, VX103088. 39 and 2/2 Bns. Cabinet maker; of Melbourne; b. Essendon, Vic, 3 Feb 1920.
[2] Pte K. F. McClelland, MM, NX83427; 2/2 Bn. Storeman and packer; of Bondi, NSW; b. Sydney, 1 May 1922.
[3] Pte G. J. Beardow, NX109755; 2/2 Bn. Farmer; of Casino, NSW; b. Lismore, NSW, 30 Aug 1917. Died of wounds 31 Mar 1945.
[4] Maj H. H. McLennan, VX60829; RMO 2/2 Bn. Medical practitioner; of Northcote, Vic; b. Northcote, 15 Aug 1915.
[5] Lieutenant Chowne was posthumously awarded the Victoria Cross.
[6] Lt L. Lee, NX28491. 2/2 MG Bn and 2/2 Bn. Schoolmaster; of Armidale, NSW; b. Goulburn, NSW, 1 Mar 1915. Killed in action 26 Mar 1945.

flank and locate the mountain gun which had again gone into action. Twenty-five yards forward of the company position this group was fired on, Lee and another being killed. The patrol was withdrawn, the artillery observer, Captain Powell, and four others remaining to direct artillery and mortar fire. The Japanese moved forward when the guns opened and seemed only 15 yards ahead in bush in which the visibility was only about five yards. Powell gave a correction to his own gunners calculated to bring shells down on his own position and then he and his men ran back down the track.

On the 27th bombers attacked these resolute Japanese and the artillery fired 500 rounds and the mortars 150, after which two platoons attacked but, at 11 a.m., encountered resistance 50 yards farther on than hitherto. A severe fight developed and after two hours and a half the company, having lost one officer killed—Lieutenant Walker,[7] who stood up to get a better view—and seven men wounded, gained a foothold on the knoll where there appeared to be some 40 Japanese well dug in with overhead cover. At this stage mortar fire was again brought down on the enemy position; one bomb dropped short and killed 2 Australians. At 5 p.m. the company withdrew, having lost 3 killed and 14 wounded in the day, and having killed 5 Japanese. These Japanese were the best troops the battalion had encountered in this campaign.

On 28th March Gilmore's company took over on 1410. Lovett's company pushed south along the track and after 1,000 yards was ambushed, losing 3 killed and 3 wounded. Patrols from Gilmore's company killed nine Japanese.

On the 30th Lieutenant Norrie[8] with eighteen men and two natives returned from a fine two-day patrol from Dagua Creek to Kauremerak Hill (2,140 feet) and thence north-east and south-east. He found a few signs of enemy movements and collected valuable information about the tracks in this area.

In preparation for a further attack on the Japanese knoll on the 1410 Feature Lieutenant Park, on 1st April, stealthily climbed an almost vertical cliff and reached a point within ten yards of the enemy. This scouting expedition took the whole day and provided Park with a detailed knowledge of the enemy's position. When he returned he planned an attack for the next day.

Thus, on 2nd April, aircraft attacked the enemy's position, then the artillery and mortars bombarded it. A party moved to a near-by knoll whence they could keep the enemy under mortar and small arms fire during the attack. At 11.30 the two attacking platoons led by Park climbed up a 60-foot cliff to a forming-up place and thence charged with fixed bayonets. At a critical moment Sergeant Finlayson[9] dashed forward and

---

[7] Lt A. J. Walker, NX72232; 2/2 Bn. Bank officer; of Port Macquarie, NSW; b. Henty, NSW, 7 Dec 1918. Killed in action 27 Mar 1945.
[8] Lt-Col J. W. Norrie, OBE, NX138174; 2/2 Bn. 3 Bn RAR Korea 1952-53. Regular soldier; b. Dyer's Crossing, NSW, 18 Apr 1922.
[9] Lt M. Finlayson, MM, NX2323. 6 Div Sigs; 2/1 MG, 2/28 and 2/2 Bns. Farm hand; of Ulmarra, NSW; b. Ulmarra, 10 Nov 1920.

overran two forward pits. Although wounded he remained in the lead and was the first to reach the main objective. The skill and courage of Park and Finlayson were the main causes of the success of this action. Two Australians were killed but 26 Japanese dead were counted. Private Jurd,[1] a stretcher bearer, attended under fire 7 of the 10 Australians who were wounded. Jurd, Private Webb,[2] who distinguished himself in this action, and 3 others were wounded next day, one mortally, when a grenade was accidentally exploded.

Derbyshire's company continued the advance towards Tokoku Pass, and on 3rd April encountered the enemy dug in on a knoll, which they took that afternoon, killing 8 and losing 2 killed and 5 wounded: so far in the campaign this company had had 40 men killed or wounded. On 5th April Derbyshire linked with the 2/3rd Battalion moving up on the west and next day with Lovett's company at the foot of the pass.

Meanwhile Lieutenant D. R. Clarke's platoon had made a three-day patrol deep to the east of the enemy's positions on Tokoku Mountain to collect information about the Japanese lines of communication to Karawop, and kill any Japanese in the area. The patrol moved south from Dagua to the Autogi and Walanduum area where twelve Japanese were seen digging in. The patrol returned along the coast finding eleven Japanese lying dead, apparently of illness, between Kofi and Dagua.

The 2/3rd Battalion had moved to a position north of the 1410 Feature on the night of 27th-28th March. Next day it advanced south, encountering several small parties of Japanese and killing eight and taking a prisoner, and bivouacked at the track and river junction south of the pass and in the midst of the enemy's area. On 29th March Major MacKenzie's[3] company moved north and encountered Japanese in well-concealed positions south of the pass. At one stage 10 Japanese attacked the rear of the company, but Sergeant Tighe[4] promptly led his section in an attack, killing 6 and dispersing the others.

Because of the air, artillery and mortar bombardment of the Japanese facing the 2/2nd Battalion, MacKenzie's company was halted until 4th April when it circled east and north and secured high ground east of the Japanese positions. There it was joined by Captain Gibbins' company and on the 5th they attacked.

The ridge occupied by the Japanese had a series of small knolls, each defended, and this necessitated a succession of platoon attacks. At dusk, in the face of enemy small arms fire from the commanding ground, the company consolidated on the highest false crest. Without artillery support any further advance would have been impossible. At first light on 6th

---

[1] Pte K. T. J. Jurd, NX111597; 2/2 Bn. Clerk; of Neutral Bay, NSW; b. Coogee, NSW, 8 Oct 1922.
[2] Pte A. Webb, MM, NX21119; 2/2 Bn. Farmer; of Wallsend, NSW; b. West Wallsend, NSW, 30 Aug 1921.
[3] Lt-Col K. M. MacKenzie, OBE, NX7596; 2/3 Bn. Regular soldier; b. Ballina, NSW, 22 Aug 1913.
[4] WO2 R. C. Tighe, NX66463; 2/3 Bn. Drover; of Paddington, NSW; b. Cobar, NSW, 9 Jul 1911.

April Lieutenant Martin,[5] the artillery observer, accompanied by an Owen gunner for protection, crawled forward and occupied a slit trench a few yards from the enemy. Ranging was extremely difficult because of the nature of the terrain, the nearness of his own troops surrounding the hill, and fire from enemy snipers. Nevertheless Martin completed ranging, with rounds falling within a few yards of his own position. Although he realised he was in the target area, he brought down 350 rounds, completely devastating the enemy defences and blowing in many of the posts. The subsequent infantry attack, which quickly followed the shelling, caught the shaken enemy by surprise, and the position was quickly taken. It extended for 500 yards and included 30 weapon-pits with overhead cover. The pass was now firmly in the Australians' hands.

During this northward advance the main body of the 2/3rd was sweeping the enemy from the area to the south. In this phase the 16th Brigade was receiving very valuable help from Lieutenant Birrell, of Angau, and about 12 native police. Day after day parties of police were sent out either with patrols or with local natives. With the troops they acted as guides; when working by themselves they brought in natives whom Birrell interrogated. One of these announced that the headquarters of Lieut-General Nakai of the *20th Division* was just east of Wonginara Mission. Among the native refugees were two who had been employed, with others, carrying Nakai about in a chair. Two companies under Captain Macdonald[6] of the 2/3rd had moved out on 2nd April and were led along a concealed route by native police and the two former chair-bearers with the object of capturing this headquarters. The leading platoon (Lieutenant J. Copeman) approached undetected to within ten yards and attacked with rapid success. In the fight a platoon that was following came under heavy fire, and its commander, Lieutenant Varley,[7] was killed. Corporal Kentwell[8] immediately led his section in a charge and overwhelmed the enemy. Round the enemy headquarters 28 out of apparently 40 Japanese were killed, including 5 officers, but not the general. The Australians lost 2 killed and 3 wounded. After this only isolated Japanese parties were found in the Mabam Valley and Wonginara Mission areas. Up to 12th April 19 more Japanese were killed by patrols.

In this period Angau officers and their native guides collected some hundreds of refugees, thus depriving the Japanese of potential labourers. The 2/3rd Battalion, as mentioned, was greatly dependent upon native guides, and to supply the battalion so far over the rugged hills demanded continuous labour for lines of carriers.

---

[5] Lt G. A. Martin, MC, QX11979; 2/2 Fd Regt. Law student; of Townsville, Qld; b. Cairns, Qld, 1 Apr 1918.

[6] Capt J. E. Macdonald, MC, NX34890; 2/3 Bn. Stock agent; of Wagga Wagga, NSW; b. Gundagai, NSW, 19 Jul 1912. Died 21 May 1958.

[7] Lt R. A. Varley, NX120685; 2/3 Bn. Bank officer; of Inverell, NSW; b. Inverell, 1 Jun 1923. Killed in action 2 Apr 1945. (Son of Brigadier A. L. Varley, MC, who died while a prisoner of the Japanese.)

[8] Sgt A. S. Kentwell, NX66620; 2/3 Bn. Shearer; of Warren, NSW; b. Warren, 21 Aug 1920.

Warrant Officer Godwin of Angau said that his line of 150 carriers had gone out over the 1410 Feature to the 2/3rd Battalion on three consecutive days carrying cargo out and wounded back and would probably go out again next day (wrote an observer on 31st March). The journey took from three to three hours and a half each way. It would kill them if it went on, Godwin declared. Among Godwin's police boys are some who know the country thoroughly and he is confident that they will clear up the area west of the present 2/2nd and 2/3rd Battalion positions very quickly and at the same time collect all the "bush kanakas" in the area so as to rob the Japs of carriers and at the same time get the women and children to a refugee camp where they can be properly fed.

As we were wading along the river towards the 2/3rd a police boy suddenly stopped like a hunting dog, announced there were some kanakas near by, disappeared into the bush, and soon reappeared with two of them, each carrying some sac sac wrapped in leaves. They offered to take the police boy out to find the rest of their group, but he was not having any, suspecting a trap. The kanakas were added to our line of carriers, and the search for the others will be made at the police party's own time.

In seven days Godwin and his men collected 250 refugees. Native guides, of whom 40 were now with the 2/3rd, had been largely responsible not only for the success of the attack on the *20th Division's* headquarters, but for other useful patrols and surprise attacks.

After having spent nearly three weeks partly resting and partly on road work, the 2/1st, as mentioned earlier, was moved forward to But on 19th March and took over responsibility for this advanced base from the 2/2nd. That evening the first barges arrived. For the next few days the men were employed partly in building a field maintenance centre and partly in patrolling the hills that overlooked the airfield.

In these hills, as elsewhere during this campaign, considerable numbers of Japanese had been left behind, out of touch with their units. During the five days to 24th March patrols of the 2/1st killed 26 Japanese including an officer. The patrolling was arduous, and when it was over the battalion's medical officer, Captain Sloss,[9] reported that in some platoons up to one quarter of the men were unfit for duty because of dermatitis, various fevers, and sprains.

In the next phase Brigadier King ordered Colonel Cullen to clear the Japanese from the hills as far south as three miles and a half from the coast and for three miles to the west. Accordingly one company with native guides moved south from But and then west, overcoming with the help of artillery and mortars a series of Japanese positions well dug in on dominating knolls. By 1st April the area had been cleared.

Meanwhile on 26th March another company, also with native guides, had moved into the hills farther east with the object of driving the Japanese from a base named Saburuman whose position was not clearly known. After several patrol clashes Lieutenant Mavay's[1] platoon on 31st March had a fight with a party of Japanese round a group of nine two-storied huts and many lean-to's—evidently Saburuman. Four Japanese and one

---

[9] Capt W. L. Sloss, VX70316; RMO 2/1 Bn. Medical practitioner; of Ballarat, Vic; b. Ballarat, 27 Jan 1918.

[1] Lt H. B. Mavay, NX3643; 2/1 Bn. Public servant; of Auburn, NSW; b. Yangan, Qld, 7 Oct 1915.

Australian were killed and other Japanese fled. Next day Mavay patrolled to Magahen. In this period the 2/1st killed 73 Japanese and captured 5 for a loss of 3 killed and 7 wounded.

Meanwhile the 2/3rd Machine Gun Battalion headquarters had been ordered to Marabus and the battalion cleared the area from Muguluwela to an area 5,000 yards east, where junction was made with the 2/1st Battalion.

The Japanese troops defending the Tokoku Pass included the *79th Regiment*, a company of the *26th Field Artillery*, and the *21st Airfield Battalion*.

As mentioned earlier all but one of the infantry regiments in the *XVIII Army* had been in action against Australians in the Salamaua and Huon Peninsula areas in 1943 and 1944. The *79th Regiment* and the *26th Field Artillery*, for example, had comprised the main part of the force that had delivered the counter-attack against the 9th Division round Scarlet Beach on the Huon Peninsula in October 1943 —perhaps the most dangerous attack on Australians in the South-West Pacific Area after the one on Wau in January and February 1943. Parts of the *26th Artillery* had fought also round Salamaua and at Kaiapit in the Ramu Valley.

Since January it had been Adachi's policy to make the Maprik district the main area of resistance because it was able to produce more food than the coastal zone. Already, as we have seen, there had been a steady movement of units from the coast into the mountains. After the loss of But the *20th Division* was ordered to move south of the mountains where it was to take under command *Miyake Force* and other units and fortify a big area to the east of the line on which the *41st Division* was fighting.

During the exacting fighting of February, March and April the Australian troops became increasingly convinced that the campaign was not worth their blood and sweat: and the fact that they had been allotted inadequate shipping, transport aircraft, and heavy engineering equipment tended to reinforce this conclusion.

Among the 16th Brigade battalions (wrote an observer in March) the tale is: "We could go straight through to Wewak if we had the equipment: a few L.S.T's and enough aircraft to drop or land the supplies needed. It's a 'Q' war and there just isn't the equipment to get forward with. But anyhow, what we are doing can't have any conceivable effect on the outcome of the war. We are wasting good lives." One comment on Forde's reported statement that the army was equipped for the task it had to do was: "Well, as we're doing ―――― all, I suppose he's right."

The conviction that the achievements did not justify the losses and the privations seemed to be far stronger in this veteran division than among the (mostly) younger and less experienced troops on Bougainville and New Britain. In the battalions of the 6th Division were many who had fought in crucial campaigns in Africa, Greece, Crete, Syria, and Papua, and who considered that no essential purpose was being served by these constant bitter platoon and company fights against a stubborn enemy who had shown that he would fight only if attacked. The fact that in this bush warfare far more than in open warfare the best and bravest were those who were killed—the forward scout and the veteran platoon and section leader—and these, painfully often, were much-admired soldiers who had survived three or four hard campaigns, made the men more bitter. At the same time a rise in the malaria rate and consequent criticism of the division and of units within it and a tightening of regulations concerning the taking of atebrin caused irritation at all levels.[2]

During the advance to Dagua and Wonginara the role of the 6th Division had been somewhat clarified. In the course of a letter to General Blamey on 27th February informing him of events in each of the First Army's areas General Sturdee had written: "I have not sought your special approval to start operations towards Wewak, as there is nothing to start. It would be more a question of stopping the constant process of advance that has gone on since we debouched across the Driniumor last November. . . . The administrative resources for operations towards Wewak are slender, but the plans made for supply will enable the operation to continue provided that there is no reduction of the two C-47's and American-owned L.C.T's. If there should be any reduction there will be no alternative but to draw back towards Aitape."

Sturdee then visited Aitape, and on 7th March (before the dash to But opened) wrote to Blamey again, giving an account of the difficulties of transport in the coastal area. He pointed out that the roads were so bad that jeeps were practically useless and even 6-wheelers were uncertain of getting forward of Dogreto Bay. But could be taken at any time if enough water transport was available, which it was not. The only American landing craft available for unloading the ships at Aitape and moving stores forward were five L.C.T's, of which not more than four were working on any day, and only one could be spared to go forward of Aitape; and 40 L.C.M's of which only 15 to 20 were serviceable daily. Often L.C.M's could not be used to unload ships because of the surf at Aitape. The original plans did not envisage the 6th Division being available at Aitape after about April, he added; consequently no provision was made for landing craft for any considerable advance towards Wewak. Big advances had been made, however, and maintenance of the road was now beyond the capacity of the engineers. Any advance beyond But would be a complete gamble unless further watercraft were made available. Yet it was desirable to seize Wewak in time to move the Aitape base thither before the north-west monsoon began again in September-October. If the 6th Division was to be withdrawn and replaced by the 8th and 23rd Brigades those brigades could more easily control the area from Wewak than from Aitape.

Sturdee then asked whether he could plan on having the 6th Division available for any specified time; whether he could anticipate that G.H.Q. would approve retention of the present watercraft at Aitape; whether he should plan to move the Aitape base to Wewak. If enough watercraft were not available should he progress beyond But?

General Blamey visited the division on 19th March, when General Stevens advanced two plans for the capture of Wewak: the first provided for an overland advance along the coastal plain and the second for a major

---

[2] See A. S. Walker, *Clinical Problems of War* (1952) and *The Island Campaigns* (1957), in the Medical series of this history.

amphibious attack at Dove Bay east of Wewak. "As there was little likelihood of obtaining the necessary requirements for the amphibious operation," wrote Blamey afterwards, "I decided that a land assault on Wewak would be undertaken."[3]

Three days later, on General Blamey's instructions, General Berryman informed G.H.Q. that it was estimated that if the 6th Division was allotted ten additional L.C.T's it could crush enemy resistance in the Wewak area in about three months. The additional craft were allotted, and Stevens learnt of this addition to his resources on 24th March.[4]

In response to a further request by Stevens for additional naval vessels, particularly as he would soon be within range of guns of up to 105-mm round Wewak and on the islands near by, the First Army informed him on 12th April that he would be allotted for the operations against Wewak the support of the sloop *Swan,* of two corvettes (*Colac* and *Dubbo*), five "Fairmile" launches, additional bombers for No. 71 Wing, three Boomerang aircraft for reconnaissance, and four Moths for communication flights. Later he was told that the corvette *Deloraine* and a sixth "Fairmile" would be added.

---

[3] Commander Allied Land Forces, Report on Operations in Australian Mandated Territory, 26 April 1944 to 15 August 1945, p. 106.

[4] On 24th February General Blamey had informed General Stevens that the Government had agreed that he should be transferred to "a very advantageous position" in the Postmaster-General's Department, in which he had held a senior post before the war. General Vasey was appointed to succeed him. Vasey, however, was killed in an aircraft accident on 5th March, and Stevens remained in command until July.

CHAPTER 14

MAPRIK AND WEWAK TAKEN

SIX weeks had passed since the 17th Brigade had been given the task of taking Maprik. After the hard fighting of February and March against a resolute enemy determined to exact a price for every Australian move into their food-producing country the time had come for the final thrust. On 3rd April Brigadier Moten issued new instructions to his two forward battalions. These allotted the 2/7th Battalion the task of capturing Maprik and the line of the Screw River from the Agricultural Station north to a point about three miles upstream in a direct line, and of securing the high ground overlooking Maprik landing ground. Hayforce was to operate on the right of this battalion and make an airstrip able to accommodate Douglas transports. As early as January, first Lieut-Colonel Parbury of the 2/7th and then Moten and Wing Commander Hall[1] of No. 8 Squadron had flown over Maprik in search of a site for an airfield and had chosen an area of kunai about eight miles south of Maprik on the Government track leading to the Sepik—the Maprik-Marui road. On the left of the brigade the 2/6th Battalion was to advance to the Screw River and prevent the enemy from moving north from Maprik.

In the early operations in the mountain area there had not been enough indentured labourers to meet all needs, and from time to time local "casual labourers" were recruited by Angau. Eventually 950 indentured labourers were allotted to the 17th Brigade. Normally 350 were allocated to a battalion, of whom 218 were in a battalion pool and 33 were allotted to each company permanently, and normally an additional 30 added when the company was on the move.

Meanwhile patrols had been pressing on from village to village. On 28th March, for example, Sergeant J. W. Hedderman, of the 2/6th, a notable leader in these as in earlier operations, had led a reconnaissance to Kulkuil and Gwanginan. Next day he led a fighting patrol which took Kulkuil with a carefully-planned surprise attack. On the 30th Lieutenant Errey's[2] platoon (16), with Hedderman as platoon sergeant, attacked Gwanginan. Hedderman confused the enemy by shouting to imaginary platoons to right and left (thus incidentally drawing fire on himself); and when the leading section was halted he brought down supporting fire and enabled it to move again. A man was wounded within 10 yards of the enemy's pits; Hedderman went forward, killed two Japanese with grenades, and dragged his comrade to safety. The enemy were 25 to 30 strong and the attack failed despite these gallant efforts. Hedderman covered the withdrawal, firing until all others had gone.

---

[1] W Cdr O. B. Hall, DFC, AFC. 6 Sqn; Comd Special Transport Flight 1942, 34 Sqn 1943, 8 Sqn 1945. Commercial pilot; of Bellevue Hill, NSW; b. 18 Jun 1908.
[2] Lt I. G. Errey, VX88613; 2/6 Bn. Schoolteacher; of Lilydale, Vic; b. Warburton, Vic, 20 Jan 1921. Killed in action 7 Apr 1945.

On 30th March a patrol found Mairoka clear of the enemy and on 4th April Lieutenant Gordon's[3] platoon established a patrol base there. On the 7th Errey's platoon attacked a village to the east of the Milak villages but without success, Lieutenant Errey being killed, and Sergeant Layfield[4] wounded. Chicanambu was occupied on the 9th.

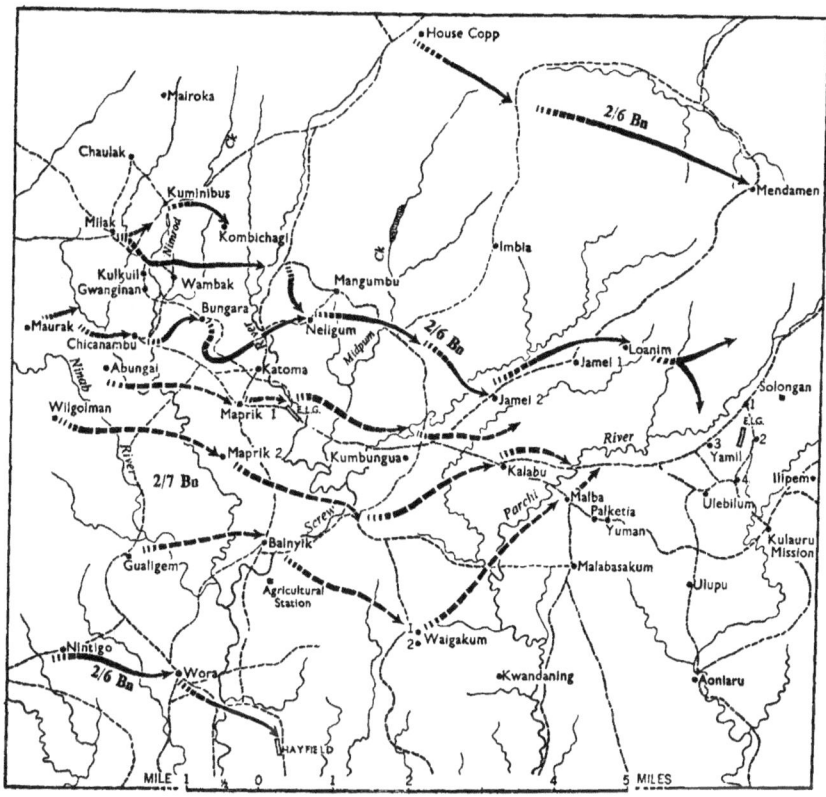

17th Brigade advance through Maprik, April-May

On the right Hayforce found Wora too strongly held on the 10th, but both it and a near-by village were empty on the 12th, the Japanese evidently having withdrawn north to Bainyik. Major Hay had thus secured the site of the proposed airstrip. It was estimated that it could be made usable in 11 days. The Pioneers of the 2/7th Battalion under Lieutenant Edwards,[5] with the help of about 200 enthusiastic natives, formed the strip, which was named Hayfield. Inevitably their only implements were hand

---

[3] Lt-Col W. J. S. Gordon, NX138183. 2/4 Armd Regt and 2/6 Bn. Regular soldier; b. Paddington, NSW, 13 Jan 1924.
[4] Lt C. R. Layfield, VX3832; 2/6 Bn. Clerk; of Prahran, Vic; b. Hawksburn, Vic, 5 Aug 1921.
[5] Lt A. D. Edwards, MBE, VX5552; 2/7 Bn. Builder; of Warrandyte, Vic; b. Warrandyte, 4 Oct 1913.

tools, with improvised graders and rollers made from bush timber and dragged by the native workers.

Meanwhile the 2/7th Battalion in the centre, pressing on, found that the enemy were well prepared to defend Maprik. The dominating ground was a long steep ridge running generally north and south through the Maprik villages and 1,000 yards west of the landing ground, and the Japanese closely guarded all approaches. Thus on 12th April a patrol to a point overlooking Maprik was ambushed and three Australians and a native were killed. On the 14th a patrol advancing from Wilgolman encountered a strong position with covered pits guarding a junction of three tracks; mortar fire failed to dislodge the enemy.

In preparation for the final attack brigade headquarters was moved to Abungai, that of the 2/6th to Kulkuil and that of the 2/7th to a point near Gualigem. On 15th April two companies of the 2/6th (Captain B. J. French's and Major A. G. S. Edgar's) began to drive eastward to the Screw River. The enemy was bombarded from the air and with mortars and machine-guns, but resisted strongly from well-dug positions.[6]

On 17th April there were three clashes in the 2/6th's area; in one of them Lieutenant Jamieson[7] and 12 others found an enemy group dug in at Wambak and killed probably ten. On the 18th there were four clashes; in the Kombichagi area Lieutenant Gordon and 12 men found the enemy dug in; one Australian, Corporal Taylor,[8] was killed in the ensuing fight. On the 19th there were two patrol clashes; and a patrol entered Bungara, hitherto strongly held, without opposition.

Parbury had issued his orders for the capture of Maprik on 12th April. In the first phase Captain Pearson's company of the 2/7th was to take a long kunai-covered spur to the north-east of Maprik 2; and next day Captain Baird's advancing from the north-west was to take Maprik 1. Each of these companies had 140 natives under command. Captain Arnold's company was to press on Bainyik, and the fourth company was in reserve. Pearson's company advanced on 15th April to the line of Nimrod Creek where they encountered heavily-defended and camouflaged pill-boxes astride the spur up which they intended to approach the kunai ridge. The advance was halted here, but the enemy's positions were closely examined, and next day the company pressed on from the north-west. Soon after the move began the leading platoon saw a Japanese manning a light machine-gun on a spur overlooking them. This position was fired on with the mortars and by 11.30 a.m. the platoon was at the kunai patch without having been fired on. Three hours later the whole company was on the kunai ridge. Patrols killed two Japanese in the area. A boy-line arrived in the afternoon. Heavy rain fell causing an intervening stream to rise until

---

[6] In this bush fighting the number of accidental injuries was becoming most disturbing. For example, in the 2/6th Battalion on 15th and 16th April: Lieutenant V. N. Maloney, a veteran, was wounded by the accidental discharge of an Owen gun; a private was wounded by a booby-trap in his own company area; and two privates were wounded by a premature explosion of a mortar bomb. In the same period, in action against the enemy, one man was killed and another fatally wounded on patrol, and an officer was wounded.

[7] Lt-Col W. D. Jamieson, VX146394; 2/6 Bn. Regular soldier; b. St. Kilda, Vic, 16 Feb 1924.

[8] Cpl A. C. Taylor, NX101509; 2/6 Bn. Truck driver; b. Randwick, NSW, 27 Apr 1920. Killed in action 18 Apr 1945.

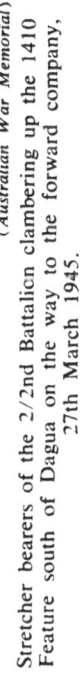

Native carriers climbing into the mountains south of Dagua with supplies for the forward troops of the 16th Brigade, 4th April 1945.

(Australian War Memorial)

Stretcher bearers of the 2/2nd Battalion clambering up the 1410 Feature south of Dagua on the way to the forward company, 27th March 1945.

(Australian War Memorial)

(Australian War Memorial)
A carrier line, with an infantry escort, taking supplies to the 2/3rd Battalion in the Wonginara Mission area, 4th April 1945.

(Australian War Memorial)
Major-General J. E. S. Stevens (G.O.C. 6th Division) and Lieut-Colonel J. A. Bishop (temporarily commanding the 19th Brigade) with the 2/8th Battalion on Mount Shiburangu, 29th June 1945.

it became a raging torrent, and as the carriers were returning one of their escort was swept away and drowned.

The leading men of Baird's company moved out at 6.30 a.m. on the 17th towards a House Tamboran (native meeting house) just north of Maprik 1. The first and second bounds were not eventful, but as soon as the third began a Japanese sentry shot and mortally wounded the leading scout. The third bound was completed by 3.30 p.m. and it was decided to occupy a defensive position at that point 300 to 400 yards from the final objective.

That night Pearson's company was mortared and next morning it was found that Japanese had dug in on both flanks, those on the north-east being on sloping ground defiladed from machine-gun fire and offering a difficult target for mortars. Three Australians were wounded, one mortally, and the flooding of the streams to the rear made it impossible to carry back the wounded or to bring forward rations.

On 18th April Baird's patrols found that the enemy was still dug in in the House Tamboran area with weapon-pits covering all approaches. They were bombarded by 4.2-inch and 3-inch mortars and Vickers guns throughout the day, as were the Japanese dug in on both sides of Pearson's company. On the fourth day—the 19th—this company made a two-platoon attack on the Japanese to the south-west. Lieutenant Clews' platoon edged forward along the direct approach while Lieutenant R. W. Saunders[9] led his men in an encircling move on the right to a spur and knoll dominating the enemy. Throughout these moves the Japanese "were plastered with mortars, Vickers, and rifle grenades and LMG fire and the final assault resulted in a veritable hail of small arms fire". The Japanese at length broke and fled leaving 10 dead. The Australians lost one man killed and 9 wounded, 7 of them only slightly. The enemy position was extensive, freshly dug, and able to hold 60 to 70 men.

Baird's company was still held up. On 20th April Lieutenant Bowden[1] led a patrol to the summit of the House Tamboran feature and drove the enemy off, killing six. One man was killed; Bowden was wounded but remained on duty. Immediately the whole company occupied the feature which gave a view of the Maprik strip, Neligum villages, Katoma village, and the hills east of the Screw.

Next day two accurate air strikes were made on the ridge between the two forward companies. Lieutenant Kilpatrick[2] led a patrol from Baird's company to the Maprik strip killing four Japanese on the way. The strip was found to be overgrown with kunai grass three feet high, but firm and well drained beneath and with only a few bomb craters. A patrol to the Bainyik area encountered three Japanese sentries, killed two, and came under fire from a well-dug position. Lance-Corporal Johnson[3] was killed

---
[9] Saunders, an aborigine and a veteran member of this battalion, had been commissioned from the O.C.T.U. a few weeks before.
[1] Lt L. F. Bowden, MC, SX4240. 2/12 and 2/7 Bns. Farmer; of Moonta, SA; b. Moonta, 30 Oct 1915.
[2] Capt W. J. Kilpatrick, VX108478; 2/7 Bn. Jackeroo; of Beaumaris, Vic; b. Armadale, Vic, 9 Feb 1919.
[3] L-Cpl N. Johnson, MM, VX58495; 2/7 Bn. Student; of Warrnambool, Vic; b. Woolsthorpe, Vic, 23 Apr 1922. Killed in action 21 Apr 1945.

and two wounded and the patrol withdrew. On the 22nd the troops were mainly engaged in patrolling to clear the Maprik area. Only at Bainyik and Maprik 2 was the enemy found still to be in occupation. Next day patrolling was continued and it was decided that the whole Maprik area west of the Screw was clear of the enemy and it was doubtful whether there were any Japanese west of the Screw south to its junction with the Ninab. The enemy was well dug in, however, at Bainyik.

On 25th April a patrol from Baird's company crossed the Screw and moved on towards Midpum Creek, came under fire 300 yards from it and withdrew. Next day a fighting patrol was sent out and it overcame a party of 7 Japanese killing 3 but later came under fire from across the Midpum.

Parbury's headquarters was established on a site above Maprik on the 28th. Next day Wing Commander Hall landed on Hayfield in an Auster and reported that, after further levelling, the strip would be able to take a Dakota.[4]

The opening of an airfield in the Torricellis would come none too soon for the toiling troops and native carriers. The march from Suain to Maprik took five hard days, with a staging camp, supplied by air dropping, at the end of each stage.[5]

For some time Angau had been maintaining a patrol base at Drekikir manned by an officer and 12 police, and to it came a number of reports of a Japanese party about 50 strong which had moved west through M'Bras to Tau, where they had settled. The natives said that they were moving against Aitape. Consequently a platoon of the 2/5th Battalion under Lieutenant C. H. Miles left Aitape on 16th April and marched five days to Drekikir and thence, accompanied by Captain D. M. Fienberg of Angau, patrolled south to find this party. Miles reported that on 24th April he had found them at Kubriwat, had killed two in the engagement there, but could not dislodge the survivors. He continued to harass them and on 3rd May the whole party surrendered: a lieut-colonel (Tagenaka), 4 other officers and 37 men. They were marched to Maprik and flown thence to Aitape.

While Hayfield was being developed the 2/6th continued its arduous task of probing forward on the northern flank. Bungara was occupied on 20th April; on the 23rd five patrols were out, setting ambushes, burning villages being used by Japanese, and locating and cutting the enemy's lines of communication. Next day there were two patrol clashes. A native reported that bombing had driven a party of 20 or 30 Japanese out of the Neligum villages but on 25th April a patrol under Lieutenant A. H. Seekamp found three there, drove these away, and burned the villages, which were occupied next day. Also on the 25th a patrol under the ubiquitous Sergeant Hedderman found Mangumbu strongly held.

---

[4] Lieutenant E. B. H. Henning of the 2/8th Field Company was flown into Balif on 23rd April and thenceforward supervised the construction of the Maprik and Hayfield strips.

[5] A vivid and humorous description of the five-day march is given in R. C. Searle, *On Your Feet* (1948), an account of the experiences of the 2nd Battery of the 2/1st Anti-Tank Regiment in this campaign.

Early in May Major Hay's company probed forward to find approaches from the north to Yentagim. Next day Lieutenant E. C. Trethewie led a platoon to attack Yentagim where about 40 Japanese, well dug in, were encountered. The attack was supported by mortars and Vickers guns and lasted an hour and a half. By this time nine Japanese dead had been counted; the Australians' ammunition was exhausted and they withdrew.

Two flame-throwers had now been received by the 2/7th and on 8th May these were used to drive the enemy from part of the narrow steepsided Kumbungua ridge. The Japanese made off, abandoning 30 weapon-pits, but engaged the Australians from a knoll farther up the ridge. That day the diarist of the 2/7th wrote:

An interesting ceremony took place on the Maprik strip at 1600 hours to commemorate the end of the war in Europe and also the capture of Maprik. This consisted of a guard in which representatives from each company were present. . . . The guard was smartly turned out having been issued with new clothes, hats and even boot-polish for the occasion. The guard marched on to the northern end of the strip where a Union Jack was flying, formed up and presented arms during the playing of the Last Post. A minute's silence then took place followed by the playing of Reveille. . . . A detachment of police boys led by a native corporal was also formed up before the flag and carried out drill movements in time with the movements of the guard.[6]

On 12th May Captain Cole of Angau arranged a native sing-sing to celebrate the fall of Maprik. Natives attended decked with flowers and paint. Cole told them that Wewak had fallen and that the natives were to help the Australians coming inland from that direction.

Flame-throwers were proving very effective. On 10th May the 2/7th occupied Waigakum 1, and on the 11th a platoon with flame-throwers attacked and took a position where the defenders abandoned 50 packs. Another platoon approached the knoll at the south end of the Kumbungua ridge from the south, attacked up a steep slope and put to flight the defenders who abandoned 25 packs and 100 sticks of gelignite. The Japanese opened fire, however, from higher up and, the ground being unsuitable for defence, the platoon withdrew.

On the 13th, after an air attack that stripped the objective of vegetation, a platoon entered central Kumbungua without opposition and found 24 covered weapon-pits. Next day 21 Beauforts made an even heavier air attack on Kumbungua—"the most effective air strike in support of our troops yet experienced". After it a platoon occupied the ridge against little resistance.

Patrols took Waigakum 2 on the 17th. On the 19th a platoon, guided by natives, surprised six Japanese in a garden south-east of Kalabu. Here Private Jenkins[7] came upon one Japanese asleep outside a weapon-pit.

---

[6] The end of the fighting in Europe on 8th-9th May seems to have caused little rejoicing in the front-line units in New Guinea. "Cessation of hostilities in Europe announced, but no excitement was felt, as it certainly made no difference to the work here," wrote one unit diarist.

[7] Cpl L. J. Jenkins, VX17060; 2/7 Bn. Butcher; of Malvern, Vic; b. Moonee Ponds, Vic, 15 Oct 1922. Jenkins had lived in Devon for seven years and had acquired a West Country accent, and was known in the unit as "Pommy" Jenkins. On enlistment Jenkins had overstated his age by four years.

As he was within feet of me (wrote Jenkins later) I thought it was an excellent opportunity to take a prisoner so I woke him with a light kick and pulled him to his feet with my left hand, keeping my Owen gun in my right. I had managed to get my prisoner some paces from his position when a slight noise alerted his mates and they opened fire on the patrol. With this the Jap broke from my grasp and I was forced to shoot him. One other Japanese was killed and the others made off.

On 26th May Lieutenant Wiles'[8] platoon of the 2/7th cleared the area north-east of Kalabu and next day attacked a ridge 1,600 yards to the east after exceptionally heavy support had been provided: 12 Beauforts attacked, then the ridge was bombarded by two field guns, by 4.2-inch and 3-inch mortars, and Vickers guns. Despite this fire the Japanese stood firm. That day Lieutenant Darryl with two Australians and two natives, in a daring reconnaissance, found the Yamil area strongly defended with all approaches guarded. Patrols also found that Malba was on the dominating ground in the area ahead, and it was heavily bombarded. It was attacked on 29th May by a platoon which gained part of the area but was forced out by intense machine-gun fire. On 31st May, however, two platoons made a brilliant attack after bombardment by artillery and mortars. Fifteen bodies and 19 rifles were found, the Australian losses being one platoon commander (Bowden) and two others wounded.

The first DC-3 aircraft landed on Hayfield on 14th May and took off four patients. Thereafter supplies, tractors, bulldozers, graders, jeeps and field guns were flown in; and practically all troops arrived in the area and departed from it by air.

With the advent of machinery via Hayfield a road was constructed to Maprik and then turned east through the trackless jungle to follow our advancing troops. Jeep transport revolutionised our supply, evacuation of casualties and native labour problems and henceforth we had no real worries in these matters.[9]

Moten instructed the 2/7th Battalion to allot one company to the task of manning the "main line of resistance". It would man nine defended localities each with not less than a section, and each section would send a patrol to the section on its right every four hours and at all times have one sentry on duty.

During May the 2/6th on the northern flank continued to patrol eastward and the enemy, harassed by patrols and by air attack, slowly moved back. Mangumbu was found to be empty of Japanese on 1st May and occupied next day. At this stage, because of the commitments round Wewak, the 17th Brigade was informed that only one air strike each day would be available to it for the next two weeks or so.

Intelligence gathered up to 11th May suggested that the enemy was strong in the Kaboibus area and round Yamil and their line of withdrawal would be towards Mount Turu. Mendamen and Jamei 2 were also firmly held. Both areas were harassed by mortar and machine-gun fire, and a patrol found a good approach to Jamei 2 along a spur. Flame-throwers

---

[8] Lt J. E. Wiles, VX16067; 2/7 Bn. Butcher; of Surrey Hills, Vic; b. Surrey Hills, 20 Mar 1915.
[9] 17th Australian Infantry Brigade Report on Operations in the Aitape-Wewak Area, November 1944-August 1945.

had now reached the 2/6th and with them Lieutenant B. W. Moloney to train teams to handle the new weapon. On the 20th a platoon attacked towards Jamei with two flame-throwers, but encountered fire from well-dug positions with overhead cover and the attack failed. Moloney and Privates Miller[1] and Ward[2] were killed and Lieutenant Fahl[3] and three others wounded. Moloney fell so close to the enemy's posts that his body could not be recovered and the flame-throwers, both damaged, fell into the enemy's hands. Twelve Beauforts attacked this position on 22nd May and for the next few days much fire was poured into the positions round Jamei; by the 25th the Japanese had had enough and the area was occupied without opposition. In preparation for an advance to Yamil Lieutenant Trethewie and 15 men of Major Hay's company, which had now rejoined the 2/6th, sought and found a suitable company position at Loanim. From there Hay moved a platoon forward to a ridge overlooking Yamil; it was attacked and he was seriously wounded.

In April and May the 2/6th had lost 11 killed and 31 wounded; it had counted 93 Japanese killed, and the natives attached to it, of whom one was killed and four wounded, had killed 65 Japanese.

The 2nd Battery of the 2/1st Anti-Tank Regiment, which had been formed into an infantry company, was sent into Hayfield early in May to protect the field and, while doing so, to patrol to the south.[4] This was the beginning of a long period of deep patrolling by these gunners turned into infantrymen. As was the general practice in the Torricellis each patrol was accompanied by a "sentry boy" who knew the country in detail. Other natives sometimes joined the patrols just for the love of it.

> They seemed to be able to sense a kill and often, when a patrol was about to get into a "blue", they would appear from nowhere, furtively, silently, like bludgers coming in for mess. They would come with long, murderous spears, with tomahawks and machetes, as keen as boxing fans to see the blood flow, and as disappointed if it didn't.[5]

On 17th May a patrol of 30 led by Captain Johnson,[6] the commander of the company, with natives, set out to attack an enemy-occupied village in the Nintigo area. They approached with stealth, formed up at the jungle edge upon a frontage of about 50 yards and attacked through the village firing as they went. They were well among the huts before they met any fire. Then Bombardier Nottingham[7] and Gunners Daley[8] and

---

[1] Pte D. Miller, NX117531; 2/6 Bn. Carton maker; of Rosebery, NSW; b. Norah Head Lighthouse, NSW, 24 Apr 1921. Killed in action 20 May 1945.

[2] Pte G. Ward, VX90799; 2/6 Bn. Fitter and turner; of Bairnsdale, Vic; b. Bairnsdale, 24 Jun 1921. Killed in action 20 May 1945.

[3] Lt R. W. Fahl, NX110899; 2/6 Bn. Clerk; of Bondi, NSW; b. Mount Morgan, Qld, 23 Feb 1918.

[4] In 1943 the anti-tank regiments were re-named tank-attack regiments, evidently with the intention of making them sound more aggressive. However, the original titles of these regiments have been preserved throughout these volumes. The regimental associations know them by those names today.

[5] Searle, p. 21.

[6] Maj C. M. Johnson, MC, DX176. 2/3 Fd Regt and 2/1 A-Tk Regt. Regular soldier; b. Ariah Park, NSW, 9 Jul 1919.

[7] Sgt S. J. Nottingham, QX2235; 2/1 A-Tk Regt. Draper; b. Mackay, Qld, 22 Apr 1919.

[8] Gnr G. H. Daley, NX193466; 2/1 A-Tk Regt. Cream carrier; of Casino, NSW; b. Moree, NSW, 12 Sep 1924.

Taylor[9] were hit, but Nottingham and Daley went on. The advance did not slacken. The attackers set fire to the huts; 14 Japanese were killed.

The doughty Johnson led out another patrol on 24th May, this time of 30 all ranks in three detachments each commanded by a lieutenant; the task was to destroy some 37 well-armed Japanese in two positions at Mikau village. After reconnaissance parties under Lieutenants Caldwell[1] and Perkins[2] had found suitable approaches to both positions, Johnson gave orders for simultaneous attacks on both before dawn next day. When preparing to attack, an Owen in Caldwell's group—the main body—was accidentally fired, and the enemy opened up. This group retired and formed a perimeter; but Perkins' group took the firing to be the signal to attack and went in and took their objective, Gunner Kitching[3] doing a fine job with the Bren gun. The main body then formed up and attacked with success, Bombardier Reed[4] playing a leading part. Thirty packs and rifles were found. Only one Australian was wounded.[5]

Early in April the remnants of the *41st Japanese Division* retreated to the northwest of Wora, but the Australians occupied Wora, thus boxing up the Japanese. Mano, however, bided his time and slipped round to the south. *Miyake Force* was still in the forward area and in late April its main line of resistance ran through Imbia-Neligum-Kumbungua-Bainyik, but in May it was withdrawn to Loanim-Yamil-Kumbungua. Orders were then received to hold a north-south line in this area until 31st May; in June the force withdrew to Ulupu and, soon afterwards, Aoniaru.

The loss of Waigakum to the 2/7th Battalion in mid-May had a very upsetting effect on the Japanese. It was the point of junction between *Miyake Force*, now 800 strong, and the *41st Division* and, according to General Yoshiwara, this loss led directly to the withdrawal from Kalabu and Loanim.

On 5th May General Yoshiwara handed over his responsibilities to General Nakai of the *20th Division*. On 11th June, however, Yoshiwara was given the task of studying the possibility of establishing a separate area of resistance, self-supporting in food, on the Sepik.

Meanwhile, in the coastal sector, the offensive against Wewak had been in progress. As a preliminary move General Stevens had decided to move the 19th Brigade and other troops forward to the growing base at But. To make room for them the main body of the 16th Brigade was concentrated east of the But River. With the 2/3rd now in the Wonginara area, Brigadier King gave Colonel Cameron of the 2/2nd the task of securing the Autogi and Walanduum areas in the hills north of the Mabam

---

[9] Gnr C. S. Taylor, QX987; 2/1 A-Tk Regt. Station hand; of Longreach, Qld; b. Barcaldine, Qld, 25 Mar 1917.

[1] Lt J. Caldwell, NX52374; 2/1 A-Tk Regt. Secretary; of Bellevue Hill, NSW; b. Sydney, 28 Nov 1902. Died 22 Aug 1945.

[2] Lt A. J. Perkins, QX4427; 2/1 A-Tk Regt. Salesman; of Brisbane; b. Ipswich, Qld, 24 May 1919.

[3] Gnr H. S. Kitching, MM, NX90538; 2/1 A-Tk Regt. Boilermaker; of Carlingford, NSW; b. Molong, NSW, 31 Oct 1919.

[4] Bdr F. L. J. Reed, MM, NX68854; 2/1 A-Tk Regt. Labourer; of Yass, NSW; b. Scone, NSW, 24 Jun 1916. Killed in action 3 Jun 1945.

[5] At this stage, in May, practically the whole of the 2/1st Anti-Tank was committed to battle, but no part of it, of course, in an anti-tank role. The 1st Battery equipped with 75-mm pack howitzers had one section with the 19th Brigade (this was later moved to Maprik) and one with the 2/6th Commando Regiment. The 2nd Battery was fighting as infantry in the Hayfield area. The 3rd had formed an infantry group, 63 strong, and two 4.2-inch mortar sections both in action about Wewak.

River, and this was achieved by 8th April. Patrols found the coast empty of Japanese as far east as Kofi.

The Japanese force in the Boiken area was now believed to number about 300, and its strongest fighting unit to be the *III/66th Battalion,* about 100 strong. Stevens on 7th April ordered King to take Karawop and Boiken and establish a beach-head across the Hawain River. Thus on 14th April the 2/1st Battalion (temporarily commanded by Major B. W. T. Catterns) moved from But to a position just in rear of the 2/2nd with orders to pass through and take the Karawop-Wisling area next day; one company was to take Karawop, one to clear the foothills to the south. On the 15th when the left company reached a point about a mile from Karawop a mortar opened fire and soon had killed 5 men and wounded four. The enemy was bombarded and patrols sent out to find the mortar, but without success. Next day the right company continued its advance through the foothills where it took an enemy outpost. In the attack Private Bartholomew[6] stepped into the open and, firing his Bren gun from the hip, stormed the enemy's position, killing a machine-gunner and dispersing the others. Having fired all his own ammunition he turned the Japanese machine-gun on the enemy. Karawop village was occupied by the battalion without opposition and then Wisling. In later clashes nine Japanese were killed. From 21st April the brigade concentrated round Karawop.

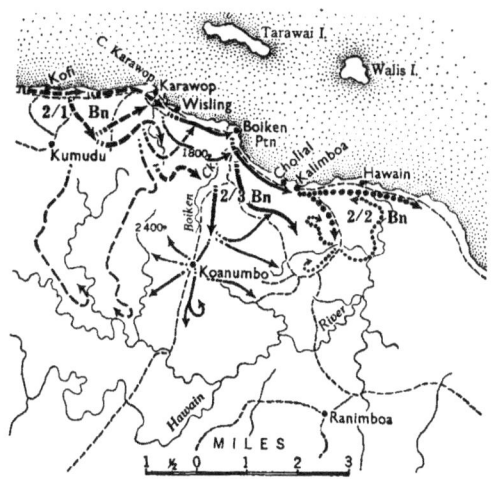

16th Brigade, 15th April-2nd May

The next task was to capture the mouth of the Hawain River. Thereupon, the 2/1st on 25th April occupied the 1800 Feature without opposition, while the 2/3rd to the north launched an attack on Boiken Plantation. The 2/3rd advanced with two companies forward—Major MacKenzie's in the foothills of 1800 and Captain Gibbins' astride the road—and with two tanks in support. About 1.30 p.m. Gibbins encountered the enemy dug in astride the road and the tanks were called forward. When Lieutenant Rumble's[7] platoon worked round the flank and the tanks attacked frontally the enemy was driven out leaving two dead. Next day in a similar

---

[6] Pte H. W. Bartholomew, MM, NX78416; 2/1 Bn. Moulder; of North Sydney; b. Kempsey, NSW, 30 Sep 1922.

[7] Lt-Col N. R. Rumble, NX139920; 2/3 Bn. Schoolteacher; of Carlingford, NSW; b. Granville, NSW, 3 Dec 1918.

fight at Cholial the enemy fled leaving three dead, and a 37-mm gun which had exploded after firing two rounds without effect.

It was quite apparent that the Nips had no stomach for the tanks for there was ample evidence where they had speedily evacuated as the tanks approached. The advance along the coast for the last three days was the fastest of the campaign—a further argument for Major Cory[8] in the use of tanks.[9]

Nineteen Indian prisoners were recovered and two more 37-mm guns captured that day in the foothills. Indian prisoners continued to come into the Australian lines in increasing numbers in the next few weeks.

We got in another goodly batch of Indians in the last few days (wrote an officer in May). They are a great race—Sikhs and Punjabis—great in adversity. It is most inspiring to see them come in. A few weeks ago a batch of 20 arrived, including a sergeant. All of them were weak and ragged, but as soon as they reached the road and were to be loaded on the lorry, the sergeant pulled them up and made them tidy their clothes to the best of their ability so that they would arrive at headquarters looking as presentable as possible. He organised them for their meal as well—the first decent one, I imagine, since February 1942, and made them wait until all were ready to begin. There is at least *something* ennobling in war, a spirit of service that seems to be so sadly lacking in so much of our country at present.

On 27th April the 2/2nd Battalion passed through the 2/3rd whose forward company was at Kalimboa and advanced to the Hawain, with Captain Lovett's company in the lead. At 10.10 a.m. Captain Oliver's[1] company and the squadron of the 2/4th Armoured Regiment crossed the river in assault boats without opposition. Meanwhile on the right small groups of Japanese were driven from the hills west of the Hawain.

The 2/2nd Battalion thus carried out the final movement of the brigade's advance. It was justly proud of its part in the thrust from Wank Creek to Karawop, and later across the Hawain. It was the swiftest advance of the campaign. There had been little resistance as far as Dagua but the fight for the mountain pass was bitter and costly, particularly in young officers and N.C.O's. Between 29th March and 6th April the battalion lost 20 killed or died of wounds and 50 wounded; 107 Japanese were killed. By 20th April only 10 of the 18 platoons were commanded by officers, and two of the companies, and the battalion itself, lacked seconds-in-command. The battalion was 246 under strength, the rifle companies being somewhat below half strength. The other battalions were not much better off.

The 2/3rd Battalion, patrolling south along Boiken Creek, now found the enemy in strength in the Koanumbo area. On 29th April a patrol led by Lieutenant F. J. Hoddinott found 15 Japanese digging in on a steep-sided spur there. On the 30th two platoons of Captain K. M. Boyer's company attacked this position. After advancing about 50 yards they were halted by intense fire. Colonel Hutchison sent forward two more

---

[8] Maj G. C. Cory, QX6086. 6 Cav Regt and 2/4 Armd Regt. Grazier; of Warwick district, Qld; b. Gordonbrook Station, via Grafton, NSW, 5 Feb 1914.
[9] *Tank Tracks—The War History of the 2/4th Australian Armoured Regimental Group*, p. 93.
[1] Capt H. A. Oliver, VX100097. 39 and 2/2 Bns. Builder and decorator; of Toorak, Vic; b. Melbourne, 12 Feb 1915. Killed in action 27 Jun 1945.

platoons and on 1st May, after artillery bombardment, the position was taken, but it was found that the Japanese were dug in 100 yards to the west. This position was attacked next day.

The attack was carried out by arming the forward section with 3 Bren LMGs and 4 OSMGs [Owens] with an infantry flame-thrower following. The secondary growth was so dense as to preclude vision for more than 10 yards. The forward section, advancing and firing on the move, encountered heavy LMG fire from dug-in positions with overhead cover . . . and here the flame-thrower [manned by Private McFarlane[2]] was brought into action. Although the density of the undergrowth limited its range to 20 yards, the effect of the weapon, combined with the continued advance and fire, caused the enemy to wildly withdraw over the precipitous sides.[3]

In this series of actions the 2/3rd lost 5 killed and 8 wounded; later a total of 28 enemy dead were found in the whole area. The extent of the field works suggested that the enemy had been about 50 strong. Patrols found that only about 15 now remained in the area and they were dug in on the 2400 Feature. These were driven out by air and artillery bombardment.

At this stage the 19th Brigade took over the advance. The 16th Brigade had been forward for more than three months and the three battalions had lost 85 killed and 192 wounded in a long series of actions. They and other units of the brigade had killed 909 Japanese and taken 27 prisoners.

The survivors in these weakened battalions were weary and often ill. The medical officer of the 2/3rd, for example, reported that early in May the men were beginning to show signs of the strain of 15 weeks in action.

The malaria rate began to rise rapidly (he wrote); skin lesions of all types were prevalent and tropical fatigue began to affect all ranks. . . . On 29th May after four weeks at Boiken—weeks of continuous patrolling and sporadic clashes with the enemy—the battalion moved on to Boram Plantation. . . . For the first three days sharp fighting ensued. . . . Exhaustion, nervous strain and malaria now became uncontrollable, and brought the battalion to its knees. All companies were affected, and by the end of the first week in June, in most cases could scarcely muster one full platoon, and of these many were carrying on the fight with temperatures over 100 degrees. The C.O. was informed that the battalion could no longer carry on, and would require at least two months' rest before they could be considered an effective fighting force again. . . . In spite of the low state of health the morale of the troops has always been high.[4]

A machine-gun officer wrote afterwards:

It is difficult to describe the utter fatigue which this campaign imposed on all ranks and how even in May when everyone seemed to be at the end of their tether we managed to keep going until the operations concluded. The 2/3rd Machine Gun Battalion was not at any stage from the Danmap to the conclusion of the campaign relieved for rest. It has always amazed me that men could, for so long, continue in these very strenuous operations without relief. The physical

---

[2] L-Cpl J. L. S. McFarlane, NX3409. 2/1 Fd Regt and 2/3 Bn. Jackeroo; of Parramatta, NSW; b. Grafton, NSW, 26 Mar 1919.

[3] 16 Aust Inf Bde Report on Operations—Aitape-Wewak Campaign, 23 Jan 45 to 8 May 45. This appears to have been the first time a flame-thrower was used in action by the Australian Army, although American troops had been using effective flame-throwers since early in 1943.

[4] Writing at the end of June, however, after three weeks' rest this medical officer reported that the men were showing signs of recovery as a result of adequate sleep, plenty of swimming, sun-bathing, and some recreation.

exhaustion and mental strain of continuous operations for many months in the jungle is beyond description.

The frequent evidence of Japanese atrocities had a remarkable effect on the morale of the troops. It developed a feeling of disgust which caused men to enter battle with a greater determination to eliminate the enemy whatever the cost.

Despite losses, weariness, and the nagging conviction that the campaign was not worth while, the men retained their pride in themselves and their leaders. In each attack young soldiers, or soldiers now in their sixth year of war, performed deeds of fine gallantry.

Had a yarn to some 2/2nd and 2/3rd Battalion men today (says a private diary). They praised their officers—all the company commanders were men and a half. Reinforcement officers who had been "given away" on the Tableland were now being "paid". The infantryman is always seeking men to praise: the stretcher bearers, the air force, the medical officers, the F.O.Os, the boongs—"you should have seen the boongs bringing in the wounded yesterday down the big hill". At the same time a recent newspaper article about how the Australians are scrounging American gear and cannibalising captured Jap equipment to keep going was quoted with glee. Someone had seen it in a newspaper dropped by one of the passing airliners.

The advance had taken the Australians through an extensive Japanese base and airfield area, and along the coastal plain and in the foothills lay an immense amount of equipment: guns, trucks, wrecked aircraft, water-carts, bombs and ammunition, machine tools, medical and signal gear, small arms, clothing, dumps of fuel. And along the tracks, in huts or in the open were hundreds of skeletons of Japanese who had died of disease and malnutrition. No systematic count was made of the skeletons lying between the Danmap and the Hawain but in one small area, about Marabus, 250 were found.

We "won" an 8 Div truck today; what is left of this Japanese army came down through Malaya and has bequeathed us a lot of junk from the Far East (wrote a soldier in a letter home). Most of its trucks are Fords or Chevs with Singapore bodies and Java tyres, but only about one in twenty go. We have done fairly well for mechanical equipment, though, since we shot through the But, Dagua and Wewak airfields.

On 30th April Generals Blamey, Sturdee, Stevens and Berryman conferred at Lae about future operations round Wewak. Both Sturdee, who had visited the forward troops round Boiken a few days earlier, and Stevens said that they had the means to take Wewak. Blamey approved orders, drawn up by Stevens on the 27th, whereby the 19th Brigade should advance from the Hawain reaching Cape Wom by 14th May; Wewak should then be attacked by the 19th Brigade, moving along the coast, and the 2/6th Commando Regiment plus other detachments landed east of Cape Moem and supported by naval bombardment. Blamey gave instructions that a battalion of the 8th Brigade, then based on Madang, should be ready to support the commando regiment if needed. The 17th Brigade was to continue patrol actions round Maprik.

At an earlier stage a landing on Muschu Island had been contemplated, but this idea was now abandoned. An effort to reconnoitre the island had led to disaster to the scouting party. This had begun on 11th April when Lieutenants Gubbay[5] and Barnes[6] and six others were taken to a point near Muschu Island in a naval motor launch and went ashore in folboats with the task of extracting one prisoner, reconnoitring the beaches in an area where a landing in force was contemplated, and reconnoitring the enemy's defensive positions generally.

The folboats overturned while landing, and all signal equipment was lost. The party hid the boats and made a base 100 yards inland. Thence they travelled east past Cape Barabar. Next morning they caught, bound and gagged a Japanese but, when a Japanese patrol was heard near by, he dragged off the gag and shouted. He was shot. When returning to their base the party detected an ambush and moved inland and thence to the coast, where they built a raft and put to sea. The raft, however, was washed on to a reef and most of the weapons were lost. Gubbay, Barnes, Lance-Corporal Walklate[7] and Private Eagleton[8] each put to sea on a log in the hope that one of them would be seen by an aircraft and be able to ask that the motor launch pick them up on 13th-14th April. The remainder under Sergeant Weber[9] moved to the east coast to await a signal or rescue but the men on the logs were not heard from again. The other men moved inland on 14th April and were attacked by a patrol; Sapper Dennis[1] killed two Japanese, but after the fight he did not see his other three companions again. Dennis went stealthily to Cape Samein, killing one Japanese and destroying a heavy machine-gun on the way. On 17th April at 7 p.m. he put to sea on a surf-board he had made, drifted to the mainland and landed just west of Cape Pus at 4 a.m. next day. He was recovered by a patrol on the Hawain River at 2 p.m. on the 20th, six days after the affray in which the last of his companions had been killed.

The strength of the enemy in the Wewak area was estimated at from 500 to 1,000, including the headquarters of the denuded *51st Division*, with parts of its *66th* and *102nd Regiments*, the *25th Airfield Battalion*, and other units under command.

Stevens' orders to the 19th Brigade were to concentrate in Boiken Plantation and thence advance and destroy the enemy from Cape Wom to Yarabos, and at Ranimboa; cut the tracks south of Wirui Mission; and then destroy the enemy in the area of Wewak Point and Cape Moem. Among the additional troops placed under Brigadier Martin's command were "C" Squadron of the 2/4th Armoured Regiment and the 2/7th Commando Squadron; in support was nearly all the artillery of the division.

---

[5] Lt A. R. Gubbay, NX82924. 11 Armd Car Regt and "Z" Special Unit. Customs officer; of Port Vila, New Hebrides; b. Noumea, New Caledonia, 19 Jan 1923. Presumed died 13 Apr 1945.

[6] Lt T. J. Barnes, VX6078; "Z" Special Unit. Labourer; of Fitzroy, Vic; b. Cootamundra, NSW, 6 Apr 1916. Presumed died 13 Apr 1945.

[7] L-Cpl S. H. Walklate, NX202843; "Z" Special Unit. Salesman; of Waverley, NSW; b. Bush Grove, NSW, 11 Jan 1918. Presumed died 13 Apr 1945.

[8] Pte R. E. Eagleton, NX92651. 2/16 Bn and "Z" Special Unit. Clerk; of Blakehurst, NSW; b. Glebe, NSW, 3 Mar 1920. Presumed died 13 Apr 1945.

[9] Sgt M. F. M. Weber, NX45386. 2/20 Bn and "Z" Special Unit. Station hand; of Scone, NSW; b. Muswellbrook, NSW, 6 Mar 1919. Killed in action 14 Apr 1945.

[1] Spr E. T. Dennis, MM, NX73110. 2/5 Indep Coy and "Z" Special Unit. Tobacco worker; of Kensington, NSW; b. Tempe, NSW, 29 Aug 1919.

"Farida Force", as the group which was to land east of Wewak was named, included the 2/6th Commando Regiment less the 2/7th Squadron, two 75-mm guns of the 1st Anti-Tank Battery, one company of the 2/3rd

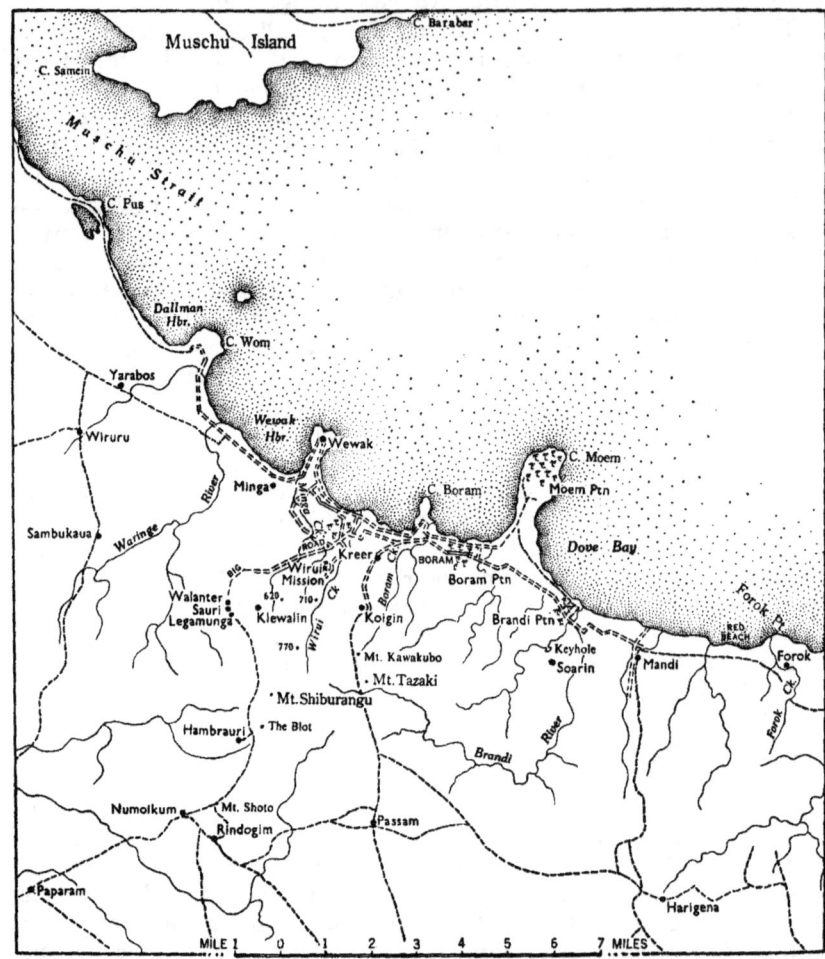

Machine Gun Battalion organised as infantry, a platoon of machine-gunners from the same battalion, two detachments of mortars, and other ancillary detachments. The total strength was 623. The troops were to be put ashore by the 43rd Landing Craft Company (Major Mitchell[2]) from one L.C.M. and nine A.L.C's, with two A.L.C's armed with mortars for

---

[2] Maj G. D. Mitchell, MC, DCM, NX156027. (1st AIF: Capt 48 Bn.) CO 43 Landing Craft Coy 1944-45. MLA NSW; of Sydney; b. Caltowie, SA, 30 Aug 1894. Died 11 Jan 1961. Author of *Soldier in Battle* (1940).

close support. D-day for this landing was to be 11th May but the 19th Brigade's advance was to begin on the 3rd. In the first phase the 2/4th Battalion was to wipe out the enemy in the Cape Wom-Yarabos area and the 2/8th to clear Ranimboa; in the second the 2/11th would cut the tracks south from Wirui Mission and take the high hill on which the mission stood, and the commando regiment would take Sauri; in the third Wewak Point would be captured.

There had been changes in the command of all battalions of the 19th Brigade since its earlier period in action. Lieut-Colonel G. S. Cox and Lieut-Colonel Green[3] (both originally officers of the 2/2nd Battalion) had been appointed to the 2/4th and 2/11th respectively, and the 2/8th was led by Major C. L. Simpson in the absence of Lieut-Colonel Howden at the Tactical School. The brigade was taken from Aitape to But in barges, and thence to Boiken in motor vehicles. On 3rd May the 2/4th with three troops of tanks advanced from the Hawain and covered six miles without opposition. Next day it

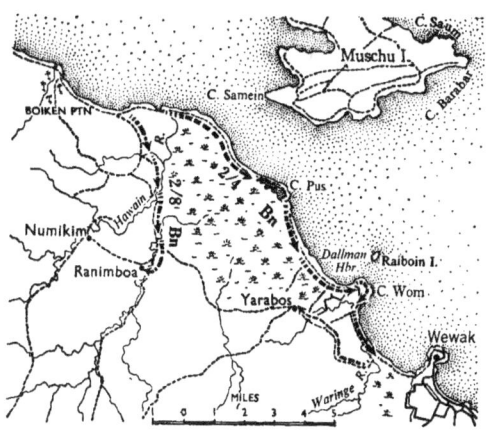

19th Brigade, 3rd-7th May

reached Wom without incident and by nightfall patrols were on the Waringe River. On the 5th and 6th a few Japanese stragglers were killed. On the night of the 6th patrols were sent forward to reconnoitre the enemy's main defences and discover whether Minga Creek was defended and whether it could be crossed by tanks. Near the objective two Japanese machine-guns opened fire, killing two Australians. Soon riflemen joined in and grenades were thrown. The Japanese withdrew but, as the enemy was on the alert, the patrol withdrew too. On the 7th Yarabos was occupied. The battalion was on the outskirts of Wewak, and the artillery was firing into Wirui Mission. Meanwhile, after a few minor clashes, the 2/8th Battalion on the right had taken Ranimboa, on 4th May, and later Numikim.

On the 7th a squadron of nine American Lightnings, sent out to strafe Wewak, attacked in error the Australian artillery positions—44 25-pounders were in the area—the tanks and 19th Brigade headquarters at Cape Wom, the next headland to the west. The aircraft killed 11 and wounded 21, more than half of the losses falling on the artillery. The

---

[3] Lt-Col C. H. Green, DSO, NX121. 2/2 Bn; CO 2/11 Bn 1945. CO 3 Bn RAR Korea 1950. Farmer; of Ulmarra, NSW; b. South Grafton, NSW, 26 Dec 1919. Killed in action, Korea, 2 Nov 1950.

2/1st Field Regiment lost 6 killed, its only fatal casualties in the whole campaign.

How the pilots mistook the two areas is beyond comprehension (wrote the 19th Brigade's diarist). Apart from the fact of Raiboin Island directly off Wom, message dropping panels were prominently displayed, jeeps, bulldozers and trucks were being used extensively while there were in the vicinity of 2,000 troops in the area. American officers held an inquiry into the tragedy but the finding was not made known to this headquarters.

On the 7th-8th in a confused clash by night between Japanese and two parties of Australians Lieutenant Hibbard[4] of the armoured squadron was mortally wounded.

It was now evident that the Japanese were abandoning their big base at Wewak and withdrawing their main forces over the Prince Alexander Mountains leaving strong rearguards to cover the exits from the Wewak area. To counter this the 2/11th Battalion and 2/7th Commando Squadron were sent on a wide encircling movement, while at the same time the 2/4th Battalion attacked Wewak Point.

On 8th May the 2/4th crossed Minga Creek in assault boats under covering fire from the artillery, mortars, tanks and machine-guns. There was some fire from bunkers beyond the creek but this was subdued by the tanks. That afternoon and next day the troops were fired on by Japanese guns from the direction of the Wewak airfield.

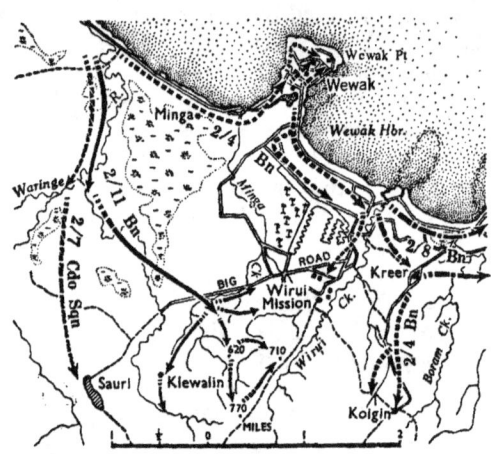

19th Brigade, 8th-25th May

Cox issued orders on 9th May for the advance through Wewak. The axis of the advance would be the coast road; the front was a narrow one between the sea and swamps. The artillery—the 2/1st Field Regiment and the 2/2nd less one battery—would fire 2,700 rounds in support of the attack.

It was raining next morning as H-hour—5.23—approached. Major Cory, commanding the tanks, told Cox that it was too dark for the tank crews to see and Cox, with Martin's approval, postponed H-hour until 6.10. The artillery opened fire at 5.55 and at 6.10 Captain Hawke's[5] company

---

[4] Lt R. G. T. Hibbard, VX117652; 2/4 Armd Regt. Salesman; of Bairnsdale, Vic; b. Leeton, NSW, 7 Sep 1917. Died of wounds 10 May 1945.

[5] Capt G. J. Hawke, MC, NX2030; 2/4 Bn. Chartered accountant; of Inverell, NSW; b. Armidale, NSW, 6 Aug 1913.

began to advance; Captain W. J. S. Atkinson's company on the left
moved off ten minutes later. Both companies advanced from a start-line
marked by masked torches 200 yards beyond the Minga; Hawke's company, with two tanks, came under fire, including a few shells, about 6.30.
Ten minutes later they had taken the knoll at the neck of Wewak Point.
On the left Atkinson's company, with Lieutenant Hall's[6] troop of tanks,
came under heavy fire from Japanese ensconced in caves in the 100-foot
escarpment of Wewak Point. These caves were dark and dirty shelters and
were connected by tunnels up to 300 feet long. By 8 a.m. all Wewak
Point had been taken.

At 12.15 Cox ordered Captain Smith's company and Hawke's to mop
up while Captain Bohle's[7] held astride the road to the east. That afternoon
a flame-thrower fired into a bunker apparently lit a dump of bombs which
blew up. Smith's company found several occupied caves and, since the
Japanese would not surrender, merely picqueted them until engineers
arrived and blew up the entrances, sealing the Japanese in. It was estimated
that about 50 perished in the caves; by midnight 65 other dead had been
counted and three 75-mm guns and two 20-mm had been captured. In a
brilliant action the Australians, supported by tanks and more than 40 field
guns, had lost only 2 killed and 17 wounded. Mopping up was continued
next day, and no live Japanese remained on the point by midday. Finally
it was estimated that from 180 to 200 Japanese had been killed.

On 11th May at Yarabos a patrol of the 2/1st Anti-Tank Regiment
under Lieutenant Stubbs[8] was ambushed: three men were killed and Stubbs
and all N.C.O's except Sergeant Leitch[9] were wounded. Leitch reorganised
the patrol, led a charge through the enemy's lines, and broke through the
Japanese. With their wounded, the men circled round through dense bush
and came to a village where natives provided carriers and guides and led
the patrol home. It was later found that the patrol had killed 21 Japanese.

On the 12th Atkinson's company advanced to the eastern end of Wewak
airfield without opposition; Smith's company on the east reached the
junction of the track to Wirui Mission.

Meanwhile, the 2/11th Battalion and the 2/7th Commando Squadron
had been operating on the inland flank. The task of the 2/7th (Captain
Lomas) was to capture Sauri villages where the enemy was considered
to have established a strong rearguard covering this exit from Wewak.
The squadron, 156 strong, began moving up the Waringe River on 8th
May accompanied by artillery and mortar parties totalling 40, and 67
natives. In the advance up the Waringe that day and the next they killed
five stragglers; on the 10th they drove an enemy group from a camp
of six huts and reached the high ground along which they were to advance
to the Sauri villages. Next day two troops advanced up a spur leading

---

[6] Lt R. W. Hall, SX12110; 2/4 Armd Regt. Improver; of Kingswood, SA; b. Adelaide, 4 Oct 1920.
[7] Capt A. H. M. Bohle, NX46374; 2/4 Bn. Regular soldier; b. Lidcombe, NSW, 31 Dec 1913.
[8] Lt J. J. Stubbs, TX667; 2/1 A-Tk Regt. Factory foreman; of King Island, Tas; b. Penguin, Tas, 14 Apr 1909.
[9] Sgt H. J. Leitch, MM, VX6526; 2/1 A-Tk Regt. Labourer; of Yackandandah, Vic; b. Yackandandah, 21 May 1913.

towards Walanter and encountered a Japanese position on a razor-back. A troop attacked with flame-throwers and with close artillery support, and after a fight lasting two hours and a half took the position, killing 16 Japanese and losing 2 killed and 5 wounded. The squadron was now at the northern end of the north-south ridge along which lay the Sauri villages. Next day the enemy were driven from the next knoll by artillery and mortar fire. "Many souvenirs captured including 2 swords which we handed to the artillery and mortar personnel as a gesture of appreciation for the fine support given by them," wrote the squadron diarist. On the 13th the squadron was held up by fire from the next knoll. Next day, after careful patrolling and accurate bombardment the enemy was driven from this knoll. Four machine-guns were captured.

A patrol to the north led by Lieutenant Shields[1] found an old hospital able to hold over 400 patients and with much medical gear lying abandoned, and moving on down the Big Road made contact with the 2/11th Battalion. This route henceforward was used as the line of supply. On the 16th one troop found an enemy group dug in at Legamunga and attacked using a flame-thrower. After a fight lasting two hours and a half Lieutenant Greer's[2] section moved in and captured the position. Ten dead Japanese were found. This completed the clearing of the Sauri villages.

During this period the 2/11th Battalion was making its encircling move towards Wirui Mission. The battalion had a grim introduction to the new area. On 10th May it

moved out of Waringe base to the Big Road. . . . The advance-guard (wrote the diarist) moved at 0700 and the main body 1 hour later. "B" Coy set off on a compass bearing to cut the Big Road at [a point a short distance west of Wirui Mission]. The march across was "bloody". The course led through a sac sac swamp up to the knees and a wide detour had to be made to avoid deeper patches. Troops carrying packs, weapons and tools were hard pushed to keep going, and Sigs, Mortars, and MMGs carrying rolls of cable, wireless sets and weapons and ammunition found the going very heavy. At 1545 "B" Coy cut the Big Road. . . . At 1630 the Bn was consolidating in a tight perimeter on very swampy ground.

While the men were digging in, three Japanese unwittingly approached the perimeter from the Wewak side and were killed.

On 11th May Captain Greenway's company of the 2/11th set out to occupy the 770 Feature but encountered Japanese dug in on a steep-sided ridge and it was decided to try again next day after artillery preparation. This it did, but came against strong opposition higher up the spur from Japanese in a T-shaped position on a steep razor-back. That day a platoon of an attached company of the 2/8th (Major Diffey's) advanced against the 710 Feature and discovered 9 or 10 huts which had evidently housed a headquarters and, farther on, killed four Japanese.

On the 13th Greenway's company attacked at dawn and took the 620 Feature killing 9 Japanese and losing one man killed. Next day Diffey's

---

[1] Maj W. R. J. Shields, VX101852; 2/7 Cdo Sqn. Regular soldier; b. Maldon, Vic, 12 Aug 1912.
[2] Lt J. H. Greer, VX50751. 2/7 Indep Coy, 2/7 Cdo Sqn. Farmer; of Rupanyup, Vic; b. Collie, WA, 9 Apr 1913.

company was sent towards the north slopes of 710, but the police boys who were guiding led them round the south where they came unexpectedly upon a strong enemy post and one man was killed and two, including Diffey, wounded.

On the 15th the 2/11th Battalion had its hardest fight so far in New Guinea. Captain Bayly's[3] company was sent against 710. The attack failed against this position which was on the top of a razor-back and held by some 40 Japanese. At 3.30, after artillery fire, the company went on, disregarding casualties, attacked again straight up the spur and took it. Promptly the Japanese counter-attacked, with much shouting, led by an officer armed with sword and shotgun, but they were beaten off, Bayly doing "a magnificent job". Sixteen Japanese were killed and seven machine-guns taken; the 2/11th lost 4 killed and 18 wounded of whom three remained on duty. The evacuation of the wounded down the precipitous slopes was an immense labour and every available man was sent out. Despite the danger, torches were used to guide the stretcher bearers, but it was 4.30 next morning before the last wounded man had been brought in. In patrol actions elsewhere that day the battalion lost one killed (Lieutenant Chidgzey[4]) and 6 wounded. On the 13th contact had been made between the 2/4th and 2/11th.

In the meantime the landing east of Wewak had taken place. It will be recalled that for some weeks the 6th Division had had the support of a tiny flotilla consisting of the sloop *Swan*, the corvettes *Dubbo* and *Colac*, and five big motor launches. The senior officer was Lieut-Commander Dovers,[5] the captain of *Swan*, and his flotilla, named Wewak Force, had been working in close cooperation with the division. The tasks of Wewak Force were varied. The corvettes searched for mines off the west coasts of Kairiru and Muschu and, later, off the east coasts and round the entrance to Wewak harbour. The motor launches took soundings in doubtful channels off Wewak and patrolled the coast westward to Muschu Strait and along the shores of Muschu and Kairiru. *Swan*, assisted where possible by the corvettes, bombarded selected targets. In the period to 3rd May *Swan* and the corvettes fired 1,440 rounds at targets ashore.

General Stevens, Group Captain Hancock and Lieut-Commander Dovers had prepared precise tables to govern air and naval support of the Dove Bay landing. It was late in the planning stage when the naval force of a size hitherto undreamt of became available—the cruisers *Hobart* and *Newfoundland* and the destroyers *Arunta* and *Warramunga* all under Commodore Farncomb.[6]

---

[3] Maj C. W. Bayly, MC, WX334. 2/11 Bn, and OC 2/8 Indep Coy 1942-43. Accountant; of Perth; b. Kew, Vic, 5 Sep 1916.

[4] Lt G. V. R. Chidgzey, BEM, WX604; 2/11 Bn. Insurance agent; of Bridgetown, WA; b. Bunbury, WA, 13 Nov 1917. Killed in action 15 May 1945.

[5] Capt W. J. Dovers, DSC; RAN. HMAS's *Canberra*, *Nestor* and *Quickmatch*; Comd HMAS *Swan* 1945. B. Eastwood, NSW, 12 Feb 1918.

[6] Rear-Admiral H. B. Farncomb, CB, DSO, MVO; RAN. (HMS *Royal Sovereign* 1917.) Comd HMAS's *Perth* 1939-40, *Canberra* 1940-41, *Australia* 1942-44, HMS *Attacker* 1944, Aust Sqn 1944-45 and 1946-49. B. Sydney, 28 Feb 1899.

Unfortunately the naval planning staff did not visit or confer with Commander 6 Aust Div and approval of the program arranged with Senior Officer Wewak Force could not be obtained. On 7th May Captain Esdaile,[7] R.A.N., Naval Officer in Charge New Guinea, called on the divisional commander and he carried the plans and full notes on the operation to the Commodore at Hollandia. On 8th May Commodore Farncomb called at Aitape on his way to join his flagship at Hollandia. There he had a discussion with the divisional commander during which the naval support plan suggested by division was approved in principle. . . . No notification of any change was received but, when the naval order was delivered on D-1, it was found that the density of fire as distributed between the targets had been altered, and that the maximum fire was not being brought down on the landing beach at the times asked for. As time to make further representations was not available, Commander 6 Aust Div decided to proceed without further amendment to the naval fire plan.[8]

The task of Farida Force, as mentioned, was to secure a beach-head on Dove Bay, at "Red Beach", with a view to cutting the Wewak-Forok road and preventing the enemy from moving east. In the first phase the beach-head was to be established, in the second the road was to be cut and patrolling begun. The assault troops were the 2/9th Commando Squadron on the right and the 2/10th on the left. Each was to advance 200 yards inland from the beach in four minutes after leaving it and form a perimeter on that line.

The naval vessels would bombard Red Beach for 55 minutes before H-hour and then lift to the area outside the perimeter. American aircraft from the reinforcement training centre at Nadzab were to bomb and strafe the beach area for 15 minutes ceasing 15 minutes before the landing, and No. 71 Wing R.A.A.F. was to be on call.

Off But on the evening of 10th May the assault troops were taken aboard *Swan*, *Dubbo* and *Colac*, in which they were to travel to the forming-up point. The convoy, including the four motor launches, the two landing craft armed with mortars, and the nine assault landing craft, sailed east during the night. At 6.45 a.m. on the 11th, when 10,000 yards off shore, the troops were loaded into the barges.

At 7.15 the naval vessels opened their bombardment, but low cloud with steady rain prevented the planned attack by American aircraft from Nadzab. However, Beauforts from Tadji bombed Brandi Plantation. The mortar barges moved in and lobbed 700 bombs into the area.

The first wave of four landing craft grounded about ten yards from the beach at 8.34 and the men waded ashore. The craft had reached the beach a little to the west of the position planned. There was sporadic enemy fire, some of it from 20-mm guns, but no effective opposition. Three minutes later the second wave, including Colonel Hennessy and his group, landed. The squadrons encountered only "very slight opposition" as they advanced and formed the perimeter. On the right were signs of recent departure. The beach-head was fully established and stores were being unloaded under some fire from both flanks by 10.24. Thus far two Japanese had been killed and one Australian wounded.

---

[7] Capt J. C. D. Esdaile, CBE; RAN. (HMAS *Australia* 1917-18.) Comd HMAS's *Penguin* 1940-42, *Adelaide* 1942-44; NOIC New Guinea Area 1944-45. B. Bendigo, Vic, 3 Oct 1899.
[8] 6th Australian Division Report on Operations—Aitape-Wewak Campaign, 26 Oct 1944-13 Sep 1945.

The squadrons sent out patrols, and a troop of the 2/10th encountered a strongly-held position on the eastern flank. Naval bombardment was called down and it drove out the Japanese—evidently about 50 men—who left a 20-mm gun and a large quantity of documents. At 5.50 a patrol cut the Wewak Road.

On the morning of the 12th Hennessy sent Captain Hewitt's infantry company (of the 2/3rd Machine Gun Battalion) to the Wewak Road-Forok Creek junction, gave the 2/10th Squadron the task of defending the perimeter, and sent the 2/9th towards the Mandi area. By the end of the day it had patrolled along the beach to a point north-west of Mandi without seeing any Japanese, but later found two stragglers farther to the west.

At 7.12 a.m. on the 13th Japanese mortared the area of "B" Troop of the 2/9th Squadron west of Mandi. The enemy was bombarded by eight bombers and by the 75-mm guns, whereupon "B" Troop attacked, took the track junction and exploited westward.

Hewitt's company patrolled to Forok on the 12th. A gun being fired into their area was bombarded by *Swan* on the 15th and by aircraft on the 16th. Patrolling continued. On 20th May Farida Force was placed under Brigadier Martin's command and ordered to be prepared to meet the leading troops of the 2/8th Battalion at Brandi, but not before the 22nd.

On 14th May, the 2/11th being heavily engaged in the foothills south of the Big Road, Martin had ordered the 2/4th to attack Wirui Mission, which was on a steep kunai-covered hill about 300 feet high dominating the airfield. Approaching from the east through tall kunai the leading company with a troop of tanks soon took the first objective—dominating ground about half way up the hill. Captain Smith's company passed through and, with the tanks, whose crews estimated that they killed about 30 Japanese, reached the top. By nightfall the top and the eastern slopes were held but the Japanese were fighting back from bunkers on the north-west slopes.

Next day Smith's company attacked these remaining bunkers. The leading section was halted by intense fire after several men had been hit. Private Kenna,[9] in the supporting section, which was firing on the bunkers at a range of only 50 yards, stood up in the kunai grass in full view of the enemy and fired his Bren at one of the Japanese machine-gun posts. The Japanese machine-gunners returned his fire but failed to hit him. Kenna then said to Private Rau[1] who was beside him that the Japanese "had a bead on him" and he asked for Rau's rifle. Still standing, he fired four rifle shots and silenced the enemy post. He then took the Bren again and opened fire on another post about 70 yards away and silenced

---

[9] Pte E. Kenna, VC, VX102142; 2/4 Bn. Plumber; of Hamilton, Vic; b. Hamilton, 6 Jul 1919.
[1] Pte E. A. Rau, VX136772; 2/4 Bn. Labourer; of Belmont, Vic; b. Geelong, Vic, 21 Jul 1922.

it too. The remaining post was then knocked out by a tank; soon the 2/4th and 2/11th were in contact.[2]

About 40 Japanese were killed and perhaps 20 escaped in the fight for the mission. Large quantities of weapons, vehicles, generators, telephones and other equipment were found there. Possession of Wirui Mission gave complete control of the Wewak coastal plain.

Captured papers made it possible to make a fairly precise estimate of the forces immediately round Wewak: *Kato Force,* built round the *25th Airfield Battalion* and about 300 strong, was holding from Sauri to Wirui Creek; *Jinka Force,* about 400 strong, was holding from Wirui Creek to the east, including Boram airfield, and south into the range as far as Passam; to the east was *Aoyama Force,* of unknown strength; the coastal plain to a depth of about 1,000 yards was not held in strength, and it was thought that there would be little opposition on the coast at least as far as Boram airfield. On 15th May the 2/8th Battalion, hitherto in reserve, was ordered to advance on Boram.

On the 16th, after Kreer and Boram had been pounded from the air and sea, the 2/8th launched a three-company attack with two troops of tanks in support. It was a complete success and by nightfall the leading company (Captain Rumley's[3]) on the coast was in contact with a company which had taken Boram unopposed. The only casualties were six who were wounded when the enemy exploded electrically-detonated bombs set in the track. Next day the advance continued. Rumley's company exploited to the mouth of Boram Creek where it encountered a strongly-held position.

Brigadier Martin next day ordered the battalion to capture Boram airfield and the foothills to the south, clear the coastal sector to the Brandi River and link with Hennessy's force. This attack went in on the 20th in heavy rain. Three companies were forward and soon the men of the centre and right companies were waist deep in water, and all three companies were halted by heavy fire from bunkers. These were pinpointed and accurately shelled and mortared in the afternoon. The left company (Captain Dwyer[4]) then moved in to mop up and the other two (Captains Gately[5] and Rumley) continued the advance. It was found that every bunker and weapon-pit had been destroyed by the bombardment, although the bunkers were roofed with three layers of coconut logs and 3 feet of spoil. Forty Japanese were killed, 28 of them by the bombardment. A patrol moving forward towards Farida Force on the 21st found 88 Indian prisoners, captured at Singapore. Next day Dwyer's company occupied Cape Moem and, as planned, made contact with Farida Force.

On 25th May the 2/4th, which had been patrolling and mopping up, sent a patrol into Koigin and took it after a fight in which eight Japanese

---

[2] Kenna was awarded the Victoria Cross.
[3] Capt L. O. Rumley, VX5479; 2/8 Bn. Salesman; of Mornington, Vic; b. Traralgon, Vic, 28 Jun 1912.
[4] Maj M. J. Dwyer, VX9768; 2/8 Bn. Clerk; of Echuca, Vic; b. Camperdown, Vic, 24 May 1919.
[5] Capt J. C. Gately, MC, VX6568; 2/8 Bn. Grocer; of Albury, NSW; b. Brisbane, 11 Feb 1911.

were killed. That day Brigadier Martin was sent to hospital with malaria, and for the next month Lieut-Colonel Bishop, Stevens' senior staff officer, temporarily commanded the brigade.

In this period the 2/11th had continued its arduous advance in the mountain area. On 17th May a party of native police patrolled to Klewalin and reported 12 Japanese in two huts there. Colonel Green ordered Captain Stoneham's[6] company to take this village, and next day it moved into the area, set an ambush with the help of the native police, and killed the 12 Japanese and took five machine-guns without loss—"a pleasant change from our other actions", the battalion diarist commented. That night 6 or 7 Japanese attacked the company's perimeter but were soon stopped.

On 20th May a patrol moved up the spur towards 770 and found it held in strength. This position and other pockets were probed in the next two days. Stoneham's company attacked an enemy pocket near Klewalin on 22nd May. One platoon thrust along the track towards this position and another was sent round to the enemy's rear. When Lance-Sergeant Fogarty's[7] section of the latter platoon was held up by a well-dug-in force Fogarty went forward and, standing, fired with his Owen gun and prevented the enemy from bringing down accurate fire. He dominated the enemy for 15 minutes, and then a flame-thrower arrived and the Japanese were overcome.

When a patrol of Major Royce's[8] company moved towards 770 on the 23rd it came under fire from a sniper; Lieutenant Anderson[9] was killed and Private Host[1] wounded; both were original members of this battalion. Most of the losses now being suffered by the Australians were at the hands of snipers sometimes firing from trees. On 24th May after an air and artillery bombardment Royce's company occupied 770, except for one post whose occupants made off that night.

The 2/11th had its last hard fight in this area on the 27th when Green ordered an attack with the intention of removing an enemy pocket south of 710 and clearing the track between it and 770. In a first phase Bayly's company, reinforced, was to clear 710, in a second Royce's company to open the track from 770. The artillery fired 2,360 rounds during 20 minutes before and 10 minutes after the attack opened at 9 a.m. Despite this concentration the Japanese resisted resolutely and it was 11.50 before the last bunker was overcome and the two companies linked. Captain Abbott[2] and one other were killed and six wounded; 15 Japanese dead were found.

---

[6] Capt A. C. Stoneham, WX358; 2/11 Bn. Clerk; of North Perth; b. North Perth, 15 Nov 1913.
[7] L-Sgt J. P. Fogarty, DCM, WX11396; 2/11 Bn. Locomotive fireman; of Witchcliffe, WA; b. Ferguson, WA, 5 Mar 1907.
[8] Maj G. E. Royce, MC, WX248; 2/11 Bn. Accountant; of Claremont, WA; b. Katanning, WA, 15 Oct 1917.
[9] Lt C. D. Anderson, WX2659. 2/16 and 2/11 Bns. Clerk; of Perth; b. Perth, 11 Jun 1919. Killed in action 23 May 1945.
[1] Pte E. J. Host, WX728; 2/11 Bn. Saddler; of Seabrook, via Northam, WA; b. Northam, 15 Sep 1919.
[2] Capt W. T. Abbott, WX3220; 2/11 Bn. Jeweller; of West Perth; b. Perth, 15 Jan 1915. Killed in action 27 May 1945.

In May the 2/11th lost 23 killed and 63 wounded, a grievously heavy loss. The casualty list reveals in some degree the extent to which the veterans who had served since 1939 were still in the front line and the extent to which this senior battalion had retained its regional character. Of the 85 killed or wounded 7 had three-figure numbers indicating that they almost certainly had enlisted in 1939, and 16 had numbers lower than 6,000. Three of the three-figure men (Lieutenant Chidgzey and Corporals McLennan[3] and Donaldson[4]) were killed. Of the 85 all but 16 had enlisted in Western Australia; on 26th May all but two of the officers were West Australians, one of the two being the commanding officer.

In the last week of May the 2/11th was only 552 strong and had only 223 riflemen instead of 397. To fill out the depleted rifle companies the Headquarters Company was drawn upon and some of its platoons reduced to skeletons. The 2/4th lacked 161 riflemen, the 2/8th 130.

At this stage the shortage of reinforcements was acute throughout the whole of the First Army. On 3rd May General Sturdee had signalled General Blamey that the First Army was 10,000 below its war establishment: "Infantry some 4,500 down and sick wastage rising. Appreciate advice what policy to be followed maintain fighting efficiency especially in 6 Div and II Corps." Next day Blamey replied that a policy direction had been given that all A.I.F. reinforcements were to be retained on the mainland pending an estimation of the operational requirements of I Corps. These were now settled, and the 6th Division was to be brought to and maintained at full establishment, and in addition 1,800 A.I.F. reinforcements were to be allotted to First Army.

The Aitape-Wewak campaign now seemed to be entering its final stage. By the end of May the 6th Division had driven most of what remained of the *XVIII Japanese Army* away from the coast, including its base at Wewak, and into the mountains, where it was enclosed between the 17th Brigade forward of Maprik to its west and the remainder of the division to its north.

While the 6th Division was advancing to Wewak the 8th Brigade, based on Madang, had continued the necessary task of patrolling the country east of the Sepik, now abandoned by all Japanese forces except some small but aggressive groups posted there to watch the *XVIII Army's* eastern flank. Early in July 1944 the operations from Madang were controlled, as they had been since January, by the 5th Division (Major-General Ramsay), which then included the 4th, 8th and 15th Brigades. The 15th Brigade departed for Australia in July and the 4th Brigade in mid-August and, as mentioned earlier, in the big redeployment that began in September, the headquarters of the 5th Division went to New Britain and the 7th Brigade, which had replaced the 15th, to Bougainville, leaving

---

[3] Cpl C. E. McLennan, WX506; 2/11 Bn. Clerk; of Perth; b. Subiaco, WA, 24 Jun 1912. Killed in action 12 May 1945.

[4] Cpl R. Donaldson, WX218; 2/11 Bn. Warehouse storeman; of Kalgoorlie, WA; b. Kalgoorlie, 16 Mar 1919. Killed in action 16 May 1945.

round Madang only the 8th Brigade, commanded since 18th August by Brigadier Fergusson.[5] The brigade had already been serving on this coast for seven months.

For the last year of the war the main role of the force east of the Sepik was to hold the Hansa Bay area, to hold an outpost at Annanberg on a knoll enclosed in a bend of the Ramu River, about 60 air miles from the mouth, and to watch any Japanese who might remain in or enter the triangle enclosed by the lower Ramu, the lower Sepik, and the

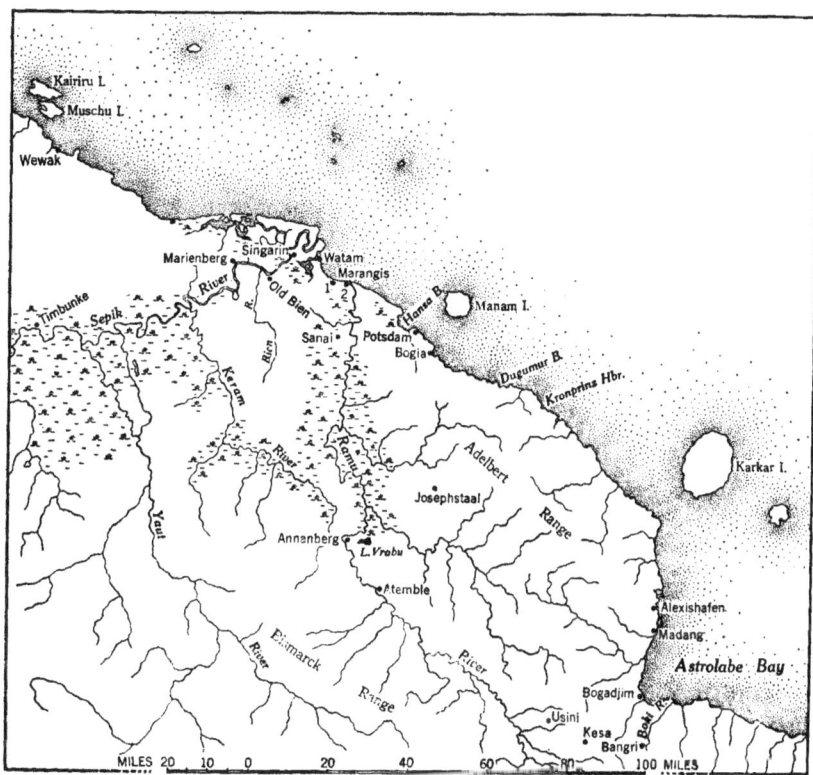

highlands. A large part of this task was performed by aircraft of No. 4 Squadron, which flew over the area almost daily at minimum altitudes reporting in detail the condition of the gardens and villages, the presence of natives, of canoes and so on. The task of patrolling the area was shared by the Australian battalions and detachments of the Papuan and the 1st New Guinea Infantry Battalions, the Royal Papuan Constabulary, and Angau. The Japanese, on their side, had recruited and armed a considerable number of friendly natives.

---

[5] Brig M. A. Fergusson, DSO, MC, ED, VX23. (1st AIF: Gnr 3 Bty AFA and Lt 4 Div Arty.) CO 6 Cav Regt 1939-41; Comd 2 Armd Bde 1942-44, 2 Bde 1944, 8 Bde 1944-45. Farmer; of Whittlesea, Vic; b. Melbourne, 5 Dec 1895.

As a rule the Australian garrison of Annanberg was built round two or three platoons, including at least one of New Guinea troops; and the Hansa Bay area was held by a company group of Australians and the greater part of a company of New Guinea troops. Patrolling was constant, arduous, widespread and sometimes eventful.

On 15th August 1944, for example, Warrant Officer Lega[6] had led out nine men of the Royal Papuan Constabulary on a routine patrol. On the 25th near Bangri villages natives reported 10 Japanese camped higher

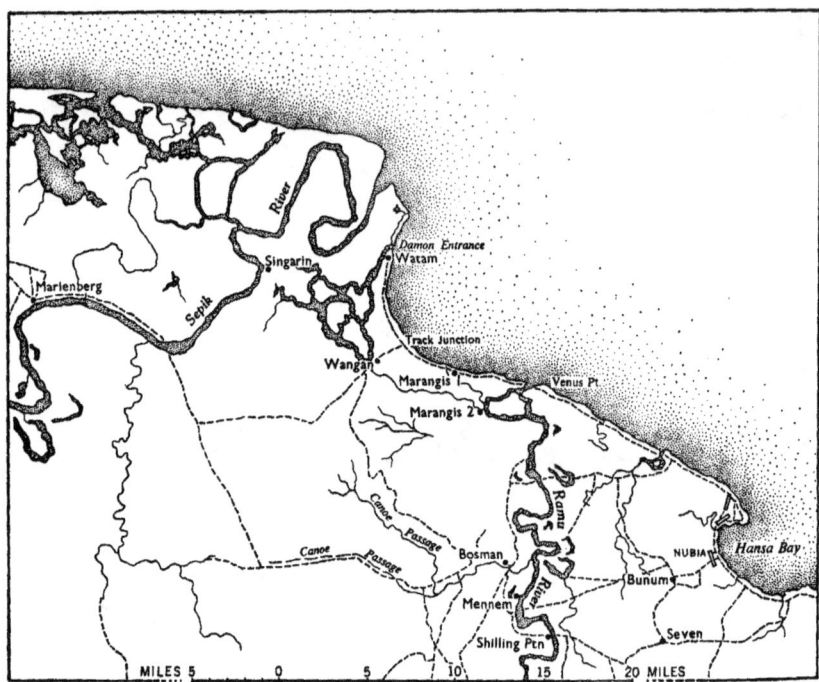

up the Boki River. Lega's party surprised and captured 3 and then led an attack on 8 more. All were killed. Lega, though wounded, led his party and their prisoners back to Madang, a three-day march.

Day after day, however, the diary of the 5th Division in this period recorded that there was "nothing to report". In June, July, August and September patrols had been along the coast as far as the Sepik mouth without finding any Japanese. In mid-October the 35th Battalion, which was then maintaining the forward company group at Hansa Bay sent out strong patrols totalling 30 Australians and 23 natives, with 8 pigeons to carry messages, to the Sepik mouth and Wangan. They found no Japanese.

---

[6] Lt T. W. J. Lega, MM, NGX385. NGVR and Angau. Winchman; of Redfern, NSW; b. Woonona, NSW, 20 May 1921.

In November, however, small forces of Japanese moved out from bases about Singarin on the Sepik west of the Watam Lagoon and established themselves at Watam and Wangan and at Bosman near the Ramu. The establishment of a post at Bosman was facilitated by developing canoe passages leading to the Ramu from the west.

In that month the 4th Battalion (Lieut-Colonel Neville[7]) was forward and its plan was to hold from Marangis on the coast along the line of the lower Ramu, and patrol forward. A strong patrol drawn from the 4th Battalion and the attached New Guinea company (Captain Keft[8]) probed to Watam and Wangan on 4th December but were attacked by 80 or more Japanese. The Australians had the better of the encounter but withdrew and established a strong position at Marangis. Heavy air strikes were delivered at Watam and Wangan and soon 130 native refugees from that area arrived in the Australian positions and reported on the enemy's numbers and dispositions. It seemed that there were some 90 Japanese round Watam and Wangan and 30 round Bosman. Henceforward, for several months the 8th Brigade was keen to go out and hit the Japanese, but from time to time was restrained by orders from First Army, which evidently did not wish the brigade to become committed to even moderately heavy operations, and was willing that the area from the Sepik to the Ramu should be a no-man's land. Thus, late in December, First Army ordered that all troops must be withdrawn east of the Ramu, though patrols might go to Marangis. When the 30th Battalion relieved the 4th early in February Lieut-Colonel W. N. Parry-Okeden of the 30th had in the forward area his tactical headquarters, one company of the 30th, one company of the 1st New Guinea Infantry Battalion, one platoon of the Papuan Infantry Battalion (at Annanberg with a platoon of the N.G.I.B.) and other detachments. The remainder of the forward battalion, as hitherto, was at Madang.

Parry-Okeden obtained permission to carry out a series of raids on the Japanese at Wangan, Watam and Bosman. A company of the 30th occupied Bosman village on 7th January, the Japanese offering little opposition. After a few days, however, the withdrawal of this outpost was ordered. Barges sent to Bosman to remove the company were attacked by 30 to 40 well-armed Japanese, who wounded three including two of the Americans who were manning the barges. The company was embarked and brought out, under spasmodic fire.

About 30 Japanese on 19th January attacked Marangis 1 but were driven off leaving eight dead. That day a patrol of the New Guinea Battalion, 9 strong, under Sergeant McDowall[9] surprised 24 Japanese preparing food at Bosman, killed all but two of them, and captured 21 rifles and a machine-gun. Only one native soldier was wounded. Thus,

---

[7] Lt-Col C. H. Neville, ED, NX104270. CO 18 Bn 1942-44, 4 Bn 1944-45. Company manager; of Mosman, NSW; b. Sydney, 17 Aug 1901.
[8] Capt J. H. Keft, NX108001; 1 NG Inf Bn. Regular soldier; b. Nowra, NSW, 8 Sep 1914.
[9] Capt A. K. McDowall, MM, VX57699. 1 and 2 NG Inf Bns. Salesman; of Camperdown, Vic; b. Camperdown, 1 Jan 1921.

in this one encounter, probably one-fifth of the Japanese in the whole area were killed.

Nevertheless small enemy patrols continued to attack the Australian outpost at Marangis 1, and it was decided to attack the enemy's position at the junction of the coastal track and the track to Wangan. This position was struck from the air, and fired into with a mortar and machine-guns mounted on a trawler. The Japanese made off.

The 30th Battalion now obtained permission to drive the enemy from Wangan and Watam, and on 7th February the forward company (Captain Simpson[1]) occupied the track junction and that day and the next sent patrols towards Wangan and Watam. These encountered well-organised positions, and bombardments by aircraft and two armed trawlers were arranged. On the 11th, however, Parry-Okeden received orders originating with First Army not to patrol forward from Marangis, and to withdraw patrols from Bosman. It was then too late to stop patrols of the New Guinea Battalion that had set out for Bosman and Mennem and one of these killed 11 Japanese near Mennem.

Parry-Okeden made it clear in his report that he did not approve of the orders from above.

> The C.O. 30 Bn was forced to adopt a passive role (he wrote) and forfeit ground which was most vital to the defence of the Hansa Bay area, namely Bosman area. This policy allows the enemy freedom of movement to form bases in the Mennem area and, seizing suitable positions, to cross the Ramu and obtain a springboard into Hansa Bay and Bogia.

During its two months in the forward area the companies of the 30th and the attached New Guinea troops killed 91 Japanese and 12 of their armed natives; only one Australian soldier and two New Guinea soldiers were killed.

In this period the Annanberg force made only occasional contacts with the enemy, of whom there appeared to be about 200 at various posts along the Keram River, with headquarters about 30 miles from Annanberg in a direct line. The natives along the Keram were cooperating with the Japanese, as they showed by drumming warning signals from village to village whenever an Australian patrol crossed the Ramu. The Australian troops were flown in and out in flying-boats which landed on Lake Vrabu, and the garrison of this remote little fortress was mainly supplied by air.

In March, April and the first half of May the 35th Battalion was the forward unit. Late in March the outposts on the Ramu were withdrawn to Bunum and Seven because the weather was making it difficult to supply posts on the river. In mid-May the 4th Battalion relieved the 35th and, as will be seen later, the 4th remained forward until the cease fire.

---

[1] Capt J. C. Simpson, MBE, NX112701; 30 Bn. Master grocer; of Kingsgrove, NSW; b. Rockdale, NSW, 13 Oct 1920.

CHAPTER 15

TAZAKI AND SHIBURANGU

SHORTAGES of shipping and aircraft and, in the ranges, the lack of an airfield for large air transports, had now been overcome, and the infantry were receiving increasingly strong support. On Hayfield, Douglas transports were landing heavy ammunition, and modest numbers of jeeps, graders, bulldozers and guns. Where formerly the heaviest weapons had been two 4.2-inch mortars with a limited supply of bombs, there were now 75-mm guns and 25-pounders were coming. Round Wewak, too, but for other reasons, artillery support was now more powerful. In that area observation for artillery fire was better than hitherto and also the opposition was more concentrated. Consequently the artillery was massed about Cape Wom, where eventually there were two field regiments plus two 155-mm and four 75-mm guns, a formidable force to concentrate on one fairly small enemy position after another.

A new shortage, however, now appeared. By 17th June only 27 aircraft loads of bombs remained at the Aitape airfields. A total of 194 Japanese bombs found at But and Dagua were carried to Aitape in barges, and about 146 tons of these were dropped on their former owners, but many failed to explode. General Stevens appealed to General Sturdee and he to General Blamey. As an outcome 780 bombs reached Aitape on 24th June and another consignment three days later. (That day, however, Stevens was informed that no further support could be given by the American Replacement Training Centre at Nadzab because it was moving north.) A small consignment of bombs arrived at Aitape on 4th July, but even so there were then only enough for 130 sorties, and air support had to be rationed. On 9th July, however, enough for 3,000 sorties arrived and thereafter No. 71 Wing could meet all demands.

In this final phase the infantry needed all the support they could be given. They were now hard against the enemy's bases, which were manned by troops who were relatively well fed, were well led, were fighting from elaborate defences, and were resolved to dispute possession of every tactically-important feature protecting the approaches to their remaining food-producing areas and the fortress in which they had been ordered to make their last stand.

In the Prince Alexander Mountains at the beginning of June the Japanese had been practically cleared from the west bank of the Parchi River as far south as the Waigakum area. Their main forces were believed to be along the tracks west of the Yamil villages, and in the Malabasakum Hamlets and about Ulupu. On the Australian side the 2/5th Battalion had now relieved the 2/7th, and its immediate task was to secure the line Solongan-Kulauru Mission. The objective of the 2/6th Battalion on the left was Yamil. Hayfield was garrisoned by the battery of the 2/1st

Anti-Tank Regiment working as infantry: these men, as mentioned, were also patrolling far to the south and east.

The defences now facing the brigade were more elaborate than those hitherto encountered. The 2/5th, whose headquarters were established at Kalabu, met strong opposition. There were evidently from 200 to 300 Japanese in the Ulupu-Yamil area with outposts forward. Lieut-Colonel Buttrose ordered Major A. C. Bennett's company to take Yamil 3, using a line of approach to the north, Captain Geer's to clear Malabasakum Hamlets and Ulupu and mop up pockets to the south, Captain Cameron's to move along the main Yamil Road and be prepared to take Yamil landing ground; Cap-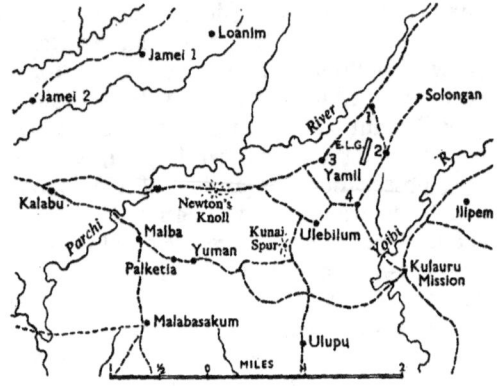tain G. McK. Fry's was in reserve with the probable future role of advancing along the main road and taking Ulebilum. The battalion now had the support of two 4.2-inch mortars and two 75-mm guns of the 2/1st Anti-Tank Regiment.

On 2nd June Geer began patrolling southward into an area where the enemy occupied many villages and gardens. In the centre "C" Company of the 2/7th was still forward at the beginning of June and on the 2nd it made a two-platoon attack on a strongly-held knoll named "Newton's Knoll", after Lieutenant T. E. Newton, about half way between Kalabu and Ulebilum, and took it at a second attempt killing seven Japanese. Here Cameron of the 2/5th took over next day and patrolled widely, pinpointing three enemy positions across his line of advance and manned apparently by about 75 Japanese. On the left Bennett's company, by vigorous patrolling, forced the enemy to withdraw from well-sited positions, and by 9th June held a position whence Yamil landing ground could be observed and the company on Newton's Knoll could be supported by flanking fire. A captured map showed the enemy's main line of resistance to run through Yamil 3-Yuman-Palketia-Malabasakum. The defenders of Palketia were driven out by mortar fire and air bombardment. On 12th June a platoon of Bennett's company took a position defending Yamil 3 and made contact with the 2/6th advancing on Yamil 1. Next day, using flame-throwers for the first time, it took Yamil 3. Fry's company, supported by mortar and artillery fire, forced the enemy out of Yuman, killing thirteen and having no casualties itself.[1] It was now evident that the Japanese

---

[1] The flame-thrower would soon, belatedly, become standard infantry equipment. It was not until 29th June 1945 that a memorandum was sent to the formations in the field from Victoria Barracks, Melbourne, explaining that flame-throwers had been adopted by the Australian Army and that 36 were being issued to each division for distribution to units.

were concentrating in Ulupu, and it was attacked by 24 aircraft. An enemy group of 50 to 60 was dug in along "Kunai Spur" north of Ulupu which the enemy was evidently determined to hold, being vital ground in the defence of Ulupu. It was harassed by artillery and mortar fire and attacked from the air.

Meanwhile the 2/6th had been fighting its way to Yamil, which was entered unopposed on 10th June after some effective air strikes and much bombardment. The defences were strong but it appeared that the Australian move from the north instead of the west had caught the enemy unprepared. Patrols advanced to the emergency landing ground, which was soon taken. The ground was quickly cleared and on 21st June a light aircraft landed and the removal of casualties by air began.

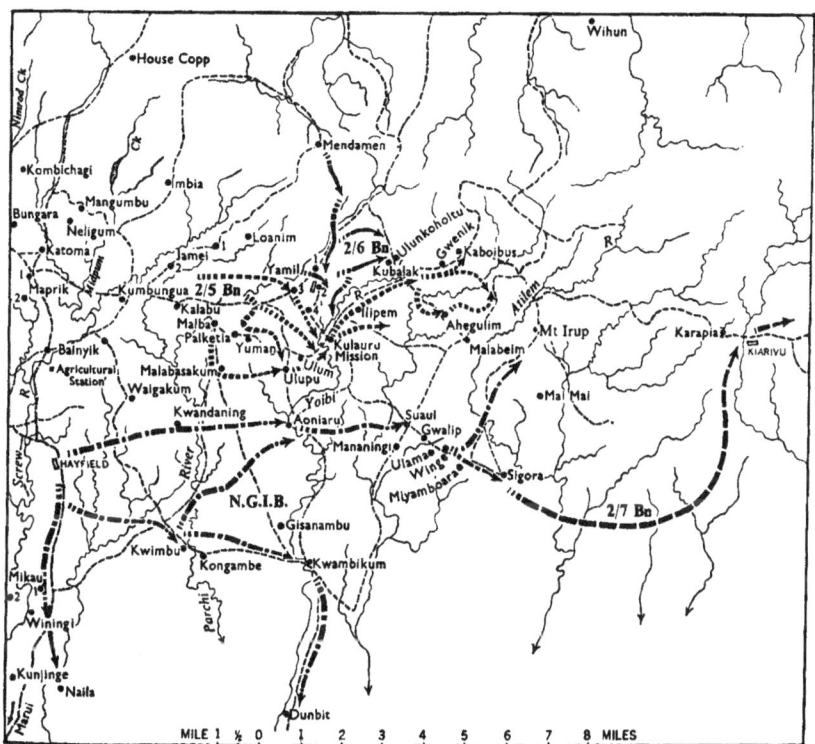

17th Brigade, June-August

The Japanese continued to defend Kunai Spur against the 2/5th with determination despite heavy bombardment. On 24th June bombardment and a flanking move forced the enemy out of Yamil 4, but Kunai Spur was still held. After more bombardment a reinforced platoon attacked the spur but was repulsed after killing 11 Japanese, losing 3 killed and 3 wounded. The spur was then bombed by 34 aircraft, but this did not dislodge the defenders.

The gunners of the 2/1st Anti-Tank Regiment patrolling as infantry on the southern flank were still very active. On 3rd June, for example, Captain Johnson sent out a fighting patrol of twenty-five under Lieutenant Savage[2] against Tuwaigum 2 where nine Japanese were reported. The patrol reached their start-line near the village undetected and attacked. The main position was taken but as a party moved out to count the dead and collect Intelligence material snipers opened fire from within and without the village killing Gunner Waterman[3] and wounding Sergeant Duncan[4] (who carried on) and Gunner King.[5] Bombardier Reed was killed while trying to bring in Waterman's body, and later Gunner Perel[6] was killed while trying to bring in a body. Another attack was made. Bombardier Arnold[7] under heavy fire recovered the bodies of Waterman and Perel and when the patrol withdrew they took these with them. In all 4 Australians died and 2 were wounded. There were not 9 but 20 to 25 Japanese in the village of whom at least 13 were killed. The attack on Tuwaigum was part of a larger operation in which a total of 52 artillerymen were involved. One group, under Johnson, attacked Mikau 2 the same day, killing 7 Japanese.

In this period Captain G. C. O'Donnell of Angau and a party of natives carried out a particularly deep patrol. He left Bana on 22nd June and travelled by way of Amam and Nilu to a point on the Screw River about three hours from Maprik, and returned by the Aramap River to Walum, where he arrived on 29th June, with much information about the enemy's deployment, the tracks, the effect of air attack, and the attitude of the natives.

As mentioned earlier General Blamey planned to give an increasingly important role to the native battalions as the operations in the New Guinea territories developed. Accordingly the 2nd New Guinea Battalion (Lieut-Colonel Murchison) was sent forward to Aitape, and it joined the 17th Brigade on 25th June. It immediately began to patrol to the south where Brigadier Moten gave it the task of destroying the remnants of the *41st Japanese Division* as far south as Kwimbu, Mikau and Kunjinge. By the end of the month the native soldiers had killed 25 Japanese, having had only 3 of their own men wounded, and were patrolling south and east from Mikau and Winingi.

---

[2] Lt N. L. Savage, PX12. 2/2 and 2/1 A-Tk Regts. Clerk; of Cairns, Qld; b. Rockhampton, Qld, 26 Jan 1914.

[3] Gnr A. J. Waterman, QX53896; 2/1 A-Tk Regt. Farm hand; of Coorparoo, Qld; b. Brisbane, 3 May 1925. Killed in action 3 Jun 1945.

[4] Sgt K. McM. Duncan, QX17113; 2/1 A-Tk Regt. Station hand; of Mitchell, Qld; b. Stanthorpe, Qld, 1 Aug 1916.

[5] Gnr J. T. King, VX148352; 2/1 A-Tk Regt. Farm hand; of Dimboola, Vic; b. Horsham, Vic, 9 Jun 1924. Died of wounds 4 Jun 1945.

[6] Gnr I. Perel, QX22561; 2/1 A-Tk Regt. Fur cutter; of Albion, Qld; b. South Brisbane, 23 May 1918. Killed in action 3 Jun 1945.

[7] Bdr J. J. Arnold, QX12488; 2/1 A-Tk Regt. Jackeroo; of Longreach, Qld; b. Sydney, 26 Aug 1917.

From 25th to 28th June General Stevens visited the inland sector and, after discussions with Brigadier Moten, instructed him to make a plan for the capture of Kiarivu with a force of not more than one battalion group.

At the beginning of July the 2/5th Battalion was meeting the stiffest resistance yet encountered in the ranges. On 3rd July, however, the Japanese abandoned Kunai Spur, where they had withstood bombardment for nearly three weeks. A platoon attack on Ulupu, however, on 4th July was repulsed. Next day a company, under cover of artillery and mortar fire, occupied Ulupu but the Japanese still held strong positions in the area; in several actions on the 4th 17 Japanese were killed.

On 8th July an attack—the decisive attack of this phase—was launched on a strongly-held knoll at the northern end of the Ulupu area. The knoll was bombarded by artillery and mortars and then by twenty-two aircraft. These employed a device that was now proving most effective: they dropped their bombs and then made dummy runs while the infantry moved in. The attack, by two platoons, succeeded. Twenty-eight Japanese were killed; one Australian was killed and four wounded, including the two platoon commanders, Lieutenants McDonald[8] and Newton[9] who had joined from the Royal Military College only three weeks before. Captain H. Busby, the medical officer, and Lieutenants Pitts,[1] the Intelligence officer, were also wounded that day. After the fight it was evident that the enemy had been ordered to hold on at all costs. They had dug an elaborate position with many pill-boxes and weapon-pits, connected by large tunnels, and had fought on until only two or three survived.

A group of about twenty-five Japanese was driven out of Ulum on 9th July by bombardment. The enemy's defence system had now been broken and the patrols of the 2/5th rapidly moved forward about 2,000 yards with only minor skirmishes to Kulauru Mission, which was occupied on 11th July, and beyond.

On the 12th, however, Cameron's company had a stiff fight lasting six hours during which six Japanese were killed. Thereafter the enemy split up into small parties and soon all known positions in the Ulupu area were found to have been abandoned. Ilipem was occupied on the 18th.[2]

The southward sweep of the 2nd New Guinea Battalion had achieved swift success, although it had involved the native troops in harder fighting

---

[8] Lt-Col B. A. McDonald, MC, VX146956; 2/5 Bn. Regular soldier; b. Geelong, Vic, 23 Mar 1925.
[9] Lt-Col K. W. Newton, MC, VX146955; 2/5 Bn. Regular soldier; b. Essendon, Vic, 17 Apr 1924.
[1] Lt D. H. Pitts, VX29262. 2/22 and 2/5 Bns. Commercial traveller; of Kew, Vic; b. Camberwell, Vic, 15 Jan 1913.
[2] A few days after the fight on 12th July Captain Cameron, for years an outstanding company commander in this battalion, was instructed to send a patrol back to battalion headquarters to escort a concert party forward. Cameron objected that he hoped to rest his weary company, which was only 75 strong instead of 129, and they needed artillery support and reinforcements not entertainment. When the order was repeated Cameron asked to be relieved of his command and paraded to higher authority. He was paraded to Brigadier Moten, who questioned him closely about the condition of the men, and finally said that he would do what he could to have more artillery and reinforcements brought in. Before rejoining his men Cameron was evacuated to the field ambulance with malaria and laryngitis. Heavier artillery pieces were evidently on the way, and on 21st July two 25-pounders were landed at Hayfield, and soon a troop of 25-pounders was in support of the 2/5th Battalion.

than was generally allotted to them, and had caused them heavier loss than the native troops were suffering on Bougainville, for example. In the Prince Alexanders, however, the native battalion was employed as a complete unit, whereas elsewhere such battalions had been employed as pools from which companies or platoons might be drawn for attachment to Australian formations or units. On 3rd July Lieutenant McDowall's platoon took Kongambe, killing six Japanese; one native soldier was killed and McDowall wounded. Another platoon took Kwandaning, killing eight and capturing documents and machine-guns; again a native soldier was killed. Captain R. S. Garland's company took Naila, killing sixteen; but three native soldiers were killed and Lieutenant Roche[3] and four men were wounded. In the day thirty-two Japanese were killed. The destruction of the Japanese on the fringes of the main force was being carried out with grim efficiency. That day Warrant-Officer Healy[4] of Angau stated that in recent patrols round Wihun in the north his native scouts had reported having killed 60 Japanese, and that he considered these claims reliable.

Captured documents showed that the next strong resistance would be met on a line Kaboibus-Ahegulim-Gwalip. Brigadier Moten's force was now poised for a big move deep into the enemy's area. On 12th July Moten had held a conference at Maprik attended by all commanding officers, his own staff, and representatives from divisional headquarters, No. 71 Wing R.A.A.F., Air Maintenance, and Angau. Moten explained that, because of the strong resistance of an enemy fighting from well-prepared defences, the advance of the 2/5th and 2/6th had been slowed down. He proposed to speed up the advance. First, the 2nd New Guinea Battalion, moving on a wide front, would converge on the Gwalip villages and secure them by 30th July. The 2/7th Battalion would be flown from Aitape, where it had been resting since 11th June, to Hayfield by the same date and would move into Gwalip whence it would advance by a circuitous route south-east of Gwalip and then strike north and take Kiarivu airfield and Karapia some ten miles behind the Japanese forward positions along the Yoibi River. The 2/7th would then establish a base round Karapia and Kiarivu, where stores and heavy weapons would be dropped from the air, and drive westward against the Japanese rear. Meanwhile the 2/5th and 2/6th would press on eastward, the 2/5th clearing the enemy from the area west of the Atilem River and the 2/6th taking Kaboibus. The 2nd Battery of the 2/1st Anti-Tank Regiment would patrol south and south-east from a base at Kunjinge Mission. After securing Gwalip the New Guinea Battalion was to turn north, attack the southern flank of the enemy's defences in the Mount Irup area and prevent any withdrawal south towards the Sepik. Native patrols were to close the escape routes leading north into the Torricellis.

---

[3] Lt R. H. Roche, QX696. 2/1 A-Tk Regt and 2 NG Inf Bn. Bank officer; of Binalong, NSW; b. Yass, NSW, 10 May 1916.

[4] WO2 T. J. Healy, NG2254. NGVR and Angau. Shoreman (mining); of Bulwa, NG; b. Herberton, Qld, 13 May 1909.

Part of "Farida Force" landing east of Wewak on 11th May 1945. (R.A.A.F.)

(Australian War Memorial)

A private of the 2/8th Battalion using a flame-thrower against Japanese positions at Wewak Point, 10th May 1945.

(Australian War Memorial)
A weapon-pit of the 2/5th Battalion on Kunai Spur in the Torricellis, 10th July 1945.

(Australian War Memorial)
Carriers climbing Mount Shiburangu on 12th July to take supplies to the 2/8th Battalion for their attack on The Blot.

On 8th July Colonel Murchison had moved his advanced headquarters forward to Kwimbu. Garland's company took Gisanambu on the 12th, killing ten. Here Garland tied inflammable material to a native spear, lit it, ran forward and threw it into the roof of a hut within which was a Japanese post. The hut was burnt down. At Dunbit on the same day Lieutenant Harris'[5] platoon was repulsed, Harris and a native soldier being killed. In the day 27 Japanese were killed. Captain Gay's[6] company to the north attacked Aoniaru with two platoons on the 18th and again on the 19th but could not break into the well-dug and well-manned defences. The battalion's headquarters was advanced to the Gwalip area on the 22nd; that day Gay's company made its third attack on Aoniaru, gaining part of the area but not all; the last Japanese were driven out after an air attack on the 24th. The whole battalion was then concentrated about Gwalip. By 27th July Sigora was taken.

On 30th July the battalion had its largest engagement so far when Gay's company was launched against Ulama where the Japanese were well entrenched on a timbered knoll. After an air strike which razed the trees and, it was discovered later, killed 21 Japanese, the company followed on and had reached the top when fire from a surviving post killed Sergeant Smith.[7] Smith's platoon commander, Lieutenant Stewart,[8] immediately crawled forward and threw a grenade at the machine-gunners, who then swung their gun round and engaged him. He threw two more grenades and silenced the gun. The advance was continued, but again came under fire which wounded Lieutenant Reed-Hankey,[9] who fell in the open. Stewart went forward under fire and carried Reed-Hankey to a bomb crater where he tried to dress the wound. Finding the field dressing insufficient, Stewart carried the wounded man back to a sheltered position where medical aid was available, then returned to the attack and carried on until the whole knoll had been secured. Sixteen Japanese were killed in the attack; others withdrew towards Suaui. By 2nd August Murchison had completed his task of securing a base for the 2/7th in the Sigora area.

Meanwhile the 2/5th had been pressing on supported by heavy air strikes and by 1st August had taken Gwenik, 1,000 yards south-west of Kaboibus, after the village had been thrice bombed by from 18 to 30 aircraft and harassed by artillery and mortars. The battalion now had the support of four 25-pounders of the 2/2nd Field Regiment with gun positions at Ulebilum. On 2nd August Bennett's company of the 2/5th advancing along the Kaboibus ridge occupied the Kaboibus villages, surprisingly against only minor opposition; about 100 weapon-pits were found abandoned.

---

[5] Lt E. W. Harris, WX13488; 2 NG Inf Bn. Schoolteacher; of Mount Hawthorn, WA; b. Maddington, WA, 5 Apr 1916. Killed in action 12 Jul 1945.

[6] Capt A. I. Gay, NX104274. 6 MG Bn and 2 NG Inf Bn. Clerk; of Como, NSW; b. Ashfield, NSW, 21 Sep 1915.

[7] Sgt F. S. Smith, VX88734. 6 Bn and 2 NG Inf Bn. Butcher; of Coburg, Vic; b. Footscray, Vic, 13 Jul 1921. Killed in action 30 Jul 1945.

[8] Capt G. F. Stewart, MC, NX579. 6 Cav Regt and 2 NG Inf Bn. Bank officer; of Beecroft, NSW; b. Manly, NSW, 9 Mar 1914.

[9] Lt J. Reed-Hankey, VX146951; 2 NG Inf Bn. Regular soldier; b. Melbourne, 17 Apr 1925. (Now Dr J. R. Hankey.)

Captain Johnson's men of the 2/1st Anti-Tank Regiment had one of their hardest-fought actions on 28th July when they attacked Jama only seven miles from the Sepik. Johnson himself led the patrol of 27, including Lieutenant Storrie[1] as second-in-command. Johnson stealthily reconnoitred and found that there were about 20 Japanese in the village and others could be heard about 50 yards away. The main position was known to contain three covered bunkers, and a pallisade surrounded it. The attackers formed up without being detected and charged the village with weapons blazing.

Complete surprise was obtained (reported Johnson afterwards) and at least half of the enemy killed died in the first rush. Volume of fire was considerably reduced while first one section and then the other broke their way through the fence. In this interval three MG opened fire. . . . The first line of trenches was seized and the occupants killed. An advance up the left flank along the crawl trenches cleared the left. . . . The right flank then moved forward and secured all but one bunker position on the right. The second line of trenches was then grenaded and occupied across the front of the position. The failure to overrun the whole position was due to the enemy holding the rear line of trenches which included three bunkers and a position in the centre . . . all with overhead cover.

The attackers began to run out of ammunition and Johnson, who had done "devastating work" with a Bren, thinned them out and eventually withdrew. They had lost four killed, including Storrie, and two wounded, all of whom were carried back; 32 Japanese dead were counted.

On the left the 2/6th Battalion probed forward during July, sending out, as a rule, five or six patrols each day. On 10th July it had established a patrol base from which to begin operations in the Kaboibus area. The heaviest clash in July was at Kubalak on the left where, on the 14th, a patrol under Lieutenant Johnson[2] attacked some 20 Japanese but was repulsed, losing 3 killed and 2 wounded. By 18th July the battalion had cleared the Ulunkohoitu Ridge. In July the battalion lost 4 killed and 14 wounded; 4 native auxiliaries were killed and 3 wounded; the natives had killed 134 Japanese and the Australians 68.

In response to these thrusts the Japanese reinforced the area with troops from both north and south. The total strength of the *20th* and *41st Divisions* was now thought to be from 1,200 to 1,600, but actually was far more; the Japanese infantry strength in the ranges was in fact more than twice the Australian. Some of the Australian units, on the other hand, had been rested from time to time, and they had the support of bombers and field guns.

Two companies of the 2/5th were now advancing on Ahegulim and Malabeim respectively. On 4th August, with the support of 25-pounders which fired 276 rounds, Geer's company drove a force of 15 to 20 Japanese out of Ahegulim. On the 7th Cameron's company overcame a force of 20 to 30 round Malabeim after a similar bombardment. East and south

---

[1] Lt J. D. Storrie, QX21544; 2/1 A-Tk Regt. Bank officer; of Windsor, Qld; b. Brisbane, 29 Mar 1921. Killed in action 28 Jul 1945.

[2] Lt F. G. Johnson, VX81838; 2/6 Bn. Grazier; of Kensington, Vic; b. Wangaratta, Vic, 24 Feb 1919.

of these positions the forward companies disposed of some small groups and patrolled to the Atilem River without opposition. For the next few days the artillery and mortars harassed enemy positions on Mount Irup. In the past two months the battalion had broken through three strongly-defended north-south defensive lines, killed 370 Japanese and taken 11 prisoners; its own losses had been 23 killed and 76 wounded.

At the end of July the 2/6th Battalion had begun moving out to Wewak for a rest having been in contact with the enemy for five months.

> During this period their advance had been generally across a series of mountain ridges densely covered with jungle and big timber. Each ridge was intersected by deep gorges dropping some 1,000 feet into the mountain streams. The fatigue of movement was immense, the problems of supply heart-breaking; it was jungle fighting at its worst.[3]

They had fought on devotedly, but in July, when the men of this battalion learned that all with five years' service, two of them being overseas, might choose to be discharged from the army, out of 176 officers and men in that category only five said that they would prefer to remain. This was probably largely a result of the feeling that they were in a backwater of the war. To have sent out all the veterans who were entitled to take their discharge in one group would have greatly disorganised this and other battalions and, in fact, the "five-and-two's" were discharged a few at a time. Thus from the 2/7th Battalion, now going into action again, were sent, as a first batch, one officer, 7 N.C.O's and 5 privates.

After a two-day march from Ulebilum through Gwalip to Sigora, the 2/7th set out on its wide movement against Kiarivu on 6th August, preceded the previous day by one of its companies and Captain Garland's company of the 2nd New Guinea Battalion which was included in Colonel Parbury's command for this operation. In three days of hard marching across undulating kunai grasslands the 2/7th met only isolated parties of Japanese, and, at 6.30 on 8th August, secured Kiarivu emergency landing ground. By 9th August Karapia and the northern end of Kiarivu were secured and two 75-mm guns had been dropped. On the 13th the first light aircraft landed and began the removal of sick and wounded. The encircling move had succeeded brilliantly.

In this phase the New Guinea Battalion to the south was taking unusually large numbers of prisoners. On 3rd August, for example, seven surrendered in three groups. At that stage the battalion had taken 11 prisoners, killed 309, and had lost 14 of its own men killed. On 10th August a captain and 12 men surrendered. These surrenders were partly the result of a special effort: supplies of surrender pamphlets were obtained and a local adaptation of the pamphlet in general use was written by the translator at brigade headquarters, who included details supplied by the New Guinea Battalion. These papers were given to local natives to leave

---
[3] 17th Australian Infantry Brigade Report on Operations in the Aitape-Wewak Area, November 1944-August 1945.

in Japanese-occupied villages, and the battalion's deep patrols put them on Japanese tracks. In addition prisoners were used

to sing out to comrades urging them to surrender. All P.W. state that because of continued harassing from the air and the unit's aggressive tactics plus the shortage of food and ammunition they decided to surrender. All had leaflets . . . when taken.[4]

In these final days the New Guinea Battalion had some hard fighting, however. When Captain E. R. Reeve's company was approaching Miyamboara a prisoner who, like many others, having once taken the drastic step and given himself up was anxious to please his captors, explained that when attacked from the air the Japanese at Miyamboara would withdraw to gardens near by. Thereupon three aircraft bombed the enemy's defences and then six made dummy runs while the native troops moved in.

Lieutenant Hodge's[5] platoon occupied a knoll near Mananingi and patrolled to the village where they were fired on. As they advanced 20 Japanese emerged from behind the huts and charged firing from the hip. Caught by surprise three native troops were wounded, two mortally. The patrol withdrew. That day in another area, however, a captain and 16 men, all with pamphlets, surrendered.

On the 12th August 62 rounds of artillery fire and 114 mortar bombs were landed into Mananingi and the Japanese fled in all directions; on the 13th, after an air attack, it was found to be abandoned. Two parties of prisoners totalling six surrendered that day. The forward troops now knew that the end of the fighting was near.

The intermittent references to the work of Angau officers and the natives whom they organised have given only an incomplete picture of their role. By this time cooperation between Angau and the army formations which it served and which served it was smooth and efficient. One task of the division was to help Angau (and A.I.B.) to gain Intelligence, establish bases and protect the local people; for their part the Angau officers of the District Services Branch had to give the divisional commander the benefit of their knowledge of the district, work with the forward troops on reconnaissance, collect information from the natives, and administer justice and relief.

Throughout the campaign a large part of the fighting force had been wholly or partly dependent on native carriers. Even where supply dropping was possible carriers were needed to take supplies farther forward and take parachutes back to a base. During the operations of the 17th Brigade an Angau network was spread deep into enemy territory, under the leadership of the Assistant District Officer, Captain Cole, and, under him, Captain C. M. O'Loghlen, Lieutenants Monk,[6] Graham,[7] Kaad,[8] and Fienberg. On the coast a similar task was done by Captain Searson,[9]

---

[4] War diary, 2nd New Guinea Infantry Battalion.
[5] Lt L. A. Hodge, QX35887; 2 NG Inf Bn. Electric welder; b. Hobart, 2 Nov 1919.
[6] Lt F. O. Monk, NGX367. NGVR and Angau. Bank officer; of Kew, Vic; b. Kew, 21 Jan 1917.
[7] Lt J. R. V. Graham, NGX123. NGVR, 2/25 Bn and Angau. Planter; of Madang, NG; b. Jondaryan, Qld, 15 Nov 1904.
[8] Lt F. P. C. Kaad, NX89868. 2/7 Bn and Angau. Student; of Potts Point, NSW; b. Brisbane, 12 Sep 1920.
[9] Capt J. J. Searson, MC, PX189; Angau. Patrol officer; of Rabaul, TNG; b. Sydney, 23 Sep 1914.

Lieutenants Gow[1] and Birrell and Warrant Officer Godwin. These were the men chiefly responsible for the events which led to frequent references in Japanese reports to the "rebellion" of natives behind their lines.

Late in July General Mano had established his headquarters at Winge with the main force at Gwalip. While at Winge some 80 Australian troops attacked. Mano was having a meal and was undressed at the time. He said after the war that if the attack had been maintained he probably would have been caught. When the Australians attacked Gwalip their patrols were between Mano's headquarters and his front line. Mano was "really surprised at the tenacity with which the Australian troops fought" in the attacks on Winge.[2]

On 25th July General Adachi issued orders for the "last stand" round Numbogua, about 20 miles south of Hayfield. Retreat to the Sepik had been considered and rejected, but at the same time, as mentioned, Yoshiwara had been put in general command there with orders to carry on guerilla warfare, and thus a way was being kept open to the Sepik.

One after another "last-stand" position had been defined in complex, ambiguous and emotional orders—and then lost to the Australians. The next orders defined yet another "last stand". A great part of most *XVIII Army* orders was taken up with reiteration of the disabilities the army suffered and generalisations about tactics and supply. Intentions and methods were not clearly defined.

In a post-mortem examination of the Australian tactics in the final months of the war the staff of the *XVIII Army* expressed the opinion that their enemy had been over-cautious. If the 17th Brigade, having thrust swiftly into the Gwalip area, at the same time had sent native troops into the Japanese rear areas the *41st Division* would have been cut off from its supplies. "If the enemy had employed the natives to guide him through our vast and weakly-manned front line and established his positions behind our lines disrupting our communications . . . and then attacked our forward positions he would have easily overrun our defences. It was unbelievable that the enemy failed to apply these tactics when it was tried over and over again in the Buna and Salamaua areas by the Australian Army with great success. . . . Had the enemy, after penetrating the Yangori sector in August, intercepted our supply route and utilised the goodwill of the natives to the fullest extent, our force would have retreated without a fight. . . . When, after the termination of hostilities, we were marched through the enemy lines we were amazed at the quantity of his marvellous mechanised equipment and material and could not help being proud of our forces fighting so valiantly against such a powerful enemy."

Meanwhile there had been severe fighting south from Wewak. On 28th May General Stevens had issued orders to Colonel Bishop of the 19th Brigade for the capture of Mount Tazaki and Mount Shiburangu. The brigade would occupy a defensive position about Koigin and patrol southward and, provided it did not involve serious fighting, advance its forward elements on to Mount Tazaki. It would then clear the track through the 770 Feature and occupy high ground to ensure control of that track. Next it would clear the area between Wewak and Sauri, and be prepared to move south via Sauri to capture Mount Shiburangu.

The approaches to both Tazaki and Shiburangu were along narrow steep-sided spurs with knolls at intervals along the spurs. As elsewhere the Japanese were well dug in on each knoll and each group of defenders was generally armed with heavy machine-guns, mainly weapons taken

---
[1] Lt A. F. Gow, MC, NGX142. 2/25 Bn and Angau. Public servant; of Shenton Park, WA; b. Subiaco, WA, 29 Dec 1915.
[2] As mentioned, the "Australian troops" round Winge were the 2nd New Guinea Battalion.

from damaged aircraft. Defending the Sauri and Shiburangu routes were the *25th Airfield Battalion,* totalling about 200, and the *III/66th Battalion* from 100 to 150 strong; from Koigin to Mount Tazaki were the *21st Airfield Battalion* and other units totalling about 400. Indeed if one Australian battalion was sent against each objective it would face a force of about equal strength in infantry.

In preparation for the new operation Bishop relieved some of the weary and depleted units then forward. A company of the 2/8th Battalion had relieved the 2/7th Commando Squadron at Sauri; the 2/8th Battalion plus gunners of the 2/1st Anti-Tank Regiment, acting as infantry, relieved the 2/11th, which went into reserve. At first the 16th Brigade was made responsible for the area west of the Big Road and east of a north-south line through Boram, but it was found that the men of this brigade were not yet fit for such a task, and Stevens decided that the 19th Brigade must take over the whole area from Wewak to Mandi. This necessitated deploying in the forward area the three battalions of the brigade, and the 2/6th Cavalry (Commando) Regiment, now to be attached again to the brigade; there was no brigade reserve.

Reinforcements for the Wewak area would soon be on the way, however. In June General Sturdee had ordered the 8th Brigade, in the Madang area, to leave one battalion to carry on the task of patrolling the area east of the Sepik and move the rest of its strength—principally the 30th and 35th Battalions, led by Lieut-Colonels Parry-Okeden and Armstrong[3] respectively—to Wewak where it was intended that the 8th Brigade would help to defend that base while other brigades followed the Japanese withdrawal into the mountains and ultimately linked with the 17th.

Before it departed from the forward area the 2/3rd Battalion had successfully attacked Hill 910, dominating the track from Boram airfield to Koigin. Captain McCrackan's[4] company advanced on this feature on 1st June. Artillery fire failed to dislodge the defenders who were in strong bunkers. Next day, with the support of devastating bombardments, the company made two more attacks, the second of which was completely successful. Of the 30 Japanese dead, 18 had been killed by the artillery, which during the day fired 3,500 rounds. At Hill 910 the only Australian casualty was McCrackan, who was wounded but carried on until the position had been taken.

In the first half of June the 2/10th Commando Squadron in the Mandi area, about two miles east of Brandi Plantation, was also still in close contact with a resolute and enterprising enemy. The Japanese had excellent observation posts overlooking Mandi and were using them to direct artillery and mortar fire. On 1st June the squadron had only 11 officers and 120 men, instead of 17 and 243; for a full squadron attack only about 70 fighting men were available. Thus the need for frequent patrols

---

[3] Lt-Col F. H. M. Armstrong, ED, WX32619. 28 Bn; CO 35 Bn 1945. Bank officer; of Wembley, WA; b. Perth, 8 Aug 1910.
[4] Capt J. A. McCrackan, MC, NX128778. 3 and 2/3 Bns. Bank officer; of Canberra; b. Casino, NSW, 12 Oct 1908.

to maintain the initiative in the hills to the south made heavy demands on the men's endurance. On 5th June a squadron attack was made on a bunker position at a junction about 1,000 yards south of the perimeter. When the attackers encountered sharp fire they were withdrawn 200 yards while the artillery observer, Lieutenant Wyburn[5] of the 2/1st Anti-Tank

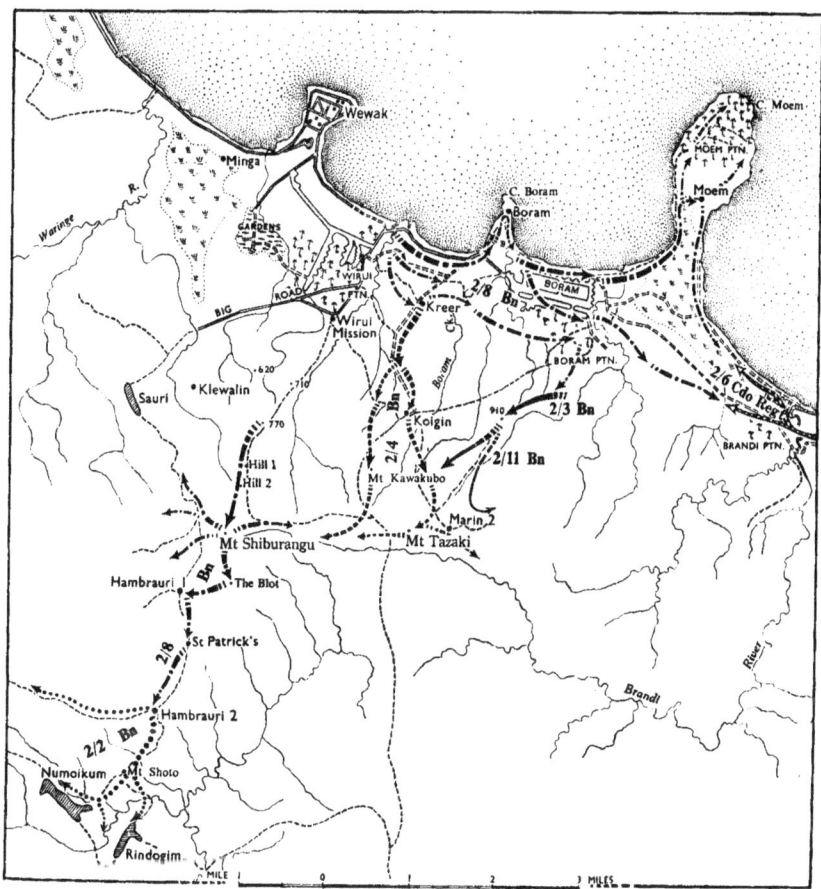

Operations south of Wewak, May-August

Regiment, ranged 16 guns of the 2/2nd Field Regiment at Boram and then poured 800 rounds into the position in less than ten minutes. The result was devastating. Out of 25 bunkers 17 were totally destroyed. It was impossible to find and count all the dead but they were estimated at about 32. On 14th June the squadron was relieved by a company of the 2/3rd Machine Gun Battalion.

[5] Lt K. T. Wyburn, NX112083; 2/1 A-Tk Regt. Public servant; of Sydney; b. Waverley, NSW, 26 Nov 1922.

In this period both the 2/8th and 2/4th Battalions patrolled on a wide front across the approaches to Shiburangu and Tazaki. For example on 6th June a patrol of the 2/8th led by Lieutenant Combes[6] encountered from five to seven Japanese south from Sauri and a brisk engagement took place.

> When the patrol contacted the enemy (wrote the battalion's diarist) Lieutenant Combes immediately got in touch with his company commander by [telephone]. During the conversation Lieutenant Combes noticed a Jap sneaking up the track towards him armed with a rifle and carrying grenades. Still continuing the conversation Lieutenant Combes gave the Jap a burst from his Owen gun which he worked with one hand and killed the Jap.

In the ensuing action Combes and two others were wounded, but Combes remained on duty. Five Japanese were killed.

By 10th June this patrolling had provided enough information to enable Bishop to give detailed orders to the units. The ruggedness of the country made the use of tanks impossible. The 2/8th was ordered to take Hills 1 and 2, and then Mount Shiburangu, to clear the spur from it to Sauri, and link with the 2/4th when that battalion had taken Mount Tazaki and the high ground to the west of it. The 2/11th, still weak—it was, for example, 16 officers short—was to protect the area from Boram airfield to Cape Moem, the 2/3rd Machine Gun to protect Brandi Plantation and Mandi and patrol vigorously to ensure against infiltration. These tasks to the rear were not sinecures since the enemy, despite his hopeless situation, was sending out raiders over a wide front; and the Australians made continual patrols into the enemy's area.

On 11th June the 2/8th had made a two-company attack on Hill 1. Eighteen Beauforts bombed the enemy and the artillery fired 2,200 rounds. Rumley's and Gately's companies took their objectives losing 2 killed and 9 wounded; also 2 officers were wounded when one of the Australian shells burst in a tree. Thirty-three Japanese were killed. Patrolling and information from natives indicated that about 100 Japanese defended Hill 2 beyond which lay Shiburangu itself.

At 8 a.m. on 16th June aircraft struck both Hill 2 and Shiburangu and then the artillery began a program in which 3,000 rounds were fired. One company began to advance on Hill 2 at 9.30. Warrant-Officer Fisk's[7] platoon, which was forward, met heavy fire from snipers on both flanks and machine-gun fire from the hills and lost one man killed and one wounded. It withdrew to the cover of the spur and moved to outflank the enemy on the left. Meanwhile at 9.45 a second company had taken the pocket without opposition.

At 10 a.m. the first company was still held. The men rested under the lip of the hill while the artillery again bombarded the enemy's positions and flame-throwers were brought forward. At 1.30 the company surged over the crest of the hill and, after close fighting in which each bunker

---

[6] Lt G. A. Combes, TX4637. 2/40 and 2/8 Bns. Dairy farmer; of Longley, Tas; b. Greymouth, NZ, 19 May 1913.

[7] WO2 K. R. C. Fisk, MBE, VX103111. 39 and 2/8 Bns. Commercial traveller; of North Melbourne; b. Brunswick, Vic, 8 Oct 1917.

was grenaded, the surviving Japanese fled leaving 38 visible dead and perhaps another 20 buried by the air and artillery bombardment. The Australians lost 2 killed and 3 wounded. "Aerial bombing coupled with artillery concentration does not deter the enemy from fighting nor unsettle him unduly," wrote the battalion diarist. "Such fanatical resistance in face of such odds makes the capturing of these strong points no light task."

On 22nd June a company attack went in against the last knoll before Shiburangu. In half an hour the Japanese were driven from covered pits in bush so dense that the men could see only three or four yards. In the course of the next few days the artillery registered on Shiburangu and the commanders of the leading companies were flown over it in light aircraft.

The onslaught on Shiburangu opened on the 27th with a strike by Beauforts, which dropped 1,000-lb, 500-lb and 250-lb bombs and almost cleared the forward slopes of timber. Then in 20 minutes guns of the 2/1st and 2/3rd Field Regiments poured 3,000 shells into the area. At 9 a.m. the forward company (Captain Dwyer) advanced with Lieutenant Westwood's[8] platoon leading. This platoon took a group of bunkers, but both it and the platoon on its left were pinned down by machine-gun fire. Lieutenant Hewit[9] brought down artillery fire but could not silence the enemy. The third platoon (Lieutenant Trethowan[1]) made an outflanking move through a deep re-entrant on the left and, at 11.30, began a 300-foot climb to the summit up an exposed slope at a grade of 60 degrees. By 12.20, however, it was astride the western spur, completely surprising the enemy and capturing a bunker before it opened fire. It pressed on with great dash and was on top by 12.35 having taken every enemy position except one bunker "manned by three Japs who had already shared seven grenades but lived long enough to cause 15 Platoon's only casualty, Private Smith,[2] who was killed". In the fight Trethowan received three bullets through his clothing and one through his hat. There were 20 bunkers on the hill, each generally manned by three men, and 44 Japanese were killed there; probably about 20 escaped to "Near Knoll" on the west and to a feature to the south. The 2/8th lost 2 killed and 4 wounded.

In the first half of June the 2/4th had pressed on towards Mount Tazaki in a series of patrol, platoon and company actions. On the 1st a patrol drove an enemy party from a razor-back above Koigin. By the 13th the battalion had cleared the eastern side of the Koigin-Tazaki track to a distance of 600 yards south of Koigin. Next day Captain Smith's company made a successful two-platoon attack on Mount Kawakubo. Here the

---

[8] Lt W. H. Westwood, VX82932; 2/8 Bn. Pastrycook; of Gardenvale, Vic; b. Stawell, Vic, 25 Jun 1919.
[9] Capt E. J. Hewit, MC, NX809; 2/1 Fd Regt. Trainee metallurgist; of Toronto, NSW; b. Newcastle, NSW, 1 Oct 1918.
[1] Capt J. M. Trethowan, MC, VX6300; 2/8 Bn. Farm hand; of Donnybrook, Vic; b. Preston, Vic, 12 Dec 1912.
[2] Pte S. J. Smith, VX53447; 2/8 Bn. Labourer; of Skipton, Vic; b. Skipton, 28 Aug 1920. Killed in action 27 Jun 1945.

enemy's position was so well concealed and in such steep country that it was very hard to locate. Smith ordered his men to dig in and remain absolutely quiet. Then he shouted "Cooee" at the top of his voice. The Japanese opened fire with all their weapons, the artillery observer saw where the machine-guns were, and brought down very effective fire. Patrolling in the next two days showed that the only suitable approach to

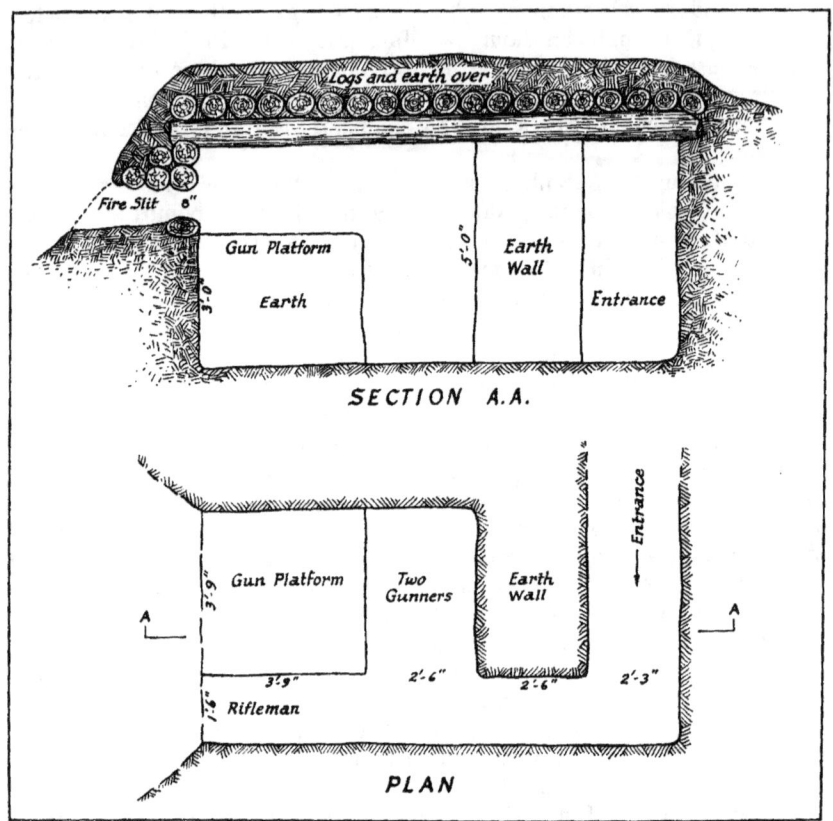

Japanese bunker, Shiburangu area

Tazaki was along the eastern track and revealed a strong enemy position at the junction of tracks south from Koigin and Hill 910. Colonels Cox and Green, after a reconnaissance from the air, planned an attack by a company of the 2/4th and one of the 2/11th for 19th June. There was an air strike and a concerted bombardment. Captain Hawke's company of the 2/4th attacked, met heavy fire, but went on, routed the enemy, and took the main position, killing 16 and losing one killed and one wounded. The attacking company of the 2/11th found its objective abandoned.

On the morning of 20th June Sergeant Hill[3] and 24 men patrolled up the slopes of Tazaki, found the next knoll abandoned, and went on up a spur into which wooden steps had been built, with, at times, a handrail. Soon fire broke out and one man was killed. Hill was wounded trying to retrieve the body. Later the enemy withdrew and the advance continued. One company advanced up Tazaki in bounds with strong artillery support —600 rounds were fired during the day—killed 14 Japanese, and penetrated to within 400 yards of the summit but were then forced back by heavy fire.

After two days of strenuous patrolling the assault on Tazaki was launched on 22nd June. It rained heavily that day. Twenty minutes before the infantry advanced the guns of the 2/1st Field Regiment began shelling the Japanese defences into which 3,000 rounds were fired before the attack and during its early stages. At 8.55 a.m. Lieutenant Mort's[4] company, with two platoons forward, advanced up the track through much debris and fallen timber to a position 200 yards from the summit without seeing any live Japanese, but passed many bunkers and five dead men. The Australians now came under machine-gun and rifle fire. The leading platoons were held; the third one moved round on the left but it too was held. The company then withdrew while the artillery poured 500 rounds on to the summit, and when, at 2.10 p.m., the attack was resumed in the same manner as before, the flanking platoon took one defended knoll but found that "the country near the top is a series of knolls and re-entrants, giving false crests and each knoll is dominated by the other making it ideal for defence".[5] Captain Hawke's company took over on this flank and captured another knoll but was held at a third. Mort had now linked with Hawke and both companies dug in for the night, and a hot meal was carried forward.

There was very heavy rain that night and the trenches were filled with water. Everyone was wet through, cold and weary. A patrol found that one position from which fire had been coming on the 22nd had been abandoned. Another patrol found some floored, well-furnished huts to be unoccupied. It seemed likely that these had been the headquarters of the *51st Division*. A third patrol under Lieutenant Gordon,[6] moved up the west flank of Tazaki and established an outpost astride the east-west track, the main enemy line of communication, and during the day killed six Japanese there.

It was still raining on the 24th. Patrols from Smith's company found that the enemy had abandoned several positions in its neighbourhood. After a mortar barrage Hawke's men, without opposition, occupied the southern crest of Tazaki, which was the commanding feature of the mountain. Patrols probed the area on the 25th, and on the 26th Mort's company moved around the only surviving Japanese—a strong pocket

---

[3] Sgt C. H. Hill, NX5963; 2/4 Bn. Farm worker; of Leeton, NSW; b. Brome, England, 14 Apr 1915.
[4] Capt T. L. Mort, NX5214; 2/4 Bn. Stock and station agent; of Mudgee, NSW; b. Balmain, NSW, 9 May 1915.
[5] War diary, 2/4th Battalion.
[6] Lt C. M. B. Gordon, QX5380; 2/4 Bn. Fire insurance inspector; of Black Rock, Vic; b. Brisbane, 26 Apr 1916.

of about 30 on a narrow razor-back spur—but could not find a usable approach. That night the Japanese stealthily departed from this stronghold probably as a result of harassing fire by the artillery. On the 27th a strong patrol found the enemy in position on a somewhat similar knoll. After further probing Colonel Cox and the commanders of the two companies between which the Japanese pocket lay, flew over it. On 1st July, which was dry and hot, an attack on the pocket was planned for the 2nd, but early that day heavy rain fell and, when it became evident that an air strike would be impossible, the attack was postponed. In the event an air strike was put on in the afternoon, and next morning, after heavy artillery fire, one company attacked and took the pocket. A patrol was ambushed farther on, however, and the regimental medical officer, Captain Williams,[7] was killed and three wounded.

The 2/8th, having taken Shiburangu, had now found that the highest ground (1,650 feet) was actually 1,000 yards farther south. This eminence was called "The Blot"—the nickname of Lieutenant Trethowan whose skilful leadership had been largely responsible for taking Shiburangu. Exploiting, the 2/8th had some sharp actions before linking with the 2/4th. On 3rd July, in torrential rain, Captain Metcalf's[8] company attacked along the western spur of the mountain supported by bombers and by the artillery, which fired 1,500 rounds. They took this objective without loss, killing 23 Japanese. On 5th July the two battalions linked.

The 2/4th continued patrolling round Tazaki and the enemy continued to fight back vigorously. Early on the 7th a raiding party of about ten Japanese struck at an outpost platoon, killed one man and wounded the commander, Lieutenant Dean,[9] but themselves lost five killed. That day the whole responsibility for the area was taken over by the 30th Battalion of the incoming 8th Brigade, and the 2/4th began resting and retraining on the beach. It was only 536 strong and of its 18 platoons only 8 were commanded by officers. At the end of the month Colonel Cox added this note to the war diary:

> During the past three months the morale of the men has been very high indeed—the result of repeated successes, vigorous battles and good supply conditions. Earlier in the campaign it was noticeable that many of the troops, and officers too, considered the campaign not worth while and consequently morale dropped. At this time, however, there were restrictions on operations and supply was not of a very high standard, and although there were many reasons for this, they were not known or appreciated by the majority of personnel.

The strength of the infantry units was indeed dwindling to a grave degree. The battalions of the 16th Brigade generally were no better off than those of the 19th. The 16th was the only brigade of the 6th Division that had fought through the bitter Kokoda-Buna battles in 1942 and 1943. It would, no doubt, have astounded the people at home to learn that

---

[7] Capt O. U. Williams, MBE, NX114064. 2/2 Fd Amb and RMO 2/4 Bn. Medical practitioner; of Killara, NSW; b. Dubbo, NSW, 29 May 1918. Killed in action 3 Jul 1945.

[8] Capt E. C. Metcalf, VX6513; 2/8 Bn. Farmer; of Tolmie, Vic; b. Shepparton, Vic, 21 Oct 1915.

[9] Lt S. Dean, DCM, NX2002; 2/4 Bn. Engineering assistant; of Inverell, NSW; b. Inverell, 26 Mar 1916.

the battalions of that brigade were in the Aitape-Wewak campaign suffering losses comparable with those in Papua in the earlier fighting. The 2/2nd Battalion lost 64 killed in action, died of wounds or died of injuries in Papua, and 54 between Aitape and Wewak. The 2/2nd had been somewhat reinforced since the hard fighting round Dagua and the 1410 Feature, but still had only 29 officers instead of 33, and 571 other ranks instead of 770. Three majors, all of whom had been with the battalion in the Middle East, had recently returned to the unit and 7 new lieutenants had either arrived from Australia or been commissioned in the field. On 23rd June the 2/3rd Battalion was only 20 plus 439 strong; there were only 139 riflemen, a deficiency of 222. Four days later 31 reinforcements arrived, where 330 were needed. There were 7 officers of the rank of captain and above instead of 13; only 10 platoons were commanded by officers. Of the 20 officers 8 had army numbers lower than NX8000, this indicating that they almost certainly had joined the battalion either in 1939 when it was being formed or very soon afterwards.

Throughout this period the Japanese were raiding boldly along the Australian-held coastal area as far west as But. In late May and early June the Japanese infiltration in the But area had assumed dangerous proportions. The 2/3rd Machine Gun Battalion garrisoning this area faced a difficult problem. As the advance progressed eastward from But it was given the task of taking over the area vacated by the advancing formation with the task of keeping the Japanese out of it. Hence the area of responsibility allotted to the battalion became very extensive, and at one period covered 25 miles of densely timbered and precipitous mountain country. At this time the battalion was reduced to a little more than half strength and one company was with the commando regiment at Dove Bay. The task of patrolling this area and keeping it free of Japanese was a very difficult one indeed. It was not hard for enemy raiding parties to descend from the hills and reach the coastal roads without being detected. There were many encounters with the Japanese raiders, some of whose bases were beyond the range of Australian patrols. The policy of the 2/3rd Machine Gun was to send natives out on long-range patrols perhaps lasting several days to find the Japanese camps. On their return the natives were questioned in front of a sand model of the area and the exact positions of the enemy camps were fixed. These were then bombarded.

As mentioned, on 3rd June the 2/3rd Machine Gun was given the task of relieving the 2/6th Cavalry (Commando) Regiment in the Mandi-Brandi area. Its task was to occupy Brandi Plantation and hold the cross-roads at Mandi with an outpost force so as to prevent the enemy moving west. Thus, on 11th June, two companies of the 2/3rd under Captain Bellair[1] relieved the 2/9th Commando Squadron at Brandi and promptly began patrolling. One patrol under Bellair encountered the enemy in some strength—about 25—at "Keyhole" and killed 3, Bellair

---
[1] Capt J. M. Bellair, VX9702. 2/1 and 2/3 MG Bns. Grazier; of Riddell's Creek, Vic; b. Hawthorn, Vic, 22 May 1909.

himself accounting for 2 of these. Next day a two-platoon attack with air and artillery support was put in at Keyhole; the bombardment drove the Japanese out.

From the beginning in this area the 2/3rd Machine Gun Battalion pursued its policy of strong offensive patrolling, ambushes and harassing fire by the artillery, and this succeeded in subduing, temporarily, the enemy's raiding tactics. On the 13th the command at Brandi passed from Colonel Rickard,[2] temporarily in command of the 2/6th Commando Regiment while Colonel Hennessy was on leave, to Colonel Gordon of the machine-gun battalion. In mid-July Rickard handed over the command of the regiment and returned to the less exacting task of commanding his anti-tank unit. At this stage of the war there must have been few men leading rifle units in action who were as old and as widely experienced as this remarkable warrior. In 1918, when 22, Rickard had been a twice-decorated major of artillery. He had served with distinction in the same rank in Syria in 1941, being then 45, and had since commanded a series of anti-tank regiments. His 21-year-old son had been killed in action at Derna four years before. Rickard was now nearly 50.

As a result of the renewal of Japanese raids in the Dagua-Boiken area the fourth company of the 2/3rd Machine Gun was held in that area where it had a more strenuous time than the companies farther forward —if the term "forward" had significance at this stage.

On 16th June in the Brandi area a platoon patrol of "A" Company which was to set an ambush on the enemy's supply route was itself ambushed on the very spot, Sergeant Parkin[3] being killed and two wounded. That night Japanese raided the same company without causing damage; indeed Private Johnson[4] captured one of the raiders, a lieutenant who was probably their leader. At this time the battalion began using its Vickers machine-guns for harassing the areas where the enemy were known to be established, spending as many as 3,000 rounds in a single fire program. The main body of the 2/3rd Machine Gun Battalion continued to thrust patrols into the features to the south and every day one or more fierce clashes occurred. On the 19th on a feature named "Steve's" there was a fight in which two Australians and four Japanese were killed. Next day there was a clash in which Corporal Nicholson[5] was killed; Sergeant Bowering[6] went forward under fire and carried in his body. Throughout this period Japanese guns shelled the area from time to time but the fire was erratic and no one was hit. The precise position of these guns proved very difficult to find, but the battalion had

---

[2] Lt-Col A. L. Rickard, DSO, MC, ED, NX438. (1st AIF: Maj 12 FA Bde.) 2/2 A-Tk Regt; CO 103 A-Tk Regt 1942-44, 106 A-Tk Regt 1944, 2/1 A-Tk Regt 1944-45. Of Wahroonga, NSW; b. Sydney, 18 Sep 1895. Died 9 Mar 1949.

[3] Sgt D. W. Parkin, WX949; 2/3 MG Bn. Breadcarter; of Roleystone, WA; b. Fremantle, WA, 3 Aug 1917. Killed in action 16 Jun 1945.

[4] Pte C. R. Johnson, SX13161; 2/3 MG Bn. Farm worker; of Parilla, SA; b. Mallala, SA, 23 May 1918.

[5] Cpl D. C. Nicholson, SX15460; 2/3 MG Bn. Baker; of Mount Gambier, SA; b. Wolseley, SA, 3 Aug 1918. Killed in action 20 Jun 1945.

[6] Sgt W. S. Bowering, SX15461; 2/3 MG Bn. Wool and skin buyer; of Millicent, SA; b. Millicent, 4 Sep 1917.

its machine-guns trained on to the general area and the duels between the machine-guns and the enemy artillery were interesting interludes. At night hungry Japanese would creep down to the gardens near Brandi Plantation to dig potatoes; few returned to their own lines, the marauders being systematically ambushed.

In the early part of July the 8th Brigade (each of its battalions about 250 below strength) relieved the 2/4th and 2/11th and took over the Wirui Creek-Mandi area on the right flank. By the 14th the 30th Battalion was holding the Koigin sector forward to Tazaki; the 2/3rd Machine Gun Battalion (now under Brigadier Fergusson's command and replacing the battalion which the 8th Brigade had left behind south of the Sepik) was round Boram and forward to Marin 2, the 35th Battalion round Brandi and Mandi and forward to Soarin. On the night of 10th-11th July the 30th had its first severe experience of Japanese attack when, without loss, it drove off a raiding group and killed thirteen.

Among the Japanese guns harassing the troops round Brandi were two which were shelling the area from a site about Soarin, and, on 12th July, after the shelling of the Angau compound had upset the natives there, General Stevens gave orders to Gordon of the 2/3rd Machine Gun Battalion that they must be captured. A raiding force was formed, led by Captain Bellair and comprising two platoons of the machine-gunners and one from the 35th Battalion, to give it experience. The raiding force moved off stealthily through the country on the east side of the Brandi River before dawn on 18th July, lay hidden all day, and in the afternoon moved across the river near where the guns were believed to be. At 11 p.m. two assault groups each of twelve men were led in to positions below the features believed to be their objectives. Early next morning the men of the first group, after a difficult climb through tangled undergrowth, were close to their objective when they heard a loud voice giving orders and men moving about. They decided that surprise had been lost and rejoined the main force. The second group found the Japanese manning their defences, opened fire, killed six and withdrew under heavy fire. That afternoon, after 540 shells had been fired into the Japanese position, a platoon attack was made but the enemy had moved forward during the artillery fire and the attack failed. It was concluded afterwards that the force defending the ridge numbered from 60 to 100 and were in a well-built position, and that a more deliberate operation would be needed to expel them. It seemed likely that they were determined to defend their gardens in this area as long as they could.

Thus in June and July the units protecting the base areas were committed to much strenuous patrolling. On 17th June the 2/1st Battalion had been ordered to relieve the 2/2nd and take over the area Big Road-Sauri-Ranimboa-Cape Pus. Colonel Cullen ordered each of three companies to establish patrol bases from which to control this wide area: Captain J. C. Burrell's at Yarabos, Captain Percival's[7] at Minga Gardens,

---

[7] Capt S. M. S. Percival, NX34855; 2/1 Bn. Assurance agent; of Wollongong, NSW; b. Lithgow, NSW, 20 Nov 1911.

Captain Givney's at Dallman Harbour. The main patrol tasks fell upon the Yarabos company which was astride the track leading inland.

After several skirmishes an enemy group was driven on 20th June from a position 3,000 yards along the track. On the 23rd Lieutenant Mavay's platoon killed 5 Japanese only about 500 yards south of Yarabos and, on the way home, was ambushed, 2 natives being killed and 3 Australians wounded. Private Krueger[8] promptly attacked the ambushers with rifle and grenades, killing 2 and wounding another, and a comrade killed a third.

It was evident that the enemy were resolved to defend the Yarabos Track at points close to the Australian base. On 26th June Mavay's platoon found Japanese dug in at a bridge just north of Wiruru. Burrell brought up another platoon and next morning, after an artillery concentration, the Japanese were driven out. From Yarabos on 5th July two platoons under Lieutenant G. MacF. Nathan attacked and entered Wiruru, a collection of 23 huts in which large quantities of equipment were found abandoned.

In order to create a diversion during the advance of the 19th Brigade, the 2/1st had been ordered to thrust along the Sambukaua Track, beginning on 14th July. Two platoons of Givney's company assembled at Wiruru on the 13th and in two clashes with the enemy killed 6 of them. Next day the company with artillery support thrust on about a mile and a half, killing 10. On the 15th the advance continued for a mile, 5 more Japanese being killed. Next day, 800 yards farther south, the enemy was driven out of another rearguard position and a native, Yaraworgy, "was ordered to climb a tree and stated that he could see Sambukaua. He then successfully directed an artillery shoot on to the village." While in this area the 2/1st and the engineers simplified the problem of supplying the Yarabos base, initially fed by native carriers toiling up from the coast, by clearing the snags from the creek leading to it and transporting supplies in launches and folding boats.

At this stage the cheerful familiarity with which the troops were treating the many native labourers was causing concern among Angau officers, and the following instructions were issued:

(a) Natives will, under no circumstances, be picked up or carried in jeeps. This in no way affects the carrying of natives in the back of larger vehicles on duty.
(b) No native will enter camp areas except on duty and then only under the supervision of Angau overseer or boss boy.
(c) Troops will not enter native compounds except on duty.
(d) Natives will not be allowed to visit picture shows or other forms of entertainment.
(e) Troops will have no dealings with natives outside the course of duty.
(f) Natives will not be given grenades or explosives for fishing.

The 2/6th Commando Regiment was now coping with daring infiltration to the west round Boiken. On 24th June five Japanese approaching

---

[8] Pte B. W. Krueger, VX116800; 2/1 Bn. Dairyman; of Hawthorn, Vic; b. Preston, Vic, 25 Mar 1919.

(Australian War Memorial)
The Blot on 14th July, the day of its capture by a company of the 2/8th Battalion. During the assault it was hit by 3,500 shells and hundreds of mortar bombs.

(Australian War Memorial)
A Vickers machine-gun crew supporting the 2/6th Battalion during its successful attack on Ulunkohoitu Ridge in the Prince Alexander Ranges on 18th July 1945.

Troops of the 2/7th Battalion, on their long flanking march to Kiarivu, pass a House Tamboran (native meeting house) in Sigora on 5th August 1945. *(Australian War Memorial)*

Weary troops of the 2/7th Battalion resting on a muddy section of the track on the way to Kiarivu. *(Australian War Memorial)*

Kiarivu, 6th August 1945. A "kai bomber" drops food for the newly-arrived troops.
(*Australian War Memorial*)

Men of the 2/7th Battalion watching for signs of Japanese movement in Kiarivu village.
(*Australian War Memorial*)

(*Australian War Memorial*)
At Kiarivu, 6th August. In the distance is Mount Turu. The 2/7th Battalion was then on the edge of the area in which the *XVIII Japanese Army* intended to make its last stand.

(*Australian War Memorial*)
Major-General H. C. H. Robertson (G.O.C. 6th Division) taking the surrender of Lieut-General Adachi, commander of the *XVIII Japanese Army,* at Cape Wom near Wewak, 13th September 1945.

along the beach entered the Angau compound at Wisling, stole 3 Owen guns, a pistol, and 3 Japanese rifles. A patrol followed these marauders, killed 2 and retrieved the weapons. Next day about 10 Japanese ambushed a party of the 2/10th Commando Squadron south of Boiken Plantation and killed Lieutenant Martin[9] and wounded 4 others; and that night about 20 stole into the plantation. On 28th June signs were found that some 35 Japanese had slept the previous night 400 yards from a commando perimeter. On 23rd July a commando patrol had a sharp clash with perhaps 40 Japanese in the hills south of Wanpea and more than 15 miles west of Wewak; 8 Japanese were killed and 4 Australians, including Lieutenant Redmond.[1]

> The Japanese were justly proud of the valour and successes of the raiding parties which harassed the Australians between Wewak and Dagua in May, June and July. Several groups were organised and trained for these enterprises, the most celebrated being led by Lieutenant Hachiro Saito of the *78th Regiment* who had first earned fame as a patrol leader in the Huon Peninsula fighting. In June his party set off to raid Maprik, but was intercepted, Saito and most of his followers being killed. From 15th June onwards two parties of raiders operated in the Karawop and Boiken areas with the object of diverting their enemy's strength away from the *51st Division* farther east. These parties, which claimed to have killed more than 100 Australians—a wild over-estimate—were the ones coped with by the 2/6th Commando Regiment. Another series of raids in late July and early August were considered less successful, because of improved Australian security measures.

Captured documents and interrogation of prisoners now indicated that the Japanese, with the *115th Regiment* and part of the *66th*, totalling 400, were defending the Big Road in strength, the main strongholds being The Blot, Hambrauri 1 and 2, Rindogim and Numoikum. On 4th July Stevens had ordered the 19th Brigade to destroy the enemy in these areas, and on 13th July Brigadier Martin, now in command again, ordered the 2/8th to take The Blot and then Hambrauri 2. For some days the 2/8th had been feeling its way towards The Blot, which was separated from Shiburangu by a deep main gorge cut with smaller steep-sided valleys between narrow spurs. The approach along the Big Road was strongly defended and the attack was made from the north-east along a more difficult but less likely route. The 2/8th's assault on The Blot opened on the morning of 14th July. Gately's company, supported by devastating artillery fire —3,500 rounds—attacked from the north-east, moved swiftly, and, while the artillery and mortars shelled the reverse slope, thrust through smashed defences and fallen trees to the summit whence the victors saw the surviving Japanese making off to the south. By 11 a.m. The Blot had been taken and soon patrols were moving down the ridges to the south and west.

Next day the 2/8th took a spur running west to the Big Road, thus gaining control of the Big Road from The Blot to Shiburangu. The rapid

---

[9] Lt G. J. Martin, VX64564; 2/10 Cdo Sqn. Cost accountant; of Sydney; b. Melbourne, 7 May 1913. Killed in action 25 Jun 1945.
[1] Lt N. T. Redmond, NX49696; 2/10 Cdo Sqn. Shipping clerk; of Mosman, NSW; b. Lindfield, NSW, 12 Mar 1922. Killed in action 23 Jul 1945.

capture of these positions disorganised the defenders and made a swift exploitation to Hambrauri 1 advisable. On 16th July a company took Hambrauri 1 without opposition. Next day patrols to the south met strong opposition on "St Patrick's", the highest ground on the spur joining the Hambrauris, and a long fire fight ensued. St Patrick's was probed by patrols and bombarded, and on 21st July Captain Dwyer's company attacked after a concentration in which 900 rounds were fired. Sergeant Gibbs'[2] platoon moving up the southern spur of St Patrick's was held by fire. Lieutenant Trethowan's moved round on its left and soon the spur was in Australian hands, 21 Japanese being killed there and elsewhere in the battalion's area that day. Hambrauri 2 was taken without opposition next day. In the advance from Shiburangu the 2/8th killed 146 and took 8 prisoners, but lost only 2 killed.

The 8th Brigade was patrolling to the south and gaining experience. On 21st July Major Serong[3] led out from the 35th Battalion a force of three platoons (including one for carrying), specialist detachments, and native police to destroy an enemy ammunition dump. They found it unguarded and started it exploding. Explosions continued for half an hour. The only opposition was some random rifle fire as the patrol withdrew. On 27th July patrols from both the 30th and 35th Battalions clashed with enemy parties and killed 8, losing 2 men wounded. Late in July the brigade area was being shelled almost daily. On 4th August there were encounters in which 7 Japanese were killed. While in the Wewak area the brigade killed 109 Japanese and took 9 prisoners, and lost 9 killed and 32 wounded.

All the infantry of the division, except the two battalions of the 8th Brigade, were now in urgent need of long rest, but the 17th Brigade most of all. On 21st July, after discussing the condition of the men with Moten, Stevens gave orders for a series of reliefs that would take more than two months to complete. The 16th Brigade would replace the 19th. The 19th after a spell would relieve the 17th, which would go into reserve. The 16th Brigade began to relieve the 19th on 25th July. Three days earlier General Stevens had ordered Brigadier King to capture Numoikum, clear Rindogim, patrol vigorously, and prepare for a further advance westward towards Paparam as soon as he could supply a force so far forward.

Consequently the 2/2nd Battalion relieved the 2/8th in the Hambrauri area on 28th July. Next day it sent out two platoon patrols which killed 5 stragglers and found 4 dead. On the 30th a patrol killed 2 Japanese officers who were in a party of 5; the others escaped. That day Lieutenant Finlayson's platoon encountered about 10 Japanese dug in on a ridge with a cleared field of fire and in the ensuing fight killed 2 and then withdrew. On the 31st Lieutenant Donoghue's[4] platoon was sent out to clear the enemy off this ridge. They found the enemy still in the

---

[2] Sgt J. J. Gibbs, VX42582; 2/8 Bn. Engineer; of South Yarra, Vic; b. Carlton, Vic, 1 May 1912.

[3] Col F. P. Serong, VX59888. 2/8 Armd Regt; 2/11 and 4 Bns. Regular soldier; b. North Fitzroy, Vic, 11 Nov 1915.

[4] Lt T. J. Donoghue, MC, MM, NX4957. 2/3 and 2/2 Bns. Electric motor driver; of Captain's Flat, NSW; b. Marrickville, NSW, 4 Jan 1918.

same position, brought down artillery fire but found it impossible to advance except in single file and withdrew. This position, occupied by a handful of men, was typical of many where small parties were now dug in and prepared to fight to the end. The narrowness of the steep ridges made these positions difficult to subdue with artillery fire—250 rounds were fired into this one—and even more difficult to attack with infantry except at heavy cost.

It now seemed evident that the enemy intended to hold fast on a ridge about a mile south-west of Hambrauri in order to defend Numoikum and protect an escape route by way of Rindogim to the south; captured documents showed that Mount Shoto was the site of a headquarters. Captain McCammon's[5] company was given the task of capturing the knolls covering Rindogim on the 1st and exploiting to Rindogim next day.

At the first of these knolls the attacking company dispersed a group of Japanese and then with one platoon advancing north and another south of the track took both knolls, losing one man killed and killing five Japanese. Beyond this point the track divided, one branch leading south-east to Rindogim and the other south-west to the Numoikum area. On the 2nd Captain Derbyshire's company was to secure the track junction and advance on Numoikum while McCammon's advanced on Rindogim. Thus on the morning of the 2nd Derbyshire's men took the track junction and successfully attacked the enemy force on Mount Shoto, killing nine; in the afternoon they patrolled forward along the track, encountered the enemy again and killed four. Meanwhile McCammon's leading platoon (Lieutenant Robertson[6]) had reached the outskirts of Rindogim, seen some 15 Japanese and had a sharp fight. In the day 19 Japanese were killed.

The 3rd August was spent in patrolling, and on the 4th Derbyshire's company was pressing on towards Numoikum and McCammon's towards Rindogim. Derbyshire's company had a series of sharp engagements and was eventually held some 700 yards from the starting-point in rugged country covered with bamboo and pit-pit. Ten Japanese were killed but 2 Australians were killed and 5 wounded, including Lieutenant Donoghue. In the course of the action Donoghue had led his platoon through precipitous country, got astride the track behind the Japanese, and led a charge against their rear. He refused to be carried out until the action was over.

Meanwhile in the afternoon McCammon's company attacked Rindogim. The forward platoon led with great dash by Sergeant Donnett attacked gallantly up a very steep slope towards the village, and then Lieutenant Lochhead's[7] platoon pressed through and completed the task. The village was secured and ten Japanese killed for a loss of one wounded.

---

[5] Lt-Col H. G. McCammon, MBE, NX34868; 2/2 Bn. Printer; of Wollongong, NSW; b. Wollongong, 3 May 1919.
[6] Lt R. W. Robertson, VX14517. 2/4 Fd Regt and 2/2 Bn. Accountant; of South Yarra, Vic; b. Brighton, Vic, 4 Nov 1916.
[7] Lt-Col A. J. Lochhead, MM, VX118202. 39 and 2/2 Bns. Clerk; of Essendon, Vic; b. Essendon, 9 Dec 1922.

The enemy continued to defend the track into the Numoikum villages with resolution and the villages were not taken until the 6th when, after a 2,000-round artillery concentration, Derbyshire's company attacked with flame-throwers, which caused the enemy to flee in panic, 18 dead being counted in the day. The enemy fire in these engagements was the most intense this battalion had encountered in the campaign.

The flame-throwers, brought into use so late, had generally been most effective, and on the 9th they were sent forward against a group of Japanese south of Rindogim. They failed to work, however, because the pressure tanks were leaking at the check valve; surprise was lost and the enemy wounded five Australians.[8] For the next six days the battalion remained on the defensive; news had come that a cease fire was imminent.

In the course of these last operations General Stevens at the Government's direction and against his own wishes had been released from the army to go to a senior appointment in the Commonwealth Public Service and, until the arrival of Major-General Robertson early in August, Brigadier King commanded the division, and Colonel Cullen the 16th Brigade.

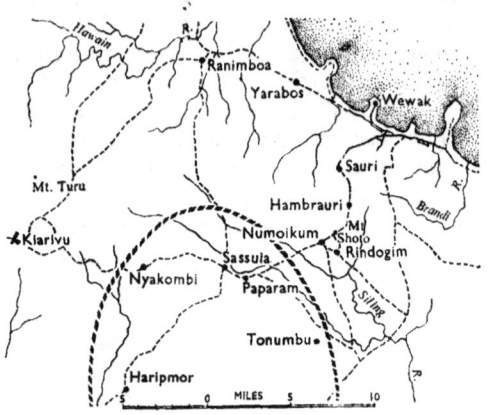

Japanese last-stand area

The main body of the *XVIII Army* was now in an arc facing north and west. The *51st Division* was on the right opposing the troops advancing from Wewak, the *20th Division* in the centre and the *41st* on the left.

Yoshiwara had now reported that the food resources of the Sepik area were less than had been believed, though there might be more in the hinterland. Already about 2,800 troops were stationed in the Sepik Valley from Marienberg to about Kanganaman and were living off the country. Adachi decided to make a last stand in the area embracing, in the north, Nyakombi and Sassuia. Here they would fight on "as long as ammunition and food are available and at least until the end of September". Liaison was to be maintained with the force in the Sepik area which was to prepare to carry on "ambush warfare" after the main force had been wiped out. This plan had been conveyed to Field Marshal Terauchi, commanding the *Southern Army*, and he approved it on 8th July.

At the same time Terauchi sent a citation to the *XVIII Army*. It was the first time that a Japanese army had been so honoured. The citation ran: "To the 18th Army and all attached units: With Lieut-General Hatazo Adachi as your commander, you have fought vigorously for three years in north-east New Guinea, where numerous epidemics prevailed and where the terrain was hitherto unknown to any Japanese. When the enemy occupied the west coast in April 1944, to cut off supplies,

---

[8] In a subsequent report Colonel Cameron wrote: "Australian tanks are roughly finished and are more prone to leak than American-made tanks. . . . It is essential that a pressure gauge is available."

you learned to live off grass and trees, and by making the best of the situation, you conquered all unfavourable conditions. Officers and soldiers alike displayed the true spirit of the Japanese Army. Wherever you encountered the enemy, you crushed them and inflicted many casualties. You have inspired fear into the hearts of the enemy and diverted their sea and air strength, thereby contributing much to the Southern Army's operations and furthermore, to all the Armies of the Empire. You were able to accomplish this through the excellent leadership, planning, fidelity and character of your Army Commander. By the sense of sincerity, loyalty and moral obligation of all the troops, you have set a model for all men to follow. I hereby present this citation and proclaim this to all the Armies."

After the war the Japanese commanders affirmed that they were spurred on round Aitape-Wewak as in Bougainville by the knowledge that their resistance was holding down troops who might otherwise have been used elsewhere. There was never any thought of surrender or precipitate retreat.

The strength of the *XVIII Army* had been greatly underestimated throughout: it was now believed to total about 8,600 whereas it was in fact about 13,500. When fighting ceased it was found that facing the 17th Brigade were 255 officers and 1,456 men of the *20th Division* and 158 and 989 of the *41st Division*. In addition, close to the 2/7th Battalion round the Mount Turu, Warimba and Haripmor areas were forces totalling 2,237. The *51st Division* was about 6,000 strong, and other units totalled about 3,000.

After the surrender the Australians were surprised at the good health and bearing of the Japanese troops, when so many who had been encountered during the fighting were sick and dirty. Account must be taken, however, of the fact that the Japanese were then rested, and were under orders, in this area as in others, to present as neat and disciplined an appearance as possible in order to impress their captors.

In the campaign 442 officers and men of the 6th Division were killed in action or died of wounds, and 1,141 were wounded.[9] The admissions to hospital because of sickness were:

Malaria	6,227
Skin diseases	1,386
Dysentery, Dengue and Scrub Typhus	1,220
Other causes	7,370
Total	16,203

Seventeen officers and 128 others died from causes other than battle wounds.

The battle casualties in this ten months' campaign were about the same as those suffered by the 7th Division in six weeks in Syria, where 416 were killed and 1,136 wounded. In the only other campaigns in which the 6th Division had fought as a complete division its casualties were:

---

[9] The battle casualties in the infantry and commando units were:

	Officers	Other Ranks		Officers	Other Ranks
16 Bde—			19 Bde—		
2/1 Bn	4	101	2/4 Bn	4	170
2/2 Bn	11	165	2/8 Bn	9	100
2/3 Bn	4	109	2/11 Bn	6	138
17 Bde—			8 Bde—		
2/5 Bn	8	138	30 Bn	1	23
2/6 Bn	9	107	35 Bn	—	17
2/7 Bn	7	122	2/6 Cav (Cdo) Regt	21	120
			2/3 MG Bn	1	93
			2 NGIB	5	41

The 2/1st Field Regiment lost 3 officers and 29 others killed or wounded; the 2/1st Anti-Tank Regiment 5 and 28.

Cyrenaica, 256 dead, 861 wounded and 21 prisoners; Greece (including corps troops), 320 dead, 494 wounded, and 2,030 prisoners.[1]

In ten months the division had advanced 70 miles along the coast, from the Driniumor to Forok Point, and, in the inland sector, 45 miles from Tong to Kiarivu, and had driven the Japanese from 3,000 square miles of territory. About 9,000 Japanese were killed and 269 taken prisoner.[2] It had been a galling campaign under most arduous conditions in heartbreaking country against a ruthless and resolute enemy. The losses suffered by the Australians, although small by comparison with those they inflicted, were made harder to bear by reason of the conviction, particularly among veteran campaigners, that the operations were of minor importance. The existence of this feeling underlines the devotion of the troops who, in spite of it, went into the attack with their usual dash until the end. The determined defence offered by the Japanese was the more admirable in view of the hopelessness of their situation and the appalling losses they were suffering, both in battle and from disease and malnutrition.

The total strength of the formations that became the *XVIII Japanese Army* was about 100,000.[3] By the time of the American landings west of Wewak, and largely as a result of the losses inflicted on the *20th, 41st* and *51st Divisions,* or parts of them, in the Australian offensives of 1943-44, they appear to have numbered about 54,000.[4] After their counter-attack on Aitape which ended in August 1944 there were, according to several accounts, 41,000; according to one account 35,000. According to another account 30,000 remained by the end of 1944. A year later only 13,300 had survived. In three years probably about 90,000 Japanese soldiers—Adachi said "more than 100,000"—had died in the area between Milne Bay and Aitape or in the hinterland. This is more than two-thirds the number of Japanese who died in the whole of the fighting in Burma, estimated at 128,000.[5]

About 300,000 Japanese, including about 20,000 civilian workers, were landed in New Guinea and the Solomons from 1942 onwards; 127,000 were alive at the surrender; of the remainder perhaps 60,000 were killed in battle and about 110,000 died of illness.

After the war Adachi was charged with war crimes, including the killing of prisoners, and on 12th July 1947 was sentenced to imprisonment for life. On 10th September that year he killed himself in his quarters in the prisoners' compound at Rabaul, having first written a number of letters.

---

[1] Detached brigades and units of the division which had fought as part of the garrison of Crete, as part of the 7th Australian and 6th British Divisions in Syria, and with Kanga Force and the 7th and 3rd Australian Divisions in New Guinea, suffered relatively heavier losses than these.

[2] It is evidence of the severity with which reports of the killing of Japanese were examined that the Australian claims totalled only 7,213 killed. It is doubtful whether at any time the Japanese staffs could have provided precise figures, but after the war estimates by their staff officers of the number killed in this period ranged from 6,400, excluding the naval forces, to 9,100 all told.

[3] General Yoshiwara says "about 105,000 including those lost at sea". Those lost at sea probably numbered about 3,500.

[4] The *XVIII Army* report gives the total strength on 1st April 1944 as 75,000. Possibly the additional 21,000 comprised the troops at Hollandia.

[5] J. Ehrman, *Grand Strategy*, Vol VI, p. 257.

In one of these, addressed to those officers and men of the *XVIII Army* who were then in the compound, he said:

I felt it a great honour to have been appointed the C-in-C in November 1942, at a time when the issue of the day was to be settled, and posted to the point of strategic importance in order to ensure that the tide of war moved in our favour. I was thankful for that appointment. However, notwithstanding the fact that my officers and men did their best in the exceptional circumstances, surmounting all difficulties, and that my superiors gave the utmost assistance, the hoped-for end was not attained, because of my inability. Thus I paved the way for my country to be driven into the present predicament. The crime deserves death.

During the past three years of operations more than 100,000 youthful and promising officers and men were lost and most of them died of malnutrition. When I think of this, I know not what apologies to make to His Majesty the Emperor and I feel that I myself am overwhelmed with shame. . . . I have demanded perseverance far exceeding the limit of man's endurance of my officers and men, who were exhausted and emaciated as a result of successive campaigns and for want of supplies. However, my officers and men all followed my orders in silence without grumbling, and, when exhausted, they succumbed to death just like flowers falling in the winds. God knows how I felt when I saw them dying, my bosom being filled with pity for them, though it was solely to their country that they dedicated their lives. At that time I made up my mind not to set foot on my country's soil again but to remain as a clod of earth in the Southern Seas with the 100,000 officers and men, even if a time should come when I would be able to return to my country in triumph.

In both Australian and Japanese history the offensives of 1945 will endure as examples of splendid fortitude, but whether they should have happened seems likely always to be in dispute.

CHAPTER 16

PLANNING FOR BORNEO—APRIL TO JUNE 1945

IN an earlier chapter the story of the higher planning of the operations against Borneo was carried as far as mid-April, when, despite General Marshall's opinion in February that such operations would have little immediate effect on the war against Japan, he and his colleagues of the Combined Chiefs of Staff had approved them and the dates had been finally fixed. One object was to secure a base for the British Pacific Fleet, and, incidentally, the operation would provide employment for the I Australian Corps. The British Chiefs of Staff, however, considered that to develop Brunei Bay in northern Borneo as a fleet base would be a waste of resources; and the Australian Commander-in-Chief, although he had expressed approval of the seizure of Tarakan Island and Brunei Bay, had made it clear that he did not favour the third and largest operation in Borneo—the attack by the 7th Division on Balikpapan.

On 1st May the Borneo campaign had opened with the landing of the 26th Australian Brigade Group at Tarakan. The second phase—the seizure of Brunei Bay by the remainder of the 9th Division—was due to begin on 10th June.

For every Allied nation but one the surrender of the German forces on 7th May signalled a great reduction of effort. Australia, however, unless plans were changed, would not diminish but rapidly intensify her efforts in the next few weeks until, from 1st July onwards, every field formation in her army would be in action. As it was, virtually all her navy and the greater part of her air force were serving in the Pacific.

For many months the Australian Government had been giving much attention to post-war problems. The prospect that its manpower would be so heavily committed in the final phase was disturbing, and now that the war in Europe had ended it seemed fair that Australia's contribution should be reduced. As mentioned, General Blamey on 16th May had suggested to the Government that the 7th Division should perhaps not be committed to the proposed attack on Balikpapan, and the Australian force employed in Borneo should be limited to the 9th Division.

On Blamey's advice the acting Prime Minister, Mr Chifley, wrote to General MacArthur on 18th May that, with the end of the war in Europe, his Government had been considering what adjustments could be made in the strength of the Australian forces in order to relieve the manpower stringencies and at the same time maintain a fighting effort of appropriate strength. The Commander-in-Chief of the Australian Army had pointed out that if there was to be a substantial reduction in the strength of that army the 7th Division should not be committed to operations on the Borneo mainland.

I shall be glad (Chifley added) if you can give urgent consideration to this matter in relation to the present stage of your plans for the Borneo campaign, and furnish me with your observations. I would add that it is the desire of the Government that Australian Forces should continue to be associated with your command in the forward movement against Japan, but the Commander-in-Chief of the Australian Military Forces advises that, if a reduction in our strength is to be made, the 7th Division should not be employed for further operations until the overall plan is known.

General MacArthur replied on 20th May:

The Borneo campaign . . . has been ordered by the Joint Chiefs of Staff who are charged by the Combined Chiefs of Staff with the responsibility for strategy in the Pacific. I am responsible for execution of their directives employing such troops as have been made available to me by the Governments participating in the Allied Agreement. Pursuant to the directive of the Joint Chiefs of Staff and under authority vested in me . . . I have ordered the 7th Division to proceed to a forward concentration area and, on a specific date, to execute one phase of the Borneo Campaign. Australian authorities have been kept fully advised of my operational plans. The concentration is in progress and it is not now possible to substitute another division and execute the operation as scheduled. The attack will be made as projected unless the Australian Government withdraws the 7th Division from assignment to the South-West Pacific Area. I am loath to believe that your Government contemplates such action at this time when the preliminary phases of the operation have been initiated and when withdrawal would disorganise completely not only the immediate campaign but also the strategic plan of the Joint Chiefs of Staff. If the Australian Government, however, does contemplate action along this line, I request that I be informed immediately in order that I may be able to make the necessary representations to Washington and London. . . . There are no specific plans so far as I know for employment of Australian troops after the Borneo Campaign. Operations in the Pacific are now under intense consideration in Washington and London. I do not know whether Australian troops are contemplated for use to the north. Consideration is being given by the Combined Chiefs of Staff to a proposal to turn over to Great Britain full responsibility for that part of the South-West Pacific Area which lies south of the Philippines. In that event undoubtedly all Australian formations would come under British Command for operations to the south.

At this distance it seems that, in his determination to squash the Australian proposal, MacArthur somewhat overstated his argument. It is not clear in what way the abandonment of the Balikpapan operation would have seriously disorganised either the local Borneo operation or "the strategic plan of the Joint Chiefs of Staff". The securing of oilfields would be achieved by the operations at Tarakan and in British Borneo. The Japanese garrison at Balikpapan had no offensive power beyond the narrow limits of the ground they occupied round a ruined refinery and a virtually-abandoned seaport. To the end, however, the Australian Government in its relations with MacArthur took the view that it was theirs not to reason why. On the day on which MacArthur's telegram arrived Chifley replied that the Government had no hesitation in agreeing to the use of the 7th Australian Division as planned. The Government fully accepted MacArthur's views, which agreed with "the Government's conception of its commitments and by which it absolutely intends to abide".

Before this decision had been reached the Government had been considering two allied problems affecting the future of the army and demanding prompt decision: what should be the size of the force which Australia would maintain in the next phase, and what principles should govern the discharge of men with long service in the army?

On 19th April Blamey had sent the Minister for the Army a detailed submission about the conditions under which men were being discharged from the army. He pointed out that it was mainly the older men who were going out, yet it had been strongly represented that men with five years of service should have the right to elect to be discharged. On 1st

March there were 12,392 of these and by the end of 1945 there would be about 40,000. He recommended that, say, one-third of future "releases to industry" should be allocated by the army and consist of

(a) men who had completed five years' service;
(b) men over 35 who had completed four years' service including two years overseas;
(c) medically "B" class personnel with disabilities which made their satisfactory employment difficult;
(d) others who applied on grounds of personal hardship.

He recommended also that the balance of the releases should be effected on recommendations from the Manpower Directorate but should be confined to "personnel with five years' service, personnel over 35 with three years' service, personnel over 45 and personnel who were medically 'B' class".

In short, whereas hitherto the main considerations had been the needs of industry and the retention of young men in the army, a main consideration should now be the future welfare of the long-service men and women. These had earned the right to be looked upon as human individuals and not merely as units of manpower.[1] The army's plan, if adopted, would presumably not have interfered with the army's efficiency; it recognised the needs of industry for men with required qualifications; from the veteran soldier's point of view the main thing was that a plan should be adopted promptly. It was then 19th April.

No decision had been made, however, when, on 30th May, Blamey sent to the acting Minister, Senator Fraser, some facts and figures about releases of men from the army which, he hoped, the Minister would make known to the War Cabinet and Parliament "in order to stifle what I consider unjustified criticism and to place the Army's ready cooperation in re-establishing the national economy in its true light". He reported that, between October 1943 and April 1945, 122,802 men and women had been discharged or released, 78,000 through normal releases and 44,000 to meet special manpower demands. In the same period 21,443 were received into the army compared with the War Cabinet allocation of 26,960. The army had been responsible for the control and maintenance of 20,000 Italian prisoners sent to rural employment. In the period the reduction in army organisations had approximated 25 per cent.

On 31st May, however, the War Cabinet decided that "all members of the Army and Air Force with operational service overseas and who have over five years' war service are to be given the option of taking their discharge". On 14th June Senator Fraser asked General Northcott to make a submission to the War Cabinet showing, among other things, how many men with five years' service who were now in operational areas could be released immediately. This suggested a drastic solution to a problem to which, two months before, Blamey had proposed a balanced one. As shown above, the number of men in the fighting formations with over five years' service was not very large but it was rapidly increasing and included a large proportion of the leaders, senior and junior. Northcott and later Blamey telegraphed to Fraser to point out that a large number of key men would be affected by such a decision and that the formations

---

[1] Most of those with five years' service or over were no longer with the fighting formations. In April 1945 the length of service of men in the main field formations was:

	Under 3 yrs	3-4 yrs	4-5	Over 5
6th Division	4,222	7,019	3,850	403
7th Division	4,890	8,129	4,459	467
9th Division	5,124	8,518	4,673	489
First Army less 6th Division	19,783	32,310	17,491	1,835

Chiefly because of the disbanding of units a majority of reinforcements in training units had over 3 years' service: 21,852 over 3 years and 12,888 under. By July 1945 the number of men with over five years' service would have greatly increased, 69,000 men having enlisted in June and July 1940.

then in action, or embarked, or soon to embark, could not afford to lose all their long-service men. The formations most affected would be the 6th, 7th and 9th Divisions. Blamey suggested that the present announcement about releases should be limited to the release of "men who enlisted in 1939 as and when the present operations permit".

The effect of the Government's proposal if rigidly applied would have been to have left the army very gravely short of leaders by the end of the year, since by that time all who enlisted in the A.I.F. up to the end of 1940 would have gone.[2] Blamey's compromise would enable commanders to retain key men and would have confined the discharges largely to the 6th Division, which contained most of those who had enlisted in 1939 and, having been in action since 1944, could better afford to spare its veterans than could the 7th and 9th which were just about to embark on large-scale operations after a long period of retraining.

Possibly the Government did not intend its proposal to include officers, but, if so, it did not indicate this either in the original inquiry or in a teleprinter message which Senator Fraser sent to General Northcott on 16th June. In the course of it he said:

My own view of the position is that full immediate effect should be given to the Government's decision to allow soldiers with previous operational service now serving in operational units or immediately due to serve in such operational units the option of taking their discharge. Desire that pending Government decision immediate instructions be issued that *no* troops who come within the Government's decision shall leave Australia for operational service.

This was a somewhat different proposal to the earlier one in that release was now to be optional. Northcott telegraphed this message to Blamey saying that he had been unable to contact Fraser to explain the impracticability of the proposals, and that he had taken no action to carry it out. Fraser continued to press that his instruction be issued. Northcott continued to insist that he could not do so.

On 18th June Northcott attended a meeting of the War Cabinet and explained the difficulties. The general effect, he said, would be to release officers, N.C.O's and specialists who by reason of length of service, training and experience had risen to positions of leadership or become key personnel. It would be impossible to begin to carry out the War Cabinet's decision until appreciable relief from present operational commitments had been obtained. The army was committed to operations to a greater extent than at any previous period.

Thereupon the War Cabinet recorded that there had been "no promise to release men with operational experience *immediately* on the attainment of five years' war service without regard to the organisation of units and the effect on operational plans", and directed the Defence Committee to

---

[2] Even the decision to release men with five years' service including two years overseas would deprive veteran units of perhaps half their officers and NCO's. For example, in the 2/6th Battalion in July, when it was in action in the inland sector south of the Aitape-Wewak coast, it was found that 14 officers and 162 other ranks were entitled to release. The other ranks included 7 warrant-officers, 27 sergeants and 31 corporals. If all had decided to accept release, the officers remaining in the battalion would have been 3 captains and 11 lieutenants; and, in fact, only one officer and four other ranks with five years of service indicated that they did not want to go.

submit a revised definition of operational service overseas with statistics to indicate its effect.

Next day (19th June) Chifley made a measured statement in Parliament in the course of which he said that the releases would be made in a graduated manner but at least 50,000 men would be released before the end of the year. This left the problem where it had been two months before when the army had made its proposals of 19th April. Finally on 28th June the War Cabinet decided that "subject to operational requirements, the option of discharge is to be given in the first place to personnel attaining five years' service, who, in the case of Army personnel and Air Force ground staff, have two years' or more operational service overseas, and, in the case of aircrew, have more than one tour of flying operations against the enemy". In this decision two other groups whom the army itself considered to deserve special consideration—"B class" men who might find it difficult to obtain employment, and others who applied on grounds of personal hardship—were left out. The Ministers had no means of knowing that it was already too late for their belated decision to substantially accelerate the release of the veterans.

To give soldiers with five years' service the choice of obtaining a discharge or remaining in the army created many personal problems, particularly among officers. Many of these felt a duty to stay with their units until the end and had misgivings about applying for discharge. On the other hand they did not wish to have to say to their wives and children that they had refused to return home, and they had also their post-war careers to consider.

Meanwhile, on 5th June 1945 the War Cabinet had decided the size of the forces which should be maintained in the later stages of the war: the navy should remain at its present strength, the operational forces of the army should be reduced to three divisions, and the air force reduced proportionately to the army. Together the army and air force were to release 50,000 men by December. This decision was communicated to Mr Bruce (the Australian High Commissioner) in London, to Mr Forde and Dr Evatt at the United Nations Conference at San Francisco, who were asked to seek the agreement of the Combined Chiefs of Staff, and to General MacArthur, who was asked, among other things, that the 7th and 9th Divisions should be replaced by other troops as soon as his plans would allow.

The Australian Ministers suggested to the Combined Chiefs that the three divisions should be employed thus:

> one brigade group in the Solomon Islands,
> one brigade group in New Guinea,
> one division in New Britain,
> one division in operations against Japan,
> probably one brigade group in south-east Asia.[3]

---
[3] At the Press conference in Perth on 9th July, mentioned earlier, Blamey was to say: "I am quite convinced in my own mind that no British troops will be allowed to participate in the move to Japan."

The Government also expressed the opinion that, if a new command was set up in the South-West Pacific, Australia should be given operational control of Australian forces in all Australian territories—a change which would merely give formal recognition to a situation which had existed since the last quarter of 1944.

One outcome of these Australian proposals was that the British Joint Planners now recommended that Borneo, Java and Celebes should be included in Admiral Mountbatten's command and that Australia should control operations elsewhere in the area. On 7th June, at the suggestion of the Americans, the boundaries were again redefined so as to remove all the Netherlands Indies from American command but retain American command in the Admiralty Islands, the eastern Solomons, Ocean and Nauru Islands.

While these proposals were still the subject of lengthy cabled discussion between Melbourne, Washington and London, Blamey instructed his staff to make plans for: one expeditionary force (probably for Japan) of one division, a second expeditionary force (probably for Malaya) of a brigade group including a tank regiment and the 1st Parachute Battalion, and a New Guinea Force including two divisions less a brigade group.

As mentioned, one reason for anxiety about manpower had long been the needs of the British Pacific Fleet. In September 1944 the British Government had informed the Australian Government that it planned to put into the Australian area by July 1945 120,000 seamen, including 29,000 ashore. The civilian labour force required by the Pacific Fleet would be 4,890 by the middle of 1945. On 7th June 1945 General Blamey received a copy of a Defence Committee minute about the works to be undertaken for this fleet. It showed that Australia was committed to spending over £25,000,000, including £1,943,000 on building or extending air stations for the Fleet Air Arm. Blamey at once wrote to Sir Frederick Shedden: "I must admit on reading it I feel very much like Bret Harte's gentleman who exclaimed: 'Am I blind? Do I see? Is there visions about?'[4] . . . Is it realised that tremendous airfields have been laid down at Moresby; there are seven of them, one or two in excellent repair. At Nadzab there are several in excellent repair and in use. Good strips have been laid down at Buna and Dobodura, all of which are 2,000 miles nearer the war at least than some of those proposed. . . . May I urge that before a decision is reached on what appears to me to be a completely absurd demand . . . a complete examination of existing facilities somewhere near the war area should be made." To Northcott he wrote: "I hope you will fight this very vigorously. It looks to me the method of conducting war in drawing rooms and hotel lounges." On 2nd July

---

[4] The opening lines of "Further Language From Truthful James" (1870) are actually:
Do I sleep? Do I dream?
Do I wonder and doubt?
Are things what they seem
Or is visions about?

Blamey's suggestion about the use of airfields in New Guinea was incorporated in a telegram to the Dominions Office.

When complaining about what he considered the extravagance of the requirements of the British Pacific Fleet Blamey may well have had in mind protests which he and other army leaders had been making in the previous two years about the lavish scale of the demands made by the American forces and their effect on the Australian manpower problem. As early as 3rd May 1943 Colonel Kemsley,[5] the Business Adviser to the Minister for the Army, wrote to the Minister that many of the demands being made by the American forces for stores, equipment and buildings seemed extravagant "to a degree far beyond any Australian or British standards". At the same time it was impossible to discover what Australia's total commitments would be for maintenance of American forces. He suggested the appointment of an additional Cabinet Minister with the task of conducting negotiations with the American representatives and the appointment to MacArthur's staff of a major-general whose approval must be obtained before any demands for purchases or construction were made. Nothing came of this.

A somewhat similar note was struck on 4th November 1944 when General Blamey wrote to Mr Curtin as Minister for Defence to point out that the American forces were building up in Australia vast reserves of food.

> Many millions of square feet of storage space are in use including wool stores and warehouses hired from industry and new buildings erected under Reverse Lend-Lease. Requests made for release of these for urgent Australian requirements, both Army and civilian, bring advice of inability to empty them because of lack of shipping to move the stores housed therein.

Blamey directed attention to a cable recently received from Washington describing American plans for bringing American industry back to normal as soon as possible after the war with Germany ended, and how to this end the American Government was already cancelling wartime contracts and reducing depot stocks. Yet, Blamey added,

> the impression is growing that stocks are being built up under Reciprocal Lease-Lend, far in excess of legitimate operational requirements, with the object of making them available in the Philippines, China or America itself, for civilian or relief purposes, thus buying favourable publicity for American interests, both Government and private, at the expense of our sadly strained and depleted Australian resources.

Blamey suggested that Australia "should immediately revise and very considerably limit Reciprocal Lease-Lend administration and commitments".

It was on top of such American demands for goods, storage space and manpower that the requirements of the British Pacific Fleet were piled. On 7th March 1945 the Quartermaster-General, Major-General Cannan,[6]

---

[5] Col A. N. Kemsley, MSM, ED, VX80892. (1st AIF: Staff Capt HQ Aust Corps 1918.) Director of Organisation AHQ 1941-43; Business Adviser to Minister for Army 1943-45. General manager, broadcasting station; of Brighton, Vic; b. Prospect, SA, 29 Mar 1896.

[6] Maj-Gen J. H. Cannan, CB, CMG, DSO, VD, VX89075. (1st AIF: CO 15 Bn 1914-16; Comd 11 Bde 1916-18.) Quartermaster-General, AMF, 1940-45. Insurance company manager; of Brisbane; b. Townsville, Qld, 29 Aug 1882.

wrote to the Chief of the General Staff pointing out that, despite a decision by the War Cabinet that services given to American forces under reciprocal Lend-Lease would have to be reduced if Australia was to meet commitments for the British Pacific Fleet, there had been reluctance to curb American demands. Cannan went on to say in effect that, because excessive quantities of supplies were occupying storage space in Australia and New Guinea, Australia was faced with the necessity of spending labour and materials on building storehouses for the British Pacific Fleet.[7]

On 4th April Cannan returned to the problem. He wrote Blamey a long minute in which he referred to "the avoidable waste of manpower and materials that went on without question [for Reciprocal Lend-Lease] and the lavishness and extravagance which characterised U.S. demands whilst Australian Army and Australian Services' demands were being subjected to rigid scrutiny and economies". He instanced three camps built for American troops at a total cost of £560,000 and never occupied; the Cairns port project, abandoned after £650,000 had been spent; an air depot at Darwin which cost £600,000 and proved unnecessary. Australia was spending about one-quarter of her war budget on services for the Allies. "Within the wide ambit of that service much could be done to effect real and justifiable economies." Throughout the war, however, the Australian Ministers showed a strong disinclination to take any action that might be looked on with disfavour by the American political and Army leaders, and the soldiers' complaints were ineffective.

The approach of the operations in British Borneo had brought forward the problem of restoring the civil administration in a British colony. Hitherto Australian troops had operated either in Australian colonial territory, with Angau officers to care for the civilians, or in Dutch Borneo, with officers of the Netherlands Indies Civil Affairs unit (N.I.C.A.) performing a similar task. For about two years, however, there had been discussions between Australian and United Kingdom authorities concerning both the general doctrines of military government being developed in London and the specific problems of Borneo.

In July 1943 the Full Cabinet, on the recommendation of the Minister for External Territories, Senator Fraser, had established a departmental committee to plan the rehabilitation of the Australian territories. G. W. Paton,[8] professor of law at Melbourne University, was appointed its chairman, and it was to contain representatives of the Departments of External Territories, Post-War Reconstruction, External Affairs, Army and the Treasury. In the second half of 1943 Paton and Major N. Penglase, of Angau, a former district officer in New Guinea, were sent abroad to study British and American doctrines of military government of occupied

---

[7] He pointed out that 900,000 tons of stores for American use had accumulated at Finschhafen, Buna-Gona and Milne Bay, and 100,000 to 110,000 tons a month were being procured on the mainland.

[8] Sir George Paton, Kt. Professor of Jurisprudence, University of Melbourne 1931-51, Vice-Chancellor since 1951. B. Geelong, Vic, 16 Aug 1902.

or re-occupied territories. They visited the American School of Military Government at Charlottesville, the United States Naval School of Military Government and Administration at Columbia University, and did the course at the War Office Civil Affairs Staff Centre in England; they had discussions with a variety of authorities including the Foreign, Dominions, Colonial and War Offices in London.[9]

Since April 1942, however, there had existed at L.H.Q. a research branch, initially attached to the Adjutant-General's branch, later to the Directorate of Military Intelligence, but since 6th October 1943 established as a directorate responsible directly to General Blamey (as were the Military Secretary, the Judge-Advocate-General and the Directorate of Public Relations). Its head was Lieut-Colonel Conlon, who had joined the former research branch at the outset.

In the five months after the establishment of the Directorate of Research, and while Paton and Penglase were either abroad or preparing their report, the directorate added to its staff a number of senior lawyers, anthropologists and economists. These included (in the order of their arrival): Major W. E. H. Stanner, an anthropologist, who had been commanding the North Australia Observer Unit; Professor Stone,[1] of the chair of international law and jurisprudence at Sydney; Professor Isles,[2] of the chair of economics at Adelaide; Dr Hogbin[3] and the Honourable Camilla Wedgwood,[4] both anthropologists; Colonel Murray,[5] a former militia battalion commander who in civil life was a professor of agriculture.[6] Those who were recruited direct from civil life came in with the rank of temporary lieut-colonel.

By February 1944 the functions of the Directorate of Research had been re-defined thus:

(1) To keep the Commander-in-Chief and certain other officers informed on current events affecting their work;
(2) To undertake specific inquiries requested by Principal Staff Officers;
(3) To assist other Government Departments in work concerning the Army.

On 20th October 1943 the Directorate was given specific duties concerned with the National Security (Emergency Control) Regulations. It is required to maintain full records at L.H.Q. of all exercise of powers and all activities by the Army under

---

[9] In October 1943 an invitation from the War Office to train up to 12 Australians for employment in the civil administration of territories to be re-occupied in north-western Europe came before the War Cabinet and was declined on the ground that Paton and Penglase were already abroad attending this course.

[1] Lt-Col J. Stone, N393191; DORCA. Professor of International Law and Jurisprudence, University of Sydney since 1942. B. Leeds, England, 7 Jul 1907.

[2] Lt-Col K. S. Isles, V514828; DORCA. Professor of Economics, University of Adelaide 1939-45. B. Bothwell, Tas, 4 Aug 1902.

[3] Lt-Col H. I. P. Hogbin, NX202820; DORCA. Anthropologist; of Sydney; b. Bawtry, England, 17 Dec 1904.

[4] Lt-Col Hon Camilla Wedgwood, VF515041; DORCA. Principal, Women's College, University of Sydney 1935-44; of Sydney; b. Newcastle-on-Tyne, England, 25 Mar 1901. Died 17 May 1955.

[5] Col J. K. Murray, OBE, QX34748. (1st AIF: Sea Transport Services and Veterinary Corps.) Staff and training appointments, and DORCA. Professor of Agriculture, University of Queensland 1927-45; Administrator of Papua and New Guinea 1945-52; b. Brighton, Vic, 8 Feb 1889.

[6] The dates of these appointments were: Stanner, 25th October 1943; Stone, Isles and Hogbin, 3rd January 1944; Camilla Wedgwood, 11th January; Murray, 7th February.

the Regulations; to effect liaison and collaborate with Federal and State authorities on matters arising out of activities by the Army under the Regulations; and to carry out such other duties in connection with the Regulations as the C-in-C may direct. . . .

A considerable proportion of the work of the Directorate has been concerned with administration and development in New Guinea.[7]

On 23rd December 1943 Lieut-Colonel Stanner had been specifically appointed "Assistant Director of Research (Territories Administration)".

Thus, in between the time of Professor Paton's appointment as chairman of the departmental committee, on which the Department of the Army was to be represented, and the presentation of his report on his and Penglase's studies abroad, a second organisation had been developed to advise the Commander-in-Chief (not the Ministers) on "civil affairs including Territories Administration". The first committee was a departmental one and thus the Army Secretariat would have had influence with it, or at least knowledge of the advice it offered. The Directorate of Research, however, was responsible directly to the Commander-in-Chief and had no direct link with the Secretariat.

This was the situation in January 1944 when Paton submitted a report describing the British doctrines of Civil Affairs and the governmental machinery so far developed, and placing before the Government the problems that, he considered, had to be faced in New Guinea. He proposed that a Civil Affairs Directorate should be established at L.H.Q. to work in cooperation with the Department of External Territories, and that a school should be set up to train additional staff for Angau. He recommended that the Director of Civil Affairs should be a person with experience of native administration and that at least some of his staff should have served in peace in the Civil Service in the territories. A War Cabinet agendum along these lines was drafted.

When the Paton proposals reached L.H.Q., Blamey, evidently on Conlon's advice, objected that he should have been consulted before the proposal went to the Cabinet, which had been

placed in the position of giving decisions on questions upon the immediate implications of which it had but little information and which obviously were not understood by those who prepared the agenda.

Blamey added that the territories would continue to be the main overseas base of operations for a considerable time and, as long as this continued, control must remain with the army. There seemed to be lack of understanding of the fact that, as the army advanced, it was setting up the former administration under army direction.

As an outcome, on the recommendation of the recently-appointed Minister for External Territories, Mr Ward, the Cabinet decided to appoint a sub-committee of Cabinet to consider post-war policy for the territories. It was to include the Ministers for the Army, Post-War Reconstruction,

---

[7] The Australian Army War Effort, February and August 1944.

External Affairs, Transport, External Territories, Health and Social Services, the Treasurer and the Attorney-General, and was to discuss its problems with the Commander-in-Chief.

When the sub-committee had its first meeting, on 10th February, Conlon accompanied Blamey, who explained that "a major part of the function of the Director of Research and his staff was to advise the Commander-in-Chief upon all matters relating to the administration in occupied or re-occupied territories". The sub-committee, on Blamey's advice, decided that the functions of the departmental committee of which Paton was chairman should be carried out by the Department of External Territories which should collaborate with Conlon.

Blamey added that the role of the Directorate of Research was in conformity with Paton's recommendation for the creation of a Directorate of Civil Affairs, and that plans for establishing a school of civil administration were ready to proceed. The Cabinet sub-committee agreed that the school should be controlled by the Director of Research. The staff of the directorate contained in the higher ranks none excepting Murray, Hogbin and Stanner who had served in a field formation, and none (except Stanner and Major Penglase, who was attached to the directorate for a month after his return from the tour with Professor Paton) fulfilled the requirement Paton had recommended by being "a person with experience of native administration".[8] In April Stanner and Major Kerr[9] (who had joined the army in 1942 as a research officer in what later became the Directorate of Research) were attached to the Australian Army Staff in London. They arrived there at the same time as General Blamey, when he attended the Prime Ministers' conference mentioned earlier. Their tasks in London were to study post-hostilities planning, Civil Affairs, the research activities of the General Staff, and "the structure of financial and other controls at the War Office". Conlon arranged that they should advise Blamey on diplomatic matters and Civil Affairs problems.

In consequence there were exploratory conversations of problems of military administration in London in May between General Smart and General Hone[1] of the War Office, and between General Blamey and Sir Frederick Bovenschen,[2] Under-Secretary of State at the War Office. In the following eight months Stanner sent reports on Civil Affairs doctrine and organisation to L.H.Q., some of them the result of study of the British Civil Affairs set-up operating in Holland, France and Belgium.

---

[8] Stanner had studied native administration in Kenya under the auspices of the Oxford Social Studies Research Committee; his review of this subject had become an official text. The other anthropologists, of course, had been close observers of native administration at work.

[9] Col J. R. Kerr, NX164481. Deputy Director, Research and Civil Affairs 1945; Chief Instructor, School of Civil Affairs 1945-46. Barrister-at-law; of Roseville, NSW; b. Rozelle, NSW, 24 Sep 1914.

[1] Maj-Gen Sir Ralph Hone, KCMG, KBE, MC, TD. Chief Legal Adviser GHQ ME 1941, Chief Political Officer 1942-43; GS War Office 1943-45; Chief Civil Affairs Officer, Malaya 1945-46. Attorney-General, Uganda; b. 3 May 1896.

[2] Sir Frederick Bovenschen, KCB, KBE. Deputy Under-Secretary for War 1936-43; Joint Permanent Under-Secretary for War and Member of Army Council 1942-45.

He had discussions with several British officers earmarked for service in Borneo.

Planning for the re-establishment of the administration in Malaya, Hong Kong and Borneo had been in progress at the Colonial Office in London since 1942.[3] In October 1943 planning had reached a stage where Mr Macaskie,[4] Chief Justice and Deputy Governor of North Borneo, was appointed Chief Planner and Chief Civil Affairs Officer designate (C.C.A.O.) for Borneo, and by early 1944 five other officers had been added to his group.

Because Borneo was likely to fall within an American or Australian area of operations, a Combined Civil Affairs Committee had been set up in Washington in July 1943. One clause of its charter read:

> When an enemy-occupied territory of the United States, the United Kingdom or one of the Dominions is to be recovered as the result of an operation combined or otherwise the military directive to be given to the Force Commander concerned will include the policies to be followed in the handling of Civil Affairs as formulated by the government which exercised authority over the territory before enemy occupation. If paramount military requirements as determined by the Force Commander necessitate a departure from those policies he will take action and report through the Chiefs of Staff to the Combined Chiefs of Staff.

In May and July 1944 a memorandum on policy in Borneo and Hong Kong, prepared by the War Office and the Colonial Office, was accepted, after slight modification, by the Combined Committee as a statement of policy under the clause quoted above. It stated the views of the United Kingdom Government that the administration of British Borneo and Hong Kong should be entrusted to a Civil Affairs staff mainly comprising British officers, mentioned that planning groups for those territories had been assembled in London, and asked that the directives to the Force commanders concerned should include instructions on these lines. A more detailed statement prepared by the Borneo group, and accepted, stated that it was intended that the C.C.A.O., British Borneo, should advise on the British Government's plans for long-term reconstruction and

> should at the discretion of the Allied Commander-in-Chief, while keeping the latter, or the military commander designated by him, informed, be authorised to communicate direct with London on questions which do not affect the Allied Commander-in-Chief's responsibilities for the military administration of British Borneo.[5]

On 14th November 1944 General Blamey, now in Australia again, cabled to General Smart in London that he had asked Sir Frederick Bovenschen to send out a Civil Affairs staff officer and that planning

---

[3] The brief account in this and later chapters of United Kingdom plans for establishing military government in Borneo and of the experiences of the British officers concerned is derived almost entirely from F. S. V. Donnison, *British Military Administration in the Far East 1943-46* (1956), a volume in the British official series, *History of the Second World War*. See pp. 135-52 and 171-96.

[4] Brig C. F. C. Macaskie, CMG. Chief Justice and Deputy Governor, North Borneo 1934-45; Chief Civil Affairs Officer BBCAU 1945-46. B. 26 Mar 1888.

[5] Donnison, p. 146.

for the administration of Borneo must begin soon. If the responsibility fell on him he wished to proceed on lines acceptable to the British authorities. It was desirable that as many suitable officers as possible with experience in Borneo should be made available. They could be given commissions and transferred to the civil administration later if desired. Smart was to take the matter up with the United Kingdom authorities.

In December 1944 a War Office liaison officer on Civil Affairs, Colonel Taylor,[6] arrived in Melbourne. Already a unit known as 50th Civil Affairs Unit, with an establishment of 145 officers and 397 other ranks, including 241 Asians, had been sanctioned by the War Office. In December Colonel Stafford,[7] Controller of Finance for the unit, left for Australia to arrange for the unit's reception; in February the advanced party under Colonel Rolleston[8] left, and in March the main party, under Brigadier Macaskie, the C.C.A.O.

Taylor had brought with him the War Office war establishment of the 50th Civil Affairs Unit. Blamey, however, on the advice of his staff, expressed the view that the war establishment prepared by the Directorate of Civil Affairs at the War Office was unsuitable and ordered the preparation of a revised establishment "more suitable for the military phase". It provided for small sections of the General Staff, Adjutant-General's and Quartermaster-General's branches to ensure proper coordination with the force to which the unit would be attached—"a valuable provision, the need for which was not realised till much later in other theatres".[9]

Telegrams were now exchanged between the War Office and L.H.Q. with the result that, on 17th March, the War Office agreed that an Australian Civil Affairs organisation should be set up with an Australian war establishment. The War Office expressed the hope that the best possible use should be made of the United Kingdom staff.

On 9th April, the Australian war establishments for Civil Affairs units having been prepared and approved by the War Office, Lieut-Colonel K. C. McMullen, Regional Commander of the Islands Region in Angau, was ordered to fly from his headquarters at Torokina to Australia to raise a detachment under the Australian Civil Affairs establishment.

That day 35 officers of the 50th Civil Affairs Unit, largely officers of the Borneo administrations, reached Australia. They found themselves faced with a baffling situation. A primarily-Australian Civil Affairs force, to be named "British Borneo Civil Affairs Unit", was being organised to do the task which they had been planning for some years and had travelled from England to perform.

---

[6] Col L. M. Taylor, DSO, MC, TD. (1914-18: King's Own Yorkshire Light Infantry.) Attached GHQ SWPA 1944-45. Solicitor; b. 18 Dec 1893. Died 19 Dec 1949.

[7] Brig F. E. Stafford, CMG, CBE. (1914-18: Queen's Regiment.) Controller of Finance, Ethiopia, and Financial Adviser to Ethiopian Government 1941-44; Controller of Finance, 50 Civil Affairs Unit 1944-45; BBCAU 1945. British Colonial Service; b. Redhill, England, 24 Aug 1895.

[8] Col W. L. Rolleston, CMG, OBE. Deputy CCAO, 50 Civil Affairs Unit, and BBCAU. Regular soldier; b. 25 Jun 1905.

[9] Donnison, p. 149.

Later in April Blamey approved the war establishment and partial raising of the British Borneo Civil Affairs Unit.[1] Authority was given to raise two "area headquarters", two "Type A detachments" (each 18 officers and 44 other ranks) and two "Type B detachments" (14 and 31). Blamey directed that his headquarters would be responsible for equipping and mobilising the unit, subject to the best possible use being made of any United Kingdom officers made available by the War Office. The unit would communicate with L.H.Q. and the Allied Intelligence Bureau through the Director of Research and Civil Affairs. The total war establishments provided for 210 officers (including a brigadier, 6 colonels and 17 lieut-colonels) and 493 other ranks, of whom 259 might be Asians.

On 23rd April Conlon, after a discussion with General Blamey, wrote General Berryman a letter about the arrangements being made for the Borneo Civil Affairs Unit. In it he made some disparaging remarks about the British unit and said:

> It will be difficult, if not impossible, to use most of [the 35 British officers] during the operational phase. . . . I have instructed that they concentrate at Ingleburn, and I have told the C.O. that we do not recognise the Colonial Office during the operational phase.

Conlon added that McMullen's detachment would be "predominantly Australian", and that he proposed that four Civil Affairs detachments be raised, with a headquarters under McMullen for attachment to corps headquarters, but that "we keep most of the present British officers at Ingleburn as a sort of rear headquarters until it is prudent to send them in". He said that Colonels Gamble[2] (of the Army Legal Corps, appointed to the directorate in April) and Stafford were going forward to confer with Berryman. Conlon sent Blamey (who was then at Morotai) a copy of his letter to Berryman. At the same time he informed Blamey that he was taking steps to form the two Type "A" and two Type "B" detachments, and had asked that Lieut-Colonels Stanner and Tasker[3] be flown from America, where since February they had been attending the School of Military Government at Charlottesville, to become detachment commanders.

The Directorate of Research and Civil Affairs, which had achieved the foregoing results, contained few officers with real military experience, yet it was organising and controlling military units, a task requiring expert

---

[1] The basic functions of B.B.C.A.U. were described thus:
1. The administration and control of all non-military individuals, whether native or otherwise, in re-occupied areas of British Borneo.
2. The distribution and control of relief supplies and services.
3. The procurement, control and employment and administration of labourers.
4. The rendering of every possible assistance to the operational forces.
(Appendix to I Aust Corps Adm Order 4 of 30 Apr 45.)

[2] Col F. B. Gamble, VX15013. LSO 7 Div 1940-42, 5 Div 1942; DDLS LHQ 1944-45; DORCA 1945. Barrister-at-law; of Melbourne; b. Sunbury, Vic, 3 Jun 1900. Died 29 May 1962.

[3] Lt-Col H. McK. Tasker, MBE, VX47925. 2/24 Bn; CO 47 Bn 1942-43; Comd Milne Bay Sub-Area 1943; BBCAU 1945. Schoolmaster; of Hawthorn, Vic; b. Seymour, Vic, 29 Sep 1900. Died Sep 1958. On 9th February the War Cabinet had approved the sending of Stanner, Tasker, Major R. G. Reynolds (a lawyer), and Captain J. Plimsoll (an economist) to Charlottesville.

staff work. At the same time the directorate was causing confusion and distress among the British Borneo officers who had arrived to perform a task for which they had long been preparing. The 50th Civil Affairs Unit became a holding centre from which its members were gradually seconded to the Australian Army. The field headquarters of B.B.C.A.U. were placed under the commander of the force invading British Borneo, and in technical matters the unit was under the control of D.O.R.C.A.

> Difficulties arose (writes the United Kingdom official historian) from . . . the facts that the C.C.A.O. was excluded from planning and preparation in the Directorate and that the Task Force was placed under the command, not of the senior officer, the D.C.C.A.O. of the British unit, but of one of his juniors, a Lieut-Colonel of the Australian unit.[4]

Blamey on 26th April instructed Conlon that the United Kingdom officers were to be used whenever reasonably qualified and that a proportion of them must be sent forward. An advanced party of B.B.C.A.U. arrived at Morotai on 2nd May, and the remainder of one Type "A" detachment began to arrive on 7th May. That day Conlon informed Blamey that the first B.B.C.A.U. detachment had embarked under the acting command of Lieut-Colonel Lohan,[5] a British officer, but that Lohan had been informed that a commanding officer would be appointed later; 12 United Kingdom officers were now attached to McMullen's group.

Blamey was also informed that a Borneo Civil Affairs mission was to be attached to General Headquarters. He cabled to Smart that he was dissatisfied with the attitude of the War Office; the matter should be left entirely in the hands of the Australian command; all details had been completed in cooperation with Stafford (who had replaced Taylor as liaison officer with the War Office). Later, however, Blamey agreed with the War Office as to the need for a joint Civil Affairs mission at G.H.Q. and Stafford joined G.H.Q. at Manila in May.

In the course of a letter to Bovenschen on 1st June Blamey explained the circumstances surrounding the decisions about B.B.C.A.U. and said that he hoped to bring Macaskie and some of the remaining officers forward as soon as possible, although he was not sure that Macaskie should not remain in Melbourne "where the major issues of policy are likely to arise".

All these decisions had been made by Blamey and his staff on their own authority. On 23rd May, however, the acting Minister for Defence had stepped in, and had written to the acting Minister for the Army seeking a fuller statement from Blamey on the matter, including any directions issued by General MacArthur. He drew attention to the recent decision to attach a United Kingdom Civil Affairs mission to G.H.Q. "to assist the Allied C-in-C (or the Military Commanders designated by

---

[4] Donnison, p. 176.
[5] Lt-Col L. G. Lohan, MBE, TD; BBCAU. Company director; b. 3 May 1910.

him) to carry out the military administration in accordance with the policy of His Majesty's Government" and expressed a desire that the administration of the Borneo colonies should be entrusted to the British Chief Civil Affairs Officer, subject to the general directions of the military commander. The only result, however, was that on 28th May the War Cabinet approved the raising of B.B.C.A.U. but expressed the view that it should have been consulted before the commitment was entered into; it limited the number of Australian officers to be attached to the unit to 50.

The work of B.B.C.A.U. in the field will be discussed in a later chapter, but some of the immediate consequences of the policy of the Directorate of Research and Civil Affairs may best be mentioned here. The report of the 9th Division says:

> Owing to the change in the task allotted to 9 Aust Div from Oboe Two (Balikpapan in Dutch Borneo) to Oboe Six, the B.B.C.A.U. party received only 24 hours notice before leaving Australia for Morotai. The advance party arrived on 30 April 45. Personnel of the unit arrived by different routes, with personal baggage only, without any unit stores, equipment or transport, and with no knowledge of the nature and area of the impending operation except that it was to be in British Borneo. The unit was equipped from Adv LHQ, I Aust Corps and Divisional resources. . . .
>
> No approved War Establishment of B.B.C.A.U. was available until 26 May, just before embarkation. The personnel available (about 29 officers and 25 other ranks) were part of a percentage of a Type 1A Detachment and a percentage of H.Q. B.B.C.A.U., but as many of the appointments had not been filled, an improvised organisation was made.[6]

On 15th June, five days after the 9th Division had landed round Brunei Bay, Lieut-Colonel McMullen appealed to the headquarters of the division for an increase in the strength of B.B.C.A.U. He pointed out that only one of the four detachments comprising the unit was then in Borneo and that the remainder were held at Ingleburn Camp, Sydney. "The rest of the U.K. personnel of the unit, mainly consisting of those designated by London for H.Q. B.B.C.A.U. are held on the strength of 50 C.A.U. (a U.K. war establishment) located at Ingleburn Camp," he wrote. He urged that the Chief Civil Affairs Officer (Brigadier Macaskie) and 13 other officers, whom he specified, including the Finance Officer, Agriculture Officer, Legal Officer, Labour Officer and others, and such other officers as Macaskie wished, should be sent forward. He considered that the military administration of British Borneo would be jeopardised if the unit was not strengthened in this way.

General Wootten, the divisional commander, concurred on the 16th, expressing the opinion to General Morshead, the corps commander, that the existing headquarters was "totally inadequate". Morshead's headquarters on Morotai did not receive Wootten's message until 24th June. On the 26th Morshead signalled L.H.Q. asking that Macaskie and his staff be flown to Labuan as soon as possible. The Adjutant-General ordered the expansion of B.B.C.A.U. on 27th June; Macaskie and five others were to fly to Labuan immediately; the movement of the main

---
[6] 9 Aust Div Report on Operation Oboe Six.

body by sea was ordered on 8th July. Macaskie took command of B.B.C.A.U. in Borneo on the 22nd. In August when the unit was almost fully staffed it had 138 Australian officers and 48 British, and six of the seven detachments were commanded by Australians.[7]

While problems concerning Borneo were absorbing much of the attention of Australian staffs MacArthur's American armies were heavily engaged far to the north-east. Throughout April, May and June fierce fighting raged on Okinawa. It was not until the last week of June that organised resistance ceased, by which time the Americans had lost 12,520 killed, and the defenders 61,000 killed and 7,400 prisoners; between July and November the number of prisoners increased to 16,000. In June heavy resistance ceased on Luzon although "sizable pockets" of resolute Japanese were still fighting. On Luzon 317,000 Japanese had been killed and 7,200 taken prisoner; the Americans had about 60,000 casualties. On Okinawa and in the Philippines at the end of June the armies were making ready for the invasion of the Japanese mainland; the President's approval had just been given for an invasion of Kyushu on 1st November, by a force of ten divisions.

---

[7] "The C.C.A.O. found that he was allowed little say in controlling the operations of the unit; as an example it may be recorded that appointments to specific posts in the unit were made, not by the C.C.A.O., but by the Director of Research and Civil Affairs 4,000 miles away in Melbourne, without experience of civil or military administration. To this may be ascribed the occasional subordination of experienced civil administrators to young officers lacking any experience of either civil administration or military staff work. Even if the earlier exclusion of the C.C.A.O. from command of the unit was desirable in the interests of integration and flexibility, this later tight subordination to the Director of Research and Civil Affairs prevented any elasticity and sealed off all local knowledge and experience." Donnison, p. 182.

CHAPTER 17

TARAKAN: TOWN AND AIRFIELD TAKEN

ON 21st March General MacArthur instructed General Morshead that, using the 26th Brigade Group, he was to seize and hold Tarakan Island, and destroy the enemy's forces there. The Netherlands Indies government was to be re-established and the oil-producing and oil-processing installations conserved. As soon as the airfield on Tarakan had been repaired squadrons of the First Tactical Air Force were to be

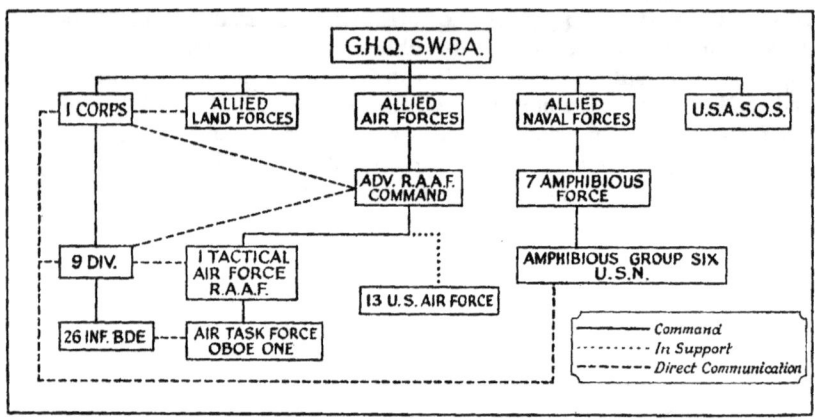

Chain of Command, Tarakan

established there: one wing of fighters by P-plus-6 day, a wing of attack bombers by P-plus-15, and staging facilities for two additional squadrons of fighters and two of attack bombers by P-plus-20. As soon as possible the brigade group was to be relieved by a garrison force and freed for operations farther west.

The chain of command for this operation by a reinforced brigade group was a long one: G.H.Q. to I Corps to 9th Division to 26th Brigade. The accompanying diagram, showing the commands concerned and the authorised channels of communication, illustrates some of the complexities of even a small amphibious operation at this stage of the war. On 24th March General Morshead gave General Wootten his outline plans for the operations against both Tarakan and Brunei Bay and the corps staff's studies were issued, whereupon planning began at the headquarters of the division. Next day the G.H.Q. staff study for Tarakan arrived, and on the 26th the G.H.Q. operation instruction. Fortunately this involved no alteration of the outline plan on which the divisional staff had then been working for two days.

By the end of March the planning headquarters of Amphibious Group Six of the American Navy (which would carry the attacking force to

Tarakan), I Corps, the 9th Division, the 26th Brigade, and Advanced R.A.A.F. Command were all on Morotai and inter-Services planning was in progress. Rear-Admiral Forrest B. Royal, U.S.N., commanding Amphibious Group Six, arrived at Morotai on his headquarters ship, *Rocky Mount,* on 6th April. The naval covering force was a "Task Group" commanded by Rear-Admiral Russell S. Berkey, U.S.N. Additional naval support was to be provided by units of the American Seventh Fleet, including Australian ships.

Brigadier D. A. Whitehead's brigade group was far stronger than the term suggests.[1] It included 40 units and sub-units, the principal ones, including those in the beach group, being:

2/23rd Battalion	2/7th Field Regiment
2/24th Battalion	53rd Composite Anti-Aircraft
2/48th Battalion	Regiment[2]
2/2nd Pioneer Battalion	2/11th Field Company
2/3rd Pioneer Battalion	2/13th Field Company
2/4th Commando Squadron	2nd Field Company
"C" Squadron 2/9th Armoured	110th Casualty Clearing Station
Regiment	2/11th Field Ambulance
"D" Company, 2/2nd Machine	
Gun Battalion	

During 1944, when American forces had landed in Dutch territory, they were accompanied by detachments of the Netherlands Indies Civil Administration (N.I.C.A.) whose task was to assist the commander on the spot to administer the civil population. It was arranged that when the Australians occupied Tarakan and Balikpapan—far larger towns than any yet regained in the Netherlands Indies—they should be accompanied in each operation not only by a N.I.C.A. group but by a company of Dutch and Indonesian troops. By August the N.I.C.A. group on Tarakan was to number 15 officers and 65 other ranks.

The island of Tarakan was 15 miles long and 11 miles wide at its widest part. The shores were muddy and often covered with mangroves, and inland, rising steeply from a swampy coastal plain, was a tangle of hills and small steep gullies covered with dense rain forest and secondary growth. Only one beach—that at Lingkas, the port of Tarakan town which lay two miles inland—was considered feasible for the landing of so large a force and it was very flat and soft and, inevitably, was commanded by strong defences. It had the advantage, however, of exit roads able to carry the heavy equipment needed to repair the only airfield, which was three miles and a half to the north-west. This field had often been cratered by Allied bombers and was now water-logged.

---

[1] The strengths of the main components were:

9th Division units	5,240
2nd Beach Group	2,605
Corps units	2,772
Base Sub-Area units	213
US and NEI troops	974
Total	11,804

[2] A composite anti-aircraft regiment was equipped with eight 3.7-in guns, eighteen 40-mm guns and eight heavy searchlights.

The two oilfields on Tarakan—Pamusian and Juata—were producing between them in 1940 some 500,000 tons a year. The Dutch had damaged the oilfield equipment before the Japanese arrived in January 1942, but the Japanese, by 1944, were reported to be producing oil at almost the pre-war rate. More recently, however, air attacks had greatly reduced the output. From Lingkas one bitumen road led to the airfield and on to the Juata oilfields, and another travelled beside a pipeline to Tarakan town. The first road was named on the Australian maps Anzac Highway, the second Glenelg Highway. In Batagau Strait between Tarakan and the mainland lies Sadau Island, about 1,200 yards by 750, and about six miles north-west of Lingkas.

It has been seen that in the New Guinea operations those knolls and ridges which became tactically important were given names when this became convenient—often the names of officers and men, or their nicknames. When planning the assaults on Tarakan and Balikpapan, where the troops would from the first day onward be fighting among a tangle of "features", the staffs systematically named each of a multitude of little hills; for example, "Essex", "Sykes", "Margy", "Essie", "Milko". This helped to make plans, orders and signals simpler and more precise.

Early in April the strength of the Japanese force on Tarakan was estimated at about 4,000 of whom 2,500 were base troops. On the eve of the attack, however, largely because of information indicating that a battalion had been moved from Tarakan to Balikpapan, it was estimated that only 1,500 to 2,000 troops remained on the island. (It was discovered later that the total was about 2,100, including some 250 civilian workers who were later incorporated in the army. The principal units were the *455th Battalion,* which had arrived in December 1944, about 860 strong, and the *2nd Naval Garrison Force,* about 900 strong, and including a company of the *Kure Special Naval Landing Force.*)

Aerial photographs showed five gun positions on the south-eastern tip of the island covering the channel along which ships normally entered Tarakan. Round Lingkas and Tarakan there seemed to be 15 anti-aircraft guns, and 9 medium and 5 light anti-aircraft guns seemed to be round the airfield.[3] The whole of Lingkas beach was protected by parallel rows of posts, rails and pipes driven into the mud and extending into the sea to a distance of 125 yards from high-water mark; and between the

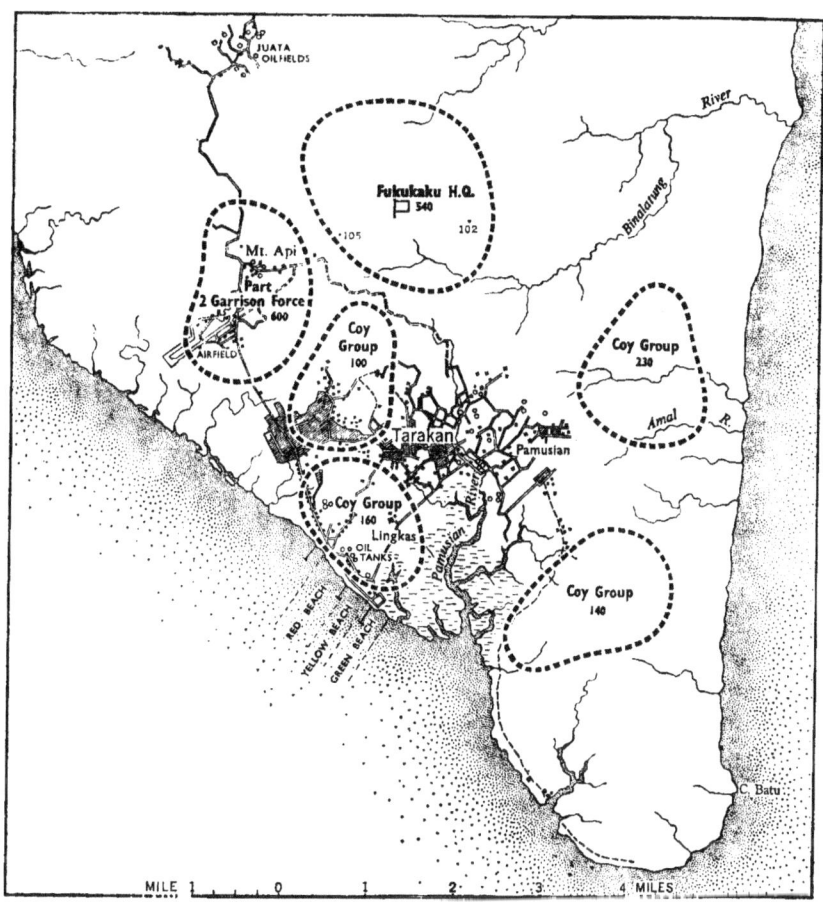

Disposition of main Japanese sub-units, 1st May 1945

beach and the road was an anti-tank ditch about 25 feet wide. A group of oil tanks was near the beach and, as it was possible that the Japanese might try to impede an attacker by flooding the oil over the sea and the swamp near the Pamusian River and setting it alight, the air force had taken pains to destroy these tanks. Field works could be seen; there were concrete pill-boxes built by the Dutch; and it was suspected that, here as elsewhere, tunnels had been dug into the hills.

---

[3] There were in fact four 3-inch coast-defence guns, six 70-mm or 75-mm field guns, and nine light anti-aircraft guns.

The initial tasks of the 26th Brigade Group were to establish a beach position to cover the landing, capture a covering position within which a beach maintenance area could be established, and seize enough ground to make possible the repair and defence of the airfield. The intention was to move two airfield construction squadrons to the airfield, and later, as mentioned, to establish there seven squadrons and other air force detachments.

When the divisional and naval staffs made a detailed study of the beach and the tides they decided that conditions would be better on 1st May than 29th April. G.H.Q. approved this change on 11th April, and the same day Morshead approved the coordinated plans of the three Services.

The air force was to attack Tarakan from 11th to 29th April, and destroy oil storage tanks, gun positions, radar stations, defences and buildings. In the same period Tawao, on the east coast of British Borneo, was to be attacked to disguise the real intention, and all airfields within range were to be bombed. Minesweeping was to begin on the 27th. Naval support was to be given by the cruiser force commanded by Rear-Admiral Berkey and including the Australian cruiser *Hobart* and destroyer *Warramunga*; air support by R.A.A.F. Command and the Thirteenth Air Force. The transport and landing craft unit of the naval force was to include:

2 L.S.I.	13 L.C.I.
1 A.K.A.	5 L.S.M.
1 L.S.D.	12 L.C.T.[4]
22 L.S.T.	

Before the main landings a party led by Captain V. D. Prentice was put ashore on Tarakan to gain information. Prentice had already led a party of six which had established an observation post and collected information on Batanta Island west of the Vogelkop in New Guinea. On 24th April Prentice's party was stealthily inserted into Tarakan and it observed enemy movements until 3rd May when it joined the invasion force and gave useful information to Brigadier Whitehead.

Two preliminary operations were to be carried out on 30th April, the day before the main landing: the 2/4th Commando Squadron and a battery of Lieut-Colonel Green's[5] 2/7th Field Regiment would land at 8 a.m. on Sadau Island and thence the artillery would support engineers as they made eight gaps in the beach obstacles. The main landing was to begin at 8.15 a.m. on 1st May on a two-battalion front: the 2/23rd Battalion on Green Beach and the 2/48th on Red Beach. The 2/24th Battalion, in reserve, would then land on Green Beach. The naval force would give covering fire until the landing craft were 400 yards off shore and the air squadrons would attack the beach-head until 15 minutes before the landing. Four B-25's and four fighters were to be over the area continuously from 7.30 a.m. to 5.30 p.m. for the first seven days.

---

[4] These types were: Landing Ship Infantry, Attack Cargo Ship, Landing Ship Dock, Landing Ship Tank, Landing Craft Infantry, Landing Ship Medium, Landing Craft Tank. The two LSI's were the Australian liners *Manoora* and *Westralia*.

[5] Lt-Col W. J. Green, DSO, ED, VX103. 2/12 and 2/8 Fd Regts; CO 2/7 Fd Regt 1943-45. Accountant; of Surrey Hills, Vic; b. Trafalgar, Vic, 7 Nov 1904. Died 4 Oct 1953.

Ashore the 2nd Beach Group (Colonel C. R. Hodgson) was to
establish and operate a beach maintenance area, and detachments from
the 1st Base Sub-Area were included in the force to assist in developing
a base which would remain on Tarakan after the departure of the beach
group, which would be needed for the north Borneo operation. At Tarakan
the 2nd Beach Group had under command the 2/2nd Pioneer Battalion,
2/11th Field Company and other units and detachments.

An alternative general plan was prepared for use if the engineers
were unable to breach the offshore obstacles or if for any other reason
the main landing failed. It provided for a landing at Juata, on the north-
west coast and an advance southward to Tarakan town.[6]

From 12th March onwards transports had landed at Morotai each
week from 6,000 to 7,000 troops of I Corps with their equipment and
stores, and by 17th April the 26th Brigade Group was complete except
for some R.A.A.F. contingents. Because of the late embarkation at Sydney
of No. 8 Airfield Construction Squadron, one of the two such units allotted
to the assault force, and other R.A.A.F. detachments, it was feared that
the ship carrying them would not arrive until too late for them to re-
embark in the assault ships. They arrived on 25th April, however, just
in time.

A rehearsal was held at Morotai on 24th April. No one was landed,
but the craft were filled, formed up, advanced to the beach in proper
order, and then turned away. The drill was carried out at good speed and
everything went well. The officers were surprised, therefore, when a
signal arrived from Admiral Royal that he was displeased with the light-
hearted attitude of the troops. It was discovered that the admiral was
annoyed to see the men in felt hats instead of helmets. In fact there
were few helmets in the brigade, and none at all in at least one battalion.
Steel helmets were seldom worn by Australians in the South-West Pacific.

The 26th Brigade Group was now about to enter its second Pacific
campaign. It had fought in the Lae-Huon Peninsula offensive from September 1943 to January 1944. Brigadier Whitehead had led this brigade since
September 1942 when it was in action at El Alamein; Lieut-Colonel
R. I. Ainslie of the 2/48th and Lieut-Colonel F. A. G. Tucker of the
2/23rd had commanded those battalions in the Huon Peninsula operations. Lieut-Colonel Warfe, who had led first an Independent Company
and then a battalion in the Salamaua operations in 1943, had taken command of the 2/24th in January 1945. The 2/3rd Pioneers (Lieut-Colonel
Anderson[7]) had fought round Finschhafen; the 2/4th Commando Squadron, under Major K. B. Garvey, had seen hard service on Timor and
in the Lae-Huon Peninsula operations in 1943.

The naval covering force arrived off Tarakan on the morning of 27th
April, and by the evening of the 29th the minesweepers had swept and

---

[6] When the Japanese took Tarakan in January 1942 they landed neither at Lingkas nor Juata but at Cape Batu, the Amal River, and a point to the north.

[7] Col J. A. Anderson, ED, NX35032. 2/3 Pnr Bn (CO 1944-45). Public servant; of Sydney; b. Sydney, 4 Mar 1905.

buoyed the approach route to within 800 yards of the beach and to Sadau Island. From 12th April onwards Liberator, Mitchell and Lightning aircraft made a total of 300 sorties over Tarakan and dropped more than 200 tons of bombs. The oilfields were set on fire and there were soon large patches of oil and soot on the sea for a distance of 20 miles from the coast. Rain and smoke obscured the town on 28th and 29th April when two cruisers bombarded targets ashore and aircraft made heavy attacks.

The force that was to land on Sadau Island and the engineers who were to breach the offshore barriers sailed from Morotai on 26th April and arrived off the island early on the 30th. At 7.40 a.m. the 2/4th Commando Squadron landed unopposed, and at 9.25, after a struggle with the muddy beach, the first gun (of the 57th Battery, Major Rungie[8]) was got ashore from an L.S.M. By 10.30 a.m. two guns were in position, by 11 o'clock five were in position and had begun to range. A few minutes later they began firing smoke shells to assist the engineers, on whose efforts the success of the accepted plan entirely depended.

The beach on which the engineers were beginning their difficult undertaking consisted of a coral shelf covered with mud which varied from fairly firm clay at high-water mark to soft mud at low-water mark. The tidal range was about nine feet and low water about 300 yards from the dune-line of the beach. There were to be two phases in the attack on the obstacles: the first was timed for half tide when there would be about one foot of water at the outer line of obstacles, but the second was to be made, at the navy's request, an hour before half tide, so that ships could be withdrawn an hour before sundown; consequently (as it was on a rising tide) about 100 yards of mud would have to be negotiated by the engineers to reach the obstacles.

The task initially given to the 2/13th Field Company (Major Foreman[9]) was to make eight gaps of not less than 30 feet each in the underwater obstacles on Red (the northern) Beach and Green (the southern one), and four of not less than 60 feet on Yellow Beach, in the centre. Later it was decided to make 60-foot gaps on Red and Green Beaches as well as Yellow.

The obstacle nearest the beach (about 50 yards from high water) was built of timber posts and old wire in poor repair, the second of a double staggered row of posts of 8 to 10 inches in diameter and about 8 feet apart, the third of single posts about 8 feet apart, the fourth (about 130 yards from high-water mark) of a double staggered row of 90 to 100-lb rails and iron pipes of 6 inches diameter 8 feet high and again 8 to 10 feet apart.

Foreman had allotted two officers and eight detachments each of six sappers to the primary attack, with a further six detachments of five

---

[8] Maj R. H. Rungie, SX2897; 2/7 Fd Regt. Salesman; of Medindie, SA; b. Adelaide, 1 Feb 1916.
[9] Maj J. G. Foreman, MC, WX11141. OC 2/13 Fd Coy 1944-45. Engineer; of Cottesloe, WA; b. Kalgoorlie, WA, 1 Mar 1904. Died of illness 13 Sep 1945.

Brigadier D. A. Whitehead (Commander of the 26th Brigade), Lieut-General Sir Leslie Morshead (G.O.C. I Corps) and Lieut-Colonel S. J. Douglas (C.O. 2/11th Field Ambulance) on Tarakan Island, 4th May 1945.

(Australian War Memorial)

View from the mast of *LST-637* as she leaves Morotai on 27th April 1945 carrying troops of the 26th Brigade for the assault on Tarakan.

(Australian War Memorial)

Engineers of the 2/13th Field Company demolishing underwater obstacles, Tarakan, 30th April 1945.

(Australian War Memorial)

Some engineers of the 2/13th Field Company on the pipeline jetty, Tarakan, on 30th April 1945 after having breached underwater obstacles in preparation for the assault. *From left*: Sappers R. A. R. Stevenson and P. Carroll, Lance-Corporal R. C. Mace, Sappers J. S. Proctor, G. E. Maxwell, A. J. McD. Clydesdale and E. S. Slee. Mace later was awarded the Military Medal and, in 1952, the British Empire Medal. Slee was killed on Tarakan on 1st July 1945.

The bombardment of Tarakan, 1st May 1945.

Tarakan, 1st May. L.S.T's beached, pontoons erected and unloading in progress.

(*Australian War Memorial*)

A machine-gun crew of the 2/23rd Battalion firing at a Japanese position across the Glenelg Highway, Tarakan, on 1st May.

(*Australian War Memorial*)

Tarakan, 1st May. Stretcher bearers of the 2/23rd Battalion bringing out a wounded man. The stretcher party is passing an oil storage tank.

sappers each as reinforcements. The first eight detachments, commanded by Lieutenant Dods,[1] were to be taken forward in L.V.T's.[2] Beginning at 11 a.m. they were to attack at Red and Green; the attack on Yellow was to open at 3.15 p.m. The attacks were thoroughly rehearsed and a drill evolved.

A naval bombardment was to begin 20 minutes before the engineers reached the objective. Aircraft were to strike targets on the beach for 30 minutes during the operation and others were to lay a smoke screen seven minutes before the engineers began work. The guns on Sadau would give support. The detachments set out on time from the line of departure in their eight L.V.T's, with Foreman ready to direct operations from an L.C.I., which carried also an officer to direct artillery fire and one to liaise with the supporting naval vessels. Because of the strong tidal set Foreman was 800 yards from the shore when command was turned over to him by the navy and the L.V.T's had drifted nearly a mile south; it was 11.15—a quarter of an hour late—before the Red Beach teams touched down. There was another mishap; no aircraft had yet arrived to lay the smoke screen. A twin machine-gun opened fire on the engineers but was soon silenced by machine-gunners on the L.V.T's.

There was no opposition for the next ten minutes, and Foreman used the discretion which had been given to him to send in the Yellow Beach parties early should the lack of opposition warrant it. These detachments, which were waiting in six L.C.V.P's[3], touched down at 11.30. By this time there was a gap of about 50 yards of mud beyond the obstacle and the sappers had to wade through it waist deep. Also at 11.30 twelve mortar bombs burst among the L.C.V.P's but without hitting anyone; and the smoke-laying aircraft arrived and put a screen 200 yards inland from the beach, making it difficult for the defenders to observe the proceedings out to sea.

When Lance-Sergeant Nixon's[4] party was ordered to withdraw until a second attack at 3 p.m. four steel rails remained intact. Nixon, doubtful whether he would be able to reach the obstacle through the mud at 3 p.m., obtained permission to remain at the job until it was finished. All matches and fuse lighters having been soaked in the mud Nixon struggled ashore, walked along the beach to the oil pipe under fire, went to the end of the jetty and obtained fresh fuse lighters from an L.C.V.P. He then returned the way he had come and completed his gap. As his L.V.T. was bogged Nixon led his party out along the beach and pier whence an L.C.V.P. picked them up. By 12.10 p.m., ten minutes after the making of gaps on Red and Green should have finished, although all gaps at Green had been made, and one at Yellow, none had been completed at Red

---

[1] Lt R. E. Dods, QX26548. 9 Div Engrs and 2/13 Fd Coy. Architect; of Ascot, Qld; b. Brisbane, 30 Nov 1912.
[2] Landing Vehicle Tracked—a bullet-proof amphibian tractor able to carry 25 men.
[3] Landing Craft, Vehicle, Personnel.
[4] L-Sgt J. Nixon, MM, NX13142; 2/13 Fd Coy. Cabinet maker; of Helensburgh, NSW; b. Helensburgh, 5 Sep 1917.

because the L.V.T's were bogged at the entrance to the gaps. Foreman and the naval commander decided to continue until 12.45. At 1 p.m. the gaps on Yellow and Red had still not been finished. At this stage two craft were bogged on Red and two on Yellow.

The crews on Green and Yellow were now withdrawn and the second attack organised. This operation was "most exhausting as the sappers had to lie flat on the mud and drag themselves to the obstacles on life-lines previously laid from each vehicle and craft engaged".[5] In an hour, however, all gaps had been completed and marked except one on Yellow, where three wooden posts were left which Foreman considered could be knocked over by the L.C.M's. There were no casualties despite sniping and mortar fire. It took 45 minutes to retrieve the exhausted sappers who had either to be dragged in through the mud or to wade ashore and come out along the oil pier. They had used 780 explosive charges during the operation.

The main convoy arrived off the south-west of Tarakan Island an hour before sunrise on 1st May. The naval bombardment opened at 6.40, the two cruisers and six destroyers firing on targets along the beach and up to half a mile inland. During this bombardment the assaulting troops embarked into their landing craft, and these were marshalled behind a line of departure marked by anchored craft and divided into sections corresponding to Red, Yellow and Green Beaches. In the Green Beach sector the L.V.T. carrying the 2/23rd Battalion assembled; in the Red Beach sector were L.C.V.P's carrying the 2/48th, which had been in the *Manoora*. The 2/24th was being disembarked from *Westralia* into L.C.V.P's which would land at Green Beach when required. Farther back L.C.M's from the L.S.D. *Rushmore,* containing engineer equipment and tanks, were being marshalled. At 7.56 craft armed with rockets and mortars set off towards Tarakan followed by the wave of L.V.T's carrying the 2/23rd to Green Beach and the wave of L.C.V.P's carrying the 2/48th to Red Beach. At 7.58 aircraft opened an attack on the beach area that was to continue until just before the leading craft beached.

"The beach appeared to be an inferno and was continually aflame from the crimson flashes of bursting bombs and shells," wrote the diarist of the 2/48th. As the craft reached the gaps which the engineers had blown in the beach obstacles, the fire was lifted from the beach to a line farther inland and in a few moments the craft ran on to the sand. There was no opposition on the beach.

Nevertheless the 2/23rd had an uncomfortable landing. The L.V.T's were halted by a 12-foot embankment along the high-water line and the troops, instead of disembarking from the rear ramp, had to scramble over the front of the craft into mud up to three feet deep. This caused a general slowing down, and there was much congestion on the shore. The two forward companies had reached their first objectives by 8.40. Then the opposition stiffened. Sharp fire came from Lingkas Hill.

---

[5] Maj J. G. Foreman, Report on Operation Oboe One, Underwater Obstacles Breaching, P-1.

On the left Major Issell's[6] company made slow progress up the Roach feature through undergrowth so thick that tracks had to be cut. At 11.45 they reached the north side of this hill and came under fire from a strong Japanese position. Issell, a platoon commander (Lieutenant Enderby[7]) and four others were hit; Lieutenant Head[8] took command until Captain Simmons[9] arrived to lead this company. They pressed on and by 6 p.m. had forced the enemy out; 15 Japanese dead lay round.

Meanwhile Captain Sedgley's[1] company, following Simmons', took two pill-boxes and a field gun and then advanced eastward down Lingkas spur; by 7.20 p.m. the spur was in their hands. This enabled the right-hand company, hitherto held by fire from Lingkas, to advance along Glenelg Highway, and to dig in on the left of the highway that night.

The 2/48th on the left had practically a dry landing—a pleasant surprise as they had been told that they would probably have to wade 100 yards. By 8.31 a.m. Captain Gooden's[2] company on the right had secured the oil tanks and was under fire from a spur of Roach; and Captain Lavan's[3] company on the left had secured the bridge over the Sibengkok and a large feature on the left of the beach. By 8.38 all the battalion's first objectives had been secured.

The enemy abandoned the pill-boxes from which fire had been brought down on Gooden's company, which was now in touch with the flanking battalion. Captain R. W. Lewin's company passed through and began to move up Finch through thick undergrowth. This company thrust forward, and by 10.20 the leading platoon was in close touch with the enemy on the crest of Finch, and heavy firing could be heard in the 2/23rd's area to the right. There were only a dozen Japanese with one machine-gun on Finch but the direct approach was along a razor-back spur; a flanking move was made, however, and by 10.55 the enemy had been overcome, nine being killed.

Colonel Ainslie, who now had his tactical headquarters on a hill with an excellent view of the front, ordered Gooden with the support of two tanks—the third tank of this troop was bogged on the beach—to move through Lavan's company on Anzac Highway and take Collins Highway ridge. The tanks could not get past a big bomb crater south of the junction with Collins Highway, but the company went on and by 1.40 p.m. held the western end of the ridge. Here they came under fire from the east.

---

[6] Maj R. W. Issell, VX14533. 2/23 Bn, and various staff appointments. Salesman; of Burwood, Vic; b. Bendigo, Vic, 5 Oct 1913.
[7] Lt E. A. Enderby, VX88699; 2/23 Bn. Bank officer; of Essendon North, Vic; b. Footscray, Vic, 24 Sep 1919.
[8] Lt A. E. Head, MC, VX39988; 2/23 Bn. Herd tester; of St Kilda, Vic; b. Melbourne, 1 Sep 1918.
[9] Capt M. A. Simmons, VX24869. 2/23 Bn and 9 Div Carrier Coy. Clerk; of Elwood, Vic; b. Geelong, Vic, 10 Oct 1918.
[1] Lt-Col J. G. Sedgley, VX61536. 2/9 Armd Regt, 2/23 Bn and staff appointments. Regular soldier; b. Brisbane, 15 Aug 1916.
[2] Capt O. D. Gooden, MC, SX9377; 2/48 Bn. Clerk; of Fullarton Estate, SA; b. Adelaide, 4 Nov 1915.
[3] Lt-Col J. F. Lavan, MC, ED, NX34687. 2/2 MG and 2/48 Bns. Bank officer; of Sydney; b. Perth, 11 Dec 1913.

Captain Johnson's[4] company then moved through Lewin's and secured Parks unopposed. By 3.15 it had cleared the main spurs of Parks, and Lieutenant Mortimer's[5] platoon had moved north along the spur leading to Collins Highway ridge and there came under heavy fire, one man being killed and Mortimer and two others wounded—the heaviest losses in a

1st-5th May

platoon of this battalion on that day. Gooden's company, with the support of mortars, pressed on, and Lieutenant T. C. Derrick's platoon established itself on dominating ground on a southern spur of Lyons. At the end of the day the 2/48th had a company on Collins Highway ridge, another astride Anzac Highway, another on Parks and another on Finch. It had counted 24 Japanese dead, and had lost 2 killed and 9 wounded.

---

[4] Capt G. E. Johnson, MBE, SX8647. 2/48 Bn and 9 Div Carrier Coy. Salesman; of Henley Beach, SA; b. Rose Park, SA, 13 Oct 1914.
[5] Lt R. G. Mortimer, SX2279. 2/27 and 2/48 Bns. Tractor driver; of Glenelg, SA; b. Mannum, SA, 27 Jun 1914.

At 5 p.m. Whitehead, who had landed at midday, ordered that the 2/48th next day should take Lyons, and the 2/24th, coming in on the left, should take Sturt and Wills. The 2/24th had begun landing, on Red Beach, at 9.20 a.m., and had remained in reserve until late in the afternoon, when Warfe received orders to move north along Anzac Highway. The eager Warfe had been irked by the inactivity of his unit, but his repeated requests for a more active role had brought from Whitehead always the same reply: "Just wait a little, you'll get plenty later." In the gathering darkness Warfe, after reconnaissance, moved two companies forward to comfortable dry ground where they could have a good night and a short approach march next day.

By nightfall the brigade held an area 2,800 yards wide at the base and up to 2,000 yards in depth. On the left the objectives had been reached, but to the east Milko, which was among the objectives, was still in the hands of the enemy.

The rear areas were still under fire from snipers. In the afternoon of the 1st a patrol of the 2/2nd Pioneer Battalion, the principal unit of the beach group, clashed with parties of Japanese near Burke Highway, and during the first night snipers or shell fire wounded six members of the battalion.

Meanwhile the beach had been a scene of strenuous and often frustrating effort. By 10 a.m. three L.S.T's had beached and thrown out pontoon causeways to connect with the solid ground. Later four others beached, but the receding tide prevented their pontoons from reaching the shore and unloading had to be delayed. The difficulty of developing the beach area was described in stark detail by Major Foreman:

From the start the beach development was hampered by the very narrow area available between the dune-line and the road, and the terrific cratering in this small space and on the east side of the road. At high water there was *no* beach at all and at low water the beach, although 500 yards to 600 yards wide, was entirely useless as it consisted of thick black mud. The whole length of the beaches was faced from seaward with a sheer clay wall approximately 8 feet high; behind this was a 3-foot deep drain, then a space varying from 10 to 30 feet in width; a further drain approximately 3 feet deep, the road (of about 16 feet available width), another 3-foot deep drain, and then rising slopes of soft clay heavily pitted with water-filled craters. The road was also extensively cratered. The soil was of a thick greasy clay with the water table about one foot to 18 inches below the natural surface of the narrow coastal strip. Mechanical equipment was successfully landed from L.C.M's but for anything but the lightest cut quickly bogged itself down. Every dozer which attacked the clay wall bogged hopelessly and had to be dragged out by other mechanical equipment.[6]

The tracked vehicles quickly made the mesh useless, but fortunately there was much round and sawn timber stacked on the beach and corduroy tracks were substituted. None of the L.S.T's could be refloated on the afternoon tide. It had been hoped to have field guns in action on the island three hours after the landing, but unloading was so difficult that none was fired until 2.50 p.m. In the first 24 hours, however, 1,562 tons of stores and equipment were unloaded.

---

[6] Report on Engineer Aspects of Operation Oboe One from P-1-day to P-plus-8-day.

On the high tide of the night of the 1st-2nd May five more L.S.T's beached beside the stranded ones, but did not drive so far inshore. Next day causeways were swung out to them. By 8 a.m. on the 3rd a total of 2,640 tons had been landed, and by 9.20 that day the unloading of the five L.S.T's of the later group was complete[7]; that morning, on the high tide and with the help of a wash created by a destroyer and some motor torpedo boats, these five were retracted, but the seven L.S.T's of the first group could not get off until the next spring tides on 11th and 12th May.

By 4th May an American Naval Construction Battalion had built a short pontoon pier at which L.C.T's and L.C.M's were unloaded, and a longer pontoon pier at which the remaining L.S.T's were unloaded. The repair of the big south pier was begun on the 1st, but there were three main gaps of 140, 50 and 35 feet, and the pier was not complete until the 4th.

The Netherlands Indies Civil Affairs unit established itself ashore on 1st May. By the end of that day it had 1,000 civilian refugees in its compound, by the end of the fifth day 5,000, and by the end of the seventh day 7,000. Many civilians were wounded by the bombardment on the 1st, so many that Australian doctors had to help the N.I.C.A. medical staff to attend them.

In the conditions encountered on Tarakan the demand for engineers to support the infantry and tanks was exceptional. They were needed to lift mines, disarm booby-traps, blow up tunnels and lay corduroy on the roads. One section of engineers was allotted to each battalion, and soon one section to each troop of tanks, a half section to the Pioneers, and a half section to the 2/4th Commando Squadron. Until the other two field companies allotted to the operation arrived this left only five sections of the 2/13th Field Company for other tasks.

Early on the morning of the 2nd Captain Wilton's[8] company of the 2/23rd on the right occupied Milko against little opposition. Simmons' company pushed on parallel to Burke Highway and reached the Lingkas Track. By 4 p.m. they had advanced a further 800 yards and were under sniper fire. The next company to the left, advancing from Pages, found the enemy to be in strength on the higher slopes of Hospital Spur in a position that included pill-boxes, tunnels and many weapon-pits.

That morning the 2/48th Battalion swiftly secured Lyons. By 6.45 a.m. Lieutenant Burke's[9] platoon had taken the southern knoll and by 9 a.m. the leading troops were on the summit. A platoon patrolling towards Burke Highway encountered an enemy post on a razor-back near the barracks. This was mortared and then attacked with flame-throwers, whereupon the enemy fled east across the road, leaving three dead.

---

[7] In the next six 24-hour periods the tonnage landed was: 4th May, 253; 5th, 566; 6th, 432; 7th, 945; 8th, 1,872; 9th, 1,507.

[8] Maj M. A. B. Wilton, VX20116. 2/23 Bn, and staff and training appointments. Bank officer; of Walla Walla, NSW; b. Sydney, 10 Feb 1909.

[9] Lt C. R. Burke, NX4473. 2/3 and 2/48 Bns. Railway employee; of Goulburn, NSW; b. Nimmitabel, NSW, 27 Apr 1913. Died of wounds 7 May 1945.

The 2/24th Battalion, which had now come in on the left, began to advance towards Sturt and Wills at 7.30 a.m. on the 2nd. Captain Eldridge's[1] and Captain Travis'[2] companies led with tanks in support. At 8 a.m. aircraft attacked Sturt and Wills but not accurately; the artillery shelled the hills from 8 a.m. and six minutes later the leading companies crossed the start-line on Collins Highway. By 9 a.m. Eldridge's had taken Sturt, where eight Japanese were killed, and by 11 a.m. were advancing towards Frank which they also took—a long and swift advance. Travis' company on the left met stiffer opposition. It reached the summit of Wills at 8.15 but then encountered Japanese in trenches, concrete pill-boxes and underground bunkers. One platoon commander, Lieutenant Scott,[3] was wounded when leading his men forward. Sergeant Wallis[4] reorganised the platoon and pressed on against intense fire, successfully assaulting a concrete pill-box, a large bunker and trench systems. When a section commander was wounded Private Rodwell[5] deployed the section and charged a pill-box which he silenced by firing his Bren through a slit.

By 8.35 a.m. the position at the south end of Wills was in the hands of the attackers except for one big bunker protected against grenading by a system of deep slit trenches. At 11.10 a.m., while intense small arms fire was poured at all the slits, Lieutenant Freame[6] moved out with a flame-thrower to a slit at the north-west side of the bunker and fired a long burst of flame into it. He then did the same at a slit on the west side whence a grenade was thrown but without harming him. The bunker then exploded and collapsed. (The ammunition stored in this bunker continued to burn for four days.)

When Warfe learnt what was happening he went forward to see whether Eldridge's company could move round Sturt to help with Wills. Warfe himself swiftly probed forward taking a patrol consisting of Eldridge and two men. About 400 yards out they found that they were in a minefield, from which they cautiously extricated themselves. Warfe now ordered Eldridge's company to continue the advance toward the airstrip through Essex and Captain Catherall's[7] to join them. In this advance one Japanese was killed and one captured. The map was found to be inaccurate and the troops had to move by compass, pacing the distances. At dusk the leading company was within several hundred yards of Essex. After dark

---

[1] Col R. T. Eldridge, OBE, VX114201; 2/24 Bn. Regular soldier; b. Northwood, NSW, 24 Jun 1917.

[2] Capt G. B. Travis, MC, VX36228; 2/24 Bn. Station manager; of Deniliquin, NSW; b. Beechworth, Vic, 25 May 1906. Killed in action 10 May 1945.

[3] Lt J. R. L. Scott, TX376. 2/12 and 2/24 Bns. Mining engineer; of Tullah, Tas; b. Launceston, Tas, 16 Dec 1915.

[4] Sgt S. Wallis, MM, VX30968; 2/24 Bn. Labourer; of Mildura, Vic; b. South Melbourne, 21 Feb 1911.

[5] WO2 E. E. Rodwell, MM, TX11365; 2/24 Bn. Clerk; of Claremont, Tas; b. Claremont, 12 Apr 1921.

[6] Lt H. W. Freame, NX177991; 2/24 Bn. Clerk; of Kentucky, NSW; b. Uralla, NSW, 5 Dec 1921. Killed in action 8 May 1945. Freame was the son of Sergeant W. H. Freame, DCM (who was half Japanese), one of the First AIF's most trusted scouts at Anzac. The son had served in the AIF as an NCO from 1942 to March 1943, when he entered the Royal Military College, Duntroon. He graduated a year later, coming top of this "special entry" class.

[7] Capt J. McP. Catherall, VX32634. 2/24 Bn and 9 Div Carrier Coy. Commercial traveller; of Hawthorn, Vic; b. Balwyn, Vic, 18 Aug 1917.

Catherall's company joined them. The prisoner, a warrant-officer, was hurried back in the dark through about 3,000 yards of jungle in which Japanese were quite likely to be encountered. The two volunteers who escorted him delivered him at battalion headquarters about 8 p.m.

Meanwhile at 4 p.m. Captain Macfarlane's[8] company began to move along the Anzac Highway towards the airfield. The road was thickly mined and covered by the fire of machine-guns on the western tip of Peningkibaru ridge. The area was bombarded by artillery and at dusk two platoons advanced at the side of the road waist deep in foul water and mud. The Japanese withdrew under cover of machine-gun fire.

That night Warfe ordered Catherall to move at 11 p.m. on to a feature a few hundred yards east of Essex. The company reached it unopposed.

An Auster aircraft of No. 16 Air Observation Post Flight was landed on a defective airstrip on the 2nd, but when it was taking off again it crashed. The pilot, Flight Lieutenant McIntyre,[9] and the Air Liaison Officer, Captain Ket,[1] were both injured, Ket fatally.[2]

Warfe issued orders for an attack on the airstrip next day; at 6 a.m. Travis' company would advance with, under command, a troop of tanks, a section of machine-guns and three 3-inch mortars. Thus by 6.45 on the morning of the 3rd this company had passed through the forward troops on the left, but it soon came under fierce fire from machine-guns and a 25-mm gun (which, when captured later, was found to have fired 11,000 rounds).

As the advance continued, with one platoon on the right of the road and one on the left, the canal on the left was flooded with oil and electrically set on fire. The platoon on that side of the road crossed the road to assault the airstrip. The tanks' advance had been halted by mines and the infantry patrols, seeking alternative lines of advance, encountered only swamps. At 8.45 Warfe ordered Catherall and Eldridge to move down the western slopes of Essex, Eldridge's company to link with Travis' and the other to exploit towards the eastern end of the strip. Catherall, checked by machine-gun fire, attacked and captured the weapon. Eldridge's company passed through and continued towards the airstrip ridge.

Meanwhile Travis moved forward of the tanks supporting his company and in the face of heavy machine-gun fire directed the tank fire at the enemy pill-boxes, neutralising them. The engineers cleared the minefields and the final assault on the ridge was led by Travis in the face of fire from 20-mm guns and snipers. Travis' and Eldridge's companies linked on the ridge at 3.30.

---

[8] Maj A. Macfarlane, VX15247; 2/24 Bn. Horticulturist; of Mildura, Vic; b. Wallasey, England, 13 Sep 1918.

[9] F-Lt J. W. O. S. McIntyre. 5 and 4 Sqns, and 16 AOP Flight. Salesman; b. Brisbane, 23 Oct 1923.

[1] Capt S. A. Ket, VX87771. 2 Fd Regt; OC 35 Sqn Air Liaison Section 1944-45. Solicitor; of Ripponlea, Vic; b. Caulfield, Vic, 15 May 1915. Died of injuries 3 May 1945.

[2] From 7th to 22nd May the remaining ALO, Captain W. T. B. Holdsworth, flew on 20 Auster sorties from this strip, and carried on although injured in a crash on 13th May.

During this attack Japanese fire was continually directed on the Anzac Highway from farther east on Peningkibaru making the road untenable. Patrols from Macfarlane's company made contact with the enemy and the company was ordered to attack at 1 p.m. Lieutenant Amiet's[3] platoon attacked the first bunker of a defensive system which was later found to include more than 250 yards of communication trenches connecting eight bunkers and many foxholes, sited on a razor-backed ridge. Immediately two men were killed and one fatally wounded. Brens were quickly sited in an endeavour to silence the enemy fire and a flame-thrower attack was pressed home, causing the enemy to retreat along a deep communication trench. Amiet's platoon gained the bunker knoll, and then Lieutenant W. G. Stretch's passed through. The only feasible line of attack followed the trench along the razor-back. Stretch adopted a bold plan: he led his Owen gunners forward, followed by the Brens and, directing withering fire, made a rapid and successful advance. Private Farmer,[4] his Bren on his hip, cleaned out a bunker and pushed forward. His Bren was shot from his grip but, though his hand was wounded and useless, he left the fighting only when a badly wounded comrade needed assisting to the rear. The razor-back narrowed to a one-man front, but Stretch still advanced, having weapons passed forward along the line. Stoppages were occurring when ammunition was fouled in oily ditches and men were stripping and cleaning guns under enemy fire. Ammunition ran out when the position was gained. The shouts for ammunition were correctly interpreted by the Japanese and they made a determined counter-attack which was held by Stretch alone while Corporal King,[5] a stretcher bearer, attended and recovered the wounded. Captain Macfarlane was evacuated here and Captain E. J. Shattock took command.

It was imperative that the strip be secured that day and at 4.38 p.m. Warfe ordered Eldridge to take Rippon overlooking it from the north. There was just time before dark to launch an attack diagonally across the east end of the airfield in open formation, reach the far side, re-form and move through jungle on to Rippon. One of the men later described the attack:

> There was no suitable forming-up place due to the terrain so the company doubled through the defile where the road passed through the dispersal bays, and fanned out into their open platoon formations at the double and then on the commander's arm signal continued the attack. However the attack had progressed about 50 yards when the right forward platoon (14 Platoon, Lt Walker[6]) had to cross the road which traversed the aerodrome diagonally. As the platoon crossed the road there were two enormous explosions and the platoon was blotted out by earth, dust and smoke. Great wooden beams about 15 feet long floated into the air, splintered and scattered everywhere. I saw one of these beams floating hori-

---

[3] Capt A. H. Amiet, VX37005; 2/24 Bn. Salesman; of North Fitzroy, Vic; b. Richmond, Vic, 17 Jul 1913.

[4] Pte C. C. Farmer, MM, WX35631; 2/24 Bn. Farmer; of Korrelocking, WA; b. Wyalkatchem, WA, 11 Oct 1923.

[5] Cpl H. G. King, MM, VX11616; 2/24 Bn. Schoolmaster; of Dromana, Vic; b. Malvern, Vic, 19 May 1909.

[6] Lt R. R. J. Walker, MC, VX113788; 2/24 Bn. Clerk; of East Brighton, Vic; b. Stawell, Vic, 27 Sep 1918.

zontally about 10 feet in the air and up with it one of our company also in the horizontal. That man lives today. When everything subsided there were only about 5 of the platoon left on their feet. The left forward platoon was ordered to continue the attack and the reserve platoon swung in behind them. 14 Pl had suffered from the Japanese exploding two large depth charges under the road and in their midst. The platoon commander, Lt Walker, got the remnants to their feet and continued, conforming to the rate of advance of the left forward platoon. Then the company ran into a belt of cross-fire from about 6 machine-guns from the far side of the aerodrome and a 75-mm gun fired at us from up the road. The shells were landing just behind us but creeping down. As the company was going to ground Sgt Cooke[7] and the company commander each raced through the forward platoons and led them into the dispersal bays on the far side. Unfortunately at this stage the company commander was shot in the head.

The company was still under heavy cross-fire and was being shelled point-blank by a 75-mm gun. Warfe, who was watching from the ridge above the strip, had seen with horror the leading platoon disappear in the big explosion. Darkness was descending and the company was completely pinned down. Sergeant Cooke assisted gallantly in organising a withdrawal and bringing out the wounded and dead. Lieutenant Gray[8] had now assumed command of the company.

On the night of the 2nd-3rd small enemy parties had probed the 2/48th's area and some were killed. On 3rd May the battalion sent out several patrols. Lieutenant Collier's[9] platoon reconnoitred Peter, found tracks, and on one of them had a sharp fight in which Collier and two others were wounded, Collier mortally. Sergeant Brock[1] took over and organised a withdrawal which was covered by Lance-Corporal Corcoran[2] who stood on the track and fired until all but he had gone back. Lieutenant J. A. R. Buckley's platoon moved north-east towards Sykes and became heavily engaged with a strong enemy group who followed up as the Australians withdrew.

On 3rd May the 2/23rd Battalion found District VI empty; an English-speaking native said that the Japanese had abandoned it three days before. Patrols were fired on from Tarakan Hill, and in the afternoon, while field and naval guns bombarded this hill, Captain Wilton's company attacked but was held up by sharp cross fire; several were hit including the leading platoon's commander, Lieutenant Edwards.[3] The company withdrew.

Platoons of one company thrust at Hospital Spur from the east and south but without success. When the first platoon attacked the Japanese charged down the spur with fixed bayonets. They were repulsed and 12 to 15 were killed, but the Australians were withdrawn. On the left

---

[7] Sgt H. A. Cooke, MM, VX44749; 2/24 Bn. Engine cleaner; of Benalla, Vic; b. Benalla, 23 Dec 1919.
[8] Capt J. C. Gray, MM, VX32559; 2/24 Bn. Driver; of Morkalla, Vic; b. Orroroo, SA, 6 Jan 1916.
[9] Lt J. M. Collier, SX1013; 2/48 Bn. Clerk; of Glenunga, SA; b. Elsternwick, Vic, 30 Mar 1920. Died of wounds 3 May 1945.
[1] Sgt P. M. Brock, SX17065; 2/48 Bn. Butcher; of Adelaide; b. Adelaide, 27 Oct 1915.
[2] L-Cpl L. J. Corcoran, SX18085; 2/48 Bn. Farm hand; of Millicent, SA; b. Tantanoola, SA, 11 Feb 1923. Killed in action 22 May 1945.
[3] Lt I. H. Edwards, VX19597; 2/23 Bn. Salesman; of Warracknabeal, Vic; b. Pinnaroo, SA, 19 Feb 1913.

another company was held up by a pill-box near Burke Highway. A flame-thrower was forward but could not be brought into range.

On the 4th patrols of the 2/23rd found Burke Ridge unoccupied. An attack by infantry and tanks on Hospital Spur was planned but it was found that the enemy had abandoned it, leaving 13 dead. On the right patrols moved through Pamusian but, to the north-east, met heavy fire, five being hit including Lieutenant Greer[4] who was killed.

Brigadier Whitehead had decided to replace the 2/23rd with the 2/3rd Pioneers and the 2/4th Commando Squadron, which had now arrived from Sadau Island, and send the 2/23rd to the left to help the 2/24th. The commando squadron was given the task of taking Tarakan Hill while the Pioneers defended the eastern area.

Thus the 2/23rd, after four days of hard fighting, set out towards more hard fighting in another sector. It had secured the beach and harbour areas and the country between Burke Highway and Pamusian was clear of the enemy. It had taken part of the eastern section of the town of Tarakan. The battalion had lost 9 killed and 31 wounded, some mortally; 90 Japanese dead had been counted.

At 4 p.m. on 3rd May the commando squadron had relieved the right-hand company of the 2/23rd on a ridge overlooking Tarakan Hill, an isolated, thickly-timbered feature commanding the lower country round about for 1,000 yards in all directions. Captain Haigh[5] planned an attack in which one troop would gain a firm base on the slopes of Tarakan Hill and a second would pass through and secure the remainder of the hill. At 9.30 a.m. on the 4th, after a naval and air bombardment, Captain Nicolay's[6] "C" Troop began to advance and by 10.15 was in a ditch that formed the start-line. Thence the leading section sprinted forward into heavy fire, gaining some protection from old concrete buildings. Soon Lieutenant Eley,[7] commanding this section, had been killed and seven others killed or wounded. Trooper O'Regan[8] took control, organised the withdrawal of the section to cover, and then went forward to help Lance-Corporal Moss[9] who had been temporarily blinded. O'Regan himself was now hit but managed to lead Moss back, and, after having his own wounds dressed, gave the squadron commander an account of what had happened. Meanwhile Sergeant Curtin[1] of the R.A.P. had dashed forward to Eley, and, finding him dead, went, still under fire, to a wounded man lying within 20 feet of the enemy post. This man died while

---

[4] Lt R. Greer, VX88979. 19 MG Regt and 2/23 Bn. Farmer; of Rupanyup, Vic; b. Collie, WA, 4 Aug 1917. Killed in action 4 May 1945.

[5] Capt P. F. Haigh, VX60728. 2/4 Indep Coy, 2/4 Cdo Sqn. Bank officer; of Melbourne; b. Coramba, NSW, 1 Oct 1915.

[6] Capt N. T. Nicolay, WX8222. 2/4 Indep Coy, 2/4 Cdo Sqn. Journalist; of Norseman, WA; b. Perth, 27 May 1916.

[7] Lt J. A. Eley, NX49281; 2/4 Cdo Sqn. Student; of Newcastle, NSW; b. Sydney, 23 Oct 1921. Killed in action 4 May 1945.

[8] Tpr K. P. O'Regan, MM, QX23962; 2/4 Cdo Sqn. Station hand; of Goomeri, Qld; b. Gayndah, Qld, 4 Nov 1920.

[9] L-Cpl K. J. Moss, QX25132; 2/4 Cdo Sqn. Stockman; of Cairns, Qld; b. Cairns, 26 Jul 1913.

[1] Sgt A. Curtin, MM, VX58373. 2/4 Indep Coy, 2/4 Cdo Sqn. Shearer; of South Melbourne; b. Ararat, Vic, 8 Dec 1917.

Curtin was looking after him. Curtin went on attending to the wounded until all were carried in.

Lieutenant Wightman's[2] section now advanced but it too was pinned down by fire, and the troop found itself lying out under fire from a well-concealed system of pill-boxes, dugouts and tunnels. Nicolay called for tanks to deal with three tunnels which had been pin-pointed. Lieutenant Burton's[3] troop was sent in on the right flank immediately and was pinned down almost at once. Captain G. C. Hart's troop was then sent in very wide on the right flank of Burton's and reached the crest of Tarakan Hill unopposed, but was then pinned down by mortar and machine-gun fire. The leading section lost their commander, Lieutenant F. W. McKittrick, and two others wounded, all by the same mortar bomb.

An hour later three tanks were forward and from 50 yards poured shells and bullets into the mouths of the tunnels. This, plus the pressure from the two commando troops, forced the Japanese out and Wightman's section advanced and took the forward slopes of the hill. The squadron now commanded three-quarters of the high ground; the remainder was dominated by two concrete pill-boxes 140 yards forward of the leading troops. Patrols knocked out both of these, one being silenced by Trooper Nugent[4] with a Pita, but rifle fire from well-concealed positions prevented the attackers from occupying the ground and Hart withdrew the forward sections to his own locality; 100 yards of the crest of the hill though cleared of the enemy was still unoccupied by the Australians.

That night (4th-5th) small parties of Japanese raiders armed with grenades, fused 75-mm shells, and spears tried to penetrate the perimeter but all were driven off; four Japanese were killed, but the squadron's medical officer, Captain Thomas,[5] and a trooper were wounded. Next morning efforts to occupy the eastern end of the hill were frustrated by snipers until the afternoon, when, about 6 p.m., Lieutenant Wilson's[6] section patrolled completely around the slopes of Tarakan Hill sealing off the many Japanese who remained in the tunnels that honeycombed the hill, their entrances hidden by undergrowth. One by one the Pioneers blew up the entrances of these caves with gelignite leaving the occupants to die; no other course was effective against an enemy who would not surrender.

The 2/48th probed forward on the 4th, moved on to Evans and dug in on its southern spur.

Shattock's company of the 2/24th was ordered to maintain pressure on Peningkibaru with the support of tanks. At 6.5 a.m. on the 4th Peningkibaru was heavily bombarded by mortars, tank howitzers and

---

[2] Lt H. K. Wightman, VX56267. 2/4 Indep Coy, 2/4 Cdo Sqn. Farmer; of Leongatha, Vic; b. Leongatha, 19 Mar 1920.

[3] Lt E. A. Burton, NX76313. 2/4 Indep Coy, 2/4 Cdo Sqn. Articled law clerk; of Bellevue Hill, NSW; b. Sydney, 21 Sep 1920.

[4] Tpr R. Nugent, QX53887; 2/4 Cdo Sqn. Fitter; of Kedron, Qld; b. Brisbane, 2 Mar 1921.

[5] Capt D. L. Thomas, NX202336; RMO 2/4 Cdo Sqn. Medical practitioner; of Neutral Bay, NSW; b. Sydney, 28 Jul 1920.

[6] Lt G. C. Wilson, WX16929. 2/5 Indep Coy, 2/4 Cdo Sqn. Labourer; of Victoria Park, WA; b. Leonora, WA, 26 Sep 1918.

machine-guns. The company attacked and gained the position in time to repel the Japanese who had withdrawn during the barrage and now tried to regain their positions. Shattock then advanced to Frank and found it unoccupied. Peningkibaru was a stronghold. A tunnel in the hillside contained 100 bunks and had evidently housed a headquarters. It contained much equipment. A very accurate Dutch map was found and was later reproduced and distributed. Twenty-four Japanese were killed here and Shattock's company lost 5 killed and 13 wounded.

At 9.30 a.m. that day Warfe arranged another attack on Rippon, again by the company that had been so severely handled there the previous afternoon; but an hour before the attack was to go in the enemy shelled the company, hitting six men, and the attack was cancelled in favour of patrolling the area. Here yet another company commander—Captain Catherall—was wounded.

In the centre Colonel Ainslie of the 2/48th ordered Captain Gooden's company on 5th May to by-pass Evans and, with a troop of tanks, to clear the road north to Otway and Sykes. The company moved out at 9 a.m. with one platoon and the tanks on the road, another pressing against Evans to the east, and the third in reserve on the road; artillery and mortars harassed Sykes and Otway. As the Australians advanced the Japanese laid booby-traps and mines ahead of them and hurled 75-mm shells at the tanks but without causing damage. Lieutenant Derrick's platoon to the east completely cleared Evans and rejoined the company. It then was sent out on a wide encircling move and cleared Otway while the tanks and other infantry fired from the south. In the afternoon Lieutenant Reed's[7] platoon passed through and came under fire from Sykes.

On the morning of the 6th a patrol reported about 30 Japanese forward of Sykes, and at 8 a.m. Captain Johnson's company took over and advanced with the tanks, cautiously, since the road ran along a cutting which, on one side, was completely dominated by Sykes—a precipitous hill with a false crest—and on the other fell away steeply "allowing no deployment whatsoever". At the south-east point of Sykes the leading platoon came under sharp fire and the Japanese hurled a shower of grenades from above and bowled 75-mm shells down at the tanks. This platoon—Sergeant Pope[8]—carried on the fight here while another moved round on the right and reached a position just east of the enemy and only about 100 yards from Pope. Thereupon Pope's platoon resolutely clambered up the slope under small arms fire and grenades, cleared the false crest, killing 8 to 10, and reached the summit, but not without losing six men killed.

The Japanese counter-attacked and forced the survivors in this platoon off the crest, but they advanced again to the top, led by Pope who, though twice wounded, fought on until hit a third time. When Pope was carried

---

[7] Lt M. T. Reed, SX23991; 2/48 Bn. Clerk; of Tarlee, SA; b. Riverton, SA, 24 May 1917.
[8] Sgt G. H. Pope, DCM, SX6915; 2/48 Bn. Salesman; of Cheltenham, SA; b. Alberton, SA, 25 Mar 1912.

out Lieutenant Allen,[9] though he too had been wounded, took command and reorganised. At the end of the day three platoons under Gooden securely held Sykes—the strongest position yet encountered by the 2/48th on Tarakan.

In the 2/24th's area on 5th May patrols had reported that only rifle fire was now coming from Rippon which had been so strongly held the day before, and by 3.30 p.m. two companies were on the feature. About 6 p.m. Warfe moved his headquarters to the airstrip and the Australian flag and the battalion's flag were hoisted over it. Having captured the airfield the 26th Brigade Group had accomplished its main task, but the Japanese still held a line of strongposts on high ground above the town and airfield.

---

[9] Capt K. F. Allen, MC, SX12498; 2/48 Bn. Insurance inspector; of Hayhurst, SA; b. Keswick, SA, 26 Apr 1915.

CHAPTER 18

TARAKAN: THE GARRISON DESTROYED

BY the evening of 6th May fairly copious information obtained from prisoners and Indonesians and from captured documents indicated that the enemy had about 390 naval troops in the Mount Api area, about 400 troops and civilians in the Fukukaku headquarters area (embracing Hills 105 and 102), 200 from Sesanip along Snags Track to Otway, 300 on Otway and in District VI, 300 in the Amal River area and 60 at Cape Juata. Having lost the airfield and the water-purifying plant and hospitals "the enemy at this time was displaying a decided disinclination to hold ground. In particular he was shunning any ground which could be subjected to heavy bombing, shelling, or attack by tanks; or against which large-scale attacks could be launched by our troops";[1] and he was directing his operations to delaying the attackers, particularly with mines, booby-traps, suicide raids, and isolated parties fighting to the death in tunnels and dugouts.

In concentrating on the main task—the capture of the airfield—the brigade had by-passed pockets of resistance such as that at Peningkibaru, whence the enemy could bring down small arms fire on 400 yards of the Anzac Highway. Also there was now need for more living space for the Indonesian refugees.

The enemy fire on the Anzac Highway had been countered by posting tanks on the road whence they used their howitzers and machine-guns. Brigadier Whitehead now decided to capture the high ground overlooking the airfield along the line of Snags Track from Mount Api to Janet, and thus secure the airfield from counter-attack, raids, or indirect fire. This task was given to the 2/23rd Battalion; at the same time the 2/24th was to exploit towards Juata oilfields and patrol the high ground between the airfield and Lyons to ensure a link with the 2/48th. In addition Whitehead proposed to clear the enemy from the high ground overlooking Tarakan town and from Districts IV and VI. To achieve this the 2/48th Battalion would gain the high ground north of the town as far as Snags Track, and the 2/4th Commando Squadron, having cleared Tarakan Hill, would advance along Snags Track towards the Sesanip oilfields. At the same time the 2/3rd Pioneers would sweep the high ground east of the town and advance along the line of John's Track to the mouth of the Amal, and the N.E.I. company would clear the enemy from the Cape Batu peninsula.

Air attack and the artillery were giving formidable support to the infantry, particularly by tearing away the vegetation covering the tangled ridges, but interrogation of prisoners indicated that most of the casualties inflicted during preliminary bombardments were being caused by mortar fire—a not unnatural event in this terrain, which was more broken than

---
[1] 26 Aust Inf Bde Report on Operation Oboe One, Tarakan, 4 May-14 Aug 45.

any this brigade had experienced. Of seven prisoners who, in the second half of May, were questioned as to what weapons were causing casualties, four said that they were caused mostly by mortar fire, another's reply was that five in his group had been killed and 8 wounded by one mortar bomb, and another declared that 300 to 400 casualties had been caused by mortar fire (where or when is not mentioned). The artillery problems on Tarakan were baffling. For example,

> each knoll on the map was exceedingly difficult to pinpoint on the ground; and, from the air, it could not be clearly identified beneath its mantle of forest, unless marked by Smoke. It could not, in most instances, be seen by the O.P.O. [observation post officer] directing fire on to it; for he was often a quarter of a mile away with the infantry on another knoll, his own visibility less than 20 yards! He relied almost entirely on sound ranging. When he "thought" by the "sound" he was "about the place", he "gave it the works", or the C.P.O. [command post officer] prepared a fire plan! If there were two or three O.P.O's on separate knolls, and each could give a sound bearing, so much the better—an unusual method of cross "observation". . . .
> When trees collapsed through constant fire and the rounds got through, it frequently depended on where the guns were sited, and at what angle, as to whether the shells hit on one side of the razor-back or the other. . . . It occasionally happened that a fire plan which started on the target began to overshoot the mark by as much as 200-300 yards when the timber started to fall, and the rounds continued unimpeded. This did not matter if our own troops were on the same side as the guns. Sometimes, however, they were on the opposite side as well.[2]

It was soon apparent that the Japanese were determined to fight for every commanding knoll. In the Mount Api area the 2/23rd met strong resistance, particularly on Tiger, a sharp ridge south of and parallel to Snags Track, which ran through the hills linking the town with the airfield. The defenders of Tiger were protected by pill-boxes and tunnels. One company took the western end of the ridge on 7th May and pressed on next day but was forced back by a counter-attack. The battalion met heavy resistance also on Crazy Ridge. A bridge on Snags Track 150 yards east of Anzac Highway had been blown and it was not possible for the engineers to replace it until the 7th because enemy weapons covered the area. This done, however, tanks came forward and on the 7th and 8th the battalion and the tanks cleared about 200 yards of the track. On the 9th a platoon patrolling towards Snags Track from the north-east of the airstrip was ambushed and six men were hit. Private Dingle[3] rushed forward and fired his Bren while the wounded were rescued.[4]

That day the 2/24th relieved the 2/23rd, which had been in constant contact with the enemy since the landing. Also on the 9th a long-distance patrol of the 2/24th under Lieutenant Walker had driven the Japanese

---

[2] D. Goodhart, *The History of the 2/7 Australian Field Regiment* (1952), pp. 315-17.

[3] Cpl N. M. Dingle, MM, QX32908; 2/23 Bn. Stockman; of Mount Perry, Qld; b. Mount Perry, 6 May 1923.

[4] After the war an officer wrote: "Throughout the operations I was most impressed with the stretcher bearers. At no time did they consider their own safety but would move through minefields and under fire to attend and remove the wounded. They were a select band who won the admiration of all. The company N.C.O's and troops selected their bearers who then reported to the company commander and asked to be appointed bearers; even the best L.M.G. member might be chosen. If a soldier knows that everything possible will be done to save him if wounded or that his body will be recovered if killed his morale is considerably fortified."

(*Australian War Memorial*)

Red Beach, Tarakan, on the day of the landing.

(*Australian War Memorial*)

Tarakan Island, 5th May 1945. Troops of the 2/24th Battalion approach a Japanese pill-box after it had been subdued by naval gunfire and a flame-thrower.

(*Australian War Memorial*)
Looking along the crest of Hill 105 on Tarakan Island, 29th May 1945.

(*Australian War Memorial*)
"H.M.A.S. Margy" bombarding the Joyce feature, Tarakan, on 10th June 1945. In support of the 2/23rd Battalion were two 25-pounders, one 3.7-inch anti-aircraft gun and the guns of three tanks. On the barrel of the 25-pounder in the foreground is painted "Tel el Eisa Tilly".

out of Juata after a skirmish. In the central sector on the night of 6th-7th May the men in the forward posts of the 2/48th heard much movement among the Japanese round Sykes, and decided that they were collecting their dead and wounded on the lower slopes. Japanese riflemen were active next day and hit three men, including Lieutenant Burke who died of his wound.

6th May-16th June

Also on the 7th Captain Lavan's company of the 2/48th, with support from artillery, mortars, machine-guns and tanks, occupied Otway without opposition. Patrols from Sykes found the enemy holding the main ridge running north in strength. Tanks could not penetrate this thickly-timbered country and, here as elsewhere, it was difficult to direct artillery fire.

Early on the morning of the 8th a Japanese raider crept into the main dressing station of the 2/11th Field Ambulance and placed an improvised bomb under a bed occupied by the gallant Lieutenant Freame of the 2/24th. When the bomb exploded it killed Freame and injured two others.

Farther to the right the 2/4th Commando by the 8th had cleared Snags Track as far as Haigh's, beyond which the tanks could not go. On 9th May a section, probing forward, was halted by sharp fire which killed two men. Mortars put down smoke to help a withdrawal, but the crews of aircraft, thinking this smoke indicated a target, bombed the area, fortunately without causing casualties. That night Japanese raiders were in the headquarters area using 12-foot spears and throwing 75-mm shells.

All nerves on edge (wrote the squadron's diarist) and men snatching some sleep in the day time. Morale of troops high but men tiring. . . . Operational rations offer no invitation to eat well.

So far this small unit had lost 7 killed and 19 wounded.

The 2/3rd Pioneers, having left one company in a defensive position on Tarakan Hill and another on Evans, moved out on 7th May to perform its task of advancing along John's Track, which followed the course of the Amal River. They met unexpectedly strong resistance. The leading platoon came under heavy fire just east of Pamusian; it attacked and one man was killed and the company commander, Captain R. L. Dunn, and one other wounded. A second attack after artillery fire—Colonel Anderson had a battery of the 2/7th Field Regiment in support—also failed. That night Anderson gave orders for an attack in which, while part of his force held the enemy in front, another part would circle round, cut the track behind the enemy and then advance westward.

This attack, by Captain Hincksman's[5] company, opened at 9 a.m. on the 8th. The platoon leading astride the track reached a point 50 yards beyond that at which the advance had been halted the previous day, and there met heavy fire. The rest of the company, sent out to encircle the enemy position, moved into very dense bush through which the men had to hack their way. They could advance only 200 yards in an hour, and, when it was evident that the movement could not be completed before nightfall, the company returned and formed a perimeter at the starting point. That night Anderson brought Major H. G. M. Rosevear forward to lead a company on a wide outflanking movement to the left.

While this was in progress accurate artillery and mortar fire was brought down on the enemy's position, one shell making a direct hit on the bunker commanding the track; and Lance-Corporal Pallister[6] brought a Vickers gun into action in a very exposed position and, until wounded, pounded the bunker with incendiary bullets. At 11 a.m. on the 9th the Japanese abandoned the bunker and at midday Rosevear's company reached the track farther east. Hincksman's then passed through and, at 1.15, came under fire at the junction of John's Track and Helen Track. A platoon sent to the flank reached a creek 30 feet wide on the opposite bank of which Japanese were dug in. Leaving a section here Lieutenant Bethell[7]

---

[5] Capt T. E. Hincksman, NX127380. 39 Bn and 2/3 Pnr Bn. Clerk; of Kogarah, NSW; b. Goulburn, NSW, 11 May 1918.

[6] L-Cpl A. W. Pallister, NX58317; 2/3 Pnr Bn. Butcher; of Kogarah, NSW; b. Glebe, NSW, 24 Apr 1923.

[7] Lt R. J. Bethell, NX59075; 2/3 Pnr Bn. Wool broker; of Roseville, NSW; b. Branxton, NSW, 5 Jun 1919.

took the rest of the platoon wide to the right and manoeuvred the enemy out of this position. The Japanese rallied 40 yards beyond, but the platoon drove them from this and another position a similar distance farther on. Their next position, however, proved too strong. In two hours and a half Bethell's platoon had fought three sharp and successful actions, and had lost four men wounded.

Next day (the 10th) a platoon was sent eastward along the track to cover this flank while Hincksman's company attacked the position on the Helen feature. The flanking platoon (Sergeant Holmes[8]) found a strongly-defended position and a second platoon was sent south of the track to outflank it. After 200 yards it came under heavy fire and two men were killed and two, including Lieutenant Keys,[9] wounded. It was now evident that the Helen feature was strongly held and was an important enemy position.

At 1.30 p.m. Colonel Anderson ordered Hincksman to advance directly on to Helen, but the men were halted by heavy fire after 50 yards and dug in. The two companies had now been in action on three successive days, and Anderson ordered the two left near Tarakan to relieve them next day. During the relief a sniper's bullet hit and detonated a grenade attached to Bethell's belt and wounded him seriously.

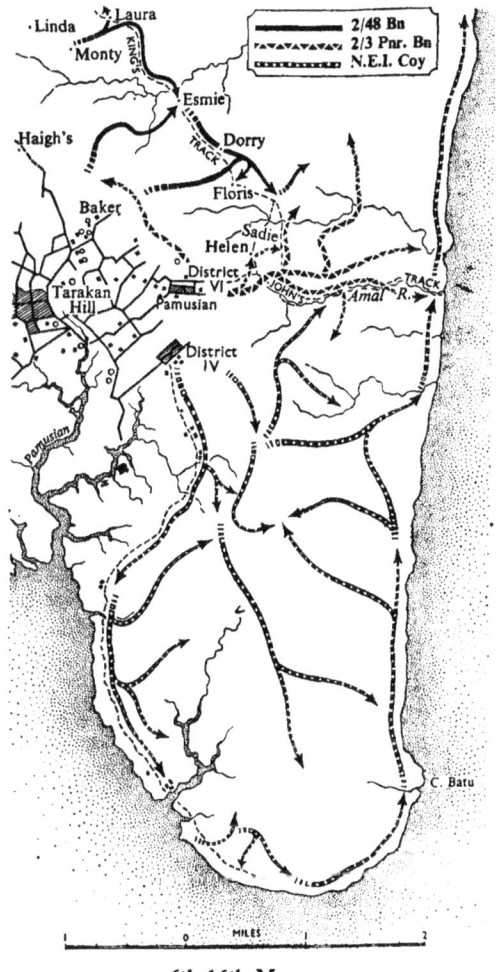

6th-16th May

At 8.25 a.m. on the 12th one of the fresh companies (Captain C. C. Knott) attacked after heavy artillery and mortar fire, directed by Captain

[8] Sgt R. W. E. Holmes, NX33348; 2/3 Pnr Bn. Sawmill worker; of Braemar, NSW; b. Sydney, 14 Jul 1914.
[9] Capt A. G. W. Keys, MC, NX104095; 2/3 Pnr Bn. 3 Bn RAR Korea 1950-51. Grazier; of Ando, NSW; b. Sydney, 2 Feb 1923.

Morish[1] and Lieutenant Whibley[2] respectively from the forward edge of the infantry position on to targets as close as 40 yards away. The objective was a long razor-backed ridge sometimes only 3 feet wide on top and with almost sheer sides. It was covered with scrub and the bombardment had thrown in the path of the attackers a tangle of fallen limbs of trees; this not only impeded the advance but also improved the defenders' field of fire.

The leading platoon (Lieutenant Travers[3]) met concentrated fire but pressed on. Corporal Mackey's[4] section which was leading was under fire from three well-sited positions at the top of an almost sheer rise. Mackey, with whom was Lance-Corporal Riedy,[5] charged the first machine-gun post, but slipped and fell into it. A Japanese seized him but he struggled free, bayoneted the Japanese, and, with Riedy, killed the others in the post. Covered by Riedy's fire, Mackey then charged another post with overhead cover containing a heavy machine-gun and threw a grenade through the firing slit, killing the gun's crew. He then borrowed Riedy's Owen gun and charged up a steep bank towards the third post, firing as he went. At the edge of the post he was hit and fell but not before he had silenced the enemy's machine-gun. He had killed at least seven Japanese and taken three machine-gun posts. When Riedy saw Mackey fall he went forward to bring him out but found him dead. Riedy remained there firing at very close quarters until he was wounded.[6]

Travers reorganised his platoon, in which every N.C.O. had now been hit, and kept up heavy fire to help another platoon (Sergeant Jones[7]) which was moving round the left. The platoon fought at close range for three hours and, when ordered to withdraw, only Travers and three others were occupying the position. Jones' men, after struggling through fallen branches and thick undergrowth, came under converging fire and were forced back. It was now midday, the fight had lasted three hours and a half and 9 had been killed and 19 wounded—half the strength of the attacking force.

On the morning of 13th May the attackers withdrew about a mile, destroyers and the 2/7th Field Regiment bombarded the feature, and Lightning aircraft dropped napalm bombs. However, none of these bombs fell on the Japanese positions and the naval fire was not very accurate. One shell hit the track less than half way back to the start-line. The Japanese were sited along the razor-back track running up the feature,

---

[1] Capt W. J. Morish, SX2898; 2/7 Fd Regt. Insurance inspector; of King's Park, SA; b. Adelaide, 13 Dec 1912.

[2] Lt H. R. Whibley, NX120650; 2/3 Pnr Bn. Cabinet-maker; of Epping, NSW; b. Cronulla, NSW, 6 Aug 1918.

[3] Capt J. E. Travers, MC, NX57155. North Australia Observer Unit and 2/3 Pnr Bn. Superintendent, assurance company; of Ashfield, NSW; b. Perth, 5 May 1913.

[4] Cpl J. B. Mackey, VC, NX20317; 2/3 Pnr Bn. Baker; of Portland, NSW; b. Leichhardt, NSW, 16 May 1922. Killed in action 12 May 1945.

[5] Cpl A. R. Riedy, DCM, QX21198; 2/3 Pnr Bn. Farm worker; of Wooroonden, via Mondure, Qld; b. Howard, Qld, 20 Sep 1920.

[6] Mackey was posthumously awarded the Victoria Cross for this action.

[7] WO2 S. W. Jones, NX69734; 2/3 Pnr Bn. Truck driver; of Willoughby, NSW; b. Sydney, 4 Jul 1920.

which from the bottom presented a series of false crests, ideal for defence since the attacking troops, after crossing a crest, could not be seen or supported from the rear.

To cope with this problem Captain Esau,[8] whose company was to renew the attack, asked for flame-throwers, the intention being to fire them from below each crest and carry out the attack to the summit in a succession of bounds.

A platoon from Knott's company acted as an advance-guard for Esau's company on its return to Knott's former position, from which the attack would be launched, but progress was so slow that the timed artillery program was finished well before Esau's company arrived at the start-line.

At 12.25 p.m. the company attacked, with one platoon assaulting, one holding astride the track in the position occupied the previous night by Knott's company, and the third platoon in reserve in the rear. Lieutenant Ormiston,[9] whose platoon led the attack, reached the scene of the hard fight on the 12th and came under heavy fire from the Japanese on the top of the next crest and from positions at the base and sides of the rise to the crest. One section, however, got to within 25 yards of the enemy and thence Corporal Shanahan[1] went forward alone firing a Bren. When this weapon jammed he went on with grenades, threw two into a pit and silenced it but was then killed. He had made the greatest advance up the track of anyone in any of the attacks. Ormiston was killed while leading another section forward, and the attackers were withdrawn, having lost 4 killed and 7 wounded. The flame-throwers unfortunately were left at the rear and not fired.

On 14th May Liberator aircraft were used in close support for the first time, the targets being the Helen and Sadie features, and Lightning fighters dropped napalm immediately after the bombing. This combination proved most effective and thereafter was the kind of air support that was always asked for.

At dawn next day a platoon was sent forward to discover whether the Helen feature was still occupied, and at 7.30 the platoon commander reported that the hill had been abandoned. So ended what the battalion considered the most protracted and difficult fight in its history—a history which included an arduous campaign in North Africa and another in New Guinea. In the course of the operation about 7,000 shells and 4,000 mortar bombs were fired.

The Japanese withdrawal from the Helen feature left John's Track unguarded and on 16th May the Pioneers reached the coast at the mouth of the Amal River. They had done their job, but at a cost of 20 killed and 46 wounded.

---

[8] Capt K. M. Esau, SX3406; 2/3 Pnr Bn. Reporter; of Hyde Park, SA; b. Mannum, SA, 22 Aug 1912.
[9] Lt F. S. Ormiston, NX133083; 2/3 Pnr Bn. Junior executive trainee; of Sydney; b. San Mateo, California, USA, 1 Mar 1921. Killed in action 13 May 1945.
[1] Cpl C. J. Shanahan, NX55081; 2/3 Pnr Bn. Clerk; of Waverton, NSW; b. Tamworth, NSW, 20 Jul 1920. Killed in action 13 May 1945.

The Japanese force on and round Helen had consisted of about 200 men under Lieutenant Fudaki. It had been guarding the beach at the Amal when the Australians landed and had then moved to the position forward of Helen. It lost heavily there on 9th May and withdrew to the Helen feature. Fudaki expected the Australians to advance along John's Track and intended to move in behind them. Bethell's platoon discovered his positions, however. Fudaki withdrew from the Helen feature after he had lost about half his force and when he seemed likely soon to be surrounded.

As the troops pushed into the more thickly timbered country greater use was made of air support. Until the 8th four Mitchells had been overhead during the daylight hours and each battalion had an air-support party with direct call on these aircraft, subject to the possible intervention of brigade headquarters, which listened in. The Mitchells proved too inaccurate against confined targets and their bomb pattern covered too wide an area to silence enemy positions. As a result these aircraft were usually directed to more distant objectives.

In the second week of May the 2/4th Commando Squadron was strenuously patrolling forward of its sector and becoming very weary. On the 13th the enemy became more aggressive in this area: about 30 attacked on the Agnes feature and were repulsed losing about 16 killed. On the 15th "B" Troop advanced farther along a spur on Agnes with the object of taking the crest of the feature, and in mid-afternoon the forward section, 16 strong, under Lieutenant Stanford,[2] was digging in on the objective when some 50 Japanese suddenly counter-attacked, making a "Banzai" charge from about 40 yards away. Again they were repulsed and mortar fire was called down on the survivors. One Japanese had got to within three feet of Trooper Collett.[3] He fired a burst from his Owen gun and the man fell. Later Trooper Nugent went out to search this body but the Japanese sprang up, hurled a grenade and made off—an occurrence the commandos attributed to the wearing of a bullet-proof vest. Next morning a patrol counted 20 dead Japanese within a few yards of the crest and 2 more farther along the track. The Australians were sure that other dead and wounded men had been carried out in the night.

After three days of strenuous patrolling the 2/48th on 12th May had set out to cut King's Track with two platoons so as to intercept Japanese who were withdrawing from the Helen and Sadie features, and to clear the heights from Sykes to Butch. The two platoons succeeded in cutting the track and by the late afternoon had each set an ambush. Captain Gooden controlled these platoons from a headquarters on Esmie. On the 13th patrols reached Dorry and Floris.

On the left the 2/24th Battalion was meeting strong resistance. A tank reconnaissance officer, Captain Austin,[4] and another were killed in an ambush on Snags Track on the 10th. Between Travis' company and

---

[2] Lt H. M. Stanford, SX21834; 2/4 Cdo Sqn. Salesman; of Fulham, SA; b. Fulham, 4 Apr 1920.
[3] Tpr A. N. Collett, NX32417. 2/4 Indep Coy, 2/4 Cdo Sqn. Storeman; of Alexandria, NSW; b. Alexandria, 28 Jul 1918.
[4] Capt A. F. Austin, NX34737. 7 Cav Regt and 2/9 Armd Regt. Station overseer; of Narrandera, NSW; b. Narrandera, 4 Dec 1914. Killed in action 10 May 1945.

Shattock's was the strongly-defended Tiger feature. Both Lieutenant Sargeant[5] from Travis' company and Lieutenant Stretch from Shattock's had led out reconnaissance patrols and made contact with the enemy. Stretch then led forward a fighting patrol but was forced to withdraw. That afternoon Travis was killed by a sniper while seeking a position from which to direct tank fire from his flank and Sargeant took command. The company made further attacks but without any success. Lieutenant Endean's[6] company was in contact that afternoon on Hill 105 which, like the position Sargeant's company was attacking, was heavily fortified and was to become the scene of a long struggle.

On the 11th a platoon of Endean's company was held up by fire from a scrub-covered knoll about 30 yards ahead. Two flame-throwers were brought up and Sergeant Campbell[7] opened fire with thin fuel and cleared all the scrub between the platoon and the enemy's post, while the riflemen advanced behind the screen of flame and smoke. Campbell next fired with thick fuel. The position was then found to have been abandoned.

Artillery was the only answer to the Tiger problem and on the 11th flares were fired into the enemy's position from both the east and west to indicate the target. After an artillery concentration a platoon of Sargeant's company dashed forward just in time to race the enemy to the positions they had vacated during the bombardment. These tactics were repeated and finally the two companies occupied the feature which was a maze of pill-boxes and foxholes.

One pill-box remained in the enemy's possession. Major Serle[8] now took command from Sargeant. Attacks with a flame-thrower next day failed to dislodge the enemy from this last position but on the night of the 12th-13th there was a great explosion and at dawn a patrol found that the enemy had blown up a big tunnel and abandoned the pill-box. Meanwhile patrols from Shattock's company had probed about 1,000 yards south-east, cutting Snags Track at several places.

On the morning of the 13th Lieutenant Freeman's[9] platoon set out to attack the knoll north of Snags Track which had now resisted attacks for two days. Lance-Corporal Casley[1] opened fire with a flame-thrower, killed two Japanese and then ran forward to the top of the knoll, but was hit by a burst from a machine-gun as he began firing again. A bullet punctured the flame-thrower and burning fuel gushed out. Casley dropped the flame-thrower and ran back with his clothes on fire; he died of his injuries. That evening after the Japanese position had been bombarded

---
[5] Lt D. H. Sargeant, VX23882. 2/32 and 2/24 Bns. Salesman; of Caulfield, Vic; b. Launceston, Tas, 25 Nov 1910.
[6] Lt D. C. Endean, NX4045. 2/4 and 2/24 Bns. Bank officer; of Concord, NSW; b. Five Dock, NSW, 15 Nov 1911.
[7] Sgt J. E. Campbell, TX12284; 2/24 Bn. Sawmiller; of Jetsonville, Tas; b. Scottsdale, Tas, 21 Oct 1915. Killed in motor-car accident 9 Apr 1954.
[8] Maj R. P. Serle, VX48826; 2/24 Bn. Insurance clerk; of Hawthorn, Vic; b. Hawthorn, 18 Nov 1914.
[9] Lt A. W. Freeman, VX131500; 2/24 Bn. Clerk; of Ivanhoe, Vic; b. Fitzroy, Vic, 26 Aug 1913.
[1] L-Cpl D. L. Casley, NX190755; 2/24 Bn. Labourer; of Tarcutta, NSW; b. Sydney, 20 Dec 1922. Died of wounds 14 May 1945. As Casley was being carried out he saw Colonel Warfe and said: "I'm O.K., skipper. They couldn't kill me with an axe."

by mortars, tanks and two 2-pounder guns, Freeman attacked and took the knoll. On the 15th Serle's company took Elbow but was forced out by fire from a 75-mm gun firing at point-blank range. This was shelled and next day Elbow was reoccupied.

By the 16th the 26th Brigade had lost 11 officers and 137 men killed, 22 officers and 353 wounded; 9 officers and 243 men were sick. As most of this loss had been suffered by the infantry, the brigade had lost the equivalent of a battalion. The counted Japanese dead numbered 479 but only five prisoners had been taken. The brigade's task was proving, in Whitehead's words, "far more difficult and tedious than anticipated", and now the enemy was holding country that was more inaccessible and rugged than the Intelligence staffs had been able to ascertain. The cover by aerial photographs had been poor, but this was offset by the capture of the excellent Dutch oil survey map which showed contours at one-metre intervals and provided detail lacking in the 1:25,000 maps with which the brigade had been equipped.

On 17th May it was estimated that 1,200 effective Japanese troops remained; no doubt more than 400 others were sick or wounded—escaped N.E.I. prisoners had reported that there were up to 300 patients in the Fukukaku hospital alone. Captured maps and other sources showed that the enemy was holding in strength Hill 105, thence along a line to the south through Margy to Janet on Snags Track, then south-east through Ostrich, Galah and Susie. A company of the *2nd Naval Garrison,* the best troops, with a company of *Tokoi Force* (the army component) were on Hill 105, Margy and Janet. It still seemed certain that the enemy's intention was to make a last stand round the Fukukaku headquarters area.

Whitehead decided to maintain pressure along the line Hill 105-Susie; to penetrate as far as possible along the valley running north-west from between Agnes and Linda toward the Fukukaku area, to patrol the high ground east of Hill 102, gain control of the main Japanese track from the Amal River to Hill 102 and close in on the Fukukaku area from the east and north-east of Hill 102, thereby cutting off escape. He would turn the defences in the north, and prevent escape in that direction, and thrust east just north of Hill 105 across the north-south track and thus cut off the forces farther north from the main defence system.

The remaining positions on Hill 105 were bombed and bombarded and on 18th May the hill was attacked by Lieutenant Ingham's[2] platoon of the 2/24th. One pill-box was still defending the area and the approach to it was along a razor-back cluttered with fallen timber. Ingham and a Bren gunner charged and took the pill-box. It was found that many Japanese in the area had been killed by bomb blast. The enemy was still holding 500 yards along the ridge. Next morning Ingham's platoon attacked this position, which could be approached only in single file. Without being seen the attackers drew close enough to roll grenades into the foxholes. One grenade was thrown back by a Japanese marine who

---

[2] Lt P. G. O. Ingham, VX4842. 2/8 and 2/24 Bns. Agent; of Ballarat, Vic; b. London, 2 Apr 1911

leapt up with bayonet fixed. He and others were shot and the remainder fled. The 105 feature was now entirely in Australian hands.

From 14th to 17th May patrols of the 2/48th had probed forward killing from 6 to 12 Japanese each day and themselves losing only 7 killed or wounded in the four days. It was decided that the enemy positions on Susie, Mamie, Freda and Clarice were too strong to be attacked by the 2/4th Commando and the 2/48th was given the task. At dawn on 19th May Lieutenant Derrick's platoon followed at 7.30 by the remainder of the company (Captain Gooden's) moved from Ossie to Agnes to attack the Freda feature—the vital ground—after an air and artillery bombardment. The aircraft attacked from 9.10 to 9.26 and the artillery went into action, as Derrick's platoon advanced. They met strong opposition before reaching Freda and pressed on, only to discover that they were on the wrong track and were approaching Clarice not Freda. Later they withdrew for the night. Meanwhile another company (Captain Lavan) occupied the Laura feature.

On 20th May, after early morning patrols from Derrick's platoon had returned, it was decided to advance along Freda from east to west. Sixteen aircraft dropped napalm on the Japanese area and the artillery bombarded it, but the attacking infantry found the feature too strongly held and again withdrew. Next day 500 mortar bombs were fired on to Freda and Track Junction Knoll but after some sharp fighting the enemy remained in possession.

It was now evident that if the Freda hill was to be taken the attack must have heavier support. Therefore, on 22nd May, 12 Liberators and 12 Lightnings were sent out with bombs and napalm, but the cloud was so low that some of the heavy bombers did not find the objective. Then the artillery and mortars fired, and a two-company attack went in, the infantry moving very close behind the barrage. Gooden's company thrust from the east, and Captain Nicholas'[3] advanced with one platoon pushing east along Snags Track towards Track Junction Knoll and another pressing north. The former platoon (Lieutenant Harvey[4]), moving through very difficult country along a razor-back so narrow that only two men could be deployed on it, edged forward under heavy fire; after losing one killed and 4 wounded and finding the enemy becoming stronger Harvey manoeuvred out of this position. It was then found that a wounded man was not with them, so Harvey and three volunteers thrust back and engaged the enemy fiercely while the wounded man was carried out.

During the day Gooden's company on the right had encountered two strongly-held knolls. Derrick's platoon succeeded in cutting the saddle between them and taking one knoll. Derrick's platoon and another launched a most courageous attack up the steep slopes of Knoll 2 in the fading light. Here, in some of the heaviest and most bitter close-in fighting of the whole campaign these two platoons finally reached the top and secured the Knoll after inflicting heavy

---

[3] Capt P. W. Nicholas, SX9840; 2/48 Bn. Fruitgrower; of Monash, SA; b. Glenelg, SA, 21 May 1918.
[4] Lt R. J. Harvey, SX2312. 2/10 and 2/48 Bns. Fisherman; of Lake Wangary, SA; b. Port Lincoln, SA, 11 Aug 1910.

casualties on the enemy. . . . [Lance-Sergeant] Fennell[5] . . . time and again . . . crawled ahead of the attacking troops, even to within five yards of the enemy, and . . . gained vital information. On one occasion, when his section was forced to ground he had charged the Jap positions with his Owen gun blazing and had silenced the enemy post, killing the occupants. In a similar manner, Private W. R. How[6] . . . found the advance of the troops checked by a well-sited pill-box, raced forward with his Owen firing until within grenade range, and then, throwing grenades, moved in for the kill until he fell wounded. He had silenced the post and killed the machine-gunner, thus allowing the advance to continue.[7]

At this stage 28 enemy dead had been counted; one Australian had been killed and 15 wounded.

Captain Hart's "B" Troop of the 2/4th Commando Squadron was ordered to move from Agnes to Freda to reinforce the company there. This was difficult as the move had to be made after dark in unfamiliar jungle. Two sections joined Derrick's platoon on Knoll 2. The Japanese evidently considered the Freda feature to be vital ground and, having been reinforced, hit back in force soon before dawn on the 23rd. In the hard and confined fighting that followed two were killed and eight wounded, including Derrick, who continued to give his orders for some hours after he had been hit in the stomach and thigh. Afterwards it was found that the platoon area was directly overlooked by a Japanese bunker on the main Freda feature—Derrick would certainly not have established his platoon there had it not been that the lateness of the successful attack the previous night had prevented him from seeing where the Japanese positions on the main feature were. The enemy was now so strong that it was decided to pull back, carrying out the wounded, and bombard the knoll again.

Next day it was learnt that Derrick had died. "This news," wrote the battalion's diarist, "had a very profound effect on the whole battalion as he had become a legend, and an inspiration to the whole unit. An original member, he had served with distinction through every campaign in which this battalion took part—Tobruk, Tel el Eisa, El Alamein, Lae, Finschhafen, Sattelberg, Tarakan. In what proved to be his last campaign he fought as ever with utmost courage and devotion to duty and his conduct and inspiration in the attack on Freda to a large extent accounted for the heavy casualties inflicted on the enemy in close-quarter hand-to-hand fighting." An officer of a neighbouring unit wrote: "His loss was not only felt by his own battalion but the whole force."

Except that they had lost Hill 105 and the Janet feature the Japanese dispositions had not changed between 14th and 22nd May. The sound of chopping and digging indicated that they were strengthening their grip. Examination of Hill 105 showed how strong the remaining defences were likely to be; it revealed a network of bunkers, trenches and shelters, many shelters being still undamaged despite bombing and shelling so heavy that the whole area was covered with a tangled mass of fallen timber.

---

[5] L-Sgt W. J. Fennell, MM, SX6832; 2/48 Bn. Labourer; of Berri, SA; b. Gawler, SA, 19 Sep 1919.
[6] L-Cpl W. R. How, MM, WX26495; 2/48 Bn. Gardener; of East Fremantle, WA; b. East Fremantle, 8 Feb 1916.
[7] J. G. Glenn, *Tobruk to Tarakan* (1960), pp. 252-3.

At this stage the *4th Company* of *Tokoi Force* plus the *1st Company* of the *2nd Naval Garrison Force* held Margy and Joyce; the *1st Company* of *Tokoi Force,* and other troops were on Hill 102. In the north was a composite group. Two 75-mm guns remained. It still seemed likely that the enemy intended to make a last stand round the Fukukaku headquarters area, but there was some evidence that they were preparing an alternative headquarters on Essie.

Whitehead now decided that the time had come to assault the enemy's last stronghold. He decided to concentrate the main effort on rolling up the Japanese from the north, where their defences were probably less well developed than elsewhere. There was no longer any need for haste, and no attack was to be made without maximum fire power being used beforehand. The general policy would be to attack each position with 18 Liberators carrying 500-lb or 1,000-lb bombs and then follow up with Lightnings carrying napalm. Since 15th May, however, it had become evident that 25-pounder ammunition would have to be used sparingly. The brigade had landed with 19,500 rounds, had been using about 800 a day, and there seemed to be no prospect of replenishment before 31st May. Consequently Whitehead took direct control of expenditure of this ammunition, which was not to exceed 500 rounds a day. As a result more mortar and machine-gun ammunition was used, and on 23rd May the use of these was also restricted.

It became evident that only one fully-supported attack could be made each day, and, because bombing by the Liberators was an essential part of the support and their arrival was dependent on the state of the weather, the decision to carry out an attack could not as a rule be made until the previous night. When this assault phase opened the plan was to use most of the fire-power resources in support of the 2/24th Battalion in its thrust along the Dutch Track from Juata oilfields towards Hill 105. At the same time patrols were to go to the north of the island to find whether the enemy was active between Fukukaku and Cape Juata and whether he was occupying the defences at Cape Juata, and patrols were to ascertain whether a track existed on the line of the Binalatung River from the coast to Fukukaku.

Captain Johnson's company of the 2/48th took over at the Freda feature. Early on the 24th the Japanese sallied out and attacked this company, using grenades and 75-mm shells, and killed or wounded 6 men. A 2/4th Commando patrol now reported the Susie feature to be unoccupied. It was evident that the Japanese had withdrawn all their strength to the Freda feature, and, on 25th May, it was given a devastating bombardment by six Liberators with 250-lb bombs and 18 Lightnings with napalm, and by artillery and mortars. Johnson's company followed the barrage closely and secured the knolls on Freda, and a company under Captain McLellan[8] took Track Junction Knoll. The bodies of 46 Japanese

---

[8] Capt N. McLellan, SX7054; 2/48 Bn. Farm worker; of Bordertown, SA; b. Wolseley, SA, 3 Feb 1913.

were buried in the area, most of them having been killed in the attack on the 23rd; in the day the 2/48th killed 21 more Japanese. For the next four days the 2/48th held the ground it had gained, and patrolled.

In the last 10 days of May the 2/23rd and 2/24th were in close contact with a resolute enemy. On 23rd May after 477 mortar bombs had been lobbed on to the Margy feature a platoon moved on to it but found the ground unfavourable and was withdrawn. That day a captured Japanese 75-mm infantry gun was assembled and sited on the edge of a cliff in full view of the Margy feature to support a company of the 2/23rd. There were two good reasons for using this relatively light gun: it was fairly easy to manhandle forward and though the supply of 25-pounder ammunition was dwindling there were some hundreds of rounds of Japanese gun ammunition. On the 24th the gun fired and virtually cleared the trees from the Margy feature. Next day it brought down very effective fire on the Japanese positions now revealed and a platoon of Captain Ferguson's[9] company of the 2/2nd Machine Gun Battalion on Elbow fired 82 belts at the hill. Patrols thrust forward and had fierce fights with the defenders, but the Japanese held on.

The 2/24th Battalion was now stretched out from Juata to Crazy Ridge, occupying and flanking the Dutch Track for a distance of 5,000 yards or more. On 23rd May a company attacked Beech 2 without prior bombardment and was halted by electrically-fired mines, which caused 11 casualties. The wounded were brought out and the position mortared and shelled.

The enemy was strongly dug in among dense vegetation on the Droop feature. Lieutenant Ludbrook's[1] platoon got astride the enemy's line of communication and held a position there during the night of the 23rd-24th, killing 12 Japanese in the course of repeated attacks. Thirty-six Liberators hit the hill on 26th May and completely cleared it of vegetation. A company then occupied the hill, advancing 1,000 yards in the day. When the advance was continued on the 27th after two strikes by Liberators, Private Christmass,[2] the leading Owen gunner, was hit in the chest by rifle fire and knocked to the ground. He staggered to his feet and with his Owen gun blazing continued to advance, killing two Japanese before being shot in the arm. His action enabled his section to gain 300 yards of valuable ground.

An Indonesian prisoner reported that the first air strike had killed no Japanese but the second had killed 10 and also, unhappily, two Indonesian prisoners employed as carriers. The infantry killed eight more Japanese. A company of the 2/23rd made another attack on the Margy feature on the 29th supported by air, artillery and mortar bombardment but was forced back, losing 3 killed and 6 wounded. Margy was now under fire from seven guns in a single row firing at point-blank range—two 25-pounders, one 3.7-inch anti-aircraft gun, the guns of three tanks, and one

---

[9] Capt G. T. Ferguson, NX15828; 2/2 MG Bn. Commercial traveller; of Roseville, NSW; b. Bangalow, NSW, 7 May 1914.

[1] Lt G. C. Ludbrook, VX50516; 2/24 Bn. Clerk; of Ballarat, Vic; b. Ballarat, 9 Aug 1919.

[2] Pte K. C. Christmass, DCM, WX22774; 2/24 Bn. Chaff cutter hand; of Northam, WA; b. Northam, 22 May 1925. Died of wounds 31 May 1945.

75-mm. On the 31st a heavier onslaught was made. In the morning 17 Liberators dropped 102 1,000-lb bombs, 16 Mitchells dropped delayed-action bombs and 15 Lightnings dropped napalm. At 11 a.m. a platoon advanced south towards Margy along a razor-back spur over much fallen timber. The first pimple was found to be unoccupied but farther on machine-gun fire halted the advance. One section moved round to the west, came in behind the enemy and cleared the intervening area and soon three of four knolls on the feature were secured. A second platoon was

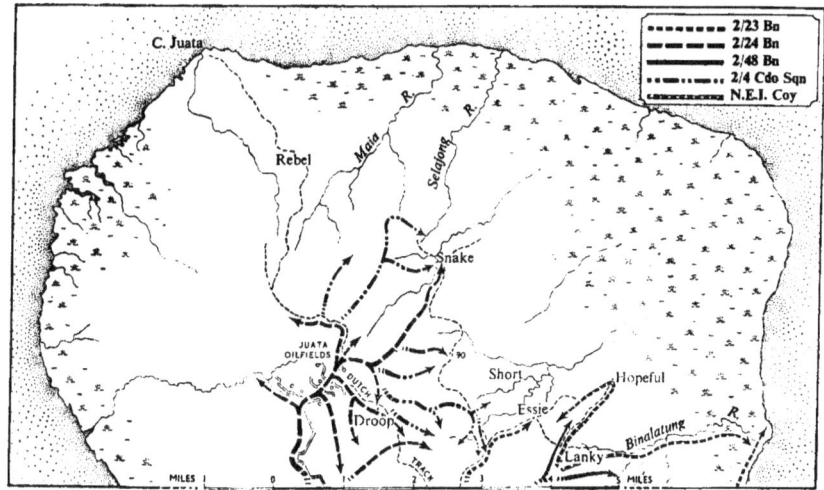

Tarakan, northern area

then sent against Margy itself. The two platoons closed in on the fourth knoll, took it, and then occupied the Margy feature without opposition. In the mopping up next day 20 Japanese were killed and others were buried in their tunnels. One wounded man was taken prisoner.

At 11 a.m., after aircraft had attacked Poker 2 and 3, Major Serle's company of the 2/24th and Captain Shattock's advanced, Serle's against Poker 2 from the north-west and Shattock's against Poker 3. There was heavy fighting on Poker 3. At midday Lieutenant Amiet's platoon attacked the dominating ground on this hill. The only approach was along a razor-back spur—a two-man front—on which were tunnels and foxholes to a depth of 100 yards. After moving four yards the leading section came under a hail of fire and four men fell. Corporal Beale[3] took his section through but it was checked immediately by grenades and small arms fire. Beale went forward, located the Japanese positions and threw grenades into one of them, then returned and sited the Bren guns of two sections. At this stage Amiet and the remaining section commander were wounded.

---
[3] Cpl L. E. Beale, DCM, VX63991; 2/24 Bn. Printer; of Bentleigh, Vic; b. Ormond, Vic, 8 Sep 1922.

Beale took over, sited the third Bren, threw phosphorous grenades, and under cover of the Bren gun fire and the smoke led a charge. The position was taken and 13 Japanese killed. Beale had been wounded in two places but carried on. Another platoon now passed through. The dauntless Beale, firing a Bren from the hip, led the forward section of this platoon until a further 200 yards of the ridge had been gained. Altogether 14 Australians were wounded; 16 enemy dead were counted. Meanwhile Serle's company could not make headway against Poker 2 that day but the Japanese abandoned it early next morning. The Dutch Track was now open from Juata to Poker 3.

On Hill 102 the Japanese facing the 2/48th were dug in on the highest point of a ridge only 20 to 30 feet wide and the only feasible approach was along a razor-back three feet wide. The defences consisted of five pill-boxes and some 30 rifle pits, with overhead cover. The hill was attacked on 1st June by 18 Liberators each with nine 500-lb bombs and 24 Lightnings with napalm. The Australians' forward positions were only 100 yards from the enemy and were brought back about 350 yards before the aircraft struck, but machine-gunners of the 2/2nd Machine Gun Battalion fired on the enemy from a flank to try to stop them from leaving their positions during the bombing or from moving forward into the Australians' positions. After the bombing, at 4.45 p.m., Lieutenant O'Rourke's[4] platoon attacked, following an artillery barrage as closely as they could, and bringing with them three flame-throwers. They gained the forward slopes without being fired on and then saw five Japanese moving towards them, evidently to re-enter their positions after the bombing. These were fired on while the flame-throwers were brought into action. One operator sprayed the slope from side to side while another fired straight up it.

> The result was devastating (said O'Rourke later). The hill was set completely ablaze to a depth of 50 yards, two of the five Japs were set on fire and the other three killed in their posts. The platoon was able to advance almost immediately through the flames, and with the help of the flame-throwers the feature was completely captured within 15 minutes of the advance commencing. The flame which was fired up a slight rise hit the trees on the crest and also sprayed the reverse slope and had the effect of completely demoralising the enemy.

On 3rd June, after an unsuccessful air attack by 49 aircraft, Lavan's company advanced on Wally from Hill 102 but found the enemy in strength across the track with a pill-box on each flank and weapon-pits farther back; fallen trees made it impossible to outflank the position. The forward scout got to within 15 yards of one pill-box but the enemy's fire was fierce and the company had to withdraw. Next day 12 Liberators again struck Wally but again the infantry found the enemy still holding in strength. They reached the conclusion that the 250-lb bombs were too light and were bursting among the branches of the big trees.

In this period the 2/23rd was engaged clearing the remaining Japanese from Margy and its neighbourhood. On 1st June patrols killed 35 Japanese

---

[4] Lt A. J. O'Rourke, NX36205; 2/48 Bn. Accounts clerk; of Wagga Wagga, NSW; b. Wagga Wagga, 16 Jun 1914.

bringing the total number killed on that hill to 118. On the 4th 36 Indonesian prisoners walked into the lines of the 2/24th waving white flags or shirts. On arrival they ran around laughing and shaking hands with the Australians; one said that 300 Indonesian prisoners who had been employed in the Fukukaku area had broken out on the night of the 2nd-3rd.

The 2/23rd was making good progress as a result of using guns sited on the Margy feature itself in close support. The unit was allotted one 3.7-inch anti-aircraft gun and two 25-pounders sited only 400 yards from the target. These guns systematically blasted the timber from the ridges and then, with the help of tank guns and a 2-pounder, battered the enemy's posts one after another.

A letter was dropped to the Japanese on 4th June addressed to Commander Kahuru (the naval commander) and Major Tokoi (the army commander). In it Whitehead expressed admiration for Japanese courage, recalled how the Japanese had refrained from attacking a hospital ship at Milne Bay, and offered to take care of Japanese wounded. He suggested that Lieut-Commander Yamagata and one man should come forward on Hill 105 at midday on the 5th carrying a white flag and wearing a white brassard and there meet an Allied medical officer and discuss arrangements for treatment of Japanese casualties. A sketch was attached showing exactly where the Japanese representative should halt. This appeal was disregarded.

On 6th June Lieutenant Herbert's[5] platoon of the 2/48th moved stealthily from Hill 102 and dug in south-east of Wally. Three Japanese who walked towards this position were shot. Lieutenant Macdonald's[6] platoon followed and sent a patrol towards the north end of the Linda spur and were 20 yards from the top when they were fired on. It was decided that this approach was not a practical one.

Also on the 6th the Roger feature was given a devastating onslaught from the air and "D" Company of the 2/24th seized it from a Japanese garrison that had been dazed by the bombardment.[7] Pressing forward from the Freda feature on the 7th a patrol of the 2/48th found the enemy in strength; Lieutenant Simper[8] and one other were killed.[9]

On the night of the 8th-9th forward posts of the 2/24th reported that the enemy "seemed to be having a regular party" in the direction of the Paddy and Melon features. There was much singing and rattling of tins.[1]

---

[5] Lt G. E. Herbert, VX104139; 2/48 Bn. Station hand; of Corryong, Vic; b. Corryong, 31 Jul 1922.
[6] Lt J. H. Macdonald, SX4253. 2/27 and 2/48 Bns. Stock clerk; of Walkerville, SA; b. Adelaide, 1 Sep 1920.
[7] One unit war diary records that this day four bottles of beer were issued "one of which is free—a gift from the Government for being in action on V-E Day".
[8] Lt C. D. Simper, SX21753. 43 and 2/48 Bns. Blacksmith; of Rosewater, SA; b. Clarendon, SA, 28 Apr 1919. Died of wounds 9 Jun 1945.
[9] Writing after the war of patrolling on Tarakan an officer said: "The forward scout was a type. It was found that certain soldiers preferred that task and that plenty volunteered. They were cool, nimble, and quick in employing their weapons. They became excellent at judging ground and recognising enemy positions or likely enemy positions, and could smell the Japanese from great distances."
[1] A prisoner later said that this was in celebration of "Navy Day".

Next day the brigade Intelligence staff warned the units that the enemy might on the 10th-11th attack over Hill 105 towards the airfield. Thereupon food and water were stored in company areas and preparations made to withstand a desperate final attack. At the same time Colonel Warfe issued orders for a general advance into the Fukukaku area if the Japanese moved out towards the airfield or beaches. A half-hearted attack was in fact made in the early morning of the 10th. There was small arms fire for half an hour and a field gun fired 11 rounds. An enemy aircraft arrived overhead and dropped three flares and one bomb. In the 2/48th's area at 3 a.m., when the Japanese aircraft flew over Hill 102 and dropped its bomb, enemy troops, firing their weapons, tried to close in on the platoon holding Wally. They sprang six booby-traps, and that was all. Later that day a platoon of the 2/48th advanced up the Linda feature from the south-east and found five abandoned pill-boxes which were later blown in. This platoon and another which approached from the north found that the enemy was firmly in position on the summit.

> Later a Japanese order for the counter-attack on 10th June was captured: at 3 a.m. on that day all troops were to open fire, the riflemen firing 30 rounds, and then make a desperate attack; seven aircraft were to support the effort. A prisoner captured on 24th June said that he knew of the order, including the mention of 30 rounds, but in fact they had carried out the order "by the firing of 5 rounds only, due to the shortage of ammunition and the appearance of one aircraft only".

In the 2/24th's area the enemy were still holding Sandy and Beech 2, two rugged, jungle-covered bastions of the headquarters fortress. Aircraft struck at these on 11th June but their bombs fell 200 to 300 yards from the target. "D" Company had withdrawn from its positions on Roger during the air strike and the Japanese, aware of this, followed up; the Australians got back to Roger only just in time to re-occupy it and drive the enemy off. Captain Eldridge's company attacked Beech 2, held by some 80 or 90 Japanese, from west and north but could make no progress. Probing on the 12th they found both features still occupied. On the 13th "A" Company found Sandy lightly held and took it, but "C" found Beech 2 still firmly defended. That night there were indications that the Japanese were withdrawing from the Fukukaku area; and early next day a patrol found Beech 2 unoccupied.

The battalions were now far below strength. In the 2/24th, for example, which had had the heaviest losses, only seven of the 12 rifle platoons were commanded by officers and there was a deficiency of 160 riflemen so that most companies were at half strength or less.

Forward of the 2/23rd bombardment was now concentrated on the Joyce feature. On 11th June 46 Liberators had made an accurate strike on targets in the Japanese headquarters area and then for 20 minutes the artillery and a troop of tanks lashed the Joyce feature. A platoon advanced close behind the artillery fire and killed five Japanese who were crouching in their pits, but a second platoon which passed through the first found the enemy still in possession farther on. On 12th June a converging attack on Joyce by two platoons of the 2/23rd failed.

The 2/48th had continued the patrolling of the Linda feature on 11th and 12th June, and on the 13th, after bombardment by artillery, mortars and machine-guns, Lieutenant Johnstone's[2] platoon advanced from Monty and thrust to within 125 yards of the top, but came to a point where further advance was across open ground strewn with fallen trees, and eventually was withdrawn. Lieutenant Macdonald's platoon from the north reached a point 60 yards from the top, but thence the approach was along a razor-back overlooked by the enemy's fortress on the summit.

Thus on the 13th the enemy was resisting strongly. On the morning of the 14th, however, patrols from the 2/24th found that the enemy on their front had made a big withdrawal. The features named Paddy, Melon and Aunty were all abandoned and much equipment lay about. On the other hand a determined force covered the Essie Track, evidently the escape route. In the 2/23rd's sector that morning a party of 87 Indonesians and 25 Chinese came forward with a white flag and a Chinese announced that the Japanese had abandoned the Fukukaku area. They bore a letter from the Japanese commander asking that they be treated well. The 2/23rd probed forward and soon was on the Joyce, Clarice and Hilda features. Eighteen stragglers were killed in the day.

The 2/48th found the Linda feature abandoned that day. On the 15th Nelly was found to be unoccupied; then Faith was taken—a big hill with twelve freshly-dug but empty positions. The platoon moved on from Faith to Dutch but there came under sharp fire from Japanese holding along a front of about 300 yards. Artillery harassed Dutch that night and next day it was found to be unoccupied.

It was learnt soon afterwards that about 8th June Major Tokoi had ordered that the Japanese force would withdraw from the Fukukaku headquarters area in an orderly way with rearguards in position during the thinning out. The force would then split up into a number of independent groups and, within an allotted area, the commander of each would choose the ground on which he and his men would fight to the death. On 13th June Tokoi issued a written order stating that the withdrawal would begin at 4 a.m. on 14th June. The wounded, the translated order said, "will be dealt with so that they will demonstrate the honour of a true soldier, if possible (hara-kiri, suicide, etc.)"; when the withdrawal was complete the main force would take measures to establish liaison. Tokoi ordered that the positions which the Australians named Faith and Nelly were to be held for a week to protect the withdrawal and Essie ridge would be held until further orders. In the event Faith was held for only two days but the withdrawal was greatly helped by this stand.

By 14th June when the pursuit of the defeated garrison opened it was estimated that about 1,000 Japanese were still unaccounted for; a captured document indicated that there were probably 800 effectives.[3]

---

[2] Lt M. Johnstone, VX115724; 2/48 Bn. Buyer, clothing factory; of Mornington, Vic; b. Wodonga, Vic, 7 Nov 1918.

[3] From this time until the end of the campaign, however, just over 1,000 Japanese were killed or captured, and others surrendered later.

At this stage it was estimated that 1,153 had been killed or captured. It was learnt from documents and prisoners that every man had been given a month's supply of rice and the remaining ammunition had been distributed.

Whitehead decided that as the enemy was on the run the pursuit should be pressed hard before they had time to establish themselves in their new positions and, in particular, that the Essie ridge should be attacked from all directions and the forces strengthened on the escape routes leading north from Essie. The forward troops of the 2/23rd and 2/24th were now advancing along the southern end of Essie ridge, and to the east the 2/48th was trying to force its way through the difficult country between Essie and Lanky.

On 14th June Lieutenant Cameron's[4] company of the 2/24th got astride the Essie Track, but the Japanese, determined to keep their escape route open, counter-attacked heavily. After a long fight the company, short of ammunition, withdrew from Essie ridge, having killed probably 23 Japanese. Next day Shattock's and Cameron's companies moved against Essie while Eldridge advanced to Short to cut the escape route to the north. Shattock, pushing swiftly down Essie ridge, ran into the heaviest fire his company had so far encountered on Tarakan, but they pressed on fast. Eldridge's company covered 2,500 yards "over razor-backed ridges, through dense undergrowth and across a knee-deep swamp"; Shattock's advanced 2,000 yards "over extremely difficult country"—"a meritorious effort", wrote the diarist.

The mopping up of Fukukaku was completed on the 16th, when 46 dead had been counted. On Essie ridge the 2/24th had found two dismantled 75's, 290 75-mm shells fused as grenades, and 87 other mines and grenades. The clashes with small groups of Japanese on this day and the next confirmed that the independent groups which had broken out of the Essie area were widely spread and were heading mainly north and east.

The role of the 2/48th, with a company of the 2/3rd Pioneers and a platoon of the N.E.I. force under command, was now to prevent the enemy from escaping east from Essie. At dusk on the 16th a patrol reported having found the tracks of perhaps 100 Japanese who had moved east across the Lanky-Hopeful track and had leaped the main track to avoid leaving footprints on it. As a result of this indication of a main escape route Captain Johnson's company was summoned from a picture show and hurriedly transported in L.C.M's to the Amal River on the east coast, and arrangements were made to ship Colonel Ainslie's tactical headquarters and a second company to the Amal next morning.

When Ainslie and the second company arrived at the Amal he learnt that Johnson had advanced without incident to the Binalatung River and consequently took his group on to that point by water. There was no contact with the enemy in the area that day.

---

[4] Lt A. Cameron, NX4714. 2/3 and 2/24 Bns. Clerk; of Cooma, NSW; b. Glenbrook, NSW, 28 Feb 1918.

The main body of the 2/48th pursued the Japanese who were escaping eastward from Essie and on the 18th caught a few but there were indications that the large group had split up into smaller parties, at least some of which probably intended to escape to the mainland: on 18th June a patrol in an L.C.M., when off Cape Juata, saw clothing hanging out to dry on the shore, landed, and found a raft, six sets of clothing and other gear, but not the owners.

By 19th June patrols were radiating east, north and west in pursuit, and at a few points Japanese were standing firm. The 2/4th Commando Squadron was held at Hill 90 and Eldridge's company of the 2/24th by a strong position west of Hill 90. Eldridge asked for artillery fire, and when he was asked how much said 2,000 rounds plus mortar fire. On the 20th after the artillery had fired 2,100 rounds and the mortars 600 the company took Hill 90 and found indications that about 200 Japanese had been driven out by the bombardment; soon afterwards patrols of the 2/4th Commando heard sounds of many Japanese moving north-east from this position.[5]

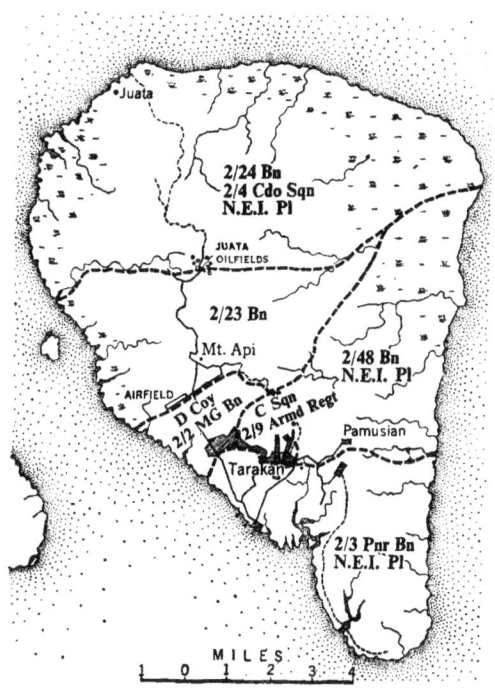

The capture of Hill 90 ended the last of organised resistance on Tarakan (wrote the diarist of the 2/24th). For 51 days the enemy had contested every yard of the approaches to Fukukaku and only on the virtual wiping out of his effective fighting troops did he cease resistance.

Farther north a patrol of the 2/24th clashed with a large enemy party on Snake and on 21st June the 2/24th attacked and took Snake after heavy artillery fire.

By 24th June 1,131 Japanese had been killed and 58 taken prisoner. It was estimated that about 250 armed effectives remained—an underestimate, as will be seen. For the mopping-up stage Whitehead now divided

---

[5] The expenditure of ammunition of the following four types on Tarakan was:
.303-inch . . 862,489
25-pounder HE . 35,384
3-inch mortar HE . 27,030
3.7-inch AA HE . 5,400

the island into six areas of responsibility as shown in the accompanying sketch. The plan was to continue to pursue the surviving Japanese, not allowing them to establish themselves anywhere or to move any food and ammunition to secluded places. There was evidence that some Japanese were making rafts on the northern and eastern coasts and the units in those areas were ordered to press on fast and prevent these Japanese from escaping. The troops were instructed to avoid casualties. On 24th June one L.C.M. began to patrol the narrow straits between Tarakan and the mainland, and another to patrol the waters off the east coast. In addition P.T. boats operated at night between Tarakan and the neighbouring islands.

The barges of the 2/3rd Pioneers were each manned by an officer and 11 other ranks, plus a crew provided by the American 593rd Engineer Boat and Shore Regiment. These barge patrols killed 78 and took 54 prisoners; one patrol took 20 prisoners in one day.

> A patrol under Lieutenant McLean[6] sighted a craft [several miles north of Tarakan] with three naked Japs aboard. . . . A burst was fired over their heads and signs made to them to surrender. They ignored the warning and continued paddling. On a second burst being fired the Jap in the centre of the craft picked up a grenade and beckoned his two companions over to him. All three knelt in the centre with their heads touching. The centre man then carefully tapped the grenade on the craft and held it under their heads. They remained in this attitude quite some time patiently waiting to join their ancestors, but the grenade was Japanese made. It failed to explode. They carefully replaced the grenade and the two paddlers calmly returned to their task. A third and final warning burst was fired, and, when they ignored it too, they were shot. A search of the craft revealed "no clothing, no food, no water and no loot".[7]

The main immediate task was now to pursue the Japanese retreating towards the Maia and Selajong Rivers in the north. Patrols of the 2/24th Battalion which had the big northern sector were slowed down by the difficult country and by enemy rearguards. On 25th June two companies of the 2/23rd passed through the depleted 2/24th and thrust northward, one company along the line of the Maia River and the other along the Selajong. By the end of the month these companies had reached the coast having overcome many groups 30 to 40 strong and generally engaged in building rafts. Other raft builders were found by the 2/48th round the Amal and Binalatung Rivers.

The 2/3rd Pioneers, patrolling the country south of John's Track found many parties on the high ground above Districts IV and VI, evidently survivors of a group pursued by the 2/48th from the Binalatung River. A company of the 2/23rd was sent into this area and in three days killed or captured 30; about 60 were killed or captured in the area south of John's Track.

The advance to the Maia and Selajong Rivers caused the Japanese there to scatter, some south, some east and some west to Cape Juata where

---

[6] Lt K. C. McLean, VX110427; 2/3 Pnr Bn. Farmer; of Galaquil East, Vic; b. Warracknabeal, Vic, 15 Aug 1916.

[7] From an interview obtained by Lieutenant W. N. Prior, Military History Section, in 1945.

they were intercepted by an N.E.I. platoon. From 20th June to the end of July the L.C.M. patrols and the crews of P.T. boats killed or captured 117 Japanese found on rafts or clinging to floating logs. Some of these rafts were substantial craft able to carry as many as ten men fully equipped, and as a rule they were camouflaged with bushes so that they resembled the little "floating islands" swept out to sea by flooded rivers. Although the gap between Tarakan and the adjoining islands was only about a mile the strong current made it almost impossible for a raft to cover the distance. Aircraft searched for rafts early each morning. The 2/2nd Machine Gun Battalion manned several prahus which patrolled the coast and the estuaries and surprised many small parties of Japanese. Carrier pigeons were used for communication with this seaborne force. So strong was the determination of some Japanese to escape that they would fight back from their rafts with rifles and grenades against heavily armed craft.

After the first week of July it became evident that the surviving Japanese were becoming very short of food, and were stealthily moving back from the north to their old defence systems such as Fukukaku and Essie, to native villages, and even Australian camps in search of food. Soon about 20 Japanese were being killed each day in these areas. As hunger increased more Japanese surrendered, some bearing pamphlets dropped by Auster aircraft or left on the tracks by patrols.

On 30th July a patrol of the 2/2nd Machine Gun Battalion led by Lieutenant Walter[8] followed a very indistinct track over the Butch feature. Suddenly Walter found himself looking at a Japanese pointing a rifle at him from five yards away and struggling to pull the trigger. Walter fired one shot from the hip and killed the Japanese. A second Jap then ran out of a concealed bunker and Walter shot him on the run. It was found that the safety catch of the rifle of the first Japanese was still applied. A further patrol in the same area found three more Japanese and killed two. These Japanese had stored away enough food to last the five of them for at least two months. It consisted mainly of Australian canned foods including tins of boiled sweets from Australian Comforts Fund parcels that had recently arrived.

From 22nd June to 14th August Australian losses were 9 killed and 27 wounded, while 418 Japanese were killed and about 200 captured—about 350 more than were believed to be effective when this period opened. The prisoners were surprised at the gentleness with which they were treated and it was evident that one reason why they had been unwilling to surrender was a belief that they would be killed or tortured. But this was certainly not the main reason. In July 1945 19 Japanese prisoners on Morotai were asked a series of questions by American Intelligence men. All said that they considered that surrender was disgraceful; having been prisoners, they could never return to Japan, and they would like to settle in America, Australia or China. Seventeen said that they thought they would be killed if they surrendered and the same number said that

---

[8] Lt P. R. Walter, SX22394; 2/2 MG Bn. Farmer; of Glenelg, SA; b. Glenelg, 17 Sep 1917.

they did not believe the propaganda pamphlets that were dropped to them. Fifteen said that they thought Japan would not win the war, but 17 would not answer the question: "Do you think Japan will lose the war?" The interrogators thought that they all believed that Japan would fight to the last man and win a spiritual victory.

By July, although patrolling continued and a few Japanese were being killed or captured every day, a majority of the troops were engaged in re-training, camp improvements and other peaceful tasks. The 2/24th opened classes for N.C.O's on 9th July. On 14th July the army census aimed at assisting post-war rehabilitation was taken and "made troops think deeply of their post-war plans". By 19th July the camp of the 2/24th was equipped with electric light, a beer garden with tables, chairs and, in the centre, a tiled floor, a concert stage, "162 signs", and a reconstructed house as a headquarters. The 2/7th Field Regiment had an art club, with two instructors, and a mathematics class; and four men were at work on a regimental history. The 2/24th had been criticised for having brought to Tarakan band instruments, a piano, and a saw-milling plant. However, all was forgiven in this period when the battalion was supplying sawn timber far and wide, training mill workers, and providing band music.

Late in July began the departure to Australia for demobilisation of men with at least five years' service, including at least two overseas. In a few weeks the 2/23rd, for example, sent away 7 officers including 3 company commanders, and 70 other ranks; the 2/7th Field Regiment soon lacked 13 officers and about one-third of those who remained had joined in July or August; the 2/24th had only 24 officers of whom 8 were newly-arrived reinforcements; the 2/48th had only 5 officers above the rank of lieutenant.

The Tarakan campaign was in some ways unique so far as Australian experience went and it produced some interesting problems.

Whitehead and his staff considered that too large an air force component had been included in the assault convoy, and after the operation Whitehead wrote that the air force component had had little or no experience of slimming to assault scales, and with its impedimenta caused serious difficulties in the allotment of the force to the available shipping, as well as greatly embarrassing the force, and especially the engineers, on landing. The army staff considered that all R.A.A.F. vehicles were too heavily laden and laden to some extent with stores not essential in the assault phase. This led to bogging of vehicles and increased the wear and tear on roads.

The size and complexity of the force, with its 13,000 troops and 5,000 men of the R.A.A.F. under command, threw a heavy burden on the small staff, which had functions more like those of a divisional than a brigade staff. Both the brigade major, Katekar,[9] and the staff captain,

---

[9] Maj H. J. Katekar, SX3079. 2/27 Bn; BM 6 and 26 Bdes. Solicitor; of Renmark, SA; b. Mile End, SA, 24 Aug 1914.

Geddes,[1] were thoroughly experienced in those appointments, but their tasks in this operation resembled those usually performed by a G.S.O.1 and A.A. & Q.M.G.

Before, during and after the landing the operations were dependent on the engineers to an unusual degree. The roads were mined and the engineers had to discover where the mines were. The ground was so boggy that roads could not be built away from the existing roadways and, particularly in the early days, repair and maintenance of roads crowded with heavy vehicles demanded great effort. There was no rock or gravel on the island and the only metal that could be obtained for road building came from the concrete foundations and floors of demolished buildings. The lack of hard standings resulted in vehicles being parked on the verge of roads where they broke the edges away.

The infantry had fought with great skill and determination. After the New Guinea campaign in 1943 and 1944 many of the older men had left the battalions as a result of wounds or illness and the ranks of the rifle companies had been filled up with young soldiers mainly aged about 19; and it was often these who led the advance as forward scouts and faced the enemy from forward section posts.

In such thickly-wooded country, with its steep slopes and sharp spurs, control of supporting weapons presented problems. However, complete confidence existed between the infantry leaders and the forward observation officers of the 2/7th Field Regiment. The gunners brought down remarkably accurate fire, often at the risk of tree bursts over the heads of the leading sections.

With accurate fire support from field guns, machine-guns, tanks and aircraft—and providing that ammunition was available—company commanders relied on blasting the enemy from their positions and on manoeuvring to the rear of their diggings rather than on head-on assault. These tactics took time to execute, specially in such tangled country. It was, however, easier than in New Guinea to pinpoint positions on the map because the Dutch had surveyed the island very accurately and placed many survey pegs along the tracks.

In the whole Australian force 14 officers and 211 others were killed and 40 officers and 629 others wounded.[2] When fighting ceased 1,540 Japanese dead had been counted and 252 had surrendered; more than 300 surrendered after the cease fire.

The main object of the Tarakan operation was to establish an air base from which to support later operations in Borneo. The airfield proved so difficult to repair that it was not ready in time for the opening of the

---

[1] Lt-Col J. O. Geddes, MBE, ED, SX2725. 9 Cav Regt and 26 Bde. Business manager; of Port Pirie, SA; b. Port Pirie, 13 Oct 1914.

[2] The battle casualties in the following units of the force were:

	Officers	OR's		Officers	OR's
2/23rd Battalion	11	147	2/4th Commando Squadron	4	52
2/24th Battalion	15	283	Squadron 2/9th Armoured		
2/48th Battalion	9	164	Regiment	1	13
2/2nd Machine Gun Battalion	—	5	2/7th Field Regiment	3	24
2/2nd Pioneer Battalion	1	11	Engineers	—	24
2/3rd Pioneer Battalion	6	88			

operation against either Brunei Bay or Balikpapan, and fighter cover for those landings was provided from Tawitawi and from aircraft carriers. Thus events demonstrated that the role allotted to the Tarakan airfield, which was strongly defended, could be performed by the Tawitawi airfield, which, with Jolo Island, had been taken by American forces without opposition early in April. Another reason why, in retrospect, the choice of Tarakan as an objective seems unfortunate is that it was an island from which the defenders had no means of withdrawal, and, since they would not surrender, they sold their lives dearly. The Australian losses on Tarakan were nearly as high as those suffered by the 6th Australian Division in the conquest of Cyrenaica early in 1941.

CHAPTER 19

OBOE SIX OPENS

WHILE the Japanese were launching their final, hopeless counter-attack against the 26th Brigade in the hills above Tarakan town the remainder of the 9th Division was landing in north Borneo. Its tasks were "to secure the Brunei Bay area of north Borneo, to permit establishment of an advanced fleet base, and to protect oil and rubber resources therein".

Brunei Bay is the best harbour on the north-west coast of Borneo. It is about 30 miles by 30 and protected by a group of islands across the northern entrance, the largest being Labuan, a triangular piece of land with sides 8 to 12 miles long. Labuan town had a population, before the war, of 8,500 and possessed some port facilities; the Japanese had made two airfields on the island. Except for about 1,500 yards of beach in Victoria Harbour (named Brown Beach for staff purposes) and a few small beaches elsewhere, the island was surrounded by reefs. On the mainland about 25 miles east of Labuan was the town of Weston from which a light railway ran north-east through Beaufort to Jesselton, 55 miles away, and at this time the site of the headquarters of the *XXXVII Japanese Army*. The main network of communication was formed, however, not by the roads and railway but by the rivers: the Papar, Klias, Padas, Trusan, Pandaruan, Limbang, Belait and Baram.

At the southern tip of Brunei Bay was Muara Island, low-lying and scrub-covered. On the south-east of the island were two beaches that were considered suitable landing places ("White" and "Red" Beaches). On the eastern point of the Brunei peninsula near Brooketon were two more beaches ("Green" and "Yellow") that were suitable for landing craft. From Brooketon a road travelled to Brunei, a town of some 12,000 people, and onwards to the coast at Tutong, and thence, skirting the shore, to the oilfields of Seria, Kuala Belait and Miri. Inland from this road the coastal plain was often swampy; a few miles from the shore the high, jungle-covered mountains began to rise.

There were three main elements in the population of north Borneo apart from the Japanese troops and the Indonesians and other civilians they had imported: the indigenous people popularly known as Dyaks,[1] who occupied the mountain country and parts of the coast; the Malays; and the Chinese of whom when the war began there were some 50,000 in British Borneo. Most of these people and in particular the Chinese and the Dyaks of the mountains were ill-disposed towards the Japanese, who had treated the townspeople harshly and had failed to reorganise an economy that had been upset by the isolation of Borneo from its usual markets.

The Japanese had conscripted many people as labourers and had bought food and other produce at low prices. Imports ceased, and the people, dependent on imported rice, in return for which they had formerly exported rubber, began to go hungry. Many Chinese buried their valuables and went farming. The inland people retreated farther into the mountains to get away from Japanese interference. In October 1943 Chinese, helped by Dyaks, carried out a well-organised rebellion, took Jesselton and held it until driven out by Japanese forces. This led to the execution of hundreds of Chinese by the Japanese, and to harsher treatment of the civilians generally, with the result that many died of disease and malnutrition.[2]

The mountainous interior of Borneo, peopled as it was by warlike tribesmen who greatly respected the British and disliked and mistrusted the Japanese, provided suitable conditions for guerilla warfare and the establishment of Intelligence parties. Long before OBOE SIX opened small parties mainly led by British officers who had worked in Borneo before the war had been at large in the interior. Among the leaders that were to be in touch with the Australians was Major Chester[3] who, with others of the "Services Reconnaissance Department", was landed from a submarine in British Borneo in October 1943 to report on shipping in the sea lanes between there and the Sulu Archipelago, and send out other Intelligence. This they did with considerable success. Later Major W. T. Jinkins (who had escaped from Ambon after the capture of the 2/21st Battalion there in February 1942) was also landed in east Borneo from a submarine to establish a coastwatching station. As an outcome of the success of these ventures, Jinkins and 10 others were attached to the American submarine force to assist in the rescue of airmen, the evacuation of people from enemy territory, and close reconnaissance of shipping.

Chester, who had been withdrawn in June 1944, was again landed in Borneo on the night of 3rd-4th March, leading a party including three other officers and three N.C.O's. They were landed from the American submarine *Tuna* at Labuk Bay. Their task, like that of later parties, was to establish a base on the east coast of British Borneo, set up a native Intelligence network, giving particular importance to information about the

---

[1] "Dyak" is a derogatory name used by the other peoples of Borneo to describe several distinct but related tribes

[2] See M. Hall, *Kinabalu Guerrillas* (Kuching, 1949).

[3] Lt-Col F. G. L. Chester, DSO, OBE; SRD. Planter; of Borneo; b. Johannesburg, South Africa, 14 Jun 1899. Died 18 Aug 1946.

prisoner camp at Sandakan, and ultimately to "organise such armed resistance by the natives as might be authorised by G.H.Q."

Chester's party, after establishing wireless contact with Australia, reconnoitred the coast and rivers in the Paitan River area in folboats, and soon Chester, who travelled 250 miles by folboat in this phase, had made contact with numbers of native people who knew him. About 10th April

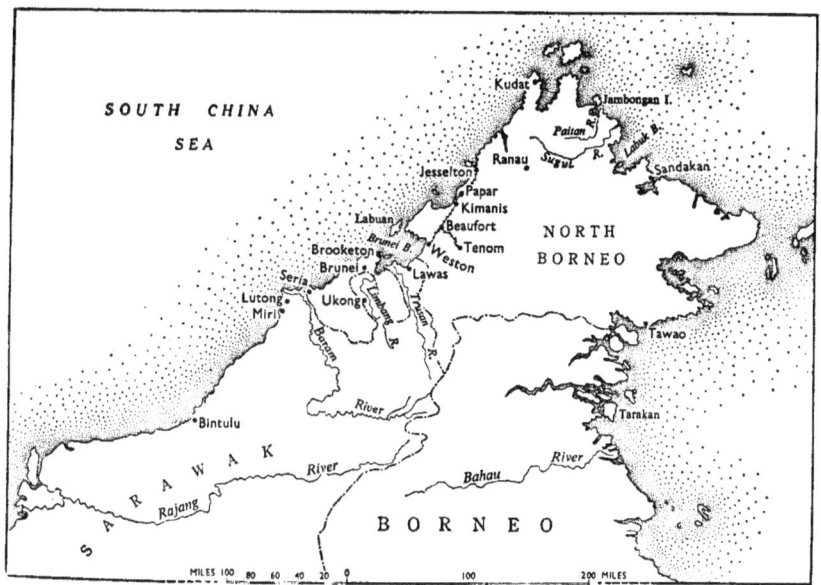

a new base was established at Jambongan Island, where stores were dropped on 20th April. On 3rd May a second group was brought in including a Chinese medical officer. By 20th May several native guerilla forces had been established. A party under Lieutenant Harlem[4] had moved into the interior and found an area for a new headquarters, and a native Intelligence network was in working order. Information sent out by the group had resulted in several destructive air raids. Chester was taken to Morotai by Catalina on 21st May to be interrogated by Intelligence officers, and it was decided to send a party into the Beaufort-Jesselton area. In consequence Chester and three others were "inserted" near Kimanis on 24th May.

Another group, led by Major Harrisson,[5] a British anthropologist who had worked in Borneo, parachuted into an upland valley some 90 miles south-east of Brunei on 25th March; a third, under Major Carter,[6] was

---

[4] Lt D. A. L. Harlem, SX1719. 2/48 Bn and "Z" Special Unit. Clerk; of Adelaide; b. St Kilda, Vic, 31 Aug 1920.
[5] Maj T. H. Harrisson, DSO, OBE; SRD. Anthropologist; of London; b. 26 Sep 1911.
[6] Lt-Col G. S. Carter, DSO; SRD. Surveyor; of Brisbane; b. Auckland, NZ, 20 Apr 1910. Carter had been an oil surveyor in Borneo.

inserted farther south in the Baram River basin on 16th April; and a fourth under Major Sochon[7] on the Rajang River in southern Sarawak. These groups, when reinforced, were each up to 50 strong, mostly Australian.

In Sarawak Harrisson was given a warm welcome and during his first day more than 500 natives had collected round him. This party established a headquarters in the mountains. After reinforcements had landed he had seven parties in the field and some 300 rifles had been distributed to natives in the river valleys from the Limbang in the west to the Bahau. In each valley a European with 15 to 25 locally-recruited "regulars" controlled a varying number of guerillas. By July the several parties had the support of more than 1,000 armed natives. An airfield was cleared in a valley in the interior and aircraft landed with men and supplies.[8]

News had reached Australia of the desperate situation of the prisoners of war in Borneo and the A.I.B. parties were given the additional task of examining the possibility of rescuing them. One such party under Flight Lieutenant G. C. Ripley, R.A.A.F., was put ashore in the Ranau area on 23rd June and at length it collected four escaped prisoners—four of the only six survivors of 2,512 who had been at Sandakan.[9]

The Japanese garrisons in Borneo were part of the *XXXVII Army* (Lieut-General Masao Baba) and were believed to include the *56th Independent Mixed Brigade* in north Borneo, the *71st Independent Mixed Brigade* in south Borneo probably with headquarters at Kuching, and perhaps the *25th Independent Regiment* at Jesselton. There were indications that the north-eastern tip of the island was being evacuated and a general westward movement of troops was in progress. The total strength of the Japanese Army forces in Borneo was believed to be 31,000. Detailed information about the enemy's deployment was at first scanty. Finally, by late May the Intelligence staffs placed about 650 Japanese on Labuan, 1,550 on the Brunei peninsula and about Seria and Miri, 6,600 round Jesselton. The main fighting units in the area to be attacked were believed to be the above-mentioned *56th Independent Mixed Brigade* of six battalions—*366th* to *371st*—and a seventh independent battalion. Of the battalions the *367th* was believed to be at Brunei, the *368th* about Beaufort, and the others moving south from Jesselton.

It was expected that although the enemy would not defend the beaches, he would fight hard to hold the Brunei Bay and oilfields areas; there were reports from natives suggesting that he might eventually withdraw inland to Ranau and Ukong and make stands at those places. The possibility of a raid by light naval forces had to be taken into account—there were

---

[7] Maj W. L. P. Sochon, DSO. SRD and BBCAU. Prison governor (formerly Asst Commissioner, Armed Constabulary and Prisons, Sarawak); of Portland, Dorset, England; b. London, 25 Dec 1904.

[8] See T. Harrisson, "The Chinese in Borneo", *International Affairs*, July 1950; and *World Within, A Borneo Story* (1959).

[9] The recovery of prisoners of war from Borneo is described in L. Wigmore, *The Japanese Thrust* (1957), in this series.

believed to be two or three cruisers and five destroyers in the Singapore-Netherlands Indies area. And since there were some 12 enemy aircraft in Borneo and 340 in the Indies, Malaya, Thailand and Indo-China harassing night attacks were considered possible.

The 9th Australian Division had returned to Australia in March 1944 after taking part in the New Guinea offensives of 1943-44, and had spent twelve months resting and retraining on the Atherton Tableland before its units began to embark for Morotai in March 1945. Its active service had now been most varied: North African campaigns, amphibious operations in New Guinea, and long and arduous jungle fighting there. The divisional and brigade commanders and four of the six infantry battalion commanders who were to serve in north Borneo had served in the same appointments during all or part of the New Guinea operations, and a majority of the troops were veterans of one, two or three campaigns. In its recent training it had concentrated particularly on jungle craft, warfare in open or semi-open country, amphibious warfare and advanced-guard tactics.

At the Manila conference in April General Morshead had learnt that OBOE ONE (Tarakan), OBOE SIX (north Borneo) and OBOE TWO (Balikpapan) were to be carried out in that order. Thirty-four L.S.T's would be allotted for OBOE SIX but had to be released by 23 days after the landing. There were other fairly severe restrictions on the vessels available: the one boat battalion of the American Engineer Boat and Shore Regiment and the one amphibian tractor battalion allotted to OBOE SIX had to be used for Balikpapan.

Morshead and his staff arrived back at Morotai from Manila on 21st April and next day the Corps issued its staff study of the north Borneo operation, and the 9th Division's staff, which from 4th to 17th April had been planning an operation against Balikpapan, began preparing an outline plan for an attack on Brunei Bay instead. This was presented to Corps and approved on 26th April; the final plan, which contained no major changes, was approved on 16th May (and will be outlined later).

Meanwhile a variety of problems had arisen at the Corps level and above. On 1st May 2,200 troops and 1,200 vehicles (including guns) of the 9th Division were still in the Cairns or Atherton areas awaiting shipment, and some of the stores and equipment were not scheduled to arrive at Morotai until 25th May, two days after the proposed date of the landing. MacArthur's headquarters were informed of this on 3rd May and on the 5th replied that the target date must be adhered to, but representatives of I Corps were required to visit G.H.Q. with alternative plans.

At that stage it appeared that, on the day of the landing, the 24th Brigade would lack some unit stores and vehicles, and the 20th Brigade would possess only one battalion; there would be no field or anti-aircraft guns, a shortage of signal vehicles and equipment, no equipment for building wharves and bulk oil storage, and neither of the casualty clearing stations allotted would be present. Morshead decided to recommend to G.H.Q. that the operation be reduced to the landing of a brigade on Labuan and only a battalion on Muara Island. To do even this it would be necessary to form a composite field artillery regiment by withdrawing a battery from Tarakan and supplementing it with 4.2-inch mortars, 75-mm pack howitzers and short 25-pounders (the latter being flown from Australia). Brigadier H. Wells, General Morshead's senior staff officer, went to Manila with this proposal on 7th May. Next day it was decided, in Manila, to postpone north Borneo until 10th June, and, tentatively, Balikpapan until 10th July. On 17th May, however, G.H.Q. informed Morshead that the Balikpapan operation would open on 1st not 10th July.

This reduction in the period between the two operations introduced new complications because certain units and equipment were required for both. Ultimately one amphibian tractor battalion was allotted to north Borneo; and, to Balikpapan, one company from another such battalion plus one company from the north Borneo battalion, after its release from that operation the day after the landing. The five A.P.D's allotted had to be returned to Morotai by 20th June and thus would not be available for coastwise operations that were being planned. Components of a squadron of tanks of the 2/1st Armoured Regiment were divided between both operations.

With its added corps troops, base troops, and R.A.A.F. units totalling 5,700, the force commanded by Major-General Wootten of the 9th Division totalled over 29,000.[1] The naval forces in the Naval Attack Force (Vice-Admiral Daniel E. Barbey), including the 6th Amphibious Group (Rear-Admiral Royal) and the Cruiser Covering Force (Rear-Admiral Berkey) possessed 3 cruisers (including H.M.A.S. *Hobart*) and 23 destroyers (including H.M.A.S. *Arunta*), 3 frigates (H.M.A.S. *Hawkesbury, Barcoo* and *Lachlan*), 12 motor torpedo boats, three Australian L.S.I's—*Westralia, Manoora, Kanimbla*—one A.K.A., one L.S.D., 7 A.P.D's,[2] 35 L.S.T's, 55 L.C.I's, 21 L.S.M's and a number of other, mostly smaller, vessels.

The minesweeping and survey units of the naval force were to begin operations three days before the landing. General air support in the preparatory and assault phases was to be given by five heavy-bomber squadrons, a fighter and an attack wing of the R.A.A.F., three bomber and one fighter groups of the U.S.A.A.F.; and a wing of the air force of the United States Marines. They were to attack airfields and other military targets, and, in particular, to destroy bridges on the railway to Jesselton to prevent reinforcements being brought to Labuan by rail.

---

[1]
9th Division	14,079
I Corps troops	3,726
Base Sub-Area	4,730
RAAF	5,729
US and UK units	1,097
	29,361

[2] Destroyer-transports.

By 30th May bombers had made the Papar River bridge unusable and thus cut this line. At length seven squadrons and other detachments from the 1st Tactical Air Force of the R.A.A.F. were to be established on Labuan Island.

The order of battle as set out in the division's report occupies 14 typewritten pages. In brief the force comprised eight main groups and they included the following principal units:

> 20th Brigade Group (Brigadier W. J. V. Windeyer)—2/13th, 2/15th, 2/17th Battalions; 2/8th Field Regiment.
> 24th Brigade Group (Brigadier S. H. W. C. Porter)—2/28th, 2/43rd Battalions; 2/11th Commando Squadron; 2/12th Field Regiment.
> Divisional reserve—2/32nd Battalion; 2/12th Commando Squadron.
> 1st Base Sub-Area—2/3rd Composite Anti-Aircraft Regiment less a battery, and 71 other units and detachments.
> 1st Beach Group—2/4th Pioneer Battalion and 30 other units or detachments.
> American units—727th Amphibian Tractor Battalion, a boat company of the 593rd Engineer Boat and Shore Regiment, and other detachments.
> British units—B.B.C.A.U., and S.R.D. (guerilla) detachments.
> R.A.A.F. units—1st T.A.F. and component units.

Appropriate detachments of the 2/9th Armoured Regiment, 2/2nd Machine Gun Battalion, engineers, signals, Army Service Corps and so on, and of the American landing craft units were distributed among the groups.

The landing at Victoria Harbour (Brown Beach), at 9.15 a.m. on 10th June, was to be made by the 24th Brigade on a two-battalion front, with the 2/43rd on the right and 2/28th on the left. Its tasks were to secure a beach-head, and a covering position to protect a beach maintenance area, capture the Labuan airfield, destroy all hostile forces on the island, and prepare for future operations in the Mempakul-Weston-Beaufort-Papar area.

On the south shore, the 20th Brigade was to land the 2/17th Battalion on Green Beach and the 2/15th on White Beach on Muara Island, reported to be held by the enemy. The brigade's initial tasks were to secure these beach-heads, capture Brooketon and the southern and western sides of Muara Island, exploit forward on the road to Brunei, seize Yellow Beach and land heavy equipment there, send a detachment including a troop of field guns in small craft to seize a position on the banks of the Brunei River to support the overland advance on Brunei, and advance on Brunei town.

After the capture of these objectives further operations would be undertaken to establish the above-mentioned air forces, occupy and defend the Brunei Bay-Beaufort area, seize and hold the Miri-Lutong-Seria areas and protect radar installations and oil and rubber resources therein, and, in general, re-establish British civil government in the occupied area.

The naval fire program and the air force bombing program for the Borneo landings had interesting features. In earlier landings the naval ships bombarded the fringe of jungle beyond the beaches, from which the enemy had usually withdrawn. Wootten, however, obtained agreement to a timed program of concentrations of naval fire which would creep inland ahead of the advancing infantry. At Brunei Bay, as at Tarakan, the area to be seized was gridded, the grid squares on Labuan Island being 300 yards, and naval and air bombardment was directed on to a grid square rather than a feature.

10th June

Such an arrangement was not accomplished without the ironing out of opposing views (wrote Brigadier Porter later). In particular, the R.A.A.F. planning staff officers questioned the wisdom of offering pilots or bomb aimers a target which consisted of "squares drawn on a map". They demanded something which could be seen to "go up in flames" when successfully engaged. Air Commodore Scherger[3] eventually saw the possibility of combining both on occasions, and of yielding to Army claims that bombs which appeared to be dropped on tree tops were often of more value than those dropped upon abandoned houses.

---

[3] Air Marshal Sir Frederick Scherger, KBE, CB, DSO, AFC. Director of Training RAAF 1938-40, 1942-43; Comd RAAF Stn, Darwin 1942-43; AOC 10 Group 1943-44, 1st TAF 1945. AOC RAF Malaya 1953-55; Chief of the Air Staff 1957-61; Chairman, Chiefs of Staff Committee since 1961. Regular air force officer; b. Ararat, Vic, 18 May 1904.

(*Australian War Memorial*)
Looking across Snags Track to the Elbow feature, Tarakan Island, 21st May 1945.

(*Australian War Memorial*)
A patrol of the 2/24th Battalion moving out on 21st June to make contact with the 2/4th Commando Squadron after the capture of Hill 90, Tarakan, on the 20th.

(U.S. Army Signal Corps)
Men of the 24th Brigade landing on Labuan Island from an L.C.I. on 10th June 1945.

(U.S. Army Signal Corps)
L.V.T's landing troops of the 20th Brigade Group on Muara Island on 10th June.

In the operations against Tarakan, British Borneo and Balikpapan—the most complex amphibious assaults carried out by Australians in the war—planning involved weeks of work by commanders and staffs who, at this stage, had reached a very high standard of skill; it demanded exact and detailed coordination between not only the arms and services (now multitudinous) of the army but also between the army, navy and air force.

For many of the troops the rehearsals at Morotai, the period after embarkation and before sailing, and the voyage itself were as uncomfortable as any experiences that followed. Because of the limited number of ships available it was necessary to load 450 or more of the assault troops into each L.S.T. and 180 to 190 into an L.C.I. At the time the commander of the 2/28th, Lieut-Colonel C. H. B. Norman, wrote a heartfelt account of the experiences of his unit (which was destined to have a heavy share of the fighting). It gives a picture of the kind of trials sometimes endured by troops taking part in amphibious operations requiring long voyages in tropical seas.

LST.637 fully loaded had 488 comprising 471 and USN Beach Party of 17. For these there were: 2 salt shower points, 12 wash basins, 6 latrines. In addition approximately 400 were compelled to sleep under or on top of the vehicles on the troop deck and were NOT allowed on the tank deck. As the ship had taken on one jeep and trailer and one 2½-ton GMC, shut-out vehicles, in addition to the full load of vehicles, conditions on the deck had to be seen to be credited.

On 1 June a dryshod rehearsal was held to check on times for loading LVT(4)s, and to ensure troops knew their craft. On 2 June a rehearsal was held for 24 Aust Inf Bde Assault Teams. Troops were loaded in LVT(4)s and took the water at 0745.

Under crowded conditions—28 to an LVT(4)—with ammunition for LVT guns, battalion ammunition, and battalion support weapons, under trying conditions of heat, they were held in their LVT(4) for 6 hours 35 minutes because USN, owing to craft faults, required the exercise to be repeated. . . .

According to R.M.O's report, 90 per cent were affected in some degree, and some suffered severely. All officers complained of the worst headaches they had ever had, and one or two, as well as a number of troops, had to receive medical attention for heat stroke. . . . Dirty, sweating and tired, with fresh water for drinking only, the troops returned to these overcrowded conditions where the only shade was that which they could get under vehicles, or under ground sheets they had erected over the hot iron deck. . . .

On 4 June the convoy left Morotai and conditions were slightly alleviated by the breeze. Night 4-5 June it commenced to rain, and on and off kept on throughout 5 and 6 June. As there were no drains in the scuppers the decks were soon awash, and conditions for the troops became such that only those who were actually in 2½-ton lorries could keep dry. Naturally these few fortunate ones were not assault troops.

Permission was secured for members to sleep on the tank deck, but these had to be cleared for night emergency drills. The only ray of sunshine was the food. The LST cooks did a splendid job using some US rations to improve our own, but this food had to be eaten in the rain and standing up. The ship's captain and staff did all they could, but the number of troops nullified their efforts.

In almost six years of war the writer has never seen troops subjected to more deplorable conditions, and on 10 June, after a fortnight of inactivity subjected to the full extent of existing climatic conditions, overcrowded, and with far less than minimum adequate sanitary and washing arrangements, they were expected to carry out an assault.

There were 83 ships in the convoy, the command ship *Rocky Mount* (16,700 tons) being by far the largest. On 8th July appeared the escorting ships: the American cruisers *Boise*, *Nashville* and *Phoenix*; the Australian cruiser *Hobart* and the destroyer *Arunta*.

While the convoy was making its 1,100-mile voyage the naval and air forces were preparing for the assault. From 7th to 9th June minesweepers swept a channel into the bay, destroying 69 mines. Air attack became intense on 5th June and reached its height on the 9th when 54 Liberators and 24 Mitchells attacked targets on Labuan, and 23 Liberators attacked the Brooketon area. On 8th and 9th June the cruisers shelled Brown, White and Green Beaches. The convoy arrived at the main channel between Labuan Island and Brunei Bluff before sunrise on 10th June and the ships containing the assault units moved to their areas.

In planning the landings by the 20th Brigade on the right Brigadier Windeyer had to take into account that it was essential to secure Yellow Beach which was the only safe all-weather beach for landing equipment but was not a suitable assault beach, the approach channel being too narrow. Control of Muara Island, reported to be held by the enemy, was essential to the use of Yellow Beach. Consequently Windeyer's plan was to make simultaneous landings on Green and White Beaches. The 2/17th would land on Green and secure a beach-head embracing the area Green Beach—Brunei Bluff—Bukit Cowie; the 2/15th would land on White Beach and secure a

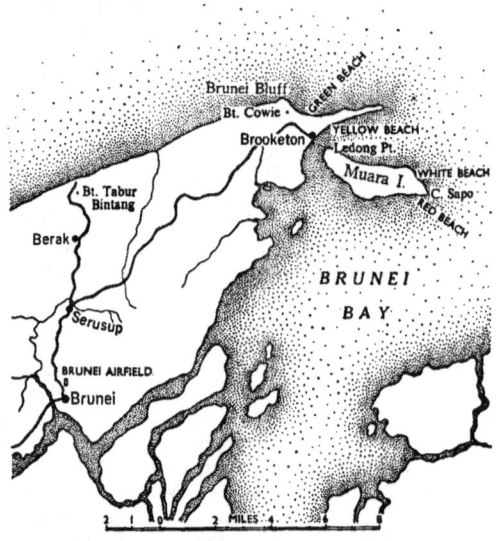

beach-head round Cape Sapo from White Beach to Red inclusive. In the second phase the brigade would take Brooketon and the southern and western side of Muara Island to Ledong Point thus opening Yellow Beach and the approach to Muara Harbour, and exploit along the road to Brunei. In the third phase heavy equipment would be landed on Yellow Beach, a detachment in small craft would be sent to seize a position on the banks of the Brunei River to enable a battery to be landed to support the advance on Brunei, and the infantry would then take Brunei town and secure the area Bukit Tabur Bintang—Berak.

The naval vessels supporting the 20th Brigade opened a bombardment at 8.15 a.m. and the L.S.I. *Kanimbla* carrying the 2/17th Battalion and an L.S.M. with a troop of tanks moved to its area off Green Beach. Landing craft were unloaded from the *Kanimbla* and the assault force assembled in three waves of L.C.V.P's and a fourth and fifth of L.C.M's behind a line of departure 2,250 yards out from Green Beach. At 9.6 a.m. the first wave moved forward, preceded by craft firing rockets and guns. Pillars of smoke were rising from Muara Island and farther south from Brunei. The first wave of the 2/17th beached at 9.18, the first wave of the 2/15th in L.V.T's at 9.15.

There was no opposition, and it did not matter that the 2/17th was put ashore 1,000 yards east of the intended spot. By dusk the 2/15th had searched the swampy Muara Island and found no Japanese. On the mainland the 2/17th met no organised opposition; five Japanese were seen and killed. By dusk the foremost troops were a few miles along the road to Brunei, and the 2/13th had landed and moved into reserve behind the 2/17th.

That night a truck containing eight Japanese drove along the road into the position of the forward company of the 2/17th. The Australians fired with machine-guns, killed seven and captured the eighth, who said to an interpreter that he had heard nothing of a landing; he had heard naval gunfire but had drawn no conclusions.

Next day the 2/17th continued its advance. It moved along the road through a defile three miles long between wooded hills and swamp—an excellent position for defence, but it was not occupied. The troop of tanks was halted by a stream and was left behind.

At 4.20 p.m. the advance-guard of the battalion saw one Japanese, and the two forward scouts fired and wounded him. All the civilians who appeared during the day were as helpful as they could be and seemed happy to see the British returning. For their part the troops were kind and polite to the civilians then and later, and got on well with them. That morning Windeyer ordered Lieut-Colonel C. H. Grace of the 2/15th to send a company in landing craft up the Brunei River, and at 3 p.m. this company landed about four miles downstream from Brunei. Next day (12th June) no Japanese were seen by the 2/17th until the forward troops had passed the road junction near Serusup; there a small party was seen in the distance, and two Indian prisoners of war were recovered. By 1 p.m. the airstrip had been occupied and some Japanese fired from the hills south of it. The leading platoon (Lieutenant Kennedy[4]) attacked and took an enemy post killing three Japanese. A second platoon (Lieutenant Trudgeon[5]) moved through on the right and, briskly attacking through high grass, overcame other posts, killing 12; one Australian was killed and four wounded.

The battalion then established itself near the south end of the strip for the night. In the darkness the Japanese fired a machine-gun and mortar

---

[4] Lt R. E. Kennedy, NX104115; 2/17 Bn. Station hand; of Berridale, NSW; b. Cooma, NSW, 7 May 1921.

[5] Lt M. P. Trudgeon, NX65621; 2/17 Bn. Schoolteacher; of Bonalbo, NSW; b. Bangalow, NSW, 4 Oct 1917.

20th Brigade, June 1945

into the area and small parties tried to infiltrate. The supporting field artillery and naval ships harassed the enemy. Next morning 13 Japanese were seen moving across the strip and all were killed. In the night and early morning two Australians, including Lieutenant Simpson,[6] were killed and three wounded.

That day Windeyer conferred with his battalion commanders and instructed them that the 2/17th would go on to Brunei and then the 2/15th would pass through and advance to Tutong. Meanwhile the company of the 2/15th on the Brunei River would cross the river and block the Limbang Road. At this stage, although opposition had been light, there could be no certainty that the Japanese were not preparing a countermove, possibly from the Limbang area. After aircraft had attacked the Japanese positions facing the 2/17th on 13th June, the enemy was found to have withdrawn. Only small parties of Japanese were encountered by the troops advancing astride the main road, and by a company which entered Brunei town, where one group of seven Japanese made a brave but hopeless charge and were all killed.

Windeyer met Lieut-Colonel J. R. Broadbent at the outskirts of Brunei soon afterwards and put him in charge of the area with orders to clear it of Japanese, prevent looting or disorder by troops or natives, and be prepared to continue the advance. Brunei consisted of an old town of native buildings on stilts in the river and a new town and a number of scattered European-style bungalows, including the British residency, on the left bank of the river. On the flagstaff near the main wharf the Australians hoisted a Union Jack.

In the first four days the 2/17th Battalion had made good its landing, advanced 17 miles into enemy-occupied territory in sweltering weather, fought one short engagement, killed 52 Japanese but met no large-scale opposition. It had control of Brunei town, and soon made contact with a detachment of the 2/15th, landed a little distance below the town.

Later an officer of the *366th Japanese Battalion* who was captured said that the air strikes on the 13th had broken the morale of the battalion, which had hitherto been resolved to defend Brunei to the last.

Brigadier Porter's plan provided that the 24th Brigade should land on Brown Beach and capture a covering position north of No. 1 Strip with a view to securing Labuan port and the airstrip as soon as possible and then preparing for future operations. The operation was to be carried out in three phases. In the first the 2/43rd Battalion on the right with two troops of the 2/9th Armoured Regiment under command would capture the aircraft park; on the left the 2/28th with one troop of tanks under command would take Flagstaff Hill and Labuan. Porter decided that the battle for the main objectives would begin early and therefore artillery, tanks and heavy mortars must be landed very promptly. Consequently two troops of the 2/12th Field Regiment were to be landed

---

[6] Lt G. Simpson, NX4302. 2/3 and 2/17 Bns. Of Arncliffe, NSW; b. Dundee, Scotland, 27 Dec 1914. Killed in action 13 Jun 1945.

with the assaulting infantry in L.V.T's; this had never been attempted before. A troop of 4.2-inch mortars was also to come ashore with the assault waves. The 2/11th Commando Squadron was to be a floating reserve with the probable role of landing on Brown Two Beach and later embarking in L.V.T's and securing Hardy's by an amphibious operation. In Phase Two the 2/43rd would capture No. 1 Strip and secure the area

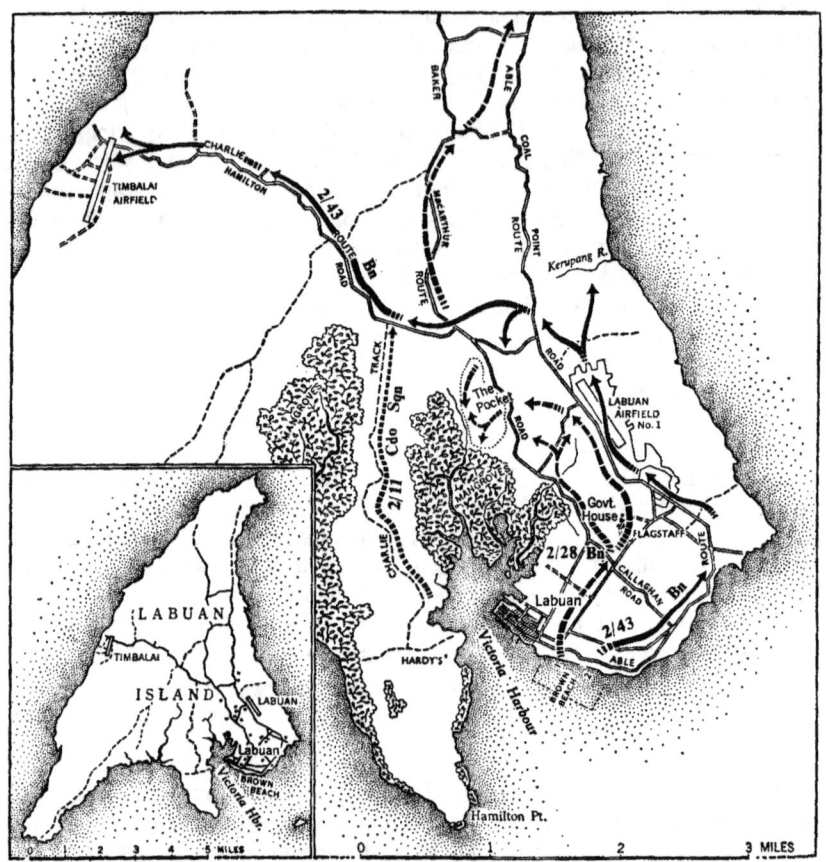

10th-21st June

from the coast at the mouth of the Kerupang River to the western edge of the strip while the 2/28th held an east-west line from the road junction near Government House to MacArthur Road. In the third phase the 2/28th was to advance to a line from the junction of MacArthur and Hamilton Roads to the junction with Charlie Track to the west, and the 2/11th Squadron was to take Hardy's and adjacent minor features.

As a result of this planning the bombardment of the enemy would be continuous. After the preliminary bombardment the naval fire would move inland; 4.2-inch mortars would cover the front until the first 25-pounders were ready for action; and then the 25-pounders would create a curtain of fire behind the naval barrage. As the leading troops moved towards the beach L.C.I's armed with rockets, light guns or mortars would make sweeps towards the shore and rake the beach and the exits from it with fire.

As was expected there was no opposition on the beaches when the two battalions of the 24th Brigade landed. The 2/43rd had its first three waves ashore by 9.20 a.m. and 20 minutes later the supporting troop of tanks landed. Soon refugees began streaming down the road into the town. Two Japanese were killed in a drain by the road just before Generals MacArthur and Morshead and a group of war correspondents and photographers arrived to inspect the scene. In the evening stronger opposition was encountered but swiftly overcome by this battalion, which moved with a speed which gave the enemy no time to recover from the bombardment and mount a counter-attack. Before the end of the day the 2/43rd held the airfield. In the day it killed 23 Japanese and had only 4 of its own men wounded.

On the left the 2/28th landed without mishap at 9.15, one company secured the town, and there was no opposition until 10.45 when the leading troops came under rifle fire just south of Flagstaff Hill. This post was by-passed and Flagstaff Hill was taken in fine style by Captain Lushington's[7] company. Here a Union Jack was found and hoisted. The opposition now increased, particularly on the left. Near the junction of Callaghan and MacArthur Roads a bridge over a canal had been demolished and heavy fire was coming across the open ground ahead. Lieutenant Woodward's[8] platoon made a dashing effort to cross. He and one section were almost across the bridge and the rest of Captain Eastman's[9] company were following when a volley of rifle fire from the high ground beyond hit five men, including Lieutenant Brown[1] of a rear platoon who was killed. Private Parsonage[2] fell wounded on the bridge. Corporal Chivas[3] ran to him but Parsonage could not move and was under accurate fire so Chivas plunged into the canal, shed his equipment, and made his way to company headquarters. He reported to Eastman and returned to his section. Parsonage was hit again and killed.

Private Walters[4] was sent to the left forward platoon to obtain support, and guided a section into position whence it could launch a flank attack. The section leader and three others were hit but Walters attacked alone, killing 5 Japanese with a sub-machine-gun and dispersing others. His

---

[7] Capt A. H. G. Lushington, VX6742. 2/6 and 2/28 Bns. Jackeroo; of Harrow, Vic; b. Ceylon, 22 Oct 1910.
[8] Lt D. P. Woodward, NX125786; 2/28 Bn. Regular soldier; b. Narrabri, NSW, 25 Oct 1913.
[9] Capt E. A. Eastman, WX11016; 2/28 Bn. Clerk; of West Perth; b. Perth, 3 Aug 1916.
[1] Lt B. N. Brown, NX128067; 2/28 Bn. Bank officer; of Artarmon, NSW; b. Rockdale, NSW, 11 Feb 1923. Killed in action 10 Jun 1945.
[2] Pte N. S. Parsonage, NX174154; 2/28 Bn. Tobacco blender; of Leichhardt, NSW; b. Parramatta, NSW, 30 Jun 1924. Killed in action 10 Jun 1945.
[3] Sgt C. W. Chivas, NX110278; 2/28 Bn. Clerk; of Bondi, NSW; b. Bondi, 18 Feb 1923.
[4] Pte R. R. Walters, DCM, WX21015; 2/28 Bn. Bogger; b. Manchester, England, 15 Apr 1920.

ammunition exhausted he pursued these, throwing grenades until he fell wounded, whereupon he shouted directions which enabled the platoon to find the enemy and continue the attack. Around the post that Walters had taken 18 dead were counted. A section of machine-guns and a mortar fired on the ridge held by the Japanese. Colonel Norman ordered forward two tanks which arrived about 2 p.m. and Sergeant Hayes[5] led them to the bridge and directed their fire. While the tanks fired, the two leading platoons advanced up the slope and hunted the Japanese riflemen out. Hayes was killed in this attack, and Corporal Gardoll[6] led the platoon in the final stages. The right flank of the 2/28th was now coming under heavy fire from positions forward of and to the left of Flagstaff Hill and was halted.

Brigadier Porter had intended to use the whole of the 2/11th Commando Squadron (Major Clements[7]) to clear the Hamilton peninsula, but in the course of the morning natives reported that there were no Japanese on the peninsula. Therefore he sent only one troop north along Charlie Track. It met no opposition. That night Porter ordered the 2/28th next day to advance to the "divisional covering position", an east-west line a mile north of the airfield, the 2/43rd to mop-up the area from their boundary with the 2/28th to the coast, and the 2/11th Squadron to stay put.

On the 11th the 2/43rd patrolled north and west and overcame some opposition, but it was evident that the main Japanese force faced the 2/28th. Its two leading companies moved off early in the morning, one to the west of Able route, the other along a spur to Baker route (MacArthur Road) and then along it. They advanced fairly swiftly against sporadic fire which caused nine casualties. By midday the left company was in contact with the 2/43rd. Then trouble began. The right company (Major L. H. Lyon) constantly lost communication with headquarters, and the indications were that it was up against Japanese who were well dug in. Then the left company was held by fire from wooded ridges. Norman decided to hold MacArthur Road—his axis—with a third company while his "B" Company pushed round the enemy. In this way they dislodged the enemy who had been holding them up, but progress this day had been slow and difficult.

By 12th June it seemed that the Japanese were strongly established in a group of positions astride MacArthur Road and to the west of it. It was evident to Porter that the enemy was not retreating across the island but to the left into what appeared to be a natural stronghold. Rather than attack this immediately Porter ordered both battalions to patrol with the object of mounting an attack supported by artillery and tanks. Patrols of the 2/43rd found that, except for one position about

---

[5] Sgt R. P. Hayes, WX14845; 2/28 Bn. Department manager; of Swanbourne, WA; b. Wallaroo, SA, 28 Nov 1909. Killed in action 10 Jun 1945.

[6] L.-Sgt E. E. Gardoll, NX122594; 2/28 Bn. Caves guide; of Wellington, NSW; b. Wellington, 25 Mar 1919.

[7] Maj J. M. Clements, SX2724. 9 Cav Regt and 2/11 Cdo Sqn. Transport contractor; of Mount Gambier, SA; b. Mount Gambier, 8 Aug 1910.

1,000 yards north-west of the airfield, the way to Hamilton Road was clear. The battalion was ordered to link with the 2/11th Squadron at the junction of Charlie Track and Hamilton Road and to take the position mentioned above.[8] By 5.40 it was in touch with the 2/11th Squadron, having met little opposition.

Meanwhile "C" Company of the 2/43rd with three tanks of the 2/9th Armoured Regiment was dealing with the position that had been by-passed by the remainder of the battalion. Several tracks led into it and these were blocked by trucks from which wires were stretched to aerial bombs, and these obstacles were covered by machine-gun fire. The tanks could advance only along the tracks as the ground fell steeply away on either side of them. Directed by Lieut-Colonel Jeanes,[9] who was forward with this company, the tanks and the infantry knocked out the Japanese machine-guns one by one. Engineers disarmed the bombs and the tanks then pushed the road-blocks off the tracks; engineers sealed the mouths of tunnels that might contain Japanese. By the end of the day the infantry had secured the whole area and hastened the enemy's retreat into his stronghold.

That day the 2/28th probed the strongly-held area just south of the one the 2/43rd was seizing. One company, with Lieutenant Avern's[1] troop of tanks, thrust west along a track towards MacArthur Road. For about 500 yards the infantry indicated targets to the tanks. Then the infantry were pinned down by fire from a heavy machine-gun and rifles, and soon the tanks were out of touch with the infantry behind them. Avern got out of his tank under fire to find the infantry officers. He was unable to do so but got an idea where the Japanese fire was coming from, re-entered his tank and pressed on after Sergeant Breaker's[2] tank, which had silenced a machine-gun. Avern now got into touch with the infantry through his third tank (Corporal Moore[3]) and was ordered to push on. He led the advance and the tank gunners killed three Japanese and fired on weapon-pits. Being still in the lead Avern reversed and while doing so a Japanese officer charged towards the tank with a bag of explosives but was shot. Avern left the tank and, finding the company commander, pointed out that it was impossible for the tanks to advance without infantry ahead and without being in contact with the leading platoon. At this stage engineers found a 250-lb bomb planted six inches from the right track of Avern's tank. The advance was then continued with one section in front of Avern's tank, which killed several Japanese; an ammunition dump exploded near by, either hit by fire from the tank's

---

[8] In the orders and reports code names were given to the roads on Labuan. Thus "Charlie route" was a combination of Rancha Road (leading north from Hamilton Point) and Hamilton Road. In this account the true names of the roads have usually been employed.

[9] Lt-Col M. R. Jeanes, DSO, MC, ED, SX9364. 2/43 Bn (CO 1945). Inspector of food and drugs; of Largs Bay, SA; b. Adelaide, 21 Dec 1911.

[1] Lt C. C. Avern, MC, NX138175; 2/9 Armd Regt. Regular soldier; b. Inverell, NSW, 12 Sep 1921. Died 9 Oct 1952, as a result of wounds received in this campaign.

[2] Sgt G. A. H. Breaker, SX14208; 2/9 Armd Regt. Salesman; b. South Payneham, SA, 9 Jul 1921.

[3] Cpl H. S. Moore, NX95879; 2/9 Armd Regt. Carrier; of New Lambton, NSW; b. Sydney, 8 Nov 1912.

howitzer or blown up by Japanese. By the evening tanks and infantry had reached MacArthur Road.

By the end of a hard day the area in which the Japanese were strongly dug in was fairly well defined. It was about 1,200 yards by 600 and consisted of a tangle of small ridges covered with trees and dense undergrowth and fringed by swamps to the west and south. By this time the brigade had lost 18 killed and 42 wounded, nearly all in the 2/28th, and had killed at least 110 Japanese.

The task for the 13th was to continue to compress the enemy in "the Pocket", as it was named, and continue mopping up the rest of the island. The 2/43rd occupied an emergency airstrip at Timbalai by 2 p.m. Lushington's company of the 2/28th pressed on along MacArthur Road with Avern's troop of tanks and made some progress. It proved impossible to withdraw the tanks at nightfall because of a crater in the road, so infantry were deployed to protect them, which proved a wise precaution as Japanese attacked in the night but were driven off.

By the end of the 14th the island was clear of enemy troops except for the Pocket, and it was evident that a strong, coordinated attack would be needed to reduce this position in which the Japanese garrison apparently intended to make a last stand.

After their conquest of Borneo in 1942 the Japanese established only small garrisons there. North Borneo, for example, was garrisoned by a force whose main component was the *4th Independent Mixed Regiment* (two battalions). The Allied advance led, in the last half of 1944, to the progressive reinforcement of the Borneo garrisons. From July 1944 onwards the *56th Independent Mixed Brigade (366th, 367th, 368th, 369th, 370th, 371st Battalions)* arrived and was deployed in the Tawao-Tawitawi area. In September the north Borneo garrisons were incorporated in a new *XXXVII Army* with headquarters at Jesselton. This army was instructed to help to establish a naval base at Brunei Bay, and four airfield units were added to the one already in north Borneo. The *25th Independent Mixed Regiment* arrived from Japan in October, and by the end of the year the *71st Independent Mixed Brigade* and two machine-gun battalions joined the *XXXVII Army,* whose area was now extended to include south Borneo.

In December the Japanese staffs decided that about March, when the Americans would probably have conquered the Philippines, the Australians would seize air bases on the east coast and at the same time land at strategic points on the west coast, specially round Brunei. Consequently they began to move units from the north-east corner of the island to the western side, a laborious process since it was almost impossible to move them by sea because of Allied air attacks, and nearly all movement was overland and on foot.

The original plan was to deploy the northern forces thus:

Jesselton, *25th Mixed Regiment* less the *II Battalion*;
Brunei Bay area, *56th Brigade (366th, 367th, 368th* and *371st Battalions)*;
Kuching-Natuna Islands, *71st Brigade*;
Tawao-Sandakan-Kudat-Miri, five battalions.

The overland journey, via Ranau, proved so slow and arduous that, when the Australians landed, not all the Japanese units had reached their destinations. In a post-war report the Japanese staffs emphasised the effectiveness of Allied air attacks on communications in and round Borneo: "By the end of March, surface transportation was at a standstill and all weapons, material, provisions and medical supplies sent to north Borneo from the Singapore area . . . remained stockpiled at Kuching.

... Inter-island sea transportation, as well as shipments from overseas, virtually came to a standstill by the end of 1944."[4]

Despite the difficulties faced by the Japanese in their re-deployment to meet the expected Australian attack, at the time of the landing the strength of the Japanese in the whole target area had in fact been somewhat higher than the 9th Division had estimated. The actual strengths were about 550 on Labuan, 850 round Brunei, 1,700 at Seria-Miri, 200 in the Weston-Beaufort area. Both the *366th* and *367th Battalions* were in the Brunei area, and the *371st* on Labuan; the *553rd Battalion* was at Miri.

---

[4] Borneo Operations 1941-1945; Japanese Monograph No. 26, prepared by Headquarters U.S. Army, Japan (1957).

CHAPTER 20

SECURING BRITISH BORNEO

BY 16th June Brunei and Labuan Island, except for the Pocket, had been won and two subsidiary operations had been ordered. One, as mentioned earlier, was the landing of a reinforced battalion about Miri. The other was the seizure of Weston, on the mainland east of Labuan. This task was given to the 2/32nd Battalion, part of the divisional reserve; it had landed on Labuan on the 12th. The 2/32nd and troops attached to it were now to land and take Weston and thence reconnoitre across country and by river towards Beaufort with a view to the eventual capture of that town by the 24th Brigade.

The principal remaining element of the divisional reserve—the 2/12th Commando Squadron — was given the task of making sure that the outlying parts of Labuan Island were cleared of Japanese, while the 2/28th Battalion, with air and artillery support, reduced the Pocket. The squadron had embarked under the command of the 2/32nd Battalion, and had now been on Labuan Island for nine days. The island was divided into troop areas and patrolling began. In the next eleven days patrols took one

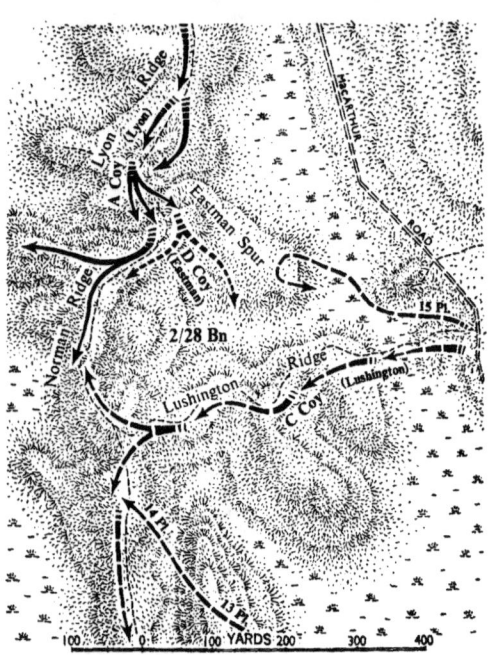

14th-21st June

prisoner and killed 27 Japanese, most of them after an enemy raid on the B.B.C.A.U. area on 24th June. On the 26th Lieutenant Johnstone's[1] section found a party of Japanese, evidently those who had made the raid, and killed 14 in a swift skirmish in which two Australians were wounded.

Meanwhile the pressure against the Pocket had continued. On the afternoon of 14th June a company of the 2/28th had attacked the Pocket after the artillery had fired 250 rounds. The company met heavy fire from mortars and machine-guns, a flanking attack failed, and it withdrew. On

---

[1] Lt W. P. Johnstone, VX100050; 2/12 Cdo Sqn. Clerk; of Colac, Vic; b. Colac, 8 Aug 1921.

the 15th the 2/12th Field Regiment continued bombarding the Pocket and in the next five days and nights hurled 140 tons of shells into it.

Within the Pocket were three main areas of high ground: Eastman Spur overlooking the northern approaches, particularly Lyon Ridge which led in from the north; Lushington Ridge which dominated the eastern approach; Norman Ridge overlooking the whole area from the west. There were only two feasible approaches: a heavily-mined track on Lyon Ridge along which it would be possible for tanks to move, and a track through swamp to the razor-backed Lushington Ridge and along it to Norman Ridge.

On 15th June the 2/11th Commando Squadron had probed from the north and reported that the track on Lyon Ridge was suitable for tanks provided a large bomb crater was filled. So, on the morning of the 16th, Major Lyon's company of the 2/28th with a troop of tanks (Lieutenant Hall[2]) attacked this side of the Pocket. The advance began at 8.45. One platoon moved forward and protected a bulldozer while it filled in the crater. Then the advance was continued, and by 10.20 the first ridge had been taken, but heavy fire from the next one pinned the infantry down and damaged a tank. Lieutenant Sweet's[3] section of the 2/11th Commando which was protecting Colonel Norman's tactical headquarters was sent forward on the left of Lyon's company. It came under sharp fire, the two leading men were killed and Sweet wounded. Corporal Carland[4] took command, coolly reorganised the men, and put them in a defensive position.

At midday Lieutenant Avern's troop of tanks relieved Hall's whose tanks remained with a fresh company (Captain Eastman) which was digging in on the ground that had been taken. The tanks pushed 150 yards ahead of the infantry and killed 8 or 10 Japanese. One tank was hit with a bomb, which jammed the turret and wounded the driver; another was bogged 50 yards ahead of the infantry. In the day the six tanks fired 268 shells and 16,000 rounds of machine-gun ammunition. In the fight, which went on all day, Lyon and Padre W. E. Holt who was helping the wounded were hit, Holt mortally. Padre Ballard,[5] who was with the 2/11th Commando, also went forward with stretcher bearers and organised the rescue of wounded. By 6.15 p.m. Eastman's company had relieved the leading company, now under Lieutenant Graffin[6]; it had lost 5 killed and 23 wounded. It was decided to continue bombarding the area until it could be taken with fewer casualties.

The field guns bombarded the Pocket heavily for two days; and on the 18th the cruiser *Shropshire* also shelled it with its 8-inch guns, a spotter

---

[2] Lt J. S. Hall, NX122887; 2/9 Armd Regt. Insurance clerk; of Roseville, NSW; b. Bondi, NSW, 3 Nov 1922.

[3] Lt J. Sweet, WX28581; 2/11 Cdo Sqn. Clerk; of Maylands, WA; b. Dwellingup, WA, 21 Dec 1919.

[4] Cpl J. G. V. Carland, MM, VX33023. 9 Cav Regt and 2/11 Cdo Sqn. Truck driver; of Nathalia, Vic; b. Nathalia, 9 Oct 1916.

[5] Chaplain Rev H. R. Ballard, MC, SX22714. 2/4 LAA Regt and 2/11 Cdo Sqn. Congregational minister; of Renmark, SA; b. Nairne, SA, 23 Sep 1910.

[6] Lt L. R. Graffin, WX18204; 2/28 Bn. Accountant; of Darwin; b. Kalgoorlie, WA, 5 Oct 1916.

in an Auster aircraft directing the fire; shell splinters weighing more than a pound fell hundreds of yards from the shell-bursts. On the 19th the infantry continued to probe the area, supported by Avern's tanks, and killed 10 Japanese, Avern, who was directing fire from the ground by walkie-talkie, and two others being wounded. On 20th June the bombardment was intensified: the 12th Battery fired 1,440 shells into the Pocket and six bombers struck it. The battery brought its fire to within 40 yards of the forward weapon-pits without mishap. It was decided that the Pocket had now been "sufficiently softened up" and would be captured next day by two companies supported by tanks, including flame-throwers.

At 4.30 a.m. next morning troops in and round Labuan town were awakened by the sound of firing close by. For an hour or two there was confused fighting in which the engineers, pioneers and other troops of the Beach Group were involved. It eventually appeared that about 50 Japanese had stealthily moved out from the Pocket through the swamps and raided the base at Labuan. One small group attacked the guard of the prisoner-of-war cage where one Australian and two Japanese, armed with swords, were killed. The detachment of the American Boat and Shore Regiment was attacked and lost 3 killed and 8 wounded. One group attacked the lines of the 2/1st Docks Operating Company. Sergeant Antill[7] organised a small party which, armed only with rifles, held the raiders off for two hours and then Antill organised a party which mopped up the remaining Japanese. This swiftly-arranged defence by a few men of a non-combatant unit probably saved heavy losses among large numbers of men sleeping in the area. Altogether 32 Japanese were killed round Labuan.

The 2/7th Field Company withstood attack by a subsidiary raiding party equipped with aerial bombs which thrust at the northern end of the airstrip, evidently with the object of destroying the Spitfires there. The engineers killed 11 and had one man killed and 4 wounded by Japanese bayonets. At 9 a.m. Colonel Norman sent a platoon into the town in trucks to help in the mopping up, but by that time they were not needed.

Meanwhile the 2/28th had opened its two-company attack on the Pocket, whose garrison had now been much reduced by the loss of the raiding parties. The artillery again bombarded the small area and at 10 a.m. on the 21st Captain Lushington's company with a troop of tanks thrust westward along the track on Lushington Ridge while Major Lyon's company with one troop of tanks and two flame-throwing Frogs thrust into the Pocket from Eastman Spur. In an hour and a half Lushington's company was half way through the Pocket and under rifle fire. They were then halted by Norman lest they come under fire from Lyon moving down from the north, and now half way into the Pocket. The Frogs then overcame all opposition.

<small>The enemy offered little resistance and appeared completely dazed as a result of the "softening up" process. Any offensive spirit which he had left was quickly</small>

---

[7] Sgt E. J. Antill, MM, NX88163; 2/1 Docks Operating Coy. Haulage contractor; of Wagga Wagga, NSW; b. Adelong, NSW, 13 Jan 1910.

lost when the Frogs commenced projecting streams of flame at medium machine-gun positions. During the day 60 Japanese were killed and a considerable quantity of equipment of all types was captured.[8]

Later in the afternoon bulldozers were burying the Japanese dead of whom about 100 were counted, about 40 of these evidently having been killed in the earlier fighting and bombardments. Only six were taken prisoner. A few days later an additional 77 dead were counted. Every Japanese in the Pocket had been accounted for except 4 officers and 7 others who had escaped. At the outset the garrison had probably been about 250 strong. At this stage 389 Japanese dead had been counted on Labuan Island and 11 prisoners taken; the 24th Brigade had lost 34 killed and 93 wounded.

By 16th June General Wootten had decided that, as the enemy was withdrawing and showing no signs of attacking, he would gain control of the high country from Mempakul and Menumbok to Cape Nosong to prevent the enemy using the track from Kota Klias to Karukan and to gain beaches for use as supply points during an advance northward. On 18th June he discussed the exploitation on the mainland with Brigadier Porter, who told him that a naval reconnaissance party had been to Mempakul and formed the opinion that there was only a standing patrol there. Wootten told Porter that he could not spare any landing craft because they were all needed south of Brunei, but Porter obtained from the commander of the American Boat and Shore Regiment a spare L.C.I. and his own headquarters craft (another L.C.I.). With these and five L.C.M's allotted to Labuan for patrolling and lightering he was able to plan a landing. Wootten approved and the 2/43rd was ordered to make an amphibious reconnaissance of the Mempakul area next day.

Meanwhile the 2/32nd Battalion had firmly established itself on the mainland farther east. A patrol under Lieutenant Billett[9] had landed at Weston from the frigate *Lachlan* on the 16th, moved 1,000 yards along the railway and found no Japanese there. The exits from the beach were very boggy; indeed the small and dilapidated town was hemmed in by swamps. The railway line leading out of the town was a single track of one-metre gauge.

The 2/32nd landed at Weston on the 17th. A few friendly natives appeared. Lieut-Colonel T. H. Scott sent one company along the railway line and by the end of the day it had a patrol in Lingkungan, having seen only three Japanese, who fled. On the 18th Lieutenant Brown's[1] platoon moved along the railway towards Maraba. Near Lingkungan they saw movement and Brown, leading a patrol forward, found 12 Japanese sitting on the railway line. In an exchange of fire Brown was killed

---
[8] 24th Australian Infantry Brigade Report on Operations—Oboe Six (British North Borneo), 10 Jun-30 Jun 1945.
[9] Lt D. L. Billett, TX446. 2/1 and 2/3 MG Bns, 2/32 Bn. Shipping clerk; of Devonport, Tas; b. Rangoon, Burma, 19 Jul 1914.
[1] Lt K. L. Brown, VX115892; 2/32 Bn. Schoolteacher; of Portland, Vic; b. Melbourne, 26 Sep 1918. Killed in action 18 Jun 1945.

and two others hit. Lieutenant Ackerly's[2] platoon, patrolling near by, joined Brown's and on Colonel Scott's orders Ackerly attacked with artillery and mortar support and drove the Japanese off.

On 19th June Captain A. P. Denness took command at Lingkungan and several patrols probed to find the enemy's positions. Natives informed

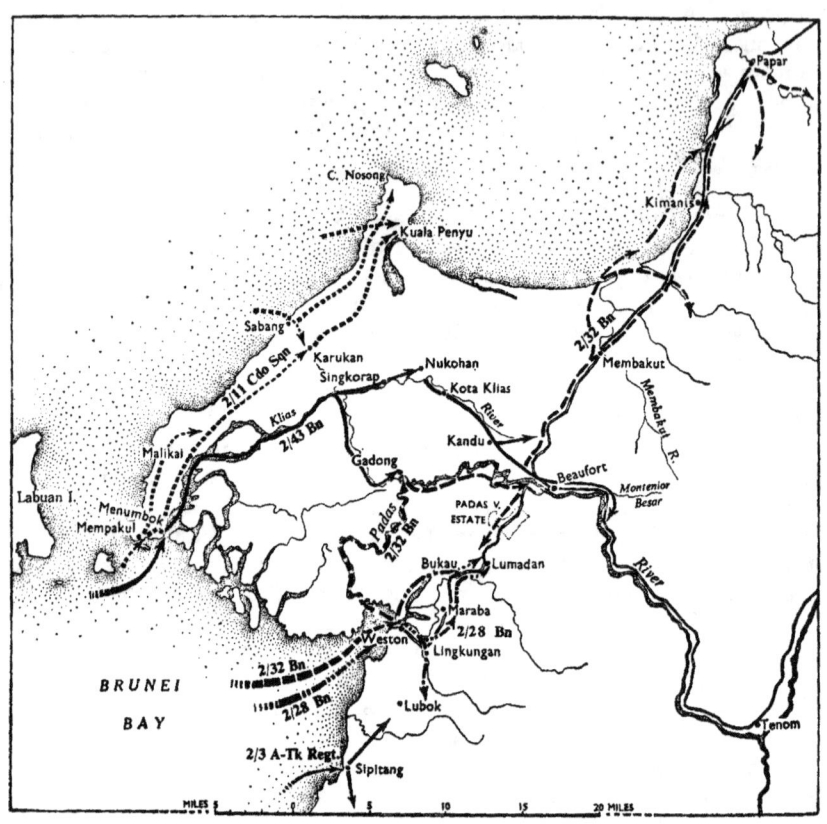

16th June-30th July

the Australians that about 1,000 Japanese had moved into the area south of Lingkungan on 24th May but had gone north probably to Bukau, about half way to Beaufort, when the air bombardment opened. On the 20th and 21st there were some clashes with parties of Japanese. One patrol along the railway reached a point north of Lingkungan where the line was bounded by swamps, and was fired on by Japanese, but after artillery fire these were driven back.

There were two main lines of approach to Beaufort: along the railway or up the wide Padas River. Porter decided that the obvious line of

[2] Lt F. E. Ackerly, NX133182; 2/32 Bn. Contractor; of Benalla, Vic; b. Yarrawonga, Vic, 7 Jun 1917.

(*Australian War Memorial*)

Left to right: Lieut-Colonel M. R. Jeanes (C.O. 2/43rd Battalion), General MacArthur and General Morshead on Labuan Island, 10th June 1945.

(*Australian War Memorial*)

Troops of the 2/43rd Battalion moving into a dispersal bay during the capture of Labuan airfield on 10th June.

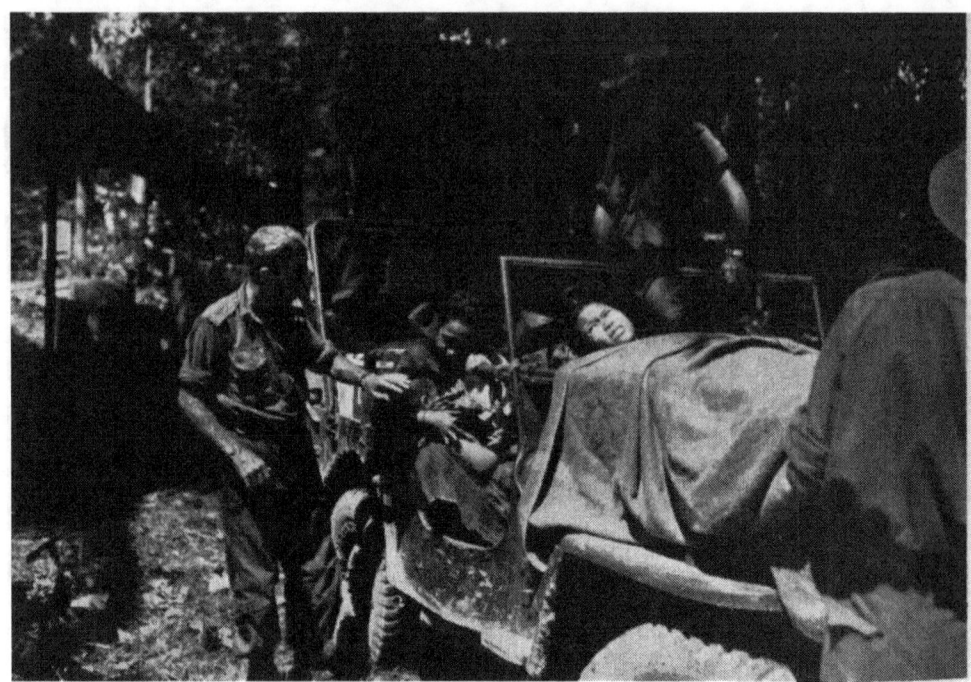

(U.S. Army Signal Corps)
Chinese girl wounded by a shell fragment near Labuan airfield being taken to hospital by a jeep ambulance, 13th June 1945.

(Australian War Memorial)
Labuan Island, 11th June. Major G. M. L. V. Gifford of the British Borneo Civil Affairs Unit questioning refugees at the headquarters of the 24th Brigade.

(*U.S. Army Signal Corps*)
Troops of the 2/17th Battalion patrolling the town of Brunei, 13th June 1945.

(*U.S. Army Signal Corps*)
Bren gun position of the 2/43rd Battalion north of Labuan airfield, 13th June.

(U.S. Army Signal Corps)

Major-General G. F. Wootten (right), commanding the 9th Division, and Air Commodore F. R. W. Scherger, commanding First Tactical Air Force, R.A.A.F., on Labuan Island 14th June, 1945.

(Australian War Memorial)

Dyaks being questioned at 20th Brigade headquarters, Brunei, 16th June 1945.

advance—along the railway—offered "unattractive prospects": it presented a series of defiles between steep hills on one side and swamps on the other, and the only rolling stock at Weston was one box van and two flat-topped trucks. A better line of approach would be the one from the west. Thus Porter, as he wrote later, "decided to conform with local practice and travel by water". He himself borrowed a launch from the Boat and Shore Regiment and prepared a water patrol program for himself and the two battalions, the ultimate object being to attack Beaufort using the waterways. The plan for patrolling the rivers was to move strong fighting patrols of about 100 men up each river in L.C.M's, with L.C.M's armed with 3-inch mortars and machine-guns, all sandbagged, in support. The patrols were to gain as much information as possible by peaceful probing, but were to fight if enemy were encountered. The type of information sought was such as would help Porter determine a line of approach for a brigade advance. Dry ground for establishing forward positions was needed, and information about the lines of communication between Beaufort and Kota Klias.

A company of the 2/32nd Battalion had established a base at Gadong on the Padas; patrols explored the surrounding country but found no Japanese. On the 23rd Colonel Scott established his tactical headquarters at Gadong, whence the 2/32nd patrolled along the Padas in small craft. If a whole company went on patrol it was normally carried in a gunboat containing the commander and others, and three L.C.M's each carrying a platoon. The craft went along the river with the gunboat 200 yards in the lead and the others at intervals of 100 yards.

By this time the 2/43rd Battalion and 2/11th Commando Squadron had secured a large area on the Klias peninsula and along the Klias River. Colonel Jeanes had landed at Mempakul with two companies on 19th June. Natives welcomed the troops as they landed and told them there were about 50 Japanese three miles away. On the same day the 2/11th Commando Squadron also landed with the task of clearing the peninsula.

The 2/43rd, on 21st June, sent an expedition up the Klias River to discover the possibilities of barge traffic along it, to find whether a force could be concentrated at Singkorap, and to learn the nature of the tracks from Singkorap, and the enemy's strength and intentions in the area. The force was embarked in one gunboat and three L.C.M's, one mounting a section of Vickers guns on the platform aft, and included a company of the 2/43rd Battalion, a platoon of the 2/2nd Machine Gun Battalion, a party of engineers, a representative of the R.A.N. beach commandos, and an interpreter. Captain Pollok[3] commanded the force. Some distance below Singkorap natives on the bank informed the patrol that two Japanese had moved upstream in a prahu 24 hours before. The craft hastened on and Pollok made a landing and established a bridgehead at Singkorap and sent out patrols. The area was very swampy and there were no foot tracks to Nukohan on the Beaufort-Kuala Penyu track—the

---

[3] Lt-Col J. A. Pollok, MC, SX8977; 2/43 Bn. Salesman; of Payneham, SA; b. Adelaide, 26 Nov 1916.

natives moved about with the help of water buffaloes. It would plainly not be practicable to base a force at Singkorap.

The flotilla moved on towards Kota Klias. Three miles from it natives informed the Australians that Japanese were in a house just round a bend in the river. The craft hastened upstream, and, while the gunboat gave covering fire, two L.C.M's each carrying a platoon beached simultaneously, the troops dashed ashore and, firing from the hip, advanced on the house. They killed ten Japanese and the survivors fled. That evening the flotilla returned to Mempakul at the mouth of the river, having ascertained that the Japanese were not in strength along the Klias.

Thereupon, on the 22nd, Colonel Jeanes with the 2/43rd Battalion less two companies set out in an L.C.M. up the Klias River from Mempakul. They travelled for five hours between banks covered with mangroves and sago palms. In the villages groups of natives stood at the salute as they passed. Near Kota Klias natives warned Jeanes that 200 Japanese were coming down the river and were about two hours away. Here the group landed in a muddy area among rubber trees and soon many natives appeared including an Indian who spoke English.

Meanwhile the 2/11th Squadron had been pressing northward along the Klias peninsula, against only slight opposition by the enemy, but through very difficult country. At Malikai a native led a patrol to a house where 8 Japanese were camped; all were killed. On 23rd June the squadron took Karukan and Sabang, and on the 27th Kuala Penyu.

The Padas River was explored by a water-borne patrol under Captain J. J. G. Davidson of the 2/32nd on 19th June. Davidson's reconnaissance led Porter to the conclusion that he could make a quick advance along the Padas to the doors of Beaufort and that the enemy was not expecting such a move. Porter now decided to concentrate his troops for the attack on Beaufort at the position where the 2/43rd, moving across from the Klias, would reach the Padas. Time was all-important and plans were quickly made and orders issued.

Porter ordered the 2/28th Battalion less two companies to take over from the 2/32nd in and forward of Weston; the other two companies of the 2/28th, under Major Jackson,[4] were to protect the axis of advance when the final approach to Beaufort began. The 2/32nd Battalion, part moving along the Padas and part along the railway, was to assemble north of the Padas Valley Estate and patrol for information south of the Padas. The 2/43rd, marching from the headwaters of the Klias, was to assemble north of the Padas and forward of Kandu and probe towards Beaufort. Brigade headquarters were to be established on the Padas just west of the battalions, but Porter's tactical headquarters would move forward in his motor launch.

On 24th June the main body of the 2/43rd toiled along a track sometimes 10 inches deep in mud, and in great heat, from their barge point on

---

[4] Brig D. R. Jackson, DSO, NX207. 2/1 Bn 1939-41; BM 24 Bde 1941-43; CO 2/28 Bn 1945. Regular soldier; b. Sunningdale, Berks, England, 12 Oct 1915.

the Klias to the Padas. That day patrols of the 2/43rd and 2/32nd met west of Kandu.

By 25th June it appeared that there were 800 to 1,000 Japanese round Beaufort, without artillery, and that their main positions were sited to protect the town from a force approaching along the railway and the Padas River and overlooked the town from the east. Porter gave orders to the 2/32nd to seize the spur running down to the river just south of Beaufort, and also the railway terminus, by outflanking moves, while the other companies guarded the railway south of the Padas. This done, the 2/43rd using two companies was to seize high ground dominating

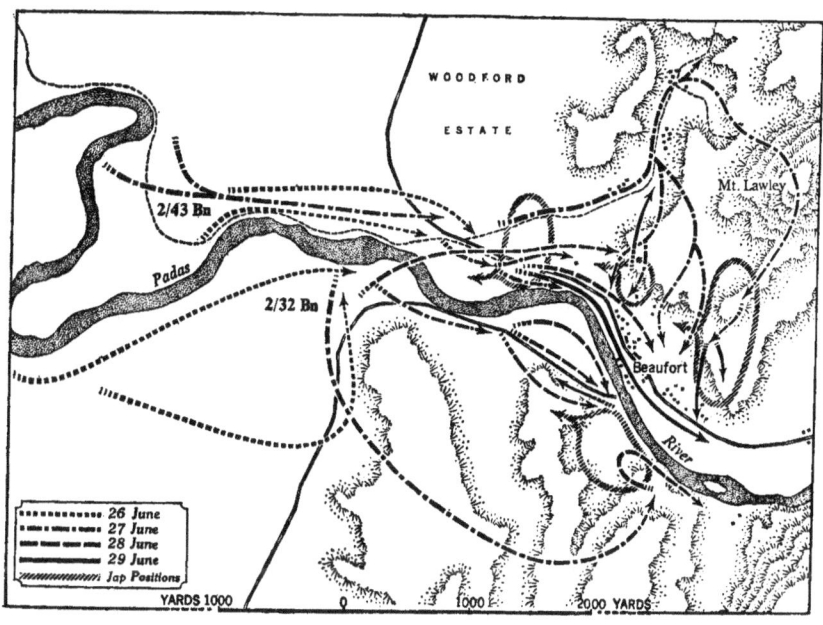

26th-29th June

Beaufort from north and east by flanking attacks from the north while a third company pressed frontally. These attacks would have the support of 14 guns of the 2/12th Field Regiment which had been brought up the Padas in barges.

The leading companies of the battalions moved forward on the 26th. Two companies of the 2/32nd moved along the river and two astride the railway. At the end of the day Captain J. J. Thornton's company of the 2/32nd was on the Padas about 2,000 yards west of the railway terminus and Captain M. H. E. C. Glover's company of the 2/43rd on the railway north of the Padas a similar distance from Beaufort. On the 27th and 28th Thornton's company took the railway terminus after meeting only slight opposition and Denness' company made a wide flanking move to the Padas just upstream from Beaufort; about 60 Japanese caught between the two companies escaped through the thick timber.

The attack by the 2/43rd opened at 2 p.m. on the 27th when Pollok's company and Glover's thrust along the Woodford Estate Road. Pollok's company swung left to high ground dominating Beaufort from the north and Glover's thrust south to the lower slopes of the same feature. Captain Lonnie's[5] company, following Glover's, took a spur to the left of Glover's axis of advance. Glover's company encountered opposition north of Beaufort, pressed on and overcame it by 6.15. It was becoming dark and there was light rain, but Glover was ordered to push on and take his objective—the high ground overlooking the town. The company took this feature at dusk and, early in the night, was in control of the town itself.

Meanwhile Pollok's company on the left had been ordered to hold the track junction with one platoon, attack south with the remainder and effect a junction with Glover's company. At 2 p.m. Pollok's men climbed to the top of Mount Lawley where they arrived at dusk weary and in drizzling rain. There were signs, however, that the Japanese were withdrawing from Beaufort so Pollok decided to push on to the junction of three tracks 2,000 yards farther on. This was done in the dark along a narrow track round the side of Lawley and took three hours. At the junction a Japanese guide, evidently posted to direct the withdrawing troops, was shot, and the company "dug in and awaited the approach of all outward bound traffic". It was soon evident that the Japanese being driven out of Beaufort by the companies to the west were making their way back through the position held by Pollok; one party after another was shot by the troops holding the track junction. That night (27th-28th) the Japanese counter-attacked both Glover's and Lonnie's companies. Glover's company was soon isolated and Glover himself wounded, but he carried on. Pollok's company was out of communication throughout the night. It came on the air again at battalion headquarters at 10.30 a.m. on the 28th and reported its position. Colonel Jeanes impressed upon Pollok the need to push on southward, where the two other companies were still being attacked, and to lend help to Glover's isolated company.

Thus Pollok left Lieutenant George's[6] platoon to hold the track junction and took the rest along a jungle pad towards Glover's company down below. After 300 yards the leading platoon (Lieutenant Kennedy[7]) found Japanese well dug in along the track. As the Japanese in the first post opened fire Private Starcevich[8] moved through the forward scouts firing his Bren gun from the hip and silenced the post.

Fired upon at once by a second LMG Starcevich, standing in full view of the gunners, coolly charged his magazine and then advanced upon this second post

---

[5] Lt-Col W. S. Lonnie, CBE, MVO, MC, WX10089; 2/43 Bn. Transport officer; of Subiaco, WA; b. Montrose, Scotland, 6 Apr 1909.

[6] Lt N. G. George, NX9124; 2/43 Bn. Clerk; of Sydney; b. Adelong, NSW, 23 Oct 1914.

[7] Lt A. Kennedy, WX10816; 2/43 Bn. Commercial traveller; of Maylands, WA; b. Perth, 17 Oct 1917.

[8] Pte L. T. Starcevich, VC, WX11519; 2/43 Bn. Farmer and gold miner; of Grass Patch, WA; b. Subiaco, WA, 5 Sep 1918.

(wrote a member of the company[9]). Starcevich [has] a method of approach which in itself must be most disconcerting to an enemy. Firmly and confidently believing that he can never be hit, he walks into an enemy post preceded by a single and unbroken stream of pellets. He is quite unmoved by returning fire and stops only when the enemy has been annihilated. The enemy in this second post must have been quite unable to "take it", for as Starcevich neared them they endeavoured to leave their foxholes, and, caught in Starcevich's fire, were at once killed. The company now proceeded along the track, meeting in a further 200 yards only single riflemen.

The company next encountered a third post. Starcevich and his No. 2, Private Porter,[1] kept the post quiet with a hail of fire while Corporal Mason[2] led a section through the bush on the right. Starcevich advanced firing his Bren and knocked out the enemy machine-gun post while Mason's section dealt with riflemen farther on.[3] Late in the afternoon the advancing company could hear Bren guns and Thompson sub-machine-guns firing close ahead, and might have walked into their fire had not a signaller speaking to battalion headquarters been told that the Japanese were using these British weapons. It was now near dusk.

All day the other two companies were hard pressed. In Lonnie's company Private Kelly[4] who was digging in by himself on the right became involved in a fierce struggle. A bullet hit him in the leg, and a Japanese slashed him with a sword on arm and shoulder, but Kelly fought on alone firing his Owen gun with one arm, and unaided drove off the enemy who left six lying dead.

Despite strenuous efforts by Pollok's company to make contact with Glover's, they were prevented from doing so by a steep gorge, and that evening, therefore, Jeanes decided to withdraw the forward companies slightly and concentrate artillery and mortar fire on the Japanese who were between them. Pollok's company withdrew to the junction where, during the day, George's platoon had killed many more Japanese who were trying to escape from Beaufort.

The engineers had been striving to get a troop of tanks forward. That evening these were landed on the river bank at the north-western end of Beaufort, but several obstacles lay between them and the forward companies, and they were not able to overcome these before the fight ended.

Bombarded by artillery and mortars throughout the night, the Japanese began to withdraw along the track held by Pollok's company, and at intervals groups of two or three walked into the company area in the darkness and were killed. Fire was strictly controlled, and one platoon was credited with having killed 21 Japanese with 21 single shots fired at ranges of from five to 15 yards. One Japanese walked on to the track

---

[9] Staff-Sergeant F. S. W. Turner (of Brompton, SA) in a lively narrative of the operations of "B" Company appended to the war diary of the 2/43rd Battalion.
[1] Pte L. L. Porter, VX82329; 2/43 Bn. Labourer; of Westbreen, Vic; b. Cranbourne, Vic, 17 Aug 1918.
[2] Cpl K. R. Mason, NX149232; 2/43 Bn. Farm worker; of Trundle, NSW; b. Parkes, NSW, 27 Feb 1922.
[3] Starcevich was awarded the Victoria Cross.
[4] Pte I. W. Kelly, MM, NX178209. 3 and 2/43 Bns. Farmer; of Adaminaby, NSW; b. Adaminaby, 3 Jul 1922.

50 yards from the foremost Australian Bren gun position and demanded the surrender of the Australians who were blocking the Japanese line of retreat. According to one observer his words were: "Surrender pliz, Ossie. You come. No?" He was promptly shot.

Pollok's company counted 81 Japanese killed with "company weapons only" round the junction and estimated that at least 35 others had been killed; six Australians were slightly wounded. By the morning of the 29th the fight was virtually over and that day was spent in mopping up a disorganised enemy force. The attack on Beaufort cost the 24th Brigade 7 killed and 38 wounded; 93 Japanese dead were counted and two prisoners taken.

Meanwhile part of the 2/28th Battalion had been moving north along the railway line. On the morning of the 29th a platoon of the 2/28th under Sergeant Weston[5] moved out along the railway line to contact the 2/32nd. In the afternoon they were at Lumadan village, which they searched. They were resting by the siding when they were fired on by riflemen and machine-gunners from high ground east of the line, from an overturned carriage near the railway, and from west of the line. Two men were wounded. They signalled to headquarters and Captain Eastman and a platoon hurried forward in rail motors and extricated them. Field guns from the Beaufort area shelled Lumadan that night, and next day no Japanese were found there, but natives said that about 100 had departed eastward in the night.

After the capture of Beaufort Brigadier Porter decided that his policy would be to pinpoint the enemy by vigorous patrolling, maintain contact, bring down maximum fire on enemy positions when they were found, and follow up fast. By these tactics the surviving Japanese, still resisting doggedly, were pushed back into the country east of Beaufort.

In the first day of July the 2/32nd was forward in the hills east of Beaufort north and south of the river, where on 3rd July Captain Denness was wounded and Lieutenant Williamson[6] killed in patrol clashes. By the next day the 2/32nd had control of the area as far as the Montenior Besar railway bridge.

From July onwards the supply of the large force round Beaufort was eased by the fact that a train drawn by a jeep was running on the Weston-Beaufort line. On 3rd July a steam train was also in operation. Part of the 2/28th Battalion, which relieved the 2/32nd at Beaufort, was taken forward from Lumadan by train.[7]

The task next given to the 24th Brigade was to take Papar, using not more than one battalion group. The object was to gain control of the coastal route from Jesselton to Beaufort and Weston. It was believed

---

[5] Sgt F. M. Weston, WX26536; 2/28 Bn. Law clerk; of Cottesloe, WA; b. Pickering Brook, WA, 18 May 1918.

[6] Lt D. D. Williamson, VX146289; 2/32 Bn. Regular soldier; b. Surrey Hills, Vic, 15 May 1924. Killed in action 3 Jul 1945.

[7] Eventually a train on the Weston-Beaufort line normally comprised one open truck and a closed passenger van, drawn by a jeep. The rails were uneven and the sleepers often worn half through. The journey to Beaufort took about two hours and a half along a line so overgrown with grass and with the bush so close on both sides that the train seemed to be moving over a lawn between walls of greenery.

that only small parties of Japanese were astride the railway line to Papar and that there would be no serious resistance until the outskirts of Papar were reached. Porter gave the work to the 2/32nd, which had not so far been engaged as heavily as the 2/28th had been on Labuan or the 2/43rd round Beaufort.

The advance to Papar did not prove a heavy undertaking. On 5th July the battalion group, which included appropriate detachments of supporting troops, set out along the railway line and that day the leading company was near Membakut. A barge point was established on the Membakut River downstream from the village and on 7th July a train was run from Beaufort to Membakut. On 10th July a company in two L.C.M's established a beach maintenance area about five miles south of Papar, and a second company which had been advancing astride the railway joined it there. On 12th July Papar was occupied, its only defenders being two Japanese with a machine-gun who made off as the Australians approached.

In the Beaufort area the 24th Brigade continued to contain the Japanese east of the town. The brigade's task was to advance only far enough along the Beaufort-Tenom railway line to secure the town and the eastern approaches to it. Porter decided that tactically the best ground to hold would be the line of the Montenior Besar, and later Wootten ordered that movement south of it be limited to protective patrols and outposts. Porter allotted areas of responsibility for patrolling to his units and instructed that contact be maintained to ensure good warning of any serious counter-offensive. The main enemy force was dug in some distance south of the Montenior Besar and remained there despite heavy artillery fire. This position was of no value to the brigade, and it was ordered not to attack it. Both Australians and Japanese patrolled vigorously. There were clashes almost every day in which two or three Japanese were killed but the Australians seldom lost a man.

Commanders now took great pains to avoid casualties. For example, Norman of the 2/28th decided that he should secure a knoll from which the Japanese were commanding one of the tracks along the ridge north of the Padas, but must do so without loss. This was achieved by a program of irregularly-timed harassing fire by the artillery lasting several days, after which the knoll was seized without a fight. Next day—3rd August—about 16 Japanese attacked. A two-man listening post forward of the platoon position established on the knoll engaged the enemy. When the fire was heard a section of five men was sent forward. They deployed and charged. One Australian was killed and another wounded, but Private Dale[8] pressed on into the enemy's position, killed three, and continued to engage the Japanese while the Australian wounded were taken out. At least 11 Japanese were killed.

As mentioned in the preceding chapter the 20th Brigade took Brunei town on 13th June. Brigadier Windeyer had considered landing the 2/13th Battalion at Tutong, but on the 13th orders arrived from General Wootten

---
[8] Pte C. E. Dale, MM, NX80997; 2/28 Bn. Farmer; of Bellingen, NSW; b. Bellingen, 25 Nov 1923.

for a wider flanking move: a battalion group built round the 2/13th, under divisional command, was to land in the Miri-Lutong area, and two companies of the 2/15th were to be in reserve to it. Thus, for a time, the available strength of the 20th Brigade would be reduced by about half.

On the 15th Windeyer established his headquarters in the Residency in Brunei. The 2/17th remained round Brunei and sent out patrols. The 2/15th probed along the river towards Limbang, where, natives said, there were 200 Japanese. A patrol of the 2/15th was ambushed on the river near Brunei and lost two men killed.

In Brunei eight natives were found chained to stakes and dead; others who had been chained up were released. The town had been severely battered by Allied bombers and Japanese demolitions. The troops were critical of the air force's practice of bombing conspicuous buildings even when they were unlikely to contain anything of military importance. In Brunei, for example, the bazaar and the cinema were destroyed, but neither was likely to have contained any Japanese men or material and their destruction and the destruction of similar buildings added to the distress of the civilians. The infantryman on the ground saw the effects of bombing at the receiving end.

> The impression was gained (says the report of the 20th Brigade) that, in the oil producing and refining centres—Seria, Kuala Belait, Lutong, Miri—much of the destruction served no military purpose. The destruction of the native bazaar and shop area in . . . Kuala Belait, Brunei, Tutong and Miri seemed wanton.

The 2/17th Battalion remained in and round Brunei, whence patrols were sent out, until 16th June when one company, with another following, moved out towards Tutong, which was entered late on the afternoon of the 16th. A ferry was established across the mouth of the Tutong River by using a pontoon and a launch and by this means the leading companies crossed and moved towards Seria. From the Tutong onwards the road was the wide beach, fringed by tall casuarinas, and on the hard sand at low and medium tides vehicles could be driven at up to 50 miles an hour.

Leaving two companies in Brunei Colonel Broadbent moved his headquarters southward on the 18th. On the morning of the 20th the 2/17th could hear the sound of the naval and air bombardment supporting the landing of the 2/13th at Lutong. The 2/17th made no contact with the enemy until the Bira River was reached late on the 20th, when there was a short skirmish in which 12 Japanese were killed. On the 21st Seria was occupied without opposition. Windeyer, who wished to concentrate the 2/17th at Seria, ordered it not to advance beyond that town until further orders.

At that stage the 2/17th had advanced 75 miles, most of it on foot, since leaving Green Beach, with frequent deployments and several small engagements on the way. It had lost 6 killed and 10 wounded and had killed and counted 85 Japanese, killed perhaps 22 more, and taken 12 prisoners.

At Seria the oil wells were ablaze. From the broken pipes that formed the head of each well the burning oil was hosing as from huge, hissing Bunsen burners. The pressure was so strong that the oil, clear as petrol, did not begin to burn until the jet was a few inches from the pipe. Then it became a tumbling cloud of flame and billowing blue-black smoke. At about 1,000 feet the plumes from more than 30 fires mixed in a single canopy of smoke. Night and day this appalling waste continued. The men round Seria went to sleep to the hiss and grumbling of an entire oilfield in flames and woke to the same din.

The Japanese had set fire to 37 wells, burnt buildings and bridges, and attempted to render vehicles, pumps and other gear useless by removing essential parts and dumping them in the rivers or burying them. Thus the Australian engineers had to tackle the job of extinguishing the fires with the help only of their own equipment plus such abandoned gear as they could put into working order, or by finding buried parts (with the help of natives who had watched the Japanese concealing them), and "by improvisation and by selective cannibalisation".[9]

Before the arrival of the Japanese in 1942 some of the wells had been sealed with cement. The Japanese had drilled out some of these and drilled sixteen new wells of their own. At some of the wells the oil now gushed from the broken pipe at the well-head at high pressure; at some the broken pipe hosed its oil horizontally. Often the ground had cracked round the well-head, blazing oil was oozing out, and the earth was on fire. In some wells the pressure was low and the oil burned less fiercely. A few such fires sanded up and went out of their own accord; a few mild fires were extinguished by enterprising troops who beat the fires out or smothered them with sand.

When Colonel Broadbent ordered a platoon of the 2/3rd Field Company under Lieutenant Underwood[1] to extinguish the fires, Underwood and his men were faced with an imposing task, particularly as they were still responsible for maintenance of the road, including two ferries between Brunei and the Baram River, for the operation of craft on rivers leading inland and other tasks; and operations, to be described later, were in progress. At first only a detachment could be spared to fight the fires, but at length more sappers were freed for this work and some 200 Malay, Dyak, Chinese and Indian tradesmen and labourers were recruited. A few days after the capture of Seria Lieutenant Beukema, an officer of the N.I.C.A. who was an oilfield engineer, arrived and provided valuable advice. He told the Australians—Underwood was a chemical engineer and had never seen an oil well before—how such a well was made. About this time the 2/58th Light Aid Detachment began repairing the workshops and fire-fighting gear.

---

[9] *The Royal Engineers Journal*, June 1946, "Fighting Oil Well Fires in Seria, Borneo" by Lieutenant E. B. Underwood, RAE. Much of what follows is drawn from this article by the officer chiefly responsible, in the early stages, for extinguishing the fires.

[1] Lt E. B. Underwood, MBE, NX40095; 2/3 Fd Coy. Chemical engineer; of Dundas, NSW; b. Newcastle, NSW, 4 Mar 1915.

Underwood and his men succeeded in extinguishing some fires by approaching them behind screens, in a favourable wind, and turning off the wheel of the master valve either by hand or with improvised long-handled tools up to 50 feet in length. Sand was then shovelled or bulldozed over any fire that remained where the oil was oozing from damaged casings. Where the flame was blazing out sideways it was sometimes made to burn vertically by shooting the damaged top off the well-head with an anti-tank gun.

Soon only the larger and fiercer fires remained, and those in which the flames had melted the pipes and valves. One was extinguished by bulldozing sand over the well-head and pumping on water which turned to steam. Having proved the effectiveness of steam Underwood set up a battery of mobile boilers and bombarded several fires with steam, extinguishing them within a few seconds. Mud was prepared at the Badas River some seven miles from Seria, pumped to Seria along a system that had been damaged but was repairable, and used to hose on to certain fires. At some fires the oil blazing round the well-head was diverted into a pit dug by a bulldozer and the blaze round the well-head, having been thus reduced, was extinguished with steam and water. Others were subdued with the help of a long-handled snuffer. When each fire had been put out the engineers renewed the well-head fittings with those salvaged elsewhere on the field.

Of the 37 wells set on fire by the Japanese, four sanded up and went out of their own accord, three were beaten out, 11 extinguished by turning off the valves, one extinguished with water, three with steam, and two chiefly by diverting the main flow of oil. From mid-July onwards other experts arrived on the scene and eventually two American experts from Texas. The Americans considered Underwood's methods of subduing the fires to be too dangerous. Under the guidance of the experts the Australians used a method whereby the well-head opening was plugged with a tapered pipe controlled by a crane, and fed with water (or mud) under pressure along a tributary pipe, and with a valve operated by remote control. Thus the flow of oil was stopped by water (or mud) pressure. Australian engineers improvised the necessary equipment and extinguished the remaining fires. A wingless aeroplane was towed close to some fires so that its propeller could blow the flame away from the crane. The work of extinguishing the fires took three months during which 7,600 man-days were worked, including 2,400 by troops.

This account of the fight against the oil fires has far outrun the story of the military operations. While the 2/17th Battalion was advancing to Seria the 2/15th was securing the Limbang area and the 2/13th taking Lutong from the sea.

The convoy of L.S.T's containing the 2/13th Battalion Group, about 1,900 strong, had moved off from Brunei Bay at 3 p.m. on 19th June. The troops were very crowded on the decks of the L.S.T's and were most uncomfortable when the wind increased and the sea became very rough.

As they were having breakfast at 5 o'clock on the 20th they could see great fires on the eastern horizon—the blazing oil wells at Seria. At 9.15, after a bombardment by three American destroyers, the first wave—two companies—moved towards the shore in American L.V.T's while three American L.C.I's fired machine-guns and launched rockets.

> The first wave hit the shore and landed without opposition (wrote the battalion diarist). Contrary to plan the LVT4's did not move straight inland but halted on the beach where they remained firing inland. The second wave followed the first ashore . . . immediately there was the spectacle of four waves of LVT's packed together on a beach some 25 yards wide. After a slight pause while pressure was being brought to bear on coxswains to proceed inland, the troops disembarked, formed up and made for their objectives on foot.

The objectives were reached without any Japanese being seen. At 11.45 General Wootten landed and repeated to Lieut-Colonel G. E. Colvin the order that Lutong was the main objective and the holding of Miri a secondary consideration; two destroyers would remain in support as long as Colvin needed them. Colvin told the general that he did not need the floating reserve—the two companies of the 2/15th—and would return them next day.

At 12.30 eight Japanese were seen in the distance near Lutong bridge but made off. In the afternoon about 90 emaciated Indian prisoners were recovered. By the end of the day all objectives were held except one position east of the Miri River which had not been crossed by L.V.T's because the approaches were so swampy. The area occupied included the whole of the Lutong refinery, the oil tank farm and the airstrip, on which were nine damaged aircraft.

The refinery proper was in ruins but a small Japanese oil-refining plant seemed to be in working order and there were undamaged storehouses containing great quantities of machinery. The oil wells had been set on fire, as at Seria, but Miri was an old field, the pressure was low, and the fires were easily put out. Natives who wandered into the Australian lines said that 400 to 500 Japanese troops had departed from Miri and Lutong in the days up to 15th June and were now astride the Riam Road seven miles from the town with a small force forward in the Miri hills.

On the 21st Colvin gave orders for an advance to the town of Miri and by 1.25 p.m. the leading sections of Captain Faulkner's[2] company had crossed the Miri River using a pontoon ferry which the engineers had contrived, and soon some jeeps were across. By the end of the day there had still been no contact with Japanese. The released Indian prisoners, most of them in a pitiful condition, now totalled 135, and more arrived on the 22nd. One group of 14 marched into battalion headquarters under an N.C.O. who halted them in front of Colvin and reported: "Fourteen Indians and one Dutch prisoner of war, sir," and then presented Colvin with a sword that he had taken from a Japanese whom he had killed.

---

[2] Maj D. F. Faulkner, NX34860; 2/13 Bn. Clerk; of Gunnedah, NSW; b. Singleton, NSW, 26 Jul 1910.

Despite their weak state their military bearing remained and they were obviously proud to report in a soldierly way to a British officer. Many patrols were out on the 22nd but found no live Japanese. By the 22nd the 2/13th knew that the 2/17th was at Seria but was unable to get into wireless touch with the sister unit.

Indian prisoners of war had also begun to reach the lines of the 2/17th at Seria on the 22nd, and by the end of June 41 had come in. They reported that on 14th June the Japanese had slaughtered some of a group of more than 100 Indian prisoners at Kuala Belait; the Australians found 24 charred bodies at Kuala Belait, and evidence that others had also been killed. "Jap motive for massacre is not clear," states a report by the 2/17th, "and whether a partial loss of rations, the waving of flags or simply Japanese brutality was responsible cannot be determined." The surviving Indians were starving and many were ill. "The loyalty and fortitude of these Indians has been amazing and is a lesson to us all," wrote Broadbent. "Even now their standard of discipline is high."

Faulkner's company of the 2/13th entered Miri on the afternoon of the 23rd and found it unoccupied. Interrogation of natives now made it appear that about 1,000 Japanese including civilians and women were withdrawing south along the Riam Road. Spitfires were strafing targets in this area and reported the destruction of vehicles. The local people, mostly Chinese, were now streaming back into Miri, where they were an embarrassment since they were in the way of the troops and were too numerous to be fed by B.B.C.A.U.

On the evening of the 26th a patrol of the 2/13th arrived at the south bank of the Baram River and one from the 2/17th, which had occupied Kuala Belait on the 24th, at the north bank. At this stage the 2/13th reverted to Windeyer's command.

The enemy's positions along the Riam Road were now being shelled from the sea and land as well as being strafed by fighters. On 27th June a platoon patrol clashed with the enemy on South Knoll. Warned by a Chinese that there were 10 Japanese on the knoll, the patrol moved in behind artillery fire. The Japanese counter-attacked and the patrol withdrew to the Riam Road but later found that four men were missing. That night Colvin ordered the platoon to search the South Knoll area next day. A second platoon was to pass through and take the knoll but, when information arrived that until a few days before up to 70 Japanese were on the knoll, the company commander, Faulkner, was told not to press home the attack against organised resistance, but to use artillery.

Before the attack opened the four missing men arrived in Miri, having found Chinese who guided them home. Soon after their return a platoon occupied the knoll, which the Japanese had abandoned. After this the 2/13th held with four platoons all the high ground astride the road overlooking the Pujut plain.

During July the 2/13th continued to patrol its area, and particularly to patrol down the Riam Road. On the 5th Colvin sent out a strong fighting patrol of one platoon (Lieutenant Breeze[3]) with detachments of mortars, machine-guns and an artillery party, to make a sortie down the Riam Road in sand-bagged jeeps, inflict casualties and take a prisoner. The patrol went some distance in the jeeps, then advanced on foot with the jeeps following. At 10.30 they were fired on and the sergeant, Pepper,[4] was killed. They brought down artillery and mortar fire and soon the enemy, evidently about 90 strong, and heavily armed, began an outflanking movement. Breeze withdrew, using all the infantry weapons to cover the movement while the artillery observer, Captain Dench,[5] directed a heavy concentration. Breeze estimated that 26 Japanese were killed. Patrolling continued. On 10th July the area where Breeze's patrol had fought was found to have been abandoned. There was a clash on the Riam Road on the 12th when a platoon was ambushed and its commander, Lieutenant Cumming,[6] wounded but he continued to command, withdrew the patrol and brought down artillery fire. From mid-July onwards the Japanese on the Riam Road were harassed by patrols, aircraft and artillery. At length they withdrew their main force southward beyond Bakam, out of artillery range.

While the 2/13th was holding the coast road the 2/17th was patrolling deeply southward from Kuala Belait and particularly along the Baram River, and the 2/15th was patrolling along the valleys of the Limbang and Pandaruan. On 16th June as part of Windeyer's plan "to make as strong a demonstration of strength as possible with the reduced forces at his disposal" a platoon of the 2/15th had been sent along the Pandaruan River in an L.C.M. to raid Limbang, or, if the commander thought fit, to land and take that village. By 18th June Limbang had been secured by a company of the 2/15th without contact with the enemy, and next day battalion headquarters and a troop of the 58th Battery landed there. Reports from natives suggested that there were fairly large bodies of Japanese beyond Limbang: one report was that 200 including some women were moving towards Mengatai; some Dyaks arrived with the heads of six Japanese, and Dyaks reported 50 Japanese six miles south-west of Limbang; another report was that 500 ill-armed and weary Japanese from Mengatai were moving to the south-east; air reconnaissance reported 300 to 400 Japanese near Mengatai. On 20th and 21st June a river patrol of the 2/15th went up the Limbang River to Ukong to investigate reports that Allied prisoners were being held there. It picked up an S.R.D. party which had been organising the Dyaks in that area but the report about prisoners proved false. Reports were now coming in daily about large bodies of Japanese moving into the mountains. The 2/15th had a somewhat anxious time at this stage. The battalion was two companies short

---

[3] Lt V. C. Breeze, NX11349. 2/31 and 2/13 Bns. Tally clerk; of Five Dock, NSW; b. Sydney, 28 Oct 1912.

[4] Sgt L. G. Pepper, NX57983; 2/13 Bn. Quarryman; of Kiama, NSW; b. Newcastle, NSW, 11 Mar 1914. Killed in action 5 Jul 1945.

[5] Capt J. R. Dench, VX50347; 2/8 Fd Regt. Insurance clerk; of North Essendon, Vic; b. Melbourne, 7 Nov 1920.

[6] Lt J. T. Cumming, NX68417; 2/13 Bn. Court reporter; of Summer Hill, NSW; b. Toowoomba, Qld, 13 Jan 1921.

until after the 2/13th had landed at Lutong on 20th June. Colonel Grace did not know whether the Japanese, who were in greater strength than he was, would or would not fight. He was greatly dependent on craft for supply and patrolling, and few were available, and sometimes the boat regiment failed to produce craft when they were ordered.

The 20th Brigade had found the townspeople generally friendly, though they gave little help of military value. On the oilfields some Chinese and Indians seemed apathetic, even hostile. On the other hand the Dyak tribes of the interior—Ibans, Muruts, Punans and others—were almost embarrassingly anxious to hunt down and slay Japanese. "Great difficulty was experienced in preventing Ibans from beheading Japanese prisoners of war and even enemy dead and it was not uncommon for them to report to our troops with one or more heads as evidence of their prowess. The Ibans and others constantly asked for arms, but were as regularly refused. Weapons captured in fight they were allowed to keep, but it was considered undesirable—looking to the future—to arm the natives."[7]

> A Dyak who reached "C" Company from the Tutong River area reported that some days ago a party of 18 Japs reached their village and asked for guides to Tutong (wrote the diarist of the 2/17th). Result: 36 Dyaks, 18 Japs less bodies arrived at destination. The Dyaks offered to deliver the heads to "C" Company but said that they would prefer to keep them as they had a party on. Permission granted to keep heads.

With the help of these Dyak allies the guerilla leaders of the S.R.D. (whose ranks ranged from major to private) had been harassing the Japanese from the flanks and rear. Among these leaders was, for example, Lieutenant Pinkerton,[8] who was parachuted into central Borneo in May as a reinforcement. He went with a party to the Trusan River area of north Sarawak and on the day of the Australian landing made a series of raids on Japanese positions and standing patrols behind Brunei Bay, and took Lawas and held it until the A.I.F. arrived.

> The Japs in the Brunei Bay area have been cut off completely from their main source of supply and are suffering seriously in consequence (reported Major Harrisson). They have sent out numerous patrols and agents to force the natives to supply the food. We have liquidated all of these, and not one man has ever returned from the interior to the coast. This success in preventing people getting back, coupled with the absolute loyalty and security of the natives, has produced the extraordinary situation by which we have continued to operate for nearly three months on an extensive scale and even right down inside Jap towns, without their being aware that any whites have deliberately entered the interior.

Although the S.R.D. parties had been provided with arms to equip Dyaks and had distributed them, Brigadier Windeyer decided that he would not do likewise. Throughout this later period the 20th Brigade was in touch with the guerillas. It was not, however, until 21st June that the brigade had made contact with them and learnt their exact dispositions

---

[7] 20 Aust Inf Bde Report on Operation Oboe Six.
[8] Lt R. J. D. Pinkerton, MC, NX43707; "Z" Special Unit. Bank officer; of Wentworthville, NSW; b. Quaker's Hill, NSW, 15 May 1921.

and capabilities. The S.R.D. provided information of Japanese movements but "SRD information was often too old to be acted upon as it generally reached this Brigade by native couriers some of whom travelled several days on foot and by canoe to deliver their messages. It is considered that a sound military training including a knowledge of how to deal with military information is as necessary for those engaged in guerilla warfare as for regular troops."[9] The S.R.D. had preached among the Dyaks that the British would soon be driving the Japanese from their country, but this was not in fact the plan and the 20th Brigade found the Dyaks somewhat disappointed to learn that the Australians had halted while the surviving Japanese roamed through Dyak territory.

The coastal strip, with its ports, oilfields and rubber plantations, was the extent of the military objective. Its occupation fulfilled the whole military purpose of the invasion of British Borneo. The 9th Division had secured the coastal area and had defeated the Japanese by breaking up their army and driving it inland. The division then set out to restore civil order in all the main settled areas under its control—a very considerable territory. Extending the boundaries of restored civil rule was a quite secondary task for the division. It had to be sure first that it really held and controlled its gains, for a great number of Japanese were at large, although the Australians kept them dispersed. By degrees the Australians greatly extended their vast area by extensive patrolling in which junior leaders and troops showed great enterprise, initiative and interest. Sometimes, however, the S.R.D's guerillas in the interior seemed to the 9th Division to think that, instead of their activities being in support of the main military purpose of the army, they were the advance-guard or front line and that the army was failing to support them. In general, however, any distant patrolling by 9th Division units was exploratory and with a view only to extending the army's influence and better securing its gains. The use of ambushes and such ruses was encouraged, but guerilla work and harassing dispersed enemy parties were mainly left to the natives— and the S.R.D.

Thus, on 27th June, with the help of Dyaks, a forward patrol base of the 2/17th was established by Captain Murphy[1] at Balai, on the Belait River, from which to keep an eye on the Japanese escape route into the mountains. By the 30th two platoons had been moved by canoe to Balai.

Also on 27th June Broadbent sent out Lieutenant Graham[2] and 14 men to patrol up the Menderam River to find whether any Japanese were there as had been reported. The Australians were taken up the Belait River in dugout canoes paddled by Dyaks. After reaching the end of navigable water they patrolled stealthily forward to within 50 yards of a Dyak village just as an aircraft appeared and a group of Japanese rushed out of the village to a hill near by. Graham decided that the ground

---

[9] 20th Brigade report.
[1] Capt P. K. Murphy, NX70701; 2/17 Bn. Clerk; of Forbes, NSW; b. Parkes, NSW, 18 May 1920.
[2] Lt L. F. Graham, NX59113; 2/17 Bn. Baker; of Hillston, NSW; b. Hillston, 10 Nov 1919.

did not favour an attack—if a man had been wounded it would have been difficult to get him out—and wisely returned to the Belait.

On 11th July Graham's platoon was sent to Ridan, three days' march away, to form a base, harass any Japanese in the area and remain out until further orders. Karin, a reliable and enterprising Dyak who had guided Graham before, and 15 other Dyaks went with him. At Mount Teraja they found signs of Japanese occupation, including women's clothing and cosmetics. At "Sandy Bar", one hour from Ridan, was another abandoned Japanese bivouac. Here Major Carter of the S.R.D. sent a messenger to Graham with news that he was in the Marudi area and that 48 Japanese had ambushed him and killed two of his Dyaks. Having learnt from a Dyak runner that Japanese were bivouacked an hour and a half on the Marudi side of Ridan, Graham took out his platoon, less eight men and plus 16 Dyaks, to set an ambush. They found Japanese in a clearing near Ridan, a section was put across the track, and soon four Japanese walked into the trap and were shot. But the Japanese promptly opened fire with a machine-gun, and there was much shooting during which each side used a light mortar. Graham, being three days' march from medical attention, eventually withdrew, having had one man slightly wounded, but having killed 4 and wounded 4, as he found later.

As a result of the news that Carter had been forced out of Marudi a company group under Major Trebeck[3] was sent to the Marudi area in L.C.M's escorted by an L.C.M. gunboat and an unarmed launch. This was an important expedition because control of the Marudi area would help in control of the maze of rivers and break up the enemy's inland communications. On the way up the Baram River on the 15th Trebeck received reports from natives that about 40 Japanese were at Ridan, and decided to make a landing there. After a strike by six Spitfires and a barrage of rockets from the gunboat two platoons landed, but found that the Japanese had gone towards Marudi. These platoons plodded to Marudi across country and the remaining troops went by barge, but again found no Japanese. The Union Jack was hoisted in Marudi. On the 17th Lieutenant Powell's[4] platoon set out to contact Graham's platoon at Ridan. On the way they encountered 40 Japanese with four machine-guns. The Australians were moving through a swamp and the Japanese were on firm ground overlooking them. After a long fight, in which five Japanese were killed and one Australian (Corporal Howard,[5] an original member of the unit) and one Dyak were killed, the platoon broke off the fight and moved back to Marudi in the dark carrying the wounded. The party of Japanese was met again on the Menderam-Ridan track by a ration party which drove them westward and then returned to the Menderam whence

---

[3] Maj N. B. Trebeck, NX12371. 2/17 Bn, and BM 26 Bde 1944. Wool buyer; of Neutral Bay, NSW; b. Sydney, 29 May 1917.

[4] Lt F. B. G. Powell, NX113719; 2/17 Bn. Shop assistant; of Grafton, NSW; b. Grafton, 15 May 1920.

[5] Cpl E. J. Howard, NX17655; 2/17 Bn. Farm worker; of Sydney; b. Hants, England, 25 May 1919. Killed in action 17 Jul 1945.

Burning oil wells at Seria, 28th June 1945.

(*Australian War Memorial*)

(Australian War Memorial)
Lutong, Borneo, 20th June. Indian troops released from captivity by the 2/13th Battalion.

(Australian War Memorial)
A patrol of the 2/13th Battalion setting out from Miri, Borneo, 6th July 1945.

a fighting patrol set out but failed to find their quarry. They were later reported east of Labi.

On 24th July a platoon was established at Bakung and patrolled thence. One section, under Corporal Lemaire,[6] patrolling near the Arang River, was ambushed in tall grass by eight Japanese on 27th July. In the fight an Australian and a Dyak guide were killed. Lemaire, who controlled his section with great resource and coolness, shot the Japanese officer in command of the ambush and one other; two other Japanese were killed and the patrol withdrew through a swamp to Bakung. Natives reported that two strong parties of Japanese were approaching and the patrol withdrew in the dark to Marudi. Patrols moved out next day but found no Japanese; one platoon and later a second one occupied the Bakung area.

When the inhabitants returned to Marudi from refuges up the river the population was about 1,000. There were large rubber plantations in the area, neglected during the Japanese regime, and a large quantity of raw rubber in store which the owners were anxious to sell. The hospital at Marudi was re-opened and soon many natives were being treated there.

The Australians found that the Japanese treated the Dyaks with well-merited respect. They did not molest them or interfere with their women, nor did they try to employ them. The Dyaks for their part avoided the Japanese but if necessary would walk calmly through their bivouacs. They seem to have regarded the Japanese as mere raiders and to have been convinced that the British would return. At every Dyak village Australian patrols were invited in by the chief and given rice wine. Of all the Asian and island peoples among whom the Australian soldier campaigned and trained in six years of war—Arabs, Palestinians, Lebanese, Ceylonese, Malays, Chinese, Indonesians, Papuans, and others—none won more respect from him than did the Dyaks, with their courage, dignity, friendliness and generosity.

> Cooperation by the natives, in particular the Dyaks, has been most helpful (wrote Broadbent in July). Many of the Dyaks have proved to be first-rate soldiers of undoubted courage with a distinct hatred for the Japs. They did much good work as scouts and were in the thick of the fighting when contact was made. Some Chinese have done very good work and have not been wanting in courage. They have been very good as interpreters. Everywhere we have been enthusiastically received by the local inhabitants irrespective of their nationality. They have all been treated harshly by the Japs and are agreeably surprised since our occupation. They are probably much more favourably inclined now towards British rule than at any other time in the past.

On 11th July the diarist of the 2/17th recorded that there was not a Japanese in its area of responsibility. It was evident that they were moving deeper into the mountains. It was soon known that their orders were to withdraw to Tenom.

In July and the first half of August the 2/15th from its base at Limbang was in contact with the S.R.D. parties about Ukong and Trusan and sent out many patrols along the rivers and tracks. There were few contacts.

---
[6] Sgt C. E. Lemaire, MM, NX65985; 2/17 Bn. Clerk; of Leeton, NSW; b. Hurstville, NSW, 5 Sep 1922.

One clash occurred east of Limbang on 7th July. Sergeant Power[7] and four others surprised from 25 to 30 Japanese in a swamp. The Australians opened fire and killed about 20. The survivors fled and blundered west into a company position of the 2/15th where two more were killed. All this firing caused some anxiety in the town of Limbang.

Next day it was decided that this party of Japanese had been the strongest surviving group of the *366th Battalion* and had included Major Sato, the commander of the battalion. This group had been traced moving from Brunei via Rangau to the Pandaruan River. It was believed that the only survivors of the clashes on the 7th were Sato and one lieutenant; the remainder of the *366th* were believed to be making off inland in twos and threes. On 10th July, however, Major Harrisson reported that at least 800 Japanese, perhaps 2,500, had moved across the lower Limbang, or in canoes by way of Rangau, far up the Trusan River to the Pa Tengoa, 30 miles upstream in a bee-line, where they were digging in and reorganising. He had got the air force to strafe them five times that day, and had 10 Europeans and 150 armed natives waylaying Japanese on the tracks leading to the Pa Tengoa. He considered that they probably intended to go to Tenom and rejoin the main force, but to do this they would have to march through a long stretch of mountain country peopled by Muruts. He planned to "give them a hard go" along the tracks to Tenom.

As we have seen, the 9th Division had reached its objectives, and it was not part of its task to extend its control throughout the hinterland or to "mop up" the broken Japanese army. The guerilla leaders on the other hand were concerned about their Dyak friends and allies, and felt some responsibility for the protection and rehabilitation of the native peoples in their areas.

By the beginning of July 1945 (wrote Major Harrisson later) many Japanese were on the move deliberately towards the interior. These were naturally our concern. More than that, it would clearly be an inexplicable thing if we let these Japanese do wide-scale damage inland or destroy the lives of these, our so loyal supporters and allies.

Thus, from this time on until the end of the war, Semut [code name of the S.R.D. groups in this area] ceased to be engaged in intelligence and sabotage, and decreasingly in administration. Instead, we devoted the greater part of all effort directly to killing Japanese. This battle was to rage and roam for hundreds of jungle and mountain miles, and continue until long after the war was over.[8]

Harrisson reached the conclusion that not only the Japanese retreating from Brunei and Sarawak but others from the east and north were making for Sapong Estate near Tenom, a well-developed but isolated rubber plantation near the head of the railway from Jesselton. This, he thought, was to be the site of their last stand round General Baba's headquarters. (In much the same way another Japanese army was preparing a last-stand position in the mountains inland from Wewak in New Guinea.)

---

[7] Sgt F. C. Power, MM, QX5639; 2/15 Bn. Overseer, sheep station; of Kurumbul, Qld; b. Texas, Qld, 2 Jan 1919.

[8] T. Harrisson, *World Within, A Borneo Story*, pp. 269-70.

Captain Edmeades[9] of Harrisson's force established a base at Tomani on the Padas south of the Sapong Estate, and deployed about 200 Dyaks about Bole astride the route of the Japanese marching over the mountains from Sarawak. Harrisson estimated that 400 Japanese were killed between Bole and the Padas River, some in despair dying by their own hands.[1]

In north Borneo as in other areas in which Australians fought in 1945 there was no anti-tank role for the anti-tank artillery and other tasks were found for them. We have seen that some anti-tank gunners in New Guinea were converted into heavy-mortar crews and others were fighting as infantry. The 9th Division's anti-tank regiment, the 2/3rd (Lieut-Colonel Argent[2]), landed in Borneo and on 3rd July relieved the 2/28th Battalion round Weston enabling that battalion to rejoin the rest of its brigade at Beaufort. The role of the 2/3rd was to protect Weston, protect and conduct the railway to Beaufort, and patrol. Its patrols had occasional clashes. It did much work in restoring the civil administration, and in July shipped 10 tons of rubber to Labuan and returned some 1,760 civilians to their homes.

On 26th July the regiment was ordered to assume responsibility for the Sipitang area south to the Mengalong River, thus forming a link with the 2/15th Battalion. A force to occupy Sipitang was formed under Captain Rennison,[3] comprising two troops and other small detachments. One troop was to hold the base at Sipitang while the other patrolled. The force made contact with a patrol of the 2/15th at Sindumin on 30th July.

By early July it was possible for the Australians to piece together the story of the Japanese forces in the Brunei Bay area. As mentioned, the infantry battalions in the area mostly belonged to the *56th Independent Mixed Brigade*, originally of six battalions. The regiment with four battalions was ordered to march west to Brunei Bay; the *369th Battalion* was sent to Bandjermasin, and the *370th* remained at Tawao. Because so many fell ill on the march westward the battalions each were only 250 to 400 strong when they arrived. The *366th* and *367th*, as mentioned, were sent to Brunei, the *368th* to Beaufort and the *371st* to Labuan. At Miri there was already the *553rd*; and at each centre there were engineers and other troops.

In the Brunei-Miri area the *367th Battalion* withdrew to the Trusan River more or less intact; the *366th* fought the rearguard action and withdrew through the Limbang area. It broke up into one group of about 40 and several smaller groups at Rangau about 14th June. Soon parties of troops and civilians of varying strength were moving up the valleys of the Baram, the Limbang and the Trusan in search of refuge, but finding none, because the Australian patrols and the air force pursued them, and the country into which they were moving was peopled, as we have seen, by hostile Dyaks, organised by officers of the S.R.D.

As the campaign proceeded the civil responsibilities of the 9th Division increased. To assist the division to re-establish British government it had

---
[9] Maj E. A. Edmeades, MC, SX11095. 2/43 Bn and "Z" Special Unit. Clerk; of North Unley, SA; b. N Bengal, India, 2 Sep 1920.

[1] In the course of the campaign Harrisson's force reported the killing of 940 Japanese troops all told, Carter's of 258, Sochon's of 227. No Europeans and only 19 Bornese allies were killed. In other parts of north Borneo S.R.D. groups reported the killing of some 390 Japanese.

[2] Col J. N. L. Argent, OBE, ED, NX12179. 2/3 Anti-Tank Regt (CO 1944-46). Building contractor; of Westmead, NSW; b. Sydney, 26 Apr 1905. Author of *"Target Tank"*, the history of this regiment.

[3] Maj A. C. Rennison, NX12581; 2/3 Anti-Tank Regt. Clerk; of Dulwich Hill, NSW; b. North Sydney, 1 Mar 1916.

under command part of the British Borneo Civil Affairs Unit, whose early history has already been described. Five officers of B.B.C.A.U. headquarters were attached to Wootten's headquarters, 11 officers to the 20th Brigade and 13 to the 24th Brigade. I Corps, in an administrative order, stated that the functions of the unit were:

(a) to relieve combat troops of the necessity of providing for civil administration;
(b) the administration and control of non-military individuals, whether native or otherwise, in re-occupied areas of north Borneo;
(c) the distribution and control of relief supplies and services;
(d) the procurement, control, employment and administration of labourers;
(e) the rendering of every possible assistance to the operational forces.

On 10th June General Morshead, acting under the authority vested in him by General MacArthur, signed a document proclaiming martial law and delegating all powers under martial law to General Wootten.

On Labuan the Civil Affairs officers had been immediately faced with the task of caring for thousands of homeless people. The bombardments had destroyed practically every building on the island and soon some 3,000 civilians including a large number of emaciated Javanese labourers were in the compound established in the beach maintenance area. Troops had to be allotted to help B.B.C.A.U. cope with these people and to handle the supplies provided for the relief of civilians.

In the opening stages two B.B.C.A.U. officers who could speak Malay were attached to each forward battalion. As the operations developed army men were increasingly engaged on work done for the benefit of the civilians: drainage, restoring sewerage and water supply, medical care of natives, collection of rubber, re-opening of schools.

Wootten considered the B.B.C.A.U. detachment far too weak in medical staff and vehicles. At the brigade level Brigadier Windeyer considered his detachment—11 officers (including one medical officer) and 13 others "hopelessly inadequate. . . . But by the enthusiasm of many members of the Brigade . . . who were detached from their normal duties to assist in the restoration of normal civilian life a very great deal was accomplished in a short time. . . . The guidance and help given . . . by those officers of BBCAU who had had experience in Borneo was invaluable."[4]

On 6th July Wootten directed the attention of the Corps Commander to the fact that B.B.C.A.U. had only three medical officers and that his division was doing most of the medical work required by B.B.C.A.U. In 17 days 7,547 civilian patients had been treated at Brooketon and Brunei, yet these were drawn from only one-third of the division's area. On 3rd August Wootten asked what action had been taken to move medical men forward and urged that they be sent in by air.

By the end of August thousands of natives were employed repairing roads, clearing plantations, getting timber and so on, and were being paid, but thousands were receiving free food and doing nothing. In the

---
[4] 20th Brigade report.

24th Brigade's area by the beginning of September the natives had consumed more rations than the troops. The rubber plantations were now mostly cleared of undergrowth but so far no trade in rubber had begun.

Miri had fallen into disrepair during the Japanese occupation because the greater part of the people had lost their employment and left the town. Drains and hygiene were neglected. Allied bombers had damaged the town, and before the Japanese departed they had blown up many buildings. When the people streamed back after the Australian occupation there were not enough houses for them, and hundreds were crowded into the oil company's barracks. Colonel Colvin put Miri out of bounds to troops off duty, and a system was established whereby a party in a jeep on which was mounted a loud speaker moved round the town giving instructions and advice or reading the news, all in Malay.

There was much work to do clearing away rubble, cleaning drains, cleaning and repairing buildings, roads and bridges. By early September much of this work had been done: the streets and back yards were clean, the debris mostly cleared away. Largely through the efforts of the 2/8th Field Ambulance a native hospital was opened at Miri, and others at Kuala Belait and Brunei. Many of the patients were Javanese labourers, neglected by the Japanese, unwanted by the people of Borneo, and often suffering from malnutrition, ulcers, malaria or dysentery.

By 26th July the 2/3rd Field Ambulance (Lieut-Colonel K. J. J. Dorney) was conducting six civil hospitals with average daily totals of 125 in-patients and 970 out-patients. The largest, at Papar, had 30 in-patients and 350 out-patients. Twenty-two civilian dressers were employed and apprentices were being trained.

By the last week of July the divisional engineers on Labuan had widened and surfaced 29 miles of road; built light timber bridges of an average span of 40 feet, and two larger temporary bridges; built a wharf able to berth Liberty ships and more capacious than any the colony had possessed before; erected 10 oil tanks with a total capacity of 705,000 gallons; made an airfield 4,800 feet long with dispersal areas for 150 aircraft. In the Brunei-Miri area 100 miles of road had been widened and surfaced, seven bridges built, and gas and water systems repaired. In several districts sawmills had been reconditioned and were operating.

Wootten considered that the approach of B.B.C.A.U. to its problems was not a sufficiently practical one. They had wanted to set up a normal administration straight away. He had been told that, in Europe, a divisional commander had a Civil Affairs officer on his staff. Wootten had replied: "The whole of B.B.C.A.U. is on my staff. This division is not in the position of a division in Europe where it would be part of a big force. This is the only force here and I am the Military Governor for the time being. In fact, I have two staffs: my military staff, and my Civil Affairs staff, which is B.B.C.A.U."

As mentioned, Brigadier Macaskie, the commander of B.B.C.A.U., did not arrive at Labuan and take command until 22nd July. He told Wootten that the unit was too large, containing, as it did, more officers than were in the Borneo administration before the war. These included a large number of Australians and these, Macaskie pointed out, would go away when the military administration ceased and the civil one took over. On two occasions Macaskie had asked for the appointment to B.B.C.A.U. of former officials of the Borneo administration who were available in Australia but L.H.Q. had not been willing to send them forward.

General Blamey had written to General Morshead on 20th July about "the background" of the formation of B.B.C.A.U. The letter was not in Blamey's normal crisp, unambiguous style, and it seems likely that it was drafted in the Directorate of Research and Civil Affairs. The letter mentioned "one or two difficulties in relation to the senior officers"; that there had been "certain delicacies in explaining the matter to the Australian Government", which was "showing some reticence in accepting the full implication of the operational responsibility which you [Morshead] carry in this respect"; a "need to proceed with care and circumspection in the interests of our relations with the U.K." There was a reference to the need for "a few minor precautions to provide for the careerists without military experience", and a reference to a proposal that an economist from the Department of Post-War Reconstruction should visit Borneo and give "an Australian appreciation of the economic position of the territories for obvious reasons"; his services could be available for only three months. In another note handed to Morshead it was stated that "L.H.Q." was not satisfied with the quality of the advisers on whom he might be asked to rely.

In the forward area, on 31st July, Macaskie wrote to Wootten that he considered that "an organisation based on a rigid Detachment War Establishment" was not suitable for B.B.C.A.U., and he asked that he be allowed to allot officers arriving in the area as he thought fit. He would later submit proposals for a revised war establishment.

Wootten wrote to Morshead on 5th August, enclosing a copy of Macaskie's letter and pointing out that so far he had not been officially supplied with a copy of the war establishment of B.B.C.A.U., although B.B.C.A.U. had lent him one. Macaskie had told him that he had not been consulted in any way about the posting of officers under his command. Wootten asked whether it was intended to make recommendations to higher authority with the object of ensuring that the organisation of B.B.C.A.U. was designed "to fit and suit British Borneo as regards the administration of civil affairs".

On 13th August Morshead in his turn signalled Land Headquarters that until that day he had not seen a copy of the war establishment of B.B.C.A.U. He asked for a list of all officers of the unit with details of the experience and qualifications of those of the rank of lieut-colonel and above. After discussions with Wootten and Macaskie he recommended that Colonel Rolleston, who was on the spot but not yet posted, should be appointed Deputy Chief Civil Affairs Officer.

In August some of the British officers were convinced that senior British officers still in Australia were being prevented from going to Borneo, and remarks which had been made suggested to them that the Australian Government hoped to take over British Borneo. It seems that such remarks were made, but that they were irresponsible; the fact remains that they were believed. The disagreements and friction within B.B.C.A.U. were unfortunate, but were almost entirely confined to the higher levels in Australia and Borneo. The achievements in the field were admirable.

There the value of those B.B.C.A.U. officers who knew the country was very great. They were able, by advice and direction, to make effective the ready cooperation of Australian officers and men released from ordinary military duties to help them. Without such assistance B.B.C.A.U. would have been virtually impotent. Some idea of the scale of the work may be gained from a report of the situation in the 20th Brigade area to 5th August. There were then 27 Eurasians, 201 Chinese, 24 Indians, 37 Malays and 1,625 Javanese in compounds at Brunei, Seria and Miri. The B.B.C.A.U. officers estimated that about 69,000 civilians were within the area of effective control, and 971 artisans and 1,730 labourers were being employed. Of these 386 were employed by or for the army. In the past week 158 civilians had been admitted to hospitals, and 8,500 treated at aid posts. Much re-building was being done; town water supplies were being restored and in Brunei, Seria and Miri were adequate. The schools throughout Brunei State were now functioning as before the war, under the direction of B.B.C.A.U. Rubber was being collected and sent to Labuan. The restoration of the oilfields was continuing.

The troops got on splendidly with the civilians—both the impassive, businesslike Chinese and the cheerful, unhurried Malays—and particularly with the children. Here and there the troops temporarily adopted abandoned children, whom they housed, fed and clothed—and spoiled—and to whom they taught slangy English. When the Australians first appeared the children had been frightened of them and would salute and bow. Gradually the bowing ceased; the salute became a cheery wave, and the frightened expression a broad grin. Soon the inhabitants were arriving at the soldiers' open-air picture shows, where the troops gave up their seats to Chinese and Malay women and sat children on their knees. They gave clothing to civilians who were in need. Trading with civilians was officially forbidden with the object of protecting the civilians from bad bargains and preventing inflation—although the Chinese in particular were not likely to come off badly in any such transactions. As a result the civilians could not legally exchange fresh food, which the troops lacked, for meat, of which the troops had plenty. In some battalion and company areas, however, trading was winked at. Some companies appointed official buyers to prevent undue bargaining and variation in prices, and systematic trading was carried on to the great satisfaction of both parties. The civilians got tinned beef; the troops fruit, poultry and eggs.

When the fighting died down the troops in several towns organised elaborate entertainments for the civilians. Typical of these was a fair organised by the 2/43rd Battalion at Beaufort. Under the guidance of Captain Lonnie of the 2/43rd a committee including Malayan, Filipino, Indian and Chinese representatives was formed. The troops and the civilians built brightly-painted see-saws, swings, slippery dips and booths. The civilians built also a pagoda-like structure for the official guests. At 10 a.m. on 8th August Brigadier Porter, Colonel Jeanes (of the 2/43rd) and Colonel Stanner (of B.B.C.A.U.) with other officers and leading civilians took their places in the pagoda. Fireworks, long hoarded by the Chinese, were set off. Porter made a speech, which an interpreter repeated in Chinese and Malay.

> The troops then took charge of the youngsters and the colourful spectacle which the costumes of the native population provided became more animated. Children were sliding down the slippery dips, swinging, drinking cordial, playing hoop-la and darts, eating sweets and buns and watching the pedestrian events. Several stages had been erected and on these Malayans, of varying ages and stages of senility, performed their shuffling national dances to the rhythm of the cymbal-like instruments which resembled more than anything else the upturned covers of a number of land mines. This Malayan music could be heard all day and few Malayans failed to tread a measure or so.[5]

Band recitals and variety acts were given on a stage by both Australian and civilian performers; there were rides in jeeps, river trips in L.C.M's, a beauty contest, an eight-hour program of athletic events, aerobatics by 24 Kittyhawks, and finally a cinema show. The food provided included the troops' allowance of canteen supplies for a week and three water buffaloes.

Comparable entertainments were organised at other places. In the 20th Brigade's area, for example, there was an aquatic carnival organised by the 2/15th Battalion at Limbang; there were concerts and sports at Kuala Belait; and similar entertainments at Miri and elsewhere.

Some of the officers who had been in Borneo before the war complained of the friendly attitude of the troops towards the natives on the ground that it would lower British prestige. These men represented the British who would live in Borneo after the Australians had gone and their opinion had to be heeded. At the same time they were astonished at the way in which the Australians were able to persuade the civilians to work really hard, and still more astonished at the strenuous way in which the Australians themselves laboured in the trying climate—and shoulder to shoulder with the Borneo people.

The Australian view was that the spectacle of Europeans doing hard physical labour might even raise European prestige, and they would not agree that playing with local children would lower the Asians' opinion of Europeans.

In Borneo as in New Guinea, as the fighting died down, the officers of the Army Education Service organised increasing numbers of classes for the troops. In the Beaufort area Brigadier Porter in August even

---

[5] Appendix to war diary of 2/43rd Battalion, August 1945.

established a boarding school at the homestead of a rubber plantation. Here several hundred pupils slept in tents and attended classes in two big storehouses. The supervisor was Captain Kennedy,[6] a former teacher. Blackboards and chalk were manufactured.

> It was strange (wrote a diarist) to see the teachers—all privates—standing in front of their classes, books in hand, and the perspiring diggers in their faded green uniforms bent over their desks. One class of four was learning to read and write. (There are also classes for illiterates in the individual battalions.) There are four English classes the most advanced of which was having the verses of Henry Lawson read to it from the new paper-covered edition. There was a class in wool-classing with no wool but only chalk and blackboard, paper and pencil; one in elementary book-keeping, one in shorthand, and one in typewriting—three machines.

By the time the cease fire was ordered a great part of the force throughout north Borneo was largely employed on non-military tasks and the demobilisation of long-service men had begun. The story of the restoration of civil government in this and other areas will be continued in a chapter about the Japanese surrenders and their immediate consequences.

In the operations in north Borneo 114 Australians were killed or died of wounds and 221 were wounded but survived.[7] In the 9th Division's operations the number of Japanese dead who were seen and counted was 1,234; it was estimated that an additional 141 were killed; 130 were taken prisoner. The S.R.D. groups believed that their guerillas killed more than 1,800 throughout north Borneo.

---

[6] Capt R. R. Kennedy, WX12543. 2/32 Bn and HQ 24 Bde. Schoolteacher; of Guildford, WA; b. Leonora, WA, 15 Dec 1922.

[7] The battle casualties in the infantry, commando and armoured units were:

	Officers	Other Ranks		Officers	Other Ranks
2/13th Battalion	1	3	2/2nd Machine Gun Battalion	—	8
2/15th Battalion	—	5	2/11th Commando Squadron	2	11
2/17th Battalion	1	23	2/12th Commando Squadron	1	2
2/28th Battalion	5	118	2/9th Armoured Regiment	2	4
2/32nd Battalion	4	20			
2/43rd Battalion	3	53			
2/4th Pioneer Battalion	—	5			

In the artillery 12 other ranks were killed or wounded; in the engineers 17.

CHAPTER 21

THE SEIZURE OF BALIKPAPAN

WHILE the 9th Division was finishing its task in north Borneo, the 7th was preparing for the attack on Balikpapan, the last large-scale Allied operation of the six years' war. The re-conquest of Luzon was now virtually completed; organised resistance had ceased on Okinawa; for nearly three months United States aircraft had been raining explosive and incendiary bombs on the major cities of Japan; in Burma, Rangoon had fallen on 3rd May.

Balikpapan was distant 2,500 miles and more from Rangoon and Okinawa, and was 1,200 miles south of Manila. Even as early as April General Blamey could see no justification for attacking Balikpapan, but the operation had been ordered by the Combined Chiefs of Staff, and the Australian Prime Minister, after having informed General MacArthur of General Blamey's opinion, had not objected.

Balikpapan, which, after Palembang in Sumatra, was the most productive oil port in east Asia, was built round the eastern headland of Balikpapan Bay. The port, with its seven piers and its warehouses, lay within the bay; the European suburb of Klandasan faced the open sea; on the steep-sided ridge in between, forming the backbone of the headland, towered the cracking plant and about 40 storage tanks. The oil was piped to the Balikpapan refinery from Sambodja and Sangasanga, 25 and 55 miles to the north-east respectively, and, in peace, oil was shipped to Balikpapan also from Java, Tarakan and Ceram. Before the war Balikpapan exported about 1,800,000 tons of cargo a year, almost all of it fuel oil and other petroleum products.

The airfields were to the east of the town on the narrow coastal plains: at Sepinggang, five miles from Balikpapan, and Manggar, about 12 miles away. The hills rose steeply from the coast to about 700 feet in the area to be covered by the troops. The country was open for several miles round Balikpapan, but farther inland, and several miles to the north along the coast, the jungle began. There was a motor road along the shore and thence inland to Sambodja, an uncompleted road to Samarinda, and a track to Bandjermasin. The Australian staffs named the coast road the Vasey Highway and the Samarinda Road the Milford Highway, and, as at Tarakan, they gave names to every hilltop in the area, thus greatly simplifying signalling, written and oral orders, and reports by reducing the use of map references.

The Japanese had assembled a fairly large force of troops and civilian workers of several nationalities in the Balikpapan-Samarinda area. In June it was estimated that there were, round Balikpapan, about 3,900 troops, of whom 1,500 were in mobile units and 2,400 in anti-aircraft, air force and base units; also 1,100 Japanese workers, 2,400 Indonesians and 1,000 Formosans. Round Samarinda there were believed to be about 1,500 troops, plus possibly a battalion recently arrived from Tarakan. Experience had taught that, in estimating the strength of the enemy's resistance, every Japanese and Formosan, whether in a fighting unit, base unit or a civilian labour group, had to be regarded as a fighting man.

It was known that at least 18 coast-defence guns were mounted round Balikpapan, principally on the ridges overlooking the sea, and there were at least 26 heavy dual-purpose and 78 medium and light anti-aircraft guns. Off shore between Klandasan and Manggar rows of stout poles had

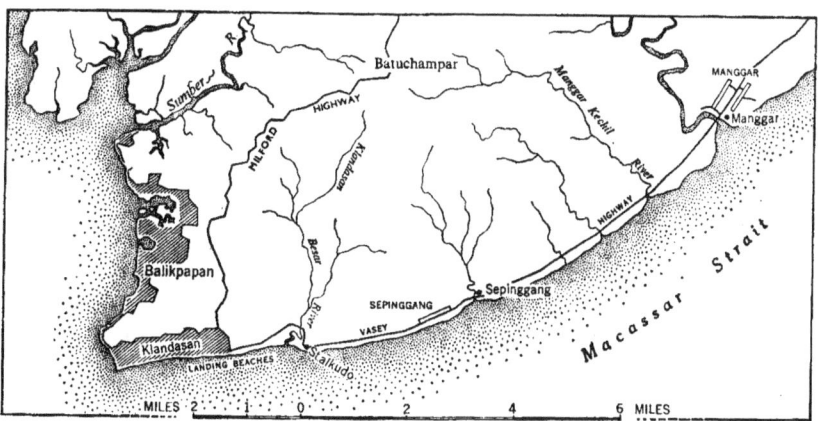

been driven into the bed of the sea and horizontally braced with timber and protected with barbed wire. An almost continuous anti-tank ditch from 12 to 14 feet wide lay above the beach from Stalkudo to Sepinggang, and extensive trench systems with many tunnel openings had been detected on the ridges overlooking Klandasan. There were also many concrete strong-posts and a continuous line of bunkers along the fringe of the beach. The area was as strongly fortified as any that the Australians had encountered anywhere in the war. Indeed Air Vice-Marshal Bostock,[1] who was in control of air support of the landing, in a letter to the Prime Minister, warned him that these carefully-prepared defences might lead to A.I.F. casualties comparable with those at the landing on Gallipoli.

The enemy appeared to have established his main defences on the slopes overlooking the beaches from Klandasan to Stalkudo. The Australian staffs considered that the Japanese would try to contain the invaders within their beach-head area as long as they could and then withdraw inland and either south to Bandjermasin or overland to Bintulu in Sarawak. It was expected that the enemy would direct burning oil down

---

[1] AVM W. D. Bostock, CB, DSO, OBE. (1st AIF, 1914-17; 48 Sqn RFC 1917-18.) Director of Operations and Intelligence RAAF HQ 1938-39; Deputy Chief of the Air Staff 1939-41; Chief of Staff AAF SWPA 1942; AOC RAAF Cd 1942-46. MHR 1949-58. Regular air force officer; b. Sydney, 5 Feb 1892.

on to the beach unless the oil tanks were destroyed in the preliminary bombardment.

As mentioned, the decision to employ the 7th Division instead of the 9th at Balikpapan was not made until 17th April, when G.H.Q. authorised the movement of the division less a brigade from Australia to Morotai, where, it was expected, the concentration of the force would be complete by 16th June. The 7th Division like the 9th had had a long period of training in combined operations.

On 30th April G.H.Q. issued a staff study which said that the preparatory naval and air bombardment would destroy enemy defences and any oil tanks whose contents might be used in the defence; in the next stage a landing would be made with the object of destroying the garrison and seizing the port and airfields; in the final stage the remaining enemy forces were to be destroyed, the N.E.I. Government re-established, and the remaining oil-producing and oil-processing installations protected. On 7th May the date of the landing was fixed at 28th June, but the delay in beginning the Brunei Bay operation caused a corresponding postponement of the landing at Balikpapan, and on 8th May this was fixed at 10th July. Nine days later, however, G.H.Q. decided that, because of the expected concentration of the force at Morotai by 19th June, the date of the landing would be 1st July. G.H.Q. provided 25 L.S.T's, in addition to ships already allotted, to hurry units from Cairns to Morotai.

The 7th Division was now going into action for the first time since it had been withdrawn from the Ramu Valley operations early in 1944. This would be its first opposed landing, the first operation since Syria in 1941 in which it would have a full array of supporting weapons, and the first operation in which it had fought as a complete formation. The division's commander, Major-General E. J. Milford, had joined it in July 1944. Milford had led the 5th Division in the final operations round Salamaua and later had been chief of staff of New Guinea Force. He was a firm leader, learned and shrewd. Primarily a gunner, he was determined to make the most of the opportunity presented by this relatively open country to use artillery. All his brigade commanders and all but two of the infantry battalion commanders had led their formations or units in the Ramu Valley.

Although it was a tried and experienced division it now contained, in the infantry, a fairly high percentage of subalterns who had come from disbanded artillery and other units and had not been in action before. Consequently, when briefing began, great emphasis was placed on the need to push on and gain ground.

Major-General Milford and his staff had begun planning the operation on 26th April and by 5th May Milford had decided to make an assault on a two-brigade front between the Klandasan Besar River and Klandasan. The infantry brigadiers, F. O. Chilton of the 18th and I. N. Dougherty of the 21st, were not informed about the operation until 11th May, and then in great secrecy. Milford told them what resources were likely to be available and that the object was to capture the town and port area. He asked the brigadiers to study the problem independently and suggest an outline plan. They studied the maps and models at divisional headquarters on the Atherton Tableland and on 18th May, in conference with Milford, each said that he favoured making the landing at Klandasan and not farther east. Milford told them that that was his plan and, after arriving at it, he had examined the appreciation already made by the 9th Division and discovered that it also had favoured Klandasan. On Chilton's representations Milford agreed to make the assault 1,000 yards east of where he had originally intended.

Three possible landing places had been considered: Manggar, Sepinggang and Klandasan, the only places where the water was deep enough, the beach long enough and the approaches suitable. Klandasan was chosen despite the fact that the minesweepers would have to operate under the enemy's coast guns and the supporting warships would have to stand farther off shore than otherwise, and that the landing would be made in the area of the enemy's strongest defences.

The following reasons in favour of landing at Klandasan were later set out in the divisional report:

(a) A successful assault against the strongest positions would considerably reduce the duration of the campaign and it was thereby hoped that casualties, which reach their highest in a long drawn out campaign which becomes a war of attrition, would be substantially reduced;

(b) The greatest fire support is required to overcome the position of greatest strength and this condition would be fulfilled on Fox Day;

(c) By attacking the centre of the enemy's defences some degree of disorganisation should result which might continue for some days if the attack were pressed with vigour;

Japanese reaction is generally slow and it was hoped to capture the vital ground commanding the harbour before he recovered from the initial bombardment;

(d) The early capture of Balikpapan Bay would ease the problem of supply over the beach and would be a safeguard against unfavourable weather;

(e) A higher degree of concentration of both fire power and man power could be effected;

(f) The full power of the force would be quickly deployed as opposed to the narrow front imposed by a coastwise advance;

(g) Defences between Balikpapan and Manggar were sited to face the East and could more readily be overcome by an advance from the West;

(h) Fewer engineering tasks of bridging and communications would be met on the vital first day;

(i) The location of defences suggested that the enemy considered a landing at Klandasan would be too hazardous an undertaking and that tactical surprise (strategic surprise was not possible with the preliminary bombardment and minesweeping) might be achieved.[2]

In short, as Milford wrote later, "why land up the coast and have to fight miles through jungle, which suits the enemy, when you can go

---

[2] 7 Aust Div Report on Operation Oboe Two.

straight in under heavy supporting fire, which the enemy can't stand, in comparatively open and favourable country".

Efforts were made to give an impression that the landing would be made at Manggar. This was done by spreading rumours, landing a reconnaissance party in that area, and demolishing some underwater obstacles at both Manggar and Sepinggang at the same time as the obstacles were breached at Klandasan.

The senior naval commander for the Balikpapan operation was Vice-Admiral Barbey, who was designated Commander of the Balikpapan Attack Force; under him Rear-Admiral Albert G. Noble commanded the attack group and Rear-Admiral Ralph S. Riggs the cruiser covering group. On 25th May the United States naval planning team arrived at Morotai and explained that they preferred a landing about Sepinggang or even farther east where their ships could stand in closer and also be away from the Japanese coast-defence guns. The leader of the naval team told Milford that the more he looked at the divisional plan the less he liked it, and that he feared that this might prove the first unsuccessful landing in the South-West Pacific.

I indicated (wrote Milford in his notebook) landing farther E was not acceptable, too far from vital town and would mean we would be restricted to advance along narrow coastal strip with enemy well prepared. The efficiency of the gun defences is doubtful and they can be blinded by smoke if very active. The difficulty is not getting the landing waves ashore but in landing heavy equipment and stores since beaches may be vulnerable to shelling.

Finally the naval team agreed to put the division ashore wherever it wished. But when Admiral Noble arrived at divisional headquarters on 28th May he expressed dislike for the choice of Klandasan with its defending guns and left a copy of a paper on the subject that he had submitted to General Morshead. Morshead, however, ruled in favour of Milford's plan.

At this stage Milford urged that the 10,500 troops of the R.A.A.F. who were to be landed by the fifteenth day after the landing be reduced by 7,000 and thus enough ships made available to include a third brigade in the assault convoy. On 31st May G.H.Q. agreed to a request by Morshead that the third brigade be included.

Finally the plan provided for the employment of the following forces in the assault:

7th Division	21,635
Corps troops	2,737
7th Base Sub-Area	4,961
R.A.A.F.	2,052
U.S. and N.E.I. units	2,061
Total	33,446

The multitude of specialist units and detachments which existed at this stage of the war is illustrated by the order of battle of the 7th Division and its supporting forces. This list contains the names of 247 headquarters, units or detachments (including 21 in the 2nd Beach Group and 67 in the 7th Base Sub-Area). Among the main units were:

Divisional Units:
2/7th Cavalry Regiment
2/4th, 2/5th and 2/6th Field Regiments; 2/2nd Anti-Tank Regiment
2/4th, 2/5th, 2/6th, 2/9th Field Companies, 2/25th Field Park Company
18th Brigade (2/9th, 2/10th, 2/12th Battalions)
21st Brigade (2/14th, 2/16th, 2/27th Battalions)
25th Brigade (2/25th, 2/31st, 2/33rd Battalions)
2/1st Pioneer Battalion, 2/1st Machine Gun Battalion
Corps and R.A.A.F. Units:
1st Armoured Regiment, less a squadron
2/1st Composite Anti-Aircraft Regiment
Nos. 1, 2, 3, 6 Airfield Construction Squadrons, R.A.A.F.
2nd Beach Group:
2/11th Field Company
2/2nd Pioneer Battalion
U.S. and N.E.I. Units:
727th Amphibious Tractor Battalion less one company
One boat company, 593rd E.B.S.R.
One company 672nd Amphibious Tractor Battalion
One company 1st N.E.I. Battalion.

By this final stage of the war the Intelligence and allied organisations within the American and Australian forces had become particularly varied, numerous and specialised. Those represented on the 7th Division's staff in the Balikpapan operation included:

Corps Intelligence
Geological engineer Intelligence
N.E.F.I.S.—Netherlands Expeditionary Forces Intelligence Service
N.I.C.A.—Netherlands Indies Civil Administration
R.A.N. Intelligence
R.A.A.F. and U.S.A.A.F. Intelligence
U.S. Naval Intelligence
A.I.B.—Allied Intelligence Bureau
S.R.D.—Services Reconnaissance Department
F.E.L.O.—Far Eastern Liaison Office
S.I.—Secret Intelligence
C.I.C.—Counter Intelligence Corps
F.S.S.—Field Security Section
F.S.S. (E.E.)—Field Security Section (Enemy Equipment)
A.T.I.S.—Allied Translator and Interpreter Section
A.A.P.I. Group—Australian Army Photographic Interpretation Group
Military History
Public Relations
M.E.I.U.—Mobile Explosive Intelligence Unit
Flakintel
U.S. naval ordnance
R.A.N. enemy equipment.

The armoured force included two squadrons of Matilda tanks, one troop of Frogs (flame-throwing tanks), one troop of tankdozers, and one bridge-laying tank. It was planned to use the tanks along roads in the following formation: gun tank, gun tank, Frog tank, Frog tank, gun tank, Frog tank. When opposition was encountered the gun tanks would engage it from the flanks while the Frogs advanced to attack frontally; the Frogs normally opened fire at ranges between 15 and 30 yards.

Changes of plan, the late inclusion of a third brigade, the distance of Morotai from north Queensland, and the inclusion in the force of many small units not under the command of the 7th Division complicated planning. The divisional headquarters had to be divided into three sections; one at Morotai engaged in planning, another at Morotai administering the troops as they arrived from Australia, and a third in Australia sending the units forward. Brigade and battalion headquarters had also to split into three similar echelons. That the planning was done swiftly and well was evidence of the high standard of staff work that had been attained at all levels after nearly six years of war.

The unit planning teams of the two leading brigades did not arrive at Morotai until 13th June, only eight days before the troops embarked for Balikpapan. On 14th June, with the landing only a fortnight away, the brigade commanders were informed in a letter from Milford's G.S.O.1, Lieut-Colonel Wilmoth,[3] that ten items of ammunition would be in short supply during the early stages of the operation. In particular, there would, until 16th July, be only 30,000 high-explosive 3-inch mortar bombs, 4,400 high-explosive 4.2-inch mortar bombs, and tank ammunition would have to be conserved.

Dougherty, who, with Chilton, had long discussed the value of "saturation" mortar bombardment as a means of saving the lives of their troops and had preached to the troops the need for generous mortar fire, immediately wrote to Milford a letter in the course of which he said:

> I do consider it criminal that Australians of any division should be asked, at this stage of the war, to go into what might well be a difficult operation, with less ammunition than that which is considered necessary by their commanders.

He asked to be paraded to General Morshead. On the 16th, however, Milford discussed the matter with Dougherty, who decided that the general had pressed similar views and no good purpose would be served by being paraded.

Before and after the landing several parties were put ashore round Balikpapan to gain information. Thus on 20th March 1945 Major Stott[4] and three others had been landed from submarines near Balikpapan to obtain Intelligence and extract natives for interrogation. On 22nd March Captain Morton[5] was landed from a submarine in the same area. He found that the presence of Stott's party was known to the enemy and was told that Stott had been captured or killed. Morton took command and led the party for six weeks, being constantly pursued. The survivors were evacuated by a prahu and a Catalina on 3rd May.

---

[3] Lt-Col E. R. Wilmoth, MC, VX206. 2/8 Bn; BM 19 Bde 1942-43; GSO1 5 Div 1943-44, 7 Div 1944-45. Law student and radio announcer; of Horsham, Vic; b. Horsham, 10 Jan 1917.

[4] Maj D. J. Stott, DSO. 5 NZ Fd Regt and SRD. Newspaper machinist; of Auckland, NZ; b. New Zealand, 23 Oct 1917. Drowned 20 Mar 1945.

[5] Capt R. McD. Morton, MC, DCM. 5 NZ Fd Regt and SRD. Postal clerk; of Nyasaland, East Africa; b. New Zealand, 3 Mar 1919.

Captain R. K. McLaren, an outstanding guerilla leader who, having escaped from captivity on Borneo, had served with guerilla forces on Mindanao for two years, led a party of five who were dropped by parachute into a village 20 miles north-west of Balikpapan on 30th June to find out whether the Japanese, when attacked, would withdraw towards Samarinda or round the bay towards Bandjermasin. One man was injured while landing and the storepedoes containing equipment and food were captured, but the party carried on. It was ambushed on 3rd July and one man was captured. McLaren took the injured man to safety and continued his task. On 6th July he extracted his party in native craft and reported to the 7th Division.

On 3rd July Captain Prentice, who had already led pre-invasion parties on Tarakan and in the Brunei Bay area, was landed with five others 35 miles west of Samarinda. They remained there until 12th August, sent useful information to the 7th Division, organised guerillas and had several successful engagements with the enemy.

The number of mines that had been laid in the sea round Balikpapan, the large area covered, and the fact that many were magnetic mines, made it necessary to begin sweeping more than two weeks before the landing, and before this could be done it was desirable to subdue the powerful array of coast and anti-aircraft guns on the high ground overlooking the minefields, which included mines laid by the Dutch in 1941, mines laid by the Japanese, and mines dropped by Allied aircraft. Since the Tarakan airfield would not be ready in time Air Vice-Marshal Bostock arranged that fighter aircraft of the American Thirteenth Air Force based on Sanga Sanga Island in the Sulu Archipelago would cover the minesweepers. All the heavy bombers of the R.A.A.F. and Thirteenth Air Force and a wing from the Fifth Air Force were made available to help subdue the enemy's defences. These bombers operated from Morotai, Zamboanga, Tawitawi, and Palawan. In addition, to ensure continuous fighter cover, particularly on the day before the landing and two days afterwards, a division of American escort carriers was made available.

The intensive bombing of the enemy defences was begun 20 days before the landing. Four days later the minesweepers arrived. During the next seven days, while waters well off shore were being swept, the supporting warships remained more than 12,000 yards from the coast and the minesweepers had a difficult time. Two were damaged by the detonation of Allied mines and one of these had to be sunk; three were hit by enemy gunfire. At this stage "the prospects of sweeping the area essential for the landing in the remaining time to meet the target date seemed somewhat doubtful".[6] On 24th June, however, when supporting destroyers came closer inshore and the air bombardment, by about 100 aircraft a day, began to make itself felt, the defenders' fire grew weaker and did not greatly hamper the minesweepers, though on 26th and 27th June two were sunk and one damaged by mine detonations.

---
[6] Commander Amphibious Group Eight, Action Report Balikpapan Operation.

On the 25th the American underwater demolition teams, working sometimes under heavy gunfire, began the finding and breaching of the underwater obstacles. Gaps of 800 yards each were blown in the Manggar and Manggar Kechil obstacles and a gap of 1,100 yards in the Klandasan obstacle.

From 4th June onwards daily air attacks had been made on the Japanese guns, on storage tanks whose oil might be used for defence and on the airfields. From 11th June the attacks were intensified and were concentrated on the gun positions. On each of the five days before the landing from 84 to 102 Liberators, 30 to 42 Mitchells and 36 to 40 Lightnings attacked.

The final plan of the 7th Division provided that the landing would be made at 9 a.m. on 1st July on a 2,000-yard section of the beach between Klandasan and Stalkudo. The beach was divided into three sections: from right to left, Green Beach, Yellow Beach, and Red Beach. The 21st Brigade was to land with one battalion forward on Green, the 18th with two battalions forward on Yellow and Red. The initial object was to secure a position covering the beach maintenance area; thence the 18th Brigade was to seize the high ground dominating the town and free the harbour for use, and the 21st was to advance along the coast and take the airstrips, where it was planned to base one fighter wing by 7th July and, as soon afterwards as possible, three bomber wings. The 25th Brigade, in reserve, was to land on the 2nd, with the probable role of thrusting inland along the Milford Highway.

The briefing of the troops, down to section leaders in the infantry, was extremely thorough. For example, in the 2/10th Battalion, which was to play a crucial part on the first day, the country over which they would attack was studied on vertical and oblique photographs, large-scale maps on which the enemy's positions were over-printed, and on a large-scale model. Lieut-Colonel Daly, who had commanded the unit since October 1944 and brought it to a high state of efficiency, had lectured all ranks, by companies, on the model, explaining "the overall strategy, the object of the operation, Div tasks, tasks of other Bdes and Bns and a detailed description of the Coy tasks, fire plan and probable subsequent developments"; the men had questioned him and all were made to realise their part in the plan. During four days company, platoon and section commanders were briefed using the model, photographs and maps. An Intelligence centre was set up containing maps, photographs, stereoscopes, Intelligence summaries, terrain studies, etc., and was open first to N.C.O's and then to all ranks. It was usually full of men all day.

The long voyages, mostly in crowded vessels, that preceded the assault somewhat reduced the fitness of the troops. The 18th Brigade, for example, was taken from Australia to Morotai in L.S.T's, a voyage of 19 days. The L.S.T's carried their normal complement of 500, which was not too many for a voyage of a day or two, but far too many for a longish voyage. After less than a week ashore the troops embarked for Balikpapan and spent another five days on overcrowded and uncomfortable craft.

There was insufficient time at the staging area for hardening and acclimatisation, or even adequately to carry out essential administration and briefing of troops. Fortunately the weather at Balikpapan was cool on F-day and subsequently, and the physical effort required of the troops was moderate only; but even so there were some casualties from exhaustion.[7]

The assault convoy, of more than 100 ships, sailed from Morotai at 1.30 p.m. on 26th June. It steamed at 7½ knots north of Halmahera and Celebes and then south along the Strait of Macassar. On the morning of the 29th the warships of the bombardment group passed the slow-moving transports. The convoy arrived at its appointed area about eight miles south-east of the landing beach an hour and a half before sunrise.

From 7 a.m. five cruisers including H.M.A.S's *Shropshire* and *Hobart* and 14 destroyers shelled the landing beaches and the defences behind them, and went on until the first waves of landing craft were within 1,300 yards of the beaches, when the fire was shifted to the flanks and rear. About an hour before the landing there was a combined rocket barrage and low-level air strike, and at 10 minutes before the landing a second rocket barrage was delivered. In the 20 days before the assault the Balikpapan-Manggar area received 3,000 tons of bombs, 7,361 rockets, 38,052 shells ranging from 8-inch to 3-inch, and 114,000 rounds from automatic weapons.

This expenditure of ammunition may, in comparison with that expended in previous operations in this theatre, appear to be excessive but examination of the captured area definitely indicates that any less effort would have proven insufficient.[8]

In the 70 minutes before 8.50 a.m. 62 Liberators attacked, and for the rest of the day flights of 4 to 8 aircraft were overhead at frequent intervals attacking pre-arranged targets or targets of opportunity.

The first and second waves of assaulting troops were carried in nine L.S.T's which moved to a line of departure 3,000 yards off shore and there launched the L.V.T's which were to put the leading troops ashore. In the rear transport area remained H.M.A.S. *Kanimbla*, 5 A.P.D's and other craft carrying the remainder of the 18th Brigade Group, and H.M.A.S's *Manoora* and *Westralia* and other craft carrying the remainder of the 21st Brigade Group and the floating reserve—the 25th Brigade.

In general terms the 18th Brigade's plan was to land the 2/12th on Yellow Beach and the 2/10th on Red whence they would secure a beach-head about half a mile in depth. Thence the 2/12th was to advance north and take a group of features of which the northernmost was Parkes, one mile inland; and the 2/10th was to advance north-west, capture Hill 87 and exploit north along Parramatta. If the 2/10th failed to take Hill 87 the 2/9th, the reserve battalion, was to capture Parramatta. This ridge at the base of the peninsula on which Balikpapan stood dominated the entire landing beach area, and was vital ground which should be seized as soon as possible.

---

[7] 18 Aust Inf Bde Report on Operation Oboe Two.
[8] Commander Amphibious Group Eight, report.

Balikpapan, 1st-5th July

One company of the 672nd American Amphibious Tractor Battalion with 51 L.V.T's was allotted to the 18th Brigade. They were to disembark their troops at high-water mark and wait in the assembly area until the engineers cleared mine-free lanes. Thereafter they would carry forward heavy weapons, ammunition, water and other things, and remove wounded men. (Their cross-country performance on the sandy coastal strip was to prove far better than that of the jeeps and trailers which were landed later.)

The plan of the 21st Brigade provided that the 2/27th Battalion would land on Green Beach and secure a covering position to a depth of 800 yards. The 2/16th would pass through and advance to Mount Malang and secure the area from Valley Road to Chilton Road. A troop of the 2/5th Commando Squadron would investigate the area east of Mount Malang. The 2/14th Battalion would come in on the right and advance across the Klandasan Besar and capture an area to the east of it; the 2/7th Cavalry (Commando) Regiment less one squadron, was to move through the 2/14th and take Sepinggang airstrip if it was not strongly held.

Before daylight the troops in the transports could see by the light of fires burning ashore. As the day broke, pillars of smoke were seen rising from the town, with fires gleaming through. Overhead wave after wave of heavy bombers flew in and dropped their bombs. Every now and then an oil tank would be hit and there would be a great burst of brilliant flame rising 1,000 feet or more into the air. The fire of the warships was continuous and deafening. Occasional splashes among the approaching craft showed that at least some Japanese guns were replying. "It was a tremendous and heartening demonstration of power—particularly to those of us who had spent a good deal of the past three years slogging it out the hard way in the jungles of New Guinea," wrote an officer later.

An incident occurred which could have resulted in opening the assault without the presence of the Corps commander and the Air Officer Commanding R.A.A.F. Command. General Morshead and Air Vice-Marshal Bostock saw the embarkation and departure of the assault troops from Morotai. On the day before the landing, with some of their senior staff officers, they left Morotai by R.A.A.F. Catalina flying-boat for Tarakan where they spent the early part of the night. The Catalina took off from the Tarakan strip before dawn, the intention being to alight on the sea beside the headquarters ship then lying off Balikpapan. It was proposed that the passengers should be transferred to the headquarters ship operations room to control and follow the assault, and then go ashore as soon as indicated. However, when the Catalina arrived over the proposed alighting area the waves were seen to be so high as to offer a serious threat to the landing step on the hull of the flying-boat and the pilot reported his fears to Group Captain Grant[9] of Bostock's staff (a former flying-boat pilot). Knowing that the aircraft would probably be wrecked

---

[9] Gp Capt A. G. Grant, OBE. Comd School of Admin 1941; SAO HQ Northern Area 1941-42, HQ North-Eastern Area 1942-43; SSOA RAAF Cd and OC RAAF Cd HQ 1943-45; SSAO and OC RAAF Cd Adv HQ, Morotai, 1945. Medical student, former regular air force officer; of Brisbane; b. Rockhampton, Qld, 11 Aug 1904.

Grant told the pilot to make the alighting. Measures were taken to lessen the shock to the people aboard and the headquarters ship was asked to arrange for a rescue launch to stand by. The aircraft was let down on to the sea where the hull immediately opened up. The occupants were rescued by the launch but the aircraft was a complete loss. General Morshead and Air Vice-Marshal Bostock and staff officers were taken to the headquarters ship. In accordance with Bostock's policy that one of his staff should take part in each R.A.A.F.-supported assault, Grant proceeded to one of the L.C.V's to take part in the landing as an "acting private" in the 18th Brigade.

As often as not, as a result of errors of navigation or some other factor, troops landed from the sea are put ashore at the wrong spot. At Klandasan the 2/27th Battalion was landed at Yellow Beach, not Green, and of the two forward companies the one on the left took Ration, which was actually an objective of the 2/12th Battalion on its left, and Romilly; the right company took Rottnest. By 10.10 a.m. the battalion held these three features and was on its first objectives, having met little opposition. It had killed 31 Japanese and lost one man killed and eight wounded. A platoon on the extreme right was halted by fire from Stalkudo.

A third company of the 2/27th now moved through and advanced along the Vasey Highway. It came under fire from Charlie's Spur when 300 yards away, but attacked and took it. That evening a strong party of Japanese tried to escape from tunnels towards Rottnest; they were fired on and, next day, 20 dead were counted.

The 2/16th also was landed some 200 yards west of the intended spot. By 11 a.m. the battalion was on Ravenshoe, whence Malang and Pigeon were visible. Advancing under sharp fire Captain Madigan's[1] company on the left took Record about 4 p.m., killing 46 Japanese. At 4.5 Captain R. H. Christian's company launched a concerted attack on Malang, supported by the fire of artillery, mortars and machine-guns, and using a flame-thrower. The hill was taken and 40 Japanese were killed. The Australians lost four killed, including the leading platoon commander, Lieutenant Armstrong,[2] and 14 wounded. By nightfall the 2/16th held a line through Malang, Pigeon and Record. It had lost 6 killed or died of wounds in the day and 24 wounded; 86 Japanese dead had been counted.

The 2/14th also was put ashore in the wrong place—on Yellow Beach instead of Green—but in 45 minutes moved into its proper areas. It found the bridge over the Klandasan Besar intact, and crossed and reached the bend in the Vasey Highway without opposition. The forward companies dug in beyond the Stalkudo ridge for the night.

At 4.30 the 2/5th Commando Squadron passed through the 2/14th Battalion and, soon afterwards, encountered heavy fire from anti-aircraft guns, mortars and machine-guns sited on the feature north-east of

---

[1] Capt E. B. Madigan, MC, WX11020; 2/16 Bn. Signwriter; of West Perth; b. Northam, WA, 14 Mar 1910.

[2] Lt L. C. Armstrong, NX113250. 3 and 2/16 Bns. Sales representative; of Coolamon, NSW; b. Coolamon, 20 Nov 1918. Killed in action 1 Jul 1945.

Stalkudo. Four were killed and Lieutenant Pearson[3] of the leading section and 6 others were wounded. The medical officer of the squadron, Captain Allsopp,[4] went forward under heavy fire and attended to the wounded. While dragging a trooper towards safety Allsopp was himself hit in the thigh and the trooper whom he was helping was mortally wounded. Allsopp continued to look after wounded and dying men until he was hit again, this time fatally. The squadron dug in for the night.

The 2/12th Battalion also was landed to the left of its appointed place —on Red Beach instead of Yellow. Two companies were put ashore in the first wave each with a detachment of mortars, a section of machine-guns and a detachment of engineers in support. The companies soon moved into their correct areas and took their first objectives without opposition, but when exploiting came under fire from Ration. As mentioned, Ration was taken by the 2/27th, although out of its area. A company of the 2/12th took over this feature, and then engaged a strong position to the north-west, which was taken at 5 p.m. after an attack in which flame-throwers were used and 25 Japanese were killed.

When the second wave landed Lieutenant Kent's[5] platoon became detached from its company, but without more ado it advanced inland along the Valley Road, under fire. At 10.20 a.m. it occupied Portee, far beyond the objective, and placed a section on Newcastle. An hour later about 60 Japanese advanced on Portee from the direction of New-castle and Australian mortar bombs began falling round the area. Kent withdrew his section from Newcastle and engaged and drove off the Japanese who were advancing on Portee, killing 36 of them. The platoon saw the 2/10th on Parramatta soon after 4 p.m. They dug in for the night on Portee and drove off four attacks in the hours of darkness.

A second platoon of this company took Parkes unopposed, but the third platoon advancing from Plug came under sharp fire. The platoon commander was wounded and the artillery observer (Lieutenant J. N. Pearson) took command, but he was killed by machine-gun fire. A troop of three tanks set off along the Valley Road towards this platoon. One bogged but the other two reached Blyth's Junction. The platoon consolidated on Plug. In the day the 2/12th lost three killed and 13 wounded and killed 103 Japanese.

The 2/10th next to the left had the crucial task of seizing the dominating Parramatta feature. Lieut-Colonel Daly's plan was that by 9.15 the two companies in the first wave should seize the high ground overlooking Red Beach and seal off the left flank. Of the two following companies, which were to land at 9.8, one was to be ready to take Petersham Junction when ordered, supported by one troop of Matilda tanks; the other was then to take Hill 87; when Hill 87 had been taken over by the company from Petersham Junction, the company it relieved would then advance

---

[3] Capt F. A. Pearson, VX4542. 2/6 Bn and 2/5 Cdo Sqn. Packer; of Hampton, Vic; b. Brighton, Vic, 6 Dec 1920.

[4] Capt R. J. Allsopp, NX104023; RMO 2/5 Cdo Sqn. Medical practitioner; of Wollongong, NSW; b. Baulkham Hills, NSW, 25 Jun 1915. Killed in action 1 Jul 1945.

[5] Lt L. A. Kent, MC, NX137809; 2/12 Bn. Schoolteacher; of Sydney; b. Sydney, 22 Jan 1917.

along Parramatta. In support Daly was allotted: the fire of U.S.S. *Cleveland*, a 6-inch gun cruiser; of eight 4.2-inch mortars, and one 6-pounder gun of the 2/2nd Anti-Tank Regiment; of a battery of the 2/4th Field Regiment; of a platoon of machine-guns, two troops of Matilda tanks of the 1st Armoured Regiment, and three Frogs.

The 2/10th landed in three waves, the first two being in L.V.T's. By 8.55 a.m. the first wave was ashore and moving up the beach towards the Vasey Highway. A few minutes later the second wave landed, 800 yards west of the intended place. This caused delay, particularly in bringing the mortar and machine-gun platoons into action. By 9.15 the two leading companies had moved fast to their objectives and sent patrols towards Prudent and Petersham Junction, both of which were found to be unoccupied.

Soon after Daly landed he was informed that the cruiser *Cleveland* had been given another task and consequently another cruiser was being allotted, but it would not have time to register Hill 87 unless the third phase was delayed.

The two companies that were to execute the second and third phases now advanced. Under some small arms fire Captain R. W. Sanderson's company ("A") occupied Petersham Junction, a small sandy plateau. Thence under fire from the higher ground to the right Lieutenant Sullivan's[6] platoon secured the lower slopes of Hill 87 to provide cover for the following company to form up and to give depth to the Petersham Junction position where Daly had his command post.

At this stage 4.2-inch mortars and a platoon of medium machine-guns were firing in support of the 2/10th, but neither the expected fire of naval guns nor of field guns was available, and the tanks were bogged near the beach.[7] Thus Daly was deprived of the three powerful supports on which he had counted in a difficult attack. He faced the choice between waiting until the supporting fire was ready and at the same time giving the Japanese time to reorganise, or attacking immediately while the Japanese were still suffering from the effects of the preliminary bombardment. He made the bold decision to attack immediately with his fourth company (Major F. W. Cook). This company ("C") reached Petersham Junction, then, at 10.10 a.m. advanced straight up Hill 87 to the point where Sullivan's platoon was established.

Lieutenant A. F. McDougall's 15 Platoon was leading, then came Lieutenant Sinclair's[8] (13), then Lieutenant Davey's[9] (14); all were under mortar fire from Parramatta and small arms fire from "The Island", a ridge on the right. By effective use of fire and movement, and screened by smoke laid by heavy mortars of the 2/2nd Anti-Tank Regiment, the leading platoon pressed on and gained a position 50 yards below the crest

---

[6] Lt A. D. K. Sullivan, MC, VX5035. 2/6 and 2/10 Bns. Repairer, Railways Dept; of Warrnambool, Vic; b. Essendon, Vic, 14 Feb 1916.

[7] The field gunners' wireless was being jammed since it was operating on a similar frequency to that of the American Air Coordinator cruising overhead.

[8] Lt I. V. R. Sinclair, QX34159; 2/10 Bn. Butcher and drover; of Chinchilla, Qld; b. Cobar, NSW, 22 Dec 1912.

[9] Lt K. J. Davey, SX12701; 2/10 Bn. Clerk; of Payneham, SA; b. Warracknabeal, Vic, 10 Oct 1920.

of Hill 87 but was pinned there by small arms and mortar fire, having lost 5 killed and 7 wounded. Cook ordered Sinclair's platoon to the left to take Green Spur. It became involved in a dogfight in which it killed 16 Japanese, of whom Lance-Corporal Copping[1] killed 6, and in which

1st July

it lost 4 killed. While this was happening McDougall's platoon, with the help of a tank, subdued the enemy fire on Hill 87 and overran it. In the final stages Private Abel,[2] from whose hands a Bren gun had been shot away, continued to lead his section, although severely wounded.

The Japanese were now returning to positions abandoned during the preliminary bombardment and the Australians were meeting stronger opposition. Thirteen in the leading platoon had now been killed or

---

[1] L-Cpl J. W. Copping, SX20021; 2/10 Bn. Grazier; of Lucindale, SA; b. Naracoorte, SA, 17 Sep 1922.

[2] Pte C. W. Abel, SX13898; 2/10 Bn. Farm worker; of Mount Torrens, SA; b. Adelaide, 18 Jul 1919.

wounded and only 17 remained, but the attack lost none of its impetus. The leading man in the final thrust on to Hill 87 was Corporal Symons.[3] Finally Symons was lying behind a heap of drums of tar wondering, as Japanese bullets hit them, whether the tar would all drain out and he would be left with no protection. The rear platoon (Lieutenant Davey) came under sharp fire from Japanese whom the leading platoons had passed by.

This was the situation when Major Ryrie[4] of the 1st Armoured Regiment arrived and said his tanks were coming. Cook told his leading platoon to hold on. By 11.40 two tanks had climbed Hill 87 and were helping to dispose of isolated pockets of Japanese. Ryrie moved about fearlessly reconnoitring for the tanks and inspired all by his coolness. As soon as the tanks appeared over the crest the Japanese on Hill 87 ceased firing. By 12.50 preparations were under way for an assault on Parramatta. Six tanks, including one Frog, were now forward and a battery of the 2/4th Field Regiment was being registered by Captain W. A. S. Whyte on targets on Parramatta. Before midday a team under Lieutenant Low[5] of the 2/2nd Anti-Tank Regiment had manhandled a 6-pounder forward to a point near Hill 87 whence L.V.T's helped it on to the hill itself.

The attack opened at 1.20 p.m. with Davey's platoon forward, each section having a tank with it. Ryrie coolly walked ahead of the leading tank which was ahead of the leading section. For the first 20 minutes there was not much opposition but then mortar fire became severe. Daly and Cook conferred and Daly asked for an air strike on the north-east end of Parramatta, and ordered Sanderson's company to move up behind Cook's and mop up the south-western slopes of Hill 87. Davey's platoon pushed on and, with the tanks, took Parramatta, and the air strike was cancelled. With flame-throwers and with the help of the tanks the rest of the company quickly dealt with tunnels and pill-boxes that had been by-passed. At 2.12 p.m. the success signal was fired. So far Cook's company had lost 9 killed and 10 wounded.

A patrol led by Sergeant A. A. Evans was sent out from Davey's platoon towards Newcastle. They silenced a bunker with a flame-thrower, and came to a house from which Japanese were firing. They overcame this position with grenades and small arms fire and then moved on to Newcastle. As Evans reached Newcastle he saw the surviving Japanese making off towards Portee.

Davey's platoon now occupied Newcastle and the other platoon took up positions on Parramatta. The seizure of Parramatta gave the 2/10th observation over the low ground to the north and the northern end of the town, and tied the battalion in with the 2/12th on Portee; the Japanese were now in a very poor position to counter-attack from the western end

---

[3] Cpl W. I. Symons, MM, SX20342; 2/10 Bn. Clerk; of Port Augusta, SA; b. Yankalilla, SA, 10 Feb 1923.

[4] Maj E. J. Ryrie, NX564. 6 Cav Regt, and 1 Armd Regt. Solicitor; of Tottenham, NSW; b. Sydney, 1 Mar 1916. Killed in action 10 Jul 1945.

[5] Lt J. R. Low, TX11204; 2/2 A-Tk Regt. Journalist; of Hobart; b. Hobart, 8 Dec 1915.

of the beach-head. Lieutenant Russack[6] of Sanderson's company led a patrol to the Cracking Plant where it silenced a Japanese pill-box. This patrol was strafed by American aircraft, but worse was to follow. At 4.55 American carrier-borne aircraft made a run over Parramatta from the west and dropped bombs and fired rockets across Hill 87, which had then been in the hands of the 2/10th for four hours and a half. Much of this fire landed in the area into which Captain Brocksopp's[7] company ("D") had moved and where Daly's command post was established. Three were killed, including Lance-Sergeant Hackett,[8] a veteran of several campaigns, and 14 wounded, including Major G. R. Miethke and two other officers. Air panels were displayed in all platoon areas after this.

Daly decided to hold that night as far forward as Newcastle, on which he placed two platoons plus a platoon of the 2/1st Machine Gun Battalion, all under Captain Bowie.[9] In the day the battalion had lost 13 killed and 30 wounded, but 216 Japanese dead were counted. That night 24 more Japanese were killed while trying to penetrate the Australians' positions and no Australian was hit. All night there were fires round about where houses were burning, and the blazing oil tanks on the Tank Plateau 600 yards to the west of the Parramatta ridge lit up the landscape.[1]

The main reasons for the success of the assault on Parramatta had been the swift advance of Cook's company up the sides of Hill 87 regardless of "mopping up", the speed and skill of the individual infantrymen and the way in which they went on despite heavy losses, Daly's action in ordering the company to press on when he had practically no reserves and little supporting fire, and the cool and courageous handling of the tanks by Ryrie and his team.

The 2/9th Battalion had remained in reserve for an hour after landing, and at 10.40 Brigadier Chilton ordered it to relieve that part of the 2/10th that was on Prudent and round Petersham Junction. It was then given the task of moving west and occupying Klandasan as far as Signal Hill. In the afternoon one company with a troop of tanks did this, clearing the houses one by one. At 6 p.m. it took Santosa Hill against light opposition, and then dug in for the night having achieved its task.

The diary of the 1st Armoured Regiment records that Lieutenant Rossiter,[2] commanding the three tanks that were with this company, on advising the infantry commander that the tanks were bogged outside the perimeter was somewhat stunned by the reply, "That's all right old man—I've finished with them."

---

[6] Lt E. K. Russack, SX21719; 2/10 Bn. Watchmaker; of Wallaroo Mines, SA; b. Kadina, SA, 2 Apr 1918.

[7] Maj W. A. Brocksopp, ED, SX1431; 2/10 Bn. Of Medindie, SA; b. Maitland, NSW, 24 Dec 1910.

[8] L-Sgt C. G. Hackett, MM, SX2448; 2/10 Bn. Labourer; of Port Elliot, SA; b. Wilmington, SA, 20 Mar 1919. Killed in action 1 Jul 1945.

[9] Maj R. A. Bowie, SX1201. 2/10 Bn; liaison duties with 18 Bde and II Corps. Shipping clerk; of Semaphore, SA; b. Semaphore, 17 Sep 1917.

[1] In the first few days most of the fighting was in fairly open country with the forward positions sometimes about 1,000 yards apart. In this phase the night-time harassing fire sought for and provided by the naval vessels included some star shell, which illuminated no-man's land so effectively that the Japanese made few attempts at infiltration.

[2] Maj N. E. L. Rossiter, NX131840; 1 Armd Regt. Regular soldier; b. Armadale, Vic, 23 Dec 1920.

At the beach-head the first L.C.T. had come ashore at 10.17 a.m. About 1 p.m. Generals MacArthur, Morshead and Milford had landed. That day G.H.Q. issued the following somewhat florid communiqué about the Balikpapan operation:

Australian ground forces have made a third major landing on the vast island of Borneo. Elements of the veteran Seventh Australian Division have secured a firm beach-head at Balik Papan, famed oil center on the southeastern coast. This area was a major source of fuel oil and aviation gasoline for the Japanese, with a total production of 15,000,000 barrels per year.

The landing was preceded by intensive air and naval bombardment and preparation of beach approaches by the Royal Australian and Far Eastern Air Forces and the United States Seventh Fleet, Royal Australian and Royal Netherlands Navies.

Assault waves swept ashore directly east of the town and rapidly advanced inland. Our losses have been very light. Swiftly following our seizure of Brunei Bay on the northwestern coast and Tarakan on the northeastern, the enemy's key Borneo defences are now isolated or crushed, and his confused and disorganised forces are incapable of effective strategic action.

The speed, surprise and shock of these three operations have secured domination of Borneo and driven a wedge south, splitting the East Indies. Strategic Macassar Strait, gateway to the Flores and Java Seas, is now controlled by our surface craft as well as by air and submarine.

Development of already existing air facilities at Balik Papan will enable our aircraft of all categories to disrupt and smash enemy communications on land and sea from Timor to eastern Sumatra. The whole extent of Java and the important ports of Surabaya and Batavia are now within easy flight range and subject to interdiction. Our shipping can now sail with land-based air cover to any point in the South-West Pacific. It is fitting that the Seventh Australian Division which, in July, three years ago, met and later turned back the tide of invasion of Australia on the historic Kokoda trail, should this same month secure what was once perhaps the most lucrative strategic target in our East Indies sector and virtually complete our tactical control of the entire South-West Pacific.

The 2/14th Battalion's task for 2nd July was to thrust along the Vasey Highway and seize the Sepinggang airstrip. This was swiftly done. The leading platoon moved off at 9 a.m. and by 10.30 was at the strip, having encountered no Japanese. By 1 p.m. the battalion was firmly established round the strip. Thus far it had found two naval guns and two 25-mm guns abandoned.

On the 2nd the 2/27th strengthened and extended its hold on the high ground north-west of Stalkudo. To the north-east the 2/3rd Commando Squadron (Major P. L. Tancred) was held by heavy fire from Lady Schofield and made little progress. Lieutenant Burzacott[3] was fatally wounded here. The 2/16th Battalion thrust north and took Resort, Owen and Oxley without loss.

In the 18th Brigade's sector the 2/12th on the 2nd took Potts and strengthened its hold on Portee, where Lieutenant Kent's platoon was now at last in touch with its own battalion. In the day the 2/12th killed 11 Japanese and lost only one man wounded. Along the brigade's front

---

[3] Lt L. B. Burzacott, SX21309; 2/3 Cdo Sqn. Ship's fireman; of Mount Barker, SA; b. Serviceton, Vic, 18 Feb 1914. Died of wounds 3 Jul 1945.

and particularly in the 2/10th's area, engineers of the 2/4th Field Company (Major Taylor[4]) and infantry blew in several tunnels in which Japanese were sheltering. It was found that the most effective way of sealing tunnels was to send engineer parties forward under covering fire to explode two 25-pound pack charges on the floor of the tunnel just inside the entrance. Normally where underground shelters or mines and booby-traps were expected or encountered six engineers, with six infantry pioneers, were attached to each attacking infantry company. In the course of the whole Balikpapan operation the engineers cooperated in destroying 110 tunnels and pill-boxes. More than 8,000 mines and booby-traps were disarmed.

During the night of 1st-2nd July the 2/10th, having thrust so deeply into a main enemy stronghold, killed about 40 Japanese who tried to infiltrate the Australians' positions. Patrols probed the Cracking Plant, Tank Plateau, Nought, Reservoir, and Nomen. At 3.30 Captain Brocksopp's company with four tanks and strong fire support occupied Mount Sepuluh and the Cracking Plant.[5]

On 3rd July one company advanced through the port, another cleared the Tank Plateau and a third the lower ground between the plateau and Parramatta. In the three days the 2/10th had lost 16 killed or died of wounds and 40 wounded, but buried 332 Japanese dead. The 2/9th, with its troop of tanks, on 3rd July took Santosa barracks which it had by-passed the previous day.

The division now held a bridgehead about five miles wide by a mile deep, and had secured one of the two airstrips; on the 3rd light aircraft began operating from it. The unloading of heavy equipment and stores was not easy and caused anxiety. There was a swell which made it difficult to transfer loads to L.C.T's and small craft, and it was impossible to run the L.S.T's on to the beach. By 6 a.m. on the 3rd, however, 985 vehicles and 1,932 tons of other equipment and stores had been landed and 16,950 men were ashore. Later that morning an L.S.T. began unloading at a pontoon jetty built on Green Beach by an American naval construction battalion.

The captured port was a collection of wrecked workshops and warehouses, with little left but rusty, twisted steel, and wrecked houses of which often only piles of rubble remained. The seven wharves for ocean-going vessels had all been burnt and none were usable. One dump of scrap iron collected by the Japanese from the ruins was 520 yards long, and opposite it was another about 150 yards long.

On 3rd July the company of the 2/14th on the right flank began moving towards the Manggar strip. Brigadier Dougherty arrived at the battalion's headquarters at 11 a.m. and ordered Lieut-Colonel P. E. Rhoden to send

---

[4] Lt-Col R. R. Taylor, DSO, NX12185. 9 Div Engrs; OC 2/4 Fd Coy 1943-45. Regular soldier; b. Adelaide, 27 Sep 1913.

[5] On the morning of 2nd July a Japanese machine-gun checking a local advance became the object of RAAF ground action. The gunner was stalked and killed by Group Captain Grant of the staff of RAAF Command who was with the RAAF Technical Air Intelligence Unit. The machine-gun had been mounted high in a tree so as to sweep one of the smaller valleys.

the whole unit forward as soon as the 2/27th had taken over the defence of the Sepinggang strip. By 12.30 this had been done and the 2/14th was on the move. A group of Japanese round the Batakan Kechil held up the advance from 1 p.m. until 6 p.m. by which time fire from naval vessels and mortars had driven the enemy out. The historian of the 2/14th records that the men of the leading platoon

> were feeling specially bitter towards the enemy at this time, because on the previous afternoon they had buried a number of native men and women who had been victims of Japanese atrocities and mutilation.[6]

Evidence was found later in other areas of the slaughter of large groups of civilians.

That morning the 2/3rd Commando Squadron found that the Lady Schofield feature, on which were five mortars and two anti-aircraft guns, had been abandoned; patrols pressed on more than a mile across the high ground overlooking the Sepinggang River.

The 25th Brigade headquarters landed on the 1st and the battalions on the 2nd. At first the brigade took over central portions of the front. It was now, on the 3rd, given the task of thrusting inland astride the Milford Highway while the 18th Brigade continued to secure the town and harbour. The brigade advanced with the 2/33rd on the right and the 2/31st on the left. The 2/33rd soon met heavy opposition in the hills above Chilton Road. At Opus the leading platoon came under heavy fire and its commander, Lieutenant Turner,[7] was hit. With the support of machine-guns Opus was taken. Then, with artillery support, two companies attacked Operator, also strongly held. Here a platoon commander, Lieutenant Hinton,[8] was mortally wounded. By dark the battalion held Opus, Operator, Oxygen and a height to the north-east, and Orange and was overlooking the next lateral track—Dougherty's Road.

The 2/31st was ordered to advance along the road and secure a line from Newsreel to Chilton Road. The two leading companies moved fast against increasing opposition. To the west of the road the leading platoon was halted by fire from two pill-boxes; Sergeant Campbell[9] dashed forward and knocked out both pill-boxes with grenades. By 9.45 the right-hand company had secured the junction of the main road and Chilton Road.

Lieut-Colonel E. M. Robson of the 2/31st ordered his leading companies to take the high ground north of Chilton Road, and Nurse, Nail and Nobody—a long stride forward. The southern slopes of Nobody were taken, but there was heavy fire from the other hills which were covered with thick undergrowth. On Nurse the Japanese were dug in in depth, with at least six machine-guns. Here, when a forward section was pinned

---

[6] W. B. Russell, *The Second Fourteenth Battalion* (1948), p. 282.

[7] Lt W. G. Turner, NX122320; 2/33 Bn. Commercial traveller; of Young, NSW; b. Goulburn, NSW, 2 Mar 1916.

[8] Lt W. A. Hinton, SX23299; 2/33 Bn. Clerk; of Quorn, SA; b. Moonta, SA, 14 May 1920. Killed in action 3 Jul 1945.

[9] Sgt G. W. Campbell, MM, WX2066; 2/31 Bn. Farm worker; of Borden, WA; b. Perth, 18 Aug 1917.

down on a narrow ridge, Private Buckley[1] dashed fifteen yards over open ground and killed four Japanese who were manning a heavy machine-gun. Later a section of a forward platoon of Captain Henderson's[2] "D" Company which was attacking Nurse was cut off by an enemy counter-attack and its commander killed. Corporal Tobin[3] took over and the men fought their way back 600 yards to the platoon.

After eight minutes of firing by Vickers guns a platoon of this company attacked in the gap between the other two platoons at 2.10 p.m. and secured a footing in the jungle below the main enemy position on Nurse. One section reached a point above the enemy and attacked downhill but were heavily engaged and all but two were killed or wounded. The survivors, Corporal Farman[4] and Private Harrison,[5] killed some 20 Japanese when they counter-attacked across open ground. The company was now under heavy fire from Nobody. Captain Henderson was wounded here but carried on.

A platoon of "A" Company now attacked from the west on to Nobody but ran into very heavy fire; in the undergrowth the sections lost contact and the attack was beaten back, the platoon losing 2 killed and 10 wounded. Sergeant Confoy[6] who had led two sections gallantly in the attack extricated them coolly and reorganised them. A section thrust forward to a ridge slightly lower than the crest of Nobody, 200 yards from the enemy. "D" Company, attacking Nurse, now had lost 4 killed and 15 wounded and three were missing, and Robson ordered it to withdraw and regroup; seven more were hit while this was being done. "A" Company took over in the forward area and at 4 p.m. artillery and one section of Vickers guns began a heavy and accurate bombardment of Nobody. In this duel one officer (Lieutenant Brennan[7]) and two others were killed and one officer wounded. Harassing fire on Nobody and Nurse was continued throughout the night. In the day the battalion had lost 13 killed and 37 wounded.

Next morning, however, at 7 a.m. a patrol under Sergeant Confoy reported that the Japanese had abandoned Nobody; they found 10 Japanese dead in one group which had been fired into by the Vickers guns. Half an hour later another patrol reported that Nurse too was unoccupied. Two missing men were found, both alive but wounded. The battalion had now reached its objective: the line Nobody-Nurse. Brigadier Eather (commanding the 25th Brigade) came forward and ordered it to hold

---

[1] Pte L. Buckley, NX26701. 2/6 Fd Regt and 2/31 Bn. Clerk; of Summer Hill, NSW; b. Homebush, NSW, 17 Jan 1920.

[2] Capt G. A. Henderson, MC, QX4144; 2/31 Bn. Company director; of Brisbane; b. Brisbane, 18 Aug 1915.

[3] Cpl G. F. Tobin, NX85775; 2/31 Bn. Farm worker; of Bundaberg, Qld; b. Bundaberg, 30 Apr 1918.

[4] Cpl F. A. Farman, VX137075. Rabaul Coast Defence Bty and 2/31 Bn. Regular soldier; b. Johore, India, 2 Aug 1918.

[5] Pte K. C. Harrison, SX29050; 2/31 Bn. Truck driver; of Adelaide; b. Adelaide, 11 Mar 1919.

[6] Sgt W. T. M. Confoy, QX16145; 2/31 Bn. Kangaroo shooter and trapper; of Brisbane; b. Sydney, 17 Apr 1918.

[7] Lt C. D. Brennan, NX110392; 2/31 Bn. Clerk; of Moree, NSW; b. Moree, 20 Jan 1919. Killed in action 3 Jul 1945.

that line and patrol forward of it. The enemy dead who had been counted now numbered 63, and others had been sealed in tunnels on Nurse, three prisoners had been taken and six medium and heavy machine-guns and a heavy mortar.

On the left the 2/12th on 3rd July had marched towards Pandansari but came under artillery and small arms fire from Nail. Nail was in the 25th Brigade area, but the 2/31st was then fully engaged at Nurse and Lieut-Colonel C. C. F. Bourne, commanding the 2/12th, sought and was given permission to take Nail. A company attacked at 6 p.m. with support from artillery and mortars and the guns of tanks which, though halted

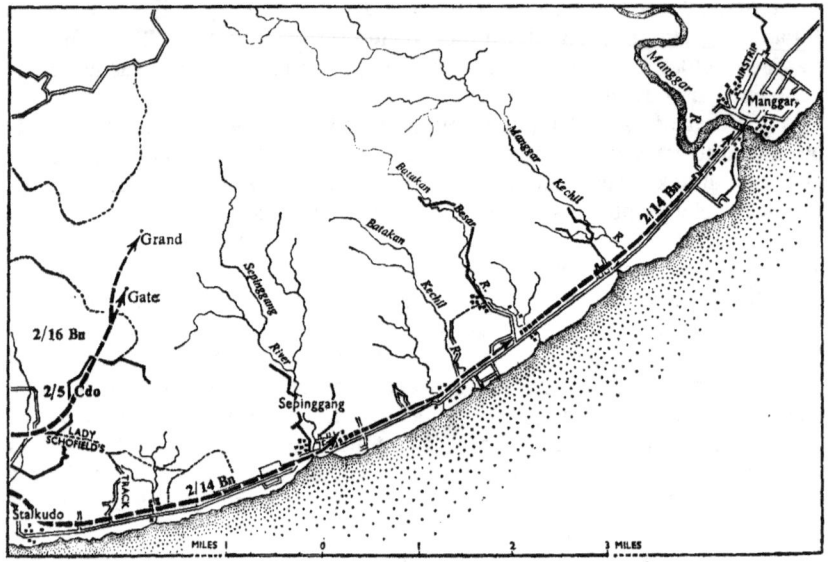

2nd-9th July

by an anti-tank ditch, gave supporting fire from that position. In a perfectly-executed attack the company took the hill, where 34 Japanese dead were counted.

Before this attack two war correspondents, John Elliott[8] and William Smith,[9] who had enlisted in the A.I.F. in 1941 and been discharged to take up their present appointments, had moved into the port area evidently not knowing that they were ahead of the forward troops. A Bren gunner saw them among the buildings south-west of Nail and, assuming they were Japanese, shot them dead.

On the morning of the 4th "C" Company of the 2/31st occupied Nail and took up a defensive position there, and patrols probed to Lodge,

---
[8] John Elliott (NX677, S-Sgt AIF 1941-43). Journalist; of Sydney; b. London, 14 Oct 1901. Killed Balikpapan 3 Jul 1945.
[9] William Smith (WX16472, Sgt AIF 1941-45). Journalist; of Merredin, WA; b. Boulder, WA, 11 Jul 1904. Killed Balikpapan 3 Jul 1945.

(Australian War Memorial)
Landing craft carrying troops of the 7th Division to the assault on Balikpapan, 1st July 1945.

(Australian War Memorial)
Men of the 2/14th Battalion landing from an L.C.I. at Balikpapan on 1st July.

(Australian War Memorial)
An L.C.V.P. landing troops at Balikpapan, 1st July.

(Australian War Memorial)
Troops moving inland at Balikpapan on 1st July.

(U.S. Army Signal Corps)
A Matilda tank advancing through Balikpapan port, 3rd July, 1945.

(U.S. Army Signal Corps)
A patrol of the 2/9th Battalion entering Penadjam village, on the west side of Balikpapan harbour, soon after landing there on 5th July.

Control tower at Manggar airfield, Balikpapan, whence Lieutenant G. M. Thorp of the 1st Naval Bombardment Group directed naval gunfire on to the Japanese stronghold on Waites' Knoll.

(Australian War Memorial)

On Parramatta feature, Balikpapan, 13th August. *From left:* Lieut-General F. H. Berryman (Chief of Staff, Advanced Land Headquarters), Major-General E. J. Milford (G.O.C. 7th Division) and General Sir Thomas Blamey.

(Australian War Memorial)

about 500 yards north of Orr's Junction. The exits of a system of tunnels on Nobody were blown in and more dead bodies and graves were found on Nurse, Nobody and Nail.

On the right flank there was heavy rain on the night of 3rd-4th July. In the morning the 2/14th advanced on Manggar, the last main objective on the east, and apparently undefended. Captain E. R. Clarke's company crossed the river and advanced 1,300 yards across the airstrip in open formation. Then Captain Mott's[1] company followed, with Brigadier Dougherty and Colonel Rhoden and his command group. Dougherty climbed half way up the 60-foot airfield control tower to survey the scene and then re-crossed the river to return to his headquarters.

Suddenly at 11.50 fire from coast-defence guns, from 75's firing airburst shells, from mortars and light quick-firing guns swept across the airfield. The fire was concentrated particularly on the bridge and the control tower. Near the tower Major Taylor,[2] commander of the 55th Battery, fell mortally wounded. Captain Chapman[3] had just begun ranging the guns of the nearest battery—the 10th—on to the Japanese guns when a shell burst killed him and Lieutenant Knight[4] of the 2/14th, mortally wounded Bombardier O'Neill,[5] and wounded Lieut-Colonel Richardson,[6] the commanding officer of the artillery regiment, Major G. O. O'Day of the 2/14th, and two artillery signallers. It also put the telephone out of action. Sergeant Ferguson[7] (of the 2/14th) went back under fire and guided forward Lieutenant Skea[8] of the 2/5th Field Regiment, who borrowed a telephone from the infantry and directed fire.

The supporting destroyer, *Eaton,* soon ranged on to the Japanese guns, its fire being directed by Lieutenant Thorp[9] of the Naval Bombardment Group who had climbed the control tower and remained there with shells bursting round him; the tower was hit twice and one of its legs shot away. The fire somewhat quietened the enemy's guns, but their bombardment lasted for an hour. The infantry, however, lost only one man killed and five wounded.

A group from the leading company, including Captain Clarke, had been forward on reconnaissance when the Japanese guns opened up and had killed three Japanese who were emerging from a shelter to man a gun

---

[1] Capt M. L. Mott, VX15274; 2/14 Bn. Sub-manager of newspaper; of Albury, NSW; b. Albury, 9 Jun 1915.

[2] Maj A. L. Taylor, QX6041. 2/1 A-Tk Regt and 2/5 Fd Regt. Accountant; of Brisbane; b. Ipswich, Qld, 21 Jan 1917. Killed in action 4 Jul 1945.

[3] Capt R. M. Chapman, NX56215; 2/5 Fd Regt. Bank officer; of Ashfield, NSW; b. Sydney, 4 Jul 1915. Killed in action 4 Jul 1945.

[4] Lt R. K. Knight, VX14408. 2/4 Fd Regt and 2/14 Bn. Clerk; of Brighton Beach, Vic; b. Glen Iris, Vic, 15 Feb 1916. Killed in action 4 Jul 1945.

[5] Bdr P. A. A. O'Neill, NX13973; 2/5 Fd Regt. Clerk; of Double Bay, NSW; b. Hindmarsh, SA, 17 Sep 1918. Killed in action 4 Jul 1945.

[6] Lt-Col F. Richardson, DSO, ED, VX106. 2/2 and 2/1 Fd Regts; CO 1 Hvy Regt 1942-43, 15 Fd Regt 1943, 2/5 Fd Regt 1943-45. Accountant; of Burwood, Vic; b. St Kilda, Vic, 23 Sep 1909.

[7] Sgt L. M. Ferguson, MM, VX16002; 2/14 Bn. Grocer; of Euroa, Vic; b. Euroa, 5 Aug 1919.

[8] Lt G. R. L. Skea, NX91104; 2/5 Fd Regt. Accountant; of Northbridge, NSW; b. North Sydney, 9 Jan 1921.

[9] Capt G. M. Thorp, MC, NX58197. 2/1 Fd Regt and 1 Naval Bombardment Group. University student; of Neutral Bay, NSW; b. 12 Jan 1920.

position; three more Japanese were killed at the north-west end of the strip. Later another party of the 2/14th destroyed a heavy machine-gun post sited to cover Vasey Highway.

At 2.30 p.m. Mott's company was withdrawn to the west side of the river and remained there until dusk when it moved forward and occupied the dispersal bays. Rhoden had the problem of taking a heavily-armed stronghold commanding the whole of the airfield area. Two troops of tanks had now been made available to him.

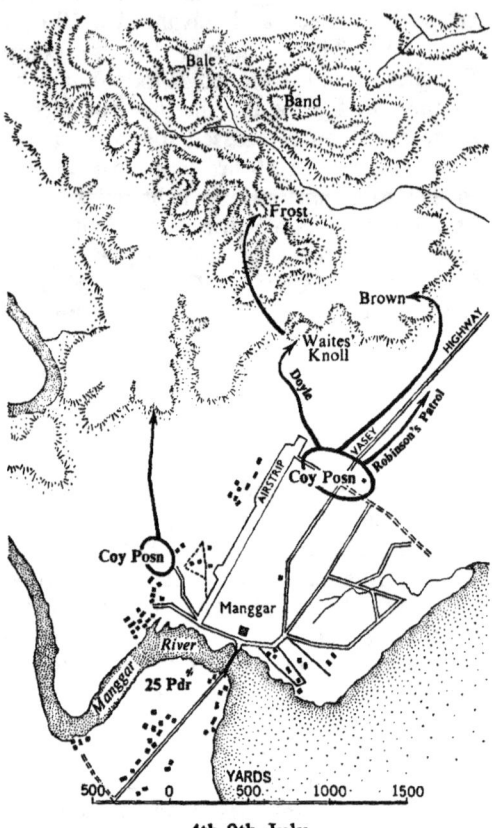

4th-9th July

By now the enemy had been driven from all positions from which interference could be caused to the unloading of stores. He had been pushed out of the town and had lost the two airstrips. It was apparent at this stage that he was trying to withdraw the remnants of his force to the Batuchampar area, and with this object in view would delay as long as possible an advance along the Milford Highway.[1]

Enemy documents captured up to 4th July showed that when the landing took place the *I Battalion* of Rear-Admiral Michiaki Kamada's *22nd Naval Base Force* was deployed from Klandasan to the Sumber River and it was this unit that had been broken on the first day. Round Manggar was the *454th Battalion* (Major Yamada), an army unit, which had arrived from Tarakan in March. Astride Milford Highway in the Batuchampar area was the *II Battalion* of the *22nd Naval Base Force*. Two companies and other detachments were in the Penadjam area, west of Balikpapan across the bay. The strength of Kamada's force was initially about 3,900; up to 5th July 665 dead had been counted and it was estimated that 132 more than that had been killed.

At first light on 5th July naval vessels bombarded the gun positions above Manggar. This was followed by air attacks by Liberators at 8.30; they attacked again twice that day. A 6-pounder anti-tank gun was brought

---

[1] 7th Division report.

forward at 11.20 a.m. to the west end of the bridge whence it fired on the coast-defence guns with armour-piercing shot at about 1,200 yards' range. (It was later found that it had made six direct hits on one coast gun and disabled it.)

At 2 p.m. L.C.M's landed a troop of three tanks on the north bank of the river at a spot where it was thought that they would be defiladed from the Japanese guns, but this was not so, and the guns destroyed two tanks and damaged the third, killing one man and wounding the troop commander and others. All day the duel continued between naval and artillery guns and aircraft on one side and the Japanese guns on the other, but the Japanese guns were not silenced.

At dusk the company that had been forward round the airfield while this duel was being fought over its head was relieved by Major O'Day's company. At 7 p.m. a 25-pounder was brought forward to the bridge ready for action at point-blank range next day. Rhoden planned to attack the Japanese guns with infantry backed by the fire of all supporting arms. Meanwhile the forward infantry were probing. At 1 a.m. on the 6th six men under Corporal Gibson[2] patrolled to within 25 yards of a barricade round the tunnel that housed one of the Japanese guns but the Japanese manned the defences within the barricade and the patrol could do nothing more.

The 25-pounder brought forward on the night of the 5th was placed under the command of Sergeant Palmer,[3] who had been one of the team manning a similar forward gun at Buna in 1942. He took 10 men with him. At dawn the gun opened fire. It fired 150 rounds and silenced two guns, one thought to be 155-mm calibre and the other 75-mm. Later Captain Tinkler[4] began to direct the fire of the two batteries of the 2/5th on to 20-mm guns in the same area, and silenced at least three.[5]

General Milford went forward to Brigadier Dougherty's headquarters on the morning of the 6th and expressed approval of the steps being taken to overcome the enemy stronghold. A fighting patrol of 13 was to move against the Japanese No. 1 gun on what was later named Waites' Knoll, and at the same time another patrol was to move north along the Vasey Highway to investigate the effects of the bombing of the guns farther on.

It was now evident that the end of the war was not far off; Dougherty was in no haste to take the 2/14th Battalion's objectives, but preferred to use all the supporting fire he could muster and minimise his losses.

The patrol to Waites' Knoll was led by Lieutenant Doyle.[6] It was to have the support of naval, field and anti-aircraft guns, of mortars and

---
[2] Sgt L. H. Gibson, WX16623; 2/14 Bn. Truck driver; of Cunderdin, WA; b. Bunbury, WA, 26 Jul 1915.
[3] Sgt K. I. Palmer, MM, NX16592; 2/5 Fd Regt. Ironworker; of Arncliffe, NSW; b. Tamworth, NSW, 8 Sep 1915.
[4] Maj N. Tinkler, NX12319; 2/5 Fd Regt. Bank officer; of Bellevue Hill, NSW; b. Sydney, 15 Oct 1917.
[5] Later one Japanese naval gun was found to be loaded and perfectly aligned on Palmer's gun, which would certainly have been hit if the Japanese had been able to fire one more shot.
[6] Lt F. C. Doyle, VX16572. 2/6 and 2/14 Bns. Cement worker; of Kew, Vic; b. Bairnsdale, Vic, 16 Nov 1915. Died of wounds 22 Jul 1945.

aircraft. The weather prevented the heavy bombers from attacking, but finally some Lightnings strafed the gun positions and dropped fire bombs. At 12.37 p.m. on the 6th Doyle led his patrol forward. The men moved through the bush for an hour and a half, and then, from a position 50 yards from the guns, they advanced firing their weapons and throwing grenades. A sapper carrying a 24-pound explosive charge was killed. Lance-Corporal Waites[7] raced forward and picked up the charge but he was mortally wounded. Corporal Lynch[8] led his section against a coast-gun on the left, threw in grenades and then climbed to the top of the emplacement and fired to cover the movement of his section. Private Sullivan[9] raced 80 yards to the other gun, forced the crew out with phosphorous smoke grenades and put them to flight. About 50 Japanese were driven off the hill and two 120-mm guns were captured. As the hill was being cleared the remainder of the platoon, under Sergeant Phefley,[1] moved in. The Australians were still greatly outnumbered, however, and Doyle sent back a request that the remainder of the company should move up; a second platoon was allotted. At this stage the company commander, Major O'Day, and others who were watching from a dispersal bay down below were wounded by mortar fire. Captain Thompson,[2] though wounded, took command and went forward to Waites'. He asked for another platoon and Lieutenant McLaren's[3] was sent forward. It was now dusk and the company dug in for the night, while the artillery and mortars registered.

It rained heavily and soon the water in the trenches was chest high. From these trenches the men had to fight off four attacks during the night. The first was made by about one company soon after darkness, and a standing patrol which had been sited some distance forward to keep away from a burning ammunition bunker which might have exploded was forced to withdraw. It was not realised until daylight next morning that the Bren gunner, Private Hamilton,[4] and his Number 2, Private Leeson,[5] had stayed behind and held their post, whence they killed eight Japanese.

In the meantime the enemy had made a very strong thrust on the left flank (said the company report). The position looked very grim as all communication with battalion had failed and no defensive fire could be called down. However the company held and the enemy were beaten back.

Interesting sidelights were: a Jap officer brandishing a sword jumping into a weapon-pit and being bayoneted for his trouble. Private (now Corporal) Dick Hill[6]

[7] L-Cpl H. A. Waites, VX50561; 2/14 Bn. Sheep station manager; of Altona, Vic; b. Wyuna, Vic, 22 Sep 1912. Killed in action 6 Jul 1945.
[8] Cpl H. J. Lynch, VX13168; 2/14 Bn. Labourer; of Geelong, Vic; b. Geelong, 25 Mar 1920.
[9] L-Cpl J. V. Sullivan, VX43480; 2/14 Bn. Labourer; of Pooncarie, NSW; b. Broken Hill, NSW, 25 Jul 1919.
[1] Sgt H. A. Phefley, VX15273; 2/14 Bn. Surveyor's assistant; of Wodonga, Vic; b. Wodonga, 26 Apr 1922.
[2] Maj R. N. Thompson, VX17954; 2/14 Bn. Book-keeper; of Clifton Hill, Vic; b. Essendon, Vic, 7 Apr 1918.
[3] Lt K. B. McLaren, VX3054; 2/14 Bn. Commercial traveller; of Elwood, Vic; b. Brighton, Vic, 17 May 1915.
[4] Cpl A. J. Hamilton, NX95970; 2/14 Bn. Butcher; of Lithgow, NSW; b. Lithgow, 21 Mar 1923.
[5] Pte A. L. C. Leeson, NX91358; 2/14 Bn. Bank officer; of Orange, NSW; b. Grafton, NSW, 11 Dec 1921.
[6] Sgt H. V. Hill, DCM, WX12808; 2/14 Bn. Truck driver; of Bayswater, WA; b. Surrey, England, 5 Nov 1920.

who, after dealing with two Japs who attacked him, was attacked by a third carrying a spear, just as he emptied his magazine. Luckily the Jap only used the spear to hit Hill and Hill's gameness in wrestling with the Jap while reloading and then killing his opponent is something still talked about. It is said that he further surprised the Jap by calling out: "Get out, you silly b———." A very serious situation now developed. Owing to the rain and mud all automatic weapons and practically all rifles failed. Grenades became the order while frantic efforts were made to clean the weapons and keep them firing. It was a company of very tired men who greeted the dawn. Ammunition had run low and the night had been full of danger but their determination to hold the position never wavered.

The patrol, under Lieutenant Robinson,[7] which had moved north along Vasey Highway, was pinned down by a gun covering the rear of the

Sketch of Waites' Knoll area, made on 10th August by Private S. Bennett, in war diary of 2/14th Battalion

Japanese position. Robinson was wounded, and the patrol withdrew in the evening.

On the morning of the 7th patrols were sent out. One of these, investigating two spurs on the left flank, came under artillery fire intended for its support and all but one of the 12 men in the patrol were killed or wounded. The Japanese attacked again next night, but the defenders were now prepared and defensive fire well organised; the 2/5th Field Regiment landed its shells only 30 to 40 yards from the forward Australian positions. The Japanese attacked five times, using petrol bombs, machine-guns and grenades, but all these attacks were driven off. On 8th July this forward company was relieved and marched to a rest area; probably 100 Japanese had been killed in the two-day fight.

On the 9th the cruiser *Shropshire* fired on the enemy positions from 8.30 onwards. At 9.30 a troop of tanks was landed by L.C.M's. From

---

[7] Lt W. G. Robinson, VX47790; 2/14 Bn. Clerk; of Bentleigh, Vic; b. Melbourne, 12 Apr 1921.

11 a.m. the enemy were bombed by Liberators and napalm was dropped. At 12.30 Rhoden decided that the Japanese stronghold had been neutralised and Captain Clarke's company and Captain H. Dalby's, supported by an artillery concentration of 600 rounds, attacked the Frost and Brown features, the sites of the remaining guns. By dusk Frost and Brown had been taken without much opposition, and the long fight round Manggar was over. A total of 107 Japanese dead were counted in the stronghold and it was thought that perhaps 150 had been buried in the tunnels that had been blown in. The guns with which the fortress was armed were found to be: two 120-mm naval guns, five 25-mm twin-barrelled guns, four 75-mm high-angle guns, four 20-mm aircraft cannons, five heavy mortars, five heavy machine-guns.

> At this stage (wrote the 2/14th Battalion's diarist) an unhappy situation arose in that our battle-exhausted troops were constantly worried by streams of war correspondents, sightseers and souvenir hunters from rear areas who not only interfered with the final stages of the campaign, but also deprived the fighting troops, who had done all the work, from securing the time-honoured trophies of a hard-fought battle. It is felt that such personnel despite their importance in the general scheme of things should be awakened to the parasitical nature of their activities and that the small prizes of war, not within the category of loot, ever have been and ever should be the reward of the combat soldier.

Meanwhile a hard fight had been in progress also at Gate where the 2/16th Battalion and the 2/5th Commando Squadron were engaged against a resolute group of Japanese. On 6th July Lieutenant Stark[8] of the 2/16th took a patrol almost to the crest of Gate, but came under heavy fire and was forced back, with the Japanese following up. The same day Lieutenant Redhead[9] of the 2/5th Commando Squadron was killed in a thrust towards the same feature. The attackers were supported by heavy fire from the 2/5th Field Regiment directed by Lieutenant Scott,[1] who, finding it difficult to get a good view, climbed a tree using an improvised ladder; five men of the 2/16th were hit by mortar fire, two fatally, while helping Scott. From his dangerous post Scott systematically bombarded Gate, and on the 8th the 2/16th took it without opposition. Next day the 2/16th took Grand after Scott had directed 300 rounds on to it from a position about 50 yards from the enemy.

Seldom in the war against the Japanese had Australians had such opportunities for clearing the way with the fire of guns as at Balikpapan, and Milford and his subordinates made the most of the opportunities. Milford had raised the 7th Divisional Artillery in 1940 and taken it to the Middle East, where it fought in Syria under another commander, Milford having been transferred to a more senior appointment in Australia. Now for the first time since Syria the regiments were in action together again.

---

[8] Lt J. A. Stark, WX8095. 2/28 and 2/16 Bns. Clerk; of Rottnest Island, WA; b. Perth, 26 Oct 1919.

[9] Lt F. A. E. Redhead, VX51729. F-O RAAF 1940-41; 2/21 Bn and 2/5 Cdo Sqn. Clerk; of Richmond, Vic; b. Tingha, NSW, 6 Dec 1920. Killed in action 6 Jul 1945.

[1] Lt-Col J. T. Scott, NX14337; 2/5 Fd Regt. Regular soldier; b. Melbourne, 8 Jun 1915.

The weight of shells fired into Balikpapan before the landing was mentioned earlier. On the day of the landing 17,250 shells and rockets were fired from the sea in the opening stage and, after the landing, the ships, at the call of officers ashore, fired 13,850 shells. In the first ten days the 25-pounders fired 41,800 rounds. In addition Air Vice-Marshal Bostock had used some 40 bomber squadrons drawn from the R.A.A.F., Fifth Air Force and Thirteenth Air Force to pound the defences.

"The operation was a lesson on the use of fire power," wrote Brigadier Dougherty in his report. "The old hands of this division remember the Owen Stanleys where they had no artillery; Gona, where 250 rounds of 25-pounder was all we could accumulate for the final assault on the Mission and where one tank would have saved 200 lives if we had only had it; the Markham and Ramu Valleys where we were an airborne division, and where the artillery support available, though on a far more liberal scale than before, was subject to the obvious limitations imposed by the need for supply by air."

CHAPTER 22

BALIKPAPAN AREA SECURED

BY 9th July both airfields were firmly in Australian hands and the 7th Division had completed its main tasks. The two forward battalions of the Japanese force had been reduced to fragments. But, meanwhile, the 25th Brigade, facing the third battalion dug in round the Batuchampar area on the Milford Highway, had become heavily engaged; and, on the extreme left, units of the 18th Brigade had become involved in a novel river war. It was now known that Rear-Admiral Kamada's headquarters were in the Batuchampar area.

On the afternoon of 4th July Brigadier Eather had held a conference at which he ordered his unit commanders to continue the northward advance on a three-battalion front. He instructed Lieut-Colonel R. H. Marson of the 2/25th to take over Nurse and Nail from the 2/31st, the object being to "seal off" the area from Orr's Junction westward to the coast and clear the country thus enclosed. All three battalions were then "to move forward slowly making utmost use of supporting arms".[1] These included those of the 2/4th Field Regiment, of a company of the 2/1st Machine Gun Battalion, some anti-tank guns, and three troops of tanks. On the right the 2/33rd had occupied Letter and Lewis on the 4th, and on the 5th pressed on against dwindling opposition to Mackay, Marshall, Mutual and Margin.

After the 2/25th had relieved the 2/31st (Lieut-Colonel Robson) on Nail and Nurse the forward companies of the 2/31st took up defensive positions on Letter and Lewis. Then Laverton was occupied, and, after a bombardment, Liverpool was taken. Heavy fire was now coming from Metal, and about 1 p.m. Robson's command post on Lodge was under heavy fire and his adjutant (Captain De Daunton[2]) and Intelligence officer (Lieutenant B. E. D. Robertson) were wounded and the wireless set shot to pieces. Robertson continued to pass information back to brigade by telephone until carried back under fire by Corporal Moorhouse,[3] who then went out again and brought in the telephone.

When it occupied its new positions on 5th July the 2/33rd was under fire from Muffle, to the east, and, like the 2/31st, from Metal. That night mortars lobbed 650 bombs on to Metal and next morning Captain Balfour-Ogilvy's[4] company took that hill, but a platoon of another company that moved towards Muffle was held up by enemy fire; in the afternoon, however, Muffle too was taken. From midday onwards Japanese guns on Joint fired on the battalion's positions. At 3.55 p.m. shells hit

---
[1] War diary, 25th Brigade.
[2] Capt F. H. De Daunton, QX20933; 2/31 Bn. Storeman and packer; of Auchenflower, Qld; b. Brisbane, 24 Mar 1920.
[3] Cpl C. A. R. Moorhouse, MM, QX16959; 2/31 Bn. 2 Bn RAR, Korea 1952-53. Labourer; of Toowoomba, Qld; b. Portsmouth, England, 2 Apr 1921.
[4] Capt J. M. Balfour-Ogilvy, SX1662; 2/33 Bn. Storeman; of Renmark, SA; b. Renmark, 10 Jul 1918.

the command post, killed the signals officer, Lieutenant Wallace,[5] and wounded the commander of the 2/33rd, Lieut-Colonel T. R. W. Cotton, and others. Cotton was taken to the dressing station and G. E. Lyon, Eather's brigade major, who had just arrived at the post, assumed command. A company probed forward towards Judge but came under heavy fire and withdrew to Marshall. On 6th July the 2/25th pressed on, took over Liverpool and occupied Huon.

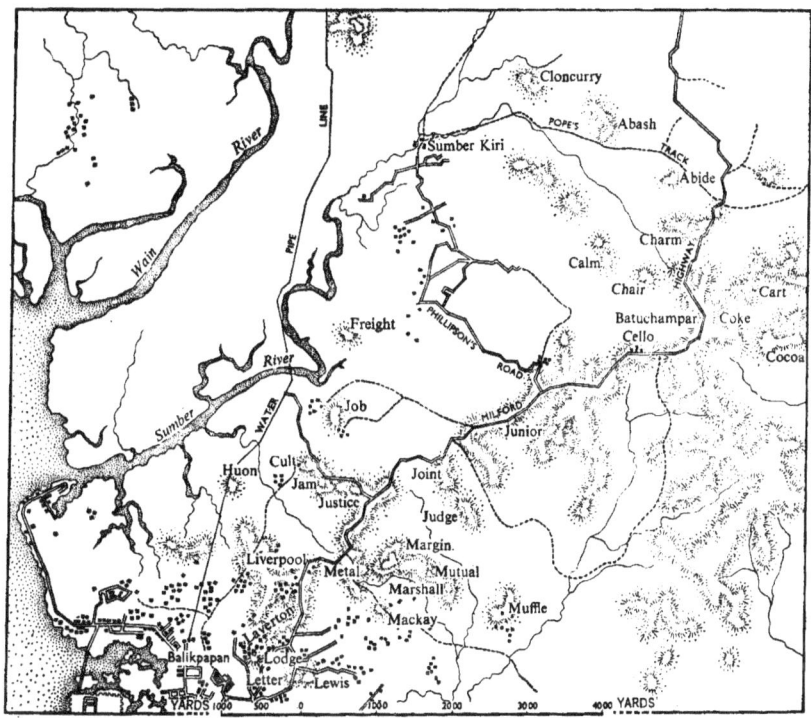

Eather's policy in this situation—the enemy resisting vigorously on naturally-strong ridges—was to use the supporting arms to the maximum and probe forward with patrols. Even so the Japanese were exacting a high price. On 5th July the brigade had lost 9 killed and 13 wounded; 31 Japanese dead were counted and 2 prisoners taken. On the 6th the brigade lost 2 killed and 32 wounded; 20 Japanese dead were counted and 3 prisoners taken.

On the morning of 7th July Lieut-Colonel Marson ordered Major C. S. Andrew's company, on Huon, to take Cult with one platoon, and if this succeeded to build up to full company strength. Lieutenant Egan[6] led

---
[5] Lt H. S. Wallace, WX26133; 2/33 Bn. Clerk; of Como, WA; b. Perth, 4 Jan 1921. Killed in action 6 Jul 1945.
[6] Lt J. M. Egan, VX105958; 2/25 Bn. Grocer; of West Richmond, Vic; b. Kew, Vic, 25 Apr 1919.

his platoon out, formed a firm base on Cult without meeting opposition, and sent a section to Jam. It came under fire from two pill-boxes and, ably led by Lance-Corporal Svenson,[7] wiped one out but then was forced back. At this stage Andrew and an artillery party arrived on Cult with the remainder of the company. It was now found that a copse between Cult and Jam was strongly held; it was kept quiet by machine-gun fire from Liverpool.

Next day the copse was shelled but patrols probing forward met sharp fire. Finally, after a very heavy concentration of fire by field guns, anti-tank guns and machine-guns, a patrol on the 9th found the copse and Jam unoccupied. On Jam and in the copse 46 enemy dead were found and there were signs that others had been buried. The 2/25th lost 3 killed and 10 wounded of whom 6 remained on duty.

Almost every night small parties of Japanese raided the Australian positions. For example, on the night of the 7th the 2/31st killed six raiders, and the headquarters of the 2/33rd was attacked by about 16 armed with rifles, machine-guns, spears and grenades. These killed the Intelligence officer, Lieutenant Melville,[8] and wounded 3; 3 Japanese officers and 9 men were killed. Eather now sent the 2/6th Commando Squadron (Captain G. C. Blainey) out on the left flank into the hills overlooking the Sumber River. Here on the 8th they occupied Job and next day found Freight and other hills unoccupied: it was evident that the Japanese had abandoned most of the garden area along Phillipson's Road.

That day after heavy bombardment the 2/33rd (now commanded by Major Bennett[9]) found Justice abandoned, and a company pressed on to Joint where 16 enemy dead and two damaged field guns were found; and to Judge. On the right flank two platoons under Lieutenants Moore[1] and Richards[2] made a converging attack on Muffle, long an isolated yet stubborn enemy outpost well to the south of their main positions, and took it; 15 Japanese dead were counted there. By the end of the day it was evident that the enemy rearguard had withdrawn about three miles along the highway to the Batuchampar area.

The effectiveness of the artillery fire—obviously a main cause of the withdrawal—was revealed by examination of the ridges that the Australians occupied on the 9th: shell holes on Muffle, Joint, Justice and Jam were only about five yards apart and many bunkers had been hit; the two field guns found on Joint had received direct hits.

For the first five days the 25th Brigade had been fighting in fairly open country in which it was able to use all available supporting weapons,

---

[7] WO2 V. P. Svenson, MBE, NX167876; 2/25 Bn. 3 Bn RAR, Korea 1950-51. Labourer; of Sydney; b. Sydney, 2 Jul 1924.

[8] Lt J. R. W. Melville, NX119431; 2/33 Bn. Bank officer; of Croydon, NSW; b. Christchurch, NZ, 17 Mar 1916. Killed in action 8 Jul 1945.

[9] Maj G. W. Bennett, MC, WX335; 2/33 Bn. Pastoral overseer; of Port Hedland-Marble Bar, WA; b. Subiaco, WA, 4 Nov 1912.

[1] Lt N. A. Moore, VX102154; 2/33 Bn. Schoolteacher; of Hamilton, Vic; b. Hamilton, 10 Aug 1918.

[2] Lt C. H. Richards, NX163759; 2/33 Bn. Clerk; of Belmore, NSW; b. Sydney, 25 Feb 1920.

but from the 9th onwards it was fighting in thick bush. The advance astride the Milford Highway to Batuchampar was allotted to the 2/31st Battalion. On the afternoon of the 9th Colonel Robson gave orders that Major C. W. Hyndman's company would be forward on the right, its objective being Junior, and Major H. F. Hayes' company on the left, its objective being a road bend due north of Junior. These were occupied without loss by 5 p.m. and at 6.25 Robson decided to move the whole battalion forward. Soon afterwards Lieutenant Lewis'[3] platoon was moving along the highway when five 500-kilo bombs lying in the open along the road were exploded around the Australians by remote control killing 3 and leaving 17 others dazed by the blast; the Japanese then opened fire with machine-guns. Corporal Mullins,[4] commanding one section, was thrown 15 feet off the road but returned, carried out a wounded man, withdrew the remainder of the bewildered men, and then went back and carried out another wounded man. That night the 2/31st formed a perimeter in this area and a patrol found the enemy dug in forward of Cello.

On the morning of the 10th Captain Lewington's[5] company secured a foothold in the buildings at Cello about 300 yards from the enemy. Robson was moving forward with a reconnaissance party when a group of depth-charges was exploded by remote control; Lewington suffered shock and the artillery observer was wounded. By 11.30, however, Cello had been secured and Japanese were seen at some fallen timber beyond, which was mortared and bombarded by the artillery.

At 12.10 p.m. Robson ordered Hayes' company to attack through the company on Cello and secure the fallen-timber area. In support was a troop of three tanks including one Frog. From 1.45 until 2.30 the artillery and 4.2-inch and 3-inch mortars fired on the area, clearing all the light timber, and the tanks, which had taken up hull-down positions on the road, fired into enemy strongpoints.

Hayes' company attacked at 2.30 with one platoon and the Frog forward. Two bunkers were soon silenced. Warrant-Officer Willson[6] advanced with one section and knocked out several Japanese machine-gun posts. He was wounded but carried on, capturing a 40-mm gun, and in 15 minutes the foremost enemy position had been taken. Twenty-five Japanese were killed and the captured weapons included one 75-mm gun, nine light anti-aircraft guns and two anti-tank guns. A patrol then probed forward and reported one machine-gun post on Coke.

Coke was a steep knoll on the right of the road carrying a tall tree every few yards and with tangled secondary growth among which lay a number of big logs 3 and 4 feet in diameter, evidently felled by timber

---

[3] Maj R. A. Lewis, NX177993; 2/31 Bn. Regular soldier; b. Wollongong, NSW, 5 Dec 1920.
[4] Cpl J. Mullins, MM, QX15555; 2/31 Bn. Tractor driver; of Tully, Qld; b. Ingham, Qld, 5 Nov 1917.
[5] Capt A. J. M. Lewington, NX12285; 2/31 Bn. Accounting clerk and wool classer; of Lindfield, NSW; b. Townsville, Qld, 18 May 1913.
[6] WO2 R. W. Willson, MM, SX1708; 2/31 Bn. Farm worker; of Penneshaw, Kangaroo Island, SA; b. Penneshaw, 21 Jan 1914.

getters. Robson, who considered that the shell of the enemy's resistance had been broken, now gave a warning order to Hyndman's company to take Coke and thrust along the road with all speed. The artillery and mortars began firing on the objective at 3 p.m. and the tanks fired from a road cutting 400 yards from the foot of Coke. There was no reply from the enemy. Lieutenant Carroll's[7] platoon attacked at 5 p.m. with three tanks (of the 2/1st Armoured Brigade Reconnaissance Squadron) and with two engineers out ahead to deal with mines. The tanks (in line ahead and about 30 yards apart) and the infantry had advanced about 100 yards without opposition when the enemy opened intense fire from several positions on Coke and also from some on the left of the road. The fire from the left killed Major Ryrie of the tanks and a signaller who were forward in the road cutting, and wounded Major K. S. Hall, second-in-command of the 2/31st, who, with Robson, was also watching from the cutting. The forward platoon lost heavily and was halted, one man, Lance-Corporal Rabjohns,[8] lying within five yards of the enemy and others within 20 yards. The posts, which numbered about seven, were dug under the big logs, which gave good overhead cover, or at the foot of big trees.

All this had happened in an instant. When the Japanese opened fire the men of Lieutenant Kelly's[9] platoon, which was to leap-frog over Carroll's when it had passed Coke, were leaning against the bank of the cutting just behind Robson, Ryrie and the others. Immediately Robson turned and shouted: "Nine platoon, get up there on the right!"

We had a grandstand view and needed no orders by the platoon commander (wrote one of them later). [Corporal Ottrey's[1]] section crossed the road first and ran into the fire that killed Ryrie. It was so quickly done that I am sure it was the same gun and the same magazine.

Ottrey and two others were hit. Lance-Corporal Cooper,[2] a former lance-sergeant in the 1st Parachute Battalion, who had heard Kelly give a shout and thought he too had been hit, collected five men, and they pressed on to the logs where Cooper grenaded two Japanese who appeared on the right. There they threw off their haversacks and fixed bayonets. Kelly now joined this group and then arrived a second platoon which Robson had sent forward. While part of the two platoons faced right Cooper sent two men up the hill in search of the machine-gun which had hit so many men on the road. The leading scout, Private Blunden,[3] fell. Cooper ran up to him and found him at the feet of a Japanese. Cooper promptly bayoneted this man, picked up Blunden's Owen gun

---
[7] Lt G. P. Carroll, NX105341; 2/31 Bn. Public servant; of Cremorne, NSW; b. Newcastle, NSW, 8 Sep 1916.
[8] L-Cpl G. A. Rabjohns, NX93647; 2/31 Bn. Station hand; of Roslyn, NSW; b. Crookwell, NSW, 13 Dec 1920.
[9] Lt A. C. Kelly, WX26075; 2/31 Bn. Farmer; of Quairading, WA; b. Quairading, 30 Apr 1917.
[1] Cpl A. J. Ottrey, QX15632; 2/31 Bn. Labourer; of Gunbower, Vic; b. Pyramid Hills, Vic, 6 Nov 1913. Died of wounds 10 Jul 1945.
[2] Maj E. J. Cooper, VX13988. 2/8 Fd Regt, 1 Parachute Bn and 2/31 Bn. Postal clerk; of Frankston, Vic; b. Mentone, Vic, 12 Oct 1920.
[3] Pte J. D. R. Blunden, VX94110; 2/31 Bn. Shop assistant; of Melbourne; b. Melbourne, 9 Jun 1925. Killed in action 10 Jul 1945.

and shot four more. Cooper held on here while the men farther down the hill beat off Japanese who were coming in from the right.

On the road, when the forward tank—the Frog—had exhausted its fuel, it went back carrying wounded, and another tank replaced it. Private Douglass,[4] a man of 39 who was normally a storeman at battalion headquarters, moved down the road under heavy fire and helped out two wounded men, then returned on a tank and remained attending to wounded men who lay in the open. The tanks could not turn on the road, and when the leading one withdrew the others had to precede it. About ten Japanese were now advancing round the lower slopes of Coke towards the wounded, but Douglass engaged them with Rabjohns' Owen gun and held them off until the wounded men had been taken out by the tank.

Corporal Murdock's[5] tank now gave supporting fire until its Besa gun was damaged and could fire only single shots and all high-explosive ammunition for its main gun was exhausted. At 5.50 Murdock was ordered to withdraw and to pass on an order to withdraw to the infantry. Murdock dismounted under fire and did this; he then directed the placing of four wounded on his tank and brought them out. Two of his crew had been wounded.

Robson's order to withdraw was passed forward from man to man. The forward infantry sections came out under spasmodic fire, helping with the wounded, and then the battalion took up a defensive position astride the road for the night. The Japanese infiltrated among the Australian posts that night and killed one man. On the 10th, 18 had been killed and 23 wounded round Coke, all but 3 killed and 9 wounded being in Hyndman's company; at the end of the day 11 of the dead had not yet been recovered.

On the left of the 25th Brigade the 2/6th Commando Squadron had been ordered by Brigadier Eather to patrol to Sumber Kiri. On the 10th a patrol under Lance-Sergeant J. McA. Brammer encountered about 60 Japanese north-east of the village. Lieutenant W. Taylor hastened forward with another section; they attacked and drove out the Japanese who left 8 dead; two Australians were killed.

There was a lull after the hard fight on Coke. The Japanese facing the 2/31st were well dug in and well armed. Next day Eather ordered the 2/25th to relieve the 2/31st. On the 12th a patrol of the 2/6th Squadron worked round through the bush to a point on Charm whence it overlooked the highway about two miles behind the forward positions. Here the men watched parties of about 30 Japanese carrying supplies and stretchers forward. A party of about 20 approached the Australians' observation post. The Australians withdrew and set an ambush which killed six; the others made off. The main body of the squadron on the 13th and 14th moved to Cloncurry and Abash. In the course of this move

---

[4] Pte H. F. Douglass, MM, NX90322; 2/31 Bn. Labourer; of Taree, NSW; b. Enfield, NSW, 18 Oct 1905.

[5] Cpl L. J. Murdock, SX17203; 2/1 Armd Bde Recce Sqn. Farmer; of Warooka, SA; b. Warooka, 24 Oct 1918.

one troop was ambushed, two bombs were detonated in its path, and Lieutenant Linklater[6] and four others were killed or mortally wounded. An N.E.I. platoon that had also been patrolling on this flank was at the Wain pumping station and probing northward.

After much patrolling on both sides of the highway, Eather, on the afternoon of 14th July, ordered the 2/25th to send a company wide on each flank: one to Cart and the other to Calm, both of which had been visited by patrols and found unoccupied. The right-hand company reached Cocoa about a mile south of Cart by dusk; the left moved through Calm to Chair. On the 15th Lieut-Colonel Marson ordered the company on the right (Captain B. G. C. Walker) to advance to Cart while another company and his own headquarters moved on to Calm. In this situation the battalion would dominate the highway from both east and west.

The enemy reacted strongly on the night of the 15th. In heavy rain from 40 to 50 raided Calm but were driven off. In this fight which lasted all night Lance-Corporal Grigg[7] moved forward alone to a log that the raiders were using as cover and threw grenades over the log at the Japanese. He was believed to have killed most of the 13 Japanese who were found dead there. The Japanese raiders moved very quietly: one of them wounded an Australian with a sword. When daylight came the Japanese withdrew about 75 yards. Marson sent up three platoons under Major Andrew at 9 o'clock next morning and these took forward ammunition, carried out the wounded and drove the Japanese away. On the 16th an enemy force occupied Cocoa, temporarily cutting the line of communication of Walker's company on Cart, and that night raiding parties attacked the headquarters of the 2/33rd near Cello causing five casualties, and attacked the N.E.I. platoon at Wain pumping station, causing it to fall back some distance.

On the 17th a company of the 2/25th occupied Charm hard by the highway and a company of the 2/33rd took over on Cart. That evening Eather gave orders for a decisive movement: the 2/6th Squadron, which was carrying out ambushes throughout its area—it killed 23 Japanese on the 16th and 17th—was to patrol in strength to the highway near the junction with Pope's Track; the 2/31st was to relieve the 2/33rd astride the highway; the 2/25th was to cut the highway at Charm; the 2/33rd was to cut the track running east from the Pope's Track junction along the valley north of Cart.

That night (the 17th-18th), which was dark and rainy, the Japanese "reacted violently to the gradual encirclement" and before dawn attacked the two companies of the 2/25th then on Charm and the headquarters of the 2/33rd. At Charm the enemy maintained constant pressure against the whole perimeter until a counter-attack drove them off at 8.30 a.m. Here three Australians and 53 Japanese were killed, many probably by

---

[6] Lt A. F. Linklater, NX68478. 2/6 Indep Coy, 2/6 Cdo Sqn. Clerk; of Willoughby, NSW; b. Willoughby, 24 Jun 1921. Killed in action 13 Jul 1945.

[7] Cpl R. F. Grigg, DCM, NX99043; 2/25 Bn. Station hand; of Wagga Wagga, NSW; b. Goulburn, NSW, 8 Dec 1922.

defensive fire brought down by the artillery. On the 19th and 20th the forward companies continued to probe on both sides of the road. There was a sharp fight on Charm on the 20th. Lieutenant Raward[8] and 12 men of Captain R. W. P. Dodd's company went out to destroy a Japanese strongpoint which was found to be far stronger than expected. Raward divided his party into two, attacked and drove the enemy out. Corporal Ford,[9] operating a flame-thrower with much daring, was largely responsible for the success. That evening a patrol of the same company under Lieutenant McCosker[1] ambushed a carrying party of 20 moving south along the highway and killed about 17. Round Charm the 2/25th killed 95 Japanese and lost 4 killed and 12 wounded. The 2/33rd on the right was now round Cart, the 2/25th on Calm, Chair, Charm and Abide.

The 2/31st was astride the highway south-south-east of Chair. The tanks moving with it along the highway had been halted by a big crater in the road. On the afternoon of the 19th, after artillery bombardment, Lewington's company advanced and attacked round the right flank, and a tank with bridging equipment moved forward to span the crater in the road and let four other tanks through. By 2 p.m. the bridge was ready and the leading tank moved up to engage the enemy; by 3 p.m. the company had its objectives, and had taken four heavy mortars. One of the tanks was temporarily disabled by a contact mine which it hit just beyond the bridge.

Patrolling continued on the morning of the 21st: the enemy was still in the same positions on both sides of the highway. In the evening, however, it was found that the forward positions had been vacated but were covered by fire from a little farther back. Patrols counted 26 dead in the abandoned posts. That night there were loud explosions round Charm and elsewhere, and next morning the enemy had gone. Against little opposition patrols pushed forward to Pope's Track and beyond.[2]

General Milford decided that, having reached the line of Pope's Track, he had his objectives and no good purpose would be served by continuing to thrust against the enemy rearguards. General Morshead agreed and Milford instructed Eather to stay put and only patrol forward of the line he then held.[3]

It was proving impossible to land the necessary tonnage of stores over the open beaches because of the sea swell and it was therefore essential to use the port, but when General Milford asked Rear-Admiral Noble to do this Noble stated firmly that he would not send even a destroyer into the bay unless he had a guarantee that the western side of it was

---

[8] Lt J. E. A. Raward, NX114055; 2/25 Bn. Shop assistant; of Murwillumbah, NSW; b. Ulmarra, NSW, 5 Nov 1921.
[9] Sgt C. H. Ford, QX9697; 2/25 Bn. Railway worker; of Dalby, Qld; b. Brisbane, 17 Jan 1912.
[1] Lt H. F. McCosker, QX37987; 2/25 Bn. Pineapple farmer; of Glass House Mountains, Qld; b. Brisbane, 30 Nov 1922.
[2] Along the highway there had been evidence of Japanese slaughter of natives; round barracks north of Abide the 2/31st found and buried the decapitated bodies of 16 Indonesians.
[3] A few days later Eather, who had led the 25th Brigade for 3 years and 7 months, departed to take command of the 11th Division. Lieut-Colonel Marson administered command of the 25th Brigade until the arrival of its new commander, Brigadier Wood, from the Torricellis.

clear of Japanese guns. Thus Milford had no alternative to sending a force across the bay. It was an interesting example of a course of aggressive action being forced on a commander by the administrative requirements.

On 4th July, therefore, Milford had given the 18th Brigade the task of landing a battalion on the western shores of Balikpapan Bay to ensure that the enemy could not interfere with the working of the port from that direction, and incidentally to assist N.I.C.A. to give aid to the natives. Brigadier Chilton gave these tasks to the 2/9th Battalion, with, under its command, a troop of the 2/7th Cavalry (Commando) Regiment, a troop of tanks, a troop of field guns, one of heavy mortars, and other detachments. This force was to land at Penadjam from L.V.T's and L.C.M's on 5th July.

The L.V.T's containing the two leading companies of the 2/9th moved off at 12.10 p.m. Milford regarded this as a ticklish operation and watched, with some anxiety, from the

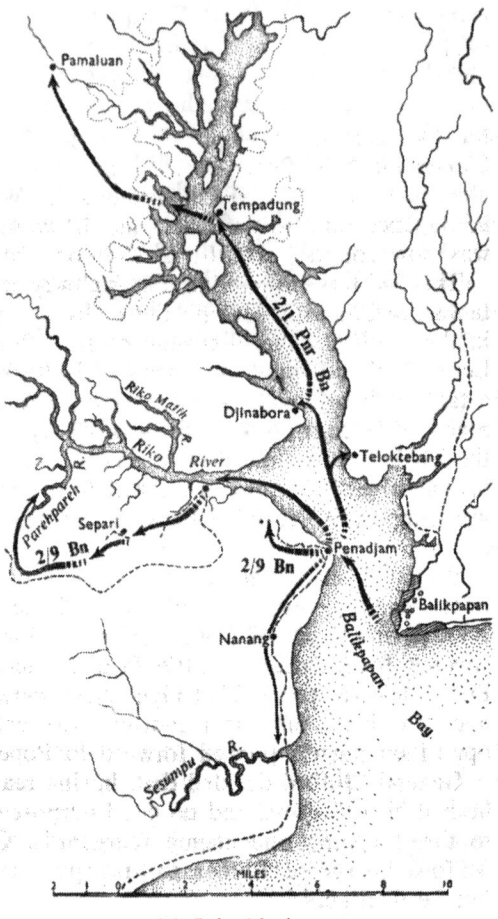

5th July-6th August

heights where the cracking plant stood. Naval vessels and field artillery bombarded the objective and at 1.35 the first troops landed without opposition. By 2.15 the whole battalion was ashore. All the tanks bogged as they landed from their L.C.M's. One company patrolled southward and found no enemy. There was random enemy artillery fire from a point three miles west of Penadjam at 3.45, but the 2/4th Field Regiment, firing across the bay, quickly silenced the gun. A second company patrolled northward and by 6.15 had reached the top of the hill to the north-west having killed one Japanese and taken a 5-inch gun intact. Five more guns were later found in this area. Just outside Penadjam five Indonesians were discovered dead with their hands tied behind their backs.

(Australian War Memorial)
Sappers of the 2/9th Field Company searching for mines, Balikpapan, 1st July.

(Australian War Memorial)
Stretcher bearers bringing in a wounded man, Balikpapan, 1st July.

A mortar crew of the 2/2nd Anti-Tank Regiment firing a 4.2 in support of the 2/10th Battalion advancing on Parramatta from a position near the Vasey Highway, Balikpapan, on 1st July.

(*Australian War Memorial*)

Directing mortar fire on to Hill 87, Balikpapan, 1st July.

(*U.S. Army Signal Corps*)

(*U.S. Army Signal Corps*)

Infantry and artillery observers pinned down by Japanese fire from Hill 87, 1st July.

(*Australian War Memorial*)

Men of the 2/12th Battalion north-east of Balikpapan, 2nd July.

(*Australian War Memorial*)

A flame-throwing tank of the 1st Armoured Regiment and men of the 2/10th Battalion attacking a Japanese bunker near the Tank Plateau, Balikpapan, 3rd July 1945.

(*U.S. Army Signal Corps*)

Troops of the 2/10th Battalion, supported by tanks, clearing the oil refinery area, Balikpapan, 3rd July.

Next day at dawn a patrol went south to Nanang village and on to the Sesumpu River which it reached by 2 p.m. No Japanese were seen but natives reported that some had passed through the previous day. The other companies and the commando troop made local patrols.

One commando patrol was ambushed near a village not far from the mouth of the Riko River and lost two men killed. A platoon of the 2/9th Battalion reinforced the commando troop and after some days of patrolling it was found that the enemy was dug in in the Separi area. On 12th July, after further probing, the enemy withdrew from this position. On 7th July a platoon under Lieutenant Gamble[4] established an artillery observation post on high ground with a view of the mouth of the Riko River.

Patrols of the 2/3rd Commando Squadron found enemy positions about four miles west-north-west of Penadjam. At the first position a patrol killed five; at the second 23, it was estimated, before enemy mortar and machine-gun fire forced the patrol of 12 to withdraw.

Captain D. C. J. Scott of the 2/9th Battalion with two platoons and mortars landed unopposed at Djinabora on the afternoon of 8th July; one platoon was left there to examine tracks in the neighbourhood; it found no Japanese.

That night Chilton ordered Lieut-Colonel A. J. Lee, the commander of the 2/9th, to land troops at Teloktebang on the eastern shore. These landed on the 9th but found no enemy. On the 11th Chilton ordered the 2/9th to maintain a platoon base at Teloktebang and patrol northward, to patrol the north bank of the Riko River to the Riko Matih and northwest along the high ground, to harass the enemy on the south bank of the Riko, and to continue patrols to the Sesumpu River and eliminate Japanese stragglers.

On 15th July natives reported that there were 30 Japanese at Separi, and patrols set out through very difficult country to find them, but when they arrived the Japanese had gone. A patrol under Lance-Corporal McKinlay[5] reported a Japanese motor vessel of 300 tons some miles up the Riko and a platoon was sent out to place a standing patrol to watch it. They found the vessel unoccupied and boarded it. During the night a big launch appeared towing a motor boat and prahu. The patrol opened fire from the motor vessel and the launch was set on fire and sank. Five Japanese were taken prisoner; the motor vessel was sailed down to the mouth of the Riko.

This kind of patrolling, by land and water, continued. A patrol led by Lieutenant Frood[6] voyaged by L.C.M. and prahu along the Parehpareh, and established a base to the west whence it probed westward to cut the enemy's line of communication. It found about 50 Japanese who were withdrawing northward. This was too large a force to be attacked in such circumstances and the patrol was withdrawn.

---

[4] Lt A. G. Gamble, NX68801; 2/9 Bn. Farmer; of Harwood, NSW; b. Harden, NSW, 9 May 1920.
[5] Cpl C. G. McKinlay, MM, NX20981. 7 Cav Regt and 2/9 Bn. Grazier; of Inverell, NSW; b. Sydney, 20 Jun 1900.
[6] Lt W. Frood, QX16591; 2/9 Bn. Clerk; of Toowoomba, Qld; b. Toowoomba, 14 May 1914.

General Milford decided on 16th July to place a reinforced company of Lieut-Colonel A. A. Buckley's 2/1st Pioneer Battalion, which had mainly been employed round the beach-head, under the command of the 18th Brigade to protect Balikpapan harbour against possible enemy attacks from the north. Milford did not know what the Japanese were doing at the top end of the bay, but the 2/9th had intercepted several small craft trying to make their way there. There was now much shipping in the port, the naval covering force had departed, and it was conceivable that the Japanese, with small craft, might make a night raid on the port.

Thus Captain Morahan's[7] company with a section of the 2/4th Field Regiment and other detachments, and with two L.C.M's, went to Djinabora and began patrolling. Its tasks included preventing enemy parties moving south to the bay and possibly engaging enemy positions to the north. On 21st July this force was enlarged to include two companies of the Pioneer battalion with detachments of heavy weapons under command and a troop of the 2/4th Field Regiment and a searchlight in support. This group was named Buckforce and was at first commanded by Major Coleman.[8] It was to establish a coast-defence position and patrol base in the Tempadung area, prevent Japanese from moving by sea to Balikpapan Bay, patrol and establish contact with the enemy, operate "such water patrols as type of craft available permits" and seek more forward patrol bases.

Buckforce patrolled widely in the next few days. Some Japanese were encountered. On 26th July the Australian frigate *Gascoyne,* placed at the disposal of Buckforce for the day, shelled Tempadung and Pamaluan, a village about 7 miles to the north-west. The latter was occupied early on the 28th; the Japanese had evidently departed a few hours before. Next day a patrol fired on a group of eight Japanese and killed three. Thick jungle and mangroves made both patrolling and the landing of water craft difficult. On 30th July two platoons under Lieutenant Blamey[9] probed east and north. One platoon encountered a bunker position and a man was killed. Artillery fire silenced this position and both platoons attacked, took three bunkers and killed seven Japanese. They dug in and at 3 a.m. on 31st July 30 Japanese attacked but were driven off by artillery and small arms fire.

Patrols were sent out on the morning of 1st August and found many signs of enemy movement but saw no Japanese. On the 2nd, however, at 8.30 p.m. a Japanese patrol attacked Captain Kitching's[1] company but was driven off leaving six dead. Soon afterwards three Japanese were killed by a booby-trap. Buckforce had now killed 30, and taken one prisoner. Lieut-Colonel Buckley took command of the force on 3rd

---

[7] Maj J. O. Morahan, NX28078; 2/1 Pnr Bn. Wool classer; of Sydney; b. Sydney, 23 Sep 1916.

[8] Col S. T. G. Coleman, OBE, NX468. 2/1 Pnr Bn. 18 Bde and staff appointments. Regular soldier; b. Sydney, 5 Feb 1916.

[9] Lt T. G. Blamey, NX52647. 2/3 and 2/1 Pnr Bns. Accountant; of Wollstonecraft, NSW; b. Wagga Wagga, NSW, 24 Oct 1917.

[1] Capt G. S. Kitching, NX51486; 2/1 Pnr Bn. Clerk; of Haberfield, NSW; b. Petersham, NSW, 7 Sep 1914.

August and the Japanese positions were bombarded by the guns of a whole battery, their fire being directed with the help of an observer in an Auster aircraft.

By 6th August the whole of the battalion was concentrated in the Tempadung area. Patrolling continued against parties of Japanese who were still disciplined and aggressive. On the 6th observers in an Auster guided a patrol to a group of 63 Indian prisoners, who were picked up by an L.C.M. next day. These had been captured in Sarawak early in 1942. The last clashes with the enemy in this area occurred on 9th August when a patrol under Lieutenant Morrow[2] killed three Japanese, and Captain Williams'[3] company, patrolling towards the Milford Highway, also killed three.

After the big withdrawal of the Japanese from the Batuchampar stronghold the 25th Brigade stayed where it was but patrolled extensively every day. On 25th July the 2/7th Cavalry (Commando) Regiment with two squadrons took over the forward positions astride the highway, and thenceforward patrolled northward; it had fairly frequent patrol clashes and set many ambushes. The last clash occurred here on 14th August when a deep patrol of the 2/25th Battalion set an ambush on the highway; 12 Japanese walked into it and 9 were killed.

While the 2/14th Battalion was overcoming the enemy stronghold above Manggar the 2/16th had been patrolling deep into the tangle of hills north-east of Balikpapan. From 8th July onwards such patrolling occupied only a few sub-units each day and much of the effort of this battalion (as of others, similarly employed) went into improving its camp, making fish traps, and engaging in other profitable and pleasant occupations.

After the Japanese positions above Manggar had been taken the 2/14th Battalion was out of contact with the enemy for a time. Hundreds of natives were then streaming into the N.I.C.A. compounds. They said that about 150 Japanese were on Bale, 2,000 yards to the north. On 10th July the 2/27th took over the left flank at Manggar, freeing the 2/14th to probe towards Sambodja. Patrols from Major C. A. W. Sims' company of the 2/27th clashed with parties of Japanese that day on Band and Frost, south of Bale; 3 Australians were killed and 9 Japanese. Lieutenant Dempsey[4] of the 2/14th led a platoon along the Vasey Highway to the Adjiraden River, made a patrol base there, and thence probed to Taratip without finding any Japanese.

On the 11th the 2/27th moved through and took over the base at the Adjiraden River and next day its command group and two companies were established at Lamaru. Natives said that there were no Japanese

---
[2] Col W. J. Morrow, OBE, VX101929; 2/1 Pnr Bn. 3 Bn RAR, Korea 1952-53; BM HQ 28 British Commonwealth Bde 1953; CO 1 RAR, Malaya 1959. Regular soldier; b. Glen Innes, NSW, 1 Jun 1921.
[3] Maj C. G. Williams, ED, NX34898; 2/1 Pnr Bn. Departmental manager; of Scone, NSW; b. Wee Waa, NSW, 23 Jun 1911.
[4] Lt L. J. Dempsey, VX81715; 2/14 Bn. Clerk; of Wodonga, Vic; b. Rutherglen, Vic, 18 Dec 1920.

even in Sambodja, and on 14th July a patrol confirmed this, and an N.E.I. patrol found Amborawang unoccupied. On the 17th Lieut-Colonel K. S. Picken of the 2/27th moved his command post forward to Amborawang and had one company there and one at Bangsal on the highway.

Thence on 18th July Picken sent two companies, 438 strong, into Sambodja. A patrol north along the pipeline encountered five stray Japanese and killed two.

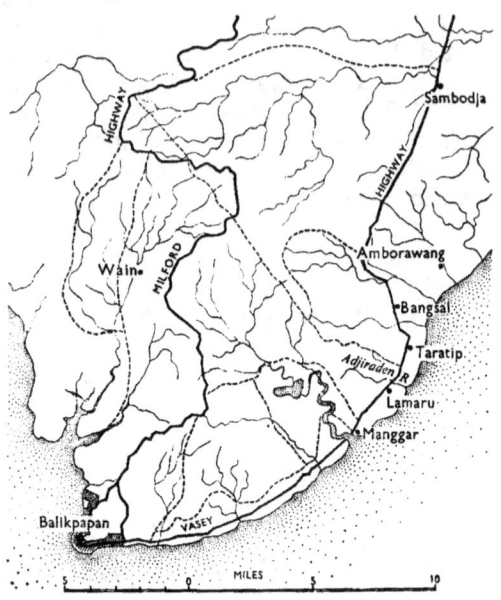

A patrol consisting of Captain Crafter's[5] company of the 2/27th less one platoon moved due west across country to the Milford Highway on the 18th. They reached a point about two miles and a half from the highway, and thence Crafter and a small party made their way forward and, having had to cut a track through thick jungle for the final 2,000 yards, reached the road at 5 p.m. They heard Japanese moving along the road and then were themselves seen and pursued. They evaded the enemy and rejoined the company, which moved back to Amborawang next day. That day (the 19th) the battalion was ordered to return to the Adjiraden and relieve the 2/14th in the country north of the airfield. It moved back in vehicles next day.

The Japanese appeared to be gradually withdrawing from the cluster of hills round Bale. On 14th July a platoon under Lieutenant Gugger[6] encountered a party of about 20 Japanese with two machine-guns on Bale. Gugger decided to withdraw under cover of smoke to allow the artillery to fire. Smoke grenades could not be fired because of the density of the bush, so Gugger crawled forward to where the screen was needed and lit the grenades with a match. The Japanese drew back farther into the hills and on 17th July the ridges north of the Bale group were found to be unoccupied except by one party, and it withdrew on the 18th.

In the next four weeks deep patrolling continued in the area north of Manggar, and there were occasional clashes. On 1st August information arrived that about 100 Japanese were moving towards Sambodja. Brigadier Dougherty ordered Lieut-Colonel F. H. Sublet to reinforce

---

[5] Maj J. G. Crafter, MBE, SX4516; 2/27 Bn. Regular soldier; b. Port Augusta, SA, 28 Jun 1914.
[6] Lt N. A. Gugger, VX118673; 2/14 Bn. Storekeeper; of Fyansford, Vic; b. Geelong, Vic, 17 Sep 1919.

Sambodja and Amborawang, and by 3rd August most of the 2/16th was concentrated at Sambodja. Long-range patrols were sent out, some remaining away five or six days, but only stragglers were found.

The 2/14th moved forward to protect the line of communication of the 2/16th and particularly to deal with ambush parties along the Vasey Highway. On 9th August Lieutenant Backhouse[7] and 20 men of the 2/14th set out on a 48-hour patrol to examine the tracks between the two forward companies. About four hours out the leading scout saw and fired on four Japanese. Backhouse put one section on the track while he and the two other sections attacked on the right and soon found themselves close behind the enemy. They had been unobserved but could now see the Japanese who appeared to be "in a large-sized panic, racing from hole to hole". "This situation," says the patrol report, "was not desirable," so the flanking group returned and a fresh attack was launched. This time two sections attacked on the left while the third held the track and watched the line of withdrawal. In close fighting seven Japanese were killed and opposition ceased. Three Australians were wounded, one mortally. It was the battalion's last engagement.

As usual the men soon found interesting employment.

> An officer of this staff is building a 15-foot sailing boat just outside his tent (wrote a visitor to the 21st Brigade in mid-August). Next door another is cleaning and polishing a set of crocodile's teeth. On the river are several sailing boats made from aircraft belly-tanks. Surf boards are in use in the 2/16th Bn area farther along the beach. There is plenty of sawn timber to be collected in the ruins of Balikpapan and bigger and better huts are going up every day.

The number of Japanese dead seen and counted in the Balikpapan operation was 1,783. It was estimated that 249 others had also been killed; 63 were captured. A total of 229 Australians were killed or died of wounds and 634 were wounded. The heaviest losses were suffered by the 25th Brigade in its advance inland along the Milford Highway, and particularly by the 2/31st Battalion.[8]

In September Milford received a copy of the report on the Oboe Two operation by the A.O.C. R.A.A.F. Command, Air Vice-Marshal Bostock. Bostock offered some criticism of the army on some interesting points

---

[7] Capt J. W. Backhouse, WX4711. 2/28 and 2/14 Bns. Shop assistant; of Perth; b. Broken Hill, NSW, 5 Jan 1915.

[8] The losses—killed and wounded—in the infantry, commando, armoured and artillery units were:

	Officers	Other Ranks		Officers	Other Ranks
2/9th Battalion	—	19	2/1st Machine Gun Battalion	1	16
2/10th Battalion	5	54	2/7th Cavalry (Commando) Regiment	9	76
2/12th Battalion	3	37	1st Armoured Regiment	1	14
2/14th Battalion	8	55	2/4th Field Regiment	5	10
2/16th Battalion	3	54	2/5th Field Regiment	3	11
2/27th Battalion	1	20	2/6th Field Regiment	1	3
2/25th Battalion	7	90	2/2nd Anti-Tank Regiment	—	6
2/31st Battalion	5	163			
2/33rd Battalion	10	85			
2/1st Pioneer Battalion	—	18			
2/2nd Pioneer Battalion	—	1			

of principle, and Milford wrote replies to this criticism into his war diary. For instance, Bostock wrote: "The local army commander, during this operation, was particularly prone to attempt to dictate the manner in which air support was to be applied. He wished to nominate classes of aircraft, types and weights of bombs and methods of attack to be employed to achieve the results he specified. This attitude is to be deprecated. It is just as illogical for a local army commander to presume to interfere with professional and technical air force aspects as it would be for him to attempt to dictate to a supporting naval force commander the classes of ships, types of guns and dispositions of naval vessels detailed to afford him support with naval bombardment."

Milford replied: "In many instances the army commander has a vital interest in the method of attack to be employed since the lives of his troops may be endangered. For targets in proximity to army troops the army commander alone knows the detailed dispositions and intention of his troops and can determine methods of attack which are safe. For distant targets the same considerations do not apply but [the] paragraph . . . does not differentiate."

Bostock also complained that "Army officers responsible for loading the First T.A.F. units were not always sympathetic to R.A.A.F. requirements . . . working with a new division, some rawness was inevitable".

Milford replied: "The allotment to ships of every man, vehicle and store of the whole force is an army responsibility. Since shipping is never available to meet all demands (and every service and unit considers its demands essential) the difficulties of a satisfactory solution are very great. As an example of army cuts, no supporting arms whatever and practically no equipment and stores for the reserve brigade could be included in the assault lift.

"The R.A.A.F., accustomed to a high standard of comfort, and not faced by the problem of fitting masses of vehicles and stores to a minimum of ships, regards as unsympathetic a reduction of air force equipment to a scale which on army standards is lavish."

Indeed, rightly or wrongly, in this and other amphibious operations, army officers considered the equipment required by the air force in the early stages excessively elaborate, and the discipline of air force ground staff capable of improvement.

The Balikpapan operation—the largest amphibious attack carried out by Australian troops—succeeded fairly swiftly. The attackers possessed the support of powerful weapons: aircraft using bombs, napalm and guns; naval guns; tanks, including flame-throwers; manhandled flame-throwers.[9] The Japanese, who were in well-prepared positions and well equipped with guns and mortars, resisted with their usual fortitude, and paid more than seven lives for each Australian life they took. Once again they

---

[9] "The air effort expended in support of the Oboe Two operation is believed to be greater than that expended directly in support of any similar operation in S.W.P.A."—R.A.A.F. Command, A.A.F., S.W.P.A., Report of Oboe Two Operation, July 1945.

demonstrated how a force of resolute men well dug in could delay a stronger force far more formidably armed.

The immediate objectives in Borneo were to establish bases and reoccupy oilfields; the long-range objective had originally been to advance westward to Java. If the attack on Java had been carried out it would have been in progress at a time when American forces were committed to an advance northward to Japan proper, and the British-Indian forces to an advance southward against Singapore. In retrospect the wisdom of embarking upon this third thrust—westward against Japanese forces isolated in the Indies—seems doubtful. Strategically the only gain would have been to the Japanese whose isolated and otherwise idle forces would be given employment; it would have been proper to place this third front on a low priority for equipment, and not improbable that it would have been plagued by shortages of men, ships and aircraft.

One result of a complex of decisions, some contradictory and some illogical, was that, in 1945, while I Australian Corps, well equipped and with powerful air and naval support, was preparing for or was fighting battles of doubtful value in Borneo, an Australian corps in Bougainville and an Australian division in New Guinea were fighting long and bitter campaigns (whose value also was doubted) in which they were short of air and naval support, and suffered such a poverty of ships and landing craft that, as a rule, the best they could do was to put ashore a company or two at a time on a hostile shore. The Japanese on the other hand could reflect with satisfaction that in this period their four depleted divisions isolated round Wewak and on Bougainville had kept three Australian divisions strenuously employed, and in Borneo three hotchpotch forces had engaged two more Australians divisions, though only briefly.

CHAPTER 23

AFTER THE CEASE FIRE

THROUGHOUT July and early August the British and Australian Governments had been discussing the part that the British Commonwealth should play in the invasion of Japan. Mr Churchill had cabled to the Australian Prime Minister on 4th July that he was considering a plan to provide a British Commonwealth force of three to five divisions supported by British naval and air forces. He asked whether an Australian division that he understood was available, the Australian Navy, and Australian air squadrons, would join the force, which might consist of "British, Australian, New Zealand, British-Indian and possibly Canadian divisions" and would form "a striking demonstration of Commonwealth solidarity".

He added that the American Joint Chiefs of Staff had proposed that they should hand over the South-West Pacific Area, less the Philippines and the Admiralty Islands bases, to British command. "They do not intend, however, to leave in this area any resources which it is possible to move farther forward, and we are therefore loath to accept responsibility for this area at the time proposed—15th August." A tentative British proposal was that the United States should transfer responsibility for the part of the South-West Pacific Area referred to as soon as practicable, probably after the recapture of Singapore, that the Australian Chiefs of Staff, linked with the Combined Chiefs of Staff through the British Chiefs, should take over that part of the area that lay east of Celebes, while the remainder should come within Admiral Mountbatten's command.

General Blamey drafted a reply to Mr Churchill's cable. In it he described the proposal for a British Commonwealth force for the invasion of Japan as "most desirable" but "unrealistic and impracticable". It would not be organised, trained and deployed before about April 1946, and he understood that the American invasion of Japan would begin at a comparatively early date. It was desired that the Australian division should take part in the main operations against Japan. "Public opinion has been restive under the allocation of our troops to secondary roles for so long and this has been cause of considerable discontent amongst forces." It did not seem to be fully appreciated that about 70,000 Japanese remained in the islands between Celebes and Australian New Guinea and separate "arduous and inglorious jungle campaigns" would be necessary to exterminate them. All the Australian divisions were employed in active operations and no Australian troops were available for their relief or replacement.

The Defence Committee approved Blamey's draft but the Ministers concerned evidently found some of its terms unacceptable, and the reply finally sent over the signature of Mr Chifley, who had become Prime Minister on 13th July, was much longer and gentler than Blamey's, but followed his draft on the main points.

This telegram reached Churchill in Berlin where he was conferring with President Truman and Marshal Stalin. He replied on 26th July that the Combined Chiefs had agreed in principle that a British Commonwealth land force and possibly a small tactical air force should take part in the main operations against Japan, and in order to resolve the problems involved "appropriate British commanders and staff should visit Admiral Nimitz and General MacArthur and draw up with them a plan for submission to the Combined Chiefs of Staff". He suggested that an Australian officer should attend this conference and another Australian officer should attend discussions soon to take place in London between the Chiefs of Staff there and Admiral Mountbatten about the reorganisation of the S.W.P.A. General Blamey and Air Vice-Marshals Jones[1] and Bostock were appointed to represent Australia at the Manila conference, and the Adjutant-General, Major-General C. E. M. Lloyd, flew to London to represent Australia at the conference there.

In a cable on 1st August to Mr Attlee, who had succeeded Churchill on 27th July, Chifley informed him of these appointments and raised the question of command.

It is noted (he said) that you refer to "British Commanders". This expression is taken to mean officers of the United Kingdom Forces and not officers of British Commonwealth Forces. . . . There are, of course, in the Australian Forces, officers who have distinguished themselves in the campaigns in the Middle East and the Pacific who have claims for consideration in the appointment of Commanders and Staffs. It was necessary to make representations on the claims of Australian senior Commanders to command formations comprising British Commonwealth Forces when the A.I.F. was serving in the Middle East.

The British Government replied that it suggested the following commanders: for the naval force, Vice-Admiral Sir William Tennant[2]; as the army commander Lieut-General Sir Charles Keightley,[3] then commanding the V Corps in Italy. For the air component, which would consist principally of Australian squadrons, an Australian should be appointed. Concerning Keightley the British cable said:

We do not think that the fact that this officer has not yet fought the Jap should be considered a handicap, since the terrain of the mainland of Japan is very different from that in which Jap has hitherto been engaged.

The surrender of Japan a few days later terminated this discussion, but it is unlikely that the Australian Government would have concurred in the appointment of an army commander who had had no experience of fighting against the Japanese when so many tried commanders far senior to Keightley were available in the Australian Army and in Burma.

Chifley received Lloyd's report on the London conference on 11th August when Japan was already suing for peace. It said that MacArthur

---

[1] Air Marshal Sir George Jones, KBE, CB, DFC. (1st AIF: 9 LH Regt 1915; 4 Sqn AFC 1916-19.) Asst Chief of the Air Staff 1939-40; Director of Training RAAF 1940-42; Chief of the Air Staff 1942-52. Regular air force officer; b. Rushworth, Vic, 11 Nov 1896.

[2] Admiral Sir William Tennant, KCB, CBE, MVO; RN. Comd HMS *Repulse* 1940-42; Flag Officer Levant and Eastern Mediterranean 1944-46. B. 2 Jan 1890.

[3] General Sir Charles Keightley, GCB, GBE, DSO. AA&QMG 1 Armd Div 1940; GOC 6 Armd Div 1942-43, 78 Div 1943-44, V Corps 1944-45. C-in-C British Middle East Land Forces 1953-56. Regular soldier; b. 24 Jun 1901.

had proposed that British participation in the operations against Japan should be limited to a corps including one British, one Canadian and one Australian division, all provided with American equipment, and functioning as a corps within an American army.

The problem was now to fix the scale of British Commonwealth participation not in a force to invade Japan but in an occupation force. On 13th August the United Kingdom Government suggested that Australia might contribute to the occupation force in Japan and to forces to be sent to Hong Kong, and should take initial responsibility for Borneo and all Japanese-occupied territory in the Indies east of Borneo. On the 17th the Australian War Cabinet decided to propose to the British Government that Australia should contribute to the force occupying Japan two cruisers and two destroyers, two brigade groups, and three fighter squadrons. It insisted, however, that this force should operate under an Australian commander who would be subject only to the Supreme Allied Commander. In addition, at the request of the Royal Navy, Australia was making six vessels available for Hong Kong to cooperate with two ships of the Royal Navy in minesweeping, but Australia would not provide other forces for the occupation of Hong Kong. Australia wished to have a share in the occupation of Singapore, however, and would make a parachute battalion available for this purpose.

> In making these contributions (the telegram added) Australia is doing so not as subsidiary but as principal Pacific power which has for so long borne the heat and burden of the struggle against Japan.

Meanwhile some doubts arose whether there would be enough volunteers to fill the proposed occupation force. After a visit to the 6th Division General Sturdee informed General Blamey on 22nd August that it would be difficult to obtain enough officers and men to form from that division a brigade to go to Japan. Only one battalion commander was willing to accept appointment. "Most 6 Div seem to be imbued with urge return Aust at earliest for release or remain in army there," his signal said.

General Blamey advised Sir Frederick Shedden that if the Government stated that the troops in the occupation force would be relieved after one year of service volunteers would probably be forthcoming from the 6th Division. It would be wise to call for volunteers from all divisions. He sought instructions whether he was to assume that the formation of the force would be approved.

After more discussion Attlee, on 1st September, cabled Chifley that his Government still considered that the general interests of the British Commonwealth would be better served if it was represented by a single force. If Australia agreed, Britain would welcome the appointment of an Australian as "inter-service Commander-in-Chief of the United Commonwealth Force of Occupation". Units of the British Pacific Fleet, however, would remain under the operational control of the Commander of the British Pacific Fleet.

General Blamey signalled Mr Forde, the Minister for the Army, on the 6th that he had come to the conclusion that the occupation force should be organised in Australia. He assumed that the Government would wish home leave to be granted before departure for Japan. New conditions of service, rates of pay and so on, would have to be considered. Shortage of shipping would delay the movement for some time.

On 21st September after more discussion the Australian Government informed the United Kingdom Government that it was agreeable to participating in a British Commonwealth force, but on the assumption that an Australian officer would command it. The strength of the Australian components would be two cruisers and two destroyers, one infantry brigade group and perhaps a second one later, and three fighter squadrons. It was agreed that on policy and administrative matters the commander of the force should be responsible to the United Kingdom and Australian Governments through a Joint Chiefs of Staff body comprising the Australian Chiefs of Staff and a representative of the United Kingdom Chiefs of Staff. (This body was formed, and named "Joint Chiefs of Staff in Australia", or, briefly, JOCOSA.)

On 1st October the British Chiefs of Staff proposed that the army component of the British Commonwealth force should be organised into one British and one British-Indian brigade formed into a group under an Indian Army officer, and one Australian and one New Zealand brigade formed into a group under an Australian or New Zealand commander, the whole force being commanded by an Australian.

Meanwhile, before the cease fire, the boundaries of the commands in the Pacific area had been re-arranged. On 1st August Chifley had received a cable from Attlee describing decisions reached at Anglo-American discussions in Berlin, one of which was that the eastern boundary of the South-East Asia Command would, if the Dutch agreed, be extended to include Borneo, Java and Celebes. For planning purposes, he said, 15th November 1946 had been adopted as the date for the end of organised resistance by Japan.

Next day the Combined Chiefs issued a directive to Mountbatten informing him that the eastern boundaries of his command were being extended to include Borneo, Java and Celebes and that it was desirable that he should take over these new areas as soon as convenient after 15th August. The area to the east of his command would be an Australian command under the British Chiefs of Staff. When the Japanese capitulated Mountbatten was ordered to take over the new area on 15th August.

On the 23rd General Northcott submitted to the Minister for the Army a proposal that in view of the fact that General MacArthur would soon relinquish command of the forces in the Australian area, a Commander-in-Chief of all Australian forces should be appointed; and on 4th September Blamey asked that he be given command of the army, navy and air forces "to ensure coordination". However, ten days later Blamey was informed that on 30th August the Government had decided that, from 2nd September, when the South-West Pacific Command ceased to exist, the command of the navy would revert to the Naval Board, of the army to the Commander-in-Chief, and of the air force to the Air Board. It was a somewhat precipitate decision in view of the fact that the formal surrender of the Japanese forces and the re-occupation of Allied territory would involve combined operations on a fairly large scale.

By this time negotiations with Japanese commanders in the areas of Australian responsibility and planning for the re-occupation of Japanese-held territory had been in progress for some weeks.

At an early stage it was evident to the Australian commanders that the process of taking surrenders throughout their vast area and of distributing occupation forces would take a long time. On 16th August MacArthur had sent a signal to his subordinates informing them that a message had been received from the Japanese Government which said:

1. His Majesty the Emperor issued an Imperial Order at 1600 hours on August Sixteenth to the entire armed forces to cease hostilities immediately.
2. It is presumed that the said Imperial Order will reach the front line and produce full effect after the following lapse of time:
   (a) In Japan proper—forty-eight hours.
   (b) In China, Manchuria, Korea and Southern Regions except Bougainville, New Guinea and the Philippines—six days.
   (c) In Bougainville—eight days.
   (d) In New Guinea and the Philippines and in the case of various local headquarters—twelve days, but whether and when the order will be received by the first line units is difficult to foresee.
3. With a view to making the august wish of His Majesty regarding the terminating of the war and the abovementioned Imperial Order thoroughly known to all concerned, members of the Imperial family will be dispatched as personal representatives of His Majesty to the Headquarters of the Kwantung Army, Expeditionary Forces in China and the forces in the southern regions respectively. The itinerary, type of aircraft, markings, etc., will be communicated later. It is accordingly requested that safe conduct for the above be granted.
4. As regards the request to dispatch a competent representative, accompanied by Service advisers, to the Headquarters of General MacArthur in Manila leaving Satu Misaki in Kyushu on August Seventeenth we feel greatly embarrassed as it is impossible for us to arrange for the flight of our representatives on August Seventeenth due to the scarcity of time allowed us. We will, however, proceed at once with necessary preparations and notify General MacArthur as to the date of the flight of such a representative which will take place as soon as possible.
5. It is proposed to make the communications with the Supreme Commander of the Allied powers in the following manner:
   (a) Sender and receiver on the Japanese side the General Headquarters of the Government.
   (b) Radio stations on the Japanese side—Tokyo station. Call sign JNP, frequency 13740 kcs.
   (c) Means of Communication—radiograph.
   (d) Language—English.
6. We fail to understand the type of airplane described in the communication received from General MacArthur. We request, therefore, that the message be repeated dealing upon the type fully and clearly. . . .

The next order set out which Japanese commanders should surrender to which Allied commanders, except that it provided that the commanders within the areas facing the S.E.A.C. and the Australian forces should surrender to

the Supreme Allied Commander South-East Asia Command or the Commanding General Australian forces the exact breakdown between Mountbatten and the Australians to be arranged between them.

After some discussion Blamey and Mountbatten agreed that the Australian area of responsibility should include all the Netherlands Indies east of and exclusive of Lombok, plus Borneo, New Guinea, New Britain, New Ireland, Nauru and Ocean Islands, Bougainville and adjacent islands. The British and Australian Governments confirmed this arrangement. It was agreed that the British would progressively extend the area under their control in the Indies until the responsibility of Australia was limited to Timor and western New Guinea. It was hoped to hand over to the British or Dutch not later than the end of October. In Dutch New Guinea Australian control would for all practical purposes be confined to Hollandia and Biak.

General MacArthur required that no surrender documents should be signed by the Japanese field commanders until the main surrender ceremony in Tokyo Bay had been performed. A series of meetings between representatives of Admiral Mountbatten and representatives of Field Marshal Terauchi opened, however, at Rangoon on 26th August. One consequence of these talks was that Mountbatten, on 30th August, instructed Terauchi to arrange for the headquarters of *II Army* (formerly *Second Area Army*) at Pinrang, in Celebes, and the *XXXVII Army* in Borneo to get into wireless contact with the Australian commander at Morotai on certain frequencies between certain hours of the day.

It soon become evident that each Japanese army commander intended punctiliously to await orders from above before surrendering. It was 7th September, after several messages had been exchanged, before the commander of the *II Army,* Lieut-General Fusataro Teshima, signalled that he had been ordered, from Saigon, to negotiate matters personally with the Australian commander.

I will be waiting at Pinrang aerodrome at [11 a.m. on the 8th] accompanied by persons designated by your order [6 officers, interpreter, 2 clerks and not more than 4 servants]. I shall be grateful if you will send one plane for our passage. I have only one heavy bomber here sufficient for carrying seven persons.

The surrender ceremony took place at Morotai on the I Corps sports ground at the sides of which troops were lined up seven ranks deep. At 10.50 a.m. on 9th September the troops and the Japanese party were in position, the Japanese standing about 10 yards from a table. At 10.58 the parade was called to attention. At 11 o'clock General Blamey arrived at the table and a guard gave the general salute. General Blamey then read the terms of surrender. General Teshima moved forward to the table and signed the document of surrender. Then Blamey signed the document and handed Teshima a written instruction—"Second Japanese Army Instruction No. 1." Teshima returned to his former position and Blamey gave an address which ended:

> In receiving your surrender I do not recognise you as an honourable and gallant foe, but you will be treated with due but severe courtesy in all matters. I recall the treacherous attack upon our ally, China, in 1938 [sic]. I recall the treacherous attack made upon the British Empire and upon the United States of America in December 1941, at a time when your authorities were making the pretence of ensuring peace. I recall the atrocities inflicted upon the persons of our nationals as prisoners of war and internees, designed to reduce them by punishment and starvation to slavery. In the light of these evils, I will enforce most rigorously all orders issued to you, so let there be no delay or hesitation in their fulfilment at your peril.

Admiral Mountbatten took the surrender of Lieut-General Seishiro Itagaki, as delegate of Field Marshal Terauchi who was ill, at Singapore on 12th September. Part of the 1st Australian Parachute Battalion took part in the surrender ceremony, and remained in Malaya performing various police duties until January 1946.[4]

Blamey delegated to Sturdee the task of accepting the surrender in the First Army area of command and at Nauru and Ocean Islands, and nominated three subordinates to accept the surrender of individual Japanese forces in British Borneo and the Dutch Indies: General Wootten was to take the surrender of the commander of the forces in British Borneo, General Milford of the commander in Dutch Borneo, Brigadier Dyke[5] of the commander of the forces in Timor or controlled from Timor. When returns were collected from the Japanese staffs it was found that there were about 190,000 Japanese, including auxiliaries, in the area controlled by the Australian headquarters at Morotai and about 150,000 in the First Army area.[6] Detailed estimates are shown in the accompanying table.

The tasks presented to the Australians in the First Army's area were relatively simple in comparison with those faced by I Corps in the Indies. As early as the morning of 11th August General Sturdee had sent signals to the commanders of his four subordinate forces—General Savige of II Corps, Brigadier King (temporarily commanding the 6th Division during the absence of General Robertson), General Eather of the 11th Division, and Lieut-Colonel Neville of the 4th Battalion (operating east

---

[4] The training of Australian Army parachutists was begun in December 1942 as an offshoot of the training of Independent Companies. The formation of the battalion began in March 1943 and in September a C.O., Major J. W. Overall, from the 9th Divisional Engineers, was appointed. By January 1944 the battalion was at full strength. Though often warned for duty in the field it never went into action.
On 26th August, however, a party of 120 members of the unit, under Major W. D. Clark, emplaned at Cairns in eight Dakotas to go to Singapore. After a wait of nine days at Labuan the party was landed at Singapore on 9th and 10th September. Later in the month 75 more officers and men were flown in and what had been "Advance 1 Aust Parachute Bn" became known as "1 Aust Parachute Bn".

[5] Maj-Gen L. G. H. Dyke, CBE, DSO, VX89. CO 2/3 Fd Regt 1941-42; CCRA II Corps 1943-44, I Corps 1944-45; Comd Timor Force 1945-46. Regular soldier; b. Adelaide, 6 Aug 1900.

[6] Within Australia in 1945 before the Japanese surrender the army had charge of 17,022 Italian prisoners of war, 5,569 Japanese and 1,567 Germans; also 2,764 Japanese internees, 1,576 Germans, 99 Italians and 73 others. In 1942 the numbers of internees had been: 4,022 Japanese, 2,661 German, 3,836 Italian, 212 others. Later a majority of these had been released.

of the Sepik)—ordering that, in view of the probability of an early end to the fighting, operations should be confined to those necessary to maintain the present main positions, and every effort should be made to avoid Australian casualties.

JAPANESE STRENGTHS IN AUSTRALIAN ARMY'S AREA OF RESPONSIBILITY, OCTOBER, 1945*

	Army	Navy	Japanese Civilians	Formosans	Other Auxiliaries	Total
First Army area:						
North-east New Guinea	12,008	950	305			13,263
New Britain	53,212	16,218	19,861		8,155	97,446
New Ireland	7,721	3,427	1,263			12,411
Solomons	15,041	6,049	2,324			23,414
From Ocean and Nauru Islands		4,046	556		541	5,143
					Total	151,677
I Corps area:						
British Borneo (and Pontianak)	17,103	183	3,490			20,776
Dutch Borneo (excluding Pontianak)	1,394	6,990	6,226			14,610
Celebes	14,873	5,406	5,694	876	3,177	30,026
Halmahera-Talaud-Sanghi	27,229	2,232	4,208	4,105	2,312	40,086
Ambon-Ceram-Buru	11,251	6,428	6,370	130	1,447	25,626
Dutch New Guinea	19,502	1,846	1,845	2,341	613	26,147
Kai-Aru-Tanimbar	9,048	772	272	1,031	1,155	12,278
Timor	1,208	792	578		657	3,235
Lesser Sundas	15,986	1,211			2,380	19,577
					Total	192,361
					Grand total	344,038

* Source: Advanced Headquarters, AMF, Weekly Operations and Intelligence Report No. 1 (to 12 Oct 1945).

With some difficulty wireless communication was established between Sturdee's headquarters and Rabaul, and on 22nd August the Japanese army and navy commanders there sent a signal to Sturdee stating that the forces on New Britain and Bougainville were trying to accomplish a cessation of hostilities but "in Bougainville on account of the dense jungle it has not been possible yet to deliver the order to . . . those units which have penetrated deep into your lines". The Rabaul commanders added that they could not open further negotiations until ordered to do so from Tokyo.

In his reply Sturdee asked that the Japanese should receive an envoy carrying a letter about certain information that he required. The Japanese declined to do this but said that they would continue to receive the Australian wireless messages. They asked Sturdee to inform his subordinates on Bougainville "who have been urging our commanders to open direct negotiations which reach beyond those necessary for the cessation of hostilities" that everything would be handled between Rabaul and Lae.

Sturdee was informed on 22nd August that the British Pacific Fleet would probably make an aircraft carrier available for the surrender of the commanders on New Britain; later he learnt that the carrier *Glory* and other vessels would be employed. His plan was then to take the surrender of the commander at Rabaul on board *Glory* about 6th September, and occupy Rabaul with troops carried in one transport.

In due course Sturdee sent General Imamura instructions to present himself aboard a warship of the Royal Navy at 9 a.m. on 6th September when the warship would be at latitude 4 degrees 17 minutes South 152 degrees 15 minutes East. Imamura was to bring a party not exceeding twelve, and including staff officers who would provide information about the Japanese forces. Here as elsewhere the instructions given to the Japanese commander included orders to provide information about dispositions, strengths, details about the sick, about Allied prisoners held, natives employed, stores and ration scales, minefields and weapon states. The Japanese were ordered to evacuate the towns of Rabaul and Kavieng and concentrate themselves and their weapons in defined areas.

On 4th September, in accordance with an arrangement made by wireless, Brigadier Sheehan, General Sturdee's senior staff officer, went from Jacquinot Bay to a point off Simpson Harbour, Rabaul. Here some Japanese envoys came on board and were given instructions for the ceremony on the 6th.

Thus Imamura—"short and stubby, hard faced, with heavy lips and generous girth"—surrendered to General Sturdee on the *Glory* on 6th September. Other ships in the convoy were the British sloops *Hart* and *Amethyst*, and the Australian ships *Vendetta, Dubbo, Townsville, Lithgow* and *Kiama*. At 10.40 a.m. the *Glory's* complement was mustered on the flight deck in a hollow box formation. General Sturdee's party took up positions behind a small table in the centre. General Imamura and Vice-Admiral Kusaka (the senior naval officer at Rabaul) were brought to the flight deck where Imamura placed his sword on the table. When General Sturdee read the instrument of surrender and instructed Imamura to sign, Imamura protested that he could sign only for the army; only Kusaka could surrender for naval forces. After a discussion between the Japanese commanders, Kusaka agreed that, although the instrument was made out only for army forces, he would accept it as including the navy provided he was allowed to sign. Imamura, Kusaka, and Sturdee then signed. Staff discussions about the administration of the surrender followed.

It was then discovered that the strength of the Japanese forces round Rabaul was far greater than had been estimated: the Australian estimate in August was 50,000 army and 5,000 navy men. There were, in fact, 57,368 army personnel including 4,156 civilian workers, and 31,923 naval

On U.S.S. *Missouri*, Tokyo Bay, 2nd September 1945. General Sir Thomas Blamey signs the surrender document on behalf of Australia. Immediately behind him, from left, are General MacArthur, Lieut-General F. H. Berryman, Air Vice-Marshal W. D. Bostock. Rear-Admiral G. D. Moore, Lieut-Colonel D. H. Dwyer. To the rear, from left, are officers representing: the American Navy. China, Royal Navy, Russia, Australia, Canada, France and the Netherlands.

(Australian War Memorial)

(*Australian War Memorial*)
After the surrender: Japanese troops dumping ammunition in the sea off Dili, Portuguese Timor, 25th September 1945.

(*Australian War Memorial*)
Tokyo, April 1947. New guard of the 65th Australian Infantry Battalion marching on to the grounds of the Imperial Palace to take over from the old guard.

personnel including 15,705 civilian workers—Rabaul had been a very big naval base. On New Ireland were 12,400 Japanese. In addition there were at Rabaul 28 European prisoners, 5,589 Indian prisoners, 1,397 Chinese, 688 Malayans and 607 Indonesians. The Japanese claimed that the Indians, Indonesians and about half the Chinese were not prisoners but had been released on parole and were working as a service corps of the Japanese Army.

The first Australians to land at Rabaul were naval officers—Captain Morris[7] and Lieutenant Hancock[8]—who went ashore from *Vendetta* unarmed and brought off the 28 European prisoners.

The Japanese at Rabaul were found to be well fed and in fairly good health. Normally the number of men in hospital ranged from 5 to 8 per cent. There was much rice, and supplementary rations included fish, eggs, poultry, beef, pork and vegetables. The Japanese had gardens aggregating thousands of acres. The port and airfield were in ruins, the town overgrown with jungle, and from the air 31 sunken ships could be seen, but the Japanese had honeycombed the hills around Rabaul with a system of tunnels totalling more than 150 miles in length and in these they lived and kept their vehicles, stores and even workshops. Some tunnels were concreted and had stairways, telephones, electric light and built-in furniture. Men's quarters were lined with tiers of bunks. Hundreds of tons of rice were in underground stores. The underground radio station was about 40 feet below the surface and 60 feet long.

A first contingent of the 4th Brigade landed at Rabaul from the *Manoora* and *Katoomba* on 10th September. Three days later General Eather's headquarters arrived. The 13th Brigade arrived on the 15th. On the 17th Eather summoned Imamura, instructed him to build thirteen compounds to hold 10,000 troops each and said that the Japanese were to cultivate their gardens and provide for themselves as far as possible. On 18th September a party of Australians visited New Ireland and instructed the senior naval officer there to concentrate the arms and ammunition in dumps ready for destruction; the 12,000 troops on the island would be taken to Rabaul. Next day Angau officers took over the administration of New Ireland with headquarters at Kavieng.

On Bougainville the first official contact with a Japanese envoy had occurred on 18th August when a Major Otsu came into the lines of the 15th Battalion on the Mivo River and was taken to Toko and there interrogated by Brigadier Garrett. It was then that the Australians learnt that there were still 23,000 Japanese on Bougainville, not 13,000 as they had estimated.

---

[7] Capt F. B. Morris, OBE; RAN. HMAS *Canberra*; comd HMAS *Nepal* 1942-44; comd HMAS *Ballarat*, and Senior Officer 21 Minesweeping Flotilla 1944-45; NOIC New Guinea Area 1945. B. Wycheproof, Vic, 22 May 1902.

[8] Lt-Cdr K. W. Hancock; RANR. Secretary to NOIC Townsville 1940-43; HMAS's *Warramunga* 1943-44, *Ballarat* 1944-45; Secretary to NOIC New Guinea Area 1945. Shipping clerk; of Fremantle, WA; b. Fremantle, 30 May 1918.

General Savige tried to persuade General Kanda to surrender promptly, but without success. He sent Kanda an order to assemble his troops in four areas: round Kahili, at Kieta, in Numa Numa Plantation, round Bonis airstrip. He himself, with the naval commander and two other officers, was to go in a barge flying a white flag to a point six miles out to sea bearing 264 degrees from Moila Point and be there at 8 a.m. on 19th August. Thence they would be taken by an Australian warship to Torokina to sign the surrender document.

On the 19th, however, the captain of H.M.A.S. *Lithgow* signalled Savige that Kanda had not turned up. Instead he had sent an officer bearing a message that Rabaul had not yet authorised him to report to Savige. Savige instructed *Lithgow* to bring the envoy to Torokina to receive a letter for delivery to Kanda. The envoy protested, but in vain, and was brought to Torokina, given the letter and returned in *Lithgow* to the rendezvous.

Another hitch occurred on the 20th when several shells were fired towards Australian minesweepers off Moila Point. Savige wrote to Kanda and threatened retaliation if this firing recurred. Next day arrived a letter, not from Kanda but from Vice-Admiral Baron Samejima, commanding the naval forces round Buin, instructing Savige that he might negotiate with the naval commander at Rabaul but until then "your naval ships may not be admissible within Shortland bay".

Finally, after the surrender off Rabaul, Kanda, Samejima and three other officers were taken on board the frigate *Diamantina* off Moila Point at 8 a.m. on 8th September, disembarked at Torokina at 11.45 and escorted to Savige's headquarters by Brigadier Field and officers of his brigade. At 12.20 Kanda, Samejima and two Japanese interpreters were taken to the "battle room" at Corps headquarters, where General Savige, six other Australian officers, Air Commodore Roberts of the R.N.Z.A.F. and Lieut-Colonel J. P. Coursey of the American Marines were present. Kanda and Samejima handed over their swords and signed the instrument of surrender.

Savige outlined the terms of the surrender of Japan and said that he would not tolerate "delay, equivocation or neglect" on Kanda's part. After the ceremony of surrender the Japanese commanders indicated that they wished to perform a bowing ceremony in honour of Australian and American dead. They then formed up in ranks, removed their head-dresses, and bowed in silence for a minute.

It was decided to concentrate the Japanese on Fauro Island or round Torokina, and by 12th October this had been done. There were 18,491 on Fauro and 8,421 at Torokina, including by that time some 3,700 from Nauru and Ocean Islands. The 7th Australian Battalion was placed on Fauro and the other Australian units concentrated round Torokina.

Throughout the First Army area huge quantities of Japanese arms and ammunition were collected and destroyed or dumped in the sea. On New Britain and New Ireland, for example, these included 136 tanks, 568 guns, 1,539,431 rounds of small arms ammunition, 107,591 75-mm shells; at

Wewak 253 heavy weapons of all types, and 181 machine-guns. On Ocean and Nauru Islands 63 guns were destroyed.

At Wewak, as on Bougainville, the Australians tried to hasten the formal surrender. The first contact with the headquarters of *XVIII Army* was made on 17th August when a party from the 6th Division's headquarters moved in *M.L.805* to within about 200 yards of Muschu Island and broadcast towards the shore with a loud speaker. After 15 minutes some Japanese came forward with a large white flag. A skiff was sent ashore, two Japanese officers returned in it, and a parley was held. On the 18th and succeeding days messages were passed to General Adachi on the mainland by means of a wireless on Kairiru Island. Adachi refused to surrender, however, without direct orders from his superiors. Eventually on 10th September Robertson demanded the surrender of Muschu and Kairiru Islands, and on that day Rear-Admiral Sato, commanding the force which occupied the islands, signed the necessary documents and handed over his sword on board *M.L.805*. On 11th September Adachi with some staff officers arrived in the area of the 2/7th Battalion at Kiarivu, and on the 13th he, an interpreter and three officers were flown from Hayfield to Wewak where, on Wom airstrip at 10 a.m., Adachi signed the surrender and handed over his sword in the presence of 3,000 troops drawn from various units of the division.

The men of the *51st Japanese Division* were marched to an assembly area at Wewak, those of the *20th* and *41st Divisions* to Boiken. They moved in parties 100 strong, except for about 300 bed-ridden patients who were brought in from the Sepik in Australian barges. The march to the assembly areas began on 18th September but it was 25th October before all but a few were concentrated on Muschu Island. The post-war report of the *XVIII Army* complains that the rations provided on Muschu by the Australians were only enough to give 1,300 to 1,500 calories per man, which was increased with locally produced supplies to an average of 1,800 a day—far too little to enable a rapid recovery by men most of whom were already suffering the effects of malnutrition. Figures in the post-war report of the *XVIII Army* suggest that more than 1,000 Japanese died during the march to the coast or on Muschu Island.

The Australian Government had been anxious to re-occupy Nauru and Ocean Islands (normally under Australian and British control respectively) so as to increase the supply of phosphates as soon as possible, and as early as July had asked the Joint Chiefs to allot shipping to carry Australian forces against the two islands. The Joint Chiefs replied that they could not spare assault shipping but would not object to the carrying out of the operation by forces available to "the commander designated for that part of the S.W.P.A.". Blamey, of course, lacked the shipping needed to carry out such an expedition.

When the surrender arrangements were announced, the British Government, on 17th August, proposed to the Australian Government that it be suggested to the United States that the Japanese on Nauru and Ocean Islands should surrender to a British commander, although they were in the area allotted to the commander of the American Pacific Fleet. The Australian Chiefs of Staff said that a suitable force could be provided from Bougainville: a frigate and two transports were available and could land a battalion group at Nauru by 2nd or 3rd September. The American Chiefs of Staff agreed that Australian forces might accept the surrenders at the two islands.

There were 3,200 Japanese and 500 Koreans on Nauru and 500 Japanese on Ocean Island. Sturdee decided that it would be desirable to

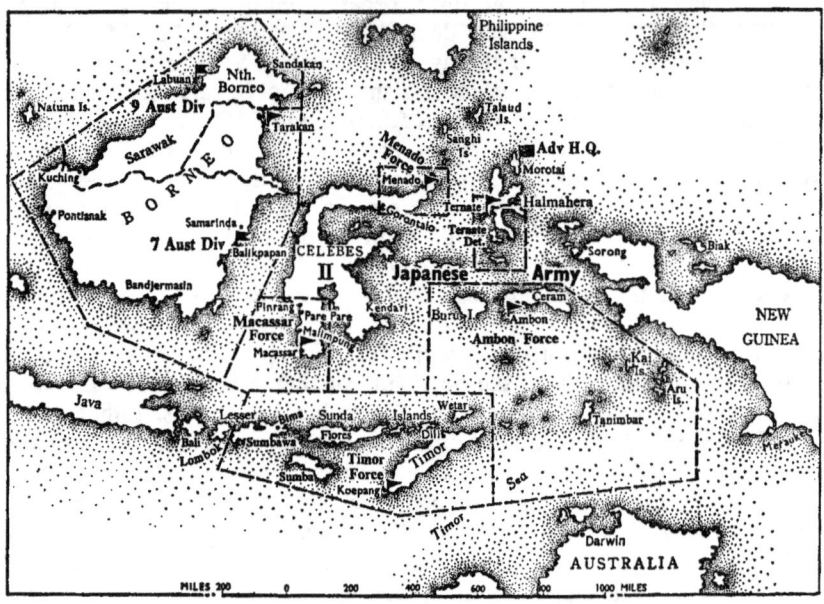

Areas of responsibility of *II Japanese Army* and Allied force commanders

remove the Japanese from the islands as otherwise it would be very difficult to supply them. He proposed to send, say, one company in each of two freighters to take the surrenders, to conduct the Japanese to the ships and to guard them on the voyage back to Bougainville where they would be confined. He would place one company on each island when most of the Japanese had been removed. The *Diamantina* would cruise round the islands while the freighters were absent.

Thus a convoy consisting of the *Diamantina* and the merchantmen *River Burdekin* and *River Glenelg* sailed from Torokina on 9th September to take the surrender of the Japanese garrisons on Nauru and Ocean Islands. The military force was commanded by Brigadier Stevenson and included some 200 men of the 31st/51st Battalion under Lieut-Colonel

Kelly. With it sailed Sir Albert Ellis[9] and Commander Phipps,[1] representing the New Zealand Government; and Mr Ridgway[2] of the Nauru Administration.

The *Diamantina* arrived off Nauru at 7 a.m. on 13th September and in response to signals a Japanese envoy and a Chinese interpreter came aboard at 7.45. The envoy was instructed to have the Japanese on Nauru ready for embarkation by 3 p.m. At 2.45 the commander of the Japanese garrison, Captain Hisayuki Soeda, and five staff officers came aboard. They handed over their swords, Stevenson read the instrument of surrender in English, and the interpreter read it in Japanese. Soeda then signed the surrender document on behalf of the troops on both islands. Parties from the 31st/51st Battalion went ashore on reconnaissance that afternoon, and next morning the occupation force landed and their supplies were unloaded. In the afternoon the Union Jack was raised at a parade ashore.

By November the Japanese and Koreans controlled by the First Army were concentrated in six areas thus:

Rabaul	95,396
Fauro Island	26,043
Torokina	704
Namatanai	6,406
Muschu Island	12,122
Nauru Island	539
Total	141,210

The 9th Australian Division was made responsible for carrying out the surrender arrangements in British Borneo, Sarawak, Brunei, Labuan Island and the Natuna Islands. The area was eventually divided into five zones of responsibility. Sandakan Force, commanded by Colonel C. J. Cummings, was to control the Sandakan area from the Dutch border to a line which, on the coast, was defined by the Sugut River. The 24th Brigade's area embraced the rest of British Borneo. The 20th Brigade's area included Brunei, and Sarawak to a line which on the coast was drawn through the mouth of the Rajang River. British territory to the south of that line was controlled by Kuching Force, commanded by Brigadier Eastick[3] and including the 2/4th Pioneer Battalion, 2/12th Commando Squadron, 2/7th Field Company and other appropriate units and detachments and totalling about 2,000 men. The Natuna Islands were

---

[9] Sir Albert Ellis, Kt, CMG. Discoverer of phosphate deposits on Nauru and Ocean Is; NZ Commissioner on Board of British Phosphate Commission 1920-51. B. Roma, Qld, 28 Aug 1869. Died 11 Jul 1951. The British Phosphate Commissioners, representing the Australian, British and New Zealand Governments, controlled the production and sale of phosphates from Nauru and Ocean Islands.

[1] Rear-Admiral P. Phipps, DSC, VRD; RNZNVR, later RNZN. Comd HMS *Bay* 1940-41; HMNZS's *Scarba* 1941-42, *Moa* 1943, *Matai* and *Arabis* (and Senior Officer 25 Minesweeping Flotilla) 1944-45. Chief of Naval Staff since 1960. Bank officer; b. Milton, NZ, 7 Jun 1909.

[2] M. Ridgway. (1st AIF: 22 Bn and 6 MG Coy.) Accountant, Nauru Admin 1938-42; Dept of War Organisation of Industry 1942-45. Administrator of Nauru I 1945-49. B. Lang Lang, Vic, 21 Dec 1891.

[3] Brig T. C. Eastick, CMG, DSO, ED, SX3295. CO 2/7 Fd Regt 1940-43; CRA 7 Div 1943-44, 9 Div 1944-46 (commanded Kuching Force 1945). Engineer; of Reade Park, SA; b. Hyde Park, SA, 3 May 1900.

to be controlled by Natuna Force, under Lieut-Colonel Argent, and comprising mainly his 2/3rd Anti-Tank Regiment.

From 19th to 23rd August leaflets were dropped by aircraft over all known areas in which Japanese were concentrated giving the general war news and news of the progress of the surrender. On 27th August letters were dropped on Tenom, Ranau, Jesselton, Riam Road and Kuching instructing the Japanese commanders to make contact with Australian commanders. At Kuching the letter contained a code of panel signals which enabled the Japanese commander to indicate that he agreed to the dropping of supplies for prisoners of war and that he would meet Australian representatives later.

At 11.45 on 3rd September a native had reported to an outpost of the 2/32nd Battalion that six Japanese pushing a hand trolley and carrying a white flag were moving down the railway from Jesselton and were then two miles away. Two officers and four armed men awaited them drawn up astride the railway line, with one officer carrying an Australian flag. A Japanese officer—a Major Mori—approached, salutes were exchanged, and the Japanese said that he was there in accordance with instructions received by letter. The Japanese were taken to a tent, the officers went in, and the escorts stood outside facing each other, at ease. At 2 p.m. Colonel Scott of the 2/32nd arrived and at 3.45 Brigadier Porter. Mori said that General Baba was at Sapong and that he (Mori) could take no executive action without Baba's authority. Meanwhile some information had been obtained from the Japanese: there were five battalions in Jesselton and groups of from 100 to 2,500 troops at eight other places in the area controlled by General Baba. The railway to Jesselton was in good repair. There was much malaria among the Japanese troops.

After communicating with the Japanese staff at Kuching Colonel Wilson,[4] G.S.O.1 of the 9th Division, landed on the Sarawak River on 5th September and conferred with the commander of the Japanese forces there, who confirmed information that there were 2,017 Allied prisoners and internees in the area.

Baba was brought to Labuan on 10th September and there he surrendered to Wootten. On the 15th Colonel Iemura, commanding the *25th Mixed Regiment* based on Jesselton, surrendered to Brigadier Porter, and on the 17th the commander of the forces in the Tenom area surrendered to him.

Thereafter the Japanese facing the Australians began to come in to the Australian lines and detached forces began to move to their destinations. The prisoners coming into Beaufort were clean and tidy and well behaved. A translated document showed that these Japanese had been instructed to conduct themselves calmly, discard all feelings of hostility, take care of their appearance, and hand their arms over in good condition. "The misconduct of one individual may adversely affect the welfare of the whole and also the fate of the Japanese Army."

---

[4] Maj-Gen A. G. Wilson, CBE, DSO, VX12398. AMLO UK 1940-43; DDSD LHQ 1944-45; GSO1 HQ 9 Div 1945. Regular soldier; b. Sydney, 29 Sep 1900.

The task of Kuching Force was to accept the surrender of and impound Japanese forces in the Kuching area; release and evacuate Allied prisoners and internees, believed to include 400 stretcher cases and 237 women and children; and establish military control. The pre-war population of Kuching had been 34,000, and a B.B.C.A.U. contingent of 20 officers and 40 other ranks accompanied the force to help with civil affairs.

Brigadier Eastick was flown in a Catalina to the mouth of the Sarawak River at Kuching on 6th September and there three Japanese officers came aboard. These said that there were about 700 troops in the area; they were instructed to prepare information under a variety of headings. On the 7th the Japanese commander of the prisoners of war at Kuching asked that two Australian medical officers be sent to care for the prisoners and internees. Immediately Lieut-Colonel Morgan[5] of the 2/12th Field Ambulance and Major Hutson[6] were flown in. They found a camp hospital of about 30 beds being conducted by Lieut-Colonel Sheppard,[7] who had been a prisoner of war, and the Kuching civil hospital being run by two other Australian medical officers.

On 8th and 9th September H.M.A.S. *Kapunda* and U.S.S. *Barnes* with Brigadier Eastick and staff officers on board sailed for Kuching. On *Kapunda* at 2.35 p.m. on the 11th Eastick took the surrender of Major-General H. Yamamura, commanding the Japanese in the area. Later that day the occupying force landed.

The 2/12th Field Ambulance took a special pride in its work among the recovered prisoners because it had been a unit of the 8th Division to which the prisoners mostly belonged. A few days before the cease fire it had applied for inclusion in a possible "Burma-Singapore" force on the grounds that it belonged to the same division as the prisoners at Singapore.[8] The diarist of the 2/12th wrote on 17th September at Kuching that perhaps the most strenuous work yet done by the unit in all its campaigns was performed during three days, when, among other achievements, with serum and blood transfusions it saved the lives of up to 50 sufferers from famine oedema.

Eight Dakota aircraft and two Catalinas were available for evacuating prisoners and internees in British Borneo; and the vessels carrying the occupation force to Kuching could take 110 stretcher cases back to Labuan. The evacuation of internees and prisoners began on 12th September and by the 14th 858 had been removed.

On the 14th, after a conference with citizens of Kuching, an order was issued fixing prices at levels based on those of 1941. A spectacular march past by the troops and processions by the civilian communities

---

[5] Lt-Col N. H. Morgan, QX6439. RMO 2/33 Bn; 2/2 and 2/11 Fd Amb, CO 2/12 Fd Amb 1943-46. Medical practitioner; of Brisbane; b. Brisbane, 9 Dec 1910.

[6] Maj A. W. M. Hutson, VX48401. 2/7 and 2/4 AGH's and 2/2 CCS. Medical practitioner; of Melbourne; b. Boonah, Qld, 12 May 1912.

[7] Lt-Col E. MacA. Sheppard, ED, NX34665. CO 2/10 Fd Amb. Medical practitioner; of Adamstown, NSW; b. Ashfield, NSW, 11 Apr 1896. Died 8 Oct 1958.

[8] As mentioned earlier the 2/14th Field Regiment, another 8th Division unit, had made a similar request.

were held on 26th September, and on 10th October the Chinese community began celebrating the Allied victory and the Chinese Republic. Brigadier Windeyer, since 22nd September acting commander of the 9th Division, and Brigadier Eastick and others, attended a dinner given by the Chinese. For three days there were concerts, dances, processions and games, including a Soccer match in which a Chinese team beat the 2/4th Pioneers four goals to two.

The main task of Natuna Force was completed on 26th September when the last of 302 Japanese were removed from the islands and taken to Kuching. By the end of October 8,034 Japanese had been concentrated in three areas, 1,388 prisoners and 597 internees had been evacuated. In December the relief of Kuching Force by an Indian garrison was carried out.

A party of Japanese from Labuan had been sent out to get into touch with the Japanese facing the 20th Brigade, and on 17th September a group of them came into the area of the 2/13th Battalion. On 20th September the commander of the Japanese forces in north Sarawak, Colonel Aikyo, surrendered to Brigadier Windeyer. Aikyo's troops were scattered over a very large area. Windeyer elicited their whereabouts in the course of a long examination of Aikyo conducted through an interpreter. One of his objects was to discover how many prisoners of war were alive in the area. Aikyo pretended ignorance, but all had in fact died.[9] Windeyer sent craft up river to collect parties of Japanese who had been told to concentrate at various points. By 18th October these were collected in a compound at Miri.

Sandakan Force was about 1,100 strong and included the 2/9th Cavalry (Commando) Regiment less two squadrons, the 2/3rd Anti-Aircraft Regiment, 14th Field Company, and 53 B.B.C.A.U. personnel. Before the force had landed at Sandakan Colonel Cummings had been invalided and Major Gannon[1] took command, the force eventually coming under the control of East Borneo Force (Lieut-Colonel England[2]) which carried out a similar task in the Tawao area. At Sandakan there were meetings with the Japanese commander from 12th September onwards. Sandakan Force disembarked at Sandakan on 17th October. The Japanese were concentrated and given a number of tasks, and before the end of the month some 1,800 of them were taken in L.S.T's to Jesselton. From the Tawao area about 2,900 were taken to Jesselton.

There remained in October one organised Japanese force in British Borneo which was showing no signs of an intention to surrender. This

---

[9] The fate of the prisoners of the Japanese is recorded in L. Wigmore, *The Japanese Thrust*, in this series of the history.
[1] Maj J. E. Gannon, NX3101. AASC 6 Div 1940-42; DAQMG 1 Aust Beach Gp 1943-45. Bank officer; of Cremorne, NSW; b. Sydney, 27 Jun 1908.
[2] Lt-Col J. A. England, ED, NX113486. CO 52 Anti-Aircraft Regt 1943-45, 2/3 Anti-Aircraft Regt 1945-46. MHR since 1960. Farmer and grazier; of Grenfell, NSW; b. Brisbane, 12 Oct 1911.

was a group some hundreds strong known to be moving up the Trusan River. By 17th September it was in the upper Limbang River area; leaflets and orders were dropped but there was no response. A Japanese officer and four other Japanese from *XXXVII Army* headquarters were sent up the Limbang to find them but apparently did not succeed. On 18th October air force pilots dropped orders to the Japanese force to remain in the upper Trusan River area where they were then believed to be but the pilots saw no Japanese there. It fell to the S.R.D. guerillas to deal with this last group. Major Harrisson with Major Rex Blow and a signals officer journeyed up the Trusan. They and other S.R.D. men who were in the mountains organised the Dyak irregulars and, after a fight, Captain Fujino on 29th October surrendered a force of 346 Japanese "still in fairly full uniform". These were concentrated in a prisoner-of-war camp organised and controlled by Blow, until they could be marched to the coast. Thus Blow, one of the very few prisoners of the Japanese who had escaped, and one who thereafter had become a famed guerilla leader, first in the Philippines and then in Borneo, for a time became "benign father of a fantastically varied flock, which included Chinese and Japanese, Indian, Javanese, Malay, Murut and Kelabit, some Kenyahs, odd Tagals, Dusun, Potok and Milau, stray Punans. Nowhere lay any trace of hatred. It was peace at the highest level! And it augured well for any residual fears . . . about our ill effects on the latent head-hunting and feuding, classic in all the interior's past."[3]

By 31st October some 21,000 Japanese troops and civilians were concentrated in British Borneo thus:

	Troops	Civilians
Jesselton	6,602	1,753
Papar	2,301	567
Beaufort	187	12
Papan Island (off Labuan)	1,200	—
Kuching	2,832	544
Bau (near Kuching)	3,292	1,226
In transit from Ledo	200	—
Trusan River	346	—

The 32nd Indian Brigade took over from the 9th Australian Division early in January 1946 and on the 10th British Borneo was formally transferred to South-East Asia Command. The story of the military government of the British areas of Borneo in the subsequent period has been told by a United Kingdom historian.[4] Briefly, between April and July 1946 military government ceased and civil government was reestablished. Sarawak was transferred to the Rajah's government on 15th April, and on 1st June the Rajah ceded his authority to the British Government and the Colony of Sarawak came into existence. The transfer of administration in North Borneo took place on 15th July, when that territory was taken over from the British North Borneo Company by the British Government and became the colony of North Borneo. Labuan,

---
[3] T. Harrisson, *World Within, A Borneo Story*, p. 333.
[4] F. S. V. Donnison, *British Military Administration in the Far East 1943-46*, pp. 183-96.

hitherto one of the Straits Settlements, was incorporated in the new colony. The hand-over in Brunei took place on 6th July. The British historian concludes his account of the military administration of British Borneo with a reference to "the debt owed by the Administration to the Australian Military Forces for aid of all kinds. In acknowledgment of this a heraldic representation of the Australian 9th Divisional sign now finds a place in the coat of arms of the new Colony of British Borneo."[5]

In Dutch Borneo there were meetings between parties of Australians and Japanese from 2nd September onwards and wireless contact was established with Vice-Admiral Kamada at Samarinda on the 4th. As a result, on 8th September Kamada and a party of officers were picked up by a flotilla of seven P.T. boats and taken to a pre-arranged rendezvous with H.M.A.S. *Burdekin* anchored 10 miles off the mouth of the Dundang River, which was about 20 miles south-east of Samarinda. Squadrons of aircraft circled overhead. The Japanese were led to a trestle table on the quarter-deck of *Burdekin* where they stood facing the four brigadiers of the 7th Division. Then General Milford arrived and, after some formal questions and answers, Kamada laid his sword in its scabbard on the table. After the ceremony, and after having told Kamada that his forces would be disarmed and treated with firmness but with humanity, Milford departed. At a subsequent conference Kamada was handed "Order Number One" giving detailed instructions.

Thus ended, off the coast of Borneo on an Australian warship, a long road for the Seventh Australian Division—a long road of war that began in Australian training camps in 1940, was continued in England, the Libyan Desert, Syria, New Guinea and entered its final phase on 1 July of this year, just over two months ago when the Division assaulted the beaches of Balikpapan. The enemy has finally been defeated.[6]

Milford sent forces to various outlying centres and arranged to concentrate the Japanese prisoners at Samarinda and Manggar. Thus the 2/25th Battalion landed at Sangasanga and marched into the town of Samarinda through lines of cheering Indonesians. It soon had everything in hand in the Samarinda area. By the end of October more than 6,600 Japanese, including 2,100 sick, were concentrated there.

The Indonesian nationalist movement which was to complicate the task of Australian occupation forces throughout the Indies became increasingly active in this town in November. The movement was less strong in the outer islands of the Indies than in Java and Sumatra. Nevertheless for the four to five months during which Australian troops were in control of Borneo and the eastern part of the archipelago some of the commanders had to cope with a variety of touchy political problems.[7]

---

[5] Donnison, p. 196.
[6] War diary, GS Branch HQ 7th Division. The history of one brigade of this division—the 18th—had in fact begun in Australian camps in 1939.
[7] An historian of the Indonesian revolution understates the problems encountered in the outer islands: "In Borneo, Celebes, the Moluccas and Lesser Sundas the Dutch encountered little difficulty in most areas and soon brought in enough troops to take over from the Australians, who had already disarmed the Japanese occupying forces." G. McT. Kahin, *Nationalism and Revolution in Indonesia* (New York, 1952), p. 145.

On 7th August, on the eve of the Japanese surrender, Field Marshal Terauchi had given the Indonesian nationalists permission to establish a committee which was to prepare to take over the government of Indonesia. Its leaders were Dr Soekarno and Dr Hatta. These found, however, that the leaders of the Indonesian underground movement, as opposed to their own above-ground movement, did not want to receive independence as a gift from the Japanese and were resolved to organise an uprising agains' the Japanese as soon as the Allies attacked Java and Sumatra. Japan surrendered before Allied troops arrived in Java and Sumatra. As mentioned, General MacArthur required that no surrender documents should be signed in outlying areas until the surrender at Tokyo, and thus in the second half of August the Japanese Army remained in control of Indonesia. The Indonesian leaders broadcast a declaration of independence on 17th August. The Japanese soon confined themselves mainly to retaining control of the cities and bigger towns while control of large outlying areas passed to groups of armed nationalists. On 31st August the nationalists formed a Cabinet; already they had proclaimed Soekarno as President of a Republic of Indonesia. Indian troops landed in Java on 29th September and soon were engaged in the distasteful task of policing a country that was in the throes of a revolution.

On 13th September Mountbatten's headquarters had warned the subordinate headquarters, including Blamey's, that some Indonesians had proclaimed independence in Java and Sumatra, and instructed that it was essential to deal only with the Japanese and to give the Indonesians no grounds for saying that their claim to independence was recognised by the occupying forces.

On 20th October Mountbatten cabled to Blamey that, because of the danger of civil war in the Indies, the British Government had instructed him to send an additional Indian division to Java and, as a result, shipping to take the Australians home from British Borneo would not be available before late December. Another consequence was that for some time no British brigade would be available to join the occupation force in Japan.

The policy followed by the Australian forces in Indonesia was expressed in the following proclamation, thousands of copies of which were printed in English, Dutch and Malay, and circulated throughout the islands:

> The forces of the United Nations have decisively defeated the Japanese by land, sea and air, and the whole Japanese nation has unconditionally surrendered to the United Nations. Troops under the command of General Sir Thomas Blamey have arrived in your country and have accepted the surrender of the Japanese forces, on behalf of the United Nations, and will protect the people and maintain Law and Order until such time as the lawful Government of the Netherlands East Indies is once again functioning.
>
> By command of General Sir Thomas Blamey, Allied commander in this area, the Netherlands East Indies laws, with which you are familiar, will be applied and enforced by the Officers of the Netherlands East Indies Civil Administration now present in your country, subject only to any further orders which the Allied Commander may be obliged, in the interests of good order, to issue.

On 12th October Army Headquarters instructed the commanders of the eight forces in the Indies that demonstrations were not to be permitted, displays of flags other than recognised national flags or wearing of emblems were to be neither authorised nor forbidden by A.I.F. commanders "who should adopt an impartial attitude in regard to internal political questions unless in their opinion the maintenance of law and order may be endangered". The maintenance of law and order was primarily a responsibility of the Netherlands Indies Civil Administration and the Netherlands East Indies companies under Australian command, and Australian forces were not to be committed unless it was necessary to prevent bloodshed or a *coup d'état,* or to safeguard essential public industries and communications.

The interpretation of these instructions was the task of a number of Australian infantry officers whose ranks ranged from major to major-general. At Samarinda, for example, when the nationalists began to demonstrate, Major A. C. Robertson, now commanding the 2/25th Battalion, forbade public political meetings but permitted such meetings in houses; forbade the display of the red and white republican flag but permitted the wearing of red and white badges on the coat. These instructions were obeyed.

At Bandjermasin the 2/31st Battalion landed on 17th September from H.M.A.S. *Burdekin* and H.M.A.S. *Gascoyne.* It was a large town with a population of about 45,000 including 8,000 Chinese. Here Major-General Uno and 2,500 Japanese surrendered to Lieut-Colonel Robson and the Australians marched through the town.

> The skirl of bagpipes mingled with the overwhelming cheers of a welcoming populace as the Battalion marched through the thronged streets of Bandjermasin. A most moving tribute was given by the Chinese community. Dressed in spotless white duck with Chinese Republic rosettes on their breasts they stood in cheering ranks behind a banner inscribed "WELCOME—CHINESE COMMUNITY", under which sat their venerable leaders, two 80-year-old men wearing black bowler hats.[8]

By 21st September the 2/31st had released 65 Indian prisoners of war, and 174 Dutch and 3 English civilians. In October the republican movement became vocal in this area also. Robson, learning that there was to be a demonstration, ordered that there were to be no raising of the republican flag, no demonstrations, and no distribution of pamphlets, and the local republican leader complied. On 18th October, its task practically done, the main body of the battalion returned to Balikpapan, leaving one company at Bandjermasin.

In all areas the Japanese strove to behave with meticulous correctness. At the same time they provided much evidence that defeat had not diminished their pride. At the Manggar prison compound

> the members of the guard [of the 2/14th Battalion] gained the following impressions of the prisoners: firstly that they were disinclined to recognise defeat, and that they believe the Emperor has only called a temporary halt necessary to save many civilians from being slaughtered by the Allies. On the first day in the compound

---

[8] War diary, 2/31st Battalion.

every opportunity was taken by the Japs to show their so-called superiority. This was done by strutting around the compound flexing their muscles and performing antics calculated to draw envious looks from the Australians.

Most Australian soldiers seem soon to have lost their animosity towards the Japanese, though in some places it was fanned into flame again by evidence of the slaughter of defenceless natives and by the accounts given by recovered prisoners and internees of killings and brutal bullying. In the 7th Division area by December it was found necessary to instruct troops not to treat the prisoners in too friendly a fashion.

Many instances noted of fraternisation with Japs which even extended to gifts of cigarettes and food (stated a rather pompous divisional instruction). This will on no account be tolerated. Strong disciplinary action will be taken against any persons who fail to treat Japs with severe justice. The following particular orders are issued. ONE. Japs will be informed that increasing failure to salute officers and general lack of smartness have been noted and will be rectified immediately. TWO. Any AUST officer or NCO who observes failure to salute or other slackness will immediately report the matter for disciplinary action to be taken against Japs even though he is not directly concerned. THREE. An officer will in no circumstances return salute of a Jap but will merely indicate that he has noted the action by a direct and severe look in the eyes of the Jap concerned. FOUR. No preferential treatment will be given to Jap personnel such as artists or interpreters who will be made to do their share of manual labour unless required for full time special duties. FIVE. Units employing Jap labour will ensure that Japs are fully employed under supervision at all times. SIX. Commanders will ensure these orders are brought to notice of all ranks.

In the Balikpapan area Indonesian nationalist agitation soon became an embarrassment. For example, on the morning of 14th November between 6,000 and 8,000 Indonesians assembled in the N.I.C.A. compound, raised banners and displayed emblems. From 10 to 15 Australian soldiers were reported to have been present inciting these Indonesians. Indonesian troops arrested some demonstrators, but the Australians had disappeared before Australian military police arrived.

The fact that the war was over did not reduce the animosity of the Dyaks in Dutch Borneo towards the Japanese, who appealed to the Australians to hasten the sending of a force to Pontianak where the Dyaks were harassing them. On 16th October a company of the 2/33rd Battalion, a company of the Royal Netherlands Indies Army and a N.I.C.A. detachment arrived and established control.

In the *II Japanese Army's* area, excluding Borneo where the 9th and 7th Divisions and the 26th Brigade between them shared responsibility for the whole island, five Australian occupation forces were created. These were initially:

> Timor Force (the islands from Sumbawa to Timor).
> Ambon Force (Buru, Ambon, Ceram, Tanimbar, Aru Islands and small adjacent islands).
> Menado Force (Menado and part of the northern peninsula of Celebes).
> Macassar Force (Macassar and the south-western peninsula of Celebes).
> Ternate Detachment (Ternate and adjacent islands of the northern Moluccas).

From its headquarters at Pinrang in Celebes the *II Army* controlled the *57th Independent Mixed Brigade* in northern Celebes, the *32nd Division* in Halmahera, the *5th* in the Ceram-Aru-Ambon area, the *35th* and *36th* in western New Guinea. Soon after the cease fire control of the *XXXVII Army* in Borneo and the *48th Division* in Timor and the Lesser Sundas was transferred to the *II Army*.

The commander of the *II Army* was informed that the Allied forces were occupying only parts of their allotted areas. Elsewhere the Japanese commanders would for the present be responsible to the local Allied commander for maintenance of law and order.

At Morotai on 21st August Brigadier Dyke, commanding the artillery of I Corps, had begun to form a force to be used to occupy some area in the Indies, as yet undecided. The staff was drawn mainly from Dyke's headquarters, and officers and men from the Advanced Reinforcement Depot, Morotai, were formed into two battalions. Dyke was sent to Darwin on 29th August to take a battalion thence to Dutch Timor, the plan then being that the remainder of his brigade would join him from Morotai.

However, on 17th September the force waiting at Morotai was informed that it would not join Dyke, as more troops were not needed on Timor, but would go to Ambon and occupy it and other islands in the Moluccas, and also the Kai, Aru and Tanimbar Islands. Brigadier W. A. B. Steele of the staff of I Corps was appointed to command what was now named the 33rd Brigade; the two battalions, numbered the 63rd and 64th, were commanded by Lieut-Colonels Ellison[9] and Costello[1] respectively.

The tasks of the 33rd Brigade were to establish headquarters on Ambon, to receive the surrender there and supervise the evacuation of the Japanese, through the *5th Japanese Division* to ensure control of Japanese forces in other areas, and to assist the re-establishment of the N.E.I. Government.

As soon as the fighting ceased an Australian naval force of six small vessels was sent to Ambon where it arrived on 16th August. One corvette entered Ambon harbour and got into touch with the Japanese commander, but he refused to negotiate and asked the corvette to depart immediately. The whole force thereupon returned to Morotai. After the surrenders of senior commanders had taken place a second naval force was sent to Ambon and on 10th September it removed all Allied prisoners of war who were there.

Brigadier Steele with a detachment totalling 100 officers and men landed at Ambon from H.M.A.S. *Glenelg* at 9 a.m. on 22nd September, twenty-four hours ahead of a convoy of four corvettes carrying 588 troops. A "follow-up force" of about 2,150 in five naval transports, including the L.S.I. *Westralia,* was to arrive later. The 64th but not the 63rd Battalion was included in this force.

---

[9] Lt-Col E. B. Ellison, SX22481. CO 1 Adv Rft Depot 1945, 63 Bn 1945-46. Regular soldier; b. Bundaberg, Qld, 31 Mar 1897. Died 26 May 1956.

[1] Lt-Col F. H. Costello, VX64666. CO 13 Motor Regt 1942-43, 2/5 Armd Regt 1943-44, 64 Bn 1945-46. Regular soldier; b. Numurkah, Vic, 21 May 1907.

The formalities on the first day were smoothly performed. The Ambonese welcomed *Glenelg,* the Australian and Dutch flags were hoisted at the control tower on the wharf, and at 10 a.m. Vice-Admiral Ichise, commanding the naval base, and Major-General Kobori, commanding the *5th Division,* reported and were given instructions. Next day the convoy arrived and the troops disembarked. That afternoon General Blamey's proclamation was read in the presence of an assembly of Ambonese, and a bamboo-flute band performed. The follow-up force arrived on 27th September.

The Japanese were "correct and most cooperative". The Australian troops found it strange that Japanese officers and other ranks saluted all Australian troops. (They did not know that Australian prisoners of the Japanese had similarly been required to salute all Japanese soldiers.)

Ichise was instructed that all his men would be concentrated on Ceram. The troops transferred from Ambon were allowed to take food, eating and cooking gear, sleeping kit, office equipment, 159 dismantled huts, and "8,378 yards of cloth for barter purposes". They were allowed five rifles and 300 rounds of ammunition for each 100 men.

Colonel Kaida, commanding the Japanese forces on Timor—a total of 3,235 men—signed the instrument of surrender in H.M.A.S. *Moresby* at midday on 11th September. That afternoon Brigadier Dyke inspected Koepang and next morning his troops, mainly the 12th/40th Battalion from the Northern Territory, disembarked.[2] The preliminary inquiries revealed that there were no Allied prisoners left on Timor, Penfui airfield was serviceable, and there was plenty of aviation fuel on the island. The Japanese had dumped their weapons and had concentrated as they had been ordered to do.

Included in the area controlled from Timor was the *48th Japanese Division.* Lieut-General Kunitaro Yamada, commander of the division, signed the instrument of surrender at Koepang on 3rd October, and was left responsible for civil administration and preservation of law and order in Sumbawa, Flores and Sumba. Meanwhile the Australian force was busy supervising the concentration of the Japanese troops into defined areas, repatriating Indonesians, organising food supplies and services, and apprehending Japanese likely to be charged with war crimes.

Late in August Blamey had asked the Minister for Defence whether he was to occupy Portuguese as well as Dutch Timor and was instructed to limit action to Dutch Timor. On 13th September Dyke signalled that the surrender off Koepang on the 11th had included the forces in Portuguese Timor, who numbered only about 150 on guard and police duties. Finally the Australian Government directed that Dyke should go to Dili, inform the Portuguese Governor of the surrender of the Japanese forces to him, arrange with the Governor for the landing of a small party to check that the terms of the surrender were effective, and arrange for the disposal of the Japanese, the recovery of any Allied prisoners, and

---

[2] It was appropriate that this Tasmanian unit should have been employed. The 2/40th had been lost on Timor in 1942.

the control of war material. He should also discuss arrangements concerning war graves and war crimes. Mr Forsyth,[3] of the Department of External Affairs, was flown to Timor to act as Dyke's political adviser.

Forsyth met the Portuguese Governor at Dili on 22nd September and satisfactory discussions were held. Next day Dyke went to Dili with Forsyth and others and a force of five corvettes. Dyke went to the Governor's house, formally apprised him of the surrender, and congratulated him on the restoration of his authority. Satisfactory arrangements were made to ensure that the surrender in Portuguese Timor was effective.

A surveillance party visited Menado on 13th September, inspected the area and collected 354 Dutch internees and took them to Morotai. A small occupation force under Lieut-Colonel R. A. C. Muir landed on 2nd October and supervised the concentration of the Japanese—on Lembeh Island and in Minahassa on the mainland—and saw to the destruction of warlike stores and the arrest of men who might be charged as war criminals. In November a company of the R.N.I.A. took over. The Japanese forces included the *57th Independent Mixed Brigade* and *8th Naval Garrison Force* and totalled 8,150. While the Australians were at Menado there was no resistance to the re-establishment of Dutch control in the immediate area but, as will be seen, there was trouble elsewhere in northern Celebes.

Small surveillance parties dealt with Halmahera, Ternate, eight areas in western New Guinea, and the Talaud Islands.

As shown earlier, the Indonesian nationalists did not greatly embarrass the Australian occupation forces in Dutch Borneo, and in British Borneo there was no revolutionary movement. In the islands to the south, however, larger problems were encountered. Until December the Indonesian revolution produced few effects in the Lesser Sundas, but in December and January disturbances began on Sumbawa, where 21,000 Japanese troops were then concentrated. There were clashes between members of the Free Indonesian movement and Japanese, whose arms the Indonesians were anxious to acquire.

On 3rd January, for example, the Japanese reported a clash with 200 Indonesians at Gempe on the night of the 1st, when four Japanese were wounded and two natives killed. At the request of the Sultan a Japanese patrol went with the Sultan's chief of police to the village and told the villagers it must not happen again. On the morning of the 3rd at Sape 400 natives attacked a Japanese post; one native was killed. Then a Japanese post of seven men near Sape disappeared. At Raba that day 80 natives assembled, and when a sentry went forward to ask them their business he was speared, his rifle seized, and his body thrown down a well. Thereupon the Japanese commander was ordered to instruct the Sultan to proclaim that attacks must cease and that the Australian Army had instructed the Japanese to shoot to kill if natives attacked them.

---

[3] W. D. Forsyth, OBE. Aust Minister to United Nations 1951-55; Ambassador to Vietnam 1959-61. Research Fellow; of Ballarat, Vic; b. Casterton, Vic, 5 Jan 1909.

Next day *Lismore* took a party to Bima to inform the Sultan that he would be removed if his control of the people did not improve.

In the next few days the Japanese arrested "253 out of 257 natives involved in Sape incident", and impounded 17 rifles: the Sultan would try all the people who had been arrested. On 13th January N.I.C.A. was installed at Bima and a company of R.N.I.A. troops landed there. N.I.C.A. now controlled all Sumbawa except the district where the Japanese were concentrated.

The Australian Army's share in the rehabilitation of the islands north of the Timor Sea ended on 19th March, when Timor Force, now under Lieut-Colonel Bartley,[4] closed its headquarters.

In November the Indonesian leader at Gorontalo in northern Celebes had gained so strong a grip that he refused to obey an order to attend a conference with the Australian authorities. Some 600 Indonesian youths were being drilled on the outskirts of the town and the Chinese and Arabs were being boycotted. On 29th November additional Dutch troops were sent to Gorontalo in H.M.A.S. *Burdekin,* an Australian officer, Major Wilson,[5] took command, the Indonesian leader was shipped off to Menado, and a satisfactory agreement was reached with his followers. By 1st December business was more or less back to normal, and control was handed over to a Dutch officer.

The nationalist movement flourished in large towns rather than small ones and it was inevitable that the Australian force that occupied south Celebes and the city of Macassar, whose population was about 90,000, should have a difficult task. Macassar Force, which was built round the 21st Brigade, had been given the tasks of recovering prisoners in southern Celebes, taking the surrender there, controlling the troops of the *II Japanese Army* in Celebes and concentrating them in one area, taking preliminary action to facilitate the re-establishment of N.E.I. Government, and helping the civil population to maintain their economy. An advanced group including a headquarters and a company arrived at Macassar in the corvettes *Barcoo* and *Inverell* on 21st September, the 2/27th Battalion was complete at Macassar on 27th September, and the remainder of the brigade group arrived between 1st and 17th October. When the first group arrived the town was quiet. The Australians were welcomed by a guard drawn from about 500 British seamen, former prisoners of war, mostly from H.M.S. *Exeter* which had been sunk off Java in 1942.

As mentioned, the *II Japanese Army* controlled the Japanese troops in Celebes, Ambon, Ceram, the Vogelkop, Timor, the Lesser Sundas and Halmahera, so that Macassar Force not only controlled south Celebes but was the liaison with the Japanese commander of forces in practically the whole of the Australian area outside Borneo.

---

[4] Col T. W. Bartley, MBE, ED, TX6157. (1st AIF: 3 AFA Bde.) CO 40 Bn 1937-45, 12/40 Bn 1945, Timor Force 1946. Master printer; of West Hobart; b. Scottsdale, Tas, 13 Jun 1897. Died 2 Mar 1963.

[5] Maj D. C. L. Wilson, NX12477. 2/16 Bn; BM 16 and 30 Bdes; GSO2 NGF, I and II Corps, Adv LHQ, 1943-45. Regular soldier; b. Melbourne, 7 May 1918.

The attitude of the Japanese could be described as one of complete "correctness". They went to extraordinary lengths to produce complete and tabulated details of their strength and locations, their holdings of arms, ammunition, food, petrol, clothing and medical supplies. . . . The impression given was that, as a beaten nation they were determined to establish themselves securely at the foot of the international ladder down which they had recently fallen, by demonstration of their unfailing desire to assist, almost to ingratiate themselves.[6]

At first Brigadier Dougherty found himself hampered by the lack of cooperation between the Japanese Army and Navy. Each claimed no knowledge of or responsibility for the other and the Navy "plainly showed their utmost contempt for the Army". Finally he insisted on dealing only with a liaison officer responsible to both Services.

Because of shortage of vehicles it took until 15th November to concentrate all Japanese forces in the selected areas near Pinrang, and it was not until 20th December that the Japanese from Kendari and south-eastern Celebes were concentrated about Malimpung.

The N.I.C.A. unit with Macassar Force was gradually increased until it was 150 strong, but it worked under great difficulty because the local rajahs and other leaders were unwilling to recognise Dutch authority. The diplomatic and political problems encountered by Macassar Force were more acute than those faced by the other Australian occupation forces, and its experiences will be described in a little more detail than those of the others.

At an assembly of townspeople at Macassar on 23rd September General Blamey's proclamation had been read and Brigadier Dougherty had given an address in the course of which he said, through a translator:

We Australians come to you as friends to help you until your government organises itself. I have seen some of the people of Macassar, and I am very pleased that you are more fortunate than the peoples of many other countries of the world. In many other countries the people's crops, animals and homes—almost everything they had —have been destroyed. In Macassar there is practically no damage at all. Elsewhere big cities twenty or thirty times the size of Macassar have been completely destroyed. . . .

In these islands of the Netherlands Indies your own government is taking over administration. I hope it will not be long before we Australians can leave a happy people here. The Netherlands Indies Government has appointed Major Wegner as Netherlands Indies Government representative here. The Japanese will continue temporarily to administer certain things. These will be taken over by N.I.C.A. as soon as possible. There will naturally be some difficulties to overcome but they will not be difficulties as great as in many other countries. From time to time while I am here as military commander I will have occasion to make decisions affecting your life and work. I have no doubt that you will give me your fullest cooperation.

From the outset, however, the Indonesian leaders refused to cooperate with N.I.C.A.; in their eyes Indonesia was now an independent republic. On 5th October the commanding officer of N.I.C.A. ordered a number of Indonesian leaders to assemble at Macassar on the 8th to confer with him. The Indonesians refused, and five of them wrote to Dougherty asking him to invite Dr Ratu Langie and Dr Tadjoeddin Noer to confer with

---

[6] Report on the Operations of Macassar Force. 22 September 1945 to 20 December 1945.

him. Ratu Langie had been appointed Governor of Celebes by the Indonesian Republican Government in Java.[7]

In a letter to the commanding officer of N.I.C.A. five Indonesian chiefs who had been summoned declared that they and their leaders were capable of carrying on the administration, that they objected to carrying it on under the guidance of Dutch officials but would carry out the orders of the Australian commander. On the 9th Dougherty addressed the village chiefs of Macassar at some length and made it clear that N.I.C.A. was the only administration that the United Nations recognised in the Indies, and therefore the only one he recognised.

The Indonesian leaders were the more ready to believe that the Australians would recognise their authority because of the sympathy that was being expressed towards the republican movement by some groups in Australia. For instance, one of those who wrote to Dougherty to say that his colleagues were willing to work under Australian Army orders but not those of the Dutch functionaries, offered the Australian commander "cordial thanks for the sympathetic attitude of a great part of the Australian people regarding the movement for national freedom of the Indonesians".

On 12th October 18 republican officials signed a letter requesting that Indonesian officials be entrusted with the administration directly under the command of the Australian Army, and again suggesting a conference with Ratu Langie. Dougherty still would not agree to treat directly with these officials.

A renewed request that he confer with Ratu Langie and the Indonesian princes and chiefs was sent in by four village chiefs on 15th October. That day in Macassar there was a clash between some Ambonese, who supported the Dutch, and some Indonesian nationalists and at least 18 people were killed and 15 wounded. No Australian troops were involved. As a result of this clash and because of the enmity between Ambonese, whom N.I.C.A. were using as police, and other Indonesians, Dougherty ordered that no Royal Netherlands Indies Army soldiers were to carry arms outside barracks unless posted on guard duty by his headquarters, no R.N.I.A. soldiers were to be used for street patrols, and no N.I.C.A. or R.N.I.A. personnel were to "interfere with or remove any badge or emblem worn by any person". And he ordered the commander of the R.N.I.A. troops to keep his men in barracks until further orders.

A further complication arose on 16th October when a Chinese leader approached Dougherty and informed him that the Indonesian nationalists had threatened that if the Chinese did not close their shops they would be dealt with as the Ambonese had been. Thereupon Dougherty himself, through N.I.C.A., issued an order that all Chinese shops were to be closed. On the morning of the 17th, however, after the men of the 2/27th

---

[7] Later a memorandum on the proposed audience was found in a house in Macassar. It stated that the Australian commander might be pro-N.I.C.A., or might favour Indonesian independence, or be neutral and passive, or might refer the problem straight away to N.I.C.A. The memorandum then set out in detail how the Indonesian delegates would respond to each of these attitudes.

Battalion had done a fine job of quiet patrolling, Dougherty ordered the immediate reopening of shops.

On 15th October Brigadier Chilton had arrived at Macassar to take over from Brigadier Dougherty, who was to be given a period of leave in Australia. In the next few days Dougherty, with Chilton beside him, gave several talks to Indonesians to whom he repeated the principles to which he was adhering. On the 16th he spoke first to a general assembly of village leaders and then to a group of "youth leaders", among whom was Dr Ratu Langie. Hitherto, as mentioned, Dougherty had taken pains not to recognise Ratu Langie in any way and now called him in merely as one member of a group claiming influence over Indonesian youths.

General Blamey arrived at Macassar on 18th October with General Milford and some staff officers. Blamey made it clear to Dougherty and Chilton that the responsibility for maintaining law and order rested with the commander of Macassar Force, that N.I.C.A. was an agent of the commander, and that if the commander arrested anybody it should only be for inciting people to interfere with law and order and not for "political reasons".

At a conference on 20th October between Brigadier Chilton (who took command of the force on the 18th) and officers of the N.I.C.A. it was agreed that Australian troops would be established at key points and would patrol and establish road-blocks to prevent movement of political agitators; N.I.C.A. representatives would accompany the Australian detachments, and under their protection would take over civil administration as far as possible.

The 2/14th Battalion had been in the Pare Pare-Pinrang area since 5th October; the 2/16th now occupied six points in the southern half of the peninsula, while the 2/27th remained in Macassar. One way in which the authority of N.I.C.A. was established was by making the local rulers go to its officers for rice and other supplies. At first the nationalists were so determined to boycott N.I.C.A. that they prevented the N.I.C.A. trucks carrying rice from moving about the country and even stole some of the vehicles. To cope with this action Dougherty, soon after his arrival, had used Australian trucks, and some trucks and coastal ships taken over from the Japanese, to transport rice.

The Indonesians continued to give trouble in small ways, and at Pare Pare on 22nd October a counter-demonstration was staged for their edification; in the presence of 400 natives, Australian machine-gunners used their weapons to clear the scrub from a knoll 2,000 yards away.

In the five months during which the 21st Brigade was in control of Celebes, with its big city population in Macassar and its closely-settled surrounding country, there was constant danger of the kind of strife and bloodshed that was occurring in Java. The Australian leaders and men were proud of the way in which they helped to preserve peace. Brigadier Chilton could justly write afterwards that

a policy of firmness in the maintenance of law and order, and our patent impartiality in regard to their political problems, succeeded and after the first few weeks there was no serious trouble. This happy result was very largely attributable to the magnificent bearing, patience and discipline of the members of the Force, at a time when their thoughts were naturally towards home, and to the innate qualities of kindness and sympathy with all sections of the community, Indonesian, Chinese and Dutch.[8]

In February Macassar Force handed over control to the 80th Indian Brigade. Before the Australians departed General Teshima on 1st February wrote to Brigadier Chilton reporting that the concentration of all Japanese at Malimpung had been completed on 20th January, and adding:

> Since the advance of your forces at Macassar, all the Japanese forces and civilians have endeavoured to obey your orders and instructions, but owing to the difference in custom and the manners, difficulties in language and different local condition, I regret very much that we have bothered you considerably. Yet you have been very lenient and patient and tried to understand us, maintaining a very fair attitude and at the same time accurate and correct in dealing with all matters and all these has won my admiration and whole-hearted confidence in you.
>
> All matters dealing with the termination of the war have almost been completed and all Japanese are now enabled to carry on their collective life in an orderly manner, as mentioned above, through your understanding and correct direction, for which we are all very grateful to you.
>
> Having fulfilled your duties here Your Excellency is leaving Celebes soon and recollecting all you have done for us, I extremely regret that you should go now: I am sure I shall miss you very much.
>
> In bidding farewell to you, I wish Your Excellency and Your Excellency's Officers and Men the best luck and every happiness.

Australia's tasks in the Indies were practically finished before her component of the British Commonwealth Occupation Force arrived in Japan.[9] The 34th Brigade Group was formed in the last part of 1945, the 65th Battalion being initially composed of men of the 7th Division, the 66th of men of the 6th and the 67th of men of the 9th.[10] At the outset more than enough volunteers were obtained, but because of the delay in sending the force to Japan more than 2,000 withdrew and the force fell below strength. As had been arranged, the commander of B.C.O.F. (British Commonwealth Occupation Force) was an Australian: Lieut-General Northcott was chosen and remained in command until June 1946 when, on his appointment as Governor of New South Wales, he was succeeded by Lieut-General Robertson.

The Australian army and air force components totalled about 11,500 officers and men, the strength of the whole of B.C.O.F. being about 36,000 at its maximum. The first Australian troops arrived in Japan in February 1946. Already, in December, Northcott had conferred with MacArthur and they had agreed that B.C.O.F. should be located in southern Honshu,

---

[8] Quoted in W. B. Russell, *The Second Fourteenth Battalion*, p. 313.

[9] There were, of course, many Australians on the American staffs. One of these, Brigadier W. M. Anderson, who was serving with the Eighth American Army as Senior Administrative Officer, in the course of a letter to General Blamey on 19th October 1945, wrote: "SCAP is exercised regarding the present Russian attitude. The Russians have withdrawn their liaison group from HQ XIV Corps in Korea and General Hodge is now without any means of communicating with the occupants of the area north of parallel 38. I have heard that U.S. planes which happen to fly north of the 38th parallel are usually fired at by Russian anti-aircraft artillery. Generally the situation in Korea is full of 'dynamite'."

[10] Later these battalions became the 1st, 2nd and 3rd Battalions, Royal Australian Regiment.

an arrangement which gave the force a good port, an area in which it was self-contained and not dispersed among American forces, and a fairly comfortable climate. Force headquarters were at Kure, and the 34th Brigade occupied the Hiroshima Prefecture.[1]

By that time the wartime army had ceased to exist. On 15th September 1945 General Blamey had addressed a memorandum to Mr Forde in

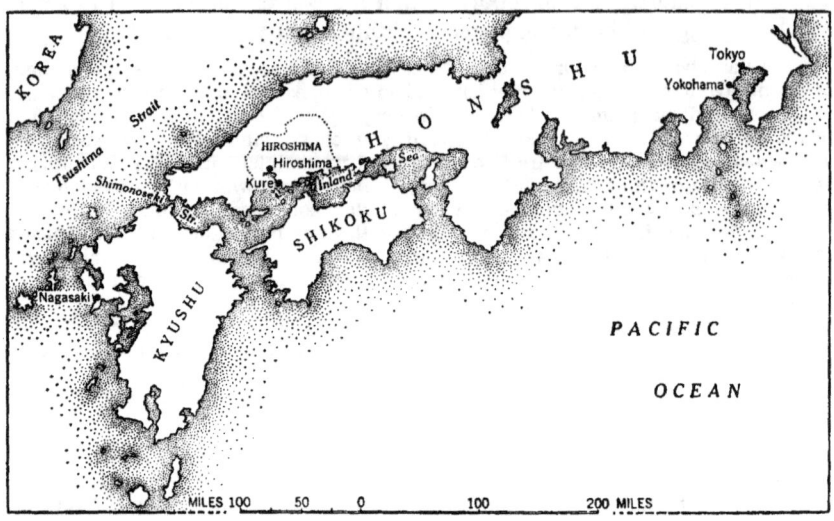

which he reported formally that he had been present at the surrender of the Japanese Empire in Tokyo Bay on 2nd September. There was no further occasion for the exercise or continuance of his powers as commander-in-chief; the residual task could be carried out under Government supervision "by the machinery of corporate control".

> I am desirous (he added) of laying down my office as early as possible in order to facilitate transition to such control. I would appreciate therefore an indication from the Government as to when this step would be acceptable.

He had, on 23rd July, conveyed to the Government his views as to the form this corporate control should take.[2]

> I feel (Blamey concluded) that I cannot lay down my high office without expressing my very great indebtedness to the late Prime Minister, the Right Honorable John Curtin. His sacrifice and devotion to Australia's cause and his wise cooperative

---

[1] An account of the Australian force's problems and experiences is contained in "History of the Australian Occupation in Japan" by Major-General R. N. L. Hopkins, *Journal and Proceedings of the Royal Australian Historical Society*, Vol XL, Part II (1954). For a detailed and critical account of the negotiations leading up to the establishment of BCOF, the command arrangements, and the force's experiences, see Rajendra Singh, *Post-War Occupation Forces: Japan and South-East Asia* (1958), a volume of the *Official History of the Indian Armed Forces in the Second World War*.

[2] These views and others concerning planning of the post-war army are part of post-war history and are not recorded in detail in this volume. To discuss the post-war planning which took place before the Japanese surrender would necessitate continuing the story into the later period of planning and decision. Once begun the narrative would need to continue at least until 1948 and 1949, and the establishment of an Australian regular army.

leadership afforded to those entrusted with the execution of the national plans the assurance of that loyal and affectionate support which made possible the measure of national cohesion necessary to overcome our difficulties.

Mr Curtin had died on 5th July. Long before Curtin's death it had been evident that, after he had gone, Blamey would not receive the same kind of support from the Ministers that he had been given in the previous four years. Blamey's letter of 23rd July was briefly acknowledged by Forde six days later. Meanwhile Shedden had informed Blamey that the Ministers were receiving advice that conflicted with Blamey's: General Lavarack, a former Chief of the General Staff, now Head of the Australian Military Mission at Washington and second in seniority in the Australian Army, had written to Mr Forde recommending that Blamey should vacate his office, that the Military Board should be re-established, and a commander be appointed for the Australian oversea forces.

It was not until 15th November that Blamey heard from Forde on the subject again. Then Forde informed Blamey that the Government had decided to re-introduce the Military Board organisation at an early date (Blamey had suggested a somewhat different organisation), and had decided that General Sturdee should be acting Commander-in-Chief from 1st December and hold that office until the introduction of the Military Board (three months later as it turned out).[3] Forde then expressed appreciation of Blamey's "outstanding services . . . to the Australian nation".

Blamey and Forde met that day. On the 17th Blamey wrote a reply thanking the Minister for his "kind remarks" but adding:

> May I express my surprise at the very short notice of the termination of my appointment and also my regret that the brief period which you have allowed me will not permit me to complete tasks which I deem to be of some importance, e.g. completion of dispatches on the latter phases of the war.

He reminded Forde that Forde had on 3rd November directed him to refuse an invitation to the Annual National Convention of the American Legion in Chicago because of "the complexity of the problems confronting the Army". "I am naturally somewhat disturbed," he added tartly, "at what appears to be a sudden and unseemly haste to meet my personal convenience." In a reply nine days later and four days before Blamey was due to be replaced Forde proposed that Blamey should complete his dispatches in a period to be added to his accumulated leave. Blamey agreed and said that he had fixed the maximum date for completion of all tasks as 31st January.

Blamey had received no honour since being made a G.B.E. in 1943 and received none now. He had had no promotion since he was made a general in September 1941, before his return from the Middle East, nor was he to receive any until, another Ministry being then in office,

---

[3] General Sturdee, who had been Chief of the General Staff from August 1940 to September 1942, resumed that appointment on 1st March 1946, with General Rowell as Vice-Chief.

he became the first Field Marshal in the Australian Army in June 1950. He was handed his baton on his death bed in the following year.

His generals were treated little better in the matter of honours. On 8th September 1945 Blamey had written to the Minister recommending that knighthoods should be conferred upon five generals whom he named and that certain other commanders should be made Commanders of the Order of the Bath (C.B.).

> There is (Blamey wrote) a genuine ground for the feeling that Australian commanders are treated far less generously than those of other parts of the Empire. Also that greater generosity was displayed when Australian forces served under British Command in the Middle East than under Australian command in the S.W.P. Area. . . . I have raised the matter from time to time and have made certain recommendations but, so far, have received no reply.

He added that he would make recommendations at a later date concerning officers who had not served in the field.

On 10th October Blamey sent the Minister the later list in which he recommended that three generals on his staff be knighted, and other senior staff officers be awarded C.B's. He pointed out that certain of these had served in the field in the Middle East and the others had spent frequent and fairly long periods in operational areas. At this point the correspondence appears to have ended. The knighthoods were not then awarded.

It is clear that the Government had been unable to decide on a clear policy towards the award of knighthoods to military commanders and others. Since it came into office General Morshead had been awarded the K.B.E. and K.C.B., General Herring the K.B.E. (in 1943), Shedden the K.C.M.G. (1943). Blamey had received the K.C.B. in 1942 and the G.B.E. in 1943. Thus if the policy was to recommend lower awards but not knighthoods it had existed only since 1943; and if the policy was to limit awards to leaders who had served in the field it had not been followed consistently. In the event only two of the awards recommended by Blamey in these lists were made within a year or two after the war; and the one army commander and the two corps commanders received no recognition of this kind in that period. In 1946 two divisional commanders, and, in 1947, a third one were awarded the C.B's for which Blamey had recommended them, but the other divisional commanders mentioned received no awards then, nor did any of the senior staff officers.[4] So far as a policy can be discerned it seems to have been this: if a field commander was already a C.B., the Government would not recommend any higher award (which would necessarily be a knighthood); and in any event the Government would not recommend any awards at all to senior staff officers not in the field formations.[5]

---

[4] The Quartermaster-General, Cannan, for example, served in that appointment, with the temporary rank of major-general, from October 1940 until after the end of the war. His substantive rank was colonel, which he had attained when appointed to command an infantry brigade in France in 1916, thirty years before when he was 34; he was awarded no honour for his service in 1940-45.

[5] In Parliament on 13th September 1945 Mr Chifley said: "The Labour Party is opposed to honours except military decorations." However, as shown above, this opposition had not been consistently applied.

After a change of government most of those whom Blamey recommended for knighthoods received that honour, either for their wartime services or for other public service performed in peace.[6]

The total strength of the Australian Army early in August 1945 was 383,000 of whom 23,000 were women. The numbers in forward areas were: New Guinea mainland and New Britain, 53,000; the Solomons, 32,000; Borneo and Morotai, 72,000. There were some 20,000 prisoners in Japanese hands.

Blamey had written to Forde on 3rd October that demobilisation had begun in accordance with the plan approved in March. He estimated that about 40,000 men and women would be discharged in that month. The army plan was based on a normal rate of dispersal of 1,965 and 125 women a day; but provision had been made to increase this to 2,948 and 187 women. He did not think the increased rate would be achieved because of lack of shipping, the anticipated inability of the civil economy to absorb such numbers and the difficulty of dealing with them at the re-establishment centres.

The general plan of demobilisation provided for the retention of an "Interim Army" to perform such duties as the occupation of territories held by the enemy, the care of equipment, and the administration of demobilisation. Otherwise troops would be demobilised at a rate decided by the Government. The principles governing discharges would be: generally speaking the existing points system would be observed; members might request a "deferred priority"; members whose service was essential could be retained regardless of priority, but members whose early return to civilian life was considered essential and members whose applications for discharge on compassionate grounds were approved would be given a special priority.

---

[6] Decorations were somewhat sparingly awarded also to more junior members of the Australian Army throughout the war. In its interim history the 2/2nd Battalion, for example, claimed with pride that, in the matter of decorations it "imposed its own standards; and those standards have been rigid to the degree of harshness". Writing in mid-1945 its chronicler said that no subaltern had been awarded an MC in this battalion, then in its fourth campaign. (Not long afterwards, however, one subaltern was awarded a VC, one a DSO and one an MC.) The following table shows the numbers of awards in a battalion of the 1st AIF, one of the 2nd AIF and one that served in Korea. The 13th and 2/13th Battalion were chosen because they were corresponding units for which precise details about awards were readily available, the 3rd Battalion RAR because it was the Australian battalion that saw most action in Korea.

	13 Bn AIF 1914-18	2/13 Bn AIF 1939-45	3 Bn RAR Korea
Deaths in action	1,045 (54 offrs)	245 (16 offrs)	287 (8 offrs)
VC	2	—	—
CB	1	—	—
CMG	3	—	—
DSO	6	3	4
Bar to DSO	1	—	—
MC	33	10	17
Bar to MC	1	—	1
OBE	—	—	6
MBE	—	1	3
DCM	31	6	4
Bar to DCM	—	—	1
MM	188	12	29
Bar to MM	7	—	1
MSM	7	—	—
m.i.d.	Approx 300	40	58
Other	9	2	7

Under the points system two points were awarded for each completed year of age at enlistment plus two points for each month of service plus, for men with dependents, an extra point for each month of service.[7]

It was calculated in September that to keep the Interim Army units in the First Army area at full strength of 46,500 only men with 178 points or more could be released at that stage. As demobilisation proceeded units that were not needed were declared "redundant" and their low-priority men transferred to Interim Army units. At length the Interim Army, its tasks completed, would merge into the Post-war Army.[8]

Thus when the 11th Division at Rabaul, for example, learnt that a ship had been allotted to take away a draft of men due for discharge, it reported the unit, rank and trade of each man in the draft. Thereupon First Army requisitioned corresponding replacements from other areas and, so far as possible, the ships landed these replacements at Rabaul before embarking the men they were replacing. It was estimated that 12,800 men would have to be moved to Rabaul from other areas to bring the garrison there up to the required strength and maintain it at that level.

Initially Australia asked London for enough shipping to lift 23,500 men a month. This, added to Australia's ability to lift 6,500 a month in her own ships and 6,000 in her aircraft, would have enabled her to move 108,000 men back to the mainland between October and December. But in fact London could provide only enough shipping to lift 12,000 a month from October to December and 10,000 thereafter. However, the use of the aircraft carriers *Implacable, Glory* and *Formidable,* and of other vessels, made it possible to move 76,000 by sea up to the end of December. At the beginning of January only about 20,000 were awaiting repatriation from the First Army areas not counting garrison forces totalling 45,000. In the later stages a number of enterprising soldiers, sometimes with the connivance of more fortunate comrades, stowed away, well knowing that they would not be returned to the islands, and regarding the subsequent fine as fair payment for the voyage home.

As the men at length moved through the depots in their home States in the process of being discharged, they were handled for the most part with commendable speed and efficiency. Dental treatment was available before discharge and medical examination and chest X-ray were obligatory. Each soldier was given the opportunity of stating before a doctor any disabilities that he considered had been a result of army service.

Dekitting, pay and the issuing of food and clothing coupons and allowances followed. The webbing and pack that had borne personal possessions to a war at first half a world away and then, nearer home, into the green jungle, went into store. The brown boots that had distinguished their wearers from most other soldiers would soon be put away, never to carry the Australian warrior to war again. For the last time the rifle number

---

[7] Thus on 1st October 1945 a married man who, when aged 30, had joined a unit of the 6th Division when it was being formed would have 276 points; a man without dependents who had enlisted two years before October 1945 aged 20 would have only 88.

[8] In the event all officers remaining in the army on 1st July 1947 were that day appointed to the Interim Army, which existed until 1952 when a new title was adopted.

was checked—hitherto a daily act of almost religious significance for the infantryman. Discharge certificates and "Returned from Active Service" badges were distributed—making a leave pass no longer a necessity. At this stage in the proceedings "Private Smith", to his astonishment, was suddenly addressed as "Mister" again.

Not only the Australians but the Japanese had to be repatriated. The first ship to remove Japanese from Rabaul was the aircraft carrier *Katsuragi*, which embarked 2,658 men on 28th February 1946. Thenceforward, until 13th June 37 ships, including some Japanese-manned American ships, embarked groups ranging from 500 to 4,554, until a total of 90,909 had departed. By Australian standards the ships were grossly overcrowded.

The embarkation of Japanese of the *XVIII Army* began at Muschu Island on 27th November when 1,130 men departed in the demilitarised cruiser *Kashima*. In January six ships took prisoners away, including one which carried 1,200 Formosan troops to Formosa. On 6th March 1946 the last man of the *XVIII Army* disembarked in Japan.

By the middle of 1946 the only Japanese in New Guinea, apart from a few stragglers, were some 550 charged with war crimes, and by the end of the year only 388 Australian troops were there.[9] From 30th October 1945 onwards a "provisional administration" had progressively taken over control of the territories, and on 24th June 1946, when it took charge in the Gazelle Peninsula, the military administration of New Guinea came to an end.

---

[9] Australian military courts tried 924 Japanese of whom 148 were sentenced to death and executed, and 496 were sentenced to imprisonment. The last 14 prisoners were released at the request of the Australian Government from Sugarno Prison, Tokyo, on 4th July 1957. For an outline of the war crimes trials see the article with that title in the *Australian Encyclopaedia* (1958), Vol 9. Appended to it is a bibliography.

CHAPTER 24

LOOKING BACK

IN this final volume of the army series it is appropriate briefly to survey the Pacific war from an Australian point of view and in the light of facts some of which could not have been set out in earlier volumes without anticipating events that were outside their period.

The initial Japanese offensive of December 1941 to March 1942 reached its objectives more swiftly than the Japanese had expected. The offensive had been carefully planned, the Japanese soon commanded the sea and the air, their leaders and men were resolute and experienced, and in every area their opponents were ill-prepared to resist them.

The Japanese tactics were much the same as those which Nimitz and MacArthur used on the return journey in 1944 and 1945: several lines of advance, leapfrog movements which usually were not too long for each landing to be backed up by land-based aircraft, support by carrier-borne aircraft whenever the distances demanded it, sealing off and by-passing of centres of stubborn resistance.

The Japanese in 1942 followed their initial successes with a period of delay at a time when they should have exploited boldly. Like the Germans in 1940 the Japanese had no plan for achieving the total defeat of their opponents but relied on attaining certain limited objectives and on the hope that their enemies would grow tired of fighting and accept a negotiated peace, advantageous to the hitherto-victorious aggressor. When the Japanese began to move forward again the Allies were readier to meet them: in the Coral Sea and off Midway the Japanese suffered their first naval setbacks, at Milne Bay one of their landings was defeated for the first time, and soon, in the Solomons and Papua, they and their opponents were locked together in what developed into campaigns of attrition in which, increasingly, the Japanese had the worst of it. The selfless devotion of the Japanese fighting men could not offset the inescapable facts that the Americans possessed a strong and expert navy and merchant marine and far faster means of augmenting both of them, and that, as soon as the Japanese lost command of the sea, their sea-girt conquests would be doomed.

Indeed, as soon as the Japanese ceased to dominate the sea and the sky above it, the loss of their new island empire was just as inevitable as the loss of the British, American and Dutch island empires off south-east Asia had been in the opening months of the war. And thenceforward the decisive struggle was the one between Nimitz's naval forces with their attendant infantry and the Japanese opposing them; the operations in the South-West Pacific and Burma became subordinate ones. In other circumstances it would have been a mistake to use more than mere holding forces in the two outlying areas, but the Allies were then so strong that they were able without risk to engage and wear down the enemy with superior land and air forces in Burma and the South-West Pacific also, without the Central Pacific forces being deprived of anything they needed.

The general shape of the strategy of each contestant in the Pacific war had been foreseen long before that war began and, indeed, had been forecast not only in the secret appreciations of the planning staffs but in books and periodicals that anybody might read. The likelihood that Japan would attack when the British fleets were elsewhere engaged and that Singapore would be taken by the Japanese from the landward side had been the subject of much public discussion. At least from the early 'thirties onwards the Americans had considered measures to defeat a surprise attack on the Hawaiian Islands.[1] And in 1940 Generalissimo Chiang Kai-shek was seeking from the American Government an air force manned by American volunteers with which to surprise and destroy the Japanese Navy in its bases—a Pearl Harbour in reverse.[2] Although some pre-war planning had pictured an all-out effort to hold the American colonial empire in the Philippines, responsible American officers had for years urged that the loss of that archipelago should be accepted, and had expressed the opinion that it would be two or three years after the outbreak of war before the American main fleet reached the Far East to fight the decisive battle.

In Australia when the Japanese war began the Ministry led by Mr Curtin had been in power only two months and few of its members had been in office before, but this inexperienced team soon proved that it contained some men of considerable drive and ability. The Ministers were disappointed to find that they were to have little say in the higher direction of the war against Japan. Despite this they not only accepted that decision but supported General MacArthur with undeviating loyalty, not only exerting political pressure in London and Washington on behalf of his command (as could be expected) but giving only qualified support to the Australian Commander-in-Chief, Blamey, when he differed with MacArthur. It is evident that this policy was adopted not merely as a matter of principle but because they had confidence in MacArthur and were greatly taken by his power of impressive and winning speech when in conference—a power which they found somewhat lacking in Blamey, although Blamey's expositions were always lucid and to the point.

Indeed in any consideration of the management of the Australian Army from 1942 to 1945 the temperament of Blamey must be reckoned with. From 1939 onwards in experience of staff and command problems he was seldom inferior and generally superior to his collaterals and seniors in the Middle East and the South-West Pacific. The clarity and wisdom of his appreciations of such problems and the logic and far-sightedness of his strategical thinking have been illustrated throughout this history. Yet

---

[1] See, for example, M. S. Watson, *Chief of Staff: Prewar Plans and Preparations* (1950), pp. 466-7, a volume in the official series *United States Army in World War II*.

[2] C. F. Romanus and R. Sunderland, *Stilwell's Mission to China* (1953), p. 9, in the U.S. official series.

on his head descended perhaps the strongest vituperation to which any military leader in that war was subjected by people on his own side, and at the end the Government terminated his appointment in a summary fashion.

Some of the reasons for Blamey's lack of popularity with several of the Ministers and part of the public can probably be discovered only by exploring traits in the Australian national character of those days; other reasons are easier to unearth. Throughout the war Blamey commanded an army whose senior appointments were shared between regular and citizen officers. In some places this created tensions and rivalry which adversely affected Blamey's reputation, through no fault of his own; also the ambiguous relationship between his headquarters and MacArthur's led to disagreements of which at least the Ministers were aware. A man of greater tact, however, could have managed these problems more smoothly. But Blamey was not a man of great tact.

When he was appointed to command the A.I.F. in 1939 he was under the shadow of charges made against him when he had been Commissioner of Police in Victoria. These charges had been investigated, with much publicity, and he was in the main exonerated but in the relatively small Australian community and one in which the front-line soldier was regarded with much respect but the general often with suspicion, it was not surprising that rumour should pursue him. If Blamey was to become a popular wartime leader it would have been necessary, from 1939 onwards, for a "public relations" campaign of some skill and persistence to be pursued, and for the man himself to cooperate by taking pains to impress on the politicians, the Press and the citizens that he was not only an efficient commander but an admirable and picturesque person. This Blamey was evidently quite unable to do; indeed some trait in his make-up—it may partly have been a distaste for humbug—led him too often to speak or act with harsh directness. Compromise is one of the essential devices of government, but compromise was not congenial to Blamey.

Some of the origins of an Australian prejudice against generals were shrewdly traced in a paper by A. N. Kemsley, one of Blamey's advisers: the widespread mistrust in Australia of a large organisation—and the army was now the biggest in the land, being bigger even than the "B.H.P." (the steel-manufacturing giant) or "the railways"; the fact that the army contained a proportion of unwilling conscripts whereas the airmen and seamen were volunteers; the awareness that if any force was to be employed in support of the civil power within the national borders it would probably be the army; the widespread conviction in the minds of many people that they could teach the generals how to do their jobs, whereas in the navy and air force there seemed to be technical mysteries baffling to the layman.

Problems of cooperation between allied armies were encountered by Australians in the Middle East, Malaya and the South-West Pacific. Discussion of them necessarily crops up in each volume of this series. It seems evident that the difficulties that arose could have been foreseen and were not sufficiently discussed between the wars either in Britain or the Dominions—or the United States. However, if answers are wanted to the special problems likely to be faced by the smaller partners in coalition wars it is the business of the smaller partners to find them, because the larger partners are unlikely to be interested until too late.

The Australian Ministers and their senior military advisers seldom influenced Allied strategy and then usually in a negative way, as when they obtained the diversion of the 7th Division from Burma to Australia, which was wise; and the withdrawal of the 9th Division first from Tobruk and then from the Middle East, which can now be seen to have been not strictly necessary. As it turned out the Australian Government was concerned rather with providing—or withholding—forces than with deciding how they were to be employed in the field.

In the matter of providing forces the Ministers and some of their advisers took an unduly long time to realise the basic principle that a nation which desires to possess effective military strength when it is most needed must produce its own military equipment. If it decides to buy or borrow its armaments from another nation it may find that such equipment is not available when most wanted. A nation which is dependent on another nation for basic military equipment is likely to find itself militarily a satellite of that country.

In the first two years of the war of 1939-45 the Australian Government was unwilling to make a maximum military effort on the scale attained in 1916-19 but sought to wage a "war of limited liability"—as some British planners had hoped to do until the setbacks of 1940. The dimensions of the Australian expeditionary forces seem to have been decided more by the rate at which citizens volunteered for service overseas than by the will of the Government, and on two occasions the Government virtually stopped the flow of volunteers into the A.I.F. The threat from Japan produced a change of mood, and the Government then did not hesitate to take stern decisions towards mobilising the full strength of the nation; and for a time it made Australian voices speak rather louder than before in London and Washington. The measures taken at home were perhaps too drastic. Australia in 1942 expanded the army to a size that she was unable to maintain after an exacting campaign in Papua even for a year, and introduced austerities that soon could be seen to be unnecessarily harsh.

For part of the last year of war the Australian Army in the field was larger in proportion to population than that of any of the Allies, except perhaps Russia. The Government's motives in maintaining the national effort at so high a level appear to have been a wish that Australia should pull her full weight, and an ambition to gain international esteem and a position of influence in the peace. It is an illusion to which small nations are prone that the policies of foreign allies, as distinct from those with whom patriotic sentiments are shared, are influenced by such emotions as gratitude for past support.

In the war of 1939-45 as in the war of 1914-18 the Australian Army soon became a force of the highest quality. Armies are not created in a social vacuum but derive their characteristics from the community from which they spring. Thus it was advantageous that the Australian community of 1939 was as homogeneous as that of any of the "new countries". The number of foreign nationals whose loyalties in war might be in conflict with those of the Australians and British-born in Australia was small. At the census of 1933 the two largest alien groups in a total population of 6,629,839 were the Italian (17,658) and Chinese (7,792). Ninety-seven per cent of the people had been born in Australia or the British Isles.

Within this community was an honoured tradition of military efficiency handed down by the men who had fought in the war of 1914-18. "The best fighting force in the fourth year of war was, by general recognition, the Australian Corps," wrote a British military critic.[3] "The A.I.F., like all other armies from the British dominions, was found to be among the most effective military forces in the war," wrote its Australian historian.[4] Anzac Day had become the national day that drew greater throngs than any other observed in Australia.

Restless enterprise and comradeship, both high military virtues, were qualities with which the Australian soldier was richly endowed. His equalitarian outlook lent itself to the development of a stronger team spirit and a more efficient sort of discipline than is likely to be achieved in armies in which there are strict social barriers and a resultant insistence on unthinking obedience.

In the early years of the war the fighting part of the Australian Army was made up entirely of volunteers and in the later years mainly so. The fact that there was always so strong a flow of volunteers was largely a result of factors mentioned above: the homogeneous community, the cherished military tradition and the restless national temperament. A volunteer force, given adequate leadership, is likely to have a stronger pride and to display more enthusiasm, enterprise and fortitude than one compulsorily enlisted.

The gradual and unhurried growth of the Second A.I.F., made possible by Australia's remoteness from the main battlefields, helped the force to maintain specially high standards. The officers of the divisions of volunteers formed in the first two years of war were selected from the large number available in the regular and citizen forces. Those chosen earliest were the first to gain valuable experience and, as has been shown, they ultimately provided most of the senior leaders of the larger army that fought against the Japanese. Wherever they fought in the first two years and a half the Australian divisions, like those of the other Dominions, were formations which, as a result of various processes of selection, were inevitably of higher quality than the Australian Army as a whole, whereas

---

[3] B. H. Liddell Hart, *Why Don't We Learn From History* (1944), p. 24.
[4] C. E. W. Bean, *Official History of Australia in the War of 1914-1918*, Vol VI, p. 1078.

the armies of their United Kingdom and Indian allies—and later their American allies—had been rapidly expanded, with a consequent dilution of the experienced soldiers and the volunteers.

In general the leaders chosen for the volunteer formations stood the test. Relatively few were relieved of their appointments; this fact combined with the steady reduction in the size of the army after 1942 meant that at senior levels promotion was far slower than in the First A.I.F., or in the British and Canadian Armies in the Second World War. In the British Army, for example, unit commanders of 1940 were commanding corps in 1942; in the Canadian Army an officer who had been a captain when war broke out was a corps commander in 1944. In Australia the reduction of the army from 1943 onwards produced a surplus of capable and tested field commanders, and some military leaders of great capacity were returned to civil life while the war was still being fought.

The Australian military contribution to the defeat of Germany, Italy and Japan was a big one in the years 1941, 1942 and 1943. In the Middle East in 1941 a series of important operations would scarcely have been possible had it not been for the presence there of the Australian corps of three divisions, and in 1942 the 9th Division played a vital part at El Alamein. In 1942, 1943 and early 1944 Australian troops first halted the Japanese and then drove them out of most of the mainland of Australian New Guinea, inflicting on them their biggest reverses on land up to that time. Thereafter the Australian Army was not needed for any major role, but was arduously employed in the series of minor campaigns which it has been the task of this volume to describe. Always a realist and therefore the more keenly aware of the probably doubtful value of the tasks to which he had been relegated, nevertheless the battlewise Australian soldier fought on to the end with much the same devotion and skill that he had shown in the decisive battles of earlier years.

APPENDIX 1

COMMAND PROBLEMS, S.W.P.A. 1942-1945

In March 1942 the Australian Government agreed eagerly to President Roosevelt's suggestion that it might nominate General MacArthur as Supreme Commander of all Allied forces in the South-West Pacific Area. The Prime Minister, Mr Curtin, was disappointed, however, to learn, on 3rd April, that his Government was to have no share in deciding the policies and plans which the new commander would be instructed to carry out: the Combined Chiefs of Staff—the British and American Chiefs—were to control the "grand strategic policy" of the S.W.P.A. as of other areas; the Joint Chiefs of Staff—the American Chiefs—were to control "operational strategy" in the S.W.P.A. The British half of the Combined Chiefs had little direct interest in the new S.W.P.A. (as distinct from the S.W.P.A. that General Wavell had commanded) and, in practice, MacArthur's instructions were formulated by the American Joint Chiefs of Staff at Washington.

The appointment of General MacArthur to the new command was politically desirable. If he had been left at Corregidor in Manila Bay he would soon have had to surrender to the Japanese, as his opposite number, General Percival, had had to do in Malaya; and the surrender of so senior a soldier—a former Chief of Staff of the United States Army—would have been a heavy blow to American prestige. (In December the American leaders had insisted that Wavell be appointed to the supreme command in the Far East partly so that an American should not be responsible for the impending disasters.[1]) If MacArthur had been ordered to escape from the Philippines and thence to go not to Australia but to the United States the blow to national prestige would also have been severe. Also MacArthur was not entirely *persona grata* with the President, the Chief of Staff (General Marshall), or with the Chief of Naval Operations (Admiral King),[2] and his seniority and autocratic disposition were likely to make him a difficult subordinate.

In fact, differences of opinion between Marshall and MacArthur soon appeared. On 18th March, the day after MacArthur's arrival in Australia, Marshall informed him that, as Supreme Commander, he would be ineligible to command directly any national force. General George H. Brett, an American, would command the Allied air forces; Vice-Admiral Herbert F. Leary, an American, the naval forces; and an Australian the ground forces—at that time by far the strongest component of the Allied forces south of the Indies. MacArthur, on 21st March, proposed, however, to appoint an American to the separate command of the American ground forces; under this arrangement there would have been both an

---

[1] R. E. Sherwood, *The White House Papers of Harry L. Hopkins*, Vol I (1948), p. 470.
[2] H. L. Stimson and McG. Bundy, *On Active Service in Peace and War* (English edn. 1949), pp. 200-5 and 281.

Australian and an American army commander under MacArthur's direct command. Marshall objected, however, pointing out that, the greater part of the land forces being Australian, the combined land forces should be under an Australian "in accordance with the policy developed for combined commands".[3] MacArthur agreed, but arranged that the two land forces should have separate "service" organisations, the American one being directly responsible to him.

It was at this stage that, on 30th March, the Joint Chiefs issued their directive to the Supreme Commander, S.W.P.A.[4] The Australian Government delayed its approval until it had established its right to control the movement of its troops outside Australian territory and the rights of its commanders to communicate with their own government.

On 18th April MacArthur assumed command—although, with Australian support, he had already, since his arrival, been acting as Supreme Commander. The same day General Blamey, who, on 27th March, had been appointed Commander-in-Chief, Australian Military Forces, became also Commander, Allied Land Forces. Admiral Leary became Commander, Allied Naval Forces; General Brett, Commander, Allied Air Forces. United States Army Forces in Australia, under Major-General Julian F. Barnes, was made responsible for administration and supply of American ground and air forces. The Australian Government assigned to MacArthur all field formations of the Australian Army,[5] all naval ships then under Admiral Leary's command, and all operational units of the air force.

A new difference of opinion now arose between Marshall and MacArthur, again without the Australian Government being aware of it. On 9th April Marshall had proposed to MacArthur that, as with General Wavell's Allied staff in Java, all the participating nations should be represented on MacArthur's staff, particularly as his chief of staff and his naval and air commanders would be Americans. The President, he added, wished Dutch and, particularly, Australian officers to be appointed to "a number of the higher positions". However, on 19th April MacArthur announced a staff on which every senior post was occupied by an American; eight of the heads of sections had served on his staff in the Philippines and had escaped from Corregidor with him and three had been on the staff of Brett's "United States Army Forces in Australia". When Marshall questioned this policy MacArthur said that his reasons were that there were no qualified Dutch officers and that the Australians did not have enough staff officers to meet the needs of their rapidly expanding army. "There is no prospect," he told Marshall on 15th June, "of obtaining

---

[3] S. Milner, *Victory in Papua* (1957), p. 19, a volume in the official series *United States Army in World War II*. The succeeding account of exchanges between Marshall and MacArthur in March and April 1942 is based on documents quoted by Milner.

[4] MacArthur chose to describe himself as "Commander-in-Chief, S.W.P.A.", and this title was accepted.

[5] These were First Army, Second Army (including the 41st American Division), III Corps, 6th Division (later Northern Territory Force), New Guinea Force.

qualified senior staff officers from the Australians."⁶ There were in fact senior Australian officers qualified both by staff college training and recent experience of active service who could have been spared to General Headquarters.⁷ MacArthur's statement is indicative either of a wish to avoid forming an Allied Staff or of lack of knowledge of the structure, standards and experience of the Australian Army, possibly of both. A few Australians of middle and junior rank were, however, appointed to G.H.Q., S.W.P.A., and several specialist branches were staffed mainly by Australians.

At the next level, the staff of Allied Land Forces, when the appointments were announced, turned out to be just as Australian as that of G.H.Q. was American. General Sturdee, who had been Chief of the General Staff in Australia since 1940, became, in effect, the Chief of the Staff of "L.H.Q."; the big change at Australian Army Headquarters—now L.H.Q.—was the replacement of a number of senior officers who had not been on overseas service in that war by their opposite numbers from A.I.F. Headquarters just returned from Egypt. Concerning his efforts at this time to form an Allied army staff Blamey wrote, in February 1945:

My requests for American officers to establish a joint staff were met with a face-saving acceptance that was completely ineffective.⁸

General Brett, the Allied Air Force commander, on the other hand organised a joint Allied air staff. His chief of staff was an Australian, the deputy chief and senior air staff officer were Americans; of the nine directors and assistant directors five were Australians and four Americans.

In the new military organisation General Blamey wore two hats just as he had done in the Middle East, when he had been Deputy Commander-in-Chief first under General Wavell and then General Auchinleck, and at the same time had been commander of the A.I.F., with the right, indeed the duty, of direct communication with both the Prime Minister and the Minister for the Army at home. He was now commander of the land forces of MacArthur who received his orders from Washington, and at the same time he was the Commander-in-Chief of the Australian Military Forces and, as such, the principal military adviser of the Australian Government.⁹

In April the important principle was established that Blamey would have direct access to the Minister for Defence (who was the Prime

---

⁶ There is no record of MacArthur having asked for senior Australian staff officers. Indeed Lieut-General Eichelberger wrote later: "I had been told before leaving Washington that General MacArthur had asked for key American officers to assist the Australians with their staff work. The Australians didn't think they needed much help from anyone. Many of the commanders I met had already been in combat with the British in North Africa, and, though they were usually too polite to say so, considered the Americans to be—at best—inexperienced theorists." (*Our Jungle Road to Tokyo*, 1950, p. 7.)

⁷ The reorganisation and slight expansion of the Australian Army in the first four months of 1942 led to promotion to the next higher grade for the great majority of staff officers who had returned from the Middle East, and for a smaller proportion of officers with staff training and experience in Australia.

⁸ Letter, Blamey to F. G. Shedden, 19th February 1945.

⁹ In the air forces there was a different allocation of responsibility. All operational units having been placed under Brett's command, the Chief of the Air Staff was made responsible only for "all matters associated with RAAF personnel, provision and maintenance of aircraft, supply and equipment, works and building and training".

Minister). In the course of a letter from Curtin to Blamey dated 25th April in which he stated this principle, Curtin wrote:

My functions as Minister for Defence relate to questions of higher Policy and important subjects, such as the strength and organisation of the Forces and appointments to higher posts, which will be submitted to War Cabinet through me. I am also the link between the Government and Commander-in-Chief, and you, as adviser to the Government on Australian Army Policy, also have direct access to me.

I do not propose at this stage to attempt to define my functions as Minister for Defence in detail in respect of the field of general administration. . . . The Service Ministers are to be responsible for the administration of Policy as laid down by War Cabinet. In the initial stages there will be . . . questions of organisation and principle which should rightly be submitted to me as Minister for Defence, or which may affect the duties and responsibilities of non-Service Ministers and of which I, as Prime Minister, should be aware.

It is therefore my desire, in questions of general administration, that the procedure should be that proposals should first be discussed with the Minister for the Army or between your officers and those of the Army Secretariat. Important questions on which agreement is reached and of which I should be aware as Minister for Defence, should be reported to me or my Department. Where agreement cannot be reached or it is desired to submit the matter for decision or confirmation of a provisional conclusion, a full statement should be forwarded to me. In short, on any administrative questions, I wish to act more in a judicial capacity than an executive one.

Though I have outlined the foregoing procedure relating to questions of administration, I wish it to be clearly understood, nevertheless, that as Minister for Defence I am most directly interested in the efficiency of the whole Army organisation, as well as Policy and associated questions, which are reserved to myself.

This system was likely to create difficulty, particularly between the secretariats concerned, because of the impossibility of defining precisely the subjects on which the Commander-in-Chief should approach the Prime Minister directly. On 12th August 1942 an effort was made to give more precise definition to the arrangement. Curtin wrote to Forde and Blamey:

The Commander-in-Chief A.M.F., by virtue of his special position, has direct access to the Minister for Defence and, in special cases, he may make written submissions direct to the Minister for Defence, at the same time forwarding a copy direct to the Minister for the Army for information. This method is to be used only in exceptional circumstances. In all other cases, the written submissions of the Commander-in-Chief will be transmitted through the Minister for the Army, who will forward them with any covering comments he may wish to make.

For the first three months of its existence G.H.Q. was situated in Melbourne, near L.H.Q. On 20th July G.H.Q. moved forward to Brisbane. Thereupon Blamey formed an "Advanced L.H.Q.", under his Deputy Chief of the General Staff, and it moved to Brisbane to keep in touch.

Despite Marshall's protests MacArthur had achieved the kind of organisation he wished except in one item: he had not achieved a separate command for his American as distinct from his Australian troops.

There being two American divisions in Australia by May 1942, Marshall decided to send out an American corps commander and staff. The VII Corps under Major-General Richardson was first chosen, but Richardson objected to serving under Australian command, and the appointment was given to Lieut-General Eichelberger, of I Corps (which had just before been warned that it was to take part in the North African landings). In February 1943, on the heels of this corps headquarters, the headquarters of the Sixth American Army, under Lieut-General Krueger, was sent to Australia, although there were then only three American divisions in the area. Blamey later wrote that "at no stage" was he given "any information as to the proposals [for the arrival of American troops and of the Sixth Army] or the development of the organisation". Blamey considered that at this stage MacArthur "took upon himself the functions of Commander, Allied Land Forces" and his own functions were limited to command of the Australian Military Forces. This position was arrived at, beyond doubt, on 26th February 1943, when, with the object of placing the Sixth Army, and thus the American corps and divisions, directly under the command of G.H.Q., the Sixth Army was named "Alamo Force" and given the status of a "task force" under MacArthur's direct command.[1] For this purpose MacArthur reconstituted "United States Army Forces in the Far East" (U.S.A.F.F.E.), his command when in the Philippines, with himself as its commander, and orders went directly from U.S.A.F.F.E. to the American formations.

Meanwhile the organisation of command within L.H.Q. had become more complex. With the development of the Japanese offensive and the Allied counter-offensive in New Guinea, New Guinea Force, from being less than a divisional command, became, in effect, an army. The titles and times of appointment of the senior commanders in New Guinea are shown in the following table:

Maj-Gen B. M. Morris:	19.5.41 to 31.7.42 (G.O.C. 8th Military District, then New Guinea Force)
Lt-Gen S. F. Rowell:	1.8.42 to 30.9.42 (G.O.C. I Corps)
Lt-Gen E. F. Herring:	1.10.42 to 29.1.43 (G.O.C. I Corps and N.G.F.)
Lt-Gen Sir Iven Mackay:	30.1.43 to 21.5.43 (Temporary G.O.C. N.G.F. and I Corps)
Lt-Gen E. F. Herring:	23.5.43 to 26.8.43 (G.O.C. N.G.F. and I Corps)
Lt-Gen Sir Iven Mackay:	28.8.43 to 19.1.44 (Temporary G.O.C. N.G.F.)
Lt-Gen Sir Leslie Morshead:	21.1.44 to 5.5.44 (G.O.C. N.G.F.)
Lt-Gen S. G. Savige:	6.5.44 to 1.10.44 (G.O.C. N.G.F.)
Lt-Gen V. A. H. Sturdee:	2.10.44 to 30.11.45 (G.O.C. First Army)

Although Major-General C. A. Clowes was appointed to command New Guinea Force on 1st August 1942, New Guinea Force at that stage was a formation junior to I Corps. It seems, according to General Herring's 1942 posting ("G.O.C. I Corps and N.G.F.") that New Guinea Force became the senior formation between this and General Mackay's January 1943 posting ("G.O.C. N.G.F. and I Corps").

From time to time in the period from September 1942 onwards Blamey maintained his own advanced headquarters in New Guinea, and on 6th November 1942 MacArthur established an Advanced G.H.Q. at Port

---
[1] See C. A. Willoughby and J. Chamberlain, *MacArthur: 1941-1951* (1954), p. 124, and W. Krueger, *From Down Under to Nippon* (1953), p. 10. Krueger considered that this arrangement created "a great many perplexing difficulties".

Moresby. By the end of November Port Moresby housed a Supreme Commander with, close by, a Commander Allied Land Forces, and over the mountains a corps commander who controlled only about a division of weary and depleted units.

When recommending changes in appointments of senior commanders consequent upon the removal of General Rowell from command in New Guinea, Blamey recommended to Curtin and MacArthur that Eichelberger be placed in command of II Australian Corps with a mixed American and Australian staff. And in fact Eichelberger for a time commanded the troops in the forward area in Papua with Major-General Berryman as his chief of staff.

Blamey's awareness of the problem created by his possession of responsibilities both at home and in the field had been illustrated by a recommendation which he made on 24th September 1942 (after the Prime Minister had instructed him to take over command in New Guinea) that the Chief of the General Staff, Lieut-General Northcott, be appointed also Deputy Commander-in-Chief. He contended that it was essential that the Chief of the General Staff should be given executive authority to ensure that the requirements of the forces in New Guinea should be "fully coordinated and supplied". Blamey pointed out that it was most undesirable that an additional officer should be appointed Deputy; from his experience as Deputy Commander-in-Chief in the Middle East he was convinced that such an appointment was not effective unless it was held by the principal staff officer.

The senior staff officer at Advanced L.H.Q. for most of this and the succeeding period was General Berryman, who was Deputy Chief of the General Staff from September 1942 to January 1944—though for part of that time he acted in other posts—and Chief of Staff of Advanced L.H.Q. from July 1944 to December 1945. During some of the time when General Mackay was commanding New Guinea Force Berryman filled the appointment of senior staff officer of New Guinea Force. Thus, from the time when G.H.Q. departed from Melbourne in July 1942, Blamey was served by two widely-separated headquarters staffs and two chiefs of staff: General Northcott in Melbourne,[2] and, as a rule, General Berryman farther forward. In September 1944, when MacArthur's headquarters moved to Hollandia, Advanced L.H.Q. threw off a small Forward Echelon, under Berryman, which established itself near G.H.Q. when it moved first to Hollandia and later to Manila. In general these two headquarters corresponded with Blamey's two roles as Commander-in-Chief of the Australian Army, which was actual, and Commander, Allied Land Forces, which was now only nominal except where Australian forces were concerned. The fact that MacArthur had taken over the role of Commander, Allied Land Forces, was underlined from December 1943 onwards when "Alamo Force" and later the Sixth American Army or the Eighth American Army, operating directly under G.H.Q., invaded New Britain and

---

[2] Northcott was Chief of the General Staff, A.M.F., and also Chief of Staff, L.H.Q.

the Admiralties, and advanced in stages along the New Guinea coast and through the Philippines.

After March 1944 the Australian forces in New Guinea, having completed their main tasks and being in need of rest, were greatly reduced. As mentioned, in July MacArthur issued preliminary orders to Blamey to relieve the American divisions then manning perimeters round bases on Bougainville and New Britain and at Aitape. When these reliefs had been completed I Australian Corps (7th and 9th Divisions) remained available for employment outside New Guinea.

Blamey refused to agree to a plan whereby each of these divisions should be employed separately in the Philippines under American corps commanders, one in November 1944 and the other in January 1945. At length, after much discussion and many changes of plan, it was decided that I Australian Corps should operate as a corps advancing westward through Borneo, and later invade Java.

In the last quarter of 1944, when various plans for employing I Corps in the Philippines were being discussed, it had been proposed to place the corps under the command of the Eighth American Army. In February 1945, after Blamey had been informed of the decision to use the corps in Borneo, it was again proposed to place the corps under the Eighth Army. Blamey protested. Thereupon, on 17th February General Chamberlin, the head of MacArthur's operations branch, informed General Berryman that in Borneo the Australian corps would be under the direct command of G.H.Q. In the course of a "frank discussion", in which Berryman pointed out reasons why Advanced L.H.Q. should continue to command I Corps just as it commanded other parts of the Australian Army, Chamberlin said

> that the question was beyond his level and that he could only act on his orders and that he thought General MacArthur would insist on dealing with one commander only and that one of the reasons for changing New Guinea Force to First Australian Army was to enable G.H.Q. to deal direct with First Australian Army.[3]

At this stage First Australian Army had taken over command of the four Australian divisions in New Guinea and the Solomons, and thus G.H.Q. proposed to remove Blamey, still nominally Commander Allied Land Forces, from the chain of command of all Australian formations fighting outside Australia. Thereupon, on 19th February, Blamey wrote a long letter to the Secretary of the Department of Defence, Sir Frederick Shedden, for the information of the Prime Minister, setting out the stages by which what he described as "the insinuation of American control and the elimination of Australian control" of Australian forces had been achieved and urging that

> the matter should be faced quite squarely, if the Australian Government and the Australian Higher Command are not to become ciphers in the control of the Australian Military Forces.

---

[3] Telegram, Berryman to Blamey, 17th February 1945.

Mr Curtin, on 27th February, wrote to MacArthur concerning, among other things, this command problem. He said:

> It was laid down in the 1914-18 war that the Australian forces serving outside Australia should be organised into and operate as a homogeneous formation appropriate to their strength, and that they should be commanded by an Australian Officer. This course was followed in the Middle East in the present war. When the South-West Pacific Area was established . . . General Blamey was appointed Commander of the Allied Land Forces which provided for the observance of the principle in respect of the command of the Australian Army.

Curtin asked for information about the operational control of I Corps and the Australian forces in New Guinea and about "the manner in which it is proposed to ensure the observance of the basic principle I have mentioned". In the course of his reply MacArthur wrote, on 5th March:

> With reference to the command organisation, we have followed a fixed pattern since the Lae operation. The Commander-in-Chief exercises personal and direct command of assault forces coordinating the action of three principal subordinates:
> (a) Naval forces under the Commander, Allied Naval Forces.
> (b) Air forces under the Commander, Allied Air Forces.
> (c) Ground forces under a Task Force Commander whose organisation is specifically prescribed according to the operation to be undertaken. These forces may vary from a Regimental Combat Team or Brigade Group to an Army. . . . In the forthcoming operation in which assault forces will include Australian troops it is contemplated that the Commander would be an Australian Officer. While General Morshead has been proposed and is entirely acceptable, I am prepared to accept another officer if designated by the Australian authorities. . . . It is considered to be impossible, however, from an operational viewpoint, for the officer so designated to be concerned with command of Australian troops in New Guinea and Australia. It is essential that the Task Force Commander remain in the field with his troops and that he have no other duties of any kind. Any other course of action would unquestionably jeopardize the success of the operation and impose a risk that could not be accepted.

No reference was made to the fact that Blamey was nominally the Commander, Allied Land Forces. Blamey met MacArthur on Leyte on 18th March and between them they arranged the compromise that, although I Corps would operate directly under MacArthur's command, "the necessary administrative functions would be performed by Advanced L.H.Q. from Morotai"; and copies of letters from G.H.Q. to I Corps were to be sent to the Forward Echelon of L.H.Q.

As for First Army, although G.H.Q. had asserted a right to exercise direct command over it, in fact it did not do so, and, indeed, implied criticism of some of the policies it followed.

These ambiguous command arrangements worked reasonably well in practice despite the disagreements on matters of principle revealed in the foregoing recapitulation. Each national army was as a rule given a separate area and this had the useful effect of avoiding the friction that may be produced when forces with different organisations, supply systems, tactical doctrines, and technical vocabularies are mingled. In effect Blamey controlled the Australian military operations in New Guinea throughout, and, in 1942 and most of 1943, the operations of all Allied land forces in the field. After late 1943 and until May 1945 MacArthur's headquarters was somewhat out of touch with the Australian Army (which still comprised about one-third of its strength) and the greater part of that army, consigned mostly to a rearward role, was seriously starved of equipment. MacArthur's staff argued, by implication, that the Australian Army in New Guinea had only a garrison role and needed only a minimum of ships and heavy equipment.

It remains to consider whether the command structure in the S.W.P.A. was faulty and, if it was, in what particulars. It differed radically from those in other theatres of war. Were those differences inevitable? Were they desirable? They produced considerable disagreement and complaint. Was this unavoidable?

In retrospect it seems evident that, from the point of view of military efficiency and smooth cooperation between allies, Roosevelt and Marshall were right when they instructed MacArthur to form a truly Allied staff and MacArthur was wrong to evade this instruction. In other theatres such staffs were formed and they worked smoothly. The existence of a joint staff is essential if the point of view of each national component is to be fairly represented and its needs fairly satisfied. For instance, in 1944 and 1945 when the two armies were operating in widely-separated areas the American Army was generously supplied with equipment and, in particular, ships, while, as mentioned, the First Australian Army was left gravely short of essentials. Under a joint staff this should not happen.

> The Supreme Command (wrote Blamey) was naturally more interested in providing the requirements of the whole of the American forces, and was able to bring great pressure to bear on the various Australian authorities. . . . The Australian Army . . . had to run the gauntlet of many and devious channels, and was always behind the Americans, and in several important matters obtained what it could from the resources of its own country after the Americans had had the pick of the market.

The metaphors were mixed, but the meaning clear.

In addition the existence of a joint staff helps to ensure that the talent and experience possessed by each component is made use of. In 1942 Australians possessed wide tactical and administrative experience gained in recent campaigns against the armies of four nations, and this could have helped at the G.H.Q. level. A proper corollary to a joint G.H.Q. staff would have been the formation, at least for the early phase of the war, of a joint L.H.Q. staff, particularly since one American division was arriving in Australia when L.H.Q. was formed, another was due to arrive in a few weeks, and there was a prospect of larger American forces eventually arriving.

The appointment of an Australian commander of all Allied land forces was appropriate in 1942 and 1943 when Australian formations did nearly all the fighting in the S.W.P.A. but it need not follow that the arrangement should have remained unaltered in the second phase, when American forces took over the advance and operated in areas far from New Guinea, yet substantial forces—inevitably Australian—were needed to cope with

Japanese armies still in New Guinea. At that stage it might have been wise to change over to a similar organisation to that employed in Europe in 1944 when General Eisenhower, as Supreme Commander, directly controlled several Army Groups or Armies. Thus at a suitable time—which would have been some time early in 1944—MacArthur might have requested that, in the changed circumstances, he should exercise direct control of three land forces: the Australian Army Group under Blamey and the Sixth and Eighth American Armies. Under such an organisation it would, incidentally, have been appropriate and efficient for the I Australian Corps in Borneo—a relatively-isolated area—to have operated under the Australian Army Group commander.

It seems unlikely that such a proposal for reorganisation, frankly placed before the Joint Chiefs and the participating governments in 1944, would have been rejected. As it was, an organisation more or less on these lines was arrived at by G.H.Q., S.W.P.A. by stealth and by the employment of subterfuges that were undignified, and at times absurd (as when the Sixth Army was renamed "Alamo Force" without L.H.Q., which this ambiguity was intended to outwit, being aware of the purpose of it).[5]

If G.H.Q. had had its way the Australian Commander-in-Chief would have been removed from the chain of command in the field and made responsible merely for the provision of two "task forces"—First Army and I Corps—serving directly under G.H.Q. Nothing substantial would have been gained by this arrangement and much would have been lost: notably the existence of a single commander who could advise the Australian Government on all the problems of its army and be answerable to that Government for the manner in which it was employed both at home and in the field.

---

[5] The reasons, in the words of General Willoughby, senior Intelligence Officer on GHQ, were "obviously bound up with international protocol: special task forces could undertake specific missions without complex inter-Allied command adjustments". (Willoughby and Chamberlain, p. 124.) Willoughby mentioned that Krueger was not told the reason for the change, but Krueger says that he guessed it.

APPENDIX 2

TOO MANY GENERALS?

Throughout the series to which this volume belongs there has been intermittent reference to the manpower problem in relation to the army. The discussion of this problem indeed forms a main theme of the story of the relations of the Government and the army during the last four years of the war. Side by side with it for two years ran another theme, a lesser one, although at times it was the subject of equally long communications. In retrospect it can be seen that the discussion of this second problem did not materially affect the war effort one way or the other, and, whatever its outcome, would not have done so. And yet, because of the manner in which character and prejudice—and some important principles—were revealed, it seems worth while to trace the course of this discussion, if only as an appendix to the main story.

A paragraph from a letter from the Minister for the Army, Mr Forde, to the Commander-in-Chief, General Blamey, on 5th August 1943 will serve as a starting point for the chronicle:

> From time to time, representations have been made to me by Ministers and Parliamentary representatives that Headquarters services which are being maintained are out of proportion to Army Organisation, with the result that senior officers who are allotted to these organisations are not fully employed, nor are they able to give efficient service in keeping with their qualifications.

The letter was written just a month before the opening on 4th September of the Australian offensive in New Guinea—the largest yet undertaken against the Japanese in this theatre. This may help to excuse the omission which made it possible for Forde on 30th October to complain that he had received no reply. He noted that an organisation diagram submitted some time before showed that the First Army, whose headquarters were in Queensland, comprised formations with a total strength of some 17,000 plus those in "three relatively minor formations"; the Second Army, with headquarters in New South Wales, possessed some 29,000 men and women. The question had arisen of replacing General Mackay as commander of the Second Army. Before the vacancy was filled Forde wished to have a comprehensive statement of the duties of these army headquarters.

This letter crossed one from Blamey recommending the appointment of General Morshead in General Mackay's place. On the 12th November Forde wrote to Blamey that the Prime Minister considered that "as the bulk of the field force is located in New Guinea and is provided with appropriate Commanders and Staffs, it is evident that the maintenance of the present Commands and Staffs established in Australia can only be justified by very strong reasons". He did not think that any further promotions to General should be made until the future organisation of the army was clear.

On the face of it the maintenance in November 1943 of two army headquarters, a Force headquarters, and three corps headquarters to control eight divisions or their equivalent, several detached forces of moderate size, and the training organisations, all spread over an area about 2,400 miles from east to west and 2,400 from north to south was a modest and economical provision; but, for reasons explored below, Australians in those days were prompt to conclude that in any army organisation there were too many generals.

At this stage Blamey had been disregarding the Minister's letters on this topic for three months. He now changed his policy and on 17th November wrote the first of what eventually became a series of characteristically lucid and emphatic statements on the principles of higher command and their particular application in Australia. He recalled the establishment at the outbreak of war of two higher command headquarters, one in New South Wales and one in Victoria, and of local commands in other States; the later separation of the base organisations from the higher-command organisations; the establishment to meet the needs of the Japanese war of a "Commander, Home Forces", of the First and Second Armies, and necessary corps headquarters; his own appointment to command Allied Land Forces. He recalled the movement forward of General MacArthur's headquarters and the establishment of a small advanced headquarters of L.H.Q. in New Guinea; the forward movement of the corps headquarters in New Guinea, and the establishment of New Guinea Force headquarters.[1] The First and Second Army headquarters would remain, however, "an essential part of the basic organisation either in the form of an Army Headquarters or a Command Headquarters during the whole period of mobilisation in Australia, and also as part of the post-war organisation". A statement of the number of troops under command at a particular time did not necessarily convey a correct appreciation of the two armies' responsibilities. The First Army controlled the units that were round Atherton under a corps headquarters, and the defence of Queensland including the Torres Strait islands, Merauke and the Gulf country. The Second Army commanded the 1st Division, miscellaneous non-divisional units, the defensive organisation of New South Wales and Victoria, and the bulk of the training organisations in Australia; its staff had been reduced to one only slightly greater than that of a corps headquarters.

A secondary consideration was that the retention of the army headquarters enabled the relief of higher commanders and staffs in New Guinea.[2] Blamey added:

> It would in my opinion be quite contrary to the principles of organisation and sound administration to reduce the higher Army organisation. . . . The most important element in the whole Army organisation is probably the headquarters of formations, etc. The failure to recognise this in the latter part of 1941 in the Middle East was

---

[1] Here Blamey somewhat over-simplified the history of NGF headquarters.
[2] Mackay of Second Army had twice relieved in New Guinea; on the other hand Lavarack had not been called forward from First Army in this way.

a prime cause of the failure of the operations against Rommel. Headquarters cannot be successfully improvised, as was attempted by the British command on that occasion. They must be trained and organised.

Forde, writing on 18th December, was "still not satisfied", asked for a chart and statistics of the formations, and noted that a report by the United States Chief of Staff stated that on 30th June 1943 there was one general to every 6,460 troops in the American Army whereas it had been stated to him that the number of generals in the Australian Army was excessive and would not stand comparison with the British and United States figures.

It must be assumed that the Minister was not unearthing these arguments and facts and figures and suppositions single-handed, but that this correspondence was evidence of a critical attitude towards Blamey within the Army Secretariat. If it was the Secretariat that advised Forde to seek comparisons between the ratio of generals to men of other ranks in the Australian, British and American Armies it advised him ill, because Blamey was able to point out that the ratios were:

	To Males	To Males and Females
British Army	1 : 8,333	1 : 9,090
United States Army	1 : 6,460	—
Australian Army	1 : 14,953	1 : 15,741

Directing his remarks not at the Minister but at his informants, Blamey wrote: "It is obvious from the above figures that your information is supplied from a thoroughly uninformed and unreliable source," which, in the circumstances, was fair comment.

Blamey then grasped the opportunity presented to him by the Minister and his informants of pointing to the relatively low pay of Australian senior officers. He illustrated this with the following table, showing daily rates of pay:

	Australian	British	United States (on duty overseas)
Lieut-General	89/3	174/9	193/6
Major-General	75/9	144/3	184/11

The figures were in Australian currency and were for an officer with one dependant.[3]

Concerning a general statement by Forde that there were "relatively large headquarters staffs" who "may not all be fully employed", Blamey said that this statement should be discredited or "evidence produced which can be examined in reference to a particular staff".

An accompanying table showed that under New Guinea Force there were 115,604 troops, and that its field formations included II Corps and four divisions. Under First Army were 90,784 men, including I Corps, and three divisions (but a total of only seven brigades). In the Queensland Lines of Communication area within the First Army area were 41,871

---

[3] It was pointed out that four Australian lieut-generals were receiving a special allowance approved by the Government, thus: Lt-Gen Morshead 38/1 a day; Lt-Gen Lavarack 21/2; Lt-Gen Bennett 4/11; Lt-Gen Sturdee (in Washington) 118/5.

men.⁴ The Second Army possessed 102,593 men including the 1st Division (two brigades), and in its two L. of C. areas were 74,115 men. In III Corps area in Western Australia were 57,916 men, and one division and one armoured brigade were under command. Northern Territory Force contained 36,997 men, and included three infantry brigades. There were 17,694 men in the South Australian L. of C. area, 7,275 in the Tasmanian; 3,859 in L.H.Q. reserve; and 17,986 in L.H.Q. units or not elsewhere included.

On 19th January 1944 Forde replied pointing out that part-time members of the Volunteer Defence Corps (85,000 in all) had been included in the above totals, and suggesting that, as brigadier-generals had been included in the American calculation, brigadiers should be included in the Australian. It still appeared to him that the headquarters should be reduced. A few days later Mr Curtin wrote to Mr Forde quoting a statement by Blamey in May 1942 that the rank of a commander of an L. of C. should be major-general where the troops under command exceeded 20,000.

Blamey's replies (on 7th and 12th February) pointed out that a brigadier in the Australian Army did not have rank or status equivalent to those of a brigadier-general in the American Army. In the latter a brigadier-general held a permanent rank and his primary role was to be second-in-command of a division (an appointment that did not exist in a British army). He added that in the calculations about the ratios of generals British and American forces equivalent to the V.D.C. had been included; and that six of the Australian generals were in fact in employment outside the Australian Army. He also pointed out that the three major-generals commanding L. of C. areas commanded 41,800, 41,800 and 32,000 troops respectively. As in an earlier letter, Blamey offered to discuss the whole question with the Prime Minister and the Minister for the Army.⁵

There the matter seems to have rested until December 1944 when it cropped up again during discussion of the proposed transfer of Second Army headquarters from the Burnside Homes near Parramatta to temporary quarters on a near-by golf links. The acting Minister, Senator Fraser, in a letter to the acting Prime Minister, now Mr Forde, on 13th December gave his "considered view" that the present war establishment of Second Army headquarters—494—was excessive; and said that he was not satisfied that there would be a need for Second Army headquarters in the post-war army. Fraser sent a copy to Blamey on 28th December.

On 4th January 1945 Blamey wrote a second long statement (of six foolscap pages) on the general organisation of command in Australia. On this occasion he went back to 1920 when a conference of senior

---

⁴ The L. of C. areas within army areas were under the army concerned for operational planning and under LHQ for general administration.

⁵ Interest in this question was evidently not confined to the Ministers. In the Senate on 28th September 1944 Senator W. E. Aylett, a Government member, asked how many generals were in the Australian Army. Senator Fraser replied that there were: one general, 10 lieut-generals, of whom only 5 were serving with the army in the South-West Pacific; and 28 major-generals, of whom 23 were serving with the army in the South-West Pacific.

commanders was convened to advise as to the most effective organisation for the army.[6] This conference recommended (i) the formation of two main field forces each of two divisions and a cavalry division to defend the vital centres, Sydney and Melbourne[7]; (ii) the necessary maintenance or base and L. of C. organisation, each State becoming an administrative area under a base commandant; and (iii) an effective system of command for the army as a whole. The components of the two field groups and the base area were provided for but considerations of economy prevented the establishment of an effective system of over-all command. In 1939, however, two principal headquarters, Eastern and Southern Command, were established to ensure command of the main field forces. In 1942, when invasion seemed imminent, the Government had "adopted without question . . . the long-standing advice as to the need for reorganising the land forces"; for Eastern Command was substituted First Army and, for Southern Command, Second Army.

> The invasion did not eventuate (Blamey continued) but the principles on which the command system had been thought out were of a nature designed to meet any changing conditions. . . . The First Army Headquarters became the operational headquarters to meet an invasion in Northern Australia. Its headquarters went first to Toowoomba and later further north to Atherton. The Second Army took over progressively the remaining functions of command and training.

After the counter-offensive in New Guinea the First Army Headquarters was again advanced, this time to New Guinea; and the area of the Second Army was extended to include Queensland up to the 20th parallel.

Basic principles of efficient army organisation were: the delegation of appropriate responsibilities to a normal maximum of six subordinate commanders; the assignment to each subordinate of one primary role; the provision for each subordinate commander of an adequate organisation and staff.[8]

There were 23 principal formations in the army, omitting schools and training units. The commanders of First Army and I Corps relieved the Commander-in-Chief of immediate control of six divisions; but the remaining formations were too numerous for efficient direct control from L.H.Q. The South Australian and Tasmanian L. of C. areas were small. The Northern Territory Force and Western Command were in the nature of detachments and must therefore remain under his direct command. But, to reduce the number of his immediate subordinates to a practical limit, it was necessary to maintain a separate principal subordinate formation to supervise the training organisation and control local defence units. It would be unsound for the L. of C. areas to carry out these functions.

---

[6] They were Lieut-Generals Chauvel and Monash and Major-Generals Legge, M'Cay, Hobbs and White. Blamey as DCGS was responsible for the preparatory studies and general staff work.

[7] The "Sydney" force was to include the troops in New South Wales and Queensland, and thus, at this stage, the principle of concentrating troops for the defence of the vital Sydney area was implied.

[8] Writing in an earlier period (in 1903) Colonel G. F. R. Henderson stated: "It is one of the first rules of organisation that eight units are as many as one commander can manage in war." —*The Science of War*, p. 427. In those days there were eight companies in an infantry battalion.

A higher formation such as the Second Army was essential for these purposes. If it was abolished he would have to institute another and less satisfactory organisation. If the functions of the Second Army were distributed among the L. of C. areas the increment needed by the area headquarters would exceed the present Second Army headquarters.

Senator Fraser's letter of 28th December had not reached Blamey when he wrote this paper. After reading that letter Blamey wrote replies to specific questions it raised, such as the extent of the telephone system of the Second Army. He gave details of the telephone system (it possessed 100 telephones), and pointed out that the war establishment of the headquarters had been decreased from 842 in 1942 to 494; during 1944, by disbanding the staffs of certain training centres, the establishment had been decreased by 138 officers and 470 others. He intended to disband the 1st Division and transfer its functions to Second Army with a further saving of 19 officers and 113 others.

Fraser's reply was to ask on 15th January 1945 for a "chart of organisation" of the Second Army. This chart, delivered on 25th January, showed that the strength on 31st December 1944 was:

Headquarters	494
Army troops	4,128
Coast and anti-aircraft defences	3,793
Training establishments	25,092
Schools	1,015
	34,522
Full-time V.D.C.	227
	34,749

In his covering letter Blamey repeated a request made three weeks before that the Prime Minister should be informed of the advice he had given on 4th January and Forde (now Minister again) did so.

As described earlier, political criticism of Blamey took a different direction about this time, and the Second Army was left alone for about four months.[9]

In May 1945 the Second Army had been without a commander for about ten months, ever since Morshead had been transferred to I Corps. Its senior General Staff Officer was Brigadier Fullarton,[1] the only general

---

[9] Meanwhile there had been criticism also of the size of the main headquarters, in Melbourne. Mr Forde discussed with General Blamey a letter in the Melbourne *Age* of 19th January 1945 alleging waste of manpower at "Victoria Barracks" where, the writer said, 7,000 were on the payroll but "business men" employed there asserted that 2,000 or 3,000 young people could be removed without any diminution of efficiency. "Post-war business," said the writer of the letter, "needs office and store space in Melbourne, and such accommodation is quite impossible to obtain, because of the huge areas still locked up by war departments which never decrease."

Blamey wrote to Forde, pointing out that not only army but naval, air and civil staffs were housed at the barracks. The army personnel at the barracks numbered 564 officers and 709 others, of whom 40 and 337 were women and 113 and 281 were men who were medically B-class. Other branches, including the personal records section, were housed at the temporary Albert Park barracks and elsewhere. The total strength of the headquarters was 1,424 officers and 3,272 other ranks, of whom a total of 1,270 were women and 1,776 were B-class.

[1] Brig I. G. Fullarton, MC, NX140112. (1st AIF: 29 Bn.) Comd Lae Base Sub-Area 1943-44; BGS Second Army 1944-45. Regular soldier; b. Orange, NSW, 2 Sep 1895. Died 6 Jun 1952.

within its organisation being Major-General H. W. Lloyd of the dwindling 1st Division. As mentioned, Blamey had decided to disband the 1st Division, and on 8th May Lloyd was appointed to administer command of the Second Army. When Fraser, now again acting Minister, was asked to approve, he said that he had decided that the Second Army should be disbanded and responsibility for administering its units taken over by the commander of the New South Wales L. of C. area (Major-General E. C. P. Plant).

> I am prepared to take full responsibility for this decision. . . . Would you please advise me of the action that has been taken to give effect to this direction.

Blamey was then on his way forward to Bougainville. On 15th June, having returned to Lae, he wrote to Fraser briefly covering some of the ground of his earlier papers, stating that the proposal was retrograde and would lead to a decline in efficiency, and that the fact of transfer of command from one particular officer to another did not affect the functions that had to be carried out. He concluded by saying that "a reversion to the ineffective system of divided control of reinforcement training" should be carried out with a minimum of friction and he was asking the Chief of the General Staff to work out a scheme.

The studies were prepared. Blamey replied to the Minister on 28th July outlining the problem and concluding with a recommendation that the title of the Second Army be altered to "Training Command". It was 16th August before Forde replied that, since hostilities had ended, no decision was necessary, *but* if the proposed establishment for the Training Command had been the same as that of the Second Army it would not have been acceptable.

To accept the general principles set out in Blamey's letters about the Second Army is not necessarily to agree that those principles were rightly applied in this instance. Among those who most keenly questioned the need for the continued existence of the Second Army in the last two years of the war were officers of all ranks who had served on that headquarters. The final proposal to alter the title of the headquarters at North Parramatta from the Second Army to Training Command might well have been brought forward about two years earlier when it had become evident that the Second Army headquarters would never go into the field. It is difficult to avoid a suspicion that Blamey was not being entirely frank and that one reason for retaining the title Second Army was that it gave him an appointment to which he could, if he wished, post a very senior officer. (He had given a hint of this in November 1943.) After July 1944, when the Second Army ceased to have a commander, and its staff dwindled until it was considerably smaller than the staff of a corps, there was insufficient justification for retaining a name that had been appropriate enough in 1942 but was now incongruous.

The persistence with which the Ministers and their advisers pursued this matter (which involved only some 500 men out of an army of nearly one thousand times as many) was indicative perhaps of the widely-held conviction of those days that armies (more than navies or air forces) wasted and misapplied their manpower, and bred senior officers who sought to enlarge the size of their commands in their own interests. Some support is provided for this belief by the fact that in August 1942, when the army in Australia and New Guinea was 443,000 strong, 18,000 were serving on various headquarters, but in August 1945 when the army was 382,000 strong, 26,000 were serving on headquarters.

Manpower is wasted in armies and armies provide scope for "Empire builders", but in Australia during the war other institutions provided similar scope, and other institutions wasted manpower, yet were not subjected to the same degree of criticism as was the army, against which in this respect there was a prejudice that was both ancient and unrelenting.

It is illuminating to compare the general attitude to sport in Australia in the first half of this century with the general attitude to the army. Bright uniforms for the army were decried, but in sport they were demanded. Army ritual was considered by many a waste of time, but in sport similar ritual was considered proper, even essential. Leaders in sport attained a popularity never approached by army leaders. Even a modest degree of idleness among the soldiery was considered scandalous, whereas the success of a game was often gauged by the number of idle spectators whom it attracted.

APPENDIX 3

GENERAL BLAMEY'S APPRECIATION OF MAY 1945

TOP SECRET
18 May 45

PART I.

APPRECIATION ON OPERATIONS OF THE AMF IN NEW GUINEA, NEW BRITAIN AND THE SOLOMON ISLANDS.

1. *Object*

To conduct operations against the enemy with a view to:

(a) Destroying the enemy where this can be done with relatively light casualties, so as to free our territory and liberate the native population and thereby progressively reduce our commitments and free personnel from the Army;

(b) Where conditions are not favourable for the destruction of the enemy, to contain him in a restricted area by the use of a much smaller force, thus following the principle of economy.

2. *American Operations*

Prior to their relief by Australian forces, American operations in NEW GUINEA, NEW BRITAIN and the SOLOMONS were designed to secure the use of air bases from which to neutralise the enemy air power, and so permit a drive to the PHILIPPINES for the purpose of liberating them from the enemy. The Americans chose as objectives small areas suitable for airfield and port development, preferably in areas where the enemy strength was weak. Having seized these objectives, airfields and port facilities were constructed and a close perimeter was established around them for protection. No effort was made to seek out and destroy the enemy forces beyond these perimeters. A policy of by-passing the enemy and leaving large undefeated forces in their rear was followed until the PHILIPPINES were reached, when there was a change of policy on the part of GHQ.

3. *Results of American Policy in Australian Territory*

The reason given for the American policy of defending their airfields by close perimeters was that the enemy would "wither on the vine" in a few months. We are well into the second year of this policy and the enemy remains a strong, well organised fighting force. The result of the policy was that the enemy outside the perimeters was left in comparative peace and developed a large measure of "self-sufficiency" by cultivating gardens and employing natives to do so, importing seeds and supplying critical items such as medical supplies and signal stores by submarine and aircraft.

4. When MOROTAI had been seized, C-in-C SWPA stated that the enemy forces by-passed in Australian territories were strategically im-

potent, but at this stage the following American forces were disposed in Australian territories:

> TOROKINA Perimeter BOUGAINVILLE—A Corps of two Divisions
> OUTER SOLOMON ISLANDS—One Division
> NEW BRITAIN (GLOUCESTER)—One Division
> NEW GUINEA (AITAPE-TADJI)—A Corps of two Divisions plus one Regimental Combat Team.

During this period the Americans were mainly confined within their perimeters and left the bulk of the patrolling to AIB, ANGAU and FIJIAN troops. At TOROKINA and AITAPE the enemy attacked the American perimeters in strength but when beaten off they were not pursued and destroyed, but allowed to re-form and pursue their policy of developing "self-sufficiency" undisturbed, thus making it possible for them to resume the offensive in future at their own free will.

5. On the initiation of planning for the PHILIPPINES campaign, GHQ SWPA requested the relief of the above American forces by equivalent Australian forces but, on my representations that such large forces were excessive, agreed to a reduction and the following Australian forces were used to relieve the American forces:

> BOUGAINVILLE and the OUTER SOLOMON ISLANDS—A Corps of one Division and two Infantry Brigade Groups
> NEW BRITAIN—One Division, since reduced to a Division of two Infantry Brigades
> NEW GUINEA (AITAPE)—One Division.

This shows a reduction on the forces used by the Americans of the equivalent of three divisions.

6. The deployment of such substantial Australian forces, under orders of GHQ, to contain these by-passed forces refutes any claim that can be raised as to their strategic impotence! Because the offensive power of these by-passed enemy forces had not been destroyed it was necessary to protect the American bases in the SOLOMONS and in NEW GUINEA with strong forces, as these bases were vital for the conduct of the PHILIPPINES campaign.

7. On reaching the PHILIPPINES the "by-passing" policy of GHQ changed, and it was decided to free all the many of these islands completely from the enemy, although only a few of the bigger islands will be developed as bases for future operations against JAPAN. However, the reason given for the complete destruction of the enemy in these islands is to ensure the security of the bases in the PHILIPPINES. It would thus appear that the difference in GHQ policy between the PHILIPPINES and the rest of the SOUTH-WEST PACIFIC AREA is based on political rather than military grounds.

8. Just as it is necessary to destroy the JAPANESE in the PHILIPPINES, so it is necessary that we should destroy the enemy in Australian territories where the conditions are favourable for such action, and so liberate the natives from JAPANESE domination. Were we to wait until

JAPAN was finally crushed, it could be said that the Americans, who had previously liberated the PHILIPPINES, were responsible for the final liberation of the natives in Australian territories, with the inevitable result that our prestige both abroad and in the eyes of the natives would suffer much harm.

As this question and its consequences are further considered in my reply to the Acting Minister's comment on the conduct of the campaigns by First Aust Army . . . and in consideration of Part II, para 2, Course C of this submission, I do not propose to repeat the details in this paper.

Part II

POLICY OF AMF ON RELIEVING US FORCES IN NEW GUINEA, NEW BRITAIN AND THE SOLOMON ISLANDS

1. *Solomon Islands*

There were three courses of action left open to me on taking over from the US Forces. These were as follows:

Course A   To take over the American defences within their perimeters as they then existed and by passive defence to protect the airfields and base installations contained within the perimeters.

Course B   To go for an all out offensive against enemy strongholds with full scale air and naval support when the latter could be developed.

Course C   By aggressive patrolling to gain information of enemy strengths and dispositions, about which little was known by American formations, and by systematically driving him from his garden areas and supply bases, forcing him into starvation and destroying him where found. Eventually to bring about his total destruction.

2. *Summary of above Courses*

Course A: To commit any troops to a passive role of defence, and particularly Australian troops, is to destroy quickly their morale, create discontent and decrease their resistance to sickness and disease. By remaining within American perimeters the defence of our airfields and bases would possibly have been achieved. The enemy would have been allowed to develop his self-sufficiency at will, to continue to receive limited essential supplies by air and submarine, to continue his domination of the natives and to inflict a steady flow of casualties on us by sporadic raids and local infiltration, a form of warfare to which he is prone. This course would lower the prestige of the Australian nation throughout the world and particularly would, in the native mind, lower the prestige of the Government to such an extent that it might be difficult to recover on the termination of hostilities.

Course B: The dispositions of the enemy throughout the SOLOMONS and NEW GUINEA were such that his destruction could not have been achieved by major operations at a few points. His forces had been dispersed to develop garden areas and to gain maximum domination of the natives whom he has used to aid him in his policy of "self-sufficiency" and in active operations against our forces. Major offensive operations with full scale air and naval support at such points as WEWAK and BUIN would have given us local control of these places just as it did at AITAPE and TOROKINA. But we would still have been obliged to follow him from the shore into the jungle to destroy him. The necessary naval forces could not be made available. The directive of C-in-C SWPA did not allow of this course.

NEW BRITAIN presented a different problem to NEW GUINEA and the SOLOMONS. Here we were faced with a force of approximately 56,000 troops, mainly located in the area immediately surrounding RABAUL with strong patrols operating throughout the GAZELLE PENINSULA and along both coasts to the SOUTH of it. The enemy defences were strong and the enemy themselves well equipped and fed. A major offensive operation with the forces at our disposal was impossible.

Course C: Following the relief by First Aust Army of the US Forces in November 1944 it was found that information of enemy strengths and dispositions was extremely limited. Apart from the enemy forces immediately in front of them the Americans could supply very little information. The morale of the air forces was reduced because their activity had been aimless. Bombing missions were carried out against areas which may or may not have contained enemy and no results of the bombing could be given by ground forces. The first task therefore, while awaiting the final deployment of the army, which was not completed until March 1945, was to gain all possible information of the enemy by active patrolling. Active patrolling enables the offensive spirit to be maintained for possible future operations and by constantly harassing the enemy gives to the troops a moral superiority over him. The information obtained showed the enemy to be distributed in definite areas in the SOLOMONS and WEWAK-AITAPE-MAPRIK areas.

To remain inactive for months while awaiting the development of full scale naval and air support is a negation of all military teaching and common sense. It reduces the morale of the troops and leads to disciplinary troubles as seen during the long stay of our troops on the mainland. It is a colossal waste of manpower, material and money. In the tropics it reduces rapidly the resistance to tropical diseases and wastage of men increases rapidly. It encourages the enemy and gives him increasing influence and control over the natives.

The only sound course of action left open was that indicated in Course C. It was therefore decided that the operations of the First Aust Army would consist of obtaining information, probing the enemy's positions and carrying out offensive operations with small forces with a view to seeking out and destroying the enemy where found.

The situation in NEW BRITAIN differed from the other areas. As it was not considered possible to destroy the enemy force at RABAUL with the forces available, it was decided to drive the enemy patrols back into the GAZELLE PENINSULA and then regain control of the major portion of NEW BRITAIN and contain a large force in the northern end of the island with a considerably smaller one. This is in accordance with the military principle: "A detachment from the main forces is justified if it contains a force superior to itself." In the situation in which I found myself taking over from the Americans, the Japanese, on their side, in certain areas justified this principle.

3. *Plan of Operations—New Guinea (Wewak-Aitape Area)*

In November 1944 an American Army Corps was concentrated in and around AITAPE, strongly entrenched behind barbed wire with the exception of one regiment which was on the DRINIUMOR River. AIB patrols were operating to the SOUTH but, through lack of support by ground troops which had been denied to them by the Americans, they were forced to yield large areas to Japanese forces.

The enemy strength in the area was approximately 24,000 to 27,000. He had suffered heavy losses in attacks on the Americans, but retained his organisation in three divisions effectively. He was spreading rapidly into the fertile and thickly populated country to the SOUTH of the TORRICELLI MOUNTAINS, where he lived largely on native gardens. In the coastal area he had considerable stocks of material in WEWAK and along the coast to BUT. Single submarines and aircraft were getting in regularly with urgently required medical and ordnance supplies.

The plan accepted was an advance east on two axes by 6th Division, operating in this area. Firstly along the coast to destroy his forces and supplies and to prevent as far as possible his movement inland and to seize WEWAK to cut his inland forces off from this area and to prevent further supplies reaching him by sea and air. Secondly to drive him from the garden area SOUTH of the TORRICELLIS, to destroy his capacity to supply his forces while destroying his organisation and personnel.

4. *New Britain*

5 Aust Division relieved 40th US Division in NEW BRITAIN. 40th Division was established at CAPE GLOUCESTER on the western end of the island and 360 miles from RABAUL. Detachments were at CAPE HOSKINS on the NORTH coast and ARAWE on the SOUTH. There was no contact between US and JAPANESE forces but AIB patrols were operating towards the GAZELLE PENINSULA.

5th Division landed at JACQUINOT BAY, 160 miles advanced beyond ARAWE, which, at the time, was the nearest anchorage to RABAUL unoccupied by the enemy. One battalion relieved the US Detachment at CAPE HOSKINS.

The plan adopted was to advance by patrols along both coasts and enemy patrols were gradually pushed back until the enemy was confined to the comparatively limited area of the GAZELLE PENINSULA.

The present situation is that some 40,000 enemy troops are being contained in the GAZELLE PENINSULA by two Australian brigades. Our losses have been 40 killed and missing and 115 wounded. 220 Japanese dead have been counted; the number of dead removed and the wounded are unknown. Many natives and large areas of country have been returned to our control.

5. Solomon Islands

When 2 Aust Corps, consisting of 3 Division and two brigade groups, took over the responsibility of the northern SOLOMONS from the 14 US Corps of three divisions in November 1944, the situation was that the bulk of American troops were concentrated within a perimeter at TOROKINA with a small force operating along the overland route to NUMA NUMA and a further force on the JABA RIVER. One US Division was occupying neighbouring islands on which there were no Japanese. This division was relieved by one brigade from 2 Aust Corps and the force has since been reduced to one battalion.

The enemy strength was estimated at 18/19,000 and they were disposed in groups throughout BOUGAINVILLE, SHORTLAND ISLAND and BUKA ISLAND, the main concentration being in SOUTH BOUGAINVILLE. In the year in which they had not been attacked, they had achieved a high degree of "self-sufficiency" by gardening and fishing. Active patrolling operations were commenced with the arrival of the first brigades in three directions. To the EAST on the NUMA TRAIL—to the NORTH towards SORAKEN and SOUTH beyond the JABA RIVER.

As a result of reconnaissance it was decided to make a stronger thrust to the SOUTH. This operation was carried out on a carefully prepared plan by advancing in small bodies and forcing the enemy to action. Already our troops have seized much of the garden area and driven on to the HONGORAI RIVER where the Jap is still resisting in an endeavour to prevent our further advance.

The move over the NUMA NUMA TRAIL has progressed to a point where our troops are overlooking NUMA NUMA and the adjacent coast line.

To the NORTH, SORAKEN PENINSULA and an island off the coast have been cleared of the enemy and our troops are now in control of the only known route from SORAKEN to the NORTH coast, thus cutting the enemy in the BUKA PASSAGE from those to the SOUTH. The whole northern sector is in process of being cleared.

General

A summary showing the comparison of casualties in all areas is attached. The increased prestige of the Australians in the native mind brought about since the commencement of offensive operations by the regaining of control of large areas of country and the releasing of thousands of natives from JAPANESE domination has been considerable. We have so far carried out our obligation to liberate a large number of our native subjects.

The release of natives from JAPANESE control has lightened the task of First Army by making them available for service in native battalions, AIB and carrier lines.

COMPARISON CASUALTIES, ETC.
TO MAY 18, 1945

	JAPANESE			OWN	
	Counted Dead	Estimated Uncounted Dead	Estimated Dead from Attrition*	Killed and Missing	Wounded
NEW GUINEA (6 Aust Div)	3,938	1,200	6,600	267	542
NEW BRITAIN (5 Aust Div)	220	100	3,700	49	131
BOUGAINVILLE (2 Aust Corps)	3,800	1,300	2,500	257	760
TOTAL	7,958	2,600	12,800	573	1,433

* This cannot be considered reliable.

Enemy wounded

No estimate can be made of enemy wounded. It is his custom to remove dead and wounded from the battlefield whenever he can.

At the same ratio as that suffered by us, viz., 1 killed 3 wounded, the Japanese wounded in relation to counted dead would be 23,874. It is believed that this would be unduly high.

PART III

FUTURE POLICY

1. *Dispositions First Aust Army as at 12 May 45*

Bougainville—
    HQ 2 Aust Corps
    3 Aust Division of three Infantry Brigades
    Two Infantry Brigades (less a Battalion)—one Battalion outer islands
    One Native Battalion, Pacific Islands Regiment
    AIB Guerilla Forces and ANGAU patrols

New Guinea—
    WEWAK-AITAPE—
      6 Aust Division
      One Native Battalion, Pacific Islands Regiment
      AIB Guerilla Forces and ANGAU patrols
    HANSA BAY-MADANG—
      8 Aust Infantry Brigade Group
      AIB Guerilla Forces and ANGAU patrols

New Britain—
    5 Aust Division, consisting of two Infantry Brigades
    One Native Battalion, Pacific Islands Regiment
    AIB Guerilla Forces and ANGAU patrols

New Ireland—
    AIB parties.

In addition two more battalions of Pacific Islands Regiment are being raised and should be available for active operations in the latter part of the year.

2. *Enemy Forces Estimated*

	26 Nov 44	12 May 45
BOUGAINVILLE	17,000	11,800*
NEW GUINEA	24,000 to 27,000	12,600*
NEW BRITAIN	56,000	50,000

* Data not reliable.

3. For the reasons given in Part II it is proposed to follow the existing policy of destroying the enemy in BOUGAINVILLE and NEW GUINEA with the object of liquidating our commitments and thereby making a progressive reduction in the strength of our forces engaged in these areas.

When enemy organisation is sufficiently destroyed and his numbers reduced, it is proposed to retain the minimum of Australian troops and to use the Pacific Islands Regiment with AIB and ANGAU elements to develop partisan fighting until the enemy is completely annihilated.

4. In NEW BRITAIN, where the reduction of RABAUL would require the use of major forces, it is proposed to continue the present economic policy of containing the enemy, but to review this policy when circumstances permit.

FORECAST OF FUTURE OPERATIONS

5. *Bougainville*

With our present aggressive policy the AIB guerillas and partisan natives are becoming increasingly effective in killing off more JAPANESE and driving them from their more isolated gardens, thus increasing the attrition rate, and forcing the enemy to move and work in greater concentrations. When the enemy is dealt with sufficiently SOUTH of the HONGORAI RIVER and in the BUIN area, a reduction in our forces from five to two infantry brigades should be possible. Thereafter a further progressive reduction should be possible until our force can be reduced to one infantry brigade and two native battalions, Pacific Islands Regiment, and, ultimately, to two native battalions, Pacific Islands Regiment.

6. *New Guinea*

When the enemy is driven from the coast, continuation of present operations should so reduce the enemy strength that a force of one infantry brigade group and two native battalions, Pacific Islands Regiment, together with partisan guerillas, should be sufficient to deal with the remnants of the enemy. After the last formed enemy bodies have been broken up two native battalions, Pacific Islands Regiment, should be sufficient to eradicate the final remnants.

7. *New Britain*

To contain the large enemy force in the GAZELLE PENINSULA, a force of one division of two infantry brigades, one native battalion, Pacific Islands Regiment, and AIB guerilla parties will be required together with a reserve of one infantry brigade, held at a convenient centre, in case the enemy should embark on offensive operations to break out of the GAZELLE PENINSULA.

New Ireland

AIB parties and guerilla activities to be conducted on a minor scale.

The policy to be followed in regard to NEW BRITAIN and NEW IRELAND will require reconsideration later.

8. *Summary*

By the end of the year it is hoped that our force can be reduced by two divisions consisting of five infantry brigade groups. If this hope is realised, the forces required will be:

WEWAK-AITAPE—One Infantry Brigade Group
BOUGAINVILLE—One Infantry Brigade Group
NEW BRITAIN—One Division of two Infantry Brigades
RESERVE—One Infantry Brigade
ALL AREAS—Ancillary and Base Troops.

This is subject to developments in NEW BRITAIN and NEW IRELAND.

(Sgd) T. A. BLAMEY
C-in-C, AMF

Melbourne,
18th May, 1945.

APPENDIX 4

THE ALLIED INTELLIGENCE BUREAU

Throughout the last three volumes of this series glimpses have been given of the Intelligence and guerilla operations of the various organisations that were directed by the Allied Intelligence Bureau. The story of these groups is complex and their activities were diverse and so widespread that some of them are on only the margins of Australian military history. They involved British, Australian, American, Dutch and Asian personnel, and officers and men of at least ten individual services. At one time or another A.I.B. controlled or coordinated eight separate organisations.

The initial effort to establish a field Intelligence organisation in what eventually became the South-West Pacific Area was made by the Australian Navy which, when Japan attacked, had a network of coastwatcher stations throughout the New Guinea territories. These were manned by people living in the Australian islands and the British Solomons. The development and the work of the coastwatchers is described in some detail in the naval series of this history and in *The Coast Watchers* (1946) by Commander Feldt, who directed their operations.

The expulsion of Allied forces from Malaya, the Indies and the Philippines, and also the necessity of establishing Intelligence agencies within the area that the enemy had conquered brought to Australia a number of Allied Intelligence staffs and also many individuals with intimate knowledge of parts of the territories the Japanese now occupied.

At the summit were, initially, the Directors of Intelligence of the three Australian Services. In March 1942 Major G. Egerton Mott of the British Army arrived in Australia from Malaya by way of Java with authority from the War Office to help Australia establish a branch of "Special Operations" to counteract sabotage and subversive activities by the enemy. He was accompanied by Major A. E. B. Trappes-Lomax. General Blamey authorised the formation of "Special Operations Australia" (S.O.A.) under Mott. In April, when General MacArthur was appointed to command the Allied forces in the S.W.P.A., his senior "G2" officer, Major-General Willoughby, became the senior Intelligence officer in the area.

Among other arrivals from Malaya were Commander Proud[1] who had worked on propaganda in Singapore, and Dr Victor Purcell, formerly Director-General of Information in Malaya. On 19th June 1942 Blamey authorised them to establish a propaganda section under the camouflaged title "Far Eastern Liaison Office" (FELO).

Also in June it was decided to form the Allied Intelligence Bureau (A.I.B.) to coordinate the existing propaganda and guerilla organisations. Colonel C. G. Roberts, who was Director of Military Intelligence at L.H.Q., was made Controller of the A.I.B., and Brigadier Rogers, who

---
[1] Cdr J. C. R. Proud, OBE, VRD; RANVR. Director, FELO 1942-45. Broadcasting officer; of Melbourne; b. Melbourne, 13 Oct 1907.

had been senior Intelligence officer with the A.I.F. in the Middle East, became D.M.I. The role of the A.I.B. was to obtain information about the enemy, "to weaken the enemy by sabotage and destruction of morale and to lend aid and assistance to local effort to the same end in enemy-occupied territories". It was divided into four sections: "A" (S.O.A. or I.S.D.—Inter-Allied Services Department), information and sabotage; "B", "secret Intelligence"; "C", field Intelligence through coastwatchers, natives, civilians, *et al.*; "D", propaganda. Mott headed "A", Captain Kendall,[2] R.N.R., "B", Commander Feldt "C", and Commander Proud "D".

The formation of the A.I.B. was necessary with so many national forces and so many separate Services operating, but for the next six months or so the lion's share of the effective work in the field was carried out by the long-established coastwatching organisation and by Angau—the New Guinea administration, now absorbed by the Australian Army. There was no lack, however, of imaginative plans for future operations: hundreds of Malayan Hadjis (pilgrims who had been to Mecca) would be recruited in Arabia and introduced into Borneo and Celebes as agents; rubber would be smuggled out of the N.E.I.; a Chinese espionage network would be established in the occupied territories; and so on.

The first long-range penetration of enemy territory was undertaken in September 1942 when Captain Van-Arcken[3] and two others were landed by night on Java from a Dutch submarine. This enterprise demonstrated the need for careful planning and training: the landing boats turned over, most of the gear was lost, and Van-Arcken was injured; the submarine surfaced next morning with the object of bringing the men off, and was probably reported to the Japanese; that night the landing party re-embarked, having collected some information. Two other parties were landed on Java in 1942 and one in Ceram. These and some other later parties were lost.

Also in 1942, while an Australian Independent company was operating in Timor, Captain Wylie[4] (a British Army officer attached to the Australian Army) led parties into other parts of Portuguese Timor.

Soon maladies from which a group of "cloak-and-dagger" organisations staffed by highly-individualistic and sometimes temperamental people seems certain to suffer began to manifest themselves. The Dutch officials informed G.H.Q. that they wanted political and economic as well as military information about the Indies and were given permission to establish a separate organisation with direct access to G.H.Q. Thereupon Roberts asked to be relieved, but his request was not granted. The separate Dutch section was not set up, but Colonel S. H. Spoor of the Dutch group was granted direct access to G.H.Q. To solve the problems created by

---

[2] Capt R. Kendall, RD; RNR. (1914-18: Merchant Navy and RNT.) Cmdre English Channel and North Sea Convoys 1940-41; Director of Secret Intelligence SWPA 1942-45. Senator since 1949. Master mariner; of Sydney; b. London, 9 Jun 1899.

[3] Capt G. G. M. Van-Arcken, VX87080. "Z" and "M" Special Units. Export sales promoter; of Melbourne; b. Batavia, Java, 4 Apr 1902. (Name changed to Vance.)

[4] Capt I. S. Wylie; "Z" Special Unit. B. Calcutta, India, 2 Mar 1910.

the existence of separate groups operating with extreme secrecy in the same areas, the bureau was re-organised on a regional instead of a functional basis into North-Eastern, N.E.I. and Philippines areas controlled by Feldt, Commander G. B. Salm, R.N.N. and Lieut-Colonel A. W. Ind (American Army) respectively; the remaining areas were directly under the A.I.B. Thus unified control was restored in the North-Eastern Area, where the most important work was then being done. It was also directed that no activities should be undertaken without the approval of Willoughby, and that, in the case of S.O.A., Blamey's approval had to be obtained for operations in the North-Eastern Area and the Dutch commander's for operations in the Indies.

Lieut-Colonel P. J. F. Chapman-Walker arrived from London to look into S.O.A., which Mott ceased to command in February 1943, and in March 1943 obtained approval for a new unit, employing S.O.A. men and equipment, to be known as the Services Reconnaissance Department (S.R.D.). It was to be available also for operations required by the South-East Asia Command.

In 1943 many bold and successful projects were carried out in the New Guinea area, as mentioned in earlier volumes of this series. There was a constant demand for reconnaissance parties, guides, air spotting and coastwatching. Parties were inserted into the Philippines to assist the guerillas there and collect information. By mid-1943 the guerilla movement in the Philippines had so developed that the Philippines section was given semi-independent status under MacArthur's Chief of Staff, and control of the section was given to Colonel Courtney Whitney, a lawyer who had spent 22 years in the Philippines.

The N.E.I. Section was renamed Netherlands Forces Intelligence Section, Division III (N.E.F.I.S. III).

The most daring S.R.D. operations of 1943 were the raid on Singapore harbour by a party led by Major I. Lyon, which is described in the naval series of this history, and those of "Mosstroops", described in this series.

The A.I.B. ventures in Borneo have been outlined in the section of this volume dealing with the operations there.

The A.I.B. continued to send parties into Timor. One group of 34, mostly Portugese and Timorese, was landed in July but was rounded up by the Japanese in September. The Japanese captured enough information to enable them to send to Australia wireless signals that appeared to come from the A.I.B. party. In this way during the rest of the war they tricked the S.R.D. into dropping supplies at places they indicated and obtained information about the insertion of later parties. As a result two later parties were captured soon after landing, and the Japanese continued to send misleading signals and to receive valuable information. Finally on 8th August 1945 a signal in the S.R.D. code arrived from "Nippon Army" expressing thanks for "information received over a long period".

In 1943 Dutch plans were handicapped by lack of suitable men and dependable submarines. Two Dutch submarines were sent out from

England for use principally on missions to the Indies, but they proved to be old and hard to refit. The most successful Dutch venture in this year was led by Lieutenant J. D. de Bruyn, who established an observation post in the Wissel Lakes area (400 miles north-west of Merauke) and held it for more than fourteen months. G.H.Q. now instructed N.E.F.I.S. to give priority to Hollandia, Wakde, Sorong, Menado, Ternate, Manokwari and Fakfak, in that order.

There were further changes in the A.I.B. organisation in 1944. The various components "were growing beyond the dimensions originally anticipated" and Willoughby sought reports on the strengths of the sections. These reports showed that, not counting the P.R.S. (Philippine Regional Section) the bureau was employing 280 officers, 1,121 other ranks and civilians, and 556 natives; of these 144 officers and 622 other ranks were in the S.R.D. The sections were showing a tendency to grow, in the manner of such private armies in wartime. Also all were tending "to set up their own mechanism regardless of economy or efficiency".[5]

At least one S.R.D. leader would have agreed with this. Later Major Harrisson wrote:

> There were several units responsible for what are nowadays known as cloak-and-dagger works in this theatre. True to the mood of the business, the secrecy they valued above all other was among themselves. Each unit appeared more concerned with preventing its "operatives" from knowing about or being in contact with any other unit, than anything else. It was heinous sin to be found in possession of knowledge of or contact with a closely related body operating in parallel with you —or, often, in conflict. One of the ultimate effects of this was that units with the best salesmanship, warmanship and political savvy tended to get the plum jobs, on a system of competitive tendering which sometimes staked claims, took risks and even made statements of fact for which there was little (or no) substance behind the cloak. A further and perhaps more important effect—for the lives of volunteers sacrificed to a group loyalty or colonel's ambition can hardly be counted in these war years—was that a lot of things which should have been done never got done properly; through lack of liaison, because no one unit was fully equipped to do it, and because (with very few exceptions) no two units were ever allowed to work together.[6]

It was decided by the War Department that the A.I.B. and the P.R.S. should be separate, and each should procure equipment from its own service: in effect this meant that the American Army would provide for the P.R.S. and the Australian provide for the several sections—Australian, British-cum-Australian, and Dutch—remaining in the A.I.B.

The lack of success of the Dutch parties and their shortage of personnel caused G.H.Q. to call upon the Australian group to undertake reconnaissance of the Hollandia area. This led to the insertion of Captain G. C. Harris' ill-fated party whose experiences are described in Volume VI of this series.

In the second half of 1944 further steps were taken towards coordinating the efforts of the A.I.B. In June 1944 it was decided that instead of the contributions of the three Governments being placed in separate

---
[5] GHQ, SWPA: Operations of the Allied Intelligence Bureau, Vol IV, p. 79. The report adds: "G2 (Willoughby) intervened time and again to coordinate and keep these prima donnas in line."
[6] T. Harrisson, *World Within, A Borneo Story*, pp. 141-2.

accounts each subject to different rules, they would be pooled. On 17th October Colonel Roberts was released to a civil appointment and Brigadier K. A. Wills, then D.D.M.I. at Advanced L.H.Q., was appointed Controller. Wills soon proposed several measures for better coordination both within the A.I.B. and between the A.I.B. and the organisations it served, and for the better equipment of the bureau. These proposals, which represented the fruits of long and hard experience, included: the placing of the headquarters of the A.I.B. and each of its sections close to G.H.Q.; that projects submitted by the A.I.B. should be judged by the Chief of Staff at G.H.Q. and not have to be channelled through the navy, the air force or the operations branch at G.H.Q.; that operational control of a project should be vested in the field commander in the area concerned; and that the A.I.B. should have a flight of aircraft for its own use. These proposals were adopted, with unimportant modifications. Six, later eight, Liberators were allotted to No. 200 Flight R.A.A.F. with nine air crews of 11 each, and a ground staff of about 450.

Major Jinkins' group, working in Borneo with the help of American submarines, achieved notable successes in 1945. A party under Captain Anderson[7] landed and damaged enemy installations on Pratas Island, and raided a railway line in Indo-China. Another group, under Lieutenant W. A. Chaffey, was also landed in Indo-China where it blew up a train.

The A.I.B. organisations contained in 1945 1,659 Australian and British personnel, 1,100 natives, 268 Dutch and 19 Americans. It possessed its own flight of aircraft, mentioned above, and its own surface craft. General Sturdee said that about half his operational Intelligence was collected by the A.I.B. parties.

In August 1945 Brigadier Wills, as Controller of the A.I.B., reported that the several special Intelligence and guerilla organisations coordinated by the bureau had, in the course of the war, killed 7,061 Japanese, taken 141 prisoners, and rescued 1,054 servicemen and civilians from enemy-occupied territory. In addition 951 enemy were reported to have surrendered as a direct result of propaganda leaflets.

The report of the A.I.B. contains a list of the field operations undertaken by the components of the bureau with a terse note on the fate of each operation. The following table shows the number of operations, the number in which the party, or a member of it, was killed or captured, and the number which were not successful although no one was killed or captured:

Organisation	Total Operations	Party Killed or Captured	Unsuccessful
S.R.D.	73	6	12
S.I.A.	15[8]	5	1
N.E.F.I.S. III	32	14	2
N.E.A.	244	10	Nil

[7] Capt C. H. Anderson, NX2374. 2/2 Bn and "Z" Special Unit. Auctioneer; of South Casino, NSW; b. Brisbane, 27 May 1920.
[8] Five of these were begun in June 1945 or later.

Comparisons between the operations of any two of these organisations should take into account the relative difficulties faced in each area, but these figures do appear to indicate that unless the local people can be relied on to help, and unless communications are reasonably secure, excursions behind the enemy's lines are unduly hazardous.

Some of the difficulties encountered by the A.I.B. stemmed from the fact that it had to coordinate four separate national groups with differing aims and allegiances; some, undoubtedly, from the fact that the kind of organisation it controlled tends to attract men who are not only adventurous but imaginative, individualistic and temperamental to an unusual degree. Such men tend also to be enthusiasts who see their own chosen activity, whether it be propaganda, sabotage, or irregular warfare, as exerting a far greater effect on the progress of the war than it actually did.[9]

After enduring a series of crises, the A.I.B. belatedly acquired a form of control that could probably not have been bettered, at least in principle: the grouping of headquarters, the channelling of proposals through the senior operational Intelligence officer to the senior operations officer, and tactical control by the field commander of any operations in his area.

The operations of the A.I.B. as a whole undoubtedly justified the expenditure of blood and effort, but that is not to say that each of its components justified itself or that every type of project it undertook was wise. Practically all the effective work done by the A.I.B. seems to have been achieved by two sorts of parties: Intelligence groups stationed in areas where they could gather information of direct interest to the commanders, and guerilla groups operating under the only conditions which justify the initiation of guerilla warfare, namely, that it be among a friendly population and in rugged or otherwise difficult country. A glowing example of the first type of activity was provided by the coastwatchers; the second was seen at its best in Bougainville, New Britain and the mainland of Australian New Guinea, in the Philippines, and in the mountains of Borneo.

---

[9] One view of the effectiveness of such groups, undoubtedly too sweeping, is expressed in the following passage from a work of fiction:

"A general in the War Office, one of the rugged sort, whose cooperation I was seeking to include two pretty A.T.S. sergeants on an Establishment, once told me that in his opinion all irregular formations and private armies like Bomfrey's Boys contributed precisely nothing to Allied victory. All they did was to offer a too-easy, because romanticised, form of gallantry to a few anti-social irresponsible individualists, who sought a more personal satisfaction from the war than that of standing their chance, like proper soldiers, of being bayoneted in a slit-trench or burnt alive in a tank. He went so far as to hint that Bomfrey's Boys in particular had caused more dislocation to its own side than it ever had to the enemy.

"I never argue with Generals. This one was much bescarred with wounds and beflagged with medals for bravery, gained fighting like a proper soldier, so I felt he was entitled to his point of view. Besides, I thought he was perfectly right"—J. Verney, *Going to the Wars* (1955), p. 147.

APPENDIX 5

THE PRISON BREAK AT COWRA, AUGUST 1944

Despite the fact that Japanese troops had been schooled to die rather than surrender there were, by August 1944, 2,223 Japanese prisoners of war in Australia, including 544 merchant seamen. There were also 14,720 Italian prisoners, mostly from the Middle East, and 1,585 Germans, mostly naval or merchant seamen.

During the years when it was known in Australia that most of the 21,000 Australian prisoners in Japanese hands were being under-fed and over-worked and that many were dying of disease and malnutrition, the Japanese prisoners in Australian camps were well fed, were living in comfortable quarters, and were thriving. By August 1944 10,200 Italian prisoners, including 200 officers, were working, without guards, on farms or in hostels; some German prisoners were employed in labour detachments, but under guard; the possibility of employing working parties of Japanese prisoners was being considered.

At this time 1,104 Japanese prisoners were in No. 12 Prisoner of War Compound near Cowra, the centre of an agricultural district in the middle west of New South Wales. This establishment was divided into four camps: "A" for Italians, "B" for Japanese, "C" for Koreans, and "D" for Indonesians. The whole compound formed an octagon about 800 yards across, and the four camps were separated by two intersecting roads and were fenced with thick barbed-wire entanglements about 8 feet high. The 22nd Garrison Battalion guarded the prisoners, its commander, Lieut-Colonel Brown,[1] holding also the appointment of commander of the "Cowra P.W. and Internment Group".

Six 30-foot observation towers overlooked the compound and at night lights from these towers swept the camps and fixed lights lit up the wire and the roads.

As the Japanese improved in health and strength as a result of their good rations, and of constant wrestling and baseball, their spirits rose. An officer of the 22nd Garrison Battalion wrote later:

They did not understand the Articles of the Geneva Convention . . . and our strict adherence to its terms merely amused them and further convinced them of our moral and spiritual weakness. They read into our humane treatment of them a desire to placate them, and this they felt sure sprang from our secret fear of them.[2]

Information was received at the Group headquarters early in August that the Japanese were discussing a mass outbreak. Additional precautions were taken, and also it was decided to move all the Japanese privates from Cowra to Hay (N.S.W.), where there was another big P.W. Group.

---

[1] Col M. A. Brown, ED, N11. (1st AIF: Lt LH. Indian Army 1917-22.) GSO1 1 Cav Div 1940-42; CO 22 Grn Bn 1942-44 and Comd Cowra PW and Internment Gp 1943-44. Secretary; of Dapto, NSW; b. Candelo, NSW, 10 Jul 1889.
[2] E. V. Timms, "The Blood Bath at Cowra", in *As You Were* (1946). Timms, a novelist, had served in the A.I.F. in 1914-17 and was a major in the 22nd Garrison Battalion.

The Geneva Convention provides that prisoners must be given 24 hours' notice of such a move, and on 4th August notice was given to the Japanese camp leader that all Japanese at Cowra except officers and N.C.O's were to go to Hay on the 7th. That night the guards were alert and tense. About 2 a.m. a Japanese ran to the camp gates and shouted what seemed to be a warning to the sentries. Then a Japanese bugle sounded. A sentry fired a warning shot. More sentries fired as three mobs of prisoners, shouting "Banzai", began breaking through the wire, one mob on the northern side, one on the western and one on the southern. They flung themselves across the wire with the help of blankets. They were armed with knives, baseball bats, clubs studded with nails and hooks, wire stilettos and garotting cords.

The Australians on guard duty were now firing into the groups of prisoners. The men not on guard, most of whom were sleeping fully clothed with rifles and 50 rounds beside them, raced out to reinforce the guard.

The strongest group of Japanese—about 400, broke through the wire on the north-west. Here Privates Hardy[3] and Jones[4] punched their way through the prisoners, manned a Vickers gun and fired it until they were knifed and clubbed to death. The Japanese swung the gun round to fire on the Australians' huts but it jammed, and its Japanese crew was killed. No Japanese succeeded in crossing the road that bisected the compound from east to west. Here the fire was so deadly that soon more than 200 Japanese were sheltering in a deep drain from which they emerged at dawn to surrender. Meanwhile Japanese who had remained in the camp had set fire to every building in it.

Some hundreds of prisoners had now broken away into the open country, where camp guards, troops from a training camp two or three miles away and two police constables were soon rounding them up. The Japanese offered no resistance in this phase. Some of them hanged themselves from trees before they were found by the searching troops.

The two policemen concerned were Constable A. P. McGovern of Mandurama and Constable C. H. R. Cooper of Woodstock. They promptly informed all residents of the two small towns and all outlying settlers what had happened and then worked long hours for several days searching for Japanese. Cooper arrested eight of them single-handed and three in company with McGovern.

Including those who killed themselves, 234 Japanese died and 108 were wounded. Thirty-one killed themselves and 12 were burnt to death in huts set on fire by Japanese. Sixteen of the wounded showed signs of attempted suicide. The 22nd Garrison Battalion lost 3 killed and 3 wounded.

---

[3] Pte B. G. Hardy, GC, N103951; 22 Grn Bn. Motor mechanic; of Willoughby, NSW; b. Marrickville, NSW, 28 Aug 1898. Killed in action 5 Aug 1944.

[4] Pte R. Jones, GC, N244527; 22 Grn Bn. Labourer; of Crookwell, NSW; b. Gorleston-on-Sea, England, 26 Sep 1900. Killed in action 5 Aug 1944.

APPENDIX 6

ORDER OF BATTLE OF THE 7TH DIVISION AT BALIKPAPAN

The following Order of Battle shows the units under the command or in support of the commander of the 7th Australian Division for the attack on Balikpapan:

ORDER OF BATTLE

PART I

7 AUST DIV UNITS

HQ UNITS
    HQ 7 Aust Div
    2 Aust Operational Report Team
    Det Directorate of Public Relations
    4 Flt 1 Aust Mobile Meteorological Sqn
    7 Aust Mil History Fd Team (LHQ Tps)

CAVALRY
    2/7 Aust Cav (Cdo) Regt

ARTILLERY
    HQ RAA 7 Aust Div
    2/4 Aust Fd Regt
    2/5 Aust Fd Regt
    2/6 Aust Fd Regt
    2/2 Aust Tk A Regt
    2/7 Aust Svy Bty

ENGINEERS
    HQ RAE 7 Aust Div
    2/4 Aust Fd Coy
    2/5 Aust Fd Coy
    2/6 Aust Fd Coy
    2/9 Aust Fd Coy
    2/25 Aust Fd Pk Coy

SIGNALS
    Sigs 7 Aust Div
    2/7 Aust Cav (Cdo) Regt Sig Tp
    2/4 Aust Fd Regt Sig Sec
    2/5 Aust Fd Regt Sig Sec
    2/6 Aust Fd Regt Sig Sec
    2/2 Aust Tk A Regt Sig Sec
    2 Aust Arty Sig Tp
    2 Aust Engr Sig Sec
    18 Aust Inf Bde Sig Sec
    21 Aust Inf Bde Sig Sec
    25 Aust Inf Bde Sig Sec
    2/42 Aust Cipher Sec

INFANTRY
    HQ 18 Aust Inf Bde
    HQ 21 Aust Inf Bde
    HQ 25 Aust Inf Bde
    2/9 Aust Inf Bn

2/10 Aust Inf Bn
2/12 Aust Inf Bn
2/14 Aust Inf Bn
2/16 Aust Inf Bn
2/27 Aust Inf Bn
2/25 Aust Inf Bn
2/31 Aust Inf Bn
2/33 Aust Inf Bn
2/1 Aust Pnr Bn
2/1 Aust MG Bn
HQ B Coy 2/1 Aust Gd Regt
5 Pl B Coy 2/1 Aust Gd Regt
6 Pl B Coy 2/1 Aust Gd Regt
7 Pl B Coy 2/1 Aust Gd Regt
8 Pl B Coy 2/1 Aust Gd Regt

INTELLIGENCE
7 Aust Div Det ATIS (GHQ Tps)
'C' Aust Fd Security Sec

SUPPLY AND TRANSPORT
HQ Comd 7 Aust Div AASC
HQ 2/6 Aust Gen Tpt Coy
2/10 Aust Tpt Pl
2/11 Aust Tpt Pl
2/12 Aust Tpt Pl
2/6 Aust Workshop Pl
HQ 2/153 Aust Gen Tpt Coy
2/7 Aust Tpt Pl
2/8 Aust Tpt Pl
2/9 Aust Tpt Pl
2/43 Aust Tpt Pl
2/153 Aust Workshop Pl
HQ 2/2 Aust Sup Dep Coy
2/5 Aust Sup Dep Pl
2/6 Aust Sup Dep Pl
2/7 Aust Sup Dep Pl
2/8 Aust Sup Dep Pl
2/9 Aust Sup Dep Pl
2/10 Aust Sup Dep Pl
2/33 Aust Sup Dep Pl
2/34 Aust Sup Dep Pl

MEDICAL
2/2 Aust CCS
2/4 Aust Fd Amb
2/5 Aust Fd Amb
2/6 Aust Fd Amb
2/101 Aust Mobile Bath Unit
2/2 Aust Malaria Control Unit (Type A)
One Laundry Increment AAMC

DENTAL
2/6 Aust Dental Unit

ORDNANCE
2/117 Aust Bde Ord Fd Pk
2/124 Aust Bde Ord Fd Pk
2/125 Aust Bde Ord Fd Pk

AEME
  2/117 Aust Bde Workshop
  2/124 Aust Bde Workshop
  2/125 Aust Bde Workshop
  2/47 Aust LAD (Type J)
  2/51 Aust LAD (Type D)
  2/52 Aust LAD (Type D)
  2/53 Aust LAD (Type D)
  2/54 Aust LAD (Type G)
  2/55 Aust LAD (Type A)
  2/56 Aust LAD (Type A)
  2/59 Aust LAD (Type J)
  315 Aust LAD (Type J)

POSTAL
  7 Aust Div Postal Unit

PROVOST
  7 Aust Div Pro Coy

AMENITIES
  113 Mobile Cinema Aust Cinema Unit
  114 Mobile Cinema Aust Cinema Unit

MISCELLANEOUS
  7 Aust Div Reception Camp
  7 Aust Div Salvage Unit
  3 Aust Visitors & Observers Sec

Part II
I AUST CORPS TROOPS AND RAAF UNITS ALLOTTED TO 7 AUST DIV

HQ UNITS
  Det 1 Aust Combined Ops Sec
  1 Aust Mil Landing Gp
  Det 11 Aust Movement Control Gp (Type E)

ARMOURED
  HQ 1 Aust Armd Regt
  2/1 Aust Armd Bde Recce Sqn less Det

ARTILLERY
  A Tp 1 Aust Naval Bombardment Gp
  2/1 Aust Comp AA Regt

SURVEY
  Det 5 Aust Fd Svy Coy

SIGNALS
  Det HQ A Aust Corps Sigs
  3 Aust Line Sec
  13 Aust Line Maintenance Sec
  1 Aust Wireless Sec (Hy)
  2 Aust Wireless Sec (Lt)
  1 Aust Armd Regt Sig Tp less Det
  2/1 Aust AA Regt (Composite) Sig Sec
  8 Aust Pigeon Sec (Type A) less Det

INTELLIGENCE
  Det 2 Army Air Photo Interpretation Gp
  35 Aust Fd Security Sec (EE)

SUPPLY AND TRANSPORT
    HQ 3 Aust Sup Dep Coy
    11 Aust Sup Dep Pl
    12 Aust Sup Dep Pl
    2/25 Aust Tpt Pl
    2/21 Aust Tpt Pl (DUKWS)
    2/3 Aust Amphibious Increment
MEDICAL
    110 Aust Adv Dep Med Stores
    2/3 Aust CCS
    21 Aust Hosp Laundry Unit (Type B)
    10 Aust Fd Amb
    2/3 Aust Mobile Bacteriological Laboratory
    4 Aust Mobile Entomological Sec
DENTAL
    2/1 Aust Dental Unit
    2/2 Aust Dental Unit less three Secs
ORDNANCE
    1 Aust Armd Regt Ord Fd Pk (LE)
    Det 4 Aust Armd Bde Ord Fd Pk
    120 Aust Bde Ord Fd Pk
AEME
    1 Aust Armd Regt Workshop (Type A) less Det
    4 Aust Armd Bde Workshop less Det
    120 Aust Bde Workshop
    2/1 Aust Comp AA Regt Workshop
    205 Aust LAD (Type H) less Det
PROVOST
    'A' Det Special Investigation Branch Det I Aust Corps
GRAVES
    24 Aust War Graves Unit
RAAF UNITS
    No. 61 Airfield Constr Wing HQ
    No. 1 Airfield Constr Sqn
    No. 2 Airfield Constr Sqn
    No. 3 Airfield Constr Sqn
    No. 6 Airfield Constr Sqn
    No. 4 Wireless Unit Det

PART III

2 AUST BEACH GROUP

HEADQUARTERS
    HQ 2 Aust Beach Group
ENGINEERS
    2/11 Aust Fd Coy
    2 Aust Mech Eqpt Pl
    2 Aust Beach Gp Stores Pl
SIGNALS
    1 Aust Beach Sig Sec
    4 Aust Beach Sig Sec
INFANTRY
    2/2 Aust Pnr Bn
INTELLIGENCE
    'B' Det 'Q' Aust Field Security Sec

SUPPLY AND TRANSPORT
  HQ 2/108 Aust Gen Tpt Coy
  2/45 Aust Tpt Pl
  2/46 Aust Tpt Pl
  2/108 Aust Wksp Pl
  235 Aust Sup Dep Pl
  58 Aust Bulk Issue Petrol Oil Depot Pl
MEDICAL
  2 AAMC Coy (Beach Gp)
  23 Aust Malaria Control Unit (Type C)
ORDNANCE
  1 Aust Ord Beach Det
AEME
  2 Aust Beach Workshop
PROVOST
  17 Aust Indep Bde Gp Provost Coy
SALVAGE
  1 Aust Armd Bde Salvage Unit
RAN UNITS ATTACHED
  B and D RAN Beach Commandos

PART IV
7 AUST BASE SUB-AREA UNITS

HEADQUARTERS
  HQ 7 Aust Base Sub Area (Type D)
  Det 2 Aust Adv 2nd Echelon
ENGINEERS
  12 CRE (Works)
  27 Aust CRE (Works)
  2/4 Aust Fd Sqn
  21 Aust Fd Coy
  9 Aust A Tps Coy
  11 Aust Workshop and Park Coy
  2/3 Aust Docks Operating Coy
  2/10 Aust Docks Operating Coy
  Det 7 Pl 1 Aust Port Maint Coy
  2/2 Aust Port Constr Coy
  1 Aust Port Constr Coy
  3 Aust Welding Pl
  5 Aust Welding Pl
  5 Aust Mech Eqpt Spare Parts Sec
  Det 11 Aust Small Ships Coy
SIGNALS
  'C' Det HQ 22 L of C Sigs
  13 Aust Line Sec
  'A' Det 9 Aust Technical Maintenance Sec
  'B' Det 94 Aust Telephone Switchboard Operating Sec
  9 Aust Telegraph Operating Sec
  3 Aust Despatch Rider Sec (less A and B Dets)
  'B' Det 4 Aust Signal Eqpt Sec
  36 Aust Cipher Sec (Type K) (less Det)
INTELLIGENCE
  'B' Det 1 Aust Fd Censorship Coy
  'B' Det 'Q' Aust Fd Security Sec

SUPPLY AND TRANSPORT
    20 Aust Fd Baking Pl
    46 Aust Fd Baking Pl
    66 Aust Bulk Issue Petrol Oil Depot Pl
    2/4 Aust Motor Ambulance Convoy Pl
    'C' Det 4 Aust Bulk Petroleum Storage Coy
MEDICAL
    2/12 Aust Gen Hosp (600 beds)
    One Surgical Team 2/12 Aust Gen Hosp
    One Surgical Team 2/2 Aust Gen Hosp
    Three Laundry Increments AAMC
    14 Aust Malaria Control Unit (Type B)
    17 Aust Malaria Control Unit (Type B)
DENTAL
    2 Sec 1 Aust Base Depot Dental Stores
ORDNANCE
    Det 17 Advanced Ordnance Depot
    Det 4 Aust Returned Stores Depot
    Det 10 Aust Ord Vehicle Park
    Det 5 Aust Ord Port Det
    Det 2/7 Aust Mobile Laundry and Forward Decontamination Unit
    Det 14 Aust LAD
    2 Aust Mobile Ammunition Repair Shop
    2/3 Aust Inf Tps Ord Fd Pk (less one Vehicle Park Sec)
AEME
    2/3 Aust Inf Tps Workshop
    5 Aust Mech Eqpt Workshop
    228 Aust LAD
    305 Aust LAD
    336 Aust LAD
    'B' Sec 10 Aust Vehicle Park Workshop
    6 Aust Mobile Gas Generating Sec
    5 Aust Mobile Tyre Repair Workshop Sec
PAY
    73 Aust Depot Cash Office
    108 Aust Depot Cash Office
POSTAL
    'A' Det 6 Aust Base Postal Unit
PROVOST
    5, 6 Secs 2/3 Aust L of C Pro Coy
PRINTING & STATIONERY
    'C' Det 11 Aust L of C Stationery Depot
CANTEENS SERVICE
    Adv Det AACS
AMENITIES
    17 Mobile Cinema Aust Cinema Unit
    20 Mobile Cinema Aust Cinema Unit
MISCELLANEOUS
    'A' Det 37 Aust L of C Salvage Sec
    28 Aust Wks Coy
    Det 10 Sec Aust Kit Store
    'B' Det 1 Aust Base Sub Area Details Depot

7TH DIVISION AT BALIKPAPAN

PART V
US, NEI AND MISCELLANEOUS UNITS

US UNITS
  727 Amphibious Tractor Bn less one Coy
  One Boat Coy Boat Bn 593 EBSR
  Det 1463 Engr Boat Maint Coy
  Det Bn HQ and one Company 672 Amphibious Tractor Bn
  Det Combat Information Centre

NEI UNITS
  1 Coy 1 Bn NEI Inf
  One NICA Unit (Dutch)

MISCELLANEOUS
  Det SRD
  Det FELO

PART VI
RAAF UNITS IN SUPPORT FOR OPERATION

Comd Post 1 TAF RAAF
No. 83 (Army Co-Op) Wing HQ Det
No. 4 Tac R Sqn Det
No. 16 Air Observation Post Flt Det
No. 9 Local Air Supply Unit Det
No. 79 (General Reconnaissance-Bomber) Wing
No. 2 (B25) Sqn
No. 18 (B24) Sqn
No. 83 Operational Base Unit
No. 28 Air Stores Pk
No. 27 Med Clearing Station
No. 18 Repair and Servicing Unit
No. 82 (H/B) Wing
No. 21 (B24) Sqn
No. 23 (B24) Sqn
No. 24 (B24) Sqn
No. 6 Repair and Servicing Unit
No. 30 Med Clearing Station
No. 24 Air Stores Pk
No. 85 Operational Base Unit
No. 18 Replenishing Centre
No. 54 (Spitfire) Sqn
No. 9 Repair and Servicing Unit Det
No. 113 Air Sea Rescue Flt Det
1 Air Support Sec and 3 Parties
8 Air Liaison Parties
No. 1 Aust Air Form Sigs Det
No. 4 Radio Installation and Maint Det
No. 2 Malaria Control Unit Det
No. 5 Replenishing Centre Det
Service Police Unit Det
No. 30 Operational Base Unit
No. 9 Transportation and Movement (Office Det)
No. 2 Airfield Defence Sqn Det
No. 110 Mobile Fighter Control Unit Assault Ech
No. 162 Radar Station
No. 302 Radar Station
No. 343 Radar Station
No. 351 Radar Station

No. 23 Air Stores Pk
No. 26 Med Clearing Station
No. 11 Postal Unit Det
TAF Telecomn Unit Det
3 Aust Comd Air Liaison Sec
21 Sqn Air Liaison Sec
25 Sqn Air Liaison Sec
28 Sqn Air Liaison Sec
35 Sqn Air Liaison Sec
55 Sqn Air Liaison Sec
56 Sqn Air Liaison Sec
'B' Det 45 Air Liaison Sec (Tac R Sqn)

PART VII

US NAVAL UNITS IN SUPPORT FOR THE OPERATION
(The list includes 21 units or detachments)

APPENDIX 7

SOME STATISTICS

EMBARKATION FOR SERVICE OUTSIDE AUSTRALIA

It is impossible to give an accurate answer to the question: How many Australian service men and women served outside Australia in the war? Many thousands embarked for oversea service more than once. Many departures by air were not recorded. Some men enlisted more than once. However, Central Army Records Office arrived at an approximate figure by adding to the numbers of "Returned from Active Service" badges issued the numbers of those who died overseas, and making other adjustments.

In this way the following totals were arrived at:

Served outside Australia
Army	. .	396,661
Navy	. .	37,061
Air Force	. .	124,077
Total	.	557,799

In the army total allowance has been made for the estimated numbers of those who died in Australia after service overseas and for those discharged for reasons that involved forfeiture of the badge. No such adjustment has been made to the navy and air force totals. On the other hand a number of persons who qualified for the badge by service at Darwin have been included. It is impossible to make any useful estimate of the number of Australians who were serving in British forces when war broke out—there were some 450 aircrew in the R.A.F. alone—or who were in Britain when war began and enlisted there, or who later proceeded to Britain and enlisted. Random perusal of school honour rolls and the like suggests that, in this war as in 1914-18, there may have been several thousands of these, including students, nurses, men gaining oversea experience in professions and trades, tourists, employees of oversea branches of Australian firms and so on.

In 1914-18 the number who embarked for army service overseas, including service in the Australian Flying Corps, was 331,781, among whom were some individuals who embarked more than once. In 1918 the number of Australians in the R.A.N. was 4,225, and some 600 other R.A.N. or R.A.N. Brigade men served at sea.

BATTLE CASUALTIES: AUSTRALIAN SERVICES, WAR OF 1939-45.

Particulars	Royal Australian Navy	Australian Army	Royal Australian Air Force	All Services
WAR AGAINST GERMANY				
Killed—				
Killed in action and missing, presumed dead	900	2,610	5,036	8,546
Died of wounds	3	700	58	761
Died of wounds while prisoner of war		56	9	65
Died of sickness, disease and injury while prisoner of war		95 ⎱		
Presumed died while prisoner of war		91 ⎰	14	200
Total killed	903	3,552	5,117	9,572
Prisoners of war escaped, recovered or repatriated	25	6,874	1,020	7,919
Wounded and injured in action (cases)	26	8,925	529	9,480
Total	954	19,351	6,666	26,971

BATTLE CASUALTIES: AUSTRALIAN SERVICES, WAR OF 1939-45.—continued

Particulars	Royal Australian Navy	Australian Army	Royal Australian Air Force	All Services
WAR AGAINST JAPAN				
Killed—				
Killed in action and missing, presumed dead	840	6,294	1,140	8,274
Died of wounds	41	1,090	65	1,196
Died of wounds while prisoner of war } Died of sickness, disease and injury while prisoner of war } Presumed died while prisoner of war	116	{ 50 5,336 2,391 }	138	8,031
Total killed	997	15,161	1,343	17,501
Prisoners of war escaped, recovered or repatriated	238	13,872	235	14,345
Wounded and injured in action (cases)	553	13,191	253	13,997
Total	1,788	42,224	1,831	45,843
ALL THEATRES OF WAR				
Killed—				
Killed in action and missing, presumed dead	1,740	8,904	6,176	16,820
Died of wounds	44	1,790	123	1,957
Died of wounds while prisoner of war } Died of sickness, disease and injury while prisoner of war } Presumed died while prisoner of war	116	{ 106 5,431 2,482 }	161	8,296
Total killed	1,900	18,713	6,460	27,073
Prisoners of war escaped, recovered or repatriated	263	20,746	1,255	22,264
Wounded and injured in action (cases)	579	22,116	782	23,477
Total	2,742	61,575	8,497	72,814

These tables do not include deaths and illnesses from natural causes. The army casualties do not include 85 Papuan and New Guinea soldiers or members of the Royal Papuan Constabulary killed in action and 201 wounded.

Casualties other than in battle suffered by the army in operational areas were·

Killed, died of injuries etc.	1,165
Wounded, injured etc. (cases)	33,396
Total	34,561

Similar casualties suffered in non-operational areas were:

Killed, died of injuries etc.	2,051
Wounded, injured etc. (cases)	121,800
Total	123,851

These figures exclude deaths and illnesses from natural causes.

Non-battle casualties suffered by the navy totalled 177 and by the air force 6,271.

The above figures are derived from tables published in the Commonwealth Year Book. The reader interested in the R.A.A.F. figures is referred to the differently organised and dissected tables of casualties published in Appendix 3 of the final volume of the Air Force series of this history.

AUSTRALIAN ARMY CASUALTIES IN THE SOUTH-WEST PACIFIC FROM 1st JULY 1944 TO THE END OF THE WAR

	Killed in action and died of wounds	Wounded	Died of Illness	Accidentally Killed
New Guinea	489	1,243	76	154
New Britain	48	134	8	35
Solomons	515	1,577	13	53
Borneo	567	1,530	45	69
Elsewhere in S.W.P.A.	69	1	—	1
Total	1,688	4,485	142	312

GROSS ARMY ENLISTMENTS BY STATES

	Gross enlistments to 29/9/45	Population in 1940 000's	Percentage of enlistments to population
Queensland	104,340	1,029	10.13
New South Wales	276,741	2,801	9.87
Victoria	205,758	1,918	10.72
South Australia	54,660	598	9.14
Western Australia	61,575	468	13.15
Tasmania	22,420	243	9.22
Northern Territory	1,049	8	13.11
	726,543	7,065	10.28

PHYSIQUE OF RECRUITS

Second Echelon, A.H.Q., examined the records of more than 25,000 men of the army with the object of discovering their average height, weight and chest measurement on enlistment. It found that the averages for men who were 21, for example, on enlistment were: height, 5 feet 7.6 inches; weight, 147 pounds; chest, 36.8 inches. The average height for various age-groups ranged from 5 feet 7 inches to 5 feet 8.4 inches (the latter for a relatively small sampling of men aged 44).

SOME COMPARATIVE FIGURES OF ARMY STRENGTHS AND CASUALTIES
1914-1918 WAR WITH 1939-1945 WAR

Casualty	1914-1918 War	1939-1945 War
Gross strength of force on continuous full time war service	416,809	727,703
Total number of personnel who served beyond the mainland of Australia	331,781	396,661
Killed in action and missing presumed dead	39,880	8,904
Died of wounds	13,393	1,790
Died of wounds while prisoner of war	288	106
Died of sickness, disease, and injuries while prisoner of war	109	7,913
Died of gas poisoning	323	—
Total battle casualty deaths	53,993	18,713
Wounded in action	137,013	22,116
Gassed	16,496	—
Shell-shock wounds	1,624	—
Prisoners of war (escaped, recovered or repatriated)	3,647	20,746
Total battle casualties	212,773	61,575
Non-battle casualty deaths from illness and other causes (a)	6,291	6,038
Sick beyond the mainland of Australia	393,155	433,587
Accidental injuries, etc. beyond the mainland of Australia	4,387	33,396
Over-all total of casualties (b)	616,606	534,596
Mortality all causes	60,284	24,751

NOTES:
(a) Includes deaths in Australia: 1914-18—1,431; 1939-45—2,658.
(b) 1914-18 War figures taken from the *Official History of the Australian Army Medical Services 1914-1918*, Vol III, Table Nos. 26 and 27.

Compiled at Central Army Records Office, MELBOURNE.

APPENDIX 8

AUSTRALIAN ARMY UNIT HISTORIES, WAR OF 1939-45

Vernon, P. V. (Editor). *The Royal New South Wales Lancers 1885-1960.* Sydney, 1961.

Kerr, Colin. *Tanks in the East: the Story of an Australian Cavalry Regiment.* (9th Divisional Cavalry Regiment.) Melbourne, Oxford University Press, 1945.

Allard, J. M., Cochrane, W. H., Maiden, M. J., Speare, J. H. *Tank Tracks: the War History of the 2/4th Australian Armoured Regimental Group.* Sydney, 1953.

"Speed and Vigilance": the Story of the 2 Aust. Tank Bn. (A.I.F.) 1939-44. Sydney.

Haywood, E. V. *Six Years in Support: Official History of 2/1st Australian Field Regiment.* Sydney, Angus & Robertson, 1959.

Cremor, W. (General Editor). *Action Front: the History of the 2/2nd Australian Field Artillery Regiment, Royal Australian Artillery A.I.F.* Melbourne, 2/2nd Field Regiment Association, 1961.

Henry, R. L. *The Story of the 2/4th Field Regiment.* Melbourne, 1950.

O'Brien, J. W. *Guns and Gunners: the Story of the 2/5th Australian Field Regiment in World War II.* Sydney, Angus & Robertson, 1950.

Goodhart, David. *The History of the 2/7 Australian Field Regiment.* Adelaide, Rigby, 1952.

"Silver John" (Argent, J. N. L.). *"Target Tank."* (The history of the 2/3rd Anti-Tank Regiment.) Parramatta, N.S.W., 1957.

The Logbook: Collected Records of the 2/7 Aust Svy Bty RAA AIF 1940-1945. Melbourne, 1946.

The Corps of Royal Australian Engineers in the Second World War 1939-45. Melbourne, 1946.

Signals: Story of the Australian Corps of Signals. Sydney, 1945.

Jacobs, J. W. and Bridgland, R. J. (Editors). *Through: the Story of Signals 8 Australian Division and Signals A.I.F. Malaya.* 8 Division Signals Association, 1950.

Mansfield, Alan (compiled by). *The Spotters: a Brief History of the New Guinea Air Warning Wireless Company (A.I.F.).* 1962.

Ross, A. R. (Editor). *The Seventeenth Brigade Magazine.* 1944.

Yeates, J. D. and Loh, W. G. *Red Platypus: a Record of the Achievements of the 24th Australian Infantry Brigade, Ninth Australian Division 1940-45.* Perth, 1946.

Marshall, A. J. (Editor). *Nulli Secundus Log.* 2/2nd Battalion, 1946.

Allchin, Frank. *Purple and Blue: the History of the 2/10th Battalion, A.I.F. (The Adelaide Rifles) 1939-1945.* Adelaide, 1958.

Fearnside, G. H. *Bayonets Abroad: a History of the 2/13th Battalion A.I.F. in the Second World War.* Sydney, 1953.

Russell, W. B. *The Second Fourteenth Battalion: a History of an Australian Infantry Battalion in the Second World War.* Sydney, Angus & Robertson, 1948.

Uren, Malcolm. *A Thousand Men at War: the Story of the 2/16th Battalion, A.I.F.* Melbourne, William Heinemann, 1959.

Ziegler, O. L. (Editor). *Men May Smoke.* Sydney, 2/18th Battalion Association, 1948.

Burns, John. *The Brown and Blue Diamond at War: the Story of the 2/27th Battalion A.I.F.* Adelaide, 2/27th Battalion Association, 1960.

Masel, Philip. *The Second 28th: the Story of a Famous Battalion of the Ninth Australian Division.* Perth, 2/28th Battalion and 24th Anti-Tank Company Association, 1961.

Penfold, A. W., Bayliss, W. C., Crispin, K. E. *Galleghan's Greyhounds: the Story of the 2/30th Australian Infantry Battalion.* Sydney, 2/30th Battalion Association, 1949.

Boss-Walker, Geoffrey. *Desert Sand and Jungle Green: a Pictorial History of the 2/43rd Australian Infantry Battalion (Ninth Division) in the Second World War 1939-1945.* Hobart, 1948.

Glenn, J. G. *Tobruk to Tarakan.* (2/48th Battalion.) Adelaide, Rigby, 1960.

Macfarlan, Graeme. *Etched in Green: the History of the 22nd Australian Infantry Battalion 1939-1946.* Melbourne, 22nd Battalion Association, 1961.

Charlott, Rupert (Editor). *The Unofficial History of the 29/46th Australian Infantry Battalion A.I.F.* Melbourne, 1952.

Benson, S. E. *The Story of the 42 Aust. Inf. Bn.* Sydney, Dymock's Book Arcade for 42nd Battalion Association, 1952.

Mathews, Russell. *Militia Battalion at War: the History of the 58/59th Australian Infantry Battalion in the Second World War.* Sydney, 58/59th Battalion Association, 1961.

Aitken, E. F. *The Story of the 2/2nd Australian Pioneer Battalion.* Melbourne, 2/2nd Pioneer Battalion Association, 1953.

Anderson, J. A. and Jackett, J. G. T. (Editors). *Mud and Sand: the Official War History of the 2/3 Pioneer Battalion A.I.F.* Sydney, 2/3rd Pioneer Battalion Association.

Fairclough, H. *Equal to the Task: the History of the Royal Australian Army Service Corps.* Melbourne, F. W. Cheshire, 1962.

In 1962 histories of the following units were known to be in preparation: the 2/3rd Battalion, 2/4th Battalion, 2/5th Battalion, 2/7th Battalion, 2/11th Battalion, 2/17th Battalion, 2/24th Battalion, 24th Battalion, 2/5th Australian General Hospital, 2/8th Field Company, R.A.E.

APPENDIX 9

ABBREVIATIONS

A—*Acting, Assistant*
AA—*Anti-Aircraft*
AAG—*Assistant Adjutant-General*
AAMC—*Australian Army Medical Corps*
AAMWS—*Australian Army Medical Women's Service*
AASC—*Australian Army Service Corps*
Admin—*Administration, Administrative*
ADMS—*Assistant Director Medical Services*
ADOS—*Assistant Director Ordnance Services*
Adv—*Advanced*
AEME—*Australian Electrical and Mechanical Engineers*
AES—*Army Education Service*
AGH—*Australian General Hospital*
AHQ—*Army Headquarters*
AIF—*Australian Imperial Force*
AMF—*Australian Military Forces*
Angau—*Australian New Guinea Administrative Unit*
AQMG—*Assistant Quartermaster-General*
Armd—*Armoured*
Arty—*Artillery*
ATIS—*Allied Translator and Interpreter Section*
A-Tk—*Anti-Tank*
AVM—*Air Vice-Marshal*
AWAS—*Australian Women's Army Service*

BBCAU—*British Borneo Civil Affairs Unit*
BCOF—*British Commonwealth Occupation Force*
Bde—*Brigade*
Bdr—*Bombardier*
BGS—*Brigadier, General Staff*
BM—*Brigade Major*
Bn—*Battalion*
Brig—*Brigadier*
Bty—*Battery*

Capt—*Captain*
CASC—*Commander, Army Service Corps*
Cav—*Cavalry*
CCRA—*Commander, Corps Royal Artillery*
Cdo—*Commando*

Cdr—*Commander*
CE—*Chief Engineer*
CEME—*Commander, Electrical and Mechanical Engineers*
CGS—*Chief of the General Staff*
C-in-C—*Commander-in-Chief*
CO—*Commanding Officer*
Col—*Colonel*
Comd—*Command, Commander, Commanded*
Coy—*Company*
Cpl—*Corporal*
CRA—*Commander, Royal Artillery*
CRE—*Commander, Royal Engineers (of a division)*
CSO—*Chief Signals Officer*
CTF—*Commander, Task Force*

DAQMG—*Deputy Assistant Quartermaster-General*
DDST—*Deputy Director Supply and Transport*
Det—*Detachment*
DGPR—*Director-General of Public Relations*
Div—*Division*
DORCA—*Directorate of Research and Civil Affairs*

EBSR—*Engineer Boat and Shore Regiment*
Engrs—*Engineers*
Eqpt—*Equipment*

Fd—*Field*
FELO—*Far Eastern Liaison Office*

Gd—*Guard*
Gen—*General*
GHQ—*General Headquarters*
Gnr—*Gunner*
GOC—*General Officer Commanding*
Gp—*Group*
GS—*General Staff*
GSO1—*General Staff Officer, Grade 1*

HQ—*Headquarters*
Hy—*Heavy*

i/c—*in command*
Indep—*Independent*
Inf—*Infantry*

LAA—*Light Anti-Aircraft*
LAD—*Light Aid Detachment*
L-Cpl—*Lance-Corporal*
LHQ—*Allied Land Forces Headquarters*
L of C—*Lines of Communication*
Lt—*Lieutenant, Light*

Maj—*Major*
MG—*Machine Gun*
MGRA—*Major-General, Royal Artillery*
MHR—*Member of the House of Representatives*
Mil—*Military*
ML—*Motor Launch*
MLC—*Member of the Legislative Council*

NCO—*Non-commissioned Officer*
NEI—*Netherlands East Indies*
NG—*New Guinea*
NGF—*New Guinea Force*
NGIB—*New Guinea Infantry Battalion*
NGVR—*New Guinea Volunteer Rifles*
NT—*Northern Territory*

OC—*Officer Commanding*
OCTU—*Officer Cadet Training Unit*
OOB—*Order of Battle*
Ops—*Operations*
OSMG—*Owen sub-machine-gun*

PIB—*Papuan Infantry Battalion*
Pk—*Park*
Pl—*Platoon*
Pnr—*Pioneer*
PT—*Patrol Torpedo (boat)*
Pte—*Private*

RAA—*Royal Australian Artillery*
RAAF—*Royal Australian Air Force*
RAE—*Royal Australian Engineers*
RAF—*Royal Air Force*
RAN—*Royal Australian Navy*
RANR—*Royal Australian Naval Reserve*
RANVR—*Royal Australian Naval Volunteer Reserve*
RAR—*Royal Australian Regiment*
Regt—*Regiment*
RFA—*Royal Field Artillery*
RMO—*Regimental Medical Officer*
RNN—*Royal Netherlands Navy*
RNZAF—*Royal New Zealand Air Force*

Sec—*Section*
Sgt—*Sergeant*
SHAEF—*Supreme Headquarters, Allied Expeditionary Force*
Sig—*Signalman*
Sigs—*Signals*
Spr—*Sapper*
Sqn—*Squadron*
S-Sgt—*Staff-Sergeant*
SWPA—*South-West Pacific Area*

Tk—*Tank*
Tpr—*Trooper*
Tps—*Troops*

USAAF—*United States Army Air Forces*
USAFFE—*United States Army Forces in the Far East*
USASOS—*United States Army Services of Supply*
USN—*United States Navy*

WO1—*Warrant-Officer, Class 1*

INDEX

ABASH (Sketch p. 533), 537
ABAU (Sketches pp. 284, 285), 277, 283-4, 286, 294
ABBOT, Col J. N., commands 26 Bn, 98
ABBOTT, Pte A. F., 108
ABBOTT, Capt W. T., 353
ABEL, Pte C. W., 517
ABIDE (Sketch p. 533), 539
ABLE ROUTE (Sketch p. 466), 468
ABOAMA (Sketch p. 284), 296, 311
ABUNGAI (Sketches pp. 302, 331), 310, 332
ACKERLEY, Lt F. E., 476
ADACHI, Lt-Gen Hatazo (Plate p. 381), 272, 291*n*, 292-4, 302, 311, 319, 327, 369, 384, 559; commands *XVIII Army*, 269; death of, 386-7
ADAMSON, Capt D. H., 259
ADELE RIVER (Map p. 91; Sketches pp. 131, 144), 128, 130-2, 153
ADJIRADEN RIVER (Sketch p. 544), 543-4
ADLER BAY (Map p. 243), 247, 268
ADMIRALTY ISLANDS (Maps pp. 3, 60), 21, 92, 394, 548, 596
AFUA (Sketch p. 276), 279
Age, The, 605*n*
AGNES (Sketch p. 429), 434, 436-8
AGRICULTURAL STATION (Sketch p. 331), 330
AHEGULIM (Sketch p. 361), 364, 366
AH MING, Chinese agent, 247
A.I.F. News, 87
AIKYO, Colonel, 564
AINSLIE, Brig R. I., 415, 425, 446; commands 2/48 Bn, 411
AIRCRAFT, Types: *Auster*, 95*n*, 152, 155, 199, 334, 420, 449, 474, 543; *Beaufort*, 246, 250, 256, 258, 275, 285, 290, 301, 309, 312, 335-7, 350, 372-3; *Boomerang*, 95*n*, 275, 329; *Catalina*, 455, 508, 513, 563; *Corsair*, 95, 109, 149, 155, 156*n*, 179, 189, 192, 194, 202, 220, 231; *Dakota*, 294, 309, 328, 334, 554*n*, 563; *Douglas*, 310, 334, 336, 359; *Kittyhawk*, 500; *Liberator*, 412, 433, 437, 439-42, 444, 462, 510-11, 526, 530, 621; *Lightning*, 345, 412, 432-3, 437, 439, 441-2, 510, 528; *Mitchell*, 410, 412, 434, 441, 462, 510; *Moth*, 329; *Piper Cub*, 304; *Spitfire*, 474, 488, 492; *Superfortress*, 28; *Wirraway*, 95*n*, 138-9, 275, 301; *Zeke*, 259*n*
AIR SUPPORT, in New Britain, 244-6, 255, 269; in Wewak campaign, 275, 306, 335-6, 359; at Tarakan, 412, 427, 433-4, 437, 439-42, 444; in north Borneo, 458-60, 462; at Balikapan, 545-6
AITA (Sketch p. 127), 127
AITAPE (Maps pp. 60, 273; Sketches pp. 271, 276), 19, 21-5, 28, 36*n*, 38-9, 44, 55, 58*n*, 61, 67-8, 76-7, 89, 96, 183, 272-6, 279-80, 291-2, 294, 296, 300, 304, 328, 334, 345, 350, 354, 359, 362, 364, 377, 385-6, 392*n*, 596; area described, 271-2, 281; HQ 6 Div opens at, 278; floods at, 314*n*
AITARA MISSION (Sketch p. 180), 186, 188
AITARA RIVER (Sketch p. 180), 188
AITARA TRACK, 188, 191
AITERAP (Map p. 273; Sketch p. 276), 276, 278
AITKEN, Lt-Col E. F., 638
AKINAGA, Lt-Gen Tsutomu, 164, 200; commands *6 Div*, 150
AKU (Sketches pp. 180, 219), 152
ALANBROOKE, Field Marshal Viscount, 8-9
ALBU CREEK (Sketch p. 284), 283
ALEXANDER, Field Marshal Earl, 4
ALLAN, Sgt D. A., 110
ALLARD, Capt J. M., 637
ALLCHIN, Lt-Col E. F., 637
ALLEN, Capt K. F., 426
ALLIED AIR FORCES, 45-6, 53*n*, 590-2, 597; in New Britain, 244, 246; in Borneo, 470-1, 484, 509-10
ALLIED INTELLIGENCE BUREAU, 67, 69, 103*n*, 263, 275, 402, 507; in Solomons, 100, 135-40, 156, 168-71, 175-6, 200-1, 205-6, 217, 227; in New Britain, 241-8, 250-2, 254-6, 269; in Wewak campaign, 276, 279, 290, 311, 342-3, 368; history of, 617-22
 —INTER-ALLIED SERVICES DEPT, 618
 —MOSSTROOPS, 619
 —NETHERLANDS FORCES INTELLIGENCE SECTION, 619-20

ALLIED INTELLIGENCE BUREAU—*continued*
 —NORTH-EASTERN AREA, 621
 —PHILIPPINE REGIONAL SECTION, 620
 —SECRET INTELLIGENCE AUSTRALIA, 621
 —SERVICES RECONNAISSANCE DEPT, 507, 619-20; in Borneo, 454-6, 459, 489, 490-5, 508-9, 565, 621
 —SPECIAL OPERATIONS AUSTRALIA, 617-19
ALLIED LAND FORCES HEADQUARTERS (L.H.Q.), 10, 28, 37, 41, 50, 73, 281, 404, 567, 593, 601, 603-4, 617, 621; Adv HQ established at Hollandia, 24; at Morotai, 47; and command problems in SWPA, 45, 53, 590-9; estimates Japanese strength in Bougainville, 101-2; deprives officers of right to censor own mail, 239; Military Government of reoccupied areas, 397-9, 401-2, 498
ALLIED NAVAL FORCES, 45-6, 590-1, 597
ALLIED TRANSLATOR AND INTERPRETER SECTION, 172*n*, 507
ALLIES, THE, 35, 65, 266, 567-8; strength of forces in 1944, 1; Australia provides services for, 396; strategy in Pacific, 584-5; problems of cooperation between armies of, 586-7
ALLSOPP, Capt R. J., 515
AMAHAUR (Sketch p. 302), 304
AMAL RIVER (Sketch p. 409), 411*n*, 427, 430, 433-4, 436, 446, 448
AMAM (Map p. 273; Sketch p. 276), 277, 279, 284, 362
AMBON ISLAND (Maps pp. 3, 28; Sketch p. 560), 11, 14, 93, 454, 569, 573; Japanese strength on, 555; surrender of, 570-1
AMBORAWANG (Sketch p. 544), 544-5
AMBUSHES: *Australian*, in Bougainville, 167-8, 185-6, 190, 199-200, 205; in New Britain, 255-6; in Wewak campaign, 283, 285, 309, 378-9; in Borneo, 492, 543. *Japanese*, in Bougainville, 168, 208-9; in Wewak campaign, 285, 308, 378; in Borneo, 492-3
AMERICA, UNITED STATES OF, 9, 13, 50, 56, 65, 70, 87, 395, 560; military contribution, 35; misconceptions about Australian war effort, 40; pre-war plans and preparations, 585
AMERICAN AIR FORCE, 28, 46, 95, 458, 507, 519; attacks Japan, 4, 502; strength in SWPA, 19*n*; in Wewak campaign, 345-6, 350
 —FORCES: *Fifth Air*, 29, 509, 531; *Thirteenth Air*, 410, 509, 531; *Twentieth Air*, 51
AMERICAN ARMY, 21, 51, 53, 65, 165, 183*n*, 237, 269, 275, 357, 359, 407*n*, 452, 550, 578, 589; Australian relations with, 1*n*, 37, 43-4, 96; in Pacific, 4-5, 19-20, 24, 27-30, 80; in Philippines, 4, 40, 45-6, 47-8, 61, 66-7, 267, 405; in Burma, 15; relieved by Australians, 25, 38, 65, 253*n*; strength, 35-6; and Borneo campaign, 50, 510; in New Guinea, 52-3, 67-8, 241, 272, 275, 291, 386; equipment of, 62, compared with Australians, 96-7; in Bougainville, 100, 103, 106, 114, 217, 241; Intelligence estimates, 101-2, 449; in New Britain, 244, 248-9, 270; makes demands on Australia for reciprocal Lend-Lease, 395-6; command problems in SWPA, 590-9; ratio of generals to strength, 602-3; and AIB, 620
 —UNITED STATES ARMY FORCES IN AUSTRALIA, 591
 —UNITED STATES ARMY FORCES IN THE FAR EAST, 594
 —UNITED STATES ARMY SERVICES OF SUPPLY, 53*n*
 —ARMIES: *Sixth*, 130*n*, 595; in Philippines, 1-2, 4, 19, 29, 55-6, 94*n*; named "Alamo Force", 594; command problems, 599. *Eighth*, 19, 28, 577*n*, 595; in Philippines, 29, 55-6, 71; role and command of I Corps, 41, 45, 47; command problems, 596, 599. *Tenth*, 27, 51
 —CORPS: *I Corps*, 19, 593-4. *VII Corps*, 593. *X Corps*, 2, 19, 29, 55. *XI Corps*, 19, 28-9, 275. *XIV Corps*, 19, 22, 90, 92-4, 101, 103, 137, 170, 281. *XXIV Corps*, 1-2, 19, 30
 —DIVISIONS: *Americal*, 30, 55; in Bougainville, 19*n*, 90, 92; relieved by 3 Aust Div, 94. *1st Cavalry*, invades Leyte, 2, 19*n*. *6th Infantry*, 19*n*. *7th Infantry*, 30; invades Leyte, 2, 19*n*. *11th Airborne*, invades Leyte, 4, 19*n*. *24th Infantry*, 30; in Philippines, 2, 19*n*, 55. *25th Infantry*, 19*n*. *31st Infantry*, 19*n*, 30, 275; in Philippines, 55. *32nd Infantry*, 275; in Philippines, 4, 19*n*. *33rd Infantry*, 19*n*. *37th*

INDEX

AMERICAN ARMY—continued
Infantry, in Bougainville, 19n, 90, 92; relief of, 94.
38th Infantry, in Philippines, 19n. 40th Infantry,
55, 241; in Philippines, 19n. 41st Infantry, 30,
591n; on Biak, 19n; in Philippines, 55. 43rd
Infantry, at Aitape, 19n, 276; relief of, 275, 278-9.
77th Infantry, 30; in Leyte, 4, 19n. 93rd Infantry,
19n, 30, 92-3. 96th Infantry, 2, 30; in Leyte, 19n.
—FORCES: *Alamo*, 594-5, 599
—REGIMENTS: 112th Cavalry, 275. 129th Infantry,
94. 132nd Infantry, 94, 106n. 145th Infantry, 94.
148th Infantry, 94. 164th Infantry, 94, 110. 172nd
Infantry, 277-8. 182nd Infantry, 94, 111-12. 185th
Infantry, 249-50. 593rd EBSR, 281, 448, 457, 459,
474-5, 477, 507. 594th EBSR, 250-1, 260
—BATTALIONS: *Amphibious Tractor*, 672 Bn, 507,
517; 727 Bn, 459, 507
AMERICAN GOVERNMENT, 35, 395, 560, 585, 587;
bombing of Japanese cities, 4; and British participation in Pacific, 7, 14, 15-18, 20; and China, 11;
supply demands on Australia, 12; policy on civil
administration of occupied territory, 400
—JOINT CHIEFS OF STAFF, 1, 6, 10-11, 27-8, 41, 46,
52, 54, 551, 559; command problems, 14-15, 394,
548, 590-1, 599; plans Borneo operations, 50-1, 389
—WAR DEPARTMENT, 620
AMERICAN NAVY, 51, 93, 104n, 507, 560, 583-5, 621;
strength, 4; role in Pacific, 12, 27-8; in Borneo
operations, 458-61, 487, 506, 521, 525
—AMPHIBIOUS GROUPS: Six, 406-7, 458. Eight, 511
—MARINE CORPS: 27, 40n, 51, 55n, 90, 418, 458,
558
—SEVENTH FLEET, 407; in Philippines, 2-4; role,
46; in Balikpapan operation, 520
—SUBMARINES, 454
Amethyst, British sloop, 556
AMI (Sketches pp. 302, 305), 303-4, 307-8
AMIET, Capt A. H., 421, 441
AMMUNITION, *Australian*, shortages in Wewak
campaign, 308; shortages at Tarakan, 439-40,
expenditure, 447; shortages at Balikpapan, 508,
expenditure, 511, 531. *Japanese*, captured in
Bougainville, 175; shortages in Wewak campaign,
291-2; destruction after surrender, 558
AMUK RIVER (Sketches pp. 302, 305), 290, 303, 305-7,
309
AMUN (Map p. 91), 106, 113
ANDAMAN ISLANDS (Map p. 3), 6
ANDERSON, Lt Allan J., 258n
ANDERSON, Lt-Col Arthur J., 178; commands 24
Bn, 99
ANDERSON, Lt C. D., 353
ANDERSON, Capt C. H., 621
ANDERSON, Capt D. O., 207-8
ANDERSON, Col J. A., 430-1, 638; commands 2/3
Pnr Bn, 411
ANDERSON, Maj-Gen W. M., 577n
ANDRESEN, Sub-Lt A. M., 100, 140
ANDREW, Maj C. S., 533-4, 538
ANNANBERG (Sketch p. 355), 355-8
ANTILL, Sgt E. J., 474
ANUMB RIVER (Map p. 273; Sketches pp. 297, 313),
272, 278, 293, 296, 300-2, 311-14, 318, 321
ANZAC HIGHWAY (Sketches pp. 416, 429), 408,
415-17, 420-1, 427-8
AONIARU (Sketches pp. 331, 361), 338, 365
AOZU, Maj-Gen Kikutaro, 293, 302, 318
APARRI (Map p. 28; Sketch p. 390), 28, 45
API, MOUNT (Sketches pp. 409, 429), 427-8
APOS (Sketch p. 276), 283, 291, 303
APPLEMAN, R. E., 27n
ARAI, Captain, 207
ARAMAP RIVER (Sketch p. 305), 362
ARANG RIVER (Map p. 464), 493
ARAVIA (Sketch p. 127), 205
ARAWA (Sketch p. 136), 169
ARAWE (Map p. 243), 130n, 241
ARCHER, Capt G. R., 247
ARGENT, Col J. N. L., 562, 637; commands 2/3 Anti-Tank Regt, 495
ARIUAI SADDLE (Sketch p. 284), 284
ARIMIMIN (Sketch p. 302), 309
ARMSTRONG, Maj A. A., 257-8
ARMSTRONG, Lt-Col F. H. M., commands 35 Bn, 370
ARMSTRONG, Pte J. L., 110n
ARMSTRONG, Lt L. C., 514

Army News, 87
ARNOLD, Capt E., 309, 332
ARNOLD, Bdr J. J., 362
ARNOTT, Brig K. M. H., 160-2, 183-4
AROHEMI (Sketches pp. 313, 315), 312-13
AROPA (Map p. 91), 200
AROPA RIVER (Sketch p. 136), 139
ARTILLERY, in Bougainville, 104, 114, 178, 192, 194-5,
198-9, 202, 211, in Wewak campaign, 353, 359,
363, 372-5, 381, 383-4, at Tarakan, 427-8, 433, 435,
437, 440-5, 447, in British Borneo, 483, 501n, at
Balikpapan, 530-1, 534; *Japanese*, in Bougainville,
125, 183, 192, at Tarakan, 408, 409n
ARTY HILL (Map p. 91; Sketches pp. 109, 111), 108,
112, 114, 116-17; attack on, 109-10
ARU ISLANDS (Map p. 28; Sketch p. 560), 555, 569-70
Arunta, Australian destroyer, 349, 458, 462
ASABA RIVER (Sketch p. 107), 109
ASANAKOR (Map p. 273; Sketch p. 302), 291, 303,
306, 309
ASHTON, Maj L. E., 311
ASIA, 11, 42, 73, 502
ASILING (Sketch p. 282), 279, 282, 289
ASINA, 169-70
ASITAVI (Sketch p. 203), 234
ASTILL, Lt D. W., 106, 227
ASTILL'S CROSSING (Sketch p. 180), 197, 229
ATALIKLIKUN BAY (Map p. 243), 242
ATARA RIVER (Sketch p. 171), 229
ATHERTON (Map p. 3), 21, 23, 47, 78, 80n, 81, 601
ATHERTON TABLELAND, 25, 58, 79, 87, 457, 505
ATILEM RIVER (Sketch p. 361), 364, 367
ATKINSON, Lt G. H., 194, 197-8
ATKINSON, Capt W. J. S., 347
ATOB RIVER (Sketch p. 305), 305
ATROCITIES, 342, 522
ATTLEE, Rt Hon Earl, 549-51
ATU (Map p. 243), 244
AUANG (Sketch p. 282), 290
AUCHINLECK, Field Marshal Sir Claude, 592
AUNTY (Sketch p. 429), 445
AUPIK (Sketches pp. 302, 305), 303, 308-10
AUSTIN, Capt A. F., 434
AUSTIN, Maj H. McP., 97n
AUSTIN, Sgt V. P., 322
AUSTRALIA, 5, 24, 30, 32, 36, 50, 52, 57, 59, 71, 75-6,
79-80, 88, 92, 170, 181, 607, 633; as base for
British forces, 7, 11, 14, 394-6; and proposed
participation of British forces in Pacific, 9, 12-13;
reciprocal Lend-Lease demands on, 12; strength of
Army in, 25; war effort, 34-5, 38, 65-6, 72, 387-8,
587-9; news censorship, 39n, 40, 238-40; command
arrangements in, 54; Service resentment of civilians,
79-80; army camps in, 81; and BCOF, 550-1;
number of POW and internees in, 554n; and
Indonesian nationalist movement, 575, 577
Australia, Australian cruiser, 29
AUSTRALIAN AIR FORCE, 35, 89, 269, 364, 388, 460
507, 521n, 586, 592n; squadrons available in
Pacific, 12; strength, 19n, 31-4; coastwatchers,
100n; in Bougainville, 143; in New Britain, 250;
in Wewak campaign, 290, 301, 303-4, 306, 312,
334-6, 372-5; release of men from, 391, 393; at
Tarakan, 412, 450; strength and role allotted in
Borneo operation, 458-9; at Balikpapan, 506, 509,
513, 520, 531, 545-6; and BCOF, 548, 550-1, 577;
number of men and women who served outside
Australia, 633; total casualties, 633-5
—AIR BOARD, 552
—CHIEF OF AIR STAFF, 10
—FIRST TACTICAL AIR FORCE, 406, 459-60, 546
—OVERSEAS HEADQUARTERS, 11n
—RAAF COMMAND, 45-6, 407, 410
—SQUADRONS: No. 1 Airfd Constr, 507; No. 2,
254-5; No. 2 Airfd Constr, 507; No. 3 Airfd Constr,
29, 507; No. 4, 275, 355; No. 5 Army Cooperation,
95n, 152n, 156n, 255, 275n; No. 6, 255; No. 6 Airfd
Constr, 507; No. 7, 275; No. 8, 275, 330; No. 8
Airfd Constr, 411; No. 36, 95n; No. 100, 275
—WINGS: No. 71, 275, 329, 350, 359, 364; No.
79, 254-5; No. 84, 95
—UNITS AND FLIGHTS: No. 5 Mobile Met Flight,
171n; No. 10 Local Air Supply Unit, 95n; No. 16
Air Observation Post Flight, 420; No. 17 AOP Flight
95n; No. 200 Flight, 621

AUSTRALIAN ARMY, 7, 10, 61-3, 72, 215-16, 226, 237, 266-7, 388, 396, 399, 501, 545, 569, 583, 585-6, 602, 618; General Blamey refuses to disperse Australian divisions among US formations, In; strength and deployment, 4, 19n, 35-6, 80n, 81-2, 217, 602-3; achievements in Pacific, 5; liaison with War Office, 8; role in SWPA, 12, 14, 20-6, 41-9, role criticised, 55-72, General Blamey's Appreciation, 608-16; reduction of, 13, 19, 31-4, 389, 390-3; and the Militia, 19-20, 76-9, 239; equipment of, 36-7, 142; GHQ communiqués on operations of, 37-8, 40; command problems, 43-4, 551-2, 590-9; plans Borneo operations, 50; and General MacArthur, 52-4; training, leadership and officering of, 73-8, 81-2, 166; staff corps, 74-6; state of, 79-81; percentage of illiteracy in, 85; relations with American troops, 96; Intelligence estimates of, 101-3, 268, 272, 280, 368, 444; and shipping shortages, 105; Japanese Intelligence of, 114-15, 268; and "psychological warfare", 181-3; liaison with Navy, 249; relations with native peoples, 262, 369, 499-500; number of generals in, 268; adopts flame-throwers, 360n; Japanese on tactics of, 369; and BCOF, 549-51, 577; areas of responsibility in surrender arrangements, 553; and Indonesian nationalist movement, 567-8, 572-3; in post-war planning, 578-9; honours and decorations, 580-1; interim army, 581-2; demobilisation, 581-3; size in proportion to population, 587; quality, traditions and achievements, 588-9; organisation and higher command, 600-7; number of men and women who served outside Australia in 1914-18 and 1939-45 wars, 633; total casualties 1939-45 war, 633-5; physique of recruits, 635; strength and casualties compared with 1914-18 war, 636
—BRANCHES AND DIRECTORATES: Adj-Gen's Branch, 397, 401; QMG's Branch, 401; Directorate of Military Intelligence, 397; Directorate of Public Relations, 39-40, 61, 238, 397, 507; publication of *Salt* and Army newspapers, 85-8; Directorate of Research and Civil Affairs, 397-9, 401-5, 498
—MILITARY BOARD, 86, 579
—ARMIES: First, 36n, 42, 47, 53n, 55, 73, 85, 90, 106, 166n, 250, 264, 268, 357-8, 391n, 558, 591n, 600-3; HQ established at Lae, 23; role of, 25-6; and GHQ SWPA, 37, 43-4, 54; staff of, 89; plans operations against Wewak, 328-9; reinforcement of, 354; Japanese surrenders to, 554-6, 561; demobilisation arrangements, 582; command problems in SWPA, 596-9; history of, 604. Second, 25, 591n, 600-1; proposed disbandment of, 603-6
—CORPS: I Corps, 19, 23, 25, 32, 71, 89, 97, 279, 354, 553-5, 594, 602, 604-5; role of, 27-8, 30, 41-50, 388, 570; and GHQ SWPA, 37, 43, 53; in Borneo operations, 404, 406-7, 411, 457, 458n, 547; states functions of BCAAU, 496; and command problems in SWPA, 596-7, 599. II Corps, 19, 85, 506-7, 554, 595, 602; role of, 24, 100; in Bougainville, 25, 55, 77, 90, 92, 94, 104-6, 113, 126, 134, 149, 157, 165, 200, 204n, 208-10, 217, 228, 240, 354, 558; staff of, 97; allotment of forces to, 99; estimates Japanese strength in Bougainville, 102-3, 177; and AIB activities, 137, 139. III Corps, 591n, 603; disbanded, 19
—COMMANDS AND MILITARY DISTRICTS: Eastern Comd, 604; Southern Comd, 604; Western Comd, 25, 604; 8th Military District, 293n
—DIVISIONS: 1st Armoured, 35, 71, 75, 80-1, 183; Support Group disbanded, 34n. 1st Infantry, 81, 601, 603; strength in 1944, 22n; disbanded in, 605-6. 2nd Infantry, 81. 3rd Infantry, 21n, 24, 81, 92, 156, 198, 248n, 386n; strength, 22n; opens HQ at Torokina, 94; in Bougainville, 97, 111, 113-14, 141, 169-70, 177, 218, 227n, 228; staff, 97n. 4th Infantry, 81, 249. 5th Infantry, 21n, 81, 249, 504; strength, 22n; in New Britain, 24-5, 55, 130n, 241-2, 245-6, 248, 250-1, 255, 262; relations with AIF, 239; casualties and achievements, 260, 269; relieved by 11 Div 265; in Madang area, 354, 356. 6th Infantry, 35, 71, 73-4, 80-1, 89, 183, 215, 376, 452, 550, 554, 577, 591n; role, 21-2, 25, 28, 30, 44, 46-9, 65, 275, 278-9, 328-9, Parliamentary and Press criticism of, 218; in Aitape-Wewak campaign, 24, 55, 77, 265, 272-4, 281, 294-5, 327, 382, 384, 559; officering of, 75-6, 274; relations

AUSTRALIAN ARMY—*continued*
with Militia, 239; naval support, 349-50; reinforcement of, 354; casualties, 385-6; release of men from, 391n, 392. 7th Infantry, 35, 43, 80-1, 386n, 393, 520, 577, 587, 596; role of, 21, 28, 30, 44-6, 48-50, 65; strength, 22n; officering of, 75; relations with Militia, 239; release of men from, 391n, 392; in Borneo planning, 388-9, 502, 504-10; at Balikpapan, 521, 532, 569; order of battle for, 625-32; Japanese surrender to, 566, 569. 8th Infantry, 35, 74, 89, 93, 266, 342, 563; officering of, 75. 9th Infantry, 35, 51, 80-1, 249, 327, 388, 393, 504-5, 562, 577, 587, 596; role, 21, 28, 30, 44-6, 48-50, 65, 453; strength, 22n, 458; moves to Morotai, 43; officering of, 75; relations with Militia, 239; release of men from, 391n, 392; and BBCAU, 404, 495-8; plans Tarakan operation, 406-7; history of, 457; in Borneo operations, 457-9, 491, 494-5, 501-2, 569; under-estimate Japanese strength, 471; Japanese surrender to, 561; relief of, 565; T-sign included in coat of arms of Colony of British Borneo, 566; achievements, 589. 10th Infantry, 81. 11th Infantry, 21n, 25, 81, 265, 268n, 539n, 554; strength, 22n; role of, 44; in Bougainville, 114; at Rabaul, 557; demobilisation, 582. 12th Infantry, 22n. 1st Motor, 81. 2nd Motor, 81.
—FORCES: Ambon, 569. Buckforce, 542. East Borneo, 564. Farida, 344, 350-2. Hayforce, 309, 330-1. Jockforce, 290-1. Kanga, 386n. Kuching, 561, 563-4. Macassar, 569, 573-7. Menado, 569. Natuna, 562, 564. New Guinea, 23-4, 42, 82, 89-90, 97, 245, 248, 591n, 594-6, 601-2. Northern Territory, 25, 81, 89, 274, 591n, 603-4. Piper, 282-3. Raffles, 199. Sandakan, 561, 564. Ternate, 569. Timor 172, 569, 573
—ARMOUR AND CAVALRY: 1st Armd Bde, 22n, 32n. 3rd Army Tk Bde, 34n. 4th Armd Bde, 22n. 6th Armd Bde, 34n. 1st Motor Bde, disbanded, 34n. 2nd Motor Bde, disbanded, 34n. 4th Motor Bde, disbanded, 34n. 1st Armd Regt, 458, 507; at Balikpapan, 516, 518-19, 521, 527, casualties, 545n. 2/4 Armd Regt, 99, 173n, 296n; in Bougainville, 156, 160-1, 183-4, 193, 196, 220, 235, casualties, 237n; in Wewak campaign, 279, 284n, 339-40, 343, 346-7; publishes history, 637. 2/6 Armd Regt, 161n, 183. 2/8 Armd Regt, 161n. 2/9 Armd Regt, 407; at Tarakan, 434, 451n; in Borneo, 459, 465, 469-70, 473-4, 501n. 9 Div Cav Regt, history published, 637. 20 Motor Regt, at Merauke, 98. 2nd Tank Bn, history published, 637. 2/1 Armd Bde Recce Sqn, at Balikpapan, 536-7, 539. 2/6 Cav (Cdo) Regt, 296n; in Wewak campaign, 274-6, 279-80, 284n, 303, 308, 338n, 342, 344-5, 350-1, 370, 377-8, 380-1, casualties, 385n. 2/7 Cav (Cdo) Regt, 540; at Balikpapan, 507, 513, 543, casualties, 545n. 2/9 Cav (Cdo) Regt, 564
—ARTILLERY, 81, 198; in Bougainville, 192, 202; in Wewak campaign, 279n, 353, 359, 363, 372-5, 381, 383-4; at Tarakan, 433, 435-7, 439-45, 447; in Borneo, 483, 501n; at Balikpapan, 530-1, 534. 2/1 Composite AA Regt, 507. 2/3 Composite AA Regt, 459, 564. 53rd Composite AA Regt, 407. *Anti-Tank Regiments:* renamed tank-attack; 337. 2/1st, in Wewak campaign, 334n, 337-8, 344, 347, 359-60, 362, 364, 366, 370-1, casualties, 385n. 2/2nd, 507, 518; at Balikpapan, 516, casualties, 545n. 2/3rd, in Borneo operations, 495; in Natuna Force, 562; history published, 637. *Field Regiments:* 2/1st, in Wewak campaign, 304, 310, 321, 346, 373, 375, casualties, 385n; history published, 637. 2/2nd, in Wewak campaign, 298, 302, 312-13, 317, 319, 321, 323, 325, 346, 365, 371; history published, 637. 2/3rd, in Wewak campaign, 279, 284n, 286, 373. 2/4th, 507; at Balikpapan, 516, 518, 532, 534, 540, 542, casualties, 545n; history published, 637. 2/5th, 507; at Balikpapan, 525, 527-30, casualties, 545n; history published, 637. 2/6th, 507, casualties at Balikpapan, 545n. 2/7th, 407; at Tarakan, 410, 412, 428, 430, 432-3, 451, casualties, 451n; demobilisation begins, 450; history published, 637. 2/8th, in Borneo, 459, 489. 2/10th, 55n. 2/11th, 165-6, 177; in Bougainville, 194-5, 198-9. 2/12th, in Borneo, 459, 465-6, 472-4, 479. 2/14th, 248n, 258, 563n; in New Britain, 250n, 252-3, 255-7, casualties, 269n; in Bougainville, 259; seeks

AUSTRALIAN ARMY—continued
inclusion in Singapore force, 266. 2nd, 99, 142n, 177n; in Bougainville, 111-12, 128, 135, 158, 180. 4th, 99, 194; in Bougainville, 106, 109, 118, 153, 171n, 210-12, 214-15, 230, 232, 234-5. 13th, movement to Bougainville delayed, 165. "U" Hvy Bty, 177n; in Bougainville, 165n, 178. 101 Hvy Mortar Coy, in Bougainville, 171n. 2 Mtn Bty, 99; in Bougainville, 123-4, 125n, 171n, 232. 2/7 Survey Bty, history published, 637
—ENGINEERS, 81, 554n; in Bougainville, 156, 185; casualties, 225n; in Wewak campaign, 380; at Tarakan, 451; in Borneo, 459, 469, 497; extinguish oil well fires, 485-6, casualties, 501n; at Balikpapan, 521; history published, 637. 7 Bomb Disposal Pl, in Bougainville, 220. Docks Operating Coy, 272n; 2/1st, in North Borneo, 474. Field Coys: 2/1st, in Wewak campaign, 314; 2/2nd, in Wewak campaign, 287; 2/3rd, in Borneo, 485-6. 2/4th, 507; at Balikpapan, 521. 2/5th, 507. 2/6th, 507. 2/7th, in Borneo, 474; in Kuching Force, 561. 2/8th, 334n, 638; in Wewak campaign, 288, 293. 2/9th, 507. 2/11th, 407, 507; at Tarakan, 411. 2/13th, 407; at Tarakan, 412-14, 417-18. 2nd, 407. 4th, in New Britain, 256. 7th, in Bougainville, 224-5. 12th, 256; in New Britain, 252. 14th, in Sandakan Force, 564. 15th, 177n; in Bougainville, 161, 181, 189, 193, 220. 16th, in Bougainville, 118, 171n, 215. 23rd, in Bougainville, 204. 2/25 Fd Park Coy, 507. Landing Craft Companies: 41st, in New Britain, 250, 260; 42nd, shortages of craft, 104-5, in Bougainville, 171n, 210-15. 43rd, in Wewak campaign, 344-5. 13 Small Ships Coy, 104. 1st Water Transport Group, 105
—COMMANDO SQUADRONS: 2/2nd, 172, 248n; in New Britain, 250n, 261. 2/3rd, at Balikpapan, 520, 522, 541. 2/4th, 407, 410; history of, 411; at Tarakan, 412, 418, 423-4, 427, 430, 434, 437-9, 447, casualties, 451n. 2/5th, 106n; at Balikpapan, 513-15, 530. 2/6th, at Balikpapan, 534, 537-8. 2/7th, 83, 276, 283; in Wewak campaign, 279-80, 282, 287, 303, 305, 308, 343-4, 346-8, 370. 2/8th, 99, 197; in Bougainville, 94, 106, 110, 122n, 129-32, 134-5, 139, 141-2, 145-6, 148, 151-3, 156-8, 167-8, 185-6, 194-5, 198-9, 204, 226-9, casualties, 237n. 2/9th, in Wewak campaign, 278-9, 287-9, 311-13, 350-1, 377. 2/10th, 289; in Wewak campaign, 277-8, 279n, 280, 303-5, 307-8, 350-1, 370-1, 381. 2/11th, in Borneo, 459, 466, 468-9, 473, 477-8, casualties, 501n. 2/12th, in Borneo, 459, 472, 561, casualties, 501n.
—INFANTRY: Brigades: 2nd, 25, 34n. 4th, 21n, 99, 248n, 354; length of service in NG, 80n; in New Britain, 250n, 261, 557. 6th, 21n, 34n, 249; NG service, 80n; in New Britain, 247-8, 250, 252-3, 255-6, malaria casualties, 260. 7th, 21n, 98, 107; NG service, 80n, 97; in Bougainville, 92, 94, 116, 133, 142, 149, 155-6, 160-2, 166-7, 177, 185, 218, 354, 558, casualties, 117n, 237n. 8th, 21n, 30, 328; at Madang, 24-5; role of, 44; NG service, 80n; in Wewak campaign, 342, 370, 376, 379, 382, casualties, 385n; east of Sepik River, 354-8. 10th, 34n. 11th, 24, 172n; NG service, 80n; in Bougainville, 92, 94, 98, 106, 113, 117-18, 141, 174n, 194, 201, 206, 208, 210, 218, casualties, 237n. 12th, 25. 13th, 21n, 248n; in New Britain, 250n, 252, 260-1. 557. 14th, 34n, 80n. 15th, 92, 94, 99, 354; NG service, 80n, 98-9; in Bougainville, 156-7, 166, 177-9, 185-8, 189n, 192-4, 196, 198, 204, 218, 228; composition, 177n; casualties, 192, 221, 237n; morale, 239-40. 16th, Middle East and NG service, 80n; in Wewak campaign, 274, 279, 287, 300, 302, 311-12, 314-15, 325, 327, 338-9, 370, 376-7, 382, 384; composition, 296, casualties, 341, 385n. 17th, 97-8; Middle East and NG service, 80n; in Wewak campaign, 274, 278-80, 282, 306, 330, 336, 342, 354, 362, 368, 370, 382, 385, tactics, 369, casualties, 385n; history published, 637. 18th, 242, 504, 507, 566n; Middle East and NG service, 80n; role, 510; at Balikpapan, 511, 513-14, 520-2, 532, 540-2. 19th, Middle East service, 80n; in Wewak campaign, 274, 278-9, 283-4, 287, 293, 296, 338, 341-3, 345-6, 369-70, 376, 380-2, casualties, 289, 385n. 20th, Middle East and NG service, 80n; role and composition, 457, 459, 462; in Borneo, 483-4, 490-1, 496, 499-500, 561, 564. 21st, 93, 507;

AUSTRALIAN ARMY—continued
Middle East and NG service, 80n; role, 504, 510; at Balikpapan, 511, 513, 527, 543-5; at Macassar, 573-7. 23rd, 21n, 92, 102, 114n, 134n, 150n, 230n, 328; role of, 24, 44; NG service, 80n, 93; in Bougainville, 94, 201, 218, 234, casualties, 237n. 24th, 461; Middle East and NG service, 80n; role and composition, 457, 459, 465-6; at Labuan, 467-8, casualties, 470, 475; in Borneo, 472, 478, 482-3, 496-7, 561; history published, 637. 25th, 97, 265, 507; Middle East and NG service, 80n; role, 510; at Balikpapan, 511, 522-4, 532-5, 537-9, 543, casualties, 545. 26th, 388, 407n, 453, 569; Middle East and NG service, 80n, 411; role and composition, 406-7, 410; at Tarakan, 426, 439, 443-4, 450-1, casualties, 436, 451-2. 28th, 34n. 29th, 21n, 92, 239; NG service, 80n; in Bougainville, 94, 98, 111-12, 128, 130, 132, 156, 166, 177, 194, 218, 221, casualties, 133, 237n. 30th, 34n, 80n, 296. 31st, 34n. 32nd, 34n. 33rd, 570-1. 34th, 577-8.
Pacific Islands Regt, 69, 82-3, 262, 264-5.
Battalions: 2/1st, in Wewak campaign, 296-8, 300-2, 318, 326-7, 339, 379-80, casualties, 385n. 2/2nd, 345; in Wewak campaign, 296, 302, 311, 313-26, 338-40, 342, 379, 382-4, casualties, 340, 377, 385n; decorations awarded to, 581n; short history published, 637. 2/3rd, 83, 98, 638; in Wewak campaign, 287-8, 298-300, 302, 311-12, 319, 324-6, 338-42, 370; strength, 377, casualties, 385n. 2/4th, 638; in Wewak campaign, 283-5, 345-7, 349, 351-2, 354, 372-6, 379, casualties, 385n. 2/5th, 638; in Wewak campaign, 282-3, 289-91, 303-6, 334, 359-66, casualties, 367, 385n. 2/6th, 83, 230; in Wewak campaign, 307-8, 330-2, 334-7, 359-61, 364, 366-7, casualties, 385n; men entitled to release, 392n. 2/7th, 77n, 78n, 230, 638; in Wewak campaign, 303, 305, 309-10, 330-6, 338, 359-60, 364-5, 367, 385, 559, casualties, 385n. 2/8th, 98; in Wewak campaign, 284, 286-8, 298, 345, 348, 351-2, 354, 370, 372-3, 376, 381-2, casualties, 385n. 2/9th, 507, 511; at Balikpapan, 519, 521, 540-2, casualties, 545n. 2/10th, 98, 507, 510-11; at Balikpapan, 515-19, 521, casualties, 545n; history published, 637. 2/11th, 249, 638; in Wewak campaign, 279, 284-6, 296, 345-9, 351-3, 370, 372, 374, 379, casualties, 354, 385n. 2/12th, 231, 507, 511; at Balikpapan, 514-15, 518, 524, casualties, 545n. 2/13th, in Borneo, 459, 463, 483-4, 486-90, 564, casualties, 501n; decorations awarded to, 581n; history published, 638. 2/14th, 507, 513-14; at Balikpapan, 520-2, 525-30, 543-5, 568, casualties, 545n; in Macassar Force, 576; history published, 638. 2/15th, 459, 462-3; in Borneo, 465, 484, 486-7, 489-90, 493-5; organises carnival, 500; casualties, 501n. 2/16th, 99, 507, 513-14; at Balikpapan, 520, 530, 543, 545, casualties, 545n; in Macassar Force, 576; history published, 638. 2/17th, 218, 459, 462, 638; in Borneo, 462-5, 484, 486, 488-9, 491-3, casualties, 501n. 2/18th, 638. 2/21st, 454. 2/23rd, 407, 410-11; at Tarakan, 414-15, 418, 422-3, 427-8, 440-6, 448; commences demobilisation, 450; casualties, 451n. 2/24th, 78n, 407, 410, 638; at Tarakan, 411, 414, 417, 419-29, 434-6, 439-48; commences demobilisation, 450; casualties, 451n. 2/25th, 507; at Balikpapan, 532-4, 537-9, 543, casualties, 545n; at Samarinda, 566, 568. 2/27th, 249, 274, 507, 513; at Balikpapan, 514-15, 520, 522, 543-4, casualties, 545n; in Macassar Force, 573, 575-6; history published, 638. 2/28th, 459, 461, 465-70; at Labuan, 472-5; in Borneo, 478, 482-3, 495, casualties, 501n; history published, 638. 2/30th, history published, 638. 2/31st, 98, 507; at Balikpapan, 522-4, 532, 534-9, casualties, 545; at Bandjermasin, 568. 2/32nd, in Borneo, 459, 472, 475-9, 482-3, 562, casualties, 501. 2/33rd, 507; at Balikpapan, 522, 532-4, 538-9, casualties, 545n; at Pontianak, 569. 2/40th, 571. 2/43rd, 459, 465-6; at Labuan, 467-70; in Borneo, 475, 477-83, 500, casualties, 501n; pictorial history published, 638. 2/48th, 77n, 407, 410-11; at Tarakan, 414-18, 422, 424-7, 429, 434, 437-9, 442-8; begins demobilisation, 450; casualties, 451n; history published, 638. 4th, in Sepik River area, 357-8, 554. 7th, on Mono and Choiseul Islands, 93, 140, 201; in Bougainville, 204, 230-4, casualties, 237n; on Fauro Island, 558.

INDEX 645

AUSTRALIAN ARMY—continued
8th, on Emirau Island, 93; in Bougainville, 201, 234-7, casualties, 237n. 9th, 139n; in Bougainville, 94, 97, 106-10, 114, 116, 142, 146-9, 151-2, 156, 159, 166-7, 179, casualties, 117n, 237n. 11th, in New Britain, 260, 269n. 12th/40th, in Timor, 571. 14th/32nd, 249; in New Britain, 250, 252-7, 259-60, casualties, 269n. 15th, in Bougainville, 98, 112, 129-31, 133, 221, 223-4, 229, 557, casualties, 237n. 16th, in New Britain, 260-1, casualties, 269n. 19th, 249; in New Britain, 256-60, casualties, 269n. 22nd, 638. 24th, 99, 177n, 638; in Bougainville, 166, 178-81, 183-5, 187, 189-93, 197-8, 219-21, 228, casualties, 237n. 25th, in Bougainville, 98, 110, 116-17, 142, 146, 149-51, 153-5, 158-63, 166, 167n, casualties, 237n. 26th, in Bougainville, 118, 121, 126, 171-5, 206, 208-10, 234, casualties, 237n. 27th, on Green Islands, 93; in Bougainville, 201-5, 230-1, 234-5, casualties, 237n. 28th, 258n; in New Britain, 260, casualties, 269n. 29th/46th, 638. 30th, in Sepik River area, 357-8; moves to Wewak, 370; in Wewak campaign, 376, 379, 382, casualties, 385n. 31st/51st, in Bougainville, 120-7, 171-2, 201, 208-16, 234, casualties, 78, 237n; at Nauru and Ocean Islands, 560-1. 35th, in Sepik River area, 356, 358; moves to Wewak, 370; in Wewak campaign, 379, 382, casualties, 385n. 36th, 268n; in New Britain, 249-54, 256, 260-1, casualties, 269n. 37th/52nd, 83; in New Britain, 260-1, casualties, 269n. 39th, 99. 42nd, 99; in Bougainville, 98, 128, 130-1, 133-5, 147, 221-4, 238, casualties, 237n; history published, 638. 47th, in Bougainville, 98, 112, 128-33, 221, 224, casualties, 237n. 55th/53rd, in Bougainville, 98, 118-20, 206-9, casualties, 237n. 57th/60th, 99, 177n, 189-90; in Bougainville, 178-80, 185, 187, 192-7, 218-21, casualties, 237n. 58th/59th, 78n, 141, 177n; in Bougainville, 166, 178, 180, 185, 187-9, 191-7, 219-21, casualties, 237n; history published, 638. 61st, in Bougainville, 98, 109-10, 130-1, 142-6, 148-9, 151-3, 156, 159-60, 163, 166, casualties, 117n, 237n. 63rd, 570. 64th, 570-1. 65th, 577. 66th, 577. 67th, 577. 1 RAR, 577n. 2 RAR, 577n. 3 RAR, 577n: decorations awarded in Korea, 581n. 1 Para, 394, 536; history of, 554. Darwin, 249. 1 NGIB, 82, 99, 142n, 177n, 248n; in Bougainville, 112, 121, 128-30, 132-3, 149-50, 153, 165, casualties, 237n; in New Britain, 248, 250, 252-3, 255, 261-2; mutinies, 262-3; employment criticised, 263-4; in Sepik River area, 355-8; casualties, 634. 2 NGIB, formation of, 82; in Wewak campaign, 362-9, 367-9, 369n, casualties, 385n. 3 NGIB, formation of, 82. 4 NGIB, 82. PIB, 82; in Bougainville, 199, 204, 209, 222, 225-6, 228-30, 233, 235-6, casualties, 237n; in Sepik River area, 355, 357, casualties, 634. Torres Strait Light, 83n. 2/1 Gd Regt, 142n, 177n. 2/2 Gd Bn, 93. 22 Grn Bn, 623-4.
—MACHINE-GUN BATTALIONS: 2/1st, 507; at Balikpapan, 519, 532, casualties, 545n. 2/2nd, 407, 442; at Tarakan, 440, 449; in Borneo, 459, 477-8, casualties, 451n, 501n. 2/3rd, 248n, 296n; in Wewak campaign, 279, 300, 311-13, 319, 327, 341-2, 344, 351, 371-2, 377-9, casualties, 385n.
—PIONEER BATTALIONS: 2/1st, 507; at Balikpapan, 542, casualties, 545n. 2/2nd, 407, 507, at Tarakan, 411, 417, casualties, 451n; at Balikpapan, 545n; history published, 638. 2/3rd, 98, 407; at Tarakan, 411, 418, 423-4, 427, 430-3, 446, 448, casualties, 451n; history, 638. 2/4th, 564; in Borneo, 459, 474, casualties, 501n; in Kuching Force, 561.
—AMENITIES SERVICE, 82, 85, 88, 96, 172n; tasks of, 88.
—AUSTRALIAN NEW GUINEA ADMINISTRATIVE UNIT, 67, 69, 81, 89, 100, 122, 126, 177n, 396, 398, 401; limits recruitment of natives, 83; in Bougainville, 135, 138-9, 142n, 145-6, 157, 168, 171n, 209, 227-8, 230; on Taiof Island, 175; on New Hanover, 201; in New Britain, 244, 557; rates of pay for native troops and labourers, 264; in Wewak campaign, 275-7, 279-80, 286, 313, 316n, 325-6, 330, 334-5, 362, 364, 368-9, 379-81; in Sepik River area, 355-6; Intelligence activities, 618.
—BEACH GROUPS: 1st, composition, 459; at Labuan, 474. 2nd, 507; at Tarakan, 407, 411
—CANTEENS SERVICE, 81, 88, 96, 296n

AUSTRALIAN ARMY—continued
—CATERING CORPS, 82
—CHAPLAINS' DEPT, 82
—DENTAL CORPS, 82; 63 Dental Unit, 177n; 72 Dental Unit, 172n
—EDUCATION SERVICE, 82, 96; formation and work of, 84-8; organises classes for troops in Borneo, 500-1
—ELECTRICAL AND MECHANICAL ENGINEERS, 81. 2/58th LAD, 485; 241 LAD, 121; 266 LAD, 177n; 102 Bde Wksp, 171n; 110 Bde Wksp, 296n; 127 Bde Wksp, 272n
—FIELD SECURITY SERVICE, 272n, 507; 25 Section, 172n
—HIRINGS SERVICE, 82
—INTELLIGENCE CORPS, 81, 507
—LABOUR SERVICE, 82; 17 Works Coy, 272n
—L OF C AND BASE SUB AREAS: NSW L of C, 606; SA L of C Area, 603-4; Qld L of C, strength in 1943, 602-3; Tas L of C, 603-4; 1st Base Sub-Area, 49, 411; strength in Borneo operation, 458n; composition in Borneo, 459; 3rd Base Sub-Area, at Aitape, 272; 4th Base Sub-Area, moves to Torokina, 92-3; 7th Base Sub-Area, 506-7
—LEGAL CORPS, 81, 402
—MEDICAL CORPS, 81. 2/5 AGH, 638; 2/11 AGH, 272n, 304; 110 CCS, 407; 2/1 Fd Amb, 301n, 314; 2/3 Fd Amb, 497; 2/7 Fd Amb, 296n; 2/8 Fd Amb, 497; 2/11 Fd Amb, 407, 429; 2/12 Fd Amb, 563; 3/14 Fd Amb, 272n; 11 Fd Amb, 142n, 177n; 19 Fd Amb, 171n, 214
—MILITARY HISTORY SECTION, 39n, 40n, 153n, 265n, 267n, 448n, 507
—MOVEMENT CONTROL, 81
—NORTH AUSTRALIA OBSERVER UNIT, 397
—ORDNANCE CORPS, 81; 19 Adv Ordnance Depot, 272n; 102 Bde Ord Fd Park, 172; 110 Bde Ord Fd Park, 296n; 15 Mobile Laundry, 272n
—PAY AND AUDIT, 81
—POSTAL SERVICE, 82; 3 Div Postal Unit, 177n
—PRINTING AND STATIONERY SERVICE, 82
—PROVOST CORPS, 81; 4 Div Provost Coy, 172n; 3 Div Provost Coy, 177n
—PSYCHOLOGY SERVICE, 82
—RECORDS, 82, 633, 636
—RECRUITING STAFF, 82
—REMOUNTS SERVICE, 82
—ROYAL MILITARY COLLEGE, DUNTROON, 75-6, 363, 419n
—SALVAGE SERVICE, 82; II Corps Salvage Unit, 172; 6 Div Salvage Unit, 296n
—SCHOOLS AND TRAINING UNITS: Cooking and Catering School, 73. Guerilla Warfare School, 73. OCTU, 73, 76-7, 333n. School of Artillery, 73. School of Military Law, 73. School of Movement and Transport, 73. Senior Staff School, 274. Tactical School, 345
—SERVICE CORPS, 81, 172n, 459; history published, 638. 126 General Tpt Coy, 272n. 2/2 Tpt Pl, 296n. 2/3 Tpt Pl, 296n. 56 Tpt Pl, 142n. 2/21 Supply Depot Pl, 296n. 2/22 SDP, 296n. 2/23 SDP, 296n. 19 SDP, 142n. 223 SDP, in Bougainville, 171n
—SIGNALS CORPS, 81, 459; history published, 637. 8 Aust Div, 637. "B" Corps Wireless Section, 171n. 7 Bde Sig Sec, 142n. 11 Bde Sig Sec, 171n. 15 Bde Sig Sec, 177n. NGAWW Coy, history published, 637. Pigeon Service, 130n. 1st Pigeon Section, 172n. 7th Pigeon Section, 172n. 1st Water Transport Signals, 171n
—SURVEY CORPS, 172n
—VETERINARY CORPS, 82
—VOLUNTEER DEFENCE CORPS, 603, 605
—WAR GRAVES SERVICE, 82
—WOMEN'S SERVICES, AWAS, 82; AAMWS, 82
AUSTRALIAN BROADCASTING COMMISSION, 39n, 238
AUSTRALIAN COMFORTS FUND, 96, 250, 449
AUSTRALIAN FLYING CORPS, 633
AUSTRALIAN GOVERNMENT, 29, 74, 105, 266, 329n, 551, 553, 559-60, 561n, 571-2, 583n; and British participation in Pacific, 5-7, 12-14, 17, 394, 548; represented at War Office, 8: appoints High Commissioner to India, 9; and command arrangements in SWPA, 17, 44, 52, 586-7, 590-9; considers reductions in Services, 19, 31-4, 35-6, 389-93; militia employment, 19-20; relations with General

INDEX

AUSTRALIAN GOVERNMENT—continued
MacArthur, 20-1, 53, 585-6; proposes fuller treatment of Australian operations in GHQ communiqués, 38; and manpower problem, 42; employment of Australian forces, 44-9; discusses conduct of operations in New Guinea, 56-72, 238-40; role of Australian forces in Borneo, 388-9, 502; military government of Borneo, 396, 398, 498-9; post-war policy in Territories, 398-9; orders command of Services to revert to Army, Navy and Air Boards, 551-2; treatment of General Blamey and other senior leaders, 578-81; and demobilisation of Australian Army, 581-2; critical of organisation of Australian Army, 600-7
—ADVISORY WAR COUNCIL, 14, 25, 63, 68-9
—ARMY, DEPARTMENT OF, 35, 265, 396, 398, 593
—CHIEFS OF STAFF, 9, 548, 551, 560; requirements of British forces based in Australia, 13-14, 17
—DEFENCE COMMITTEE, 31, 392, 394; on British forces available for Pacific, 12; and BCOF, 548
—DEFENCE DEPARTMENT, 20, 63, 596
—EXTERNAL AFFAIRS, DEPARTMENT OF, 396, 572
—EXTERNAL TERRITORIES, DEPARTMENT OF, 264-5, 396, 398-9
—FULL CABINET, 396
—INFORMATION, DEPARTMENT OF, 39-40, 88
—MANPOWER DIRECTORATE, 391
—MILITARY MISSION, Washington, 89, 579
—POSTMASTER-GENERAL'S DEPARTMENT, 329n
—POST-WAR RECONSTRUCTION, DEPARTMENT OF, 396, 498
—TREASURY, DEPARTMENT OF, 62, 265, 396
—WAR CABINET, 40n, 42, 397n, 398, 593; command arrangements in SWPA, 14; on strength of Australian Army, 31-5; prohibits public statements by members of Services, 63-4; and General Blamey, 65-6, 69; agrees to dispatch of AWAS to New Guinea, 82; approves scheme for Army Education Service, 84; and army journal *Salt*, 85-6; distribution of army canteens funds, 88; authorises release of members of Services, 391-3; and reciprocal Lend-Lease, 396; and BCOF, 550
—WAR ORGANISATION OF INDUSTRY, DEPARTMENT OF, 182n
AUSTRALIAN IMPERIAL FORCE, FIRST, 73-4, 588
AUSTRALIAN LABOUR PARTY, 580n
AUSTRALIAN NATIONAL AIRWAYS, 296n
AUSTRALIAN NAVY, 35, 45, 52, 100, 507, 570, 586; strength of, 4, 393; in Philippine operations, 38, 388; role of Australian Squadron, 46; and coastwatchers, 100n, 617; in attack on Wewak, 349-50; in Borneo operations, 458-69, 477, 511, 520; and BCOF, 548, 550-1; strength of personnel who served outside Australia, 633; total casualties, 633-5
—CHIEF OF NAVAL STAFF, 10
—NAVAL BOARD, 522
AUSTRALIAN NEWSPAPER PROPRIETORS' ASSOCIATION, 38
AUSTRALIAN WAR MEMORIAL, 40n, 87
AUTOGI (Sketch p. 320), 324, 338
AVERN, Lt C. C., 469-70, 473-4
AVIANG (Sketch p. 111), 121
AWUL (Map p. 243), 242, 244, 247
AYLETT, W. E., 603n

BABA, Lt-Gen Masao, 494, 562; commands XXXVII Army, 456
BABIANG (Map p. 273; Sketch p. 276), 276-80, 283-4, 288
BACKHOUSE, Capt J. W., 545
BACON HILL (Sketch p. 257), 259-60
BADAS RIVER (Map p. 464), 486
BAGANA, MOUNT (Map p. 91; Sketch p. 95), 94, 110
BAHAU RIVER (Sketch p. 455), 456
BAHR, Pte E. J., 233
BAI (Sketch p. 315), 315-16
BAIA (Map p. 243; Sketch p. 253), 247, 251, 253, 267
BAIEN (Map p. 243), 242, 244
BAIN, Capt W. H., 259
BAINYIK (Sketch p. 331), 331-4, 338
BAIRD, Capt V. C., 309, 332-4
BAK, Lt C. J., 125
BAKAM (Map p. 464), 488
BAKER, Cpl E. E., 166

BAKER ROUTE (Sketch p. 466), 468; *see also* MACARTHUR ROAD
BAKER'S BROW (Sketch p. 116), 116-17
BAKUNG (Map p. 464), 493
BALAGA (Sketch p. 302), 303
BALAI (Map p. 464), 491
BALAM CREEK (Sketch p. 297), 301
BALANGABADABIL (Sketch p. 302), 306, 309
BALBI, MOUNT (Map p. 91), 92
BALE (Sketch p. 526), 543-4
BALFOUR-OGILVY, Capt J. M., 532
BALIF (Map p. 273; Sketches pp. 282, 302), 272, 282, 289-90, 293, 303-4, 309, 311, 334n
BALIKPAPAN (Maps pp. 28, 512; Sketches pp. 503, 544), 29, 404, 407, 452, 566, 568-9; plans for attack on, 41, 49-50, 65, 388-9, 408, 457-8, 461, 504-8; area described, 502; strength of Japanese forces and defences at, 502-3; operations against, 509-47, casualties, 545; 7 Div OOB at, 625-32
BALIKPAPAN BAY (Sketch p. 540), 502, 505, 540, 542
BALIMA RIVER (Map p. 243), 248, 251-2
BALLARD, Chaplain Rev H. R., 473
BALUP (Sketch p. 276), 278
BANA (Sketch p. 302), 362
BAND (Sketch p. 526), 543
BANDJERMASIN (Map p. 28; Sketches pp. 453, 560), 495, 502-3, 509, 568; plans for attack on, 29, 41, 49-50
BANDUNG (Map p. 3), 49
BANGRI (Sketch p. 355), 356
BANGSAL (Sketch p. 544), 544
BANKS, Sgt H. H., 236
BANYAN KNOLL (Sketch p. 109), 109-10
BARABAR, CAPE (Sketch p. 344), 343
BARAM RIVER (Map p. 464; Sketch p. 455), 453, 456, 485, 488-9, 492, 495
BARANGABANDANGI (Sketch p. 302), 303-4
BARARA (Sketch p. 144), 150-3, 159, 162
BARBEY, Vice-Adm Daniel E., 458, 506
Barcoo, Australian frigate, 250, 458, 573
BARGES, Pte E., 108n
BARGES' HILL (Sketch p. 107), 108n, 118, 204, 231
BARHAM, Maj-Gen L. De L., 26
BARILO (Sketch p. 171), 171
BARKER, Brig L. E. S., 89n
BARLING, Lt-Col G. W., 97n
BARNDEN, Maj C. V. I., 274n
Barnes, American ship, 563
BARNES, Maj J., 198
BARNES, Maj-Gen Julian F., 591
BARNES, Pte L., 184, 187
BARNES, Lt T. J., 343
BARRETT, Maj A. G., 186, 195
BARRETT'S TRACK (Sketch p. 190), 195-6
BARTHOLOMEW, Pte H. W., 339
BARTLEY, Col T. W., 573
BARTON, Pte P. B., 110n
BARTON'S KNOLL (Sketch p. 116), 110
BASE 5 (Sketch p. 207), 236-7
BASE POINT 3 (Sketch p. 203), 203-4, 230
BASKERVILLE, Lt N. T., 231
BATAGAU STRAIT (Sketch p. 408), 408
BATAKAN KECHIL RIVER (Sketch p. 524), 522
BATANTA ISLAND, 410
BATAVIA (Map p. 3; Sketch p. 390), 49, 520
BATES, Maj C. D., 244
BATHGATE, Sgt H., 316
BATU, CAPE (Sketch p. 409), 411n, 427
BATUCHAMPAR (Sketches pp. 503, 533), 526, 532, 534-5, 543
BAU, 565
BAUMAN, Capt C. H., 193
BAWABU RIDGE (Sketch p. 107), 108-9
BAYLISS, W. C., 638
BAYLY, Maj C. W., 349, 353
BEALE, Cpl L. E., 441-2
BEAN, Dr C. E. W., 39n, 84, 588n
BEARDOW, Pte G. J., 322
BEASLEY, Rt Hon J. A., 63-4, 69
BEAUFORT (Map p. 28; Sketches pp. 460, 476, 479), 453, 455-6, 459, 471-2, 476-8, 483, 495, 500-1, 562, 565; operations against, 479-82
BEAVIS, Maj-Gen L. E., 24n
BEECH, Maj A. T., 149
BEECH 2 (Sketch p. 429), 440, 444
BEECHEY, CAPE (Map p. 243), 244

INDEX

BEECH'S CROSSING (Sketch p. 131), 142, 149
BEENIE, Lt P. C., 290
BEGG, Lt C. E., 300
BEHM, Capt W. J., 257-8
BELAIT RIVER (Map p. 464), 453, 491-2
BELL, Sub-Lt S. G. V., 100
BELLAIR, Capt. J. M., 377, 379
BEMBITOK (Sketch p. 305), 304
BENGAL, BAY OF (Map p. 3), 5-7, 10, 12, 16
BENNETT, Sgt A. A., 231
BENNETT, Maj A. C., 360, 365
BENNETT, Maj G. W., 534
BENNETT, Lt-Gen H. Gordon, 57, 64, 70-1, 602n
BENSON, Cpl S. E., 96n, 222n, 238n, 638
BERAK (Sketch p. 462), 462
BERKEY, Rear-Adm Russell S., 407, 410, 458
BERLIN, Allied conference at, 549, 551
BERNARD, Maj H. R. C., 248n, 252
BERRY, Maj H. J., 234
BERRYMAN, Lt-Gen Sir Frank (Plate p. 525), 1n, 28, 43, 48, 105, 329, 342, 402, 595-6; becomes Chief of Staff, Adv LHQ, 24; on employment of AIF, 30, 41-2, 44-5, 52
BERRY'S HILL (Sketches pp. 111, 203), 202, 230
BETHELL, Lt R. J., 430-1, 434
BEUKEMA, Lieutenant, 485
BIAK ISLAND (Map p. 28), 19, 553
BIALLA (Map p. 243), 252
BIERWIRTH, Lt-Gen R., 89, 166n
BIG ROAD (Sketches pp. 344, 346), 348, 351, 370, 379, 381
BILLETT, Lt D. L., 475
BIMA (Sketch p. 560), 573
BINALATUNG RIVER (Sketch p. 441), 439, 446, 448
BINTULU (Sketch p. 453), 503
BIRA RIVER (Map p. 464), 484
BIRCH, Pte S. G., 167
BIRI, Corporal, 192
BIROSI (Sketch p. 144), 146
BIRRELL, Lt J. A., 286, 316n, 325, 369
BISHOP, Maj-Gen J. A. (Plate p. 333), 274, 369-70, 372; temporarily commands 19 Bde, 353
BIWAM (Sketch p. 318), 318-19
BLABY, Maj K., 233
BLACK, Capt G. B., 244-5
BLAINEY, Capt G. C., 534
BLAMEY, Field Marshal Sir Thomas (Plates pp. 525, 556), 28-30, 93, 102, 239, 248, 268, 275, 354, 359, 362, 397, 559, 567, 571, 574, 576, 577n, 617, 619; employment of Australian divisions with American Army, 1n, 41-2; on control and employment of British Commonwealth forces, 7-10; confers with British Chiefs of Staff, 11-13; participation of British forces in Pacific, 17, 393n, 394-5; relations with General MacArthur, 21-3, 37-8, 43-4, 52-4; forms advanced LHQ, 24; defines role of First Army, 25-6; on army strength and proposed reductions, 31-3; defends DPR, 39; role of I Corps, 44-9; conduct of operations examined, 57-72; presents Appreciation of 18 May 1945 to War Cabinet, 66, 608-16; appoints committee to make recommendations on RMC, Duntroon, 75; employment and pay of native battalions, 82-3, 264-5; on army newspapers and amenities, 87-8; seeks additional shipping, 105, 269; visits Bougainville, 166, 193; in Wewak campaign, 328-9, 342; Borneo operations, 388, 396, 502; on release of army personnel, 390-2; administration of surrendered territories, 398-403, 498; and BCOF, 548-51; takes surrender at Morotai, 553-4; appointment terminated, 578-9; seeks recognition of senior officers, 580-1; relations with Australian Government, 585-6; command problems, 591-9; organisation and command of Australian Army, 600-6
BLAMEY, Lt T. G., 542
BLANCH, Maj J. A., 109, 147
BLONDELL, S-Sgt G. P., 215
BLOT, THE (Sketch p. 371), 376, 381
BLOW, Maj R., 55n, 565
BLUNDEN, Pte J. D. R., 536
BLYTH'S JUNCTION (Map p. 512), 515
BOASE, Lt-Gen A. J., commands 11 Div, 25
BOGIA (Sketches pp. 271, 355), 248n, 358
BOHLE, Capt A. H. M., 347
BOIKEN (Map p. 273; Sketches pp. 339, 345), 291, 321, 339, 341-3, 345, 378, 380-1, 559

BOIKEN CREEK (Sketch p. 339), 340
Boise, American cruiser, 462
BOISEN, Capt F. N., 139n
BOKI RIVER (Sketch p. 355), 356
BOLE (Sketch p. 460), 495
BOLTON, Sgt P. F., 167
BOMBETA (Sketch p. 302), 303-4, 309
BOMBISIMA (Sketch p. 282), 290
BONDE, Lt R. R., 231, 233
BONIN ISLANDS (Map p. 3), 27-8
BONIS PENINSULA (Map p. 91; Sketch p. 127), 113, 175, 207-8, 212, 215, 217, 234, 558
BORAM (Sketches pp. 344, 371), 341, 352, 370-2, 379
BORAM CREEK (Sketches pp. 344, 371), 352
BORNEO (Map p. 28; Sketches pp. 390, 453), 20, 62, 70, 72, 77, 394, 451, 509, 550-1, 553, 565, 570, 573, 581, 596, 599, 618-19, 621-2; plans for operations in, 11, 14, 28, 30, 41, 44, 46-51, 53, 65; relations of people with Japanese, 454, 484, 522, 539n, 569, with Australians, 490, 493, 496-7, 499-500; strength and disposition of Japanese forces, 456, 470; campaign in, 406-547; and Indonesian nationalist movement, 566-9; Australian casualties in, 635
BORNEO, BRITISH (Map p. 28; Sketches pp. 453, 455), 41, 410-11, 453, 502, 564, 567, 572; plans for operations in, 388-9, 457-61; military government in, 396, 400-5, 495-9, 565-6; AIB operations in, 454-6; campaign in, 462-501; Australian casualties in, 501; surrender arrangements in, 554, 561; Japanese strength in, 555, 565; evacuation of POW and internees from, 563
BORNEO, DUTCH (Sketches pp. 390, 453), 396, 404, 554, 569, 572; operations in, 41, 50, 509-47; Japanese strength in, 555; surrender in, 566
BOSMAN (Sketch p. 356), 357-8
BOSS-WALKER, G., 638
BOSTOCK, Air Vice-Marshal W. D., 503, 509, 513-14, 531, 549; criticises Army in Balikpapan operation, 545-6
BOSWELL, Cpl J. W. H., 187
BOTT, Capt F. McC., 198
BOUGAINVILLE (Maps pp. 3, 60, 91; Sketch p. 22), 1, 21-2, 24-6, 36, 39, 40n, 55-6, 58n, 59, 61, 63, 65, 68-9, 71-2, 77-8, 80n, 85, 89, 93-4, 95n, 97-9, 105, 114, 122, 241, 244, 247, 262-4, 266, 268-9, 327, 354, 364, 385, 547, 559-60, 596, 606, 622; Japanese strength in, 23, 38, 101-3; native people of, 26, 83, 106, 128-9, 136-40, 145, 168-71, 176, 205-6, 227-9; described, 90-2; AIB operations in, 100; campaign in, 106-237; casualties, 237; value of campaign examined, 238-40; surrender in, 552-3, 555, 557-8
BOURNE, Brig C. C. F., commands 2/12 Bn, 524
BOVENSCHEN, Sir Frederick, 399-400, 403
BOWDEN, Lt L. F., 333, 336
BOWER, Lt R. R., 316
BOWERING, Sgt W. S., 378
BOWIE, Maj R. A., 519
BOYD, Capt D. G., 278
BOYER, Maj K. M., 340
BRAHATIS, WO2 S., 152
BRAMMER, L-Sgt, J. McA., 537
BRANDI (Sketches pp. 344, 371), 350-1, 370, 372, 377-9
BRANDI RIVER (Sketches pp. 344, 371), 352, 379
BREAKER, Sgt G. A. II., 469
BREEZE, Lt V. C., 489
BREHENY, Maj D. J., 97n
BRENNAN, Lt C. D., 523
BRENNAN, Lt-Col J. G., 260
BRETT, Lt-Gen George H., 590-2
BREWSTER, Maj D. J., 188
BRIDGE, Lt K. W. T., 100, 127-8, 170, 205
BRIDGEFORD, Lt-Gen Sir William (Plate p. 125), 111-12, 130, 132-3, 141-2, 148-9, 151-2, 155-6, 158, 160, 166, 177, 185, 194, 199, 218, 221, 227; commands 3 Div, 92; opens HQ at Torokina, 94; service of, 97
BRIDGES, in Wewak campaign, 314
BRIDGLAND, Lt-Col R. J., 637
BRINK BASE (Sketch p. 144), 143
BRINKLEY, Lt F. R., 143n
BRISBANE, 23, 34n, 80n, 98, 274, 593
BRITAIN, GREAT, 33, 35, 56, 65, 568; participation of forces in Pacific Theatre, 4-10, 12-13, 15; Australians serving with forces of, 633

BRITISH AIR FORCE, 86; liaison staff in Australia, 9; role in Far East, 12-13, 18; Australians in, 633
BRITISH ARMY, 40n, 53, 56, 567, 617; in Burma, 4; proposed participation in Pacific Theatre, 6, 12-13; liaison staff in Australia, 9; strength required to maintain one division, 36; Australian officers lent to, 74n; relations between regular and citizen soldiers in, 76; civil affairs, 401-4; promotion of officers in, 589; ratio of generals to men, 602-3
—V CORPS, 549
—DIVISIONS: 6th, 386n; 51st Highland, 74n
BRITISH BORNEO, COLONY OF, 566
BRITISH BORNEO CIVIL AFFAIRS UNIT, 459, 472, 488, 563-4; formed, 401; functions and establishment, 402-5; work of, 496-500
BRITISH COMMONWEALTH, 6, 53, 57; relationship and control of forces, 7-10; plans for joint force for participation in war against Japan, 15, 17-18, 548-9
BRITISH COMMONWEALTH OCCUPATION FORCE, 550-1, 577-8
BRITISH GOVERNMENT, 8, 16, 266, 389, 553, 559-60, 561n, 585, 587; cooperation with Dominions in military affairs, 9; participation of forces in Pacific, 10, 13, 15, 17-18, 394-5, 548-9; administration of reoccupied areas, 398-401, 403-4, 565; and BCOF, 550-1
—ADMIRALTY, 9, 11, 13, 104n
—AIR MINISTRY, 9
—CHIEFS OF STAFF, 51-2; plans for participation of British forces in Pacific, 5-7, 10-18, 548-9, 551; and Borneo operations, 50-1, 388; on command of forces in SWPA, 394, 590
—COLONIAL OFFICE, 397, 400, 402
—DEFENCE COMMITTEE, 6
—DOMINIONS OFFICE, 395, 397
—FOREIGN OFFICE, 5-6, 397
—H.M. STATIONERY OFFICE, 40n
—INFORMATION, MINISTRY OF, 40n
—JOINT PLANNING STAFF, 52
—WAR CABINET, 404
—WAR OFFICE, 9, 36, 105, 399; liaison with SWPA, 8; civil administration of reoccupied areas, 397, 400-3
BRITISH NAVY, 86, 104n, 105, 550, 556, 573; participation in war against Japan, 4-7, 10, 12-14, 15-18, 49; bases in Australia, 33, 42, 394-6
—FLEET AIR ARM, 394
—FLEETS: *Eastern*, 5; *Mediterranean*, 5; *Pacific*, 4, 388, 550, 556; role of, 46: in planning for Borneo operations, 50-1; bases in Australia, 394-6
BROADBENT, Brig J. R., 74n, 484-5, 488, 491, 493; commands 2/17 Bn, 465
BROCK, Sgt P. M., 422
BROCKSOPP, Maj W. A., 519, 521
BROOKE, General Sir Alan; *see* ALANBROOKE, Field Marshal Viscount
BROOKES, Capt J. D., 189
BROOKETON (Map p. 464; Sketches pp. 455, 460), 453, 459, 462, 496
BROWN (Sketch p. 526), 530
BROWN, Lt B. N., 467
BROWN, S-Sgt H. J., 225
BROWN, Lt K. L., 475-6
BROWN, Col M. A., 623
BROWN BEACH (Sketch p. 466), 459, 462, 465-6; *see also* VICTORIA HARBOUR
BRUCE, Rt Hon Viscount, 393
BRUCE, Maj W. F., 116-17
BRUNEI (Map p. 464; Sketches pp. 460, 462), 463, 470, 472, 475, 483, 485, 494, 496-7, 499; Japanese strength at, 456, 471, 495; plans for capture, 459, 462; occupied, 465, 484
BRUNEI, STATE OF, 494, 566; restoration work in, 499; surrender arrangements in, 561
BRUNEI BAY (Map p. 464; Sketch p. 460), 404, 452-3, 456, 470, 486, 490, 504, 509, 520; plans for capture, 30, 49-51, 388, 406, 457, 459-60; described, 453; landings in, 462-3; Japanese strength at, 495
BRUNEI BLUFF (Sketch p. 460), 462
BRUNEI RIVER (Sketch p. 460), 459, 462-3, 465
BRYCESON, Col E. W., 97n
BUCKLEY, Lt-Col A. A., 542
BUCKLEY, Lt J. A. R., 422
BUCKLEY, Pte L., 523

BUCKNER, Lt-Gen Simon B., 27
BUDDEN, Pte H. G., 167
BUIN (Maps pp. 60, 91; Sketch p. 171), 90, 92, 101, 128, 133, 138-9, 141, 154, 168, 170, 194, 227, 240, 558; Japanese strength at, 217
BUIN ROAD (Map p. 91; Sketches pp. 144, 180), 153-4, 157-61, 163, 166, 178-9, 185-96, 199-200, 218-20, 222, 224, 227, 229
BUKA ISLAND (Maps pp. 60, 91; Sketch p. 22), 92-3, 113, 127, 212, 215; people of, 199; Japanese strength on, 217, 234
BUKA PASSAGE (Maps pp. 60, 91; Sketch p. 127), 93, 175, 208, 234
BUKAU (Sketch p. 476), 476
BUKIT COWIE (Sketch p. 462), 462
BUKIT TABUR BINTANG (Sketch p. 462), 462
BULAMITA (Sketches pp. 276, 282), 290-1, 293
BULOLO (Map p. 60), 9n
BULUS RIVER (Sketch p. 245), 260
BUNA (Map p. 60), 40n, 66, 76, 89, 183, 369, 376, 394, 396n
BUNDY, McG., 590n
BUNGARA (Sketches pp. 305, 331), 307, 332, 334
BUNUM (Sketch p. 356), 358
BUOI (Sketch p. 207), 208-10, 235
Burdekin, Australian frigate, 566, 568, 573
BURITSIOTORARA (Sketches pp. 111, 203), 121, 230, 233
BURKE, Lt C. R., 418, 429
BURKE HIGHWAY (Sketch p. 416), 417-18, 423
BURKE RIDGE, 423
BURMA (Map p. 3), 1, 13, 19, 56, 386, 502, 549, 563, 584-5; strength and deployment of Allied forces in, 4; Allied plans for operations in, 10-11, 14-16
BURMA ROAD, 16
BURNS, Sgt J. H., 638
BURNS, J. M., 27n
BURNS, Cpl T. C., 193
BURNS, Capt W. M., 204
BURRELL, Lt-Col J. C., 379-80
BURROWS, Maj D. S. I., 274n
BURSTON, Maj-Gen Sir Samuel, 24n
BURTON, Lt E. A., 424
BURUI (Sketch p. 271), 294
BURU ISLAND (Map p. 28), 555, 569
BURZACOTT, Lt L. B., 520
BUSBY, Capt H., 363
BUSH, Sgt J. W., 188
BUT (Maps pp. 60, 273; Sketches pp. 315, 318), 272, 278, 293-4, 300-1, 314, 317-19, 326-8, 338-9, 342, 345, 350, 359, 377; 16 Bde advance to, 315-16
BUTCH (Sketch p. 429), 434, 449
BUT RIVER (Sketch p. 318), 317-18, 338
BUTTROSE, Brig A. W., 289-90, 293, 303, 360; commands 2/5 Bn, 283
BYRNE, Maj E. F., 280
BYRNE, Lt-Col J. H., 133, 238; commands 42 Bn, 98

CAIRNS (Map p. 3), 43, 98, 105, 396, 457, 504, 554n
CAIRO, Allied Conference at, 5-7
CAKE HILL (Sketch p. 257), 256, 258
CALDWELL, Lt J., 338
CALDWELL, Lt-Col W. B., 74n, 252, 259; commands 14/32 Bn, 249
CALLAGHAN ROAD (Sketch p. 466), 467
CALLINAN, Lt-Col B. J., 171n, 174, 209; commands 26 Bn, 172
CALM (Sketch p. 533), 538-9
CALWELL, Hon A. A., 39
CAMBRIDGE, Capt R. C., 126-7, 175
CAMERON, Lt A., 446
CAMERON, Hon A. G., 57n, 61, 63
CAMERON, Lt-Col A. G., 313, 315-17, 321-2, 338, 384n; commands 2/2 Bn, 296
CAMERON, Pte C. J., 147
CAMERON, Col Hon D. A., 301n
CAMERON, Lt K. R., 317
CAMERON, Capt L. A., 289, 305, 360, 363, 366
CAMERON, Capt W. O., 231-2
CAMERON'S HILL (Sketch p. 203), 232
CAMPBELL, Maj D. L., 102
CAMPBELL, Sgt G. W., 522
CAMPBELL, Sgt J. E., 435
CAMPBELL, Lt L. J., 120
CANADIAN ARMY, 548, 550, 589

INDEX 649

CANNAN, Maj-Gen J. H. (Plate p. 268), 24n, 395-6, 580n
CANNIBALISM, 278
CANUNGRA, Qld, 73, 98
CAPE YORK PENINSULA (Map p. 3), 98
CARINS, Capt T. J., 287
CARLAND, Cpl J. G. V., 473
CARNELL, Sgt E. J., 313
CARR, Lt J. W., 308
CARRIERS, NATIVE, in Wewak campaign, 325-6, 368
CARROLL, Lt G. P., 536
CARSTAIRS, Lt-Col J. D., 74n
CART (Sketch p. 533), 538-9
CARTER, Lt-Col G. S., 455, 492, 495n
CARTER, Cpl W. E., 116
CASLEY, L-Cpl D. L., 435
CASUALTIES, in Papuan and New Guinea Battalions, 82-3, 129. *American* in the Philippines, 4, 56, 405; on Iwo Jima, 51; on Okinawa, 405. *Australian*, 61, 68; in Bougainville, 117n, 133n, 221, 237, 260; in New Britain, 269; in Wewak campaign, 289, 354, 385; at Tarakan, 436, 451-2; on Labuan, 475; in British Borneo, 501; at Balikpapan, 545; in war of 1939-45, 633-5; compared with those of war of 1914-18, 636. *Japanese*, 61, 68; in the Philippines, 4, 405; in Bougainville, 90, 101-3, 133n, 163-4, 167n, 169-70, 201, 230, 237; in Wewak campaign, 341-2, 386; on Okinawa, 405; at Tarakan, 446-7, 449, 451; on Labuan, 475; in British Borneo, 495, 501; at Balikpapan, 526, 545; inflicted by AIB parties, 621
CATER, Lt R. B., 304-5
CATHERALL, Capt J. McP., 419-20, 425
CATTERNS, Maj B. W. T., 339
CAYLEY, Lt-Col W. C., 97n
CEBU (Map p. 28), 29, 55
CELEBES (Maps pp. 3, 28; Sketch p. 560), 11, 394, 511, 548, 551, 553, 566n, 569-70, 572, 577, 618; Japanese strength, 555; surrender in, 573-4; Indonesian nationalist movement, 574-7
CELLO (Sketch p. 533), 535, 538
CENSORSHIP, in Australia, 39n, 64-5, 86
CENTRAL PACIFIC AREA (Sketch p. 16), 1, 18-19, 28, 104n, 585
CENTRE HILL (Sketch p. 203), 232
CERAM (Map p. 3; Sketch p. 560), 502, 569-71, 573, 618; strength of Japanese forces, 555
CHABAI (Sketch p. 207), 216
CHAFFEY, Capt W. A., 621
CHAIR (Sketch p. 533), 538-9
CHALLEN, Lt-Col H. B., 97n
CHAMBERLAIN, J., 594n, 599n
CHAMBERLIN, Lt-Gen Stephen J., 21, 30, 41-2, 45, 596
CHAMBERS, Lt A. L. E., 121
CHAPMAN, Cpl J. W., 320
CHAPMAN, Capt R. M., 525
CHAPMAN-WALKER, Col P. J. F., 619
CHARLIE CREEK (Sketch p. 203), 233
CHARLIE ROUTE (Sketch p. 466), 469n; *see also* HAMILTON ROAD
CHARLIE'S SPUR (Map p. 512), 514
CHARLIE TRACK (Sketch p. 466), 466, 468-9
CHARLOTT, R., 638
CHARM (Sketch p. 533), 537-9
CHAULAK (Sketch p. 305), 307
CHAUVEL, General Sir Harry, 604n
CHEESEMAN, Cpl A., 158
CHEM (Sketch p. 276), 280
CHESTER, Lt-Col F. G. L., 454-5
CHESTERMAN, Lt-Col C. D. R., 105
CHESTERTON, Lt J., 117, 155, 159-62
CHIANG KAI-SHEK, Generalissimo, 585
CHICANAMBU (Sketch p. 331), 331
CHIDGZEY, Lt G. V. R., 349, 354
CHIFLEY, Rt Hon J. B., 62-3, 65, 74, 388-9, 393, 548-51, 580n
CHILTON, Brig F. O., 505, 508, 519, 540-1, 576-7; commands 18 Bde, 504
CHILTON ROAD (Map p. 512), 513, 522
CHINA (Map p. 3; Sketch p. 16), 1, 4, 15, 55, 90, 395, 552; Allied plans in, 10-11, 14, 16, 27, 41; Japanese forces in, 18-19
CHINDAWON (Sketch p. 127), 175, 209-10
CHINDWIN RIVER, 1, 14

CHINESE, in Bougainville, 137-9; at Tarakan, 445; in Borneo, 454, 485, 488, 490, 493, 499-500, 564, 568; at Rabaul, 557; in Celebes, 575, 577; in Australia, 588
CHIVAS, Sgt C. W., 467
CHOISEUL ISLAND (Sketch p. 22), 93, 100, 137n, 140, 170, 201
CHOLIAL (Sketch p. 339), 340
CHOP CHOP TRAIL (Sketch p. 111), 128
CHOWNE, Lt A., VC, 321-2
CHRISTIAN, Capt R. H., 514
CHRISTIE, Lt K. MacN., 121
CHRISTMASS, Pte K. C., 440
CHURCHILL, Rt Hon Sir Winston, 11, 36; participation of British forces in Pacific, 5-10, 12, 15-18; command arrangements in SWPA, 14; plans for British Commonwealth invasion force, 548-9
CHUSAN ISLAND (Sketch p. 16), 41
CLARICE (Sketch p. 429), 437, 445
CLARK, Lt C. E., 147
CLARK, Cpl F. E. J., 184
CLARK, Maj W. D., 554n
CLARK BASE (Sketch p. 144), 143, 145
CLARKE, Lt D. R., 324
CLARKE, Capt E. R., 525, 530
CLARKSON, Lt A. G., 143n
CLEARY, Lt J. S., 87
CLEMENTS, Maj J. M., 468
CLENNETT, Maj B. G., 319
Cleveland, American cruiser, 516
CLEWS, Lt G. W., 309, 333
CLIFTON, Lt D. M., 186, 199
CLOHESY, Sgt L. J. B., 232-3
CLONCURRY (Sketch p. 533), 537
CLOWES, Lt-Gen C. A., 57n, 594
COASTWATCHERS, 100, 170, 201, 617-19, 622; *Japanese*, 188, 241-2
COCHRANE, Maj W. H., 637
COHEN, Brig H. E., 88
COHEN, Capt P. R., 285
COKE (Sketch p. 533), 535-7
Colac, Australian corvette, 204n, 329, 349-50
COLE, Capt R. R., 277, 280, 335, 368
COLEBATCH, Lt-Col G. T., 79
COLEMAN, Col K. R. G., 172-5, 209
COLEMAN, Col S. T. G., 542
COLLETT, Tpr A. N., 434
COLLEY, WO2 D., 170
COLLIER, Lt J. A., 133
COLLIER, Lt J. M., 422
COLLINS HIGHWAY (Sketch p. 416), 415-16, 419
COLVIN, Lt-Col G. E., 488, 497; commands 2/13 Bn, 487
COLVIN, Admiral Sir Ragnar, 11
COMBES, Brig B., 75
COMBES, Lt G. A., 372
COMBINED CHIEFS OF STAFF, 6, 10, 12, 16-17, 54, 393, 400, 502, 548-9, 551; and reduction of Australian forces, 13, 19, 31; command problems in SWPA, 14-15, 590; plans for Borneo operations, 49, 388-9
COMMAGER, H. S., 40n
COMMANDO RIDGE (Sketch p. 144), 152
COMMANDO ROAD (Sketches pp. 144, 190), 167-8, 178, 180, 185-6, 189, 194, 198, 218, 226-7
COMMO RIDGE (Sketch p. 207), 235
COMMUNIQUES, GHQ, 2n; lack news of Australian operations, 37-8, 40, 53; on Balikpapan operations, 520
COMPTON, Lt J. W., 174
COMPTON RIVER (Sketch p. 173), 172-5
CONFOY, Sgt W. T. M., 523
CONLON, Col A. A., 84, 398-9, 402-3; Director of Research, LHQ, 397
CONWAY, Pte A. W., 322
COOK, Lt-Col F. W., 516-19
COOKE, Sgt H. A., 422
COOMBES, Lt-Col C. J. A., 98
COOMBES' CROSSING, 161
COOPER, Cpl A., 193
COOPER, Constable C. H. R., 624
COOPER, Maj E. J., 536-7
COOPER, W Cdr E. W., 275
COOPER, L-Sgt R. W. F., 133
COPEMAN, Maj J., 325
COPPING, L-Cpl J. W., 517
CORAL SEA (Map p. 60), 88, 90, 584

CORBOULD, Capt R. W., 150
CORCORAN, L-Cpl L. J., 422
CORE, Pte M. J., 321
CORMORAN, CAPE (Map p. 243), 244, 247
CORONET OPERATION, 52
CORREGIDOR (Map p. 28), 590-1
CORY, Maj G. C., 340, 346
CORY, Capt G. E., 298-9
CORY, F-Lt G. R. I., 138-9
CORY'S SPUR (Sketch p. 297), 299-300
COSTELLO, Lt-Col F. H., 570
COTTON, Lt-Col T. R. W., 533
COURSEY, Lt-Col J. P., 558
COURTNEY, Lt D. A., 133
COWRA PRISONER-OF-WAR COMPOUND, 623-4
COX, Brig A. R. B., 24n
COX, Brig G. S., 346-7, 374, 376; commands 2/4 Bn, 345
COYLE, Maj G., 317
CRACKING PLANT (Map p. 512), 519, 521
CRAFTER, Maj J. G., 544
CRAWFORD, Cpl W. J., 213-14
CRAZE, Cpl W. A. C., 170
CRAZY RIDGE (Sketch p. 429), 428, 440
CREMOR, Brig W. E., 97, 637
CRISPIN, K. E., 638
CROMPTON, Lt-Col D. H., 257
CROSS, Sgt A. F., 200
CROWDEN, Lt C. W., 298
CROWN PRINCE RANGE (Map p. 91; Sketch p. 111), 135
CULLEN, Maj-Gen P. A., 297-8, 301, 318, 326, 379, 384; commands 2/1 Bn, 296
CULT (Sketch p. 533), 533-4
CUMMING, Lt J. T., 489
CUMMINGS, Col C. J., 561, 564
Current Affairs Bulletin, 86-7, 96
CURTIN, Sgt A., 423-4
CURTIN, Rt Hon John, 11, 62, 70, 105, 395, 585, 590, 593, 595, 603; participation of British forces in the Pacific, 6-7, 9, 12, 15, 17; reduction of Australian forces, 13, 31-4; command problems in SWPA, 14, 597; on employment of Australian forces, 20, 42-50, 57; and General Blamey, 59-61, 64-5, 578-9
CUTARP (Map p. 243), 245, 252
CUTHBERTSON, Capt C. C., 195

DAGUA (Map p. 273; Sketches pp. 318, 320), 272, 293-4, 300, 316-20, 324, 328, 340, 342, 359, 377-8, 381
DAGUA CREEK (Sketch p. 320), 323
DALBY, Capt H., 530
DALE, Pte C. E., 483
DALEY, Gnr G. H., 337-8
DALLMAN HARBOUR (Sketch p. 344), 380
DALY, Maj-Gen T. J., 74, 515-16, 518-19; commands 2/10 Bn, 510
DAMPIER, CAPE (Map p. 243), 242
DANDRIWAD RIVER (Sketch p. 276), 277, 280, 288
DANIEL, Admiral Sir Charles, 11, 13
DANMAP RIVER (Map p. 273; Sketches pp. 284, 297), 277-80, 283-5, 287-9, 291, 293, 297, 311, 314, 341-2
DANMUL RIVER (Sketch p. 285), 287
DARENA (Sketch p. 136), 138
DARRYL, Lt L. J., 310, 336
DARWIN (Map p. 3; Sketch p. 560), 14, 34n, 44, 58n, 93, 250n, 266, 396, 570, 633
DAVEY, Lt K. J., 516, 518
DAVIDSON, Maj J. J. G., 478
DAVIES-GRIFFITHS, L-Sgt O. L., 122
DAVIS, Lt A. L., 118
DAWE'S CREEK (Sketch p. 179), 178-9
DAWSON, Lt-Col B. G., 262-4; commands 1 NGIB, 261
DEACON, Capt J., 108
DEACON, MOUNT (Sketch p. 107), 108-9
DEAN, Lt S., 376
DE BRUYN, Lt J. D., 620
DECORATIONS, awarded to Pacific Islands Regt and Royal Papuan Constabulary, 83n; awarded to Australian Army, 581n
DE DAUNTON, Capt F. H., 532
Deloraine, Australian corvette, 329
DEMPSEY, Lt L. J., 543
DENCH, Capt J. R., 489

DENGUE FEVER, in Bougainville, 237n, in Wewak campaign, 385
DENNESS, Maj A. P., 476, 479, 482
DENNIS, Spr E. T., 343
DENNISTON, Lt-Col J. A. Y., 89n
DENT, Capt G. C., 193
DERBYSHIRE, Lt-Col M., 316-17, 320, 322, 324, 383-4
DERRICK, Lt T. C., VC, 77n, 416, 425, 437-8
DEVONSHIRE, Capt J. W., 312
DEW, Tpr L. F., 196
DEWAR, Lt R., 286
DEWING, Maj-Gen R. H., 8, 9n, 10
DEXTER, Lt-Col W. R., 145; commands 61 Bn, 98
Diamantina, Australian frigate, 204n, 558, 560-1
DICKIE, Capt R. M., 184
DIETRICH, Maj P. W., 195
DIFFEY, Maj S. C., 287, 348-9
DILI (Sketch p. 560), 571-2
DINGLE, Cpl N. M., 428
DIO DIO (Sketch p. 171), 227
DISTRICT IV (Sketches pp. 416, 431), 427, 448
DISTRICT VI (Sketches pp. 416, 431), 422, 427, 448
DJINABORA (Sketch p. 540), 541-2
DOBODURA, 255, 394
DODD, Lt-Col R. W. P., 539
DODS, Lt R. E., 413
DOGRETO BAY (Map p. 273; Sketches pp. 284, 297), 283, 286, 294, 296, 300, 311, 314, 328
DOIABI RIVER (Sketch p. 111), 104, 106, 109
DOIABI VALLEY (Sketch p. 111), 108
DONADABU (Map p. 60), 9n
DONALDSON, Cpl R., 354
DONELEY, Lt A. R., 283
DONNETT, Sgt A. H., 317, 383
DONNISON, F. S. V., 400n, 401n, 403n, 405n, 565n, 566n
DONOGHUE, Lt T. J., 382-3
DORNEY, Lt-Col K. J. J., 497
DORRY (Sketch p. 431), 434
DOUGHERTY, Maj-Gen I. N., 508, 521-2, 525, 527, 531, 544, 574-6; commands 21 Bde, 504
DOUGLASS, Pte H. F., 537
DOVE BAY (Map p. 273; Sketch p. 344), 329, 377; landing at, 349-50
DOVERS, Capt W. J., 349
DOWLING, Maj L. E., 286
DOWNS, Capt H. C., 125-6, 210-13
DOWNS' RIDGE (Sketches pp. 127, 173), 126, 172-3
DOYLE, Lt F. C., 527-8
DRAPER, Cpl M. L. W., 215
DREKIKIR (Sketch p. 282), 334
DRINIUMOR RIVER (Map p. 273; Sketch p. 276), 68, 276, 278-9, 289, 291, 293, 314, 328, 386
DROOP (Sketch p. 441), 440
Dubbo, Australian corvette, 204n, 329, 349-50, 556
DULAG (Map p. 28), 2
DUNBIT (Sketch p. 361), 365
DUNCAN, Sgt K. McM., 362
DUNCAN, Prof W. G. K., 86
DUNDANG RIVER, 566
DUNKLEY, Lt-Col H. L. E., 231, 233-4; commands 7 Bn, 230
DUNLOP, Cpl R. A., 304
DUNN, Capt R. L., 430
DUNSHEA, Capt C. J. P., 145, 168, 198-9
DUNSTAN, Maj A. R., 193
DUNSTAN, Tpr T. E., 196
DUTCH (Sketch p. 429), 445
DUTCH, THE, 408-9, 451, 568, 572, 575, 577
DUTCH ARMY, 407, 487, 591
DUTCH GOVERNMENT, 551, 553, 566n, 572
DUTCH NAVY, 618-20
DUTCH TRACK (Sketch p. 441), 439-40, 442
DWYER, Maj M. J., 352, 373, 382
DYAKS, relations with Japanese, 454, 569; assist Australians, 485, 489-95, 565
DYKE, Maj-Gen L. G. H., 570-2; commands Timor Force, 554
DYSENTERY, in Bougainville, 237n, in Wewak campaign, 385

EA EA (Map p. 243), 248, 251-4, 267
EAGLETON, Pte R. E., 343
EASON, Brig R. T., 312-13
EASTICK, Brig T. C., 563-4; commands Kuching Force, 561

INDEX 651

EASTMAN, Capt E. A., 467, 473, 482
EASTMAN SPUR (Sketch p. 472), 473-4
EATHER, Maj-Gen K. W., 265, 532-4, 537-9, 557; commands 25 Bde, 523, 11 Div, 554
Eaton, American destroyer, 525
EDGAR, Maj A. G. S., 332
EDGAR, Brig C. R. V., 248*n*
EDGAR, Lt-Gen H. G., 97*n*, 148, 227*n*
EDMEADES, Maj E. A., 495
EDWARDS, Lt A. D., 331
EDWARDS, Lt I. H., 422
EGAN, Maj C. J., 189
EGAN, Lt J. M., 533
EGAN'S RIDGE (Sketch p. 190), 187, 189-90, 192
EHRMAN, J., 5*n*, 6*n*, 18*n*, 51*n*, 386*n*
EICHELBERGER, Lt-Gen Robert L., 40*n*, 592*n*, 593, 595; commands Eighth Army, 19
EISENHOWER, General of the Army Dwight D., 1, 4, 37, 599
EJIMA, Colonel Yoshiyuki, 164
ELBOW (Sketch p. 429), 436, 440
ELDRIDGE, Col R. T., 419-21, 444, 446-7
ELEY, Lt J. A., 423
ELLIOTT, John, 524
ELLIOTT, Pte K., 119
ELLIOTT, Lt M. H., 232
ELLIOTT-SMITH, Lt-Col S., 204
ELLIS, Sir Albert, 561
ELLISON, Lt-Col E. B., 570
EMBREY, Lt-Col F. J., 261
EMIRAU ISLAND (Maps pp. 3, 60), 21-2, 24, 89-90, 93, 201
EMPEROR RANGE (Map p. 91), 114
EMPRESS AUGUSTA BAY (Map p. 91; Sketches pp. 131, 144), 90, 128, 130, 135
ENDEAN, Lt D. C., 435
ENDERBY, Lt E. A., 415
ENGLAND, Lt-Col J. A., 564
ENGLISH, Capt W. M., 244
EQUIPMENT, American, compared with Australian, 62, 95. *Australian*, 36-7, 59, 61-2, 142, 314, 327, 457-8, 587, 598. *Japanese*, 163, 174-5, 291-2, 317, 342, 352, 558-9
ERBS, Sgt A. R., 198
ERIWEL, Private, 248*n*
ERREY, Lt I. G., 330-1
ESAU, Capt K. M., 433
ESCREET, Pte H. G., 289
ESDAILE, Capt J. C. D., 350
ESMIE (Sketch p. 431), 434
ESSEX (Sketches pp. 416, 429), 408, 419-20
ESSIE (Sketch p. 441), 408, 439, 445-7, 449
ESSIE TRACK (Sketch p. 441), 445-6
EVANS (Sketch p. 416), 424-5, 430
EVANS, Sgt A. A., 518
EVANS, Capt J. A., 316
EVANS, Lt W. F. P., 121
EVANS, L-Cpl W. J., 232
EVATT, Rt Hon H. V., 56, 393
Exeter, British cruiser, 573
BYERS, Lt-Col E. S., 97*n*

FAHL, Lt R. W., 337
FAIRCLOUGH, Lt-Col H., 638
FAIRFAX-ROSS, Maj B., 242-7
FAISI (Map p. 60), 101
FAITH (Sketch p. 429), 445
FAKFAK (Map p. 28), 620
FAR EAST, 1, 5-6, 12, 15, 20, 56-7, 342
FAR EASTERN LIAISON OFFICE, 121, 181-3, 507, 617
FARGHER, Lt-Col L. W., 97*n*
FARMAN, Cpl F. A., 523
FARMER, Pte C. C., 421
FARNCOMB, Rear-Adm H. B., 349-50
FAUL, Lt H. J., 258
FAULKNER, Maj D. F., 487-8
FAURO ISLAND (Map p. 60; Sketch p. 22), 92, 133, 217, 558, 561
FAUX, L-Sgt H. L., 232
FEARNSIDE, Lt G. H., 288, 638
FEATURE 620 (Sketch p. 346), 348
FEATURE 710 (Sketches pp. 344, 346), 348-9, 353
FEATURE 770 (Sketches pp. 344, 346), 348, 353, 369
FEATURE 800 (Sketch p. 297), 298, 300
FEATURE 1410 (Sketches pp. 318, 320), 319, 321-4, 326, 377

FEATURE 1800 (Sketch p. 339), 339
FEATURE 1860 (Sketch p. 318), 318
FEATURE 2400 (Sketch p. 339), 341
FELDT, Cdr E. A., 201, 617-19
FENNELL, L-Sgt W. J., 438
FERGUSON, Capt G. T., 440
FERGUSON, Lt K., 316, 322
FERGUSON, Sgt L. M., 525
FERGUSSON, Brig M. A., 379; commands 8 Bde, 355
FERTIG, Colonel Wendell, 55*n*
FIELD, Brig J., 97, 108, 130, 142-3, 147, 149-50, 153, 155-6, 158, 160-1, 558; commands 7 Bde, 92
FIELDS, Miss Gracie, 226*n*, 266
FIENBERG, Capt D. M., 334, 368
FIJI DEFENCE FORCE, 67, 92
FINCH (Sketch p. 416), 415-16
FINLAYSON, Lt M., 323-4, 382
FINSCHHAFEN (Map p. 60), 40, 89, 102, 268, 396*n*
FISHER, Col H. M., 274*n*
FISK, WO2 K. R. C., 372
FITZ-GERALD, Maj A. T., 224
FLAGSTAFF HILL (Sketch p. 466), 465, 467-8
FLAME-THROWERS, 341, 360*n*, 384, 442
FLEMING, Capt R. S., 280
FLETCHER, Col J. W., 89*n*
FLORES (Map p. 3), 571
FLORES SEA, 520
FLORIS (Sketch p. 431), 434
FOGARTY, L-Sgt J. P., 353
FOLL, Hon H. S., 57-8
FORBES, Lt A. J. de B., 124, 125*n*
FORD, Lt A. J. T., 118-19
FORD, Sgt C. H., 539
FORDE, Rt Hon F. M., 24*n*, 38, 39*n*, 56, 64, 88, 327, 393, 551, 578-9, 581, 593; on employment of Australian Army, 58-9; on organisation and higher command of Australian Army, 600-3, 605-6
FOREMAN, Maj J. G., 413-14, 417; commands 2/13 Fd Coy, 412
FORMA (Sketch p. 136), 138-9, 168
Formidable, British aircraft carrier, 582
FORMOSA (Map p. 3; Sketch p. 16), 6, 10, 14-15, 27-8, 35, 583
FORMOSANS, 503, 555
FOROK (Sketch p. 344), 350-1
FOROK CREEK (Sketch p. 344), 351
FOROK POINT (Sketch p. 344), 386
FORSYTH, W. D., 572
FRANK (Sketch p. 416), 419, 425
FRASER, Lt D. W. H., 196
FRASER, Hon J. M., 59, 61-3, 391-2, 396, 603, 605-6
FRASER, Lt H. W., 419, 429
FREAME, Lt A. W., 435-6
FREAME, Sgt W. H., 419*n*
FREDA (Sketch p. 429), 437-41, 443
FREEMAN, Lt A. W., 435-6
FREIGHT (Sketch p. 533), 534
FREMANTLE, 34*n*
FRENCH, Maj B. J., 332
FROOD, Lt W., 541
FROST (Sketches pp. 526, 529), 530, 543
FRY, Maj G. McK., 360
FRY, Lt-Col W. G., 159; commands 47 Bn, 221
FUDAKI, Lieutenant, 434
FUJINO, Captain, 565
FUKUDA, Major, 229-30
FUKUKAKU (Sketch p. 409), 427, 436, 439, 443-7, 449
FULLARTON, Brig I. G., 605

GABEL, Lt-Col C. P., 116-17
GADONG (Sketch p. 476), 477
GAIRDNER, General Sir Charles, 29*n*
GALAH (Sketch p. 429), 436
GALVIN, Pte P. J., 153
GAMBLE, Lt A. G., 541
GAMBLE, Col F. B., 402
GANLY, Chaplain Rev D. A., 148
GANNON, Maj J. E., 564
GARDENS, JAPANESE, in Bougainville, 151-2, 154-5, 186
GARDOLL, L-Sgt E. E., 468
GARLAND, Maj R. S., 364-5, 367
GARRETT, Lt-Gen Sir Ragnar (Plate p. 236), 137, 166*n*, 183*n*, 557; BGS II Corps, 97
GARVEY, Maj K. B., 411
Gascoyne, Australian frigate, 542, 568
GATE (Sketch p. 524), 530

652   INDEX

GATELY, Capt J. C., 352, 372, 381
GAUL, Maj A. J. F., 147
GAY, Capt A. I., 365
GAY, Lt H. W., 187, 194
GAZELLE HARBOUR (Sketches pp. 131, 144), 103, 114
GAZELLE PENINSULA (Map p. 243), 25, 55, 68-9, 244-5, 247, 251, 260, 270, 583; described, 241; strength of Japanese forces on, 242, 268
GEAI, Corporal, 225-6
GEDDES, Lt-Col J. O., 451
GEER, Capt A. S., 289-90, 303, 360, 366
GEMPE, 572
GENERAL HEADQUARTERS, SWPA, 21, 23, 29, 39n, 93, 137, 274, 291n, 403, 406, 410, 455, 457-8, 504, 506; communiqués, 2n, 37-8, 40, 53, 520; moves to Hollandia, 24; role of I Aust Corps, 28, 30, 41-2, 49-50; relations with General Blamey, 37, 52, 71-2; command problems, 43-5, 47, 53-4, 590-9; estimates of Japanese strength on Bougainville differ from Australian, 101-2; shortage of shipping, 105, 165, 269, 281, 328-9; and Allied Intelligence Bureau, 618, 620-1
GENEVA CONVENTION, 623-4
GENGA RIVER (Sketches pp. 123, 173), 122-6, 175, 215
GEORGE (Sketches pp. 107, 108), 106-9
GEORGE, Lt N. G., 480-1
GERMAN ARMY, 1, 35, 182
GERMANS, 554n
GERMANY, 5-7, 12-13, 18, 41-2, 50, 65, 72, 182, 388, 589, 633; strength of army, 35
GIBBINS, Capt G. W., 299, 324, 339
GIBBS, Sgt J. J., 382
GIBSON, Capt J. McL., 172-4
GIBSON, Sgt L. H., 527
GILL, Pte L. W., 288
GILLIES, Cpl M. J., 110n
GILLIGAN, Sgt D. M. R., 203
GILLMAN RIVER (Sketch p. 173), 124-5, 172
GILMORE, Maj J. C. S., 316, 319, 321, 323
GISANAMBU (Sketch p. 361), 365
GIVNEY, Capt E. C., 300, 380
GLARE, Gnr E. W., 215
GLASS, Lt R. L. Barnet, 224
GLASSOP, S-Sgt L., 87
Glenelg, Australian corvette, 570-1
GLENELG HIGHWAY (Sketch p. 416), 408, 415
GLENN, J. G., 438n, 638
Glory, British aircraft carrier, 556, 582
GLOUCESTER, CAPE (Map p. 243), 241
GLOVER, Capt M. H. E. C., 479-80
GODWIN, Maj J. B., 313, 326, 369
GOEBBELS, Dr J., 182
GOOBULU CREEK (Sketch p. 245), 256
GOLDSMITH, Capt O. D., V., 317, 320
GONA (Map p. 60), 396n
GOODE, Maj A. L., 282; commands 2/7 Cdo Sqn, 280
GOODEN, Capt O. D., 415-16, 425-6, 434, 437
GOODHART, D., 428n, 637
GOODWIN, Lt L. F., 119-20, 206
GOOLEY, Sgt B. V., 299
GORDON, Lt C. M. B., 375
GORDON, Maj-Gen R. R., 312, 378-9; commands 2/3 MG Bn, 311
GORDON, Lt-Col W. J. S., 331-2
Gorgon, British ship, 274
GORONTALO (Sketch p. 560), 573
GORRIE, Lt R. M., 258n
GOTTS, Lt R. J., 298
GOVERNMENT HOUSE, Labuan (Sketch p. 466), 466
GOW, Lt A. F., 369
GRACE, Col C. H., 490; commands 2/15 Bn, 463
GRAFFIN, Lt L. R., 473
GRAHAM, Capt A. G., 215
GRAHAM, Lt C. A., 197
GRAHAM, Lt J. R. V., 368
GRAHAM, Lt L. F., 491-2
GRAHAM, Sgt R. D., 301
GRAHAM, Col S. C., 179, 190, 197-8
GRAND (Sketch p. 524), 530
GRANT, Gp Capt A. G., 513-14, 521n
GRAY, Capt J. C., 422
GREEN, Lt-Col C. H., 74n, 353, 374; commands 2/11 Bn, 345
GREEN, Bdr K. E., 158
GREEN, Lt-Col W. J., 410

GREEN BEACH, Balikpapan (Map p. 512), 510, 513-14, 521
GREEN BEACH, Brunei Bay (Sketches pp. 460, 462), 453, 459, 462-3, 484
GREEN BEACH, Tarakan (Sketches pp. 409, 416), 410, 412-14
GREEN ISLANDS (Map p. 60; Sketch p. 22), 21-2, 24, 90, 92-3, 201
GREENSHIELDS, WO2 F. T., 120
GREEN SPUR (Sketch p. 517), 517
GREENWAY, Capt G. J., 286, 348
GREER, Lt J. H., 348
GREER, Lt R., 423
GREGORY, Maj R. C., 132
GRIFF, Lt-Col E. M., 193
GRIGG, Cpl R. F., 538
GRISWALD, Rev Father, 171
GRISWOLD, Lt-Gen Oscar W., 94
GUADALCANAL (Sketch p. 22), 90
GUALIGEM (Sketches pp. 302, 331), 310, 332
GUBBAY, Lt A. R., 343
GUERIN, WO2 J. F., 200
GUGELER, R. A., 27n
GUGGER, Lt N. A., 544
Guinea Gold, 87, 96
GULAGULA (Sketch p. 254), 252
GULCHER, MOUNT (Sketch p. 171), 200
GULLEY, Pte T., 190
GUNDO, 247
GURSKI, Cpl D. W., 155
GWALIP (Sketch p. 361), 364-5, 367, 369
GWANGINAN (Sketches pp. 305, 331), 307, 330
GWENIK (Sketch p. 361), 365

HACKETT, L-Sgt C. G., 519
HAIGH, Capt P. F., 423
HAIGH'S (Sketch p. 431), 430
HAINAN ISLAND (Maps pp. 3, 28), 41, 51
HAINES, Pte E. J., 151
HALIKAMOK RIVER (Sketches pp. 318, 320), 317-18
HALL, WO2 E. D., 213-14
HALL, Lt J. S., 473
HALL, Maj K. S., 536
HALL, M., 454n
HALL, W Cdr O. B., 330, 334
HALL, Sgt P. J., 160-1
HALL, WO1 R. E., 301
HALL, Lt R. W., 347
HALMAHERA (Map p. 28; Sketch p. 560), 12, 511, 555, 570, 572-3
HALSEY, Fleet Admiral William F., 1-2, 29, 54
HAMBINI (Sketch p. 282), 290
HAMBRAURI (Sketches pp. 344, 371), 381-3
HAMILTON, Cpl A. J., 528
HAMILTON, Maj J. McK., 244
HAMILTON PENINSULA (Sketch p. 466), 468
HAMILTON POINT (Sketch p. 466), 469n
HAMILTON ROAD (Sketch p. 466), 466, 469
HAMMER, Maj-Gen H. H. (Plate p. 125), 99, 183n, 187, 189, 193, 196, 200, 219, 221, 239-40; commands 15 Bde, 98; estimate of, 177-8
HAMMER JUNCTION, 225
HAMSUK (Sketch p. 320), 319
HANCOCK, Lt-Cdr K. W., 557
HANCOCK, Air Marshal Sir Valston, 349; commands No. 71 Wing RAAF, 275
HANEMO (Sketch p. 111), 110, 139
HANKEY, J. R.; see REED-HANKEY, Lt J.
HANSA BAY (Sketch p. 356), 355-6, 358
HANSEN, Sgt F. J., 314
HANUNG (Sketch p. 180), 225
HARDING, Lt B. A., 265n, 266n
HARDY, Pte B. G., 624
HARDY'S (Sketch p. 466), 466
HARECH RIVER (Map p. 273), 276, 282
HARI (Sketch p. 190), 157
HARIPMOR (Sketch p. 384), 385
HARI RIVER (Map p. 91; Sketches pp. 180, 190), 114, 152-3, 155-6, 170, 177-8, 183n, 186-8, 192-5, 197, 200
HARLEM, Lt D. A. L., 455
HARMON, Lt-Gen Millard F., 27
HARRIS, Lt E. W., 365
HARRIS, Capt G. C., 620
HARRIS, Capt M. N. J., 124-5
HARRISON, Pte K. C., 523

HARRISSON, Maj T. H., 455-6, 490, 494-5, 565, 620
HARROP, Capt C. O., 280
Hart, British sloop, 556
HART, Capt G. C., 424, 438
HARVEY, Lt R. J., 437
HASSETT, Maj-Gen F. G., 227-8
HATAI (Sketch p. 144), 155, 161
HATAI TRACK, 158, 185
HATTA, Dr, 567
HATTORI, Colonel Takushiro, 103, 291*n*
HAWAII, 1
HAWAIIAN ISLANDS, 585
HAWAIN RIVER (Sketches pp. 339, 345), 339-40, 342-3, 345
HAWKE, Capt G. J., 346-7, 374-5
Hawkesbury, Australian frigate, 458
HAY, Lt-Col D. O., 307, 309, 331, 335
HAYDON, Lt J. B., 297
HAYDON KNOLL (Sketch p. 297), 297-8, 300
HAYES, Maj H. F., 535
HAYES, Lt-Col J. M., 195
HAYES, Sgt R. P., 468
HAYFIELD (Map p. 273; Sketches pp. 331, 361), 331, 334, 336-7, 338*n*, 359, 363*n*, 364, 369, 559
HAYWOOD, Major E. V., 637
HEAD, Lt A. E., 415
HEALEY, Lt D. G., 285
HEALY, WO2 T. J., 364
HEATH, Miss D., 291*n*
HEDDERMAN, Lt J. W., 330, 334
HEGARTY, Capt V. H., 165
HELEN (Sketch p. 431), 431, 433-4
HELEN TRACK, 430
HELY, Air Vice-Marshal W. L., 95
HENDERSON, Capt G. A., 523
HENDERSON, Col G. F. R., 604*n*
HENDERSON, L-Cpl R. H., 224
HENNESSY, Lt-Col E. C., 276, 280, 303, 306, 308, 350-2, 378; commands 2/6 Cav (Cdo) Regt, 275
HENNING, Lt E. B. H., 334*n*
HENRY, Capt R. L., 637
HENRY, Lt-Col T. H., 206
HENRY REID BAY (Map p. 243; Sketch p. 245), 242, 245, 247, 252-3, 256
HENRY REID RIVER; *see* WULWUT RIVER
Herald, The, 40
HERBERT, Lt G. E., 443
HERRING, Lt-Gen Hon Sir Edmund, 57*n*, 64, 70, 580, 594
HEWIT, Capt E. J., 373
HEWITT, Capt J. S., 312, 319, 351
HIBBARD, Lt R. G. T., 346
HIBBERD, Lt-Col H. D., 132
HILDA (Sketch p. 429), 445
HILL, Sgt C. H., 375
HILL, Sgt H. V., 528-9
HILL 1 (Sketch p. 371), 372
HILL 2 (Sketch p. 371), 372
HILL 87 (Map p. 512; Sketch p. 517), 511, 515-19
HILL 90 (Sketch p. 441), 447
HILL 102 (Sketch p. 409), 427, 436, 439, 442-4
HILL 105 (Sketch p. 409), 427, 435-9, 443-4
HILL 910 (Sketch p. 371), 370, 374
HINCKSMAN, Capt T. E., 430-1
HINTON, Lt W. A., 522
HIROSHIMA (Sketch p. 578), 578
HIRU HIRU (Sketches pp. 144, 179), 152, 154, 179
HIXON BAY (Map p. 243), 247
Hobart, Australian cruiser, 349, 410, 458, 462, 511
HOBBS, Maj-Gen Sir Talbot, 604*n*
HOCKING, Capt L. J., 191
HODDINOTT, Capt F. J., 340
HODGE, Lt-Gen J. R., 577*n*
HODGE, Lt L. A., 368
HODGSON, Col C. R., 411
HOGBIN, Lt-Col H. I. P., 397, 399
HOLDSWORTH, Maj W. T. B., 420*n*
HOLE, Tpr H. E., 189
HOLLANDIA (Maps pp. 28, 60), 19, 26, 30, 37, 41, 48, 296*n*, 350, 386*n*, 553, 620; GHQ at, 24, 595
HOLMES, Sgt R. W. E., 431
HOLT, Chaplain Rev W. E., 473
HONE, Maj-Gen Sir Ralph, 399
HONE, Lt-Col R. B., 248*n*; commands 2/14 Fd Regt, 252
HONG KONG (Maps pp. 3, 28), 11, 400, 550

HONGORAI RIVER (Map p. 91; Sketches pp. 144, 180), 141, 152-3, 155, 156-7, 165, 167, 177, 179, 181, 183-9, 191, 224
HONOLULU, 27
HONSHU ISLAND (Sketch p. 578), 577
HOOPER, F-Lt C. F., 244
HOPEFUL (Sketch p. 441), 446
HOPKINS, Maj-Gen R. N. L., 578*n*
HORINU 2 (Sketch p. 144), 153, 167
HORLEY, Lt-Col R. J., 260
HORSESHOE KNOLL (Sketch p. 173), 174
HOSKINS, CAPE (Map p. 243; Sketch p. 254), 241, 248-9, 251-2, 254-5
HOSPITAL SPUR (Sketch p. 416), 418, 422-3
HOST, Pte E. J., 353
HOUSE COPP (Sketch p. 305), 305, 308
HOW, L-Cpl W. R., 438
HOWARD, Cpl E. J., 492
HOWDEN, Lt-Col W. S., 287, 345; commands 2/8 Bn, 286
HUDA RIVER (Sketch p. 190), 185, 189
HUGHES, Rt Hon W. M., 69
HUIO RIVER (Sketch p. 144), 166
HUNGERFORD, Sgt T. A. G., 106*n*, 156-7, 171*n*
HUNT, Capt L. E. E., 230
HUNTER, Lt R., 258
HUNT's HILL (Sketch p. 203), 202
HUON (Sketch p. 533), 533
HUON GULF (Map p. 60), 40*n*
HUON PENINSULA (Map p. 60), 66, 291, 327, 381, 411
HUPAI RIVER (Sketches pp. 131, 144), 128, 132-3, 141-2, 146-7, 149
HUPAISAPANI, 133
HUTCHINSON, Maj T. C., 153
HUTCHISON, Lt-Col I., 296, 298, 340; commands 2/3 Bn, 287
HUTCHISON, MOUNT, 298
HUTSON, Maj A. W. M., 563
HYAKUTAKE, Lt-Gen Haruyoshi, 114, 133-4, 150, 269; commands *XVII Army*, 101
HYNDMAN, Maj C. W., 535-7

IBU (Sketches pp. 111, 203), 122, 230, 233-4
ICHISE, Vice-Admiral, 571
IDAKAIBUL (Sketch p. 285), 284, 287-8
IEMURA, Colonel Shinshichi, 562
ILAHETA (Sketch p. 302), 303, 309
ILAHOP (Sketch p. 302), 303-4, 306, 309
ILAP (Sketch p. 297), 296
ILIPEM (Sketches pp. 360, 361), 363
IMAMURA, General Hitoshi, 114, 241, 266-7, 269-70, 556-7; commands *Eighth Area Army*, 90
IMBIA (Sketch p. 331), 338
IMPHAL, 14
Implacable, British aircraft carrier, 582
IND, Lt-Col A. W., 619
INDIA (Map p. 3), 6-7, 12-13, 70
INDIAN ARMY, 4-5, 53, 65, 311, 548, 551, 564, 567, 589; prisoners of war recovered, 106, 127, 215, 283, 340, 352, 463, 487-8, 543, 557, 568
—BRIGADES, 32nd, 565; 80th, 577
INDIAN OCEAN (Map p. 3), 4-5, 7, 10
INDIANS, in Borneo, 485, 490, 499-500
INDO-CHINA (Map p. 3), 557, 621
INDONESIANS, 215, 440, 443, 445, 502, 539*n*, 540, 557, 571; and nationalist movement, 566-9, 572-3, 574-6
INGHAM, Lt P. G. O., 436
INIMBI (Sketch p. 302), 309
INTELLIGENCE, *Allied*, of strength of Japanese forces, 23, 101-2, 113. *American*, 103, 449. *Australian*, 103, 280; of strength of Japanese forces, 26, 209, 272. *Japanese*, 114-15, 268
INUS (Sketch p. 127), 137, 176, 205
INUS POINT, 232
Inverell, Australian corvette, 573
IP RIVER (Sketch p. 245), 253, 255
IRAI (Sketch p. 219), 199
IRUP, MOUNT (Sketch p. 361), 364, 367
IRVING, Brig R. G. H., 293*n*
ISAACHSEN, Lt-Col O. C., 251-4; commands 36 Bn, 249
ISLAND, THE (Sketch p. 517), 516
ISLES, Lt-Col K. S., 397
ISMAY, General Rt Hon Lord, 7
ISSELL, Maj R. W., 415
ITAGAKI, Lt-Gen Seishiro, 554

ITALIAN ARMY, 1, 182, 391
ITALIAN NAVY, 5
ITALIANS, 554n, 588
ITALY, 4, 549, 589
IVANA RIVER (Sketch p. 219), 199, 219-20
IWO JIMA (Sketch p. 16), 27-8, 51

JABA RIVER (Map p. 91; Sketches pp. 131, 134), 94, 103-4, 111-14, 128-31, 143, 146
JACK, Capt R. L., 259
JACKETT, J. G. T., 638
JACKSON, Brig D. R., 478
JACKSON, Lt H. H., 317, 321
JACOBS, Maj J. W., 637
JACQUINOT BAY (Map p. 243; Sketch p. 254), 89, 96, 244-8, 250, 252, 254-5, 261, 263, 265-6, 556
JAM (Sketch p. 533), 534
JAMA (Map p. 273), 366
JAMBONGAN ISLAND (Sketch p. 455), 455
JAMEI (Sketch p. 331), 311, 336-7
JAMIESON, Lt-Col W. D., 332
JAMMER BAY (Map p. 243; Sketch p. 254), 247, 260-1, 268
JANET (Sketch p. 429), 427, 436, 438
JAPAN (Map p. 3; Sketch p. 578), 5, 12, 40n, 49, 56, 66, 90, 181-3, 266, 387-9, 393-4, 450, 547, 567, 585, 589; Allied plans for defeat of, 1, 4, 6-7, 10, 16, 27, 50, 52, 548-50; strength of forces in, 18-19, 35; surrenders, 69, 237, 265, 549, 578; bombing of, 502; occupation forces in, 550-1, 577-8; forces repatriated, 583
JAPANESE AIR FORCE, 37, 92, 457; in Philippines, 2, 4, 29; in New Britain, 241-2, 259; in Borneo, 444, 502
—6TH AIR DIVISION, 292
—63RD AIR REGIMENT, 310
—AIRFIELD BATTALIONS: 21st, in Wewak campaign, 318-19, 327, 370. 25th, in Wewak campaign, 343, 352, 370
JAPANESE ARMY, 1-2, 20, 51, 53, 58, 71, 101, 128, 405, 450, 621; organisation compared with British, 2n; in Philippines, 4, 55; in Burma, 14-16; strength and deployment, 18-19, 23, 272; losses, 38, 61, 501; in New Britain, 49, 68, 241-2, 247, 252-3, 260, 267-70; in Wewak campaign, 68, 283, 289, 296, 310, 340, 343, 359, 367-8, 386; in Bougainville, 90, 100-3, 126, 129, 133-4, 140, 163-4, 167n, 169-71, 175-7, 186, 205-6, 217, 221, 230, 234, 237-8, 240, 386; defects in staff work and communications, 150-1; response to "psychological warfare", 181-3; relations with native peoples, 227-9, 262, 306, 454, 493; at Balikpapan, 389, 502-3, 530, 545; at Tarakan, 408, 427, 436, 443, 445-7, 449, 451; in Borneo, 456, 470-1, 475, 485, 488, 492, 494-5, 501; achievements, 547; surrender of, 553-4, 556-65, 567-9; strength in Australian area of responsibility, 555; and Indonesian nationalist movement, 572-4; repatriation of, 583; strategy and tactics in Pacific theatre, 584-5; prison break at Cowra, 623-4
—AREA ARMIES: Second, 90, 553. Eighth, at Rabaul, 90, 241, 266-70. Fourteenth, in Philippines, 2. Kwantung, 552. Southern, 2, 90, 384-5
—ARMIES: II, 553-4, 569-70; in Celebes, 573-4, 577. XVII, in Bougainville, 72, 90, 101, 156, 217n, 269; lacks Intelligence of Aust Army, 114-15; changes in command, 150; casualties, 237n. XVIII, 90; in Wewak campaign, 72, 269, 311, 319, 327, 354, 369, 384-5, 387; strength and dispositions, 272, 291-3, 384; casualties, 386; surrenders, 559; repatriated, 583. XXXV, in the Philippines, 2. XXXVII, in Borneo, 453, 456, 470, 553, 565, 570
—DIVISIONS: 1st, 4. 5th, 570-1. 6th, 241; in Bougainville, 90, 101, 103, 111, 113-14, 158, 164-5, 185, 200; changes in command, 150. 8th, 4. 16th, 2. 17th, on New Britain, 90, 241-2, 266; strength, 268. 20th, strength and dispositions, 272, 278, 319, 366, 385; in Wewak campaign, 291, 302, 311, 325-7, 338, 384; state of, 307; casualties, 386; surrenders, 559. 26th, 4. 30th, 2, 4. 32nd, 570. 35th, 570. 36th, 570. 38th, 90; on New Britain, 241-2, 267-8. 41st, strength and dispositions, 272, 289, 291, 293, 366, 385; in Wewak campaign, 278, 310-11, 327, 338, 362, 369, 384; casualties, 386; surrenders, 559. 48th, 570-1. 51st, 241;

JAPANESE ARMY—continued
strength and dispositions, 272, 278, 293, 385; in Wewak campaign, 291, 311, 343, 375, 381, 384; casualties, 386; surrenders, 559. 100th, 2. 102nd, 2, 4.
—FORCES: Aoyama, in attack on Wewak, 352. Jinka, strength and dispositions, 352. Kato, strength and dispositions, 352. Miyake, in Wewak campaign, 327; strength of, 338. Ozihara, strength and dispositions, 293. Tokoi, at Tarakan, 436, 439
—BRIGADES AND REGIMENTS: 4th Indep Mixed Regt, 470. 13th Regt, in Bougainville, 103, 112, 114, 147n, 150, 153, 159, 164, 198, 229, 237-8. 14th Regt, in New Britain, 242n, 269. 20th Regt, 293. 23rd Regt, in Bougainville, 103, 158, 162-4, 188, 199, 229, 238. 25th Indep Mixed Regt, in Borneo, 456, 470, 562. 34th Regt, in New Britain, 242n, 269. 35th Regt, in New Britain, 242n, 269. 38th Indep Mixed Bde, 101; in Bougainville, 103, 114, 117, 121, 234. 39th Bde, in New Britain, 242, 268-9. 40th Indep Bde, in New Ireland, 242n. 45th Regt, in Bougainville, 103, 156, 229, 238. 54th Regt, in New Britain, 266. 56th Indep Mixed Bde, in Borneo, 456, 470, 495. 57th Indep Mixed Bde, 570, 572. 65th Bde, in New Britain, 241, 242n, 269. 66th Regt, in Wewak campaign, 291, 293, 339, 343, 370, 381. 71st Indep Mixed Bde, in Borneo, 456, 470. 78th Regt, in Wewak campaign, 293, 311, 381. 79th Regt, in Wewak campaign, 293, 319, 327. 80th Regt, in Wewak campaign, 293, 318-19. 81st Regt, in Bougainville, 103, 114, 117, 123, 175, 238. 102nd Regt, in Wewak campaign, 293, 343. 115th Regt, in Wewak campaign, 293, 303, 319, 381. 237th Regt, in Wewak campaign, 278, 284, 289, 291, 293, 296, 319. 238th Regt, in Wewak campaign, 278, 284, 289, 291, 293. 239th Regt, in Wewak campaign, 278, 284, 289, 291, 293, 312
—ARTILLERY, 192, 408, 409n. 4th Medium Regt, 186. 6th Field, 147n, 238. 26th Field, 327
—CAVALRY: 6th Regt, 229
—ENGINEERS, 495. 19th Regt, 229, 237-8
—GARRISON UNITS: 4th South Seas, 229. 54th, 293
—INFANTRY BATTALIONS: 366th, in Borneo, 456, 465, 470-1, 494-5. 367th, in Borneo, 456, 470-1, 495. 368th, in Borneo, 456, 470, 495. 369th, in Borneo, 456, 470, 495. 370th, in Borneo, 456, 470, 495. 371st, in Borneo, 456, 470-1, 495. 454th, 526. 455th, 408. 553rd, 471, 495
JAPANESE NAVY, 10, 37, 92, 311, 386n, 456, 566, 574, 585; in Philippines, 2, 4; in Bougainville, 90, 113, 199, 209, 215-17, 229, 234; strength, 237-8; strength in New Britain, 241-2, 268-9; at Tarakan, 427, 436-7; at Balikpapan, 526, 527n; surrender of, 555-8
—EIGHTH FLEET, 229
—ENGINEER REGIMENT: 5th Shipping, 310
—GARRISON FORCES: 2nd, 408, 436, 439. 8th, 572. 82nd, 238. 87th, 113, 215-16, 238. 88th, 238
—NAVAL BASE FORCES: 22nd, 526. 27th, 293
—SPECIAL NAVAL LANDING FORCES, 408. 6th Saseho, 113, 238. 7th Kure, 113, 238
JARVIE, Lt J., 317
JAVA (Map p. 3; Sketch p. 16), 71, 342, 394, 502, 551, 566-7, 573, 576, 591, 596; plans for capture, 41, 46-50, 72; AIB landings in, 618
JAVANESE, 496, 499
JAVA SEA, 520
JEANES, Lt-Col M. R. (Plate p. 476), 477-8, 480-1, 500; commands 2/43 Bn, 469
JEFFERIES, Capt R. D. K., 154-5
JENKINS, Cpl L. J., 335-6
JESSELTON (Map p. 28; Sketches pp. 453, 455), 30, 453-6, 458, 470, 482, 494, 562, 564-5
JESSER, Maj H. J., 236
JILLETT, Brig C. A., 89n
JINKINS, Maj W. T., 454, 621
JOB (Sketch p. 533), 534
JOHNS, Lt D. H., 300
JOHNSON, Capt C. K., 244-5
JOHNSON, Maj C. M., 337-8, 362, 366
JOHNSON, Pte C. R., 378
JOHNSON, Lt F. G., 366
JOHNSON, Capt G. E., 416, 425, 439, 446
JOHNSON, Capt L. R. P., 112, 128
JOHNSON, L-Cpl N., 333

JOHNSTON, Col S., 97n
JOHNSTONE, Lt M., 445
JOHNSTONE, Lt W. P., 472
JOHN'S TRACK (Sketch p. 431), 427, 430, 433-4, 448
JOINT (Sketch p. 533), 532, 534
JOLO ISLAND (Map p. 28), 28, 452
JONES, Air Marshal Sir George, 549
JONES, Lt-Col J. S., 83
JONES, Pte R., 624
JONES, WO2 S. W., 432
JORGENSEN, L-Cpl C. C., 124
JORGENSEN, Sgt E. N., 160
JOSEP, Sergeant-Major, 246
JOYCE (Sketch p. 429), 439, 444-5
JUATA (Sketch p. 408), 411
JUATA, CAPE (Sketch p. 441), 427, 439, 447-8
JUATA OILFIELD (Sketches pp. 408, 441), 408, 427, 429, 439-40, 442
JUDGE (Sketch p. 533), 533-4
JUNIOR (Sketch p. 533), 535
JUNKERS, Rev Father, 171
JURD, Pte K. T. J., 324
JUST, Col M. E., 116-17, 149-50, 154-5, 160-3
JUSTICE (Sketch p. 533), 534

KAAD, Lt F. P. C., 368
KABOIBUS (Map p. 273; Sketch p. 361), 336, 364-6
KAHILI (Map p. 91), 558
KAHIN, G. McT., 566n
KAHURU, Commander, 443
KAIAPIT (Map p. 60), 327
KAIDA, Colonel, 571
KAI ISLANDS (Sketch p. 560), 555, 570
KAINO (Sketch p. 136), 138, 170
KAIRIRU ISLAND (Map p. 273; Sketches pp. 271, 355), 272, 293, 301, 349, 559
KALABU (Sketch p. 331), 335-6, 338, 360
KALAI (Sketch p. 245), 255-6, 266
KALEWA, 15
KALIMBOA (Sketch p. 339), 340
KAMADA, Vice-Adm Michiaki, 532, 566; commands *22 Naval Base Force*, 526
KAMANDRAN (Map p. 243; Sketch p. 245), 246-7, 255-6
KAMTI (Sketch p. 276), 276, 278
KANAURA (Sketch p. 180), 227, 229
KANDA, Lt-Gen Masatane (Plate p. 236), 164, 229-30, 234, 558; commands *6 Div*, 114; commands *XVII Army*, and estimate of, 150
KANDU (Sketch p. 476), 478-9
KANEKO, Colonel Atsushi, 114
KANGANAMAN (Sketch p. 271), 384
Kanimbla, Australian ship, 458, 462-3, 511
KAPANA (Sketch p. 190), 152, 186, 194, 196-7
KAPIKAVI NATIVES, 136, 139, 169
Kapunda, Australian ship, 563
KARA (Sketch p. 171), 229
KARAPIA (Sketch p. 361), 364, 367
KARAWOP (Map p. 273; Sketch p. 339), 272, 324, 339-40, 381
KARIN, 492
KARUKAN (Sketch p. 476), 475, 478
Kashima, Japanese cruiser, 583
KATEKAR, Maj H. J., 450
KATH, Capt N. S., 258
KATH'S HILL (Sketch p. 257), 258-60
KATO, Captain, 215-16
KATOMA (Sketch p. 331), 333
Katoomba, Australian ship, 557
Katsuragi, Japanese aircraft carrier, 583
KATSUWA (Sketch p. 180), 197, 229
KAUK (Sketches pp. 313, 315), 301, 316
KAUKAUAI (Map p. 91), 114
KAUMALA (Sketch p. 305), 305
KAUREMERAK HILL (Sketch p. 318), 323
KAVIENG (Map p. 60), 556-7
KAVRATA (Map p. 91), 113
KAWAKAMI, Captain, 175
KAWAKUBO, MOUNT (Sketch p. 371), 373
KAWANO, Lt-Col Takatsugu, 163-4
KAYROOZ, Lt L. S., 120
KEED, Cpl B. K., 132
KEENAN'S RIDGE (Sketch p. 107), 118, 120
KEFT, Capt J. H., 357
KEIGHTLEY, General Sir Charles, 549
KEKEMONA (Map p. 91), 169

KEKERE (Map p. 91), 200
KELLY, Lt A. C., 536
KELLY, Pte I. W., 481
KELLY, Lt-Col J. L. A., 74, 98, 122, 561; commands *31/51 Bn*, 120
KEMP, Tpr G. R., 185-6
KEMSLEY, Col A. N., 395, 586
KENDALL, Capt C. McI., 298
KENDALL, Capt R., 618
KENDARI (Sketch p. 560), 574
KENNA, Pte E., VC, 351-2
KENNEDY, Lt A., 480
KENNEDY, Lt R. E., 463
KENNEDY, Capt R. R., 501
KENSINA (Map p. 243), 244
KENT, Lt L. A., 515, 520
KENTWELL, Sgt A. S., 325
KEOPILI, 232
KERAM RIVER (Sketch p. 355), 358
KERAVAT RIVER (Map p. 243), 242, 267-8
KERO CREEK (Sketches pp. 163, 179), 160-2
KERR, C., 637
KERR, Col J. R., 399
KERRIDGE, Capt J. C., 147n
KERUPANG RIVER (Sketch p. 466), 466
KET, Capt S. A., 420
KEYHOLE (Sketch p. 344), 377-8
KEYS, Capt A. G. W., 431
Kiama, Australian corvette, 204n, 245, 556
KIARIVU (Map p. 273; Sketch p. 361), 363-4, 367, 386, 559
KIEP (Map p. 243; Sketch p. 245), 253
KIETA (Map p. 91; Sketch p. 136), 92, 100, 103-4, 114, 135, 137, 140, 156, 169-70, 200-1, 217, 229, 558
KIJIMA, Maj-Gen Kesao, 215, 234; commands *38 Indep Mixed Bde*, 117
KIKIMOGO (Sketch p. 171), 228
KILIPAIJINO (Sketch p. 171), 227
KILLEN, Lt B. G. L., 167, 199
KILLEN'S TRACK (Sketch p. 219), 219
KILPATRICK, Capt W. J., 333
KIMANIS (Sketch p. 455), 455
KING, Lt B. W., 154-5
KING, Fleet Admiral Ernest J., 18, 27-8, 590
KING, Cpl H. G., 421
KING, Gnr J. T., 362
KING, Maj-Gen R., 296, 300-1, 311, 315, 317-19, 326, 338-9, 382, 554; commands *16 Bde*, 274; commands *6 Div*, 384
KINGORI (Sketches pp. 180, 190), 186, 194-8, 228
KING'S TRACK (Sketch p. 431), 434
KINKAID, Vice-Adm Thomas C., 2
KITCHING, Capt G. S., 542
KITCHING, Gnr H. S., 338
KLANDASAN (Map p. 512; Sketch p. 503), 502-6, 510, 514, 519, 526
KLANDASAN BESAR RIVER (Map p. 512; Sketch p. 503), 504, 513-14
KLEIN, Brig B. E., 97n
KLEWALIN (Sketch p. 346), 353
KLIAS PENINSULA (Sketch p. 460), 477-8
KLIAS RIVER (Sketches pp. 460, 476), 453, 477-9
KNIGHT, Sgt J. A. C., 190-1
KNIGHT, Lt J. D., 260
KNIGHT, Lt R. K., 525
KNOTT, Maj C. C., 431, 433
KNOX, D. W., 40n
KOANUMBO (Sketch p. 339), 340
KOAS, CAPE (Map p. 243), 248, 251
KOBORI, Major-General, 571
KOCH, Capt A. M., 153
KOEPANG (Sketch p. 560), 571
KOFI (Sketches pp. 318, 320), 324, 339
KOGIMARA, Sergeant, 248n
KOIGIN (Sketches pp. 346, 371), 352, 369-70, 373-4, 379
KOKOPA (Sketch p. 180), 227
KOMBICHAGI (Sketch p. 331), 332
KOMBIO (Sketch p. 276), 277
KONGAMBE (Sketch p. 361), 364
KOOPANI RIVER (Sketch p. 219), 219-20
KOREA (Sketch p. 16), 35, 552, 577n, 581n
KOROKO RIVER (Sketch p. 180), 197
KOROMIRA (Map p. 91), 169
KOTA KLIAS (Sketch p. 476), 475, 477-8

INDEX

KOVIDAU (Sketch p. 136), 138, 168
KREER (Sketch p. 344), 352
KRUEGER, Pte B. W., 380
KRUEGER, General Walter, 27, 594, 599n; commands Sixth Army, 19
KUALA BELAIT (Map p. 464), 453, 484, 488-9, 497, 500
KUALA PENYU (Sketch p. 476), 477-8
KUALIGEM (Sketch p. 302), 304
KUBALAK (Sketch p. 361), 366
KUBRIWAT (Sketch p. 276), 334
KUCHING (Map p. 28; Sketch p. 560), 30, 456, 470, 562, 565; Japanese surrender at, 563-4
KUDAT (Map p. 28; Sketch p. 455), 28, 470
KUKUGAI (Sketch p. 171), 227
KULAURU MISSION (Sketch p. 360), 359, 363
KULKUIL (Sketch p. 331), 330, 332
KUMBUN (Sketch p. 276), 280
KUMBUNGUA (Sketches pp. 331, 361), 335, 338
KUMILIOGU (Sketch p. 171), 171
KUMINIBUS (Sketch p. 305), 307
KUNAI SPUR (Sketch p. 360), 361, 363
KUNAMATORO (Sketches pp. 123, 127), 122, 125-6
KUNJINGE (Sketch p. 361), 362, 364
KUPON (Sketches pp. 131, 144), 112, 132, 135, 142, 144-5
KUPON ROAD, 128
KURAIO (Map p. 91; Sketch p. 123), 104, 106, 122
KURE (Sketch p. 578), 578
KURILE ISLANDS (Sketch p. 16), 18
KUSAKA, Vice-Admiral, 556
KWANDANING (Sketch p. 361), 364
KWIMBU (Sketch p. 361), 362, 365
KYUSHU ISLAND (Sketches pp. 16, 578), 28, 405, 552

LABI (Map p. 464), 493
LABUAN (Sketches pp. 460, 466), 453, 459, 465, 474
LABUAN ISLAND (Map p. 28; Sketches pp. 460, 466), 49, 404, 462, 483, 495, 499, 554n, 561-6; plans for attack on, 28, 458-60, 465-6; described, 453; strength of Japanese forces at, 456, 471; capture of, 467-75; rehabilitation and restoration work in, 496-7
LABUK BAY (Sketch p. 455), 454
Lachlan, Australian frigate, 458, 475
LADY SCHOFIELD (Sketch p. 524), 520, 522
LAE (Map p. 60), 9n, 23, 36, 46, 58n, 64-5, 92, 96, 105, 166n, 250n, 264, 268, 272, 291, 342, 411, 438, 556, 606; First Army HQ at, 25, 89-90
LAE, Sergeant, 175
LAGOONS (Sketch p. 219), 223
LAGUAI (Sketch p. 171), 171
LAHINGA (Sketch p. 302), 303, 309-10
LAIDLAW, Maj G. G., 248n
LAITARO (Sketch p. 171), 229
LAKIRI (Map p. 243), 242, 244, 246
LALUM (Sketches pp. 123, 173), 122, 172
LAMARIEN (Sketch p. 245), 261
LAMARU (Sketch p. 544), 543
LAMBERT, WO2 C. H., 166
LAMBERT, CAPE (Map p. 243), 266
LAMBOM, 248n
LAMBUAIN (Sketch p. 276), 282
LAMPARAN (Sketch p. 136), 135
LAMSHED, Lt S. M., 260
LANCEY, Pte R., 198
LANDING CRAFT, in Bougainville campaign, 104-6, 142, 210-15; in New Britain, 250; in Wewak campaign, 281, 328-9, 344, 350; at Tarakan, 410, 413-14, 417-18, 448-9; in Borneo, 457-8, 461, 463, 466, 475, 477, 486-7; at Balikpapan, 511, 521, 540
LANG, Lt-Col J. T., 272
LANGEIA (Map p. 243), 248
LANGIE, Dr Ratu, 574-6
LANGTRY, Maj J. O., 187, 198
LANKY (Sketch p. 441), 446
LARUMA RIVER (Map p. 91; Sketches pp. 95, 111), 104, 106-7, 118, 139n
LARUMA RIVER VALLEY (Sketch p. 111), 109, 113
LASHIO, 15
LAU (Map p. 243), 244
LAULI (Sketch p. 254), 254, 256
LAURA (Sketch p. 431), 437
LAVAN, Lt-Col J. F., 415, 429, 437, 442
LAVARACK, Lt-Gen Sir John, 57, 64, 70-1, 579, 601n, 602n

LAVERTON (Sketch p. 533), 532
LAWAS (Map p. 464), 490
LAWLEY, MOUNT (Sketch p. 479), 480
LAWN, Lt B. E., 181
LAWSON-DOOK, Lt R., 157, 227
LAYFIELD, Lt C. R., 331
LAZY CREEK (Sketch p. 285), 284-6
LEAFLETS, 233, 237, 562, 565
LEAHY, Fleet Admiral William D., 18, 27n
LEARY, Vice-Admiral Herbert F., 590-1
LE BRETON, Rev Father, 171
LE BRUN, Tpr N. S., 278
LEDO (Sketch p. 453), 565
LEDONG POINT (Sketch p. 462), 462
LEE, Lt-Col A. J., 541
LEE, Lt H., 206
LEE, Lt L., 322-3
LEESON, Pte A. L. C., 528
LEGA, Lt T. W. J., 356
LEGAMUNGA (Sketch p. 344), 348
LEGGE, Lt-Gen J. G., 604n
LEITCH, Sgt H. J., 347
LEMAIRE, Sgt C. E., 493
LEMBEH ISLAND, 572
LEMINGI (Map p. 243), 245, 247, 268
LEND-LEASE, 12, 62, 395-6
LESLIE, Capt A. S., 212
LESSER SUNDA ISLANDS (Sketch p. 560), 555, 566n, 570, 572-3
LETHBRIDGE MISSION, 9
LETTER (Sketch p. 533), 532
LEWIN, Capt R. W., 415-16
LEWINGTON, Capt. A. J. M., 535, 539
LEWIS (Sketch p. 533), 532
LEWIS, Maj R. A., 535
LEYTE (Maps pp. 3, 28), 1-2, 4, 19, 27, 29, 37, 41, 45, 53n, 55, 58n, 94, 281, 597; casualties in, 56
LIDDELL HART, B. H., 588n
LIGHT, Lt M. E., 132
LILES, Lt N. J., 305
LIMBANG (Map p. 464; Sketch p. 460), 465, 484, 486, 489, 493-5, 500
LIMBANG RIVER (Map p. 464; Sketch p. 455), 453, 456, 489, 494-5, 565
LIMBANG ROAD, 465
LINDA (Sketches pp. 429, 431), 436, 443-5
LINDSAY, Lt D. C., 133
LINEHAN, Lt D. W., 180
LINGAYEN (Map p. 28), 28, 45
LINGAYEN GULF (Map p. 28), 28-9, 45, 94n
LINGKAS (Sketches pp. 408, 416), 407-9, 411n, 415
LINGKAS HILL (Sketch p. 416), 414
LINGKAS TRACK, 418
LINGKUNGAN (Sketch p. 476), 475-6
LINKLATER, Lt A. F., 538
Lismore, Australian corvette, 573
Lithgow, Australian corvette, 204n, 556, 558
LITTLE GEORGE (Sketches pp. 107, 108), 106-10, 114
LITTLE HUNT'S HILL (Sketch p. 203), 202
LITTLE SIWI RIVER (Sketch p. 171), 229
LIVERPOOL (Sketch p. 533), 533-4
LLOYD, Maj-Gen C. E. M., 24n, 549
LLOYD, Maj-Gen H. W., 606
LOANIM (Sketch p. 331), 316n, 337-8
LOCHHEAD, Lt-Col A. J., 383
LODGE (Sketch p. 533), 524, 532
LOGAN, Brig E., 274n
LOH, W. G., 637
LOHAN, Lt-Col L. G., 403
LOLOBAU ISLAND (Map p. 243), 252
LOMAS, Maj F. J., 305, 347
LOMBOK (Map p. 3; Sketch p. 560), 553
LOMBOK STRAIT, 49
LONDON, 5, 9-10, 13-14, 21, 58n, 102, 393-4, 396, 399, 549; Prime Ministers' Conference in, 11, 399
LONE TREE HILL (Sketch p. 257), 257
LONGMORE, Lt F. R., 231
LONG RIDGE (Sketch p. 297), 287, 298
LONGWORTH, Lt S. P., 259
LONNIE, Lt-Col W. S., 480-1, 500
LOUGHRAN, Col L. J., 234n
LOVEGROVE, Capt H. A., 286
LOVELL, Lt-Col D. J. H., 98
LOVETT, Capt K. H., 320-4, 340
LOVETT-CAMERON, Lt H. E., 200
Low, David, 86

INDEX

Low, Lt J. R., 518
LST-637, 461
LUAGOA (Sketch p. 171), 229
LUAIN (Sketches pp. 276, 285), 278, 287, 289
LUDBROOK, Lt G. C., 440
LUDWIG, Sister, 171
LUDWINA, Sister, 171
LUKYN, Maj A. F. P., 202
LULUAI RIVER (Map p. 91; Sketch p. 136), 138
LULUAI VALLEY (Map p. 91), 200
LUMADAN (Sketch p. 476), 482
LUMSDEN, Lt-Gen H., 8, 29
LUMSIS (Sketch p. 127), 205
LUSHINGTON, Capt A. H. G., 467, 470, 474
LUSHINGTON RIDGE (Sketch p. 472), 473-4
LUTONG (Map p. 464; Sketch p. 453), 459, 484, 486-7, 490
LUWAITE (Sketch p. 282), 290, 310
LUZON (Maps pp. 3, 28), 2, 10, 27-9, 40, 45, 48, 77, 94n, 502; operations in, 55-6, casualties, 405
LYNCH, Cpl H. J., 528
LYON, Maj G. E., 533
LYON, Capt H. McM., 248n, 252, 255
LYON, Lt-Col I., 619
LYON, Maj L. H., 468, 473-4
LYON RIDGE (Sketch p. 472), 473
LYONS (Sketch p. 416), 416-18, 427

MABAM RIVER (Sketch p. 320), 319, 338-9
MABAM VALLEY (Sketch p. 320), 325
MACADIE, Brig T. F. B., 83
MACARTHUR, General of the Army Douglas (Plates pp. 476, 556), 1, 4, 8-9, 12-13, 15, 17-18, 27, 55-6, 59-60, 65, 66n, 67, 69-72, 94, 114, 201, 269, 395, 403, 405-6, 457, 467, 496, 502, 520, 549-51, 567, 577, 584, 601, 617, 619; his communiqués, 2n, 37-8, 40; and command problems, 14, 43-9, 51, 54, 590-9; strength and disposition of forces, 19; relations with Australian Government, 20, 585; employment of Australian forces, 21-3, 28-30, 33-4, 41-2, 52-3, 388-9, 393; establishes advanced HQ at Hollandia, 24; and Japanese surrender arrangements, 552-3
MACARTHUR ROAD (Sketch p. 466), 466-70
MACASKIE, Brig C. F. C., 400-1, 403-5, 497-8
MACASSAR (Map p. 28; Sketch p. 560), 569, 573, 577; Indonesian nationalist movement at, 574-6
MACASSAR, STRAIT OF (Map p. 28), 511, 520
MCBRIDE, Maj I. H., 282, 290, 303
MCCABE, Sgt F. J., 313
MCCAFFREY, Maj R. K., 97n
MACCALLUM, Maj M. B., 85-6
MCCAMMON, Lt-Col H. G., 383
MCCARTHY, Lt L. D., VC, 190n
MCCARTHY, Sgt L. N., 190n
M'CAY, Lt-Gen Hon Sir James, 604n
MCCLELLAND, Pte K. F., 322
MCCOLL, Lt K. H., 311
MCCOSKER, Lt H. F., 539
MCCRACKAN, Capt J. A., 370
MCDONALD, Lt-Col B. A., 363
MCDONALD, Col H. H., 98
MACDONALD, Capt J. E., 325
MACDONALD, Lt J. H., 443, 445
MCDONALD, Brig S. M., 129, 221
MCDONALD, Brig W. D., 225
MACDOUGAL, Lt B. H., 302
MCDOUGALL, Lt-Col A. F., 516-17
MCDOWALL, Capt A. K., 357, 364
MCEVOY, Sgt D. G., 100, 127
MACFARLAN, G., 638
MACFARLANE, Maj A., 420-1
MACFARLANE, Maj C. W., 83
MCFARLANE, L-Cpl J. L. S., 341
MACFIE, Lt H. H., 312
MCGEE, Capt T. W., 202
MCGOVERN, Constable A. P., 624
MCGRATH, Brig P. S., 89n
MCGRATH, Pte S. W., 162
MCGREEVY, Sgt F. B., 290
MCGRUER, Cpl J., 200
MCINNES, Maj R. D., 154-5, 159-63
MCINNES, Capt W. O., 232
MCINNES HILL (Sketch p. 203), 233
MCINTYRE, F-Lt J. W. O. S., 420
MACKAY (Sketch p. 533), 532

MACKAY, Lt-Gen Sir Iven, 9, 57n, 594-5, 600, 601n
MCKENNA, Maj J. I., 165n
MCKENZIE, Brig E. G. H., 248n, 261; commands 13 Bde, 260
MACKENZIE, Lt-Col K. M., 324, 339
MACKEY, Cpl J. B., VC, 432
MACKIE, Maj J. H., 205, 217
MCKINLAY, Cpl C. G., 541
MCKINNA, Brig J. G., 117, 150, 154-5, 158, 160-3; commands 25 Bn, 98
MCKINNA BRIDGE, 162
MACKINNON, Capt A. G., 278
MCKINNON, Sgt C. D., 207
MCKINNON'S RIDGE (Sketch p. 207), 206-7
MCKITTRICK, Lt F. W., 424
MCLAREN, Lt K. B., 528
MCLAREN, Capt R. K., 509
MCLEAN, Lt K. C., 448
MCLEAY, Hon G., 57
MCLELLAN, Lt C. J., 224
MCLELLAN, Capt N., 439
MCLENNAN, Cpl C. E., 354
MCLENNAN, Pte F. D., 185
MCLENNAN, Maj H. H., 322
MCLEOD, D., 59
MCMULLEN, Col K. C., 401-4
MCNAIR, Capt S. H. H., 172-4, 209
MCNAMARA, Col E. G., 97n
MCNEIL, Lt L., 298
MCNEIL'S CREEK (Sketch p. 297), 298, 300
MCNICOLL, Capt D. R., 87
MCNICOLL, Maj-Gen R. R., 74n
MCPHEE, Lt G. J., 100, 127
MCPHEE, Lt N. H., 233
MADANG (Map p. 60; Sketch p. 355), 24-5, 36n, 89, 130n, 161n, 183, 250n, 262-3, 342, 354-7, 370
MADGWICK, Col R. B., 84-5
MADIGAN, Capt E. B., 514
MAGAHEN (Sketch p. 320), 320, 326
MAHARINGI (Sketch p. 282), 289
MAIA RIVER (Sketch p. 441), 448
MAIDEN, Capt M. J., 637
MAI MAI (Map p. 273), 276
MAIROKA (Sketch p. 331), 331
MAITLAND, Brig G. B. G., 97n
MAITLAND, Lt-Col J. A., 256
MAKAKU (Sketch p. 144), 150
MAKAPEKA (Sketch p. 144), 148, 151
MAKAPEKA RIVER (Sketch p. 144), 146, 151-2
MAKOTOWA (Sketches pp. 131, 144), 128, 133, 147-8
MAKRU (Map p. 273), 276
MAKUIR (Sketch p. 276), 280
MALABANG (Map p. 28), 55n
MALABASAKUM (Sketch p. 360), 359-60
MALABEIM (Sketch p. 361), 366
MALACCA, STRAIT OF (Map p. 3), 12
MALAHUN (Sketch p. 302), 303-5, 309
MALANG, MOUNT (Map p. 512), 513-14
MALARIA, in Bougainville, 237n; in New Britain, 260; in Wewak campaign, 327-8, 341, 385; in Borneo, 562
MALAYA (Map p. 3; Sketch p. 16), 5-7, 10, 18, 30, 34, 48-9, 52, 56-7, 60, 79n, 394, 400, 457, 554, 590; Allied plans for recovery, 11
MALAYANS, 454, 485, 499-500, 557
MALBA (Sketch p. 331), 336
MALBUAIN (Sketch p. 282), 283, 291
MALIKAI (Sketch p. 476), 478
MALIMPUNG (Sketch p. 560), 574, 577
MALIN (Map p. 273; Sketches pp. 276, 284), 277, 279, 283-4, 287, 289, 294, 296, 311
MALONEY, Lt V. N., 332n
MAMAGOTA (Sketch p. 180), 186, 188
MAMAMARINO (Sketch p. 171), 228
MAMIE (Sketch p. 429), 437
MANANINGI (Sketch p. 361), 368
MANCHURIA (Sketch p. 16), 18, 19, 226, 552
MAN CREEK (Sketch p. 318), 319
MANDI (Sketch p. 344), 351, 370, 372, 377, 379
MANGGAR (Sketches pp. 503, 524), 502-3, 505-6, 510-11, 521, 525-6, 530, 543-4, 566, 568-9
MANGGAR KECHIL RIVER (Sketch p. 503), 510
MANGUMBU (Sketch p. 305), 334, 336
MANIB CREEK (Sketch p. 315), 316, 318
MANILA (Maps pp. 3, 28), 2, 4, 28-9, 45, 47-8, 403, 457-8, 502, 549, 552, 595

MANILA BAY (Map p. 28), 56, 590
MANN, Brig J., 97n, 225
MANO, Lt-Gen Goro, 291n, 293, 310, 338, 369; commands *41 Div*, 272
MANOKWARI (Map p. 28), 620
Manoora, Australian ship, 410n, 414, 458, 511, 557
MANPOWER, in Australia, 12, 31-3, 35, 42, 45, 388, 391, 394-5, 600, 607
MANSFIELD, A., 637
MANUS ISLAND (Map p. 60), 92, 130n
MAPIA (Sketch p. 203), 204
MAPRIK (Maps pp. 60, 273; Sketches pp. 302, 331), 271-2, 279, 284, 293-4, 300, 303, 306-7, 311, 327, 335-6, 338n, 342, 354, 362, 364, 381; capture of 330, 332-4
MAPS, in Bougainville operations, 106, 147-8, 173; in Tarakan operations, 425, 436
MARABA (Sketch p. 476), 475
MARABUS (Sketch p. 315), 327, 342
MARANGIS (Sketch p. 356), 357-8
MARAVERA, Corporal, 236
MARCH, Lt C. V., 301
MARCHANT, Capt J. L., 206
MARGIN (Sketch p. 533), 532
MARGY (Sketch p. 429), 408, 436, 439-43
MARIANAS (Map p. 3), 1, 4
MARIENBERG (Sketch p. 355), 384
MARIN (Sketch p. 371), 379
MARIROPA RIVER (Map p. 91; Sketch p. 131), 112
MARSHALL (Sketch p. 533), 532-3
MARSHALL, Capt A. J., 290, 637
MARSHALL, General of the Army George C., 29, 41, 50, 388; and command problems, 590-3, 598
MARSHALL ISLANDS (Map p. 3), 101
MARSON, Col R. H., 533, 538, 539n; commands 2/25 Bn, 532
MARSTON, Lt-Col R. R., 99
MARTIN, Lt G. A., 325
MARTIN, Lt G. J., 381
MARTIN, Lt J. A. A., 121
MARTIN, Brig J. E. G., 284, 291n, 343, 346, 351-3, 381; commands 19 Bde, 274
MARTIN, Pte K., 108n
MARTIN, Capt R. D., 227
MARTIN, Capt R. M., 196
MARTIN, Cpl W. C., 259-60
MARUDI (Map p. 464), 492-3
MARUI (Sketch p. 271), 272, 310, 330
MASALANGA (Map p. 273), 290
MASEL, Brig P., 638
MASON, Cpl K. R., 481
MASON, Lt P. E., 100, 135-40, 168-70, 186, 200-1
MASSAU (Map p. 243), 244
MASSAVA BAY (Map p. 243), 266
MATALAILI RIVER (Sketch p. 253), 254, 268
MATAPAU (Sketch p. 285), 285-6
MATATOGA (Sketch p. 254), 252
MATHESON, Cpl A. L., 196
MATHEWS, Capt R. L., 191n, 192, 197n, 638
MATSUNAMI, Captain, 175
MATSUNKEI (Sketch p. 144), 149
MATTHEW, Maj W. D., 209n
MATTHEWS, Lt-Col G. R., 108-9, 139n, 147, 167; commands 9 Bn, 97
MATTHEWS, Cpl J., 139
MATTHEWS' JUNCTION (Sketch p. 131), 149
MATTINGLEY, Pte L. F., 224
MATTNER, Senator E. W., 57-8
MAU (Sketch p. 136), 138, 168
MAURAK (Sketch p. 305), 307-8
MAVAY, Lt H. B., 326-7, 380
MAVELO (Map p. 243; Sketch p. 253), 253, 267
MAVELO RIVER (Sketch p. 253), 251, 253-4
MAWARAKA (Map p. 91; Sketches pp. 131, 144), 104, 111, 130, 132-4, 141-2, 147, 152
MAXWELL, Maj K. J., 151-2
MAXWELL'S CROSSING, 152
MAYBERRY, Lt-Col W. M., 178, 194; commands 58/59 Bn, 141
MAYBERRY'S CROSSING (Sketch p. 190), 191
M'BRAS (Sketch p. 302), 303, 306, 334
MEDITERRANEAN SEA, 13
MEIVO TRACK (Sketch p. 144), 149
MELBOURNE, 24, 58n, 61, 63, 69, 99, 394, 593, 595, 604
MELON (Sketch p. 429), 443, **445**
MELVILLE, Lt J. R. W., 534

MELVILLE, Lt-Col W. S., 260
MEMBAKUT (Sketch p. 476), 483
MEMBAKUT RIVER (Sketch p. 476), 483
MEMPAKUL (Sketches pp. 460, 476), 459, 475, 477-8
MENADO (Map p. 28; Sketch p. 560), 11, 569, 572-3, 620
MENCE, Lt-Col W. H., 274n
MENDAI (Sketches pp. 131, 144), 132, 135, 142, 145-6
MENDAI TRACK (Sketch p. 131), 129, 131
MENDAMEN (Sketch p. 331), 336
MENDERAM RIVER (Map p. 464), 491-2
MENGALONG RIVER (Map p. 464), 495
MENGATAI (Map p. 464), 489
MENNEM (Sketch p. 356), 358
MENUMBOK (Sketch p. 476), 475
MENZIES, Rt Hon Sir Robert, 56, 58, 60-2
MERAUKE (Maps pp. 3, 60; Sketch p. 560), 24, 58n, 98, 601, 620
MERIDAU (Sketch p. 136), 168
MERRITT, Maj W. G. T., 97n
METAL (Sketch p. 533), 532
METCALF, Capt E. C., 376
MEVELO RIVER (Sketch p. 254), 256-7
MIDDLE EAST, service of Australian brigades in, 80n, of army leaders in, 73-4, 76; Australian Army's contribution to operations in, 589
MIDGLEY, Sgt H. K., 233
MIDPUM CREEK (Sketch p. 331), 334
MIDWAY ISLAND, 88, 584
MIELL, Lt-Col L. D., 249
MIETHKE, Maj G. R., 519
MIKAU (Sketch p. 361), 338, 362
MIKON CREEK (Sketch p. 297), 302
MILAK (Sketch p. 305), 307-8, 311, 331
MILES, Lt C. H., 334
MILES, L-Cpl D. T. G., 124
MILFORD, Maj-Gen E. J. (Plate p. 525), 505-6, 508, 520, 527, 530, 539-40, 542, 554, 566, 576; commands 7 Div, 504; on RAAF in Balikpapan operations, 545-6
MILFORD HIGHWAY (Sketches pp. 503, 533), 502, 510, 522, 526, 532, 535, 543-5
MILIM (Map p. 243; Sketch p. 245), 242, 244-6, 253
MILITARY GOVERNMENT, plans for establishment in British Borneo, 396-405
MILITIA, 76-9; brigades in Bougainville, 97-9; and attitude to AIF, 239
MILKO (Sketch p. 416), 408, 417-18
MILLER, Pte D., 337
MILLER, Cpl G. C., 124
MILLS, Lt L. C., 202
MILLS, Lt-Col T., 183
MILNE BAY (Map p. 60), 89, 97-8, 107, 386, 396n, 584
MILNER, S., 591n
MILTON, Lt E. J., 304
MIMA CREEK (Sketch p. 297), 288, 298-9
MIMBIOK (Sketch p. 276), 280, 282
MINAHASSA, 572
MINANGI (Sketch p. 305), 307
MINCHIN, WO2 R. F., 223
MINDANAO (Maps pp. 3, 28), 1-2, 28-30, 55, 71, 509
MINES, 181, 190-1, 220, 420
MINESWEEPING, 410-11, 462, 509
MINGA (Sketch p. 346), 379
MINGA CREEK (Sketch p. 346), 345-7
MIRI (Map p. 464; Sketch p. 453), 30, 453, 456, 459, 470-2, 484, 487-8, 495, 497, 499-500, 564
MIRI RIVER (Map p. 464), 487
MISIM (Sketch p. 282), 289
MISSIONARIES, 171, 185, 247
MITCHELL, Maj G. D., 344
MIVO RIVER (Map p. 91; Sketches pp. 180, 219), 157, 171, 186, 194, 197-200, 218-30, 557
MIYAKAWA, Lt-Col Kiyoshi, 237n
MIYAKE, Maj-Gen Sadahiko, 291n, 311
MIYAMBOARA (Sketch p. 361), 368
M.L.802, 250
M.L.805, 559
M.L.825, 259n
M.L.827, 250
MOBIAI RIVER (Sketches pp. 180, 219), 185, 196-7, 199-200, 218-20, 226-7, 229
MOEM, CAPE (Sketch p. 344), 342-3, 352, 372
MOILA POINT (Sketch p. 171), 218, 558
MOLE, Lt C., 108
MOLLOY, Brig A. D., 89n

INDEX

MOLONEY, Lt B. W., 337
MOLTKE, CAPE (Map p. 91), 113
MOLUCCAS, 566n, 569, 570
MONAGHAN, Brig R. F., 111-12, 129-33; commands 29 Bde, 98
MONASH, General Sir John, 604n
MONEY, Capt W. A., 251
MONK, Lt F. O., 368
MONO ISLAND (Sketch p. 22), 92-3, 140, 201
MONOITU (Sketches pp. 180, 190), 152, 156, 186, 198
MONOREI (Sketch p. 180), 198
MONTAGU BAY (Map p. 243), 244
MONTENIOR BESAR RIVER (Sketch p. 476), 482-3
MONTY (Sketch p. 429), 445
MOONDEI RIVER (Sketch p. 245), 256, 260
MOORE, Capt E. H., 174
MOORE, Cpl H. S., 469
MOORE, Lt K. W., 130
MOORE, Lt N. A., 534
MOORHOUSE, Cpl C. A. R., 532
MOOSE HILL (Sketch p. 257), 257
MORAHAN, Maj J. O., 542
MORALE, of Australians in Wewak campaign, 341-2, 376
MORAN, Maj M. B., 234
Moresby, Australian sloop, 571
MORETON'S REST (Sketch p. 107), 118
MORGAN, Lt-Col N. H., 563
MORI, Major, 562
MORISH, Capt W. J., 432
MORISON, S. E., 40n
MOROKAIMORO (Sketch p. 180), 199, 228-9
MORONI (Map p. 91), 170
MOROTAI (Maps pp. 3, 28; Sketch p. 560), 1, 19, 30, 41, 43, 49-50, 55, 58n, 67, 93, 402-4, 407, 411-12, 449, 455, 457-8, 461, 504, 506, 508-11, 513, 570, 572, 581, 597; surrender ceremony at, 553-4
MORRIS, Maj-Gen B. M., 594
MORRIS, Pte E. G., 321
MORRIS, Capt F. B., 557
MORROW, Col W. J., 543
MORSHEAD, Lt-Gen Sir Leslie (Plates pp. 412, 476), 21, 41, 45-6, 50, 52, 57n, 73-4, 87, 404, 406, 410, 467, 496, 498, 508, 513-14, 520, 539, 580, 594, 597, 600, 602n, 605; commands I Corps, 19; and planning for Borneo operations, 457-8, 506
MORT, Capt T. L., 375
MORTIMER, Lt R. G., 416
MORTIMER, Lt W. A., 286
MORTON, Capt R. McD., 508
MOSIGETTA (Map p. 91; Sketches pp. 131, 144), 111, 114, 141-3, 146-52, 159, 162
MOSIGETTA ROAD (Sketch p. 144), 133, 147-8
MOSINA (Sketches pp. 131, 144), 112, 132, 135, 141-2, 144-5
MOSS, L-Cpl K. J., 423
MOTEN, Brig M. J., 282, 289-90, 291n, 300, 303, 306-9, 330, 336, 362-4, 382; commands 17 Bde, 274
MOTT, Lt-Col G. E., 617-19
MOTT, Capt M. L., 525-6
MOTUPENA POINT (Map p. 91; Sketches pp. 131, 144), 133, 135, 149, 153
MOULD, L-Cpl E. W., 301
MOUNTBATTEN, Admiral of the Fleet Rt Hon Earl, 6, 10-11, 14-16, 29, 394, 548-9, 551, 553-4, 567; Supreme Allied Cdr SEAC, 4
MOYLE, Sgt E. F., 193
MUARA ISLAND (Sketches pp. 460, 462), 453, 458-9, 462-3
MUDA, Colonel Toyoharu, 164, 229
MUFFLE (Sketch p. 533), 532, 534
MUGULUWELA (Sketch p. 318), 318-19, 327
MUIR, Lt-Col R. A. C., 572
MULCAHY, Capt E. R., 149
MULIKO RIVER (Sketch p. 171), 228-9
MULLALY, Lt A. E. C., 132-3
MULLER, Rev Father, 169
MULLINS, Cpl J., 535
MUNDA (Sketch p. 22), 24, 90, 93, 201
MURCHISON, Brig A. C., 83, 365; commands 2 NGIB, 362
MURDOCH, Maj R. L. A., 260
MURDOCK, Cpl L. J., 537
MU RIVER (Sketch p. 245), 246
MURPHY, Capt J., 233
MURPHY, Capt J. J., 247

MURPHY, Capt P. K., 491
MURPHY, Lt-Col W. C., 274
MURRAY, Capt A. D. B., 298
MURRAY, Col J. K., 397, 399
MUSARAKA (Sketch p. 180), 194, 197, 219
MUSCHU ISLAND (Map p. 273; Sketches pp. 271, 345), 272, 291n, 293, 342-3, 349, 559, 561, 583
MUSCHU STRAIT (Sketch p. 344), 349
MUSENDAI (Sketch p. 276), 291
MUSIMBE (Sketch p. 282), 280, 282-3
MUSINAU (Sketch p. 276), 283, 289
MUSIYAMA, 145
MUSU (Sketch p. 282), 279-80, 282, 289
MUTINY, of native soldiers on New Britain, 262-3
MUTUAL (Sketch p. 533), 532
MYITKYINA, 15

NADZAB (Map p. 60), 275, 350, 359, 394
NAGAM RIVER (Sketch p. 173), 173-5, 206
NAGIPEM (Sketch p. 305), 305
NAHARO (Sketch p. 171), 171
NAIL (Map p. 512), 522, 524-5, 532
NAILA (Sketch p. 361), 364
NAKAI, Lt-Gen Masutaro, 291n, 325, 338; commands 20 Div, 272
NAKAMURA, Lt-Col Shinzo, 126, 175, 215
NAKANO, Lt-Gen Hidemitsu, 291n; commands 51 Div, 272
NAMATANAI (Map p. 60), 561
NAMBUT CREEK (Sketch p. 297), 300-1
NAMBUT HILL (Sketch p. 284), 297-8, 300-2
NAMI MOUNTAIN (Sketch p. 315), 319
NANANG (Sketch p. 540), 541
NANTAMBU; *see* EA EA
NANU RIVER (Map p. 273; Sketch p. 302), 290, 303, 306-7
NARAKAS, Corporal, 169
NASH, S-Sgt B. F., 100, 139
Nashville, American cruiser, 462
NASISIPOK (Sketch p. 203), 233
NATHAN, Lt G. MacF., 380
NATUNA ISLANDS (Sketch p. 560), 470, 561-2
NAURU (Map p. 3,) 394, 553-5, 558-61
NEEDHAM, Lt B., 298
NEEDHAM, Col J. G.,, 181
NEELSSEN, Sgt H. E., 210n
NEGROS (Map p. 28), 29
NELIGUM (Sketch p. 331), 333-4, 338
NELLY (Sketch p. 429), 445
NELSON, Maj G. J. S., 252, 256
NETHERLANDS EAST INDIES (Map p. 3), 5-7, 10-11, 14, 18, 28, 30, 52, 56, 60, 255, 394, 406-7, 457, 504, 520, 550, 570, 573-7, 590, 620; plans for operations in, 46-7, 49, 51; civil administration in, 396, 407, 418, 485, 507, 540, 543, 569, 573-6; surrender arrangements, 553-4; nationalist movement, 566-9; AIB operations, 618-19
—AIR FORCE: No. 18 Sqn, 254-5; No. 120 Sqn, 254-5
—ARMY, 427, 436, 446, 449, 538, 544, 569, 572-3, 575, 1 Bn, 507; NEFIS, 507, 619-21
—NAVY, 520, 619
NEVATO, 236
NEVILLE, Lt-Col C. H., 357, 554
NEVILLE, Lt K. C., 232
NEW BRITAIN (Maps pp. 3, 60, 243), 1, 19, 30, 36n, 55, 58n, 61-2, 65-9, 71, 76, 89, 92, 105, 170, 327, 354, 393, 553, 558, 595, 622; Japanese strength in, 23, 38, 90, 555; campaign in, 21-2, 24-5, 241-70; mutiny of NGIB soldiers in, 262-3; surrender of, 265-6, 556; Australian strength and casualties in, 581, 635; General Blamey's Appreciation, 608-16
NEW BRITAIN, NATIVE POPULATION OF, 83, 241-5, 247-8, 262
NEWCASTLE (Map p. 512; Sketch p. 517), 515, 518-19
Newfoundland, British cruiser, 349
NEW GEORGIA (Sketch p. 22), 22, 90
NEW GUINEA (Maps pp. 3, 60; Sketch p. 16), 1, 9, 11-12, 18-19, 36n, 46-9, 52-3, 55, 76, 77n, 81, 87, 89-90, 92, 97-9, 105, 130n, 135, 165, 178, 180, 183, 241-2, 246, 249, 255, 266, 274, 276, 278, 283, 296, 349, 384, 393-6, 398, 408, 513, 547-8, 570, 572, 581, 583, 589, 594-6, 599-601, 604, 617, 619, 622; operations in, 20-6, 44, 271-387; lack of publicity about, 37-40, 238; Japanese strength and

660 INDEX

New Guinea—*continued*
  casualties in, 38, 268-70, 385-6, 555; command problems, 43-6, 54; criticism of conduct of operations, 56-72, 218, 239; Australian casualties, 72, 385, 635; service of Australian brigades in, 80n; cease fire, 552-3; General Blamey's Appreciation, 608-16
New Guinea, Dutch (Maps pp. 3, 28), 1, 37, 77, 98; Japanese strength in, 555
New Guinea, Native Population of, 71, 82-3, 264, 275, 306, 310-11, 325-6, 330, 335, 337, 356-8, 380
New Guinea Constabulary, 246, 335, 353, 382
New Hanover (Map p. 60), 100, 201
New Ireland (Maps pp. 3, 60), 1, 90, 137n, 242n, 248n, 553, 558; strength of Japanese forces in, 23, 268, 555, 557
New Mexico, American battleship, 29
New Sahik (Sketch p. 282), 283
New South Wales, proportion of army leaders from, 79n; militia battalions from, 99n; gross army enlistments, 635
Newsreel (Map p. 512), 522
Newton, Lt-Col K. W., 363
Newton, Lt T. E., 360
Newton's Knoll (Sketch p. 360), 360
New York Herald-Tribune, 2n
New Zealand, 5, 17, 33, 56, 561
New Zealand Air Force, 12, 93-5, 109, 128-9, 140, 149, 156n, 178, 194, 202, 205, 220, 231, 558
  —Squadrons: No. 14, 179, 189. No. 16, 189. No. 19, 261. No. 20, 261. No. 21, 261. No. 22, 179, 189. No. 26, 179, 189
New Zealand Army, 4, 40n, 53, 90, 548, 551
Nialu (Sketch p. 276), 280
Niap (Sketch p. 285), 285-6
Nicholas, Capt P. W., 437
Nicholson, Cpl D. C., 378
Nicholson, Lt G. L., 140
Nicobar Islands (Map p. 3), 6
Nicolay, Capt N. T., 423-4
Nigitan (Sketches pp. 131, 144), 132, 135, 141-2, 144
Nihero (Sketch p. 144), 145, 156, 168
Nilu (Sketch p. 302), 303, 362
Nimbum Creek (Sketches pp. 284, 297), 286-7, 297
Nimitz, Fleet Admiral Chester W., 4, 19, 27-8, 40n, 51, 549, 584; commands Pacific Ocean Area, 1
Nimrod Creek (Sketch p. 331), 332
Ninab River (Sketches pp. 302, 305), 306, 310, 334
Ninahau River (Sketches pp. 313, 315), 311, 314-15, 318-19, 321
Ningpo, 41
Nintigo (Sketch p. 302), 337
Nisbet, Brig T. G., 312; commands 2/9 Cdo Sqn, 287
Nixon, L-Sgt J., 413
Noble, Rear-Admiral Albert G., 506, 539-40
Nobody (Map p. 512), 522-3, 525
Noer, Dr Tadjoeddin, 574
Nomen (Map p. 512), 521
Norman, Pte A. W., 167
Norman, Brig C. H. B., 468, 473-4, 483; commands 2/28 Bn, 461
Norman Ridge (Sketch p. 472), 473
Norrie, Lt-Col J. W., 323
Northcott, General Sir John (Plate p. 268), 21, 24n, 31, 34, 239, 264, 391-2, 394, 551, 595; Chief of the General Staff, 10; commands BCOF, 577
Northern Territory, gross army enlistments in, 635
North Hill (Sketch p. 203), 232
Nosong, Cape (Sketch p. 476), 475
Nosworthy, Maj J. R., 274n
Nott, Sgt A. H., 179
Nottingham, Sgt S. J., 337-8
Nought (Map p. 512), 521
Noumea, 19n
Nugent, Tpr R., 424, 434
Nukohan (Sketch p. 476), 477
Numango (Sketch p. 302), 303
Numa Numa (Map p. 91; Sketches pp. 111, 127), 94, 100, 103-4, 106-7, 108n, 110, 113-14, 119, 121-2, 127, 138, 141, 143, 165, 175, 204-6, 208-9, 215, 230, 232, 234, 558; Japanese strength at, 217
Numbogua (Map p. 273), 369
Numikim (Sketch p. 345), 345
Numoikum (Map p. 273; Sketch p. 371), 381-4
Nungagua (Map p. 273), 311

Nuremberg, 35
Nurse (Map p. 512), 522-5, 532
Nyakombi (Sketch p. 384), 384

Oamai River (Sketch p. 219), 186, 224, 227, 229
Oaveta, 235-6
Oboe Operation, 49-50, 404, 454, 457, 545
O'Brien, Maj-Gen J. W., 637
Ocean Island (Map p. 3), 394, 553-5, 558-61
O'Connell, Brig K. E., 198
O'Connor, Cpl O. G. J., 187
O'Day, Lt-Col G. O., 525, 527-8
Odgers, G., 45n
O'Donnell, Capt G. C., 362
Ogden, Capt R. C., 235
Ogorata River (Sketches pp. 180, 190), 193-5, 200
Okema (Sketch p. 171), 171
Okinawa (Sketch p. 16), 28, 30, 51, 405, 502
Oldfield, Maj A. S., 222
Old German Road (Sketches pp. 315, 318), 277-8, 285-6, 301-2, 313, 317
O'Leary, Lt S. H., 87
Oliver, Cfn A. R. S., 162
Oliver, Capt H. A., 340
O'Loghlen, Capt C. M., 368
O'Loughlin, Lt-Col B. J., 97n
Olsson, Maj R. C., 321
Olympic Operation, 52
O'Neill, Bdr P. A. A., 525
Opai (Sketch p. 144), 148
Open Bay (Map p. 243; Sketches pp. 253, 254), 24, 251, 261, 267
Operator (Map p. 512), 522
Opus (Map p. 512), 522
Orami (Sketch p. 136), 135, 137-8, 168-9
Orange (Map p. 512), 522
O'Regan, Tpr K. P., 423
Orford, Cape (Map p. 243), 259n
Ormiston, Lt F. S., 433
O'Rourke, Lt A. J., 442
Orr's Junction (Map p. 512), 525, 532
Oso (Sketches pp. 144, 180), 158, 185-6, 192
Ossie (Sketch p. 429), 437
Ostrich (Sketch p. 429), 436
Otsu, Major, 557
Ottrey, Cpl A. J., 536
Otway (Sketch p. 416), 425, 427, 429
Overall, Lt-Col J. W., 554n
Owen (Map p. 512), 520
Oxley (Map p. 512), 520
Oxley, Lt-Col P. H. G., 131n
Oxley Ambush (Sketch p. 131), 131
Oxygen (Map p. 512), 522

Pacific Theatre (Map p. 3; Sketch p. 16), 1, 32, 40n, 41, 48, 51-2, 72, 189, 255, 388-9, 551, 584-5; participation of UK forces in, 4-10, 12, 15, 17-18; plans for operations in, 27-30
Pacific War Council, 14
Padas River (Sketches pp. 460, 476), 453, 476-80, 483, 495
Padas Valley Estate (Sketch p. 476), 478
Paddy (Sketch p. 429), 443, 445
Paff, Pte T. E., 285
Pagana River (Sketches pp. 131, 144), 129, 141-2
Page, Rt Hon Sir Earle, 68, 71
Page, Lt-Col L. C., 97n
Pages (Sketch p. 416), 418
Paice, Pte M. F., 119
Paitan River (Sketch p. 455), 455
Palau Islands (Map p. 28), 1
Palauru (Sketch p. 276), 276, 278
Palawan (Map p. 28), 29, 48, 55, 509
Palembang, 502
Pali River (Sketch p. 253), 254
Palketia (Sketch p. 360), 360
Pallister, L-Cpl A. W., 430
Palmalmal (Map p. 243), 242
Palmer, Sqn Ldr B. M. H., 156n
Palmer, Sgt K. I., 527
Pamaluan (Sketch p. 540), 542
Pamusian (Sketches pp. 408, 416), 408, 423, 430
Pamusian River (Sketch p. 409), 409
Panay (Map p. 28), 29, 55
Pandansari (Map p. 512), 524

INDEX

PANDARUAN RIVER (Map p. 464; Sketch p. 460), 453, 489, 494
PANDI RIVER (Map p. 243), 247-8, 251-2
PAPAN ISLAND, 565
PAPAR (Sketches pp. 455, 460), 459, 482-3, 497, 565
PAPARAM (Sketch p. 384), 382
PAPAR RIVER (Sketch p. 460), 453, 459
PAPUA (Map p. 60), 79n, 161n
PAPUAN CONSTABULARY, ROYAL, 122n, 282, 355-6, 634; strength, casualties and decorations, 83
PARANG (Map p. 28), 55n
PARBURY, Lt-Col P. K., 78n, 306, 309-10, 330, 332, 334, 367; commands 2/7 Bn, 305
PARCHI RIVER (Sketches pp. 331, 360), 359
PAREHPAREH RIVER (Sketch p. 540), 541
PARE PARE (Sketch p. 560), 576
PARK, Lt-Col E. N., 315-16, 321-4
PARKER, Col A. E. H., 128
PARKES (Map p. 512), 511, 515
PARKIN, Sgt D. W., 378
PARKINSON, Sgt F. F., 288
PARKS (Sketch p. 416), 416
PARRAMATTA (Map p. 512; Sketch p. 517), 511, 515-16, 518-19, 521
PARRY-OKEDEN, Lt-Col W. N., 358, 370; commands 30 Bn, 357
PARSONAGE, Pte N. S., 467
PART RIDGE (Sketch p. 207), 237
PARTRIDGE, Pte F. J., VC, 236-7
PASSAM (Sketch p. 344), 352
PA TENGOA RIVER (Map p. 464), 494
PATERSON, Capt H. T., 190
PATON, Sir George, 396-9
PATROLS, in Bougainville, 26, 71, 106, 119-21, 187, 199, 222-4, 232-3; in New Britain, 260-1; in Wewak campaign, 277-8, 326, 330, 337, 362, 377-80, 382; in Tarakan, 443n; in Borneo, 491; in Balikpapan operations, 540-5; Japanese, in Bougainville, 234-5
PATTERSON, Lt J. G., 121, 213, 215
PAY, of senior Australian Army officers, 602
PEAR HILL (Sketch p. 116), 117
PEARL RIDGE (Sketches pp. 111, 116), 109-10, 113, 118, 121-2, 201, 204; attack on, 116-17
PEARSON, Col C. M. I., 309, 332-3
PEARSON, Capt F. A., 515
PEARSON, Maj J. A., 195
PEARSON, Lt J. N., 515
PEELER, Pte D., 130n
PEELER, S-Sgt W., VC, 130n
PEELER'S POST (Sketch p. 131), 129, 130n
PEGG, Maj F. J., 285
PELNANDU (Sketch p. 282), 290
PENADJAM (Sketch p. 540), 526, 540-1
PENFOLD, A. W., 638
PENFUI, 571
PENGLASE, Maj N., 396-9
PENINGKIBARU (Sketch p. 416), 420-1, 424-5, 427
PEPERU RIVER (Sketch p. 190), 193
PEPPER, Sgt L. G., 489
PERCIVAL, Lt-Gen A. E., 590
PERCIVAL, Capt S. M. S., 379
PEREI ROAD (Sketch p. 131), 135
PEREL, Gnr I., 362
PEREMBIL (Map p. 273), 283, 289, 291
PERKINS, Lt A. J., 338
PERKINS, Lt K. C., 307
PERRY, L-Cpl J. W., 299
PERRY, Lt L. G., 258
PERRY, Lt R. W., 151, 200
PERRY'S KNOLL (Sketch p. 257), 258-9
PETATS ISLAND (Map p. 91), 126-7
PETER (Sketch p. 416), 422
PETERSHAM JUNCTION (Sketch p. 517), 515-16, 519
PHEFLEY, Sgt H. A., 528
PHILIPPINE ISLANDS (Maps pp. 3, 28), 1-2, 4, 6, 12, 19-21, 24, 37-9, 42, 44-5, 49, 51, 53, 58n, 61, 66-7, 266-7, 389, 395, 405, 470, 548, 552, 585, 590-1, 594, 596, 622; Allied advance to, 27-8; operations in, 29-30, 55-6; proposed employment of Australian forces in, 38, 44-8, 52, 56; AIB operations in, 619-20
PHILLIPSON'S ROAD (Sketch p. 533), 534
PHIPPS, Rear-Adm P., 561
Phoenix, American cruiser, 462
PIARINO (Sketch p. 180), 227

PIATERAPAIA (Sketches pp. 107, 111), 106-7
PICKEN, Lt-Col K. S., 544
PIGEON (Map p. 512), 514
PIGEONS, CARRIER, 130, 147, 223, 356, 449
PIKE, Maj W. A., 188, 191, 194-5
PINKERTON, Lt R. J. D., 490
PINNEY, Cpl P. P., 87, 106n, 135n
PINRANG (Sketch p. 560), 553, 570, 574, 576
PITTS, Lt D. H., 363
PLANT, Maj-Gen E. C. P., 606
PLIMSOLL, Maj J., 402n
PLUG (Map p. 512), 515
POCKET, THE (Sketch p. 466), 470; attack on, 472-5
POKER (Sketch p. 429), 441-2
POLLOK, Lt-Col J. A., 477, 480-2
PONDO (Map p. 243), 266, 268
PONTIANAK (Sketch p. 560), 555, 569
POPE, Lt-Col A., 204, 235; commands 27 Bn, 202
POPE, Sgt G. H., 425
POPE, Lt K. R., 298-9
POPE'S TRACK (Sketch p. 533) 538-9
PORA PORA (Sketches pp. 127, 207), 172, 175, 206-7
POROREI RIVER (Sketch p. 190), 185, 187, 189-90
PORROR RIVER (Sketch p. 180), 164
PORTAL, Marshal of the RAF Viscount, 18
PORTEE (Map p. 512), 515, 518, 520
PORTER, Pte L. L., 481
PORTER, Maj-Gen S. H. W. C., 460, 465-6, 468, 475-9, 482-3, 500-1, 562; commands 24 Bde, 459
PORT MORESBY (Maps pp. 3, 60), 36n, 82, 89, 394, 594-5
PORTON PLANTATION (Map p. 91; Sketch p. 207), 207-8, 234; landing at, 210-16
POTAITI RIVER (Sketch p. 253), 254
POTTS (Map p. 512), 520
POTTS, Brig A. W., 94, 201-2, 234-5; commands 23 Bde, 93
POWELL, Lt F. B. G., 492
POWELL, Capt R. L., 321, 323
POWER, Sgt F. C., 494
PRATAS ISLAND (Map p. 28), 621
PRENTICE, Capt V. D., 410, 509
PRESS, AUSTRALIAN, 52; and General Blamey, 59-60, 70-1; criticises Australian operations in Bougainville, 218, 230; fails to publicise Australian campaigns, 238
PRICE, Capt E. W. A., 308
PRINCE ALEXANDER MOUNTAINS (Map p. 273), 292, 346, 359, 364
PRIOR, Capt C. J., 298, 301
PRIOR, Lt W. N., 267n, 448n
PRISONERS OF WAR, 557, 562-3; in prison break at Cowra, 623-4
PROBY, Lt L. S., 220
PROUD, Cdr J. C. R., 617-18
PROVAN, Maj D., 112
PRUDENT (Sketch p. 517), 516, 519
PUGH, Lt J. N., 259
PUJUT (Map p. 464), 488
PULVER, Maj-Gen B. W., 97
PURCELL, Dr V. V. M., 617
PURIATA RIVER (Sketches pp. 144, 180), 113, 128, 141-2, 146, 148-55, 158, 161-2, 164, 168, 178-9
PUS, CAPE (Sketch p. 345), 343, 379
PUTNAM, Lt P. E., 191
PUTO (Sketches pp. 123, 127), 125-6, 171
PUT PUT (Map p. 243), 242, 247, 268

QUEBEC, 1, 18
QUEENSLAND, proportion of army leaders from, 79n; militia battalions from, 99; gross army enlistments in, 635

RABA, 572
RABAUL (Maps pp. 60, 243), 49, 90, 92-3, 114, 241-2, 256, 259n, 261, 266-9, 386, 555, 558, 561, 582-3; surrender ceremony at, 556; *Japanese*, strength at, 556-7
RABJOHNS, L-Cpl G. A., 536-7
RABOIN ISLAND (Sketch p. 345), 346
RADFORD, Capt D. P., 110n
RAJANG RIVER (Sketch p. 455), 456, 561
RAJENDRA SINGH, 578n
RALSTON, Maj A. C., 210n
RAMAZON RIVER (Sketch p. 127), 205

INDEX

RAMSAY, Maj-Gen Sir Alan (Plate p. 268), 250-4, 256, 260, 269, 354; commands 5 Div, 25, 248-9; commands 11 Div, 265
RAMU RIVER (Map p. 60; Sketch p. 355), 355, 357-8
RANAU (Sketch p. 455), 456, 470, 562
RANCHA ROAD, 469n
RANG (Map p. 243,) 244
RANGAU (Map p. 464), 494-5
RANGOON (Map p. 3), 15-16, 502, 553
RANIMBOA (Sketch p. 345), 343, 345, 379
RANKEN, Lt J. B., 246
RANKIN, Maj-Gen G. J., 63-4
RASMUSSEN, Brig J. H., 61, 85-6
RATION (Map p. 512), 514-15
RATSUA (Sketch p. 127), 175, 206-10, 215
RATSUA ROAD, 235
RATTEY, Sgt R. R., VC, 155
RAU, Pte E. A., 351
RAUA (Sketch p. 127), 205
RAVENSHOE (Map p. 512), 514
RAWARD, Lt J. E. A., 539
RECORD (Map p. 512), 514
RED BEACH, Balikpapan (Map p. 512; Sketch p. 517), 510-11, 515
RED BEACH, Brunei Bay (Sketch p. 462), 453, 462
RED BEACH, Tarakan (Sketches pp. 409, 416), 410, 412-14, 417
RED BEACH, Wewak (Sketch p. 344), 350
REDDISH, Brig J., 274n
REDHEAD, Lt F. A. E., 530
REDMOND, Lt N. T., 381
REED, Bdr F. L. J., 338, 362
REED, Lt M. T., 425
REED, Capt S. J., 235
REED-HANKEY, Lt J., 365
REES, Maj K. P., 97n
REEVE, Capt E. R., 368
REEVE, Col R. C., 97n
REINFORCEMENTS, in Bougainville, 183, 354. *Japanese*, 114, 293, 307
REITER, Lt F. A., 120-1, 215
REITER'S RIDGE (Sketch p. 107), 120-1
RENNISON, Maj A. C., 495
RESERVOIR (Map p. 512), 521
RESORT (Map p. 512), 520
REYNOLDS, Lt-Col R. G., 402n
RHOADES, Lt-Cdr F. A., 140
RHODEN, Lt-Col P. E., 74n, 525-7, 530; commands 2/14 Bn, 521
RIAM ROAD (Map p. 464), 487-9, 562
RICHARDS, Lt C. H., 534
RICHARDSON, Lt-Col F., 525
RICHARDSON, Lt-Gen Robert C., 27, 593
RICHARDSON, Lt R. R., 301
RICKARD, Lt-Col A. L., 378
RIDAN (Map p. 464), 492
RIDGWAY, M., 561
RIEDY, Cpl A. R., 432
RIGGS, Rear-Adm Ralph S., 506
RIKO RIVER (Sketch p. 540), 541
RIKO MATIH RIVER (Sketch p. 540), 541
RIL (Map p. 243), 245, 255, 261
RINDOGIM (Sketches pp. 371, 384), 381-4
RIPLEY, F-Lt G. C., 456
RIPPON (Sketches pp. 416, 429), 421, 425-6
River Burdekin, Australian ship, 560
River Glenelg, Australian ship, 560
ROACH (Sketch p. 416), 415
ROADS, in Bougainville, 103-4, 156, 177, 206, 225; in Wewak campaign, 293, 328; in Tarakan, 451
ROBERTS, Col C. G., 617-18, 621
ROBERTS, Air Cmdre G. N., 95, 558
ROBERTS, Capt R., 231
ROBERTS, Pte R. C., 167
ROBERTSON, Maj A. C., 568
ROBERTSON, Maj B. E. D., 532
ROBERTSON, Lt-Gen Sir Horace (Plate p. 381), 25, 57, 70-1, 75, 269, 384, 554, 559; commands 5 Div, 265; commands BCOF, 577
ROBERTSON, Lt R. W., 383
ROBERTSON, Lt-Col W. T., 74n
ROBIN, Lance-Corporal, 247
ROBINSON, Maj E. D., 205, 247-8, 251-2
ROBINSON, Capt G. A., 308
ROBINSON, Lt H. D., 144
ROBINSON, Sqn Ldr R. A., 100, 136-7
ROBINSON, Lt W. G., 529
ROBSON, Lt-Col E. M., 523, 532, 535-7, 568; commands 2/31 Bn, 522
ROCHE, Lt R. H., 364
Rocky Mount, American ship, 407, 462
ROCKY POINT (Sketch p. 285), 284-5
ROCKY POINT ROAD, 293
RODWELL, WO2 E. E., 419
ROGER (Sketch p. 429), 443-4
ROGERS, Brig J. D., 101-2, 617-18
ROLLESTON, Col W. L., 401, 498
ROMANUS, C. F., 585n
ROMILLY (Map p. 512), 514
ROMMEL, Field Marshal Erwin, 602
RONAN, Gnr T. M., 87
RONDAHL HARBOUR (Map p. 243), 247
ROODAKOFF, Lt A., 122
ROOKE, Capt A. N., 309
ROOSEVELT, President Franklin D., 7, 10, 18, 27, 590, 598
ROROVANA (Sketch p. 136), 170, 201
ROSEVEAR, Maj H. G. M., 430
ROSS, A.; *see* ROODAKOFF, Lt A.
ROSS, Capt A. R., 637
ROSS, Sqn Ldr J. M. S., 95n
ROSS, Capt W. A., 189
ROSSITER, Maj N. E. L., 519
ROTTNEST (Map p. 512), 514
ROUBAII, 169
ROWBOTTOM, Pte N. K., 223
ROWELL, Lt-Gen Sir Sydney, 57, 70, 579n, 594-5
ROYAL, Rear-Adm Forrest B., 407, 411, 458
ROYCE, Maj G. E., 285-6, 353
RUGEN PLANTATION (Sketch p. 127), 205
RUKUSSIA (Sketch p. 123), 122
RUMBLE, Lt-Col N. R., 339
RUMIKI (Sketches pp. 144, 180), 155-6, 167, 178-9, 185
RUMLEY, Capt L. O., 352, 372
RUNAI (Sketch p. 180), 188, 229
RUNGIE, Maj R. H., 412
RURI (Sketch p. 207), 175
RURI BAY (Map p. 91; Sketch p. 207), 156n, 205, 208-9, 215, 236
RURI BAY ROAD, 235n
RUSEI (Sketches pp. 180, 190), 193-6, 229
RUSH, Lt G., 233
Rushmore, American ship, 414
RUSSACK, Lt E. K., 519
RUSSELL, L-Sgt A. G., 236
RUSSELL, Cpl O., 129n
RUSSELL, Maj W. B., 522n, 577n, 638
RUSSELL ISLANDS (Sketch p. 22), 183n
RUSSIA, 18, 41, 182, 226
RUSSIAN ARMY, 1, 577n, 587
RUTHERFORD, Lt G. A., 130
RYAN, Lt J. S., 118-19
RYLAH, Maj A. G., 266
RYRIE, Maj E. J., 518-19, 536
RYUKYU ISLANDS (Sketch p. 16), 19, 27-8

SABANG (Sketch p. 476), 478
SABURUMAN (Sketch p. 315), 326
SADAU ISLAND (Sketch p. 408), 408, 410, 412-13, 423
SADIE (Sketch p. 431), 433-4
SAIDOR (Map p. 60), 21, 130n
SAIGON (Map p. 3), 11, 553
ST PATRICK'S (Sketch p. 371), 382
SAI RIVER (Map p. 243; Sketch p. 253), 251, 253-4, 267
SAITO, Lt Hachiro, 381
SAKAI, Lt-Gen Yasushi, 266
SALAMAUA (Map p. 60), 64, 229
SALATA (Sketch p. 276), 289, 293, 303, 310
SALM, Capt G. B., 619
Salt, 85-6, 96
SALVATION ARMY, 96
SAMARINDA (Sketch p. 453), 502-3, 509, 566, 568
SAMARINDA ROAD; *see* MILFORD HIGHWAY
SAMBODJA (Sketch p. 544), 502, 543-5
SAMBUKAUA (Sketch p. 344), 380
SAMBUKAUA TRACK (Sketch p. 344), 380
SAMEIN, CAPE (Sketch p. 344), 343
SAMEJIMA, Vice-Admiral Baron (Plate p. 236), 229, 558
SAMISAI (Sketch p. 282), 289
SAMPSON, Lt J. C., 245-6
SAMPSON, Maj R. G., 127, 212

SAMPUN (Map p. 243), 252-3
SAN BERNARDINO STRAIT (Map p. 28), 2
SANDAKAN (Map p. 28; Sketches pp. 455, 560), 30, 55n, 455-6, 470, 561, 564
SANDERSON, Capt R. W., 516, 518-19
SANDFORD, F-Lt N. C., 100, 127, 170, 175-6, 205-6, 230
SANDOVER, Brig R. L., 73, 248n, 250-3, 256, 259, 263; commands 6 Bde, 249
SANDY (Sketch p. 429), 444
SANGASANGA (Sketch p. 453), 466, 502
SANGA SANGA ISLAND (Map p. 28), 509
SANGHI ISLAND (Map p. 28), 555
SANSAPOR (Map p. 28), 19
SANTOSA BARRACKS, 521
SANTOSA HILL (Map p. 512), 519
SAPE, 572-3
SAPO, CAPE (Sketch p. 462), 462
SAPONG ESTATE (Sketch p. 460), 494-5, 562
SAPOSA ISLAND (Sketch p. 207), 175, 209
SARAWAK (Sketches pp. 453, 455), 456, 490, 494-5, 503, 543, 561, 564-5
SARAWAK RIVER, 562-3
SARGENT, Lt D. H., 435
SASSUIA (Sketch p. 384), 384
SATO, Major, 494
SATO, Rear-Admiral, 559
SATU MISAKI, 552
SAUNDERS, Capt R. W., 77n, 333
SAURI (Sketches pp. 344, 371), 345, 347-8, 352, 369-70, 372, 379
SAUTELLE, Capt J. B., 312
SAVAGE, Lt N. L., 362
SAVIGE, Lt-Gen Sir Stanley (Plates pp. 125, 236), 23-5, 64, 73, 90, 93-4, 97, 106, 110-11, 117, 122, 124, 137, 141-2, 146, 148-9, 152, 156, 165-6, 177, 183, 186, 194, 201, 204, 208, 217-18, 227, 230, 233-5, 239, 248, 554, 594; commands II Corps, 19; compiles manual of jungle warfare, 99; takes surrender in Bougainville, 558
SCHERGER, Air Marshal Sir Frederick (Plate p. 477), 460
SCHIELE, WO2 V. G., 232
SCHURR, Sgt C. H., 231
SCOTT, Capt D. C. J., 541
SCOTT, Lt J. R. L., 419
SCOTT, Lt-Col J. T., 530
SCOTT, Lt R. G., 179, 191, 235
SCOTT, Brig T. H., 476-7, 562; commands 2/32 Bn, 475
SCOTT, Maj W. H., 194-6
SCREW RIVER (Sketches pp. 271, 331), 305, 330, 332-4, 362
SCRUB TYPHUS, 237n, 385
SEARLE, Gnr R. C., 334n, 337n
SEARLES, Maj S. G., 172-5, 209
SEARSON, Capt J. J., 368
SEBBENS, Capt E. R., 207
SEDGLEY, Lt-Col J. G., 415
SEEKAMP, Lt A. H., 334
SEILLER, Rev Father, 171
SELAJONG RIVER (Sketch p. 441), 448
SELMES, Sgt J. G., 140
SELNAUA (Sketch p. 282), 289
SELNI (Sketch p. 282), 310
SEPARI (Sketch p. 540), 541
SEPIK RIVER (Map p. 60; Sketches pp. 271, 355), 90, 130n, 271-2, 275, 292, 306, 311, 330, 338, 354-7, 364, 366, 369-70, 379, 384, 555, 559
SEPIK VALLEY (Map p. 60), 294-5, 384
SEPINGGANG (Sketches pp. 503, 524), 502-3, 505-6, 520, 522
SEPINGGANG RIVER (Sketch p. 524), 522
SEPULUH, MOUNT (Map p. 512), 521
SERAGI (Map p. 243), 247
SERIA (Map p. 464; Sketch p. 455), 453, 456, 459, 471, 484, 488, 499; oil fires at, 485-7
SERLE, Maj R. P., 435-6, 441-2
SERONG, Col F. P., 382
SERUSUP (Sketch p. 462), 463
SERVICES RECONNAISSANCE DEPARTMENT; see ALLIED INTELLIGENCE BUREAU
SESANIP (Sketch p. 429), 427
SESUMPU RIVER (Sketch p. 540), 541
SETON, Capt C. W., 170, 200-1, 248
SEVEN (Sketch p. 356), 358

SHANAHAN, Cpl C. J., 433
SHANAHAN, Lt J., 313
SHATTOCK, Capt E. J., 421, 424-5, 435, 441, 446
SHAVE, Lt-Col L. K., 89n
SHAW, Lt B. A., 116, 154
SHAW, Lt L. C., 222-3
SHEARGOLD, Capt R. W., 236
SHEDDEN, Sir Frederick, 20, 43, 394, 550, 579-80, 592n, 596
SHEEHAN, Maj-Gen E. L., 89, 556
SHEPHERD, Pte F. W., 301
SHEPPARD, Lt-Col E. MacA., 563
SHERWOOD, R. E., 20n, 27n, 590n
SHIBURANGU, MOUNT (Sketch p. 371), 369-70, 372-3, 376, 381-2
SHIELDS, Maj W. R. J., 348
SHILTON, Capt A. L., 123-4, 210
SHIPPING, 54, 72, 582; shortage in operations, 41, 48, 89, 104-6, 134, 165, 250n, 269, 272, 294, 327, 359
SHISHIGATERO (Sketch p. 219), 219, 229
SHISSO MOUNTAIN (Sketch p. 318), 318
SHORT (Sketch p. 441), 446
SHORT, Capt L. T., 277-8
SHORTLAND ISLANDS (Maps pp. 60, 91; Sketch p. 22), 92-3, 133, 217, 558
SHOTO, MOUNT (Sketch p. 371), 383
Shropshire, Australian cruiser, 473, 511, 529
SHWEBO, 15
SIARA (Sketch p. 207), 175, 209
SIBENGKOK RIVER (Sketch p. 416), 415
SIGNAL HILL (Map p. 512), 519
SIGORA (Sketch p. 361), 365, 367
SIKIOMONI (Sketch p. 171), 170, 200
SILEIMBEP (Sketch p. 276), 290
SILIBAI RIVER (Map p. 91; Sketch p. 171), 164, 171, 194, 218, 227, 229-30
SIMBI CREEK (Sketch p. 313), 313-14
SIMMONS, Capt M. A., 415, 418
SIMPER, Lt C. D., 443
SIMPSON, Maj-Gen C. H., 24n
SIMPSON, Lt-Col C. L., 345
SIMPSON, Lt G., 465
SIMPSON, Capt J. C., 358
SIMPSON, Col J. T., 89n
SIMPSON, Maj-Gen N. W., 221, 239; commands 29 Bde, 218
SIMPSON HARBOUR, 556
SIMS, Brig C. A. W., 543
SINAHAU (Sketch p. 302), 303, 307, 309
SINANAI (Sketch p. 144), 157
SINAVINA, Corporal, 175
SINCLAIR, Capt E. B., 259
SINCLAIR, Lt I. V. R., 516-17
SINDOU CREEK (Sketch p. 179), 179
SINDUMIN (Map p. 464), 495
SINGAPORE (Map p. 3; Sketch p. 16), 10, 29, 51, 56-7, 66, 266, 342, 352, 457, 470, 547-8, 550, 554, 563, 585, 619
SINGARIN (Sketch p. 356), 356
SINGKORAP (Sketch p. 476), 477-8
SIPAAI (Sketch p. 123), 122
SIPITANG (Sketch p. 460), 495
SIPURU (Sketch p. 136), 136, 168, 201
SISIRUAI (Sketches pp. 131, 144), 128, 132-3, 135, 142, 146
SISIVIE (Sketches pp. 111, 203), 106-8, 120, 202, 230, 233
SIWAI DISTRICT (Sketch p. 180), 139, 168
SKEA, Lt G. R. L., 525
SKIN DISEASES, 237n, 385
SKINNER, Maj R. I., 242
SLATER, Pte C. R., 153
SLATER'S KNOLL (Map p. 91; Sketches pp. 144, 163), 153-4, 166-7, 184-5, 205, 237; action at, 158-65
SLOSS, Capt W. L., 326
SMART, Lt-Gen E. K., 10, 399-401, 403
SMILES, Lt J., 322n
SMITH, Capt E. P. A., 284-5, 347, 351, 373-5
SMITH, Sgt F. S., 365
SMITH, Capt G. L., 199
SMITH, Lt K. H., 110
SMITH, Pte L. H., 118
SMITH, Lt N. J., 212, 215n
SMITH, Lt P. V., 222
SMITH, Lt S. H., 226
SMITH, Pte S. J., 373

SMITH, William, 524
SMITH'S HILL (Sketch p. 107), 118, 121
SNAGS TRACK (Sketches pp. 416, 429), 427-8, 430 434-7
SNAKE (Sketch p. 441), 447
SOARIN (Sketch p. 344), 379
SOCHON, Maj W. L. P., 456, 495*n*
SOEDA, Capt Hisayuki, 561
SOEKARNO, President, 567
SOLOMON ISLANDS (Map p. 3; Sketch p. 22), 19, 21-2, 25, 30, 37-8, 60, 66-9, 72, 90, 95, 140, 239, 244, 246, 255, 386, 393-4, 584, 596, 617; Japanese strength in, 555; Australian Army strength in, 581; General Blamey's Appreciation, 608-16; Australian casualties in, 635
SOLONGAN (Sketch p. 360), 359
SORAKEN (Map p. 91; Sketches pp. 123, 173), 122, 125, 174, 209, 234
SORAKEN HARBOUR (Sketch p. 123), 122, 175
SORAKEN PENINSULA (Sketch p. 173), 174-5, 206, 208, 210, 215-16
SORONG (Sketch p. 560), 620
SOUTH AUSTRALIA, proportion of army leaders from, 79*n*; militia battalions from, 99*n*; gross army enlistments in, 635
SOUTH CHINA SEA (Map p. 28), 48, 51
SOUTH-EAST ASIA COMMAND, 5-6, 10, 15, 17, 29, 51, 56, 66, 551, 553, 565, 567, 619
SOUTH KNOLL (Map p. 464), 488
SOUTH PACIFIC AREA, 245
SOUTH-WEST PACIFIC AREA (Sketch p. 16), 5-6, 8 20, 31, 51-2, 54, 56, 66, 80, 88, 241, 268, 327, 389, 394, 506, 546*n*, 548-9, 551, 559, 580, 584, 603*n*; plans for operations in, 1-2, 21, 41-6; participation of British forces in, 9-18; Allied forces in, 19; communiqués on, 37-8, 40, 520; command problems in, 590-9; AIB operations in 617-22; Australian Army casualties in, 635
SOVELE (Sketch p. 144), 135, 141, 145-6, 169
SOWOM (Sketch p. 297), 301, 303, 316*n*
SPARK, Lt D. F., 211-12
SPEARE, J. H., 637
SPEARS, used by Japanese, 424, 430
SPEED, Col F. W., 89*n*
SPENDER, Hon Sir Percy, 38, 56-7, 60, 69
SPENDLOVE, Lt N. J., 179, 190
SPITZ, Cpl L. E., 151-2
SPOOR, Lt-Gen S. H., 618
STAFFORD, Brig F. E., 401
STAINLAY, Maj D. R., 257
STALIN, Marshal Joseph, 549
STALKUDO (Sketch p. 503), 503, 510, 514-15, 520
STANFORD, Lt H. M., 434
STANLEY, Maj M., 85-6
STANNER, Lt-Col W. E. H., 397-400, 402, 500
STANTKE, Maj-Gen V. P. H., 84
STARCEVICH, Pte L. T., VC, 480-1
STARK, Lt J. A., 530
STEELE, Maj-Gen Sir Clive (Plate p. 268), 24*n*
STEELE, Maj-Gen W. A. B., 570
STEIGRAD, Brig J., 89*n*
STEINHEUER, Sgt H. B., 224
STEINHEUER, Lt P. E., 133, 222
STEPHENS, Capt K. H. R., 185
STEVENS, J., 27*n*
STEVENS, Maj-Gen Sir Jack (Plate p. 333), 73, 275-9, 280-4, 287, 290, 294-6, 300, 306, 328-9, 338-9, 342-3, 349-50, 353, 359, 363, 369-70, 379, 381-2, 384; commands 6 Div, 25; service of, 274
STEVENSON, Maj-Gen J. R., 117, 122, 124, 126, 143, 206, 208, 210, 560-1; commands 11 Bde, 98
STEVENSON, Maj W. R. D., 232
STEVE'S FEATURE, 378
STEWART, Col A. J., 97*n*
STEWART, Capt G. F., 365
STEWART, Lt R. K., 155
STILWELL, Lt-Gen Joseph W., 15
STIMSON, H. L., 590*n*
STONE, Lt-Col J., 397
STONEHAM, Capt A. C., 353
STORRIE, Lt J. D., 366
STOTT, Maj D. J., 508
STRETCH, Lt W. G., 421, 435
STRETCHER BEARERS, 428*n*
STRONG, Lt-Col J. A. R. K., 317
STUART, F-O R., 168, 170-1, 185-6, 197, 200, 227-8

STUBBS, Lt J. J., 347
STUBBS, L-Cpl S. B. A., 316
STURDEE, Lt-Gen Sir Vernon (Plate p. 125), 25-6, 37, 44, 70, 73, 90, 93, 165-6, 201, 218, 239, 250-1, 256, 264-5, 268, 275-6, 279, 281, 294-5, 300, 328, 342, 354, 359, 370, 550, 554, 560, 579, 592, 594, 602*n*, 621; commands First Army, 23; service of, 89; takes surrender at Rabaul, 555-6
STURT (Sketch p. 416), 417, 419
SUAIN (Sketch p. 276), 277-8, 283-4, 334
SUANI, Constable, 122*n*
SUAUI (Sketch p. 361), 365
SUBIANA (Sketch p. 127), 175
SUBIC BAY (Map p. 28), 51
SUBLET, Lt-Col F. H., 544
SUGARNO PRISON, 583*n*
SUGUT RIVER (Sketch p. 455), 561
SULLIVAN, Lt A. D. K., 516
SULLIVAN, L-Cpl J. V., 528
SULU ARCHIPELAGO (Map p. 28), 30, 454, 509
SUMATRA (Map p. 3; Sketch p. 16), 5-6, 10, 502, 520, 566-7
SUMBA (Sketch p. 560), 571
SUMBAWA (Sketch p. 560), 569, 571, 572-3
SUMBER KIRI (Sketch p. 533), 537
SUMBER RIVER (Sketch p. 533), 526, 534
SUM SUM (Map p. 243), 247
SUMUL (Sketch p. 282), 289, 291
SUNDERLAND, R., 585*n*
SUNIN RIVER (Sketch p. 190), 192
SUPILI, 232*n*
SUPPLY, in Australia, 12, 13-14, 105; in Bougainville, 117-18, 177, 186, 196, 204, 222; in New Britain, 242; in Wewak campaign, 281, 289, 296, 308-9, 314, 327-8, 368, 380; reserves built up by Americans, 395-6; in Tarakan, 417-18; in Borneo, 457-8; at Balikpapan, 539-40. *Japanese*, in Bougainville, 103, 113-14, 215; in New Britain, 242, 557; in Wewak campaign, 291-2, 317, 336, 384-5; in Borneo, 490
SURABAYA (Map p. 3), 29, 49, 520
SURANGO (Sketch p. 127), 176
SURIGAO STRAIT (Map p. 28), 2
SUSIE (Sketch p. 429), 436-7, 439
SUTHERLAND, Lt-Gen Richard K., 28, 30, 48
SVENSON, WO2 V. P., 534
Swan, Australian sloop, 246, 250, 254, 301 329, 349-51
Swartenhondt, Dutch ship, 249
SWEET, Lt-Col H. G., 188
SWEET, Lt J., 473
SYDNEY, 6, 34*n*
Sydney Morning Herald, 39, 60, 63
SYDNEY UNIVERSITY, 84, 86-7
SYKES (Sketches pp. 416, 429), 408, 422, 425-6, 429, 434
SYMINGTON, Maj N. M., 274*n*
SYMONS, Cpl W. I., 518
SYRETT, Lt J., 190-1

TAAR RIVER (Sketch p. 180), 168
TABAGO (Sketch p. 171), 229
TABARATA (Sketch p. 131), 138-9
Table Tops, 87
TACLOBAN (Map p. 28), 2
TADJI (Sketch p. 276), 275, 279, 290, 294, 350
TADOLINA (Sketch p. 144), 135, 142
TAGENAKA, Lieut-Colonel, 334
TAGESSI RIVER (Map p. 91), 130, 133*n*, 135
TAIOF ISLAND (Map p. 91; Sketch p. 127), 125, 175, 209, 212
TAITAI (Sketches pp. 144, 180), 156, 186, 197-8, 229
TAKAHASI, Col T., 267*n*
TALASEA (Map p. 243), 241, 248-9, 251
TALAUD ISLANDS (Map p. 28), 555, 572
TALBOT, Vice-Adm A. G., 104*n*
TALBOT, Lt-Col J., 274*n*
TAME, Capt S. A., 122
TANAKA, Colonel, 291*n*
TANCRED, Col P. L., 520
TANIMBAR ISLAND (Sketch p. 560), 555, 569-70
TANIMBAUBAU (Sketch p. 127), 127, 175
TANK PLATEAU (Sketch p. 517), 519, 521
TANK TACTICS, in Bougainville, 235
TARAKAN (Sketches pp. 408, 416), 407-8, 411, 423, 427, 431, 453

INDEX 665

TARAKAN HILL (Sketch p. 416), 422-4, 427, 430
TARAKAN ISLAND (Map p. 28; Sketches pp. 408, 447), 28, 30, 41, 49-50, 62-3, 388-9, 457-8, 460-1, 502-3, 509, 513, 520, 526; attack on, 406, 409-52; described, 407-8; casualties, 451-2
TARATIP (Sketch p. 544), 543
TARBUT (Sketch p. 207), 207-8, 215
TARLENA (Sketch p. 207), 175, 208, 215
TAROMI RIVER (Sketch p. 190), 167, 189
TARR, Lt H. A., 180
TASHIRO, Japanese officer, 137
TASKER, Lt-Col H. McK., 402
TASMANIA, proportion of army leaders from, 79n; militia battalions from, 99n; gross army enlistments in, 635
TATIMBA (Sketch p. 302), 309
TAU (Sketch p. 276), 334
TAVERA RIVER (Sketches pp. 131, 134), 128-9, 131, 141-2, 146
TAWAO (Sketch p. 455), 410, 470, 495, 564
TAWITAWI ISLAND (Map p. 28), 452, 470, 509
TAYLOR, Cpl A. C., 332
TAYLOR, Maj A. L., 525
TAYLOR, Gnr C. S., 338
TAYLOR, Lt C. W., 236-7
TAYLOR, Col L. M., 401, 403
TAYLOR, Lt-Col R. R., 521
TAYLOR, Lt W., 537
TAYLOR, Lt W. J., 161
TAZAKI, MOUNT (Sketches pp. 344, 371), 369-70, 379; attack on, 372-6
TELOKTEBANG (Sketch p. 540), 541
TEMPADUNG (Sketch p. 540), 542-3
TENNANT, Admiral Sir William, 549
TENOM (Sketch p. 476), 483, 493-4, 562
TEOPASINO (Sketch p. 127), 175, 205
TERAJA, MOUNT (Map p. 464), 492
TERAUCHI, Field Marshal Count, 90, 384-5, 553-4, 567; commands *Southern Army*, 2
TERNATE ISLAND (Sketch p. 560), 569, 572, 620
TESHIMA, Lt-Gen Fusataro, 554, 577; commands *II Army*, 553
THAILAND (Map p. 3; Sketch p. 16), 457
THOMAS, Capt D. L., 424
THOMAS, Capt J. C., 184
THOMAS, Lt R. R., 314
THOMPSON, Maj C. W., 236
THOMPSON, Cpl N. D., 139
THOMPSON, Maj R. N., 528
THOMSON, Lt-Col C. R., 274n
THORN, Sgt C., 305
THORNTON, Capt J. J., 479
THORP, Capt G. M., 525
TIDDIM, 14
TIERNAN, Lt J. A., 203-4
TIERNAN'S SPUR (Sketch p. 203), 204
TIGER (Sketch p. 429), 428, 435
TIGER ROAD (Sketch p. 180), 185-6, 198
TIGHE, WO2 R. C., 324
TIMBALAI (Sketch p. 466), 470
TIMMS, Maj E. V., 623n
TIMOR (Map p. 3; Sketch p. 560), 11-12, 93, 520, 553-4, 569-73, 619; Japanese strength in, 555
TIMOR, DUTCH, 570-1
TIMOR, PORTUGUESE, 77, 571-2, 618
TIMOR SEA (Sketch p. 560), 573
TINKLER, Maj N., 527
TINPUTZ (Sketch p. 127), 175-6, 205, 217
TITLEY, Maj T. H. A., 122-3
TOBIN, Cpl G. F., 523
TOBOREI (Sketch p. 136), 140
TOIMONAPU (Map p. 91), 169, 200
TOKINOTU (Sketch p. 144), 154-6, 158, 167
TOKO (Sketch p. 144), 150-1, 153, 156, 158-9, 161, 164, 165n, 177, 185, 210, 557
TOKOI, Major, 443, 445
TOKOKU MOUNTAIN, 324
TOKOKU PASS (Sketches pp. 318, 320), 319, 324, 327
TOKUA (Sketch p. 203), 203, 230, 233
TOKUAKA (Sketch p. 171), 227
TOKYO (Map p. 3; Sketch p. 16), 4, 60, 85, 238-9, 291n, 552, 555, 567, 583n
TOKYO BAY, surrender at, 553, 578
TOL (Map p. 243; Sketches pp. 245, 254), 253n, 256, 260-1, 266-7, 270
TOLMER, Maj A. R., 262-3

TOMANI (Sketch p. 460), 495
TOMKINS, Maj R. C., 97n
TON (Sketch p. 127), 175
TONG (Map p. 273; Sketch p. 282), 276-7, 279-80, 282, 293, 386
TORIU (Map p. 243; Sketch p. 253), 267
TORIU RIVER (Map p. 243; Sketch p. 253), 254, 266-7
TOROBIRU RIVER (Sketch p. 190), 190
TOROKINA (Maps pp. 60, 91; Sketches pp. 95, 111), 19, 67-8, 85, 89-90, 96-8, 100-1, 104-6, 111, 114, 127-8, 130n, 135-8, 153, 156-7, 165n, 166, 168-70, 177-8, 201, 204-5, 217, 225, 226n, 234, 401, 558, 560-1; area described, 92; HQ 3 Div opens at, 94
TOROKORI ISLAND (Sketch p. 207), 207, 209, 215
TORR, Brig A. G., 89n
TORRES STRAIT (Map p. 60), 24, 34n, 601
TORRICELLI MOUNTAINS (Maps pp. 60, 273; Sketch p. 271), 68, 77, 130n, 276-8, 280, 282, 289-91, 294-5, 296n, 303, 306, 309, 334, 337, 364, 539n; area described, 271-2
TOTOKEI (Sketch p. 123), 122
TOWNSLEY, Sgt C. J., 160
TOWNSVILLE, Qld, 43, 80n, 98, 165
Townsville, Australian corvette, 556
TRACK JUNCTION KNOLL (Sketch p. 429), 437, 439
TRAPPES-LOMAX, Maj A. E. B., 617
TRAVERS, Lt-Col B. H., 99
TRAVERS, Capt J. E., 432
TRAVIS, Capt G. B., 419-20, 434-5
TREASURY ISLANDS (Map p. 60; Sketch p. 22), 22, 24, 90, 92, 201
TREBECK, Maj N. B., 492
TRETHEWIE, Lt E. C., 335, 337
TRETHOWAN, Capt J. M., 373, 376, 382
TRIBOLET, Lt-Col L. N., 274n
TRUDGEON, Lt M. P., 463
TRUMAN, Harry S., 549
TRUSAN (Map p. 464), 493
TRUSAN RIVER (Map p. 464; Sketch p. 455), 453, 490, 494-5, 565
TSIMBA (Sketches pp. 123, 127), 123, 125
TSIMBA RIDGE (Map p. 91; Sketch p. 125), 123-6
TUCKER, Lt-Col F. A. G., 411
TUCKER, Cpl G. J., 224
TUCKER, F-Lt W. H., 138-9
TUGIOGU (Sketch p. 180), 227, 229
TUJU RIVER (Sketches pp. 131, 134), 112, 128, 131
TUM (Map p. 28), 19n
Tuna, American submarine, 454
TURNBULL, Lt A. W. J., 287
TURNER, S-Sgt F. S. W., 481n
TURNER, Lt W. G., 522
TURU, MOUNT (Map p. 273; Sketch p. 384), 336, 385
TUTONG (Map p. 464), 453, 465, 483-4
TUTONG RIVER (Map p. 464), 484, 490
TUWAIGUM (Sketch p. 302), 362
TYNDALE, Capt W., 304, 310
TYRES, Lt B. W. E., 309

UBILI (Map p. 243; Sketch p. 254), 251
UEBERGANG, Pte E. A., 237
UGUIMO RIVER (Sketch p. 171), 229
UKONG (Map p. 464; Sketch p. 455), 456, 489, 493
ULAGAMAGIN CREEK (Sketch p. 297), 286
ULAMA (Sketch p. 361), 365
ULAMONA (Map p. 243; Sketch p. 254), 248, 251-2, 267
ULEBILUM (Sketches pp. 331, 360), 360, 365, 367
ULTAN (Sketches pp. 315, 318), 316
ULUM (Sketch p. 361), 363
ULUNKOHOITU RIDGE (Sketch p. 361), 366
ULUPU (Sketches pp. 331, 361), 338, 359-61, 363
UMUM (Sketch p. 127), 175
UMUM TRACK, 235
UNA CREEK (Sketch p. 297), 300
UNANAI (Sketches pp. 144, 190), 157
UNDERWOOD, Lt E. B., 485-6
UNITED NATIONS, 12, 42, 393, 567, 575
UNO, Major-General, 568
UREN, M., 638
USO (Sketch p. 190), 186
UTUMUGU (Sketch p. 302), 309

VALENTIN, Lt G., 208
VALLEY ROAD (Map p. 512), 513, 515
VAN-ARCKEN, Capt G. G. M., 618
VARLEY, Brig A. L., 325n

INDEX

VARLEY, Lt R. A., 325
VASEY, Maj-Gen G. A., 75, 329n
VASEY HIGHWAY (Map p. 512; Sketches pp. 503, 517), 502, 514, 516, 520, 526-7, 529, 543, 545
VENABLES, Lt H., 259n
Vendetta, Australian destroyer, 244, 250, 556-7
VERNEY, J., 622n
VERNON, Maj P. V., 637
VERNON, F-Lt W. R., 152n
VERNON STRIP, 152n
VICTORIA, proportion of army leaders from, 79n; militia battalions from, 99n; gross army enlistments in, 635
VICTORIA HARBOUR (Sketches pp. 460, 466), 453, 459; *see also* BROWN BEACH
VISAYAN ISLANDS (Map p. 28), 28-9, 55, 71
VITO (Map p. 91), 200
VOGELKOP PENINSULA (Map p. 28), 410, 573
VOWLES, Brig E. L., 92
VRABU, LAKE (Sketch p. 355), 358

WADE-FERRELL, Lt-Col D. H., 129
WAHEP CREEK (Sketch p. 315), 319
WAIGAKUM (Sketch p. 331), 335, 338, 359
WAIN (Sketch p. 544), 538
WAITAVALO (Map p. 243; Sketch p. 245), 242, 246-7, 251, 256-7, 260, 266-7, 269
WAITES, L-Cpl H. A., 528
WAITES' KNOLL (Sketch p. 526), 527-9
WAKDE ISLAND (Map p. 28), 620
WAKIP RIVER (Sketch p. 284), 286
WAKUNAI RIVER (Sketches pp. 111, 203), 121-2, 205, 230-2, 234
WAKUNAI VALLEY (Sketch p. 111), 230
WALAHUTA (Sketch p. 305), 303-4
WALANDUUM (Sketch p. 320), 324, 338
WALANTER (Sketch p. 344), 348
WALENDE (Sketch p. 282), 289
WALHIGA (Sketch p. 305), 305
WALKER, Lt A. J., 323
WALKER, Col A. S., 328n
WALKER, Capt B. G. C., 538
WALKER, Sir Ronald, 182n
WALKER, Lt R. R. J., 421-2, 428-9
WALKLATE, L-Cpl S. H., 343
WALL, Lt J. D. S., 209
WALLACE, Col F. K., 97n
WALLACE, Lt H. S., 533
WALLACE, Sir Robert, 84
WALLIS, Sgt S., 419
WALLY (Sketch p. 429), 442-4
WALSH, Sgt W., 231
WALTER, Lt P. R., 449
WALTERS, Pte R. R., 467-8
WALTERS, Maj V. M., 289-90, 303
WALUM (Sketches pp. 276, 285), 277, 279, 282, 284, 287, 289, 294, 296, 311, 362
WAMBAK (Sketches pp. 305, 331), 307, 332
WANGAN (Sketch p. 356), 356, 358
WANIMBIL (Sketch p. 302), 309
WANK CREEK (Sketch p. 297), 300-1, 314, 340
WANN, Cpl A. C., 153n, 158n
WANPEA (Sketch p. 320), 381
WAPIAI RIVER (Sketch p. 219), 224
WARANGOI RIVER (Map p. 243), 242, 247, 267-8
WARAPA (Sketch p. 144), 145
WAR CORRESPONDENTS, 40, 530
WAR CRIMES TRIALS, 583
WARD, Hon E. J., 264, 398
WARD, Pte G., 337
WARD, Sgt K. R., 211, 213
WARFE, Col G. R., 78n, 99, 417, 419-22, 425-6, 435n, 444; commands 2/24 Bn, 411
WARIMBA (Map p. 273), 385
WARINGE RIVER (Sketch p. 344), 345, 347-8
WARNER, Sgt K. O., 135, 169
Warramunga, Australian destroyer, 349, 410
WASHINGTON, DC, 13-14, 17, 20, 28-30, 32, 34, 42-3, 52, 57, 58n, 70, 102, 389, 394-5, 400, 590; Australian Military Mission to, 89, 579
WATAM (Sketch p. 356), 357-8
WATERFALL BAY (Map p. 243), 242, 246
WATERMAN, Gnr A. J., 362
WATSON, Pte C. C., 180
WATSON, M. S., 585n
WATSON, Capt R., 145

WATU POINT (Sketch p. 254), 254
WAU (Map p. 60), 89
WAVELL, Field Marshal Rt Hon Earl, 590-2
WEARNE'S HILL (Sketch p. 203), 203-4, 230-2
WEBB, Pte A., 324
WEBB, Lt R. G., 235
WEBER, Sgt M. F. M., 343
WEBSTER, Lt-Col P. G. C., 190, 195-6; commands 57/60 Bn, 178
WEDGWOOD, Lt-Col Hon Camilla, 397
WEGNER, Maj J. G., 574
WEIR, Lt-Col S. P., 298-9
WELLS, Lt-Gen Sir Henry, 458
WELSH, Capt N. B., 278
WEPPNER, Maj R., 158-9
WERDA, Lt E. C., 147
WERDA'S KNOLL (Sketch p. 116), 116
WEST, L-Cpl A. F., 167
WESTERN AUSTRALIA, 25, 71, 354; proportion of army leaders from, 79n; militia battalions from, 99n; gross army enlistments in, 635
WESTON (Map p. 464; Sketches pp. 460, 476), 453, 459, 471-2, 475, 477-8, 482, 495
WESTON, Sgt F. M., 482
Westralia, Australian ship, 410n, 414, 458, 511, 570
WESTWOOD, Lt W. H., 373
WEWAK (Maps pp. 60, 273; Sketches pp. 346, 371), 21, 24, 39, 49, 55, 61, 63, 68, 71-2, 90, 265, 269, 277-9, 283, 292, 300, 327, 335-6, 338, 367, 381-2, 384-6, 392n, 494, 547; Japanese deployment, 23, 291, 293, 343, 352; capture of, 328-9, 342-54; surrender ceremony at, 559
WEWAK CAMPAIGN, 271-387
WEWAK POINT (Sketch p. 346), 343, 345-7
WEWAK ROAD (Sketch p. 344), 351
WHATLEY, Sgt R. S., 184
WHEELER, Lt A. B., 192
WHEELER, Lt-Col K. E., 97n
WHIBLEY, Lt H. R., 432
WHITE, Sgt B., 135, 139, 169, 200-1
WHITE, General Sir Brudenell, 604n
WHITE, Lt G. J., 244
WHITE, Pte S. C., 160n
WHITE BEACH (Sketches pp. 460, 462), 453, 459, 462
WHITEBROOK, Capt F. C., 197
WHITEHEAD, Brig D. A. (Plate p. 412), 410-11, 417, 423, 427, 436, 439, 443, 446-8, 450; commands 26 Bde, 407
WHITELAW, Lt-Col J., 214
WHITELAW, Maj-Gen J. S., 24n
WHITNEY, Brig-Gen Courtney, 619
WHITTON, Cpl S. A. R., 223-4
WHYTE, Lt-Col W. A. S., 518
WIDE BAY (Map p. 243; Sketches pp. 245, 254), 24, 244-5, 250, 252, 254-5, 266
WIGHTMAN, Lt H. K., 424
WIGLEY, Sgt J. H., 100, 127, 139, 168, 170
WIGMORE, L., 456n, 564n
WIHUN (Sketch p. 361), 364
WILES, Lt J. E., 336
WILGOLMAN (Sketch p. 331), 310, 332
WILKIE, Maj W. H., 189
WILLIAM, D. M., 247
WILLIAMS, Maj C. G., 543
WILLIAMS, Lt F. D., 312
WILLIAMS, Capt O. U., 376
WILLIAMS, Maj-Gen T. R., 70
WILLIAMSON, Lt D. D., 482
WILLIS, Capt J. G., 189
WILLOUGHBY, Maj-Gen Charles A., 101-2, 594n, 599n, 617, 619-20
WILLS (Sketch p. 416), 417, 419
WILLS, Brig Sir Kenneth, 621
WILLSON, WO2 R. W., 535
WILMOT, R. W. W. (Chester), 64
WILMOTT, Lt-Col E. R., 508
WILSON, Maj-Gen A. G., 562
WILSON, Lt A. J., 304, 310
WILSON, Maj D. C. L., 573
WILSON, Lt-Col E. H., 97n, 102-3, 137
WILSON, Lt G. C., 424
WILTON, Maj M. A. B., 418, 422
WINCHESTER, Lt-Col T. H. F., 97n
WINDEYER, Maj-Gen Rt Hon Sir Victor, 462-3, 465, 483-4, 488-91, 496, 564; commands 20 Bde, 459
WINGE (Sketch p. 361), 369

INDEX

WININGI (Sketch p. 361), 362
WINNING, Maj N. I., 134-5, 142, 145-6, 148, 157, 185, 199, 226-9; commands 2/8 Cdo Sqn, 106
WINNING, Brig R. E., 263; commands 13 Bde, 261
WINTER, Sgt K. N., 223
WINTER, Lt R. B., 222-3
WINTON, Capt J. H., 195
WIRUI CREEK (Sketches pp. 344, 346), 352, 379
WIRUI MISSION (Sketches pp. 344, 346), 343, 345, 347-8, 351-2
WIRURU (Sketch p. 344), 380
WISLING (Sketch p. 339), 339, 381
WISSEL LAKES, 620
WOGIA (Map p. 273), 290
WOLFE, Maj C. C., 118, 124
WOLFENDEN, Lt D. J., 202
WOLHUK CREEK (Sketch p. 297), 300
WOM (Sketch p. 276), 277, 559
WOM, CAPE (Sketches pp. 344, 345), 342-3, 345-6, 359
WOMEN, in Australian Services, 19n, 32
WOMISIS (Sketches pp. 276, 305), 278-9, 282
WOMSAK (Sketch p. 282), 282, 289, 293
WONGINARA (Sketches pp. 318, 320), 320-1, 325, 328, 338
WONGINARA TRACK (Sketch p. 318), 321-2
WONG YOU, 137-8
WOOD, Brig F. G., 539n; commands 2/6 Bn, 308
WOODFORD ESTATE ROAD (Sketch p. 479), 480
WOODHOUSE, Capt M. C., 277, 289, 304
WOODWARD, Lt D. P., 467
WOODWARD, Capt W. C., 220
WOOLBANK, L-Cpl R. B., 180
WOOTTEN, Maj-Gen Sir George (Plate p. 477), 73, 404, 406, 458-60, 475, 483, 487, 496-8, 554, 562; commands 9 Div, 50
WORA (Sketch p. 331), 331,338
WORTHINGTON, Lt S., 258
WRAY, Maj C. H. W., 277
WRIGLEY, Air Vice-Marshal H. N., 11
WULWUT RIVER (Sketches pp. 245, 257), 256-7, 259, 266-7
WYBURN, Lt K. T., 371
WYLIE, Lt A., 121
WYLIE, Capt I. S., 618
WYNTER, Lt-Gen H. D., 24n, 57n

YAKAMUL (Sketch p. 276), 279-80
YALAMINUNI (Sketch p. 320), 319
YALENGE (Sketch p. 282), 290

YALOM (Map p. 243), 266
YALTA, Allied conference at, 41
YAMADA, Major, 526
YAMADA, Lt-Gen Kunitaro, 571
YAMAGATA, Lieut-Commander, 443
YAMAMURA, Maj-Gen H., 563
YAMASHITA, General Tomoyuki, 2
YAMBES (Map p. 273; Sketch p. 276), 277, 280, 282-3, 290, 294, 311
YAMIL (Map p. 273; Sketches pp. 331, 360), 311, 318, 336-8, 359-61
YAMIL ROAD (Sketch p. 360), 360
YAMULE RIVER (Map p. 243), 251
YANATONG (Sketch p. 276), 280, 282
YAP ISLAND (Map p. 28; Sketch p. 16), 1, 27
YAPUNDA (Sketch p. 276), 276, 279
YARABOS (Sketches pp. 344, 345), 343, 345, 347, 379-80
YARABOS TRACK (Sketch p. 344), 380
YARAWORGY, 380
YARET (Sketch p. 245), 246
YASILE (Sketch p. 282), 280
YASUAR MISSION (Sketch p. 282), 277, 280
YAUWIGA, Warrant-Officer, 100, 127-8
YEATES, Lt J. D., 637
YELLOW BEACH, Balikpapan (Map p. 512), 510-11, 514-15
YELLOW BEACH, Brunei Bay (Sketches pp. 460, 462), 453, 459, 462
YELLOW BEACH, Tarakan (Sketches pp. 409, 416), 412-14
YENTAGIM (Sketch p. 302), 335
YOIBI RIVER (Sketch p. 361), 364
YORATH, Lt L. W., 184
YOSHIWARA, Lt-Gen Kane, 291n, 306, 311, 338, 369, 384, 386n
YOTT, Maj B. A., 232
YOUNG, Lt D. H., 224
YOUNG, Capt R. A., 258
YOUNG MEN'S CHRISTIAN ASSOCIATION, 96
YOUNG'S HILL (Sketch p. 257), 258
YOURANG (Sketch p. 282), 280
YUBANAKUOR (Sketch p. 302), 303, 306, 309
YUMAN (Sketch p. 360), 360
YUNNAN (Sketch p. 16), 16

ZAMBOANGA (Map p. 28), 55, 509
ZIEGLER, O. L., 638
ZUNGEN POINT (Sketch p. 245), 256

www.ingramcontent.com/pod-product-compliance
Lightning Source LLC
Chambersburg PA
CBHW070752300426
44111CB00014B/2385